TEACHER'S EDITION

AGS

World Literature

AGS®

American Guidance Service, Inc.
Circle Pines, Minnesota 55014-1796
1-800-328-2560
www.agsnet. com

Original cover art: Connie Hayes

Literature Consultant

Jack Cassidy, Ph.D.
Texas A&M University
Corpus Christi, TX

The publisher wishes to thank the following for their helpful comments during the review process for *AGS World Literature.* Their assistance has been invaluable.

Thor Carlson
News Director
Monticello Times
Monticello, MN

Susan Hentges
Language Arts Instructor
Mounds View Senior High
Arden Hills, MN

Katherine Meyers
Teacher
Chippewa Middle School
Shoreview, MN

Marsha O'Brien
Cochair, English Department
Eden Prairie High School
Eden Prairie, MN

Alice C. Richardson
Special Education Teacher
Central High School
Detroit, MI

Timothy Welshons
Cochair, English Department
Eden Prairie High School
Eden Prairie, MN

Printed in the United States of America

ISBN 0-7854-1829-6

Product Number 93032

A 0 9 8 7 6 5 4 3 2 1

Table of Contents

Overview

Lesson Plans

Unit 6 Humorous Literature 367

Appendixes

Indexes

Teacher's Resources

World Literature

Reading Level: 7-10 Fry

Student Text

World Literature opens the door to culturally diverse writers from around the world. Complete works and excerpts capture student interest and encourage engagement with the text. An Atlas and Student Passport to World Cultures in the student text help students understand the culture by providing location and background of various countries.

Vocabulary Workbook

Consumable workbook contains 37 activities that teach and reinforce the vocabulary for each selection. Also available on the Teacher's Resource Library (62 pages). Answer Key is also available.

Student Workbook

Consumable workbook contains 72 activities that reinforce and extend the selections from the text. Also available on the Teacher's Resource Library (91 pages). Answer Key is also available.

Teacher's Wraparound Edition

This full-color Teacher's Edition includes the complete student text with teaching strategies presented at point of use. Also includes the answers to all questions in the student's text.

Teacher's Resource Library CD-ROM (TRL) for Windows™ and Macintosh® TRL

Contains all the activities referenced in the teacher's edition. Over 400 activities are available to help teachers tailor instruction to meet the needs of their class. Includes answers to all activities.

Audiocassettes

The entire text is available on audiocassette for your auditory learners and students who need added reinforcement.

Transparencies

Overhead transparencies offer valuable teaching aids, including activities showing various types of graphic organizers.

Exploring Literature and *American Literature*

Reading Level: 7-10 Fry

Two inviting, full-color texts from AGS help make the vast world of fine literature available to your students.

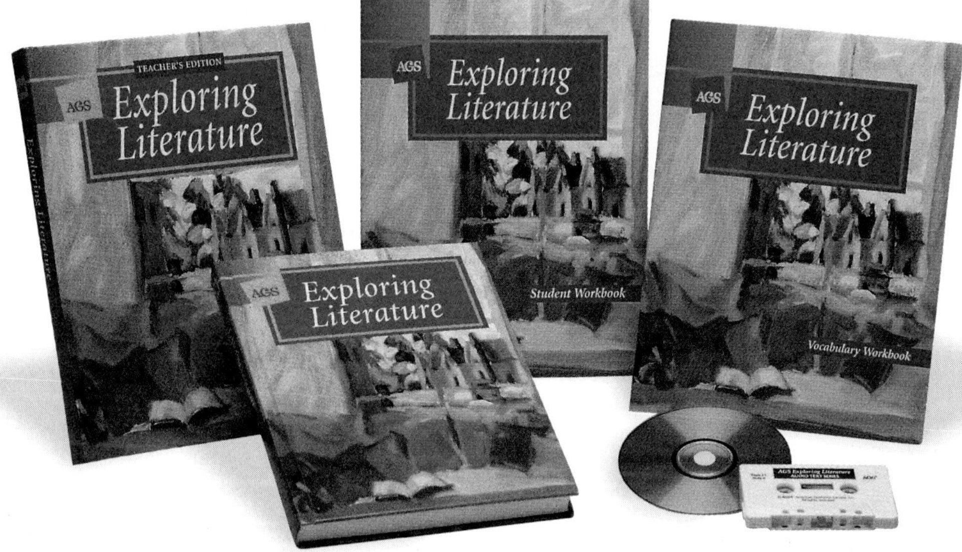

In *Exploring Literature,* students become acquainted with several genres and styles by reading tall tales, short stories, drama, and ballads. Works by Ray Bradbury, Gwendolyn Brooks, W. W. Jacobs, William Carlos Williams, and other outstanding writers introduce students to a diverse range of literature.

American Literature explores our literary heritage from the age of sail to the era of cyberspace. Selections are presented in chronological sequence to provide historical overviews. Literary periods and timelines illustrate the events occurring while the selections were written.

Both student texts are accompanied by valuable, carefully constructed support materials. The wraparound Teacher's Edition features skill charts, point-of-use teaching strategies, bibliographies, and unit planning guides. The comprehensive Teacher's Resource Library (TRL) on CD-ROM is available for Macintosh and Windows and allows you to review a multitude of activities—just select and print the materials you need. The TRL offers graphic organizers, selection glossaries, quizzes, genre-related activities, study guides, and testing materials.

In addition, a Student Workbook is available in print or on CD-ROM to help students with comprehension, literary analysis, interpretation, and study skills. A Vocabulary Workbook also is available in print or on CD-ROM. Featuring over 60 pages of vocabulary activities, this workbook helps students become familiar with key words.

Other support materials include recorded versions of the text to accommodate auditory learners or reluctant readers, and teaching transparencies that can be used to introduce selections, teach vocabulary, and show students how to organize information meaningfully.

AGS Classic Literature Series Extends Instruction

AGS Illustrated Classics

Reading Level: 3.8–4.8

To supplement your literature program, AGS offers a comprehensive collection of classic literature ideally suited for students reading below grade level. *AGS Illustrated Classics* is a wide-range collection of 72 books offered in six sets. The easy-reading books feature artwork on every page to capture and hold students' attention.

The collection includes works by many famous authors, including Mark Twain, H. G. Wells, Nathaniel Hawthorne, Helen Keller, Charles Dickens, Thomas Hardy, Jack London, Fyodor Dostoyevsky, Jane Austen, and also includes an entire set of the works of Shakespeare. For a complete list of all the titles in this series, please contact AGS.

Support materials include an 80-page Student Exercises Book and Read-Along Cassettes—word-for-word readings of the stories.

The *AGS Illustrated Classics* series makes it possible for more students to explore the world of classic literature at a reading level best suited to their needs.

AGS Classics Classroom Reading Plays

Reading Level: 3–4

AGS Classics Classroom Reading Plays offer students with lower-level reading abilities an entertaining alternative to silent reading. Students enjoy valuable practice in oral reading while acting out some of the greatest plays of all times.

This collection of 24 plays is divided into three categories—British, American, and Shakespeare. Each playscript is 32 pages and takes about one hour to perform.

The plays include *Treasure Island,* Robert Louis Stevenson; *Frankenstein,* Mary Shelley; *A Christmas Carol,* Charles Dickens; *Jane Eyre,* Charlotte Bronte; *Tom Sawyer,* Mark Twain; *The Last of the Mochicans,* James Fenimore Cooper; and *King Lear* and *Othello,* William Shakespeare. For a complete list, please contact AGS.

Teacher's Notes are included with each set of eight plays, and a sampler set also is available that includes one copy of each of the 24 playscripts.

AGS Classic Short Stories

Reading Level: 3–4

AGS Classic Short Stories provide an entertaining and nonthreatening opportunity for students to enjoy excellent literature at an easier reading level.

This collection of 150 stories in 50 books offers an abundance of illustrations that provide a visual reference of the characters and settings. Each book includes a biographical sketch of the author and discussion questions.

The *AGS Classic Short Stories* set is organized into five collections: *Great American Short Stories Collections 1, 2,* and *3; Stories from Great Britain and Ireland;* and *Stories from Around the World.*

Classic Short Stories are an ideal supplement to your literature program. Some of the famous authors included are:

Great American Short Stories Collection 1—Washington Irving, Nathaniel Hawthorne, Mark Twain, Willa Cather, Edgar Allan Poe

Great American Short Stories Collection 2—O. Henry, Stephen Crane, Edith Wharton, Ambrose Bierce, Jack London

Great American Short Stories Collection 3—Theodore Dreiser, Edna Ferber, Ring Lardner, Henry James, Mary Wilkins Freeman

Stories from Great Britain and Ireland—Sir Arthur Conan Doyle, Saki, Rudyard Kipling, Katherine Mansfield, Thomas Hardy, James Joyce

Stories from Around the World—Guy de Maupassant, Leo Tolstoy, Mori Ogwai, Rabindranath Tagore, Anton Chekhov

For a complete list of all the authors and titles, please contact AGS.

Students will enjoy reading such well-known stories as *Rip Van Winkle, The Tell-Tale Heart, The Gift of the Magi, The Ransom of Red Chief, The Yellow Cat, Araby, The Phantom Rickshaw,* and *The Necklace*—to name a few.

Student Text Highlights

Many special features in the student text enhance learning by making the content relevant to students.

- Students learn how to read various types of literature in a step-by-step method.
- A special section, "How to Use This Book," at the beginning of the text helps your students become more independent learners. Study skills taught in this section can be applied to all other subjects.
- Vocabulary strategies are offered to increase students' comprehension.

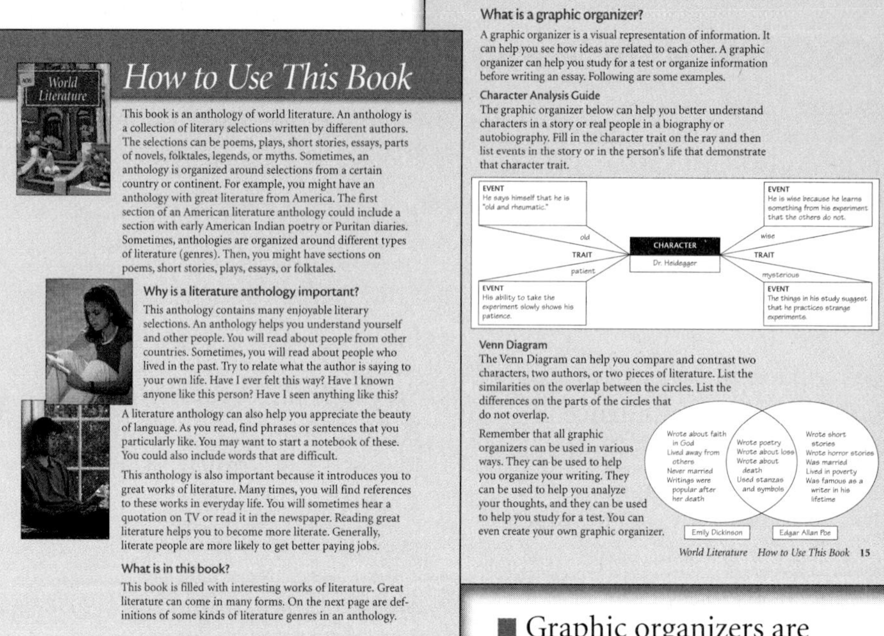

How to Use This Book

This book is an anthology of world literature. An anthology is a collection of literary selections written by different authors. The selections can be poems, plays, short stories, essays, parts of novels, folktales, legends, or myths. Sometimes, an anthology is organized around selections from a certain country or continent. For example, you might have an anthology with great literature from America. The first section of an American literature anthology could include a section with early American Indian poetry or Puritan diaries. Sometimes, anthologies are organized around different types of literature (genres). Then, you might have sections on poems, short stories, plays, essays, or folktales.

Why is a literature anthology important?

This anthology contains many enjoyable literary selections. An anthology helps you understand yourself and other people. You will read about people from other countries. Sometimes, you will read about people who lived in the past. Try to relate what the author is saying to your own life. Have I ever felt this way? Have I known anyone like this person? Have I seen anything like this?

A literature anthology can also help you appreciate the beauty of language. As you read, find phrases or sentences that you particularly like. You may want to start a notebook of these. You could also include words that are difficult.

This anthology is also important because it introduces you to great works of literature. Many times, you will find references to these works in everyday life. You will sometimes hear a quotation on TV or read it in the newspaper. Reading great literature helps you to become more literate. Generally, literate people are more likely to get better paying jobs.

What is in this book?

This book is filled with interesting works of literature. Great literature can come in many forms. On the next page are definitions of some kinds of literature genres in an anthology.

What is a graphic organizer?

A graphic organizer is a visual representation of information. It can help you see how ideas are related to each other. A graphic organizer can help you study for a test or organize information before writing an essay. Following are some examples.

Character Analysis Guide

The graphic organizer below can help you better understand characters in a story or real people in a biography or autobiography. Fill in the character trait on the ray and then list events in the story or in the person's life that demonstrate that character trait.

EVENT
He says himself that he is "old and rheumatic."
EVENT
He is wise because he learns something from his experiment that the others do not.
old
TRAIT
CHARACTER
Dr. Heidegger
wise
TRAIT
patient
mysterious
EVENT
His ability to take the experiment slowly shows his patience.
EVENT
The things in his study suggest that he practices strange experiments.

Venn Diagram

The Venn Diagram can help you compare and contrast two characters, two authors, or two pieces of literature. List the similarities on the overlap between the circles. List the differences on the parts of the circles that do not overlap.

Remember that all graphic organizers can be used in various ways. They can be used to help you organize your writing. They can be used to help you analyze your thoughts, and they can be used to help you study for a test. You can even create your own graphic organizer.

Wrote about faith in God
Lived away from others
Never married
Writings were popular after her death
Wrote poetry
Wrote about loss
Wrote about death
Used stanzas and symbols
Wrote short stories
Wrote horror stories
Was married
Lived in poverty
Was famous as a writer in his lifetime
Emily Dickinson
Edgar Allan Poe

World Literature How to Use This Book 15

- Graphic organizers are introduced as a way to help students better understand the selections.

UNIT 1 *Fiction*

How long have people told stories? Probably as long as they have been able to talk. People made up stories to explain things like why the sky is blue or ducks have webbed feet. They created stories to entertain themselves. Some stories are scary. Some are funny. Some are short. Others are very long. No matter where in the world you go, people tell stories and have always told stories. In this unit, you will enjoy stories from the nine different countries shown on the map on the next page.

"You know that fiction...is possibly the roughest trade of all in writing...You have the sheet of blank paper, the pencil, and the obligation to invent truer than things can be true."
—Ernest Hemingway

"It is not a bad thing in a tale that you understand only half of it."
—Isak Dinesen

Unit 1 Selections Page

Fiction Unit 1

Europe

422 *Appendix B World Atlas*

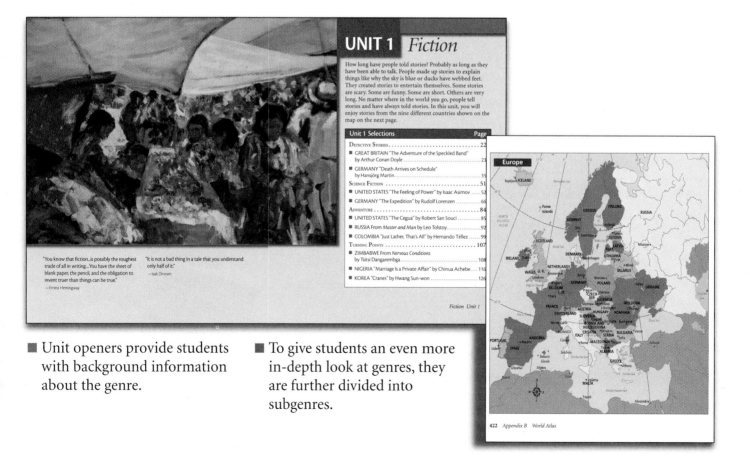

- Unit openers provide students with background information about the genre.
- To give students an even more in-depth look at genres, they are further divided into subgenres.

- Students are introduced to the selection with a picture of the author and a brief explanation about the author's life.
- Culturally diverse authors address a wide range of topics.
- Literary terms are highlighted to help students comprehend the selection.
- A brief explanation is provided to set the stage for reading.
- Inset maps help students identify where an author's country is. This helps students find the maps quickly in the World Atlas.

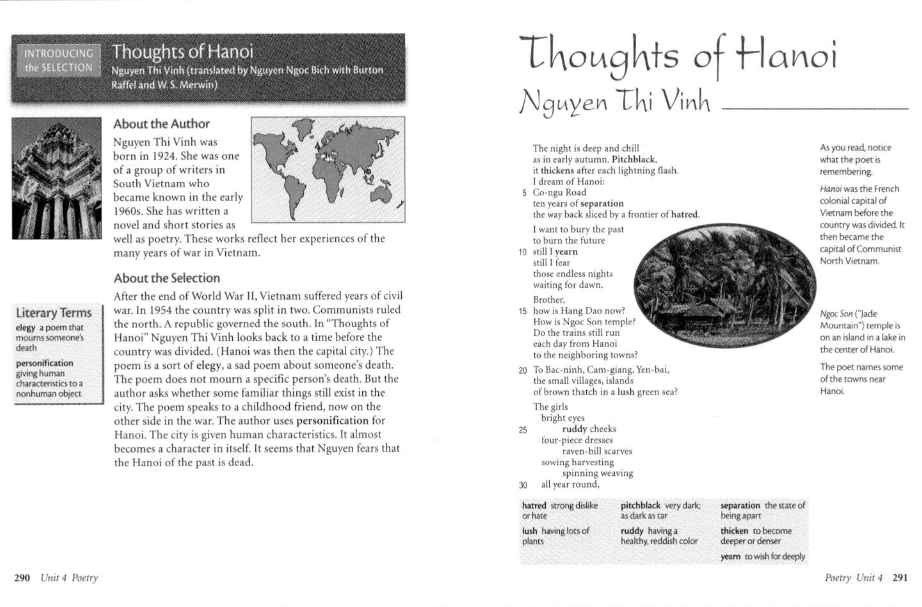

INTRODUCING the SELECTION

Thoughts of Hanoi

Nguyen Thi Vinh (translated by Nguyen Ngoc Bich with Burton Raffel and W. S. Merwin)

About the Author

Nguyen Thi Vinh was born in 1924. She was one of a group of writers in South Vietnam who became known in the early 1960s. She has written a novel and short stories as well as poetry. These works reflect her experiences of the many years of war in Vietnam.

About the Selection

After the end of World War II, Vietnam suffered years of civil war. In 1954 the country was split in two. Communists ruled the north. A republic governed the south. In "Thoughts of Hanoi" Nguyen Thi Vinh looks back to a time before the country was divided. (Hanoi was then the capital city.) The poem is a sort of **elegy**, a sad poem about someone's death. The poem does not mourn a specific person's death. But the author asks whether some familiar things still exist in the city. The poem speaks to a childhood friend, now on the other side in the war. The author uses **personification** for Hanoi. The city is given human characteristics. It almost becomes a character in itself. It seems that Nguyen fears that the Hanoi of the past is dead.

Literary Terms

elegy a poem that mourns someone's death

personification giving human characteristics to a nonhuman object

290 *Unit 4 Poetry*

Thoughts of Hanoi

Nguyen Thi Vinh

The night is deep and chill
as in early autumn. **Pitchblack,**
it **thickens** after each lightning flash.
I dream of Hanoi:
Co-ngu Road
ten years of **separation**
the way back sliced by a frontier of **hatred.**

I want to bury the past
to burn the future
still I **yearn**
still I fear
those endless nights
waiting for dawn.

Brother,
how is Hang Dao now?
How is Ngoc Son temple?
Do the trains still run
each day from Hanoi
to the neighboring towns?
To Bac-ninh, Cam-giang, Yen-bai,
the small villages, islands
of brown thatch in a **lush** green sea?

The girls
bright eyes
ruddy cheeks
four-piece dresses
raven-bill scarves
sowing harvesting
spinning weaving
all year round,

As you read, notice what the poet is remembering.

Hanoi was the French colonial capital of Vietnam before the country was divided. It then became the capital of Communist North Vietnam.

Ngoc Son ("Jade Mountain") temple is on an island in a lake in the center of Hanoi.

The poet names some of the towns near Hanoi.

hatred strong dislike or hate

lush having lots of plants

pitchblack very dark; as dark as tar

ruddy having a healthy, reddish color

separation the state of being apart

thicken to become deeper or denser

yearn to wish for deeply

Poetry Unit 4 291

- Reader's Response marginal notes promote better comprehension by reminding students of various aspects of the selection.
- Vocabulary words are in bold and defined at the bottom of the page for easy reference. The Glossary at the back of the book also includes these words with their definitions.

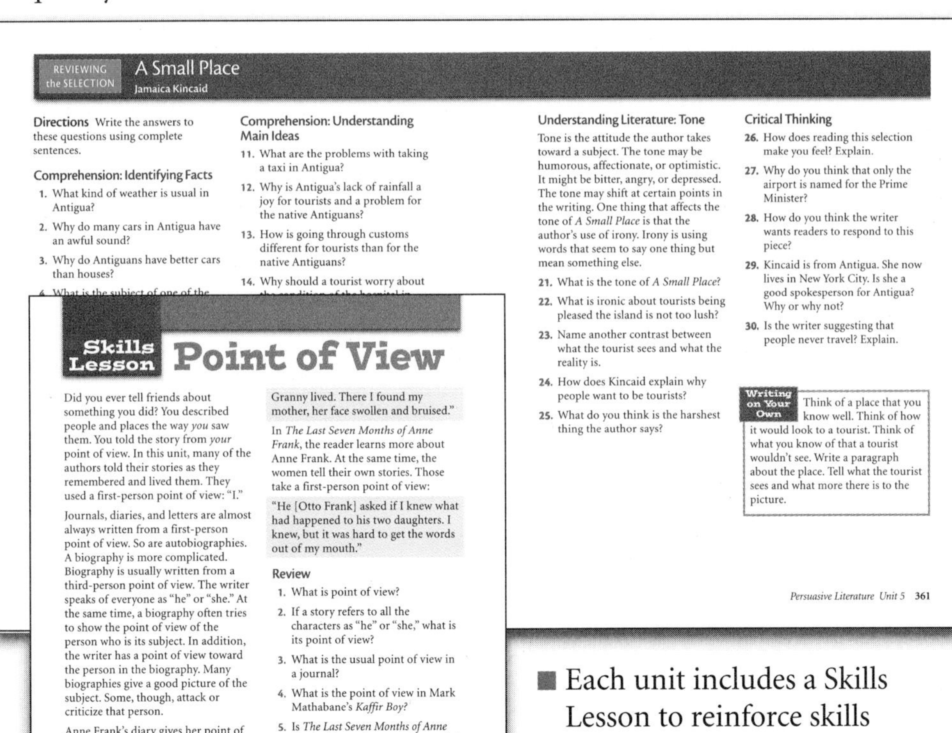

REVIEWING the SELECTION

A Small Place

Jamaica Kincaid

Directions Write the answers to these questions using complete sentences.

Comprehension: Identifying Facts

1. What kind of weather is usual in Antigua?
2. Why do many cars in Antigua have an awful sound?
3. Why do Antiguans have better cars than houses?
4. What is the subject of one of the

Comprehension: Understanding Main Ideas

11. What are the problems with taking a taxi in Antigua?
12. Why is Antigua's lack of rainfall a joy for tourists and a problem for the native Antiguans?
13. How is going through customs different for tourists than for the native Antiguans?
14. Why should a tourist worry about

Understanding Literature: Tone

Tone is the attitude the author takes toward a subject. The tone may be humorous, affectionate, or optimistic. It might be bitter, angry, or depressed. The tone may shift at certain points in the writing. One thing that affects the tone of *A Small Place* is that the author's use of irony. Irony is using words that seem to say one thing but mean something else.

21. What is the tone of *A Small Place*?
22. What is ironic about tourists being pleased the island is not too lush?
23. Name another contrast between what the tourist sees and what the reality is.
24. How does Kincaid explain why people want to be tourists?
25. What do you think is the harshest thing the author says?

Critical Thinking

26. How does reading this selection make you feel? Explain.
27. Why do you think that only the airport is named for the Prime Minister?
28. How do you think the writer wants readers to respond to this piece?
29. Kincaid is from Antigua. She now lives in New York City. Is she a good spokesperson for Antigua? Why or why not?
30. Is the writer suggesting that people never travel? Explain.

Writing on Your Own Think of a place that you know well. Think of how it would look to a tourist. Think of what you know of that a tourist wouldn't see. Write a paragraph about the place. Tell what the tourist sees and what more there is to the picture.

Persuasive Literature Unit 5 361

Skills Lesson

Point of View

Did you ever tell friends about something you did? You described people and places the way *you* saw them. You told the story from *your* point of view. In this unit, many of the authors told their stories as they remembered and lived them. They used a first-person point of view: "I."

Journals, diaries, and letters are almost always written from a first-person point of view. So are autobiographies. A biography is more complicated. Biography is usually written from a third-person point of view. The writer speaks of everyone as "he" or "she." At the same time, a biography often tries to show the point of view of the person who is its subject. In addition, the writer has a point of view toward the person in the biography. Many biographies give a good picture of the subject. Some, though, attack or criticize that person.

Anne Frank's diary gives her point of view:

"Margot and I are getting a bit tired of our parents."

The reader sees Mark Mathabane's school and family through his eyes, too:

"I ran, without stopping, all the way to the other end of the township where Granny lived. There I found my mother, her face swollen and bruised."

In *The Last Seven Months of Anne Frank*, the reader learns more about Anne Frank. At the same time, the women tell their own stories. Those take a first-person point of view:

"He [Otto Frank] asked if I knew what had happened to his two daughters. I knew, but it was hard to get the words out of my mouth."

Review

1. What is point of view?
2. If a story refers to all the characters as "he" or "she," what is its point of view?
3. What is the usual point of view in a journal?
4. What is the point of view in Mark Mathabane's *Kaffir Boy?*
5. Is *The Last Seven Months of Anne Frank* a biography or autobiography?

Writing on Your Own Write a short paragraph about something you have done. Use the first-person point of view. Underline the words in the paragraph that show your point of view.

228 *Unit 2 Nonfiction*

- At the end of each selection students are asked a variety of questions to check for understanding, including:
  - –Comprehension: Identifying Facts
  - –Comprehension: Understanding Main Ideas
  - –Understanding Literature
  - –Critical Thinking
- A "Writing on Your Own" writing activity accompanies each selection.
- Each unit includes a Skills Lesson to reinforce skills taught during the unit.
- Students are encouraged to apply these skills in a writing exercise.

Teacher's Edition Highlights

UNIT 3 Planning Guide

Drama

	Selection Features					
	Student Pages	About the Author	About the Selection	Literary Terms	Reviewing the Selection	Writing on Your Own
■ ENGLAND From *Macbeth* by William Shakespeare	237–249	✔	✔	✔	✔	✔
■ SOUTH AFRICA From *"Master Harold"... and the Boys* by Athol Fugard	251–264	✔	✔	✔	✔	✔
■ SWEDEN *The Stronger* by August Strindberg	266–275	✔	✔	✔	✔	✔
■ SKILLS LESSON: Characterization; UNIT REVIEW	276, 278–279			✔		✔

	Teaching Strategies							Language Skills			
	Viewing the Art	Career Connection	Environmental Connection	Cross-Curricular Connection	Diversity Connection	Community Connection	Transparencies	Grammar	Literary Elements	Comprehension	Writing Connection
■ ENGLAND From *Macbeth* by William Shakespeare	238, 241	241		242				240	243	246	247
■ SOUTH AFRICA From *"Master Harold"... and the Boys* by Athol Fugard			255	254	260	262			252		259
■ SWEDEN *The Stronger* by August Strindberg	269	268	269	271	270			273		272	
■ SKILLS LESSON: Characterization; UNIT REVIEW							9				

	Learning Styles					TRL Teacher's Resource Library					
	Auditory	Visual	Tactile/Kinesthetic	Group Learning	LEP/ESL	Vocabulary Workbook	Selection Glossary	Student Study Guide	Activities	Workbook	Writing Activities
■ ENGLAND From *Macbeth* by William Shakespeare	239	244		245		23	23	29	37	37	**25**
■ SOUTH AFRICA From *"Master Harold"... and the Boys* by Athol Fugard			254	261	256	24	24	30	39	39	**26**
■ SWEDEN *The Stronger* by August Strindberg						25	25	31	41	41	**27**
■ SKILLS LESSON: Characterization; UNIT REVIEW									42	42	**28**

Unit Features

Student Text
Drama
Classical Drama
Realistic Drama
Expressionistic Drama
Skills Lesson: Characterization
Unit Summary

Teacher's Resource Library
Activity 35: Drama
Workbook 35: Drama
Activity 36: Classical Drama
Workbook 36: Classical Drama
Activity 38: Realistic Drama
Workbook 38: Realistic Drama
Activity 40: Expressionistic Drama
Workbook 40: Expressionistic Drama

Assessment Features

Student Text
Unit 3 Review

Teacher's Resource Library
Activity 42: Unit 3 Review, pages 1–2
Workbook 42: Unit 3 Review, pages 1–2
Selection Quizzes 23–25
Unit 3 Mastery Tests A and B, pages 1–2
Midterm Mastery Test, pages 1–4

TRL Alternative Selection

The Alternative Selection can be found in the Teacher's Resource Library.

Alternative Selection 3:
Macbeth by William Shakespeare

232A *Unit 3 Drama*

Drama Unit 3 232B

Unit Planning Guides

- The AGS Planning Guides save valuable preparation time by organizing all materials in each unit.
- Contains a complete listing of all lessons so you can preview the units quickly.
- Assessment options are highlighted for easy reference. These include:
  –review activities
  –selection quizzes
  –unit mastery tests, forms A and B
  –midterm mastery test
  –end-of-book mastery test
- Alternative selections are listed as options to help you tailor instruction to meet your students' needs.
- All activities from the Teacher's Resource Library CD-ROM are listed. These include:
  –selection activities
  –student study guides
  –workbook activities
  –mastery tests
  –vocabulary activities
  –selection glossary
  –writing activities
  –selection quizzes
- Learning styles: teaching strategies are provided to help teachers meet the needs of students with diverse learning styles. Modalities included are:
  –Visual activities
  –Tactile/kinesthetic activities
  –Auditory activities
  –ESL/LEP activities
  –Group learning

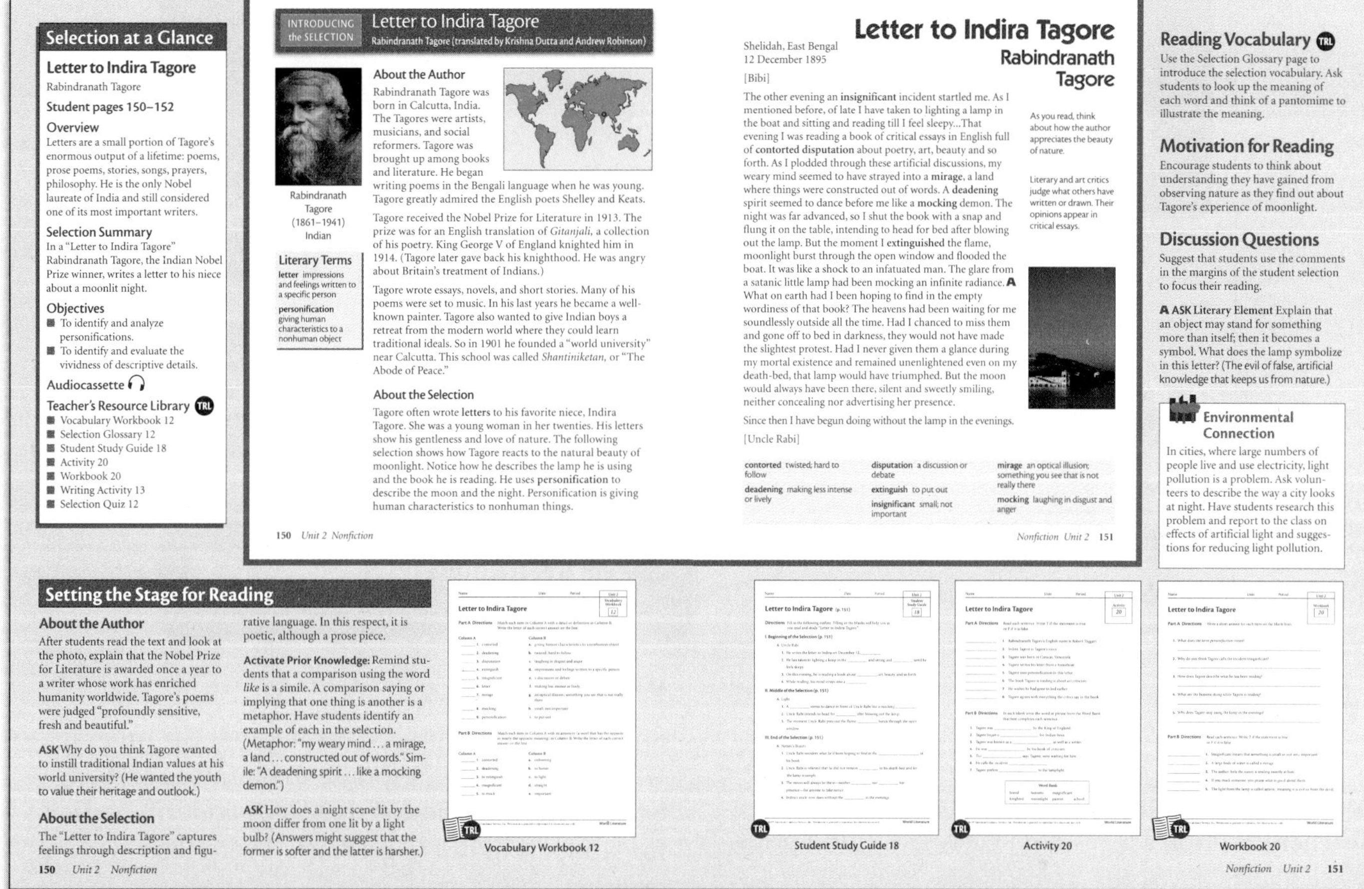

Selection at a Glance

Letter to Indira Tagore
Rabindranath Tagore
Student pages 150–152

Overview
Letters are a small portion of Tagore's enormous output of a lifetime: poems, prose poems, stories, songs, prayers, philosophy. He is the only Nobel laureate of India and still considered one of its most important writers.

Selection Summary
In a "Letter to Indira Tagore" Rabindranath Tagore, the Indian Nobel Prize winner, writes a letter to his niece about a moonlit night.

Objectives
- To identify and analyze personifications.
- To identify and evaluate the vividness of descriptive details.

Audiocassette

Teacher's Resource Library TRL
- Vocabulary Workbook 12
- Selection Glossary 12
- Student Study Guide 18
- Activity 20
- Workbook 20
- Writing Activity 13
- Selection Quiz 12

INTRODUCING the SELECTION **Letter to Indira Tagore**
Rabindranath Tagore (translated by Krishna Dutta and Andrew Robinson)

Rabindranath Tagore (1861–1941) Indian

About the Author
Rabindranath Tagore was born in Calcutta, India. The Tagores were artists, musicians, and social reformers. Tagore was brought up among books and literature. He began writing poems in the Bengali language when he was young. Tagore greatly admired the English poets Shelley and Keats.

Tagore received the Nobel Prize for Literature in 1913. The prize was for an English translation of *Gitanjali*, a collection of his poetry. King George V of England knighted him in 1914. (Tagore later gave back his knighthood. He was angry about Britain's treatment of Indians.)

Tagore wrote essays, novels, and short stories. Many of his poems were set to music. In his last years he became a well-known painter. Tagore also wanted to give Indian boys a retreat from the modern world where they could learn traditional ideals. So in 1901 he founded a "world university" near Calcutta. This school was called *Shantiniketan*, or "The Abode of Peace."

Literary Terms
letter impressions and feelings written to a specific person
personification giving human characteristics to a nonhuman object

About the Selection
Tagore often wrote **letters** to his favorite niece, Indira Tagore. She was a young woman in her twenties. His letters show his gentleness and love of nature. The following selection shows how Tagore reacts to the natural beauty of moonlight. Notice how he describes the lamp he is using and the book he is reading. He uses **personification** to describe the moon and the night. Personification is giving human characteristics to nonhuman things.

150 *Unit 2 Nonfiction*

Letter to Indira Tagore
Rabindranath Tagore

Shelidah, East Bengal
12 December 1895
[Bibi]

The other evening an **insignificant** incident startled me. As I mentioned before, of late I have taken to lighting a lamp in the boat and sitting and reading till I feel sleepy...That evening I was reading a book of critical essays in English full of **contorted disputation** about poetry, art, beauty and so forth. As I plodded through these artificial discussions, my weary mind seemed to have strayed into a **mirage**, a land where things were constructed out of words. A **deadening** spirit seemed to dance before me like a **mocking** demon. The night was far advanced, so I shut the book with a snap and flung it on the table, intending to head for bed after blowing out the lamp. But the moment I **extinguished** the flame, moonlight burst through the open window and flooded the boat. It was like a shock to an infatuated man. The glare from a satanic little lamp had been mocking an infinite radiance. **A** What on earth had I been hoping to find in the empty wordiness of that book? The heavens had been waiting for me soundlessly outside all the time. Had I chanced to miss them and gone off to bed in darkness, they would not have made the slightest protest. Had I never given them a glance during my mortal existence and remained unenlightened even on my death-bed, that lamp would have triumphed. But the moon would always have been there, silent and sweetly smiling, neither concealing nor advertising her presence.

Since then I have begun doing without the lamp in the evenings.
[Uncle Rabi]

As you read, think about how the author appreciates the beauty of nature.

Literary and art critics judge what others have written or drawn. Their opinions appear in critical essays.

contorted twisted; hard to follow
deadening making less intense or lively
disputation a discussion or debate
extinguish to put out
insignificant small; not important
mirage an optical illusion; something you see that is not really there
mocking laughing in disgust and anger

Nonfiction Unit 2 151

Reading Vocabulary TRL
Use the Selection Glossary page to introduce the selection vocabulary. Ask students to look up the meaning of each word and think of a pantomime to illustrate the meaning.

Motivation for Reading
Encourage students to think about understanding they have gained from observing nature as they find out about Tagore's experience of moonlight.

Discussion Questions
Suggest that students use the comments in the margins of the student selection to focus their reading.

A ASK Literary Element Explain that an object may stand for something more than itself; then it becomes a symbol. What does the lamp symbolize in this letter? (The evil of false, artificial knowledge that keeps us from nature.)

Environmental Connection
In cities, where large numbers of people live and use electricity, light pollution is a problem. Ask volunteers to describe the way a city looks at night. Have students research this problem and report to the class on effects of artificial light and suggestions for reducing light pollution.

Setting the Stage for Reading

About the Author
After students read the text and look at the photo, explain that the Nobel Prize for Literature is awarded once a year to a writer whose work has enriched humanity worldwide. Tagore's poems were judged "profoundly sensitive, fresh and beautiful."

ASK Why do you think Tagore wanted to instill traditional Indian values at his world university? (He wanted the youth to value their heritage and outlook.)

About the Selection
The "Letter to Indira Tagore" captures feelings through description and figurative language. In this respect, it is poetic, although a prose piece.

Activate Prior Knowledge: Remind students that a comparison using the word *like* is a simile. A comparison saying or implying that one thing is another is a metaphor. Have students identify an example of each in the selection. (Metaphor: "my weary mind . . . a mirage, a land . . . constructed out of words." Simile: "A deadening spirit . . . like a mocking demon.")

ASK How does a night scene lit by the moon differ from one lit by a light bulb? (Answers might suggest that the former is softer and the latter is harsher.)

150 *Unit 2 Nonfiction*

Vocabulary Workbook 12

Student Study Guide 18

Activity 20

Workbook 20

Nonfiction Unit 2 151

Selections

- Quick overviews of the units and selections save teacher-planning time.
- Each *Selection at a Glance* lists all materials and objectives of the lesson for quick reference.
- Teaching strategies are highlighted.
- Career applications are listed for easy reference.
- Comprehension questions and answers are provided to stimulate discussion.
- Objectives are listed for easy reference.
- Page references are provided for convenience.
- All materials needed for the selections are listed.
- Audiocassettes are referenced with lessons and are available for students who need added reinforcement.
- Transparencies are referenced with appropriate lessons.
- An introductory discussion or activity opens each lesson by activating prior knowledge and setting the stage for learning.
- Answers are provided for all questions.
- Activity pages from the Teacher's Resource Library (TRL) are featured at point of use.
- Discussion questions are provided to help students understand the selections.

Teacher's Resource Library

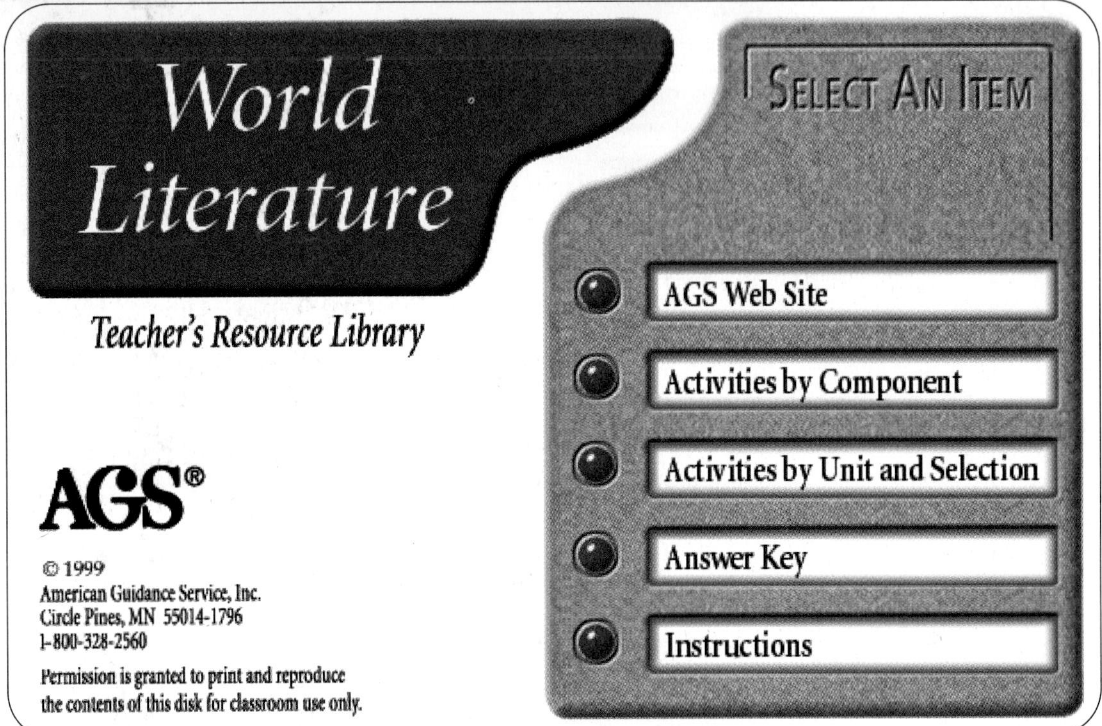

World Literature
Teacher's Resource Library
AGS®
© 1999
American Guidance Service, Inc.
Circle Pines, MN 55014-1796
1-800-328-2560
Permission is granted to print and reproduce the contents of this disk for classroom use only.
SELECT AN ITEM
AGS Web Site
Activities by Component
Activities by Unit and Selection
Answer Key
Instructions

TRL All the activities you'll need to reinforce and extend the text are conveniently located on the AGS Teacher's Resource Library (TRL) CD-ROM. All the reproducible activities featured in the Teacher's Edition are ready to view, select, and print.

Vocabulary Workbook

Vocabulary activities to accompany all selections are included. Also available in workbook format.

Selection Glossary

To further help your students comprehend each selection, all potentially difficult terms are included in the selection glossary.

Student Study Guide

Provide your students with an organized method to take notes and organize their reading with this outline for each selection.

Activities

Selection activities are available to reinforce and extend skills and comprehension questions from the selections.

Workbook

Activities that reinforce and extend the selections are included. Also available in workbook format.

Writing Activities

Students are encouraged throughout the program to write frequently in response to literature and to extend themes. These activities provide an outline for students to use to get started with their writing projects.

Selection Quizzes

Teachers may reproduce the selection quizzes from each selection.

Mastery Tests

Unit, midterm, and end-of-book mastery tests are conveniently referenced.

Alternative Selections

With some selections teachers have the option of using an alternative selection to the one in the student's text. These are adaptations of selections in the text, or adaptations of other works by these authors. They are intended for use with students having difficulty with the regular text. The entire alternative selection is included in the TRL for quick retrieval.

World Literature Scope and Sequence of Skills

- ✔ Reading Comprehension
- ✔ Literary Skills
- ✔ Critical Thinking
- ✔ Composition
- ✔ Speaking and Listening
- ✔ Process Writing
- ✔ Study Skills

Reading Comprehension	Unit 1	Unit 2	Unit 3	Unit 4	Unit 5	Unit 6
Analyzing Information	X	X	X	X	X	X
Antagonist	X	X	X	X	X	X
Author's Purpose	X	X	X	X	X	X
Author's Use of Language	X	X	X	X	X	X
Cause and Effect			X			
Character Traits	X					
Comparing and Contrasting	X				X	
Details	X	X	X	X	X	X
Drawing Conclusions	X	X	X	X	X	X
Evaluations	X	X	X	X	X	X
Facts and Opinions	X	X	X	X	X	X
Figurative Language				X		
Finding Evidence	X	X	X	X	X	X
Generalizations	X	X	X	X	X	X
Humor	X		X			X
Inferences	X	X	X	X	X	X
Letters		X			X	
Main Ideas	X	X	X	X	X	X
Making Judgments	X	X	X	X	X	X
Predicting	X	X	X	X	X	X
Protagonist	X	X	X	X	X	X
Sentence Meanings	X	X	X	X	X	X
Sequence	X	X	X	X	X	X
Speech/Oration					X	
Summarizing	X	X	X	X	X	X
Symbols	X			X		
Verifying Conclusions	X	X	X	X	X	X
Vocabulary	X	X	X	X	X	X

World Literature Scope and Sequence of Skills

Literary Skills	Unit 1	Unit 2	Unit 3	Unit 4	Unit 5	Unit 6
Action	X					
Anecdote						X
Antagonist	X	X	X	X	X	X
Autobiography		X				
Biography		X				
Characterization			X			
Comparison and Contrast	X	X	X	X	X	X
Conflict	X	X	X	X	X	X
Denouement	X					
Dialogue		X	X			X
Diary/Journal		X				
Drama			X			
Essay		X			X	
Exaggeration		X				X
Fiction	X					
Figurative Language	X	X	X	X	X	X
Figures of Speech		X		X	X	
First Person	X	X	X	X	X	X
Flashback	X		X			
Foreshadowing	X	X	X		X	X
Free Verse				X		
Genre	X	X	X	X	X	X
Imagery				X	X	
Irony	X				X	X
Letter		X				
Metaphor				X	X	
Mood				X		
Moral				X		

World Literature Scope and Sequence of Skills

Literary Skills, Continued	Unit 1	Unit 2	Unit 3	Unit 4	Unit 5	Unit 6
Mystery/Suspense	X					
Myth		X				
Nonfiction		X			X	
Novel	X					
Personification		X		X		
Plot	X	X	X			X
Poetry				X		
Point of View	X	X				
Prose				X		
Protagonist	X	X	X	X	X	X
Rhyme				X		
Rhythm				X		
Rising Action	X					
Sarcasm						X
Satire		X				X
Science Fiction	X					
Sequence	X					
Setting	X	X	X	X	X	X
Short Story	X					
Simile				X		
Speeches					X	
Style/Technique	X			X	X	
Surrealism				X		
Symbol	X			X		
Theme	X	X				X
Third Person		X				
Tone					X	X
Turning Point	X	X				

World Literature Scope and Sequence of Skills

Critical Thinking	Unit 1	Unit 2	Unit 3	Unit 4	Unit 5	Unit 6
Analyzing Author's Purpose	X	X	X	X	X	X
Analyzing Effect of Setting	X	X	X	X	X	
Analyzing Point of View	X	X				
Analyzing Sequence in a Story	X					
Applying Information	X	X	X	X	X	X
Classifying/Categorizing	X	X	X	X	X	X
Comparing and Contrasting	X	X	X	X	X	X
Drawing Conclusions	X	X	X	X	X	X
Evaluating Biographical Subjects	X	X	X	X	X	X
Evaluating Inferences	X					
Finding Relevant Evidence	X	X	X	X	X	X
Identifying Cause/Effect			X	X		
Identifying Exaggeration						X
Improving Reading Comprehension	X	X	X	X	X	X
Inductive/Deductive Reasoning	X	X	X	X	X	X
Interpreting Figurative Language				X		
Interpreting Sensory Words				X		
Interpreting Symbols	X			X	X	
Making Comparisons	X	X	X	X	X	X
Making Inferences	X	X	X	X	X	X
Making Observations	X	X	X	X	X	X
Organizing Information	X	X	X	X	X	X
Paraphrasing Poetry				X		
Predicting Outcomes	X	X	X	X	X	X
Recognizing Persuasive Techniques					X	
Recognizing Relationships	X	X	X	X	X	X
Recognizing Relevant Details		X				
Recognizing Sequence/Order		X				
Separating Details		X				
Separating Fact/Assumption	X	X	X	X	X	X
Summarizing an Essay/Poem				X	X	
Supporting Opinions with Facts	X	X	X	X	X	X
Understanding Main Ideas	X	X	X	X	X	X

World Literature Scope and Sequence of Skills

Composition	Unit 1	Unit 2	Unit 3	Unit 4	Unit 5	Unit 6
Characterization			X			
Creative Writing	X	X	X	X	X	X
Descriptive Paragraphs	X	X				
Dialogue						X
Drama			X			
Essays	X					
Fiction	X					
Humorous Writing						X
Imagery				X		
Journalism		X				
Nonfiction		X			X	
Personification		X				
Persuasive Writing					X	
Plot	X					
Poetry				X		
Point of View	X	X				
Setting					X	
Style				X		
Speaking and Listening	**Unit 1**	**Unit 2**	**Unit 3**	**Unit 4**	**Unit 5**	**Unit 6**
Dialogue	X	X	X			
Dramatic Reading				X	X	
Essay or Composition		X				
Fiction Analysis	X					
Legend		X				
Play/Scene			X			
Plot/Theme Discussion	X	X	X	X	X	X
Poem				X		
Speech		X			X	X
Process Writing	**Unit 1**	**Unit 2**	**Unit 3**	**Unit 4**	**Unit 5**	**Unit 6**
Prewrite	X	X	X	X	X	X
Write	X	X	X	X	X	X
Revise	X	X	X	X	X	X
Proofread	X	X	X	X	X	X
Evaluate	X	X	X	X	X	X
Study Skills	**Unit 1**	**Unit 2**	**Unit 3**	**Unit 4**	**Unit 5**	**Unit 6**
Graphic Organizers	X	X	X	X	X	X
Reader Response Notes	X	X	X	X	X	X
Test-Taking Strategies	X	X	X	X	X	X
Vocabulary	X	X	X	X	X	X

Dictionary of Basic English

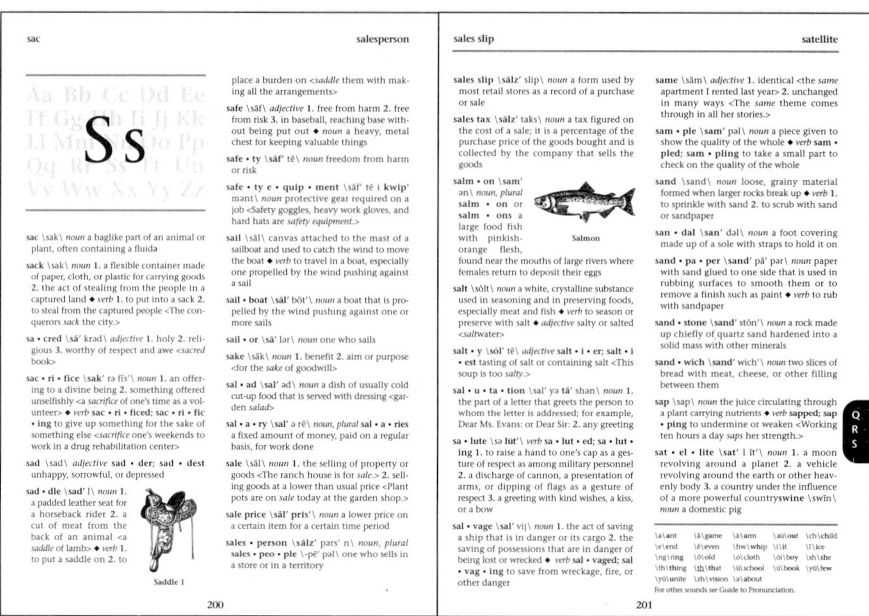

sac | salesperson

Ss

sac \sak\ *noun* a baglike part of an animal or plant, often containing a fluida

sack \sak\ *noun* **1.** a flexible container made of paper, cloth, or plastic for carrying goods **2.** the act of stealing from the people in a captured land ◆ *verb* **1.** to put into a sack **2.** to steal from the captured people <The conquerors *sack* the city.>

sa • cred \sā' krəd\ *adjective* **1.** holy **2.** religious **3.** worthy of respect and awe <*sacred* book>

sac • ri • fice \sak' rə fīs'\ *noun* **1.** an offering to a divine being **2.** something offered unselfishly <a *sacrifice* of one's time as a volunteer> ◆ *verb* **sac • ri • ficed; sac • ri • fic • ing** to give up something for the sake of something else <*sacrifice* one's weekends to work in a drug rehabilitation center>

sad \sad\ *adjective* **sad • der; sad • dest** unhappy, sorrowful, or depressed

sad • dle \sad' l\ *noun* **1.** a padded leather seat for a horseback rider **2.** a cut of meat from the back of an animal <a *saddle* of lamb> ◆ *verb* **1.** to put a saddle on **2.** to place a burden on <*saddle* them with making all the arrangements>

Saddle 1

safe \sāf\ *adjective* **1.** free from harm **2.** free from risk **3.** in baseball, reaching base without being put out ◆ *noun* a heavy, metal chest for keeping valuable things

safe • ty \sāf' tē\ *noun* freedom from harm or risk

safe • ty e • quip • ment \sāf' tē i **kwip'** mənt\ *noun* protective gear required on a job <Safety goggles, heavy work gloves, and hard hats are *safety equipment.*>

sail \sāl\ canvas attached to the mast of a sailboat and used to catch the wind to move the boat ◆ *verb* to travel in a boat, especially one propelled by the wind pushing against a sail

sail • boat \sāl' bōt'\ *noun* a boat that is propelled by the wind pushing against one or more sails

sail • or \sā' lər\ *noun* one who sails

sake \sāk\ *noun* **1.** benefit **2.** aim or purpose <for the *sake* of goodwill>

sal • ad \sal' əd\ *noun* a dish of usually cold cut-up food that is served with dressing <garden *salad*>

sal • a • ry \sal' ə rē\ *noun, plural* **sal • a • ries** a fixed amount of money, paid on a regular basis, for work done

sale \sāl\ *noun* **1.** the selling of property or goods <The ranch house is for *sale*.> **2.** selling goods at a lower than usual price <Plant pots are on *sale* today at the garden shop.>

sale price \sāl' prīs'\ *noun* a lower price on a certain item for a certain time period

sales • person \sālz' pərs' n\ *noun, plural* **sales • peo • ple** \-pē' pəl\ one who sells in a store or in a territory

200

sales slip | satellite

sales slip \sālz' slip\ *noun* a form used by most retail stores as a record of a purchase or sale

sales tax \sālz' taks\ *noun* a tax figured on the cost of a sale; it is a percentage of the purchase price of the goods bought and is collected by the company that sells the goods

salm • on \sam' ən\ *noun, plural* **salm • on** or **salm • ons** a large food fish with pinkish-orange flesh, found near the mouths of large rivers where females return to deposit their eggs

Salmon

salt \sölt\ *noun* a white, crystalline substance used in seasoning and in preserving foods, especially meat and fish ◆ *verb* to season or preserve with salt ◆ *adjective* salty or salted <*salt*water>

salt • y \söl' tē\ *adjective* **salt • i • er; salt • i • est** tasting of salt or containing salt <This soup is too *salty*.>

sal • u • ta • tion \sal' yə **tā'** shən\ *noun* **1.** the part of a letter that greets the person to whom the letter is addressed; for example, Dear Ms. Evans: or Dear Sir: **2.** any greeting

sa • lute \sə **lüt'**\ *verb* **sa • lut • ed; sa • lut • ing** **1.** to raise a hand to one's cap as a gesture of respect as among military personnel **2.** a discharge of cannon, a presentation of arms, or dipping of flags as a gesture of respect **3.** a greeting with kind wishes, a kiss, or a bow

sal • vage \sal' vij\ *noun* **1.** the act of saving a ship that is in danger or its cargo **2.** the saving of possessions that are in danger of being lost or wrecked ◆ *verb* **sal • vaged; sal • vag • ing** to save from wreckage, fire, or other danger

same \sām\ *adjective* **1.** identical <the *same* apartment I rented last year> **2.** unchanged in many ways <The *same* theme comes through in all her stories.>

sam • ple \sam' pəl\ *noun* a piece given to show the quality of the whole ◆ *verb* **sam • pled; sam • pling** to take a small part to check on the quality of the whole

sand \sand\ *noun* loose, grainy material formed when larger rocks break up ◆ *verb* **1.** to sprinkle with sand **2.** to scrub with sand or sandpaper

san • dal \san' dəl\ *noun* a foot covering made up of a sole with straps to hold it on

sand • pa • per \sand' pā' pər\ *noun* paper with sand glued to one side that is used in rubbing surfaces to smooth them or to remove a finish such as paint ◆ *verb* to rub with sandpaper

sand • stone \sand' stōn'\ *noun* a rock made up chiefly of quartz sand hardened into a solid mass with other minerals

sand • wich \sand' wich'\ *noun* two slices of bread with meat, cheese, or other filling between them

sap \sap\ *noun* the juice circulating through a plant carrying nutrients ◆ *verb* **sapped; sap • ping** to undermine or weaken <Working ten hours a day *saps* her strength.>

sat • el • lite \sat' l īt'\ *noun* **1.** a moon revolving around a planet **2.** a vehicle revolving around the earth or other heavenly body **3.** a country under the influence of a more powerful country**swine** \swīn\ *noun* a domestic pig

Q R S

\a\ant	\ā\game	\ä\arm	\aù\out	\ch\child
\e\end	\ē\even	\hw\whip	\i\it	\ī\ice
\ng\ring	\ō\old	\ó\cloth	\ói\boy	\sh\she
\th\thing	\th\that	\ü\school	\ú\book	\yü\few
\yù\unite	\zh\vision	\ə\about		

For other sounds *see* Guide to Pronunciation.

201

Reading Level: 4.2 Spache

This up-to-date new resource from AGS carefully explains the most essential and frequently used words in the English language. With more than 5,000 entries, the *Dictionary of Basic English* features short, clear definitions to make learning easier for lower-level readers.

The entries in the *Dictionary* include the words that are most important for students to understand—words that will help them gain a stronger hold on English. The *Dictionary* includes examples of how words are used in phrases and sentences, and also includes glossary words from popular AGS textbooks—*Life Skills English, English to Use,* and *English for the World of Work.*

Students can easily gain valuable dictionary skills by using the *Dictionary of Basic English.* And with both English-Spanish and Spanish-English indexes, it's also an ideal resource for Spanish-speaking students learning English as a second language.

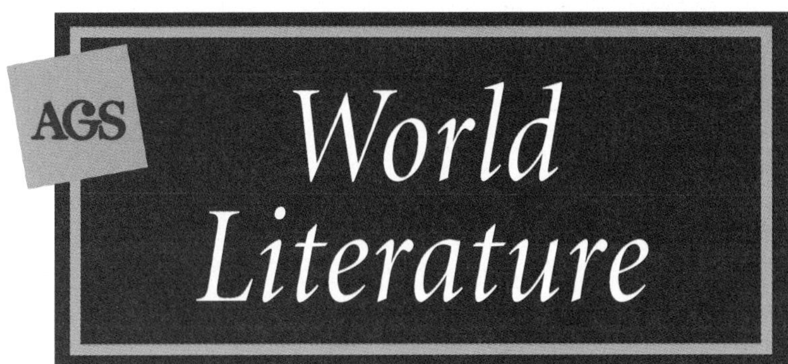

AGS®
American Guidance Service, Inc.
Circle Pines, Minnesota 55014-1796
800-328-2560

Literature Consultant

Jack Cassidy, Ph.D.
Texas A&M University
Corpus Christi, Texas

Original Cover Art

Connie Hayes

Printed in the United States of America

ISBN 0-7854-1828-8

Product Number 93030

A 0 9 8 7 6 5 4 3 2 1

Contents

World Literature Contents 3

World Literature Contents 5

World Literature Contents **7**

Using This Section

How to Use This Book

Student Pages 10–17

Overview

This section may be used to introduce the study of world literature, to preview the book's features, to introduce the use of graphic organizers in the study of literature, and to review vocabulary and test-taking skills.

Objectives

- To introduce the study of world literature.
- To preview literary genres and terms.
- To preview the student anthology.
- To review word-attack skills.
- To review test-taking skills.

Transparencies 1–6 

Teacher's Resource Library TRL

- Student Study Guide, pages 1–6
- Workbook 73

How to Use This Book

This book is an anthology of world literature. An anthology is a collection of literary selections written by different authors. The selections can be poems, plays, short stories, essays, parts of novels, folktales, legends, or myths. Sometimes, an anthology is organized around selections from a certain country or continent. For example, you might have an anthology with great literature from America. The first section of an American literature anthology could include a section with early American Indian poetry or Puritan diaries. Sometimes, anthologies are organized around different types of literature (genres). Then, you might have sections on poems, short stories, plays, essays, or folktales.

Why is a literature anthology important?

This anthology contains many enjoyable literary selections. An anthology helps you understand yourself and other people. You will read about people from other countries. Sometimes, you will read about people who lived in the past. Try to relate what the author is saying to your own life. Have I ever felt this way? Have I known anyone like this person? Have I seen anything like this?

A literature anthology can also help you appreciate the beauty of language. As you read, find phrases or sentences that you particularly like. You may want to start a notebook of these. You could also include words that are difficult.

This anthology is also important because it introduces you to great works of literature. Many times, you will find references to these works in everyday life. You will sometimes hear a quotation on TV or read it in the newspaper. Reading great literature helps you to become more literate. Generally, literate people are more likely to get better paying jobs.

What is in this book?

This book is filled with interesting works of literature. Great literature can come in many forms. On the next page are definitions of some kinds of literature genres in an anthology.

Introduction to the Book

Why is a literature anthology important?

Have students read the first two sections of the introduction silently. Help them discuss reasons to study world literature. Point out that reading literature by and about people from many cultures and many countries can affect readers in the following ways:

- Lead to a greater understanding of themselves, others, and relationships among people.
- Give them more knowledge and understanding of a place, an event, or a culture.
- Provide enjoyment of words and images.
- Stimulate thinking about an important idea.

Have volunteers describe works of literature they have read that have affected them in these ways.

Genre Definitions

autobiography A person's life story written by that person.

biography The story of a person's life written by someone else. You will find many biographies in this book.

diary A record of personal events, thoughts, or private feelings. People usually write in a diary every day or weekly. Mostly, people write diaries for themselves. Sometimes an author will create a fictional diary.

drama A play that often involves intense emotional conflict. Usually, a drama is serious.

essay A written work that expresses a writer's opinions on some basic or current issue.

fable A short story or poem with a moral, often with animals who act like humans. Aesop was a famous author of fables.

fiction Writing that is made up and often intended to entertain. Fiction is usually in prose form. Short stories, novels, folktales, myths, legends, and most plays are works of fiction.

folktale A story that has been handed down from one generation to another. The characters are usually either good or bad. Folktales make use of rhyme and repetitive phrases. Sometimes, they are called tall tales, particularly if they are humorous and exaggerated. They are also called folklore.

journal Writing that expresses an author's feelings or first impressions about a subject. A journal is like a diary, but it expresses more of the author's feelings. Sometimes, students keep journals to record their feelings about what they have read.

legend A traditional story that at one time was told orally and handed down from one generation to another. Legends are like myths, but they do not have as many supernatural forces. Usually, they have some historical base.

myth A story designed to explain the mysteries of life. A myth explains natural events, such as the change of seasons. Like fables and folktales, myths were first oral stories. Most early cultures have myths.

nonfiction Writing about real people and events. Nonfiction is usually designed to explain, argue, or describe. Essays, speeches, diaries, journals, autobiographies, and biographies are all usually nonfiction.

novel Fiction that is book-length and has more plot and character details than a short story.

poem A short piece of literature that usually has rhythm and paints powerful or beautiful impressions with words. Poems often have sound patterns such as rhyme. Songs are poetry set to music. Prose is the opposite of poetry.

prose Written language that is not verse. Short stories, novels, autobiographies, biographies, diaries, journals, and essays are examples of prose.

science fiction A type of literature that deals with people, places, and events that could not happen in our reality. However, science fiction is sometimes based on projected scientific developments. Most stories are set in the future. Stories about space are examples of science fiction. Jules Verne was one of the first science fiction authors.

short story A brief prose narrative. Short stories are designed to create unified impressions forcefully. Edgar Allan Poe was a great writer of short stories.

World Literature *How to Use This Book* **11**

Genre Definitions

Explain that literature comes in many different forms, or genres. Each genre has a specific purpose and style and specific conventions. For example, a play is written to be performed by actors on a stage; it is written almost entirely in dialogue. In a short story, an author creates a fictional world in which one or more characters are involved in a conflict that is resolved in the course of the story. An essay, on the other hand, expresses the ideas and opinions of the writer about aspects of the real world.

Have volunteers read each genre name and definition aloud. Ask other class members to mention examples of each genre that they have read or written. Suggest that students refer to this list of definitions as they read the various genres in the anthology.

Name Date Period

Units 1–6

Workbook 73

Sample Note Cards for a Research Project

Directions Use index cards to take notes for a research project. Study the following sample note cards for a bibliography entry for a book, an encyclopedia, or a magazine or periodical. Note the information included on each card.

1. Write the topic or subtopic at the top of each card.
2. Include all information and punctuation as shown in the sample cards below. Write the last name of the author first. If the name of the author is not known, begin with the next item. Underline titles of books, encyclopedias, and magazines. Use quotation marks around titles of chapters or articles.
3. Write your notes for your research project below each bibliography entry.

Topic: ____________
Last name of author, First name of author. Date of publication. Title of Book. Place of publication: Publisher.

Book Entry

Magazine Entry

Topic: ____________
Last name of author, First name of author. "Title of Article." Title of Magazine. Volume number (Date): Page numbers.

Topic: ____________
Title of Encyclopedia, Number of edition, volume number: Page numbers.

Encyclopedia Entry

World Literature

TRL

Workbook 73

Workbook 73 is a helpful tool that students can use as a guide when preparing research note cards. Before students begin a research project, remind them that they must credit their reference sources used in research reports. Then display Workbook 73. Identify the bibliographic information students should record before they begin taking notes summarizing the source's content. Explain that they can use their notes to prepare their research paper.

What is a literary term?

Suggest that students read the boxes in the margins of each selection before reading the selection. These contain important information about the selection and key literary terms for the selection. Have students turn to page 35 and read aloud the Literary Terms in the box at the beginning of the selection. The literary term or terms will call their attention to aspects of the selection they should focus on as they read. Also point out that the genre definition will help them understand the purpose, style, and conventions of the selection as they begin reading it.

Discuss each term in the box titled "Key Literary Term Definitions." Explain that the elements defined here will be found in many genres such as poems, legends, biographies, and short stories. You may wish to illustrate each term by having students recall a well-known folktale such as "Goldilocks and the Three Bears." Suggest that students describe the characterization, the conflict, the plot, the setting, and the themes of the story.

Lead a discussion about the reasons for identifying the elements of a literary work. Point out that readers can enjoy a piece of literature without identifying its parts. However, doing so helps readers better understand and remember a work, especially a complex one. It also helps readers recognize and appreciate how a writer creates a work of literature. This can help students in their own writing.

What is a literary term?

Literary terms are words or phrases used to study and discuss works of literature. These terms describe the devices that an author uses to help us enjoy and understand what we are reading. Some of the terms also describe a genre. In this anthology, you will see shaded boxes on the side of the Introducing the Selection pages that define some literary terms. These terms are important in understanding and discussing the selection being read. By understanding these literary terms, you can appreciate the author's craft.

> **Literary Terms**
>
> **autobiography** a story about a person's life written by that person
>
> **setting** the place and time in a story

The following are literary terms that apply to all works of literature. You should be familiar with these terms as you read this anthology. All of the literary terms used in this book can be found on page 436 in the Handbook of Literary Terms.

Glossary of Key Literary Terms

characterization The devices authors use to reveal characters. Characters are revealed by their actions, speech, appearance, others' comments, or the author's comments.

conflict The struggle the main character of a story faces. Conflict is an important part of the plot of a short story or novel. Main characters can struggle against themselves, other people, society, or nature. The four types of conflict are defined as person-against-person, person-against-self, person-against-society, and person-against-nature.

plot The series of events in a story. The plot shows what happens to the characters. Plots have conflict and resolutions to that conflict. Plots are very important in stories. Plots should have rising action, foreshadowing, a climax, and falling action.

setting The time and place in a story. Sometimes authors describe the setting in detail. Sometimes, the setting is left unclear so the reader can imagine it. A setting can even be a person's mind.

theme The idea that holds the whole piece of literature together. A theme is a generalization about humankind that the author wants to make. Themes are underlying statements about a topic. A theme is the topic of a piece of literature and the author's opinion about that topic.

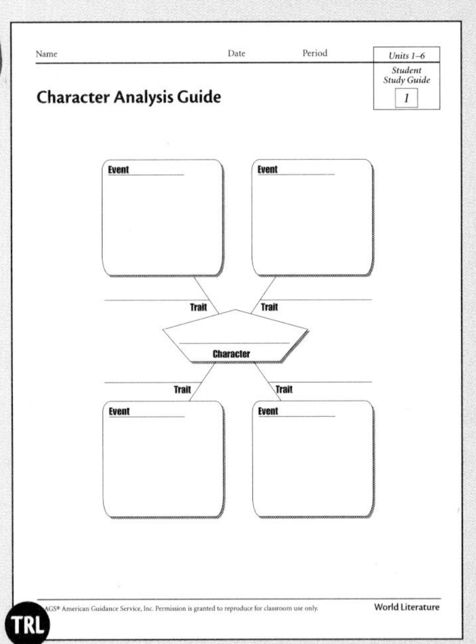

Student Study Guide 1

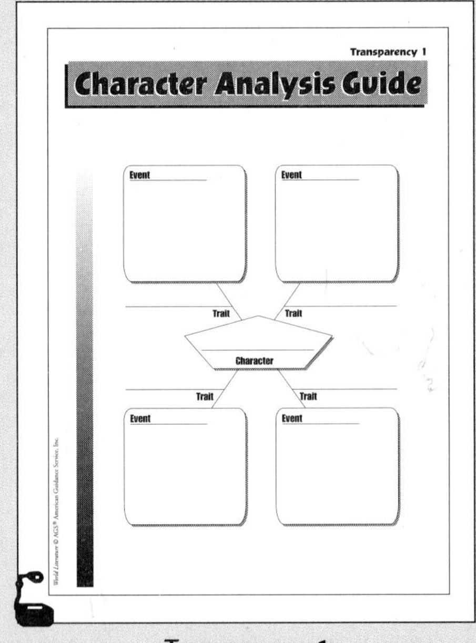

Transparency 1

How do I read this book?

Different works of literature can be read in different ways. However, you can use some strategies with all works of literature.

Before beginning a unit:

- Read the unit title and selection titles.
- Read any introductory paragraphs about the unit.
- Look at the pictures and other graphics in the unit. There may be maps to help you.
- Think about the unit's main topic.
- Think about what you want to learn about this topic.
- Think about what you already know about the unit.
- Develop questions in your mind that you think will be answered in this unit.

Before beginning the reading of a selection:

- Read the selection's title.
- Look at the pictures and other visuals.
- Read the background material included in About the Author and About the Selection.
- Predict what you think the selection is going to be about.
- Ask yourself questions about the material.

INTRODUCING the SELECTION

The History of Plymouth Plantation

William Bradford

William Bradford
1590–1657

About the Author

William Bradford was born in England in 1590 the son of a farmer. As a young boy, Bradford joined a church that separated from the Church of England. The members of Bradford's church were not treated well by those of other religions, and eventually moved to Holland.

Although Bradford had no formal schooling, he was well educated. The church members were university trained. Bradford learned languages, literature, and the Bible.

The church members, later called Pilgrims, decided to go to America to set up a new religious colony. Bradford joined them. They traveled on the ship the *Mayflower* and landed at Plymouth, Massachusetts, in December of 1620. After the landing on Plymouth, John Carver was elected governor of the colony. After Carver died, Bradford was chosen governor. He led the colony for many years. Bradford's **diary** is one of the few remaining accounts of what happened on the Pilgrims' voyage and on their settlement in America. A diary is a daily record of personal events, thoughts, or feelings. It is **nonfiction**. Nonfiction is writing that explains or describes real events and is not meant to entertain.

Literary Terms

diary a daily record of personal events, thoughts, or feelings

nonfiction writing that explains or describes real events and is not meant to entertain

This map shows the route the Pilgrims took to America. The Pilgrims left Plymouth, England, in September of 1620. They landed in Plymouth, Massachusetts, in December of 1620.

About the Selection

The *History of Plymouth Plantation* is a diary written by William Bradford beginning in 1620. Bradford explains the feelings of the early settlers, the Pilgrims, as they land in America for the first time. This selection tells of the landing at Cape Cod, Massachusetts, after the sickness and hardship of a long sea trip.

12 *Unit 1 Forging America's Literary Tradition*

As you read the selections:

- Think about the predictions that you made before reading. Were they right?
- Make new predictions as you read.
- Read the notes in the side columns. These will help you understand and think about the main concepts.
- Think of people or events in your own life that are similar to those described.
- Reread sentences or paragraphs that you do not understand.
- Refer to the definitions at the bottom of the page for words you do not know.
- In a notebook or on note cards, record definitions of words that you do not know. Also, record words defined in the text that you find interesting or unusual.

affirm to state positively	**miseries** things that cause one to suffer	**tedious** tiresome; boring

World Literature How to Use This Book 13

How do I read this book?

Have students read the points under "Before beginning a unit" silently. Then have them turn to the first unit opener on pages 18–21. Point out the variety of information available. Identify the selection titles and countries of origin for the unit listed on page 19. Examine the quotations and the pictures on pages 18–19. Note the genre information on pages 20–21 that helps put the literature in perspective. Ask students to write two questions they hope to learn answers to while studying the unit. Have volunteers read their questions aloud. Point out that questions at the beginning of Unit 1 may be as simple as "How are short stories from different countries alike?"

Before Reading

Have students read the points under "Before beginning the reading of a selection" silently. Then have students turn to the first selection opener on page 23. Ask them how looking at a picture of an author and learning about his or her life might improve a reader's understanding of a literary work. Have them discuss what they learn from the picture of Arthur Conan Doyle. Then have students write a sentence predicting what the selection will be about. Have volunteers read their predictions aloud.

After students read the points under "As you read the selections" silently, discuss the following questions:

- In what ways is reading literature an active process?
- In what ways is reading a work of literature similar to reading a science or history textbook? In what ways does it differ?
- In what ways is reading a work of literature similar to reading a romance novel? In what ways does it differ?

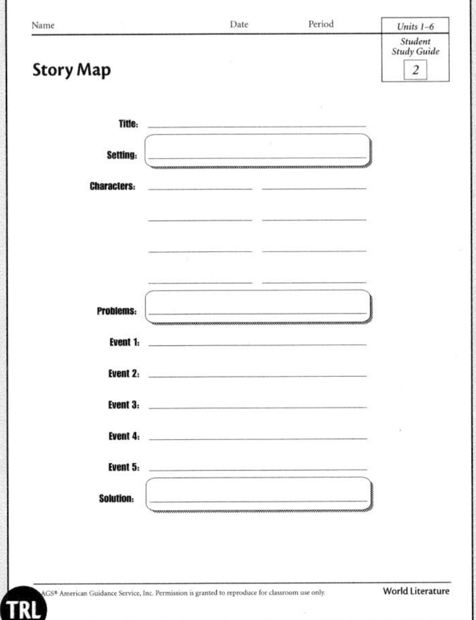
Name Date Period

Units 1–6
Student Study Guide
2

Story Map

Title:

Setting:

Characters:

Problems:

Event 1:

Event 2:

Event 3:

Event 4:

Event 5:

Solution:

World Literature

Student Study Guide 2

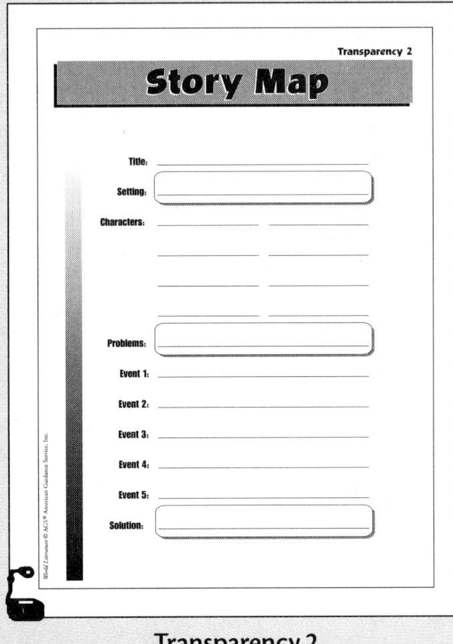
Transparency 2

Story Map

Title:

Setting:

Characters:

Problems:

Event 1:

Event 2:

Event 3:

Event 4:

Event 5:

Solution:

Transparency 2

After Reading

Have students read "After reading the selections" and discuss the importance of reflecting on a work of literature after reading it. Ask students to think about the last movie they saw with friends. Did they discuss the movie when it was over? How did discussion affect their enjoyment of the film? Point out that even more than most films, literary works may have interesting characters, settings, and themes that become clearer when they are considered and discussed.

How do I read specific types of literature?

Have students refer to the list of literary genres on page 11. Explain that because different genres have different purposes, styles, and conventions, a reader must use a variety of strategies when reading them.

Have students turn to a poem such as "Mindoro" on page 294. Ask a volunteer to read the items under "When reading poetry" aloud. Point out and demonstrate the items as students read the poem. Explain that much of a poem's enjoyment exists in appreciating its sounds and imagery.

Have a volunteer read aloud the items under "When reading essays." After students turn to an essay such as *A Small Place* on page 348, have them describe how this selection differs in appearance from the poem they looked at previously. (It is longer and denser; it is written in sentences and paragraphs instead of lines and stanzas.) Point out that the strategies listed help a reader understand the opinions stated in an essay.

Have a volunteer read aloud the items under "When reading plays." Explain that plays consist almost entirely of dialogue written after each character's name.

Suggest that students refer to this list when reading any one of the three kinds of literature discussed.

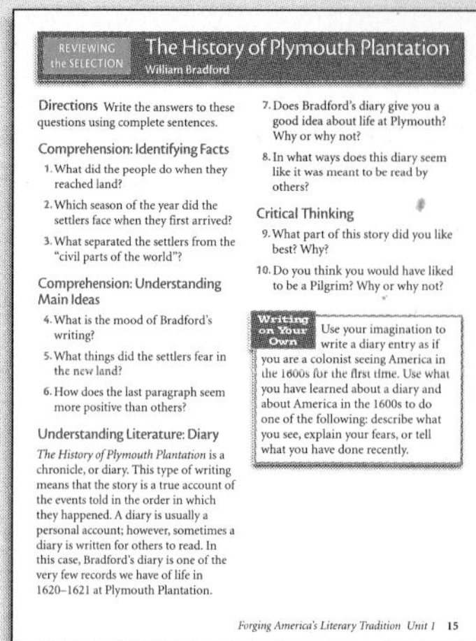

REVIEWING the SELECTION **The History of Plymouth Plantation**
William Bradford

Directions Write the answers to these questions using complete sentences.

Comprehension: Identifying Facts

1. What did the people do when they reached land?
2. Which season of the year did the settlers face when they first arrived?
3. What separated the settlers from the "civil parts of the world"?

Comprehension: Understanding Main Ideas

4. What is the mood of Bradford's writing?
5. What things did the settlers fear in the new land?
6. How does the last paragraph seem more positive than others?

Understanding Literature: Diary

The History of Plymouth Plantation is a chronicle, or diary. This type of writing means that the story is a true account of the events told in the order in which they happened. A diary is usually a personal account; however, sometimes a diary is written for others to read. In this case, Bradford's diary is one of the very few records we have of life in 1620–1621 at Plymouth Plantation.

7. Does Bradford's diary give you a good idea about life at Plymouth? Why or why not?
8. In what ways does this diary seem like it was meant to be read by others?

Critical Thinking

9. What part of this story did you like best? Why?
10. Do you think you would have liked to be a Pilgrim? Why or why not?

Writing on Your Own Use your imagination to write a diary entry as if you are a colonist seeing America in the 1600s for the first time. Use what you have learned about a diary and about America in the 1600s to do one of the following: describe what you see, explain your fears, or tell what you have done recently.

Forging America's Literary Tradition Unit 1 15

After reading the selections:

- Think about the questions that you asked yourself before you read. Were your answers to these questions right?
- Reread interesting or difficult parts of the selection.
- Reflect on what you have learned.
- Write the answers to the review questions in Reviewing the Selection.
- Use graphic organizers to help you organize and remember information. (See "What is a graphic organizer?" on page 15 to get some ideas.)

How do I read specific types of literature?

The strategies already described will work for all kinds of literature, but some types of literature need specific strategies.

When reading poetry:

- Read the poem aloud.
- Listen to the sounds of the words.
- Picture the images the author is describing.
- Reread poems over and over again to appreciate the author's use of language.

When reading essays:

- Review the questions in Reviewing the Selection before you begin reading.
- Use the questions to help you make your own predictions before reading.
- Remember that essays usually express an author's opinions. Try to understand how the author arrived at these opinions.

When reading plays:

- Picture the setting of the play. There is usually not much description. Try to relate it to what you have seen before.
- Pay attention to the dialogue. How does the dialogue reveal the characters' personality? Have you ever known anyone like this? Are you like this?

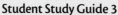

14 *How to Use This Book World Literature*

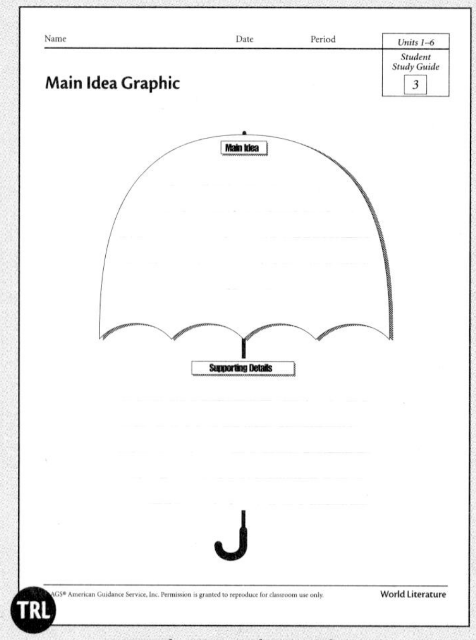

Name Date Period

Units 1–6
Student Study Guide
3

Main Idea Graphic

Main Idea

Supporting Details

AGS® American Guidance Service, Inc. Permission is granted to reproduce for classroom use only. World Literature

TRL

Student Study Guide 3

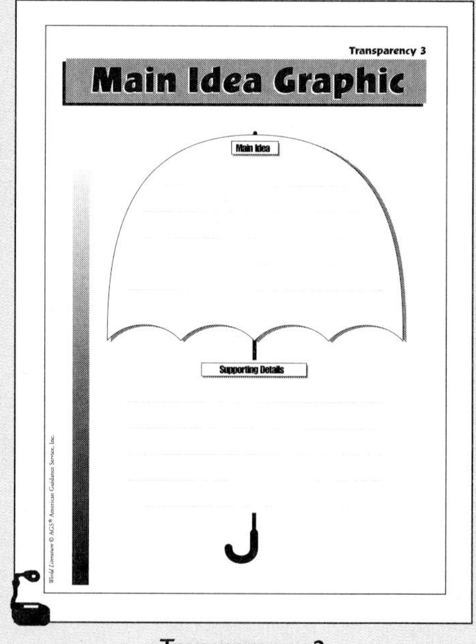

Transparency 3

Main Idea Graphic

Main Idea

Supporting Details

World Literature © AGS® American Guidance Service, Inc.

Transparency 3

What is a graphic organizer?

A graphic organizer is a visual representation of information. It can help you see how ideas are related to each other. A graphic organizer can help you study for a test or organize information before writing an essay. Following are some examples.

Character Analysis Guide

The graphic organizer below can help you better understand characters in a story or real people in a biography or autobiography. Fill in the character trait on the ray and then list events in the story or in the person's life that demonstrate that character trait.

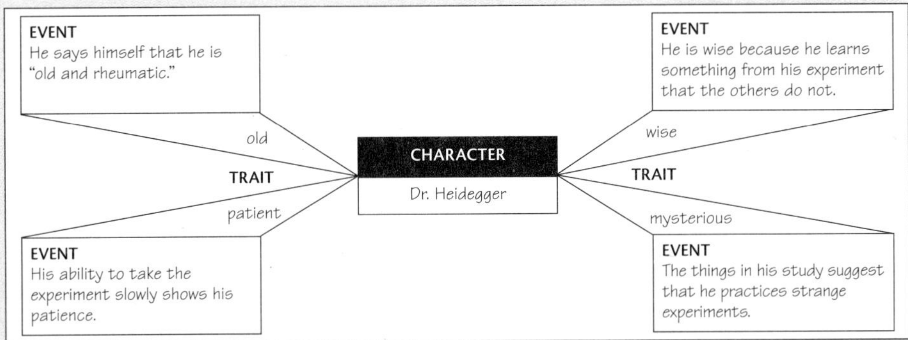

Venn Diagram

The Venn Diagram can help you compare and contrast two characters, two authors, or two pieces of literature. List the similarities on the overlap between the circles. List the differences on the parts of the circles that do not overlap.

Remember that all graphic organizers can be used in various ways. They can be used to help you organize your writing. They can be used to help you analyze your thoughts, and they can be used to help you study for a test. You can even create your own graphic organizer.

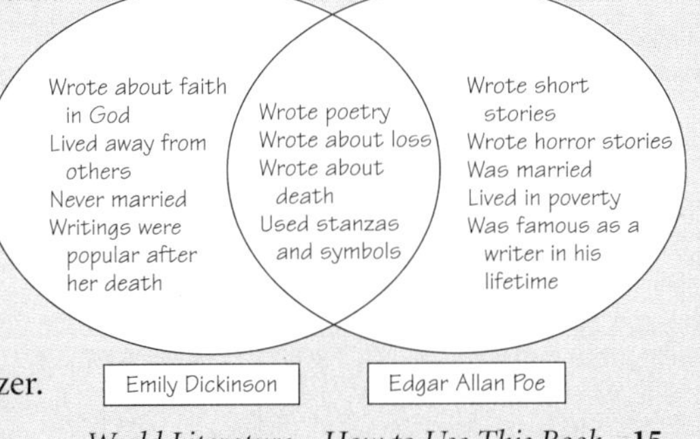

World Literature *How to Use This Book* **15**

What is a graphic organizer?

Have students examine the Character Analysis Guide. Point out that each character trait is supported by a specific example from the story. Explain that in taking tests and writing essays on literature, students should make generalizations supported by specific facts from the work. A graphic organizer like this one can help students formulate and support generalizations.

As students examine the Venn Diagram, discuss how it can help a reader organize ideas on similarities and differences. Point out that students can use many other kinds of graphic organizers. For example, a concept map can be used to indicate the kinds of imagery used in a poem. A story map can be used to identify the major parts and events of a story. Display and complete Transparency 2 to illustrate the use of a story map. Use it to analyze story parts in a story students have read or a folktale such as "Cinderella."

Transparencies 1–6 offer graphic organizers that can help students analyze reading selections. As the class discusses selections, project a transparency and explain one way the organizer can be used to identify story elements. Remind them that each organizer can be used in a variety of ways. Then distribute copies of the matching Student Study Guide. Have students work individually or in pairs or small groups to analyze a selection using the graphic organizer. Encourage them to share their insights.

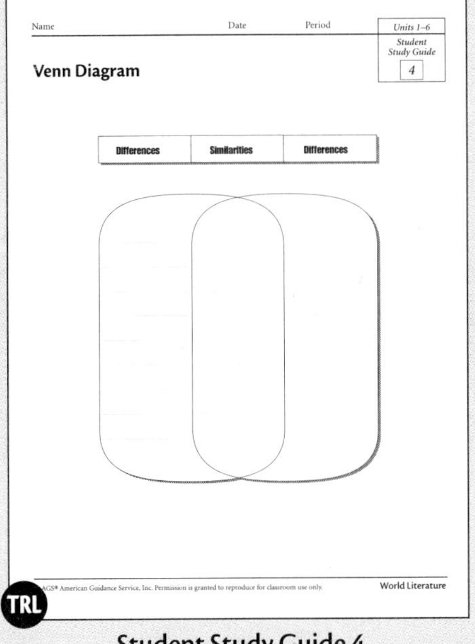

Student Study Guide 4

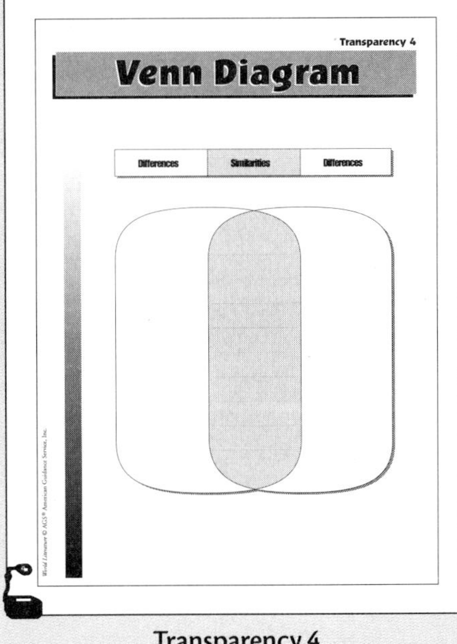

Transparency 4

What strategies should I use when I encounter a word that I don't know?

Discuss each point after a volunteer has read it aloud. Point out a boldface word on one of the selection pages. Have a student read the sentence in which it appears and then read the definition at the bottom of the page.

Demonstrate figuring out the meaning of a word through context. For example, you might write on the board the following from Jonathan Swift's "A Modest Proposal."

> … This prodigious number of children in the arms or on the backs or at the heels of their mothers, and frequently of their fathers, is in the present deplorable state of the kingdom a very great additional grievance. …

Ask students to discuss ways they might determine the meaning of *prodigious* if they do not know it. Have them first read the excerpt. Point out that the context, with the word *number* being modified by *prodigious,* indicates that the term has something to do with amounts. In addition, the context indicates that the children surround their parents. Students can also separate the base word, *prodigy,* from the suffix *-ous.* From the context clues and the meaning of the base word, students may surmise that *prodigious,* means "large," "enormous," or "extraordinary." If students are unable to determine meaning from context or base words, suggest that they look the word up in the dictionary.

Have volunteers read the Word Study Tips. Discuss the reasons why it is important for students to understand the meaning of words they read:

- Each word is important in communicating the precise meaning of a literary work.
- Each word is important in creating an artistic effect, especially in poetry or other writing with many images and figures of speech.
- Learning new words will help readers progress to more difficult literary works and increase their speaking and writing vocabularies.

What strategies should I use when I encounter a word that I don't know?

- If the word is boldface, look for the definition of the word at the bottom of the page.
- If the word is not boldface, read to the end of the sentence and maybe the next sentence. Can you determine the unknown word now?
- If your teacher has given you a Selection Glossary, use it to look up additional terms that are not boldface.
- Look at the beginning sound of the unknown word.
- Ask yourself, "What word would make sense here that begins with this sound?"
- Sound out the syllables of the word.
- If you still cannot determine the unknown word, see if you know any parts of the word: prefixes, suffixes, or roots.
- If this does not work, write the word on a note card or in a vocabulary notebook and look it up in the dictionary after you have finished reading the selection.
- If the word is necessary to understand the passage, look it up in a dictionary or glossary immediately.

Word Study Tip

- Start a vocabulary file with note cards to use for review.
- Write one word on the front of each card. Write the unit number, selection title, and the definition on the other side.
- You can use these cards as flash cards by yourself or with a study partner to test your knowledge.

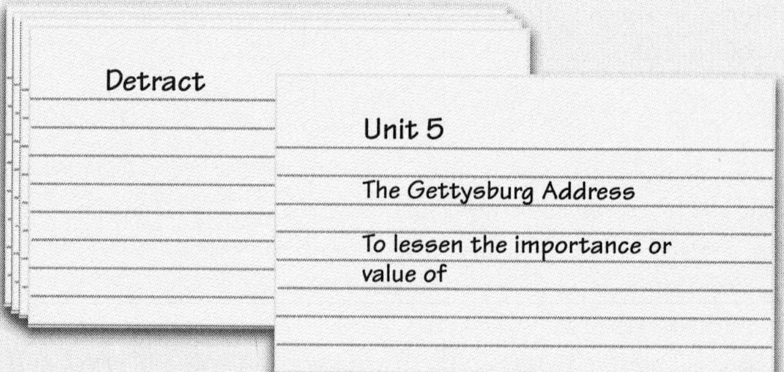

Detract
Unit 5
The Gettysburg Address
To lessen the importance or value of

16 How to Use This Book World Literature

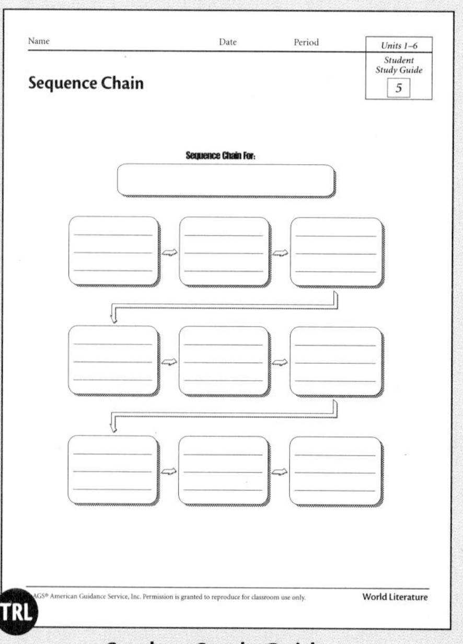

Name Date Period

Units 1–6 Student Study Guide 5

Sequence Chain

Sequence Chain For:

©AGS® American Guidance Service, Inc. Permission is granted to reproduce for classroom use only. World Literature

Student Study Guide 5

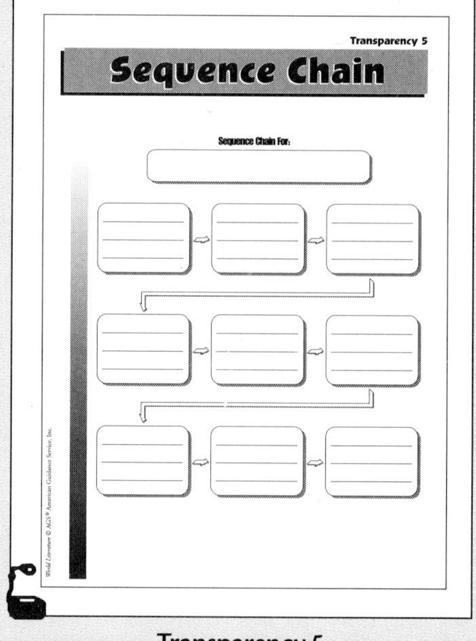

Transparency 5

Sequence Chain

Sequence Chain For:

Transparency 5

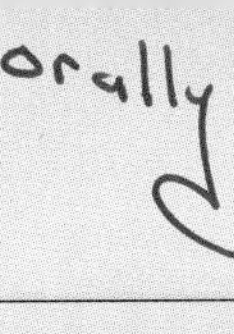

What should I know about taking a test on literature?

Before the test day:

- Read all the works assigned.
- Review your class notes, the Unit Summary, and the Unit Review.
- Ask your teacher what kinds of questions will be on the test.
- Review any notes that you have taken or graphic organizers you have developed.
- Try to predict what questions will be asked and develop answers to those questions.
- Review the Test-Taking Tips at the bottom of the Unit Review pages in this book.

UNIT 1 SUMMARY

Unit 1 covers 1620 to 1849. The development of new colonies, the struggle between Europeans and American Indians, and the American Revolution took place during this time.

Four styles of literature—native, colonial, revolutionary, and early national—represent early America. Native literature in this unit includes American Indian poems and a myth that had been passed down orally. Colonial literature in this unit includes the works of William Bradford, Anne Dudley Bradstreet, and Benjamin Franklin. These writings copied European styles. The revolutionary literature in this unit is by Thomas Paine, a writer during the American Revolution. Early national literature came about in the 1800s. Two professional writers, Washington Irving and Edgar Allan Poe, were part of this movement. They studied the inner workings of people and society. Early national literature began to replace letters, essays, and speeches that were popular in the past.

- "To My Dear and Loving Husband" by Anne Dudley Bradstreet is a love poem from a wife to her husband.
- The selection from *Poor Richard's Almanac* by Benjamin Franklin is a list of aphorisms, or clever sayings.
- *The American Crisis, Number 1* by Thomas Paine is a pamphlet that expresses the desire for freedom and urges Americans to continue their struggle against England.
- "Wouter Van Twiller" by Washington Irving is a sketch that uses satire and exaggeration to poke fun at a man's undeserved fame.
- Three American Indian poems by the Omaha, Sioux, and Chippewa express American Indian attitudes toward death and love for the land.
- "The Origin of Plumage" is an Iroquois myth, or story that explains how something in the natural world came to be. This myth explains how all birds got their feathers.
- "The Black Cat" by Edgar Allan Poe is a horror short story about one man's madness and his cat.
- "Annabel Lee" by Edgar Allan Poe is a poem about the grief caused by the death of a lover.

America's Literary Tradition Unit 1 61

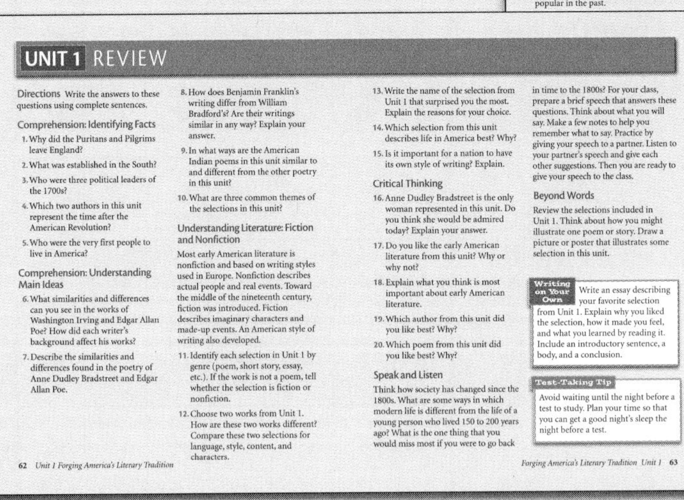

UNIT 1 REVIEW

Directions Write the answers to these questions using complete sentences.

Comprehension: Identifying Facts

1. Why did the Puritans and Pilgrims leave England?
2. What was established in the South?
3. Who were three political leaders of the 1700s?
4. Which two authors in this unit represent the time after the American Revolution?
5. Who were the very first people to live in America?

Comprehension: Understanding Main Ideas

6. What similarities and differences can you see in the works of Washington Irving and Edgar Allan Poe? How did each writer's background affect his works?
7. Describe the similarities and differences found in the poetry of Anne Dudley Bradstreet and Edgar Allan Poe.
8. How does Benjamin Franklin's writing differ from William Bradford's? Are their writings similar in any way? Explain your answer.
9. In what ways are the American Indian poems in this unit similar to and different from the other poetry in this unit?
10. What are three common themes of the selections in this unit?

Understanding Literature: Fiction and Nonfiction

Most early American literature is nonfiction and based on writing styles used in Europe. Nonfiction describes actual people and real events. Toward the middle of the nineteenth century, fiction was introduced. Fiction describes imaginary characters and made-up events. An American style of writing also developed.

11. Identify each selection in Unit 1 by genre (poem, short story, essay, etc.). If the work is not a poem, tell whether the selection is fiction or nonfiction.
12. Choose two works from Unit 1. How are these two works different? Compare these two selections for language, style, content, and characters.
13. Write the name of the selection from Unit 1 that surprised you the most. Explain the reasons for your choice.
14. Which selection from this unit describes life in America best? Why?
15. Is it important for a nation to have its own style of writing? Explain.

Critical Thinking

16. Anne Dudley Bradstreet is the only woman represented in this unit. Do you think she would be admired today? Explain your answer.
17. Do you like the early American literature from this unit? Why or why not?
18. Explain what you think is most important about early American literature.
19. Which author from this unit did you like best? Why?
20. Which poem from this unit did you like best? Why?

Speak and Listen

Think how society has changed since the 1800s. What are some ways in which modern life is different from the life of a young person who lived 150 to 200 years ago? What is the one thing that you would miss most if you were to go back in time to the 1800s? For your class, prepare a brief speech that answers these questions. Think about what you will say. Make a few notes to help you remember what to say. Practice by giving your speech to a partner. Listen to your partner's speech and give each other suggestions. Then you are ready to give your speech to the class.

Beyond Words

Review the selections included in Unit 1. Think about how you might illustrate one poem or story. Draw a picture or poster that illustrates some selection in this unit.

Writing on Your Own Write an essay describing your favorite selection from Unit 1. Explain why you liked the selection, how it made you feel, and what you learned by reading it. Include an introductory sentence, a body, and a conclusion.

Test-Taking Tip Avoid waiting until the night before a test to study. Plan your time so that you can get a good night's sleep the night before a test.

62 Unit 1 Forging America's Literary Tradition

Forging America's Literary Tradition Unit 1 63

During the test:

- Come to the test with a positive attitude.
- Preview the test and read the directions carefully.
- Plan your time.
- Answer the essay questions and the questions that you know first.
- Go back and answer the more difficult questions.
- Allow time to reread all of the questions and your answers.
- Put your name on the paper.

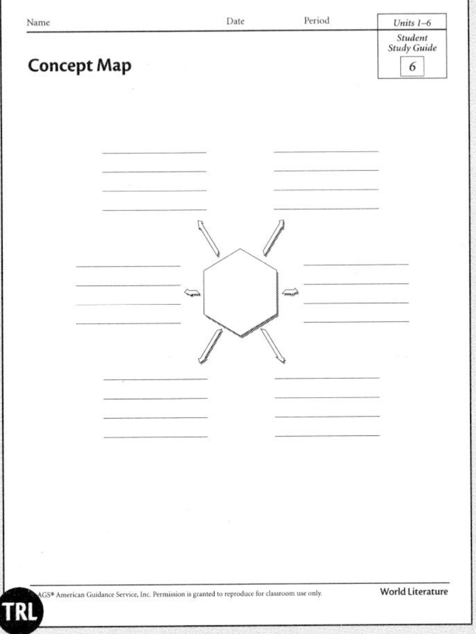

Student Study Guide 6

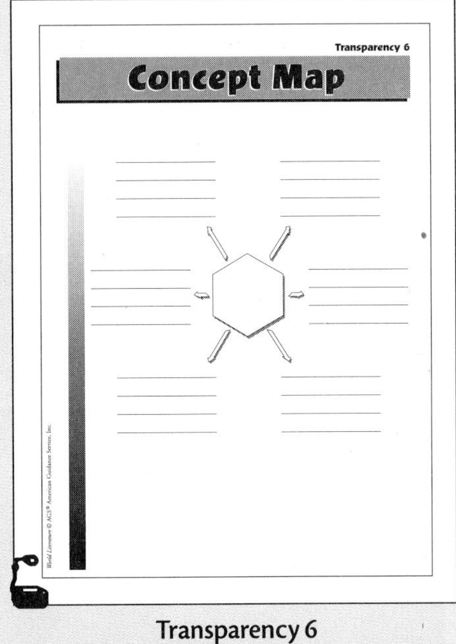

Transparency 6

What should I know about taking a literature test?

Have students silently read the list of items to do before the test day. You may wish to use the following questions to lead students in a discussion about taking literature tests.

- How are literature tests different from tests in other subjects? (Tests in other subjects may require students to recall facts they have memorized. Literature tests do not require a memorization of facts. They call for a memory and understanding of the important elements of a work. They may also require independent thinking to synthesize the important elements of a work.)
- Why is a careful reading of the assigned selections particularly important in preparation for a literature test? Point out that teachers' lectures or explanations may be the primary way of getting information in some subjects. However, in a literature class the literary selections themselves are the primary texts.
- What methods can help you remember the specific details of literary works before you take a test? Review the importance of graphic organizers, discussions, and answering review questions in helping readers remember literary works. Turn to the Test-Taking Tip on page 137. Point out that one of these tips appears in each Unit Review in the book.

Have students silently read the list of items under "During the test." Point out that in students' answers to essay questions in a literature test, teachers usually do not look for one correct answer. They look for thoughtful answers, the use of specific examples from the selections, and evidence that students have carefully read the selections.

UNIT 1 Planning Guide

Fiction

	Student Pages	About the Author	About the Selection	Literary Terms	Reviewing the Selection	Writing on Your Own
■ GREAT BRITAIN "The Adventure of the Speckled Band" by Arthur Conan Doyle	23–34	✔	✔	✔	✔	✔
■ GERMANY "Death Arrives on Schedule" by Hansjörg Martin	35–50	✔	✔	✔	✔	✔
■ UNITED STATES "The Feeling of Power" by Isaac Asimov	52–65	✔	✔	✔	✔	✔
■ GERMANY "The Expedition" by Rudolf Lorenzen	66–83	✔	✔	✔	✔	✔
■ UNITED STATES "The Cegua" by Robert D. San Souci	85–91	✔	✔	✔	✔	✔
■ RUSSIA From *Master and Man* by Leo Tolstoy	92–98	✔	✔	✔	✔	✔
■ COLOMBIA "Just Lather, That's All" by Hernando Téllez	99–106	✔	✔	✔	✔	✔
■ ZIMBABWE From *Nervous Conditions* by Tsitsi Dangarembga	108–115	✔	✔	✔	✔	✔
■ NIGERIA "Marriage Is a Private Affair" by Chinua Achebe	116–125	✔	✔	✔	✔	✔
■ KOREA "Cranes" by Hwang Sun-won	126–133	✔	✔	✔	✔	✔
■ SKILLS LESSON: Plot UNIT REVIEW	134, 136–137			✔		✔

Selection Features: columns above.

Unit Features

Student Text
About Fiction
Detective Stories
Science Fiction
Adventure
Turning Points
Skills Lesson: Plot
Unit Summary

Teacher's Resource Library
Activity 1: About Fiction
Workbook 1: About Fiction
Activity 2: Detective Stories
Workbook 2: Detective Stories
Activity 5: Science Fiction
Workbook 5: Science Fiction
Activity 8: Adventure
Workbook 8: Adventure
Activity 12: Turning Points
Workbook 12: Turning Points

Teaching Strategies							Language Skills				Learning Styles					TRL Teacher's Resource Library					
Viewing the Art	Career Connection	Environmental Connection	Cross-Curricular Connection	Diversity Connection	Community Connection	Transparencies	Grammar	Literary Elements	Comprehension	Writing Connection	Auditory	Visual	Tactile/Kinesthetic	Group Learning	LEP/ESL	Vocabulary Workbook	Selection Glossary	Student Study Guide	Activities	Workbook	Writing Activities
90			26, 31	28			25, 27, 29								24	1	1	7	3	3	1
	48		40, 46		38		37, 41	44	45			42				2	2	8	4	4	2
	54	60	56, 58						59	62			55	63		3	3	9	6	6	3
	75	71	72		68			73	70, 76	77		69	81			4	4	10	7	7	4
	89									90		88			86	5	5	11	9	9	5
		94	96				95, 97									6	6	12	10	10	6
100, 103	102							105				101	103	104		7	7	13	11	11	7
				110							114					8	8	14	13	13	8
			119				122	118			121					9	9	15	14	14	9
132			128, 131									129		132		10	10	16	15	15	10
						7													16	16	11

Assessment Features

Student Text

Unit 1 Review

Teacher's Resource Library

Activity 16: Unit 1 Review, pages 1–2
Workbook 16: Unit 1 Review, pages 1–2
Selection Quizzes 1–10
Unit 1 Mastery Tests A and B, pages 1–2

TRL Alternative Selection

The Alternative Selection can be found in the Teacher's Resource Library.

Alternative Selection 1:
"The Adventure of the Speckled Band"
by Arthur Conan Doyle
Alternative Selection 2:
"How Much Land Does a Man Need?"
by Leo Tolstoy

Unit at a Glance

(Answer Keys for the Teacher's Resource Library begin on page 468 of this Teacher's Edition.)

"You know that fiction...is possibly the roughest trade of all in writing....You have the sheet of blank paper, the pencil, and the obligation to invent truer than things can be true."

—Ernest Hemingway

"It is not a bad thing in a tale that you understand only half of it."

—Isak Dinesen

Other Resources

Books for Teachers

Asimov, Isaac. *Asimov on Science Fiction.* Garden City, NY: Doubleday, 1981.

Doyle, Arthur Conan. *The Annotated Sherlock Holmes.* New York: C. N. Potter. Distributed by Crown Publishers, 1967.

Tolstoy, Leo. *Anna Karenina.* New York: Knopf. Distributed by Random House, 1992.

Books for Students

Achebe, Chinua. *Chike and the River.* Cambridge University Press: 1966.

Asimov, Isaac. *100 Great Fantasy Short Stories.* Garden City, NY: Doubleday, 1984.

2041 A.D.: Twelve Stories About the Future by Today's Top Science Fiction Writers. New York: Delacorte Press, 1991.

UNIT 1 Fiction

How long have people told stories? Probably as long as they have been able to talk. People made up stories to explain things like why the sky is blue or ducks have webbed feet. They created stories to entertain themselves. Some stories are scary. Some are funny. Some are short. Others are very long. No matter where in the world you go, people tell stories and have always told stories. In this unit, you will enjoy stories from the nine different countries shown on the map on the next page.

Unit 1 Selections — **Page**

Introducing the Unit

Ask volunteers to read aloud the quotations on page 18. If necessary, identify Hemingway and Dinesen as well-known novelists. Have students discuss the quotations.

ASK What do you think Hemingway meant when he said someone writing fiction had to "invent truer things than can be true"? (Perhaps he meant that fiction writers must write so well that they bring out the essential truth about people or life.)

ASK Could Dinesen really have meant that a reader doesn't have to understand half of a story? Why do you think as you do? (She may have felt that the reader could not always understand everything the writer intended.)

Point out that the universality of storytelling makes stories uniquely interesting to everyone in any time or any place. However, not all stories are meant simply to entertain. Many were originally intended as ways to explain the natural world to people whose knowledge of science was rudimentary. Others were meant to explain the principles of acceptable behavior or religious belief.

ASK What are some of your favorite stories? (Allow brief discussion, reminding students if necessary that some favorite stories are those that people remember from their childhood.)

Review the Unit 1 selection genres and titles. Discuss the different genres.

Viewing the Art

Draw students' attention to the painting, *Market Place, Guatemala*, by John Hollis Kaufmann. Invite them to notice its colors and its sense of movement and activity.

ASK How do you think this painting might connect to a unit about fiction and stories? (Allow students to speculate, but many will see that people getting together, as in the marketplace, often told stories to each other.)

Video

The Adventures of Sherlock Holmes: The Speckled Band. Botsford, CT: Filmic Archives, 1983.

Chinua Achebe. Princeton, NJ: Films for the Humanities and Sciences.

The 39 Steps. Los Angeles: Janus Films/Voyager Press, 1985.

Software

Sherlock Holmes. CD-ROM. Fairfield, CT: Queue.

About Fiction

Ask students to read the text on page 20. You may want to invite volunteers to take turns reading paragraphs aloud.

ASK What are the three elements of all works of fiction? (character, setting, and plot)

Point out to students that works of fiction can also differ in their emphasis of one or more of the elements. For example, character development might be the main focus of a short story, showing how one person changes or develops in a certain situation. Another story might emphasize the plot, or what happens. Often "action" movies, for example, emphasize plot over character. Sometimes, as in much science fiction, for example, the setting—time and place—is the most important element that drives the plot and characters.

ASK What works of fiction have you read or seen on television or movies that emphasize plot? characters? setting? (Answers will vary, but make sure students can explain or defend their choices.)

UNIT 1 ■ ABOUT FICTION

orally

Writing about events that did not really happen is called fiction. Some fiction is realistic and may seem like it is from a newspaper. Other fictional stories describe far-off planets, alien life forms, or the future.

All works of fiction share three elements: character, setting, and plot. Characters perform the action. They are usually people, but they can be animals or even objects. Some examples of nonhuman characters are the magic mirror in *Snow White* and the rabbits Hazel and Fiver in *Watership Down.* Plot is the action in a story. As characters act and react, they move the plot along. Plot changes the characters and reveals their true nature and hidden feelings. The plot of *A Christmas Carol,* for instance, is about Ebenezer Scrooge. He changes from being cheap and lonely to generous and friendly. Setting is a country or the special place or time in which a story happens. For example, the setting of *Star Wars* is "a long time ago in a galaxy far, far away."

Fiction can be grouped by the length of the work. Short stories are short enough to read in one sitting. They usually center on one character or situation. Novels are longer works. They can explore more than one character or situation over a longer period of time.

Fiction can also be grouped by where the stories take place or where the authors come from. Gabriela Mistral, Pablo Neruda, and Gabriel García Márquez are from different countries. But all may be discussed as Latin American writers.

The fiction in Unit 1 is arranged by genre, or type of story. The authors use setting, character, and plot to create many kinds of stories. Libraries often place the stories they have in special sections so you can find them easily. Look for sections of detective stories, science fiction, or other genres. You may also find the complete work from which a selection in this unit was taken.

The following countries are represented in this unit: Great Britain, the United States, Germany, Russia, Colombia, Zimbabwe, Nigeria, and Korea.

Draw students' attention to the world map on page 21 showing the countries represented in this unit.

ASK What are the countries represented in this unit? (Great Britain, the United States, Germany, Russia, Colombia, Zimbabwe, Nigeria, and Korea) Which countries are represented by two stories? (the United States and Germany)

Name Date Period | *Unit 1* | *Activity* 1

About Fiction

Part A Directions Read each sentence. Write *T* if the statement is true or *F* if it is false.

_______ 1. Three elements of fiction are: character, plot, and time.
_______ 2. Some fiction is realistic.
_______ 3. Novels are not fiction.
_______ 4. A main character may be an animal.
_______ 5. Plot is the exact place where the action happens.

Part B Directions Circle the letter of the answer that correctly completes each sentence.

1. Genre means
   a. gentle. b. science fiction. c. type of story. d. library.
2. _____ may be grouped by where the stories take place.
   a. Songs b. Poem c. Fiction d. Cookbooks
3. Authors use _____ to create stories.
   a. setting b. plot c. character d. all of these
4. Some fictional stories describe
   a. aliens. b. today's news. c. a current event. d. your family.
5. Plot lets us see _____ of the characters.
   a. houses b. hidden feelings c. cars d. a special place

 World Literature

TRL

Activity 1

Name Date Period | *Unit 1* | *Activity* 1

About Fiction

Part A Directions Read each sentence. Write *T* if the statement is true or *F* if it is false.

_______ 1. Three elements of fiction are: character, plot, and time.
_______ 2. Some fiction is realistic.
_______ 3. Novels are not fiction.
_______ 4. A main character may be an animal.
_______ 5. Plot is the exact place where the action happens.

Part B Directions Circle the letter of the answer that correctly completes each sentence.

1. Genre means
   a. gentle. b. science fiction. c. type of story. d. library.
2. _____ may be grouped by where the stories take place.
   a. Songs b. Poem c. Fiction d. Cookbooks
3. Authors use _____ to create stories.
   a. setting b. plot c. character d. all of these
4. Some fictional stories describe
   a. aliens. b. today's news. c. a current event. d. your family.
5. Plot lets us see _____ of the characters.
   a. houses b. hidden feelings c. cars d. a special place

Guidance Service, Inc. Permission is granted to reproduce for classroom use only. World Literature

TRL

Workbook 1

Detective Stories

Ask students to read the text on page 22, or have them take turns reading it aloud. Invite volunteers to read the two quotations aloud. Explain that Raymond Chandler and P. D. James are both very famous writers of detective stories.

ASK Why do you think a writer of detective stories would say that a good detective never gets married? (Probably because the writer wants the detective story to concentrate on the plot. If he or she wrote about a detective who got married, it would be necessary to write about the personal life of the detective—an unimportant side issue to most detective stories.)

ASK What do you think P. D. James meant by the story being about the restoration of order? (A murder is messy and a startling turn of events. A detective story writer needs to explain how order is restored by solving the murder.)

Point out to students that detective-story writers often invent a specific detective who becomes the main character in a series of books. V. I. Warshawski and Miss Marple are examples, among many others. These main characters are like the characters in a detective series on television, such as *Law and Order.* The same main characters appear in each book or episode, but a different crime or problem to be solved is presented in each one.

ASK Why do you think a writer might continue to write about the same detective? (The character becomes very familiar to readers, who develop an affectionate interest in the detective. Also, the emphasis can be on the development of the puzzling story.)

Detective Stories

- "A really good detective never gets married." —Raymond Chandler
- "What the detective story is about is not murder but the restoration of order." —P. D. James

Detective stories are sometimes called mysteries or "whodunits." They present a crime and a protagonist, or main character. The protagonist is usually a detective. He or she watches and questions the other characters. The detective finds clues and reveals the criminal.

Detectives originally observed and commented without being part of the plot. Today, they are right in the middle of the action. V. I. Warshawski, with her hard Chicago attitude, or the English busybody Miss Marple are detectives with strong personalities. Over a cup of tea or a glass of something stronger they reveal the "bad guy."

Detectives dodge bullets and plunge into fights. Sometimes they take the place of the law. They may protect the innocent or punish the guilty. All this action often attracts any handsome or beautiful person involved in the crime. Modern detectives do not always stay away from such temptations. Characters like Easy Rawlins of Los Angeles are much like their antagonists, or opponents. Only their sense of decency and justice separates them from the criminals. Much of the fun in reading a detective story is in spotting the criminal before the detective explains everything.

22 *Unit 1 Fiction*

Name Date Period

Unit 1 *Activity* 2

Detective Stories

Part A Directions Read each sentence. Write *T* if the statement is true or *F* if it is false.

______ 1. Another name for detective stories is "you-dunnits."
______ 2. Detectives look for clues to reveal the criminal.
______ 3. Detectives usually take the law into their own hands.
______ 4. Beautiful and handsome characters often turn away from detectives.
______ 5. Detectives in early detective stories often observed the action without taking part.
______ 6. The protagonist in detective stories is usually the next-door neighbor.
______ 7. Readers cannot use clues in detective stories to figure out the criminal.
______ 8. According to Raymond Chandler, "Really good detectives never get married."
______ 9. P. D. James said that detective stories should only be about murder.
______ 10. Many modern detectives are similar in many ways to the "bad guys."

Part B Directions Circle the word or phrase in parentheses that best completes each sentence.

1. The main character in a detective story is the (antagonist, protagonist).
2. According to the text, detectives dodge (bullets, the police) and plunge into fights.
3. Sometimes detectives give in to (temptations, their conscience).
4. Criminals and detectives may be (brought together, separated) by their sense of decency and justice.
5. A detective watches and (admires, questions) the other characters.

 World Literature

TRL

Activity 2

Name Date Period

Unit 1 *Workbook* 2

Detective Stories

Part A Directions In each blank write the word or phrase from the Word Bank that best completes each sentence.

1. Detective stories are sometimes called ______ or mysteries.
2. The ______ is the main character of the story.
3. Detectives may protect the ______ or punish the guilty.
4. The real criminal in a plot might be the ______.
5. Sometimes it is hard to tell the bad character from the good. But their sense of ______ and justice helps us.

Word Bank	
antagonist	decency
innocent	protagonist
whodunits	

Part B Directions Read each sentence. Write *T* if the statement is true or *F* if it is false.

______ 1. A detective in a story is always the antagonist.
______ 2. Detectives shoot bullets and never fight, according to the text.
______ 3. Some modern detectives are much like their opponents.
______ 4. Detectives find criminals, they do not question or punish them.
______ 5. In stories today, a detective will usually just observe the action.

 World Literature

TRL

Workbook 2

INTRODUCING the SELECTION

The Adventure of the Speckled Band

Arthur Conan Doyle

Arthur Conan Doyle (1859–1930) British

Literary Terms

character a person, animal, or object who performs the action in a fictional work

first-person using "I" to tell a story; told from the narrator's point of view

narrator the person telling the story

put into notebook

p. 422, 434

About the Author

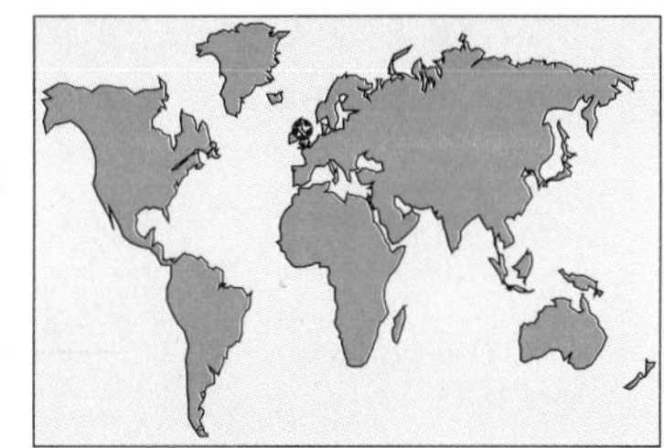

Sir Arthur Conan Doyle was trained as a doctor. He quit medicine to write. The first Sherlock Holmes story was "A Study in Scarlet," which came out in 1887. From 1891 on, Doyle wrote many more Holmes stories. To many, the **characters** of Holmes and his friend Dr. John Watson seemed real. Characters are people or objects in a story who do the action. The Sherlock Holmes stories have been made into films and television shows. You can even find fan clubs such as the "Baker Street Irregulars," named for Holmes's London address, 221-B Baker Street. "The Hounds of the Internet" are on the World Wide Web. Doyle wrote other books, too. In fact, he grew very tired of Holmes. He killed off the detective in an 1893 story. People were so upset that Doyle had to bring him back to life. A final book of Holmes stories came out in 1927. Doyle was made a knight in 1902 for his work during the Boer War.

About the Selection

Sherlock Holmes is one of the greatest fictional detectives. He lived and worked in the city of London in the late 1800s. When many people think of detectives, they think of Holmes. He is usually shown with deerstalker cap, a pipe, and a magnifying glass. The admiring Dr. Watson is the **narrator** for almost all the adventures. He writes in the **first-person.** This means Watson writes as "I," as though he is watching the action. In the following selection, Holmes looks into a mysterious death. Notice his attention to details.

Selection at a Glance

The Adventure of the Speckled Band

Arthur Conan Doyle

Student pages 23–34

Overview

Arthur Conan Doyle invented Sherlock Holmes, whose uncanny and infallible powers of observation and deduction solved many mysterious crimes. Holmes appeared in more than fifty short stories and several novels.

Selection Summary

In "The Adventure of the Speckled Band" by Arthur Conan Doyle, Sherlock Holmes solves the murder of a young woman.

Objectives

- To understand the first-person point of view in stories.
- To appreciate a classic detective story.

Audiocassette

Teacher's Resource Library

- Vocabulary Workbook 1, pages 1–3
- Selection Glossary 1
- Student Study Guide 7, pages 1–2
- Activity 3, pages 1–2
- Workbook 3, pages 1–2
- Writing Activity 1
- Selection Quiz 1

Discuss:

Setting the Stage for Reading

About the Author

Have students read this section and look at the photograph of Arthur Conan Doyle. You may want to mention that Doyle's medical practice turned out to be a failure; he took up writing while he was waiting for patients, who never appeared. However, his medical knowledge helped him develop certain important details in many of his stories. He also wrote plays, historical novels, and even some romances.

ASK What is another example of people developing fan clubs about fictional heroes? (various "Trekkies," or fans of the *Star Trek* television and movie series) Why do you suppose people join such fan clubs? (It is one way to stay involved with stories or characters they have especially enjoyed.)

About the Selection

This selection is a slightly excerpted version of the original, which is one of the most widely read of the Sherlock Holmes stories.

Activate Prior Knowledge: Discuss with students other examples of detective stories they have read (or seen on television or the movies), including other Sherlock Holmes stories.

ASK Why might Arthur Conan Doyle tell the Sherlock Holmes stories through the voice and eyes of a character named Dr. Watson? (Dr. Watson may be a stand-in for Doyle himself, observing the tales of Sherlock Holmes with a doctor's eye.)

Reading Vocabulary TRL

Help students preview the selection's vocabulary words by giving them copies of the Selection Glossary. Review the words and ask pairs of students to take turns saying the words and providing the matching definitions.

Motivation for Reading

Ask students to theorize what the "speckled band" might be. Remind them that Arthur Conan Doyle probably wanted the titles of his stories to seem as mysterious as the stories themselves. Suggest they read the story to find out what the speckled band is.

Discussion Questions

Suggest that students read the entire selection before answering the questions in the margins of the student selection.

A ASK Comprehension Remember that the story was written over 100 years ago in England, and therefore some situations, terms, and words may seem unfamiliar. How can you figure out what unfamiliar terms might mean? (by depending on the context, or other words and sentences around the terms)

B ASK Literary Element What is the setting of this story? (the year 1883 in the living quarters of Sherlock Holmes and Dr. Watson in London)

A The Adventure of the Speckled Band

Arthur Conan Doyle

As you read, watch for clues that lead to a solution.

This story takes place in April 1883.

To *knock up* is British slang for *to wake by knocking at the door.*

Mrs. Hudson is the landlady and housekeeper for Holmes and Watson.

B It was early in April in the year '83 that I woke one morning to find Sherlock Holmes standing, fully dressed, by the side of my bed. He was a late riser, as a rule, and as the clock on the mantelpiece showed me that it was only a quarter-past seven, I blinked up at him in some surprise, and perhaps just a little resentment, for I was myself regular in my habits.

"Very sorry to knock you up, Watson," he said, "but it's the common lot this morning. Mrs. Hudson has been knocked up, she retorted upon me, and I on you."

"What is it, then—a fire?"

"No; a **client.** It seems that a young lady has arrived in a considerable state of excitement, who insists upon seeing me. She is waiting now in the sitting-room. Now, when young ladies wander about the **metropolis** at this hour of the morning, and knock sleepy people up out of their beds, I presume that it is something very pressing which they have to communicate. Should it prove to be an interesting case, you would, I am sure, wish to follow it from the **outset.** I thought, at any rate, that I should call you and give you the chance."

"My dear fellow, I would not miss it for anything."

I had no keener pleasure than in following Holmes in his professional **investigations,** and in admiring the rapid **deductions,** as swift as **intuitions,** and yet always founded on a **logical** basis, with which he unravelled the problems which were submitted to him. I rapidly threw on my clothes and was ready in a few minutes to accompany my friend down to the sitting-room. A lady dressed in black and heavily veiled, who had been sitting in the window, rose as we entered.

client a customer; a person for whom one does a professional service

deduction an answer found by reasoning

intuition a way of knowing without proof

investigation a study to get facts

logical reasonable

metropolis a city

outset the beginning

Learning Styles

LEP/ESL Students struggling with the use of English may have difficulty with some of the Englishisms and old-fashioned usage found throughout any Sherlock Holmes story. Point out to them that they need to depend on context clues—the words and sentences around the difficult word or phrase—to get an idea of its meaning. Remind them, too, that often it is unnecessary to understand exactly what the word or phrase means. They should try skipping over it to get a general sense of the meaning of the whole paragraph or even the whole page. You may also want to explain that in some detective stories, such as this one, a mysterious word or phrase may be part of the story. For example, in this story, no one can know what "speckled band" means until the end of the story. The phrase is part of the mystery itself.

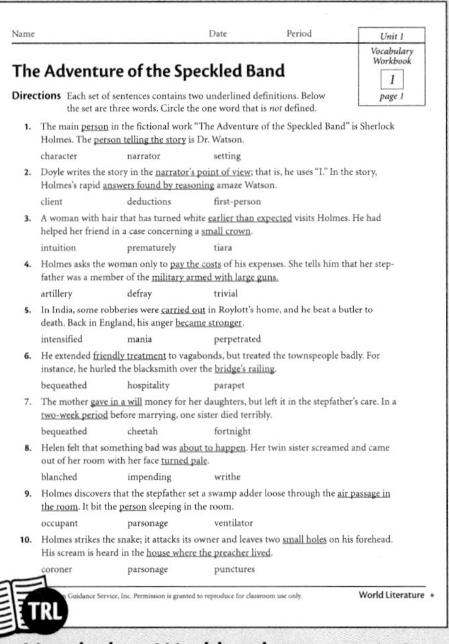

Name Date Period

Unit 1 — *Vocabulary Workbook* 1 *page 1*

The Adventure of the Speckled Band

Directions Each set of sentences contains two underlined definitions. Below the set are three words. Circle the one word that is *not* defined.

1. The main person in the fictional work "The Adventure of the Speckled Band" is Sherlock Holmes. The person telling the story is Dr. Watson.
   character narrator setting
2. Doyle writes the story in the narrator's point of view; that is, he uses "I." In the story, Holmes's rapid answers found by reasoning amaze Watson.
   client deductions first-person
3. A woman with hair that has turned white earlier than expected visits Holmes. He had helped her friend in a case concerning a small crown.
   intuition prematurely tiara
4. Holmes asks the woman only to pay the costs of his expenses. She tells him that her stepfather was a member of the military armed with large guns.
   artillery defray trivial
5. In India, some robberies were carried out in Roylott's home, and he beat a butler to death. Back in England, his anger became stronger.
   intensified mania perpetrated
6. He extended friendly treatment to vagabonds, but treated the townspeople badly. For instance, he hurled the blacksmith over the bridge's railing.
   bequeathed hospitality parapet
7. The mother gave in a will money for her daughters, but left it in the stepfather's care. In a two-week period before marrying, one sister died terribly.
   bequeathed cheetah fortnight
8. Helen felt that something bad was about to happen. Her twin sister screamed and came out of her room with her face turned pale.
   blanched impending writhe
9. Holmes discovers that the stepfather set a swamp adder loose through the air passage in the room. It bit the person sleeping in the room.
   occupant parsonage ventilator
10. Holmes strikes the snake; it attacks its owner and leaves two small holes on his forehead. His scream is heard in the house where the preacher lived.
    coroner parsonage punctures

 World Literature

TRL **Vocabulary Workbook 1, pages 1–3**

"Good-morning, madam," said Holmes cheerily. "My name is Sherlock Holmes. This is my intimate friend and associate, Dr. Watson, before whom you can speak as freely as before myself. Ha! I am glad to see that Mrs. Hudson has had the good sense to light the fire. Pray draw up to it, and I shall order you a cup of hot coffee, for I observe that you are shivering." **C**

"It is not cold which makes me shiver," said the woman in a low voice, changing her seat as requested.

"What, then?"

"It is fear, Mr. Holmes. It is terror." She raised her veil as she spoke, and we could see that she was indeed in a **pitiable** state of **agitation**, her face all drawn and gray, with restless, frightened eyes, like those of some hunted animal. Her features and figure were those of a woman of thirty, but her hair was shot with **premature** gray, and her expression was weary and **haggard**. Sherlock Holmes ran her over with one of his quick, all-**comprehensive** glances. **D**

"You must not fear," said he soothingly, bending forward and patting her forearm. "We shall soon set matters right, I have no doubt. You have come in by train this morning, I see."

"You know me, then?"

"No, but I observe the second half of a return ticket in the palm of your left glove. You must have started early, and yet you had a good drive in a **dog-cart**, along heavy roads, before you reached the station."

A *dog-cart* is a small, horse-drawn wagon.

The lady gave a violent start and stared in bewilderment at my companion.

"There is no mystery, my dear madam," said he, smiling. "The left arm of your jacket is **spattered** with mud in no less than seven places. The marks are perfectly fresh. There is no vehicle save a dog-cart which throws up mud in that way, and then only when you sit on the left-hand side of the driver."

This is an example of Holmes's amazing deductions.

"Whatever your reasons may be, you are perfectly correct," said she. "I started from home before six, reached Leatherhead at twenty past, and came in by the first train to Waterloo. Sir, I can stand this strain no longer; I shall go mad if it continues. I have no one to turn to—none, save only one, who cares for me, and he, poor fellow, can be of little aid. I have heard of you, Mr. Holmes; I have heard of you from Mrs. Farintosh, whom you helped in the hour of her sore

Leatherhead is a town south of London. *Waterloo* is a train station in London.

agitation strong emotion; disturbance

comprehensive knowing

dog-cart a cart pulled by one horse with room for two passengers

haggard looking worn because of worry

pitiable causing a feeling of pity

premature earlier than expected

spatter to splash

C ASK Comprehension What did Holmes mean when he said that Mrs. Hudson had had the good sense to light a fire? (England in the 1880s did not have central heating. Mrs. Hudson lit the fire in the fireplace, which was the method of heating the room.)

D ASK Critical Thinking A deduction is an answer found by reasoning from facts. Holmes is especially expert in observing closely to identify facts. Often even information that seems inconsequential turns out to be very important to Holmes. How can careful observation of details help a detective? (Even tiny details can be clues to what has happened.)

G Grammar

Who and Whom Near the top of this page, Holmes says, "… Dr. Watson, before whom you can speak. …" Most speakers of English have difficulty with knowing when (and when not) to use the word *whom*. The word *whom* is the form of the word *who* that is used as the object of a verb or of a preposition. Holmes used *whom* correctly in the quotation, as the object of the preposition *before*. However, many educated people disregard the use of *whom* and use *who* freely where a strict interpretation of grammatical rules might demand the use of *whom* instead. One of these was Shakespeare! The word *whom* is usually not used in everyday speech and is instead relegated mostly to very formal writing. Assure students that they usually need not worry about using the word *whom,* therefore, although it is important that they understand it when they read or hear it.

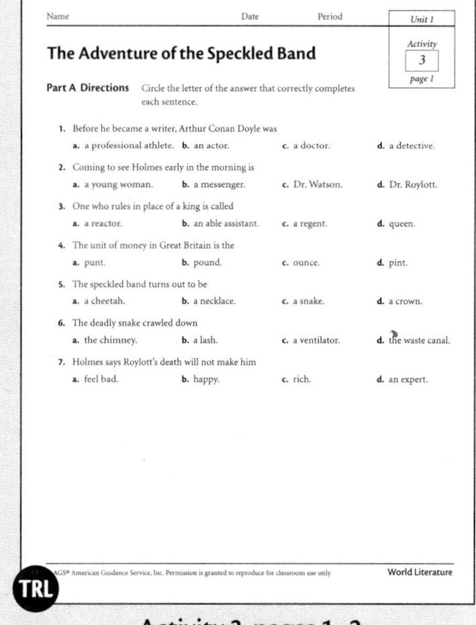

Name Date Period

Unit 1 — Student Study Guide 7 — page 1

The Adventure of the Speckled Band (pp. 24–32)

Directions Fill in the following outline. Filling in the blanks will help you as you read and study "The Adventure of the Speckled Band."

I. Beginning of the Selection (pp. 24–26)

A. Sherlock Holmes
1. He wakes Watson at quarter-past ________ in the morning.
2. A lady has arrived and is waiting for him in the ________.
3. Watson admires the rapid ________ with which he solves problems.

B. The Woman
1. Her face is drawn and ________, with restless, ________ eyes.
2. To get to Holmes, she rode in a ________ to the station and then took a ________ to Waterloo.
3. She heard of Holmes from her friend Mrs. ________.
   a. Mrs. ________ had seen Holmes because of an opal ________.
4. Her name is Helen ________.

II. Middle of the Selection (pp. 26–30)

A. Dr. Roylott
1. He is Helen's ________ and the last survivor of the ________ of Stoke Moran.
2. He beat his native ________ to death and had to serve a long term in prison.
3. When he married Helen's mother, Helen and her twin sister ________ were ________ years old.
4. He moved back to ________ ________ and shut himself in his house.
5. He has a passion for Indian animals; he owns a ________ and a baboon.

 World Literature

TRL

Student Study Guide 7, pages 1–2

Name Date Period

Unit 1 — Activity 3 — page 1

The Adventure of the Speckled Band

Part A Directions Circle the letter of the answer that correctly completes each sentence.

1. Before he became a writer, Arthur Conan Doyle was
   a. a professional athlete. **b.** an actor. **c.** a doctor. **d.** a detective.
2. Coming to see Holmes early in the morning is
   a. a young woman. **b.** a messenger. **c.** Dr. Watson. **d.** Dr. Roylott.
3. One who rules in place of a king is called
   a. a reactor. **b.** an able assistant. **c.** a regent. **d.** queen.
4. The unit of money in Great Britain is the
   a. punt. **b.** pound. **c.** ounce. **d.** pint.
5. The speckled band turns out to be
   a. a cheetah. **b.** a necklace. **c.** a snake. **d.** a crown.
6. The deadly snake crawled down
   a. the chimney. **b.** a lash. **c.** a ventilator. **d.** the waste canal.
7. Holmes says Roylott's death will not make him
   a. feel bad. **b.** happy. **c.** rich. **d.** an expert.

 World Literature

TRL

Activity 3, pages 1–2

Discussion Questions

A ASK Critical Thinking Why do you think the author included this bit about the opal tiara case being before Watson's time? (He wanted to establish the connection between Holmes and Miss Stoner, but the case is not one he has written about—so it had to take place in the reader's imagination of Holmes' past before Watson was part of his life.)

B ASK Comprehension Why do you suppose Miss Stoner mentions that her stepfather is the last of one of the oldest Saxon families in England? (Family ancestry has always been important in England, particularly that of royal families or those of important heritage. She is establishing with Holmes that her stepfather comes from an important family—and, as it turns out, he recognizes the family name.)

Cross-Curricular Connection

History In nineteenth-century England, society was somewhat different from what it is today in the United States and elsewhere. This is especially true of the accepted roles for women. Point out that in the story, Miss Stoner explains that she will have control of her own income when she gets married; yet it is clear she lives currently with her stepfather, who apparently is providing for her. Women were considered unlikely candidates for taking care of themselves, and any inheritance, as with Miss Stoner's, was always in control of a male family member. Women often could not own property or guide their own affairs. This was accepted custom among middle- and upper-class people and was often upheld by local laws as well as standard practice. Although women of lower classes who had to work for a living often were able to be more independent, their very independence was often the subject of scorn and pity. You may want to allow interested students to find out more about the ways in which women's roles have changed. If so, have them report the results to the rest of the class.

need. It was from her that I had your address. Oh, sir, do you not think that you could help me, too, and at least throw a little light through the dense darkness which surrounds me? At present it is out of my power to reward you for your services, but in a month or six weeks I shall be married, with the control of my own income, and then at least you shall not find me ungrateful."

Holmes turned to his desk and, unlocking it, drew out a small case-book, which he consulted.

"Farintosh," said he. "Ah yes, I recall the case; it was concerned **A** with an opal **tiara**. I think it was before your time, Watson. I can only say, madam, that I shall be happy to devote the same care to your case as I did to that of your friend. As to reward, my profession is its own reward; but you are at liberty to **defray** whatever expenses I may be put to, at the time which suits you best. And now I beg that you will lay before us everything that may help us in forming an opinion upon the matter."

"Alas!" replied our visitor, "the very horror of my situation lies in the fact that my fears are so vague, and my suspicions depend so entirely upon small points, which might seem **trivial** to another, that even he to whom of all others I have a right to look for help and advice looks upon all that I tell him about it as the fancies of a nervous woman. He does not say so, but I can read it from his soothing answers and **averted** eyes. But I have heard, Mr. Holmes, that you can see deeply into the **manifold** wickedness of the human heart. You may advise me how to walk amid the dangers which encompass me."

Miss Stoner is speaking of her fiancé here.

About 1,500 years ago, Germanic people from Europe conquered and settled parts of England. They were *Angles* and *Saxons*.

"I am all attention, madam."

B "My name is Helen Stoner, and I am living with my stepfather, who is the last survivor of one of the oldest Saxon families in England, the Roylotts of Stoke Moran, on the western border of Surrey."

Holmes nodded his head. "The name is familiar to me," said he.

"The family was at one time among the richest in England, and the estates extended over the borders into Berkshire in the north, and Hampshire in the west. In the last century, however, four **successive** heirs were of a **dissolute** and wasteful disposition, and the family ruin was eventually completed by a gambler in the days of the Regency. Nothing was left save a few acres of ground, and the two-hundred-year-old house, which is itself crushed under a

In English history, the *Regency* lasted 1811–1820. In this period, King George III had a mental illness. His son ruled as *regent* in his place.

averted looking away
defray to pay the costs
dissolute wicked; of bad character
manifold of many kinds
successive following
tiara a small crown
trivial not important

26 *Unit 1 Fiction*

Name Date Period

Unit 1 Workbook 3 page 1

The Adventure of the Speckled Band

Part A Directions Match each item on the left with the correct item on the right. Write the correct letter on each line.

____	1. deductions	a. not important
____	2. metropolis	b. about to happen
____	3. parapet	c. conclusions
____	4. fortnight	d. to twist in pain
____	5. trivial	e. a railing along the edge of a bridge
____	6. hubbub	f. a city
____	7. writhe	g. spotted
____	8. speckled	h. a period of two weeks
____	9. puncture	i. confusion
____	10. impending	j. a small hole caused by a sharp object

Part B Directions In each blank write the word or phrase that best completes each sentence.

1. Dr. Watson tells "The Adventure of the Speckled Band" in the ________________-person.
2. Helen lives with her ________________ at the estate named Stoke Moran.
3. Dr. Roylott allowed a ________________ and a baboon to roam freely around the estate.
4. Several nights before Julia died, she had heard a ________________ that woke her up.
5. The last person that the speckled band killed was ________________.

 World Literature

TRL

Workbook 3, pages 1–2

heavy mortgage. The last squire dragged out his existence there, living the horrible life of an **aristocratic** pauper; but his only son, my stepfather, seeing that he must adapt himself to the new conditions, obtained an advance from a relative, which enabled him to take a medical degree and went out to Calcutta, where, by his professional skill and his force of character, he established a large practice. In a fit of anger, however, caused by some robberies **C** which had been **perpetrated** in the house, he beat his native butler to death and narrowly escaped a capital sentence. As it was, he suffered a long term of imprisonment and afterwards returned to England a **morose** and disappointed man.

Calcutta is a large city in India. India was a colony of Britain when this story was written.

"When Dr. Roylott was in India he married my mother, Mrs. Stoner, the young widow of Major-General Stoner, of the Bengal **Artillery.** My sister Julia and I were twins, and we were only two years old at the time of my mother's re-marriage. She had a considerable sum of money—not less than £1000 a year—and this she **bequeathed** to Dr. Roylott entirely while we resided with him, with a provision that a certain annual sum should be allowed to each of us in the event of our marriage. Shortly after our return to England my mother died—she was killed eight years ago in a railway accident near Crewe. Dr. Roylott then abandoned his attempts to establish himself in practice in London and took us to live with him in the old ancestral house at Stoke Moran. The money which my mother had left was enough for all our wants, and there seemed to be no obstacle to our happiness.

The unit of money in Great Britain is the pound. Its symbol is £.

"But a terrible change came over our stepfather about this time. Instead of making friends and exchanging visits with our neighbours, who had at first been overjoyed to see a Roylott of Stoke Moran back in the old family seat, he shut himself up in his house and seldom came out save to indulge in ferocious quarrels with whoever might cross his path. Violence of temper approaching to **mania** has been hereditary in the men of the family, and in my stepfather's case it had, I believe, been **intensified** by his long residence in the tropics. A series of disgraceful brawls took place, two of which ended in the police-court, until at last he became the terror of the village, and the folks would fly at his approach, for he is a man of immense strength, and absolutely uncontrollable in his anger.

D
Neighbour is a British spelling of the American word *neighbor.* Do you see other British spellings in this story?

aristocratic of high social class

artillery branch of the military armed with large guns

bequeath to give to, as in a will

intensify to become stronger

mania an intense, almost insane, excitement

morose gloomy

perpetrate to carry out

C ASK Literary Element Foreshadowing is a literary technique in which an author plants hints about what will happen later in the story. What situations or descriptions on this page might be elements of foreshadowing? (The descriptions of the violent temper and nature of Miss Stoner's stepfather hint that he may be part of her problem.)

D There are few other British spellings in the story, though there are many examples of dated and/or British vocabulary and terms, such as "take a medical degree," "railway," "the old family seat," and "police-court" on this page.

G Grammar

Quotations and Quotation Marks
Much of this Sherlock Holmes story is provided by Miss Stoner telling Holmes and Watson about her situation. Make sure students understand the importance of paying attention to the quotation marks that indicate who is speaking. In some cases, the author does not provide words that tell exactly who is talking. For example, on page 26, the sentence "I am all attention, madam" is not attributed to anyone. Point out that students must use their logic to figure out that this is what Holmes said to Miss Stoner, since she is the one who has just finished speaking and he is the one who must listen carefully. Indicate the opening quotation marks at the beginning of the last paragraph on page 26 that show she is beginning to speak. Then direct students' attention to the end of that paragraph and the beginning of the second paragraph on page 27. Explain that the omission of closing quotation marks at the end of the paragraph indicates that the speaker has not finished talking. The opening quotation marks at the beginning of the following paragraph indicate that the same speaker continues to speak.

Discussion Questions

A The villagers might be afraid of a cheetah and a baboon because they are unfamiliar animals to the British. Also, both are wild animals, and it probably was wise of the people to be afraid of them.

B It was common belief that great shock or emotional difficulty could cause a person's hair to turn white, often "over night." This has now been scientifically disproved, but for Doyle it was another way to plant a clue in the story that he thought his readers would understand.

Diversity Connection

The Gypsies mentioned in the story have an interesting history. (Note that technically, the word should be capitalized, as it is the proper name of a group of people.) Gypsies are known for their itinerant ways. Their ancestors are thought to have been from India as early as the 1300s. Although some have moved to North America, many are located in North Africa, Egypt, Syria, and Europe. Most live a nomadic existence according to their own laws, although they often adopt local customs. Some tribes of Gypsies speak a unique language based on Sanskrit. In Spain, some Gypsies live in a group of caves near the city of Granada. Many are famous for their musical skills and have become professional singers and dancers. Thousands of Gypsies were murdered in Nazi concentration camps during World War II.

A
Why would the villagers be afraid of a *cheetah* and a *baboon*?

B
Why do you think the hair of the two women turned white so early?

"Last week he hurled the local blacksmith over a **parapet** into a stream, and it was only by paying over all the money which I could gather together that I was able to avert another public exposure. He had no friends at all save the wandering gypsies, and he would give these vagabonds leave to encamp upon the few acres of bramble-covered land which represent the family estate, and would accept in return the **hospitality** of their tents, wandering away with them sometimes for weeks on end. He has a passion also for Indian animals, which are sent over to him by a correspondent, and he has at this moment a **cheetah** and a **baboon**, which wander freely over his grounds and are feared by the villagers almost as much as their master.

"You can imagine from what I say that my poor sister Julia and I had no great pleasure in our lives. No servant would stay with us, and for a long time we did all the work of the house. She was but thirty at the time of her death, and yet her hair had already begun to whiten, even as mine has."

"Your sister is dead, then?"

"She died just two years ago, and it is of her death that I wish to speak to you. You can understand that, living the life which I have described, we were little likely to see anyone of our own age and position. We had, however, an aunt, my mother's maiden sister, Miss Honoria Westphail, who lives near Harrow, and we were occasionally allowed to pay short visits at this lady's house. Julia went there at Christmas two years ago, and met there a half-pay major of marines, to whom she became engaged. My stepfather learned of the engagement when my sister returned and offered no objection to the marriage; but within a **fortnight** of the day which had been fixed for the wedding, the terrible event occurred which has deprived me of my only companion."

Sherlock Holmes had been leaning back in his chair with his eyes closed and his head sunk in a cushion, but he half opened his lids now and glanced across at his visitor.

"Pray be precise as to details," said he.

"It is easy for me to be so, for every event of that dreadful time is **seared** into my memory. The **manor**-house is, as I have already said, very old, and only one wing is now inhabited. The bedrooms in this wing are on the ground floor, the sitting-rooms being in the

baboon a large monkey

cheetah a wild spotted cat

fortnight a period of two weeks

hospitality the friendly treatment of guests

manor the main house on an estate

parapet a railing along the edge of a roof or wall

sear to burn

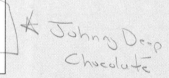

central block of the buildings. Of these bedrooms the first is Dr. Roylott's, the second my sister's, and the third my own. There is no communication between them, but they all open out into the same corridor. Do I make myself plain?"

"Perfectly so."

"The windows of the three rooms open out upon the lawn. That fatal night Dr. Roylott had gone to his room early, though we knew that he had not retired to rest, for my sister was troubled by the smell of the strong Indian cigars which it was his custom to smoke. She left **C** her room, therefore, and came into mine, where she sat for some time, chatting about her approaching wedding. At eleven o'clock she rose to leave me, but she paused at the door and looked back.

"'Tell me, Helen,' said she, 'have you ever heard anyone whistle in the dead of the night?'

"'Never,' said I.

"'I suppose that you could not possibly whistle, yourself, in your sleep?'

"'Certainly not. But why?'

"'Because during the last few nights I have always, about three in the morning, heard a low, clear whistle. I am a light sleeper, and it has awakened me. I cannot tell where it came from—perhaps from the next room, perhaps from the lawn. I thought that I would just ask you whether you had heard it.'

"'No, I have not. It must be those **wretched** gypsies in the plantation.'

"'Very likely. And yet if it were on the lawn, I wonder that you did not hear it also.'

"'Ah, but I sleep more heavily than you.'

"'Well, it is of no great **consequence**, at any rate.' She smiled back at me, closed my door, and a few moments later I heard her key turn in the lock."

"Indeed," said Holmes. "Was it your custom always to lock **D** yourselves in at night?"

"Always."

"And why?"

"I think that I mentioned to you that the doctor kept a cheetah and a baboon. We had no feeling of **security** unless our doors were locked."

consequence importance

security safety

wretched worthless; seen with scorn

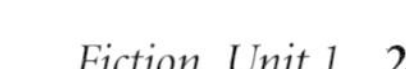

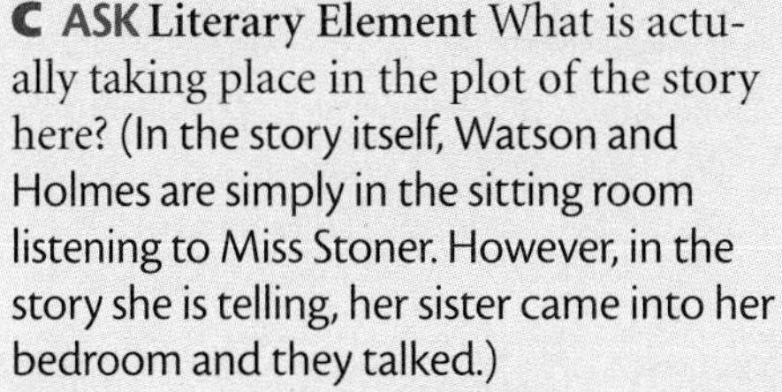

C ASK Literary Element What is actually taking place in the plot of the story here? (In the story itself, Watson and Holmes are simply in the sitting room listening to Miss Stoner. However, in the story she is telling, her sister came into her bedroom and they talked.)

D ASK Comprehension Why do you think it was important to Holmes that the two sisters locked their bedroom doors at night? (It meant that no person could simply walk into their bedrooms. It is another clue that will be important as the story resolves.)

Grammar

Single Quotation Marks Read aloud several paragraphs on page 29 beginning with "The windows of the three rooms… " and ending with the paragraph beginning with "'Because during the last few nights. …" Then draw students' attention to the quotation marks that signal a change of speaker. Point out the double quotation marks indicate that Miss Stoner is speaking, and the absence of them at the end of the first paragraph you read indicates that she continues to speak. But the beginning of the following paragraph includes double quotation marks and a single opening quotation mark. The double quotation marks show that Miss Stoner continues to speak, but the single quotation mark shows that she is quoting someone else—in this case, her sister. A quote within a quote is indicated by single quotation marks, which follow the same rules that double quotation marks do. Tell students that paying close attention to quotation marks can help them keep straight who is talking in the story.

Discussion Questions

A The question of what happened to Julia is, of course, the heart of the mystery. Let students speculate. Remind them to rely on clues they have read so far in the story. It is unlikely that they will at this point figure out what the speckled band is or determine its involvement in Julia's death.

B ASK Vocabulary In the sentence "There was something else which she would *fain* have said, . . ." what do you think the word fain means? (*Fain* is an archaic word that means "compelled." Students should be able to figure out from context that she badly wanted to say something more.)

"Quite so. Pray proceed with your statement."

"I could not sleep that night. A vague feeling of **impending** misfortune impressed me. My sister and I, you will recollect, were twins, and you know how subtle are the links which bind two souls which are so closely allied. It was a wild night. The wind was howling outside, and the rain was beating and splashing against the windows. Suddenly, amid all the **hubbub** of the gale, there burst forth the wild scream of a terrified woman. I knew that it was my sister's voice. I sprang from my bed, wrapped a shawl round me, and rushed into the corridor. As I opened my door I seemed to hear a low whistle, such as my sister described, and a few moments later a **clanging** sound, as if a mass of metal had fallen. As I ran down the passage, my sister's door was unlocked, and revolved slowly upon its hinges. I stared at it horror-**stricken**, not knowing what was about to issue from it. By the light of the corridor-lamp I saw my sister appear at the opening, her face **blanched** with terror, her hands groping for help, her whole figure swaying to and fro like that of a drunkard. I ran to her and threw my arms around her, but at that moment her knees seemed to give way and she fell to the ground. She **writhed** as one who is in terrible pain, and her limbs were dreadfully **convulsed**. At first I thought that she had not recognized me, but as I bent over her she suddenly shrieked out in a voice which I shall never forget, 'Oh, my God! Helen! It was the band! The speckled band!' There was something else which she would fain have said, and she stabbed with her finger into the air in the direction of the doctor's room, but a fresh convulsion seized her and choked her words. I rushed out, calling loudly for my stepfather, and I met him hastening from his room in his dressing-gown. When he reached my sister's side she was unconscious, and though he poured brandy down her throat and sent for medical aid from the village, all efforts were in vain, for she slowly sank and died without having recovered her consciousness. Such was the dreadful end of my beloved sister."...

A
What do you think happened to Julia?

B

[Holmes takes the case. Holmes and Watson travel to the house and examine Miss Stoner's rooms. At night, they are waiting in the dark in the room where her sister died. Holmes has not told Watson why. Suddenly they see a small light and hear a very gentle sound. Holmes jumps up and yells.]

"You see it, Watson?" he yelled. "You see it?"

blanch to turn pale
clanging ringing
convulsed shaken or pulled jerkily
hubbub confusion
impending about to happen
stricken struck; strongly affected
writhe to twist as in pain

But I saw nothing. At the moment when Holmes struck the light I heard a low, clear whistle, but the sudden glare flashing into my weary eyes made it impossible for me to tell what it was at which my friend lashed so savagely. I could, however, see that his face was deadly pale and filled with horror and **loathing**.

He had ceased to strike and was gazing up at the **ventilator** when suddenly there broke from the silence of the night the most horrible cry to which I have ever listened. It swelled up louder and louder, a hoarse yell of pain and fear and anger all mingled in the one dreadful shriek. They say that away down in the village, and even in the distant **parsonage**, that cry raised the sleepers from their beds. It struck cold to our hearts, and I stood gazing at Holmes, and he at me, until the last echoes of it had died away into the silence from which it rose.

"What can it mean?" I gasped.

"It means that it is all over," Holmes answered. "And perhaps, after all, it is for the best. Take your pistol, and we will enter Dr. Roylott's room."...

On the wooden chair, sat Dr. Grimesby Roylott, clad in a long gray dressing-gown, his bare ankles **protruding** beneath, and his feet thrust into red heelless Turkish slippers. Across his lap lay the short stock with the long lash which we had noticed during the day. His chin was cocked upward and his eyes were fixed in a dreadful, rigid stare at the corner of the ceiling. Round his brow he had a peculiar yellow band, with brownish speckles, which seemed to be bound tightly round his head. As we entered he made neither sound nor motion.

"The band! the speckled band!" whispered Holmes.

I took a step forward. In an instant his strange headgear began to move, and there reared itself from among his hair the squat diamond-shaped head and puffed neck of a **loathsome** serpent.

"It is a swamp *adder*!" cried Holmes; "the deadliest snake in India. He has died within ten seconds of being bitten." **C**

[Later Holmes explained,] "It became clear to me that whatever danger threatened an **occupant** of the room could not come either from the window or the door. My attention was **speedily** drawn, as I have already remarked to you, to this ventilator, and to the bell-rope which hung down to the bed. The discovery that this was a dummy, **D**

Adders are highly poisonous snakes in the viper family.

loathing intense dislike

loathsome disgusting

occupant a person who lives or stays in a certain place

parsonage a house where a church minister lives

protruding sticking out

speedily quickly

ventilator a passage in a house that air is blown through

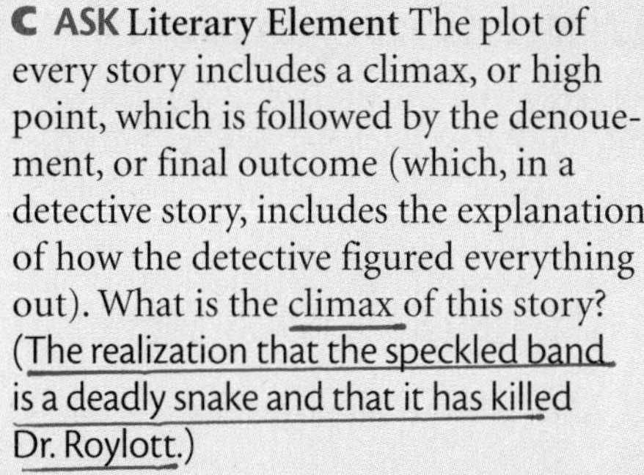

C ASK Literary Element The plot of every story includes a climax, or high point, which is followed by the denouement, or final outcome (which, in a detective story, includes the explanation of how the detective figured everything out). What is the climax of this story? (The realization that the speckled band is a deadly snake and that it has killed Dr. Roylott.)

D ASK Critical Thinking What do you predict will be the explanation for a deadly snake being in Dr. Roylott's house? (No matter what other explanation there is, the connection between Dr. Roylott and India, including his habit of importing exotic animals from there, has previously been established. So we assume that it is he who brought the snake into the house, presumably not with the intention of having it kill himself.)

Cross-Curricular Connection

Science Some students will be fascinated by the idea of poisonous snakes. Encourage them to do some research and report on what they find. Help them draft a list of questions to answer, such as (1) What viper snakes are found in the United States? (2) Can a swamp adder or other snake really be trained, as in this story? (3) What provokes a poisonous snake to bite? (4) Can a snake's venom be identified in a victim?

Discussion Questions

A ASK Critical Thinking After inspecting Dr. Roylott's chair, Holmes figured out that Dr. Roylott had the habit of standing on it. What clues might he have observed? (dirt or other debris that matched that on his shoes or slippers)

B ASK Critical Thinking Holmes does not explain Dr. Roylott's motive for killing Miss Stoner's sister and for presumably attempting to kill her as well. Why do you think he did it? (He probably did it for the money that was the legacy of their mother, mentioned early in the story as his only current income. It was also made clear earlier that the money would go to the sisters as soon as they were married. So this was his last chance before Miss Stoner married.)

and that the bed was clamped to the floor, instantly gave rise to the suspicion that the rope was there as a bridge for something passing through the hole and coming to the bed. The idea of a snake instantly occurred to me, and when I coupled it with my knowledge that the doctor was furnished with a supply of creatures from India, I felt that I was probably on the right track. The idea of using a form of poison which could not possibly be discovered by any chemical test was just such a one as would occur to a clever and **ruthless** man who had had an Eastern training. The **rapidity** with which such a poison would take effect would also, from his point of view, be an advantage. It would be a sharp-eyed **coroner**, indeed, who could distinguish the two little dark **punctures** which would show where the poison fangs had done their work. Then I thought of the whistle. Of course he must **recall** the snake before the morning light **revealed** it to the victim. He had trained it, probably by the use of the milk which we saw, to return to him when summoned. He would put it through this ventilator at the hour that he thought best, with the certainty that it would crawl down the rope and land on the bed. It might or might not bite the occupant, perhaps she might escape every night for a week, but sooner or later she must fall a victim.

"I had come to these conclusions before ever I had entered his
A room. An inspection of his chair showed me that he had been in the habit of standing on it, which of course would be necessary in order that he should reach the ventilator. The sight of the safe, the saucer
B of milk, and the loop of whipcord were enough to finally **dispel** any doubts which may have remained. The metallic clang heard by Miss Stoner was obviously caused by her stepfather hastily closing the door of his safe upon its terrible occupant. Having once made up my mind, you know the steps which I took in order to put the matter to the proof. I heard the creature hiss as I have no doubt that you did also, and I instantly lit the light and attacked it."

"With the result of driving it through the ventilator."

"And also with the result of causing it to turn upon its master at the other side. Some of the blows of my cane came home and roused its snakish temper, so that it flew upon the first person it saw. In this way I am no doubt indirectly responsible for Dr. Grimesby Roylott's death, and I cannot say that it is likely to weigh very heavily upon my conscience."

5. J
6. K or L

coroner the official who decides the cause of death

dispel to make disappear

puncture a small hole caused by a sharp object

rapidity speed

recall to call back; remember

reveal to show

ruthless cruel

REVIEWING the SELECTION

The Adventure of the Speckled Band

Arthur Conan Doyle

Directions Write the answers to these questions using complete sentences.

Comprehension: Identifying Facts

1. How did Helen Stoner travel to London?
2. Who does Helen Stoner live with when she comes to see Sherlock Holmes?
3. How long has her sister been dead when Helen Stoner comes to see Holmes?
4. What change had happened in Julia's life a few weeks before she died?
5. What sound did Julia tell her sister she heard in the night?
6. What words did Julia say just before she died?
7. What wild animals roam the estate?
8. What is the speckled band?
9. How did the speckled band get into Julia's room?
10. Who is the speckled band's final victim?

Comprehension: Understanding Main Ideas

11. What facts about Helen Stoner does Holmes learn just by observing her?
12. How do you know that the story takes place in the 1800s?
13. Why does Helen Stoner look tired and older than her age?
14. Why does Helen think she can trust only Holmes?
15. What happened to Dr. Roylott before his return to England?
16. Where did the family's money come from?
17. What causes Dr. Roylott's terrible temper?
18. Why didn't the Stoner sisters ever have company?
19. Why was Julia Stoner killed?
20. How does Holmes feel about Dr. Roylott's death?

Review Continued on Next Page

1. step Father
2. afraid?
3. India
4. snake
5. stepFather

Reviewing the Selection

Answer Key

Comprehension: Identifying Facts

1. She traveled by dog-cart and then by train.

2. She lives with her stepfather.

3. Her sister has been dead for two years.

4. Julia had become engaged to be married a few weeks before she died.

5. Julia heard a whistle in the night.

6. She said, "Oh, my God! Helen! It was the band! The speckled band!"

7. A baboon and a cheetah roam the estate.

8. The speckled band is a swamp adder—a deadly snake.

9. The speckled band got into Julia's room through a hole in the ceiling from the ventilator, then down a rope.

10. The final victim of the speckled band is Dr. Roylott.

Comprehension: Understanding Main Ideas

11. Holmes learns that she is very tense and upset and that she is prematurely gray. He also observes details that tell him how she traveled to see him.

12. The story begins with Holmes identifying the year as "'83," and we presume it was 1883 rather than 1983 because we know that Doyle was not alive in 1983.

13. She has been frightened and under great strain.

14. Her fiancé does not seem to take her seriously, she is afraid of Dr. Roylott, and his behavior has cut her off from most other people. In addition, she knows of Holmes through his help for a friend of hers.

15. He had a successful medical practice and married Miss Stoner's mother. However, he beat a servant to death and was imprisoned.

16. The family's money came from Miss Stoner's mother.

17. Miss Stoner believes that Dr. Roylott's temper is hereditary.

18. They had no company because Dr. Roylott behaved so badly no one wanted to associate with them.

19. The story doesn't specifically say why Julia Stoner was killed, but we deduce that Dr. Roylott killed her so she would not get married, which would mean that she would take some of the family income from him.

20. Holmes is not sorry that Dr. Roylott died, even though he was somewhat responsible for his death.

Understanding Literature: First-Person

21. We know that Watson was regular in his habits and took great pleasure in following Holmes in his investigations.

22. Holmes explains that Watson is his "intimate friend and associate."

23. If Holmes were the narrator, we would know what he was thinking as events took place—and that would spoil the suspense of the story.

24. If the story were told by a third-person narrator, Watson's role would be a minor one.

25. Answers will vary, but students should realize that most stories are told in the third-person.

Critical Thinking

26. She probably led a very nice life; she would marry her fiancé, have the income from her mother's estate, and probably also inherit her stepfather's property.

27. Answers will vary, but invite students to present the reasons for their opinions.

28. All students may not agree, but most will feel that the title is suitable.

29. Many students will have found the death of Julia scary.

30. Make sure they can defend their ideas with specific examples from the story.

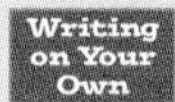

You may want to suggest that students visit the library or a bookstore to read several examples of the back covers of detective stories.

Selection Quiz

The Teacher's Resource Library includes a Selection Quiz for "The Adventure of the Speckled Band" that may be given following the Selection Review.

REVIEWING the SELECTION

The Adventure of the Speckled Band *(Continued)*

Understanding Literature: First-Person

A story told in first-person uses pronouns such as *I, me, my,* and *we.* It is told from the point of view of the narrator—the person telling the story. In the Sherlock Holmes stories, the narrator is his friend Watson. We know only what Watson knows. We do not know what Sherlock Holmes is thinking. We can be as puzzled as Watson is during the case.

21. Watson tells us a little bit about himself. Describe one thing about Watson.
22. How does Holmes explain to the woman why Watson is in the room?
23. Would the story work as well if Holmes were the narrator? Explain.
24. Imagine the story told in the third-person. A third-person narrator knows the thoughts and acts of all the characters. What role would Watson have? Explain.
25. Think of other stories you have read. Do you prefer first-person stories or third-person stories? Explain.

Critical Thinking

26. What do you think life was like for Helen Stoner after Dr. Roylott's death?
27. Do you think you could be a detective like Sherlock Holmes? Why or why not?
28. Is "The Adventure of the Speckled Band" a good title for this story? Why or why not?
29. What was the scariest part of the story for you?
30. Did you like this story? Why or why not?

Writing on Your Own

Imagine you are writing the text for a paperback book cover to attract readers. Write two paragraphs about the mysterious murder of Julia Stoker without giving the story away.

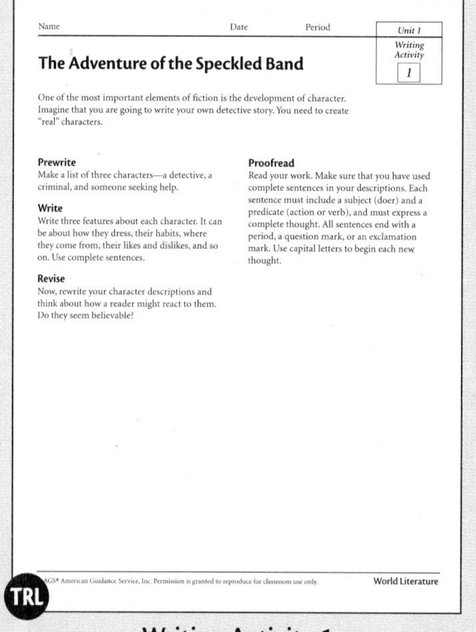

Name Date Period | *Unit 1* *Writing Activity* 1

The Adventure of the Speckled Band

One of the most important elements of fiction is the development of character. Imagine that you are going to write your own detective story. You need to create "real" characters.

Prewrite
Make a list of three characters—a detective, a criminal, and someone seeking help.

Write
Write three features about each character. It can be about how they dress, their habits, where they come from, their likes and dislikes, and so on. Use complete sentences.

Revise
Now, rewrite your character descriptions and think about how a reader might react to them. Do they seem believable?

Proofread
Read your work. Make sure that you have used complete sentences in your descriptions. Each sentence must include a subject (doer) and a predicate (action or verb), and must express a complete thought. All sentences end with a period, a question mark, or an exclamation mark. Use capital letters to begin each new thought.

 World Literature

TRL

Writing Activity 1

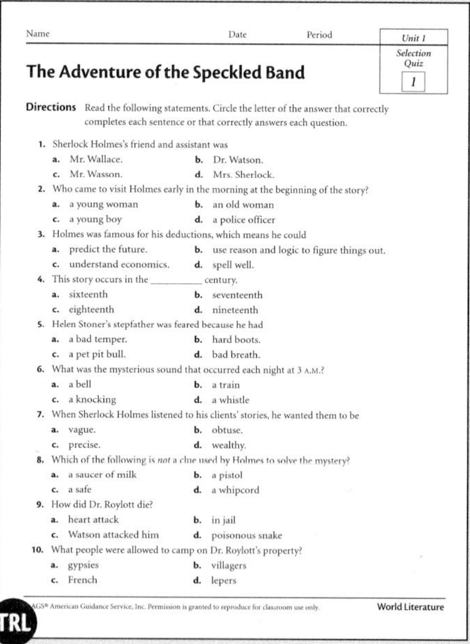

Name Date Period | *Unit 1* *Selection Quiz* 1

The Adventure of the Speckled Band

Directions Read the following statements. Circle the letter of the answer that correctly completes each sentence or that correctly answers each question.

1. Sherlock Holmes's friend and assistant was
   a. Mr. Wallace. b. Dr. Watson.
   c. Mr. Wasson. d. Mrs. Sherlock.
2. Who came to visit Holmes early in the morning at the beginning of the story?
   a. a young woman b. an old woman
   c. a young boy d. a police officer
3. Holmes was famous for his deductions, which means he could
   a. predict the future. b. use reason and logic to figure things out.
   c. understand economics. d. spell well.
4. This story occurs in the __________ century.
   a. sixteenth b. seventeenth
   c. eighteenth d. nineteenth
5. Helen Stoner's stepfather was feared because he had
   a. a bad temper. b. hard boots.
   c. a pet pit bull. d. bad breath.
6. What was the mysterious sound that occurred each night at 3 A.M.?
   a. a bell b. a train
   c. a knocking d. a whistle
7. When Sherlock Holmes listened to his clients' stories, he wanted them to be
   a. vague. b. obtuse.
   c. precise. d. wealthy.
8. Which of the following is *not* a clue used by Holmes to solve the mystery?
   a. a saucer of milk b. a pistol
   c. a safe d. a whipcord
9. How did Dr. Roylott die?
   a. heart attack b. in jail
   c. Watson attacked him d. poisonous snake
10. What people were allowed to camp on Dr. Roylott's property?
   a. gypsies b. villagers
   c. French d. lepers

 World Literature

TRL

Selection Quiz 1

INTRODUCING the SELECTION

Death Arrives on Schedule

Hansjörg Martin (translated by Charles E. Pederson)

About the Author

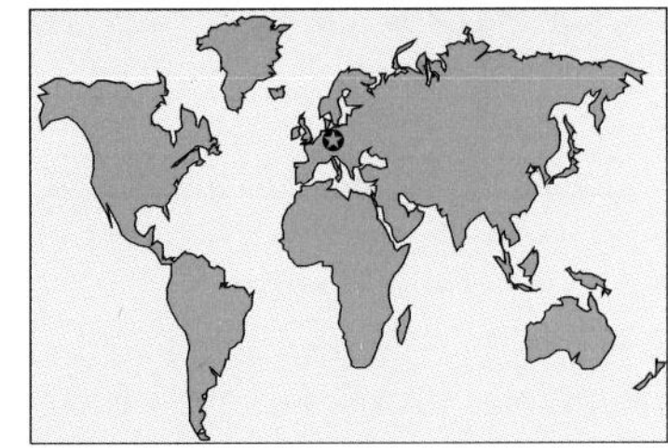

Hansjörg Martin was born in 1920 in Leipzig, Germany. He served in the German army during World War II. After the war he held many jobs. He was an artist, clown, decorator, stage set builder, editor, and teacher. In 1962, he became a full-time writer. He moved with his family to a province in northern Germany, where he still lives.

Martin has been called the "founder of the modern German **detective story.**" A detective story is one in which the main character usually solves a crime. Martin's work has several **themes,** or main ideas. One is that crime is not entirely a person's own fault. It is also a result of social pressure. Martin's mysteries may not always have a careful plot or well-developed characters. But he always presents a problem in an entertaining way. He has written more than seventy **novels** and books of short stories. A novel is fiction with more plot and character details than a short story has. His books have been translated into at least fourteen languages, with millions of copies sold. His writing has also won many awards.

Literary Terms

detective story a story in which the main character usually solves a crime

novel a literary work of fiction having more plot and character details than a short story

theme the main idea of a literary work

About the Selection

One of Martin's idols is Raymond Chandler, a well-known American mystery writer. Martin especially loves Chandler's use of natural language. The following selection uses similarly short sentences and everyday language. Martin's theme of social pressure appears, as well. But the story does not have the usual dead body, with no clues about "whodunnit." Instead, it follows the criminal as he plans and commits his crime. But the luck of this bad guy is about to run out. "Death Arrives on Schedule" was first published in 1974.

Selection at a Glance

Death Arrives on Schedule

Hansjörg Martin
(translated by Charles E. Pederson)

Student pages 35–50

Overview

Hansjörg Martin's work is well liked and well-known in his native Germany. He is particularly noted for his detective stories.

Selection Summary

In "Death Arrives on Schedule" by Hansjörg Martin, a killer has bad luck with well-laid plans.

Objectives

- To read and understand the genre of detective stories.
- To appreciate the element of surprise in detective stories.

Audiocassette 

Teacher's Resource Library 

- Vocabulary Workbook 2, pages 1–3
- Selection Glossary 2
- Student Study Guide 8, pages 1–3
- Activity 4, pages 1–2
- Workbook 4, pages 1–2
- Writing Activity 2
- Selection Quiz 2

Setting the Stage for Reading

About the Author

Have students read this section. Mention that Hansjörg Martin has written children's books and radio plays in addition to the detective stories for which he is especially well-known.

ASK How might Martin's varied career history have helped his writing? (His exposure to different kinds of people and situations is likely to have contributed to his knowledge of people and how they act.)

About the Selection

The story is written from the third-person (or "omniscient") point of view. Nevertheless, the unknown narrator's style is informal, as is the dialogue of the characters. Despite this, some students may have difficulty with the references to unfamiliar places.

Activate Prior Knowledge: Have students recall other modern detective stories they are familiar with.

ASK You know that this is a detective story. What does that lead you to expect? (That there will be a character who solves a crime, and that, presumably, there will be some suspense.)

Reading Vocabulary TRL

Help students preview the selection's vocabulary words by giving them copies of the Selection Glossary. Have pairs of students take turns making up a sentence using one of the words.

Motivation for Reading

Remind students that in this story the criminal and the crime are known to the reader. Suggest they read the story to find out what the mystery is and who solves it.

Discussion Questions

Suggest that students skim the selection to find the answers to notes in the margin of the student text.

A ASK Literary Element Three characters are introduced on these two pages. Who are they? (Alfred Algernissen, Loni Leisegang, and her husband, Helfried Leisegang)

B ASK Comprehension What do you predict will be the crime? (the murder of Helfried Leisegang) Who will commit the crime? (probably Alfred Algernissen)

Death Arrives on Schedule

Hansjörg Martin

As you read, think about why the characters act as they do.

At a time in his life when he possessed almost **A** everything a man could want, Alfred Algernissen's eyes fell on Loni Leisegang. And his heart beat as it never had before. His wealth, his luxury limousine, his **exclusive bungalow** home, everything became unimportant—everything but Loni Leisegang, whose **B** looks (and this must be said both to explain and to defend Alfred Algernissen's behavior) had already caused many other men to lose their heads in the same way. Besides, it's understandable why men might lose their heads over Loni. After all, chestnut-red hair and green eyes like Loni's are the best guarantee of **masculine** head loss. And when such hair and eyes crown a **regally** curvy shape, men might even become **aggressive**. Alfred Algernissen became aggressive.

It was not Loni Leisegang's fault (or **merit**, if you prefer) that she met Alfred Algernissen at a party. It's not her fault that she led him to understand that she certainly was not against aggressiveness, or at least not against

aggressive ready to do combat

bungalow a low, one-story house

exclusive not letting others participate

masculine relating to men

merit a positive quality

regally in a royal way

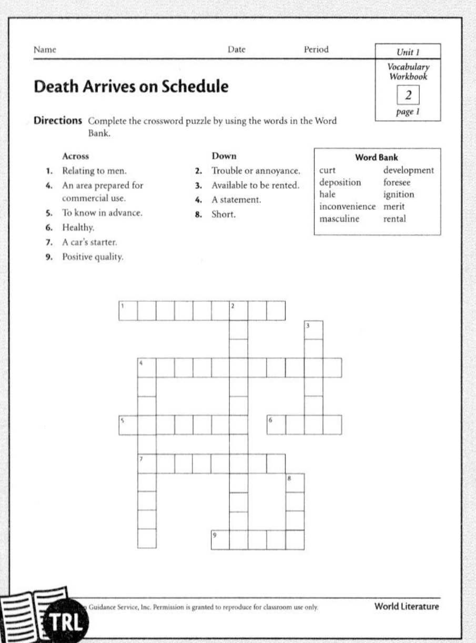

Name Date Period

Unit 1 Vocabulary Workbook 2 page 1

Death Arrives on Schedule

Directions Complete the crossword puzzle by using the words in the Word Bank.

Across
1. Relating to men.
4. An area prepared for commercial use.
5. To know in advance.
6. Healthy.
7. A car's starter.
9. Positive quality.

Down
2. Trouble or annoyance.
3. Available to be rented.
4. A statement.
8. Short.

Word Bank	
curt	development
deposition	foresee
hale	ignition
inconvenience	merit
masculine	rental

 World Literature

TRL Vocabulary Workbook 2, pages 1–3

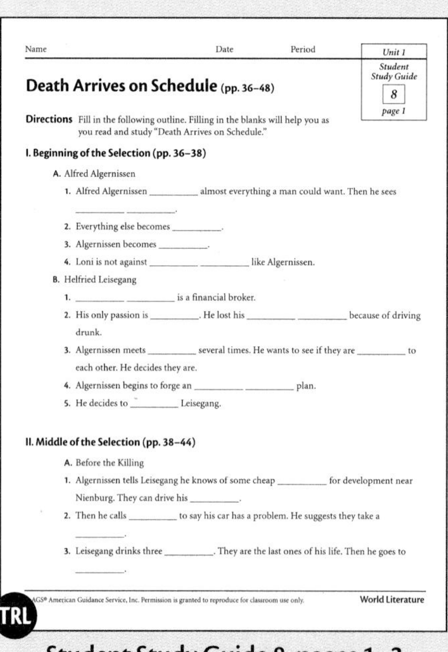

Name Date Period

Unit 1 Student Study Guide 8 page 1

Death Arrives on Schedule (pp. 36–48)

Directions Fill in the following outline. Filling in the blanks will help you as you read and study "Death Arrives on Schedule."

I. Beginning of the Selection (pp. 36–38)

A. Alfred Algernissen
1. Alfred Algernissen ______ almost everything a man could want. Then he sees ______ ______.
2. Everything else becomes ______.
3. Algernissen becomes ______.
4. Loni is not against ______ ______ like Algernissen.

B. Helfried Leisegang
1. ______ ______ is a financial broker.
2. His only passion is ______. He lost his ______ ______ because of driving drunk.
3. Algernissen meets ______ several times. He wants to see if they are ______ to each other. He decides they are.
4. Algernissen begins to forge an ______ ______ plan.
5. He decides to ______ Leisegang.

II. Middle of the Selection (pp. 38–44)

A. Before the Killing
1. Algernissen tells Leisegang he knows of some cheap ______ for development near Nienburg. They can drive his ______.
2. Then he calls ______ to say his car has a problem. He suggests they take a ______.
3. Leisegang drinks three ______. They are the last ones of his life. Then he goes to ______.

 World Literature

TRL Student Study Guide 8, pages 1–3

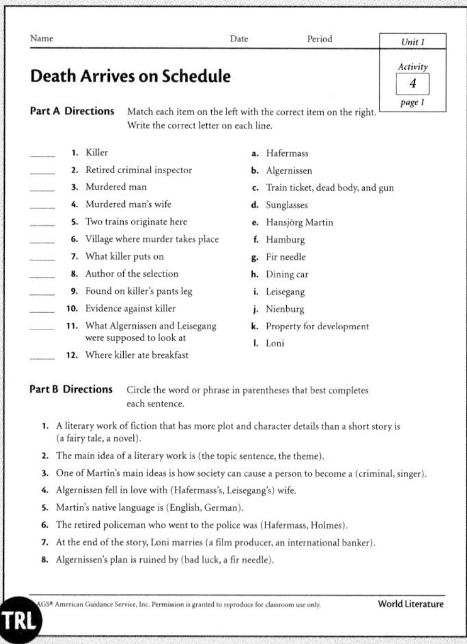

Name Date Period

Unit 1 Activity 4 page 1

Death Arrives on Schedule

Part A Directions Match each item on the left with the correct item on the right. Write the correct letter on each line.

____	1. Killer	a. Hafermass
____	2. Retired criminal inspector	b. Algernissen
____	3. Murdered man	c. Train ticket, dead body, and gun
____	4. Murdered man's wife	d. Sunglasses
____	5. Two trains originate here	e. Hansjörg Martin
____	6. Village where murder takes place	f. Hamburg
____	7. What killer puts on	g. Fir needle
____	8. Author of the selection	h. Dining car
____	9. Found on killer's pants leg	i. Leisegang
____	10. Evidence against killer	j. Nienburg
____	11. What Algernissen and Leisegang were supposed to look at	k. Property for development
____	12. Where killer ate breakfast	l. Loni

Part B Directions Circle the word or phrase in parentheses that best completes each sentence.

1. A literary work of fiction that has more plot and character details than a short story is (a fairy tale, a novel).
2. The main idea of a literary work is (the topic sentence, the theme).
3. One of Martin's main ideas is how society can cause a person to become a (criminal, singer).
4. Algernissen fell in love with (Hafermass's, Leisegang's) wife.
5. Martin's native language is (English, German).
6. The retired policeman who went to the police was (Hafermass, Holmes).
7. At the end of the story, Loni marries (a film producer, an international banker).
8. Algernissen's plan is ruined by (bad luck, a fir needle).

 World Literature

TRL Activity 4, pages 1–2

certain *kinds* of aggressiveness—and especially not against rich **aggressors** such as Alfred Algernissen obviously was. **C** In any case, it cannot be proven whether Loni's **inclination** toward violence included at this point the idea of her becoming a widow.

D Do you think Loni wants her husband to be killed?

Financial broker Helfried Leisegang, Loni's husband, was far too healthy for thoughts of widowhood, anyway.

aggressor an aggressive person

financial broker one who helps others invest money

inclination a way of thinking

C ASK Literary Element Every story plot has a conflict or problem. What do you think is the conflict in this story? (Alfred Algernissen is attracted to Loni Leisegang, but she has a husband.)

D Students' opinions may vary on whether Loni wants her husband to be killed. We get the feeling that she flirted with Alfred Algernissen, but we don't know much else yet.

G Grammar

Italics Draw students' attention to the italicized word *kinds* on page 37. Discuss with students that italicizing words can mean several things. Here it is used as it is most commonly—to indicate that the word is to be emphasized in the reader's mind. To demonstrate this, read the sentence aloud (beginning on page 36) with expression, first emphasizing the word *kinds* and then rereading it without the emphasis. Help students realize how the emphasis changes the meaning slightly. Point out that when students do their own writing, they can use underlining for the same purpose. You may want to explain that professional editors and typographers use underlining in manuscripts to indicate the use of italics, although most computer word processing programs now allow writers to use italics directly.

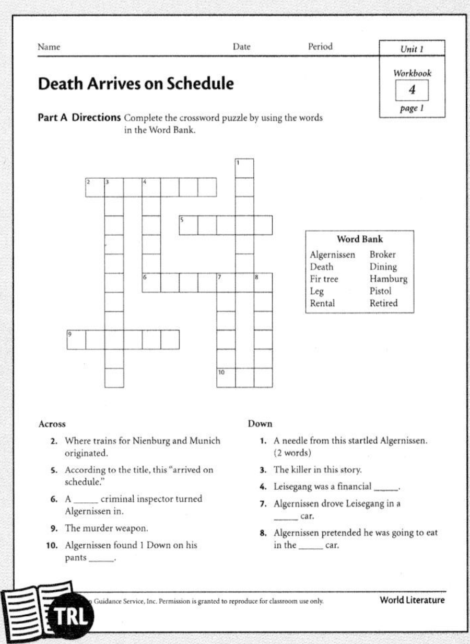

Name Date Period

Unit 1 *Workbook* 4 *page 1*

Death Arrives on Schedule

Part A Directions Complete the crossword puzzle by using the words in the Word Bank.

Word Bank

Algernissen	Broker
Death	Dining
Fir tree	Hamburg
Leg	Pistol
Rental	Retired

Across

2. Where trains for Nienburg and Munich originated.
5. According to the title, this "arrived on schedule."
6. A _____ criminal inspector turned Algernissen in.
9. The murder weapon.
10. Algernissen found 1 Down on his pants _____.

Down

1. A needle from this startled Algernissen. (2 words)
3. The killer in this story.
4. Leisegang was a financial _____.
7. Algernissen drove Leisegang in a _____ car.
8. Algernissen pretended he was going to eat in the _____ car.

World Literature

TRL

Workbook 4, pages 1–2

Discussion Questions

A ASK Critical Thinking What does the phrase "an almost-perfect murder" suggest will happen? (The murder will happen, but something will go wrong.)

B Hints like the phrase "an almost-perfect murder" make it seem unlikely that Algernissen will get away with his plan.

Community Connection

Many places, among them Germany and the United States, have laws against drunk driving. Those who break the law may be punished by having their driving privileges taken away, as happened to Leisegang. Discuss with students why this is so. Make sure they realize that alcohol affects a person's physical capabilities as well as his or her intellectual judgment. This is what makes driving dangerous to the driver, other passengers in the car, as well as people in other cars. Point out that the campaign to name a designated driver and not drive when you have had a drink of alcohol is intended to save lives.

If possible, acquire information about such organizations as MADD (Mothers against Drunk Driving) and SADD (Students against Drunk Driving). If there are chapters in your community, invite a representative to speak to the class. Alternatively, ask a police officer or a judge to speak to you about the consequences of drinking and driving.

Herr is German for *Mr.*

Herr Leisegang's only real **passion** was whiskey. Because of this passion, he had lost his driver's license several months before. That his passion had put him on the quickest path to losing his wife, too, had not yet become clear to him. And that shortly, he would lose his life—well, he could hardly **foresee** that.

Fourteen days after that first party, however, the fate of the whiskey lover Herr Leisegang was sealed. In those two weeks Alfred Algernissen had found three opportunities to test whether he and Loni were suited to each other. They found themselves so well suited, in fact, that Algernissen decided to win his lover completely. It was certain that Leisegang would never freely release his Loni. So Algernissen began to forge a plan that would help him sweep away, risk free, the only **barrier** to Loni's release: Helfried Leisegang himself. And because Algernissen was a self-confident and clear-thinking man, and because he had no taste for a years-long visit to jail, the plan grew slowly, was altered, rethought, and improved. Finally, it was so good that it **A** led to an almost-perfect **murder**. And this is what happened:

B Do you think Algernissen will get away with his plan?

Alfred Algernissen knew that Leisegang's company (Leisegang & Co., Building Contractors) provided Helfried Leisegang enough profits that he wanted to **invest** in property. So one beautiful evening, Algernissen called up the **hale** and healthy husband and said he had

barrier something that blocks

foresee to know in advance

hale healthy

invest to use money for later profit

murder a killing of another

passion an object of deep interest

available 12,000 square meters of land to sell. Prime land for **development**. **Favorable** location in the country. Cheap. Inside tip.

12,000 square meters is about three acres.

Leisegang was extremely interested.

Algernissen gave him a few other tempting **tidbits**. The very healthy candidate for death promptly took the bait.

C
Why is Leisegang called a *very healthy candidate for death?*

They agreed to take a look at the property the day after tomorrow. Algernissen told Leisegang that it lay near Nienburg, about a hundred kilometers, or an hour's drive, outside the city. Naturally, Leisegang swore himself to **absolute secrecy**—if only in his own interest. Algernissen offered to pick him up by car—yes, early in the morning, how did seven-thirty sound? That's okay with you? Great, thank you!

100 kilometers is about 60 miles.

The evening before the meeting, Algernissen called again: "Sorry, Leisegang, slight problem. This afternoon I went out to the property and . . ."

"What has happened?" Leisegang interrupted, shocked. "Has the property been sold?"

"No, no, of course not. It's just that—well, my car went on strike! Something with the **ignition**. I don't know anything about cars. I just dropped it off at the repair shop. They said they'll drive it over to the Nienburg train station by tomorrow morning. I have a second key. We'll have to—if you're still interested, as I assume you

D
Do you think Algernissen's car is really *at the repair shop?*

absolute complete

development an area prepared for commercial use

favorable promoting success

ignition a car's starter

secrecy the condition of being hidden

tidbit a small bit of knowledge

C Leisegang is called a "very healthy candidate for death" because he was going to die despite the fact that there was nothing physically wrong with him.

D It is unlikely that his car is really at the repair shop. Clearly he is trying to set up a plan, and he doesn't want the two of them to be in his car until the Nienburg train station.

Fiction Unit 1 **39**

Discussion Questions

A Comprehension How does the fact that Leisegang has lost his driver's license fit into Algernissen's plan? (Leisegang cannot have a car along, which might be difficult for Algernissen to get rid of.)

B The story doesn't tell us enough about Loni to make clear what she knows. However, earlier we found out that she and Algernissen had met privately on several occasions, so she may have some sense that he is going to do something about her husband.

Cross-Curricular Connection

Geography Provide students with a map of Germany or direct volunteers to find such a map to share with the class. Help them follow Algernissen's plan on the map. Make sure they find Nienburg, Hamburg, Frankfurt, Hannover, Würzburg, and Munich. Ask them to speculate where in Germany Algernissen and Leisegang live, using clues from the story.

Hamburg is a large seaport in northern Germany.

are?—we'll have to take the train over, and then drive back to Hamburg in my car. Sorry about the **inconvenience** . . ."

"Don't worry about it," said Leisegang, "it's no trouble at all. Maybe taking a **rental** car to pick up your car would be best . . .?"

"I can't drive two cars at once," Algernissen patiently explained. "And you have no driver's license, if I remember correctly."

A "That's right," Leisegang said with a curse. "Then we'll take the train. Have you already looked into connections, or should I?"

Algernissen had already done so. In fact, he had found a fine connection. He had sat for almost two hours studying the timetables until he had found exactly the right train—or rather, the right trains. He told Leisegang that a train left the central Hamburg train **terminal**, track 11, at 8:24 the next morning, arriving in Nienburg at 9:58. They could meet on the track 11 platform.

B
Do you think Loni really *knew nothing*?

Leisegang had three more whiskeys—the last ones in this life—and went to sleep next to Loni about eleven. He fell asleep right away while she read. It can be assumed that she knew nothing, though perhaps she had a feeling something was going to happen.

inconvenience trouble or annoyance

rental available to be rented

terminal station

Algernissen, meanwhile, had packed a small suitcase and laid out and rechecked his train tickets and schedule. He loaded his small pistol, set the safety, and pocketed it in his loose, double-sided jacket. He had bought the gun a week earlier from a dealer in Frankfurt. In the morning, shortly before eight, Algernissen boarded the express train for Munich, which **originated** in Hamburg, and which—as he had found out by asking careful questions—was always ready a half hour before departure.

Frankfurt is a large city in central Germany. *Munich* is far to the south.

He walked down the corridor of the still-empty train, said a few friendly words to the conductor, and finally **C** found a second-class **compartment** in which an **elderly** couple sat. They were full of travel fever. **D**

Algernissen lifted his suitcase into the luggage rack above the vacant third seat and chatted with the elderly couple. He made fun of himself for always being too early, always too excited at the prospect of traveling, and now they had a half hour before departure—but better thirty minutes too early than thirty minutes too late, right? Ha ha!

Algernissen is "proving" he will be on the train.

He asked the elderly pair to watch his suitcase, saying he was just going to slip out for a quick smoke and a magazine, then head over to the dining car for a bit of breakfast. "At the latest, I'm sure I'll be back by the time we reach Hannover, full and contented," he said after hearing that they were going only as far as Würzburg.

On its way to Munich, the train will stop in *Hannover.* Nienburg is about twenty miles away. *Würzburg* is farther south.

compartment an enclosed space

elderly old

originate to start

C ASK Critical Thinking Why did Algernissen stop only when he found people already on the train? (He clearly wanted witnesses to the fact that he is on the train.)

D ASK Vocabulary What do you think the sentence "They were full of travel fever" means? (They seemed eager to travel, to get going.)

Grammar

Hyphenated Compound Words

Draw students' attention to the several hyphenated compound words on page 41. You may want to list the phrases on the board: *double-sided jacket, still-empty train, second-class compartment.* Point out that hyphens are often used to prevent confusion on the part of a reader. For example, two words that together make one adjective are usually hyphenated so they will not be misread. The examples cited all fall into this classification. Sometimes the parts of a compound word are used so often together that they become used as a "solid compound," or a single word. There are several examples on these two pages that you may want to share with students: *timetable* and *something* on page 40 and *suitcase* and *breakfast* on page 41.

Discussion Questions

A **ASK Critical Thinking** What do you think the picture on this page has to do with the story? (It depicts the scene described on page 43, where the two men drive into a small forest of trees.)

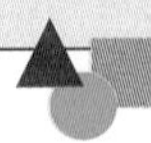

Learning Styles

Visual Visually oriented students may appreciate the picture on this page, which sets the scene for the death of Leisegang at the "prime land for development" he thinks he has come to see.

ASK How does this picture compare to the description of the place on page 43? (It is pretty close, showing a somewhat open area surrounded by trees. We surmise that Algernissen has chosen a lonely spot, and the picture shows a place without people around.)

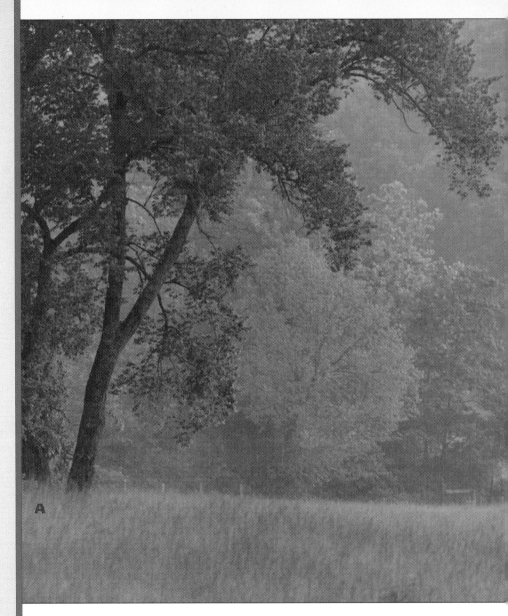

A

42 *Unit 1 Fiction*

At 8:13, twenty minutes before the express was to depart, he stepped off the train. He crossed to track 11, putting on sunglasses as he went—although even outside there was no sun to speak of, and certainly none inside the train terminal. He greeted Leisegang, who was already nervously waiting for him. They climbed aboard this train, which was bound for Nienburg. That train left the terminal three minutes later, with him and Leisegang on board. Crossing from the express train to the Nienburg train, Algernissen had turned his jacket inside out—now the light-colored side faced in and the dark side faced out. And he was still wearing the same dark jacket and sunglasses as he got off the train again with Leisegang at the end of the line.

B
Why does Algernissen turn *his jacket inside out* and put on sunglasses?

Five minutes later they sat in a car.

Algernissen rented this car. His own car is parked in Hamburg, as you will see.

Ten minutes later they were leaving the village of Nienburg.

Fourteen minutes later Algernissen turned the car off the highway into a small woods, drove a couple hundred meters along a small forest path among the beech trees, birches, and firs, and stopped the car.

"Here?" Leisegang sounded **irritated**. "But this is certainly not 'prime land for development,' Herr Algernissen, is it?"

"Of course it is," said Algernissen. "Get out. I'll show you." **C**

irritated annoyed

B He is trying to disguise himself so casual observers would not think he is the same person.

C **ASK Comprehension** What is about to happen? (Algernissen is about to murder Leisegang.)

Discussion Questions

A ASK Comprehension Why did Algernissen reverse his jacket again? (He wanted to look the way he did when he got on this train earlier.)

B ASK Literary Element We know what the crime is and we know who committed it. What is the suspense about? (whether he will get away with it)

Literary Elements

Plot, Setting, and Characters Often in short stories one of these elements seems more important than the others. Some authors emphasize plot and provide little insight into character development, for example. In other stories it is the development of one or more characters that seems to be the plot. In most detective stories, plot drives the story more than does character development. This is true of "Death Arrives on Schedule," too. Nevertheless, students may benefit from discussing what they know of the character of Algernissen and how they know it. Help them realize that the character really does not change throughout the story.

Leisegang hesitated—maybe it was an instinct that warned him of danger, or maybe he felt a sudden distrust of Algernissen. But finally he got out.

Algernissen had also left the car. He now approached Leisegang and smoothly drew his pistol, shooting Leisegang twice. He was surprised that it was not louder. He had feared it would be much worse. In the basement of his lovely home, where he had practiced for so many hours, it had seemed almost to roar.

Leisegang had no time for any other doubts. He died immediately.

Algernissen pulled him beneath a bushy blue spruce tree, hurriedly brushing over the tracks they had made as he dragged the body. He got back in the car and quickly drove back to the highway, which was empty—and from the highway to the freeway, where he got from the car everything its motor was capable of. He reached the Hannover train station at the same time a voice on the loudspeaker announced, "Attention on track 3. The express train for Munich will arrive in several minutes. Stand back on the platform, please."

Algernissen wants to reach Hannover before the Hamburg-to-Munich train arrives.

Algernissen grinned. He stood behind a pillar on the platform until the train had arrived. Then he stepped up into the dining car, took off the jacket—which he **A** had reversed again so that the light side was facing out—and sat down at an empty table.

He must have returned the rental car.

B He took a deep breath, ordered an egg, coffee, and cold cuts with double butter on the bread—and with a start saw a fir needle stuck to the leg of his pants. He discovered it as he bent to **retrieve** his lighter, which had fallen from his pocket. He quickly picked the needle from his pants.

The *fir needle* comes from the spot where he killed Leisegang. Why might he be startled? **C**

After a good, relatively hasty breakfast, he strolled back to the compartment where he had left his suitcase in the care of the elderly married couple.

The woman slept. The man gave a **curt** nod to his greeting and to his "Thanks very much for watching my things" and then went on reading the thick book he held in his hands.

Algernissen carefully hung up his double-sided jacket and settled himself comfortably in his corner. He would have liked to sleep too, but he couldn't. After ten minutes, he stood, went to the toilet, and then remained standing in the corridor to smoke a cigarette.

D Why can't Algernissen sleep?

The married couple left the train in Würzburg with friendly good-byes. In Munich, Alfred Algernissen climbed from the train. There he experienced a severe shock: his pistol had disappeared. He could have sworn that after using it on Leisegang, he had stuck it back in his jacket pocket. But it was not there now.

He forced himself to calm down. It was probably in his car, which stood in the parking lot at the Hamburg train terminal. He would find it when he went back tomorrow.

curt short

retrieve to pick up

C He is probably startled because he has been so careful to cover his tracks and make sure there is no way to connect him to the crime.

D He can't sleep because he is nervous and excited.

Comprehension

Predicting Explain to students that one way they can become better readers is to predict throughout a story what will happen next. To do this, they need to use clues they have been reading and put them together to make a prediction. This can be fun with detective stories, especially, and is what many people like about reading such stories. After students have read the last paragraph on page 45, ask them to stop and predict before they turn the page.

ASK What might have happened to the gun? Do you think Algernissen is right that it is in his car? (Students will have to speculate based on what they know of Algernissen and his behavior. He has been so careful that it is probably unlikely that he has lost it or misplaced it—or forgotten what he did with it. Encourage them to conclude that this in itself may be a clue about what will happen.)

Cross-Curricular Connection

Art Showing perspective can be tricky in drawing and painting. Use the photograph on this page as a start for a discussion of perspective. Point out that the train tracks are obviously parallel and never meet. Nevertheless, in the picture it seems that the lines point to each other and therefore will meet eventually. Invite students with drawing skill to demonstrate how perspective can be shown in drawing by varying the size of objects as well as plane.

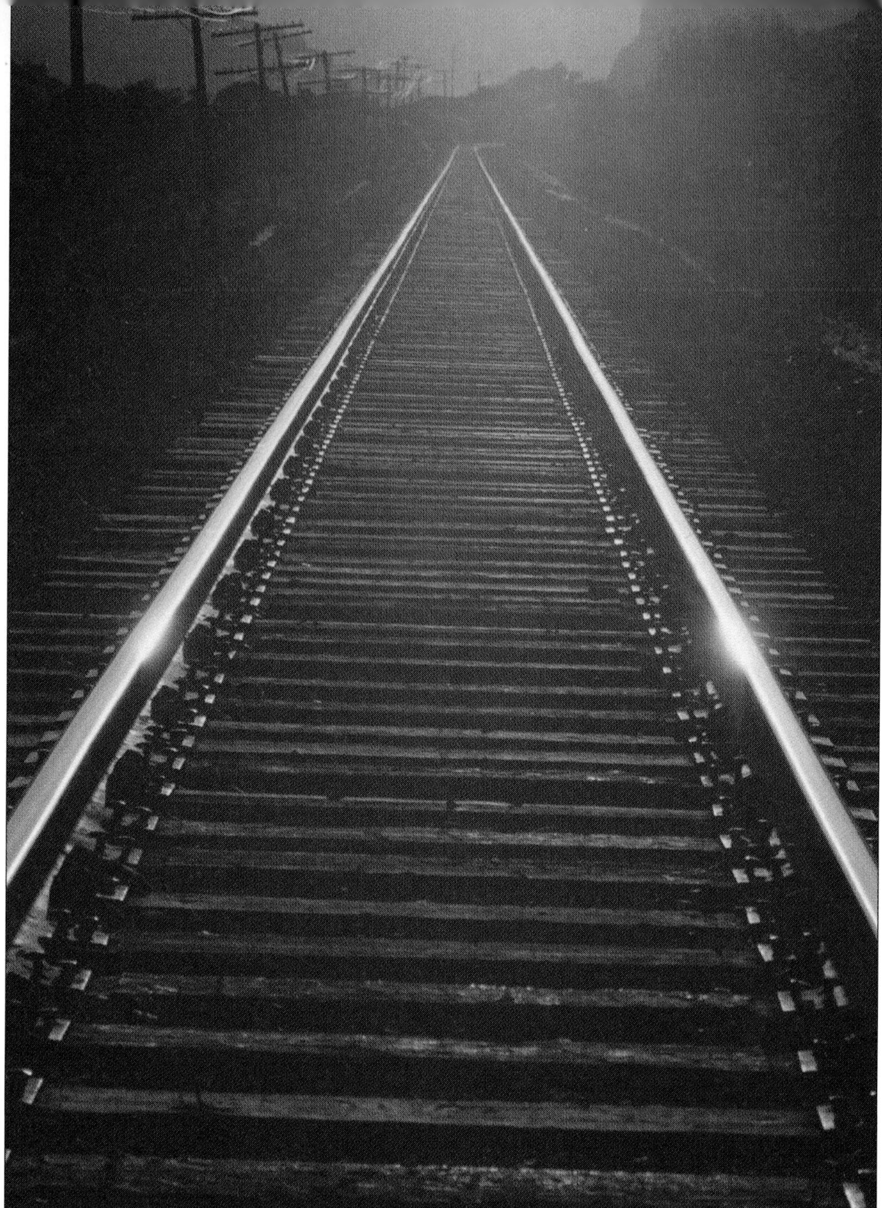

46 *Unit 1 Fiction*

The next afternoon in Hamburg, as Algernissen unlocked his car, he was arrested. **A**

The following police **deposition** had led to his arrest: **B**

> I happened to follow the man, since I wanted a newspaper before our express for Munich left. I was surprised that he put on sunglasses and took off the light-colored jacket to put it on again with the dark side out. It also surprised me that he did not go to the newsstand, as he had said he was going to, but instead ran over to a different platform. There he greeted another man and to my astonishment climbed with him into another train, which left immediately. As our train pulled in to Hannover, the man was standing on the platform. He wore the jacket with the light side facing out again and no sunglasses, although the sun was brightly shining there. He got into the dining car and half an hour after that returned to our compartment. He acted as though he had been in the train the entire time. The man was not calm. When he left for the toilet, I searched his jacket. I found his car's **registration** papers, including its license number and, in the left-hand inside pocket a 7.65 caliber Smith and Wesson revolver. I was able to **ascertain** that it had been fired shortly before then. Along with that I found a train ticket for Nienburg.

ascertain to find out

deposition a statement

registration an official document

Discussion Questions

A Comprehension Were you surprised that Algernissen was arrested? Why or why not? (Students may disagree here; some may be surprised because everything seemed to be going so well; others may not be surprised because they assumed from the beginning that the mystery would be solved somehow.)

B Critical Thinking Who do you think is the writer of the police deposition? What makes you think so? (Many students will guess correctly that one of the elderly passengers with whom Algernissen tried to establish an alibi is the writer of the deposition.)

Discussion Questions

A Critical Thinking It may have been bad luck that Algernissen met a retired police inspector at the wrong time. But he was being very careful. Why do you suppose he did not suspect that the elderly couple might pose a problem? (Students may see that often elderly people are not respected enough for someone to think they would be capable enough for suspicion.)

B Answers may vary; make sure students can defend their opinions with evidence from the story.

Career Connection

Many students may express interest in police or detective work as a possible career. Since their models are usually those shown on television, in movies, or described in detective stories, their view may be unrealistic. Invite a representative of your local police force to visit the class to talk about careers in police work. Have students develop a list of questions and topics in advance. Make sure your guest talks specifically about educational preparation and steps students can follow, including types of classes to take in school that are especially helpful. That may give them a new appreciation for their classes in math, English, and science!

Hafermass is the *elderly man*. Bad luck for Algernissen to meet a retired policeman.

The deposition, dated at Würzburg on May 26, 19——, was given into the criminal records, signed by the elderly man from the train: Heinrich Hafermass, Criminal Inspector (retired).

Leisegang's body was found and shown to Alfred Algernissen. In light of the pistol, the train ticket, and **A** the statement of the retired criminal inspector, Algernissen confessed to the killing. He was convicted and sentenced to life in prison.

B Did this ending surprise you?

Nothing could be proven against the attractive Loni L., and a short time later she married a film producer who promised to make her a movie star. Instead, he wasted her fortune before dying of a heart attack.

REVIEWING the SELECTION

Death Arrives on Schedule

Hansjörg Martin

Directions Write the answers to these questions using complete sentences.

Comprehension: Identifying Facts

1. Why is everything suddenly unimportant to Algernissen?
2. What is Herr Leisegang's passion?
3. Why does Herr Leisegang have no driver's license?
4. What kind of danger is Leisegang in?
5. There are two trains. Which cities are they bound for?
6. How does Algernissen change his looks when going to track 11?
7. Why does Leisegang hesitate to get out of the car?
8. In the dining car, what does Algernissen find that startles him?
9. What does the elderly man find in Algernissen's jacket pocket?
10. Describe Algernissen's plan to kill Leisegang.

Comprehension: Understanding Main Ideas

11. Describe Loni Leisegang.
12. There are two trains. How does Algernissen use them?
13. Why does Algernissen ask the elderly couple to watch his bags?
14. Where is Algernissen arrested?
15. Why does he confess when shown Leisegang's body?
16. What was Heinrich Hafermass's profession before retiring?
17. Does Hafermass follow Algernissen on purpose?
18. Name the three things that surprise Hafermass.
19. What prison sentence does Algernissen receive?
20. Whom does Loni Leisegang marry?

Review Continued on Next Page

Reviewing the Selection

Answer Key

Comprehension: Identifying Facts

1. He was so attracted to Loni that nothing else seemed important.

2. Herr Leisegang's passion is whiskey.

3. He lost his driver's license because of his drinking.

4. Leisegang is about to be murdered.

5. One train is bound for Nienburg, the other for Munich.

6. He turns his reversible coat inside out and puts on sunglasses.

7. He is suddenly suspicious and afraid.

8. He finds a fir needle stuck to his pants.

9. The elderly man finds the gun in Algernissen's pocket.

10. Algernissen sets up an alibi for himself by showing the elderly couple that he is on the train to Munich with them. He gets off the train, changes his appearance, gets on another train with Leisegang, picks up a rented car, drives Leisegang to the woods ostensibly to see property for sale, and shoots Leisegang. He returns the rented car, changes his appearance back to the way it was, and meets the Munich-bound train. He gets on and proceeds as if he had been on board the whole time.

Comprehension: Understanding Main Ideas

11. She is beautiful, with chestnut-red hair, green eyes, and a good figure.

12. He begins by establishing his presence on one train, gets off and gets on another, then returns to the first train as if he had never left it.

13. He wants to make sure they know he is on the train, and he believes they will think it very unlikely that he would get off the train without taking his bags with him.

14. He is arrested in Hamburg as he is unlocking his car.

15. He confesses when he realizes the police not only have the evidence of the body, they also have his pistol, train ticket, and the statement of the retired police inspector.

16. He had been a police criminal inspector.

17. Hafermass follows Algernissen by accident, as he got off the train briefly to get a newspaper.

18. Hafermass is surprised that Algernissen changes his appearance; that instead of going to the newsstand as he said he would, Algernissen met someone else; and that he got on another train.

19. He was sentenced to life in prison for the murder.

20. She marries a film producer.

Understanding Literature: Detective Story

21. The good guy in this story is the retired police inspector, Hafermass.

22. The bad guy is Algernissen.

23. The main character, Algernissen, is the bad guy.

24. He had the police arrest Algernissen because he suspected Algernissen had committed a crime, as evidenced by the pistol that had just been fired and other suspicious behavior.

25. His deposition is believable because he is a retired police criminal inspector.

Critical Thinking

26. Algernissen's carefully worked out plan involved trains running on schedule, which they did—enabling him to carry out the murder on schedule.

27. Algernissen did not really have property for sale, and he did not want anyone to know that he was taking Leisegang somewhere.

28. He becomes suspicious of Algernissen's behavior and later realizes Algernissen must have committed a crime.

29. Students' answers may vary; make sure they can defend their conclusions with what they know from the story.

30. Answers will vary. Make sure students can defend their opinions with examples from the story.

Writing on Your Own Suggest that students emphasize either the plot or the characters as they describe the reasons for their preference.

Selection Quiz

The Teacher's Resource Library includes a Selection Quiz for "Death Arrives on Schedule" that may be given following the Selection Review.

REVIEWING the SELECTION

Death Arrives on Schedule *(Continued)*

Understanding Literature: Detective Story

Detective stories are also called mysteries. There is a good reason for that name. If the writer is clever enough, the reader will find it hard to solve the puzzle. The answer will be a mystery for most of the story. Detective stories also have good guys and bad guys. The good guys win in the end, but not before facing danger.

21. Who is the good guy in this story?
22. Who is the bad guy or bad guys?
23. Is the main character a good guy or bad guy?
24. What are the elderly man's reasons for having the police arrest Algernissen? Does he have good reason to suspect Algernissen of a crime?
25. Is the elderly man's police deposition believable? Why or why not?

Critical Thinking

26. How does the title of the story apply to the story's action?
27. What is Algernissen's real reason for swearing Leisegang to secrecy?
28. Why does Hafermass, the elderly man, decide to become involved?
29. Do you think Loni Leisegang knows her husband will be killed? Explain your answer.
30. Did you like the ending to this story? Why or why not?

Writing on Your Own Which detective story did you prefer, "The Adventure of the Speckled Band" or "Death Arrives on Schedule"? Write a sentence telling which story you liked better. Then, write at least three sentences about why you prefer that story.

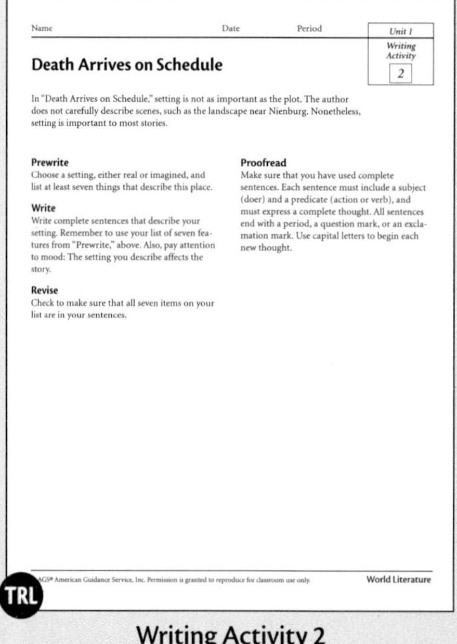

Name Date Period

Unit 1 *Writing Activity* 2

Death Arrives on Schedule

In "Death Arrives on Schedule," setting is not as important as the plot. The author does not carefully describe scenes, such as the landscape near Nienburg. Nonetheless, setting is important to most stories.

Prewrite
Choose a setting, either real or imagined, and list at least seven things that describe this place.

Write
Write complete sentences that describe your setting. Remember to use your list of seven features from "Prewrite," above. Also, pay attention to mood: The setting you describe affects the story.

Revise
Check to make sure that all seven items on your list are in your sentences.

Proofread
Make sure that you have used complete sentences. Each sentence must include a subject (doer) and a predicate (action or verb), and must express a complete thought. All sentences end with a period, a question mark, or an exclamation mark. Use capital letters to begin each new thought.

 World Literature

TRL

Writing Activity 2

Name Date Period

Unit 1 *Selection Quiz* 2

Death Arrives on Schedule

Directions Read the following statements. Circle the letter of the answer that correctly completes each sentence or that correctly answers each question.

1. In this story, who was the victim of the crime?
   a. Algernissen **b.** Loni **c.** Leisegang **d.** Hafermass
2. Algernissen is the
   a. police officer. **b.** engineer. **c.** killer. **d.** conductor.
3. Nothing else mattered when Algernissen met
   a. Loni. **b.** Hafermass. **c.** Mrs. Hafermass. **d.** his match.
4. The story is set in
   a. Switzerland. **b.** Germany. **c.** Haagen Dazs. **d.** Amsterdam.
5. Near which village did Algernissen commit murder?
   a. Nienburg **b.** Hamburg
   c. Munich **d.** He did not commit murder
6. Algernissen planned his crime for
   a. eight years. **b.** months.
   c. two days. **d.** the middle of the night.
7. What evidence convinced Hafermass to call the police?
   a. Algernissen said good morning. **b.** He found a gun in Algernissen's coat.
   c. He saw Algernissen kill Leisegang. **d.** Algernissen had a fir needle on his jacket.
8. Algernissen was arrested in
   a. the middle of the night. **b.** the rental car.
   c. Hamburg. **d.** Munich.
9. How did "death arrive on schedule"?
   a. The television program was on. **b.** The killer used a television magazine.
   c. The airplane was right on time. **d.** The killer took a train.
10. At the end of the story, Loni married a
   a. film producer. **b.** rocket scientist. **c.** financial broker. **d.** killer.

 World Literature

TRL

Selection Quiz 2

Science Fiction

- "If science fiction is the mythology of modern technology, then its myth is tragic."
  —Ursula K. Le Guin
- "Space or science fiction has become a dialect for our time." —Doris Lessing

Science fiction deals with people, places, and events that didn't happen. Not only that, but they couldn't—at least in life as we know it. Science fiction is often divided into "sci-fi" and fantasy. Sci-fi may try to tell exactly what the world will be like. Fantasy includes tales in which objects can talk or characters save the day with powerful words. Each describes a world with certain rules. The characters in these stories help us understand our world more clearly. That is because good, evil, power, love, stupidity, and fear affect these imaginary beings and places. They affect us here and now in the same way.

Writers view their imaginary settings in many ways. Some science fiction is hopeful. Arthur C. Clarke (the *Space Odyssey* books) and Isaac Asimov believe that humanity will improve. The future will be a better place. Work will be less boring. There will be more excitement and challenge. Other writers, though, see a loss of personal freedom. George Orwell's *1984* shows such a grim world. C. J. Cherryh in her *Alien* series and Frank Herbert in *Dune* see the future as a mixture of challenge and danger. They raise thought-provoking and entertaining questions. These writers write about good and evil and excite our imaginations. As you sample science fiction, you may find authors who share your view of the future. Many libraries and bookstores have special science fiction sections. Look there to find more stories like these.

Science Fiction

Ask students to read page 51. You may want to have several volunteers share reading the page aloud to the rest of the class.

Discuss the two quotations at the top of the page, pointing out, if necessary, that both people quoted are writers of science fiction. You may want to remind students that mythology is a group of stories people told to explain the world around them.

ASK What might Le Guin mean that science fiction might be the tragic myth of modern technology? (She might mean that the stories of science fiction cannot match the reality of modern technology, that if people assume science fiction is the same as modern technology, they should recall that science fiction is no more than myth.)

Point out to students that the word *dialect* means a version of a language spoken by a small group of people who understand each other.

ASK What could Doris Lessing mean by that quotation? (Lessing may have meant that in our technologically oriented time, science fiction is a language we can all understand.)

Open a discussion about science fiction. Invite students to mention stories or novels they have read or television shows or movies they have seen. Encourage them to acknowledge the imagination involved in the writers' forecasts of future worlds. You may want to mention that many science fiction writers have a great deal of background knowledge of science, and that enables them to extend what they know into the realm of the possible. Often this gives the fiction these writers provide a certain aura of plausibility.

ASK Why do you think people who know a great deal about science might want to write science fiction stories? (It may be because their imaginations can see where scientific knowledge could take us.)

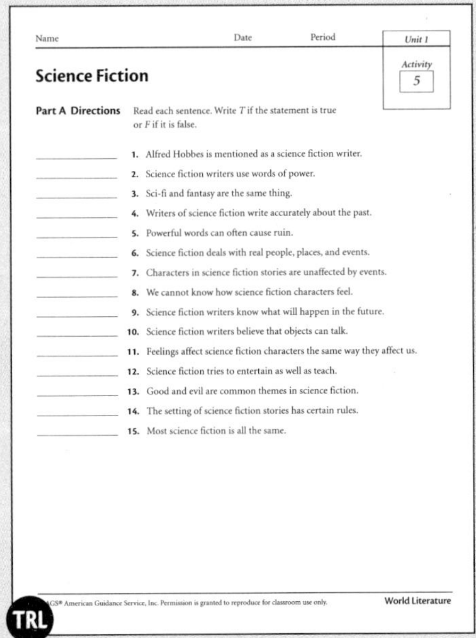

Name ______ Date ______ Period ______

Unit 1 — *Activity* 5

Science Fiction

Part A Directions Read each sentence. Write *T* if the statement is true or *F* if it is false.

______ 1. Alfred Hobbes is mentioned as a science fiction writer.
______ 2. Science fiction writers use words of power.
______ 3. Sci-fi and fantasy are the same thing.
______ 4. Writers of science fiction write accurately about the past.
______ 5. Powerful words can often cause ruin.
______ 6. Science fiction deals with real people, places, and events.
______ 7. Characters in science fiction stories are unaffected by events.
______ 8. We cannot know how science fiction characters feel.
______ 9. Science fiction writers know what will happen in the future.
______ 10. Science fiction writers believe that objects can talk.
______ 11. Feelings affect science fiction characters the same way they affect us.
______ 12. Science fiction tries to entertain as well as teach.
______ 13. Good and evil are common themes in science fiction.
______ 14. The setting of science fiction stories has certain rules.
______ 15. Most science fiction is all the same.

 World Literature

TRL

Activity 5

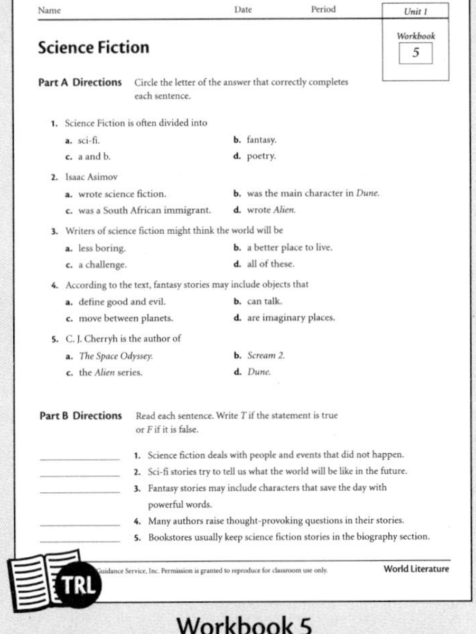

Name ______ Date ______ Period ______

Unit 1 — *Workbook* 5

Science Fiction

Part A Directions Circle the letter of the answer that correctly completes each sentence.

1. Science Fiction is often divided into
   a. sci-fi. b. fantasy.
   c. a and b. d. poetry.
2. Isaac Asimov
   a. wrote science fiction. b. was the main character in *Dune*.
   c. was a South African immigrant. d. wrote *Alien*.
3. Writers of science fiction might think the world will be
   a. less boring. b. a better place to live.
   c. a challenge. d. all of these.
4. According to the text, fantasy stories may include objects that
   a. define good and evil. b. can talk.
   c. move between planets. d. are imaginary places.
5. C. J. Cherryh is the author of
   a. *The Space Odyssey*. b. *Scream 2*.
   c. the *Alien* series. d. *Dune*.

Part B Directions Read each sentence. Write *T* if the statement is true or *F* if it is false.

______ 1. Science fiction deals with people and events that did not happen.
______ 2. Sci-fi stories try to tell us what the world will be like in the future.
______ 3. Fantasy stories may include characters that save the day with powerful words.
______ 4. Many authors raise thought-provoking questions in their stories.
______ 5. Bookstores usually keep science fiction stories in the biography section.

 World Literature

TRL

Workbook 5

Selection at a Glance

The Feeling of Power

Isaac Asimov

Student pages 52–65

Overview

Isaac Asimov wrote more than 400 books and many short stories. He wrote his famous *Foundation Trilogy* in 1951–1953, several years before "The Feeling of Power" presented here.

Selection Summary

In "The Feeling of Power" by Isaac Asimov, a technician in a world run by computers learns the power of the human mind.

Objectives

- To identify and understand irony.
- To read and appreciate science fiction.

Audiocassette 

Teacher's Resource Library TRL

- Vocabulary Workbook 3, pages 1–3
- Selection Glossary 3
- Student Study Guide 9, pages 1–2
- Activity 6, pages 1–2
- Workbook 6, pages 1–2
- Writing Activity 3
- Selection Quiz 3

INTRODUCING the SELECTION

The Feeling of Power

Isaac Asimov

Isaac Asimov (1920–1992) American

Literary Terms

autobiography a story about a person's life written by that person

irony the use of words that seem to say one thing but mean the opposite

parody an exaggerated look at a situation

science fiction literature that deals with people, places, and events that could not happen in our reality

About the Author

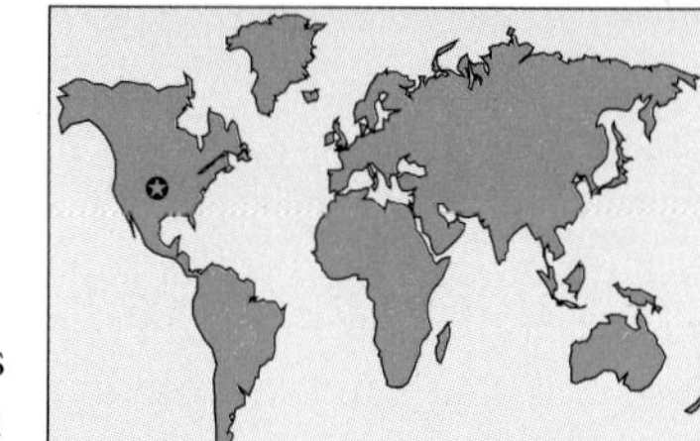

Born in Russia, Isaac Asimov came to America when he was a small child. As a teenager, he began to write **science fiction** stories for magazines. He earned a Ph.D. in chemistry and taught at Boston University. Later, he became a full-time writer of both fact and fiction. Asimov wrote hundreds of books on every subject from Shakespeare to the Bible. One of the most famous is his *Foundation Trilogy.* It is a series of science fiction stories and novels. They trace the history of a space empire started by earth people. Asimov wrote many stories about robots. One collection is *I, Robot* (1950). It is the fictional **autobiography** of a designer of robots. (An autobiography is a person's life story told by that person.) In it, Asimov sets up three "laws of robotics." This set of rules seems to control the behavior of most artificial life forms in modern science fiction.

About the Selection

"The Feeling of Power" is a humorous look at the future. Society is so advanced and technical that it depends completely on computers. People find human abilities strange. This story is also a **parody** of the arms race between the United States and the former Soviet Union. Parody is an exaggerated look at a situation. The arms race was a major issue in 1957, when the story was written. The story uses **irony** to point out the humor of the situation. Irony is using an idea or image in the opposite way from its ordinary meaning.

52 *Unit 1 Fiction*

Setting the Stage for Reading

About the Author

Have students read the section and look at the picture of Isaac Asimov. Point out that he lived until 1992. Explain that he was one of the most prolific writers ever. He is especially famous for his science fiction, but he also wrote nonfiction, usually about scientific topics. He coined the word *robotics.* He was called "the great explainer" by one critic because he was a popularizer of scientific subjects. Asimov was known for his nurturing personality, which often was apparent in his work involving concern about humanity's future.

ASK How might being a scientist, as Asimov was, help a writer of science fiction? (A person's scientific knowledge could help him or her imagine what might really be possible, and that in turn could make the stories sound like a reasonable forecast of life in the future.)

About the Selection

Like many other writers of science fiction, Asimov often incorporated current political situations into his imaginative future worlds.

Activate Prior Knowledge: Have students recall other science fiction stories they have read or seen.

ASK Why might a writer use what was going on at the time the story was written as part of the story? (Perhaps because it forms what the writer knows at the time and is an issue that the writer knows readers will also know about.)

The Feeling of Power

Isaac Asimov

Jehan Shuman was used to dealing with the men in authority on **A** long-**embattled** Earth. He was only a civilian but he **originated** programming patterns that resulted in self-directing war computers of the highest sort. Generals **consequently** listened to him. Heads of congressional committees, too.

As you read, watch for ways in which the author uses irony.

There was one of each in the special **lounge** of New Pentagon. General Weider was space-burnt and had a small mouth puckered almost into a **cipher**. Congressman Brant was smooth-cheeked and clear-eyed. He smoked Denebian tobacco with the air of one whose patriotism was so notorious, he could be allowed such liberties.

The story takes place on earth in the future. Earth is at war with *Deneb,* a planet the author has invented. The war is being carried on by computers.

Shuman, tall, distinguished, and Programmer-first-class, faced them fearlessly.

He said, "This, gentlemen, is Myron Aub."

Consider how important a *Programmer-first-class* would be in a world run by computers.

"The one with the unusual gift that you discovered quite by accident," said Congressman Brant **placidly**. "Ah." He inspected the little man with the egg-bald head with **amiable** curiosity.

The little man, in return, twisted the fingers of his hands anxiously. He had never been near such great men before. He was only an aging low-grade Technician who had long ago failed all tests designed to smoke out the gifted ones among mankind and had settled into the rut of unskilled labor. There was just this hobby of **B** his that the great Programmer had found out about and was now making such a frightening fuss over.

amiable friendly

cipher a zero

consequently as a result

embattled locked in a struggle

lounge a room in which to wait or relax

originate to begin

placidly calmly

Reading Vocabulary TRL

Have students preview the selection's vocabulary words by giving them copies of the Selection Glossary. Have students work in small groups to take turns choosing words randomly, giving their definitions, and identifying the word chosen.

Motivation for Reading

Ask students to imagine a time when people have turned over much of their thinking to computers. Suggest that they read the story to find out what that might be like.

Discussion Questions

Use the questions in the margins of the student selection to help students focus and check their reading.

A ASK Literary Element One characteristic of science fiction is that it deals with situations that could not happen in life as we know it. What is the first clue in this story that it is science fiction? (In the first sentence, the reference to "long-embattled Earth" implies that the whole Earth is in a battle with some other entity.)

B ASK Comprehension What do you think might be Technician Aub's hobby? (Let students speculate. There are few clues so far, but it is clear what-ever his "unusual gift" or "hobby" is, it has come to the attention of some very pow-erful people.)

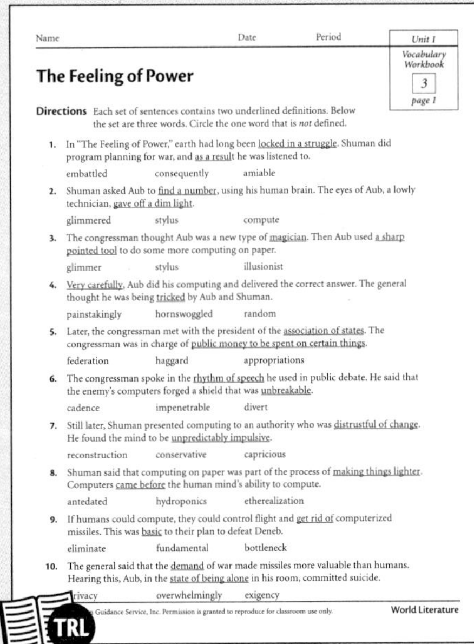

Name Date Period

Unit 1 *Vocabulary Workbook* 3 *page 1*

The Feeling of Power

Directions Each set of sentences contains two underlined definitions. Below the set are three words. Circle the one word that is *not* defined.

1. In "The Feeling of Power," earth had long been locked in a struggle. Shuman did program planning for war, and as a result he was listened to.
   embattled consequently amiable
2. Shuman asked Aub to find a number, using his human brain. The eyes of Aub, a lowly technician, gave off a dim light.
   glimmered stylus compute
3. The congressman thought Aub was a new type of magician. Then Aub used a sharp pointed tool to do some more computing on paper.
   glimmer stylus illusionist
4. Very carefully, Aub did his computing and delivered the correct answer. The general thought he was being tricked by Aub and Shuman.
   painstakingly hornswoggled random
5. Later, the congressman met with the president of the association of states. The congressman was in charge of public money to be spent on certain things.
   federation haggard appropriations
6. The congressman spoke in the rhythm of speech he used in public debate. He said that the enemy's computers forged a shield that was unbreakable.
   cadence impenetrable divert
7. Still later, Shuman presented computing to an authority who was distrustful of change. He found the mind to be unpredictably impulsive.
   reconstruction conservative capricious
8. Shuman said that computing on paper was part of the process of making things lighter. Computers came before the human mind's ability to compute.
   antedated hydroponics etherealization
9. If humans could compute, they could control flight and get rid of computerized missiles. This was basic to their plan to defeat Deneb.
   eliminate fundamental bottleneck
10. The general said that the demand of war made missiles more valuable than humans. Hearing this, Aub, in the state of being alone in his room, committed suicide.
   rivacy overwhelmingly exigency

 World Literature

TRL

Vocabulary Workbook 3, pages 1–3

Name Date Period

Unit 1 *Student Study Guide* 9 *page 1*

The Feeling of Power (pp. 53–63)

Directions Fill in the following outline. Filling in the blanks will help you as you read and study "The Feeling of Power."

I. Beginning of the Selection (pp. 53–55)

A. Mathematics in the Future
1. At New Pentagon, Jehan Shuman is talking to General __________ and Congressman __________ about Myron Aub.
2. Myron Aub is an aging, low-grade __________.
3. Aub is able to compute __________ times seven in his head without using a computer.
4. Aub surprises Weider and Brant further by writing the numbers __________ and twenty-three on a piece of paper.
5. Congressman Brant doesn't believe that __________ times __________ will always be twenty-one.

II. Middle of the Selection (pp. 56–59)

A. Taking Multiplication to the President
1. General Weider thinks Aub's system of multiplying is too complicated to be anything but __________.
2. Aub tells Weider his system of multiplying will work for __________ numbers.
3. Congressman Brant learns the system of multiplying and shows his new skills to the President of the __________ __________.
4. It takes Brant one __________ to get the hang of multiplying.

B. A Secret Project
1. Brant suggests going beyond the computer by combining the mechanics of computation with __________ __________.
2. Brant tells the President to establish a secret project on human computation and call it __________ __________.

 World Literature

TRL

Student Study Guide 9, pages 1–2

Discussion Questions

A The people probably need a computer to do simple multiplication because they have always depended on the computers to do it and have not learned to do it themselves.

Career Connection

Most students will know that currently people have jobs called computer programmers, though few are as powerful as Jehan Shuman, the Programmer in the story. There are many careers in the computer industry, and most jobs elsewhere require some basic knowledge of computer use. Invite someone from your area who works as a programmer and/or with computer technology to address your class about career paths in computers. Have students prepare a list of questions and topics in advance, which you may share with the presenter before he or she visits. Make sure students talk to the person about educational requirements in both high school and college.

General Weider said, "I find this atmosphere of mystery childish."

"You won't in a moment," said Shuman. "This is not something we can leak to the firstcomer. — Aub!" There was something **imperative** about his manner of biting off that one-syllable name, but then he was a great Programmer speaking to a mere Technician. "Aub! How much is nine times seven?"

Aub hesitated a moment. His pale eyes **glimmered** with a feeble anxiety. "Sixty-three," he said.

Congressman Brant lifted his eyebrows. "Is that right?"

A

Why do you think these people needed a computer to do simple multiplication?

"Check it for yourself, Congressman."

The congressman took out his pocket computer, nudged the milled edges twice, looked at its face as it lay there in the palm of his hand, and put it back. He said, "Is this the gift you brought us here to demonstrate. An **illusionist**?"

"More than that, sir. Aub has memorized a few operations and with them he **computes** on paper."

"A paper computer?" said the general. He looked pained.

"No, sir," said Shuman patiently. "Not a paper computer. Simply a sheet of paper. General, would you be so kind as to suggest a number?"

"Seventeen," said the general.

"And you, Congressman?"

"Twenty-three."

"Good! Aub, multiply those numbers and please show the gentlemen your manner of doing it."

"Yes, Programmer," said Aub, ducking his head. He fished a small pad out of one shirt pocket and an artist's hairline **stylus** out of the

smoke out to find; to make known

compute to find a number; to work mathematical problems

glimmer to give off a dim light

illusionist a magician

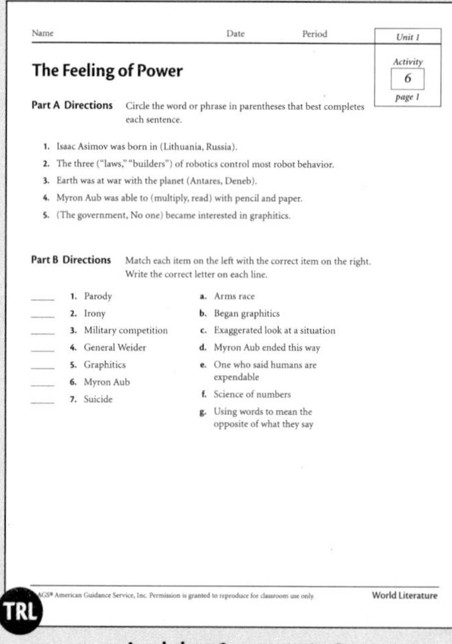

Name Date Period

Unit 1 — Activity 6 — page 1

The Feeling of Power

Part A Directions Circle the word or phrase in parentheses that best completes each sentence.

1. Isaac Asimov was born in (Lithuania, Russia).
2. The three ("laws," "builders") of robotics control most robot behavior.
3. Earth was at war with the planet (Antares, Deneb).
4. Myron Aub was able to (multiply, read) with pencil and paper.
5. (The government, No one) became interested in graphitics.

Part B Directions Match each item on the left with the correct item on the right. Write the correct letter on each line.

____	1. Parody	a. Arms race
____	2. Irony	b. Began graphitics
____	3. Military competition	c. Exaggerated look at a situation
____	4. General Weider	d. Myron Aub ended this way
____	5. Graphitics	e. One who said humans are expendable
____	6. Myron Aub	f. Science of numbers
____	7. Suicide	g. Using words to mean the opposite of what they say

 World Literature

TRL

Activity 6, pages 1–2

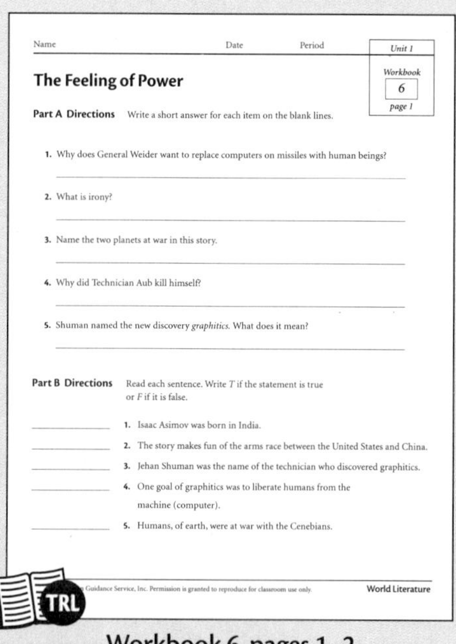

Name Date Period

Unit 1 — Workbook 6 — page 1

The Feeling of Power

Part A Directions Write a short answer for each item on the blank lines.

1. Why does General Weider want to replace computers on missiles with human beings?
2. What is irony?
3. Name the two planets at war in this story.
4. Why did Technician Aub kill himself?
5. Shuman named the new discovery *graphitics.* What does it mean?

Part B Directions Read each sentence. Write *T* if the statement is true or *F* if it is false.

____ 1. Isaac Asimov was born in India.

____ 2. The story makes fun of the arms race between the United States and China.

____ 3. Jehan Shuman was the name of the technician who discovered graphitics.

____ 4. One goal of graphitics was to liberate humans from the machine (computer).

____ 5. Humans, of earth, were at war with the Cenebians.

 World Literature

TRL

Workbook 6, pages 1–2

other. His forehead **corrugated** as he made **painstaking** marks on the paper.

General Weider interrupted him sharply. "Let's see that."

Aub passed him the paper, and Weider said, "Well, it looks like the figure seventeen."

Congressman Brant nodded and said, "So it does, but I suppose anyone can copy figures off a computer. I think I could make a passable seventeen myself, even without practice."

"If you will let Aub continue, gentlemen," said Shuman without heat.

Aub continued, his hand trembling a little. Finally he said in a low voice, "The answer is three hundred and ninety-one."

Congressman Brant took out his computer a second time and flicked it, "By Godfrey, so it is. How did he guess?" **B**

Do you think earthlings used computers for all writing as well as all mathematics? **C**

"No guess, Congressman," said Shuman. "He computed that result. He did it on this sheet of paper."

"Humbug," said the general impatiently. "A computer is one thing and marks on paper are another."

"Explain, Aub," said Shuman.

"Yes, Programmer. —Well, gentlemen, I write down seventeen and just underneath it, I write twenty-three. Next, I say to myself: seven times three—"

The congressman interrupted smoothly, "Now, Aub, the problem is seventeen times twenty-three."

"Yes, I know," said the little Technician earnestly, "but I start by saying seven times three because that's the way it works. Now seven times three is twenty-one."

"And how do you know that?" asked the congressman.

"I just remember it. It's always twenty-one on the computer. I've checked it any number of times."

"That doesn't mean it always will be, though, does it?" said the congressman. **D**

imperative commanding

corrugate to wrinkle

painstaking very careful

stylus a sharp pointed tool

B ASK Critical Thinking Why is Aub's ability to multiply numbers so amazing to the others? (Simply because they have depended on computers to do such figuring for them, they have forgotten or never knew that the human mind could figure out the problems.)

C In the story, it seems that people do depend heavily on computers to do writing as well as mathematics. The main clue here is that the congressman thinks he too could make a "passable seventeen ... even without practice." This probably means that he rarely writes with a pen or pencil on paper.

D ASK Comprehension How do you know that the congressman has never memorized the multiplication tables? (Because he can't figure out how Aub knows that seven times three is twenty-one and that it is always the same answer.)

Learning Styles

Tactile/Kinesthetic Some students will benefit from working out the arithmetic problems in the story themselves. Encourage them to do so as the characters do—with paper and pencil, checking all answers with a calculator or computer. For fun, have them check the answers they get against the ones provided in the story.

Discussion Questions

A The process of multiplication is parodied, or exaggerated for effect, to make very clear how dependent on computers the people are for even the simplest action.

B ASK Comprehension What does Aub mean when he says that the "rules are quite simple and will work for any numbers"? (He is referring to the method of multiplying, which sounded so complicated to the general but will indeed work for any numbers.)

Cross-Curricular Connection

Mathematics A major point in the story is the extreme reliance by the future characters on computers, to the point that they do not know how to do the simplest arithmetic computations themselves. Discuss with students whether they think this can be a problem for them as they participate in their math classes. Are they too dependent on the use of calculators? Do they rely on calculators only to speed up their calculations, or do they have trouble working out the problems without the calculators? Encourage students to give thoughtful attention to this situation in light of what they have read in the story. Why is it important for people to learn basic arithmetic skills?

"Maybe not," stammered Aub. "I'm not a mathematician. But I always get the right answers, you see."

"Go on."

"Seven times three is twenty-one, so I write down twenty-one. Then one times three is three, so I write down a three under the two of the twenty-one."

"Why under the two?" asked Congressman Brant at once.

"Because—" Aub looked helplessly at his superior for support. "It's difficult to explain."

Shuman said, "If you will accept his work for the moment, we can leave the details for the mathematicians."

Brant **subsided**.

A Why do you think the author makes a parody of the process of multiplying?

Aub said, "Three plus two makes five, you see, so the twenty-one become a fifty-one. Now you let that go for a while and start fresh. You multiply seven and two, that's fourteen, and one and two, that's two. Put them down like this and it adds up to thirty-four. Now if you put the thirty-four under the fifty-one this way and add them, you get three hundred and ninety-one and that's the answer."

There was an instant's silence and then General Weider said, "I don't believe it. He goes through this **rigmarole** and makes up numbers and multiplies and adds them this way and that, but I don't believe it. It's too **complicated** to be anything but **hornswoggling**."

"Oh no, sir," said Aub in a sweat. "It only seems complicated **B** because you're not used to it. Actually, the rules are quite simple and will work for any numbers."

GI stands for "Government Issue." It refers to a soldier or to equipment issued by the military.

"Any numbers, eh?" said the general. "Come then." He took out his own computer (a severely styled GI model) and struck it at **random**. "Make a five seven three eight on the paper. That's five thousand seven hundred and thirty-eight."

"Yes, sir," said Aub, taking a new sheet of paper.

"Now," (more punching of his computer), "seven two three nine. Seven thousand two hundred and thirty-nine."

"Yes, sir."

"And now multiply those two."

complicated not simple
hornswoggling tricking someone
random by chance; without purpose
rigmarole nonsense
subside to become quiet

56 *Unit 1 Fiction*

"It will take some time," quavered Aub.

"Take the time," said the general.

"Go ahead, Aub," said Shuman crisply.

Aub set to work, bending low. He took another sheet of paper and another. The general took out his watch finally and stared at it. "Are you through with your magic-making, Technician?"

"I'm almost done, sir. —Here it is, sir. Forty-one million, five hundred and thirty-seven thousand, three hundred and eighty-two." He showed the scrawled figures of the result.

General Weider smiled bitterly. He pushed the multiplication contact on his computer and let the numbers whirl to a halt. And then he stared and said in a surprised squeak, "Great Galaxy, the fella's right."

The President of the **Terrestrial Federation** had grown **haggard** in **C** office and, in private, he allowed a look of settled melancholy to appear on his sensitive features. The Denebian war, after its early start of vast movement and great popularity, had trickled down into a **sordid** matter of maneuver and countermaneuver, with discontent rising steadily on Earth. Possibly, it was rising on Deneb, too.

And now Congressman Brant, head of the important Committee on Military **Appropriations** was cheerfully and smoothly spending his half-hour appointment spouting nonsense.

"Computing without a computer," said the president impatiently, **D** "is a **contradiction** in terms."

"Computing," said the congressman, "is only a system for handling **data**. A machine might do it, or the human brain might. Let me give you an example." And, using the new skills he had learned, he **E** worked out sums and products until the president, despite himself, grew interested.

"Does this always work?"

"Every time, Mr. President. It is foolproof."

"Is it hard to learn?"

"It took me a week to get the real hang of it. I think you would do better."

appropriations public money to be spent on certain things

contradict saying both one thing and its opposite

data information

federation an association of states

haggard looking thin and tired

sordid dirty; selfish

terrestrial referring to the earth and its people

C ASK Comprehension Time has passed since the meeting Aub had with the others. How do you know that? (There is a little extra space on the page above the paragraph that begins "The President of the Terrestrial Federation. . . ." And the President was not part of that earlier meeting, so we can tell that the scene has shifted to include him.)

D ASK Vocabulary What does the word *computing* mean? (figuring out arithmetically) Then do you think computers are aptly named? Why or why not? (no, because they do much more then simple computing)

E ASK Critical Thinking What has the congressman done in the time between the two meetings? (He has apparently practiced the skill of multiplying and adding.)

Discussion Questions

A The irony is exactly as the question implies: it is computer games that were used as entertainment, not using pencil and paper.

B Critical Thinking Is there additional irony in the congressman saying "there is nothing the computer can do that the human mind cannot do"? (Yes, because many people today say there is nothing the human mind can do that a computer cannot eventually be programmed to do.)

Cross-Curricular Connection

Social Studies War has engaged human beings probably since their very beginnings. In this futuristic story, war still dominates the attention of people. Ask interested students to do some minimal research into the issues in current wars around the world. Individuals may want to address such famous wars as World Wars I and II, the American Civil War, the Vietnam War, or others in particular. Let students share what they discover about causes of war through a panel discussion.

What is the irony here? Did some people once think that using computers was just for entertainment whereas using pencil and paper was more useful? **A**

"Well," said the president, considering, "it's an interesting parlor game, but what is the use of it?"

"What is the use of a newborn baby, Mr. President? At the moment there is no use, but don't you see that this points the way toward liberation from the machine. Consider, Mr. President," the congressman rose and his deep voice automatically took on some of the **cadences** he used in public debate, "that the Denebian war is a war of computer against computer. Their computers forge an **impenetrable** shield of counter-missiles against our missiles, and ours forge one against theirs. If we advance the efficiency of our computers, so do they theirs, and for five years a **precarious** and profitless balance has existed.

"Now we have in our hands a method for going beyond the computer, leapfrogging it, passing through it. We will combine the mechanics of computation with human thought; we will have the **equivalent** of intelligent computers; billions of them. I can't predict what the consequences will be in detail but they will be **incalculable**. And if Deneb beats us to the punch, they may be unimaginably **catastrophic**."

The president said, troubled, "What would you have me do?"

"Put the power of the administration behind the establishment of a secret project on human computation. Call it Project Number, if you like. I can vouch for my committee, but I will need the administration behind me."

"But how far can human computation go?"

"There is no limit. According to Programmer Shuman, who first introduced me to this discovery—"

"I've heard of Shuman, of course."

B "Yes. Well, Dr. Shuman tells me that in theory there is nothing the computer can do that the human mind cannot do. The computer merely takes a **finite** amount of data and performs a finite number of operations upon them. The human mind can duplicate the process."

The president considered that. He said, "If Shuman says this, I am inclined to believe him—in theory. But, in practice, how can anyone know how a computer works?"

cadence a rhythm of speech

catastrophic terrible

equivalent something that is equal

finite limited

impenetrable not able to be pierced or broken

incalculable not possible to measure in advance

precarious dangerous

Brant laughed genially. "Well, Mr. President, I asked the same question. It seems that at one time computers were designed directly by human beings. Those were simple computers, of course, this being before the time of the **rational** use of computers to design more advanced computers had been established."

"Yes, yes. Go on."

"Technician Aub apparently had, as his hobby, the **reconstruction** of some of these ancient devices and in so doing he studied the details of their workings and found he could imitate them. The multiplication I just performed for you is an imitation of the workings of a computer."

"Amazing!"

The congressman coughed gently, "If I may make another point, Mr. President— The further we can develop this thing, the more we can **divert** our Federal effort from computer production and computer maintenance. As the human brain takes over, more of our energy can be directed into peacetime pursuits and the **impingement** of war on the ordinary man will be less. This will be most advantageous for the party in power, of course."

"Ah," said the president, "I see your point. Well, sit down, Congressman, sit down. I want some time to think about this. — But meanwhile, show me that multiplication trick again. Let's see if I can't catch the point of it."

Programmer Shuman did not try to hurry matters. Loesser was **C** **conservative**, very conservative, and liked to deal with computers as his father and grandfather had. Still, he controlled the West European computer combine, and if he could be persuaded to join Project Number in full enthusiasm, a great deal would be accomplished.

But Loesser was holding back. He said, "I'm not sure I like the idea of relaxing our hold on computers. The human mind is a **capricious** thing. The computer will give the same answer to the same problem each time. What guarantee have we that the human mind will do the same?"

"The human mind, Computer Loesser, only **manipulates** facts. It **D** doesn't matter whether the human mind or a machine does it.

capricious acting on impulse; hard to predict

conservative not liking change

divert to turn aside

impingement the act of intruding or disturbing

manipulate to handle or manage

rational based on reason

reconstruction the rebuilding of something

C ASK Comprehension There is another shift of scene on this page. Where is it? How do you know? (It is right above the paragraph beginning "Programmer Shuman." It is signaled by a little extra space above the paragraph. And we know that Shuman was not part of the previous scene between the congressman and the president.)

D ASK Vocabulary What does the fact that Shuman addresses Loesser as "Computer Loesser" tell you? (Loesser may actually be a computer.)

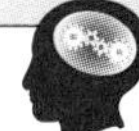

Comprehension

Classifying Part of the appeal of good science fiction is its verisimilitude, or sense that the situations could really happen. One way a writer does this is to weave throughout the story elements recognizable from current "real" life. Ask students to make a chart with two columns, one headed Fiction and one headed Fact. Have them list in the columns elements from the story that fit each heading. Point out that when Asimov wrote this story in 1957, much of our current dependence on computers was yet to happen. Suggest that students put a check mark by each item in their columns that they think Asimov was only predicting at the time he wrote the story but is now possible or commonplace.

Discussion Questions

A Many, many words are based on the root *graph-* or *-graph* among them *photograph, telegraph, autograph, geography, bibliography, biography, paragraph, graphic.*

B The technology has become so advanced that food is no longer grown in soil, and people do not believe that fire can be made by rubbing pieces of flint together.

Environmental Connection

Students may not realize that hydroponics is a method of growing crops that takes place today. It entails growing the crops in water without soil. Necessary nutrients are added to the water, and the plants are monitored scientifically. The method was developed over a century ago but was not used seriously until fairly recently. If possible, have someone address the class to describe the actual use of hydroponics in farming. Or you may suggest that interested students do some research to find out more about the use of hydroponics, especially its impact on the environment.

They are just tools."

"Yes, yes. I've gone over your ingenious demonstration that the mind can duplicate the computer but it seems to me a little in the air. I'll grant the theory but what reason have we for thinking that theory can be converted to practice?"

"I think we have reason, sir. After all, computers have not always existed. The cave men with their **triremes**, stone axes, and railroads had no computers."

"And possibly they did not compute."

"You know better than that. Even the building of a railroad or a **ziggurat** called for some computing, and that must have been without computers as we know them."

A
What other words can you think of that are also based on the root *graph-*?

"Do you suggest they computed in the fashion you demonstrate?"

"Probably not. After all, this method—we call it 'graphitics,' by the way, from the old European word 'grapho' meaning 'to write'—is developed from the computers themselves so it cannot have **antedated** them.Still, the cave men must have had some method, eh?"

"Lost arts! If you're going to talk about lost arts—"

"No, no. I'm not a lost art enthusiast, though I don't say there may not be some. After all, man was eating grain before **hydroponics**, and if the primitives ate grain, they must have grown it in soil. What else could they have done?"

B
What does this tell you about life on earth during the time of this story?

"I don't know, but I'll believe in soil-growing when I see someone grow grain in soil. And I'll believe in making fire by rubbing two pieces of flint together when I see that, too."

Shuman grew **placative**. "Well, let's stick to graphitics. It's just part of the process of **etherealization**. Transportation by means of bulky **contrivances** is giving way to direct mass-transference. Communications devices become less massive and more efficient constantly. For that matter, compare your pocket computer with the massive jobs of a thousand years ago. Why not, then, the last step of doing away with computers altogether? Come, sir, Project Number is a going concern; progress is already headlong. But we

antedate to come before

contrivance a mechanical device

etherealization making things lighter

hydroponics a method of growing plants in water

placative calming; ready to ease another person's mind

trireme an ancient Greek or Roman warship

ziggurat an ancient tower built something like a pyramid

want your help. If patriotism doesn't move you, consider the **intellectual** adventure involved."

Loesser said **skeptically**, "What progress? What can you do beyond multiplication? Can you integrate a transcendental function?"

"In time, sir. In time. In the last month I have learned to handle division. I can determine, and correctly, integral quotients and decimal quotients."

"Decimal quotients? To how many places?"

Programmer Shuman tried to keep his tone casual. "Any number!"

Loesser's jaw dropped. "Without a computer?"

"Set me a problem."

"Divide twenty-seven by thirteen. Take it to six places."

Five minutes later, Shuman said, "Two point oh seven six nine two three."

Loesser checked it. "Well, now, that's amazing. Multiplication didn't impress me too much because it involved **integers** after all, and I thought trick manipulation might do it. But decimals—" **C**

"And that is not all. There is a new development that is, so far, top secret and which, strictly speaking, I ought not to mention. Still— We may have made a **breakthrough** on the square root front."

"Square roots?"

"It involves some tricky points and we haven't licked the bugs yet, but Technician Aub, the man who invented the science and who has an amazing **intuition** in connection with it, maintains he has the problem almost solved. And he is only a Technician. A man like yourself, a trained and talented mathematician, ought to have no difficulty."

"Square roots," muttered Loesser, attracted.

"Cube roots, too. Are you with us?"

Loesser's hand thrust out suddenly, "Count me in."

General Weider stumped his way back and forth at the head of the room and addressed his listeners after the fashion of a savage **D**

This conversation is about various kinds of mathematical processes. A *quotient* is the answer in a division problem. It can be a whole number (*integral*) or a *decimal.*

breakthrough a major accomplishment

integer a whole number such as 1, 2, 3

intellectual having to do with the mind

intuition a way of knowing without proof

skeptically with doubt

C ASK Critical Thinking What is another clue here that Loesser may actually be a computer? (He checks Shuman's computation and is satisfied that it is correct.) Could he be human instead of a computer? Why or why not? (He might be human. Later on the page he is identified as a mathematician, who is intrigued by the idea that a human might be able to learn to do cube roots.)

D ASK Comprehension There is another scene shift on this page. Where is it? (Near the bottom of the page, right above the paragraph beginning "General Weider.") How do you know? (The general was not part of the previous scene between Shuman and Loesser, and there is a little extra space above the paragraph.)

Discussion Questions

A ASK Literary Element What is ironic about Aub's social position here? (He is the one who has been smarter than everyone else, with his self-taught ability to "do math," yet he is still treated—and thinks of himself—as not equal to the others.)

B ASK Comprehension Why are the computers on the missiles "limited in intelligence"? (In order to make them smarter, they would have to be bigger. That would make them too expensive and the missiles too heavy.)

Writing Connection

Suggest to students that they write a new ending to the story. Let them choose either to begin their new ending right before Technician Aub commits suicide, or to begin it after the last line on page 63. Remind them that they should stay true to the plot, setting, and characters so that their ending seems a logical extension of the story. Some students may benefit from working together to brainstorm before doing their writing. You may even want to allow several students to cooperatively write a single ending.

teacher facing a group of **recalcitrant** students. It made no difference to the general that they were the civilian scientists heading Project Number. The general was the over-all head, and he so considered himself at every waking moment.

He said, "Now square roots are all fine. I can't do them myself and I don't understand the methods, but they're fine. Still, the Project will not be sidetracked into what some of you call the **fundamentals**. You can play with graphitics any way you want to after the war is over, but right now we have **specific** and very practical problems to solve."

A In a far corner, Technician Aub listened with painful attention. He was no longer a Technician, of course, having been relieved of his duties and assigned to the project, with a fine-sounding title and good pay. But, of course, the social distinction remained and the highly placed scientific leaders could never bring themselves to admit him to their ranks on a footing of **equality**. Nor, to do Aub justice, did he, himself, wish it. He was as uncomfortable with them as they with him.

The general was saying, "Our goal is a simple one, gentlemen; the replacement of the computer. A ship that can navigate space without a computer on board can be constructed in one fifth the time and at one tenth the expense of a computer-**laden** ship. We could build fleets five times, ten times, as great as Deneb could if we could but **eliminate** the computer.

"And I see something even beyond this. It may be fantastic now; a mere dream; but in the future I see the manned missile!"

There was an instant murmur from the audience.

B The general drove on. "At the present time, our chief **bottleneck** is the fact that missiles are limited in intelligence. The computer controlling them can only be so large, and for that reason they can meet the changing nature of anti-missile defenses in an unsatisfactory way. Few missiles, if any, accomplish their goal and missile warfare is coming to a dead end; for the enemy, fortunately, as well as for ourselves.

"On the other hand, a missile with a man or two within, controlling flight by graphitics, would be lighter, more mobile, more intelligent.

bottleneck something that slows progress

eliminate to get rid of

equality state of being equal

fundamentals the basics

laden loaded with; heavy

recalcitrant stubborn; resisting authority

specific particular

62 Unit 1 Fiction

It would give us a lead that might well mean the margin of victory. Besides which, gentlemen, the **exigencies** of war **compel** us to remember one thing. A man is much more **dispensable** than a computer. Manned missiles could be launched in numbers and under **circumstances** that no good general would care to undertake as far as computer-directed missiles are concerned—"

He said much more but Technician Aub did not wait.

What is the irony of saying that it is easier to lose a human than a computer?

Technician Aub, in the **privacy** of his quarters, labored long over the note he was leaving behind. It read finally as follows:

"When I began the study of what is now called graphitics, it was no more than a hobby. I saw no more in it than an interesting **amusement**, an exercise of mind.

"When Project Number began, I thought that others were wiser than I; that graphitics might be put to practical use as a benefit to mankind, to aid in the production of really practical mass-transference devices perhaps. But now I see it is to be used only for death and destruction.

"I cannot face the responsibility involved in having invented graphitics."

He then deliberately turned the focus of a protein-depolarizer on himself and fell instantly and painlessly dead.

The *protein-depolarizer* is a weapon of science fiction.

They stood over the grave of the little Technician while tribute was **D** paid to the greatness of his discovery.

Programmer Shuman bowed his head along with the rest of them, but remained unmoved. The Technician had done his share and was no longer needed, after all. He might have started graphitics, but now that it had started, it would carry on by itself **overwhelmingly**, triumphantly, until manned missiles were possible with who knew what else.

Nine times seven, thought Shuman with deep satisfaction, is sixty-three, and I don't need a computer to tell me so. The computer is in my own head.

And it was amazing the feeling of power that gave him.

amusement entertainment

circumstances conditions

compel to force

dispensable not necessary

exigency something demanding immediate attention

overwhelmingly with strength impossible to resist

privacy state of being alone, away from others

C It is exactly the opposite of what we might think today would be something we would want to do. We would want to replace the human beings with computers in order to keep the human beings safe.

D ASK Literary Element Were you surprised by the way the story ended? Why or why not? (Answers may vary, but many students will express surprise and dismay that Aub killed himself. Make sure students understand Asimov's trademark optimism that is shown by Shuman's final thoughts in the story.)

Learning Styles

Group Learning There is much dialogue in this story, and Asimov doesn't always give "dialogue carriers" to make clear who is speaking. Students may benefit from reading the story aloud, with volunteers taking the parts of the various characters. You may even want to allow them to wear signs with their character's name and act out the story a bit. This can be especially helpful to clarify scene changes.

Reviewing the Selection

Answer Key

Comprehension: Identifying Facts

1. The characters include Jehan Shuman, General Weider, Congressman Brant, Myron Aub, the President of the Terrestrial Federation, and Computer Loesser.

2. He can do arithmetic by computing with pencil and paper.

3. He has also learned to compute in his head and with pencil and paper.

4. It is called graphitics.

5. He wants to train human beings to use the skill so they can replace the computers on missiles.

6. He is a "low-grade technician."

7. He uses pencil and paper to use a process we call multiplying.

8. Earth is at war with the mythical planet Deneb.

9. The general thinks Aub is an illusionist.

10. Aub commits suicide.

Comprehension: Understanding Main Ideas

11. The first sentence tells us the story takes place in the future when it points out that Earth is at war with another planet.

12. Aub is most important because he starts everything rolling with his skills in arithmetic.

13. It is the plan to teach many people to compute the way Aub could.

14. He was head of the congressional Committee on Military Appropriations.

15. He developed the computer programming patterns that guided the war computers.

16. He wants graphitics to be used to benefit people.

17. They are amazed because they have never seen a human being do such things; in their experience computers do this kind of work.

18. Human beings are not making new computers because computers make new computers.

19. He thinks grains were grown in soil at one time because he knows that people ate grain before hydroponics was invented.

20. The leaders think humans are cheaper and easier to lose than the computers.

REVIEWING the SELECTION

The Feeling of Power

Isaac Asimov

Directions Write the answers to these questions using complete sentences.

Comprehension: Identifying Facts

1. List the characters.
2. What unusual skill has Myron Aub developed?
3. By the end of the story, what has Jehan Shuman learned to do?
4. What is doing math with pencil and paper called in this story?
5. How does the general want to use Aub's skill?
6. What kind of job does Myron Aub have?
7. How does Aub find the answer to 23 times 17? What do we call the process he used?
8. With whom is earth at war?
9. When General Weider first sees Aub at work, what does he say Aub is doing?
10. What finally happens to Aub?

Comprehension: Understanding Main Ideas

11. Name one point that tells you the story takes place in the future.
12. How important is Aub compared with the other characters?
13. What is Project Number?
14. What does Congressman Brant have to do with the military?
15. Why does Shuman's job make him so important in the government?
16. What does Aub hope that graphitics would be used for?
17. Why are the congressman and the general amazed that Aub can solve multiplication problems?
18. Why aren't humans making new computers at the time of the story?
19. Why does Shuman think that at one time grains were grown in soil?
20. Why do the leaders want to put humans into missiles?

Understanding Literature: Irony

Irony is using an idea or image in the opposite way from its ordinary meaning. For instance, we depend on computers to do what we can't. It is irony when General Weider wants to use people to do what computers can't. It is also irony that officials would rather lose a human life than a computer.

21. Find one statement about graphitics in which you could substitute the word *computers* to sound like today's attitudes.
22. What is ironic about Brant's statement that multiplication is an imitation of how a computer works?
23. What is ironic about General Weider's wanting to replace the computers on missiles?
24. Why is Aub's fate ironic?
25. Shuman feels powerful because he can multiply. What is ironic about that?

Critical Thinking

26. Which person in this story did you like best? Explain.
27. Choose one of the characters. List some of the emotions he shows.
28. Does the author think that everything about technology is good? Explain.
29. Choose one of the characters who has to be persuaded to support Project Number. Tell what arguments win him over.
30. Would you want to live during this time? Why or why not?

Writing on Your Own Write at least two sentences explaining why you think Aub doesn't want his skills to become Project Number.

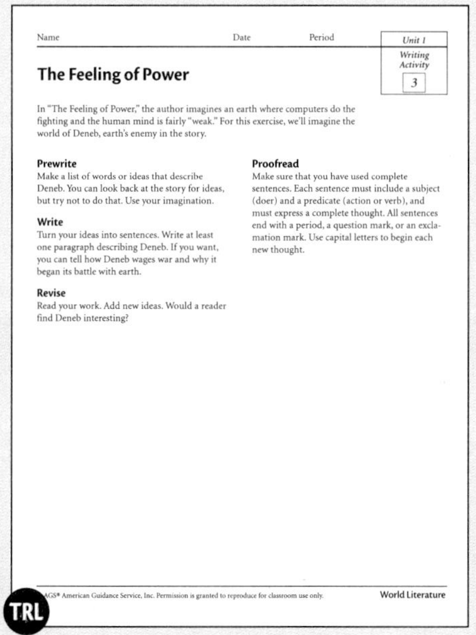
Name Date Period

Unit 1 *Writing Activity* 3

The Feeling of Power

In "The Feeling of Power," the author imagines an earth where computers do the fighting and the human mind is fairly "weak." For this exercise, we'll imagine the world of Deneb, earth's enemy in the story.

Prewrite
Make a list of words or ideas that describe Deneb. You can look back at the story for ideas, but try not to do that. Use your imagination.

Write
Turn your ideas into sentences. Write at least one paragraph describing Deneb. If you want, you can tell how Deneb wages war and why it began its battle with earth.

Revise
Read your work. Add new ideas. Would a reader find Deneb interesting?

Proofread
Make sure that you have used complete sentences. Each sentence must include a subject (doer) and a predicate (action or verb), and must express a complete thought. All sentences end with a period, a question mark, or an exclamation mark. Use capital letters to begin each new thought.

 World Literature

TRL

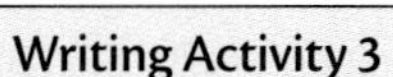
Writing Activity 3

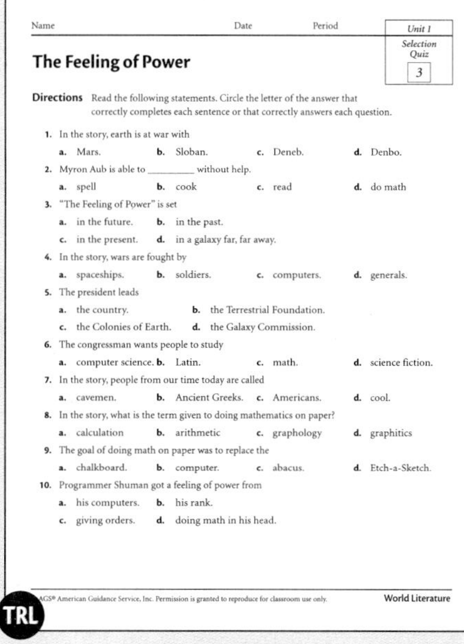
Name Date Period

Unit 1 *Selection Quiz* 3

The Feeling of Power

Directions Read the following statements. Circle the letter of the answer that correctly completes each sentence or that correctly answers each question.

1. In the story, earth is at war with
   a. Mars. b. Sloban. c. Deneb. d. Denbo.
2. Myron Aub is able to ________ without help.
   a. spell b. cook c. read d. do math
3. "The Feeling of Power" is set
   a. in the future. b. in the past. c. in the present. d. in a galaxy far, far away.
4. In the story, wars are fought by
   a. spaceships. b. soldiers. c. computers. d. generals.
5. The president leads
   a. the country. b. the Terrestrial Foundation. c. the Colonies of Earth. d. the Galaxy Commission.
6. The congressman wants people to study
   a. computer science. b. Latin. c. math. d. science fiction.
7. In the story, people from our time today are called
   a. cavemen. b. Ancient Greeks. c. Americans. d. cool.
8. In the story, what is the term given to doing mathematics on paper?
   a. calculation b. arithmetic c. graphology d. graphitics
9. The goal of doing math on paper was to replace the
   a. chalkboard. b. computer. c. abacus. d. Etch-a-Sketch.
10. Programmer Shuman got a feeling of power from
    a. his computers. b. his rank. c. giving orders. d. doing math in his head.

 World Literature

TRL

Selection Quiz 3

Understanding Literature: Irony

21. One example might be the general's comment (on page 62) that "You can play with graphitics any way you want to ... but right now we have specific and very practical problems to solve."

22. It is ironic because, of course, it was human beings who knew multiplication who originally programmed computers to do it.

23. His intention is ironic because ordinarily people would be trying to replace humans with computers to save the human beings.

24. It is ironic because he has started a revolution but does not realize it.

25. He is a very powerful programmer of extremely powerful computers. It seems unthinkable to us that such a person would not know simple arithmetic.

Critical Thinking

26. Answers will vary, but make sure students can support their opinions with elements from the story.

27. Students will choose different characters. Insist that they defend their lists with evidence from the story.

28. Apparently the author believes that technology is not always good because he has presented computers being used to wage war.

29. Loesser, for example, has to be persuaded to join Project Number. He is finally won over by the prospect of being able to learn to do square roots and cube roots without a computer.

30. Students' answers will vary. Their reasons should be sensible based on the story.

Writing on Your Own Students may want to skim the story again before they write their sentences.

Selection Quiz

The Teacher's Resource Library includes a Selection Quiz for "The Feeling of Power" that may be given following the Selection Review.

Selection at a Glance

The Expedition

Rudolf Lorenzen
(translated by Charles E. Pederson)

Student pages 66–83

Overview

Rudolf Lorenzen's work is well-known in his native Germany, especially his work for television and movies.

Selection Summary

In "The Expedition" by Rudolf Lorenzen, four astronauts and their descendants make a space expedition but learn little from it.

Objectives

- To identify conflict in a short story.
- To understand characterization.

Audiocassette

Teacher's Resource Library TRL

- Vocabulary Workbook 4, pages 1–3
- Selection Glossary 4
- Student Study Guide 10, pages 1–2
- Activity 7, pages 1–2
- Workbook 7, pages 1–2
- Writing Activity 4
- Selection Quiz 4

INTRODUCING the SELECTION

The Expedition

Rudolf Lorenzen (translated by Charles E. Pederson)

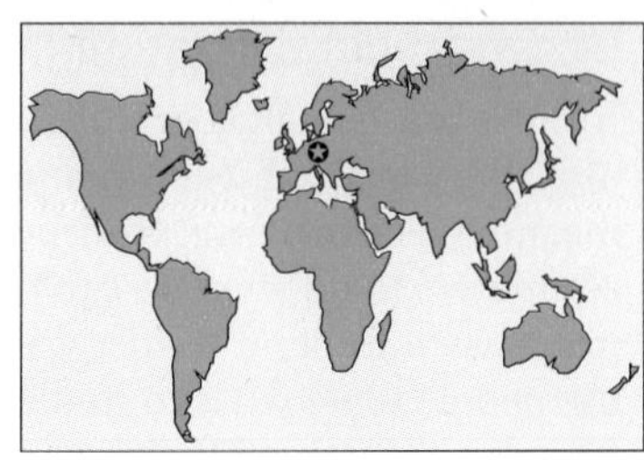

About the Author

Rudolf Lorenzen was born in 1922 in Lübeck, a seaport in northern Germany. His first jobs were in the shipping industry. He wrote many short stories and newspaper articles before publishing his best-known work, *Anything but a Hero,* in 1959. This book has been translated into English. It has also been made into a movie. "The Expedition" has also been translated into Japanese. Lorenzen has written novels, short stories, screen and television plays, and documentary movie scripts. He currently lives in Berlin, Germany, with his second wife, Bettina.

Literary Terms

conflict a struggle the main character of a story has

denouement the resolution to a story

protagonist the main character in a story

About the Selection

"The Expedition" was published in 1974. It tells the story of four astronauts on a space journey to Cerberus, an imaginary planet. The voyage will take about eighty years. The travelers expect to have children and die before their spaceship can return to earth. They depend on the children to take over. The characters experience **conflict** with each other and their children. Conflict is a struggle the **protagonist**, or main character, has. The group must also struggle against boredom and meaninglessness. The author avoids a real **denouement**, or resolution to the story.

Setting the Stage for Reading

Ask students to read the text on page 66. Rudolf Lorenzen is a prolific writer, at home in several different media.

ASK What might a person who writes movies and television plays do differently when he or she is writing a story? (Let students speculate, but many should see that in a short story the writer must describe surroundings rather than expect them to be shown, for example.)

About the Selection

This two-part story covers a very long time span—three generations of people.

Activate Prior Knowledge: Ask students what other stories they have read (or seen on television or in the movies) that cover such long periods of time in the lives of people.

ASK Why might an author write about such a long time span? (Perhaps the writer's theme is carried out by seeing people through their lives and beyond.)

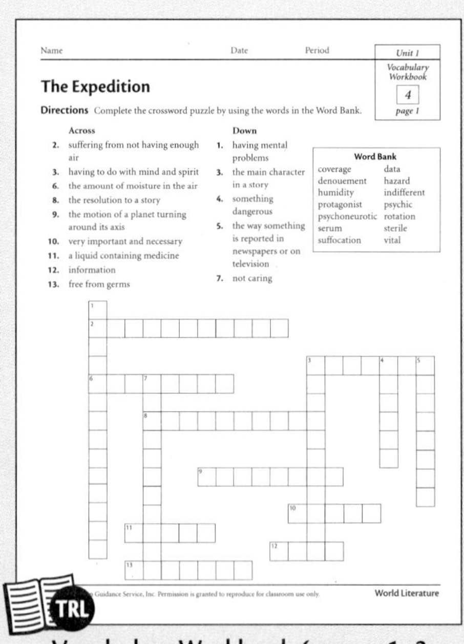

Name Date Period

Unit 1
Vocabulary Workbook 4 *page 1*

The Expedition

Directions Complete the crossword puzzle by using the words in the Word Bank.

Across
2. suffering from not having enough air
3. having to do with mind and spirit
6. the amount of moisture in the air
8. the resolution to a story
9. the motion of a planet turning around its axis
10. very important and necessary
11. a liquid containing medicine
12. information
13. free from germs

Down
1. having mental problems
3. the main character in a story
4. something dangerous
5. the way something is reported in newspapers or on television
7. not caring

Word Bank

coverage	data
denouement	hazard
humidity	indifferent
protagonist	psychic
psychoneurotic	rotation
serum	sterile
suffocation	vital

 World Literature

Vocabulary Workbook 4, pages 1–3

THE EXPEDITION

Rudolf Lorenzen

Part I

They came together for the experiment. Strictly speaking, visiting Cerberus, the outermost of the known planets, was no longer an experiment. The result of an exact **calculation** had already assured success. Both men and the two women who had come together were good calculators.

They met at the space station *Halifax*. One of the men was an engineer, the other, a chemist. They had known each other since they were schoolboys. Cerberus was thirteen light hours, eight minutes distant from earth. Nothing was known about its volume, density, or **rotation**. Leichrieder had discovered the planet two years ago. He expected to find methane and ammoniac gas on it. The two women came from Springfield. They were medical students in their eighth semester. They had become acquainted with their fellow travelers at a ball. They had danced well together. Now they wanted to go to Cerberus with the men.

All four **participants** were healthy. Knowing this fact was **B** important, because the distance of Cerberus to earth was so great that there was almost no chance any of them would reach their goal. The trip depended on children, and those children depended on their children to bring back to earth the results of the expedition.

A
As you read, watch for *conflicts* among the people on the spaceship.

Cerberus is not a real planet. The most distant known planet in the solar system today is Pluto. Many other stars and planets mentioned in the story are real, however.

Frozen gases surround the biggest planets in the solar system—Jupiter, Saturn, Neptune. They are mainly helium, hydrogen, *methane*, and *ammonia*.

C
How does the trip depend on children?

calculation a mathematical process or answer

participant one who takes part in something

rotation the motion of a planet turning around its axis

Reading Vocabulary TRL

Help students preview the selection's vocabulary words by giving them copies of the Selection Glossary. Review the words by having pairs of students take turns saying sentences using the words.

Motivation for Reading

Ask students to imagine that they and several friends are going on a space exploration so long that they will never live to return. Suggest that they read the story to find out one writer's vision of such a journey.

Discussion Questions

Suggest that students use the questions in the margins of the student selection to check their understanding as they read.

A ASK Literary Element What does the word *conflict* mean in terms of a story? (It is the struggle the main character has that sets up the plot, or what happens in the story.)

B The trip will take more than a human lifetime; therefore, the children born to the people who begin the trip will have to have children of their own to guide the ship back to earth.

C ASK Critical Thinking What are some of the assumptions these people are making about their trip? (Let students draw reasonable conclusions. Among them might be that the people would have children, that the trip will be worthwhile, and so on.)

Name Date Period | Unit 1 | Student Study Guide 10 page 1

The Expedition (pp. 67–81)

Directions Fill in the following outline. Filling in the blanks will help you as you read and study "The Expedition."

I. Part I (pp. 67–75)

A. Preparation

1. Leichrieder expects to find __________ and ammoniac gas on Cerberus.
2. The children's children will bring back to Earth the __________ of the expedition.
3. They pack many supplies, including plenty of __________ for the grandchildren.
4. Bruno says they won't be any more __________ than they would be on earth.

B. Leaving Earth

1. In addition to the technical inspector, the inspector general of space station __________ says good-bye to the four adventurers.
2. Heat, air pressure, and __________ are all self-regulating on the ship.
3. During film period, first-grade children make trips to __________.
4. Melanie records the last news reports they could hear in __________ on tinted cardboard.

C. Life on the Ship

1. Vera trains Astraea to care for the test __________.
2. Melanie and Bruno know that their second child will be a girl because __________ __________ and the predetermination of gender are reliable.
3. Olaf dies at the age of fifty-nine years due to dystrophy of the __________.
4. When Astraea dreams, she __________ her duty.

D. Landing on Cerberus

1. Bruno begins to suffer from __________ __________.
2. Astraea enters Bruno's death in the __________.
3. While everyone else practices __________ procedures, Vera is left with her logbook and a pot of moss because she is expecting a __________.

 World Literature

TRL

Student Study Guide 10, pages 1–2

Name Date Period | Unit 1 | Activity 7 page 1

The Expedition

Part A Directions Circle the word or phrase in parentheses that best completes each sentence.

1. In this story, (Cerberus, Monokeros) is the planet farthest from the sun.
2. (Four, Eight) children were born during the expedition.
3. The spaceship was named the *(Galaxis, Halifax)*.
4. The first child born on the expedition was (Astraea, Vera).
5. (Bruno, Olaf) was the first to die on the expedition.
6. The children are all named after (cities on earth, heavenly bodies).

Part B Directions Read each sentence. Write *T* if the statement is true or *F* if it is false.

__________ 1. The author of this story is from Argentina.
__________ 2. The author's name is Rudolf Valentino.
__________ 3. The expedition to Cerberus takes about eighty years.
__________ 4. Two men and three women started the expedition.
__________ 5. The space travelers were very worried about being bored on the expedition.
__________ 6. Astraea killed herself at the end of the story.
__________ 7. On Cerberus, the travelers were surprised to hear the news about earth.

 World Literature

TRL

Activity 7, pages 1–2

Discussion Questions

A ASK Critical Thinking Why do you think the main characters seem so uncaring about their families and their home on earth? (The implication is that at this time in the future only the scientific explorations were considered important, and even they were somewhat routine.)

B Bruno is the protagonist in this part of the story. That means he is the main character. Make sure students understand that the protagonist in a story can change, especially in one like this that covers such a long time.

Community Connection

The small crew on the spaceship formed a closed community, with no possibility of outsiders entering except their own children and grandchildren. Some groups of people in our modern age choose to be part of a closed community. Their motives may be religious or political. (In some places certain groups find themselves isolated by geography, but these are not deliberate choices.) Suggest that students find out about such groups as the Shakers and the Amish, both examples of closed communities in the United States, or others. Have them share what they discover with their classmates.

They went into the station bar before departing from Halifax. **A** They were jolly. It made no difference to them that this was to be their last departure ever. To them, such expressions as "homesickness" and "Mother Earth" were foreign. They laughed at their parents, who were not **indifferent** where they died. "My father," said the engineer, "wants to die on the terrace of his summer home, with the sight of the Alps before his eyes." They all laughed. Even the barkeeper laughed. "Have you packed enough toothbrushes for eighty-six years?" he asked, but no one answered him. They had heard similar jokes ever since they had begun preparing for the trip. They had thought of everything. They even had plenty of diapers for the grandchildren. These had been placed in **sterile** packing, entered as Item 53 in the **inventory** list. Melanie, who was responsible for **administering** the supplies, knew the items by heart.

B
In this part of the story, who is the protagonist?

Their spaceship was named *Galaxis.* Bruno, the engineer, was commander. At the moment, he was being interviewed by two reporters who had entered the bar to report on the start of the *Galaxis* for Cerberus. Bruno was annoyed that it was only two reporters. In the old days, such events had received huge **coverage**.

"You are counting on dying before reaching Cerberus," said one reporter, the one who wrote for a news agency. Bruno answered, "That seems certain. Under such conditions, who could live longer than seventy?"

"Aren't you afraid of being bored until the day you die?" the reporter went on.

Bruno answered, "We won't be any more bored than we would be on earth. Aren't you a little bit bored?"

"Sometimes, yes," said the reporter. Then he turned to questions about technical **data** and amount of supplies.

administer to manage

coverage the way something is reported in newspapers or on television

data information

indifferent not caring

inventory the stock of supplies

sterile free from germs

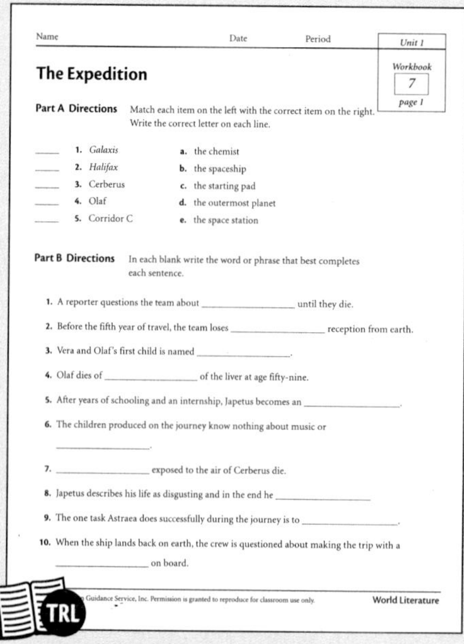

Name Date Period

Unit 1 Workbook 7 page 1

The Expedition

Part A Directions Match each item on the left with the correct item on the right. Write the correct letter on each line.

____	1. *Galaxis*	a. the chemist
____	2. *Halifax*	b. the spaceship
____	3. Cerberus	c. the starting pad
____	4. Olaf	d. the outermost planet
____	5. Corridor C	e. the space station

Part B Directions In each blank write the word or phrase that best completes each sentence.

1. A reporter questions the team about ____________ until they die.
2. Before the fifth year of travel, the team loses ____________ reception from earth.
3. Vera and Olaf's first child is named ____________.
4. Olaf dies of ____________ of the liver at age fifty-nine.
5. After years of schooling and an internship, Japetus becomes an ____________.
6. The children produced on the journey know nothing about music or ____________.
7. ____________ exposed to the air of Cerberus die.
8. Japetus describes his life as disgusting and in the end he ____________
9. The one task Astraea does successfully during the journey is to ____________.
10. When the ship lands back on earth, the crew is questioned about making the trip with a ____________ on board.

 World Literature

TRL

Workbook 7, pages 1–2

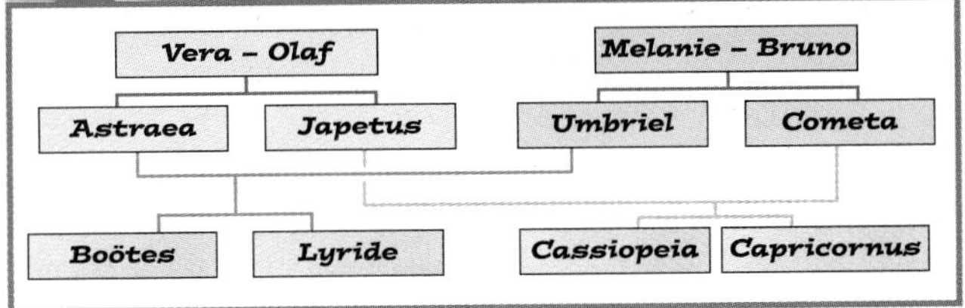

C

Olaf, the chemist, was just dancing with Vera on the small dance floor. "As I left early this morning," said Vera, "my mother asked when I was coming back. I said, 'Read about it in tomorrow's paper.' Then she asked where she could write me."

"I would definitely never make such a trip," said the other reporter to Bruno. "Just thinking that I could never again lie on the beach in the sun makes me uncomfortable."

"Has lying in the sun on the beach ever made you happy?" asked Bruno.

The reporter considered. "Sometimes, yes," he said. "Sometimes, no."

"There you are then," said Bruno, adding that the time had come, and he paid their bar tab.

They went down Corridor C to the starting pad. The two **D** reporters followed them. They noted that besides the technical inspector, the inspector general of space station *Halifax* accompanied them to take leave of the four adventurers as they started this journey, which after all was still uncommon. The inspector general shook the hand of each. As the rocket left the base, the reporters went to the radio station to file their reports with their home office.

The ship was large and comfortable. It had come from last year's production at the Clavenna Works. All difficulties with handling had been reduced to a minimum. Heat, air pressure, and **humidity** were **self-regulating**. It was hardly necessary to touch the instruments. Still, Bruno never neglected to make his **rounds** every eight hours, as recommended in the training

humidity the amount of moisture in the air

rounds a pattern of assigned duties

self-regulating making adjustments without outside help

C ASK Comprehension What does the chart at the top of this page tell you? (Apparently it is a family tree and shows the children the couples will have. The four people at the top of the chart—Vera, Olaf, Bruno, and Melanie—are those about to take the journey.)

D ASK Critical Thinking Note that two reporters followed the four to the starting pad. Then the reporters filed their reports with their home offices. How is this different from the way it would be done if this journey were starting today? (Today there would be thousands of reporters, television cameras, and so on. The media coverage described is tiny compared with what would be likely today.)

Learning Styles

Visual Visually oriented students will benefit from referring to the chart on this page as they proceed to read the rest of the story. They may find it helpful to copy it and add notes to it about the people and when they are born in relation to each other. They can also add information regarding which people marry each other, who their offspring are, and some identifying characteristics of each one.

Fiction Unit 1 **69**

Discussion Questions

A The people do not seem very excited about the idea of traveling in space. The story explains that such travel is routine, with even first-grade children taking "field trips" to Mars regularly. It is the trip beyond that is unusual.

B ASK Vocabulary The Greek word *astron,* meaning "star," is the root of many English words including *asteroid* and, in the story, the name of Astraea. What are some others? (*astronomy, astrodome, astrodynamics, astronaut, asterisk,* as well as *disaster*—from "ill-starred")

C Yes, the crew members are apparently completely on their own once they are beyond radio contact with earth.

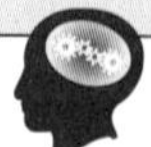

Comprehension

Drawing Conclusions Ask students to compare what they do in their free time to what the characters in the story do. What are some common activities the story characters do not do? (They don't seem to read, watch television or movies, or certainly play sports.) Do you think they would be interesting people to talk to ? Why or why not? (Probably not because they have so little experience in doing things, they would have little to talk about or share.)

Meteors are small pieces of rock in space. Because the spacecraft is moving very fast, even a small object could cause damage.

course. During his rounds, he also checked for meteor damage. But meteor damage was rare.

Mostly, the company sat in the main room of the ship, played cards, and listened to music from earth's radio stations. They looked through the portholes only now and again. They had all seen the pictures of a space trip in countless films—the ever-shrinking earth, the **waning** earth, the half earth, the crescent earth, the orange of Mars, the green spots on its surface. There was nothing new to it. First-grade children made trips to Mars all the time during school film period.

A
Do the people seem excited about traveling in space?

Asteroids are pieces of rock, smaller than a planet, that orbit the sun. Most are found in the asteroid belt, between the orbits of Mars and Jupiter.

B At the far edge of the asteroid belt, Vera had a child. It was a girl, and the company named her Astraea, after the asteroid that was closest to them in the belt. Bruno entered the event in the logbook, along with the exact time and their universal position.

Are the crew members completely on their own now?
C

After four years, radio reception with earth was weakening, three-quarters of a year later it faded out altogether. The last news reports that they could hear, Melanie recorded in **calligraphy** on a piece of tinted cardboard. In Nepal, there was a temporary truce. The post office had raised its rates. An heir to the Bourbons had married an Ostrowski in San Sebastian. The couple had ridden in a coach drawn by horses, a spy was executed in the electric chair, European beer **consumption** continued to rise. Melanie framed the reports and hung them next to the ship's rules and regulations. She had good taste in such artistic matters.

As they crossed Neptune's orbit, Astraea had already passed astronautical mathematics. She had learned to make entries in the logbook and to read the instruments. For the past year, she had been responsible for the care of the test plants. Her mother had trained her, urging her to take **conscientious** care of the continued **pollination**. In the following year, her medical training would begin.

calligraphy fine handwriting

conscientious careful to do things right

consumption the process of eating or drinking

pollination transfer of pollen to make plants fertile

waning growing smaller, as the visible part of the moon

Astraea's brother, Japetus, born in the vicinity of Saturn, had begun being able to read in his primer at this time. "The planet is beautiful. The moons are beautiful too. Our rocket is fast. I like to live on a rocket."

Melanie and Bruno's son, named for Uranus's moon Umbriel, still lay next to the map cabinet in the bunk that had been **designated** for newborns. A fourth child, Melanie's daughter, was due to be born. But there was no doubt that it would come on time. There also was no doubt that it would be a girl. Birth control and the **predetermination** of **gender** were **reliable**. One used Ryders-Schelde's tables, which were the most dependable, being based on hundreds of experiments.

Six years after exiting the angle of the **ecliptic** of Pluto, Olaf died. The ship was shortly to cross the orbit of Monokeros, a small, **eccentrically** orbiting planet. Monokeros, like Cerberus, had been little researched. Its brightness varied. Melanie and Vera agreed about time and cause of death. Bruno had Astraea enter the death in the logbook. Astraea wrote, "At kilometer position 7,862,447,350, on 30 October 2145, at 0:43:15, Olaf Tyde died at **D** the age of fifty-nine years. Cause of death: **dystrophy** of the liver. Nothing else to report. No meteor damage. He was a good husband, friend, and father to us all." Bruno judged that the last sentence did not belong in the logbook.

Neptune, Saturn, Uranus, and *Pluto* are the outer planets in the solar system. *Monokeros* is imaginary.

E
What conflict is developing among the characters here?

Olaf's body was released into space through the airlock in Opening D.

designate to select for a role
dystrophy illness caused by poor nutrition
eccentrically oddly, not in an expected way
ecliptic circle formed where the plane of earth's orbit and another object cross
gender sex; male or female
predetermination deciding in advance
reliable to be trusted

D ASK Critical Thinking Note that Astraea records the date as the year 2145. How long is that from now? Is it likely that some of the things in this story would be really possible in the year 2145? Why or why not? (Have students compute the number of years accurately. Let them theorize about the possibility of some aspects of the story. It is unlikely that such a space journey will be technically possible by 2145.)

E The conflict that seems to be developing among the characters is over the human commentary beyond the scientific facts. Bruno feels that the personal observations about Olaf's contributions are irrelevant to the scientific record of his death.

Environmental Connection

The people in this futuristic spaceship can and do carefully control their population growth, including choosing the gender of each baby. Uncontrolled population growth is a problem in many parts of the world now, especially in developing countries that have fewer industrial resources and income per capita than developed countries do. For example, many of the poorest nations are expected to triple their populations by the middle of the twenty-first century, according to the Population Institute, a United States research organization, late in 1998. Among these countries are Afghanistan, Ethiopia, Mali, Somalia, and Uganda. The population of Liberia will probably quadruple in that same period. Ask interested students to find out about this problem and why many people consider it a serious one for the environment.

Discussion Questions

A Let students volunteer their opinions about the value of the children's educations compared to their parents'. Many will feel that the children's education is missing something important because of its concentration on science to the exclusion of the humanities.

B ASK Comprehension Have students turn back to page 69 and look at the chart of the family trees again. Provide a copy of the chart for everyone or ask a volunteer to copy it on the chalkboard. Who are Cometa's parents? (Melanie and Bruno) What other children have been born to the original four travelers? (Astraea, Umbriel, Japetus, and now Cometa)

C Astraea's personality seems to be different from the others. She is not as scientifically driven and is instead given to dreaminess, for example. Point out to students that the characterization of the main people in the story can contribute to what happens in a story.

Cross-Curricular Connection

Science/Astronomy Many planets and constellations are mentioned in this story. Have students work together to list all that are mentioned and note which ones are real and which made up only for the story. If possible, obtain maps of the night sky that show some of the constellations mentioned. Some interested students may want to show the constellations to the rest of the class.

After five years of elementary school, eight years of technical schooling, and six years of **internship**, Japetus was **certified** as an engineer. Bruno presented his diploma, which Japetus hung at the head of his bunk. The education of all the children on the trip was one-sided, but thorough in the specialties. They learned from their parents, and then from books in the various fields. At the end of their education, they knew somewhat more than their parents. They knew nothing of geography, history, or foreign languages. They had no experience of art, literature, or music. Even their parents had forgotten what they had known of literature, art, and music. But they did not miss it.

A
Do you think the children's education was better or worse than their parents' education?

B When Cometa was born, they had only ten years until arrival at Cerberus. Umbriel and Astraea had been engaged for a year. They wanted to marry within the next year. Astraea was the oldest of the second-generation children. Bruno had looked forward to the day when he could hand over command of the ship to her. But Astraea seemed to lack the **aptitude** for the position. She was more inclined to dream. When she dreamed, she neglected her duty. One day, some of the test plants in her care died, and the cause was pinpointed as **negligence**. Bruno removed the duty from Astraea. The remaining plants came under Umbriel's care. In place of the plants, Astraea administered the wash, **disbursed** the dry soap, and distributed the vitamins. Only a pot of moss with boat-shaped leaves was left to her.

C
How is *Astraea* different from the others on the ship?

Sirius is also called the Dog Star. It is about the same size as our sun but gives off about 30 times as much light.

Cometa learned to recognize the sun as a tiny spot among the other stars. The sun lay in the **constellation** Great Dog (Canis Major) and was outshone by Sirius. Earth could no longer be seen with the ship's telescope. When Cometa asked what was happening on earth, her mother answered, "What does it matter? Everything is the same there as it is here on board, only larger. Be happy that we will be on Cerberus in a couple of years."

One day Bruno began to suffer from panic attacks, although they were not based in his **psychic** nature. He imagined he could not

aptitude an natural ability or talent

certify to confirm that standards have been met

constellation a pattern of stars that form a picture

disburse to pay out or hand out

internship a time of supervised training

negligence carelessness

psychic having to do with mind and spirit

get his breath. Many times a day, he staggered to the instruments, stared at them. He pounded his fists against the glass of the air pressure monitor and screamed, "Air! I can't get any air. The instrument is broken." The instruments were **functioning** perfectly. It was guessed that Bruno had a mild heart condition; but the medicine that Vera gave him did not help. The fear of **suffocation** constantly grew in Bruno, until one day he dashed into the air lock and also into the lockless Exit A, to get some air. He had to be overpowered by Japetus and Umbriel. **D**

When Bruno's condition did not improve and he threatened to become a general **hazard**, the company decided he had to be killed. Vera gave him an injection. Japetus oversaw removal of the body through Opening D. While entering the death into the logbook, Astraea was watched by her mother, so that no **extraneous** remarks would find their way into the official record. Astraea did not write that Bruno was a good husband, father, and friend, but only entered the position, time, and kilometer position. She wrote, "Bruno Perneder died at the age of seventy-one years. Cause of death: complications of **psychoneurotic** disturbances. No evidence of organic disease. Since early today, Cerberus clearly visible at 2° 12' to starboard. Nothing else to report."

When Melanie died eleven months later, Vera overtook sole command of the ship. She handed over complete technical supervision to her son, Japetus. **E**

As you read, notice a change in the protagonist.

Four years before arrival at Cerberus, Japetus and Umbriel had begun daily preparations for the landing. They practiced the maneuvers, learned the regulations by heart. "Power units on. Approaching **tangential**. Rotate the machine. Stern forward. Check pressure suits before exiting ship." Every three days they held a general exercise to practice emergency **procedures**. Vera and little Cometa had to take part in these exercises too. Only Astraea was left in peace, with her logbook and her pot of moss. She was expecting a child.

extraneous not necessary

function to work properly

hazard something dangerous

procedure a way of doing something

psychoneurotic having mental problems

suffocation suffering from not having enough air

tangential a point or line that touches, but doesn't cross, another

D ASK Literary Element How has Bruno changed since the beginning of the story? (His panic attacks seem to show he is less trusting of the scientific control of his environment than he was earlier, although this seems unfounded.)

E ASK Comprehension Which of the original four travelers lived the longest? (Vera)

Literary Elements

The main elements of stories are setting, plot, and characters. Some stories emphasize one element more than others, but all stories have these elements. Discuss with students what the setting, plot, and characters are in this story.

ASK Which of these story elements is the most important in this story? (The setting is most important; it governs everything that happens with the plot and the characters.)

Discussion Questions

A ASK Vocabulary Use a dictionary to look up the name of the constellation Boötes. How is it pronounced? (boh-OH-teez) What does the diacritical mark called a dieresis over the second *o* in the word tell you about how to pronounce it? (It indicates that the second *o* has its own separate sound.)

B The work on Cerberus seems neither interesting nor valuable. According to the story, there don't seem to be any specific important questions the crew is to try to answer about Cerberus.

C ASK Critical Thinking Remember that *irony* is the expression of something that is the opposite of what is expected. How is the work on Cerberus ironic? (The travelers in the spaceship have made great sacrifices and lived their whole lives for the purpose of getting to Cerberus. For the work there to be neither interesting nor valuable is ironic. Make sure students understand that the true irony, however, is that the characters do not seem disappointed or concerned about the results of their time on Cerberus.)

Boötes is the name of a constellation.

A The child that Astraea had was a boy. She called him Boötes. He lay in the bunk next to the map cabinet. Every twenty-four hours Astraea prayed with him, "Deliver us from meteors. And protect our equipment. Let us not suffer lack of oxygen, moisture, and vitamins. Lead us not into false calculations. And turn your eyes to us when we land."

As *Galaxis* reached Cerberus, Boötes was three years old. As the stay on the planet was to last two years and the child couldn't be denied a chance to go outside the ship and play a little, his mother made a little protective suit for him. With a small oxygen tank on his back, he sat in it at the foot of a **pumice** hill, building little **pyramids** of stones. Now and then his mother called him when it was time to eat his pills or his oxygen should be topped up. She said, "Be careful of your spacesuit! If you tear it, poison gas will come in and make you very sick!" At the same time, the two men undertook **excursions** over a wide area. They made measurements and tested the rocks and atmosphere. Leichrieder had been correct about methane and ammoniac gas on the planet. The period of rotation was one and a half days, the angle of the elliptic was nineteen degrees. These results had **C** no practical value, as their distance from the sun was so great that day and night, summer and winter were unnoticeable. The test plants that were exposed to Cerberus died.

B Does the work on Cerberus seem interesting or valuable?

Only in the afternoons would Cometa watch the measurements. In the mornings she had school. She solved simple astronautical problems, studied scientific laws, and wrote compositions. Astraea gave her the topic "A Beautiful Day in My Life." Cometa wrote:

> "A beautiful day in my life was when we landed on Cerberus. My father and mother gave a me holiday from school on this day, and I did not have to study. When our ship stood firmly on the ground, I was allowed to put on my new protective suit and breathe oxygen from a bottle. That was very fun. Then I

excursion a trip

pumice a light rock from a volcano

pyramid a figure with four triangles for sides

74 *Unit 1 Fiction*

was allowed to jump outside through Exit D. I held little Boötes's hand. I played outside all day long, until Mother called and I had to go to bed. That was a beautiful day. When I get big, I will tell my children about it."

Part II

Almost two years later, the time that Bruno had calculated arrived. It was the best time to leave Cerberus and begin the return trip. Japetus followed Uncle Bruno's instructions to the letter, laid out in many carefully **compiled** notebooks. On the day before liftoff, little Boötes celebrated his fifth birthday. His parents gave him building blocks and puzzles. From Grandma Vera he received a picture book, "Hansi and Möpsi in the Milky Way." For the evening meal, Boötes got $C_6H_{12}O_6$ tablets—as many as he wanted. He was allowed to stay up two hours past his bedtime.

D
The writer gives the chemical formula for fructose, a sugar. Why do you suppose he doesn't just say "sugar"?

Ten years later, at his fifteenth birthday, Boötes's father gave him a do-it-yourself electric motor and a biography of explorers, called *Look Forward!* But Boötes did not like to read, and he also disliked building things, and was definitely not a stay-at-home type. His favorite thing was to play ball in the forward cabin of the ship with Lyride, his little sister, who had been born eight years earlier, and little Cassiopeia, Cometa's daughter.

Sometimes, when the children were too loud, Japetus came to the forward cabin and scolded them, "Pay a little more attention to your lessons. What will you do when we are all gone? Boötes, you don't even know how to regulate the heat and measure the air pressure!" But the children did not listen, they had no technical interests, they preferred to play ball. "What would your grandmother say if she saw you," said Cometa. But Grandmother Vera did not see them. She had been dead seven years. She had died shortly before the start of the return trip. No **E**

compile to put together information into a record

D The writer gives the chemical formula instead of simply saying "sugar" because on the trip the travelers' food was tablets chemically manufactured to provide the nutrients they needed. Apparently they did not eat "real" food.

E **Literary Element** Remember that *foreshadowing* is a literary technique that gives the reader hints about what might take place later. You can use these clues to predict what might happen. What do you think the descriptions of the latest generation of children might foreshadow? (These children are not very interested in scientific knowledge or their studies. That may mean trouble ahead.)

Career Connection

Point out to students that the people in this story clearly have different talents. The first generation was made up of scientists, but their children are not necessarily interested in science. Explain that everyone has different aptitudes, talents, and interests that guide them into different careers and hobbies. If possible, have students find out about aptitude testing or interview a local career counselor or a high school guidance counselor.

Discussion Questions

A Japetus's words indicate the conflict between the generations. Japetus feels that the trip has been pointless and only taken so that the children can one day land on earth. However, the children do not seem to understand that this is important, nor do they appreciate the sacrifice their parents have made.

B The derogatory comparison "one spoon short of a silverware drawer" indicates that Capricornus does not seem to comprehend the world around him very well at all.

Comprehension

Compare and Contrast The three generations on the spaceship were different, but so were the individuals within those groups. Ask students to consider what they know from the story about the characters and to compare them to each other. Invite them to ask questions about the characters such as: Which person was the best engineer? (probably Bruno) or Which character do we know best? (Astraea)

one was left alive of the first generation that had planned the expedition fifty-four years ago back on earth.

The company's worries about the children grew. Little Cassiopeia could not even understand the multiplication table, and Lyride refused even the simplest task her parents set her. She messed the supply rooms and mixed up their **vital** pills. At fourteen she still chewed her fingernails. Her brother Boötes was not expected ever to pass the engineering tests.

So all hopes came to rest on Capricornus, the youngest, born to Cometa sixteen years after leaving Cerberus. Capricornus was a strong baby, and his father, Japetus, often sat for hours at the infant's bunk next to the map cabinet, speaking to the newborn. "Your parents," he said, "live only for you. They have never seen earth, and never will. When our ship arrives there, we will all be dead. Only you will be alive, and your sister, and Boötes and Lyride. But they are all ungrateful and can't see that we live only for all of you, they don't understand the sacrifice that we have made for you. We take on ourselves the gloomy, disgusting life of this miserable steel casing, the **monotonous** days on this pointless trip, the uselessness of our daily **manipulations**, so that all of you can one day land on earth. Boötes, Lyride, and your sister Cassiopeia do not understand that. So we live only for you, Capricornus."

A
What conflicts do Japetus's words show?

Six years later, Japetus was still saying the same things to Capricornus. He sat at his son's bunk and said, "Our daily activities are useless, our life is disgusting, and this trip makes no sense." But Capricornus did not understand his father. He understood nothing, took in nothing that happened around him, did not speak, only made little gurgling sounds. His look was numb. If he did move around the ship, he crawled on all fours. Capricornus was one spoon short of a silverware drawer.

B
What does this phrase tell you about Capricornus?

When there clearly was no hope of improvement for his son, Japetus killed himself. He injected himself with a poison **serum**.

manipulation the action of controlling or operating

monotonous dull, boring

serum a liquid containing medicine

vital very important and necessary

He felt no pain. Umbriel dispatched the body through the air lock. Boötes **sullenly** helped him with this procedure.

Astraea entered her brother's death in the logbook. Making entries in the logbook was one of the few duties that had been left to her. She was the oldest on board, but the company was **reluctant** to give her other assignments. Her **tendency** to dream, which she had shown early in life, became stronger with every passing year. She was now sixty-four years old. In her youth, there had still been light outside the porthole, the sun was a small, glowing ball, one could see earth through the telescope. Astraea remembered hearing the radio when she was four years old. The programs from earth had sometimes come weakly and unclearly, often accompanied by static. On other days, clear and pure, came music. Sometimes someone spoke on the radio and reported happenings on earth. The last reports, which had been received sixty years ago on the outward voyage, Aunt Melanie had **transcribed** in calligraphy, framed, and hung next to the house **C** rules and regulations. The document still hung there. A Bourbon had married an Ostrowski. That was in San Sebastian, and the couple had ridden in a coach pulled by horses. Truce in Nepal, higher rates at the post office. In Europe, beer consumption continued to rise, and a spy was sent to the electric chair.

Astraea sat at her place near the porthole, looking into the darkness and the stars. She dreamed that the sun was a small glowing ball, and outside, everything shone with brightness. She dreamed of stepping up to the telescope and seeing the earth as a big, round disk, half dark, half lighted by the sun. She dreamed that music came from the radio, and that a voice on the radio said postage rates had gone down again and that the spy had been pardoned. She sat at the porthole, looking into the darkness. The moss with the boat-shaped leaves, which her Uncle Bruno had given her as a present, had died thirty years ago. The empty pot still stood next to her bunk.

D

Are Astraea's feelings about life different from the others' feelings?

reluctant not willing

sullenly in a gloomy or sulky way

tendency a pattern of doing things a certain way

transcribe make a copy of

C ASK Critical Thinking Do you think the last radio reports hanging on the wall mean anything to anyone but Astraea? Why or why not? (Probably not, because they refer to happenings on earth that no one on the ship knows anything about. Astraea, in fact, only remembers them as the radio broadcast; she probably has little understanding of what they mean.)

D Astraea's feelings about life are definitely different from the others' feelings. She remembers the sun and the music from the radio, which no one else does. And she may be keeping the empty plant pot for sentimental reasons because her Uncle Bruno had given it to her. Such sentimentality does not seem to be a characteristic of the others.

Writing Connection

Astraea is the character readers know the most about. Ask students to write a brief character sketch describing her. Encourage them to add details of their own about her without changing the kind of person she was.

Discussion Questions

A ASK Literary Element Think about the youngest people on board. What kind of people are they? How do you know? (They have little understanding or patience for Astraea, as demonstrated by their attitude toward her when she remarked on the anniversary of her father's death and her recording of human commentary in the logbook. They seem to be uncaring about the purpose of their journey or making sure it happens properly; one clue is their attitude toward keeping up the logbook.)

B ASK Critical Thinking What might it mean that the youngest generation plays such primitive card games? (Their education and studies have not taught them to think very critically or about strategies.)

C ASK Literary Element What might the comment about the primitive card playing foreshadow? (It may mean that this generation is not intellectually capable of doing what needs to be done to guide the spaceship.)

One day Astraea surprised the company with the news that **A** **precisely** at this point on the outward trip, her father had died and been **dispatched** into space. Umbriel and Cometa were not able to convince Astraea that their Uncle Olaf had not died on this spot. "We have taken a completely different return path," said Umbriel, and Cometa added, "Dear Astraea, you're wrong, your father died six years beyond Pluto. And we are now a year and a half inside Pluto's orbit." Astraea would not listen to reason. She sat at the porthole, looked out, and waited to meet her father's body. But she saw nothing.

Between the orbits of Pluto and Neptune, Cometa contracted a lung infection. She had chills, fever, and chest pains. Her **sputum** left no doubt about the diagnosis, and everyone wondered where such germs had come from. In twelve days, Cometa was dead. Umbriel took care of **disinfection**, and in the logbook, Astraea wrote, "Cometa died at age thirty-nine. She always had weak health. She was a good mother, sister, sister-in-law, and aunt to us all." When, only a few years later, Astraea's husband, Umbriel, followed his sister in death, she added a similar line in the logbook. No one stopped her from such personal entries anymore. Her children, Boötes and Lyride, and her niece, Cassiopeia, did not care what she did. Making entries in the logbook seemed **superfluous** to the young people. They left such games to Astraea, who had reached the age of seventy-one.

With the third generation, a new era came to *Galaxis.* The youngsters did not possess the strict outlook that their parents had, nor the sporting spirit of their grandparents. They lived only for the moment, expecting nothing of the future. Mostly the three of them sat in the main room of the ship and played cards.
B Astraea, watching them, was surprised at how **primitive** their
C card-playing was. The players constantly chose several random cards from the pile, threw them down on the table, and laughed. It was nothing compared to the **complicated** games with which

complicated not easy to understand

disinfection getting rid of germs that can cause diseases

dispatch to send out

precisely exactly

primitive simple or crude

sputum spit

superfluous more than needed

their grandparents had occupied themselves, back in the days of the outward trip. But Astraea said nothing, stayed out of it, was happy that her children and nieces left her in peace.

She sat at the porthole, watching the stars. Capricornus chewed at her feet. He still could not speak, could not run. This year he turned fourteen. Slowly over years, the sun emerged from the constellation Hydra. It became larger, gave light, soon was the size of a screw head, DIN M 8. "Day by day, I feel it getting warmer," Astraea said, but her children laughed. "The inside temperature is always the same," they said. "You're imagining things." But Astraea was not to be talked out of what she felt. "For seventy years, I've frozen," she said. "Finally, I feel better."

Hydra is a constellation of stars in the southern sky of earth.

DIN M 8 is an industrial measurement.

A couple of years later, it was possible to receive radio signals from earth. But the company made no use of the privilege. The music hurt their ears, the news was meaningless to them. Only Astraea would have liked to listen now and then, but her hearing was failing. Soon she would be eighty. She was also unable to see earth's disk through the telescope, her eyes were too weak. She sat at the porthole again, watching the sun through the protective glass and imagining that she could feel the warmth on her skin.

D
Why do they realize they are nearing the earth?

Think about the ways in which Astraea is the protagonist in the story. Why do you think she decides to stay on the ship?

Would the company have gone back to playing cards if Bruno or Japetus were in command?
E

At Jupiter's orbit, the company gradually considered it might become necessary to learn how to land the ship. Lyride looked in her grandfather's papers and found a notebook that precisely described the landing **maneuvers** and all possible dangers that came with it. It is true that the notes were for landing on Cerberus; but Boötes thought that the difference of landing on earth couldn't be that much. They practiced the necessary manipulations and also **improvised** a way to use the radio. When they believed they had mastered everything, they went back to playing cards until they reached earth's vicinity.

The *Galaxis* landed, following radioed commands, at space station *Wellington.* At touchdown, there was some slight

maneuver a change in course or position

improvise to invent or put together on the spur of the moment

D They apparently can see both the sun and the earth. And evidently they have received radio signals from earth, although they have decided not to listen to them.

E From what we know about Bruno and Japetus, the company would certainly not have gone back to playing cards if either had been in command at this point. Those two men were conscientious scientists who tried to make sure everything was run "by the book."

Fiction Unit 1 **79**

Discussion Questions

A ASK Literary Element Were the foreshadowing hints that you picked up accurate? Why or why not? (The hints seemed to point to impending disaster caused by the crew's lack of interest in their own training. However, they managed to pull it together and land on the space station without incident.)

B ASK Critical Thinking How is the uneventful landing ironic? (The crew was not as rigorously trained as the original crew was, yet they managed the landing anyway. Also, the whole intent of the journey was to bring both the last generation of people and the results of their trip back to earth, and the people on earth don't seem to know or care anything about it.)

C Astraea stays on the ship because it is home to her. She is sentimental and not a scientist. She has little interest in going back to earth, and she thinks the experiences she has had were enough for her.

D No one on earth seems to understand where the expedition has been or why.

damage, but the company did not bother about it. They left the **A** ship and followed the directions of the ground crew, who sent them down Corridor C to register. Boötes carried his cousin Capricornus on his shoulders, Lyride and Cassiopeia carried the crates of rock samples from Cerberus and the test tube samples of its atmosphere. They carried all the papers that had been issued almost ninety years ago: permission to depart, Bruno's commission, their grandparents' health certificates, and the **B** logbook kept by Astraea. They were uncertain what might be asked of them. They had no experience with the **formalities** of a space station on earth.

Astraea remained behind in the ship. She had no wish to climb out and make acquaintance with the ground that her parents had left. A few years ago she had often thought, while sitting in her place at the porthole, what a space station might be like, or even how earth itself might look. She had looked at the sun and dreamed that she walked down corridor after endless corridor.

C
Think of how Astraea is the protagonist. Why does she stay on the ship?

But the dream had ceased, and with the dream, her last wishes had disappeared. Astraea was eighty-four years old. As her children **debarked**, she said, "Leave me at my place. From here I've seen everything. I've seen all the stars, and I've seen the sun as it disappeared and came back again. As a child I saw the earth as a tiny point, and now as a great round disk. What else is there? What else don't know I about?"

D
The doctor does not understand how long the *Galaxis* has been gone. Does anyone on earth seem to understand this expedition?

So the children went without mother and aunt. At the end of Corridor C they found the registration office. They heard that their papers were no longer valid and if they wished to renew them, a certain fee was required. From registration they were sent for a technical inspection, and from the technical inspection to a physical inspection. The doctor gave them trouble about Capricornus. "How could you make a space journey with a mentally retarded boy?" the doctor scolded them, and Boötes had

debark to get off, as from a ship

formalities official rules; customs

to describe in detail that the *Galaxis* had just finished a long journey and that his cousin had been born underway.

With the formalities taken care of, the four of them went to Counter G, where they could buy shuttle tickets for earth. Counter G was busy, a tour group had just arrived from the moon. The people stood in a long line before the counter. They had been underway for several days and were in a hurry because after the Easter holiday, they had to be at their workplaces promptly the next day. Joining the line, the crew of the *Galaxis* briefly attracted the attention of these Easter vacationers. The tourists poked each other and laughed. They joked about Lyride and Cassiopeia, about their hairstyles and clothes. The tour group also joked about Capricornus, who sat drooling on the floor.

Meanwhile, a mechanic entered the *Galaxis*. He had been sent to inspect the damage done at landing. He met Astraea in the main room. "Well, Grandma, did you have a nice trip?" But Astraea did not understand him. The mechanic repeated his question. "Yes, yes," said Astraea. "The sun is getting warmer. I've frozen for eighty years." The mechanic laughed, tapping his forehead behind Astraea's back as he left.

Not long afterward, an inspector arrived at the *Galaxis*'s landing place. The mechanic reported the damage he had found. "An old grandma is sitting inside," he added. "She must be older than eighty. I always wonder what use these old people have with flying around in space."

"Yeah," answered the inspector. "I always think the same thing. We live in crazy times."

The mechanic said, "You're right about that, sir. Crazy times." Then he took a pencil and the pad of forms to write down the damage he had found.

E
Why don't the inspector and the mechanic know that Astraea was born in space?

F
This story stops without following the characters to an end. In the conflict with boredom, what has won?

E The inspector and the mechanic don't know that Astraea was born in space because they don't know anything about the trip the spaceship and its crew have been on.

F In the conflict with boredom, which was foreshadowed by the original reporter's questions, boredom has certainly won. Not only are the people from the spaceship supremely bored with what they have experienced, but so are the people on earth. The whole journey seems to have been totally pointless—the great irony of the story.

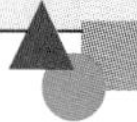

Learning Styles

Tactile/Kinesthetic Toward the end of the story, a mechanic makes fun of Astraea behind her back by making a gesture in which he taps his forehead, indicating that she might not be thinking quite straight. Point out to students that we communicate a great deal with gestures and facial expressions in addition to words and tone of voice. Suggest that they watch people for a day and keep a list of gestures, expressions, and what they think such motions mean. Have them act out the gestures and expressions for the class.

Reviewing the Selection

Answer Key

Comprehension: Identifying Facts

1. The expedition will take more than twenty-six light hours, sixteen minutes, which is the distance to Cerberus and back.

2. For his daily rounds, Bruno checks all the instruments, and he looks for meteor damage.

3. Olaf is the first person on board to die.

4. Vera takes over after Melanie dies.

5. She stays aboard the spaceship.

6. Bruno was an engineer; Olaf was a chemist; Vera and Melanie were both medical students.

7. The first child born on board was Astraea, whose parents were Vera and Olaf.

8. Bruno and Melanie's son was Umbriel.

9. His parents are Astraea and Umbriel.

10. He suffers from panic attacks.

Comprehension: Understanding Main Ideas

11. Bruno does not want to include such comments because he is a scientist and thinks only the facts should be recorded.

12. He is not interested in studying or learning, and Japetus is an engineer.

13. Japetus felt that the three members of the younger generation were ungrateful, and he worried that they were unschooled. He placed all his hopes on the youngest child, Capricornus. When he realized that Capricornus was mentally retarded, he committed suicide in despair.

14. The grandchildren do not seem to care about the ship's mission or their part in it.

15. They realized they were getting close enough to earth that they would have to land on the nearby space station.

16. She could record personal information about Cometea because at this point no one else cared what was written in the logbook.

17. His behavior had become a hazard to them all.

18. The birthday presents would not be up to date because they were all so far from earth that they would not know what was going on there. On the other hand, they may have made the birthday gifts so that they were as up to date regarding their own surroundings as possible.

19. Results of her daydreaming include that she likes to put personal comments in the logbook, neglects her plants, and so on. Her daydreams later include memories of the sun's shine and brightness and the music and news from the radio.

20. Her death is very strange because she dies of an infection, meaning that she had contracted germs. Their life was so carefully controlled scientifically that the source of germs was extremely mysterious.

REVIEWING the SELECTION

The Expedition

Rudolf Lorenzen

Directions Write the answers to these questions using complete sentences.

Comprehension: Identifying Facts

1. How long will the expedition to Cerberus take?
2. What does Bruno check for on his daily rounds?
3. Who is the first person to die on board?
4. Who takes over control of the ship after Melanie dies?
5. What does Astraea do when the ship first returns to earth?
6. List the four people who start the trip. What are their professions?
7. Who gives birth to the first child?
8. Who is Bruno and Melanie's son?
9. Who are Boötes's parents?
10. What does Bruno suffer from?

Comprehension: Understanding Main Ideas

11. Why doesn't Bruno want to include the words about Olaf being a good husband, friend, and father in the logbook?
12. What is one way in which Boötes is different from his uncle Japetus?
13. Why does Japetus kill himself?
14. How are the grandchildren born on the trip different from their parents?
15. Why do the grandchildren finally learn how to make landings?
16. Why could Astraea put personal information about Cometa in the logbook?
17. Why does the company have to kill Bruno?
18. Would Boötes's birthday presents be up to date? Explain.
19. Give examples of the forms that Astraea's daydreaming takes.
20. What is strange about Cometa's death?

Understanding Literature: Conflict

Conflict is the struggle that the main character in the story has. (In this story, the main character changes from time to time.) The conflict may force the character to grow or change. The conflict may be with something outside the character. It may take place in the character's head or heart.

21. Think about the four who started the expedition. Do they seem to have conflicts between the adventure and what they will leave behind? Give an example to support your answer.
22. What conflict arises over what should be put in the logbook?
23. What is the conflict between what Bruno wants for Astraea and Astraea's ways?
24. What is the conflict between Japetus and Boötes?
25. Give an example of conflict between Astraea and the younger people.

Critical Thinking

26. Why do Vera and Melanie make the expedition? Do you think this is a good reason?
27. Does this story make living in a spaceship sound like something you would like to do? Why or why not?
28. Is it wise for the parents not to teach their children about art, literature, and music? Why or why not?
29. Which group would you rather be in: parents, children, or grandchildren? Explain your reasons.
30. Was the trip worth it for anyone? Why or why not?

Writing on Your Own Think about the people who do get back to earth. Write a paragraph about one of them telling what life will be like later for him or her.

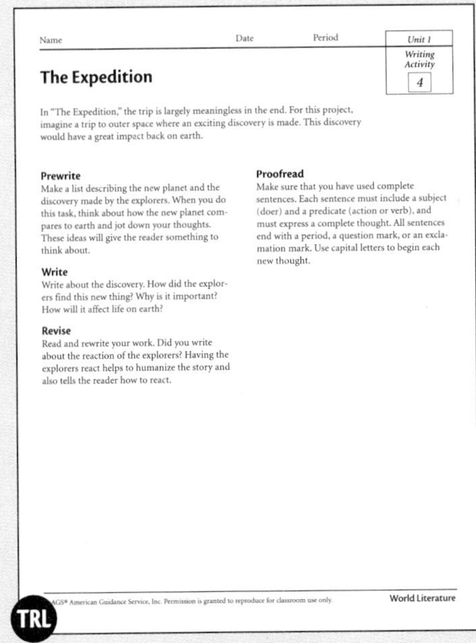

Name Date Period | *Unit 1* *Writing Activity* 4

The Expedition

In "The Expedition," the trip is largely meaningless in the end. For this project, imagine a trip to outer space where an exciting discovery is made. This discovery would have a great impact back on earth.

Prewrite
Make a list describing the new planet and the discovery made by the explorers. When you do this task, think about how the new planet compares to earth and jot down your thoughts. These ideas will give the reader something to think about.

Write
Write about the discovery. How did the explorers find this new thing? Why is it important? How will it affect life on earth?

Revise
Read and rewrite your work. Did you write about the reaction of the explorers? Having the explorers react helps to humanize the story and also tells the reader how to react.

Proofread
Make sure that you have used complete sentences. Each sentence must include a subject (doer) and a predicate (action or verb), and must express a complete thought. All sentences end with a period, a question mark, or an exclamation mark. Use capital letters to begin each new thought.

 World Literature

TRL

Writing Activity 4

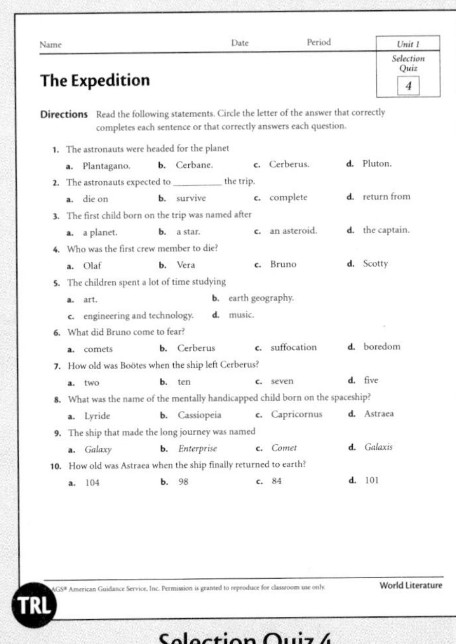

Name Date Period | *Unit 1* *Selection Quiz* 4

The Expedition

Directions Read the following statements. Circle the letter of the answer that correctly completes each sentence or that correctly answers each question.

1. The astronauts were headed for the planet
   a. Plantagano. b. Cerbane. c. Cerberus. d. Pluton.
2. The astronauts expected to ________ the trip.
   a. die on b. survive c. complete d. return from
3. The first child born on the trip was named after
   a. a planet. b. a star. c. an asteroid. d. the captain.
4. Who was the first crew member to die?
   a. Olaf b. Vera c. Bruno d. Scotty
5. The children spent a lot of time studying
   a. art. b. earth geography. c. engineering and technology. d. music.
6. What did Bruno come to fear?
   a. comets b. Cerberus c. suffocation d. boredom
7. How old was Boötes when the ship left Cerberus?
   a. two b. ten c. seven d. five
8. What was the name of the mentally handicapped child born on the spaceship?
   a. Lyride b. Cassiopeia c. Capricornus d. Astraea
9. The ship that made the long journey was named
   a. *Galaxy* b. *Enterprise* c. *Comet* d. *Galaxis*
10. How old was Astraea when the ship finally returned to earth?
   a. 104 b. 98 c. 84 d. 101

 World Literature

TRL

Selection Quiz 4

Understanding Literature: Conflict

21. The four didn't seem to feel any conflict between the idea of the adventure and what they were leaving behind. Evidence of this is their attitude before they leave toward their parents.

22. Astraea wrote personal comments in the logbook, but Bruno did not think such things belonged there.

23. Bruno wants Astraea to be the leader of the spaceship, but she is not interested in becoming a scientist.

24. The conflict between Japetus and Boötes is similar; Japetus is an engineer who wants Boötes to follow in his footsteps, but the younger man is not interested.

25. Astraea is interested in the earth and the sun, but the younger people are not. Nevertheless, they decide to get off the ship and go to earth, but she declines.

Critical Thinking

26. They liked Bruno and Olaf and danced well with them. This does not seem to be a very good reason but foreshadows the lack of emotional commitment shown later throughout the story.

27. Answers may vary, but most students will think that the life sounds uninteresting and pointless according to this story.

28. Students may express different viewpoints about this, but some will see that knowing something about art, literature, or music might have made the journey both more interesting and more valuable to the people making it.

29. Students will make different choices. Make sure they can defend their decision with reasons reflecting what they know from the story.

30. The trip didn't seem worth it for anyone. No one seemed to care that the people had gone, and what they discovered on Cerberus seemed very unimportant.

Writing on Your Own Ask students to consider not only what they know of the personalities of the people who get back to earth, but also what might have changed on earth since their grandparents left it.

Selection Quiz

The Teacher's Resource Library includes a Selection Quiz for "The Expedition" that may be given following the Selection Review.

Adventure

Ask students to read the text on page 84, or have them take turns reading it aloud. Draw attention to the two quotations at the top of the page.

ASK Do you agree with Eldridge Cleaver? Why or why not? (Answers may vary, but many students will be astute enough to realize that Cleaver was right—hate leads to self-disrespect and even self-hate.)

ASK Faith Popcorn sounds like a fan of adventure stories. According to what she said, why do people like such stories? (because they can live an exciting life through the story but still be safe at home in their own routine)

Adventure stories are among the oldest types of stories. People have always been entranced by the larger-than-life adventures of heroes. Thousands of years after the first tales of Odysseus were told, for example, the *Odyssey* is being read and even made into television shows and movies. In fact, action/adventure stories form a whole genre of movies and television shows. Sometimes part of their appeal is that the heroes survive many perils and usually outwit their antagonists.

ASK What are some adventure stories you have liked? (Let students offer their favorites from books, television, or movies. Encourage them to provide a few examples of the types of heroes or adventures they like.)

Adventure

- "The price of hating other human beings is loving oneself less." —Eldridge Cleaver
- "Send me out into another life. But get me back for supper." —Faith Popcorn

Adventure stories are like those you have read so far, but their appeal comes from plot. Exciting, fast-paced, dangerous events are the trademark of certain authors. For instance, John Grisham makes sure someone tries to kill his main characters at least once in every book. Plot rather than symbolism defines each character. Symbolism gives places, people, and objects a larger meaning.

The action in adventures rarely changes the characters. They may go broke, fall in love, or betray friends. Danger brings out the protagonist's basic strengths and values. For this reason, adventures often make effective TV or film series—even computer games. You can always count on Captain Picard and the trusty crew of the starship *Enterprise* or "Tomb Raider" Lara Croft to save the day. They might even have to die and come back to life to finish the job. Westerns, spy stories, and war stories all appeal to readers of adventures.

The selections in this section all include other elements besides adventure. Each story has brave, clever protagonists. They try to survive by using their wits as well as their strength.

84 *Unit 1 Fiction*

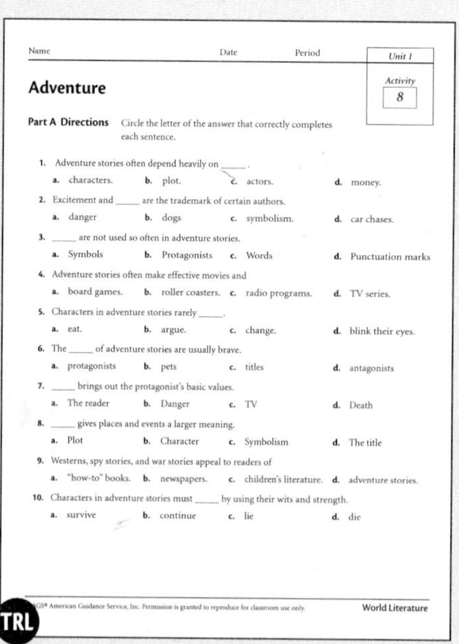

Name Date Period | *Unit 1* | *Activity* 8

Adventure

Part A Directions Circle the letter of the answer that correctly completes each sentence.

1. Adventure stories often depend heavily on _____ .
   a. characters. b. plot. c. actors. d. money.
2. Excitement and _____ are the trademark of certain authors.
   a. danger b. dogs c. symbolism. d. car chases.
3. _____ are not used so often in adventure stories.
   a. Symbols b. Protagonists c. Words d. Punctuation marks
4. Adventure stories often make effective movies and
   a. board games. b. roller coasters. c. radio programs. d. TV series.
5. Characters in adventure stories rarely _____.
   a. eat. b. argue. c. change. d. blink their eyes.
6. The _____ of adventure stories are usually brave.
   a. protagonists b. pets c. titles d. antagonists
7. _____ brings out the protagonist's basic values.
   a. The reader b. Danger c. TV d. Death
8. _____ gives places and events a larger meaning.
   a. Plot b. Character c. Symbolism d. The title
9. Westerns, spy stories, and war stories appeal to readers of
   a. "how-to" books. b. newspapers. c. children's literature. d. adventure stories.
10. Characters in adventure stories must _____ by using their wits and strength.
    a. survive b. continue c. lie d. die

 World Literature

TRL

Activity 8

Name Date Period | *Unit 1* | *Workbook* 8

Adventure

Part A Directions In each blank write the word or phrase from the Word Bank that best completes each sentence.

1. The appeal of adventure stories comes from the _______________.
2. _______________ events are the trademark of certain authors.
3. Some adventure stories are turned into _______________ games.
4. Main characters use their _______________ as well as their strength to survive.
5. _______________ gives places, people, and objects a larger meaning.

Word Bank	
computer	Dangerous
plot	Symbolism
wits	

Part B Directions Circle the letter of the answer that correctly completes each sentence.

1. John Grisham makes sure someone tries to _____ his main character.
   a. marry b. meet c. contain d. promote
2. Some protagonists _____ and come back to life, to finish the job.
   a. scream b. die c. read d. eat
3. Characteristics of adventure stories include excitement and fast-paced
   a. horses. b. regionalisms. c. action. d. pictures.
4. Each story has a brave and clever
   a. title. b. statue. c. antagonist. d. protagonist.
5. _____, rather than symbolism, defines the characters.
   a. Plot b. A dictionary c. Science fiction d. A first and last name

 World Literature

TRL

Workbook 8

INTRODUCING the SELECTION

The Cegua

Robert D. San Souci

Robert D. San Souci (1946–) American

About the Author

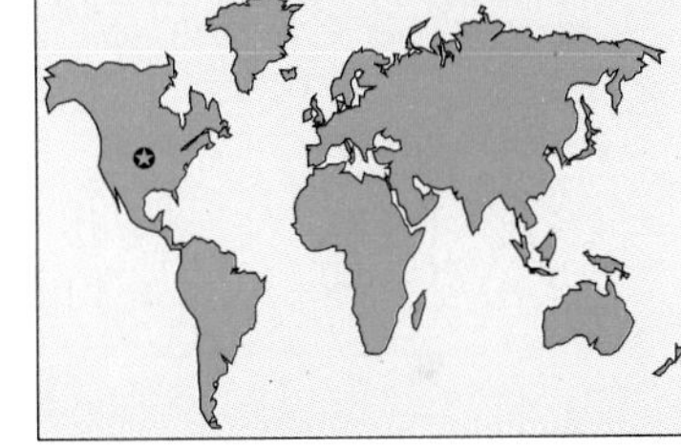

Robert D. San Souci has written more than fifty books and has won many awards. *The Talking Eggs* won both a Caldecott Honor and a Coretta Scott King Honor. He also won an award from the Smithsonian. San Souci lives in the San Francisco Bay area of California.

Literary Terms

action what goes on in a story

regionalism a word or phrase that comes from a particular area

setting the time and place in a story

About the Selection

In this story from Costa Rica, a young man is traveling alone on horseback. He is warned about a terrible monster—the Cegua. It lures careless travelers into giving it a ride and then kills the rider or drives him mad. The story takes place in the rural countryside near San José, the capital city of Costa Rica, which is its **setting**. The author uses **regionalisms**, or words that are found in that area. These words help set the mood for the **action**. The action is what happens in the story. The traveler has a terrifying trip. Did it really happen? You decide.

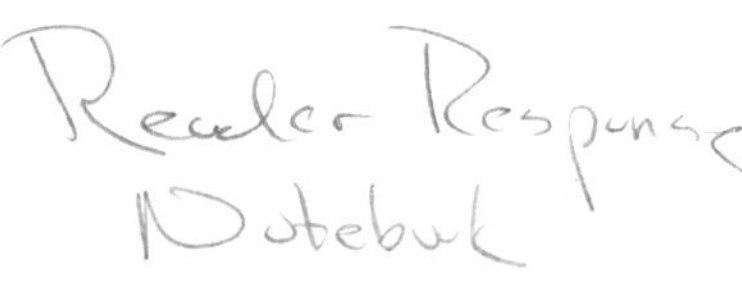

Selection at a Glance

The Cegua

Robert D. San Souci

Student pages 85–91

Overview

"The Cegua" is one of many stories based on folk tales that Robert D. San Souci has written. In fact, most of his work has been based on stories he has heard around the world.

Selection Summary

In "The Cegua" by Robert D. San Souci, a lone traveler has a frightening experience on the road.

Objectives

- To read and enjoy an adventure story.
- To understand and appreciate regionalisms in story.

Audiocassette 

Teacher's Resource Library TRL

- Vocabulary Workbook 5
- Selection Glossary 5
- Student Study Guide 11
- Activity 9
- Workbook 9
- Writing Activity 5
- Selection Quiz 5

Setting the Stage for Reading

About the Author

Explain that Robert D. San Souci has written many, many stories—most of them based on folk tales from around the world. He is particularly well-known as a writer for children, and he has won many awards for his writing. He enjoys the celebration of various cultures.

ASK How can reading stories from another place and time be useful to us? (It can help us understand the people who invented the stories.)

About the Selection

The story offers a frightening scenario that may or may not have really happened. It has similarities to horror stories and movies.

Activate Prior Knowledge: Discuss horror stories and movies with students. Most students will have experienced examples.

ASK What is the appeal of scary stories? Why do people like them? (Answers will vary. Some students will believe that part of the appeal is simply the vicarious thrills and excitement.)

Name Date Period

Unit 1 *Vocabulary Workbook* 5

The Cegua

Directions For each definition below, circle the word being defined.

1. What happens in a story is its ______________.
   action regionalism setting
2. The time and place of a story is its ______________.
   action regionalism setting
3. A word or phrase from a particular area is ______________.
   an action a regionalism a setting
4. In the story, the owner, or ______________, talked to the young man.
   quench proprietor woe
5. The young man wanted to satisfy, or ______________, his thirst.
   quench proprietor woe
6. He sat at a rough, or ______________, table with the proprietor.
   woe unsuspecting rude
7. He heard about a Cegua. It was a tale of misfortune, or ______________.
   rude woe unsuspecting
8. The tavern owner told the story to ______________, or trusting, travelers.
   unsuspecting proprietor quench
9. Sensing the Cegua, a horse would bolt in wild excitement, or ______________.
   frenzy abruptly landscape
10. Before that, the horse would become hard to handle, or ______________.
    frenzy woe restive
11. As he rode, the man noticed the scene, or ______________, before him.
    razor quench landscape
12. Suddenly, or ______________, his horse broke into a gallop.
    frenzy abruptly woe
13. He felt the Cegua's teeth as sharp as ______________, or instrument for shaving.
    a razor unsuspecting lingered
14. Coming to his destination, he looked around quickly, or ______________.
    lingering rudely hastily
15. The Cegua was gone, but its smell of sulfur ______________, or stayed on.
    lingered quenched restively

 World Literature

TRL

Vocabulary Workbook 5

Reading Vocabulary TRL

Help students preview the selection's vocabulary words by giving them copies of the Selection Glossary. Review the words, and ask pairs of students to take turns saying the words and providing the matching definitions.

Motivation for Reading

Ask students if they have ever found themselves walking or riding alone somewhere in the dark. Suggest they read the story to find out one man's adventure in that kind of situation.

Discussion Questions

Ask students to read the entire story before answering the question in the margin of the student selection.

A ASK Literary Element What are some clues, or foreshadowing, here that hint at what is to come? (The friend's ranch is described as being in a lonely area; the traveler is not sure of his way; the proprietor of the *cantina* warns him of the danger of the Cegua.)

Learning Styles

LEP/ESL Providing pronunciations and definitions of non-English terms gives an opportunity for students from another culture to share part of their culture with other students.

If any students in your class speak Spanish, ask them to pronounce the Spanish words and define them for the rest of the class as they go along.

The Cegua

Robert D. San Souci

As you read, picture the settings in your mind.

A One evening, a young man from San José, the capital of Costa Rica, rode into a small town north of the city. He was on his way to visit the ranch of a friend situated in a lonely area, but he wasn't sure which road to take out of the town.

The word *cantina* is Spanish for a tavern.

He decided to stop in the local *cantina* to **quench** his thirst and ask directions.

When the **proprietor** brought him a mug of beer, he told the traveler he still had a fair distance to cover. "But," the proprietor warned, "no one travels these roads after dark. Stay here: I have a room I will let for a few *pesos*—then you can finish your journey in the morning."

A *peso* is a unit of money.

The young man shook his head. "I have to reach my friend's ranch tonight."

The older man shook his head. "Only a fool would risk meeting the *Cegua*."

"The *Cegua!*" the traveler exclaimed. "What kind of creature is *that?*"

Señor means "mister" in Spanish.

The *cantina* owner smiled, as if he was unable to believe such ignorance existed. "*Señor*," he said, "don't folks in San José know

proprietor the owner of a business

quench to satisfy; to put out

Name ______ Date ______ Period ______

Unit 1 — *Student Study Guide* 11

The Cegua (pp. 86–90)

Directions Fill in the following outline. Filling in the blanks will help you as you read and study "The Cegua."

I. Beginning of the Selection (pp. 86–88)

A. The Traveler at the *Cantina*

1. He is on his way to visit a friend at his ______.
2. The proprietor tells him he is a ______ to risk meeting the *Cegua*.
3. Men have gone ______ from the sight of the *Cegua*.
4. The *Cegua* first appears as a beautiful ______.
   a. After she turns into a creature, her eyes burn fiery ______ and her breath stinks like ______.

II. Middle of the Selection (pp. 88–89)

A. The Journey

1. The night is calm, without any ______ to stir the ______.
2. On the side of the road, the traveler sees a beautiful girl with curly black hair, huge ______ eyes, and ______ red lips.
3. The woman wants the traveler to take her to ______.
4. The traveler tries to talk to the woman, but she ______ ______.
5. The horse gives a cry and charges down the road as if something is ______ them.

III. End of the Selection (pp. 89–90)

A. The *Cegua*

1. The collar of his ______ saves the traveler's skin from sharp ______.
2. The traveler sees fingers that are too ______ clutching him.
3. Ahead of him, the traveler sees his friend's ranch, and ______ ______, signaling his arrival.
4. Both riders fall from the horse, and the traveler is knocked ______.
5. His friend tells him the *Cegua* is a story told to ______ ______, nothing more.

 World Literature

TRL

Student Study Guide 11

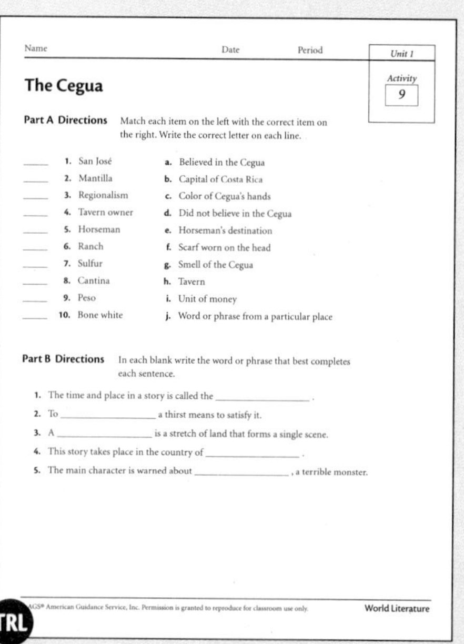

Name ______ Date ______ Period ______

Unit 1 — *Activity* 9

The Cegua

Part A Directions Match each item on the left with the correct item on the right. Write the correct letter on each line.

______	1. San José	a. Believed in the Cegua
______	2. Mantilla	b. Capital of Costa Rica
______	3. Regionalism	c. Color of Cegua's hands
______	4. Tavern owner	d. Did not believe in the Cegua
______	5. Horseman	e. Horseman's destination
______	6. Ranch	f. Scarf worn on the head
______	7. Sulfur	g. Smell of the Cegua
______	8. Cantina	h. Tavern
______	9. Peso	i. Unit of money
______	10. Bone white	j. Word or phrase from a particular place

Part B Directions In each blank write the word or phrase that best completes each sentence.

1. The time and place in a story is called the ______.
2. To ______ a thirst means to satisfy it.
3. A ______ is a stretch of land that forms a single scene.
4. This story takes place in the country of ______.
5. The main character is warned about ______, a terrible monster.

 World Literature

TRL

Activity 9

what the *Cegua* is? She is a demon—and heaven keep you from meeting her on the road!" **B**

"I've never heard of such a thing," said the young man. "Bring me another mug of beer, and please explain what you know about this *Cegua*."

When the older man returned with the beer the traveler had ordered, he brought a second mug for himself. He sat down across the **rude** wooden table and said, "No one who sees the *Cegua* is left with a sound mind. Strong men, in the peak of health, have gone mad from the sight. Some have even died of fright." He began to rattle off the names of locals who had lost their minds or lives because of this monster.

But the younger man interrupted him, saying, "If she is such a terrible devil, why haven't I heard of her before?"

"She prefers certain parts of our country; we have the misfortune to be one such place," explained the proprietor patiently. "For that reason, no one here rides alone after dark. If someone must travel after nightfall, he always goes with a companion."

"Why? Doesn't she like crowds?" laughed the young man, who was beginning to feel the effects of his long ride and the beer.

"The *Cegua* only appears to someone who travels alone," said the older man gravely, finishing his own beer and starting to rise. "She appears as a beautiful *señorita,* smiling sadly and fluttering her eyes, pleading for a ride—but **woe** to the traveler who stops to help her! If the **unsuspecting** rider sits her in front, she turns her head. If he has placed her behind him, she will make him turn to look at her. In either case, his doom is sealed."

"How so?" traveler asked. **C**

The name of the *Cegua* is an example of a regionalism. The term—and the legend—are found only in certain places.

A *señorita* is a young woman.

rude rough; crudely made

unsuspecting trusting; not suspicious

woe misfortune; great sorrow

B ASK Comprehension Does the Cegua seem to be real or imaginary? What clues do you have so far? (She may or may not be real, although the fear about her makes her seem to be a fantasy.)

C ASK Critical Thinking What do you think just hearing the stories would make the traveler feel? (Probably fear that it might happen to him.)

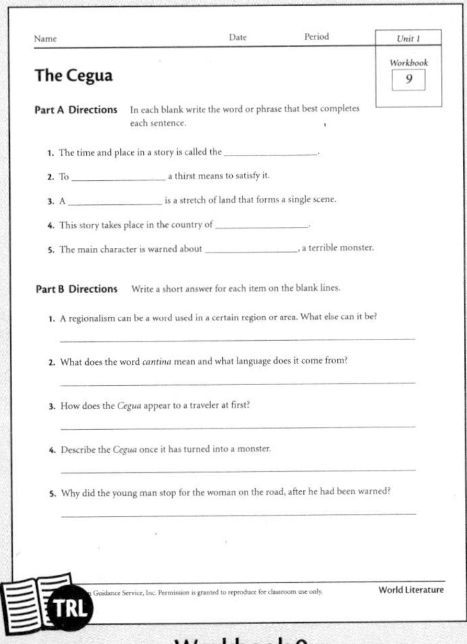

Name Date Period | *Unit 1* | *Workbook* 9

The Cegua

Part A Directions In each blank write the word or phrase that best completes each sentence.

1. The time and place in a story is called the ________________.
2. To ________________ a thirst means to satisfy it.
3. A ________________ is a stretch of land that forms a single scene.
4. This story takes place in the country of ________________.
5. The main character is warned about ________________, a terrible monster.

Part B Directions Write a short answer for each item on the blank lines.

1. A regionalism can be a word used in a certain region or area. What else can it be?
2. What does the word *cantina* mean and what language does it come from?
3. How does the *Cegua* appear to a traveler at first?
4. Describe the *Cegua* once it has turned into a monster.
5. Why did the young man stop for the woman on the road, after he had been warned?

 World Literature

TRL

Workbook 9

Discussion Questions

A ASK Critical Thinking Put yourself into the story. Would you have set off for your friend's place that night? Why or why not? (Most students will say they would not, but they will also realize that there would be no story if the protagonist didn't go.)

B ASK Comprehension The author does not give us a clue about the traveler's thoughts or feelings here. Why do you suppose he agrees to take the young woman, even though that is exactly how the terrifying legend of the Cegua begins? (Some students will suspect that the traveler feels the Cegua will not really happen to him and that this is really a woman in trouble.)

Learning Styles

Visual The description of the Cegua will appeal to visually oriented students. Some may want to volunteer to sketch or paint the Cegua as described in the story. Make space on the bulletin board for a display of their efforts.

Sulfur is often associated with the devil. It has a smell like rotten eggs.

"When he looks, the beautiful *señorita* is gone. The creature riding with him has a huge horse's head, with monstrous fangs. Her eyes burn fiery red, like hot coals, and her breath stinks like *sulfur.* With a hiss, she will bury her claws in the shoulders of the rider and hang on like a wild animal. A horse, sensing that he is being ridden by a demon, will bolt in such a **frenzy** that no one can stop him."

"What then?" asked the younger man, no longer smiling quite so broadly.

"Those who are found the next day, if they are still alive, will have gone mad from the sight of her."

"Nonsense," said the traveler, suddenly standing up and tossing down a few *pesos* to pay for the beer. "I must be on my way, if I'm to reach my friend's ranch tonight."

The older man shrugged, gathered up the coins, and turned away. Clearly, he thought to himself, there is no arguing with a fool.

A The little town square was deserted. The traveler untied his horse from the hitching post and set out along the road the *cantina*'s proprietor had pointed out to him earlier.

It was a warm night. Not a breath of wind stirred the leaves in the trees on either side of the road. Nothing disturbed the silence, except the *clop-clop* of his horse's hoofs on stones in the roadway.

As you read, note the action.

Suddenly, around the bend, when the town was out of sight behind him and no other building was visible, he saw a slender figure standing in the thick shadows where the trees overhung the road.

A *mantilla* is a scarf worn over the head.

Slowing his horse, the young man discovered a beautiful girl, with a pale face framed by the black-lace *mantilla* that covered her head, and which she held under her chin with her left hand. In the moonlight he could see she had curly black hair, huge dark eyes, and deep red lips.

"*Señor,*" she began. Her voice was sweet, but so weak and weary that he feared she must be near fainting. "I am so tired, but I must go to see my mother, who is ill. Would you take me to Bagaces?"

B "Of course," he said, bringing his horse to a stop and climbing down. Bowing slightly and removing his hat, he said, "My friend's

frenzy a wild excitement

ranch is just south of that town. You can spend the night there. In the morning I will escort you the rest of the way."

"You are very kind, *señor,*" she said, in such a faint whisper that he had to lean close to make out her words. Then he helped her onto the horse—which had grown **restive** during their halt—behind his saddle. He mounted himself, and they took off at a good trot.

A breeze had arisen to freshen the still air and flutter the leaves on the nearby trees. The moon and stars tinted the **landscape** pale silver. Several times the traveler tried to make conversation with the woman, but she didn't answer. She only leaned her head against his back and clung to his shoulders with her hands, as if she were afraid of fainting and tumbling from his horse.

Abruptly his horse, without any prodding, broke into a gallop. The woman dug her fingers into his shoulder, clearly afraid of falling. The young man was too polite to tell her that her nails were digging into his skin.

The horse gave a cry and charged down the dark road as though something terrible were pursuing them. The traveler pulled back on the reins and shouted, but it did no good. His horse only galloped faster.

Suddenly he felt **razor**-sharp teeth **C** lock onto his neck so that only the collar of his coat saved his skin. An instant later, he heard a cry that came from no human throat as the awful teeth suddenly pulled away a mouthful of his coat collar.

He wrapped the ends of the reins around the fingers of one hand, and with his free hand he struggled to pry loose the fingers that were clamped on his shoulder. As shadow, then moonlight, then shadow again, washed over the horse and its two riders, the young man saw that the fingers clutching him were too pale—they were **D** the white of bone, rather than fair skin.

abruptly suddenly

landscape a stretch of land forming a single scene

razor an instrument used for shaving

restive hard to handle

C ASK Literary Element This is the climax of the plot—the traveler is actually experiencing the Cegua, just as he had been warned he might. What do you think might happen next? (Answers may vary, but many students will expect something terrible to happen but the traveler to somehow escape.)

D ASK Critical Thinking Visualize the Cegua. What do you see in your mind's eye? (Let students describe the monster. Make sure their ideas reflect what has been stated in the text.)

Career Connection

Many visually talented people turn to jobs in the movie-making industry where they can tell stories with pictures. Students in many schools are learning to use video cameras for experiments in such creative thinking. "The Cegua" is a story that lends itself to this medium. Students may especially be able to visualize the gradual attack of the Cegua described on pages 89 and 90. Ask them how they might film this transformation and what it might look like. Students may be interested in exploring what jobs are available in movies and television and what kind of schooling or training is helpful to get into this field.

Discussion Questions

A ASK Literary Element Remember that the resolution of the plot is called the denouement. It is the way the incidents of the plot are "tied up." How is the problem of the Cegua resolved? (She simply disappears.)

B The Cegua may have been real. On the other hand, the traveler may have fallen asleep as he was riding and had a terrible dream of the Cegua, reflecting the story he had been told.

Writing Connection

President Franklin Delano Roosevelt once said that "We have nothing to fear but fear itself." Ask students to think about this statement in connection with the story of the Cegua. Then suggest that they write a paragraph or two explaining the role that fear might play in the legend of the Cegua.

He heard another screech and smelled the creature's foul breath. He felt his strength giving out, while the bony fingers pulling at him seemed to grow stronger. The jaws snapped at the back of his neck, this time drawing blood.

A *hacienda* is a ranch house.

Then, ahead, he could see his friend's ranch. He thought he could hear dogs barking, to signal his arrival. Lights were burning in the *hacienda.* There were figures running up the road toward him, carrying torches.

There was a final, ear-splitting scream from the demon behind him. He felt his whole body jerked backward. The hand that was tangled in the reins pulled backward suddenly, causing his horse to rear up, then fall sideways. Both riders fell with the animal.

The traveler was knocked senseless for a moment. When he came to, his friend, holding a torch, was staring at him, asking if he was all right. He nodded, still shaking from his near-brush with death. When he touched his hand to the stinging at the back of his neck, his fingers came away bloody. He looked around **hastily**, but all he saw was a crowd of friendly-looking *campesinos,* countrymen, watching him. One was calming his horse, which was on its feet again.

"Where is it—the creature?" he asked his friend.

"What creature?"

A "The *Cegua.*"

"My friend," laughed the other man, "you stayed too long at some *cantina,* I think. The *Cegua* is a story to frighten children, nothing more. Still, next time you ride at night, be sure you travel with a companion. These lonely roads can be dangerous in the dark."

B What do you think really happened?

The young man said nothing, but he shivered just a little when the night breeze brought the **lingering** odor of sulfur to his nostrils.

hastily quickly

lingering lasting a long time; staying on

90 *Unit 1 Fiction*

REVIEWING the SELECTION

The Cegua

Robert D. San Souci

Directions Write the answers to these questions using complete sentences.

Comprehension: Identifying Facts

1. Where is the young man from?
2. Where is the young man traveling to?
3. Where does he stop to ask directions?

Comprehension: Understanding Main Ideas

4. Why does the proprietor tell the young man not to travel alone after dark?
5. The young man tries to talk to the woman. What happens?
6. What is the traveler's experience on the road?

Understanding Literature: Regionalism

A regionalism is a word or term used in a certain region or area. Regionalisms can include a region's habits, folk tales, and customs. Regionalisms help give a story a local flavor. They help us understand the setting and the characters.

7. How does the writer give us an idea of the language of the region?
8. How is the *Cegua* an example of regionalism?

Critical Thinking

9. Do you think the traveler actually met the Cegua? Why or why not?
10. Would you have stayed the night at the cantina? Why or why not?

Writing on Your Own Think of a time in your life when you were afraid of something. Write a paragraph about that event. Was it really something scary or did it turn out to be nothing to fear?

Reviewing the Selection

Answer Key

Comprehension: Identifying Facts

1. He is from San José.

2. He is traveling to a friend's ranch north of the city.

3. He stops at a *cantina,* or tavern.

Comprehension: Understanding Main Ideas

4. The proprietor warns him not to travel alone because of the Cegua.

5. She does not answer his attempts at conversation.

6. He has a nightmarish experience with the young woman apparently turning into the Cegua, as he had been warned.

Understanding Literature: Regionalism

7. He uses several words of Spanish in the story.

8. The Cegua is a story told locally to frighten children. It is not a legend that people out of that area would probably have heard before.

Critical Thinking

9. Answers may vary. Some students will think so; others will believe that it was the traveler's imagination or a bad dream. Accept opinions that students can defend by using examples from the story.

10. Students will have different answers to whether they would have stayed the night at the *cantina.* Of course it would have been sensible to do so, but there would be no story if the traveler had stayed at the *cantina.*

Writing on Your Own Ask students to consider the role of their imaginations in the scary episode they describe.

Selection Quiz

The Teacher's Resource Library includes a Selection Quiz for "The Cegua" that may be given following the Selection Review.

Name Date Period | Unit 1 | Writing Activity 5

The Cegua

Think about a time when you were scared of something—like a monster. Maybe someone told you a scary story when you were younger. If you can't remember a story or a time when you were scared, then make one up. Your imagination can probably help you think of something scary.

Prewrite
Make a list of details that describe your monster or the thing you feared. Also, place your "monster" in a certain setting, like under a bed, in a haunted house, and so on.

Write
Write your description of the monster and the setting. When you do this, imagine you are telling someone this story—just like the tavern owner in "The Cegua."

Revise
Read and rewrite your work. Try to make your story sound scary. Read your work aloud to someone. See if they are scared.

Proofread
Make sure that you have used complete sentences. Each sentence must include a subject (doer) and a predicate (action or verb), and must express a complete thought. All sentences end with a period, a question mark, or an exclamation mark. Use capital letters to begin each new thought.

 World Literature

TRL

Writing Activity 5

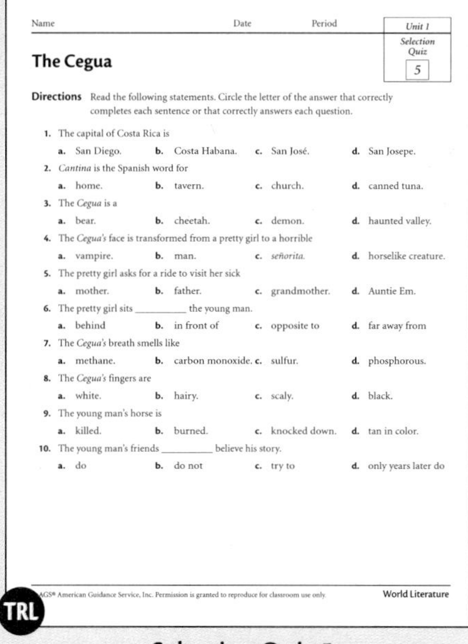

Name Date Period | Unit 1 | Selection Quiz 5

The Cegua

Directions Read the following statements. Circle the letter of the answer that correctly completes each sentence or that correctly answers each question.

1. The capital of Costa Rica is
 a. San Diego. **b.** Costa Habana. **c.** San José. **d.** San Josepe.
2. *Cantina* is the Spanish word for
 a. home. **b.** tavern. **c.** church. **d.** canned tuna.
3. The *Cegua* is a
 a. bear. **b.** cheetah. **c.** demon. **d.** haunted valley.
4. The *Cegua's* face is transformed from a pretty girl to a horrible
 a. vampire. **b.** man. **c.** *señorita.* **d.** horselike creature.
5. The pretty girl asks for a ride to visit her sick
 a. mother. **b.** father. **c.** grandmother. **d.** Auntie Em.
6. The pretty girl sits ________ the young man.
 a. behind **b.** in front of **c.** opposite to **d.** far away from
7. The *Cegua's* breath smells like
 a. methane. **b.** carbon monoxide. **c.** sulfur. **d.** phosphorous.
8. The *Cegua's* fingers are
 a. white. **b.** hairy. **c.** scaly. **d.** black.
9. The young man's horse is
 a. killed. **b.** burned. **c.** knocked down. **d.** tan in color.
10. The young man's friends ________ believe his story.
 a. do **b.** do not **c.** try to **d.** only years later do

 World Literature

TRL

Selection Quiz 5

Selection at a Glance

From *Master and Man*

Leo Tolstoy
(translated by Paul Foote)

Student pages 92–98

Overview

Leo Tolstoy's most famous works are his novels *War and Peace* and *Anna Karenina.* The novel *Master and Man* also demonstrates Tolstoy's keen interest in how people interact with each other and their environment.

Selection Summary

In the selection from *Master and Man* by Leo Tolstoy, a rich man looks for help after he and his servant are stranded in a snowstorm.

Objectives

- To read and understand an adventure story in which nature acts as a main character.
- To understand and appreciate the use of naturalism in a story.

Audiocassette

Teacher's Resource Library TRL

- Vocabulary Workbook 6
- Selection Glossary 6
- Student Study Guide 12
- Activity 10
- Workbook 10
- Writing Activity 6
- Selection Quiz 6

INTRODUCING the SELECTION

Master and Man

Leo Tolstoy (translated by Paul Foote)

Leo Tolstoy
(1828–1910)
Russian

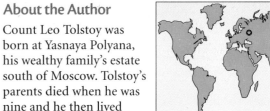

Literary Term

naturalism a literary movement focused on the survival of the fittest against nature. It features helpless characters against events beyond human control and understanding

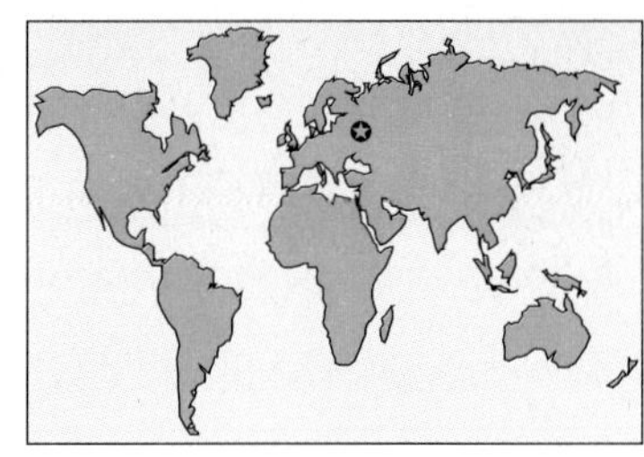

About the Author

Count Leo Tolstoy was born at Yasnaya Polyana, his wealthy family's estate south of Moscow. Tolstoy's parents died when he was nine and he then lived with relatives. He attended but did not finish college. Tolstoy later became a soldier and took part in the Crimean War. He began to write stories after the war. Tolstoy married in 1896 and had a large family. While managing his estates, he wrote two of the greatest modern novels. *War and Peace* was written in 1865–1868; *Anna Karenina* was written about eight years later. Tolstoy worked to make life better for the peasants on his land. In later life, he wrote about morals and religion.

About the Selection

Master and Man takes place in 1870's Russia. The "master" is Vasilii Andreich and the "man" is his servant, Nikita. Vasilii Andreich is a rich businessman who will let nothing stop him from gaining more money. On a winter's day, Vasilii Andreich takes a horse-drawn sleigh to see a piece of valuable property he wants to buy. Nikita goes with him. Master and man both become lost in a severe snowstorm. Money does not matter to the storm. Tolstoy uses **naturalism** in this story, his characters are helpless against nature. Events are beyond human control. In the following selection, Vasilii Andreich takes the horse to try to find help.

Setting the Stage for Reading

About the Author

Have students read this section and note the picture of Tolstoy. Leo Tolstoy is often considered one of the world's greatest writers. He was also well-known as a social reformer and a philosopher. About twenty years before his death, Tolstoy had a religious experience. He gave up all his worldly goods and never again owned anything material. His wife managed his affairs. His philosophical views often caused conflict with his family and even the government. He continued to write, but his later works reflected his changed outlook, and they are not as popular as his earlier ones.

ASK Tolstoy's two famous novels have been translated into many languages and read and appreciated by people around the world. How do you think it is possible that people elsewhere can enjoy a book about a place and time so foreign to them? (Probably because Tolstoy, like other great writers such as Shakespeare, wrote about people and situations that are universal.)

About the Selection

This selection is an excerpt from *Master and Man,* in which Tolstoy describes an incident that shows the insignificance of human beings and their possessions in the face of forces of nature.

Activate Prior Knowledge: Ask students to discuss briefly their experiences with dramatic forces of nature such as storms or floods.

ASK Why might a writer like Tolstoy choose to write about a conflict between people and nature? (Such a conflict can be dramatic, the situation is universal, and people react very differently to crises.)

Master and Man

Leo Tolstoy

A

Meanwhile Vasilii Andreich was driving the horse on with feet and reins towards where for some reason he supposed the forest and the keeper's hut to be. He was blinded by the snow, the wind seemed anxious to hold him back, but **relentlessly** he drove the horse on, crouching forward and continually drawing his coat across him and tucking it between himself and the small cold saddle which stopped him sitting properly. Though with difficulty, the horse obediently went at an **ambling** pace along the way he was made to go. B

As you read, watch how *Vasilii Andreich* struggles against nature.

For some five minutes Vasilii Andreich rode as he thought in a straight line, seeing nothing but the horse's head and the white wilderness, hearing nothing but the wind whistling past the horse's ears and the collar of his fur top-coat.

There was suddenly something dark ahead. His heart thumped with joy and he headed towards this dark something, already seeing it as the walls of houses in the village. But the dark shape did not keep still, it kept

ambling slow-moving

relentlessly without yielding

Reading Vocabulary TRL

Give students copies of the Selection Glossary. Suggest that they write sentences for the words in the Glossary.

Motivation for Reading

Suggest that students think about the ways people combat storms and other forces of nature. Have them read the story to find out what one man does.

Discussion Questions

Have students use the questions in the margins of the student selection to help them focus their thinking.

A ASK Comprehension Remind students that this is an excerpt from a larger work. What has happened right before the beginning of this story? (Vasilii Andreich and his servant, Nikita, have become lost in a snowstorm. Vasilii Andreich has gone off alone on his horse to try to find help.)

B ASK Comprehension Do you think that Vasilii Andreich did the right thing by going off alone in the storm? Why or why not? (We do not know all the previous circumstances, but it does seem somewhat foolish for someone to go off alone in such a storm.)

Name Date Period | *Unit 1* | *Vocabulary Workbook* 6

Master and Man

Directions Each set of sentences is missing two words. On the blanks, fill in the letters of the two correct words from the three given beneath the sentences.

1. *Master and Man* is an example of ______________, or literature focused on survival against nature. As it begins, Vasilii Andreich's horse moves slowly, or ______________.
   a. naturalism b. ambles c. relentlessly
2. Without yielding, or ______________, Vasilii Andreich drives the horse on. The wind is cruel, or ______________.
   a. compass b. merciless c. relentlessly
3. When Vasilii Andreich sees dark ahead, he is delighted, or ______________. But it is not the village, for he has gone in a limited area, or small ______________.
   a. overjoyed b. unaccountable c. compass
4. The tossing weeds mysteriously, or ______________, terrify Vasilii Andreich. He hears the unclear, or ______________, howl of a wolf or dog.
   a. askew b. indistinct c. unaccountably
5. He thinks this is his imagination, or ______________. Then Dapple, the horse, collapses and the strap holding the harness, or the ______________, twists.
   a. indistinct b. fancy c. breeching
6. This twists the saddle to one side, or ______________. The horse bolts with the rough, coarse cloth, or ______________, trailing behind.
   a. wethers b. sackcloth c. askew
7. Left behind, Vasilii Andreich thinks of his small woods, or ______________. He also thinks of his sheep, or ______________.
   a. coppice b. askew c. wethers
8. In the dark, cold night, he remembers his property held by lease, or ______________. Lost and alone, he feels that death is sure to happen, or ______________.
   a. leasehold b. inevitable c. compass
9. He calls on Saint Nicholas who taught the way of self-denial, or ______________. But he knows he is in a desperate ______________, or has a serious problem.
   a. sackcloth b. abstinence c. plight
10. The horse leads him correctly, or ______________. Vasilii Andreich's plan, or ______________, is to follow, and soon he discovers himself only fifty yards from where he started.
   a. aright b. abstinence c. intention

 World Literature

TRL

Vocabulary Workbook 6

Name Date Period | *Unit 1* | *Student Study Guide* 12

Master and Man (pp. 93–97)

Directions Fill in the following outline. Filling in the blanks will help you as you read and study *Master and Man*

I. Beginning of the Selection (pp. 93–94)

A. Vasilii Andreich
1. He is on his way to the forest and the keeper's __________.
2. He can see nothing but the horse's head and the white __________.
3. He thinks he might see the village, but it turns out to be a patch of __________.
4. The horse tries to go to the __________, but he keeps making the horse go __________.

II. Middle of the Selection (pp. 94–95)

A. The Horse
1. Again, Vasilii Andreich comes across the same __________, and realizes he's been going in a __________.
2. The horse's name is __________.
3. The horse lets out a deafening cry for good __________ or as a cry for __________.
4. Vasilii Andreich doesn't realize he now has the wind __________ him and not in his __________.

III. End of the Selection (pp. 95–97)

A. Back to the Sledge
1. The horse __________ under Vasilii Andreich, and when Vasilii Andreich jumps off the horse, the horse runs off, disappearing from sight.
2. The snow is numbing Vasilii Andreich's __________ hand.
3. Vasilii Andreich begs Holy Father __________ to save him and promises to offer prayers and __________ to him.
4. After Vasilii Andreich tarts to follow the horse tracks, he finds Dapple and the sledge and the upright __________ with his kerchief.

 World Literature

TRL

Student Study Guide 12

Name Date Period | *Unit 1* | *Activity* 10

Master and Man

Part A Directions In each blank write the word or phrase from the Word Bank that best completes each sentence.

1. Leo Tolstoy was from __________________ .
2. Tolstoy was a soldier in the __________________ War.
3. "Master and Man" takes place in Russian in the __________________
4. One protagonist is __________________ .
5. Nikita is Vasilii Andreich's __________.
6. The __________________ , Dapple, carries Vasilii Andreich through the storm.
7. Vasilii Andreich __________________ makes it to the village.
8. Dapple fell into a __________________.
9. Vasilii Andreich and the horse walk in a __________________ .
10. The snow and cold caused Vasilii Andreich's hand to become __________________ .

Word Bank				
1870s	circle	Crimean	horse	never
numb	Russia	servant	snowdrift	Vasilii Andreich

Part B Directions Read each sentence. Write *T* if the statement is true or *F* if it is false.

__________ 1. Naturalism is a style of singing.
__________ 2. Tolstoy worked to make life better for Russian peasants.
__________ 3. Tolstoy graduated from college with honors.
__________ 4. The two main characters are lost in a hurricane.
__________ 5. Vasilii Andreich is never frightened.

 World Literature

TRL

Activity 10

Discussion Questions

A Probably the horse is the one who knows the way. Instinct may guide the animal better than the man, who cannot see anything, can do.

B The hoof-prints tell Vasilii Andreich that he has been going in circles in the storm.

Environmental Connection

As described in the story, snowstorms can be very dangerous. And heavy snow can stop even a large city in its tracks, as has happened in cities like Chicago. However, snow is also a prime ingredient of winter sports such as skiing. Suggest that students do some research as necessary and hold a panel discussion about the positive and negative effects of snow. They may also be interested to find out how places that frequently get a great deal of snow have learned to cope with it. What do cities like Buffalo do to keep themselves operating during heavy snowfalls?

Wormwood is a tall weedy plant that has a bitter flavor.

moving, and it was not the village but a tall patch of wormwood that had grown up along the edge of a field and stood up clear of the snow, frantically tossing in the wind, which bent it over and whistled through it. For some reason the sight of this wormwood tormented by the **merciless** wind made Vasilii Andreich shudder and he hastily urged the horse on, not noticing that in going towards the wormwood he had completely changed course and was now pointing the horse in a quite different direction, though he still supposed he was heading for where the keeper's hut should be. But the horse kept pulling to the right and Vasilii Andreich continually had to make him go left.

A
Which do you think knows the way, the man or the horse?

Once more there was something dark ahead. He was **overjoyed**, certain that this really must now be the village. But again it was a field-boundary with wormwood growing along it. The tall dry weeds tossed and swayed as frantically as ever and **unaccountably** terrified Vasilii Andreich. But it was not only that the weeds were the same—alongside ran hoof-prints partly covered with blown snow. Vasilii Andreich stopped and bent to take a closer look: it was the lightly covered tracks of a horse and it could be no one else's but his own. He had evidently been going in a circle and in quite a small **compass**. This way I'm done for! he thought, but so as not to give way to his fear he drove the horse on more urgently than before, peering ahead into the snowy white gloom in which shining dots seemed to appear, only to vanish the moment he tried to focus on them. Once

B
What do the *hoof-prints* tell Vasilii Andreich

compass limited area

merciless cruel; without mercy

overjoyed delighted; very happy

unaccountably mysteriously; without explanation

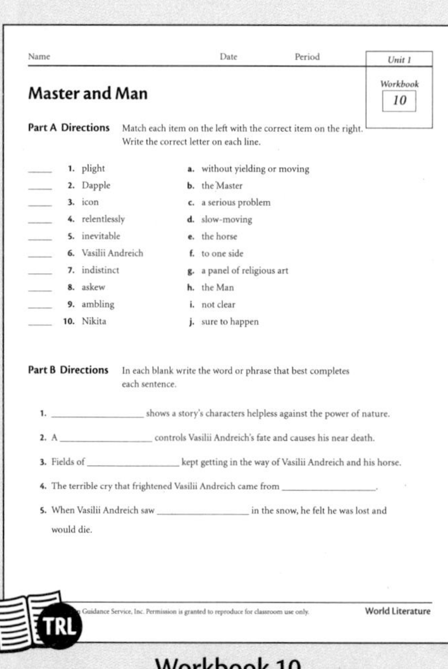

Name Date Period

Unit 1

Workbook 10

Master and Man

Part A Directions Match each item on the left with the correct item on the right. Write the correct letter on each line.

_____ 1.	plight	a.	without yielding or moving
_____ 2.	Dapple	b.	the Master
_____ 3.	icon	c.	a serious problem
_____ 4.	relentlessly	d.	slow-moving
_____ 5.	inevitable	e.	the horse
_____ 6.	Vasilii Andreich	f.	to one side
_____ 7.	indistinct	g.	a panel of religious art
_____ 8.	askew	h.	the Man
_____ 9.	ambling	i.	not clear
_____ 10.	Nikita	j.	sure to happen

Part B Directions In each blank write the word or phrase that best completes each sentence.

1. ________________ shows a story's characters helpless against the power of nature.
2. A ________________ controls Vasilii Andreich's fate and causes his near death.
3. Fields of ________________ kept getting in the way of Vasilii Andreich and his horse.
4. The terrible cry that frightened Vasilii Andreich came from ________________.
5. When Vasilii Andreich saw ________________ in the snow, he felt he was lost and would die.

World Literature

TRL

Workbook 10

he thought he heard the bark of a dog or the howl of a wolf, but the sound was so faint and **indistinct** that he could not tell if he had actually heard it or if it was just his **fancy**, so he stopped to listen.

All at once there was a terrible deafening cry right in his ears and everything shuddered and shook beneath him. Vasilii Andreich grabbed the horse's neck, but that too was shuddering and the terrible cry was more terrifying than before. For some seconds Vasilii Andreich could not collect himself and realize what it was. In fact all that had happened **C** was that Dapple—for good cheer or as a cry for help—had let out a loud, well-tuned neigh. 'Cursed horse! Proper put the wind up me!' said Vasilii Andreich to himself. But even though he now knew what had caused his fear he could not shake it off.

To *put the wind up* is to be startled or alarmed.

I've got to come to and get a grip on myself, he thought, but still he could not help himself and pressed the horse on, without noticing that he now had the wind behind him and **D** not in his face. His body, especially in the crutch, where it was exposed and touched the saddle, was chilled through and aching, his arms and legs trembled, his breath came in gasps. He could see that he would perish in this awful waste of snow and saw no way of escape.

Suddenly the horse collapsed under him. It was deep in a drift and began to struggle, falling over on its side. Vasilii Andreich sprang off. In doing so he pulled over the **breeching** which supported his foot and twisted **askew** the saddle to which he held while jumping off. No sooner had Vasilii Andreich sprung clear than the horse found its feet again and plunged ahead. It gave a couple of leaps, let out another neigh and disappeared from sight, trailing the

askew to one side

breeching strap of harness behind a horse's rear legs

fancy imagination

indistinct not clear

C ASK Comprehension What startled Vasilii Andreich? (the horse's neigh) Why do you suppose that frightened him so much? (probably because he could hear no other sounds through the storm and he could not for a moment imagine what made the sound)

D ASK Critical Thinking Why did Vasilii Andreich not notice such clues as the direction of the wind? (He was becoming too frightened and confused to pay attention.)

Grammar

Single Quotation Marks Draw students' attention to the single quotation marks used to show Vasilii Andreich's thoughts in the second paragraph on this page. Explain that single quotation marks are commonly used this way to indicate something a character is thinking rather than saying aloud. Remind students that single quotation marks are also used to show one person's remarks quoted by another person, as *"I heard him say, 'Come in' as I approached the door," Mary reported.*

Fiction Unit 1 95

Discussion Questions

A ASK Critical Thinking Why does Vasilii Andreich suddenly begin to think about his possessions? (The reality of the danger he is in becomes clear to him, so he wonders what will happen to the other elements of his life if he does not return to them.)

B ASK Literary Element How important is the setting in this story? (The setting virtually is the story. The snowstorm provides the plot and the conflict and even acts like a major character in the story.)

Cross-Curricular Connection

Art Many icons of Eastern Orthodox churches are fine art. Examples can be found in many art museums throughout the world. Interested students may want to do some research to find examples in art books or catalogs, or even go to local museum exhibits to find some. If there is an Eastern Orthodox church in your vicinity, students may be able to arrange to visit it to see the icons it has on display.

sackcloth and breeching behind and leaving Vasilii Andreich alone in the snowdrift. Vasilii Andreich dashed after it, but the snow was so deep and his fur coats so heavy that with every step he sank in over his knees and after running some twenty yards he was out of breath and stopped. What will **A** become of it all? he thought. The **coppice**, the **wethers**, the **leasehold**, my shop and taverns, my metal-roofed house and barn, my son and heir? What's going on? It just can't be true! And for some reason he remembered the wormwood tossing in the wind which he had twice passed and experienced such a feeling of terror that he did not believe that this was actually happening to him. He thought it must all be a dream and tried to wake up, but there was no other, waking world. It was real snow which lashed his face and settled on him and numbed his right hand whose glove he had lost; **B** and this was a real wilderness, this place where he was now alone, like the wormwood, waiting for death, **inevitable**, swift and pointless.

Vasilii Andreich is thinking of his wealth and property.

Mother of Heaven, Holy Father Nicholas, thou who teachest the way of **abstinence**... he recalled the prayers said the day before, and the icon with the black face framed in the golden riza, [robe] and the candles he sold for lighting to this icon which were then promptly returned to him and stored away in a bin, scarcely used. And he begged this same Nicholas the miracle-worker to save him, and promised to offer prayers and candles to him. But at the same time he realized clearly and certainly that the face on the icon, the frame, the candles, the priest and the prayers were all very important and necessary *there,* in church, but that where he was they could do nothing for him, and that there was not and could not be any possible connection between these candles and prayers and his present desperate **plight**. I must not despair,

Icons are religious paintings, usually of Jesus or saints. They are considered holy images in Eastern Orthodox churches.

abstinence stopping oneself from doing something; self-denial

coppice a dense growth of bushes; a small wood

inevitable sure to happen

leasehold property held by lease

plight a serious problem

sackcloth rough, coarse cloth

wethers sheep

aright correctly

he thought. And he had an idea. I must follow the tracks of **C** the horse before they get covered. The horse will lead me **aright**. I might even catch him. The great thing is not to hurry or I'll get tired out and be worse off still. But despite his **intention** to go slowly, he hurried on and ran, continually falling and getting up and falling again. The horse tracks were already hard to see where there was no depth of snow. I'm done for, thought Vasilii Andreich. I can't follow the tracks and I'll never catch up with the horse. But at that very moment as he looked ahead he saw something black. It was Dapple—and not only Dapple, but also the sledge and the upright shafts with his kerchief. With the breeching and sackcloth pulled over to one side Dapple now stood where he had been before, only nearer the shafts; he was shaking his head, which was held down by the reins caught up in his leg. It turned out that Vasilii Andreich had got stuck in the same gully where he and Nikita had got stuck earlier; the horse was taking him back to the sledge **D** and where he had jumped off was no more than fifty yards away from it.

Kerchief is another form of *handkerchief*.

intention aim; plan

C ASK Comprehension What good idea did Vasilii Andreich finally have? (to follow the tracks so he could find the horse)

D ASK Critical Thinking What progress did Vasilii Andreich make through the snow? (Apparently he made no progress at all, as the implication is that he is now back at the sledge where he and his servant originally got stuck.)

G Grammar

Word Origins Point out to students that the word *kerchief* as a shortened form of *handkerchief* is an example of one way in which people form new words in English. This method is called "clipping" because the new word is "clipped" from the old. Often, though not always, both the old and the new forms of the word remain in use at the same time, like *bike* and *bicycle, phone* and *telephone*. Some clipped words are considered to be informal language, for example, and the shorter forms are not used in formal writing. Examples are *ad* from *advertisement* and *champ* from *champion*. In other cases, the original long word is hardly known once the shortened form has taken over. Who knows that the word *bus* really is *omnibus* or that *lunch* is *luncheon?*

Reviewing the Selection

Answer Key

Comprehension: Identifying Facts

1. He is trying to reach a village to get help.

2. The loud cry he hears is his horse's neigh.

3. He begs Saint Nicholas (Holy Father Nicholas) to save him.

Comprehension: Understanding Main Ideas

4. The storm has made him lose his bearings so he is not traveling in the direction he should be.

5. He finally finds himself back where he started, at the sledge where he and Nikita originally got stuck.

6. At one point in the story, he thinks he will die in the storm. Later he apparently thinks finding the horse again will save him.

Understanding Literature: Naturalism

7. The setting is a very bad snowstorm.

8. He struggles against nature in many ways. Perhaps the most obvious is his insistence that the horse go where Vasilii Andreich wants the horse to go rather than allowing the horse to lead.

Critical Thinking

9. Answers will vary, but many students will find that he is stubborn and too sure of himself.

10. Students will have different opinions, but encourage them to refer to the story as they discuss them.

Students who have not experienced a natural disaster directly may refer to newspaper accounts of a recent flood, hurricane, or other disaster to describe its power.

Selection Quiz

The Teacher's Resource Library includes a Selection Quiz for *Master and Man* that may be given following the Selection Review.

REVIEWING the SELECTION

Master and Man

Leo Tolstoy

Directions Write the answers to these questions using complete sentences.

Comprehension: Identifying Facts

1. What is Vasilii Andreich trying to reach?
2. What is the loud cry that he hears?
3. Whom does Vasilii Andreich beg to save him?

Comprehension: Understanding Main Ideas

4. Why isn't Vasilii Andreich getting where he wants to go?
5. Where does Vasilii Andreich finally find himself?
6. What does Vasilii Andreich think is going to happen?

Understanding Literature: Naturalism

Naturalism is a form of literature that deals with life's realities. Characters struggle against forces of nature. The strong survive and the weak do not. In some fiction of this type, the characters are helpless against events that are beyond their control. Nature is more powerful than humans.

7. What natural event is the setting for this story?
8. Point out an action showing how Vasilii Andreich struggles against nature.

Critical Thinking

9. What do you think of Vasilii Andreich as a person?
10. How does this story make you feel about the power of nature?

Writing on Your Own Think of a real natural disaster you know about or have been through. (It might be a flood, storm, or hurricane.) Write a paragraph about the power of the event.

98 *Unit 1 Fiction*

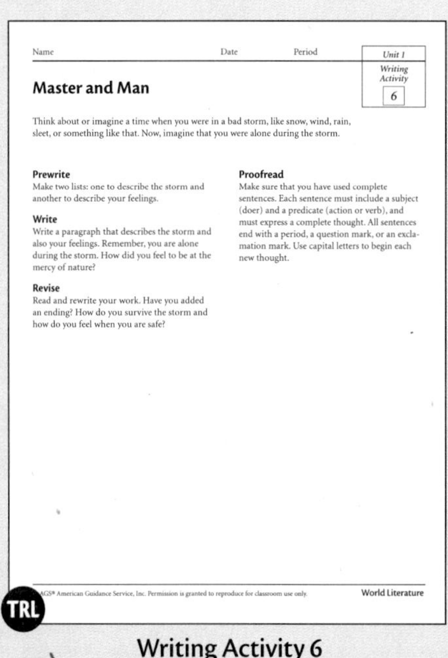

Name Date Period

Unit 1 Writing Activity 6

Master and Man

Think about or imagine a time when you were in a bad storm, like snow, wind, rain, sleet, or something like that. Now, imagine that you were alone during the storm.

Prewrite
Make two lists: one to describe the storm and another to describe your feelings.

Write
Write a paragraph that describes the storm and also your feelings. Remember, you are alone during the storm. How did you feel to be at the mercy of nature?

Revise
Read and rewrite your work. Have you added an ending? How do you survive the storm and how do you feel when you are safe?

Proofread
Make sure that you have used complete sentences. Each sentence must include a subject (doer) and a predicate (action or verb), and must express a complete thought. All sentences end with a period, a question mark, or an exclamation mark. Use capital letters to begin each new thought.

 World Literature

TRL

Writing Activity 6

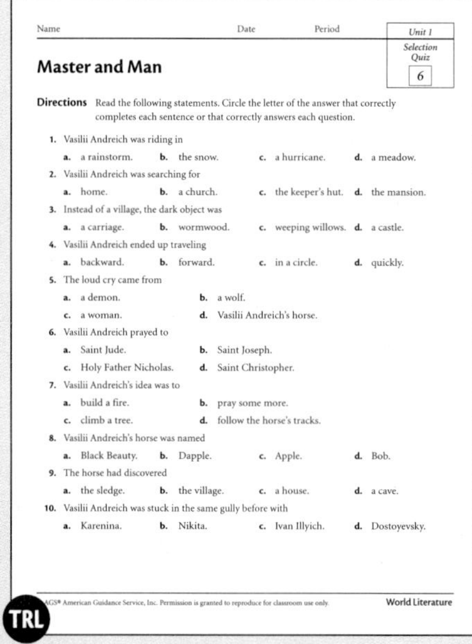

Name Date Period

Unit 1 Selection Quiz 6

Master and Man

Directions Read the following statements. Circle the letter of the answer that correctly completes each sentence or that correctly answers each question.

1. Vasilii Andreich was riding in
   a. a rainstorm. **b.** the snow. **c.** a hurricane. **d.** a meadow.
2. Vasilii Andreich was searching for
   a. home. **b.** a church. **c.** the keeper's hut. **d.** the mansion.
3. Instead of a village, the dark object was
   a. a carriage. **b.** wormwood. **c.** weeping willows. **d.** a castle.
4. Vasilii Andreich ended up traveling
   a. backward. **b.** forward. **c.** in a circle. **d.** quickly.
5. The loud cry came from
   a. a demon. **b.** a wolf. **c.** a woman. **d.** Vasilii Andreich's horse.
6. Vasilii Andreich prayed to
   a. Saint Jude. **b.** Saint Joseph. **c.** Holy Father Nicholas. **d.** Saint Christopher.
7. Vasilii Andreich's idea was to
   a. build a fire. **b.** pray some more. **c.** climb a tree. **d.** follow the horse's tracks.
8. Vasilii Andreich's horse was named
   a. Black Beauty. **b.** Dapple. **c.** Apple. **d.** Bob.
9. The horse had discovered
   a. the sledge. **b.** the village. **c.** a house. **d.** a cave.
10. Vasilii Andreich was stuck in the same gully before with
   a. Karenina. **b.** Nikita. **c.** Ivan Illyich. **d.** Dostoyevsky.

 World Literature

TRL

Selection Quiz 6

INTRODUCING the SELECTION

Just Lather, That's All

Hernando Téllez (translated by Donald A. Yates)

Hernando Téllez (1908–1966) Colombian

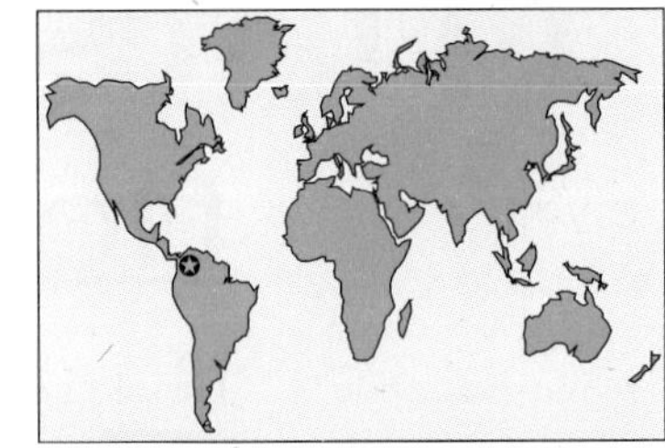

About the Author

Hernando Téllez was born in Bogotá, Colombia, in 1908. He worked for several magazines and newspapers. Téllez also was active in the politics of Colombia. He served as a diplomat and a senator. As a writer, he is best known for a book of short stories *Ashes for the Wind and Other Tales* published in 1950. Téllez also wrote essays. "Just Lather, That's All" was made into a movie with the name "Just Lather, Please."

Literary Term

rising action the buildup of excitement in a story

About the Selection

The following story is set during a civil war. Captain Torres leads soldiers who hunt down rebels. He executes them in public. The barber is a secret member of the rebel group. He gets the perfect chance to kill his enemy, Captain Torres. The adventure takes place in the barber's mind. The **rising action** builds with every stroke of his razor against the captain's unprotected neck. The suspense builds and the reader feels the mood of violence in the town. Will the barber let the captain go? Will he kill him? What will happen if he does? What will happen if he doesn't?

Selection at a Glance

Just Lather, That's All

Hernando Téllez
(translated by Donald A. Yates)

Student pages 99–106

Overview

Hernando Téllez's work reflects his region's frequent rebel uprisings and military overthrows of governments.

Selection Summary

"Just Lather, That's All" by Hernando Téllez tells of a barber who is a secret rebel and has a chance to murder the captain whose soldiers have been killing his friends.

Objectives

- To read and appreciate an action story.
- To recognize rising action in the plot development of a story.

Audiocassette 

Teacher's Resource Library TRL

- Vocabulary Workbook 7
- Selection Glossary 7
- Student Study Guide 13
- Activity 11
- Workbook 11
- Writing Activity 7
- Selection Quiz 7

Setting the Stage for Reading

About the Author

Hernando Téllez has been both a politician and a writer—a mutually supportive combination of talents, some would say. Both fields have shown his talent for understanding human nature.

ASK How do you think a person's talent for politics might also be used in writing? (Encourage students to theorize. Many will see that both professions can benefit from observation and understanding of people.)

About the Selection

This suspenseful story involves a single incident in which a barber struggles with a moral dilemma—should he cut the throat of his enemy who sits in his barber chair?

Activate Prior Knowledge: Ask students to recall stories they have read or movies they have seen that were full of suspense.

ASK How do you think a writer creates suspense in a story? (By making sure readers know something will happen but not giving the readers any clues about what it will be.)

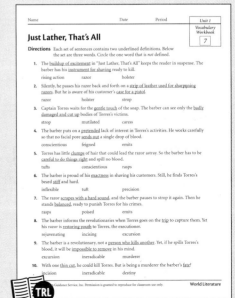

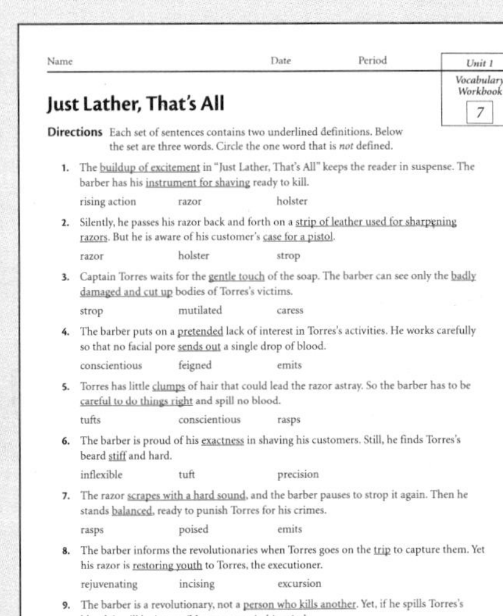

Name Date Period

Unit 1 *Vocabulary Workbook* 7

Just Lather, That's All

Directions Each set of sentences contains two underlined definitions. Below the set are three words. Circle the one word that is *not* defined.

1. The buildup of excitement in "Just Lather, That's All" keeps the reader in suspense. The barber has his instrument for shaving ready to kill.
   rising action razor holster
2. Silently, he passes his razor back and forth on a strip of leather used for sharpening razors. But he is aware of his customer's case for a pistol.
   razor holster strop
3. Captain Torres waits for the gentle touch of the soap. The barber can see only the badly damaged and cut up bodies of Torres's victims.
   strop mutilated caress
4. The barber puts on a pretended lack of interest in Torres's activities. He works carefully so that no facial pore sends out a single drop of blood.
   conscientious feigned emits
5. Torres has little clumps of hair that could lead the razor astray. So the barber has to be careful to do things right and spill no blood.
   tufts conscientious rasps
6. The barber is proud of his exactness in shaving his customers. Still, he finds Torres's beard stiff and hard.
   inflexible tuft precision
7. The razor scrapes with a hard sound, and the barber pauses to strop it again. Then he stands balanced, ready to punish Torres for his crimes.
   rasps poised emits
8. The barber informs the revolutionaries when Torres goes on the trip to capture them. Yet his razor is restoring youth to Torres, the executioner.
   rejuvenating incising excursion
9. The barber is a revolutionary, not a person who kills another. Yet, if he spills Torres's blood, it will be impossible to remove in his mind.
   excursion ineradicable murderer
10. With one thin cut, he could kill Torres. But is being a murderer the barber's fate?
    incision ineradicable destiny

 World Literature

TRL **Vocabulary Workbook 7**

Reading Vocabulary TRL

Help students preview the selection's vocabulary words by giving them copies of the Selection Glossary. Review the words, and ask pairs of students to take turns saying the words and providing the matching definitions.

Motivation for Reading

Suggest that students put themselves in the place of the barber in the story. As they read, have them consider what they would do in his place.

Discussion Questions

Suggest that students read the entire selection before answering the questions in the margins of the student selection.

A The story is being told in the first person, meaning the narrator refers to himself as "I."

B ASK Literary Element The rising action and suspense begin right away. What are some clues to the problem of the story? (The man who comes to the barber is an enemy; he is vulnerable because he takes off his gun. He asks the barber to shave him, which will mean his throat will be open to the barber's razor.)

Viewing the Art

Draw students' attention to the illustration *In the Barbershop* on page 100. Point out that the artist did not paint this picture in order to illustrate this story. Ask them to compare the barbershop envisioned by the artist with that described by the author of the story.

ASK How is the barbershop in the picture like the one you imagine in the story? How is it different? (Let students offer their own interpretations.)

Visually oriented people may point out the unusual perspective in the painting. If so, invite them to consider why the artist might have used such a perspective.

Just Lather, That's All

Hernando Téllez

As you read, notice how the suspense builds. That is the rising action.

Is this story being told in first person or third person?

A

He said nothing when he entered. I was passing the best of my **razors** back and forth on a **strop**. When I recognized him I started to tremble. But he didn't notice. Hoping to conceal my emotion, I continued sharpening the razor. I tested it on the meat of my thumb, and then held it up to the light.

B At that moment he took off the bullet-studded belt that his gun **holster** dangled from. He hung it up on a wall hook and placed his military cap over it. Then he turned to me, loosening the knot of his tie, and said, "It's hot as hell. Give me a shave." He sat in the chair.

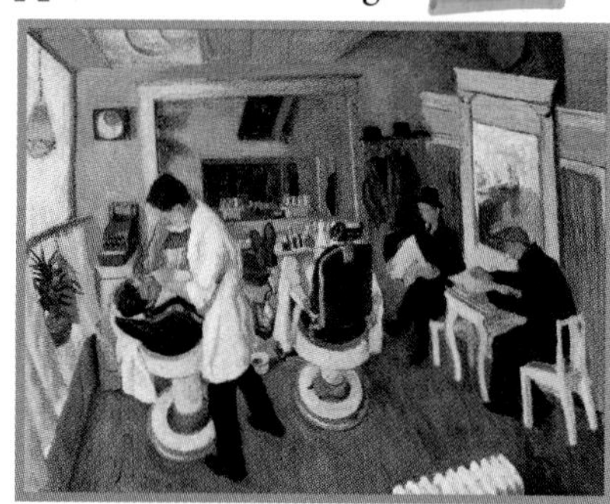

In the Barbershop, **Ilya Bolotowsky, 1934. Estate of Ilya Bolotowsky/Licensed by VAGA, New York, NY.**

I estimated he had a four-day beard—the four days taken up by the latest expedition in search of our troops. His face seemed reddened, burned by the sun. Carefully, I began to prepare the soap. I cut off a few slices, dropped them into the cup, mixed in a bit of warm water, and began to stir with the brush. Immediately the foam began to rise. "The other boys in the group should have this much beard, too," he remarked. I continued stirring the lather.

holster a case for a pistol

razor an instrument used for shaving

strop a strip of leather used for sharpening razors

Name _______ Date _______ Period _______

Unit 1 — *Student Study Guide* 13

Just Lather, That's All (pp. 100–105)

Directions Fill in the following outline. Filling in the blanks will help you as you read and study "Just Lather, That's All."

I. Beginning of the Selection (pp. 100–101)

A. Recognition

1. The man entering the shop hangs his bullet-studded belt and his __________ __________ on a wall hook.
2. The barber realizes the man probably thinks he's in __________ with his party.
3. The man had ordered the whole town to see four __________ rebels hanging there.

II. Middle of the Selection (pp. 101–103)

A. Applying the Soap

1. Captain Torres had held __________ __________ on the bodies of the hanging naked rebels.
2. The barber is both a secret __________ and a conscientious __________.
3. Torres tells the barber to come to the school at __________ o'clock.
4. When the barber glances at the clock, it is __________ in the afternoon.
5. The barber thinks about a tiny __________ opening up and issuing forth its pearl of __________.

III. End of the Selection (pp. 103–105)

A. Executioners and Barbers

1. Torres does not know the barber is his __________.
2. The barber worries about having to explain why he let Torres go __________ and __________.
3. The barber wonders what he would do with the __________ and where he would __________ it.
4. Before Torres leaves, he tells the barber that they'd told him the barber would __________ him, and he'd come to find out.

 World Literature

TRL

Student Study Guide 13

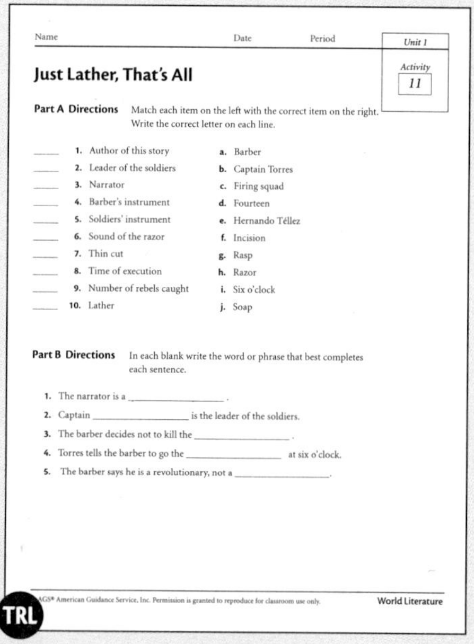

Name _______ Date _______ Period _______

Unit 1 — *Activity* 11

Just Lather, That's All

Part A Directions Match each item on the left with the correct item on the right. Write the correct letter on each line.

_____	**1.** Author of this story	**a.** Barber
_____	**2.** Leader of the soldiers	**b.** Captain Torres
_____	**3.** Narrator	**c.** Firing squad
_____	**4.** Barber's instrument	**d.** Fourteen
_____	**5.** Soldiers' instrument	**e.** Hernando Téllez
_____	**6.** Sound of the razor	**f.** Incision
_____	**7.** Thin cut	**g.** Rasp
_____	**8.** Time of execution	**h.** Razor
_____	**9.** Number of rebels caught	**i.** Six o'clock
_____	**10.** Lather	**j.** Soap

Part B Directions In each blank write the word or phrase that best completes each sentence.

1. The narrator is a __________________.
2. Captain __________________ is the leader of the soldiers.
3. The barber decides not to kill the __________________.
4. Torres tells the barber to go the __________________ at six o'clock.
5. The barber says he is a revolutionary, not a __________________.

 World Literature

TRL

Activity 11

"But we did all right, you know. We got the main ones. We brought back some dead, and we got some others still alive. But pretty soon they'll all be dead."

"How many did you catch?" I asked.

"Fourteen. We had to go pretty deep into the woods to find them. But we'll get even. Not one of them comes out of this alive, not one."

He leaned back on the chair when he saw me with the lather-covered brush in my hand. I still had to put the sheet on him. No doubt about it, I was upset. I took a sheet out of a drawer and knotted it around his neck. He wouldn't stop talking. He probably thought I was in sympathy with his party.

C
Why was the barber upset? Who were the people the other man been hunting?

"The town must have learned a lesson from what we did," he said.

"Yes," I replied, securing the knot at the base of his dark, sweaty neck.

"That was a fine show, eh?"

"Very good," I answered, turning back for the brush.

The man closed his eyes with a gesture of fatigue and sat waiting for the cool **caress** of the soap. I had never had him so close to me. The day he ordered the whole town to file into the patio of the school to see the four rebels hanging there, I came face to face with him for an instant. But the sight of the **mutilated** bodies kept me from noticing the face of the man who had directed it all, the face I was now about to take into my hands.

It was not an unpleasant face, and the beard, which made him look a bit older than he was, didn't suit him badly at all. His name was Torres—Captain Torres. A man of imagination, because who else would have thought of hanging the naked rebels and then holding target practice on their bodies?

D
What does this detail tell you about *Captain Torres*?

caress a gentle touch

mutilated cut up; badly damaged

C The barber is very upset because his enemy has just described his latest victory over the people whom the barber supports in this fight. The people the man had been hunting were the rebels.

D The horrifying detail of the captain's public treatment of the rebels reveals that he is more than just a man of imagination, as the barber observes. He is also a sadistic bully.

Learning Styles

Visual There are two very graphic scenes described on these two pages—the one in the barber shop and the briefer one of the rebels hanging in the patio of the school. Visually oriented students will be able to "see" these scenes in their minds. Ask volunteers to imagine each scene in detail and describe each one in his or her own words to the rest of the class. Allow them to add descriptive details of their own imagining as long as they are logical to the scene.

Name Date Period

Unit 1

Workbook *11*

Just Lather, That's All

Directions Circle the letter of the answer that correctly completes each sentence.

1. The narrator and main character of this story is
   a. a general. **b.** a barber. **c.** a soldier. **d.** none of these.
2. _____ is an enemy of the main character.
   a. Téllez **b.** Sanistra **c.** Torres **d.** Roderico
3. The physical setting of this short story is in a
   a. barber shop. **b.** tavern. **c.** church. **d.** none of these.
4. For _____ the soldiers have hunted and killed the rebel group.
   a. one month **b.** two weeks **c.** four days **d.** three days
5. The captain is said to be a man of _____ for hanging rebels naked and shooting at their dead bodies.
   a. evil **b.** greatness **c.** imagination **d.** wickedness
6. "I was a rebel, but also a conscientious _____ says the narrator to the reader.
   a. worker **b.** citizen **c.** leader **d.** barber
7. When the Captain is finished, the narrator thinks he must feel
   a. rejuvenated. **b.** preferred. **c.** dethroned. **d.** repentant.
8. "My _____ depends on the edge of this blade. Murderer or hero?" thinks the narrator.
   a. future **b.** life **c.** destiny **d.** village
9. In his own mind, the narrator is
   a. a revolutionary. **b.** a rebel. **c.** a barber. **d.** all of these.
10. As the Captain leaves, he says to the narrator, _____ isn't easy."
    a. Killing **b.** Murdering **c.** Hanging **d.** Shooting

World Literature

TRL

Workbook 11

Fiction Unit 1 **101**

Discussion Questions

A The barber faces the problem of how to treat this unusual customer. Should the barber behave as the conscientious professional he is? Or should he treat him as his enemy?

B ASK Literary Element Notice the careful detail the author provides as the barber begins to shave the captain. How does this contribute to the suspense? (It makes the reader follow the action one minute at a time, which slows down the action and builds up the excitement of what will happen.)

Career Connection

Discuss with students the skill and conscientious attention to detail that the barber shows in his work. It is clear that he takes pride in and really likes what he does for a living. Invite further discussion of this enjoyment as a key ingredient of doing a good job no matter what a person does. Tell students that this is one reason why career counselors try to find out what students' aptitudes and interests are before suggesting various fields they might go into.

I began to apply the first layer of soap. With his eyes closed, he continued. "Without any effort I could go straight to sleep," he said, "but there's plenty to do this afternoon."

I stopped the lathering and asked with a **feigned** lack of interest, "A firing squad?"

"Something like that, but a little slower."

I got on with the job of lathering his beard. My hands started trembling again. The man could not possibly realize it, and this was in my favor. But I would have preferred that he hadn't come. It was likely that many of our faction had seen him enter. And an enemy under one's roof imposes certain conditions.

A What problem is the barber facing?

B I would be obliged to shave that beard like any other one, carefully, gently, like that of any customer, taking pains to see that no single pore **emitted** a drop of blood. Being careful to see that the little **tufts** of hair did not lead the blade astray. Seeing that his skin ended up clean, soft, and healthy, so that passing the back of my hand over it I couldn't feel a hair. Yes, I was secretly a rebel, but I was also a **conscientious** barber, and proud of the **precision** required of my profession.

I took the razor, opened up the two protective arms, exposed the blade, and began the job—from one of the sideburns downward. The razor responded beautifully. His beard was **inflexible** and hard, not too long, but thick. Bit by bit the skin emerged. The razor **rasped** along, making its customary sound as fluffs of lather, mixed with bits of hair, gathered along the blade.

I paused a moment to clean it, then took up the strop again to sharpen the razor, because I'm a barber who does things properly. The man, who had kept his eyes closed, opened them now, removed one of his hands from under the sheet, felt the spot on his face where the soap had been cleared off, and said, "Come to the school today at six o'clock."

conscientious careful to do things right
emit send out
feign to pretend
inflexible stiff; rigid
precision exactness
rasp scrape with a harsh sound
tuft a small clump of hair

102 *Unit 1 Fiction*

"The same thing as the other day?" I asked, horrified.

"It could be even better," he said.

"What do you plan to do?"

"I don't know yet. But we'll amuse ourselves." Once more he leaned back and closed his eyes. I approached with the razor **poised.**

"Do you plan to punish them all?" I ventured timidly.

"All."

The soap was drying on his face. I had to hurry. In the mirror I looked towards the street. It was the same as ever—the grocery store with two or three customers in it. Then I glanced at the clock—2:20 in the afternoon.

The razor continued on its downward stroke. Now from the other sideburn down. A thick, blue beard. He should have let it grow like some poets or priests do. It would suit him well. A lot of people wouldn't recognize him. Much to his benefit, I thought, as I attempted to cover the neck areas smoothly.

C Why might Torres not want to be recognized?

There, surely, the razor had to be handled masterfully, since the hair, although softer, grew into little swirls. A curly beard. One of the tiny pores could open up and issue forth its pearl of blood, but a good barber prides himself on never allowing this to happen to a customer.

How many of us had he ordered shot? How many of us had he ordered mutilated? It was better not to think about it. Torres did not know that I was his enemy. He did not know it **D**

poised held up; balanced

C Torres might not want to be recognized when he was among his enemies for his own protection. It also might enable him to learn more about what was going on with his enemies if they did not know who he was.

D ASK Critical Thinking Why does the barber feel that Torres does not know that the barber is his enemy? (He probably assumes that if Torres suspected it, Torres would not have come into the barber shop and trusted the barber to shave him.)

Learning Styles

Tactile/Kinesthetic The description of the way the barber goes about shaving his customer will appeal very much to students with heightened tactile/kinesthetic senses. Ask volunteers to role-play the scene.

Viewing the Art

Rural Landscape (Paisaje Campestre) by Susana Gonzalez-Pagliere shows a small town surrounded by mountains. The setting of the story could very well have taken place in such a setting.

ASK How does the painting reinforce the setting of the story? (The painting helps provide a visual setting for the type of community—small rural town—where the story could take place.)

Discussion Questions

A ASK Critical Thinking Why should the barber kill the captain? (The captain is his enemy, and other revolutionaries will wonder why he didn't take the opportunity when he had it.) Why shouldn't the barber kill the captain? (The barber is not a murderer and does not believe in people killing each other.)

B ASK Comprehension Why is the barber sorry that the captain has come into his shop? (He would have preferred not to be faced with this moral dilemma of whether to kill the captain.)

Learning Styles

Group Learning Clearly the two groups of people mentioned in this story disagreed over some issue, although we don't know what it is. They have carried that disagreement to a violent confrontation. Invite discussion of ways in which people can "agree to disagree" and get along without violence. Have groups of students explore the issue of violence between groups and how it sometimes erupts into war. Have them address possible alternatives of conflict resolution such as negotiation and arbitration and why they sometimes do not work.

nor did the rest. It was a secret shared by very few, precisely so that I could inform the revolutionaries of what Torres was doing in the town and of what he was planning each time he undertook a rebel-hunting **excursion.**

A So it was going to be very difficult to explain that I had him right in my hands and let him go peacefully—alive and shaved.

The beard was now almost completely gone. He seemed younger, less burdened by years than when he had arrived. I suppose this always happens with men who visit barber shops. Under the stroke of my razor Torres was being **rejuvenated**—rejuvenated because I am a good barber, the best in the town, if I may say so.

How hot it is getting! Torres must be sweating as much as I. But he is a calm man, who is not even thinking about what he is going to do with the prisoners this afternoon. On the other hand I, with this razor in my hands—I stroking and restroking this skin, can't even think clearly.

B Damn him for coming! I'm a revolutionary, not a **murderer.** And how easy it would be to kill him. And he deserves it. Does he? No! What the devil! No one deserves to have someone else make the sacrifice of becoming a murderer. What do you gain by it? Nothing. Others come along and still others, and the first ones kill the second ones, and they the next ones—and it goes on like this until everything is a sea of blood.

I could cut this throat just so—*zip, zip!* I wouldn't give him time to resist and since he has his eyes closed he wouldn't see the glistening blade or my glistening eyes. But I'm trembling like a real murderer. Out of his neck a gush of blood would sprout onto the sheet, on the chair, on my hands, on the floor. I would have to close the door. And the blood would keep inching along the floor, warm, **ineradicable**, uncontainable, until it reached the street, like a little scarlet stream.

excursion a trip; an expedition

ineradicable impossible to erase or remove

murderer someone who kills another person

rejuvenate to restore youth or energy

I'm sure that one solid stroke, one deep **incision**, would prevent any pain. He wouldn't suffer. But what would I do with the body? Where would I hide it? I would have to flee, leaving all I have behind, and take refuge far away. But they would follow until they found me. "Captain Torres' murderer. He slit his throat while he was shaving him—a coward."

And then on the other side. "The avenger of us all. A name to remember. He was the town barber. No one knew he was defending our cause."

Murderer or hero? My **destiny** depends on the edge of this blade. I can turn my hand a bit more, press a little harder on the razor, and sink it in. The skin would give way like silk, like rubber. There is nothing more tender than human skin and the blood is always there, ready to pour forth.

But I don't want to be a murderer. You came to me for a shave. And I perform my work honorably...I don't want blood on my hands. Just lather, that's all. You are an executioner and I am only a barber. Each person has his own place in the scheme of things.

C Why does the barber decide not to kill the captain?

climax

Now his chin had been stroked clean and smooth. The man sat up and looked into the mirror. He rubbed his hands over his skin and felt it fresh, like new.

"Thanks," he said. He went to the hanger for his belt, pistol, and cap. I must have been very pale; my shirt felt soaked. Torres finished adjusting the buckle, straightened his pistol in the holster, and after automatically smoothing down his hair, he put on the cap. From his pants pocket he took out several coins to pay me for my services and then headed for the door.

In the doorway he paused for a moment and said, "They told me that you'd kill me. I came to find out. But killing isn't easy. You can take my word for it." And he turned and walked away.

D Does the ending surprise you?

denouement

destiny fate **incision** a thin cut

C The barber decides not to kill the captain because the barber simply does not see himself as a murderer.

D Most students will find the ending surprising, as they would not have expected that the captain knew the barber was an enemy. Invite discussion about the other element of surprise—that the captain says "killing isn't easy."

Literary Elements

Plot and Climax The rising action of a plot finally comes to a head, or a part of the story called the climax. After the climax, the story winds down to an end that usually ties up the loose ends of the plot.

ASK What is the climax of this story? (The point on page 105 when the barber realizes he does not want to be a murderer. This solves the tension of whether he would slit the throat of the captain or not.)

Reviewing the Selection

Answer Key

Comprehension: Identifying Facts

1. He wants a shave.

2. He has hunted and murdered them.

3. He has been hunting the rebels.

Comprehension: Understanding Main Ideas

4. The barber has to decide whether to murder the captain while he sits in the barber's chair.

5. The captain and his forces will "put on a show," which may be the same kind of horrible display they did earlier with the dead bodies of some of the rebels.

6. He decides not to murder the captain because the barber is not a murderer.

Understanding Literature: Rising Action

7. The conflict is within the barber: should he murder the captain or not?

8. The turning point comes when the barber admits to himself that he is not a murderer.

Critical Thinking

9. Answers may vary, but many students will feel the barber did the right thing. Others may feel that the barber should have taken vengeance and murdered the captain. Make sure students defend their opinions with evidence from the story.

10. Captain Torres tells the barber that he knew the barber was his enemy. More importantly, he tells the barber that "killing isn't easy."

Writing on Your Own Remind students to use evidence from the story to make their own ending logical.

Selection Quiz

The Teacher's Resource Library includes a Selection Quiz for "Just Lather, That's All" that may be given following the Selection Review.

REVIEWING the SELECTION

Just Lather, That's All

Hernando Tellez

Directions Write the answers to these questions using complete sentences.

Comprehension: Identifying Facts

1. What does Captain Torres want in the barber shop?
2. What has Captain Torres done to the barber's political friends?
3. Where has he been for four days?

Comprehension: Understanding Main Ideas

4. What does the barber have to decide?
5. What will happen at the school at six o'clock?
6. Why does the barber make the decision he makes?

Understanding Literature: Rising Action

Rising action is the build-up of excitement in the story. It takes place as the story introduces a conflict. The action then builds to a climax or turning point.

7. What is the conflict in this story?
8. What is the turning point in this story?

Critical Thinking

9. Do you think the barber did the right thing? Why or why not?
10. What does Captain Torres say as he leaves? What do you think he means?

Writing on Your Own What if the barber had killed Torres? Write a paragraph telling what might have happened.

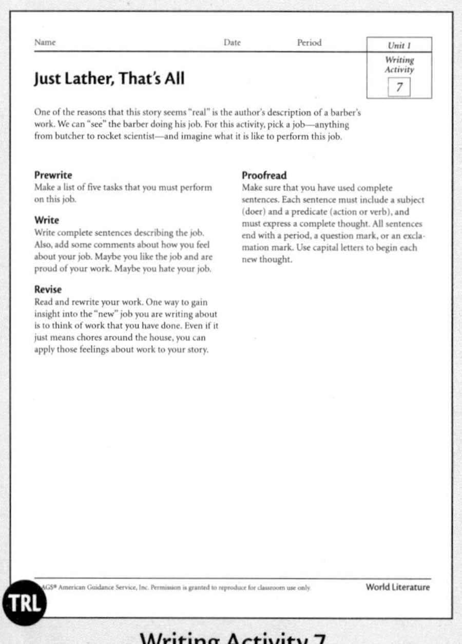
Name Date Period Unit 1 Writing Activity 7

Just Lather, That's All

One of the reasons that this story seems "real" is the author's description of a barber's work. We can "see" the barber doing his job. For this activity, pick a job—anything from butcher to rocket scientist—and imagine what it is like to perform this job.

Prewrite
Make a list of five tasks that you must perform on this job.

Write
Write complete sentences describing the job. Also, add some comments about how you feel about your job. Maybe you like the job and are proud of your work. Maybe you hate your job.

Revise
Read and rewrite your work. One way to gain insight into the "new" job you are writing about is to think of work that you have done. Even if it just means chores around the house, you can apply those feelings about work to your story.

Proofread
Make sure that you have used complete sentences. Each sentence must include a subject (doer) and a predicate (action or verb), and must express a complete thought. All sentences end with a period, a question mark, or an exclamation mark. Use capital letters to begin each new thought.

 World Literature

TRL

Writing Activity 7

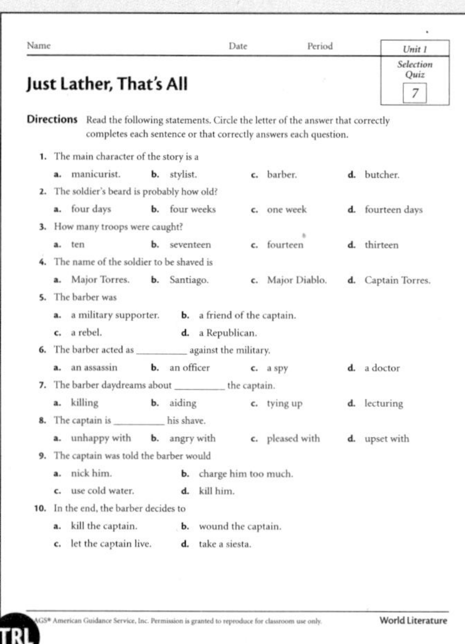
Name Date Period Unit 1 Selection Quiz 7

Just Lather, That's All

Directions Read the following statements. Circle the letter of the answer that correctly completes each sentence or that correctly answers each question.

1. The main character of the story is a
 a. manicurist. b. stylist. c. barber. d. butcher.
2. The soldier's beard is probably how old?
 a. four days b. four weeks c. one week d. fourteen days
3. How many troops were caught?
 a. ten b. seventeen c. fourteen d. thirteen
4. The name of the soldier to be shaved is
 a. Major Torres. b. Santiago. c. Major Diablo. d. Captain Torres.
5. The barber was
 a. a military supporter. b. a friend of the captain. c. a rebel. d. a Republican.
6. The barber acted as _______ against the military.
 a. an assassin b. an officer c. a spy d. a doctor
7. The barber daydreams about _______ the captain.
 a. killing b. aiding c. tying up d. lecturing
8. The captain is _______ his shave.
 a. unhappy with b. angry with c. pleased with d. upset with
9. The captain was told the barber would
 a. nick him. b. charge him too much. c. use cold water. d. kill him.
10. In the end, the barber decides to
 a. kill the captain. b. wound the captain. c. let the captain live. d. take a siesta.

 World Literature

TRL

Selection Quiz 7

Turning Points

- "Youth was serious, but not entirely fatal." —Rosario Castellanos
- "Now it seems to me...that one can *choose* to become an adult, but only at given moments." —Nick Hornby

The experiences of characters often move the plot toward an exciting ending, or denouement. Or an experience may show an important part of their personalities. When an experience changes a character's life, the story belongs to a genre called turning points.

Turning points are often events that, at the time, seem frightening or confusing. The character does not understand the event's importance right away; only later does he or she understand. For this reason, the narrator's point of view is important in these stories. Point of view refers to who is telling the story. If the events happen to the narrator, the first-person point of view is used. This point of view has limits, such as the narrator's age or intelligence. Sometimes a story is told by someone who is not part of it. This known as the third-person point of view.

Turning points seem to have the most effect on young people. For that reason, turning points about young people are sometimes called "coming of age" or "initiation" stories. Only as adults can these characters finally see what a childhood experience meant. They can then understand and explain it.

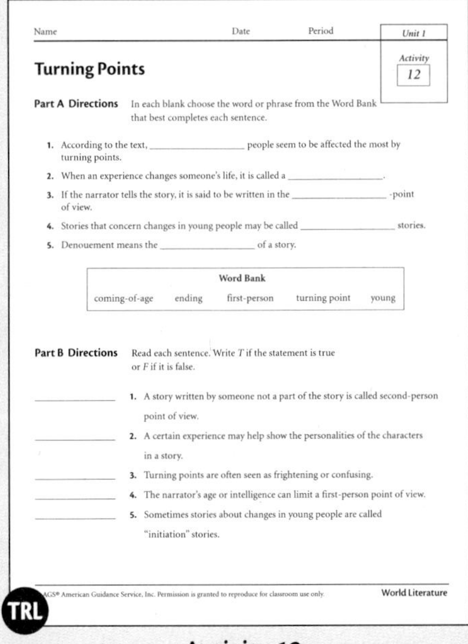

Name Date Period — *Unit 1* — *Activity* 12

Turning Points

Part A Directions In each blank choose the word or phrase from the Word Bank that best completes each sentence.

1. According to the text, ________________ people seem to be affected the most by turning points.
2. When an experience changes someone's life, it is called a ________________.
3. If the narrator tells the story, it is said to be written in the ________________ -point of view.
4. Stories that concern changes in young people may be called ________________ stories.
5. Denouement means the ________________ of a story.

Word Bank

coming-of-age ending first-person turning point young

Part B Directions Read each sentence. Write *T* if the statement is true or *F* if it is false.

________ 1. A story written by someone not a part of the story is called second-person point of view.

________ 2. A certain experience may help show the personalities of the characters in a story.

________ 3. Turning points are often seen as frightening or confusing.

________ 4. The narrator's age or intelligence can limit a first-person point of view.

________ 5. Sometimes stories about changes in young people are called "initiation" stories.

 World Literature

TRL

Activity 12

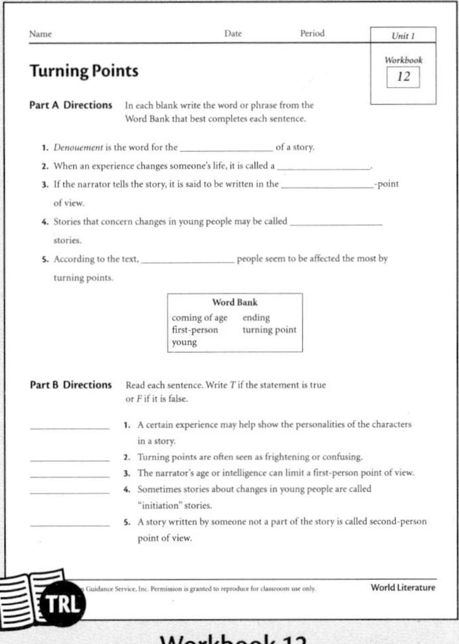

Name Date Period — *Unit 1* — *Workbook* 12

Turning Points

Part A Directions In each blank write the word or phrase from the Word Bank that best completes each sentence.

1. *Denouement* is the word for the ________________ of a story.
2. When an experience changes someone's life, it is called a ________________.
3. If the narrator tells the story, it is said to be written in the ________________-point of view.
4. Stories that concern changes in young people may be called ________________ stories.
5. According to the text, ________________ people seem to be affected the most by turning points.

Word Bank

coming of age ending
first-person turning point
young

Part B Directions Read each sentence. Write *T* if the statement is true or *F* if it is false.

________ 1. A certain experience may help show the personalities of the characters in a story.

________ 2. Turning points are often seen as frightening or confusing.

________ 3. The narrator's age or intelligence can limit a first-person point of view.

________ 4. Sometimes stories about changes in young people are called "initiation" stories.

________ 5. A story written by someone not a part of the story is called second-person point of view.

 World Literature

TRL

Workbook 12

Turning Points

Ask students to read the text on page 107, or have them take turns reading it aloud. Then turn their attention to the two quotations at the top of the page.

ASK As a young person, what do you think the first quotation about youth means? (Let students discuss their ideas. Some will see the humor in the quotation. Many will understand that the quotation implies that youth is a difficult time, but most people survive it.)

ASK Do you feel that you can choose to be an adult at certain times? (Again let students discuss their opinions. This quotation is especially meaningful for students, whose early adolescence makes them vulnerable to being a child one minute and an adult the next. Perceptive students may see this. Many will assert that they think they are adults now.)

Point out that all people go through the adolescent time of life that students are now experiencing. That time is often one that includes a turning point. Most people like stories about turning points because they can sympathize, or deeply understand, what the character is going through even though the specific details are different for everyone.

ASK Why do you think many people, including characters in stories, do not understand that they have experienced a turning point until later in their lives? (It is hard to have perspective when you are living through something. Later in your life you can realize what an impact something had on you.)

Selection at a Glance

Nervous Conditions

Tsitsi Dangarembga

Student pages 108–115

Overview

Having experienced personally the differences between two cultures, Tsitsi Dangarembga finds fertile ground for her writing in various media.

Selection Summary

In *Nervous Conditions* by Tsitsi Dangarembga, a young girl in Zimbabwe makes a choice between tradition and the chance for a good education.

Objectives

- To read and appreciate a coming-of-age story.
- To identify and understand first-person point of view.

Audiocassette 

Teacher's Resource Library TRL

- Vocabulary Workbook 8
- Selection Glossary 8
- Student Study Guide 14
- Activity 13
- Workbook 13
- Writing Activity 8
- Selection Quiz 8

INTRODUCING the SELECTION

Nervous Conditions

Tsitsi Dangarembga

Tsitsi Dangarembga
(1959–)
Zimbabwean

Literary Term

coming-of-age story a story that tells how a young person matures

About the Author

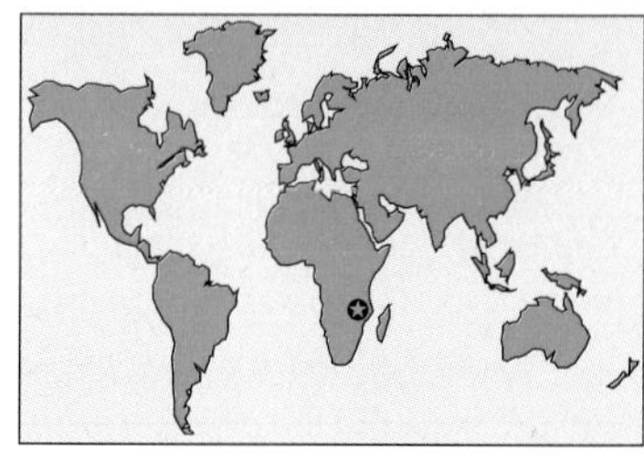

Tsitsi Dangarembga was born in 1959 in Zimbabwe (then called Rhodesia.) She spent her childhood in England, where her parents were studying. In 1965, she returned to Zimbabwe and went to a mission school. Dangarembga went back to England to study medicine at Cambridge University. She also studied psychology at the University of Zimbabwe. She then became a full-time writer. *Nervous Conditions* was written when Dangarembga was twenty-five years old. It was not published immediately. It won the Commonwealth Writers Prize in 1989. She has also written three plays. Dangarembga now lives in Germany. She is studying film and working on another novel.

About the Selection

This **coming-of-age story** is about Tambudzai, a young black girl who lives in 1960's Rhodesia. Babamukuru, her rich uncle, offers her a chance to go to school. She wants a better education. But each step weakens her ties to her family and way of life. The story explores many themes. One theme is power. In her family, some members have power over others. In the culture, men have power over women. Colonial schools conflict with traditional ways.

In the following selection, Tambudzai is talking with her cousin Nyasha. Nyasha's parents lived in England, where Nyasha grew up. Now Nyasha feels at home nowhere. She seems too English to be accepted by her relatives at home. White society does not accept her either. Nyasha warns Tambudzai against going to a school run by whites. Her uncle has some doubts. Tambudzai must decide what to do.

Setting the Stage for Reading

About the Author

Tsitsi Dangarembga's writing talent showed itself early, although she experimented with other fields such as medicine and psychology.

ASK What special problems do you think someone might have growing up in two different cultures? (Let students who have personal experience contribute whatever insights they choose. Others may see that cultural expectations of growing up may be different, and someone may feel torn between the two.)

About the Selection

In this novel, Tambudzai is the main character. But her cousin Nyasha also plays a part in this episode from the book. Nyasha has lived in England, as we know the author did.

Activate Prior Knowledge: Consider whether people who write coming-of-age stories may have personal knowledge of similar turning points.

ASK How do you think the author might be able to write convincingly about a young African girl who has lived in England? (because it mirrors her own experience)

Going to the convent was a chance to lighten those burdens by entering a world where burdens were light. I would take the chance. I would lighten my burdens. I would go. If Babamukuru would let me. **C**

Still Nyasha was not impressed. "Really, Tambudzai," she said severely when I had finished **glorifying** my interests, "there'll always be brothers and mealies and mothers too tired to clean latrines. Whether you go to the convent or not. There's more to be done than that." This was typical of Nyasha, this **obstinate idealism**. But she could afford it, being my **affluent** uncle's daughter. Whereas I, I had to take whatever chances came my way.

Babamukuru was of the opinion **D** that enough chances had come my way, and on another level he agreed with Nyasha that the experience would not be good for me. From his armchair opposite the fireplace he told me why I could not go to the convent.

"It is not a question of money," he assured me. "Although there would still be a lot of expense on my part, you have your scholarship, so the major **financial** burden would be lifted. But I feel that even that little money could be better used. For one thing, there is now the small boy at home. Every month I put away a little bit, a very little bit, a very little bit every month, so that when he is of school-going age everything will be provided for. As you know, he is the only boy in your family, so he must be provided for. As for you, we think we are providing for you quite well. By the time you have finished your Form Four you will be able to take

Boys and girls were not treated equally at this time and this place.

affluent rich; having plenty of money

glorify to give honor or high praise

obstinate stubborn

financial having to do with money

idealism belief that things can be perfect

C ASK Critical Thinking Babamukuru is the uncle who runs the local mission school. He is also Nyasha's father. Why do you think he has a role in deciding whether Tambudzai goes to the convent school? (He apparently contributes to the upkeep of Tambudzai's family and seems to have a powerful role in the family.)

D ASK Literary Element Even in stories that are not suspense stories, the plot leads up to a climax, or high point of resolution. What do you think that might be in this story? (probably when the decision is made whether Tambudzai can go to the convent school)

Discussion Questions

A ASK Vocabulary The word *marvellous* was pointed out on page 109 as a British spelling. What others have you noticed? (*sceptical* on page 110, *behaviour* and *leant* on page 112)

B Tambudzai is surprised that her aunt speaks up, as this is clearly a male-dominated society in which women play a secondary role.

your course, whatever it is that you choose. In time you will be earning money. You will be in a position to be married by a decent man and set up a decent home. In all that we are doing for you, we are preparing you for this future life of yours, and I have observed from my own daughter's **A** behaviour that it is not a good thing for a young girl to associate too much with these white people, to have too much freedom. I have seen that girls who do that do not develop into decent women."

Marriage. I had nothing against it in principle. In an **abstract** way I thought it was a very good idea. But it was **irritating** the way it always cropped up in one form or another, stretching its tentacles back to bind me before I had even begun to think about it seriously, threatening to **disrupt** my life before I could even call it my own. Babamukuru had lost me with his talk of marriage. I inspected my dressing-gown for fluff, waiting for the session to end. "This," continued my uncle, "is what I shall tell your father: if he wishes to send you there to that school, he may do so if he can find the money. Myself, I would not consider it money well spent. Mai," he concluded, turning to my aunt, "is there anything that you would wish to say?"

B
Why is Tambudzai surprised when her aunt chooses to speak?

"Yes, Baba," Maiguru spoke up softly from the sofa. My inspection came to an abrupt end. I listened **incredulously**.

"You do!" exclaimed Babamukuru and, recovering himself, invited her to continue. "Speak freely, Mai. Say whatever you are thinking."

There was a pause during which Maiguru folded her arms and leant back in the sofa. "I don't think," she began easily in her soft, soothing voice, "that Tambudzai will be **corrupted** by going to that school. Don't you remember, when we went to

abstract not practical; not related to real life

disrupt to upset or interfere

incredulously in surprise; not believing

corrupt spoil; to make less honest or moral

irritating annoying

South Africa everybody was saying that we, the women, were loose." Babamukuru winced at this **explicitness**. Maiguru continued. "It wasn't a question of **associating** with this race or that race at that time. People were **prejudiced** against **C** educated women. Prejudiced. That's why they said we weren't decent. That was in the fifties. Now we are into the seventies. I **D** am disappointed that people still believe the same things. After all this time and when we have seen nothing to say it is true. I don't know what people mean by a loose woman—sometimes she is someone who walks the streets, sometimes she is an educated woman, sometimes she is a successful man's daughter or she is simply beautiful. Loose or decent, I don't know. All I know is that if our daughter Tambudzai is not a **F** decent person now, she never will be, no matter where she goes to school. And if she is decent, then this convent should **G** not change her. As for money, you have said yourself that she has a full scholarship. It is possible that you have other reasons why she should not go there, Babawa Chido, but these—the question of decency and the question of money—are the ones I have heard and so these are the ones I have talked of."

E
Is Nyasha included in this description of *loose women*?

There was another pause during which Maiguru unfolded her arms and clasped her hands in her lap.

Babamukuru cleared his throat. "Er, Tambudzai," he asked **tentatively**, "do you have anything to say?"...

It was on New Year's Eve that my uncle and my father discussed my future. The discussion took place in the house. I was obliged to **eavesdrop**.

"It may change her character for the worse...these Whites, you know...you never know," mused Babamukuru.

"No," agreed my father. "How could you know with these ones? You never know. With Whites! No. You never know."

associating being with; keeping company

explicitness a very frank or clear statement

tentatively with hesitation

eavesdrop to listen secretly

prejudice an unfair strong feeling toward a group

C ASK Critical Thinking Why do you think people were prejudiced against educated women? (In this society, men have power over women. A woman who is educated is very likely to threaten that power.)

D ASK Literary Element You know the setting of this story is in the country of Rhodesia. What decade is it when this incident takes place? (the 1970s)

E Nyasha is probably not included in the description of loose women. However, her aunt wants Tambudzai to be educated, and her aunt feels that often it is educated women who are characterized as "loose."

F ASK Comprehension Why do you think Maiguru refers to Tambudzai, who is her niece, as her daughter here? (Probably because she thinks of her as a daughter.)

G ASK Literary Element What was the climax of the plot of this story? (The point in Maiguru's speech in which she explained that Babamukuru's objections did not really apply to Tambudzai.)

Discussion Questions

A ASK Critical Thinking Babamukuru told Tambudzai that he did not think he would allow her to go to the convent school. Why do you think he changed his mind? (His wife pointed out that his reasons were groundless.)

B ASK Critical Thinking Why did Tambudzai consider the opportunity to go to the convent school a step toward freedom? (She believed that a good education would enable her to overcome some of the restrictions and poor conditions in which her people lived.)

Learning Styles

Auditory Several episodes of dialogue in this story lend themselves to rich oral interpretation. Ask volunteers to take parts of the different characters and read with expression the one with Babamukuru and Maiguru (and Tambudzai, who is silent) on pages 111 through 113 and the one between Babamukuru and Tambudzai's father on pages 113 through 114.

"On the other hand," continued my uncle, "she would receive a first-class education."

"Ah, ya, Mukoma, first class. First class," my father **enthused.**

"I did not want her to go to that school..." said Babamukuru.

"What for, Mukoma? Why should she go there? Your mission is first class."

A "...because of the reasons I have told you," continued my uncle. "But then, considering that this is a fine opportunity for the girl to receive the finest education in Rhodesia, I think she must not be denied the opportunity. I have decided to let her go."

Rhodesia is now called Zimbabwe.

My father went down on one knee. Bo-bo-bo. "We thank you, Chirandu, we thank you, Muera bonga, Chihwa" he **intoned.** "Truly, we would not **survive** without you. Our children would not survive without you. Head of the family, princeling, we thank you."

This is how it was settled. I was to take another step upwards **B** in the direction of my freedom. Another step away from the flies, the smells, the fields and the rags; from stomachs which were seldom full, from dirt and disease, from my father's **abject obeisance** to Babamukuru and my mother's **chronic lethargy**. Also from Nyamarira that I loved.

abject humble; without self-respect

chronic constant; continuing

enthuse to show excitement or interest

intone to speak in a chant

lethargy drowsiness; slowness

obeisance a respectful gesture or attitude

survive to stay alive

REVIEWING the SELECTION

Nervous Conditions

Tsitsi Dangarembga

Directions Write the answers to these questions using complete sentences.

Comprehension: Identifying Facts

1. Who runs the school Tambudzai wants to go to?
2. Who is Babamukuru?
3. Who speaks up in favor of the school?

Comprehension: Understanding Main Ideas

4. What is Tambudzai's family discussing?
5. Why does Tambudzai want to go away to school?
6. Why does Nyasha think Tambudzai should not go to the convent school?

Understanding Literature: Coming-of-Age Story

This is a coming-of-age story. The main character, Tambudzai, experiences new events that help her grow up. She learns that choosing a school is not just about whether her family can afford it. She learns about the power of those who make decisions. She also learns about prejudice.

7. How does Tambudzai find out what the family is saying about her and the school?
8. What does Tambudzai learn about herself when her uncle talks about marriage?

Critical Thinking

9. Why is it Babamukuru who makes the decision about the school?
10. Why does Babamukuru finally say Tambudzai can go to the convent school?

Writing on Your Own Write a brief description of a person who learns something important. This can be the beginning of a coming-of-age story. It might be about yourself or someone you know. Or, it can be entirely made up. Think about how the character will change because of the experience.

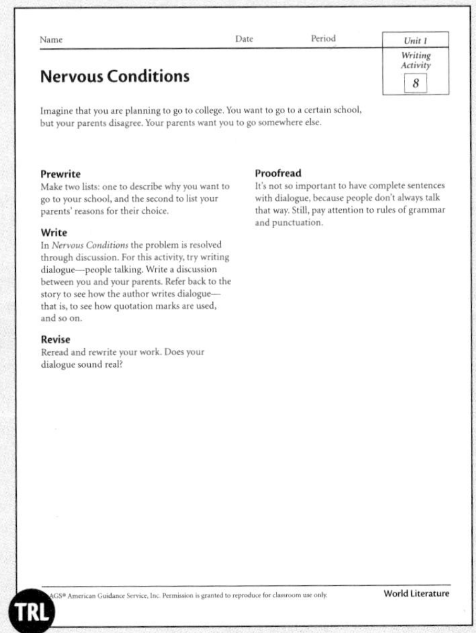

Name Date Period

Unit 1 *Writing Activity* 8

Nervous Conditions

Imagine that you are planning to go to college. You want to go to a certain school, but your parents disagree. Your parents want you to go somewhere else.

Prewrite
Make two lists: one to describe why you want to go to your school, and the second to list your parents' reasons for their choice.

Write
In *Nervous Conditions* the problem is resolved through discussion. For this activity, try writing dialogue—people talking. Write a discussion between you and your parents. Refer back to the story to see how the author writes dialogue—that is, to see how quotation marks are used, and so on.

Revise
Reread and rewrite your work. Does your dialogue sound real?

Proofread
It's not so important to have complete sentences with dialogue, because people don't always talk that way. Still, pay attention to rules of grammar and punctuation.

 World Literature

TRL

Writing Activity 8

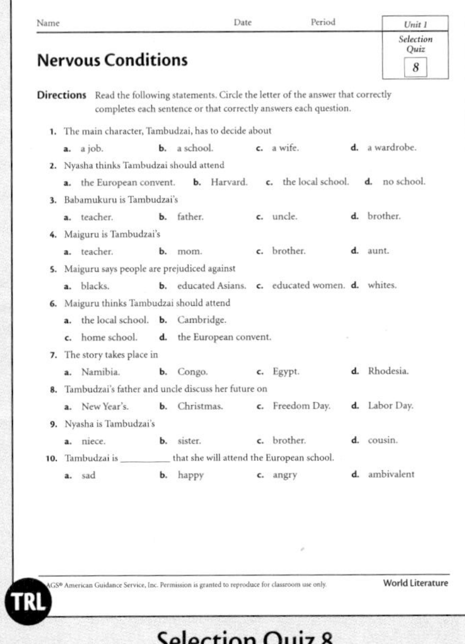

Name Date Period

Unit 1 *Selection Quiz* 8

Nervous Conditions

Directions Read the following statements. Circle the letter of the answer that correctly completes each sentence or that correctly answers each question.

1. The main character, Tambudzai, has to decide about
   a. a job. **b.** a school. **c.** a wife. **d.** a wardrobe.
2. Nyasha thinks Tambudzai should attend
   a. the European convent. **b.** Harvard. **c.** the local school. **d.** no school.
3. Babamukuru is Tambudzai's
   a. teacher. **b.** father. **c.** uncle. **d.** brother.
4. Maiguru is Tambudzai's
   a. teacher. **b.** mom. **c.** brother. **d.** aunt.
5. Maiguru says people are prejudiced against
   a. blacks. **b.** educated Asians. **c.** educated women. **d.** whites.
6. Maiguru thinks Tambudzai should attend
   a. the local school. **b.** Cambridge.
   c. home school. **d.** the European convent.
7. The story takes place in
   a. Namibia. **b.** Congo. **c.** Egypt. **d.** Rhodesia.
8. Tambudzai's father and uncle discuss her future on
   a. New Year's. **b.** Christmas. **c.** Freedom Day. **d.** Labor Day.
9. Nyasha is Tambudzai's
   a. niece. **b.** sister. **c.** brother. **d.** cousin.
10. Tambudzai is __________ that she will attend the European school.
   a. sad **b.** happy **c.** angry **d.** ambivalent

 World Literature

TRL

Selection Quiz 8

Reviewing the Selection

Answer Key

Comprehension: Identifying Facts

1. Missionary nuns run the school that Tambudzai wants to go to.

2. Babamukuru is her uncle who runs the local mission school.

3. Nyasha, Babamukuru's daughter, speaks in favor of the school he runs.

Comprehension: Understanding Main Ideas

4. The family discusses whether she should go the convent school.

5. She knows she will get a better education.

6. Nyasha is afraid that Tambudzai will forget her own people.

Understanding Literature: Coming-of-Age Story

7. Both Nyasha and Babamukuru tell her their concerns.

8. She realizes that she does not even want to think about marriage for herself because she is afraid it will disrupt her life even before she begins living it.

Critical Thinking

9. He is clearly the head of the family and the most powerful person in it.

10. His wife persuades him that his reasons for keeping Tambudzai home are not valid.

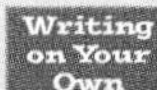

Point out to students that a turning point is usually when a person learns something important about themselves, even though the situation may be prompted by another person or situation.

Selection Quiz

The Teacher's Resource Library includes a Selection Quiz for *Nervous Conditions* that may be given following the Selection Review.

Selection at a Glance

Marriage Is a Private Affair

Chinua Achebe

Student pages 116–125

Overview

Chinua Achebe's work has won many awards. He was one of the founders of the "new Nigerian literature" that reflected the oral tradition and rapidly changing society.

Selection Summary

In "Marriage Is a Private Affair" by Chinua Achebe, a Nigerian family is split when a man marries a woman who is not of his tribe.

Objectives

- To identify and understand third-person point of view.
- To appreciate a turning-point story set in a different culture.

Audiocassette

Teacher's Resource Library TRL

- Vocabulary Workbook 9, pages 1–2
- Selection Glossary 9
- Student Study Guide 15, pages 1–2
- Activity 14, pages 1–2
- Workbook 14, pages 1–2
- Writing Activity 9
- Selection Quiz 9

INTRODUCING the SELECTION

Marriage Is a Private Affair

Chinua Achebe

Chinua Achebe
(1930–)
Nigerian

Literary Term

third-person a point of view that refers to characters as "he" or "she" and expresses some characters' thoughts

About the Author

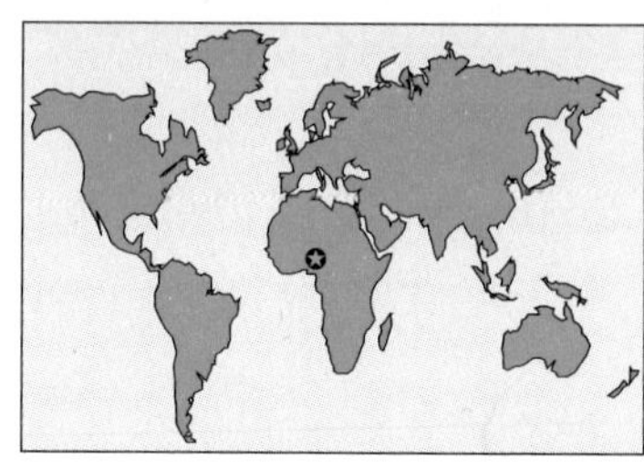

Chinua Achebe is one of Nigeria's most popular writers. He was born in Ogidi, Nigeria, on November 16, 1930. He graduated from the University College at Ibadan in 1953. He was a teacher and has worked in radio. Achebe often writes about a conflict between traditional African culture and new ideas. His first novel, in 1958, was *Things Fall Apart*. Others are *No Longer at Ease* and *A Man of the People*. He also writes poems and short stories. Achebe writes in English. His books have been translated into many other languages.

About the Selection

Achebe looks at conflicts between customs. A young Nigerian, Nnaemeka, plans to marry Nene. She is city-bred and from another tribe. Back in his home town, Nnaemeka's father Okeke has already chosen a wife for Nnaemeka. Nnaemeka still marries Nene. Okeke believes in tradition and is angry when his son defies his wishes. He will have nothing to do with the new wife. The son and father in this story are Ibos, which is one of Nigeria's many large tribal groups. (The author is also Ibo.) The story reveals how old customs continue. It is told in **third-person**.

116 *Unit 1 Fiction*

Setting the Stage for Reading

About the Author

Explain that Chinua Achebe is one of Nigeria's finest novelists. He has worked as a writer in broadcasting and has also been a publisher. He believes that "any good story, any good novel, should have a message, should have a purpose."

ASK Do you agree that a story should have a purpose or message? (Let students discuss this. Some will feel that stories and novels should entertain, but most will agree that stories might seem meaningless without a message.)

About the Selection

In this story, a man who is loyal to the traditional ways of doing things almost loses sight of what is more important to him—his family.

Activate Prior Knowledge: Invite students to discuss briefly other stories they have read about individuals who have a conflict within themselves.

ASK What might it be like to have a conflict within yourself? (You might feel torn because you feel two different ways about something.)

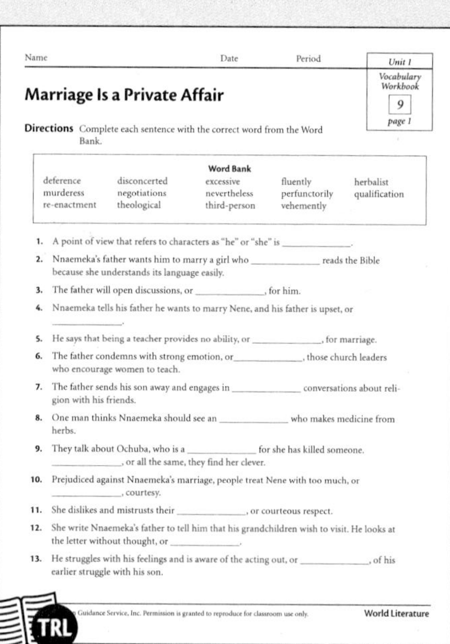

Name Date Period

Unit 1
Vocabulary Workbook
9
page 1

Marriage Is a Private Affair

Directions Complete each sentence with the correct word from the Word Bank.

Word Bank				
deference	disconcerted	excessive	fluently	herbalist
murderess	negotiations	nevertheless	perfunctorily	qualification
re-enactment	theological	third-person	vehemently	

1. A point of view that refers to characters as "he" or "she" is ____________.
2. Nnaemeka's father wants him to marry a girl who ____________ reads the Bible because she understands its language easily.
3. The father will open discussions, or ____________, for him.
4. Nnaemeka tells his father he wants to marry Nene, and his father is upset, or ____________.
5. He says that being a teacher provides no ability, or ____________, for marriage.
6. The father condemns with strong emotion, or ____________, those church leaders who encourage women to teach.
7. The father sends his son away and engages in ____________ conversations about religion with his friends.
8. One man thinks Nnaemeka should see an ____________ who makes medicine from herbs.
9. They talk about Ochuba, who is a ____________ for she has killed someone. ____________, or all the same, they find her clever.
10. Prejudiced against Nnaemeka's marriage, people treat Nene with too much, or ____________, courtesy.
11. She dislikes and mistrusts their ____________, or courteous respect.
12. She write Nnaemeka's father to tell him that his grandchildren wish to visit. He looks at the letter without thought, or ____________.
13. He struggles with his feelings and is aware of the acting out, or ____________, of his earlier struggle with his son.

 World Literature

TRL **Vocabulary Workbook 9, pages 1–2**

Marriage Is a Private Affair

Chinua Achebe

"Have you written to your dad yet?" asked Nene one afternoon as she sat with Nnaemeka in her room at 16 Kasanga Street, Lagos.

"No. I've been thinking about it. I think it's better to tell him when I get home on **leave**!"

"But why? Your leave is such a long way off yet—six whole weeks. He should be let into our happiness now."

Nnaemeka was silent for a while, and then began very slowly as if he groped for his words: "I wish I were sure it would be happiness to him."

"Of course it must," replied Nene, a little surprised. "Why shouldn't it?"

"You have lived in Lagos all your life, and you know very little about people in remote parts of the country."

"That's what you always say. But I don't believe anybody will be so unlike other people that they will be unhappy when their sons are engaged to marry."

A "Yes. They are most unhappy if the engagement is not arranged by them. In our case it's worse—you are not even an Ibo."

B This was said so seriously and so bluntly that Nene could not find speech immediately. In the **cosmopolitan** atmosphere of the city it had always seemed to her something of a joke that a person's tribe could determine whom he married.

As you read, notice when the writer seems to know the thoughts of a character.

Lagos is the largest city in Nigeria.

Nigeria has many different ethnic groups, each with its own customs and language. The *Ibo* are one of the largest. As you will see, tribal differences are still important, especially in rural areas.

cosmopolitan including people from many places

leave a vacation; permission to be away from work

Reading Vocabulary TRL

Help students preview the selection's vocabulary words by giving them copies of the Selection Glossary. Have pairs of students take turns making up a sentence using one of the words.

Motivation for Reading

Nnaemeka has a conflict with his father. But his father has an even greater conflict. Suggest that students read the story to find out what that conflict is and how it is resolved.

Discussion Questions

Suggest that students skim the selection to find the answer to the question in the margin of the student text.

A ASK Literary Element What is the basic conflict in this story? (Nnaemeka's father disapproves of his marriage to Nene because fathers always choose brides for their sons from their own tribe, and neither of those conditions has been met.)

B ASK Comprehension Why does Nene have trouble understanding Nnaemeka's father's objections? (She has lived in a large city all her life and has not really learned about the power of the tribal customs.)

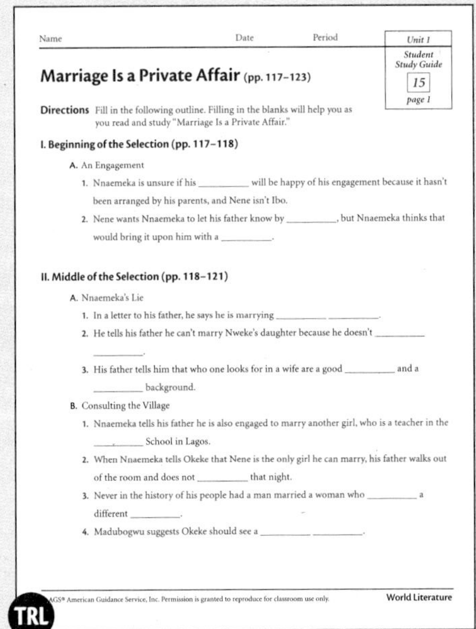

Name Date Period Unit 1 Student Study Guide 15 page 1

Marriage Is a Private Affair (pp. 117–123)

Directions Fill in the following outline. Filling in the blanks will help you as you read and study "Marriage Is a Private Affair."

I. Beginning of the Selection (pp. 117–118)

A. An Engagement
1. Nnaemeka is unsure if his ________ will be happy of his engagement because it hasn't been arranged by his parents, and Nene isn't Ibo.
2. Nene wants Nnaemeka to let his father know by ________, but Nnaemeka thinks that would bring it upon him with a ________.

II. Middle of the Selection (pp. 118–121)

A. Nnaemeka's Lie
1. In a letter to his father, he says he is marrying ________ ________.
2. He tells his father he can't marry Nweke's daughter because he doesn't ________ ________.
3. His father tells him that who one looks for in a wife are a good ________ and a ________ background.

B. Consulting the Village
1. Nnaemeka tells his father he is also engaged to marry another girl, who is a teacher in the ________ School in Lagos.
2. When Nnaemeka tells Okeke that Nene is the only girl he can marry, his father walks out of the room and does not ________ that night.
3. Never in the history of his people had a man married a woman who ________ a different ________.
4. Madubogwu suggests Okeke should see a ________ ________.

 World Literature

TRL Student Study Guide 15, pages 1–2

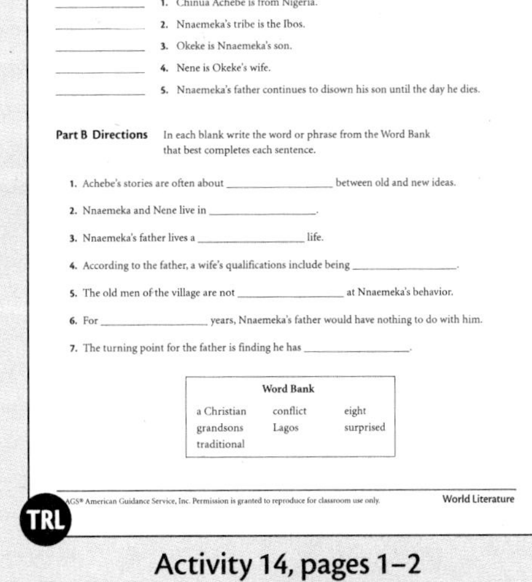

Name Date Period Unit 1 Activity 14 page 1

Marriage Is a Private Affair

Part A Directions Read each sentence. Write *T* if the statement is true or *F* if it is false.

________ 1. Chinua Achebe is from Nigeria.
________ 2. Nnaemeka's tribe is the Ibos.
________ 3. Okeke is Nnaemeka's son.
________ 4. Nene is Okeke's wife.
________ 5. Nnaemeka's father continues to disown his son until the day he dies.

Part B Directions In each blank write the word or phrase from the Word Bank that best completes each sentence.

1. Achebe's stories are often about ________ between old and new ideas.
2. Nnaemeka and Nene live in ________.
3. Nnaemeka's father lives a ________ life.
4. According to the father, a wife's qualifications include being ________.
5. The old men of the village are not ________ at Nnaemeka's behavior.
6. For ________ years, Nnaemeka's father would have nothing to do with him.
7. The turning point for the father is finding he has ________.

Word Bank		
a Christian	conflict	eight
grandsons	Lagos	surprised
traditional		

 World Literature

TRL Activity 14, pages 1–2

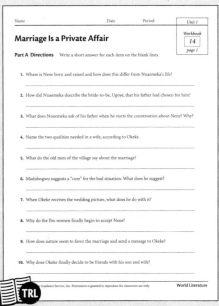

Name Date Period Unit 1 Workbook 14 page 1

Marriage Is a Private Affair

Part A Directions Write a short answer for each item on the blank lines.

1. Where is Nene born and raised and how does this differ from Nnaemeka's life?
2. How did Nnaemeka describe the bride-to-be, Ugoye, that his father had chosen for him?
3. What does Nnaemeka ask of his father when he starts the conversation about Nene? Why?
4. Name the two qualities needed in a wife, according to Okeke.
5. What do the old men of the village say about the marriage?
6. Madubogwu suggests a "cure" for the bad situation. What does he suggest?
7. When Okeke receives the wedding picture, what does he do with it?
8. Why do the Ibo women finally begin to accept Nene?
9. How does nature seem to favor the marriage and send a message to Okeke?
10. Why does Okeke finally decide to be friends with his son and wife?

 World Literature

TRL Workbook 14, pages 1–2

Discussion Questions

A ASK Comprehension Why is Nnaemeka especially hesitant to write his father a letter about Nene? (He has received a letter from his father saying that his father has picked out a bride for him from their own tribe.)

B ASK Comprehension How does knowing something about Greek mythology sometimes help you understand what you are reading? (Often writers make references to characters or situations from Greek mythology in order to describe something they are writing about, as does Chinua Achebe with his comparison of Nnaemeka's intended bride to an Amazon. That tells us immediately that she is strong, tough, and probably also physically large.)

Literary Elements

Allusions Greek and Roman mythology provide a rich source of literary references. In fact, people without some knowledge of mythology can miss allusions and comparisons made by many writers. Ask volunteers to do some research and make a brief list of some of the most important Greek and Roman gods and goddesses and their attributes. Suggest that students watch for references to the gods and goddesses in their reading and, in fact, in advertisements they see and hear. You may want to start them off by suggesting they find out why someone would want to name a car Mercury.

At last she said, "You don't really mean that he will object to your marrying me simply on that account? I had always thought you Ibos were kindly disposed to other people."

"So we are. But when it comes to marriage, well, it's not quite so simple. And this," he added, "is not peculiar to the Ibos. If your father were alive and lived in the heart of Ibibio-land he would be exactly like my father."

"I don't know. But anyway, as your father is so fond of you, I'm sure he will forgive you soon enough. Come on then, be a good boy and send him a nice lovely letter..."

In Nnaemeka's tribe, parents chose marriage partners for their children. This is called an arranged marriage.

A "It would not be wise to break the news to him by writing. A letter will bring it upon him with a shock. I'm quite sure about that."

"All right, honey, suit yourself. You know your father."

As Nnaemeka walked home that evening he turned over in his mind the different ways of overcoming his father's opposition, especially now that he had gone and found a girl for him. He had thought of showing his letter to Nene but decided on second thoughts not to, at least for the moment. He read it again when he got home and couldn't help smiling to himself. He remembered Ugoye quite well, an Amazon of a girl who used to beat up all the **B** boys, himself included, on the way to the stream, a complete **dunce** at school.

In Greek mythology, an *Amazon* was a woman warrior.

I have found a girl who will suit you admirably—Ugoye Nweke, the eldest daughter of our neighbour, Jacob Nweke. She has a proper Christian upbringing. When she stopped schooling some years ago her father (a man of sound judgment) sent her to live in the house of a ***pastor*** *where she has received all the training a wife could need. Her Sunday School teacher has told me that she reads her Bible very*

dunce a stupid person

pastor a Christian minister

fluently. I hope we shall begin ***negotiations*** *when you come home in December.*

On the second evening of his return from Lagos Nnaemeka sat with his father under a cassia tree. This was the old man's retreat where he went to read his Bible when the **parching** December sun had set and a fresh, reviving wind blew on the leaves.

"Father," began Nnaemeka suddenly, "I have come to ask forgiveness."

"Forgiveness? For what, my son?" he asked in amazement.

"It's about this marriage question."

"Which marriage question?"

"I can't—we must—I mean it is impossible for me to marry Nweke's daughter."

"Impossible? Why?" asked his father.

"I don't love her."

"Nobody said you did. Why should you?" he asked. **C**

"Marriage today is different..."

"Look here, my son," interrupted his father, "nothing is different. What one looks for in a wife are a good character and a Christian background."

Nnaemeka saw there was no hope along the present line of argument.

"Moreover," he said, "I am engaged to marry another girl who has all of Ugoye's good qualities, and who . . ."

His father did not believe his ears. "What did you say?" he asked slowly and **disconcertingly.**

"She is a good Christian," his son went on, "and a teacher in a Girls' School in Lagos."

"Teacher, did you say? If you consider that a **qualification** for a good wife I should like to point out to you, Emeka, that no **D** Christian woman should teach. St. Paul in his letter to the Corinthians says that women should keep silence." He rose slowly from his seat and paced forwards and backwards. This was his pet

St. Paul wrote letters to the church at Corinth. They make up two books of the New Testament of the Christian Bible.

disconcertingly in an upsetting way

fluently using language easily

negotiations discussions leading to an agreement

parching very dry

qualification an ability that suits a person for a certain task

C ASK Comprehension Why does Nnaemeka's father not consider it a problem that Nnaemeka does not love Ugoye, the woman his father wants him to marry? (Clearly love is not important to an arranged marriage in the customary tradition of the tribe.)

D ASK Critical Thinking Do you think most people in the United States today would agree with Nnaemeka's father that "no Christian woman should teach"? (No, because most teachers are women and many people in the United States consider themselves to be Christians.)

Cross-Curricular Connection

Science Remind students that this story takes place in Nigeria, a country in Africa. Point out the reference near the top of page 119 to "the parching December sun." Ask volunteers to use their knowledge of Nigeria's location on Earth and what causes the seasons to explain why it is hot in Nigeria in December.

Fiction Unit 1 **119**

Discussion Questions

A ASK Comprehension Why does Nnaemeka's father seem uninterested in Nene and why does he ask only about her family? (In their custom, people marry only within the tribe where presumably they know everyone's family. Nene is not only a stranger to him but also a member of another tribe.)

B ASK Vocabulary The word *behavior* usually does not have the letter *u* in it. Why is it spelled *behaviour* in the last line on this page? (That is the British spelling. You may want to explain to students that many Africans, like this author, were educated in schools influenced by the British because of the British occupation of much of Africa in years past.)

subject, and he condemned **vehemently** those church leaders who encouraged women to teach in their schools. After he had spent his emotion on a long **homily** he at last came back to his son's engagement, in a seemingly milder tone.

Note that the father is not interested in the woman herself. He only wants to know about her family.

A "Whose daughter is she, anyway?"

"She is Nene Atang."

"What!" All the mildness was gone again. "Did you say Neneataga, what does that mean?"

"Nene Atang from Calabar. She is the only girl I can marry." This was a very **rash** reply and Nnaemeka expected the storm to burst. But it did not. His father merely walked away into his room. This was most unexpected and perplexed Nnaemeka. His father's silence was **infinitely** more menacing than a flood of threatening speech. That night the old man did not eat.

When he sent for Nnaemeka a day later he applied all possible ways of **dissuasion**. But the young man's heart was hardened, and his father eventually gave him up as lost.

"I owe it to you, my son, as a duty to show you what is right and what is wrong. Whoever put this idea into your head might as well have cut your throat. It is Satan's work." He waved his son away.

"You will change your mind, Father, when you know Nene."

"I shall never see her," was the reply. From that night the father scarcely spoke to his son. He did not, however, cease hoping that he would realize how serious was the danger he was heading for. Day and night he put him in his prayers.

Nnaemeka, for his own part, was very deeply affected by his father's grief. But he kept hoping that it would pass away. It if had occurred to him that never in the history of his people had a man married a woman who spoke a different tongue, he might have been less optimistic. "It has never been heard," was the verdict of an old man speaking a few weeks later. In that short sentence he spoke for all of his people. This man had come with others to **commiserate** with Okeke when news went round about his son's **B** behaviour. By that time the son had gone back to Lagos.

commiserate to express sorrow and sympathy

dissuasion discouraging someone from an action

homily a sermon

infinitely without any limits

rash bold; hasty

vehemently with strong emotion

120 *Unit 1 Fiction*

"It has never been heard," said the old man again with a sad shake of his head. **C**

Note that the entire village is concerned.

"What did Our Lord say?" asked another gentleman. "Sons shall rise against their Fathers; it is there in the Holy Book."

"It is the beginning of the end," said another.

The discussion thus tending to become **theological**, Madubogwu, a highly practical man, brought it down once more to the ordinary level.

"Have you thought of consulting a native doctor about your son?" he asked Nnaemeka's father.

"He isn't sick," was the reply.

"What is he then? The boy's mind is diseased and only a good **herbalist** can bring him back to his right senses. The medicine he requires is *Amalile,* the same that women apply with success to recapture their husbands' straying affection."

"Madubogwu is right," said another gentleman. "This thing calls for medicine."

"I shall not call in a native doctor." Nnaemeka's father was known to be **obstinately** ahead of his more superstitious neighbours in these matters. "I will not be another Mrs. Ochuba. If my son wants to kill himself let him do it with his own hands. It is not for me to help him."

Nnaemeka's father does not hold with every tradition among the Ibo.

"But it was her fault," said Madubogwu. "She ought to have gone to an honest herbalist. She was a clever woman, **nevertheless**."

"She was a wicked **murderess**," said Jonathan who rarely argued with his neighbours because, he often said, they were **incapable** of reasoning. "The medicine was prepared for her husband, it was his name they called in its preparation and I am sure it would have been perfectly **beneficial** to him. It was wicked to put it into the herbalist's food, and say you were only trying it out."

Six months later, Nnaemeka was showing his young wife a short letter from his father: **D**

beneficial doing good; helpful

herbalist a person who makes medicines from herbs

incapable without the ability

murderess a woman who kills someone

nevertheless all the same

obstinately stubbornly

theological related to the study of religion

C ASK Comprehension Why do you suppose the whole village shares Nnaemeka's father's concern about Nnaemeka's marriage? (They all feel the same way about marrying out of the tribe, and they worry about the old ways being lost.)

D ASK Literary Element Who do you think has the more serious conflict, Nnaemeka or his father? (Probably his father. Nnaemeka gets married, anyway, to the woman he loves. But his father still faces the conflict between accepting Nnaemeka's behavior and insisting on the tribal ways.)

Learning Styles

Auditory This story lends itself well to a readers' theater. Ask students to take the parts of the various characters including the narrator. Have them read the story aloud, using the tone of voice and expression they think each character would in the circumstances of the story.

Discussion Questions

A **ASK Literary Element** From what you know of Nnaemeka's father, do you think he is stubborn, prideful, loyal, or perhaps all three? (He is probably all of those things. He is stubborn because he has made up his mind and is sticking to it. He is prideful because he refuses to change his mind. And he is very loyal to his tribal customs.)

B Most students will agree that Nnaemeka and Nene are strong people because they are going on to make their own lives as happy as possible despite Nnaemeka's father.

Grammar

Quoted Material Point out to students that in this story the quotations from the letters written by several characters are indicated by the use of italics. Explain that more often such quoted excerpts might be indicated by the use of opening and closing quotation marks and, perhaps, bigger margins on one or both sides of the quoted material. Explain that such conventions of the written language need mainly to be clear to the reader. Sometimes there are several acceptable ways of doing things, as this example shows.

It amazes me that you could be so unfeeling as to send me your wedding picture. I would have sent it back. But on further thought I decided just to cut off your wife and send it back to you because I have nothing to do with her. How I wish that I had nothing to do with you either.

When Nene read through this letter and looked at the **mutilated** picture her eyes filled with tears, and she began to sob.

"Don't cry, my darling," said her husband. "He is essentially good-natured and will one day look more kindly on our marriage." But years passed and that one day did not come.

A For eight years, Okeke would have nothing to do with his son, Nnaemeka. Only three times (when Nnaemeka asked to come home and spend his leave) did he write to him.

"I can't have you in my house," he replied on one occasion. "It can be of no interest to me where or how you spend your leave—or your life, for that matter."

The prejudice against Nnaemeka's marriage was not confined to his little village. In Lagos, especially among his people who worked there, it showed itself in a different way. Their women, when they met at their village meeting were not **hostile** to Nene. Rather, they paid her such **excessive deference** as to make her feel she was not one of them. But as time went on, Nene gradually broke through some of this prejudice and even began to make friends among them. Slowly and **grudgingly** they began to admit that she kept her home much better than most of them.

B
Do you think that Nnaemeka and Nene are strong people? Why or why not?

The story eventually got to the little village in the heart of the Ibo country that Nnaemeka and his young wife were a most happy couple. But his father was one of the few people who knew nothing about this. He always displayed so much temper whenever his son's name was mentioned that everyone avoided it in his presence. By a tremendous effort of will he had succeeded in pushing his son to the back of his mind. The strain had nearly killed him but he had **persevered**, and won.

Then one day he received a letter from Nene, and in spite of himself he began to glance through it **perfunctorily** until all of a

deference courteous respect
excessive too much
grudgingly unwillingly
hostile angrily opposed to
mutilated cut up; damaged
perfunctorily without thought or care
persevere to carry on in spite of difficulties

122 *Unit 1 Fiction*

sudden the expression on his face changed and he began to read more carefully.

...Our two sons, from the day they learnt that they have a grandfather, have insisted on being taken to him. I find it impossible to tell them that you will not see them. I ***implore*** *you to allow Nnaemeka to bring them home for a short time during his leave next month. I shall remain here in Lagos....* **C**

The old man at once felt the resolution he had built up over so many years falling in. He was telling himself that he must not give in. He tried to steel his heart against all emotional appeals. It was a **re-enactment** of that other struggle. He leaned against a window and looked out. The sky was overcast with heavy black clouds and a high wind began to blow filling the air with dust and dry leaves. It was one of those rare occasions when even Nature takes a hand in a human fight. Very soon it began to rain, the first rain in the year. It came down in large sharp drops and was accompanied by the lightning and thunder which mark a change of season. Okeke was trying hard not to think of his two grandsons. But he knew he was now fighting a losing battle. He tried to hum a favourite hymn but the pattering of large rain drops on the roof broke up the tune. His mind immediately returned to the children. How could he shut his door against them? By a curious mental process he imagined them standing, sad and **forsaken,** under the harsh angry weather—shut out from his house.

D
How is the weather like what is going on in Okeke's heart?

symbol

That night he hardly slept, from **remorse**—and a vague fear that he might die without making it up to them.

RRAS JurL

forsaken abandoned; left alone

implore to beg

re-enactment acting out something that happened once before

remorse regret for having done something harmful

C ASK Critical Thinking Why do you think Nene finally wrote a letter to her father-in-law? (She wanted her sons to meet their grandfather, and she may have been kind enough to want the rift between her husband and his father to end, as well.)

D In an apt comparison, the tension of the buildup of the storm and the final release of the rain mimics the feelings of Okeke's heart. Additionally, the storm makes him somehow picture his grandsons shut out in it because he will not let them in. He knows he must allow them into the house—and into his heart.

Reviewing the Selection

Answer Key

Comprehension: Identifying Facts

1. They live in the city of Lagos. Nene has always lived there, but Nnaemeka previously lived in a village of his tribe.
2. His tribe is the Ibo.
3. He wants to tell his father in person because he has found out that his father has plans for him to marry someone else.
4. Nnaemeka's father wants him to marry a woman named Ugoye Nweke, the daughter of a neighbor.
5. The two things his father thinks are important in a wife are good character and a Christian background.
6. Okeke cuts Nene out of the wedding picture.
7. The village eventually heard that Nene and Nnaemeka were very happy together.
8. Okeke doesn't know about the story because he refuses to listen to anything about his son.
9. Nene writes to Okeke to ask him to see her sons, his grandsons.
10. Okeke worries that night that he might die before he can make up to his grandsons what he has done by not being involved in their lives.

Comprehension: Understanding Main Ideas

11. She believes that he can simply tell his father about their relationship.
12. She assumes the tribal difference doesn't matter if they are happy together.
13. Okeke expects to find a wife for his son.
14. He asks for Okeke's forgiveness because he does not want to marry the woman Okeke has chosen for him.
15. He objects because St. Paul, in the Bible, wrote that women should be silent.
16. Nnaemeka hardens his heart to his father's grief and goes ahead with his marriage.
17. They are just as worried about it as Okeke is.
18. He does not agree with some of their superstitions about their native medicine.
19. They eventually accept her and make friends with her.
20. The idea of seeing his grandsons changes his mind.

REVIEWING the SELECTION

Marriage Is a Private Affair

Chinua Achebe

Directions Write the answers to these questions using complete sentences.

Comprehension: Identifying Facts

1. Where do Nnaemeka and Nene live? Have they always lived there?
2. What is Nnaemeka's tribe?
3. Why does Nnaemeka want to tell his father about their engagement in person?
4. Whom does Nnaemeka's father want him to marry?
5. What two things does the father say are important in a wife?
6. What does Okeke, the father, do with the wedding picture?
7. What story gets back to the village about Nene and Nnaemeka?
8. Why doesn't Okeke know about the story?
9. Why does Nene write to Okeke?
10. What does Okeke worry about that night?

Comprehension: Understanding Main Ideas

11. Why does Nene think Nnaemeka should write to his father?
12. Why does Nene think the tribal difference won't matter?
13. How does Okeke expect his son to get a wife?
14. Why does Nnaemeka ask for his father's forgiveness?
15. Why does Okeke object to women being teachers?
16. How does Nnaemeka react to his father's grief?
17. How do the other men in the village feel about Nnaemeka's marriage?
18. In what way is Okeke less traditional than other men in the village?
19. How does Nene get along with the Ibo women in Lagos?
20. What changes Okeke's mind about the marriage?

124 *Unit 1 Fiction*

Understanding Literature: Third-Person

"Marriage Is a Private Affair" is a third-person story. The writer speaks of all the characters as "he" or "she." The reader knows the thoughts and actions of the major characters. A third-person story can show what is going on in Lagos with Nene and Nnaemeka. It can also show what is going on in the village with Okeke and his friends. The ideas of all the main characters are clear. So are the ideas of some less important characters.

21. Whose thoughts does the reader know about?
22. Who is the first person whose thoughts the reader knows? Who is the last?
23. How does the reader know what the villagers think?
24. If the story were told in the first-person, who would the narrator probably be? Explain.
25. Who writes the letters in the story?

Critical Thinking

26. How was Nnaemeka's boyhood different from the way Nene grew up?
27. How does Nnaemeka feel about the letter from his father?
28. In what way is Nnaemeka surprised by his father's reaction?
29. What happened when the village woman consulted the herbalist?
30. How does Okeke feel at the end of the story?

Writing on Your Own Write the beginning of a story. Use the third-person. In your beginning, show that there will be several characters and situations. Share your story beginning with a partner.

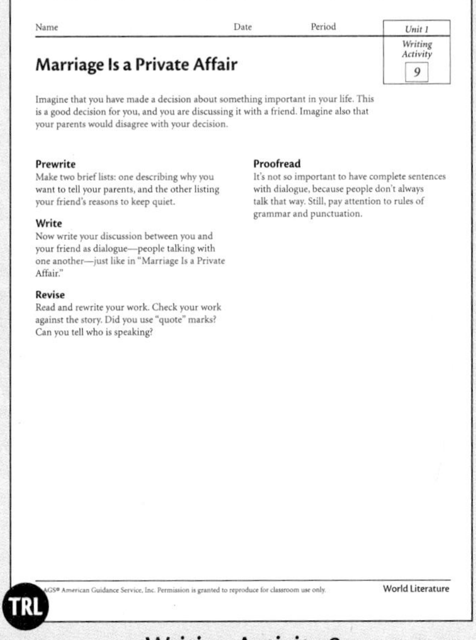

Name Date Period

Unit 1
Writing Activity
9

Marriage Is a Private Affair

Imagine that you have made a decision about something important in your life. This is a good decision for you, and you are discussing it with a friend. Imagine also that your parents would disagree with your decision.

Prewrite
Make two brief lists: one describing why you want to tell your parents, and the other listing your friend's reasons to keep quiet.

Write
Now write your discussion between you and your friend as dialogue—people talking with one another—just like in "Marriage Is a Private Affair."

Revise
Read and rewrite your work. Check your work against the story. Did you use "quote" marks? Can you tell who is speaking?

Proofread
It's not so important to have complete sentences with dialogue, because people don't always talk that way. Still, pay attention to rules of grammar and punctuation.

 World Literature

TRL

Writing Activity 9

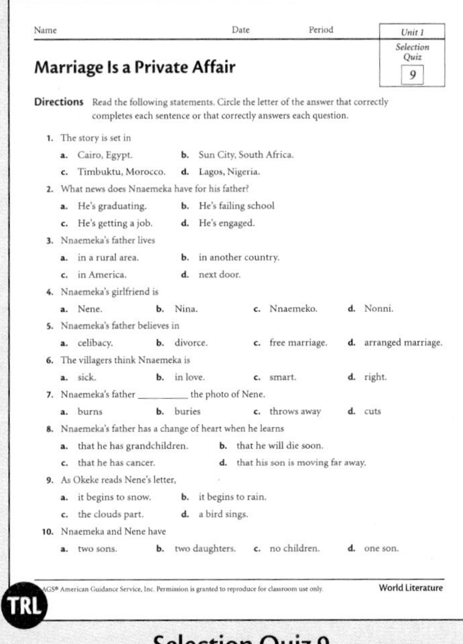

Name Date Period

Unit 1
Selection Quiz
9

Marriage Is a Private Affair

Directions Read the following statements. Circle the letter of the answer that correctly completes each sentence or that correctly answers each question.

1. The story is set in
   a. Cairo, Egypt. b. Sun City, South Africa. c. Timbuktu, Morocco. d. Lagos, Nigeria.
2. What news does Nnaemeka have for his father?
   a. He's graduating. b. He's failing school c. He's getting a job. d. He's engaged.
3. Nnaemeka's father lives
   a. in a rural area. b. in another country. c. in America. d. next door.
4. Nnaemeka's girlfriend is
   a. Nene. b. Nina. c. Nnaemeko. d. Nonni.
5. Nnaemeka's father believes in
   a. celibacy. b. divorce. c. free marriage. d. arranged marriage.
6. The villagers think Nnaemeka is
   a. sick. b. in love. c. smart. d. right.
7. Nnaemeka's father ________ the photo of Nene.
   a. burns b. buries c. throws away d. cuts
8. Nnaemeka's father has a change of heart when he learns
   a. that he has grandchildren. b. that he will die soon. c. that he has cancer. d. that his son is moving far away.
9. As Okeke reads Nene's letter,
   a. it begins to snow. b. it begins to rain. c. the clouds part. d. a bird sings.
10. Nnaemeka and Nene have
    a. two sons. b. two daughters. c. no children. d. one son.

 World Literature

TRL

Selection Quiz 9

Understanding Literature: Third-Person

21. In a story told from the third-person point of view, like this one, the reader can know the thoughts of all the characters.

22. In this story, the first person whose thoughts the reader understands is Nene during her confusion over Nnaemeka's worry about his father's reaction to their marriage. The last person whose thoughts the reader understands is Okeke.

23. The reader knows the villagers thoughts primarily through what they say in their conversation with Okeke.

24. The narrator would probably be Okeke because the major conflict is within his heart. Some students might choose Nnaemeka as the first-person narrator because the plot revolves around him.

25. The first letter quoted (on page 118) is written by Okeke. Okeke and Nnaemeka write to each other later (page 122). Nene writes the last letter in the story, as quoted on page 123.

Critical Thinking

26. Nnaemeka grew up in the tribal village, but Nene grew up in the city of Lagos.

27. Nnaemeka is bemused by the letter his father writes to tell him he has found a bride for Nnaemeka. In response to his father's letter about the wedding picture, Nnaemeka comforts his wife and insists that his father will eventually change his mind.

28. He is surprised that his father maintains the rift between them because he feels his father is good hearted and will eventually give up.

29. Apparently the woman tried the prescribed medicine on the herbalist himself, and the herbalist died.

30. Okeke feels remorseful at the end of the story, and he is clearly determined to change things.

Writing on Your Own Students may benefit from brainstorming story ideas with their partners before they begin writing.

Selection Quiz

The Teacher's Resource Library includes a Selection Quiz for "Marriage Is a Private Affair" that may be given following the Selection Review.

Selection at a Glance

Cranes

Hwang Sun-won
(translated by J. Martin Holman)

Student pages 126–133

Overview

The experience of war has been the subject of many writers. Hwang Sun-won's "Cranes" shows us not only the horror of war but also its impact on personal relationships and even childhood memories.

Selection Summary

In "Cranes" by Hwang Sun-won, a South Korean soldier meets a boyhood friend who has been taken prisoner as an enemy.

Objectives

- To recognize and appreciate an author's style.
- To understand how a character is revealed in a story.

Audiocassette 

Teacher's Resource Library TRL

- Vocabulary Workbook 10
- Selection Glossary 10
- Student Study Guide 16
- Activity 15
- Workbook 15
- Writing Activity 10
- Selection Quiz 10

INTRODUCING the SELECTION

Cranes

Hwang Sun-won (translated by J. Martin Holman)

Hwang Sun-won
(1915–)
Korean

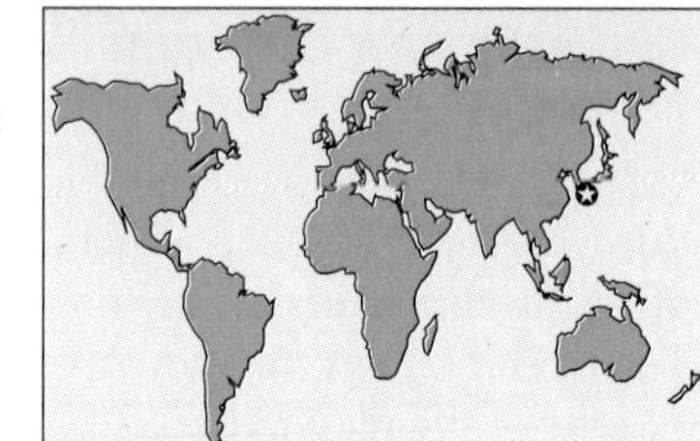

About the Author

Hwang Sun-won was born near Pyongyang, Korea. After World War II, Korea was divided. In 1946, his family moved from the Soviet-occupied north to South Korea. Hwang Sun-won lived through the Korean War in the 1950s. These wartime experiences affected his writing. Hwang Sun-won is a major figure in modern Korean literature. From 1957 to 1993, he taught Korean literature at Kyung Hee University in Seoul, South Korea. He is known as a master of the short story. He has also written novels and poems. His novel *Trees on the Cliff* won a major award in Korea. It has been published in English. Hwang Sun-won lives in Seoul with his wife.

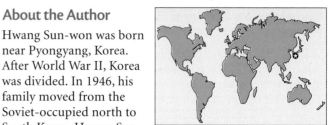

Literary Terms

style an author's way of writing

symbol a person, place, or thing that represents an idea or thought

About the Selection

"Cranes" is the story of friends divided by war. Its setting is divided Korea. One man, Tok-jae, is a North Korean communist. He has been taken prisoner by the South Korean army. The other is a South Korean soldier, Song-sam. Song-sam is to take Tok-jae for questioning. But he recognizes an old childhood friend. The two grew up together, but the war separated them. Song-sam is full of hatred toward his old friend.

"Cranes" has many **symbols**. Think about the divided country and the Demilitarized Zone. Notice the symbol of the captured crane and its flight. Also pay attention to the author's **style**. It is simple but says much more than the words. Hwang Sun-won's understanding of people comes through clearly.

126 *Unit 1 Fiction*

Setting the Stage for Reading

About the Author

Ask students to read page 126. Point out that the author lived through a war fought in his country and experienced its division into two countries with very different kinds of government.

ASK Why might a person who has been through a war choose to write about it rather than try to forget it? (Writers may want to share their experience with those who did not experience the war. They may also simply want to tell the stories that they experienced.)

About the Selection

The terrible irony of friends and families divided by war has been a topic of many stories and novels. In this one, it is the Korean War that has separated two childhood friends who meet again as enemies.

Activate Prior Knowledge: Have students briefly discuss other stories they have read or seen about war and its effects on people.

ASK Why would it be especially difficult to meet a childhood friend who is now your enemy in war? (In war, people need to believe they hate those on the other side. Finding that a friend is suddenly an enemy would be a terrible emotional conflict.)

CRANES

Hwang Sun-won

The village just north of the thirty-eighth parallel was quiet beneath the clear, **lofty** autumn sky.

A white **gourd** lay where it had tumbled, leaning against another on the dirt-floored space between the rooms of an **abandoned** house.

An old man Song-sam happened to meet put his long tobacco pipe **A** behind his back. The children, as children would, had already fled from the street to keep their distance. Everyone's face was masked with fear.

Overall, the village showed few signs of the **conflict** that had just ended. Still, it did not seem to Song- **B** sam to be the same village where he had grown up.

He stopped walking at a grove of **chestnut** trees on the hill behind the village. He climbed one of the trees. In his mind, from far away, he could hear the shouts of the old man with a **wen**. Are you kids climbing my chestnut tree again?

Had that old man died during Song-sam's absence? He had not seen him among the men he had met so far in the village. Hanging onto the

As you read, notice the author's style, or way of writing.

The *thirty-eighth parallel*, or line of latitude, is the dividing line between North and South Korea.

abandoned no longer lived in

chestnut a type of tree that has nuts enclosed in a prickly casing

conflict a battle; the fighting

gourd a kind of vegetable that grows on a vine

lofty high

wen a small growth on the skin

Reading Vocabulary TRL

Help students preview the selection's vocabulary words by giving them copies of the Selection Glossary. Have students work in small groups. One student chooses one of the words at random. The group member who defines the word correctly can choose another word for the group to define.

Motivation for Reading

Suggest that students read the story to find out how two childhood friends react to each other when they meet as enemies in war.

Discussion Questions

Use the questions in the margins of the student selection to help students focus and check their reading.

A ASK Critical Thinking How can you tell that this village is now on the opposite side of the war? (We know that Song-sam is a soldier for South Korea. People in the village seem afraid of him as he walks through. That indicates that they consider him to be their enemy.)

B ASK Comprehension You know that Song-sam is a South Korean soldier. Do you think it has been a while since he has been in this village where he grew up? Why do you think as you do? (Yes, it has been a while since Song-sam was in the village. It all looks different to him, and his climbing the chestnut tree and remembering a childhood incident is a clue that he has not been here for quite some time.)

Name Date Period

Unit 1

Vocabulary Workbook *10*

Cranes

Directions If the sentence is true, circle *T*. If the sentence is false, circle *F*.

1. Style is the setting of a novel. T F
2. A symbol is a person, place, or thing that represents an idea or thought. T F
3. An abandoned house is no longer lived in. T F
4. A chestnut is a type of calendar. T F
5. If I am in conflict with someone, I am in battle. T F
6. A gourd is a kind of electrical device used in plumbing. T F
7. A lofty ambition is a high one. T F
8. A wen is a small insect in China. T F
9. A burr is a rough or prickly covering around a movie star. T F
10. To dash away is to walk slowly and deliberately. T F
11. A detachment of soldiers is a small military unit. T F
12. To recall something is to remember it. T F
13. To be taken aback by something is to be startled by it. T F
14. If I'm cowed by something, I'm frightened. T F
15. Fodder is a type of airplane. T F
16. A mission is a task or an assignment. T F
17. The spine of a chestnut is one of its thorns. T F
18. Stubble is a type of breakfast food in Minnesota. T F
19. To invade a country is to enter it by force. T F
20. A prig is a type of musical instrument. T F
21. To stifle something is to hold it back. T F
22. Generally, a suspicious happening arouses your mistrust. T F
23. To till the land means to build a house on it. T F
24. A widower is a woman whose husband has died. T F
25. To avert your eyes is to wear contact lenses. T F
26. To hesitate is to hold back. T F
27. A ruckus is a quiet tea party at a hotel. T F
28. To snare an animal is to trap it. T F
29. A specimen is an example of a group of things. T F
30. To do something abruptly is to do it all of a sudden. T F

 World Literature

TRL

Vocabulary Workbook 10

Name Date Period

Unit 1

Student Study Guide *16*

Cranes (pp. 127–32)

Directions Fill in the following outline. Filling in the blanks will help you as you read and study "Cranes."

I. Beginning of the Selection (pp. 127–129)

A. Song-sam

1. When he appears in the village, the __________ have already fled.
2. He finds Tok-jae bound tightly with rope in the __________ __________ Office.
3. As boys, he and Tok-jae sometimes shared a smoke of dried __________ leaves.
4. He decides not to __________ anymore while he is escorting Tok-jae.

II. Middle of the Selection (pp. 129–130)

A. Tok-jae

1. Song-sam asks him how many people he has __________.
2. He tells Song-sam that first and last, he is the son of a __________ farmer.
3. He is married to __________.

III. End of the Selection (pp. 129–132)

A. Remembering Childhood

1. Tok-jae had thought he would carry his __________ on his back.
2. Song-sam's father had said the same thing as Tok-jae's—how could a __________ flee and leave his work behind?
3. Song-sam sees a flock of cranes in the __________ __________ at the thirty-eighth parallel.

B. Freedom

1. When Song-sam and Tok-jae were young, they set a snare and caught a __________.
   a. People from __________ came to hunt cranes.
2. Song-sam tells Tok-jae he wants to go catch a __________.
3. Two cranes soar against the high, blue __________ sky.

 World Literature

TRL

Student Study Guide 16

Discussion Questions

A ASK Critical Thinking Why do you think Song-sam decides to take Tok-jae himself? (He may feel he wants to talk to his old friend, even though they are now enemies.)

B The phrase "a guy like this" in this context sounds negative. Song-sam is thinking of Tok-jae as his enemy here. Yet Song-sam is obviously torn in his feelings toward his old friend, as he wonders whether Tok-jae would like a smoke, too.

Cross-Curricular Connection

History The Korean War took place in the early 1950s. It is sometimes thought of as the first "police action" in which a group of other nations worked together against one nation. It was a very bloody conflict with huge numbers of casualties, many of them civilians. Interested students may want to find out more about North Korea and South Korea, which have remained permanently divided into two countries since the war.

Read on to see why *Song-sam* has been away from the village.

tree, Song-sam looked up at the clear autumn sky. Though he did not shake the branch, some of the remaining chestnut **burrs** burst open, and the nuts fell to the ground.

When he reached the house that was being used temporarily as the Public Peace Office, he found someone there bound tightly with rope. This was the first young man he had seen in the village. As Song-sam drew closer and examined his face, he was **taken aback.** It was none other than his boyhood friend Tok-jae.

Song-sam asked one of the security guards from his **detachment** who had accompanied him from Ch'ont'ae what the situation was. The guard answered that the prisoner had been vice-chairman of the Communist Farmers' Alliance and that he had just been captured while hiding in his own house here in the village.

Song-sam squatted by the house and lit a cigarette. Tok-jae was to be escorted to Ch'ongdan by one of the young security guards.

After a while Song-sam lit a cigarette from the one he had been smoking, then stood up.

A "I'll take the guy myself."

Tok-jae kept his face turned away; he did not even glance at Song-sam.

They left the village.

B Why does Song-sam think of Tok-jae as *a guy like this*?

Song-sam kept smoking, but he could not taste the tobacco. He just sucked and puffed. He suddenly realized that Tok-jae might like a smoke. He **recalled** when they were boys how they had shared a smoke of dried pumpkin leaves, hiding from the adults in the corner of the wall around the house. But how could he offer a guy like this a cigarette?

Once, when they were boys, he had gone with Tok-jae to steal chestnuts from the old man with the wen. Song-sam was taking his turn climbing the tree when suddenly they heard the old man shouting. Song-sam slid down the tree and got chestnut burrs stuck in his rear end. Yet he **dashed** off without doing anything about them. Once they had run far enough that the old man could

burr a rough or prickly covering around a nut

dash to run quickly

detachment a small military unit of soldiers

recall to remember

taken aback startled

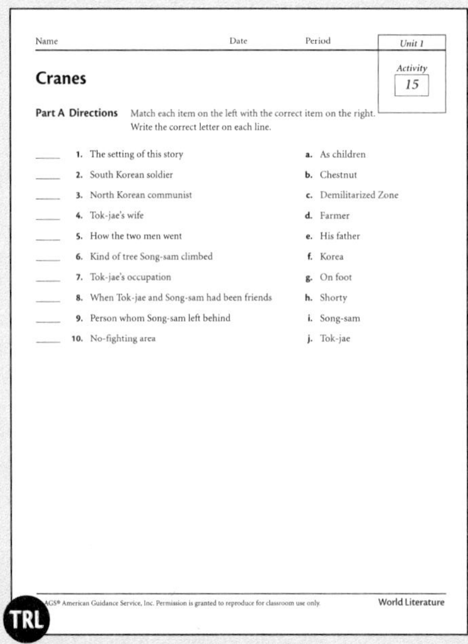

Name Date Period

Unit 1 *Activity* 15

Cranes

Part A Directions Match each item on the left with the correct item on the right. Write the correct letter on each line.

____	1. The setting of this story	a. As children
____	2. South Korean soldier	b. Chestnut
____	3. North Korean communist	c. Demilitarized Zone
____	4. Tok-jae's wife	d. Farmer
____	5. How the two men went	e. His father
____	6. Kind of tree Song-sam climbed	f. Korea
____	7. Tok-jae's occupation	g. On foot
____	8. When Tok-jae and Song-sam had been friends	h. Shorty
____	9. Person whom Song-sam left behind	i. Song-sam
____	10. No-fighting area	j. Tok-jae

 World Literature

TRL

Activity 15

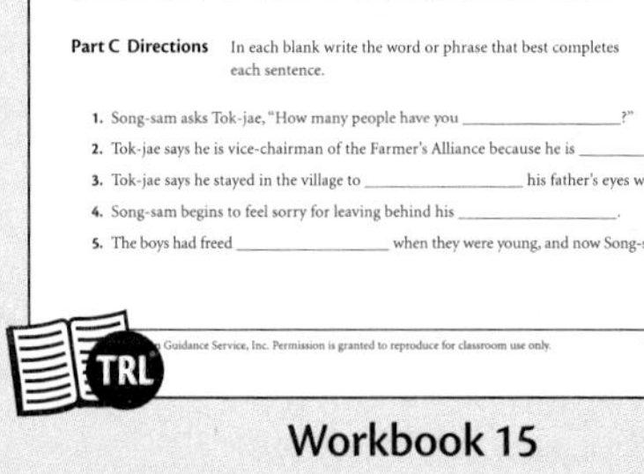

Name Date Period

Unit 1 *Workbook* 15

Cranes

Part A Directions Circle the word or phrase in parentheses that best completes each sentence.

1. In the captured village, everyone's face was masked with (war paint, fear).
2. The (Territorial Jail, Public Peace Office) was the name of the building where prisoners were kept.
3. (Song-sam, Tok-jae), the main character, is in the South Korean army.
4. The Demilitarized Zone is also called the (Thirty-Eighth parallel, a zone of latitude).
5. Tok-jae and Song-sam had (grown up in the same village, met each other in college).

Part B Directions Read each sentence. Write *T* if the statement is true or *F* if it is false.

________ 1. The two main characters came from rural, farming families.
________ 2. Both men had left their families behind to serve their countries.
________ 3. Song-sam volunteered to take Tok-jae to make sure he was punished for his crimes.
________ 4. Tok-jae had cried as a youngster when he got prickly spines in his backside.
________ 5. Tok-jae's wife was expecting their first child very soon.

Part C Directions In each blank write the word or phrase that best completes each sentence.

1. Song-sam asks Tok-jae, "How many people have you ____________?"
2. Tok-jae says he is vice-chairman of the Farmer's Alliance because he is ____________.
3. Tok-jae says he stayed in the village to ____________ his father's eyes when he dies.
4. Song-sam begins to feel sorry for leaving behind his ____________.
5. The boys had freed ____________ when they were young, and now Song-sam frees Tok-jae.

 World Literature

TRL

Workbook 15

not catch them, he turned his backside toward Tok-jae. It hurt even more to have the prickly chestnut **spines** pulled out. Tears ran freely down Song-sam's face. Tok-jae held out a fistful of his own chestnuts, then thrust them into Song-sam's pocket.

Song-sam had just lit a cigarette from the last one he had smoked, but he tossed it away. He made up his mind not to smoke anymore while he was escorting...Tok-jae.

They reached the mountain ridge road. He had often come to the ridge with Tok-jae to cut **fodder** before Song-sam moved to the area around Ch'ont'ae, south of the thirty-eighth parallel, two years before the Liberation in 1945.

The 1945 *Liberation* freed Korea from Japanese rule. Japan had been defeated in World War II. American troops occupied the south, below the thirty-eighth parallel. Soviet troops occupied the north.

Song-sam felt an **inexplicable** urge. He burst out shouting. "...How many people have you killed?" **C**

Tok-jae glanced toward Song-sam, then looked away again.

"How many people have you killed?"

Tok-jae turned his face toward Song-sam and glared. The light in his eyes grew fierce and his mouth, which was surrounded by a **stubble** beard, twitched.

"So, is that what you've been doing? Killing people?"

...Still, Song-sam felt a clearing in the center of his chest, as if something caught there had been released. But then he said, "Why wouldn't someone like the vice-chairman of the Farmers' Alliance try to escape? You must have been hiding out because you had been given some assignment."

Tok-jae did not respond.

"Well? Answer me. What kind of **mission** were you hiding out to do?"

Silent, Tok-jae just kept walking. The guy certainly seems **cowed**. At a time like this, it would be good to get a look at his face. But Tok-jae did not turn toward Song-sam again.

Song-sam took hold of the pistol in his belt. **D**

"It's no use trying to explain your way out of it. You'll have to be shot anyway, so go ahead and tell the truth."

cowed frightened by threats

fodder dry food for farm animals

inexplicable not possible to explain

mission a task; an assignment

spine a thorn

stubble short, stiff growth

C ASK Literary Element Think about what kind of man Song-sam is. Why does he shout at Tok-jae about how many people he has killed right after he has been remembering some of the fun he and Tok-jae had together as children? (He is feeling very much in conflict about Tok-jae. His question is intended to make him remember that Tok-jae is his enemy and he should hate him for killing people on Song-sam's side of the war.)

D ASK Comprehension What do you predict will happen? Will Song-sam shoot Tok-jae? Why do you think as you do? (Let students provide their own predictions based on what they have read so far. Most will not believe that Song-sam will actually shoot Tok-jae because of Song-sam's fond memories of their boyhood together.)

Learning Styles

Visual Visually oriented students will benefit from looking at a map of North and South Korea and identifying the Demilitarized Zone. They may be able to locate Ch'ongdan, where Song-sam was supposed to take Tok-jae, and other places mentioned in the story. Have them show the rest of the class what they find.

Discussion Questions

A Most students will probably agree that Song-sam believes Tok-jae, mainly because the story makes clear that Song-sam remembers Tok-jae's father so well that Tok-jae's story about him seems logical.

B Shorty sounds like a person who pays attention to everything around her—"the breadth of the earth"—but not much beyond herself—"the height of the sky."

Tok-jae began to speak. "I'm not trying to get out of anything. First and last, I'm the son of a dirt farmer. I was made vice-chairman of the Farmers' Alliance because they said I was a hard worker. If that's a crime worthy of death, there is nothing I can do. The only skill I've got is **tilling** the ground." After a moment he continued. "My father is sick in bed at home. It's been six months now."

A
Do you think Sam-song believes Tok-jae?

Tok-jae's father was a **widower**, a poor farmer who had grown old with only his son by his side. Seven years ago his back had already been bent, and his face had dark age spots.

"Are you married?"

"Yes," Tok-jae answered after a moment.

"Who to?"

"To Shorty."

B
What does this sentence tell you about *Shorty's* personality?

Not Shorty! Now that's interesting. Shorty, a fat little girl who knew the **breadth** of the earth but not the height of the sky. Always such a **prig**. Song-sam and Tok-jae had hated that about her. They were always teasing and laughing at her. So that's who Tok-jae had married.

"And how many kids do you have?"

"Our first is due this fall."

Song-sam tried to **stifle** a smile that rose to his lips in spite of himself. Asking how many children Tok-jae had and having him answer that the first was due in autumn was so funny he could not stand it. Shorty—holding up her armload of a belly on that little body. But Song-sam realized that this was not the place to laugh or joke about such things.

"Anyway, don't you think it looks **suspicious** that you stayed behind and didn't flee?"

"I tried to go. They said if there was an **invasion** from the south, every last man who was a man would be captured and killed, so all the men between seventeen and forty were forced to head north. I really didn't have any choice. I thought I would carry my father on my back and go. But he wouldn't stand for it. He said if a farmer

breadth width; extent

invasion an entering by force

prig a person who is easily offended

stifle to hold back

suspicious arousing distrust

till to make land ready for growing crops

widower a man whose wife has died

130 *Unit 1 Fiction*

leaves the fields he has already tilled and planted, where can he go? My father has always depended on me alone. He's grown old farming all these years, and I have to be the one to close his eyes when the end comes. The truth is, people like us who just till the ground wouldn't be any better off even if we *did* flee..."

Song-sam himself had fled the past June. One night he secretly spoke to his father about escaping, but his father had said the same thing as Tok-jae's. How could a farmer flee and leave his work behind? Song-sam fled alone. As he wandered along the strange roads through strange towns in the south, he never stopped thinking of the farm work he had left to his old parents and his wife and children. Fortunately, then as now, his family was healthy.

They crossed the ridge. Now, somehow, Song-sam was the one who kept his eyes **averted**. The autumn sun was hot on his forehead. What a perfect day this would be for harvesting, he thought.

C Does Song-sam wonder whether he should have stayed with his family like Tok-jae did?

After they had gone down the far side of the ridge, Song-sam **hesitated**.

It looked like a group of people wearing white clothes were stooped over working in the middle of the field. It was actually a flock of cranes, here in the so-called Demilitarized Zone at the thirty-eighth parallel. Even though people were no longer living here, the cranes remained as before.

The *Demilitarized Zone* was a no-fighting zone on either side of the boundary dividing the two sides.

Once when Song-sam and Tok-jae were about twelve years old, **D** they had secretly set a **snare** and caught a crane. They even bound its wings with a straw rope. The two boys came out to the place they kept the crane almost every day; they would hold the crane around the neck and raise a **ruckus** trying to ride on its back. Then one day they heard the adults in the village talking in whispers. Some people had come from Seoul to hunt cranes. They had special permission from the Japanese governor-general to collect **specimens** of some kind. When they heard this, the two boys raced off to the field. They were not worried about being caught by the adults and scolded. Now they had only one thought: their crane must not die. Without stopping to catch their breath, they

Korea was under Japanese rule until 1945.

averted turned away
hesitate to hold back
ruckus a noisy disturbance
snare a trap
specimen an example of a group of things

C Yes, clearly Song-sam is wondering which of the two of them did the right thing in terms of staying with their families or leaving to serve in the army.

D ASK Comprehension The incident with the cranes that Song-sam remembers becomes a symbol for something else in the story. What do you think it might be? (Let students speculate. The captured crane that the boys let go is the symbol in Song-sam's mind of Tok-jae's situation.)

Cross-Curricular Connection

Science Some students will be interested to find out more about the cranes described in the story. Mention that various kinds of cranes are common in Asia and elsewhere. They are often very large birds, some with a wingspread of six to eight feet. Let students share the results of their research with the rest of the class.

Discussion Questions

A ASK Critical Thinking Do you think Song-sam really wants the two of them to try to catch another crane? (Probably not. He is probably using that as an excuse or cover up to untie Tok-jae and let him go without having to explain why.)

B The two cranes flying and free are a symbol of the two men, who now can also be free.

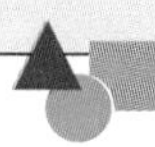

Learning Styles

Group Learning Organize students into three groups. Assign each group one of the main literary elements: plot, characters, and setting. Have each group discuss and summarize their assigned element in the story. Then have each group report to the class as a whole.

Viewing the Art

Cranes and Pine Tree is by a Japanese artist. Here the artwork provides visual support for a story about Korea, once ruled by Japan. Japan and Korea are neighboring East Asian countries.

ASK Is it appropriate to have a Japanese drawing of cranes here? (At the time the boys released their crane in the story, Japan governed Korea. The story mentions that the boys released their crane because it was endangered by a Japanese order.)

scrambled through the weeds. They took the snare off the crane's leg and loosened the straw rope from its wings. But the crane could hardly walk, probably because it had been tied up for so long. The boys held the crane up between them and tossed it into the air. They heard a gunshot. The bird flapped its wings two, three, four times, but fell back to the ground. It was hit! But in the next instant, another crane in the grass nearby spread its wings. Their own crane, which had been lying on the ground, stretched out its long neck, gave a cry, and rose into the sky, too. They circled over the boys' heads, then flew off into the distance. The boys could not take their eyes off the spot in the blue sky where the cranes had disappeared.

A "Let's go catch a crane," Song-sam said **abruptly**.

Tok-jae was bewildered. He did not know what was going on.

"I'll make a snare out of this, and you drive the cranes this way." Song-sam untied Tok-jae's bonds and took the cord. Before Tok-jae knew it, Song-sam was crawling through the grass.

At once, Tok-jae's face went white. The words "you'll have to be shot" flashed through his mind. At any moment a bullet would come from wherever Song-sam had crawled.

Some distance away, Song-sam rose and turned toward Tok-jae. "What do you mean standing there like an idiot! Go drive some cranes this way!"

Only then did Tok-jae realize what was happening. He started crawling through the weeds.

B What are the *cranes* a symbol of?

Above, two cranes were soaring, their vast wings spread against the high, blue autumn sky.

abruptly all of a sudden

REVIEWING the SELECTION

Cranes

Hwang Sun-won

Directions Write the answers to these questions using complete sentences.

Comprehension: Identifying Facts

1. Who are the two main characters? How do they know each other?
2. Why is Tok-jae tied up?
3. What is supposed to happen to Tok-jae in Ch'ongdan?

Comprehension: Understanding Main Ideas

4. What is Song-sam thinking about as he enters the village?
5. What does Song-sam remember about Tok-jae?
6. As boys, what did they do with the crane they had captured?

Understanding Literature: Style

The style in "Cranes" is simple but tells a powerful story. The style is matter-of-fact. The author does not describe the characters' feelings. He just states the actions and the words. He also draws on the power of visual symbols.

7. When in the story does the author tell about Song-sam crying? Describe the event.
8. The author gives strong, simple visual pictures of the village. Point one out.

Critical Thinking

9. How are Song-sam and Tok-jae alike?
10. Why do you think Song-sam releases Tok-jae?

Writing on Your Own This story contains some strong but simple pictures drawn with words. Look, for example, at the first two sentences. Write three sentences of your own in which you create a vivid word picture.

Reviewing the Selection

Answer Key

Comprehension: Identifying Facts

1. Song-sam and Tok-jae grew up together.

2. Tok-jae has been captured and tied up by Song-sam's forces, who are on the opposite side of Tok-jae in the war.

3. He will be shot.

Comprehension: Understanding Main Ideas

4. He is thinking about his childhood there.

5. Song-sam remembers the wonderful times he and Tok-jae had together as children, especially in the chestnut grove and capturing the crane.

6. They let it go when they realized it was in danger of being killed.

Understanding Literature: Style

7. Song-sam cried when Tok-jae pulled the prickly chestnut spines out of his backside when they were children. Tok-jae gave Song-sam some of his own chestnuts.

8. One description of the village opens the story on page 127. Life there is described several times, especially when Song-sam is remembering his childhood.

Critical Thinking

9. They are both basically simple farmers who did not want to serve as soldiers. They are good-hearted, as witnessed by their desire to save the crane and their concern about their families.

10. His fond memories of his friend would not let him hurt Tok-jai. And he realized that Tok-jai was not really his enemy but had been forced by circumstances to be a soldier on the other side.

Writing on Your Own Tell students to think of appealing to one or more of the five senses—seeing, hearing, smelling, touching, or tasting—in their word pictures.

Selection Quiz

The Teacher's Resource Library includes a Selection Quiz for "Cranes" that may be given following the Selection Review.

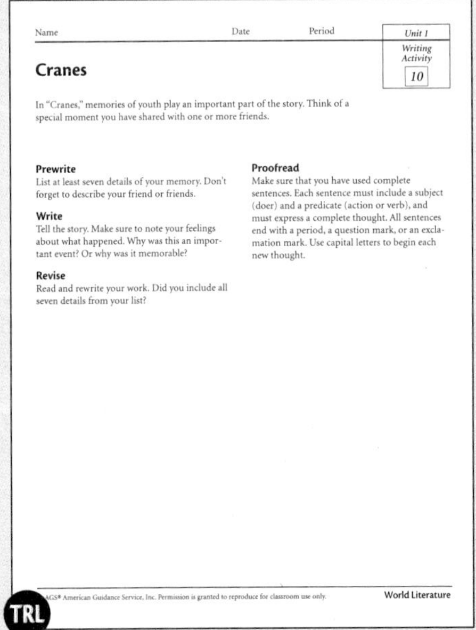

Name Date Period

Unit 1 — Writing Activity 10

Cranes

In "Cranes," memories of youth play an important part of the story. Think of a special moment you have shared with one or more friends.

Prewrite
List at least seven details of your memory. Don't forget to describe your friend or friends.

Write
Tell the story. Make sure to note your feelings about what happened. Why was this an important event? Or why was it memorable?

Revise
Read and rewrite your work. Did you include all seven details from your list?

Proofread
Make sure that you have used complete sentences. Each sentence must include a subject (doer) and a predicate (action or verb), and must express a complete thought. All sentences end with a period, a question mark, or an exclamation mark. Use capital letters to begin each new thought.

 World Literature

TRL Writing Activity 10

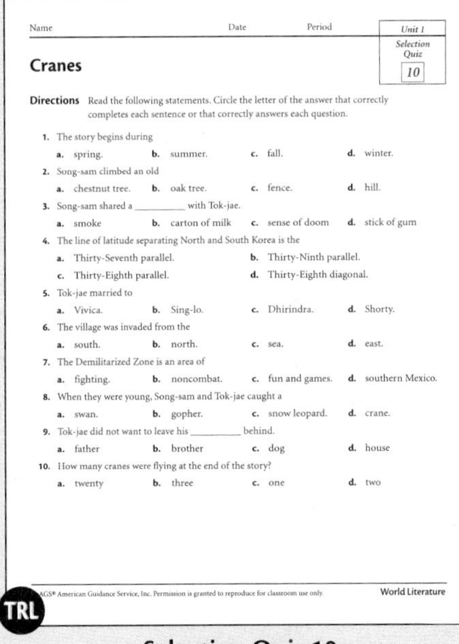

Name Date Period

Unit 1 — Selection Quiz 10

Cranes

Directions Read the following statements. Circle the letter of the answer that correctly completes each sentence or that correctly answers each question.

1. The story begins during
   a. spring. b. summer. c. fall. d. winter.
2. Song-sam climbed an old
   a. chestnut tree. b. oak tree. c. fence. d. hill.
3. Song-sam shared a ________ with Tok-jae.
   a. smoke b. carton of milk c. sense of doom d. stick of gum
4. The line of latitude separating North and South Korea is the
   a. Thirty-Seventh parallel. b. Thirty-Ninth parallel.
   c. Thirty-Eighth parallel. d. Thirty-Eighth diagonal.
5. Tok-jae married to
   a. Vivica. b. Sing-lo. c. Dhirindra. d. Shorty.
6. The village was invaded from the
   a. south. b. north. c. sea. d. east.
7. The Demilitarized Zone is an area of
   a. fighting. b. noncombat. c. fun and games. d. southern Mexico.
8. When they were young, Song-sam and Tok-jae caught a
   a. swan. b. gopher. c. snow leopard. d. crane.
9. Tok-jae did not want to leave his ________ behind.
   a. father b. brother c. dog d. house
10. How many cranes were flying at the end of the story?
   a. twenty b. three c. one d. two

 World Literature

TRL Selection Quiz 10

Skills Lesson: Plot

This Skills Lesson focuses on the definition of plot with some examples.

Review Answers

1. A plot is the action or the main events in a story.

2. The beginning of the plot and story presents the puzzle to be solved.

3. Holmes figures out about the snake at the end of the plot and story.

4. Holmes explains what he has learned at the end of the story.

5. Answers may vary, although most students will admit they found the plot of "The Adventure of the Speckled Band" interesting. Make sure they support their conclusion with logical reasons from the story.

Writing on Your Own Students may work in pairs or small groups to come up with a story plot. Make sure they remember that the beginning, middle, and end have to be logical and develop the idea of the problem or puzzle of the plot.

Skills Lesson Plot

Plot is the action or the main events in a story. Each plot has a beginning, middle, and end. It might begin with a puzzle. Action starts when the characters learn about the puzzle. The middle tells the events as they try to solve the puzzle. The end solves the puzzle. For example:

Beginning
- a puzzle
- event: finding out about the puzzle

Middle
- event: trying to solve the puzzle
- event: characters face problems

End
- event: the puzzle is solved

Below is a list of events in "The Adventure of the Speckled Band." They are divided into parts of the plot:

Beginning
- Helen Stoner calls on Sherlock Holmes. She asks him to solve her sister's death.
- Holmes takes the case.

Middle
- Holmes and Watson visit the manor house. They wait in the dark.
- Holmes hears something. He hits at it with his cane.
- The stepfather screams. He is found dead. The "speckled band" around his head is a deadly snake.

End
- Holmes shows how the stepfather caused the snake to bite the sister. Holmes has scared the snake and sent it back through the air vent. Then the snake bit the stepfather.
- Holmes also explains why the stepfather wanted Julia Stoner dead.

Review

1. What is a plot?
2. Which part of a plot gives the puzzle to be solved?
3. In which part of the plot does Holmes figure out about the snake?
4. In which part does Holmes explain what he has learned?
5. Did Doyle use a plot that kept you interested? Why or why not?

Writing on Your Own Make up your own plot. What will be the beginning, middle, and end? Write two sentences for each part of the plot.

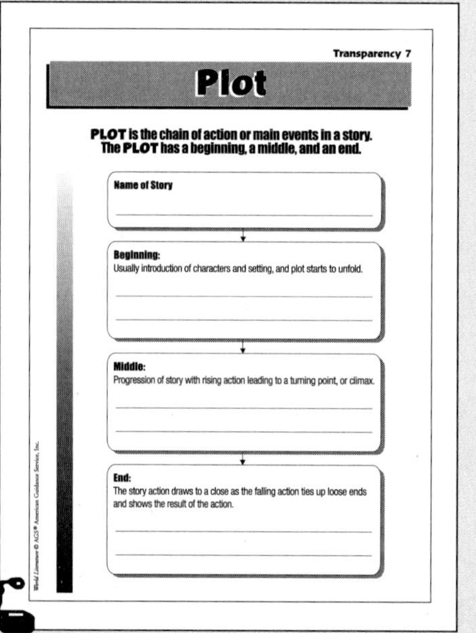

Transparency 7

Plot

PLOT is the chain of action or main events in a story. The PLOT has a beginning, a middle, and an end.

Name of Story

Beginning:
Usually introduction of characters and setting, and plot starts to unfold.

Middle:
Progression of story with rising action leading to a turning point, or climax.

End:
The story action draws to a close as the falling action ties up loose ends and shows the result of the action.

Transparency 7

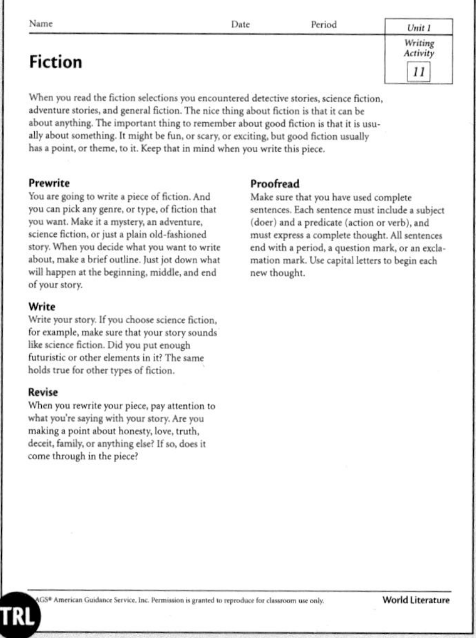

Name Date Period

Unit 1 Writing Activity 11

Fiction

When you read the fiction selections you encountered detective stories, science fiction, adventure stories, and general fiction. The nice thing about fiction is that it can be about anything. The important thing to remember about good fiction is that it is usually about something. It might be fun, or scary, or exciting, but good fiction usually has a point, or theme, to it. Keep that in mind when you write this piece.

Prewrite
You are going to write a piece of fiction. And you can pick any genre, or type, of fiction that you want. Make it a mystery, an adventure, science fiction, or just a plain old-fashioned story. When you decide what you want to write about, make a brief outline. Just jot down what will happen at the beginning, middle, and end of your story.

Write
Write your story. If you choose science fiction, for example, make sure that your story sounds like science fiction. Did you put enough futuristic or other elements in it? The same holds true for other types of fiction.

Revise
When you rewrite your piece, pay attention to what you're saying with your story. Are you making a point about honesty, love, truth, deceit, family, or anything else? If so, does it come through in the piece?

Proofread
Make sure that you have used complete sentences. Each sentence must include a subject (doer) and a predicate (action or verb), and must express a complete thought. All sentences end with a period, a question mark, or an exclamation mark. Use capital letters to begin each new thought.

 World Literature

TRL

Writing Activity 11

UNIT 1 SUMMARY

In Unit 1 you have read several types of fiction. They were detective, science fiction, adventure, and turning point stories. In a detective story, the protagonist looks for clues to solve a crime. Science fiction deals with unreal places and events. It is usually set in the future or in far-off places. The protagonist in an adventure story survives by wits and luck. Turning points are about experiences that change a character's life. Some turning points are "coming of age" stories. A young person makes a decision, only later does he or she understand its importance.

Selections

- "The Adventure of the Speckled Band" by Arthur Conan Doyle. Sherlock Holmes solves the murder of a young woman.
- "Death Arrives on Schedule" by Hansjörg Martin. A killer has bad luck with well-laid plans.
- "The Feeling of Power" by Isaac Asimov. In a world run by computers, a technician learns the power of the human mind.
- "The Expedition" by Rudolf Lorenzen. Four astronauts and their descendants make a space expedition but learn little from it.
- "The Cegua" by Robert D. San Souci. A lone traveler has a frightening experience on the road.
- *Master and Man* by Leo Tolstoy. A rich man looks for help after he and his servant are stranded in a snowstorm.
- "Just Lather, That's All" by Hernando Téllez. A barber, who is a secret rebel, has a chance to murder the captain whose soldiers have been killing his friends.
- *Nervous Conditions* by Tsitsi Dangarembga. A young girl in Zimbabwe makes a choice between tradition and the chance for a good education.
- "Marriage Is a Private Affair" by Chinua Achebe. A Nigerian family is split when a man marries a woman who is not of his tribe.
- "Cranes" by Hwang Sun-won. A South Korean soldier meets a boyhood friend who has been taken prisoner as an enemy.

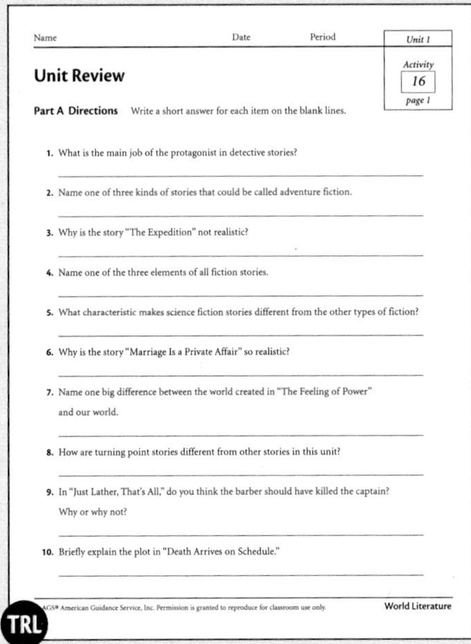

Name Date Period | *Unit 1* | *Activity* 16 *page 1*

Unit Review

Part A Directions Write a short answer for each item on the blank lines.

1. What is the main job of the protagonist in detective stories?
2. Name one of three kinds of stories that could be called adventure fiction.
3. Why is the story "The Expedition" not realistic?
4. Name one of the three elements of all fiction stories.
5. What characteristic makes science fiction stories different from the other types of fiction?
6. Why is the story "Marriage Is a Private Affair" so realistic?
7. Name one big difference between the world created in "The Feeling of Power" and our world.
8. How are turning point stories different from other stories in this unit?
9. In "Just Lather, That's All," do you think the barber should have killed the captain? Why or why not?
10. Briefly explain the plot in "Death Arrives on Schedule."

 World Literature

TRL

Activity 16, pages 1–2

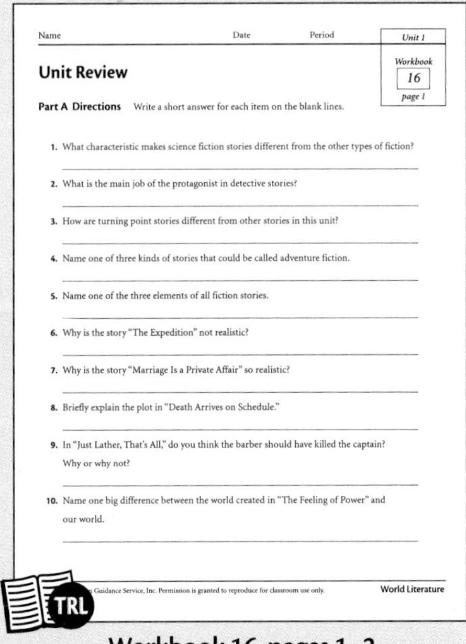

Name Date Period | *Unit 1* | *Workbook* 16 *page 1*

Unit Review

Part A Directions Write a short answer for each item on the blank lines.

1. What characteristic makes science fiction stories different from the other types of fiction?
2. What is the main job of the protagonist in detective stories?
3. How are turning point stories different from other stories in this unit?
4. Name one of three kinds of stories that could be called adventure fiction.
5. Name one of the three elements of all fiction stories.
6. Why is the story "The Expedition" not realistic?
7. Why is the story "Marriage Is a Private Affair" so realistic?
8. Briefly explain the plot in "Death Arrives on Schedule."
9. In "Just Lather, That's All," do you think the barber should have killed the captain? Why or why not?
10. Name one big difference between the world created in "The Feeling of Power" and our world.

 World Literature

TRL

Workbook 16, pages 1–2

Unit Summary

Ask volunteers to read the selection descriptions and identify each selection's type of fiction—detective story, science fiction, adventure story, or turning point story.

ASK How do you know that "The Adventure of the Speckled Band" is a detective story? (The protagonist, Sherlock Holmes, looks for clues to solve a crime.)

ASK We know who the killer is in "Death Arrives on Schedule." So what's the mystery? (whether he will get caught and how)

ASK The sophisticated computer programmers in "The Feeling of Power" do not know how to do something that you do. What is it? (arithmetic such as multiplication and division)

ASK Was the purpose of the space journey in "The Expedition" realized? Was it important? (Yes, the explorers got to the planet that was their target, and they did the research they were sent to do. However, it turned out that neither they nor anyone else cared about it at all.)

ASK Is the Cegua real or imaginary? Explain your answer. (Many students will believe that it is imaginary.)

ASK What lesson does the rich man learn in the selection from *Master and Man?* (His riches and wealth cannot help him find his way through a storm.)

ASK Why does the barber not kill his enemy in "Just Lather, That's All"? (The barber realizes that he is not a murderer.)

ASK Do you think the main character, Tambudzai, made the right decision in the selection from *Nervous Conditions?* (Most students will agree that she made the right decision about going to a better school.)

ASK Is the family split in "Marriage Is a Private Affair" eventually healed? How? (Yes, when Nene, the wife, writes to her father-in-law about his grandsons, the grandfather realizes he must see them.)

ASK How is the conflict in "Cranes" finally resolved? (One soldier lets another, who is his prisoner and childhood friend, go free.)

Unit 1 Review

The Teacher's Resource Library includes two parallel forms of the Unit 1 Mastery Test. The difficulty level of the two forms is equivalent. You may wish to use one form as a pretest and the other form as a posttest.

Answer Key

Comprehension: Identifying Facts

1. The four types of fiction are detective stories, science fiction, adventure stories, and turning point stories.

2. The countries represented are Great Britain, the United States, Germany, Russia, Colombia, Zimbabwe, Nigeria, and Korea.

3. Stories whose setting is a long time ago include "The Adventure of the Speckled Band," *Master and Man,* and "Cranes."

4. Both science fiction stories are set in the future: "The Feeling of Power" and "The Expedition."

5. Make sure students recognize that the protagonist is the main character in the story and usually the one who addresses the problem or puzzle of the plot.

Comprehension: Understanding Main Ideas

6. The most obvious difference is that science fiction stories are set in the future. Some science fiction stories may be detective stories, but none occurs in this unit.

7. The turning point comes with Nene's letter to her father-in-law about her sons, his grandsons.

8. Sherlock Holmes solves the mystery of the "speckled band," which has mysteriously been the agent of death for Miss Stoner's sister.

9. They are alike because they both are exciting with dangerous events and are from Latin American countries. They are different in that one is about a possibly imaginary legend and the other is about a very real disagreement within a country.

10. They both face the conflict between old ways of doing things and new lives in other places.

Understanding Literature: Fiction

11. The setting of both science fiction stories is very important because without the timing the plots would not work. The setting of *Master and Man* is the storm out in the country, which is the point of the story. The three "turning point" stories that end the unit are all dependent on their settings.

12. Students might choose "Death Arrives on Schedule," *Master and Man,* "Just Lather, That's All," *Nervous Conditions,* "Marriage Is a Private Affair," or "Cranes" as realistic stories. Make sure their explanations reflect the stories.

13. "The Adventure of the Speckled Band," "The Feeling of Power," "The Expedition," and "The Cegua" are not realistic. Accept students' logical explanations.

14. Examples of stories in which the main character's feelings change include *Master and Man,* "Just Lather, That's All," "Marriage Is a Private Affair," and "Cranes." Students' identification of the change should reflect the stories.

UNIT 1 REVIEW

Directions Write the answers to these questions using complete sentences.

Comprehension: Identifying Facts

1. What four types of fiction are in this unit?
2. Name two countries in which these stories take place.
3. Name one story whose setting is a long time ago.
4. Name one of the stories that is set in the future.
5. Name the protagonist of one story. Tell what story he or she is in.

Comprehension: Understanding Main Ideas

6. Explain at least one difference between a detective story and a science fiction story.
7. What is the turning point in "Marriage Is a Private Affair"?
8. What is the mystery that Sherlock Holmes solves?
9. "The Cegua" and "Just Lather, That's All" are adventure stories. How are they alike? How are they different?
10. Tambudzai in *Nervous Conditions* and the young couple in "Marriage Is a Private Affair" face similar conflicts. How are those conflicts alike?

Understanding Literature: Fiction

Stories that did not happen are called fiction. Some fiction seems very real. Other fiction is clearly not real. Science fiction, for example, is often set in the future. We know it could not have happened. Fiction is made up of characters, setting, and plot. Characters are the people, animals, or things in the story. They perform the action. Setting is the time and place where the story takes place. Plot is the action in the story.

11. Name a story from the unit in which the setting is very important. Tell why it is important.
12. Name one story that is realistic. Tell what makes it realistic.
13. Name a story that is not realistic. Tell why it is not.
14. Some of these stories show a change in the main character's feelings. Name one of these stories. Tell what the change was.

15. Choose one story. Briefly tell what happens in the plot.

Critical Thinking

16. Which genre of fiction do you like best? Why?
17. Which story did you like best? Why?
18. Name a story that has a moral, or lesson. Tell what the moral is.
19. Choose a character from this unit that you like. Tell why you like the person.
20. Choose a character from this unit that you do not like. Tell why.

Speak and Listen

Choose a story that has dialogue, or characters talking to each other. Work with a partner. Each of you will choose one of the characters. Practice reading each character's words aloud. Think about how that person would speak. Try to make your words sound like a real conversation. Read the dialogue for the class.

Beyond Words

Imagine that one of these stories has been made into a movie. Think of an exciting scene from the story. Think about its setting and action. What characters are in it? Draw a poster of that scene to advertise the movie version. Your poster should make people want to see the movie.

Writing on Your Own

Endings can be very important to stories. Write an essay about why the ending of a story is often the most important part. Begin your essay with a general statement about endings. Add statements to support your idea. Use stories from this unit for examples.

Test-Taking Tip

Prepare for a test by making a set of flash cards. Write a word on the front of each card. Write the definition on the back. Use the flash cards in a game to test your knowledge.

15. Answers will vary. Make sure students accurately summarize the main points of the plot of the story they choose.

Critical Thinking

16. Opinions will vary. Make sure students can defend their opinions with references to the stories in the unit.

17. Answers will vary, but make sure students can defend their choices.

18. *Master and Man, Nervous Conditions,* "Marriage Is a Private Affair," and "Cranes" are the most obvious choices, although some students may find morals in either science fiction story. Make sure they identify the moral in a way that is true to the story.

19. Answers will vary. Make sure students can defend their answers.

20. Students should explain their choices with reasons from the story.

Speak and Listen

Let pairs present their readings to the class as a whole. Some scenes with good dialogue will require more than two students. Let pairs work with other students as necessary for those scenes.

Beyond Words

You may want to allow some students to work together to produce a poster. In many cases, students will benefit from brainstorming with a small group to come up with the idea for the poster first.

Writing on Your Own Suggest that students begin by choosing two or three stories from this unit whose endings they especially liked. Then they can write their essays with those particular stories in mind.

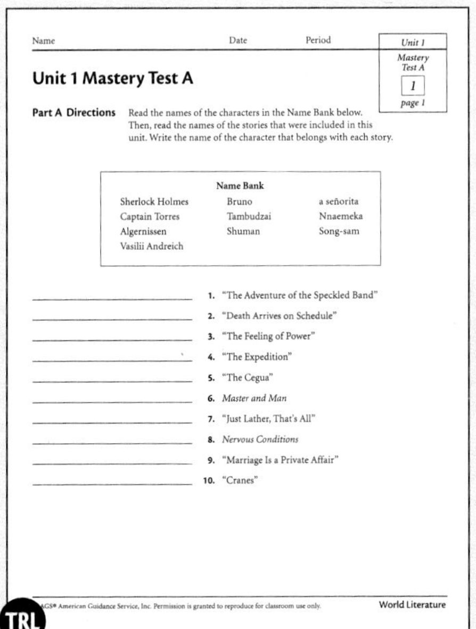

Name Date Period

Unit 1 Mastery Test A 1 page 1

Unit 1 Mastery Test A

Part A Directions Read the names of the characters in the Name Bank below. Then, read the names of the stories that were included in this unit. Write the name of the character that belongs with each story.

Name Bank

Sherlock Holmes	Bruno	a señorita
Captain Torres	Tambudzai	Nnaemeka
Algernissen	Shuman	Song-sam
Vasilii Andreich		

1. "The Adventure of the Speckled Band"
2. "Death Arrives on Schedule"
3. "The Feeling of Power"
4. "The Expedition"
5. "The Cegua"
6. *Master and Man*
7. "Just Lather, That's All"
8. *Nervous Conditions*
9. "Marriage Is a Private Affair"
10. "Cranes"

 World Literature

TRL

Unit Mastery Test A, page 1

Name Date Period

Unit 1 Mastery Test A 1 page 2

Unit 1 Mastery Test A, continued

Part B Directions From the Word Bank, identify the type of fiction of each selection included in this unit, along with each author. Write the type of fiction on the lines next to each author.

Word Bank

Detective Story Science Fiction Adventure Turning Point

1. Hwang Sun-won
2. Hernando Téllez
3. Rudolf Lorenzen
4. Hansjörg Martin
5. Chinua Achebe
6. Leo Tolstoy
7. Isaac Asimov
8. Arthur Conan Doyle
9. Tsitsi Dangarembga
10. Robert D. San Souci

Part C Directions Read each sentence. Write *T* if the statement is true or *F* if it is false.

1. Sherlock Holmes's partner was named Mr. Warner. ("The Adventure of the Speckled Band")
2. Hafermass is a retired criminal inspector. ("Death Arrives on Schedule")
3. Nyasha thinks Tambudzai should attend Harvard. (*Nervous Conditions*)
4. Nnaemeka's girlfriend is Nene. ("Marriage Is a Private Affair")
5. The line of latitude separating North and South Korea is the Thirty-Eighth Parallel. ("Cranes")

 World Literature

TRL

Unit Mastery Test A, page 2

UNIT 2 Planning Guide

Nonfiction

	Student Pages	About the Author	About the Selection	Literary Terms	Reviewing the Selection	Writing on Your Own
■ NETHERLANDS *Anne Frank: The Diary of a Young Girl* by Anne Frank	143–149	✔	✔	✔	✔	✔
■ INDIA "Letter to Indira Tagore" by Rabindranath Tagore	150–152	✔	✔	✔	✔	✔
■ UNITED STATES "Letter to the Reverend J. H. Twichell" by Mark Twain	153–156	✔	✔	✔	✔	✔
■ VIETNAM *When Heaven and Earth Changed Places* by Le Ly Hayslip	158–164	✔	✔	✔	✔	✔
■ INDIA "By Any Other Name" by Santha Rama Rau	165–174	✔	✔	✔	✔	✔
■ SOUTH AFRICA *Kaffir Boy* by Mark Mathabane	175–194	✔	✔	✔	✔	✔
■ UNITED STATES *China Men* by Maxine Hong Kingston	196–200	✔	✔	✔	✔	✔
■ NETHERLANDS *The Last Seven Months of Anne Frank* by Willy Lindwer	201–207	✔	✔	✔	✔	✔
■ PAKISTAN "Account Evened With India, Says PM" by M. Ziauddin From *Dawn*	209–213	✔	✔	✔	✔	✔
■ INDIA "Tests Are Nowhere Near India's: Fernandes" From *The Times of India*	214–219	✔	✔	✔	✔	✔
■ GREAT BRITAIN "Pakistan Nuclear Moratorium Welcomed" From the *BBC Online Network*	220–223	✔	✔	✔	✔	✔
■ NETHERLANDS "The Frightening Joy" From *De Volkskrant* POLAND "Building Atomic Security" by Tomasz Wroblewski From *Zycie Warszawy*	224–227	✔	✔	✔	✔	✔
■ SKILLS LESSON: Point of View; UNIT REVIEW	228, 230–231			✔		✔

Unit Features

Student Text
About Nonfiction
Journals and Letters
Autobiography
Biography
Journalism
Skills Lesson: Point of View
Unit Summary

Teacher's Resource Library
Activity 17: About Nonfiction
Workbook 17: About Nonfiction
Activity 18: Journals and Letters
Workbook 18: Journals and Letters
Activity 22: Autobiography
Workbook 22: Autobiography
Activity 26: Biography
Workbook 26: Biography
Activity 29: Journalism
Workbook 29: Journalism

Teaching Strategies							Language Skills				Learning Styles					TRL Teacher's Resource Library					
Viewing the Art	Career Connection	Environmental Connection	Cross-Curricular Connection	Diversity Connection	Community Connection	Transparencies	Grammar	Literary Elements	Comprehension	Writing Connection	Auditory	Visual	Tactile/Kinesthetic	Group Learning	LEP/ESL	Vocabulary Workbook	Selection Glossary	Student Study Guide	Activities	Workbook	Writing Activities
							145			147						11	11	17	19	19	12
		151														12	12	18	20	20	13
													155			13	13	19	21	21	14
			160								162					14	14	20	23	23	15
	167			172			169		170					168	171	15	15	21	24	24	16
175			179	180	180		177	182, 185, 187	192		188	178			183	16	16	22	25	25	17
				198											199	17	17	23	27	27	18
			206					205								18	18	24	28	28	19
										212					211	19	19	25	30	30	20
	217								218							20	20	26	31	31	21
		222														21	21	27	32	32	22
												225				22	22	28	33	33	23
						8													34	34	24

Assessment Features

Student Text

Unit 2 Review

Teacher's Resource Library

Activity 34: Unit 2 Review, pages 1–2
Workbook 34: Unit 2 Review, pages 1–2
Selection Quizzes 11–22
Unit 2 Mastery Tests A and B, pages 1–2

Unit at a Glance

Unit 2: Nonfiction

pages 138–231

About Nonfiction
pages 140–141

Selections

- NETHERLANDS *Anne Frank: The Diary of a Young Girl* by Anne Frank, pages 143–149
- INDIA "Letter to Indira Tagore" by Rabindranath Tagore, pages 150–152
- UNITED STATES "Letter to the Reverend J. H. Twichell" by Mark Twain, pages 153–156
- VIETNAM *When Heaven and Earth Changed Places* by Le Ly Hayslip, pages 158–164
- INDIA "By Any Other Name" by Santha Rama Rau, pages 165–174
- SOUTH AFRICA *Kaffir Boy* by Mark Mathabane, pages 175–194
- UNITED STATES *China Men* by Maxine Hong Kingston, pages 196–200
- NETHERLANDS *The Last Seven Months of Anne Frank* by Willy Lindwer, pages 201–207
- PAKISTAN "Account Evened With India, Says PM" by M. Ziauddin, pages 209–213
- INDIA "Tests Are Nowhere Near India's: Fernandes," pages 214–219
- GREAT BRITAIN "Pakistan Nuclear Moratorium Welcomed," pages 220–223
- NETHERLANDS "The Frightening Joy"; POLAND "Building Atomic Security" by Tomasz Wroblewski, pages 224–227

Unit Skills Lesson: Point of View
page 228

Unit Summary page 229

Unit Review pages 230–231

Audiocassette

Transparency 8

Teacher's Resource Library TRL

- Activity 17 and 34, pages 1–2
- Workbook 17 and 34, pages 1–2
- Unit 2 Mastery Tests A and B, pages 1–4

(Answer Keys for the Teacher's Resource Library begin on page 468 of this Teacher's Edition.)

"The challenge of nonfiction is to marry art and truth."
—Phyllis Rose

"Facts don't lie—not if you've got enough of 'em."
—John Stephen Strange

Other Resources

Books for Teachers

Hudson, Yeager, ed. *Emerson and Tagore: The Poet as Philosopher* (West and the Wider World Series, Vol 1). Notre Dame, IN: Cross Cultural Publications, 1987.

Hong Kingston, Maxine. *Conversations with Maxine Hong Kingston* (Literary Conversations Series). Jackson, MS: University Press of Mississippi, 1998.

Rittner, Carol, ed. *Anne Frank in the World: Essays and Reflections.* Armonk, NY: M. E. Sharpe, 1997.

Books for Students

Mathabane, Mark. *Kaffir Boy in America: An Encounter With Apartheid.* New York: Scribner's, 1989.

Twain, Mark. *Life on the Mississippi.* New York: Random House, 1994.

Hayslip, Le Ly. *Child of War, Woman of Peace.* New York: Doubleday, 1993.

UNIT 2 *Nonfiction*

Nonfiction by authors all over the world gives us new perspectives. Their letters, autobiographies, biographies, and articles are a valuable resource for learning about our world.

Unit 2 Selections — Page

Introducing the Unit

Read aloud the quotations on page 138. Ask students to name some works of nonfiction they have enjoyed. Point out that both quotes describe the use of words to tell true stories.

ASK What nouns in the first quotation describe nonfiction? (*challenge, truth, art*)

ASK Why is it difficult to "marry art and truth"? (Because art is often fanciful, and the truth is factual. Also, purely factual accounts may be uninteresting.)

ASK What does the second quotation say about facts? (They reveal truth.)

ASK What does the number of facts have to do with their truth? (The more facts you have about a subject, the more readily readers accept what you say as truth.)

Explain that nonfiction takes many forms. The one characteristic they all share is that they are based on real-life people and events.

Review the Unit 2 selection genres and titles. Discuss the different genres.

Viewing the Art

Have students look at the picture on pages 138–139. In *Day's End*, Abdim Dr No depicts a native couple returning to their village. Their bare feet, the man's shouldered spear, and a baby slung on the woman's back suggest a simple, mobile lifestyle in direct contact with the earth. The rounded huts of the village suggest simplicity, fertility, and unity with the earth.

ASK What mood or feeling about everyday life does this picture convey? Why is art that suggests day-to-day life appropriate for a unit on nonfiction? (Answers may include the simple, open feel of the village or the humble, calm manner of village life. Since most people of the world live humble, simple lives, this picture about the daily lives of such people fits the "real" nature of global nonfiction.)

Video

The Diary of Anne Frank. (150 minutes) Botsford, CT: Filmic Archives, 1959.

The Stories of Maxine Hong Kingston (52 minutes) Princeton, NJ: Films for the Humanities and Sciences.

Software

The Last Days of Apartheid. Sunbury, OH: Fas-Track Computer Products.

About Nonfiction

Ask students to silently read the text on pages 140 and 141, or have students take turns reading aloud.

ASK Why are diaries, journals, and letters so personal? (They are a private record of thoughts and feelings. People will write things they would never say to others.)

Poll students to see how many keep a diary or journal. Ask how many write letters to friends or family (including e-mail, notes, and letters). Point out that in earlier times, letter writing was a necessary art; people took pride in writing vivid, interesting letters. With the advent of the telephone, letter writing became less popular as a means of communicating. Now, with the computer and e-mail, people communicate instantly in writing. Ask students to comment about the quality of the writing in e-mails they receive and send.

ASK How is an autobiography different from a biography? (An autobiography gives a first-hand account of the author's life which is colorful and personal. A biography tells about someone else's life on the basis of the author's research.)

Have students list their favorite biographies and autobiographies. Discuss reasons why people like to read about others' lives. (They are curious about famous people, or they want to understand how a person became successful or accomplished goals so they can do the same.)

UNIT 2 ■ ABOUT NONFICTION

Nonfiction literature is about real people, settings, and events. It can be divided into several genres. The most personal kinds of nonfiction are diaries, journals, and letters. Sometimes diaries or collected letters are published. A diary is more personal than a journal because the writer expresses feelings. Journals and letters record a writer's first impressions and reactions about places and events as well as emotions.

Nonfiction about a person's life can be an autobiography or a biography. When people tell their own stories they are autobiographies. An autobiography describes events, people, places, and feelings from the author's own life. It often gives a colorful picture of the author. Biographies are not written by the person whom the book is about. Instead, they are written by authors who are interested in that person. They don't talk about feelings as much as autobiographies.

Journalism is another type of nonfiction. It answers the "who," "what," "where," "when," and "how" of an event clearly and quickly. It tells readers what has happened. The first reports of journalists are news stories. These are the kind of stories you see on the front page or cover of newspapers and magazines. Feature stories come after the first reports. They analyze, explain, and judge the importance of the news. Sometimes feature stories grow into books as their authors collect information and opinion. The Internet is having an effect on journalism; some newspapers are putting their stories online. Two of the journalism selections in this unit were first published on the Internet.

The following countries are represented in this unit: the Netherlands, India, the United States, Vietnam, South Africa, Pakistan, Great Britain, and Poland.

ASK What is journalism? (It is nonfiction writing that reports news.)

ASK What is the difference between a news story and a feature? (A news story is all fact; a feature often adds the writer's opinions and personal perspective.)

Discuss students' preferred ways of absorbing news stories. Find out how many students read newspapers and what information they seek out daily. Explain that besides newspapers and television broadcasts, they can find journalism online, in news magazines, and on the radio. Many newspapers and magazines are now reproduced on the Internet.

Have students think of other types of nonfiction writing with which they are familiar. (Topic-specific trade books, criticism, and books explaining processes or historic events are examples. How-to and personal improvement books are popular today.)

Draw a continuum on the chalkboard, labeling the left end as personal and emotional and the right as factual and impersonal. Ask students to place each kind of nonfiction in order on the continuum and tell why they placed it there. Explain that these forms of nonfiction have existed for many centuries, so they all meet human needs for self-expression, information, and understanding.

Name ______ Date ______ Period ______ *Unit 2* *Activity* *17*

About Nonfiction

Part A Directions Circle the word or phrase in parentheses that best completes each sentence.

1. Personal (letters, pictures) that are published are considered a type of nonfiction.
2. Nonfiction literature is about (real, pretend) people, settings, and events.
3. A (news story, diary) is a very personal form of nonfiction.
4. (Biographies, autobiographies) are written about one person, by a different person.
5. You will find nonfiction articles by journalists in (short story collections, magazines).

Part B Directions In each blank choose the word or phrase from the Word Bank that best completes each sentence.

1. A personal ______ or diary, when published, is a form of nonfiction.
2. Nonfiction is divided into several ______, each different in style.
3. Journalism answers "who," "______," "where," "when," "why," and "how" of an event.
4. Biographies are written by someone who is ______ in that person and his or her life.
5. A diary deals with the writer's personal ______.
6. When a person writes his or her own story it is called ______.
7. ______ stories, in journalism, analyze and explain the news.
8. The ______ is having a serious effect on journalism today.
9. A feature news story may become a ______ if the writer collects more information.
10. Nonfiction is a valuable ______ for learning about the world.

Word Bank

autobiography	book	Feature	feelings	genres
interested	Internet	journal	resource	what

 World Literature

TRL

Activity 17

Name ______ Date ______ Period ______ *Unit 2* *Workbook* *17*

About Nonfiction

Part A Directions Circle the word or phrase in parentheses that best completes each sentence.

1. Nonfiction literature is about (real, pretend) people, settings, and events.
2. A (news story, diary) is a very personal form of nonfiction.
3. (Biographies, autobiographies) are written about one person, by a different person.
4. You will find nonfiction articles by journalists in (short story collections, magazines).
5. Personal (letters, pictures) that are published are considered a type of nonfiction.

Part B Directions In each blank write the word or phrase from the Word Bank that best completes each sentence.

1. Nonfiction is divided into several ______, each different in style.
2. Journalism answers "who," "______," "where," "when," "why," and "how" of an event.
3. A diary deals with the writer's personal ______.
4. When a person writes their own story it is called ______.
5. ______ stories, in journalism, analyze and explain the news.
6. A personal ______ or diary, when published, is a form of nonfiction.
7. Biographies are written by someone who is ______ in that person and his or her life.
8. A feature news story may become a ______ if the writer collects more information.
9. Nonfiction is a valuable ______ for learning about the world.
10. The ______ is having a serious effect on journalism today.

Word Bank

autobiography	book	Feature	feelings	genres
interested	Internet	journal	resource	what

 World Literature

TRL

Workbook 17

Journals and Letters

Have students read the quotes on page 142 and decide which one best captures their feelings about keeping a journal. Violet Weingarten looks at it as an adventure; Jacqueline Onassis, as less important than living well. Encourage students to think of ways a journal or diary might prove useful in the future. (It might give perspective on personal growth or become raw material for a book.)

ASK Why do you think most people do not want to share their diaries with anyone? (Diaries contain secret thoughts and feelings that are deeply personal and could embarrass or hurt the writer or reader.)

ASK Why do people write fewer letters today than they did about one hundred years ago? (Technology has made other forms of communication much more immediate.)

ASK What has been lost in the switch to telephone and electronic mail? (A lasting record of written expression, directed specially at the receiver.)

Journals and Letters

- "A journal is a leap of faith. You write without knowing what the next day's entry will be—or when the last." —Violet Weingarten
- "I never even kept a journal. I thought, 'I want to live my life, not record it.'" —Jacqueline Kennedy Onassis

The most personal form of writing is the journal or diary. The diary is often like an imaginary friend. It gives the writer a chance to express anger, fear, or jealousy. These emotions might be embarrassing if told to the wrong person. Diaries are popular with people trying to sort out life and their feelings as they grow and change.

Journals are another personal writing form. They focus more on events than feelings. People may keep journals to remind themselves of interesting events, sights, or ideas. The ideas in journals, diaries, and letters may appear in later writing. But the events and people in them usually have been changed. This is because the author has thought about how to use the experiences effectively. These early looks into a personality can sometimes help a reader better understand the writer.

Letters also can discuss feelings or events, but they communicate with a real person. The writer keeps that person in mind while writing, which helps the letter "speak" effectively. Today, handwritten communication is less popular than it once was. Most people use telephones or computers to reach others. But perhaps you have discovered a packet of love letters or an old diary. You will agree that the written word holds a special charm and force that can't be reproduced electronically.

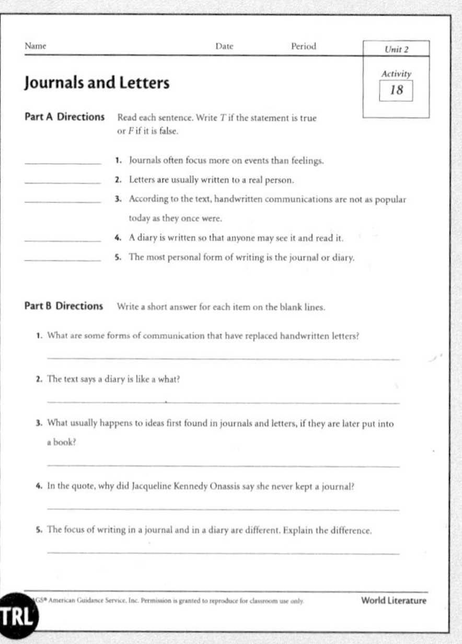

Name Date Period

Unit 2 Activity 18

Journals and Letters

Part A Directions Read each sentence. Write *T* if the statement is true or *F* if it is false.

______ 1. Journals often focus more on events than feelings.

______ 2. Letters are usually written to a real person.

______ 3. According to the text, handwritten communications are not as popular today as they once were.

______ 4. A diary is written so that anyone may see it and read it.

______ 5. The most personal form of writing is the journal or diary.

Part B Directions Write a short answer for each item on the blank lines.

1. What are some forms of communication that have replaced handwritten letters?
2. The text says a diary is like a what?
3. What usually happens to ideas first found in journals and letters, if they are later put into a book?
4. In the quote, why did Jacqueline Kennedy Onassis say she never kept a journal?
5. The focus of writing in a journal and in a diary are different. Explain the difference.

 World Literature

Activity 18

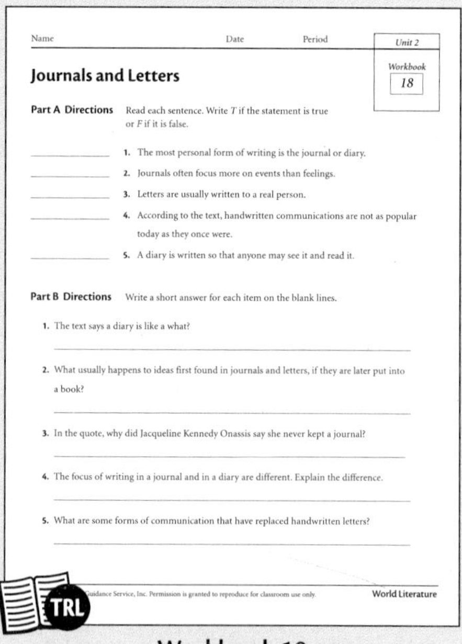

Name Date Period

Unit 2 Workbook 18

Journals and Letters

Part A Directions Read each sentence. Write *T* if the statement is true or *F* if it is false.

______ 1. The most personal form of writing is the journal or diary.

______ 2. Journals often focus more on events than feelings.

______ 3. Letters are usually written to a real person.

______ 4. According to the text, handwritten communications are not as popular today as they once were.

______ 5. A diary is written so that anyone may see it and read it.

Part B Directions Write a short answer for each item on the blank lines.

1. The text says a diary is like a what?
2. What usually happens to ideas first found in journals and letters, if they are later put into a book?
3. In the quote, why did Jacqueline Kennedy Onassis say she never kept a journal?
4. The focus of writing in a journal and in a diary are different. Explain the difference.
5. What are some forms of communication that have replaced handwritten letters?

 World Literature

Workbook 18

INTRODUCING the SELECTION

Anne Frank: The Diary of a Young Girl

Anne Frank (translated by B. M. Mooyaart)

Anne Frank
(1929–1945)
Dutch

About the Author

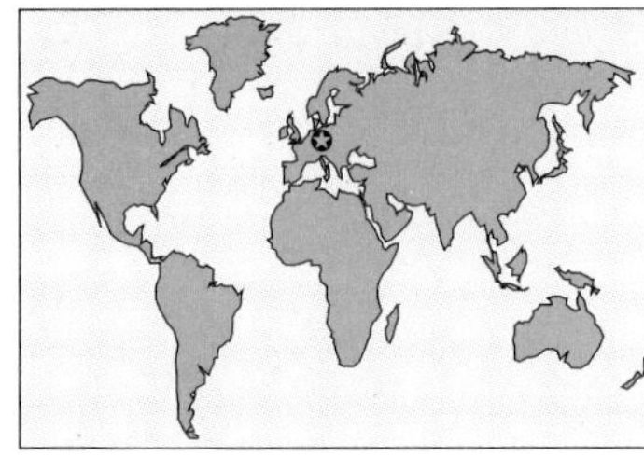

Anne Frank was the younger of two daughters in a wealthy Dutch Jewish family. A month after she turned thirteen, Adolf Hitler began his campaign to destroy all Jews in Europe. The Frank family and four others hid in a small apartment above her father's office. She called it the "secret annex." After two years, the Nazis discovered the group. They were all sent to concentration camps. In 1945, shortly before the end of World War II, Anne Frank died of typhus in the Bergen-Belsen camp. She was fifteen.

Literary Term

diary a record of personal events, thoughts, or private feelings

About the Selection

Anne Frank received a **diary** for her thirteenth birthday in 1942. A diary is a personal record. She thought of it as a secret friend. (She even called it "Kitty.") Her diary records the boredom of daytime silence. It tells of quarrels with her family. Anne dreams of a romance with Peter, a sixteen-year-old boy hiding with them. Through the diary we learn that she loves American movie stars and misses her friends.

After World War II, Anne Frank's father returned to Amsterdam. There he found his daughter's diary. He decided to share it with the world in a book. The book was later made into a play and a film. Here are selections from three entries in that diary.

Selection at a Glance

Anne Frank: The Diary of a Young Girl

Anne Frank (translated by B. M. Mooyaart)

Student pages 143–149

Overview

These entries from *Anne Frank: The Diary of a Young Girl* represent her impressions, thoughts, and feelings about herself, about being "captive" in the hiding place, and about the people with whom she lives in such close quarters.

Selection Summary

In these three excerpts from a Dutch Jewish girl's diary, the writer, Anne Frank, reveals her thoughts during World War II.

Objectives

- To analyze the diary as a personal genre.
- To identify and analyze a teenage girl's reactions to life and confinement.

Audiocassette 

Teacher's Resource Library TRL

- Vocabulary Workbook 11
- Selection Glossary 11
- Student Study Guide 17
- Activity 19
- Workbook 19
- Writing Activity 12
- Selection Quiz 11

Setting the Stage for Reading

About the Author

Ask students to read the text and look at the photo. Anne Frank at first wrote in her diary for herself alone. In 1944 she heard a radio broadcast suggesting a collection of eyewitness accounts of the suffering endured during the war. Then Anne began to edit and rewrite the diary. She also wrote essays, memoirs, and short stories, which were later collected in the book *Anne Frank's Tales from the Secret Annex.*

ASK Why did Anne revise her diary? (She felt it would be published and wanted it to be polished.)

About the Selection

The diary entries of Anne Frank are polished and eloquent. They show a mature grasp of the significance of her position in history.

Activate Prior Knowledge: Remind students that diary entries are frequently addressed to an imaginary someone (or at least to "Dear Diary"). Have students explain why this convention is helpful.

ASK Why is it important for a young person to have privacy in some part of his or her life? (Answers might focus on the process of discovering one's own values and beliefs and gaining a sense of independence necessary for adult life.)

Reading Vocabulary TRL

Use the Selection Glossary page to acquaint students with vocabulary words they need to know. Have students work with partners to practice pronouncing the words, defining them, and using them in sentences.

Motivation for Reading

Invite students to imagine how they would react to being in prison, without television, mail, or visitors. What would be their most pressing concerns? What one possession or object would they consider indispensable?

Discussion Questions

Suggest that students use the questions in the margins of the student selection to focus their reading.

A ASK Critical Thinking Have students look at the photo on page 145. Point out that this small hiding place is shared by eight people—two families and one single man. Why do you think Anne feels "shoved about"? (Simply being so crowded and never being alone could cause tension and hard feelings.)

B ASK Comprehension What details show that Anne is suffering from lack of privacy and a "space of her own"? (She goes to the attic often to be alone. She keeps everything to herself and feels she cannot "be herself.")

Anne Frank: The Diary of a Young Girl

Anne Frank

As you read, remember that Anne Frank is writing in the small hiding place she shares with her family and several other people.

Thursday, 16 March 1944

Dear Kitty,

The weather is lovely, **superb,** I can't describe it; I'm going up to the attic in a minute.

Now I know why I'm so much more **restless** than Peter. He has his own room where he can work, dream, think, and
A sleep. I am shoved about from one corner to another. I hardly spend any time in my "double" room and yet it's
B something I long for so much. That is the reason too why I so frequently escape to the attic. There, and with you, I can be myself for a while, just a little while. Still, I don't want to moan about myself, on the contrary, I want to be brave. Thank goodness the others can't tell what my inward feelings are, except that I'm growing cooler towards Mummy daily, I'm not so **affectionate** to Daddy and don't tell Margot a single thing. I'm completely closed up. Above all, I must maintain my outward reserve, no one must know that war

affectionate showing loving, fond feelings for someone

restless never still or motionless

superb of unusually high quality

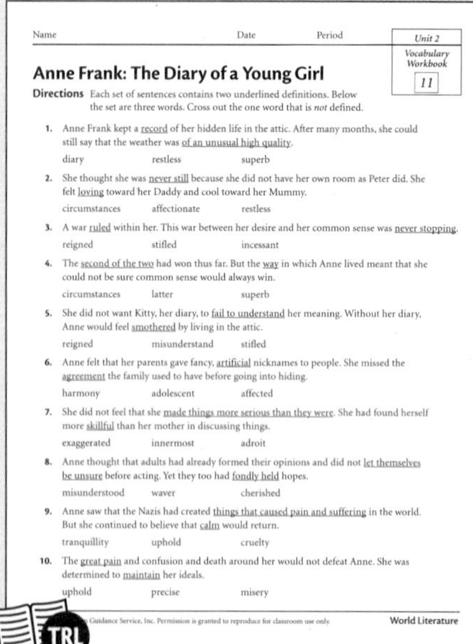

Name Date Period

Unit 2 *Vocabulary Workbook* 11

Anne Frank: The Diary of a Young Girl

Directions Each set of sentences contains two underlined definitions. Below the set are three words. Cross out the one word that is *not* defined.

1. Anne Frank kept a record of her hidden life in the attic. After many months, she could still say that the weather was of an unusual high quality.
   diary restless superb
2. She thought she was never still because she did not have her own room as Peter did. She felt loving toward her Daddy and cool toward her Mummy.
   circumstances affectionate restless
3. A war ruled within her. This war between her desire and her common sense was never stopping.
   reigned stifled incessant
4. The second of the two had won thus far. But the way in which Anne lived meant that she could not be sure common sense would always win.
   circumstances latter superb
5. She did not want Kitty, her diary, to fail to understand her meaning. Without her diary, Anne would feel smothered by living in the attic.
   reigned misunderstand stifled
6. Anne felt that her parents gave fancy, artificial nicknames to people. She missed the agreement the family used to have before going into hiding.
   harmony adolescent affected
7. She did not feel that she made things more serious than they were. She had found herself more skillful than her mother in discussing things.
   exaggerated innermost adroit
8. Anne thought that adults had already formed their opinions and did not let themselves be unsure before acting. Yet they too had fondly held hopes.
   misunderstood waver cherished
9. Anne saw that the Nazis had created things that caused pain and suffering in the world. But she continued to believe that calm would return.
   tranquillity uphold cruelty
10. The great pain and confusion and death around her would not defeat Anne. She was determined to maintain her ideals.
    uphold precise misery

 World Literature

TRL

Vocabulary Workbook 11

Name Date Period

Unit 2 *Student Study Guide* 17

Anne Frank: The Diary of a Young Girl (pp. 144–48)

Directions Fill in the following outline. Filling in the blanks will help you as you read and study *Anne Frank: The Diary of a Young Girl.*

I. Thursday, 16 March 1944 (pp. 144–45)

A. Anne Frank
1. She goes to the __________ so that she can be herself for a little while.
2. She battles a war between desire and __________ __________.
3. She finds it difficult not to say anything to __________, but she feels he is the one who must begin.

II. Friday, 17 March 1944 (pp. 145–47)

A. Parents and Daughters
1. At the moment, Anne can't get along with __________.
2. Anne doesn't think that her parents are strict, because she's allowed to __________ nearly everything.
3. Anne's parents are not pleased that Anne doesn't give lots of __________ any more.
4. __________ means that the girls are treated as children over outward things, and they are older than most girls of their age inwardly.
5. Anne feels more of a __________ than a child.
6. To love someone, Anne must have __________ and respect for them.

III. Saturday, 15 July 1944 (pp. 147–48)

A. Anne's Beliefs
1. Older people have already formed their __________ about everything.
2. The difficulty in these times is that __________, dreams, and hopes are shattered when met with the horrible __________.
3. Everything will come out right, the cruelty will end, and __________ and __________ will return.

 World Literature

TRL

Student Study Guide 17

Name Date Period

Unit 2 *Activity* 19

Anne Frank: The Diary of a Young Girl

Part A Directions Circle the word or phrase in parentheses that best completes each sentence.

1. Anne Frank was (a teenager, a young girl) when she was in hiding.
2. Frank's family was from (the Netherlands, the Ukraine).
3. (Margot Frank, Otto Frank) published the diary after the war.
4. The Frank family was in hiding in (Amsterdam, Rotterdam).
5. Frank calls her diary (Dearie, Kitty).
4. Frank writes about living in (the attic, the basement).
7. The Franks had to hide because they (hated the government, were Jews).

Part B Directions Read each sentence. Write *T* if the statement is true or *F* if it is false.

__________ 1. Frank wishes she was closer to Peter.
__________ 2. Peter is Frank's brother.
__________ 3. Frank likes to show affection for her parents.
__________ 4. Frank's sister is named Margot.
__________ 5. Frank is not aware that Jews are being killed.
__________ 6. Frank enjoys living closely with so many people.
__________ 7. As she writes, Frank is seventeen.
__________ 8. Frank believes being old is harder than being young.

 World Literature

TRL

Activity 19

The building that Anne Frank and her family lived in is now a museum.

still **reigns incessantly** within. War between desire and common sense. The **latter** has won up till now; yet will the former prove to be the stronger of the two? Sometimes I fear that it will and sometimes I long for it to be! **C**

Oh, it is so terribly difficult never to say anything to Peter, but I know that the first to begin must be he; there's so much I want to say and do, I've lived it all in my dreams, it is so hard to find that yet another day has gone by, and none of it comes true! Yes, Kitty, Anne is a crazy child, but I do live in crazy times and under still crazier **circumstances.**

But, still, the brightest spot of all is that at least I can write down my thoughts and feelings, otherwise I would be absolutely **stifled**! ...

Yours, Anne

D
Why does writing in her diary make Anne Frank feel better?

Friday, 17 March 1944

Dear Kitty, ...

Margot and I are getting a bit tired of our parents. Don't **misunderstand** me, I can't get on well with Mummy at the moment, as you know. I still love Daddy just as much, and Margot loves Daddy and Mummy, but when you are as old as we are, you do want to decide just a few things for yourself, you want to be independent sometimes. **F**

E
Remember that *Kitty* is Anne's name for her diary, as if it were a friend.

circumstances the way someone lives

incessantly without stopping

latter the second of two things mentioned

misunderstand to fail to understand correctly

reign to rule or dominate

stifled choked or smothered

C ASK Vocabulary What is the meaning of the term *incessantly* as it is used in the first line on page 145? (constantly) What does it describe? (the war of emotions inside Anne)

D Students may suggest that the diary has become a substitute friend and confidante or that writing about one's frustrations airs them in much the same way as talking about them does.

E ASK Critical Thinking Invite students to describe the friend "Kitty" that they think Anne envisions as she writes. What sort of person do they think the name suggests? (It is a nickname that sounds friendly and may remind of former pets. They may suggest that Anne wants a friend her age, who understands her feelings and is a reliable sounding board.)

F ASK Literary Element This diary entry begins with a confession of negative feelings. Why can Anne write this but not say it aloud? (She has to be confined in close quarters with her parents in miserable circumstances. She does not want resentment to bloom into a full-blown conflict. Noise must be avoided, and she does not want to hurt her parents.)

Grammar

Run-on Sentences Explain that two complete sentences written as though they were one is an error called a run-on. Two main clauses need to be connected by a semicolon or separated by a period and capital. You may want to emphasize that Anne Frank was writing the diary for herself and was probably more concerned with recording her thoughts than with being concerned about punctuation. Point out the sentences "Above all, I must maintain my outward reserve, no one must know that war still reigns incessantly within." Ask students how they would correct the run-on. (reserve. No one or reserve; no one) Have students locate other run-on sentences on page 145.

Name Date Period | *Unit 2* | *Workbook* *19*

Anne Frank: The Diary of a Young Girl

Part A Directions Match each item on the left with the correct item on the right. Write the correct letter on each line.

____	**1.** calm	**a.** harmony
____	**2.** to maintain; to keep	**b.** innermost
____	**3.** correct; proper	**c.** uphold
____	**4.** choked or smothered	**d.** exaggerate
____	**5.** kept fondly in mind	**e.** cherished
____	**6.** to make something greater or more serious than it is	**f.** precise
		g. tranquility
____	**7.** never still or motionless	**h.** incessantly
		i. restless
____	**8.** most personal; deepest	**j.** stifled
____	**9.** agreement	
____	**10.** without stopping	

Part B Directions In each blank write the word or phrase that best completes each sentence.

1. Anne dreams about ________________, a young man who lives with her and her family.
2. Anne describes the times she is living in as ________________.
3. ________________ is the name Anne gives to her diary.
4. Anne believes that ________________ is a lonelier time of life than old age.
5. Anne feels her hopes and dreams are shattered daily by the horrible ________________.

 World Literature

TRL

Workbook 19

Discussion Questions

A Students may suggest that irritations and conflicting feelings become magnified out of proportion because people cannot get away from each other.

B ASK Critical Thinking Why do you think Anne's parents keep such close, anxious watch over their daughters in the hiding place? (They may be perceiving the girls as children to comfort themselves or to live in the past; they probably are terrified of outbursts and medical problems that could not be handled because of their isolation and need for silence.)

C ASK Comprehension Why do Anne and her sister resent the way their parents are treating them? (They are treated as though they are younger than their chronological age, while they are in fact more mature than most of their age.)

A
Remember that the Franks are living in a small space. How might this affect Anne and her sister's point of view?

If I go upstairs, then I'm asked what I'm going to do, I'm not allowed salt with my food, every evening regularly at a quarter past eight Mummy asks whether I ought not to start undressing, every book I read must be inspected. I must admit that they are not at all strict, and I'm allowed to read nearly everything, and yet we are both sick of all the remarks plus all the questioning that go on the whole day long.

B Something else, especially about me, that doesn't please them: I don't feel like giving lots of kisses any more and I think fancy nicknames are terribly **affected.** In short, I'd really like to be rid of them for a while. Margot said last evening, "I think it's awfully annoying, the way they ask if you've got a headache, or whether you don't feel well, if you happen to give a sigh and put your hand to your head!"

C It is a great blow to us both, suddenly to realize how little remains of the confidence and **harmony** that we used to have at home. And it's largely due to the fact that we're all "skew-wiff" here. By this I mean that we are treated as children over outward things, and we are much older than most girls of our age inwardly.

Although I'm only fourteen, I know quite well what I want, I know who is right and who is wrong, I have my opinions, my own ideas and principles, and although it may sound pretty mad from an **adolescent,** I feel more of a person than a child, I feel quite independent of anyone.

I know that I can discuss things and argue better than Mummy, I know I'm not so **prejudiced,** I don't **exaggerate** so much, I am more precise and adroit and because of this—you may laugh—I feel superior to her over a great

adolescent a teenager or young person

affected artificial; assumed to impress others

exaggerate to make something greater or more serious than it really is

harmony agreement

prejudice feeling of hatred for a particular group

146 *Unit 2 Nonfiction*

many things. If I love anyone, above all I must have admiration for them, admiration and respect. Everything would be all right if only I had Peter, for I do admire him in many ways. He is such a nice, good-looking boy! **D**

Yours, Anne

Saturday, 15 July 1944

Dear Kitty,

... "For in its **innermost** depths youth is lonelier than old age." I read this saying in some book and I've always remembered it, and found it to be true. Is it true then that grownups have a more difficult time here than we do? No. I know it isn't. Older people have formed their opinions about everything, and don't **waver** before they act. It's twice as hard for us young ones to hold our ground, and maintain our opinions, in a time when all ideals are being shattered and destroyed, when people are showing their worst side, and do not know whether to believe in truth and right and God. **E**

Anyone who claims that the older ones have a more difficult time here certainly doesn't realize to what extent our problems weigh down on us, problems for which we are probably much too young, but which thrust themselves upon us continually, until, after a long time, we think we've found a solution, but the solution doesn't seem able to resist the facts which reduce it to nothing again. That's the difficulty in these times: ideals, dreams, and **cherished** hopes rise within us, only to meet the horrible truth and be shattered.

F
As a Jew during World War II, what might Anne mean about *the horrible truth*?

cherished kept fondly in mind

innermost most personal; deepest

waver to be unsure

D ASK Comprehension What feelings does Anne say a loved one must inspire? For whom does she have these feelings? (admiration and respect; Peter)

E ASK Critical Thinking Do you agree with Anne that "youth is lonelier than old age"? Why or why not? (Those who agree may cite the lost feelings of teenagers who are questioning their parents' values and seeking to validate their own ideals. The weight of greater uncertainty and inexperience only add to the burden.)

F The horrible truth is that throughout Europe, the Nazis are trying to exterminate the Jews, whom they hate and consider racially inferior.

Writing Connection

Anne has a hard time maintaining her belief in "truth and right and God" because of the evil going on all around Europe. Imagine that you are Kitty and can write a letter to Anne. Persuade her to keep her ideals. Remember that a good persuasive argument shows understanding of the audience's point of view and gives sound logical reasons for a course of action.

Discussion Questions

A ASK Literary Element Explain that an author creates irony when what happens is the opposite of what is expected. How is Anne's belief "that people are really good at heart" ironic? (Her actions and whole life are being dictated by the racist cruelty and hate that force her and her family into hiding; ultimately, people who are not good at heart will cause her death. Her experience should teach her that people are evil, less than human. Also, it is looking at "the heavens"—which are not living—that reinforces her ideals and brings her peace.)

B ASK Comprehension Explain that a writer may describe two very different feelings, events, objects, or people so that readers will contrast them. What does Anne contrast with the peace and tranquillity she hopes will return? (the confusion, misery, and death she sees all around her)

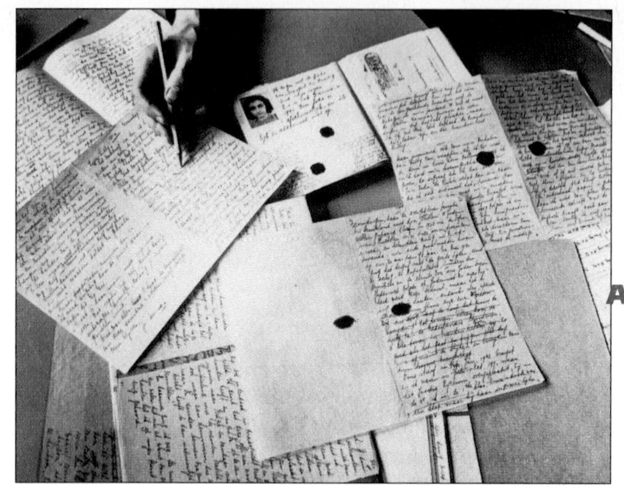

The actual pages from Anne Frank's diary are on view at the Anne Frank museum in Amsterdam.

It's really a wonder that I haven't dropped all my ideals, because they seem so absurd and impossible to carry out. Yet I keep them, because in spite of everything I still believe that people are **A** really good at heart. I simply can't build up my hopes on a foundation consisting of confusion, **misery**, and death. I see the world gradually being turned into a wilderness, I hear the ever approaching thunder, which will destroy us too, I can feel the suffering of millions and yet, if I look up into the **B** heavens, I think that it will all come right, that this **cruelty** too will end, and that peace and **tranquillity** will return again.

In the meantime, I must **uphold** my ideals, for perhaps the time will come when I shall be able to carry them out.

Yours, Anne

cruelty something that causes pain or suffering

misery great pain

tranquillity calm

uphold to maintain; to keep

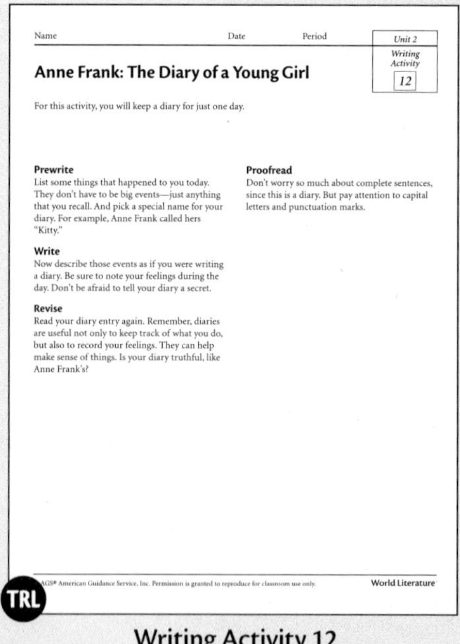

Name Date Period

Unit 2 Writing Activity 12

Anne Frank: The Diary of a Young Girl

For this activity, you will keep a diary for just one day.

Prewrite
List some things that happened to you today. They don't have to be big events—just anything that you recall. And pick a special name for your diary. For example, Anne Frank called hers "Kitty."

Write
Now describe those events as if you were writing a diary. Be sure to note your feelings during the day. Don't be afraid to tell your diary a secret.

Revise
Read your diary entry again. Remember, diaries are useful not only to keep track of what you do, but also to record your feelings. They can help make sense of things. Is your diary truthful, like Anne Frank's?

Proofread
Don't worry so much about complete sentences, since this is a diary. But pay attention to capital letters and punctuation marks.

 World Literature

TRL

Writing Activity 12

REVIEWING the SELECTION

Anne Frank: The Diary of a Young Girl

Anne Frank

Directions Write the answers to these questions using complete sentences.

Comprehension: Identifying Facts

1. How has hiding changed Anne Frank?
2. Who else is getting tired of her parents?
3. What does Anne Frank think about Peter?

Comprehension: Understanding Main Ideas

For more than two years, Anne Frank lived in a small, crowded apartment. She could not leave for fear of being seen. Everyone had to be quiet during the day. People worked in the office below them during the day. They did not know there was a hiding place above the office.

4. Problems must have occurred in such a situation. List four.
5. Why do her parents' questions bother Anne Frank?
6. Why does Anne Frank write in her diary?

Understanding Literature: Diary

A diary holds people's private thoughts and feelings. Diaries are usually written in the form of a letter addressed to "Dear Diary." Anne Frank writes to an imaginary friend called "Kitty."

7. List one advantage of writing to a person rather than a book.
8. Did Anne Frank know that others would read what she wrote? Why do you think so?

Critical Thinking

On July 15, 1944, Anne Frank wondered about this question: "Is it true that grownups have a more difficult time here than we do?"

9. Do you agree with her answer? Why or why not?
10. List the most important problems Anne Frank faced.

Writing on Your Own The last two paragraphs of Anne Frank's July 15 entry explain her beliefs. They also predict what will happen in the future. Write a paragraph explaining which predictions came true and which parts were wrong.

Reviewing the Selection

Answer Key

Comprehension: Identifying Facts

1. She has become more reserved and inward; she becomes resentful of her parents' controlling behavior.

2. Her sister, Margot, is also tired of their parents' behavior.

3. She admires him and thinks him "nice" and "good-looking."

Comprehension: Understanding Main Ideas

4. Students may cite lack of privacy, inadequate food and health care, trouble scheduling to use the bathroom, and stress from the unnatural stillness that must be enforced, no matter what.

5. She feels a need to be independent and have her own space; her parents seem to deny that she has a mind or a right to make some decisions herself.

6. It gives her a safe way to express the conflicts and think through the confusions with which she is wrestling. The diary always listens, is never offended, and will not start a dangerous argument.

Understanding Literature: Diary

7. By visualizing the person, the writer creates a more earnest, human communication and can feel comforted by a human response.

8. She talks about philosophical issues and what the war means to humanity in well-crafted language. She appears to have hoped that her words would survive.

Critical Thinking

9. Most students will agree that young teenagers are struggling to establish just what they do (or can) believe in. It is hard to believe in one's heart what one has not experienced or observed in "real life."

10. It is hard for her to hold on to ideals, to hold her inmost thoughts and feelings inside, to have no personal space that is all her own, and to endure being treated like a little girl.

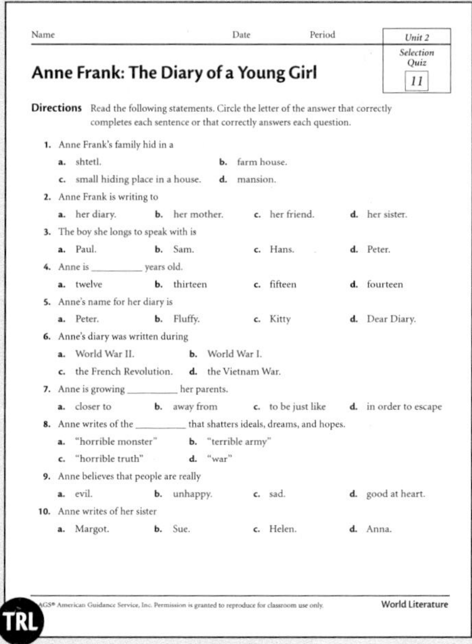

Name Date Period

Unit 2 Selection Quiz 11

Anne Frank: The Diary of a Young Girl

Directions Read the following statements. Circle the letter of the answer that correctly completes each sentence or that correctly answers each question.

1. Anne Frank's family hid in a
   a. shtetl. b. farm house.
   c. small hiding place in a house. d. mansion.
2. Anne Frank is writing to
   a. her diary. b. her mother. c. her friend. d. her sister.
3. The boy she longs to speak with is
   a. Paul. b. Sam. c. Hans. d. Peter.
4. Anne is __________ years old.
   a. twelve b. thirteen c. fifteen d. fourteen
5. Anne's name for her diary is
   a. Peter. b. Fluffy. c. Kitty d. Dear Diary.
6. Anne's diary was written during
   a. World War II. b. World War I.
   c. the French Revolution. d. the Vietnam War.
7. Anne is growing __________ her parents.
   a. closer to b. away from c. to be just like d. in order to escape
8. Anne writes of the __________ that shatters ideals, dreams, and hopes.
   a. "horrible monster" b. "terrible army"
   c. "horrible truth" d. "war"
9. Anne believes that people are really
   a. evil. b. unhappy. c. sad. d. good at heart.
10. Anne writes of her sister
   a. Margot. b. Sue. c. Helen. d. Anna.

 World Literature

TRL

Selection Quiz 11

Writing on Your Own Review with students the structure for a paragraph: The topic sentence should state the predictions. The supporting detail sentences should explain what happened in each case. A concluding sentence should evaluate Anne's understanding. Students may find it helpful to address their paragraphs to an audience whose government is on the brink of war.

Selection Quiz

The Teacher's Resource Library includes a Selection Quiz for *Anne Frank: The Diary of a Young Girl* that may be given following the Selection Review.

Selection at a Glance

Letter to Indira Tagore

Rabindranath Tagore

Student pages 150–152

Overview

Letters are a small portion of Tagore's enormous output of a lifetime: poems, prose poems, stories, songs, prayers, philosophy. He is the only Nobel laureate of India and still considered one of its most important writers.

Selection Summary

In a "Letter to Indira Tagore" Rabindranath Tagore, the Indian Nobel Prize winner, writes a letter to his niece about a moonlit night.

Objectives

- To identify and analyze personifications.
- To identify and evaluate the vividness of descriptive details.

Audiocassette

Teacher's Resource Library TRL

- Vocabulary Workbook 12
- Selection Glossary 12
- Student Study Guide 18
- Activity 20
- Workbook 20
- Writing Activity 13
- Selection Quiz 12

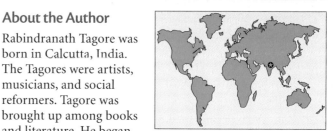

INTRODUCING the SELECTION

Letter to Indira Tagore

Rabindranath Tagore (translated by Krishna Dutta and Andrew Robinson)

Rabindranath Tagore (1861–1941) Indian

Literary Terms

letter impressions and feelings written to a specific person

personification giving human characteristics to a nonhuman object

About the Author

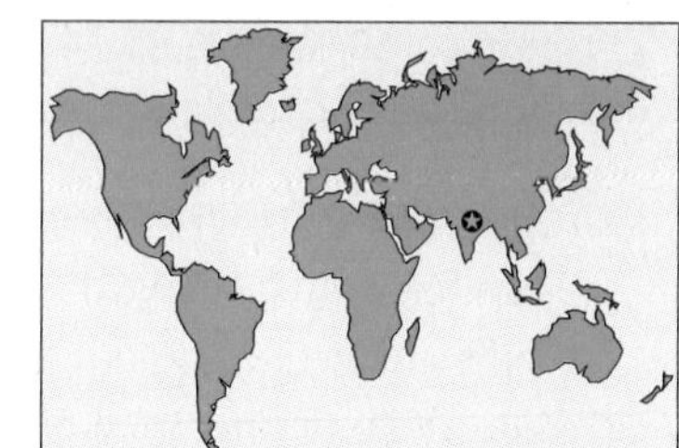

Rabindranath Tagore was born in Calcutta, India. The Tagores were artists, musicians, and social reformers. Tagore was brought up among books and literature. He began writing poems in the Bengali language when he was young. Tagore greatly admired the English poets Shelley and Keats.

Tagore received the Nobel Prize for Literature in 1913. The prize was for an English translation of *Gitanjali,* a collection of his poetry. King George V of England knighted him in 1914. (Tagore later gave back his knighthood. He was angry about Britain's treatment of Indians.)

Tagore wrote essays, novels, and short stories. Many of his poems were set to music. In his last years he became a well-known painter. Tagore also wanted to give Indian boys a retreat from the modern world where they could learn traditional ideals. So in 1901 he founded a "world university" near Calcutta. This school was called *Shantiniketan,* or "The Abode of Peace."

About the Selection

Tagore often wrote **letters** to his favorite niece, Indira Tagore. She was a young woman in her twenties. His letters show his gentleness and love of nature. The following selection shows how Tagore reacts to the natural beauty of moonlight. Notice how he describes the lamp he is using and the book he is reading. He uses **personification** to describe the moon and the night. Personification is giving human characteristics to nonhuman things.

Setting the Stage for Reading

About the Author

After students read the text and look at the photo, explain that the Nobel Prize for Literature is awarded once a year to a writer whose work has enriched humanity worldwide. Tagore's poems were judged "profoundly sensitive, fresh and beautiful."

ASK Why do you think Tagore wanted to instill traditional Indian values at his world university? (He wanted the youth to value their heritage and outlook.)

About the Selection

The "Letter to Indira Tagore" captures feelings through description and figurative language. In this respect, it is poetic, although a prose piece.

Activate Prior Knowledge: Remind students that a comparison using the word *like* is a simile. A comparison saying or implying that one thing is another is a metaphor. Have students identify an example of each in the selection. (Metaphor: "my weary mind . . . a mirage, a land . . . constructed out of words." Simile: "A deadening spirit . . . like a mocking demon.")

ASK How does a night scene lit by the moon differ from one lit by a light bulb? (Answers might suggest that the former is softer and the latter is harsher.)

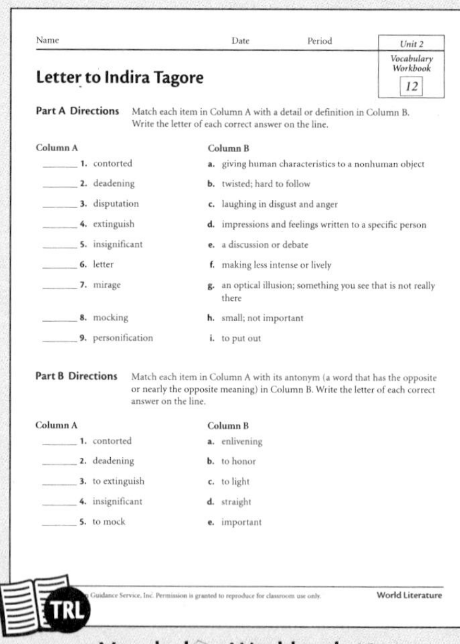

Name Date Period

Unit 2 Vocabulary Workbook 12

Letter to Indira Tagore

Part A Directions Match each item in Column A with a detail or definition in Column B. Write the letter of each correct answer on the line.

Column A	Column B
______ 1. contorted	a. giving human characteristics to a nonhuman object
______ 2. deadening	b. twisted; hard to follow
______ 3. disputation	c. laughing in disgust and anger
______ 4. extinguish	d. impressions and feelings written to a specific person
______ 5. insignificant	e. a discussion or debate
______ 6. letter	f. making less intense or lively
______ 7. mirage	g. an optical illusion; something you see that is not really there
______ 8. mocking	h. small; not important
______ 9. personification	i. to put out

Part B Directions Match each item in Column A with its antonym (a word that has the opposite or nearly the opposite meaning) in Column B. Write the letter of each correct answer on the line.

Column A	Column B
______ 1. contorted	a. enlivening
______ 2. deadening	b. to honor
______ 3. to extinguish	c. to light
______ 4. insignificant	d. straight
______ 5. to mock	e. important

World Literature

TRL

Vocabulary Workbook 12

Letter to Indira Tagore

Rabindranath Tagore

Shelidah, East Bengal
12 December 1895

[Bibi]

The other evening an **insignificant** incident startled me. As I mentioned before, of late I have taken to lighting a lamp in the boat and sitting and reading till I feel sleepy...That evening I was reading a book of critical essays in English full of **contorted disputation** about poetry, art, beauty and so forth. As I plodded through these artificial discussions, my weary mind seemed to have strayed into a **mirage**, a land where things were constructed out of words. A **deadening** spirit seemed to dance before me like a **mocking** demon. The night was far advanced, so I shut the book with a snap and flung it on the table, intending to head for bed after blowing out the lamp. But the moment I **extinguished** the flame, moonlight burst through the open window and flooded the boat. It was like a shock to an infatuated man. The glare from a satanic little lamp had been mocking an infinite radiance. **A** What on earth had I been hoping to find in the empty wordiness of that book? The heavens had been waiting for me soundlessly outside all the time. Had I chanced to miss them and gone off to bed in darkness, they would not have made the slightest protest. Had I never given them a glance during my mortal existence and remained unenlightened even on my death-bed, that lamp would have triumphed. But the moon would always have been there, silent and sweetly smiling, neither concealing nor advertising her presence.

Since then I have begun doing without the lamp in the evenings.

[Uncle Rabi]

As you read, think about how the author appreciates the beauty of nature.

Literary and art critics judge what others have written or drawn. Their opinions appear in critical essays.

contorted twisted; hard to follow

deadening making less intense or lively

disputation a discussion or debate

extinguish to put out

insignificant small; not important

mirage an optical illusion; something you see that is not really there

mocking laughing in disgust and anger

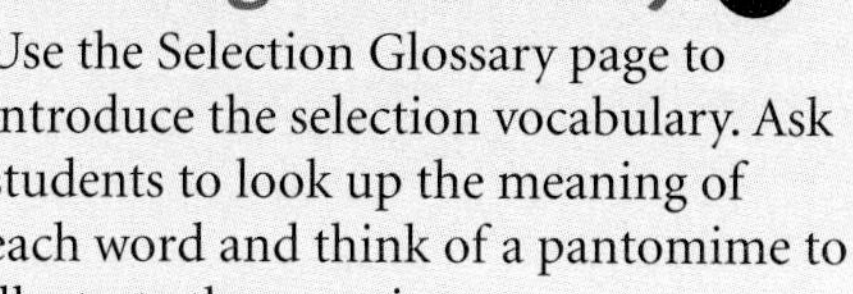

Reading Vocabulary TRL

Use the Selection Glossary page to introduce the selection vocabulary. Ask students to look up the meaning of each word and think of a pantomime to illustrate the meaning.

Motivation for Reading

Encourage students to think about understanding they have gained from observing nature as they find out about Tagore's experience of moonlight.

Discussion Questions

Suggest that students use the comments in the margins of the student selection to focus their reading.

A ASK Literary Element Explain that an object may stand for something more than itself; then it becomes a symbol. What does the lamp symbolize in this letter? (The evil of false, artificial knowledge that keeps us from nature.)

Environmental Connection

In cities, where large numbers of people live and use electricity, light pollution is a problem. Ask volunteers to describe the way a city looks at night. Have students research this problem and report to the class on effects of artificial light and suggestions for reducing light pollution.

Name Date Period | Unit 2 | Student Study Guide 18

Letter to Indira Tagore (p. 151)

Directions Fill in the following outline. Filling in the blanks will help you as you read and study "Letter to Indira Tagore."

I. Beginning of the Selection (p. 151)

A. Uncle Rabi
1. He writes the letter to Indira on December 12, ________.
2. He has taken to lighting a lamp in the ________ and sitting and ________ until he feels sleepy.
3. On this evening, he is reading a book about ________, art, beauty, and so forth.
4. While reading, his mind strays into a ________.

II. Middle of the Selection (p. 151)

A. Light
1. A ________ seems to dance in front of Uncle Rabi like a mocking ________.
2. Uncle Rabi intends to head for ________ after blowing out the lamp.
3. The moment Uncle Rabi puts out the flame, ________ bursts through the open window.

III. End of the Selection (p. 151)

A. Nature's Beauty
1. Uncle Rabi wonders what he'd been hoping to find in the ________ ________ of his book.
2. Uncle Rabi is relieved that he did not remain ________ to his death-bed and let the lamp triumph.
3. The moon will always be there—neither ________ nor ________ her presence—for anyone to take notice.
4. Indira's uncle now does without the ________ in the evenings

 World Literature

TRL

Student Study Guide 18

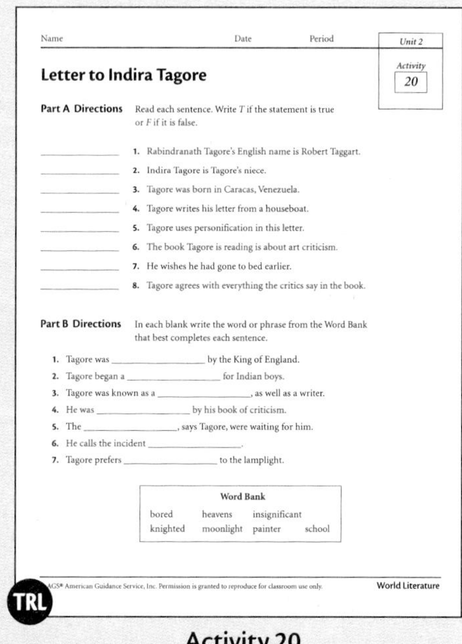

Name Date Period | Unit 2 | Activity 20

Letter to Indira Tagore

Part A Directions Read each sentence. Write *T* if the statement is true or *F* if it is false.

________ 1. Rabindranath Tagore's English name is Robert Taggart.
________ 2. Indira Tagore is Tagore's niece.
________ 3. Tagore was born in Caracas, Venezuela.
________ 4. Tagore writes his letter from a houseboat.
________ 5. Tagore uses personification in this letter.
________ 6. The book Tagore is reading is about art criticism.
________ 7. He wishes he had gone to bed earlier.
________ 8. Tagore agrees with everything the critics say in the book.

Part B Directions In each blank write the word or phrase from the Word Bank that best completes each sentence.

1. Tagore was ________ by the King of England.
2. Tagore began a ________ for Indian boys.
3. Tagore was known as a ________, as well as a writer.
4. He was ________ by his book of criticism.
5. The ________, says Tagore, were waiting for him.
6. He calls the incident ________.
7. Tagore prefers ________ to the lamplight.

Word Bank
bored heavens insignificant
knighted moonlight painter school

 World Literature

TRL

Activity 20

Name Date Period | Unit 2 | Workbook 20

Letter to Indira Tagore

Part A Directions Write a short answer for each item on the blank lines.

1. What does the term *personification* mean?
2. Why do you think Tagore calls the incident insignificant?
3. How does Tagore describe what he has been reading?
4. What are the heavens doing while Tagore is reading?
5. Why does Tagore stop using the lamp in the evenings?

Part B Directions Read each sentence. Write *T* if the statement is true or *F* if it is false.

________ 1. Insignificant means that something is small or not very important.
________ 2. A large body of water is called a mirage.
________ 3. The author feels the moon is smiling sweetly at him.
________ 4. If you mock someone, you praise what is good about them.
________ 5. The light from the lamp is called satanic, meaning it is evil or from the devil.

 World Literature

TRL

Workbook 20

Nonfiction Unit 2 151

Reviewing the Selection

Answer Key

Comprehension: Identifying Facts

1. It is probably well after midnight.
2. He is in a boat, probably a houseboat, as it has a window and is large enough to sleep in.
3. He is reading criticism judging which human works are beautiful and worthy.

Comprehension: Understanding Main Ideas

4. He is shocked by its overwhelming presence.
5. It offers "infinite radiance," peace, understanding from the heavens but never hides or proclaims its presence; the lamp light is glaring, "satanic," and mocking.
6. Students may point out that Tagore finds spiritual enlightenment in the whole presence of nature, whereas the words of people are just so much empty noise that frets the spirit and causes us to miss the deeper satisfactions of life.

Understanding Literature: Personification

7. The moon is like a loving person, "silent and sweetly smiling," always sending "infinite radiance" from the heavens.
8. The heavens are like an enlightened master, waiting patiently to offer understanding to the receptive soul.

Critical Thinking

9. His spirit is fed, or enlightened, by nature, not by empty words.
10. He wants her to be attentive and receptive to nature, too, and not put too much faith in intellect.

Writing on Your Own Encourage students to brainstorm to list all the sounds, sights, smells, tastes, and tactile sensations of the natural event they have chosen. Then they can think of what sort of person and situation could embody these traits. They may find it helpful to imagine that this person has a specific attitude toward them.

Selection Quiz

The Teacher's Resource Library includes a Selection Quiz for "Letter to Indira Tagore" that may be given following the Selection Review.

REVIEWING the SELECTION

Letter to Indira Tagore

Rabindranath Tagore

Directions Write the answers to these questions using complete sentences.

Comprehension: Identifying Facts

1. At what time of day do the events in the letter take place?
2. Where is Tagore when the events are taking place?
3. What is he doing?

Comprehension: Understanding Main Ideas

Tagore has been reading. He does not notice the moonlight until he blows out his lamp.

4. What is Tagore's first reaction to the moonlight?
5. How does the lamplight compare with the moonlight?
6. Tagore says this was "an insignificant incident." However, it clearly means a lot to him. Describe its significance in your own words.

Understanding Literature: Personification

Personification is giving human qualities to objects, animals, or ideas. Tagore's letter has several examples of this figure of speech. For instance, he writes "... that lamp would have triumphed." Can a lamp feel victory or failure? No, a lamp is an object. It cannot feel an emotion. Tagore is using personification to describe it.

7. Explain how Tagore uses personification to describe the moon.
8. Explain how he uses personification to describe the heavens.

Critical Thinking

9. What discovery does Tagore make?
10. What do you think Tagore wants his niece to do?

Writing on Your Own Think about something in nature that surprises or delights you. Use personification to describe its qualities. For example, you might write about a winter storm that cries and howls outside your window.

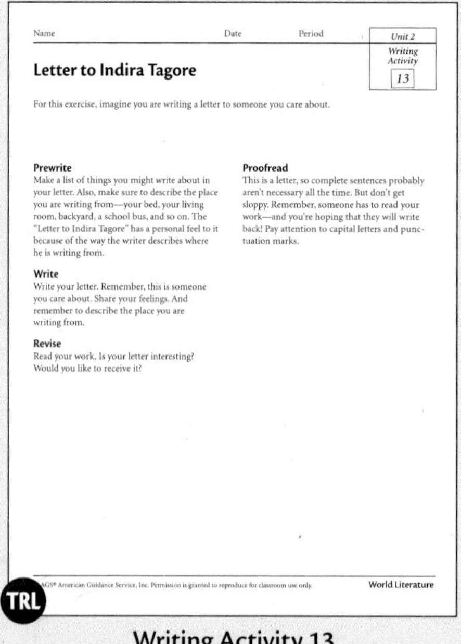

Name Date Period | *Unit 2* *Writing Activity* 13

Letter to Indira Tagore

For this exercise, imagine you are writing a letter to someone you care about.

Prewrite
Make a list of things you might write about in your letter. Also, make sure to describe the place you are writing from—your bed, your living room, backyard, a school bus, and so on. The "Letter to Indira Tagore" has a personal feel to it because of the way the writer describes where he is writing from.

Write
Write your letter. Remember, this is someone you care about. Share your feelings. And remember to describe the place you are writing from.

Revise
Read your work. Is your letter interesting? Would you like to receive it?

Proofread
This is a letter, so complete sentences probably aren't necessary all the time. But don't get sloppy. Remember, someone has to read your work—and you're hoping that they will write back! Pay attention to capital letters and punctuation marks.

 World Literature

TRL

Writing Activity 13

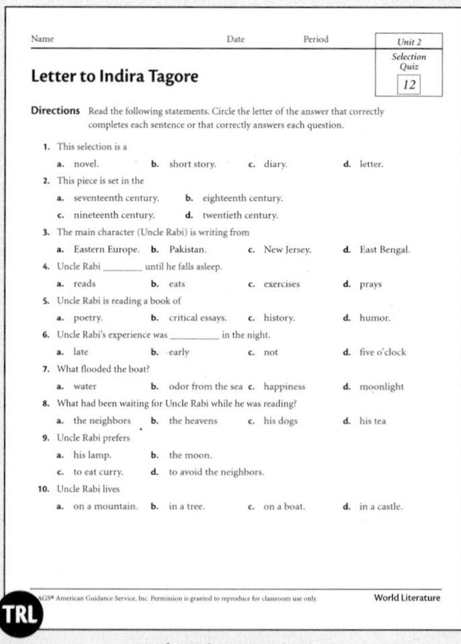

Name Date Period | *Unit 2* *Selection Quiz* 12

Letter to Indira Tagore

Directions Read the following statements. Circle the letter of the answer that correctly completes each sentence or that correctly answers each question.

1. This selection is a
   a. novel. b. short story. c. diary. d. letter.
2. This piece is set in the
   a. seventeenth century. b. eighteenth century.
   c. nineteenth century. d. twentieth century.
3. The main character (Uncle Rabi) is writing from
   a. Eastern Europe. b. Pakistan. c. New Jersey. d. East Bengal.
4. Uncle Rabi ________ until he falls asleep.
   a. reads b. eats c. exercises d. prays
5. Uncle Rabi is reading a book of
   a. poetry. b. critical essays. c. history. d. humor.
6. Uncle Rabi's experience was ________ in the night.
   a. late b. early c. not d. five o'clock
7. What flooded the boat?
   a. water b. odor from the sea c. happiness d. moonlight
8. What had been waiting for Uncle Rabi while he was reading?
   a. the neighbors b. the heavens c. his dogs d. his tea
9. Uncle Rabi prefers
   a. his lamp. b. the moon.
   c. to eat curry. d. to avoid the neighbors.
10. Uncle Rabi lives
    a. on a mountain. b. in a tree. c. on a boat. d. in a castle.

 World Literature

TRL

Selection Quiz 12

INTRODUCING the SELECTION

Letter to the Reverend J. H. Twichell

Mark Twain

Mark Twain
(1835–1910)
American

Literary Terms

pen name a false name used for writing

pun humorous use of words or phrases

satire humorous writing that makes fun of foolishness or evil

theme the main idea of a literary work

About the Author

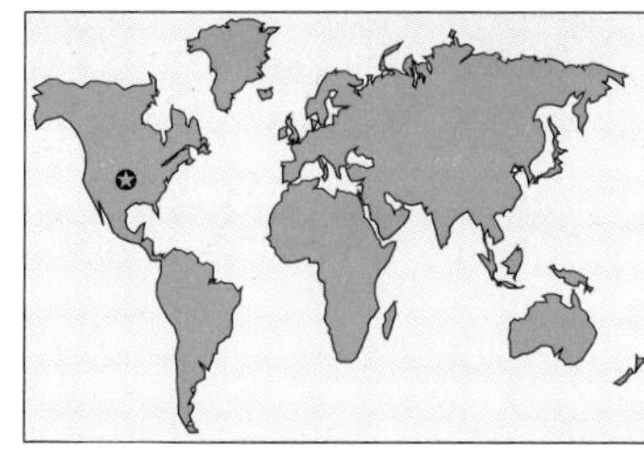

Mark Twain was born Samuel L. Clemens in a small Missouri town. As a young man, he was a Mississippi riverboat pilot. Later he was a gold miner in Nevada and a printer. For his writing he chose the **pen name** "Mark Twain." A pen name is a false name used by an author. Twain's humorous stories about American life quickly made him popular. He is regarded as one of the first truly American writers. He uses **themes** (topics), language, and ideas gathered during his travels. His major works are *The Adventures of Tom Sawyer* and *The Adventures of Huckleberry Finn.* Both combine **satire** with fiction. Satire is humor that makes fun of foolishness or evil.

Late in life, Twain lost most of his wealth in bad investments. In 1895 he started a long lecture tour to earn money to repay debts. During the tour, one of his daughters died. Shortly after he returned, his wife and another daughter also died. These losses, as well as continuing disappointment in humans, affected his mood. Later satires like *The Mysterious Stranger* are more intense and serious than earlier works.

About the Selection

After his writing became popular, Twain married and moved to Connecticut. There he began a friendship with a local minister, the Reverend Joseph H. Twichell. Twain loved to travel. He went to Germany in the late 1870s. From Munich he wrote the following letter to Twichell. It is the kind you might enjoy getting from a friend who happens to be writer. It contains many funny images. Twain also used **puns**—humorous use of words or phrases.

Selection at a Glance

Letter to the Reverend J. H. Twichell

Mark Twain

Student pages 153–156

Overview

This letter was written after Twain had established himself as a comic master but before he wrote his greatest masterpiece, *The Adventures of Huckleberry Finn.* The letter's sense of humor and yarn-spinner style are typical of Twain's gift.

Selection Summary

Unable to sleep, Twain rises and dresses in the dark, trying not to wake his wife. He cannot find one sock and in his disorientation knocks the wash bowl off its stand, curses a blue streak, and wakes Livy.

Objectives

- To identify the puns in a letter.
- To analyze tone in a writing.

Audiocassette X 

Teacher's Resource Library TRL

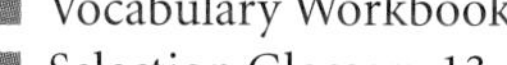

- Vocabulary Workbook 13
- Selection Glossary 13
- Student Study Guide 19
- Activity 21
- Workbook 21
- Writing Activity 14
- Selection Quiz 13

Setting the Stage for Reading

About the Author

Have students read the text and look at the photo. Twain's love of travel gave him much material for his writings and served him well later in life, when his publishing business went bankrupt. He embarked on a world lecture tour, paid off his debts, and reestablished himself financially.

ASK What qualities of his writing do you think made Twain so popular in his time? (Answers may include his use of humor or his uniquely American perspective and subjects.)

About the Selection

During the nineteenth century, the United States was a growing, "upstart" nation that Europeans considered rather primitive socially. One way of becoming "educated" in the social graces was travel abroad. Twain used his travels instead to write books, letters, and essays mocking aristocracy and poking fun at many American characteristics.

Activating Prior Knowledge: Ask students to recall a time when they had to try to accomplish a task without waking someone sleeping in the same room. Have volunteers describe what they did.

ASK What would have been different about a hotel room in 1879? (It would have lacked electricity, running water, and direct heat, unless it had a fireplace.)

Reading Vocabulary TRL

Distribute the Selection Glossary page and review it orally. Have students work in pairs to make a crossword puzzle using the words. After exchanging puzzles, students can complete them.

Motivation for Reading

Ask students to imagine trying to perform a task in darkness. Encourage them to describe their movements and state of mind as they make their way in a strange, dark place.

Discussion Questions

Suggest that students use the comments and questions in the margins of the student selection to review and predict as they read the story.

A ASK Critical Thinking Be sure students understand that "warmed to" means he began to like or sympathize with the swearing butcher. What was this story about? Why might the minister have told it to Twain? (It probably told about some way the butcher hurt himself or was frustrated in a task. The minister knows Twain has similar reactions to frustration.)

B ASK Comprehension For what reasons does Twain include the sentences about the butcher? (The answer to a letter should acknowledge the content of the letter. More importantly, he uses them to introduce his own experience, which reduced him to swearing, and to set a humorous tone.)

C ASK Literary Element Explain that Twain is famous for assuming an innocent, serious tone when he intends to make readers laugh. What descriptive details help to create a comic tone for this letter? (He compares swearing to praying. He describes his movements in animal terms throughout, even though his clumsiness and emotional responses are all too human. His "catlike stealthiness," crawling around on the floor, holding in his temper only to collide with the wash stand and erupt in anger create humorous images.)

Letter to the Rev J. H. Twichell

Mark Twain

To the Reverend J. H. Twichell
Munich, January 26, 1879
Dear Old Joe:

As you read, watch for clues to help you determine who *Livy* is.

Twain is referring to a story he read in a letter from Twichell.

Sunday. Your **delicious** letter arrived exactly at the right time. It was laid by my plate as I was finishing breakfast at 12 noon. Livy and Clara [Spaulding] arrived from church 5 minutes later. I took a pipe and spread myself out on the **A** sofa and Livy sat by and read, and I warmed to that butcher **B** the moment he began to swear. There is more than one way of praying and I like the butcher's way because the **petitioner** is so apt to be **in earnest**. I was peculiarly alive to his performance just at this time for another reason, **to wit:** Last night I awoke at 3 this morning and after raging to myself for 2 **interminable** hours, I gave it up. I rose, assumed **C** a catlike **stealthiness**, to keep from waking Livy, and proceeded to dress in the **pitch** dark. Slowly but surely I got on garment after garment—all down to one sock; I had one slipper on and the other in my hand. Well, on my hands and knees I crept softly around, pawing and feeling and scooping along the carpet and among chair-legs for that missing sock;

delicious delightful
in earnest sincere
interminable endless
petitioner one who asks for help
pitch completely black
stealthiness secretive actions
to wit an expression meaning "that is to say"

154 *Unit 2 Nonfiction*

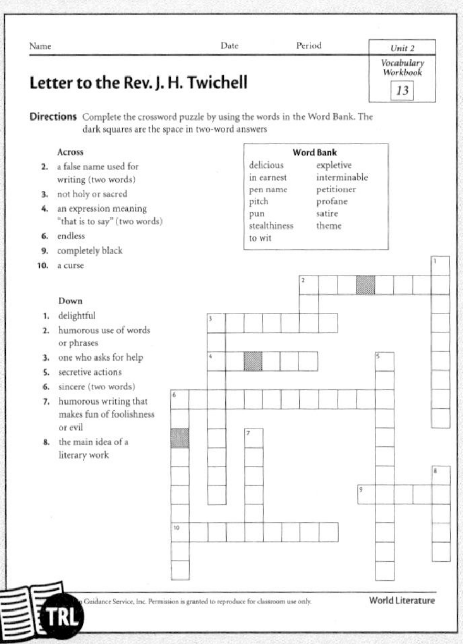
Name Date Period
Unit 2 *Vocabulary Workbook* 13

Letter to the Rev. J. H. Twichell

Directions Complete the crossword puzzle by using the words in the Word Bank. The dark squares are the space in two-word answers

Across
2. a false name used for writing (two words)
3. not holy or sacred
4. an expression meaning "that is to say" (two words)
6. endless
9. completely black
10. a curse

Down
1. delightful
2. humorous use of words or phrases
3. one who asks for help
5. secretive actions
6. sincere (two words)
7. humorous writing that makes fun of foolishness or evil
8. the main idea of a literary work

Word Bank
delicious, in earnest, pen name, pitch, pun, stealthiness, to wit, expletive, interminable, petitioner, profane, satire, theme

World Literature

Vocabulary Workbook 13

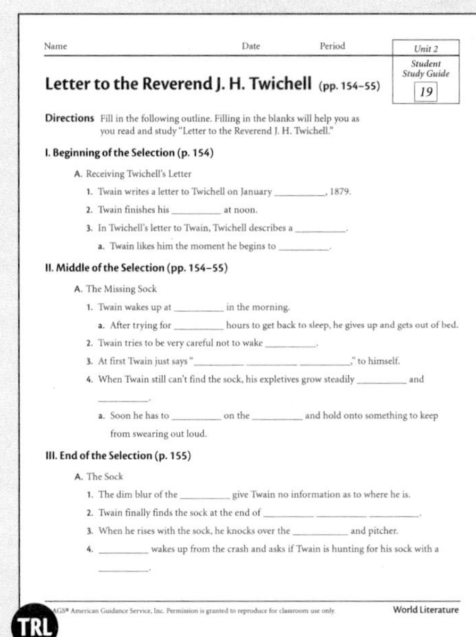
Name Date Period
Unit 2 *Student Study Guide* 19

Letter to the Reverend J. H. Twichell (pp. 154–55)

Directions Fill in the following outline. Filling in the blanks will help you as you read and study "Letter to the Reverend J. H. Twichell."

I. Beginning of the Selection (p. 154)

A. Receiving Twichell's Letter
1. Twain writes a letter to Twichell on January ________, 1879.
2. Twain finishes his ________ at noon.
3. In Twichell's letter to Twain, Twichell describes a ________.
   a. Twain likes him the moment he begins to ________.

II. Middle of the Selection (pp. 154–55)

A. The Missing Sock
1. Twain wakes up at ________ in the morning.
   a. After trying for ________ hours to get back to sleep, he gives up and gets out of bed.
2. Twain tries to be very careful not to wake ________.
3. At first Twain just says "________ ________ ________," to himself.
4. When Twain still can't find the sock, his expletives grow steadily ________ and ________.
   a. Soon he has to ________ on the ________ and hold onto something to keep from swearing out loud.

III. End of the Selection (p. 155)

A. The Sock
1. The dim blur of the ________ give Twain no information as to where he is.
2. Twain finally finds the sock at the end of ________ ________ ________.
3. When he rises with the sock, he knocks over the ________ and pitcher.
4. ________ wakes up from the crash and asks if Twain is hunting for his sock with a ________.

World Literature

Student Study Guide 19

I kept that up;—and still kept it up and *kept* it up. At first I only said to myself "Blame that sock," but that soon ceased to answer; my **expletives** grew steadily stronger and stronger and at last, when I found I was *lost,* I had to sit flat down on the floor and take hold of something to keep from lifting the roof off with the **profane** explosion that was trying to get out of me. I could see the dim blur of the window, but of course it was in the wrong place and could give me no information as to where I was. But I had one comfort, I had not waked Livy; I believed I could find that sock in silence if the night lasted long enough. So I started again and softly pawed all over the place, and sure enough at the end of half an hour I laid my hand on the missing article. I rose joyfully up and butted the wash-bowl and pitcher off the stand and simply raised - - - - so to speak. Livy screamed, then said, "Who is that? what *is* the matter? I said, "There ain't anything the matter—I'm hunting for my sock." She said, "Are you hunting for it with a club?"...

D Twain is writing in the late 1800s. The hotel room didn't have a bathroom or running water. Instead, they were given water in a pitcher and a bowl to pour it in. Both sat on the washstand.

E

F

8 **expletive** a curse

9 **profane** not holy or sacred

D ASK Critical Thinking How do you know that Twain is a man with a temper? (He "rages" to himself about being unable to sleep. As he becomes more and more frustrated with his search, he has more and more trouble resisting the urge to curse.)

E ASK Comprehension What prevents Twain from venting his frustration in an outburst of profanity? (He does not want to wake his wife.)

F ASK Critical Thinking Why does the incident with the wash-bowl and the pitcher make Twain lose his temper? (He hurts his head, makes a mess, wakes his wife despite all his efforts, and probably spills cold water on himself and the floor.)

Learning Styles

Tactile/Kinesthetic Have students work in groups to brainstorm about real-life comic experiences in darkness. For each situation, encourage students to pantomime the actions it entails. Remind them to show emotions as well as actions in order to establish the desired mood.

Name Date Period *Unit 2* *Activity* *21*

Letter to the Rev. J. H. Twichell

Part A Directions Read each sentence. Write *T* if the statement is true or *F* if it is false.

_______ 1. Samuel Clemens is the pen name of Mark Twain.

_______ 2. Twain was married three times.

_______ 3. Twain writes about staying in a hotel room.

_______ 4. Twain was looking for his socks and a broom.

_______ 5. Livy never awoke during Twain's search.

Part B Directions Circle the letter of the answer that correctly completes each sentence.

1. Twain
   - **a.** traveled widely. **b.** visited the doctor nearly every day.
   - **c.** worked at one job his whole life. **d.** hated his next-door neighbor.
2. Twain lost most of his money
   - **a.** gambling. **b.** in bad investments.
   - **c.** because of holes in his pockets. **d.** driving down the street.
3. The Reverend Twichell was from
   - **a.** Connecticut. **b.** New York.
   - **c.** Munich. **d.** Canada.
4. Twain wrote this letter from
   - **a.** Connecticut. **b.** New York.
   - **c.** Munich. **d.** Canada.
5. Twain's wife was named
   - **a.** Livy. **b.** Clara.
   - **c.** Spaulding. **d.** Wanda.

 World Literature

TRL

Activity 21

Name Date Period *Unit 2* *Workbook* *21*

Letter to the Reverend J. H. Twichell

Part A Directions In each blank write the word or phrase from the Word Bank that best completes each sentence.

1. Twain refers to Twichell's letter as ______________.
2. Swear words are called ______________ in Twain's letter.
3. As Twain searches for his sock, he is ______________, or feeling and scooping along the carpet.
4. The text calls quiet catlike action ______________.
5. Twain is finishing ______________ when Twichell's letter arrives.
6. To keep from waking Livy, Twain tries to dress in the ______________.
7. Twichell's letter talked about the butcher's way of ______________.
8. At ______________ Twain wakes up and cannot get back to sleep.
9. Livy wakes up when Twain bumps the ______________ and the pitcher.
10. Mark Twain is a ______________ for Samuel L. Clemens.

Word Bank				
3 A.M.	breakfast	dark	delicious	expletives
pawing	pen name	praying	stealthiness	wash-bowl

Part B Directions Circle the word or phrase in parentheses that best completes each sentence.

1. Twain says he is peculiarly (alive, sympathetic) to the performance of the butcher.
2. For (thirty minutes, two hours) Twain lies awake before he gets up to dress.
3. Twain tries to be quiet so as not to wake up (Livy, Lacey).
4. Twain finds all his clothes, save one (shoe, sock).
5. When his wife awakes with a scream, she asks if he is using a (club, gun) to hunt.

 World Literature

TRL

Workbook 21

Reviewing the Selection

Answer Key

Comprehension: Identifying Facts

1. Livy is her name.
2. He wakes at 3 A.M.
3. He does not want to wake Livy.

Comprehension: Understanding Main Ideas

4. 3, 1, 4, 2
5. Students may reason that it would be considered bad manners and a sin, and he is addressing a minister. By not using the words, he increases readers' involvement as they imagine what they were.
6. He uses a dash for each letter in the word he omits. He describes his internal cursing using neutral synonyms such as expletives.

Understanding Literature: Puns

7. He uses *hunting* to mean "searching"; Livy uses it to mean "preying on" or "trying to kill for food."
8. Yes; it refers to both the taste of food and the enjoyment the letter gives.

Critical Thinking

9. Students may suggest that written communication is now primarily for business and consumer information, while personal feelings and experiences are expressed in speech. Informal speech tends to lack the careful thought and quality of expression that one would put into a letter.
10. Fewer personal experiences will be preserved in writing for future generations. It may be more difficult in future centuries to understand the daily concerns and enjoyments of average people in the twentieth century.

Writing on Your Own Encourage students who choose to summarize the narrative to list events in order using their own words. They can then use the list to draft their paragraphs. Students who contrast the letters should first create a table to describe differences in such elements as type of language used, character of the writer, tone, etc.

Selection Quiz

The Teacher's Resource Library includes a Selection Quiz for "Letter to the Rev J. H. Twichell" that may be given following the Selection Review.

REVIEWING the SELECTION

Letter to the Reverend J. H. Twichell

Mark Twain

Directions Write the answers to these questions using complete sentences.

Comprehension: Identifying Facts

1. What is the first name of Twain's wife?
2. What time does Twain wake up?
3. Why is Twain trying to dress in the dark?

Comprehension: Understanding Main Ideas

4. Put these events in the correct order.
   - Twain bumps his head.
   - Livy wakes up.
   - Twain can't sleep.
   - Twain loses his temper.

Twain may have used bad language during the night he described, but he doesn't in this letter.

5. List one reason why he doesn't.
6. What does he use in the letter to show bad language?

Understanding Literature: Puns

A pun is a humorous play on words or phrases. The joke depends on different meanings. For instance, a film called *Family Plot* contains a pun on the word *plot*. The movie is about a plan to murder various relatives. (That's a plot to kill the family). They will then be buried in the family's section of the cemetery, which is called the family plot.)

7. What is the pun in the last line of Twain's letter?
8. Is Twain's use of "delicious" in the first sentence another pun?

Critical Thinking

Letters tell us much of what we know about life in earlier times. People from all walks of life wrote letters. They wrote to family members, and to friends. The telephone and low-cost long distance service has changed this. People now call instead of writing.

9. How has this change affected the type of information people exchange?
10. What effect will this have on recorded history?

Writing on Your Own Write two paragraphs about one of these topics.

- Explain what happens to Mark Twain during the night described in his letter.
- Contrast the purpose of Twain's letter with that of Tagore's.

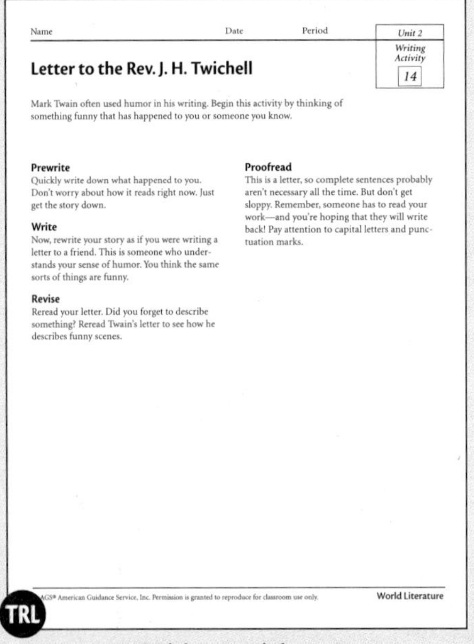

Name Date Period | *Unit 2* *Writing Activity* 14

Letter to the Rev. J. H. Twichell

Mark Twain often used humor in his writing. Begin this activity by thinking of something funny that has happened to you or someone you know.

Prewrite
Quickly write down what happened to you. Don't worry about how it reads right now. Just get the story down.

Write
Now, rewrite your story as if you were writing a letter to a friend. This is someone who understands your sense of humor. You think the same sorts of things are funny.

Revise
Reread your letter. Did you forget to describe something? Reread Twain's letter to see how he describes funny scenes.

Proofread
This is a letter, so complete sentences probably aren't necessary all the time. But don't get sloppy. Remember, someone has to read your work—and you're hoping that they will write back! Pay attention to capital letters and punctuation marks.

 World Literature

TRL

Writing Activity 14

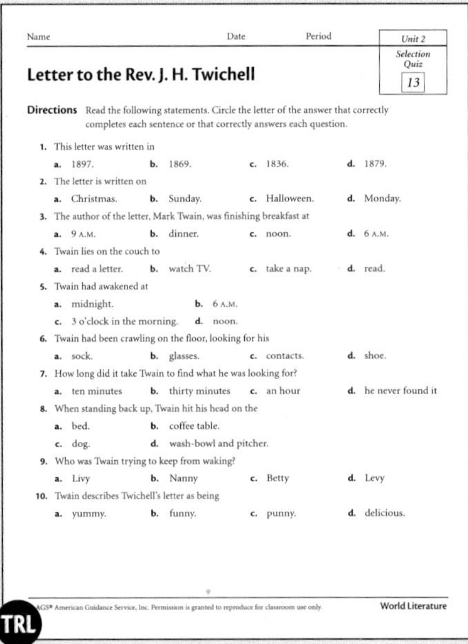

Name Date Period | *Unit 2* *Selection Quiz* 13

Letter to the Rev. J. H. Twichell

Directions Read the following statements. Circle the letter of the answer that correctly completes each sentence or that correctly answers each question.

1. This letter was written in
   a. 1897. b. 1869. c. 1836. d. 1879.
2. The letter is written on
   a. Christmas. b. Sunday. c. Halloween. d. Monday.
3. The author of the letter, Mark Twain, was finishing breakfast at
   a. 9 A.M. b. dinner. c. noon. d. 6 A.M.
4. Twain lies on the couch to
   a. read a letter. b. watch TV. c. take a nap. d. read.
5. Twain had awakened at
   a. midnight. b. 6 A.M.
   c. 3 o'clock in the morning. d. noon.
6. Twain had been crawling on the floor, looking for his
   a. sock. b. glasses. c. contacts. d. shoe.
7. How long did it take Twain to find what he was looking for?
   a. ten minutes b. thirty minutes c. an hour d. he never found it
8. When standing back up, Twain hit his head on the
   a. bed. b. coffee table.
   c. dog. d. wash-bowl and pitcher.
9. Who was Twain trying to keep from waking?
   a. Livy b. Nanny c. Betty d. Levy
10. Twain describes Twichell's letter as being
   a. yummy. b. funny. c. punny. d. delicious.

 World Literature

TRL

Selection Quiz 13

Autobiography

- "Few books are more thrilling than certain confessions, but they must be honest, and the author must have something to confess." —Simone de Beauvoir
- "Hiring someone to write your autobiography is like hiring someone to take a bath for you." —Mae West

Writing one's own life story is known as an autobiography. If talented enough, the person may write the story alone. Or the person may choose to write the book "as told to" someone. A ghost writer may be paid to write the book and let its subject take credit. In any case, the author shapes and arranges the life experiences. Some events will be pointed out, others ignored. This helps the reader share the author's view of his or her life.

Authors of autobiographies try to be honest, then write about all of their life, good and bad. Or they may look only at what they think is most important. Whatever the choice, these authors must leave out some personal experiences. They can talk about their life only from their own point of view.

An author's personal knowledge and viewpoint limit an autobiography. A good autobiography balances those limits. It does so by offering a personal glimpse at the author's mistakes and the decisions that shaped his or her life. In this section you will learn how people react to something in their lives. As you read, think about how these people are the same as or different from you.

Autobiography

Have students take turns reading the text on page 157 aloud or read it silently.

ASK If a person wants to tell the world his or her story, why do so many people seek help in writing (or let others write) their autobiographies? (They may lack confidence in their ability to express themselves or lack experience in writing.)

ASK Explain why an autobiography might omit certain of the person's life experiences. (The writer may exclude incidents that seem unimportant or boring or may be unwilling to share some of the most intimate details. The writer includes only the facts and descriptions that are relevant to the overall impression he or she wants to create.)

ASK Why do you think a writer might include unflattering details and mistakes in an autobiography? (Students may mention a desire to purge a guilty conscience, to get attention, to create a truthful image of himself or herself, or to help others learn from his or her experience.)

Have students read the quotes at the top of page 157 and explain why they agree or disagree with each.

Name Date Period — Unit 2, Activity 22

Autobiography

Part A Directions Circle the letter of the answer that correctly completes each sentence.

1. A _____ may be hired to do the actual writing of an autobiography.
   a. news reporter **b.** singer **c.** lawyer **d.** ghost writer
2. If you write your own life story, it is called
   a. autobiography. **b.** biography. **c.** fiction. **d.** journal.
3. An author's knowledge and _____ may limit the story.
   a. skills **b.** viewpoint **c.** talents **d.** partner
4. Every author of an autobiography usually leaves out some _____ experiences.
   a. critical **b.** personal **c.** life-threatening **d.** fictional
5. Most autobiographical authors try to be _____ when writing their own life stories.
   a. funny **b.** personal **c.** honest **d.** serious

Part B Directions Read each sentence. Write *T* if the statement is true or *F* if it is false.

_____ 1. The author of a news piece shapes and arranges their life.
_____ 2. A person may choose to write a book "as told to" someone.
_____ 3. The reader dislikes the author's view of his or her life.
_____ 4. Some authors include only events they consider important.
_____ 5. A good autobiography tries to make its subject look good, even if he or she wasn't.

 World Literature

TRL

Activity 22

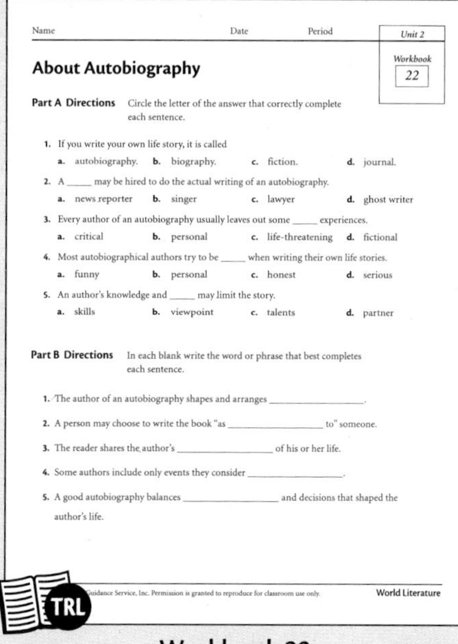

Name Date Period — Unit 2, Workbook 22

About Autobiography

Part A Directions Circle the letter of the answer that correctly complete each sentence.

1. If you write your own life story, it is called
   a. autobiography. **b.** biography. **c.** fiction. **d.** journal.
2. A _____ may be hired to do the actual writing of an autobiography.
   a. news reporter **b.** singer **c.** lawyer **d.** ghost writer
3. Every author of an autobiography usually leaves out some _____ experiences.
   a. critical **b.** personal **c.** life-threatening **d.** fictional
4. Most autobiographical authors try to be _____ when writing their own life stories.
   a. funny **b.** personal **c.** honest **d.** serious
5. An author's knowledge and _____ may limit the story.
   a. skills **b.** viewpoint **c.** talents **d.** partner

Part B Directions In each blank write the word or phrase that best completes each sentence.

1. The author of an autobiography shapes and arranges _____________.
2. A person may choose to write the book "as _____________ to" someone.
3. The reader shares the author's _____________ of his or her life.
4. Some authors include only events they consider _____________.
5. A good autobiography balances _____________ and decisions that shaped the author's life.

 World Literature

TRL

Workbook 22

Selection at a Glance

When Heaven and Earth Changed Places

Le Ly Hayslip

Student pages 158–164

Overview

This excerpt comes from the memoir of life in war-time Vietnam that moved director and Vietnam War veteran Oliver Stone to fund the building of a clinic for homeless children in Le Ly's village in Da Nang.

Selection Summary

This excerpt explains the importance of rice to the Vietnamese peasants and describes the sequence of painstaking jobs required to ready the paddies, sprout and plant the seedlings, care for the rice crop, and harvest and sort it.

Objectives

- To understand and explain the meaning of a legend.
- To read about and understand another culture.

Audiocassette

Teacher's Resource Library TRL

- Vocabulary Workbook 14
- Selection Glossary 14
- Student Study Guide 20
- Activity 23, pages 1–2
- Workbook 23, pages 1–2
- Writing Activity 15
- Selection Quiz 14

INTRODUCING the SELECTION

When Heaven and Earth Changed Places

Le Ly Hayslip

Le Ly Hayslip
(1949–)
Vietnamese

Literary Terms

legend a traditional story that was told orally and handed down from one generation to another

sequence the order of events in a literary work

About the Author

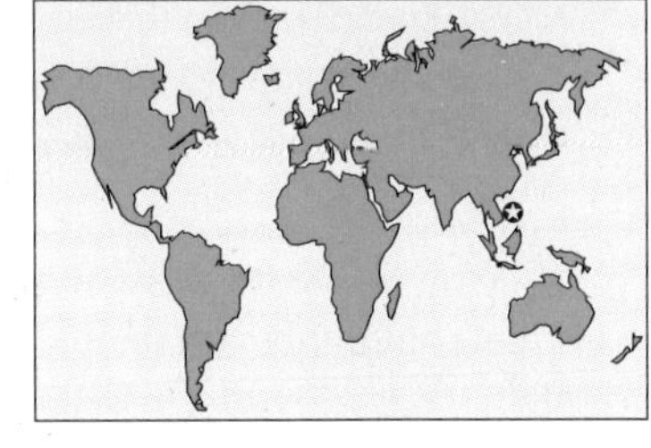

Le Ly Hayslip was born in central Vietnam. She was the youngest girl in a peasant family. The country was a French colony, but some Vietnamese were fighting for independence. The fighters were led by Communists in the north. As a result, Americans later became involved. Villages like Ky La were caught between the armies. In 1969 Hayslip married an older American who worked in Vietnam. They moved to the United States. She became a citizen. In 1973 her husband died and Hayslip was left to make her own way. In 1987 she founded the East Meets West Foundation, which tries to help Vietnam rebuild from the war. Another goal of the foundation is to improve cultural relations between Vietnam and the United States.

About the Selection

When Heaven and Earth Changed Places is Hayslip's story of life in Vietnam. Her wartime life was full of love and hate and fear. This selection describes the hard work that goes into planting and harvesting rice.

The order of events in a story is called **sequence**. Hayslip's story carefully shows the sequence of work in raising a rice crop. Look for the steps in this sequence as you read.

Hayslip retells a Vietnamese legend in her story. A **legend** is a traditional story that was once told orally. It was handed down from one generation to another. Notice how the legend adds interest and humor to the story.

Setting the Stage for Reading

About the Author

Have students read the text and look at the photo. Hayslip's books have helped to heal the wounds of war, but they were only her first step. Her East Meets West Foundation helps Vietnamese children and promotes healing among those who fought in Vietnam. She urges guilt-stricken American soldiers to take positive action by rebuilding Vietnamese schools and medical facilities and so gain peace of mind.

ASK Why do you think someone who was hurt by the war would try to help those who hurt her? (She knows the power of positive action to heal wounds and has forgiven the enemies.)

About the Selection

Much of *When Heaven and Earth Changed Places* is difficult reading, with accounts of torture, torment, and suffering of innocent victims of war. However, this excerpt focuses on the daily lives and spirit of Vietnamese people.

Activate Prior Knowledge: Le Ly gives detailed descriptions of the processes involved in raising rice, a crucial and life-giving activity for the community. Have students think of an activity in which their whole community (or family) takes part frequently that is important to their lives.

ASK How are the farming techniques of the Vietnamese peasants different from those used in the United States? (They are laborious, primitive, and exhausting, whereas U.S. technology and machinery make farming a big business.)

When Heaven and Earth Changed Places

Le Ly Hayslip

Twice a year, in May and October, we villagers **A** prepared the land for planting. Because these months followed the winter and summer **monsoons**, it meant we had a variety of natural (as well as war-made) disasters to repair: from floods and high winds to **plagues** of grasshoppers and the wearing out of the soil itself.

As you read, notice that the author is telling about simple, everyday events. Even in wartime, they are essential to life in the village.

Although we grew many crops around Ky La—sweet potatoes, peanuts, cinnamon, and **taro**—the most important by far was rice. Yet for all its long history as the staff of life in our country, rice was a **fickle** provider. First, the spot of ground on which the rice was thrown had to be just right for the seed to sprout. Then, it had to be protected from birds and animals who needed food as much as we did. As a child, I spent many hours with the other kids in Ky La acting like human scarecrows—making noise and waving our arms—just to keep the raven-like *se-se* birds away from our future supper.

About 200 to 400 pounds per person of rice is eaten per year in Asia, compared with 6 pounds per person in North America.

According to legend, god did not mean for us to work so hard for our rice. My father told me the story of *ong trang bu hung*, the spirit messenger who had been entrusted by god to bring rice—the heavenly food—to earth for humans to enjoy. God gave the messenger two magic sacks. "The seeds in the first," god said, "will grow when they touch the ground and give a plentiful harvest, anywhere, with no effort. The seeds in the second sack, however, must be **nurtured**; but, if tended properly, will give the earth great beauty."

The author uses words from the Vietnamese language throughout her story to remind you of the setting.

fickle not faithful; not reliable

monsoon seasonal winds that bring rain to southern Asia

nurture to care for

plague the sudden arrival of something destructive; a nuisance

taro a plant grown for its edible, starchy root

Nonfiction Unit 2 **159**

Reading Vocabulary 

Distribute the Selection Glossary page and ask students to scan it and star any words they already know. Pair students and have them explain to one another the meanings of words they have starred, then look up the definitions of the rest.

Motivation for Reading

Encourage students to imagine how it would feel to have to work many long, hard hours to have food to eat as they read about the laborious and exhausting processes of raising rice in Vietnam.

Discussion Questions

Suggest that students use the comments and questions in the margins of the student selection to focus their reading.

A ASK Comprehension Why do the villagers expose themselves to the dangers of war? (They have no choice; if they are to have food, they must ready the fields and plant rice.)

Name Date Period

Unit 2 *Vocabulary Workbook* *14*

When Heaven and Earth Changed Places

Directions If the sentence is true, circle *T*. If the sentence is false, circle *F*.

1. A legend is a traditional story that was first told orally and then handed down from one generation to another. T F
2. The sequence of events means the place they happened. T F
3. If I am fickle, then I am reliable and faithful. T F
4. A monsoon takes places once every hundred years in Greenland. T F
5. To nurture children is to care for them. T F
6. A plague is the sudden arrival of something destructive. T F
7. People eat taro, which is an edible plant. T F
8. A person could never throw a clod of dirt because it is too big. T F
9. To convey news is to keep it secret and tell no one. T F
10. My karma is my fate or my destiny. T F
11. I could use a mallet to pound a nail into a wooden board. T F
12. When I become mature, I will be fully grown. T F
13. To transplant something is to arrange it for the piano. T F
14. To heighten something is to make it less intense. T F
15. A leech is a type of tree that grows fruit. T F
16. Farmers use manure to fertilize their crops. T F
17. If something is monotonous, we never get tired of it. T F
18. A parcel of land is a fence. T F
19. A receptive person is unwilling to accept anything. T F
20. If something is sensual, it is pleasing to the senses. T F
21. A ritual is a type of furbearing animal. T F
22. If I run the race adequately, I do it well enough. T F
23. Communion is a sharing of feelings. T F
24. A divine is a type of sofa or couch for the living room. T F
25. A gemstone is a type of jewel. T F
26. A laborious task is one that I can do easily, with little work. T F

ishes and silverware need nutrients for cleaning. T F

 World Literature

Vocabulary Workbook 14

Name Date Period

Unit 2 *Student Study Guide* *20* *page 1*

When Heaven and Earth Changed Places (pp. 159–63)

Directions Fill in the following outline. Filling in the blanks will help you as you read and study *When Heaven and Earth Changed Places.*

I. Beginning of the Selection (pp. 159–60)

A. The Land

1. In ________ and October villagers prepare the land for planting.
2. The most important crop grown in ________ ________ is rice.
3. Legend says that ________ gave the spirit ________ two sacks of seeds.
   a. The messenger got the sacks ________ ________.
   b. God turned the messenger into a hard-shelled ________.

II. Middle of the Selection (pp. 160–61)

A. Planting Rice

1. It is replanted into ________ after the seeds grow into ________.
2. To test the texture of the soil, villagers lift a handful to see if the watery ________ oozes through their fingers like ________.
3. When the women transplant rice stalks, there is a sensual contact between their ________ and feet, the baby ________, and the wet, receptive ________—connecting women to the land.
4. To fertilize the plants, villagers shovel ________ from ________ pens.

 World Literature

Student Study Guide 20, pages 1-2

Discussion Questions

A ASK Literary Element Explain that a legend, or myth, often serves to explain some natural event. What natural phenomenon does this legend explain? (It provides a supposedly historical reason why rice requires hard work to grow, while grass does not. Students may be surprised to learn that the rice plant is actually a type of aquatic grass.)

B ASK Comprehension Call attention to the photograph on page 160, which shows women working in rice paddies. Ask students to use it and the text to describe the rice paddies. (Each paddy is contained within earth ridges, or terraces, to hold in place the water in which the rice must grow. The water is knee-deep and muddy.)

Cross-Curricular Connection

Social Studies Ask students to contrast the daily activities of women and children in the village with those of women and children in the United States. Suggest that they consider questions like the following:

- Why don't children labor in the United States?
- What is considered "women's work" in the United States?
- How might rice be planted in the United States?
- What dangers might arise from the long hours standing in mud and muddy water?

A Of course, god meant for the first seeds to be rice, which would feed millions with little effort; and the second to be grass, which humans couldn't eat but would enjoy as a cover for bare ground. Unfortunately, the heavenly messenger got the sacks mixed up, and humans immediately paid for his error: finding that rice was hard to grow whereas grass grew easily everywhere, especially where it wasn't wanted.

When god learned of this mistake, he booted the messenger out of heaven and sent him to earth as a hard-shelled beetle, to crawl on the ground forever lost in the grass to dodge the feet of the people he had so carelessly injured. This harsh **karma,** however, did nothing to make life easier for farmers.

A rice *paddy* is a field, usually small, surrounded by banks of dirt that serve as dams to hold the water when the field is flooded.

When the seeds had grown into stalks, we would pull them up—*nho ma*—and replant them in the paddies—the place where the rice **matured** and our crop eventually would be harvested.

After the hard crust had been turned and the **clods** broken up with **mallets** to the size of gravel, we had to wet it down with water **conveyed** from nearby ponds or rivers. Once the field had been flooded, it was left to soak for several days, after which our buffalo-powered plows could finish the job. In order to accept the seedling rice, however, the ground had to be *bua ruong*—even softer than the richest soil we used to grow vegetables. We knew the texture was right when a handful of watery mud would ooze through our fingers like soup.

B **Transplanting** the rice stalks from their "nursery" to the field was primarily women's work. Although we labored as fast as we could, this chore involved bending over for hours in knee-deep, muddy water. No matter how practiced we

clod a lump or chunk of dirt

convey to bring or carry

karma fate; destiny

mallet a short-handled, heavy hammer

mature to become fully grown

transplant to lift and replant in another area

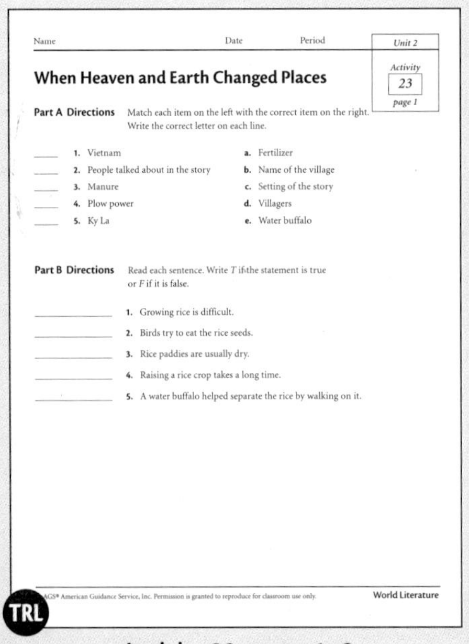

Name Date Period

Unit 2 Activity 23 page 1

When Heaven and Earth Changed Places

Part A Directions Match each item on the left with the correct item on the right. Write the correct letter on each line.

____ 1. Vietnam — a. Fertilizer
____ 2. People talked about in the story — b. Name of the village
____ 3. Manure — c. Setting of the story
____ 4. Plow power — d. Villagers
____ 5. Ky La — e. Water buffalo

Part B Directions Read each sentence. Write *T* if the statement is true or *F* if it is false.

______ 1. Growing rice is difficult.
______ 2. Birds try to eat the rice seeds.
______ 3. Rice paddies are usually dry.
______ 4. Raising a rice crop takes a long time.
______ 5. A water buffalo helped separate the rice by walking on it.

 World Literature

TRL

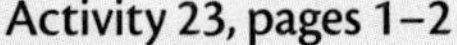

Activity 23, pages 1–2

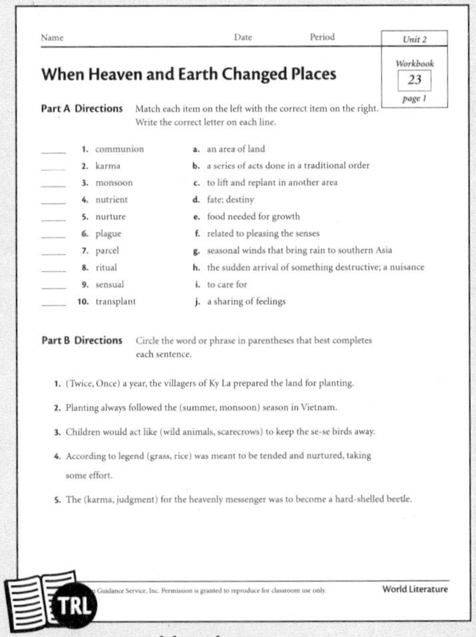

Name Date Period

Unit 2 Workbook 23 page 1

When Heaven and Earth Changed Places

Part A Directions Match each item on the left with the correct item on the right. Write the correct letter on each line.

____ 1. communion — a. an area of land
____ 2. karma — b. a series of acts done in a traditional order
____ 3. monsoon — c. to lift and replant in another area
____ 4. nutrient — d. fate; destiny
____ 5. nurture — e. food needed for growth
____ 6. plague — f. related to pleasing the senses
____ 7. parcel — g. seasonal winds that bring rain to southern Asia
____ 8. ritual — h. the sudden arrival of something destructive; a nuisance
____ 9. sensual — i. to care for
____ 10. transplant — j. a sharing of feelings

Part B Directions Circle the word or phrase in parentheses that best completes each sentence.

1. (Twice, Once) a year, the villagers of Ky La prepared the land for planting.
2. Planting always followed the (summer, monsoon) season in Vietnam.
3. Children would act like (wild animals, scarecrows) to keep the se-se birds away.
4. According to legend (grass, rice) was meant to be tended and nurtured, taking some effort.
5. The (karma, judgment) for the heavenly messenger was to become a hard-shelled beetle.

 World Literature

TRL

Workbook 23, pages 1–2

were, the constant search for a foothold in the sucking mud made the tedious work exhausting. Still, there was no other way to transplant the seedlings properly; and that **sensual** contact between our hands and feet, the baby rice, and the wet, **receptive** earth, is one of the things that preserved and **heightened** our connection with the land. While we worked, we sometimes sang to break the **monotony** and raise our spirits. One song my mother taught me went: **C**

We love the *hoa binh;*
Hoa binh means peace—first *hoa,* then *binh:*
Hoa means "together" and *binh* means "all the same."
When we're all together, no one is parted.
When we're the same, no one's at war.
Peace means no more suffering,
Hoa binh means no more war.

D
Why do you think the author included this song in her story?

When the planting was done, the ground had to be watered every other day and, because each **parcel** had supported our village for centuries, fertilized as well. Unless a family was very wealthy, it could not buy chemicals for this purpose, so we had to shovel **manure** from the animal pens and carry it in baskets to the fields where we would cast it evenly onto the growing plants. When animals became scarce later in the war, we sometimes had to add human waste collected from the latrines outside the village. And of course, wet, fertile ground breeds weeds and pulling them was the special task of the women and children. The first big weeding was called *lam co lua di,* followed a month later by a second "weeding party" called *lam co lua lai.* The standing water was also home for mosquitoes, **leeches,** snakes, and freshwater crabs and you were never too sure just what you would come up with in the next handful of weeds. It was backbreaking, unpleasant labor that ran fourteen hours a day for many days.... **E** **F**

#3 E or F

heighten to make more intense

leech a blood-sucking worm

manure animal waste used as fertilizer

monotony sameness

parcel an area of land

receptive ready to accept

sensual pleasing to the senses

C ASK Comprehension What main idea about the villagers' values do the details in this paragraph support? (The villagers love feeling connected to the land and to each other; they long for peace and harmony.)

D The song adds human interest and illustrates how the Vietnamese long for peace. It reminds of the war that is going on around them as they plant and harvest.

E ASK Comprehension What are the steps in planting and raising rice? (1. Sprout the seeds. 2. Prepare and flood the paddy. 3. Transplant the sprouts. 4. Water and fertilize the crop often.)

F ASK Critical Thinking Why do you think the women and children do such hard work and work such long hours? (Students can infer that women and children must work like this in order to have enough food; they also apparently are lower in social standing than the men.)

Discussion Questions

A ASK Critical Thinking Why did the author include the legends in this writing? (She wanted to show the character of the people—their simplicity, humor, and superstition—and give a flavor of their daily lives.)

B ASK Literary Element How has the author used humor here to make a point about life in Vietnam? (Her wry joke shows the people can laugh about their difficulties. At the same time, the comment reminds that hardship and the threat of starvation are the way of life for the peasants.)

C ASK Comprehension How are the water buffalo helpful to the villagers? (They pull the plows in the fields and trample the cuttings to separate rice grains and stalks.)

Learning Styles

Auditory Ask volunteers to read aloud the legend about how rice came to earth, beginning with the last paragraph on page 159, continuing through the third paragraph on page 160, and finishing with the second paragraph on page 162. Encourage them to use imaginative expression and gestures to help listeners visualize the action.

But planting was only part of village life. Like daylight and darkness, wakefulness and sleep, the labors and **rituals** of harvest defined the other half of our existence.

The author refers back to the legend telling the story of how rice came to earth.

A According to legend, human problems with rice didn't end with the forgetful beetle. When god saw that the mix-up in magic sacks had caused so much trouble on earth, he commanded the rice to "present itself for cooking" by rolling up to each home in a ball. Of course, the rice obeyed god and rolled into the first house it was supposed to serve. But the housewife, unprepared for such a sight, became frightened and hit it with a broom, scattering the rice ball into a thousand pieces. This so angered the rice that it went back outside and shouted, "See if I come back to let you cook me! Now you'll have to come out to the fields and bring me in if you want your supper!"

B That was the closest any Vietnamese ever came to a free bowl of rice.

Beginning in March, and again in August, we would bring the mature rice in from the fields and process it for use during the rest of the year. In March, when the ground was dry, we cut the rice very close to the soil—*cat lua*—to keep the plant alive. In August, when the ground was wet, we cut the plant halfway up—*cat gat*—which made the job much easier.

The separation of stalk and rice was done outside in a special smooth area beside our house. Because the rice was freshly cut, it had to dry in the sun for several days. At this stage, we called it *phoi lua*—not-yet rice. The actual separation was **C** done by our water buffalo, which walked in lazy circles over a heap of cuttings until the rice fell easily from the stalks. We gathered the stalks, tied them in bundles, and used them to fix roofs or to kindle our fires. The good, light-colored rice,

ritual a series of acts done in a traditional order

162 *Unit 2 Nonfiction*

called *lua chet,* was separated from the bad, dark-colored rice—*lua lep*—and taken home for further processing. The very best rice, of course, we gave back to Mother Earth. This seed rice was called *lua giong* and we put it into great jars which we filled with water. The wet rice was then packed under a haystack to keep warm. The **nutrients**, moisture, and heat helped the rice seeds to sprout, and after three days (during which we watered and fertilized the seedbed like a garden), we recovered the jars and cast the fertile *geo ma* seeds onto the ground we had prepared. But this was rice we would enjoy another day... **D**

The villagers made use of everything they grew and harvested. The stalks were used to patch roofs, the best rice as seeds for replanting, and the rest of the rice for food.

#4 Aork

We always blamed crop failures on ourselves—we had not worked hard enough or, if there was no other explanation, we had failed to **adequately** honor our ancestors. Our solution was to pray more and sacrifice more and eventually things always got better. Crops ruined by soldiers were another matter. We knew prayer was useless because soldiers were human beings, too, and the god of nature meant for them to work out their own karma just like us. **E**

In any event, the journey from seedling to rice bowl was long and **laborious** and because each grain was a symbol of life, we never wasted any of it. Good rice was considered god's **gemstone**—*hot ngoc troi*—and was cared for accordingly on pain of **divine** punishment. Even today a peasant seeing lightning will crouch under the table and look for lost grains in order to escape the next bolt. And parents must never strike children, no matter how naughty they've been, while the child is eating rice, for that would interrupt the sacred **communion** between rice-eater and rice-maker. Like my brothers and sisters, I learned quickly the advantages of chewing my dinner slowly. **F** **G**

climax

humorous

#5 Jork

#6 om

adequately well enough	**divine** coming from a god	**laborious** requiring long, hard work
communion a sharing of feelings	**gemstone** a jewel	**nutrient** food needed for growth

D ASK Critical Thinking Look at the Vietnamese words on these pages. What must *lua* mean? (Students should infer that it means rice.)

E ASK Comprehension What did crop failures cause the peasants to do? (Pray and sacrifice to be more worthy of a good crop.) Why didn't they react the same way to soldiers ruining crops? (Soldiers were not sent by gods; they were simply working out their fate.)

F ASK Critical Thinking How do you know rice had spiritual or sacred meaning to the villagers? (They considered it a gift from the gods; they believed not caring for it would bring divine punishment and eating rice established a "sacred communion.")

G ASK Literary Element Explain that a metaphor compares two things by saying one thing is the other. What metaphor do the Vietnamese have about good rice? Why is this comparison a good one? (It is "god's gemstone," which suggests something precious and beautiful. Rice and the rituals around it are valued greatly.)

Reviewing the Selection

Answer Key

Comprehension: Identifying Facts

1. They plant rice after preparing the paddies, probably in April and September; they harvest it when it matures, in March and August.

2. Two crops are harvested.

3. Women transplant the rice.

Comprehension: Understanding Main Ideas

4. They have used the same land over and over for centuries, so they must replace the nutrients in the soil.

5. They lack the money for tractors, and they would only get stuck in the mud, anyway.

6. Without rice, they would starve. It's also an integral part of their spiritual community.

Understanding Literature: Legend

7. They have to work very hard to raise and harvest the crop.

8. The messenger was turned into a hard-shelled beetle who had to worry about being stepped on. This harsh fate seems just, since the people are the ones who suffer for his mistake.

Critical Thinking

9. They seem to accept what comes and not to blame anyone. Although their life is hard, they seem to find happiness in small things.

10. She quips that the legend of the rice ball the housewife smashed is "the closest any Vietnamese ever came to a free bowl of rice" and confesses she ate slowly so her rice would last to avoid punishment.

Encourage students to list in two columns all the pluses and minuses they can think of. They can then evaluate each column and select the three most important in each. Encourage students to explain why they chose these advantages and disadvantages.

Selection Quiz

The Teacher's Resource Library includes a Selection Quiz for *When Heaven and Earth Changed Places* that may be given following the Selection Review.

REVIEWING the SELECTION

When Heaven and Earth Changed Places

Le Ly Hayslip

Directions Write the answers to these questions using complete sentences.

Comprehension: Identifying Facts

1. When do the villagers plant rice? When do they harvest the crop?
2. How many crops of rice do they harvest in one year?
3. Whose job is it to transplant the rice stalks?

Comprehension: Understanding Main Ideas

4. Why do the villagers need to fertilize the rice paddies?
5. Why do they use water buffaloes instead of tractors to plow the paddies?
6. Why is the rice crop so important to the villagers?

Understanding Literature: Legend

Hayslip retells the legend of how rice came to earth. A legend is a traditional story. It is passed on, often orally, from one generation to another. This legend tells how a heavenly messenger mixed up the sacks of grass seeds and rice seeds.

7. How do humans have to pay for the messenger's mistake?
8. What happened to the messenger? Was it a punishment that fit his crime?

Critical Thinking

Planting, caring for, and harvesting a rice crop is hard work. It required the help and time of everyone in the village. Hayslip writes that it defined their existence.

9. Do you think the villagers are happy or unhappy about their life?
10. Hayslip includes humor, the funny side of things, in her story. Give two examples of humor from the story.

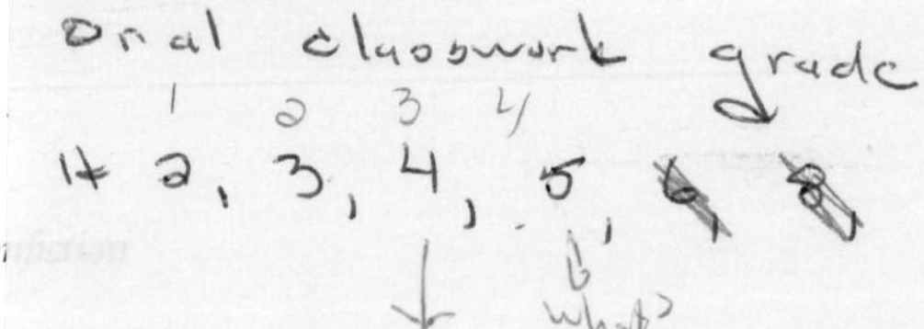

Writing on Your Own What do you think life was like for a child in Hayslip's village? Make a list of three advantages and three disadvantages of growing up in her village.

164 *Unit 2 Nonfiction*

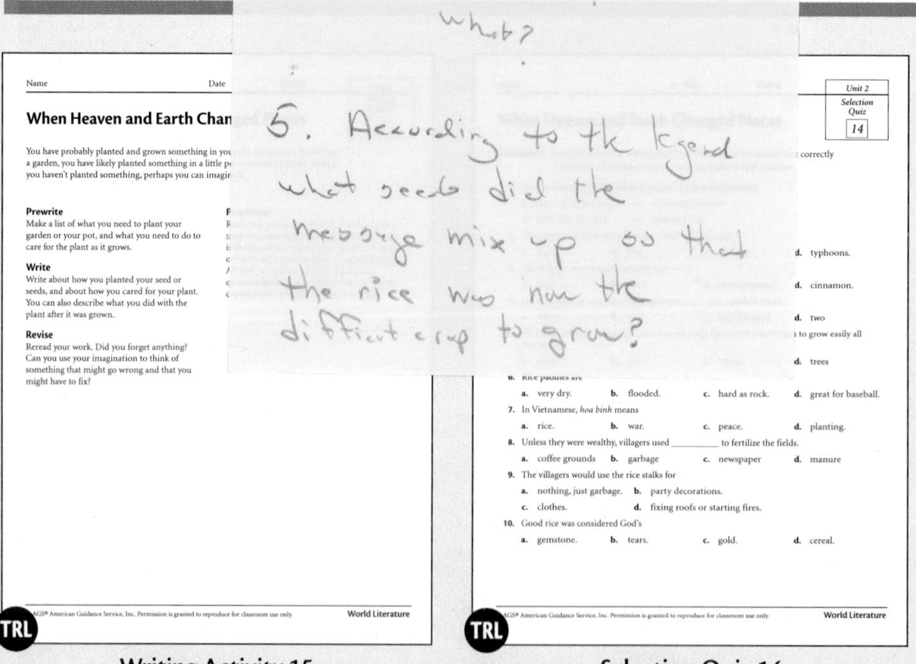

Name Date

When Heaven and Earth Chan

You have probably planted and grown something in you… a garden, you have likely planted something in a little p… you haven't planted something, perhaps you can imagi…

Prewrite
Make a list of what you need to plant your garden or your pot, and what you need to do to care for the plant as it grows.

Write
Write about how you planted your seed or seeds, and about how you cared for your plant. You can also describe what you did with the plant after it was grown.

Revise
Reread your work. Did you forget anything? Can you use your imagination to think of something that might go wrong and that you might have to fix?

AGS® American Guidance Service, Inc. Permission is granted to reproduce for classroom use only. World Literature

Unit 2 Selection Quiz 14

correctly

d. typhoons.

d. cinnamon.

d. two

to grow easily all

d. trees

6. Rice paddies are
a. very dry. b. flooded. c. hard as rock. d. great for baseball.
7. In Vietnamese, *hoa binh* means
a. rice. b. war. c. peace. d. planting.
8. Unless they were wealthy, villagers used _______ to fertilize the fields.
a. coffee grounds b. garbage c. newspaper d. manure
9. The villagers would use the rice stalks for
a. nothing, just garbage. b. party decorations.
c. clothes. d. fixing roofs or starting fires.
10. Good rice was considered God's
a. gemstone. b. tears. c. gold. d. cereal.

AGS® American Guidance Service, Inc. Permission is granted to reproduce for classroom use only. World Literature

TRL Writing Activity 15

TRL Selection Quiz 14

INTRODUCING the SELECTION

By Any Other Name

Santha Rama Rau

Santha Rama Rau
(1923–)
Indian

Literary Terms

autobiography a person's life story written by that person

first-person written as if the author is telling the story

point of view the position from which the author or storyteller tells the story

sketch a brief written work that often runs from subject to subject and is often humorous

About the Author

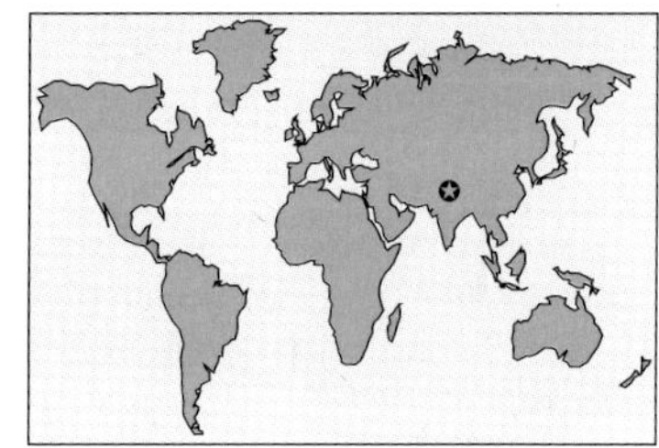

Santha Rama Rau was born in Madras, India in 1923. Her father held an important job in the British colonial government. His job took him many different places. His family moved with him. As a child, Rau lived in many parts of India. She also lived in England and South Africa. Rau went to college in the United States. She attended Wellesley College in Massachusetts. In her early twenties, she wrote an **autobiography**, a story of her life. It was called *Home to India*. The book was about her childhood and growing-up years. She went on to write several more books of autobiography. She also wrote fiction and articles about her travels.

About the Selection

In 1961, Rau published a book titled *Gifts of Passage.* It was a collection of **sketches** about her life. A sketch is a short piece of writing. It moves from subject to subject. A sketch is often humorous. The next selection is one of those sketches. It is written from a **first-person point of view.** This means that Rau is telling her own story just as she saw it. She tells about her experiences as a new student in a British school.

Selection at a Glance

By Any Other Name

Santha Rama Rau

Student pages 165–174

Overview

Santha Rama Rau's keen intelligence and literary skill are evident in this sketch about the negative beginning of her formal education. Ironically, she went on to obtain an excellent education. Her writing skill helped her tell the world about her beloved India.

Selection Summary

"By Any Other Name" is an autobiographical sketch that tells about two Indian girls who do not fit in at the British colonial school.

Objectives

- To read and understand an autobiographical sketch.
- To understand the use of first-person point of view.

Audiocassette 

Teacher's Resource Library 

- Vocabulary Workbook 15, pages 1–2
- Selection Glossary 15
- Student Study Guide 21, pages 1–2
- Activity 24, pages 1–2
- Workbook 24, pages 1–2
- Writing Activity 16
- Selection Quiz 15

Setting the Stage for Reading

About the Author

Ask students to read the text and look at the photo of Santha Rama Rau. She also adapted E. M. Forster's novel *A Passage to India* for the stage; her version had successful runs in London and New York. From 1971 to 1974 she taught English at Wellesley, a private college in the United States where she had been educated. Truly a citizen of the world, Rama Rau lived in South Africa, the United States, and Japan.

ASK Why do you think Rama Rau always wrote about India, despite the fact that she lived elsewhere much of her adult life? (Answers may include that her heritage was there, that she was proud of her family and culture, and that she wanted the world to know about India.)

About the Selection

Rama Rau's deep respect and love for her family and her culture are communicated through this anecdotal sketch, whose principle theme is the crippling nature of British racism.

Activate Prior Knowledge: Ask students to think of an occasion on which someone outside their family looked at them with suspicion or dislike, for no apparent reason. Invite volunteers to describe how this makes one feel.

ASK Why might British-run schools have existed in India in the 1920s? (India was a British colony until 1947.)

Reading Vocabulary TRL

Review the words on the Selection Glossary page. Have students look up the meaning and part of speech of each. Encourage them to find illustrations or photos showing what each person or thing looks like.

Motivation for Reading

Invite students to imagine and explain how they would feel the first day at a new school if teachers and students felt they were inferior.

Discussion Questions

Suggest that students use the comments and questions in the margins of the student selection to focus their reading.

A ASK Literary Element Remind students that the setting includes the place and time. Have them identify both and describe what it is like where the girls live. (In Zorinabad, India, it is hot and dry in September, just after the monsoon season. Their home is comfortable but the British-run school has been made less so by English touches.)

B ASK Critical Thinking What does the headmistress's attitude toward the girls' names reveal? (They are "foreign" and not pretty; she believes she is improving them by making them British. Her attitude reveals racism.)

C ASK Literary Element What do you think Premila's "stubborn silence" indicates? What clues to the girls' character do you have so far? (She doesn't like the headmistress's actions or attitude. Premila is proud and assumes the role of protector for her sister. Santha is timid and wants to please.)

By Any Other Name

Santha Rama Rau

As you read, think about when you were new in school.

The term *Anglo-Indian* usually meant a person from Britain living in India. It could also mean a person of English and Indian descent. This school is run by the British.

At the Anglo-Indian day school in Zorinabad to which my sister and I were sent when she was eight and I was five and **A** a half, they changed our names. On the first day of school, a hot, windless morning of a north Indian September, we stood in the **headmistress's** study and she said, "Now you're the *new* girls. What are your names?"

My sister answered for us. "I am Premila, and she"—nodding in my direction—"is Santha."

The headmistress had been in India, I suppose, fifteen years or so, but she still smiled her helpless **inability** to **cope** with Indian names. Her rimless half-glasses glittered, and the **precarious** bun **B** on the top of her head trembled as she shook her head. "Oh, my dears, those are much too hard for me. Suppose we give you pretty English names. Wouldn't that be more jolly? Let's see, now—Pamela for you, I think." She shrugged in a **baffled** way at my sister. "That's as close as I can get. And for *you*," she said to me, "how about Cynthia? Isn't that nice?"

C My sister was always less easily **intimidated** than I was, and while she kept a stubborn silence, I said, "Thank you," in a very tiny voice.

We had been sent to that school because my father, among his responsibilities as an officer of the **civil service**, had a tour of duty to perform in the villages around that steamy little provincial town, where he had his headquarters at that time. He used to make his shorter inspection tours on horseback, and a week before, in the stale heat of a

baffled confused

civil service civilian workers of the government

cope to manage successfully

headmistress female principal of a school

inability lack of ability

intimidated frightened

precarious insecure

166

Name Date Period

Unit 2 Vocabulary Workbook 15 page 1

By Any Other Name

Directions Each set of sentences below is missing two words. On the blanks, fill in the letters of the two correct words from the three given beneath the sentences.

1. Santha Rama Rau wrote her life story, or ____________, when she was young. *By Any Other Name* is an example of a ____________, or short piece of writing.
   a. sketch b. point of view c. autobiography
2. In her sketch, the author had a position, or ____________, from which to tell her story. She told it from the ____________, or her own, point of view.
   a. point of view b. first-person c. autobiography
3. Her father worked in the ____________ as a civilian worker for the government. Her mother felt that the British were ____________, or limited in their outlook.
   a. Hindi b. insular c. civil service
4. The author went to the British school and met the ____________, the woman principal. She left behind her books written in ____________, an Indian language.
   a. Hindi b. precarious c. headmistress
5. This happened in the ____________ season, which comes after the rainy season. The ____________, or roofed porch, of the British school was not typical.
   a. veranda b. postmonsoon c. valid
6. One young Indian girl at the school wore ____________, or makeup, around her eyes. She seemed to understand the series of events, or ____________, in the class.
   a. proceedings b. palpitate c. kohl
7. The word *apple* was not understandable, or was _____, to Santha Rama Rau at five and a half. Nor did she understand winning in _____ sports.
   a. competitive b. incomprehensible c. curry
8. For lunch, she had ____________, a highly seasoned food dish. She missed the smell of ____________, from the vines around her home.
   a. jasmine b. accordance c. curry
9. ____________, the British were not friends with the Indians. The child understood, for she was different and wore a ____________ draped around her body.
   a. apparently b. sari c. eucalyptus
10. On the way home, she smelled the leaves of the ____________ tree. She also saw a few ____________, who were the unskilled workers in India.
    a. collies b. sari c. eucalyptus

 World Literature

TRL Vocabulary Workbook 15, pages 1–2

Name Date Period

Unit 2 Student Study Guide 21 page 1

By Any Other Name (pp. 166–72)

Directions Fill in the following outline. Filling in the blanks will help you as you read and study "By Any Other Name."

I. Beginning of the Selection (pp. 166–69)

A. The Family
1. Santha and Premila go to an Anglo-Indian day school in __________.
2. The headmistress changes Premila's name to __________ and Santha's name to __________.
3. The girls' father is an officer of the __________ __________.
4. __________ health breaks down, so the girls are sent to the Anglo-Indian school.

B. The School
1. Santha develops a form of dual __________.
2. Indian verandas are usually __________, with stone floors; in tradition of British schools, the School verandas were painted dark brown and had __________ on the floors.
3. Santha sits next to an Indian girl wearing a __________ dress, Indian jewelry, and her hair in braids.
4. When the teacher asks Santha to stand and tell the class her __________, she says "I don't know."

II. Middle of the Selection (pp. 169–70)

A. Lunch
1. Santha watches a __________ clinging to the ledge of a window behind the teacher's head.
2. Premila and Santha are the only children eating __________ food.
   a. They eat chapatties, vegetable __________, and buttermilk.
3. After lunch, Santha is sleepy, because she usually takes a __________ at this time of day, when she's at home.

 World Literature

TRL Student Study Guide 21, pages 1–2

typically **postmonsoon** day, we had waved good-by to him and a little procession—an assistant, a secretary, two bearers, and the man to look after the bedding rolls and luggage: They rode away through our large garden, still bright green from the rains, and we turned back into the twilight of the house and the sound of fans **D** whispering in every room.

Up to then, my mother had refused to send Premila to school in the British-run establishments of that time, because, she used to say, **E** "you can bury a dog's tail for seven years and it still comes out curly, and you can take a Britisher away from his home for a lifetime and he still remains **insular**." The examinations and degrees from entirely Indian schools were not, in those days, considered **valid.** In my case, the question had never come up, and probably never would have come up if Mother's **extraordinary** good health had not broken down. For the first time in my life, she was not able to continue the lessons she had been giving us every morning. So our **Hindi** books were put away, the stories of the Lord Krishna as a little boy were left in mid-air, and we were sent to the Anglo-Indian school.

That first day at school is still, when I think of it, a remarkable one. At that age, if one's name is changed, one develops a curious form of dual personality. I remember having a certain detached and **F** disbelieving concern in the actions of "Cynthia," but certainly no responsibility. Accordingly, I followed the thin, erect back of the headmistress down the **veranda** to my classroom feeling, at most, a passing interest in what was going to happen to me in this strange, new atmosphere of School.

The building was Indian in design, with wide verandas opening onto a central courtyard, but Indian verandas are usually whitewashed, with stone floors. These, in the tradition of British schools, were painted dark brown and had matting on the floors. It gave a feeling of extra intensity to the heat.

I suppose there were about a dozen Indian children in the school—which contained perhaps forty children in all—and four of them were in my class. They were all sitting at the back of the room, and I went to join them. I sat next to a small, solemn girl who didn't smile at me. She had long, glossy-black braids and wore a cotton

The girls' mother believes that the British always act as if they were still in England although they are really living and working in India.

Lord Krishna is revered as a Hindu deity or god. His triumph over a demon god is celebrated each year in a festival of lights.

The dark paint and mats absorbed the heat from the sun. The whitewashed floors reflected it and were therefore cooler

extraordinary remarkable

Hindi languages widely spoken in India

insular limited in outlook and experience

postmonsoon after the rainy season

valid completely acceptable; genuine

veranda a roofed porch running along the outside of a building

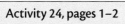

D ASK Literary Element Explain that an author may give a more vivid impression of a place or thing by personifying it, or giving it human characteristics. Have students identify what is personified. What impression of the house does it create? (The fans are personified as whispering people. It gives the impression of quiet and coolness.)

E ASK Literary Element The mother's analogy here compares the British attitude to a long-buried dog's tail. Help students to understand that the comparison is intended to show how the British retain an unchanging attitude of superiority about their culture no matter how long they are exposed to others.

F ASK Comprehension Why does Santha not feel nervous or excited about school now? (Since her real identity was taken from her, she does not feel responsible for "Cynthia's" actions; the school experience seems to be happening to someone else.)

Career Connection

Civil Service Explain that civil service jobs are salaried positions with a government agency. There are literally hundreds of thousands of civil service jobs in the United States, ranging from office work at state universities to many different careers with the federal government, in Washington, D.C., and other locations. Have students research careers in civil service at the state or federal level and find out how employees are chosen, what opportunities are available, and what education is required.

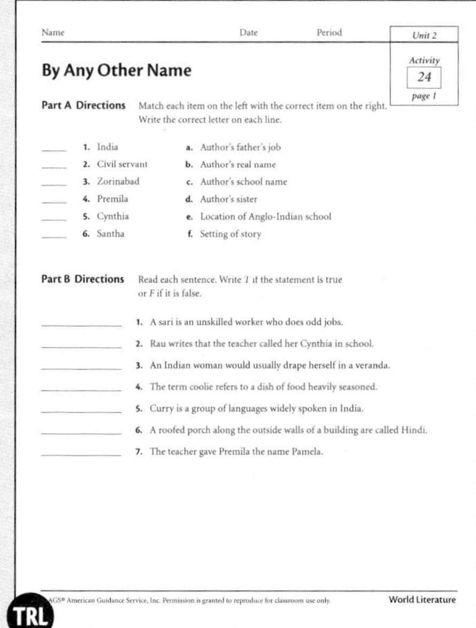

Name Date Period | Unit 2 | Activity 24 page 1

By Any Other Name

Part A Directions Match each item on the left with the correct item on the right. Write the correct letter on each line.

_____ 1. India — a. Author's father's job
_____ 2. Civil servant — b. Author's real name
_____ 3. Zorinabad — c. Author's school name
_____ 4. Premila — d. Author's sister
_____ 5. Cynthia — e. Location of Anglo-Indian school
_____ 6. Santha — f. Setting of story

Part B Directions Read each sentence. Write *T* if the statement is true or *F* if it is false.

_____ 1. A sari is an unskilled worker who does odd jobs.
_____ 2. Rau writes that the teacher called her Cynthia in school.
_____ 3. An Indian woman would usually drape herself in a veranda.
_____ 4. The term coolie refers to a dish of food heavily seasoned.
_____ 5. Curry is a group of languages widely spoken in India.
_____ 6. A roofed porch along the outside walls of a building are called Hindi.
_____ 7. The teacher gave Premila the name Pamela.

 World Literature

TRL

Activity 24, pages 1–2

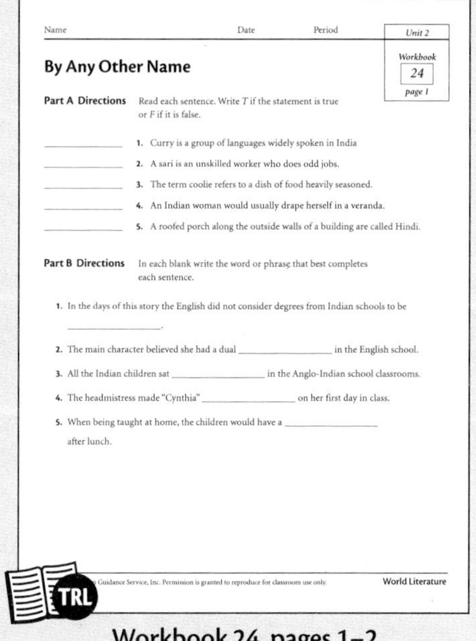

Name Date Period | Unit 2 | Workbook 24 page 1

By Any Other Name

Part A Directions Read each sentence. Write *T* if the statement is true or *F* if it is false.

_____ 1. Curry is a group of languages widely spoken in India
_____ 2. A sari is an unskilled worker who does odd jobs.
_____ 3. The term coolie refers to a dish of food heavily seasoned.
_____ 4. An Indian woman would usually drape herself in a veranda.
_____ 5. A roofed porch along the outside walls of a building are called Hindi.

Part B Directions In each blank write the word or phrase that best completes each sentence.

1. In the days of this story the English did not consider degrees from Indian schools to be _____.
2. The main character believed she had a dual _____ in the English school.
3. All the Indian children sat _____ in the Anglo-Indian school classrooms.
4. The headmistress made "Cynthia" _____ on her first day in class.
5. When being taught at home, the children would have a _____ after lunch.

 World Literature

TRL

Workbook 24, pages 1–2

Nonfiction Unit 2 **167**

Discussion Questions

A ASK **Comprehension** What details show that the girl has had to change her identity to attend the school? (She wears a western style dress; she is subdued and seems sad.)

B ASK **Critical Thinking** How does Santha react to the laughter of the English children? Why does Santha want to "dry" her eyes? (Their laughter shames her. Humiliated, she begins to cry. She does not want the English to realize she is crying, as they would if she wiped her eyes with her hand.)

C Apples are not native to India. *Apple* is one of the first words English children learn in school, and the teacher is approaching the class as if everyone is (or should be) English.

Learning Styles

Group Learning Have students participate in small group discussions about ways a teacher can meet individual needs of students and show respect for diverse cultures in the classroom. Encourage them to describe specific learning situations, including situations in which they failed to understand something new. Suggest alternative ways to learn a subject, besides traditional lecture and discussion. Invite students to describe their experiences of other cultures.

A dress, but she still kept on her Indian jewelry—a gold chain around her neck, thin gold bracelets, and tiny ruby studs in her ears. Like most Indian children, she had a rim of black **kohl** around her eyes. The cotton dress should have looked strange, but all I could think of was that I should ask my mother if I couldn't wear a dress to school, too, instead of my Indian clothes.

I can't remember too much about the **proceedings** in class that day, except for the beginning. The teacher pointed to me and asked me to stand up. "Now, dear, tell the class your name."

I said nothing.

"Come along," she said, frowning slightly. "What's your name, dear?"

"I don't know," I said, finally.

The English children in the front of the class—there were about eight or ten of them—giggled and twisted around in their chairs to **B** look at me. I sat down quickly and opened my eyes very wide, hoping in that way to dry them off. The little girl with the braids put out her hand and very lightly touched my arm. She still didn't smile.

Most of that morning I was rather bored. I looked briefly at the children's drawings pinned to the wall, and then concentrated on a lizard clinging to the ledge of the high, barred window behind the teacher's head. Occasionally it would shoot out its long yellow tongue for a fly, and then it would rest, with its eyes closed and its belly **palpitating**, as though it were swallowing several times quickly. The lessons were mostly concerned with reading and writing and simple numbers—things that my mother had already taught me—and I paid very little attention. The teacher wrote on the easel blackboard words like "bat" and "cat," which seemed babyish to me; only "apple" was new and **incomprehensible**.

C
Why didn't Santha know what an apple was? Why did the teacher present it as a word to learn?

Chapatties are delicate flatbreads served with almost every meal in India. They may be used in place of a fork or spoon to scoop up bites of food.

When it was time for the lunch recess, I followed the girl with braids out onto the veranda. There the children from the other classes were assembled. I saw Premila at once and ran over to her, as she had charge of our lunchbox. The children were all opening packages and sitting down to eat sandwiches. Premila and I were the only ones who had Indian food—thin wheat chapatties, some

kohl dark powder used as eye makeup

incomprehensible not capable of being understood

proceedings series of events

palpitate to beat rapidly

vegetable **curry**, and a bottle of buttermilk. Premila thrust half of it into my hand and whispered fiercely that I should go and sit with my class, because that was what the others seemed to be doing.

The enormous black eyes of the little Indian girl from my class looked at my food longingly, so I offered her some. But she only **D** shook her head and plowed her way solemnly through her sandwiches.

I was very sleepy after lunch, because at home we always took a **siesta**. It was usually a pleasant time of day, with the bedroom darkened against the harsh afternoon sun, the drifting off into sleep with the sound of Mother's voice reading a story in one's mind, and, finally, the shrill, fussy voice of the ayah waking one for tea.

At school, we rested for a short time on low, folding cots on the veranda, and then we were expected to play games. During the hot part of the afternoon we played indoors, and after the shadows had begun to lengthen and the slight breeze of the evening had come up we moved outside to the wide courtyard.

I had never really grasped the system of **competitive** games. At **E** home, whenever we played tag or guessing games, I was always allowed to "win"—"because," Mother used to tell Premila, "she is the youngest, and we have to allow for that." I had often heard her say it, and it seemed quite reasonable to me, but the result was that I had no clear idea of what "winning" meant.

When we played twos-and-threes that afternoon at school, in **accordance** with my training, I let one of the small English boys catch me, but was naturally rather puzzled when the other children did not return the **courtesy**. I ran about for what seemed like hours without ever catching anyone, until it was time for school to close. Much later I learned that my attitude was called "not being a good sport," and I stopped allowing myself to be caught, but it was not for years that I really learned the spirit of the thing.

When I saw our car come up to the school gate, I broke away from my classmates and rushed toward it yelling, "Ayah! Ayah!" It seemed like an eternity since I had seen her that morning—a

An *ayah* in India is a person who cares for young children. In America, the person would be called a nanny.

accordance agreement

competitive involving the effort to win

courtesy an act of politeness

curry a food dish seasoned with curry powder

siesta a rest, usually taken after the noonday meal

D ASK Critical Thinking Help students draw a conclusion from this reaction to lunch from an Indian child attending the British school. What does her longing reveal? (She would prefer to eat this familiar food than the foreign sandwiches. Her refusal shows that she feels she must mimic the English in order to be accepted in school and escape ridicule.)

E ASK Comprehension Have students compare and contrast the "rules" of games in the two cultures. Why doesn't Santha understand competition? What does her family value more? (British games stress skill and winning by outperforming others; Santha's mother stresses building good feelings and a positive self-image. One is self-centered and one considers others. One creates conflict of a sort between playmates, and the other fosters kindness and caring about other's feelings. The idea of winning is completely foreign to Santha.)

Grammar

Adverbs Point out the phrase "frowning slightly" on page 168. Explain that *slightly* is an adverb, a word used to modify, or describe, a verb, adjective, or other adverb. *Slightly* tells how the teacher was frowning. Adverbs may also tell when, where, and to what extent. Many adverbs are formed by adding *-ly* to an adjective form of a word. Have students scan pages 168 and 169 to find ten more examples of adverbs and the words they modify. (can't remember too much; said, finally; sat down quickly; very lightly touched; occasionally would shoot; swallowing quickly; mostly concerned; had already taught; whispered fiercely; looked longingly; plowed solemnly; very sleepy; had never really grasped; had often heard; was naturally rather puzzled; ran about; really learned)

Discussion Questions

A She does not want to give the English any chance to criticize their behavior. She wants to blend in. Santha's impulsive outburst lacks the dignity Premila wants to maintain.

B ASK Literary Element Point out that this paragraph shows more of Santha's character. What sort of girl is she? How would you describe her personality? What is different about the way she acted at school? (She is energetic, happy, and bubbly at home, where she knows she is well loved. She is playful, argumentative, and joyfully involved. At school, she was confused, quiet, and inattentive.)

C Although she says it is for Santha's benefit, Premila is the one who cares. She wants to fit in. Their Indian food and dress make her and Santha stand out, and for an Indian, that is not good.

Comprehension

Word Meaning Remind students that when they come upon an unfamiliar word in reading, they should first reread the sentence in which it occurs and one or two sentences before and after it for context clues. These details often help to define the word. For example, in the sentence "Premila followed more sedately," students may not know the meaning of *sedately.* Point out that her manner of walking is contrasted with Santha's, described in the paragraph's first sentence. Santha races to the car in excitement, yelling at her Ayah. Premila's movements are opposite, so *sedately* must mean calmly, slowly, and with dignity.

wizened, affectionate figure in her white cotton **sari** giving me dozens of urgent and useless instructions on how to be a good girl at school. Premila followed more **sedately,** and she told me on the way home never to do that again in front of the other children.

A
Why did Premila criticize Santha's behavior?

B When we got home we went straight to Mother's high, white room to have tea with her, and I immediately climbed onto the bed and bounced gently up and down on the springs. Mother asked how we had liked our first day in school. I was so pleased to be home and to have left that peculiar Cynthia behind that I had nothing whatever to say about school, except to ask what "apple" meant. But Premila told Mother about the classes, and added that in her class they had weekly tests to see if they had learned their lessons well.

I asked, "What's a test?"

Premila said, "You're too small to have them. You won't have them in your class for donkey's years." She had learned the expression that day and was using it for the first time. We all laughed enormously at her wit. She also told Mother, in an aside, that we should take sandwiches to school the next day. Not, she said, that *she* minded. But they would be simpler for me to handle.

C
Did Premila really want to take sandwiches because that's what all the other students ate? Did she want to do it in order to fit in?

That whole lovely evening I didn't think about school at all. I **sprinted** barefoot across the lawns with my favorite playmate, the cook's son, to the stream at the end of the garden. We quarreled in our usual way, waded in the **tepid** water under the lime trees, and waited for the night to bring out the smell of the **jasmine.** I listened with fascination to his stories of ghosts and demons, until I was too frightened to cross the garden alone in the semidarkness.

jasmine a vine or bush with fragrant flowers

sari a draped outer garment of lightweight cloth traditionally worn by Indian women

sedately calmly; with dignity

sprint to run a short distance at top speed

tepid slightly warm

wizened dried up; wrinkled

170 *Unit 2 Nonfiction*

The ayah found me, shouted at the cook's son, scolded me, hurried me in to supper—it was an entirely usual, wonderful evening.

It was a week later, the day of Premila's first test, that our lives changed rather abruptly. I was sitting at the back of my class, in my usual inattentive way, only half listening to the teacher. I had started a rather guarded friendship with the girl with the braids, whose name turned out to be Nalini (Nancy, in school). The three other Indian children were already fast friends. Even at that age it was **apparent** to all of us that friendship with the English or Anglo-Indian children was out of the question. Occasionally, during the class, my new friend and I would draw pictures and show them to each other secretly. **D**

Notice that Nalini has also been given an English name to use in school.

The door opened sharply and Premila marched in. At first, the teacher smiled at her in a kindly and encouraging way and said, "Now, you're little Cynthia's sister?" **E**

Premila didn't even look at her. She stood with her feet planted firmly apart and her shoulders **rigid**, and addressed herself directly to me. "Get up," she said. "We're going home."

I didn't know what had happened, but I was aware that it was a crisis of some sort. I rose obediently and started to walk toward my sister. **F**

"Bring your pencils and your notebook," she said.

I went back for them, and together we left the room. The teacher started to say something just as Premila closed the door, but we didn't wait to hear what it was.

In complete silence we left the school grounds and started to walk home. Then I asked Premila what the matter was. All she would say was "We're going home for good."

It was a very tiring walk for a child of five and a half, and I dragged along behind Premila with my pencils growing sticky in my hand. I can still remember looking at the dusty hedges, and the tangles of thorns in the ditches by the side of the road, smelling the faint **fragrance** from the **eucalyptus** trees and wondering whether we would ever reach home. Occasionally a horse-drawn **tonga** passed **G**

apparent easily understood

eucalyptus a tall tree with strong-smelling leaves

fragrance sweetness of smell

rigid stiff

tonga a wagon

D ASK Comprehension How is Santha different at school than she is at home? (She is inward and withdrawn and pays little attention to the teacher. She is tentative in her friendship with Nalini, in contrast to her exuberant friendship with the cook's son. Cynthia is a different child from Santha.)

E ASK Critical Thinking Students should be able to read Premila's body language to tell her mood. How do you know that Premila is furious when she enters Santha's classroom? (She opens the door with a snap, marches in, and stands in a stiff posture, with legs braced as though to take on an enemy. She also complete ignores the teacher, being deliberately rude.)

F ASK Literary Element Remind students that this story is written from a first-person point of view. We watch Premila through Santha's eyes and learn what Santha thinks about this extraordinary behavior. Invite a volunteer to describe Santha's point of view about this incident. (She knows immediately that something is very wrong, so she obeys her sister without asking questions.) How would it differ if Premila were telling the story? (She would describe her humiliation and fury and how the students, teacher, and her sister looked at her.)

G ASK Literary Element Explain that writers use images, vivid word pictures, to help readers enter into an experience. By involving the senses, they encourage readers to see, hear, feel, smell, and taste the scene. Have students review this last paragraph on the page to find images that appeal to the senses of touch, smell, and sight. (Touch: sticky pencils, dusty hedges, hottest; smell: eucalyptus fragrance; sight: dragged along, tangles of thorns, pink or green silks, women carrying baskets of vegetables on their heads.)

Learning Styles

LEP/ESL Students who are learning English may not understand idiomatic expressions. Explain that some phrases act like a single word; they have a meaning different from the literal meanings of the words in the phrase. For example, in the first paragraph on page 171, three Indian children are "fast friends." This means they are close and loyal to one another, not that they move quickly. Tell students that often the meaning of an idiom is given in the dictionary at the end of the entry for the main word in the phrase. Ask students to find the idioms "out of the question" and "for good" on this page and decide or look up their meanings. (impossible; permanently)

Discussion Questions

A ASK Critical Thinking Why does Premila tell her sister to put her notebook on her head? What good will this do? (Students should be able to infer that the notebook will block the sun's rays. Since the sun is directly overhead, the book will also create a little shade over Santha's body so she will stay cooler.)

B Students should infer that the mother is thinking angrily and bitterly that she was right about the British being rigid and insular. She is also worried about how her daughters will react to being treated as inferiors.

C ASK Critical Thinking Have students analyze Santha's reaction to her experience at school. Why isn't she upset? (She never became involved emotionally because, as the strange Cynthia, she was not herself. The racism and humiliation happened to someone in whom she was not "particularly interested." Unscathed, Santha can resume her happy life at home.)

Diversity Connection

The majority of Indians are Hindu. Encourage students to learn more about Indian culture and the Hindu religion by reading other books. *The Cooking of India* provides many descriptions and insights into the daily lives of Rama Rau's family when she was growing up in India—in addition, of course, to many recipes and photographs of Indian food. (Alexandria, VA: Time-Life Books, 1975.)

us, and the women, in their pink or green silks, stared at Premila and me trudging along on the side of the road. A few **coolies** and a line of women carrying baskets of vegetables on their heads smiled at us. But it was nearing the hottest time of day, and the road was almost **deserted.** I walked more and more slowly, and shouted to Premila, from time to time, "Wait for me!" with increasing **A** **peevishness.** She spoke to me only once, and that was to tell me to carry my notebook on my head, because of the sun.

When we got to our house the ayah was just taking a tray of lunch into Mother's room. She immediately started a long, worried questioning about what are you children doing back here at this hour of the day.

Mother looked very startled and very concerned, and asked Premila what had happened.

Premila said, "We had our test today, and She made me and the other Indians sit at the back of the room, with a desk between each one."

Mother said, "Why was that, darling?"

"She said it was because Indians cheat," Premila added. "So I don't think we should go back to that school."

B What was Mother thinking? Remember what she said about the British earlier in the story.

Mother looked very distant, and was silent a long time. At last she said, "Of course not, darling." She sounded displeased.

We all shared the curry she was having for lunch, and afterward I was sent off to the beautifully familiar bedroom for my siesta. I could hear Mother and Premila talking through the open door.

Mother said, "Do you suppose she understood all that?"

Premila said, "I shouldn't think so. She's a baby."

Mother said, "Well, I hope it won't bother her."

C Of course, they were both wrong. I understood it perfectly, and I remember it all very clearly. But I put it happily away, because it had all happened to a girl called Cynthia, and I never was really particularly interested in her.

coolie an unskilled worker who does odd jobs

deserted empty

peevishness annoyance; bad temper

172 *Unit 2 Nonfiction*

REVIEWING the SELECTION

By Any Other Name

Santha Rama Rau

Directions Write the answers to these questions using complete sentences.

Comprehension: Identifying Facts

1. Although Rau's school is in India, who runs the school?
2. Rau's sister has two names in the story. What are they?
3. What English name does the teacher give Santha Rama Rau?
4. What does Rau's father do for a living?
5. Why are Rau and her sister sent to school?
6. Are most of the children in the school English or Indian?
7. Why doesn't Rau pay attention in class on her first day?
8. How is the lunch that Rau and her sister brought different from the other childrens' lunches?
9. What kind of clothes does Rau wear to school?
10. How long do Rau and her sister go to this school?

Comprehension: Understanding Main Ideas

11. Rau's mother taught the girls at home instead of sending them to school. Why?
12. Rau says the new name gave her a dual personality. What does she mean?
13. What makes the school look like a British school?
14. The teacher asks Rau her name. She answers, "I don't know." Why?
15. Why doesn't Rau understand competitive games?
16. After her first day, Rau is happy to be home and "to have left that peculiar Cynthia behind." What does she mean when she says that?
17. Why does Rau's sister ask to take sandwiches for lunch? What is her real reason?
18. Does Rau make friends with the English students? Why or why not?
19. What happens to make Rau's sister decide to leave the school?
20. Why does Premila tell her sister to carry her notebook on her head?

Review Continued on Next Page

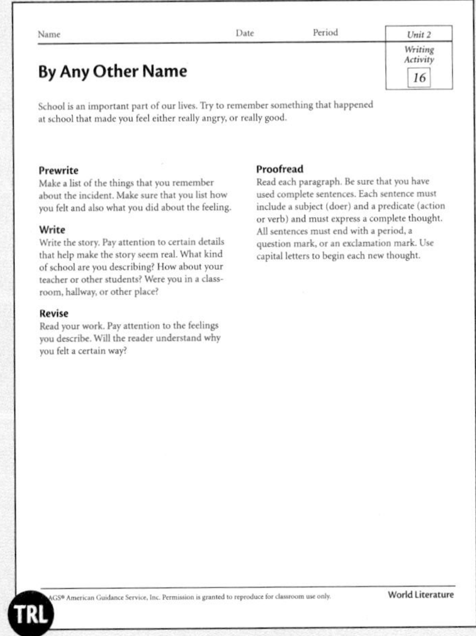

Name Date Period

Unit 2 *Writing Activity* 16

By Any Other Name

School is an important part of our lives. Try to remember something that happened at school that made you feel either really angry, or really good.

Prewrite
Make a list of the things that you remember about the incident. Make sure that you list how you felt and also what you did about the feeling.

Write
Write the story. Pay attention to certain details that help make the story seem real. What kind of school are you describing? How about your teacher or other students? Were you in a classroom, hallway, or other place?

Revise
Read your work. Pay attention to the feelings you describe. Will the reader understand why you felt a certain way?

Proofread
Read each paragraph. Be sure that you have used complete sentences. Each sentence must include a subject (doer) and a predicate (action or verb) and must express a complete thought. All sentences must end with a period, a question mark, or an exclamation mark. Use capital letters to begin each new thought.

 World Literature

TRL

Writing Activity 16

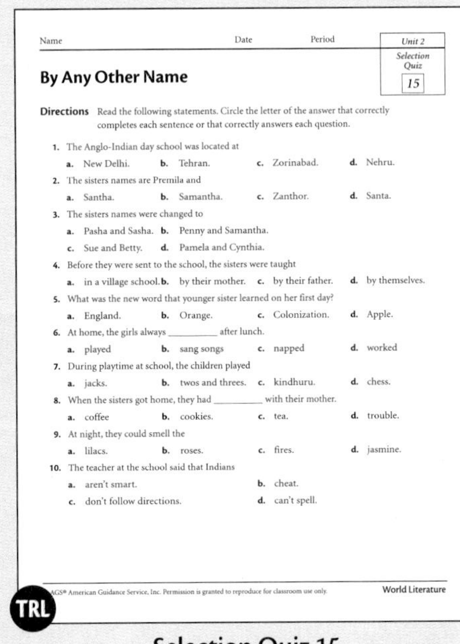

Name Date Period

Unit 2 *Selection Quiz* 15

By Any Other Name

Directions Read the following statements. Circle the letter of the answer that correctly completes each sentence or that correctly answers each question.

1. The Anglo-Indian day school was located at
   a. New Delhi. b. Tehran. c. Zorinabad. d. Nehru.
2. The sisters names are Premila and
   a. Santha. b. Samantha. c. Zanthor. d. Santa.
3. The sisters names were changed to
   a. Pasha and Sasha. b. Penny and Samantha.
   c. Sue and Betty. d. Pamela and Cynthia.
4. Before they were sent to the school, the sisters were taught
   a. in a village school. b. by their mother. c. by their father. d. by themselves.
5. What was the new word that younger sister learned on her first day?
   a. England. b. Orange. c. Colonization. d. Apple.
6. At home, the girls always __________ after lunch.
   a. played b. sang songs c. napped d. worked
7. During playtime at school, the children played
   a. jacks. b. twos and threes. c. kindhuru. d. chess.
8. When the sisters got home, they had __________ with their mother.
   a. coffee b. cookies. c. tea. d. trouble.
9. At night, they could smell the
   a. lilacs. b. roses. c. fires. d. jasmine.
10. The teacher at the school said that Indians
    a. aren't smart. b. cheat.
    c. don't follow directions. d. can't spell.

 World Literature

TRL

Selection Quiz 15

Reviewing the Selection

Answer Key

Comprehension: Identifying Facts

1. British teachers and administrators run the school.
2. Premila is her real name; Pamela is the name she is given at school.
3. Santha is called Cynthia.
4. He is a civil service officer of some importance, working for the British government.
5. Their mother is ill and can no longer give them their lessons.
6. Three-fourths are English students.
7. The material being taught is too easy for her, and she is off-balance because of her new identity.
8. They bring traditional Indian food; all the others bring western-style sandwiches.
9. She probably wears a sari.
10. They stay one week.

Comprehension: Understanding Main Ideas

11. She wanted them to learn Indian culture and values. More importantly, she did not want to subject them to the racism shown by the English teachers.
12. She felt as though she became someone else at school.
13. The floors are painted dark brown and have mats on them.
14. She is confused and uncertain. She is not really Cynthia, but the English do not want her to be Santha. She wants to do the "right thing," but is caught between a lie and saying something that may make the teacher angry.
15. She has always been allowed to "win" games at home because she is youngest.
16. The feelings she has at school and the way she must act are uncomfortable and foreign to her.
17. Premila says it is to make lunch easier for Santha. Really she wants to blend in by eating what the others eat.
18. No, she knows the English consider her inferior and were not her friends.
19. Her teacher makes the Indian students sit at the back with desks between them so they won't cheat.
20. She knows the notebook will shade Santha's head and make her cooler.

Understanding Literature: Autobiography and First-Person Point of View

21. The narrator uses the pronoun *I* and tells how she is feeling inside.

22. It deals intimately with the life of the narrator.

23. On page 167, she says that she feels "at most a passing interest in what was going to happen." On page 169, she is "puzzled when the other children" do not let her catch them. On page 170, she is "pleased to be home and have left that peculiar Cynthia behind." On page 172, she puts the school incident "happily away."

24. It would not report directly on Santha's feelings. Observations would be attuned to the age, sex, and upbringing of the narrator.

25. Since it records Santha's life, the story is most effectively and authentically told by her. Only she knows how she felt about events and can give them a personal slant.

Critical Thinking

26. Santha seems confused and feels detached from the person called "Cynthia." Premila seems angry and resentful.

27. She insists on taking sandwiches for lunch and sits with her class rather than her sister at lunch.

28. She feels mistrust toward the Indian students and superiority over them.

29. She is silent and restrained but evidently angry and bitter.

30. Because she is a separate person from the strange "Cynthia" character, it is easy for Santha to put the school experience behind her.

Writing on Your Own Have students begin by making a concept map with details of their experience. Ask them to decide on the appropriate order for presenting these details—most probably chronological order. After they write a draft, suggest to students that they review their work to see where they might replace explanation with dialogue.

REVIEWING the SELECTION

By Any Other Name

(Continued)

Understanding Literature: Autobiography and First-Person Point of View

"By Any Other Name" is an autobiographical sketch. Santha Rama Rau tells a brief story about one subject in her life. She tells it from the first-person point of view. This means the author is a character in the story. She uses the pronouns "I," "me," and "my" in telling the facts. This lets us know the story happened to the writer. It also tells how she felt about it.

21. "Most of that morning I was rather bored." How do you know from this sentence that the story is told from the first person point of view?
22. How do you know the story is an autobiography?
23. Find three examples from the story where Rau tells how she feels. List them.
24. If this story was told from another point of view, how would it be different?
25. Do you think the story is more effective because it is told in the first person? Why or why not?

Critical Thinking

In the Anglo-Indian school, the Indian students are expected to behave like the English students. However, they are not treated like the English students. For example, Rau is called by an English name. Yet she joins the Indian students sitting at the back of the classroom.

26. At first, how does Rau feel about being called by an English name? How does her sister feel about it?
27. Name two things Premila does to try to fit in.
28. What does the teacher's behavior show about her attitude toward Indians?
29. How does their mother react to the news of the teacher's treatment of the Indian children?
30. What lasting effect does this school experience have on Rau?

Writing on Your Own Write a sketch about a time when you were the new person in town, in class, or on the team. Tell about how others reacted to you and how you felt. Refer to the selections for ideas.

Selection Quiz

The Teacher's Resource Library includes a Selection Quiz for "By Any Other Name" that may be given following the Selection Review.

INTRODUCING the SELECTION

Kaffir Boy

Mark Mathabane

About the Author

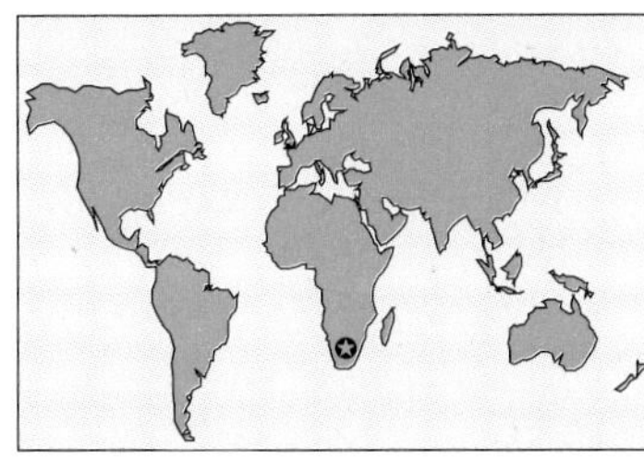

White South Africans created a system called *apartheid.* It used the law to keep the different races apart. Apartheid was a government policy. Under it, blacks had few rights. Many lived in dismal slums. Mark Mathabane was born in 1960 in Alexandra, which was one of Johannesburg's worst slums. His early life was full of gangs, police raids, and death. Then he found he had a talent for tennis. His playing continued to improve. He began to hope for a life outside Alexandra. Finally, he was allowed to play in tournaments for whites. Later, he received a tennis scholarship to an American college. In the United States, Mathabane became a fine tennis player. He also found the freedom to write about his life in the apartheid system.

Literary Terms

narrator the teller of a story

turning point a story about an experience that changes a literary character's life

About the Selection

Kaffir Boy is a remarkable story of courage. It tells how Mathabane survived eighteen years in Alexandra. He got his start with a good head on his shoulders. His mother and grandmother lent him their strength as well. They insisted that he go to school. Mathabane himself at first wanted to be a *tsotsi.* That was the term for a member of a South African gang. Mathabane believed his decision to attend school was a **turning point** in his life. A turning point is an experience that changes a character's life. In the following selection Mathabane is the **narrator.** He tells the story of his first visit to school at the age of seven and a half.

Selection at a Glance

Kaffir Boy

Mark Mathabane

Student pages 175–194

Overview

This excerpt clearly shows both the horrific brutality of life for black South Africans under apartheid and the strength of will needed to survive and gain knowledge.

Selection Summary

In *Kaffir Boy* by Mark Mathabane, a young black South African describes his life in a Johannesburg slum.

Objectives

- To analyze and explain why a story marks a turning point.
- To be aware of the narrator's voice in a story.

Audiocassette 

Teacher's Resource Library TRL

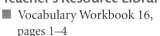

- Vocabulary Workbook 16, pages 1–4
- Selection Glossary 16
- Student Study Guide 22, pages 1–2
- Activity 25, pages 1–2
- Workbook 25, pages 1–2
- Writing Activity 17
- Selection Quiz 16

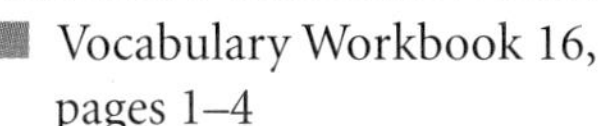

Setting the Stage for Reading

About the Author

Have students read the text. Explain that, for Mathabane, life in Alexandra meant living penniless and hungry and terrified of police raids and brutality.

ASK Why do you think Mathabane wanted to tell this painful story? (Answers may include that he wanted to educate the world about apartheid or to give hope to those facing a seemingly impossible task.)

About the Selection

In some communities, there have been attempts to ban *Kaffir Boy* because of its brutal, graphic language (although none have succeeded to date). The word *kaffir* is the derogatory name some white South Africans call a black person.

Activate Prior Knowledge: Mathabane's book describes the horrors of life under South African apartheid. Ask students to explain what they know about apartheid and describe the feelings of someone on the receiving end of discrimination, racism, and hatred.

ASK Mathabane believes his extended family helped him survive apartheid. Why might extended family help children survive? (Answers might include that there are more people to support each other.)

Viewing the Art

Have students look at the sculpture on page 175. This bust of an African head draws your eye to the pure, beautiful features of the young African. The expression is sorrowful and thoughtful.

ASK Why do you think the sculptor represented this person with the eyes closed? (Answers may include that the artist wants to suggest the world of possibility in the imagination or the need to shut out cruelty, violence, and hatred.)

Reading Vocabulary TRL

Take time for students to become familiar with the selection's vocabulary. Assign each student 3–5 words from the Selection Glossary page. Have him or her define each word and use it in a useful context. Ask students to share their definitions and sentences with the class.

Motivation for Reading

Have students read the quote at the top of the page and explain whether they agree or disagree. What sorts of doors might the speaker be talking about?

Discussion Questions

Suggest that students use the questions and comments in the margins of the student selection to focus their reading.

A ASK Comprehension How does the narrator's opinion of education differ from the quote? (School is worthless, "a waste of time," in the narrator's borrowed opinion, whereas the quote values education and points out its miraculous ability to transform life.)

B ASK Literary Element Every story contains conflict. Ask students to name two conflicts introduced on this page and describe them. (The narrator is in conflict with his mother about going to school and associating with gangs. Their battles are verbal and their differences stem from different points of view.)

C ASK Critical Thinking Why do you think the narrator believes school is useless? Is this his opinion or one he is parroting? (No one around him, except his mother, talks about school as a valuable tool. His older gang friends, whom he idolizes, have formed this opinion, and he is happy to accept it.)

Kaffir Boy

Mark Mathabane

"Education will open doors where none seem to exist."

As you read, think about the quote at the beginning of the story. Mathabane has placed it there to tell you that it's what his story will be about.

A When my mother began dropping hints that I would soon be going to school, I vowed never to go because school was a waste of time. She laughed and said, "We'll see. You don't know what you're talking about." My **philosophy** on school was that of a gang of ten-, eleven- and twelve-year-olds whom I so **revered** that their every word seemed that of an **oracle**.

Shebeens were illegal drinking places. They made their own liquor and beer. That was illegal because it took business away from government-run beer halls.

These boys had long left their homes and were now living in various neighbourhood junkyards, making it their own. They slept in abandoned cars, smoked glue and **benzene**, ate **pilchards** and brown bread, sneaked into the white world to caddy and, if unsuccessful, came back to the township to steal beer and soda bottles from shebeens, or goods from the Indian traders on First Avenue. Their life-style was exciting, **B** adventurous and full of surprises; and I was attracted to it. My mother told me that they were no-gooders, that they would amount to nothing, that I should not associate with them, but I paid no heed. What does she know? I used to tell myself. One thing she did not know was that the gang's way of life had **captivated** me wholly, particularly their philosophy on school: they hated it and considered an education a waste of time.

C They, like myself, had grown up in an environment where the value of an education was never emphasized, where the first thing a child learned was not how to read and write and spell, but how to fight and steal and rebel; where the money to send children to school was grossly lacking, for survival was first **priority**. I kept my membership in the gang, knowing that for as long as I was under its influence, I would never go to school.

benzene a colorless, flammable liquid

captivate to fascinate; to interest deeply

oracle a person who gives wise advice

philosophy a basic theory; a viewpoint

pilchard a small fish related to the herring

priority order of importance

revere to honor and respect

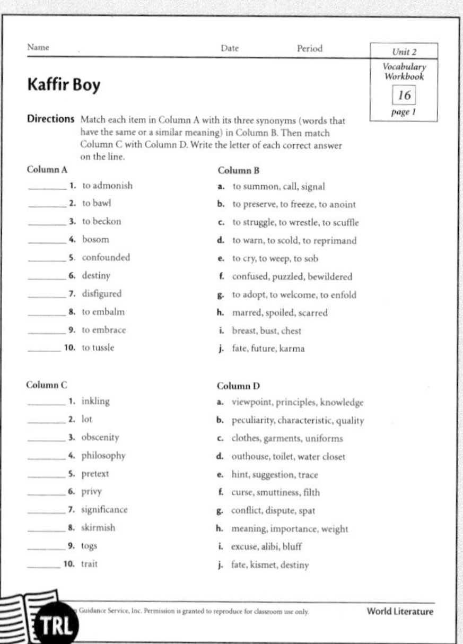

Name Date Period

Unit 2 Vocabulary Workbook 16 page 1

Kaffir Boy

Directions Match each item in Column A with its three synonyms (words that have the same or a similar meaning) in Column B. Then match Column C with Column D. Write the letter of each correct answer on the line.

Column A	Column B
______ 1. to admonish	a. to summon, call, signal
______ 2. to bawl	b. to preserve, to freeze, to anoint
______ 3. to beckon	c. to struggle, to wrestle, to scuffle
______ 4. bosom	d. to warn, to scold, to reprimand
______ 5. confounded	e. to cry, to weep, to sob
______ 6. destiny	f. confused, puzzled, bewildered
______ 7. disfigured	g. to adopt, to welcome, to enfold
______ 8. to embalm	h. marred, spoiled, scarred
______ 9. to embrace	i. breast, bust, chest
______ 10. to tussle	j. fate, future, karma

Column C	Column D
______ 1. inkling	a. viewpoint, principles, knowledge
______ 2. lot	b. peculiarity, characteristic, quality
______ 3. obscenity	c. clothes, garments, uniforms
______ 4. philosophy	d. outhouse, toilet, water closet
______ 5. pretext	e. hint, suggestion, trace
______ 6. privy	f. curse, smuttiness, filth
______ 7. significance	g. conflict, dispute, spat
______ 8. skirmish	h. meaning, importance, weight
______ 9. togs	i. excuse, alibi, bluff
______ 10. trait	j. fate, kismet, destiny

 World Literature

Vocabulary Workbook 16, pages 1–4

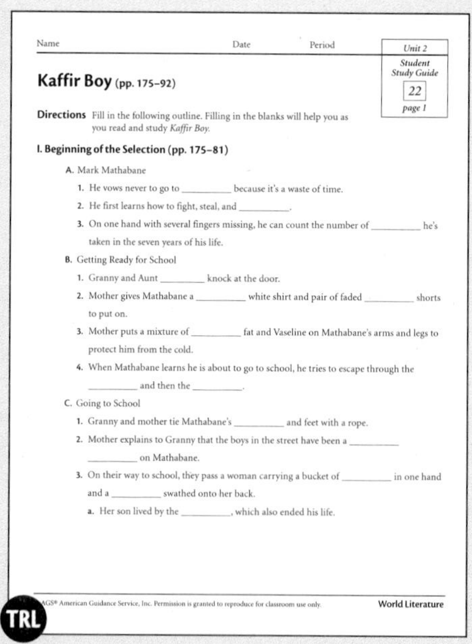

Name Date Period

Unit 2 Student Study Guide 22 page 1

Kaffir Boy (pp. 175–92)

Directions Fill in the following outline. Filling in the blanks will help you as you read and study *Kaffir Boy.*

I. Beginning of the Selection (pp. 175–81)

A. Mark Mathabane
1. He vows never to go to ______ because it's a waste of time.
2. He first learns how to fight, steal, and ______.
3. On one hand with several fingers missing, he can count the number of ______ he's taken in the seven years of his life.

B. Getting Ready for School
1. Granny and Aunt ______ knock at the door.
2. Mother gives Mathabane a ______ white shirt and pair of faded ______ shorts to put on.
3. Mother puts a mixture of ______ fat and Vaseline on Mathabane's arms and legs to protect him from the cold.
4. When Mathabane learns he is about to go to school, he tries to escape through the ______ and then the ______.

C. Going to School
1. Granny and mother tie Mathabane's ______ and feet with a rope.
2. Mother explains to Granny that the boys in the street have been a ______ ______ on Mathabane.
3. On their way to school, they pass a woman carrying a bucket of ______ in one hand and a ______ swathed onto her back.
   a. Her son lived by the ______, which also ended his life.

 World Literature

Student Study Guide 22, pages 1–2

One day my mother woke me up at four in the morning.

"Are they here? I didn't hear any noises," I asked in the usual way.

"No," my mother said. "I want you to get into that washtub over there."

Mathabane's family and others like them lived in fear of the police. They often treated blacks harshly while enforcing South Africa's apartheid laws.

"What!" I **balked**, upon hearing the word *washtub*. I feared D taking baths like one feared the plague. Throughout seven years of **hectic** living the number of baths I had taken could be counted on one hand with several fingers missing. I simply had no natural inclination for water; cleanliness was a **trait** I still had to acquire. Besides, we had only one bathtub in the house, and it constantly sprung a leak.

Granny holds a great-grandchild.

"I said get into that tub!" My mother shook a finger in my face.

Reluctantly, I obeyed, yet wondered why all of a sudden I had to take a bath. My mother, armed E with a **scropbrush** and a piece of Lifebuoy soap, **purged** me of years and years of grime till I ached and bled. As I howled, feeling pain shoot through my limbs as the thistles of the brush encountered stubborn callouses, there was a loud knock at the door.

Instantly my mother leaped away from the tub and headed, on F tiptoe, toward the bedroom. Fear seized me as I, too, thought of the police. I sat frozen in the bathtub, not knowing what to do.

"Open up, Mujaji [my mother's maiden name]," Granny's voice came shrilling through the door. "It's me."

balk to stop and refuse to go
hectic confused; full of fast activity
purge to cleanse; to purify
reluctantly unwillingly
scropbrush a brush to scrub with
trait a quality of character, a peculiarity

D ASK Critical Thinking The narrator states that he has had only a few baths in his seven years of life. What reasons could he have for including this detail? (Answers might include that he is illustrating their poverty and how wild he has run, that it suggests how filthy he is and explains why his mother must scrub him so hard.)

E ASK Comprehension The bath is a painful ordeal. Have students point out details that support this main idea. (The scrub brush makes him ache and bleed; the scrubbing bristles cause sharp pains.) Why is this description shocking? (Answers may include that students associate bathing with social acceptance, warmth, comfort, and relaxation, yet this bath offers none of these. The mother's approach is rough, and the narrator's suffering is intense.)

F ASK Comprehension How do you know the mother is afraid of the knock at the door? What does she fear? (She leaps away from the task she is determined to complete and moves soundlessly to a hiding place. She fears that police may be staging a raid.)

Grammar

Irregular Past Tense Remind students that usually the past tense of a verb has an *-ed* ending, as in *balked, feared,* and *purged.* Some verbs form the past tense in irregular ways. The past tense of *say* is *said,* of *wake* is *woke.* Remind students that the dictionary entry for a verb will show how its tenses are formed. Have students list three more irregular verbs from this page, including present and past tenses. (have, had; spring, sprung; bleed, bled; is or am, was; sit, sat; come, came)

Name Date Period

Unit 2 *Activity* 25 *page 1*

Kaffir Boy

Part A Directions Write a short answer for each item on the blank lines.

1. What did Mrs. Mathabane mean when she said, "Education will open doors"?
2. Why was Johannes (the narrator) attracted to the life of the *tsotsi?*
3. What happened to make Johannes's father become so violent against his mother?
4. What was Mrs. Mathabane's dream for her son and herself?
5. What was apartheid and why was it created?

Part B Directions Read each sentence. Write *T* if the statement is true or *F* if it is false.

_____ 1. There were government laws about which tribal children could go to certain schools.
_____ 2. Mrs. Mathabane wanted to buy her freedom from marriage, but had no job or money.
_____ 3. The grandmother refused to give her daughter the money she needed.
_____ 4. Johannes finally decided he wanted to go to school after he saw his mother beaten so badly.
_____ 5. Mr. Mathabane thought his Johannes should have an education.

 World Literature

TRL

Activity 25, pages 1–2

Name Date Period

Unit 2 *Workbook* 25 *page 1*

Kaffir Boy

Part A Directions Write a short answer for each item on the blank lines.

1. What is apartheid and why was it created?
2. What did Mrs. Mathabane mean when she said, "Education will open doors"?
3. Why was Johannes (the narrator) attracted to the life of the *tsotsi?*
4. What happened to make Johannes's father become so violent against his mother?
5. What was Mrs. Mathabane's dream for her son and herself?

Part B Directions Read each sentence. Write *T* if the statement is true or *F* if it is false.

_____ 1. Mr. Mathabane thought his Johannes should have an education.
_____ 2. Johannes finally decided he wanted to go to school after he saw his mother beaten so badly.
_____ 3. There were government laws about which tribal children could go to certain schools.
_____ 4. Mrs. Mathabane wanted to buy her freedom from marriage, but had no job or money.
_____ 5. The grandmother refused to give her daughter the money she needed.

 World Literature

TRL

Workbook 25, pages 1–2

Discussion Questions

A ASK Comprehension What causes the boy to be confused? (His mother's behavior, his grandmother's presence, and the unusually early hour are extraordinary to him. This is a new experience, and he doesn't know what it means.)

B ASK Critical Thinking Have students read the dialogue between mother and son aloud, using the expression they think each person would use. What do her words and actions show about the mother's attitude? (She is determined and will not take no for an answer.) Do you think she is too hard on her son? (Accept students' opinions.)

Learning Styles

Visual In the second half of this page, the narrator describes how he looks dressed in adult clothes. Ask students to picture him in the mind's eye. Then invite them to create a sketch that captures this image and suggests the boy's mood.

My mother heaved a sigh of relief; her tense **limbs** relaxed. She turned and headed to the kitchen door, unlatched it and in came Granny and Aunt Bushy.

"You scared me half to death," my mother said to Granny. "I had forgotten all about your coming."

"Are you ready?" Granny asked my mother.

"Yes—just about," my mother said, **beckoning** me to get out of the washtub.

A She handed me a piece of cloth to dry myself. As I dried myself, questions raced through my mind: What's going on? What's Granny doing at our house this **ungodly** hour of the morning? And why did she ask my mother, "Are you ready?" While I stood debating, my mother went into the bedroom and came out with a stained white shirt and a pair of faded black shorts.

"Here," she said, handing me the **togs**, "put these on."

"Why?" I asked.

B "Put them on I said!"

I put the shirt on; it was grossly loose-fitting. It reached all the way down to my ankles. Then I saw the reason why: it was my father's shirt!

"But this is Papa's shirt," I complained. "It don't fit me."

"Put it on," my mother insisted. "I'll make it fit."

"The pants don't fit me either," I said. "Whose are they anyway?"

"Put them on," my mother said. "I'll make them fit."

Moments later I had the garments on; I looked ridiculous. My mother started working on the pants and shirt to make them fit. She folded the shirt in so many **intricate** ways and stashed it inside the pants, they too having been folded several times at the waist. She then choked the pants at the waist with a piece of **sisal**

beckon to summon by gesturing

intricate complex; difficult to arrange

limb a leg or arm

sisal a long, strong durable white fiber used to make ropes and twine

togs clothes

ungodly wicked or outrageous

rope to hold them up. She then **lavishly** smeared my face, arms and legs with a mixture of pig's fat and Vaseline. "This will insulate you from the cold," she said. My skin gleamed like the morning star and I felt as hot as the centre of the sun and I smelled God knows like what. After **embalming** me, she headed to the bedroom. **C**

Centre is the British spelling for the word *center.* Look for other British spellings in this story.

"Where are we going, Gran'ma?" I said, hoping that she would tell me what my mother refused to tell me. I still had no idea I was about to be taken to school.

"Didn't your mother tell you?" Granny said with a smile. "You're going to start school."

"What!" I gasped, leaping from the chair where I was sitting as if it were made of hot lead. "I am not going to school!" I **blurted** out and raced toward the kitchen door.

My mother had just reappeared from the bedroom and guessing what I was up to, she yelled, "Someone get the door!"

Aunt Bushy immediately barred the door. I turned and headed for the window. As I leaped for the windowsill, my mother lunged at me and brought me down. I **tussled**, "Let go of me! I don't want to go to school! Let me go!" but my mother held fast onto me. **D** **E**

"It's no use now," she said, grinning triumphantly as she pinned me down. Turning her head in Granny's direction, she shouted, "Granny! Get a rope quickly!"

Granny grabbed a piece of rope nearby and came to my mother's aid. I bit and clawed every hand that grabbed me, and howled **protestations** against going to school; however, I was no match for the two determined **matriarchs.** In a jiffy they had me bound, hands and feet.

"What's the matter with him?" Granny, bewildered, asked my mother. "Why did he suddenly turn into an imp when I told him you're taking him to school?"

blurt to say suddenly and without thinking

embalm to preserve

lavishly generously; using more than is necessary

matriarch a woman who rules a family

protestation a strong objection

tussle to struggle; to wrestle

C ASK Literary Element Remind students that a simile is a comparison using the word *like* or *as.* Have students identify two similes in the first paragraph. ("skin gleamed like the morning star" and "as hot as the centre of the sun") Why do you think the narrator uses these comparisons? (To emphasize the comic and extraordinary nature of what is happening to him. Ordinary, earthly objects are not adequate.)

D ASK Critical Thinking Why do you think his mother asked Granny and Aunt Bushy to come to her house today? (She knew he would struggle and try to escape, and she wanted all the help she could get. She also would need someone to watch her other children.)

E ASK Literary Element Explain that the conflict grows through a story. How does the conflict between the mother and son change at this point? (It becomes a physical battle instead of a strictly verbal one.)

Cross-Curricular Connection

Science Mathabane's mother rubs fat and oil on him to insulate him from the cold. Explain that insulation is a material that prevents heat loss because it does not conduct heat well. She is trying to prevent the loss of body heat to cold air. Have students work in groups to brainstorm a list of materials they think would make good insulators. Then have each student take one or two of them to research or experiment with and report back to the class.

Discussion Questions

A ASK Comprehension What does Mathabane's mother think of the gangs most boys belong to? (She blames the gangs for her son's unwillingness to go to school. She thinks them a "bad influence.")

B ASK Comprehension After students read the third paragraph, have them summarize the sort of life it describes. How do the people in Alexandra live? What is the principle attitude? (Young and old are aimless, uneasy, and preoccupied with police raids. Fear, hunger, and despair dominate the scene.)

C ASK Critical Thinking Does Mathabane's reaction to going to school seem normal or unusual? (The other children being taken to school are also trying to escape. His reaction is the norm.)

Diversity Connection

Mathabane describes his mother and grandmother as matriarchs, women who head a family. In some societies, women have greater authority, status, and rights than men. In such matriarchies, descent and kinship are traced through the mother. Mathabane uses the term *matriarch* in a limited sense to show that these women are firmly in control of him. Have students research and report on past and present matriarchal communities.

Community Connection

Schools are often the focal point of communities. They not only provide education for children but may also provide educational, social, and career-oriented opportunities for adults in a community. Encourage children to conduct interviews and research information to find out about the role of their school or the school district in the community. How does the school help meet the needs of community members?

Mathabane learned to play tennis on a court like this in Alexandra.

"You shouldn't have told him that he's being taken to school," my mother said. "He doesn't want to go there. That's why I requested you come today, to help me take him there. Those boys in the streets have been a bad influence on him." **A**

As the two matriarchs hauled me through the door, they told Aunt Bushy not to go to school but stay behind and mind the house and the children.

B The sun was beginning to rise from beyond the **veld** when Granny and my mother dragged me to school. The streets were beginning to fill with their everyday traffic: old men and women, **wizened,** bent and ragged, were beginning to assemble in their usual **coteries** and head for shebeens in the backyards where they discussed how they escaped the morning pass raids and **contemplated** the conditions of life amidst intense beer drinking and vacant, uneasy laughter; young boys and girls, some as young as myself, were beginning their aimless wanderings along the narrow, dusty streets in search of food, carrying **bawling** infants piggyback.

Apartheid laws required black South Africans to carry a government-issued passbook with papers stating where they were assigned to live and work. The police often conducted *pass raids* during the night to look for people who were not where they were supposed to be.

As we went along some of the streets, boys and girls who shared the same fears about school as I were making their feelings **C** known in a variety of ways. They were howling their protests and trying to escape. A few managed to break loose and make a mad dash for freedom, only to be recaptured in no time, **admonished** or whipped, or both, and ordered to march again.

As we made a turn into Sixteenth Avenue, the street leading to the tribal school I was being taken to, a short, chubby black woman came along from the opposite direction. She had a **scuttle** overflowing with coal on her *doek*-covered (cloth-

admonish warn; to scold with a warning

bawling crying loudly

contemplate to look at thoughtfully

coterie a group of people who meet often

scuttle a pail for carrying coal

veld the South African grassland

wizened dried up

covered) head. An infant, bawling deafeningly, was loosely **swathed** with a piece of sheepskin onto her back. Following closely behind the woman, and picking up pieces of coal as they fell from the scuttle and placing them in a small plastic bag, was a half-naked, potbellied and thumb-sucking boy of about four. The woman stopped **abreast**. For some reason we stopped too.

"I wish I had done the same to my oldest son," the strange woman said in a **regretful** voice, gazing at me. I was **confounded** by her stopping and offering her **unsolicited** opinion.

"I wish I had done that to my oldest son," she repeated, and **D** suddenly burst into tears; amidst sobs, she continued, "before ...the street claimed him ...and ...turned him into a *tsotsi*."

Granny and my mother offered consolatory remarks to the **E** strange woman.

A *tsotsi* is a gang member.

"But it's too late now," the strange woman continued, tears now streaming freely down her puffy cheeks. She made no attempt to dry them. "It's too late now," she said for the second time, "he's beyond any help. I can't help him even if I wanted to. *Uswile* [He is dead]."

"How did he die?" my mother asked in a sympathetic voice.

"He shunned school and, instead, grew up to live by the knife. And the same knife he lived by ended his life. That's why whenever I see a boy-child refuse to go to school, I stop and tell the story of my dear little *mbitsini* [heartbreak]."

F
How did the strange woman's son die?

Having said that, the strange woman left as mysteriously as she had arrived.

"Did you hear what that woman said!" my mother screamed into my ears. "Do you want the same to happen to you?"

I dropped my eyes. I was confused.

"Poor woman," Granny said **ruefully**. "She must have truly loved her son."

abreast side by side; in an even line

confounded confused; puzzled

regretful remembering with sorrow or grief

ruefully expressing regret or pity

swathe to wrap with a band of material

unsolicited not requested

D ASK Critical Thinking This episode at first seems like a distraction from the story. Why might the author have included it? Why does he go to such trouble to describe the strange woman? (She tells a story about what happened to her boy, who stayed with the gangs. This incident helps give Mathabane an "education" about why it is important for him to go to school. The description shows that she is as poor as they and creates sympathy for her.)

E ASK Critical Thinking Granny and the mother respond to the woman with sympathy. What do you think they are feeling? Why does Granny decide the woman "must have truly loved her son"? (They empathize with her despair, for it is just such an end they fear for their boy. She shows deep sorrow for his loss and for not having forced him to go to school.)

F He was stabbed and died "by the knife," as he had lived.

Discussion Questions

A ASK Comprehension This is the first description of people who dress and live differently than the narrator and his family. How does the appearance of the principal and assistant compare with that of the average black in Alexandra? (They are stylishly, showily dressed—despite the shabby, unpleasant feel of the office. Their prosperity and dignity contrast markedly with the ragged group before them.)

B ASK Critical Thinking Ask students to describe what they think the boy's classroom will be like and explain why they picture it this way. (Descriptions may include adjectives such as *hot, stuffy, smelly, dusty,* and *oppressive.*)

Literary Elements

Descriptive Details to Create an Impression The author provides a vivid description of the principal's office, for it is his first glimpse of a school and memorable for him. Have students study the details and point out which appeal to the senses of sight, sound, smell, and touch. Ask students to describe their first impression of a place or person that is important to them. Encourage students to make notes about details they want to include and to present their descriptions orally, as though telling a story.

Finally, we reached the school and I was **ushered** into the principal's office, a tiny **cubicle** facing a row of **privies** and a patch of yellowed grass.

A "So this is the rascal we'd been talking about," the principal, a tall, **wiry** man, **foppishly** dressed in a black pin-striped suit, said to my mother as we entered. His **austere**, shiny face, inscrutable and imposing, reminded me of my father. He was sitting behind a brown table upon which stood piles of dust and cobweb-covered books and papers. In one upper pocket of his jacket was arrayed a variety of pens and pencils; in the other nestled a lily-white handkerchief whose presence was more decorative than utilitarian. Alongside him stood a disproportionately portly black woman, fashionably dressed in a black skirt and a white blouse. She had but one pen, and this she held in her hand. The **B** room was hot and stuffy and buzzing with flies.

"Yes, Principal," my mother answered, "this is he."

"I see he's living up to his notoriety," remarked the principal, noticing that I had been bound. "Did he give you too much trouble?"

"Trouble, Principal," my mother sighed. "He was like an imp."

"He's just like the rest of them, Principal," Granny sighed. "Once they get out into the streets, they become wild. They take to the many vices of the streets like an infant takes to its mother's milk. They begin to think that there's no other life but the one shown them by the *tsotsis*. They come to hate school and forget about the future."

"Well," the principal said. "We'll soon remedy all that. Untie him."

"He'll run away," my mother cried.

"I don't think he's that foolish to attempt that with all of us here."

austere stern and serious

cubicle a small room

foppishly vainly; overly proud of one's looks

privy an outhouse

usher to conduct; to escort

wiry slender yet muscular

Mathabane attended Bovet Community School.

"He *is* that foolish, Principal," my mother said as she and Granny began untying me. "He's tried it before. Getting him here was an ordeal in itself."

The principal rose from his seat, took two steps to the door and closed it. As the door swung closed, I spotted a row of canes of different lengths and thicknesses hanging behind it. The principal, seeing me staring at the canes, grinned and said, in a manner suggesting that he had wanted me to see them, "As long as you behave, I won't have to use any of those on you."

Use those canes on me? I gasped. I stared at my mother—she smiled; at Granny—she smiled too. That made me abandon any **inkling** of escaping. **C**

"So they finally gave you the birth certificate and the papers," the principal addressed my mother as he returned to his chair.

"Yes, Principal," my mother said, "they finally did. But what a battle it was. It took me nearly a year to get all them papers together." She took out of her handbag a neatly wrapped package and handed it to the principal. "They've been running us around for so long that there were times when I thought he would never attend school, Principal," she said. **D**

inkling a hint; a suggestion

C ASK Comprehension What causes Mathabane to give up his ideas of escaping? (The principal implies that attempted escape will be punished with a caning. The boy doesn't want to get a beating.]

D ASK Critical Thinking The mother and principal refer to "they"—the people who have given her the papers. Who might "they" be? (Answers might include white South Africans who don't want black children to be educated or officials of the government, who put obstacles in the way until parents give up on getting an education for their children.)

Learning Styles

LEP/ESL The story contains difficult vocabulary and many long sentences with intricate syntax. Students whose English is limited may have difficulty reading paragraphs such as the second one on page 182. Pair students with more English-proficient students and have them read through this paragraph sentence by sentence, stopping after each to rephrase its content in their own words. Encourage students learning English to ask questions about words or phrases they do not understand.

Discussion Questions

A ASK Critical Thinking The principal attaches great importance to these papers. Why might he need to read them closely? (Students should infer that he also is liable to checks by the police, who are universally feared. If the legal paperwork is not in order, then he will shoulder the blame. In a society that deals with blacks so harshly and unfairly, he might be injured, imprisoned, or fired.)

B ASK Comprehension What reason does the principal give to justify the "piece of paper"? Tell whether you agree with his viewpoint and why. (He explains that the law requires the papers, and he must abide by it. Students who disagree with this viewpoint may mention the unfairness and oppressiveness of the laws, which were designed to prevent blacks from having any power or decent standard of living.)

C ASK Literary Element Explain that a paradox is a statement that seems to contradict itself yet is true. What does Granny understand? What doesn't she understand? (Answers may include that she understands the helplessness of the principal, who wants to live peacefully; she does not understand the cruelty of the system that makes unfair demands of some people, throws up obstacles to their progress, and mistreats them using the law as a cover.)

South Africa has three capital cities. *Pretoria* is the administrative capital; Cape Town the legislative capital; and Bloemfontein the judicial capital.

"That's pretty much standard procedure, Mrs. Mathabane," the principal said, unwrapping the package. "But you now have the papers and that's what's important.

A "As long as we have the papers," he continued, **minutely perusing** the contents of the package, "we won't be breaking the law in admitting your son to this school, for we'll be in full **compliance** with the requirements set by the authorities in Pretoria."

Granny mispronounces the name *Pretoria.*

"Sometimes I don't understand the laws from Pitori," Granny said. "They did the same to me with my Piet and Bushy. Why, Principal, should our children not be allowed to learn because of some piece of paper?"

B "The piece of paper you're referring to, Mrs. Mabaso," the principal said to Granny, "is as important to our children as a pass is to us adults. We all hate passes; therefore, it's only natural we should hate the regulations our children are subjected to. But as we have to live with passes, so our children have to live with the regulations, Mrs. Mabaso. I hope you understand, that is the law of the country. We would have admitted your grandson a long time ago, as you well know, had it not been for the papers. I hope you understand."

"I understand, Principal," Granny said, "but I don't understand,"
C she added **paradoxically**.

One of the papers caught the principal's eye and he turned to my mother and asked, "Is your husband a Shangaan, Mrs. Mathabane?"

The people of South Africa belong to many tribes and ethnic groups, which speak different languages.

"No, he's not, Principal," my mother said. "Is there anything wrong? He's Venda and I'm Shangaan."

The principal reflected for a moment or so and then said, concernedly, "No, there's nothing seriously wrong. Nothing that we can't take care of. You see, Mrs. Mathabane, technically, the fact that your child's father is a Venda makes him **ineligible** to

compliance yielding to a demand

ineligible not qualified

minutely paying attention to small details

paradoxically self-contradictory

peruse to read carefully

attend this tribal school because it is only for children whose parents are of the Shangaan tribe. May I ask what language the children speak at home?" **D**

"Both languages," my mother said worriedly, "Venda and Shangaan. Is there anything wrong?

The principal coughed, clearing his throat, then said, "I mean which language do they speak more?"

"It depends, Principal," my mother said, swallowing hard. "When their father is around, he wants them to speak only Venda. And when he's not, they speak Shangaan. And when they are out at play, they speak Zulu and Sisotho."

"Well," the principal, heaving a sigh of relief. "In that case, I think an exception can be made. The reason for such an exception is that there's currently no school for Vendas in Alexandra. And should the authorities come asking why we took in your son, we can tell them that. Anyway, your child is half-half." **E**

Everyone broke into a nervous laugh, except me. I was bewildered by the whole thing. I looked at my mother, and she seemed greatly relieved as she watched the principal register me; a broad smile broke across her face. It was as if some enormously heavy burden had finally been lifted from her shoulders and her conscience. **F**

"Bring him back two weeks from today," the principal said as he saw us to the door. "There're so many children registering today that classes won't begin until two weeks **hence.** Also, the school needs repair and cleaning up after the holidays. If he refuses to come, simply notify us, and we'll send a couple of big boys to come fetch him, and he'll be very sorry if it ever comes to that."

As we left the principal's office and headed home, my mind was still against going to school. I was thinking of running away from home and joining my friends in the junkyard. **G**

I didn't want to go to school for three reasons: I was reluctant to surrender my freedom and independence over to what I heard every school-going child call "**tyrannous discipline.**" I had heard

discipline punishment given as a correction | **hence** from this time | **tyrannous** unfair; severe; cruel

D ASK Literary Element As the plot, or action, of a story unfolds, new complications arise. This rising action increases tension and suspense. What new problem arises for Mathabane? Why? (His mixed tribal heritage may prevent him from registering. Officials require the children to be Shangaan, and he is half Venda.)

E ASK Comprehension How is the problem resolved? What shows the principal really wants the boy to attend school? (The principal reasons that the boy's Shangaan blood and language and the absence of a school for Vendas make his school the logical choice. He believes the authorities will accept these reasons. He is willing to take some risk to register the boy.)

F ASK Critical Thinking What "enormously heavy burden" do you think has been lifted from the mother's shoulders? (She has succeeded at last in registering her son for school. Students may suggest that the burden is the long, difficult struggle against stubborn obstacles to get the boy in school or her fears and doubts that she could succeed in doing so.)

G ASK Comprehension Everyone is happy except the registrant himself. What is his reaction? (He is so unhappy and desperate that he considers running away.)

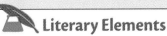

Literary Elements

Dialogue Remind students that a storyteller uses dialogue to make the action immediate, like a drama. Discuss how the dialogue between Mathabane's mother and the principal of the school adds tension and realism to this scene. Then invite students to work with a partner to write a dialogue in which one person's request may be denied or granted by the other.

Discussion Questions

A He fears beatings and long school hours; he feels loyalty to the gang, which is against schooling.

B He doesn't want to end up dead like many gang members. He doesn't want his mother's struggle to have been for nothing; he doesn't want to let her down.

C **ASK Literary Element** Remind students that this story's purpose is to illustrate a turning point in the author's life. This sentence that stands on its own, near the middle of the story, alerts them to watch for the incident that causes a big change. Ask students to predict what will happen that might change Mathabane's mind. (Students may predict that he will have a narrow scrape on the streets or that some event that makes him see things differently will occur. The story so far should suggest to them that the incident will involve violence.)

What are Mathabane's three reasons against going to school?

A

many bad things about life in tribal school—from daily beatings by teachers and mistresses who worked you like a mule to long school hours—and the sight of those canes in the principal's office gave **ample credence** to rumors that school was nothing but a torture chamber. And there was my allegiance to the gang.

B

What are two reasons Mathabane lists for going to school?

But the thought of the strange woman's **lamentations** over her dead son presented a somewhat strong case for going to school: I didn't want to end up dead in the streets. A more **compelling** argument for going to school, however, was the vivid **recollection** of all that **humiliation** and pain my mother had gone through to get me the papers and the birth certificate so I could enroll in school. What should I do? I was torn between two worlds.

C But later that evening something happened to force me to go to school.

I was returning home from playing soccer when a neighbour **accosted** me by the gate and told me that there had been a bloody fight at my home.

"Your mother and father have been at it again," the neighbour, a woman, said.

"And your mother left."

I was stunned.

"Was she hurt badly?"

"A little bit," the woman said. "But she'll be all right. We took her to your grandma's place."

I became hot with anger.

"Is anyone in the house?" I stammered, trying to control my rage.

"Yes, your father is. But I don't think you should go near the house. He's raving mad. He's armed with a meat cleaver. He's

accost to approach and speak to in challenging way

ample enough to satisfy

compelling forceful

credence belief; proof

humiliation the state of being disgraced or shamed

lamentation a cry of grief or sorrow

recollection something remembered

chased out your brother and sisters, also. And some of the neighbours who tried to **intervene** he's threatened to carve them to pieces. I have never seen him this mad before."

This is a typical ghetto yard.

I brushed aside the woman's **D** warnings and went. Shattered windows convinced me that there had indeed been a **skirmish** of some sort. Several pieces of broken bricks, evidently broken after being thrown at the door, were lying about the door. I tried opening the door; it was locked from the inside. I knocked. No one answered. I knocked again. Still no one answered, until, as I turned to leave:

"Who's out there?" my father's voice came growling from inside.

"It's me, Johannes," I said...

I went to the broken window and screamed **obscenities** at my **E** father, daring him to come out, hoping that if he as much as ever stuck his black face out, I would pelt him with the half-a-loaf brick in my hand. He didn't come out. He continued launching a **tirade** of obscenities at my mother and her mother... He was drunk, but I wondered where he had gotten the money to buy beer because it was still the middle of the week and he was dead broke. He had lost his entire wage for the past week in dice and had had to borrow bus fare.

"I'll kill you someday for all you're doing to my mother," **F** I threatened him, overwhelmed with rage. Several nosey neighbours were beginning to **congregate** by open windows and doors. Not wanting to make a spectacle of myself, which was

There had been other disagreements in Mathabane's house. The neighbors had seen other spectacles.

congregate to collect or gather

intervene to come in between

obscenities curses

skirmish a conflict or dispute

tirade a long, violent, scolding speech

D ASK Comprehension Is Mathabane in danger? Why do you think this? (Yes, his father could hurt him badly. The warning and the broken windows show that his father is violent; the locked door indicates the man is still enraged.)

E ASK Critical Thinking From this description, what can you infer about the father's habits and character? How do you think the family feels about him? (He has a drinking as well as a gambling problem and a violent, quick temper. These things make him unreliable as a provider and, when present, a dangerous man to be avoided. His family must resent and dislike him for making their lives miserable.)

F ASK Literary Element Mathabane shows a new side of his character. How does his reaction to his father change your view of the boy? (He stands up to his father, even threatening him, showing he has courage and feels both love and protectiveness for his mother. The incident shows how he has had to act like an adult in some ways, though only seven.)

Literary Elements

Conflict Point out that the story so far has involved a struggle between the boy and his mother, sometimes mental and sometimes physical. Explain that a story is constructed to increase in conflict up to a crisis point. Ask students to write several sentences explaining how this incident with Mathabane's father increases the conflict. (Answers may include that it makes the physical conflict very violent and life threatening or that it illustrates how the father is part of the family's difficulties.)

Discussion Questions

A ASK Comprehension Clearly, the boy is used to conflicts between his parents. What is there about this fight that upsets him so much? (It was a worse fight. His father has never beaten his mother like this before.)

B ASK Critical Thinking What is suggested about the relationship of the mother and Granny in this description? (They are close; although the mother is a woman of conviction and capable of determined action to get what she wants, this secret makes her doubt herself. She still looks to her own mother for support and guidance about difficult family issues.)

C ASK Literary Element Point out that still another conflict is revealed here. About what are the parents in conflict? What does this conflict mean to the boy's education? (The father is determined that his son will not get an education, which is worthless in his eyes; the mother is even more resolved that he will, for it is of great value in her eyes. If his father is stronger than his mother, then he will remain ignorant.)

Learning Styles

Auditory Have volunteers read the dialogue on pages 188 and 189, taking the parts of Mama, Granny, and the boy. You may want to have another student read the paragraph of narration on page 188. Encourage students to express the feelings of each character through tone, pace, and expression. If possible, record the reading and make it available for use by students who want to listen.

something many of our neighbors seemed to always expect from our family, I **backtracked** away from the door and vanished into the dark street. I ran, without stopping, all the way to the other end of the township where Granny lived. There I found my mother, her face swollen and bruised and her eyes puffed up to the point where she could scarcely see.

A "What happened, Mama?" I asked, fighting to hold back the tears at the sight of her **disfigured** face.

"Nothing, child, nothing," she mumbled, almost apologetically, between swollen lips. "Your papa simply lost his temper, that's all."

"But why did he beat you up like this, Mama?" Tears came down my face. "He's never beaten you like this before."

B My mother appeared reluctant to answer me. She looked searchingly at Granny, who was pounding **millet** with pestle and mortar and mixing it with **sorghum** and nuts for an African **delicacy**. Granny said, "Tell him, child, tell him. He's got a right to know. Anyway, he's the cause of it all."

"Your father and I fought because I took you to school this morning," my mother began. "He had told me not to, and when I told him that I had, he became very upset. He was drunk. We started arguing, and one thing led to another."

"Why doesn't he want me to go to school?"

C "He says he doesn't have money to waste paying for you to get what he calls a useless white man's education," my mother replied. "But I told him that if he won't pay for your schooling, I would try and look for a job and pay, but he didn't want to hear that, also. 'There are better things for you to work for,' he said. 'Besides, I don't want you to work. How would I look to other men if you, a woman I owned, were to start working?' When I asked him why shouldn't I take you to school, seeing that you

backtrack to go back the way one came

delicacy a special, enjoyable food

disfigured marred or spoiled

millet a cereal grain whose small seeds are used for food

sorghum cereal grain ground into fine meal or made into a sweet syrup

because times have changed somewhat. Though our **lot** isn't any better today, an education will get you a decent job. If you can read or write you'll be better off than those of us who can't. Take my situation: I can't find a job because I don't have papers, and I can't get papers because white people mainly want to register people who can read and write. But I want things to be different for you, child. For you and your brother and sisters. I want you to go to school, because I believe that an education is the key you need to open up a new world and a new life for yourself, a world and life different from that of either your father's or mine. It is the only key that can do that, and only those who seek it earnestly and **perseveringly** will get anywhere in the white man's world. Education will open doors where none seem to exist. It'll make people talk to you, listen to you and help you; people who otherwise wouldn't bother. It will make you soar, like a bird lifting up into the endless blue sky, and leave poverty, hunger and suffering behind. It'll teach you to learn to **embrace** what's good and **shun** what's bad and evil. Above all, it'll make you a somebody in this world. It'll make you grow up to be a good and proud person. That's why I want you to go to school, child, so that education can do all that, and more, for you."

A long, awkward silence followed, during which I reflected upon the **significance** of my mother's lengthy speech. I looked at my mother; she looked at me.

Finally, I asked, "How come you know so much about school, Mama? You didn't go to school, did you?"

"No, child," my mother replied. "Just like your father, I never went to school." For the second time that evening, a mere statement of fact had a thunderous impact on me. All the confusion I had about school seemed to leave my mind, like darkness giving way to light. And what had previously been a dark, yawning **void** in my mind was suddenly transformed into a beacon of light that began to grow larger and larger, until it

embrace to adopt; to welcome

lot fate; state in life

perseveringly keeping at something in spite of difficulties

shun to avoid

significance meaning

void a feeling of emptiness

D ASK Comprehension How do whites control the job market and keep blacks from holding good jobs? (They require the black citizens to have papers permitting them to work but then do not give papers to those who lack education.)

E ASK Comprehension What one thing is most important to the mother? What is she willing to give to get this? (She is determined to give her son an education and with it a better life, mind, and heart. She is willing to sacrifice her own health and safety.)

F ASK Comprehension Students should recognize this sentence "Education will open doors where none seem to exist," which appears as a prologue before the story. Ask them to explain why they think the author attaches so much importance to this statement. (This is his mother's main point, and his point in telling the story has been to describe the closed walls of his childhood world and the turning point at which he recognized that he must escape this prison to live.)

G ASK Literary Element As awareness comes to Mathabane, he compares his understanding to "a beacon of light." Explain what effect this simile has on the mood of the story. (It is like light in that it destroys the darkness of confusion that has prevented him from seeing the truth about his parents' life and his gang involvement.)

Discussion Questions

A ASK Critical Thinking What "things and facts" do you think the boy now understands? (Answers may include his mother's determination, his father's violence and failure, and the self-destructive path he has taken up until now.)

B ASK Literary Element Review the kinds of conflict readers have observed through the story: Mathabane struggles with his mother physically and mentally; his parents fight over his schooling; he attacks his father verbally; his mother struggles with the apartheid system and backward tribal customs. By the story's end, what conflict or struggle remains for Mathabane? (He must fight traditions and white discrimination that would hold him down.)

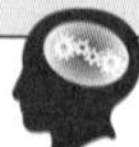

Comprehension

Author's Purpose Remind students that they should think about the author's purpose as they read a story, and note how the details help carry out that purpose. The purpose is the reason for writing, or what the author wants the reader to understand. Authors may state their purpose or it may be up to the reader to discover it. Point out that in this excerpt from *Kaffir Boy,* the author's purpose is not fully understood until the end. As they finish reading the story, ask students to work in pairs to draft a statement explaining the author's purpose. (Wording will vary, but students should infer that the author wants readers to understand how his mother's determined efforts and his own realization about his future made him want to go to school and thus changed his life for the better.)

had swallowed up, blotted out, all the blackness. That beacon of
A light seemed to reveal things and facts, which, though they must have always existed in me, I hadn't been aware of up until now.

"But unlike your father," my mother went on, "I've always wanted to go to school, but couldn't because my father, under the **sway** of tribal traditions, thought it unnecessary to educate females. That's why I so much want you to go, child, for if you do, I know that someday I too would come to go, old as I would be then. Promise me, therefore, that no matter what, you'll go back to school. And I, in turn, promise that I'll do everything in my power to keep you there."

With tears streaming down my cheeks and falling upon my mother's **bosom,** I promised her that I would go to school "forever." That night, at seven and a half years of my life, the battlelines in the family were drawn. My mother on one side, **illiterate** but determined to have me drink, for better or worse, from the well of knowledge. On the other side, my father, he too illiterate, yet determined to have me drink from the well of
B ignorance. Scarcely aware of the **magnitude** of the decision I was making, or, rather, the decision which was being emotionally thrusted upon me, I chose to fight on my mother's side, and thus my **destiny** was forever altered.

bosom the breast of a human

illiterate not knowing how to read or write

sway influence

destiny a person's fate or future

magnitude greatness; importance

192 *Unit 2 Nonfiction*

REVIEWING the SELECTION — Kaffir Boy

Mark Mathabane

Directions Write the answers to these questions using complete sentences.

Comprehension: Identifying Facts

1. Where did Mark Mathabane live as a child?
2. What does Mathabane want to do? Why? What does his mother want him to do?
3. Who comes to help Mathabane's mother take him to school?
4. What is wrong with the clothes his mother finds for him?
5. When he hears he is going to school, what does Mathabane do?
6. Whom did they meet on the way to school? What does she say?
7. What does the principal look like?
8. What makes Mathabane give up any idea of escaping from the principal's office?
9. What tribe is the school for? How does Mathabane qualify?
10. What happens to Mathabane's mother when his father returns home?

Comprehension: Understanding Main Ideas

11. What papers are needed to enroll in school? Why are they hard to get?
12. Why does Mathabane's father lose his temper? List two reasons.
13. What does Mathabane's father think of education?
14. Why doesn't Mathabane's mother leave her husband?
15. Why can't she borrow the money from her parents?
16. How is Mathabane's mother different from other women in her tribe?
17. Why does Mathabane's mother want him to go to school?
18. Why can't Mathabane's mother get a job?
19. How could Mathabane's mother finally get an education?
20. What does Mathabane finally decide to do?

Review Continued on Next Page

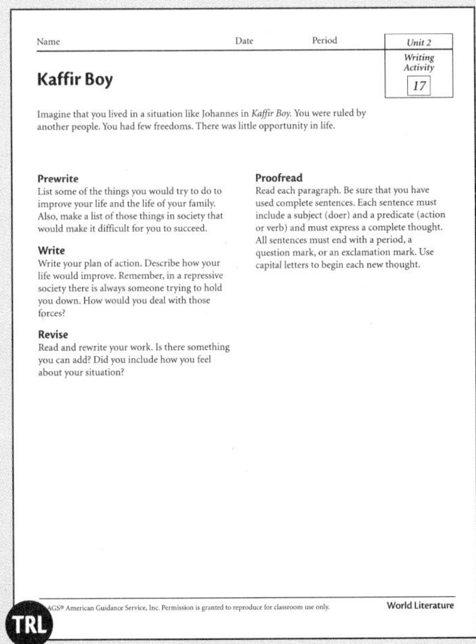

Name Date Period | *Unit 2* *Writing Activity* *17*

Kaffir Boy

Imagine that you lived in a situation like Johannes in *Kaffir Boy*. You were ruled by another people. You had few freedoms. There was little opportunity in life.

Prewrite
List some of the things you would try to do to improve your life and the life of your family. Also, make a list of those things in society that would make it difficult for you to succeed.

Write
Write your plan of action. Describe how your life would improve. Remember, in a repressive society there is always someone trying to hold you down. How would you deal with those forces?

Revise
Read and rewrite your work. Is there something you can add? Did you include how you feel about your situation?

Proofread
Read each paragraph. Be sure that you have used complete sentences. Each sentence must include a subject (doer) and a predicate (action or verb) and must express a complete thought. All sentences must end with a period, a question mark, or an exclamation mark. Use capital letters to begin each new thought.

 World Literature

TRL

Writing Activity 17

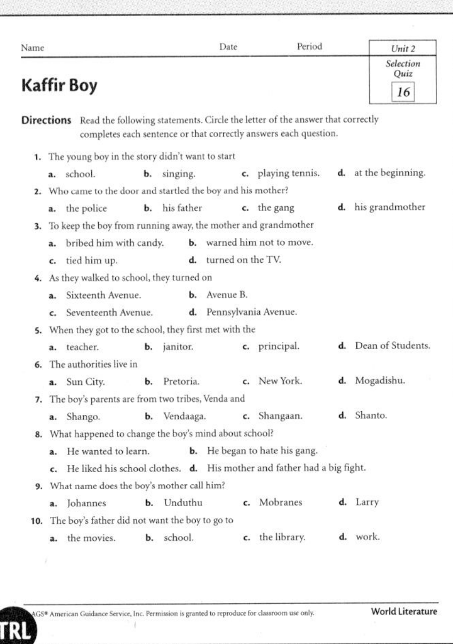

Name Date Period | *Unit 2* *Selection Quiz* *16*

Kaffir Boy

Directions Read the following statements. Circle the letter of the answer that correctly completes each sentence or that correctly answers each question.

1. The young boy in the story didn't want to start
   a. school. b. singing. c. playing tennis. d. at the beginning.
2. Who came to the door and startled the boy and his mother?
   a. the police b. his father c. the gang d. his grandmother
3. To keep the boy from running away, the mother and grandmother
   a. bribed him with candy. b. warned him not to move. c. tied him up. d. turned on the TV.
4. As they walked to school, they turned on
   a. Sixteenth Avenue. b. Avenue B. c. Seventeenth Avenue. d. Pennsylvania Avenue.
5. When they got to the school, they first met with the
   a. teacher. b. janitor. c. principal. d. Dean of Students.
6. The authorities live in
   a. Sun City. b. Pretoria. c. New York. d. Mogadishu.
7. The boy's parents are from two tribes, Venda and
   a. Shango. b. Vendaaga. c. Shangaan. d. Shanto.
8. What happened to change the boy's mind about school?
   a. He wanted to learn. b. He began to hate his gang. c. He liked his school clothes. d. His mother and father had a big fight.
9. What name does the boy's mother call him?
   a. Johannes b. Unduthu c. Mobranes d. Larry
10. The boy's father did not want the boy to go to
   a. the movies. b. school. c. the library. d. work.

 World Literature

TRL

Selection Quiz 16

Reviewing the Selection

Answer Key

Comprehension: Identifying Facts

1. He lived in Alexandra, a slum of Johannesburg, South Africa.

2. He wants to remain a gang member because he finds their lifestyle exciting and interesting. His mother wants him to go to school instead.

3. Granny comes to help take him to school. His aunt babysits for his siblings.

4. They are adult clothes and much too big; they are also stained and worn.

5. He tries to escape.

6. A woman whose son died violently says she wished she had forced her son to go to school.

7. He is tall, slenderly muscular, well dressed, and serious; he shows little emotion on his face.

8. He realizes that if he escapes, he will be caught and beaten with a cane.

9. This is a school for Shangaans. He is half Shangaan and speaks the language, and there is no nearby Venda school.

10. Her husband beats her severely.

Comprehension: Understanding Main Ideas

11. The authorities require a birth certificate and permit papers which they issued, much as they issued passes to adult blacks.

12. His wife disobeyed him, and he opposes his son going to school.

13. He thinks it's a waste of time, and it instills white man's values. He believes that the school will brainwash his son and make him a pawn of the white rulers.

14. She is legally bound to him.

15. Her father has used up the "bride price" that was paid to him for her and deserted his wife. Granny has no money.

16. She has an independent spirit.

17. She knows it is his only chance to have a decent job, understanding, and good values. She believes it is vital to improving his life and, indirectly, perhaps her own.

18. She is illiterate, and work passes are given to those who can read and write.

19. The boy could teach his mother.

20. He decides to fight on his mother's side and to get all the education he can.

Understanding Literature: Turning Point

21. He will no longer run with the gang boys, so he will not be involved in theft, drug abuse, and violence with them.

22. He will have to struggle with his father, but he will have a strong ally in his mother. He will be gone all day, so avoiding some of the conflict and tension of the home.

23. His mother has hoped and prayed for him to choose school. She believes that it will improve his life, maybe even save it.

24. His father is furious because he believes his son will be "in enemy hands" in a white-controlled school, and the family will waste scarce money.

25. Students will agree. They may reason that he makes an about-face in thinking that profoundly affects his future. Or they may point to his literal turning away from the gangs and accepting school.

Critical Thinking

26. He believed, like his father, that the whites would only teach him to be more subservient and take more freedom from him.

27. The social climate is changing; now with an education, a black can get a decent job.

28. Because he will have poise, understanding, and ability to express himself, those around him will notice and take him seriously. They will consider him "worthwhile" and therefore be more willing to help him rise above poverty.

29. It gives hope, which is uplifting, and it literally raises the standard of living by giving a way to make a living. The simile also refers to the liberating potential of the trained mind.

30. While the odds are against her, the woman's determination and courage make it seem that, if anyone can, she can.

Writing on Your Own Encourage students to develop their ideas using clustering technique. Have them write "The Value of My Education" in the center of a piece of paper. As related ideas pop into their minds, they write them down around the topic, circle them, and draw lines to show how they relate to the topic or to the first tier of ideas. For example, one advantage of education might be described as "making me open-minded." Related to this, students might list, "willing to try new things" and "more tolerant of others."

REVIEWING the SELECTION

Kaffir Boy

(Continued)

Understanding Literature: Turning Point

A turning point story is a story about an experience that changes a person's life. Mathabane's decision to attend school is a turning point in his life. That decision would change his life forever.

21. How would Mathabane's life in the neighborhood be different?
22. How would his life in his family be different?
23. Does his mother agree with his choice? Why or why not?
24. Does his father agree with his choice? Why or why not?
25. Do you agree that this is a turning point story? Explain your answer.

Critical Thinking

Reread the long speeches Mathabane's mother makes near the end of the story. She is explaining why education is important.

26. Why didn't his father attend school as a boy?
27. Why does his mother think it will be different for her sons?
28. She says, "It'll make people talk to you, listen to you and help you..." What does she mean?
29. She says education is "...like a bird lifting up into the endless blue sky..." What does she mean?
30. Do you think his mother will achieve her goal of going to school? Explain your answer.

Writing on Your Own Reread the quote at the beginning of the story. Find it again in Mathabane's mother's speech near the end of the story. Think about how it applies to your life, too. Write two or three paragraphs about what you hope education will do for you. How will it make your life different?

194 *Unit 2 Nonfiction*

Selection Quiz

The Teacher's Resource Library includes a Selection Quiz for *Kaffir Boy* that may be given following the Selection Review.

Biography

- "Biography is all about cutting people down to size. Getting an unruly quart into a pint pot." —Alan Bennett
- "A biography is considered complete if it merely accounts for six or seven selves, whereas a person may well have as many as a thousand." —Virginia Woolf

In some ways, a biography is like an autobiography. It tells all or part of someone's life. But biographies are not written by the subjects themselves. They are written by people who are interested in their subject. They can't know the subject's thoughts. These writers must rely on conversations with the subject or those who knew him or her. The author usually uses information from several places. The writer tries to judge how the subject's actions affect others. An authorized biography will probably be kind to its subject. That is because most of the information in it comes from the subject, or people speaking for the subject.

Until recently, most biographers wrote about their subject by choosing facts, quotations, and anecdotes that supported the biographer's opinion. Carl Sandburg wrote a three-part biography of Abraham Lincoln. In it, Sandburg makes Abraham Lincoln into an almost godlike figure. Sandburg obviously admired Lincoln. He wanted his readers to admire him too. Modern Lincoln biographers write about Lincoln's mistakes and weaknesses as well as his greatness.

Biographers today have often been journalists. This background trained them to use many sources to present a balanced picture of the subject. Biographers often show their opinions of their subject by deciding which events and relationships are most important in that person's life.

Biography

Ask students to read the text on page 195 silently, or have them take turns reading aloud.

ASK How is a biography different from an autobiography? (It is written from the point of view of someone other than the subject. The author can't know the subject's actual thoughts and feelings.)

ASK What do you think an authorized biography is? (Answers may suggest that it is written with the active input and blessing of the subject, if living, or the subject's close relatives or that it is biased in favor of its subject.)

ASK Why might today's biographers try to provide a more balanced portrait of their subjects, including both bad and good? (Answers may include that they are trained to be fair and unbiased in reporting, or that today's society expects realism, not glorification.)

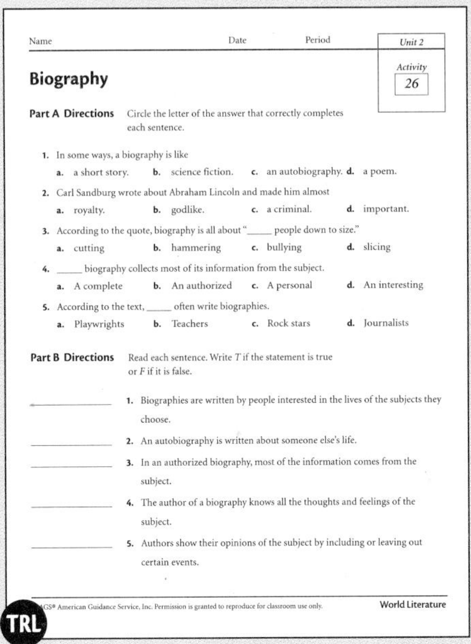

Name Date Period | *Unit 2* | *Activity* 26

Biography

Part A Directions Circle the letter of the answer that correctly completes each sentence.

1. In some ways, a biography is like
   a. a short story. **b.** science fiction. **c.** an autobiography. **d.** a poem.
2. Carl Sandburg wrote about Abraham Lincoln and made him almost
   a. royalty. **b.** godlike. **c.** a criminal. **d.** important.
3. According to the quote, biography is all about "_____ people down to size."
   a. cutting **b.** hammering **c.** bullying **d.** slicing
4. _____ biography collects most of its information from the subject.
   a. A complete **b.** An authorized **c.** A personal **d.** An interesting
5. According to the text, _____ often write biographies.
   a. Playwrights **b.** Teachers **c.** Rock stars **d.** Journalists

Part B Directions Read each sentence. Write *T* if the statement is true or *F* if it is false.

_______ 1. Biographies are written by people interested in the lives of the subjects they choose.

_______ 2. An autobiography is written about someone else's life.

_______ 3. In an authorized biography, most of the information comes from the subject.

_______ 4. The author of a biography knows all the thoughts and feelings of the subject.

_______ 5. Authors show their opinions of the subject by including or leaving out certain events.

 World Literature

TRL

Activity 26

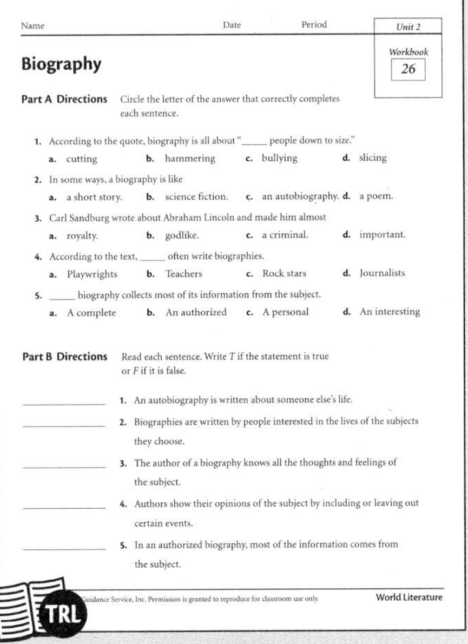

Name Date Period | *Unit 2* | *Workbook* 26

Biography

Part A Directions Circle the letter of the answer that correctly completes each sentence.

1. According to the quote, biography is all about "_____ people down to size."
   a. cutting **b.** hammering **c.** bullying **d.** slicing
2. In some ways, a biography is like
   a. a short story. **b.** science fiction. **c.** an autobiography. **d.** a poem.
3. Carl Sandburg wrote about Abraham Lincoln and made him almost
   a. royalty. **b.** godlike. **c.** a criminal. **d.** important.
4. According to the text, _____ often write biographies.
   a. Playwrights **b.** Teachers **c.** Rock stars **d.** Journalists
5. _____ biography collects most of its information from the subject.
   a. A complete **b.** An authorized **c.** A personal **d.** An interesting

Part B Directions Read each sentence. Write *T* if the statement is true or *F* if it is false.

_______ 1. An autobiography is written about someone else's life.

_______ 2. Biographies are written by people interested in the lives of the subjects they choose.

_______ 3. The author of a biography knows all the thoughts and feelings of the subject.

_______ 4. Authors show their opinions of the subject by including or leaving out certain events.

_______ 5. In an authorized biography, most of the information comes from the subject.

 World Literature

TRL

Workbook 26

Selection at a Glance

China Men

Maxine Hong Kingston

Student pages 196–200

Overview

Hong considers *China Men* along with her earlier *The Woman Warrior* to be "one big book" based on the history and myth imparted to her by her family and other "story-talkers."

Selection Summary

In *China Men,* Maxine Hong Kingston's father, a Chinese immigrant, shows New York City to his wife.

Objectives

- To analyze dialogue as a clue to character
- To infer the characters' vision of the American Dream from dialogue and action.

Audiocassette

Teacher's Resource Library TRL

- Vocabulary Workbook 17
- Selection Glossary 17
- Student Study Guide 23
- Activity 27
- Workbook 27
- Writing Activity 18
- Selection Quiz 17

China Men

Maxine Hong Kingston

Maxine Hong Kingston (1940–) American

Literary Term

dialogue the conversation between characters in a story; the words that characters in a play speak

About the Author

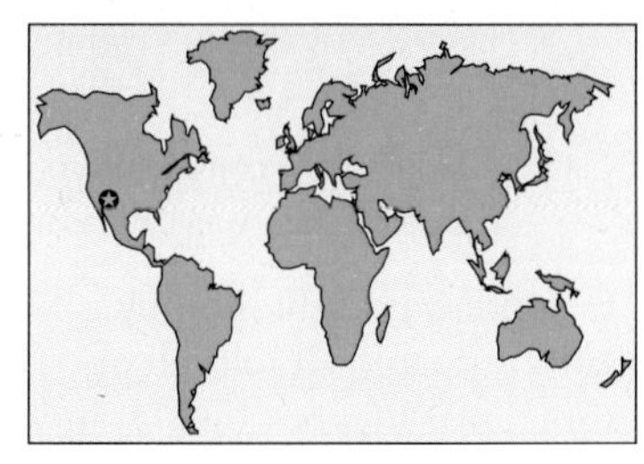

Maxine Hong Kingston was born in California. Her parents were Chinese immigrants. For a time she taught English in California and Hawaii. Kingston felt the conflict between her Asian heritage and the American culture around her. Her family had a strong tradition of storytelling. She also wanted to talk about her family's experiences. For those reasons, she began a writing career. Another of her books is *The Woman Warrior*. It focuses on Chinese American women.

About the Selection

China Men is the story of the men in Kingston's family. It tells how they came to America. It also tells how they tried to succeed in the "Land of the Gold Mountain." At the same time, they tried to keep their Chinese identity. They kept many old attitudes and ideas. Kingston describes how these ideas made it hard to fit in.

The following selection focuses on Kingston's father, Ed. With three other immigrants, he started a laundry in New York City. He then sent for his wife. The selection takes place in the 1930s. Dressed in their best clothes, Ed and his wife are exploring the city. Kingston was not born at the time of this story. Still, she uses **dialogue,** or conversations between characters. These help make her characters come alive. They seem like real people. The dialogue comes from the writer's imagination. As you read, think about the "American dream" and what it means.

Setting the Stage for Reading

About the Author

After students read the text and look at the picture, read the following quote by Kingston: "I am saying, 'No, we're not outsiders, we belong here, this is our country, this is our history, and we are a part of America. . . . If it weren't for us, America would be a different place.'"

Her writings have been described as blending "myth, legend, history and autobiography into a genre of her own invention."

ASK How do you think Kingston was able to create realistic dialogue for her parents? (Answers may include that she knew their speech patterns and habits well or that she had spent many years hearing stories about their early years in New York.)

About the Selection

In China, Kingston's father had been a scholar, and her mother, a medical practitioner and midwife. In this country, they became laundry workers and field hands. Nonetheless, they found much to admire in their adoptive country.

Activating Prior Knowledge: Remind students that many nationalities have immigrated to the United States. Have them describe the pattern experienced by most immigrants, regardless of their race. Point out that, while many arrived with little and took menial jobs, they tended through hard work and tenacity to build successful lives and gradually were accepted into the mainstream.

ASK In the 1930s, what was the tallest building in New York City? What feature drew the most tourists? (the Empire State Building; the Statue of Liberty)

China Men

Maxine Hong Kingston

They strolled in their **finery** along Fifth Avenue. "I washed all these windows," he told her. "When I first came here, I borrowed a **squeegee** and rags and a bucket, and walked up and down this street. I went inside each store and asked if they wanted the windows washed. The white foreigners **A** aren't so hard to get along with; they nod to mean Yes and shake their heads to mean No, the same as anybody." New York glittered and shined with glass. He had liked pulling **B** the water off the panes and leaving brief rainbows. While working, he had looked over the displays of all the wonderful clothes to own and wear. He had made the money to **pool** for starting the laundry. "In the spring," he promised her, "we'll buy you white cotton gloves."...

As you read, notice Ed's mixed feelings about his new country. For instance, he still calls white Americans *foreigners.*

"You ought to put your earrings in the safe deposit box at **C** the bank. Pierced ears look a little **primitive** in this country." He also told her to buy makeup at a drugstore. "American people don't like oily faces. So you ought to use some powder. It's the custom. Also buy some **rouge**. These foreigners dislike yellow skin."

In the 1930s and 1940s, few American women had pierced ears.

finery elegant, dressy clothing

pool to combine one's money with others in a group project

primitive too simple or crude

rouge reddish powder used to add color to the face

squeegee a tool used to scrape water from a flat surface

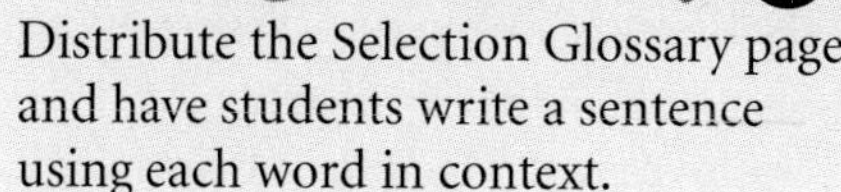

Reading Vocabulary TRL

Distribute the Selection Glossary page and have students write a sentence using each word in context.

Motivation for Reading

Have students describe a busy, prosperous American city. Encourage them to imagine how it would impress someone who had never seen buildings, technology, or size like that.

Discussion Questions

Suggest that students use the marginal comments and questions to focus their reading.

A ASK Critical Thinking What does his comment about the "white foreigners" reveal about the author's father? (He is anxious to accept and be accepted in his new country; he is looking for common humanity with people whose culture is very different.)

B ASK Critical Thinking Why do you think he likes cleaning windows? (Making them shine and sparkle with rainbows casts the city in a favorable light as a place where dreams can come true.)

C ASK Comprehension What main idea is he communicating to his wife with these suggestions? (Try to change yourself every way possible to fit in with what Americans do and like.)

Name Date Period

Unit 2 *Vocabulary Workbook* 17

China Men

Part A Directions Match each item in Column A with a detail or definition in Column B. Write the letter of each correct answer on the line.

Column A	Column B
______ 1. dialogue	a. a tool used to scrape water from a flat surface
______ 2. electric eel	b. the conversation between characters in a story
______ 3. finery	c. to beat or to strike
______ 4. Gold Mountain	d. kinds or a way of doing something
______ 5. immortal	e. elegant and dressy clothing
______ 6. manner	f. one who lives forever
______ 7. to pool	g. the name Chinese immigrants give to the United States
______ 8. primitive	h. a wise person
______ 9. resourceful	i. reddish power used to add color to the face
______ 10. rouge	j. to combine one's money with others in a group project
______ 11. sage	k. too simple or crude
______ 12. squeegee	l. a long thin fish that can produce an electric current
______ 13. to thrash	m. able to find ways to get things done
______ 14. uncluttered	n. empty; not filled with things

Part B Directions Write one original sentence for each of the following words: *dialogue, finery, immortal, resourceful, rouge,* and *uncluttered.*

1. ______
2. ______
3. ______
4. ______
5. ______
6. ______

 World Literature

TRL

Vocabulary Workbook 17

Name Date Period

Unit 2 *Student Study Guide* 23

China Men (pp. 197–99)

Directions Fill in the following outline. Filling in the blanks will help you as you read and study *China Men.*

I. Beginning of the Selection (p. 197)

A. Ed
1. He tells his wife he borrowed a squeegee and rags and a bucket and asked each store owner if they wanted their ______ washed.
2. He promises his wife he'll buy her white ______ ______ in the spring.
3. He tells his wife to put her ______ in the safe deposit box and to wear ______ and rouge.

II. Middle of the Selection (p. 198)

A. Ed's wife
1. To look American, she buys a rat of hair to roll her own hair over for an ______ hairdo.
2. Ed takes her to see the Statue of Liberty and the ______ ______ ______.
   a. She tells him she has now been on the tallest building in the world, and that she has seen ______.

III. End of the Selection (pp. 198–99)

A. Everything's Possible
1. Ed tells his wife that he's danced with ______.
2. At the free aquarium they see electric ______ and ______ fish.
3. At the movies they see *Young* ______ ______.
4. Ed explains that he named himself after the successful ______.

 World Literature

TRL

Student Study Guide 23

Name Date Period

Unit 2 *Activity* 27

China Men

Part A Directions Circle the word or phrase in parentheses that best completes each sentence.

1. The wife wondered when they would travel to (California, China).
2. The wife bought (rouge, lipstick) so her skin would not look so yellow.
3. America was called the (Gold Mountain, Mecca) in this story.
4. Ed told his wife that (curly hair, pierced ears) were primitive in America.
5. The husband and wife walked along Fifth Avenue in their (flannel shirts, finery).

Part B Directions In each blank choose the word or phrase from the Word Bank that best completes each sentence.

1. The wife packed away all her ______ clothes and never wore them again.
2. Ed saved money from ______ to start the laundry.
3. He wanted to buy white ______ for his wife in the spring.
4. Ed explained that Americans disliked people with ______.
5. From the top of the Empire State Building, they looked at an ______ sky.
6. Ed called New York ______.
7. The wife had her ______ cut and done up to look more American.
8. Ed had named himself after Thomas Edison, and in Chinese "Eh-da-Son" meant ______.
9. Ed had danced with ______, who were considered demonesses by the Chinese.
10. The "fish house" was really the city's ______.

Word Bank				
aquarium	blonde women	cotton gloves	hair	his city
saint	silk	uncluttered	washing windows	yellow skin

 World Literature

TRL

Activity 27

Discussion Questions

A He is familiar with it and has enjoyed some success in its business world. This gives him a proud feeling of belonging and being able to introduce it to his wife.

B ASK Comprehension What can you tell about the character of the woman and man from their dialogue? (She is thrilled and somewhat overwhelmed. She still filters her perceptions through Chinese understanding. He is optimistic, positive, and proud.)

C ASK Literary Element The Chinese compare the United States to a gold mountain. What does this show about how they look at their new country? (They look up to its lofty heights; it is difficult to scale to the top; and it offers a wealth of opportunities.)

D ASK Critical Thinking What do her question and comment suggest about her state of mind? (She is homesick.) What does his response suggest? (He gently silences her questions. He knows how she feels but also knows that she will adjust, as he has.)

Diversity Connection

Historians point to the diversity of cultures and races in the United States as a reason for the country's strength. Immigration to the United States has occurred in waves since 1820, spurred by economic hardships or political oppression in other nations. From 1905 to 1914, an average of more than a million immigrants entered the country every year. Have students find out more about Chinese immigration and the contributions of Chinese Americans and share what they learn in a poster.

Some women's hair styles in the 1930s and early 1940s used false hairpieces, called *rats.* Another hair style, the *marcel,* had tight curls.

She also bought a long black rat of hair to roll her own hair over for an upswept hairdo. At a beauty parlor, she had her wavy hair cut and curled tighter with a marcel. She washed, ironed, and wrapped her silk pants and dresses and never wore them again.

A
Why do you think Ed thinks of New York as *his city?*

He took her to see the Statue of Liberty. They climbed the ladder, she in high heels, up the arm to the torch, then the stairs to the crown. "Now we're inside her chin. This part must be the nose." From the windows of the crown, he showed her his city.

In the 1930s, the *Empire State Building* was the tallest building in the world.

They also went to the top of the Empire State Building, took the second elevator to the very top, the top of the world. Ed loved the way he could look up at the **uncluttered** sky. They put money in the telescopes and looked for the laundry and **B** their apartment. "So I have been on the tallest building in the world," she said. "I have seen everything. Wonderful. Wonderful. Amazing. Amazing."

Chinese immigrants called white Americans "ghosts" or "demons." A *demoness* is a female demon.

C "Yes," he said. "Everything's possible on the **Gold Mountain**. I've danced with blondes." "No, really?" she said. "You didn't. You're making that up, aren't you? You danced with demonesses? I don't believe it."

Her favorite place to go was the free aquarium, "the fish house," where all **manner** of creatures swam. Walking **D** between the lighted tanks, she asked, "When do you think we'll go back to China? Do you think we'll go back to China?" "Shh," he said. "Shh." The **electric eels** glowed in their dark tank, and the talking fish made noises. "There are bigger fish in China," she said.

electric eel a long, thin fish that can produce an electric current

Gold Mountain Chinese immigrants' name for the United States

manner kinds

uncluttered empty; not filled with things

Name Date Period

Unit 2
Workbook 27

China Men

Part A Directions Circle the word or phrase in parentheses that best completes each sentence.

1. The husband and wife walked along Fifth Avenue in their (suits, finery).
2. Ed told his wife that (curly hair, pierced ears) were primitive in America.
3. The wife bought (rouge, lipstick) so her skin would not look so yellow.
4. America was called the (Gold Mountain, Mecca) in this story.
5. The wife wondered when they would travel to (California, China).

Part B Directions In each blank write the word or phrase from the Word Bank that best completes each sentence.

1. Ed saved money from ________________ to start the laundry.
2. He wanted to buy white ________________ for his wife in the spring.
3. Ed explained that Americans disliked people with ________________.
4. The wife packed away all her ________________ clothes and never wore them again.
5. Ed called New York ________________.
6. The wife had her ________________ cut and done up to look more American.
7. From the top of the Empire State Building, they looked at an ________________ sky.
8. Ed had danced with ________________, who were considered demonesses by the Chinese.
9. The "fish house" was really the city's ________________.
10. Ed had named himself after Thomas Edison, and in Chinese "Eh-da-Son" meant ________________.

Word Bank				
aquarium	blondes	cotton gloves	hair	his city
saint	silk	uncluttered	washing windows	yellow skin

 World Literature

TRL

Workbook 27

They went to the movies and saw *Young Tom Edison* with Mickey Rooney. They both liked the scene where the mother took Eh-Da-Son into the barn, but only pretended to **thrash** him; she faked the slaps and crying and scolding to fool the strict father, the father "the severe parent," according to Confucius, and the mother "the kind parent." ...After the movie, Ed explained to his wife that this cunning, **resourceful,** successful inventor, Edison, was who he had named himself after. "I see," she said. "Eh-Da-Son. Son as in ***sage*** or ***immortal*** or *saint.*"

E F G

Mickey Rooney was a popular movie actor in the 1940s. He appeared in *Young Tom Edison* in 1940.

Confucius—(551?– 479 B.C.) was an important Chinese philosopher. His teachings are called Confucianism. They state that people's behavior should be based on duty and virtue.

New York City streets were filled with people and automobiles even in the early 1900s.

immortal one who lives forever

resourceful able to find ways to get things done

sage a wise person

thrash to beat or strike

E ASK Comprehension Why do they like this scene in the movie? How do they explain the mother's behavior? (They enjoy the mother's clever way of sparing her son and satisfying her husband. The incident confirms a truth of their culture and reassures by giving something common between the old and new countries.)

F ASK Comprehension Why is Thomas Edison a role model for Ed? (He "beat the odds" using his inner qualities to succeed; Ed thinks of himself as resourceful and cunning as well.)

G ASK Critical Thinking How does his wife make sense of Ed's admiration for Edison? In fact, how does she interpret all the new ideas and information he gives her? (She relates it to Chinese beliefs, culture, or language. In this case, the name Son means wisdom or saintliness.)

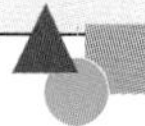

Learning Styles

LEP/ESL Students unfamiliar with English may not be used to its rules of capitalization. Explain that proper nouns are capitalized because they name a specific person, place, thing, or idea. Watching for these capitalized words or phrases within a sentence will clue them that a particular site, work of art, etc., should be pictured. Ask students to locate the proper nouns on pages 198–199. Display illustrations of as many as possible. (Statue of Liberty, Empire State Building, Gold Mountain, China, Young Tom Edison, Mickey Rooney, Eh-Da-Son, Edison, Confucius, Ed.)

Reviewing the Selection

Answer Key

Comprehension: Identifying Facts

1. He washed windows for business people along prosperous Fifth Avenue.

2. They tour the Statue of Liberty, the Empire State Building, and the aquarium.

3. She asks when they can go to China.

Comprehension: Understanding Main Ideas

4. He wants her to fit in and adopt the ways of her new country.

5. They want to experience these symbols of freedom and towering strength and to enjoy the views. They look for their business and home in order to place themselves within this magic network.

6. He uses part of Edison's name to honor the American inventor and remind himself to emulate him.

Understanding Literature: Dialogue

7. On page 197: "The white foreigners aren't so hard to get along with; they . . . the same as anybody," "American people don't like oily faces," and "These foreigners dislike yellow skin."

8. Students may include for the wife: "You danced with demonesses? I don't believe it." For Ed: "Everything's possible on the Gold Mountain."

Critical Thinking

9. It seems to them a mountain in its majesty and the "heights" of society and business they are welcome to climb; it is gold because of the wealth and freedom they can "mine" if they put forth enough effort. That the whole mountain is gold implies that the country represents values that are precious.

10. He became very successful despite humble beginnings, and he made many worthwhile contributions to his country.

Writing on Your Own Before students write, have them create a word web about the concept *success*.

Selection Quiz

The Teacher's Resource Library includes a Selection Quiz for *China Men* that may be given following the Selection Review.

REVIEWING the SELECTION

China Men

Maxine Hong Kingston

Directions Write the answers to these questions using complete sentences.

Comprehension: Identifying Facts

1. How did Ed earn money to start the laundry?
2. List two things Ed and his wife see in New York.
3. What does his wife keep asking at the aquarium?

Comprehension: Understanding Main Ideas

4. Why does Ed want his wife to put her earrings away and wear makeup?
5. Why do they go up in the Statue of Liberty and the Empire State Building? What do they look for through the telescopes?
6. Why has Kingston's father chosen *Ed* as his American name?

Understanding Literature: Dialogue

Kingston can't know exactly what her parents said long ago. Still, she uses dialogue in this biography. Dialogue is the conversation between characters in a story. It gives the actual words they said. What a character says is often a clue to his or her personality. It can also reflect feelings and attitudes.

7. Point out several sentences in which Ed describes his feelings about white Americans.
8. Kingston uses dialogue to show the individual personalities of Ed and his wife. Give an example.

Critical Thinking

9. Why do you think that Chinese immigrants called America "the Gold Mountain"?
10. What do you think were the qualities about Thomas Edison that made the Chinese admire him?

Writing on Your Own In two or more sentences, explain how you know Ed feels successful in America. If possible, include quotations from his own words.

200 *Unit 2 Nonfiction*

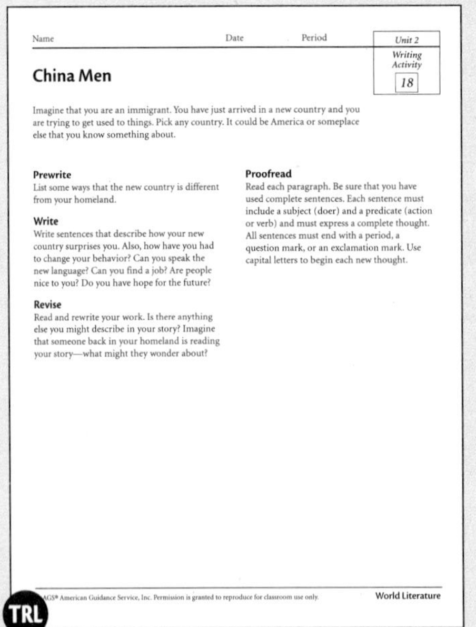

Name Date Period | *Unit 2* *Writing Activity* *18*

China Men

Imagine that you are an immigrant. You have just arrived in a new country and you are trying to get used to things. Pick any country. It could be America or someplace else that you know something about.

Prewrite
List some ways that the new country is different from your homeland.

Write
Write sentences that describe how your new country surprises you. Also, how have you had to change your behavior? Can you speak the new language? Can you find a job? Are people nice to you? Do you have hope for the future?

Revise
Read and rewrite your work. Is there anything else you might describe in your story? Imagine that someone back in your homeland is reading your story—what might they wonder about?

Proofread
Read each paragraph. Be sure that you have used complete sentences. Each sentence must include a subject (doer) and a predicate (action or verb) and must express a complete thought. All sentences must end with a period, a question mark, or an exclamation mark. Use capital letters to begin each new thought.

 World Literature

TRL

Writing Activity 18

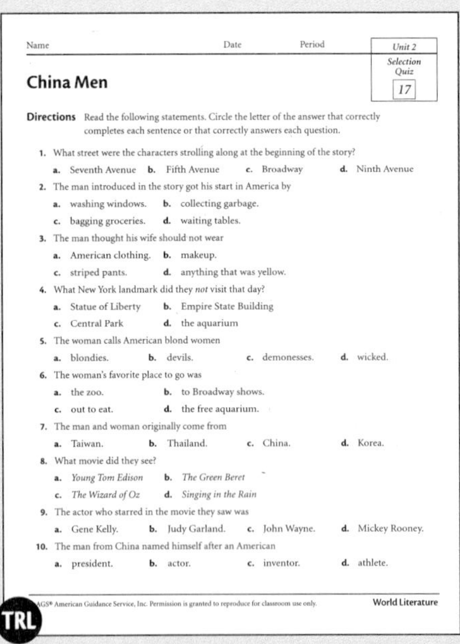

Name Date Period | *Unit 2* *Selection Quiz* *17*

China Men

Directions Read the following statements. Circle the letter of the answer that correctly completes each sentence or that correctly answers each question.

1. What street were the characters strolling along at the beginning of the story?
   a. Seventh Avenue **b.** Fifth Avenue **c.** Broadway **d.** Ninth Avenue
2. The man introduced in the story got his start in America by
   a. washing windows. **b.** collecting garbage.
   c. bagging groceries. **d.** waiting tables.
3. The man thought his wife should not wear
   a. American clothing. **b.** makeup.
   c. striped pants. **d.** anything that was yellow.
4. What New York landmark did they *not* visit that day?
   a. Statue of Liberty **b.** Empire State Building
   c. Central Park **d.** the aquarium
5. The woman calls American blond women
   a. blondies. **b.** devils. **c.** demonesses. **d.** wicked.
6. The woman's favorite place to go was
   a. the zoo. **b.** to Broadway shows.
   c. out to eat. **d.** the free aquarium.
7. The man and woman originally come from
   a. Taiwan. **b.** Thailand. **c.** China. **d.** Korea.
8. What movie did they see?
   a. *Young Tom Edison* **b.** *The Green Beret*
   c. *The Wizard of Oz* **d.** *Singing in the Rain*
9. The actor who starred in the movie they saw was
   a. Gene Kelly. **b.** Judy Garland. **c.** John Wayne. **d.** Mickey Rooney.
10. The man from China named himself after an American
    a. president. **b.** actor. **c.** inventor. **d.** athlete.

 World Literature

TRL

Selection Quiz 17

INTRODUCING the SELECTION

The Last Seven Months of Anne Frank

Willy Lindwer

Willy Lindwer
(1946–)
Dutch

About the Author

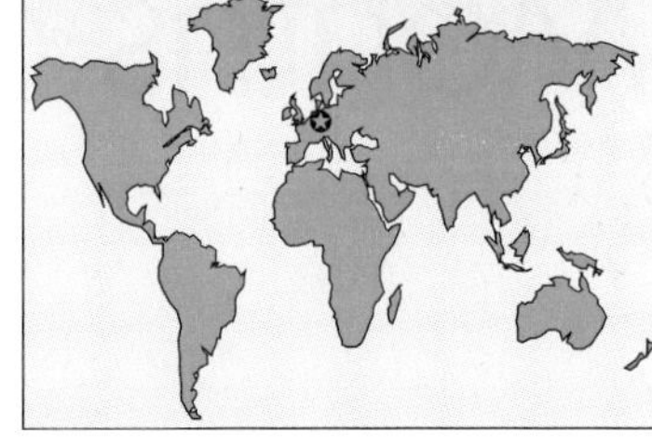

Willy Lindwer is a Dutch filmmaker. He was born in Amsterdam just after World War II. His Jewish parents survived the war by hiding. His grandmother, though, was killed by the Nazis in Poland. As an adult, Lindwer has concentrated on making documentary films. A documentary is a nonfiction movie. It tells the true stories of real people.

Literary Term
excerpt a short passage from a longer piece of writing

About the Selection

Earlier in this unit you read excerpts from Anne Frank's diary. *The Last Seven Months of Anne Frank* picks up Frank's story where her diaries end. In August 1944, four days after the last diary entry, the Nazis arrested the family. Lindwer made a documentary film about the last months of Frank's life. He found six women who had known Anne Frank and her family. Some were childhood friends. Others knew the Franks only in the Nazi concentration camps. Lindwer's interviews of these women went into his documentary. The film was first shown on television in 1988. But Lindwer found he could use only short pieces, or **excerpts,** in the film. So he published the full interviews in a book.

The women in Lindwer's book recount their memories of the Frank family. They also tell their own stories. And they tell how they feel today about that past suffering. All spent some time in the camps. The following selections are excerpts. An excerpt is a short passage take from a longer work. These are taken from longer interviews with several of the women.

Selection at a Glance

The Last Seven Months of Anne Frank

Willy Lindwer

Student pages 202–207

Overview

The book, published in 1992, was first a film that won an Emmy Award for best documentary in 1988.

Selection Summary

In *The Last Seven Months of Anne Frank,* Willy Lindwer, a Dutch filmmaker, interviews women who knew the Frank family.

Objectives

- To use excerpts of a longer work of nonfiction to gain perspective.
- To get a feel for the mood and purpose of a longer work.

Audiocassette 

Teacher's Resource Library 

- Vocabulary Workbook 18
- Selection Glossary 18
- Student Study Guide 24
- Activity 28
- Workbook 28
- Writing Activity 19
- Selection Quiz 18

Setting the Stage for Reading

About the Author

Both historian and filmmaker, Willy Lindwer has extensively researched and investigated all the subjects of his documentaries. His passion is exploring the problems of human suffering, especially that of Jewish subjects.

ASK What do you think inspired Lindwer to make his films? (Answers may include that he knew about the suffering of the Jews in World War II firsthand, that he felt he owed it to his parents, and that he hopes to enlighten the world community.)

About the Selection

Each woman's voice is different in its perspective and tone, as each shares a different moment in the lives of the Frank family. Each voice also reveals something of the character of the speaker.

Activate Prior Knowledge: Ask students if they have read scripts of interviews before. Invite them to describe the differences between reading and hearing an interview. Discuss pluses of hearing and viewing the interviewees firsthand, such as getting clues from tone and body language, and the pluses of reading the account, such as having time to reread and think about comments in depth.

ASK What might have made the production of this film a difficult task? (Answers might include the emotional stress, the difficulty of finding survivors, and the trauma of remembering the Holocaust experience.)

Reading Vocabulary TRL

Review the words on the Selection Glossary page. Present the words with letters scrambled at the top of a sheet of paper. Write a sentence using each word in context, but leave a blank where the word belongs. Have students work in pairs to unscramble and write the words in the blanks.

Motivation for Reading

Invite students to predict the sorts of adjectives Anne's friends and acquaintances will use to describe her in these excerpts.

Discussion Questions

Point out that the questions and comments in the margins will increase students' understanding of the selection.

A ASK Comprehension When did Pick-Goslar spend time with Anne Frank? (During their childhood and up until Anne went into hiding, she and Anne were friends.)

B ASK Literary Element In what sense is this passage biographical? How is it unlike Anne Frank's diary? (It reports on details in the experiences of someone's life. Unlike the diary, it cannot express what Anne is thinking or feeling.)

The Last Seven Months of Anne Frank

Willy Lindwer

As you read, remember what you have already learned about Anne Frank and her family from reading her diary.

Hannah Elisabeth Pick-Goslar (Pick-Goslar was Frank's childhood friend. In Frank's published diary, she is called "Lies Goosens."):

Anne was given a diary on her thirteenth birthday. There **A** was a party in the afternoon and we saw that she had gotten a very beautiful diary from her parents. I don't know if it was the first or second one that she had, because I remember that Anne was always writing in her diary, **shielding** it with her hand, even at school during the break. Everybody could see that she was writing. But no one was allowed to see what she had written. And I **B** thought that she was writing entire books. I was always very curious to know what was in the diary, but she never showed it to anyone.

Hannah Elisabeth Pick-Goslar

I never could find out what was in it, but I have thought that there must have been much more than there was in the published diary. Maybe they never found all that she wrote

shielding hiding

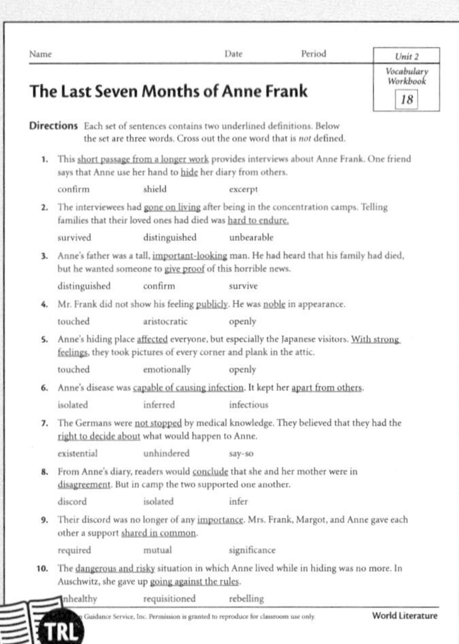

Name Date Period | Unit 2 | *Vocabulary Workbook* 18

The Last Seven Months of Anne Frank

Directions Each set of sentences contains two underlined definitions. Below the set are three words. Cross out the one word that is *not* defined.

1. This short passage from a longer work provides interviews about Anne Frank. One friend says that Anne use her hand to hide her diary from others.
   confirm shield excerpt
2. The interviewees had gone on living after being in the concentration camps. Telling families that their loved ones had died was hard to endure.
   survived distinguished unbearable
3. Anne's father was a tall, important-looking man. He had heard that his family had died, but he wanted someone to give proof of this horrible news.
   distinguished confirm survive
4. Mr. Frank did not show his feeling publicly. He was noble in appearance.
   touched aristocratic openly
5. Anne's hiding place affected everyone, but especially the Japanese visitors. With strong feelings, they took pictures of every corner and plank in the attic.
   touched emotionally openly
6. Anne's disease was capable of causing infection. It kept her apart from others.
   isolated inferred infectious
7. The Germans were not stopped by medical knowledge. They believed that they had the right to decide about what would happen to Anne.
   existential unhindered say-so
8. From Anne's diary, readers would conclude that she and her mother were in disagreement. But in camp the two supported one another.
   discord isolated infer
9. Their discord was no longer of any importance. Mrs. Frank, Margot, and Anne gave each other a support shared in common.
   required mutual significance
10. The dangerous and risky situation in which Anne lived while in hiding was no more. In Auschwitz, she gave up going against the rules.
   unhealthy requisitioned rebelling

 World Literature

Vocabulary Workbook 18

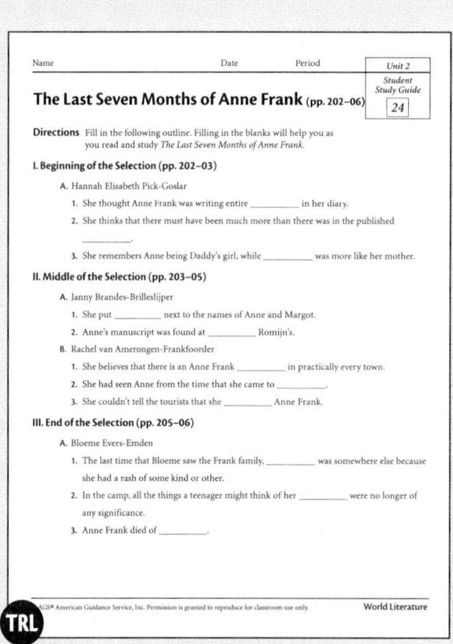

Name Date Period | Unit 2 | *Student Study Guide* 24

The Last Seven Months of Anne Frank (pp. 202–06)

Directions Fill in the following outline. Filling in the blanks will help you as you read and study *The Last Seven Months of Anne Frank.*

I. Beginning of the Selection (pp. 202–03)

A. Hannah Elisabeth Pick-Goslar
   1. She thought Anne Frank was writing entire __________ in her diary.
   2. She thinks that there must have been much more than there was in the published __________.
   3. She remembers Anne being Daddy's girl, while __________ was more like her mother.

II. Middle of the Selection (pp. 203–05)

A. Janny Brandes-Brilleslijper
   1. She put __________ next to the names of Anne and Margot.
   2. Anne's manuscript was found at __________ Romijn's.

B. Rachel van Amerongen-Frankfoorder
   1. She believes that there is an Anne Frank __________ in practically every town.
   2. She had seen Anne from the time that she came to __________.
   3. She couldn't tell the tourists that she __________ Anne Frank.

III. End of the Selection (pp. 205–06)

A. Bloeme Evers-Emden
   1. The last time that Bloeme saw the Frank family, __________ was somewhere else because she had a rash of some kind or other.
   2. In the camp, all the things a teenager might think of her __________ were no longer of any significance.
   3. Anne Frank died of __________.

 World Literature

Student Study Guide 24

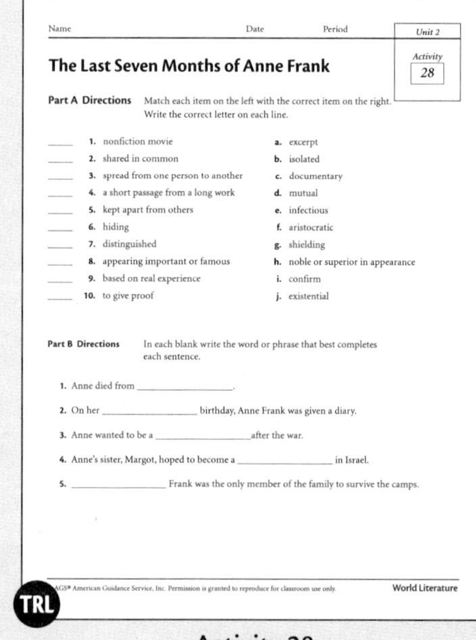

Name Date Period | Unit 2 | *Activity* 28

The Last Seven Months of Anne Frank

Part A Directions Match each item on the left with the correct item on the right. Write the correct letter on each line.

_____	1. nonfiction movie	a. excerpt
_____	2. shared in common	b. isolated
_____	3. spread from one person to another	c. documentary
_____	4. a short passage from a long work	d. mutual
_____	5. kept apart from others	e. infectious
_____	6. hiding	f. aristocratic
_____	7. distinguished	g. shielding
_____	8. appearing important or famous	h. noble or superior in appearance
_____	9. based on real experience	i. confirm
_____	10. to give proof	j. existential

Part B Directions In each blank write the word or phrase that best completes each sentence.

1. Anne died from __________________.
2. On her __________________ birthday, Anne Frank was given a diary.
3. Anne wanted to be a __________________ after the war.
4. Anne's sister, Margot, hoped to become a __________________ in Israel.
5. __________________ Frank was the only member of the family to survive the camps.

 World Literature

Activity 28

before she went into hiding—she had already been writing for a couple of years—I remember that very well.

She did write in the diary that if she had a choice after the war, she wanted to become a writer in the Netherlands.

As I remember it, she was a bit spoiled, particularly by her **C** father. Anne was her Daddy's girl; Margot was more like her mother. It's a good thing there were only two children. Mrs. Frank was a little religious, and Margot went in that direction too. Margot always said that after the war, if she could choose, she wanted to be a nurse in Israel.

Many European Jews moved to *Israel* in the 1920s and 1930s. It was a place where Jews could live in safety. Israel became a nation in 1948.

Janny Brandes-Brilleslijper (Brandes-Brilleslijper met the Frank family in the Amsterdam central train station. They all were waiting to be sent away to Auschwitz.): **D**

Auschwitz was a Nazi concentration camp in Poland.

In those days, I also went immediately to the Red Cross to look at the lists that showed who had **survived** and who had died. And I put a cross next to the names of those who I knew had actually died.

I also put a cross next to the names of Anne and Margot. **E** Much later, in the summer of 1945, a tall, thin, **distinguished** man stood on the sidewalk. He looked through our window and Bob (my husband) opened the door, because he often protected me. In the beginning, I had to deal so much with family members whom I had to tell that their sons, daughters, and husbands would not be coming back. That was often **unbearable**. And it was especially difficult to deal with because I had survived and had come back.

F This woman has been in a concentration camp herself. Why would that make it harder for her to meet family members?

And there stood Otto Frank. He asked if I knew what had happened to his two daughters. I knew, but it was hard to get the words out of my mouth. He had already heard from the Red Cross, but he wanted to have it **confirmed**....I had to **G** tell him that...that his children were no more.

confirm to give proof

distinguished appearing important or famous

survive to go on living

unbearable painful; hard to endure

C ASK Comprehension Compare this observation to Anne's diary entry in which she talks about her parents. Does Pick-Goslar's assessment agree with Anne's? (Yes. Anne recognized that she loved her father more than her mother and could express that love more easily; her impatience toward her mother and her affection for her father both suffered with the strain of captivity.)

D ASK Critical Thinking Brandes-Brilleslijper lived in a concentration camp with the Franks. What was the life they shared like? (It was brutal and deadly. A majority of the Jews who were incarcerated died of starvation, exposure, or disease, if they were not gassed.)

E ASK Comprehension Brandes-Brilleslijper does not describe the deaths of Anne and Margot. How do you know she was there when they died? (She put a cross by their names. She could only be sure of the deaths she witnessed.)

F She knows firsthand how they suffered and fought for life. She grieves for them, too, and feels guilty that she survived. Telling the families reopens the wound.

G ASK Literary Element Point out the ellipses and explain that they generally indicate that material has been left out. In the interview, they are more likely to show that the speaker pauses at these points. Why does she pause? (It is emotional and hard for her to report now, as it was then, that the girls had died. Note that she still avoids using the word *dead*.)

Name Date Period *Unit 2* *Workbook* 28

The Last Seven Months of Anne Frank

Part A Directions Match each item on the left with the correct item on the right. Write the correct letter on each line.

____	**1.** nonfiction movie	**a.**	excerpt
____	**2.** shared in common	**b.**	isolated
____	**3.** spread from one person to another	**c.**	documentary
____	**4.** a short passage from a long work	**d.**	mutual
____	**5.** kept apart from others	**e.**	infectious
____	**6.** hiding	**f.**	aristocratic
____	**7.** distinguished	**g.**	shielding
____	**8.** appearing important or famous	**h.**	noble or superior in appearance
____	**9.** based on real experience	**i.**	confirm
____	**10.** to give proof	**j.**	existential

Part B Directions In each blank write the word or phrase that best completes each sentence.

1. On her ________________ birthday, Anne Frank was given a diary.
2. Anne wanted to be a ________________ after the war.
3. Anne's sister, Margot, hoped to become a ________________ in Israel.
4. ________________ Frank was the only member of the family to survive the camps.
5. Anne died from ________________.

 World Literature

TRL

Workbook 28

Discussion Questions

A ASK Comprehension Why did Brandes-Brilleslijper and Mr. Frank see each other often? (He was alone and probably felt better seeing someone who knew how he felt and who had seen his daughters right before they died. They had mutual friends, and the Jewish community clung to one another after the war.)

B ASK Critical Thinking What effect has Anne Frank had on people? (Her experience and thoughts have captured the imagination and hearts of Jewish people and people around the world. While a real person, she has also become larger than life.)

C ASK Comprehension Why is the visit to the Anne Frank house so difficult for van Amerongen-Frankfoorder? (She was so traumatized by her experience in concentration camps that she has forced it from her mind and does not want the memories to surface again.)

He took it very hard. He was a man who didn't show his feelings **openly**, he had tremendous self-control. He was a **A** tall, thin, **aristocratic** man. Later, we saw him frequently. By a remarkable chance, Anne's manuscript (her diary) was found at Annie Romijn's. And Annie Romijn was in our circle of friends. That's really amazing. And later he came often. He always stayed at the Hotel Suisse on Kalverstraat, where my relatives from Brussels always stayed. I always found that so nice.

Kalverstraat is a street in Amsterdam. *Brussels* is a city in Belgium, a country next to the Netherlands.

Rachel van Amerongen-Frankfoorder (van Amerongen-Frankfoorder first knew the Frank family while they were in a detention camp near Amsterdam.):

B In Israel, where we live, Anne Frank is a legend, and at the same time, a living girl. People are very interested in her. I believe that there is an Anne Frank Street in practically every town. Her diary has been translated into modern Hebrew.

Hebrew is one of the languages spoken in Israel.

People think that she is very special. Once, when my daughter was in the Netherlands with her twin daughters, one of the first things they wanted me to show them was the **C** Anne Frank House. I didn't feel up to it; actually, I didn't want to go at all. For more than forty years, I had pushed that aside because I really wanted to live normally, and I didn't want to talk about it anymore.

The house where Anne and her family hid is a place that many tourists in Amsterdam visit.

Nonetheless, I went to the Anne Frank House, and I had a very special feeling there. I had seen her, after all, from the time that she came to Westerbork. People took pictures there of every corner, every plank, everything; especially the Japanese, who you would suppose wouldn't be as **emotionally touched** as the Europeans. My daughter panicked, because she knew that I had known Anne. She

Westerbork was a Nazi detention camp near Amsterdam. It was the first stop for people being taken to the concentration camps.

aristocratic noble or superior in appearance

emotionally with strong feelings

openly publicly; in front of others

touched affected

looked around and she said, "Mama, shouldn't you tell these people that you knew her? Shouldn't you do something? Tell them, tell them."

I couldn't do it; I absolutely couldn't. I wouldn't have known how to tell it.

Rachel van Amerongen-Frankfoorder

Bloeme Evers-Emden (Evers-Emden got to know Anne and Margot Frank at a Jewish school in Amsterdam.): **D**

I especially remember the last time I saw the Frank family [in Auschwitz]. Another selection had taken place. I spoke to Mrs. Frank, who was with Margot. Anne was somewhere else; she had *Krätze* (scabies). She had a rash of some kind or other. The Germans, **unhindered** by medical knowledge—at least the Germans who had the **say-so** over our lives—were terribly afraid because it might be **infectious** and she had to be **isolated**. As a result, Anne couldn't go with our group. Mrs. Frank, echoed by Margot, said, "We are, of course, going with her." I remember that I nodded, that I understood that.

In the camps, a *selection* divided people into groups. Some were moved to other places; some were killed.

Scabies is an itchy skin disease.

That was the last time I saw them.

Before that, we naturally saw each other regularly, and I talked with them. They were always together—mother and daughters. Whatever **discord** you might **infer** from the diary **E** was swept away now by **existential** need. They were always together. It is certain that they gave each other a great deal

discord arguments, disagreements

existential based on real experience

infectious capable of causing infection

infer to conclude

isolated kept apart from others

say-so the right to decide

unhindered not prevented or stopped

D ASK Comprehension What two different connections did Evers-Emden have with Anne and Margot? (She knew them in school and was interned at Auschwitz with the Frank family.)

E ASK Critical Thinking Why do you think the mother and daughters were close here, while they did not get along when hiding together? (They are united against the common enemies of Nazism, disease, and death. Now they know every day could be their last. In such circumstances, people generally cherish their loved ones.)

Literary Elements

Identifying Character Traits As they talk about their lives, people reveal much about their character. Ask students what traits they think these four witnesses for the Frank family share. (Answers may include compassion and grief for the suffering of others, a strong sense of belonging and community with other Jews, or strong moral fiber and will to live.) Compare these traits to the traits Anne revealed in her diary.

Discussion Questions

A ASK Comprehension What helped the Franks survive as long as they did? (They supported each other physically, mentally, and spiritually. Each knew as long as the others were alive, she had someone to live for.)

Cross-Curricular Connection

Social Studies The horrifying experience of the Holocaust made the European Jewish community determined to create their own nation, Israel. Throughout history, the Jewish people have often been mistreated and periodically been the objects of brutal oppression and murder. Because of this discrimination, they have often settled in communities together, creating their own "community within a community." Invite students to explain why this has been necessary and helpful to the Jewish people.

of support. All the things that a teenager might think of her mother were no longer of any **significance.**

What I mean is that there are people who talk about the war, whose bike was **requisitioned**, how terrible that was, and then they stop. For them, that was the very worst that happened. If you say, "Yes, but there are people who went into hiding, and, much worse, there were also people in the camps."

"Oh yes, that was too bad, but I had to give up my bike."

I think it was that way with Anne. When she was in hiding, which was a very **unhealthy** situation, her mother was someone against whom she **rebelled.** But in the camp, all of that actually completely fell away. By giving each other **A** **mutual** support, they were able to keep each other alive—although no one can fight typhus.

Typhus is a serious illness, from which Anne Frank died. It is carried by fleas and other tiny insects. Typhus is common in places such as the camps, where living conditions are bad.

Bloeme Evers-Emden

mutual shared in common

requisitioned demanded, required

unhealthy dangerous, risky

rebel to go against rules or authority

significance importance

REVIEWING the SELECTION

The Last Seven Months of Anne Frank

Willy Lindwer

Directions Write the answers to these questions using complete sentences.

Comprehension: Identifying Facts

1. Which of the women was a close childhood friend of Anne Frank?
2. Where do the other women meet the Frank family?
3. Which member of the Frank family survived the camps?

Comprehension: Understanding Main Ideas

4. These women and Anne Frank all share certain experiences. Describe them.
5. How do people in Israel today think about Anne Frank?
6. How did Anne's relationship with her mother change in the camps?

Understanding Literature: Excerpts

This selection is made up of excerpts. An excerpt is a short passage from a longer piece of writing. These excerpts are taken from much longer interviews with several women who knew Anne Frank. Each of them gives you an idea of how the speaker knew the Frank family. They also give you more information about her life and death.

7. How many different women are represented in these excerpts?
8. Which excerpt describes a visit from Anne Frank's father?

Critical Thinking

9. Why do you think visitors to Amsterdam go to the Anne Frank House?
10. One of these women at first did not want to talk about Anne Frank. Later she said, "It was much more difficult to remain silent." Why do you think that was true?

Writing on Your Own You have now seen Anne Frank from two different points of view. Earlier, you read parts of her diary. Now you have heard from others who knew her. Now it's your turn. Write one or two paragraphs explaining what you think about Anne Frank. Why is her story so important to so many people?

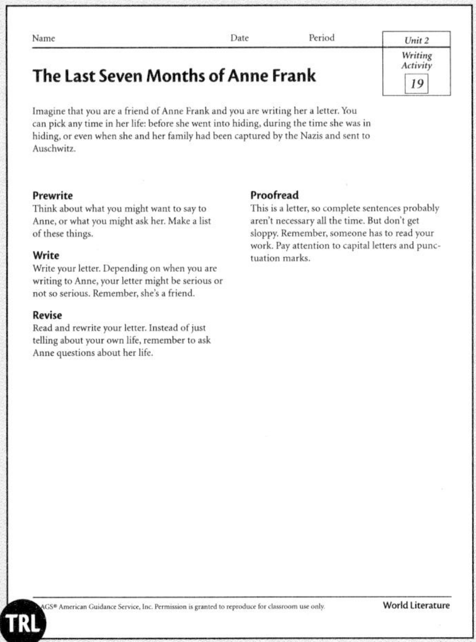

Name Date Period

Unit 2 *Writing Activity* 19

The Last Seven Months of Anne Frank

Imagine that you are a friend of Anne Frank and you are writing her a letter. You can pick any time in her life: before she went into hiding, during the time she was in hiding, or even when she and her family had been captured by the Nazis and sent to Auschwitz.

Prewrite
Think about what you might want to say to Anne, or what you might ask her. Make a list of these things.

Write
Write your letter. Depending on when you are writing to Anne, your letter might be serious or not so serious. Remember, she's a friend.

Revise
Read and rewrite your letter. Instead of just telling about your own life, remember to ask Anne questions about her life.

Proofread
This is a letter, so complete sentences probably aren't necessary all the time. But don't get sloppy. Remember, someone has to read your work. Pay attention to capital letters and punctuation marks.

 World Literature

TRL

Writing Activity 19

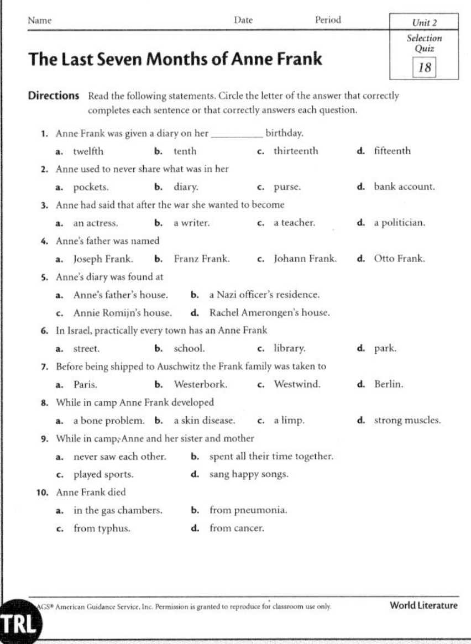

Name Date Period

Unit 2 *Selection Quiz* 18

The Last Seven Months of Anne Frank

Directions Read the following statements. Circle the letter of the answer that correctly completes each sentence or that correctly answers each question.

1. Anne Frank was given a diary on her ________ birthday.
   a. twelfth b. tenth c. thirteenth d. fifteenth
2. Anne used to never share what was in her
   a. pockets. b. diary. c. purse. d. bank account.
3. Anne had said that after the war she wanted to become
   a. an actress. b. a writer. c. a teacher. d. a politician.
4. Anne's father was named
   a. Joseph Frank. b. Franz Frank. c. Johann Frank. d. Otto Frank.
5. Anne's diary was found at
   a. Anne's father's house. b. a Nazi officer's residence.
   c. Annie Romijn's house. d. Rachel Amerongen's house.
6. In Israel, practically every town has an Anne Frank
   a. street. b. school. c. library. d. park.
7. Before being shipped to Auschwitz the Frank family was taken to
   a. Paris. b. Westerbork. c. Westwind. d. Berlin.
8. While in camp Anne Frank developed
   a. a bone problem. b. a skin disease. c. a limp. d. strong muscles.
9. While in camp, Anne and her sister and mother
   a. never saw each other. b. spent all their time together.
   c. played sports. d. sang happy songs.
10. Anne Frank died
    a. in the gas chambers. b. from pneumonia.
    c. from typhus. d. from cancer.

 World Literature

TRL

Selection Quiz 18

Reviewing the Selection

Answer Key

Comprehension: Identifying Facts

1. Hannah Elizabeth Pick-Goslar was a childhood friend.

2. The others meet the Franks in concentration camps; one also knew the girls at a school.

3. Otto Frank survived.

Comprehension: Understanding Main Ideas

4. They shared the hardships and horrors of life in a concentration camp, where death was almost certain and mistreatment was the norm. They shared the understanding that they were the target of racial hatred and of a group that wanted them all to die.

5. They revere her and honor her wherever possible; she is a legend but also someone real to them.

6. Anne forgot her rebellious feelings; they supported each other completely.

Understanding Literature: Excerpts

7. Four women are represented.

8. Janny Brandes-Brilleslijper describes her encounter with Otto Frank when she confirms that his family members are dead.

Critical Thinking

9. Some may be drawn by the charismatic and tragic feeling surrounding the girl's life and death. Others may feel a need to experience this sad chapter of history. Still others may be paying tribute to her bravery and spirit.

10. Answers may include that she realizes the world must not forget or try to gloss over what happened, that her memories haunted her, or that she realized she could not heal her emotional wounds until she rid herself of the torment.

Writing on Your Own You may want to suggest that students develop one paragraph describing the character of Anne Frank and a second one explaining what made this character extraordinary in her situation.

Selection Quiz

The Teacher's Resource Library includes a Selection Quiz for *The Last Seven Months of Anne Frank* that may be given following the Selection Review.

Journalism

Read the opening sentence of the first paragraph aloud and have students list as many journalistic media as possible. (Answers may include newspapers, TV and radio newscasters, weekly news magazine writers and editors, and specialized media such as sportscasts, show business reports, etc.)

Have students take turns reading aloud the paragraphs on page 208. Then ask them to read the quotes at the top of the page and paraphrase them to focus on their main ideas.

ASK What responsibility does a journalist have to readers? (He or she is responsible for presenting information that is clear and factual and covers every point of view.)

ASK What sort of story have you read or heard that is an example of "breaking news"? (Answers might include coverage of a hostage situation while it is in progress, combat reporting, or stories broadcast from the scene of a jailbreak or election.)

ASK Why do journalists sometimes include a sidebar next to a feature article? (To give the reader background or related information that helps them get the big picture or understand a situation better.)

ASK How has the Internet benefited news reporting? (It permits worldwide coverage immediately and provides instantaneous updates.)

Activity 29

Journalism

- "You should always believe all you read in newspapers, as this makes them more interesting." —Rose Macaulay
- "In journalism there has always been a tension between getting it first and getting it right." —Ellen Goodman

Journalism is the gathering and communicating of news to the public. The Constitution guarantees freedom of the press to American journalists. This lets them keep the public well informed. Along with freedom comes the responsibility to report fairly and accurately. Imagine there is a fight between two public officials. A reporter covering the story should talk to both sides before writing the story. He or she might also need to talk to other witnesses. The story should use all these different points of view.

Some journalists report immediate news. Such "breaking news" is in newspapers and on TV as an event happens. Staff reporters often cover these stories. (They don't sign their articles or get public credit for putting the story together.) Feature articles and sidebars come later. They analyze the news. Sidebars are short articles running next to the main story. They may provide more background, or they may report related issues. This is called "in-depth" reporting.

One of the most immediate news sources is the Internet. It is a worldwide network of computers. Anyone connected to the Internet can get information from all over the world at any time. Many newspapers, big and small, have a Web site. A newspaper's Web site has material that the paper puts on the Internet for the public to read. Putting news on the Internet shortens the news cycle. The news cycle starts when a news item is printed. It ends when an update or reaction to it is printed.

The following articles represent news stories and editorials about a world event. As you read, notice how much of each article reports facts and how much is analysis. Several of the selections were taken from the Internet edition of a newspaper. You might not be able to find these newspapers at your local newsstand. But you might find them on the Internet.

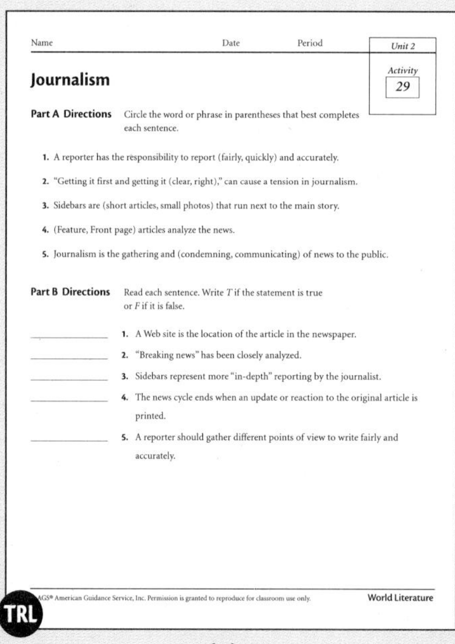

Name Date Period | Unit 2 | Activity 29

Journalism

Part A Directions Circle the word or phrase in parentheses that best completes each sentence.

1. A reporter has the responsibility to report (fairly, quickly) and accurately.
2. "Getting it first and getting it (clear, right)," can cause a tension in journalism.
3. Sidebars are (short articles, small photos) that run next to the main story.
4. (Feature, Front page) articles analyze the news.
5. Journalism is the gathering and (condemning, communicating) of news to the public.

Part B Directions Read each sentence. Write *T* if the statement is true or *F* if it is false.

_______ 1. A Web site is the location of the article in the newspaper.
_______ 2. "Breaking news" has been closely analyzed.
_______ 3. Sidebars represent more "in-depth" reporting by the journalist.
_______ 4. The news cycle ends when an update or reaction to the original article is printed.
_______ 5. A reporter should gather different points of view to write fairly and accurately.

 World Literature

TRL

Activity 29

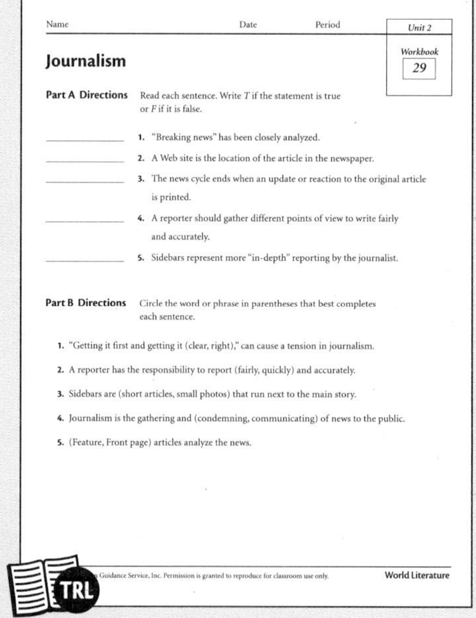

Name Date Period | Unit 2 | Workbook 29

Journalism

Part A Directions Read each sentence. Write *T* if the statement is true or *F* if it is false.

_______ 1. "Breaking news" has been closely analyzed.
_______ 2. A Web site is the location of the article in the newspaper.
_______ 3. The news cycle ends when an update or reaction to the original article is printed.
_______ 4. A reporter should gather different points of view to write fairly and accurately.
_______ 5. Sidebars represent more "in-depth" reporting by the journalist.

Part B Directions Circle the word or phrase in parentheses that best completes each sentence.

1. "Getting it first and getting it (clear, right)," can cause a tension in journalism.
2. A reporter has the responsibility to report (fairly, quickly) and accurately.
3. Sidebars are (short articles, small photos) that run next to the main story.
4. Journalism is the gathering and (condemning, communicating) of news to the public.
5. (Feature, Front page) articles analyze the news.

 World Literature

TRL

Workbook 29

INTRODUCING the SELECTION

Account Evened With India, Says PM

M. Ziauddin, From *Dawn* (Friday, 29 May 1998)

Dawn
(established 1947)
Pakistani

Literary Terms

news story the first reports of an event; mainly covers the basic facts

Web site a place on the Internet where information is published

About the Newspaper

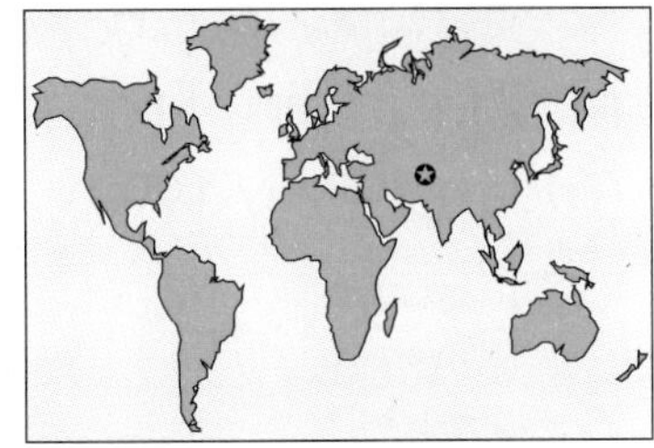

Dawn is an English-language morning paper. It is one of the leading papers in Pakistan. Before independence, it was published in Delhi. Today it is published in Karachi and Lahore, Pakistan. Those are Pakistan's largest cities. Karachi has more than five million people. Pakistan has many newspapers in English. Pakistanis also speak many other languages. Many papers are published in those languages, especially Urdu and Sindh.

You will find articles from *Dawn* on its **Web site.** *Dawn Online* (http://dawn.com/) is the Internet address of *Dawn.* Other foreign newspapers also have Web sites.

About the Selection

Early in May 1998, India held tests of nuclear weapons. They were the first in the region. A few weeks later, Pakistan held its own tests. The two countries have been rivals and enemies for more than fifty years. Until 1947, all of South Asia was the British colony of India. It then split into two independent countries. Most Pakistanis are Muslim. India's people are more varied and Hindus are the main religious group.

This selection is a **news story** from Pakistan. It reports that Pakistan has just made its first nuclear tests. The prime minister has announced them. He also predicted that other nations would punish Pakistan. Why? Most people in Pakistan were proud of their country's decision. At the same time, Pakistanis knew that the tests would bring trouble. Other nations with nuclear weapons have agreed to stop testing them. The Indian and Pakistani tests frightened many people.

Selection at a Glance

Account Evened With India, Says PM

M. Ziauddin, From *Dawn* (Pakistan)

Student pages 209–213

Overview

This article, reporting nuclear tests by Pakistan, is clearly intended to answer India's nuclear tests of two weeks prior, which Pakistan read as a direct threat from India.

Selection Summary

The article relies heavily on quotes from Pakistan's Prime Minister Nawaz Sharif.

Objectives

- To identify the basic facts of a news story.
- To recognize the slant or point of view implied by statements of an article.

Audiocassette 

Teacher's Resource Library TRL

- Vocabulary Workbook 19
- Selection Glossary 19
- Student Study Guide 25
- Activity 30
- Workbook 30
- Writing Activity 20
- Selection Quiz 19

Setting the Stage for Reading

About the Newspaper

Dawn has the widest circulation of any English-language newspaper in Pakistan and is read by policy makers and decision makers in both public and private sectors. Its Internet edition is accessed by fifty thousand readers in seventy-two countries across six continents.

ASK Why might the Prime Minister of Pakistan want his statements to appear in *Dawn?* (People in leadership positions must be informed about what has happened and the government stance on it.)

About the Selection

When India detonated its nuclear weapons early in May 1998, an outcry went up around the world. Pakistan felt challenged and threatened by India on the one hand and was besieged by pressure from world superpowers to ignore the tests and not to retaliate.

Activate Prior Knowledge: Discuss the destruction and long-term health hazards caused by nuclear blasts. Remind students that the World War II blasts caused such death and destruction that it became clear humans had invented a weapon powerful enough to destroy civilization.

ASK Why have world powers such as the United States, Russia, and Germany signed agreements not to test nuclear weapons? (They want to hold the growth of this type of military potential in check. They want to lessen the threat of nuclear weapons on the world.)

Reading Vocabulary TRL

Use the Selection Glossary page to acquaint students with vocabulary. You may want to suggest that students skim the article before reading to locate other new words. Ask students to familiarize themselves with meanings of all these words before they read.

Motivation for Reading

Have students read the headline and predict what attitude the prime minister of Pakistan will have about his nation's tests.

Discussion Questions

Point out to students that notes in the margins provide explanations that are helpful to understanding the article and the history of India-Pakistan relations.

A ASK Literary Element The opening paragraph explains what has happened and why. Have students give this information in their own words. (Pakistan conducted nuclear tests to ensure it can defend itself against India.)

B ASK Comprehension What does the prime minister warn the nation to be ready for? What does he seem to think will happen? (He warns that the world will make Pakistan "pay a price." He expects punishment from other countries.)

Account Evened With India, Says PM

M. Ziauddin, From *Dawn*

(Friday, 29 May 1998)

Pakistani citizens demonstrated in the streets to show their support of the nuclear tests.

A ISLAMABAD: Pakistan on Thursday joined the exclusive club of nuclear nations by conducting five nuclear tests of varying **intensity** in Chagai hills, a remote region of Balochistan desert near the border with Iran and Afghanistan. Announcing the successful **completion** of a series of tests in response to those conducted by India on May 11–13, Prime Minister Nawaz Sharif told the nation on radio and television that he took the decision in the interest of national security and **integrity**.

Keep in mind that India and Pakistan have been rivals since the two nations were formed. *Islamabad* is Pakistan's capital.

Only a few countries have nuclear weapons. The writer calls them the *exclusive club of nuclear nations.*

B He, however, warned the nation to be prepared to pay the price for taking this decision in the face of immense world pressure. The prime minister said in a few days time he would present to the nation a complete national **agenda** for meeting the **anticipated** hardships. He announced a number of official austerity measures to meet the challenges of the expected sanctions and asked the nation to reciprocate by trying to live within its means.

The prime minister also served final notice on the country's tax **evaders** and **corrupt** tax collectors, cautioning them to

agenda a list of things to be done

anticipated expected

completion ending

corrupt dishonest

evader a person who avoids doing something

integrity completeness

intensity strength

210 *Unit 2 Nonfiction*

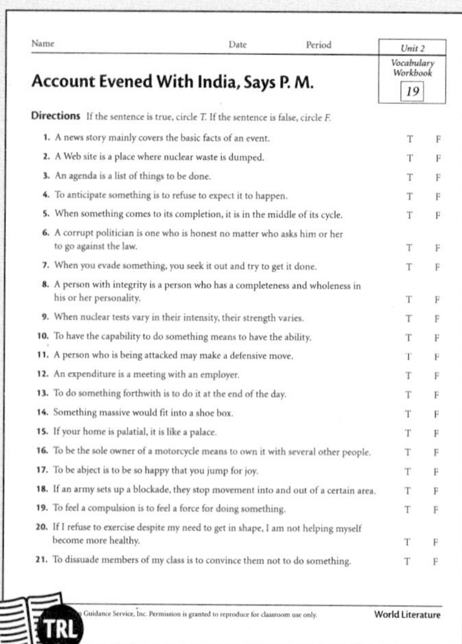

Name Date Period

Unit 2 — Vocabulary Workbook 19

Account Evened With India, Says P. M.

Directions If the sentence is true, circle *T.* If the sentence is false, circle *F.*

1. A news story mainly covers the basic facts of an event. T F
2. A Web site is a place where nuclear waste is dumped. T F
3. An agenda is a list of things to be done. T F
4. To anticipate something is to refuse to expect it to happen. T F
5. When something comes to its completion, it is in the middle of its cycle. T F
6. A corrupt politician is one who is honest no matter who asks him or her to go against the law. T F
7. When you evade something, you seek it out and try to get it done. T F
8. A person with integrity is a person who has a completeness and wholeness in his or her personality. T F
9. When nuclear tests vary in their intensity, their strength varies. T F
10. To have the capability to do something means to have the ability. T F
11. A person who is being attacked may make a defensive move. T F
12. An expenditure is a meeting with an employer. T F
13. To do something forthwith is to do it at the end of the day. T F
14. Something massive would fit into a shoe box. T F
15. If your home is palatial, it is like a palace. T F
16. To be the sole owner of a motorcycle means to own it with several other people. T F
17. To be abject is to be so happy that you jump for joy. T F
18. If an army sets up a blockade, they stop movement into and out of a certain area. T F
19. To feel a compulsion is to feel a force for doing something. T F
20. If I refuse to exercise despite my need to get in shape, I am not helping myself become more healthy. T F
21. To dissuade members of my class is to convince them not to do something. T F

 World Literature

TRL

Vocabulary Workbook 19

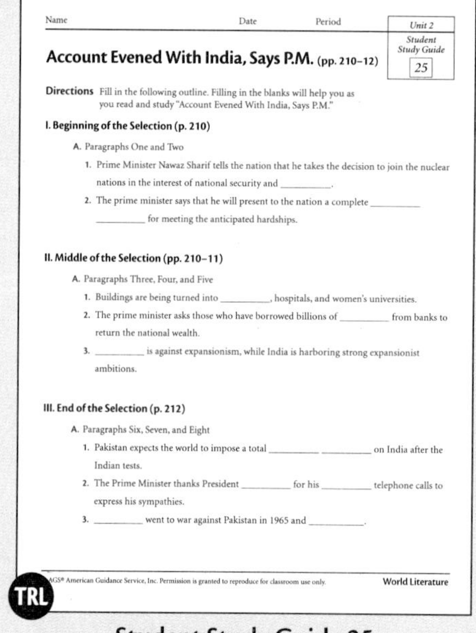

Name Date Period

Unit 2 — Student Study Guide 25

Account Evened With India, Says P.M. (pp. 210–12)

Directions Fill in the following outline. Filling in the blanks will help you as you read and study "Account Evened With India, Says P.M."

I. Beginning of the Selection (p. 210)

A. Paragraphs One and Two
1. Prime Minister Nawaz Sharif tells the nation that he takes the decision to join the nuclear nations in the interest of national security and ________.
2. The prime minister says that he will present to the nation a complete ________ ________ for meeting the anticipated hardships.

II. Middle of the Selection (pp. 210–11)

A. Paragraphs Three, Four, and Five
1. Buildings are being turned into ________, hospitals, and women's universities.
2. The prime minister asks those who have borrowed billions of ________ from banks to return the national wealth.
3. ________ is against expansionism, while India is harboring strong expansionist ambitions.

III. End of the Selection (p. 212)

A. Paragraphs Six, Seven, and Eight
1. Pakistan expects the world to impose a total ________ ________ on India after the Indian tests.
2. The Prime Minister thanks President ________ for his ________ telephone calls to express his sympathies.
3. ________ went to war against Pakistan in 1965 and ________.

 World Literature

TRL

Student Study Guide 25

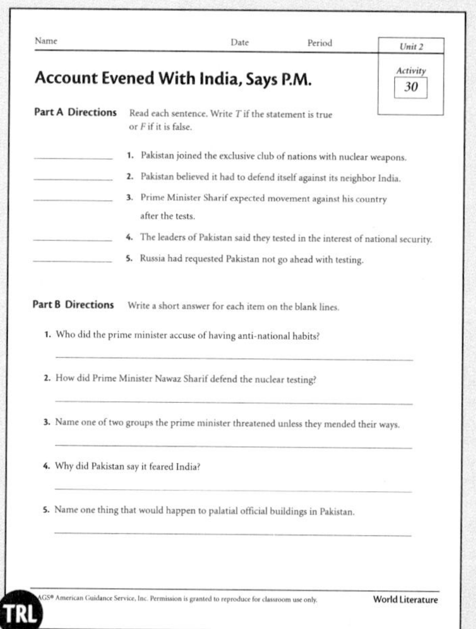

Name Date Period

Unit 2 — Activity 30

Account Evened With India, Says P.M.

Part A Directions Read each sentence. Write *T* if the statement is true or *F* if it is false.

________ 1. Pakistan joined the exclusive club of nations with nuclear weapons.
________ 2. Pakistan believed it had to defend itself against its neighbor India.
________ 3. Prime Minister Sharif expected movement against his country after the tests.
________ 4. The leaders of Pakistan said they tested in the interest of national security.
________ 5. Russia had requested Pakistan not go ahead with testing.

Part B Directions Write a short answer for each item on the blank lines.

1. Who did the prime minister accuse of having anti-national habits?
2. How did Prime Minister Nawaz Sharif defend the nuclear testing?
3. Name one of two groups the prime minister threatened unless they mended their ways.
4. Why did Pakistan say it feared India?
5. Name one thing that would happen to palatial official buildings in Pakistan.

 World Literature

TRL

Activity 30

mend their ways; otherwise he warned that the government would not spare them. He assured the nation that the government would stop **forthwith** all of its demonstrative and wasteful **expenditures** and said all **palatial** official buildings would be pressed into the service of the nation. Some of these **C** buildings would be turned into schools, some into hospitals and some others into women's universities. And some would be sold to retire debts. The prime minister announced that he **D** would not use the Prime Minister's Secretariat and said the government has decided to observe complete austerity at the official level.

The prime minister expects other countries to impose *sanctions* because they oppose the nuclear tests. That is, they will stop or cut down trade and aid to Pakistan.

The *Secretariat* is a large government building in Islamabad.

He said the president was in complete agreement with these decisions and all provincial governors, chief ministers, federal ministers, chiefs of navy, army, and air-force and high civil and military officials will join the nation in its sacrifices and austerity efforts. He asked those who had borrowed billions of rupees from the banks to return the national wealth and warned tax evaders to give up their anti-national habits. Describing the nuclear tests as a **defensive** step, the prime minister said these tests were conducted **solely** in the interest of national security and integrity.

Pakistan is divided into four provinces. Each has a *provincial governor.*

The *rupee* is the unit of money in both India and Pakistan.

Prime Minister Nawaz Sharif said every time Pakistan **E** brought to the world attention India's **massive** arms build-up, New Delhi attributed it to Chinese threat to India's security. But he said despite its tremendous superiority in defensive **capability,** China was against expansionism while India had proven on more than one occasion that it **F** harboured strong expansionist ambitions. Under the circumstances it was natural for Pakistan, Mr. Nawaz Sharif said, to feel concerned and in order to ward off the threat to national security, the country had even proposed that **G** America, Russia and China should mediate and save Asia from arms race.

capability the ability to do something

defensive done to defend oneself

expenditure spending

forthwith immediatel

massive huge

palatial elaborate; like a palace

solely only

Name Date Period

Unit 2

Workbook 30

Account Evened With India, Says P.M.

Part A Directions Circle the word or phrase in parentheses that best completes each sentence.

1. Pakistan joined the (exclusive club, private circle) of nations with nuclear weapons.
2. Pakistan believed it had to defend itself against its neighbor (China, India).
3. Prime Minister Sharif expected (sanctions, movement) against his country after the tests.
4. The leaders of Pakistan said they tested in the interest of national (security, defense).
5. (Russia, America) had requested Pakistan not go ahead with testing.

Part B Directions Write a short answer for each item on the blank lines.

1. How did Prime Minister Nawaz Sharif defend the nuclear testing?
2. Name one of two groups the prime minister threatened unless they mended their ways.
3. Name one thing that would happen to palatial official buildings in Pakistan.
4. Who did the prime minister accuse of having anti-national habits?
5. Why did Pakistan say it feared India?

 World Literature

TRL

Workbook 30

C ASK Vocabulary The word *pressed* often means "to squeeze" or "to iron." What other meaning does it have as used here? (Its meaning is "forced" or "compelled.")

D ASK Critical Thinking Why do you think the prime minister is giving up his government offices? (He is leading by example. He shows how serious the sanctions might be and what sacrifices may be required.)

E ASK Comprehension How do India and Pakistan differ in their view of China's role, according to the prime minister? (Pakistan believes India wants to take over land on its borders; India says it only seeks to protect itself from Chinese aggression.)

F ASK Literary Element How does this information go beyond reporting the facts? (It states that India has "proven" it wants to expand its borders but gives no proof. The statement is an opinion.)

G ASK Comprehension What does Pakistan want the world powers to do? (Step in and convince India to stop nuclear weapons development; Pakistan's cooperation is implied.)

Learning Styles

LEP/ESL The author of the article uses a complex writing style. Many sentences are long; some phrases are inserted in unusual places. Encourage students to attack confusing sentences by breaking them down into clear units of meaning. For example, look at the sentence "(Prime Minister Nawaz Sharif said) every time Pakistan brought *to the world attention* India's massive arms buildup, New Delhi attributed it to Chinese threat to India's security." The words in parentheses indicate the speaker, and the italicized words can be moved after "buildup." Encourage students to check understanding by stating what pronouns represent: *it = the buildup.*

Discussion Questions

A ASK Comprehension For what does the prime minister blame the world? (He implies that the failure of powerful nations to pressure India to change its policies and actions has left Pakistan in a precarious, dangerous position.)

B ASK Critical Thinking Do you think Japan praised or criticized Pakistan for the tests? (Answers should note that Japan must have protested the tests by both India and Pakistan, since it wants to avoid the suffering of nuclear war.)

C ASK Vocabulary Explain that the noun *hegemony* means "dominance of one state or nation over others." The adjective form of the word is *hegemonic*. What are India's "hegemonic designs"? (Its strategies and plans for dominating Pakistan.)

Writing Connection

Ask students to state the purpose of a newspaper article. (To communicate the facts of a news event and, at times, to analyze its meaning.) Discuss students' reactions to the tone and content of this article. Do they feel it remains objective in its analysis? What principle impression does it make? (Answers may include that it attempts to give Pakistan's perspective on events, not necessarily the facts, and to justify Pakistan's actions as a response to an unfair and hostile world.) Have students write a paragraph defending an action they have been criticized for.

He said if Pakistan had wanted it would have conducted nuclear tests 15–20 years ago but the **abject** poverty of the people of the region **dissuaded** Pakistan from doing so. But **A** the world, he said, instead of putting pressure on India not to take the destructive road imposed all kinds of sanctions on Pakistan for no fault of her [own]. He said after the Indian tests, Pakistan had expected the world to impose a total economic **blockade** on India but unfortunately no such action was taken.

Near the end of World War II, the United States dropped atomic bombs on *Hiroshima* and *Nagasaki*, Japan. Japan today opposes nuclear weapons.

Prime Minister Nawaz Sharif praised China for its support **B** during "this hour of crisis" and said Pakistan was proud of its great neighbour. Stating that Japan's position on the nuclear issue was based on the highest human principles, he, however, thought if Japan had had its own nuclear capability Hiroshima and Nagasaki would not have suffered destruction. He thanked President Clinton for his five telephone calls to express his sympathies following Indian explosions but said he expected the American president to appreciate Pakistan's **compulsions** for carrying out its own tests **despite** American advise against it.

The *big bomb* refers to a nuclear weapon. *Kashmir* is a disputed region on the Indian border.

The prime minister said Pakistan has taken the extreme step without bothering about the expected sanctions and spurning promises of all kinds of gifts and goodies. He said the world should not believe India when it says that it would use the 'big bomb' only if attacked because both in 1965 and 1971 India went to war against Pakistan accusing it of committing aggression and even today New Delhi was accusing Pakistan of keeping Azad Kashmir under its occupation. He asked the world to see Pakistan's nuclear tests in the context of India's **C** aggressive and hegemonic designs but said if even then the world decided to impose sanctions on the country then Pakistan would accept these as the will of God.

abject miserable

blockade something that stops movement in and out of an area

compulsion the force or reason behind an action

despite in spite of

dissuade to persuade someone not to take a certain action

REVIEWING the SELECTION

Account Evened With India, Says PM

M. Ziauddin, From *Dawn* (Friday, 29 May 1998)

Directions Write the answers to these questions using complete sentences.

Comprehension: Identifying Facts

1. What is the name of the prime minister of Pakistan?
2. What are Pakistan's reasons for conducting nuclear tests?
3. What other country seems to have supported Pakistan's actions?

Comprehension: Understanding Main Ideas

4. How does the prime minister expect other countries to react to Pakistan's tests? How will that affect the country?
5. What does the prime minister want the people of Pakistan to do to help the country?
6. What specific actions will the Pakistani government take to cut down spending?

Understanding Literature: News Story

A news story presents the basic facts about an event. It answers the questions "who, what, when, why, how, and where." The first sentence of this story answers some of those questions. This is called the "lead." The rest of the news story reports on the prime minister's speech to the country. In it, he explains more of the "why" of the story.

7. Reread the first sentence of the news story. How does it answer the questions "when" and "where"?
8. Several paragraphs of the story are meant for a world audience, not just Pakistan. Which paragraphs are they?

Critical Thinking

9. What can you tell about Pakistan's relations with India from the tone of this article?
10. Do you think that Pakistan is a rich or a poor country?

Writing on Your Own Think of a recent event—in your city or in the world. Now write one or two sentences that would be the "lead" of a news story about that event. Your sentences should answer the basic questions: who, what, when, where, how, why?

Reviewing the Selection

Answer Key

Comprehension: Identifying Facts

1. The prime minister is Nawaz Sharif.
2. Pakistan wanted to show it had the same defensive capability as India and assure that it could defend itself.
3. China offered support.

Comprehension: Understanding Main Ideas

4. He believes they will punish Pakistan by imposing economic and political sanctions.
5. He wants them to repay government loans, consume goods more modestly, and give up luxuries to conserve money.
6. The government will eliminate all unessential spending and convert offices into public service facilities.

Understanding Literature: News Story

7. It states that Pakistan conducted nuclear tests on Thursday in the Chagai hills.
8. The final three lines on page 211 and all three paragraphs on page 212 are directed at world powers which Pakistan considers "guilty."

Critical Thinking

9. The two countries rattle sabers and conflict with each other in political and military ways often. Relations between them are tense and unpredictable.
10. Sharif's reference to "the abject poverty" of people in the Chagai hills and the fact that he must ask that loans be returned to the government show that the country is poor.

Writing on Your Own Encourage students to scan several news stories, highlighting the *who, what, when, where, how,* and *why* information. Then have them write the answers to each of these questions for their story in table form before they write their sentences.

Selection Quiz

The Teacher's Resource Library includes a Selection Quiz for "Account Evened With India, Says P.M." that may be given following the Selection Review.

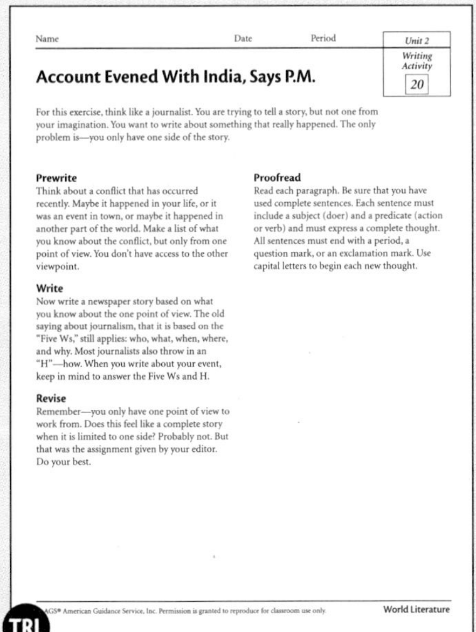

Name Date Period

Unit 2 *Writing Activity* 20

Account Evened With India, Says P.M.

For this exercise, think like a journalist. You are trying to tell a story, but not one from your imagination. You want to write about something that really happened. The only problem is—you only have one side of the story.

Prewrite
Think about a conflict that has occurred recently. Maybe it happened in your life, or it was an event in town, or maybe it happened in another part of the world. Make a list of what you know about the conflict, but only from one point of view. You don't have access to the other viewpoint.

Write
Now write a newspaper story based on what you know about the one point of view. The old saying about journalism, that it is based on the "Five Ws," still applies: who, what, when, where, and why. Most journalists also throw in an "H"—how. When you write about your event, keep in mind to answer the Five Ws and H.

Revise
Remember—you only have one point of view to work from. Does this feel like a complete story when it is limited to one side? Probably not. But that was the assignment given by your editor. Do your best.

Proofread
Read each paragraph. Be sure that you have used complete sentences. Each sentence must include a subject (doer) and a predicate (action or verb) and must express a complete thought. All sentences must end with a period, a question mark, or an exclamation mark. Use capital letters to begin each new thought.

 World Literature

TRL

Writing Activity 20

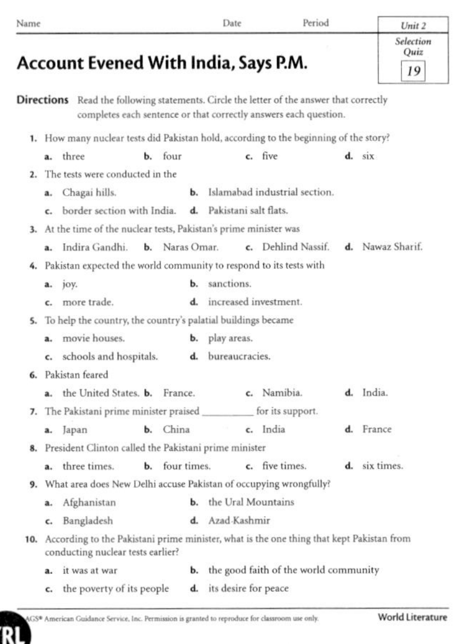

Name Date Period

Unit 2 *Selection Quiz* 19

Account Evened With India, Says P.M.

Directions Read the following statements. Circle the letter of the answer that correctly completes each sentence or that correctly answers each question.

1. How many nuclear tests did Pakistan hold, according to the beginning of the story?
   a. three b. four c. five d. six
2. The tests were conducted in the
   a. Chagai hills. b. Islamabad industrial section. c. border section with India. d. Pakistani salt flats.
3. At the time of the nuclear tests, Pakistan's prime minister was
   a. Indira Gandhi. b. Naras Omar. c. Dehlind Nassif. d. Nawaz Sharif.
4. Pakistan expected the world community to respond to its tests with
   a. joy. b. sanctions. c. more trade. d. increased investment.
5. To help the country, the country's palatial buildings became
   a. movie houses. b. play areas. c. schools and hospitals. d. bureaucracies.
6. Pakistan feared
   a. the United States. b. France. c. Namibia. d. India.
7. The Pakistani prime minister praised ________ for its support.
   a. Japan b. China c. India d. France
8. President Clinton called the Pakistani prime minister
   a. three times. b. four times. c. five times. d. six times.
9. What area does New Delhi accuse Pakistan of occupying wrongfully?
   a. Afghanistan b. the Ural Mountains c. Bangladesh d. Azad Kashmir
10. According to the Pakistani prime minister, what is the one thing that kept Pakistan from conducting nuclear tests earlier?
   a. it was at war b. the good faith of the world community c. the poverty of its people d. its desire for peace

 World Literature

TRL

Selection Quiz 19

Selection at a Glance

Tests Are Nowhere Near India's: Fernandes

From *The Times of India*

Student pages 214–219

Overview

The Times of India is a sophisticated newspaper with contacts all over the world, as this article's extensive quotes and facts suggest.

Selection Summary

The article evaluates Pakistan's nuclear tests as insignificantly small compared to those of India.

Objectives

- To identify sources of information for journalism.
- To analyze the types of information included in an article.

Audiocassette 

Teacher's Resource Library TRL

- Vocabulary Workbook 20
- Selection Glossary 20
- Student Study Guide 26
- Activity 31
- Workbook 31
- Writing Activity 21
- Selection Quiz 20

INTRODUCING the SELECTION

Tests Are Nowhere Near India's

From *The Times of India* (Monday, 1 June 1998)

The Times of India (established 1838) Indian

Literary Term

journalism the gathering and communicating of news to the public

About the Newspaper

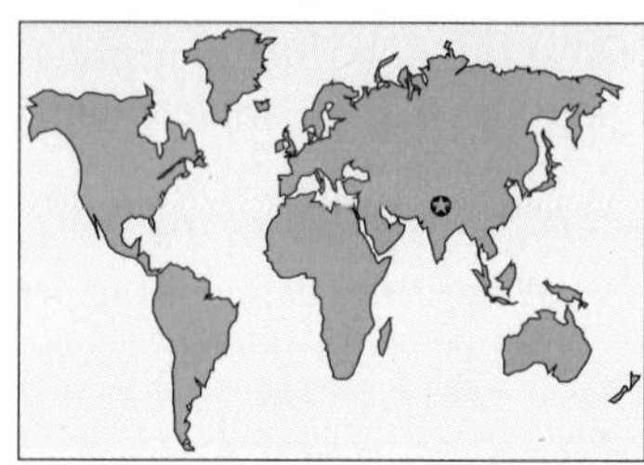

This newspaper first appeared in Bombay, India, in 1838. It was originally called *The Bombay Times and Journal of Commerce.* It was a paper mainly by and for the British residents who ran India's colonial government. Today *The Times of India* is published in New Delhi. It is the most widely circulated English-language daily newspaper in India. It is part of a large Indian publishing group that also prints newspapers in Indian languages. Every day more than a million copies are sold from its printing plants in Mumbai, Delhi, Bangalore, Ahmedabad, Lucknow, and Patna. The *Times* is published every day including Sunday. It is a well-established newspaper with a good reputation for objective reporting.

The Times of India Online (http://www.timesofindia.com) is the Internet version of *The Times of India.*

About the Selection

People who work in **journalism** have the job of finding, collecting, and communicating news. The news reported in this story adds more information about India and Pakistan's nuclear tests. It is based mainly on a TV interview during which an Indian government official compared the two countries' tests. India had made the first tests. Pakistan had made tests a few weeks later. The official, George Fernandes, also discusses India's future nuclear plans. Besides reporting the speech, this journalist added other information. The article quotes scientists in the United States. Giving such "background information" is also part of a journalist's job.

Setting the Stage for Reading

About the Newspaper

Point out that *The Times of India* has been publishing since 1838, when India was under British rule. Have students compare this to the date that *Dawn* (source of the preceding selection) was established. (1947) Point out that in 1947 India and Pakistan gained independence. Disputes over territory and religious persecution of minorities have resulted in conflicts ever since. By comparison to *Dawn, The Times* has much greater history and finesse.

ASK Why might *The Times* and *Dawn* have opposite points of view on a political story? (They represent India and Pakistan, respectively, and these countries are enemies.)

About the Selection

The article "Tests Are Nowhere Near India's" was published several days after the *Dawn* article and reports more completely on specifics about the Pakistani tests, citing more sources.

Activate Prior Knowledge: Remind students of military intelligence organizations that cover the globe and worldwide communication between scientists. Ask them to identify a U.S. agency they know that monitors activities around the world. (Answers may include the CIA, U.S. Geological Society, etc.)

ASK: What does a seismologist analyze? (Shock waves from earthquakes.) Why might a seismologist know about nuclear tests? (The bomb sets off shock waves.)

214 *Unit 2 Nonfiction*

TESTS ARE NOWHERE NEAR INDIA'S: FERNANDES

From *The Times of India*

(Monday, 1 June 1998)

As you read this newspaper article, keep in mind that it gives India's point of view about the Pakistani tests.

NEW DELHI: Defence minister George Fernandes has asserted that Pakistan's nuclear blasts were "nowhere near" the Indian tests and said New Delhi exercised its nuclear **option** without holding **strategic** defence review because "scientists did feel that the tests were needed." In an interview to a private TV channel, Mr Fernandes said, "Everything that we have learnt about their [Pakistani] **A** nuclear tests show that they are nowhere near where we are. In terms of our tests we [also] went in for low-intensity sub-kiloton tests. They are the most important tests in any kind of nuclear testing."

New Delhi is India's capital city.

India was a British colony for many years. Indian newspapers use British spellings such as *defence* for *defense*.

Nuclear weapons are measured in *kilotons*, a force equal to the explosion of 1,000 tons of TNT. TNT is an explosive compound.

Asked if Islamabad's claim that it conducted tests similar to **B** those by India was "mistaken and **deliberately** wrong," he said, "that's the general understanding that we have." Noting that New Delhi's concerns were much bigger and it had acted on those bigger concerns, he said there had been no testing since 1974 despite a lot of **development** in the nuclear science area and its **application** and "the scientists wanted to test it."

application a way to use something

deliberately on purpose

development growth; progress

option a choice

strategic related to military planning

Reading Vocabulary TRL

Have students review the words on the Selection Glossary page. Assign one or two words to each student and have him or her write a sentence using the word in context. When they read their sentences aloud, students can leave the words out and classmates fill in the blanks.

Motivation for Reading

Remind students that India detonated nuclear devices first. Ask students how they think India will justify its nuclear tests and respond to Pakistan's.

Discussion Questions

Refer students to the marginal notes, which explain some of the background for the article and interpret some of the statements.

A ASK Critical Thinking Why does the defense minister think it important that Pakistan's tests were inferior? (Pakistan is an enemy with whom India has frequent conflicts. If it has a nuclear arsenal as strong as India's, there is more danger for India.)

B ASK Comprehension How does this statement answer the Pakistani prime minister's comments in the preceding article? (It implies that Pakistan's representative lied in order to mislead India and the world.)

Name Date Period | Unit 2 | *Vocabulary Workbook* 20

Tests Are Nowhere Near India's: Fernandes

Part A Directions Match each item in Column A with a detail or definition in Column B. Write the letter of each correct answer on the line.

Column A	Column B
____ 1. deployment	a. different types of weapons seen as a group
____ 2. executive	b. the branch of government that carries out the laws
____ 3. journalism	c. the gathering and communicating of news to the public
____ 4. militarisation	d. the front part of a missile or bomb that contains the explosive
____ 5. seismology	e. the spreading of troops or weapons in a larger area
____ 6. warhead	f. the study of earthquakes
____ 7. weaponry	g. the process of being taken over or used by the military

Part B Directions Match each item in Column C with its three synonyms (words that have the same or a similar meaning) in Column D. Write the letter of each correct answer on the line.

Column C	Column D
____ 1. to air	a. doorsill, entrance, beginning
____ 2. application	b. armory, storehouse, stockpile
____ 3. arsenal	c. to oversee, to measure, to supervise
____ 4. context	d. to discuss, to confess, to broadcast
____ 5. deterrent	e. impediment, obstacle, blockage
____ 6. to monitor	f. setting, situation, framework
____ 7. option	g. utilization, use, employment
____ 8. threshold	h. choice, selection, substitution

Part C Directions Match each item in Column E with its antonym (a word that has the opposite or nearly the opposite meaning) in Column F. Write the letter of each correct answer on the line.

Column E	Column F
____ 1. to alarm	a. thoughtlessly
____ 2. backbreaking	b. unimportant
____ 3. deliberately	c. decline
____ 4. development	d. to deny
____ 5. global	e. danger
____ 6. to maintain	f. easy
____ 7. security	g. local
____ 8. strategic	h. to calm

 World Literature

TRL

Vocabulary Workbook 20

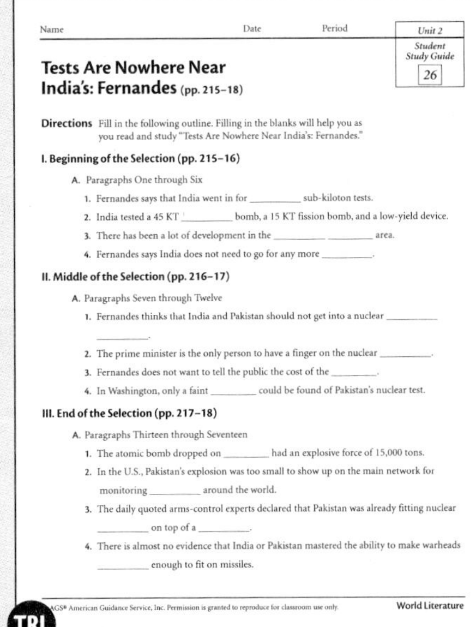

Name Date Period | Unit 2 | *Student Study Guide* 26

Tests Are Nowhere Near India's: Fernandes (pp. 215–18)

Directions Fill in the following outline. Filling in the blanks will help you as you read and study "Tests Are Nowhere Near India's: Fernandes."

I. Beginning of the Selection (pp. 215–16)

A. Paragraphs One through Six

1. Fernandes says that India went in for __________ sub-kiloton tests.
2. India tested a 45 KT __________ bomb, a 15 KT fission bomb, and a low-yield device.
3. There has been a lot of development in the __________ __________ area.
4. Fernandes says India does not need to go for any more __________.

II. Middle of the Selection (pp. 216–17)

A. Paragraphs Seven through Twelve

1. Fernandes thinks that India and Pakistan should not get into a nuclear __________ __________.
2. The prime minister is the only person to have a finger on the nuclear __________.
3. Fernandes does not want to tell the public the cost of the __________.
4. In Washington, only a faint __________ could be found of Pakistan's nuclear test.

III. End of the Selection (pp. 217–18)

A. Paragraphs Thirteen through Seventeen

1. The atomic bomb dropped on __________ had an explosive force of 15,000 tons.
2. In the U.S., Pakistan's explosion was too small to show up on the main network for monitoring __________ around the world.
3. The daily quoted arms-control experts declared that Pakistan was already fitting nuclear __________ on top of a __________.
4. There is almost no evidence that India or Pakistan mastered the ability to make warheads __________ enough to fit on missiles.

 World Literature

TRL

Student Study Guide 26

Name Date Period | Unit 2 | *Activity* 31

Tests Are Nowhere Near India's: Fernandes

Part A Directions Circle the word or phrase in parentheses that best completes each sentence.

1. India believed its (nuclear tests, army personnel) were greater in number and larger in strength.
2. (Asia, India) said that national security was one reason for the testing.
3. Only the Defense Minister in India will be allowed to push the (elevator, nuclear) button.
4. American experts tracking (earthquakes, missiles) could tell both countries had performed tests.
5. The article said there is evidence that Pakistan and India can fit nuclear warheads on (missiles, tractors).

Part B Directions Match each item on the left with the correct item on the right. Write the correct letter on each line.

____ 1. deterrent	a. different types of weapons seen as a group
____ 2. deployment	b. at first
____ 3. warhead	c. a storehouse for weapons
____ 4. arsenal	d. related to military planning
____ 5. strategic	e. greatness in size or power
____ 6. preliminary	f. something that prevents or discourages an action
____ 7. weaponry	g. the study of earthquakes
____ 8. seismology	h. the front part of a missile that contains the explosive
____ 9. magnitude	i. the spreading out of troops or weapons in a larger area
____ 10. militarization	j. the process of being taken over or used by the military

 World Literature

TRL

Activity 31

Discussion Questions

A ASK Comprehension Why did India make the tests, according to Fernandes? (They felt a need to catch up with the world in military technology and see if their applications of nuclear science worked in fact. They also wanted to show the world they were nuclear "players.")

B ASK Comprehension Does the defense minister say there will not be more tests? (He says there will be no more tests for accuracy, but he implies that they will use their nuclear power if necessary to defend their nation.)

C ASK Comprehension What does India hope will happen next? (Judging from Fernandes's remarks, India hopes to negotiate with Pakistan from a position of strength.)

D ASK Critical Thinking Why does he not rule out a nuclear weapons build-up, if India does not want a "nuclear race"? (India and Pakistan are locked in a conflict in which both are afraid to appear the weaker, for that might result in attack.)

These are different types and sizes of nuclear devices.

India had tested a 45 kiloton (KT) hydrogen bomb, a 15 KT fission bomb and a low-yield device on May 11 and two sub-kiloton devices on May 13. Pakistan conducted its tests on May 28 and 30.

The Central Intelligence Agency (CIA) is an American government agency. It gathers information about foreign governments.

Maintaining that Pakistan had carried out only one test on May 28, he said, "We got a bit of information that in fact there may not have [been] five tests. The US agency, the CIA, has put out a piece of information that the number five is only to match India's five. The general feeling is that there was only one."

A Admitting that India carried out the Pokhran tests without holding a strategic defence review, he said, "There has been a lot of development in the nuclear science area. There has been **militarisation** of nuclear **weaponry.** We have to show not only to ourselves, but tell the world we [too] are there."

Asked whether India would conduct more tests, Mr **B** Fernandes said, "We do not need to go for any more testing, whatever we needed to know we got it," but also added "in terms of a country's **security** concerns one does not say the last word at any point of time."

Fernandes is talking about whether India will now build nuclear weapons. To *weaponize* is to adapt something for use as a weapon.

To a question if India would go in for weaponisation, the minister noted "What I have said is that any nuclear tests without weaponising do not make sense.

Here *across the border* means Pakistan.

"Whether one needs to weaponise in the **context** of what has happened across the border is a matter on which in Parliament the Prime Minister had made a public offer to **C** Pakistan that we should sit together, we should talk and we should not get into any kind of a nuclear weapon race. **D** Therefore, it is going to be a two-way traffic and I hope Pakistan responds to the Prime Minister's appeal," he said.

context the setting or situation

maintaining declaring, insisting

militarisation (Amer. militarization) the process of being taken over or used by the military

security safety

weaponry different types of weapons seen as a group

Name Date Period

Unit 2

Workbook 31

Tests Are Nowhere Near India's: Fernandes

Part A Directions Read each sentence. Write *T* if the statement is true or *F* if it is false.

_______ 1. India believed its nuclear tests were greater in number and larger in strength.

_______ 2. India said that national security was one reason for the testing..

_______ 3. Only the Defense Minister in India will be allowed to push the nuclear button.

_______ 4. Experts tracking earthquakes in the United States could tell both countries had performed tests.

_______ 5. The article said there is evidence that Pakistan and India can fit nuclear warheads on missiles.

Part B Directions Match each item on the left with the correct item on the right. Write the correct letter on each line.

____	1. arsenal	a. different types of weapons seen as a group
____	2. deterrent	b. at first
____	3. deployment	c. a storehouse for weapons
____	4. warhead	d. related to military planning
____	5. preliminary	e. greatness in size or power
____	6. strategic	f. something that prevents or discourages an action
____	7. militarization	g. the study of earthquakes
____	8. weaponry	h. the front part of a missile that contains the explosive
____	9. seismology	i. the spreading out of troops or weapons in a larger area
____	10. magnitude	j. the process of being taken over or used by the military

World Literature

TRL

Workbook 31

Asked about control and command structure Mr Fernandes said "there will be the same kind of control which exist in those countries which have nuclear weaponry. They cannot be any different." Observing that the Prime Minister will be the only person to have his finger on the nuclear button, he said, "In India the Prime Minister is the **executive** head of government...And it shall be the Prime Minister."

Control and command structure means the government and military officials who are in charge of nuclear weapons.

On nuclear **deterrent,** he said, "The Army is happy that it has it and the Army believes that no one can push us around." **E**

Mr Fernandes refused to give details on the size of deterrent **F** that India required or the cost of creating it saying "these are matters which I do not believe can be **aired** in public." He said that the cost of developing a deterrent and an appropriate delivery system would not be "**backbreaking**" and added "a delivery system is something that we always had. Your aircraft are there. Your missiles are there. India is producing missiles."

In military language, a *delivery system* is the device, such as a missile, that carries a weapon to its target.

Meanwhile, in Washington, the **global** network that tracks earthquakes and underground atomic blasts found only a faint echo from Saturday's Pakistan nuclear test that could mean the test was successful, but small or that the test was a failure and produced relatively few shock waves, says the *New York Times* quoting US experts. "It's a small event," said **G** Terry Wallace, a seismologist at the University of Arizona, who works with the incorporated research institutions for **seismology,** a scientific group in Washington.

Here the New Delhi paper quotes an American newspaper and American scientists.

Mr Wallace said the blast had a preliminary magnitude of 4.3 equal to about 1,000 tons of high explosive; by contrast, the atomic bomb dropped on Hiroshima in 1945 had an explosive force of 15,000 tons.

The shock waves from nuclear tests are measured with the Richter scale. This is the same scale used to measure earthquakes.

air to discuss in public

backbreaking very difficult

deterrent something that prevents or discourages an action

executive the branch of government that carries out the laws

global worldwide

seismology the study of earthquakes

E ASK Critical Thinking Why might the Army believe "no one can push us around"? (They feel confident that their nuclear weapons are larger, stronger, and more effective than Pakistan's.)

F ASK Critical Thinking Fernandes gives very few specific facts. Why do you think he avoids them? (Answers may include that his main goal is to communicate confidence and strength or that he does not want to give Pakistan a number to try to outdo.)

G ASK Literary Element This news article gives a lot of specifics and has drawn facts from a number of sources. What are those sources? (It uses the *New York Times,* which in turn used seismologists' and independent research expert analysis; the CIA was an indirect source.)

Career Connection

Seismologist A seismologist is an earth scientist specializing in study of earthquakes. By studying movements along faults in the earth's crust and reading data collected by seismographs, seismologists determine the location and strength of earthquakes. Have students learn more about this career by writing to the Seismological Society of America, El Cerrito Professional Building, Suite 201, El Cerrito, CA 94530 or accessing the society's Internet site at www.seismosoc.org.

Discussion Questions

A ASK Comprehension How does the Pakistan blast compare in strength to most nuclear warheads? (It is thousands of times smaller; it did not even produce shock waves that could be sensed on the other side of the globe.)

B ASK Comprehension What is frightening to India about Pakistan's response? (Pakistan appears to be forging ahead with plans for nuclear missiles, although the country apparently has not mastered the basics of nuclear bombs. Pakistan appears to be out of control.)

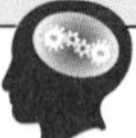

Comprehension

Summarizing Point out to students that if they have read with understanding, they should be able to state the main ideas of the article in a few original sentences. Ask students to write a paragraph summarizing the main points of the article.

A The main Pakistani blast on Thursday was **monitored** as having magnitude of 4.8, equal to 8,000 to 15,000 tonnes. Such bombs are considered relatively small by the standards of world **arsenals,** where the explosive power of **warheads** can exceed millions of tonnes. Saturday's explosion was too small to show up on the government's main network for monitoring earthquakes around the world. "We've searched everything we have and we don't see anything." said Waverly Person, a spokesman at the national earthquake informations centre, in Golden, Colo. "We didn't record anything at all."

Nawaz Sharif is prime minister of Pakistan.

The daily quoted arms-control experts as saying that the **B** truly **alarming** thing that prime minister Nawaz Sharif's government announced on Thursday was not that Pakistan had successfully conducted its own tests. Rather it was the declaration that Pakistan was already fitting nuclear warheads on top of a missile.

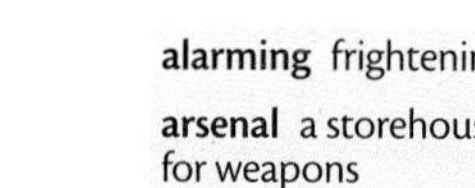

Indian Prime Minister Vajpayee (center) pays a visit to the site of the Indian blast.

Michael Krepon, president of the Henry L. Stimson Centre, an independent research institute, said, "A crucial **threshold** has been crossed, if it's true and that means we have only two thresholds left. **Deployment** and use."

The daily says India is said to have enough fissile material for perhaps 50 nuclear devices, maybe more. Pakistan has enough for perhaps 12. There is almost no evidence that either country has mastered the ability to make warheads small enough to fit on missiles, though not for lack of trying. It says senior administration officials cast doubt on Pakistan's claims to have already fitted its longest range missile with nuclear warheads. "That would be a fateful and foolish [decision]," one official said on condition of anonymity.

alarming frightening

arsenal a storehouse for weapons

deployment the spreading of troops or weapons in a larger area

monitor to measure with an instrument or device

threshold an entrance or beginning

warhead the front part of a missile or bomb that contains the explosive

218 *Unit 2 Nonfiction*

Name Date Period

Unit 2 *Writing Activity* *21*

Tests Are Nowhere Near India's: Fernandes

In the previous activity you wrote a journalistic account of a story based on one viewpoint. For this exercise, you will write the story from the other point of view.

Prewrite
Make a list of points that the "other side" would probably make in the story. Remember, even though the two sides don't agree, some of the points will be the same.

Write
Write the story. Use your previous work to remind yourself of some of the details. And remember, you're a journalist. Even though you only have one side of the story, you still have to write the article.

Revise
Did you remember the "Five Ws" and the "H": who, what, when, where, why, and how? And don't forget, the point of view in this story should disagree in some way with the views of your previous article.

Proofread
Read each paragraph. Be sure that you have used complete sentences. Each sentence must include a subject (doer) and a predicate (action or verb) and must express a complete thought. All sentences must end with a period, a question mark, or an exclamation mark. Use capital letters to begin each new thought.

 World Literature

TRL

Writing Activity 21

REVIEWING the SELECTION

Tests Are Nowhere Near India's

From *The Times of India* (Monday, 1 June 1998)

Directions Write the answers to these questions using complete sentences.

Comprehension: Identifying Facts

1. What is the main point of the Indian official's speech?
2. When did the Indian and Pakistani tests take place?
3. What expert is quoted late in the article? What is his specialty?

Comprehension: Understanding Main Ideas

4. What evidence does Fernandes offer about the actual number of Pakistani tests?
5. What does Fernandes say about India's plans to do more testing?
6. How did scientists monitor Pakistan's tests?

Understanding Literature: Journalism

The article from *The Times of India* illustrates some of the things a journalist does. This story reports on an interview with a government official. It then adds background material. It brings in facts and figures from experts. Another part of journalism is communicating with people. News may appear in a newspaper article. It may be on the Internet, as this one was. Radio and TV broadcasting are still another kind of journalism.

7. Where was Fernandes' interview originally given?
8. What are the other sources of information used in the article?

Critical Thinking

9. Why do you think this Indian newspaper quotes American scientists?
10. The official says that only the prime minister will "have his finger on the nuclear button." What does he mean?

Writing on Your Own Make a list of each journalistic source you use. (Remember that journalism includes radio, TV, newspapers, and magazines.) Then write a sentence about each type telling what kind of news or information you get from it. For example, where do you get sports news?

Selection Quiz

The Teacher's Resource Library includes a Selection Quiz for "Tests Are Nowhere Near India's: Fernandes" that may be given following the Selection Review.

Name Date Period | *Unit 2* *Selection Quiz* 20

Tests Are Nowhere Near India's: Fernandes

Directions Read the following statements. Circle the letter of the answer that correctly completes each sentence or that correctly answers each question.

1. The name of the defense minister quoted at the beginning of the story is
   a. George Foreman. **b.** George Fernandes. **c.** Jorge Fernandez. **d.** Giorgio Fernando.
2. Regarding nuclear testing, the minister from India says Pakistan is ________ India.
   a. ahead of **b.** behind **c.** south of **d.** tied with
3. Which country tested its nuclear weapons first in the month of May 1998?
   a. India **b.** Pakistan **c.** Canada **d.** the Netherlands
4. In India, who will be in control of a nuclear launch?
   a. the president **b.** the military leader
   c. the parliament **d.** the prime minister
5. The story quotes an American scientist from the University of
   a. Washington. **b.** Southern California.
   c. Arizona. **d.** Montana.
6. The Indian nuclear blast had a preliminary magnitude of
   a. 4.3 **b.** 3.4 **c.** 1,000,550 **d.** 82
7. In 1945, the atomic bomb dropped on ________ had an explosive force of 15,000 tons.
   a. Nagasaki **b.** Hiroshima **c.** Tokyo **d.** Seoul
8. According to one source, the dangerous thing about Pakistan's actions was that
   a. it was an unstable country.
   b. it didn't know enough about nuclear weapons.
   c. it was already fitting nuclear weapons to missiles.
   d. it was aiming its weapons at the United States.
9. Michael ________ is the president of the Henry L. Stimson Centre.
   a. Keaton **b.** Krepe **c.** Klingon **d.** Krepon
10. India is said to have enough material for ________ nuclear devices.
    a. fifty **b.** five hundred **c.** five **d.** fifteen

 World Literature

TRL

Selection Quiz 20

Reviewing the Selection

Answer Key

Comprehension: Identifying Facts

1. His main point is that Pakistan does not have nuclear capability, at least nothing nearly as powerful as India has.

2. The Indian tests took place on May 11 and 13, 1998. The Pakistani tests took place on May 28 and 30.

3. Seismologist Terry Wallace is cited as saying that the blast was small—some fifteen times less powerful than Hiroshima's blast. Wallace reads the waves produced by earthquakes.

Comprehension: Understanding Main Ideas

4. Fernandes cites the CIA response that it believes there was only one test.

5. He says they have found out all they needed to know but will not rule out further activity if needed for defense.

6. They read the shock waves produced by the blasts, using a seismograph.

Understanding Literature: Journalism

7. The original interview was on a New Delhi television station.

8. Information has also been gathered from the *New York Times*, the CIA, the national earthquake information center in Colorado, and the Henry L. Stimson Center, an independent research institute.

Critical Thinking

9. Students may suggest that the information provided by the United States would be given credence by the world and believed. In addition, a scientist is trained to be objective; his or her analysis is not biased by political motives, also giving credibility to the defense minister's words.

10. He implies that control will be strict; the military will not be allowed to respond rashly. He wants to reassure the world community that India will act responsibly.

Writing on Your Own Students' data could be compiled and graphed to show student preferences for specific types of news, such as sports, politics, entertainment, health, and space exploration.

Selection at a Glance

Pakistan Nuclear Moratorium Welcomed

From the *BBC Online Network*

Student pages 220–223

Overview

This report's perspective is more objective about each country's actions, but the relief it expresses speaks to the larger world community's concerns.

Selection Summary

Pakistan has announced a halt to nuclear testing and a scheduled summit between India's and Pakistan's prime ministers. The two nations' moratoriums and public postures of conciliation seem intended to offset world condemnation and sanctions.

Objectives

- To understand the news cycle and analyze this cycle.
- To identify paragraphs that review facts that came to light earlier in the news cycle.

Audiocassette 

Teacher's Resource Library TRL

- Vocabulary Workbook 21
- Selection Glossary 21
- Student Study Guide 27
- Activity 32
- Workbook 32
- Writing Activity 22
- Selection Quiz 21

INTRODUCING the SELECTION

Pakistan Nuclear Moratorium Welcomed

From the *BBC Online Network* (Friday, June 12, 1998)

About the News Source

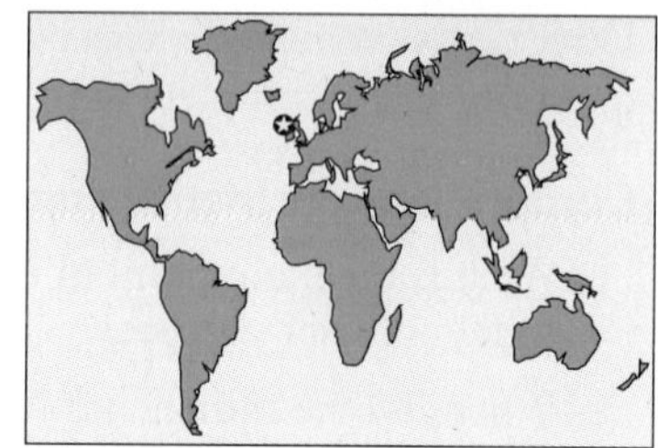

Radio listeners around the world know the voice of the *BBC*. Those letters stand for British Broadcasting Corporation. It was set up by the British government in 1927. It operates independently, though. In the 1930s the BBC began to send short-wave radio programs to all the countries in the British Empire. In 1967 it started the first regular color TV service in Europe. Today the BBC sends radio and TV programs to audiences all over the United Kingdom. Local programs include music, sports, plays, and news. BBC radio news and other programs are heard all over the world. The network has reporters in many foreign countries. It broadcasts in English and thirty-five other languages.

Like other world news sources, the BBC posts articles and information on its Web site. The Internet address is *BBC Online Network* (http://www.bbc.co.uk/home/today/index .html).You may be able to hear the BBC on your local public radio station.

Literary Term

news cycle the length of time between the publishing of a news item and an update or reaction to the item

About the Selection

The Indian and Pakistani tests were world news. Other countries then reacted. Some praised the tests, but others punished the two countries. They cut down trade and financial help. The **news cycle** is the timing of news stories that follow an event. You have already read Indian and Pakistani stories that react to the tests. This news story appeared on-line about two weeks after Pakistan's tests. It followed another new event in the on-going story.

Setting the Stage for Reading

About the News Source

Have students read the text and look at the photo. The BBC is the world's foremost source of international news on radio, television, and online. In a December 1998 statement about the BBC's aims for the future, Chairman Bland called the organization "a civilising force" that has "been a voice of reason" and "a buttress for democracy." A key goal is to continue to enable all sides to join the debate about significant issues.

ASK In what sense is the BBC a public service organization? (It provides unbiased information from all available sources to help listeners/readers/viewers make informed decisions.)

About the Selection

This article exemplifies BBC policy to provide balanced information needed to make informed decisions. It quotes UN Secretary Annan and spokespersons from the White House and Pakistan's foreign ministry. It recaps the basics of the story that has been unfolding for weeks. It presents brief analysis by a BBC correspondent on the scene in Asia.

Activate Prior Knowledge: Condemnation and protest of a nation's aggressions or human rights violations have been tools of powerful nations in recent years. Such actions make a point without intervening militarily. Ask students to recall a world event they remember that resulted in the United States invoking sanctions against another nation. For example, the United States imposed trade sanctions against South Africa in opposition to its system of apartheid.

ASK Why is it important to review the sequence of events leading up to the moratorium announced in the article? (The moratorium is a result of the preceding events. It needs to be understood in context.)

Pakistan Nuclear Moratorium Welcomed

From the *BBC Online Network*

(Friday, June 12, 1998)

Pakistan's announcement of a **unilateral** moratorium on nuclear testing has been welcomed by the United States and the United Nations. UN Secretary General Kofi Annan hailed the move as an "important step in joining the international **norm** of nuclear testing and non-proliferation." A White **A** House spokesman said the decision would help to limit **tensions** in the area.

As you read, keep in mind the rivalry between India and Pakistan.

A *moratorium* is a temporary pause or delay in an action—in this case, more nuclear tests.

A statement issued by Pakistan's foreign ministry said the country was ready to arrive at a "no-nuclear test agreement with India, as an important confidence-building measure at the regional level." "We are ready to engage **constructively** with India and other members of the international community to **formalise** this arrangement," the statement said. Pakistan hopes India will **reciprocate** and contribute towards a 'durable peace' in South Asia. Pakistan's Prime Minister, Nawaz Sharif, and his Indian counterpart, Atal Bihari Vajpayee, are due to meet at a regional summit in Sri Lanka.

India and Pakistan are part of the larger area, or region, of Asia. A *regional summit* is a meeting between the heads of government of the countries in a region.

India and Pakistan provoked world condemnation last **B** month by carrying out nuclear tests, which triggered economic sanctions against them by the US, Japan and other states.

constructively helpfully

formalise (Amer. formalize) to make official; to sign an agreement

norm the usual pattern

reciprocate to respond to another's actions

tension an uneasy or angry relationship

unilateral involving only one side in an issue

Reading Vocabulary TRL

Help students learn the selection vocabulary after passing out copies of the Selection Glossary. Have students write a sentence for each word. Then as they read sentences aloud, have them substitute the definition for the word in the sentence. Classmates can decide which word belongs in the sentence.

Motivation for Reading

Ask students to consider how a poor nation would respond to wealthy nations' threats to stop sending aid.

Discussion Questions

Remind students to read the marginal comments to get important explanations about the article's content.

A ASK Vocabulary Point out the term *non-proliferation.* Ask students to explain the meaning of *prolific.* (producing many or much) Remind them that the prefix *non-* means "not." Encourage students to surmise the longer word's meaning from the context and these clues. (a limiting of production of nuclear weapons, especially by international agreement)

B ASK Literary Elements Why does the article give a summary? (It summarizes the events because they occurred long enough before this article was printed that people need to review the facts.)

Name Date Period

Unit 2 *Vocabulary Workbook* 21

Pakistan Nuclear Moratorium Welcomed

Directions Complete the crossword puzzle by using the words in the Word Bank. The dark square is the space in a two-word answer.

Across

1. Control over actions or feelings
3. the usual pattern
8. helpfully
9. a plan to do something
10. to make official; to sign an agreement (British spelling)
11. to stop change; to make steady (British spelling)

Down

2. weapons
3. the length of time between the publishing of a news item and an update or reaction to the item (two words)
4. an explosion
5. an uneasy or angry relationship
6. involving only one side in an issue
7. to respond to another's actions

Word Bank

arms	constructively
detonation	formalise
intention	news cycle
norm	reciprocate
restraint	stabilise
tension	unilateral

 World Literature

TRL

Vocabulary Workbook 21

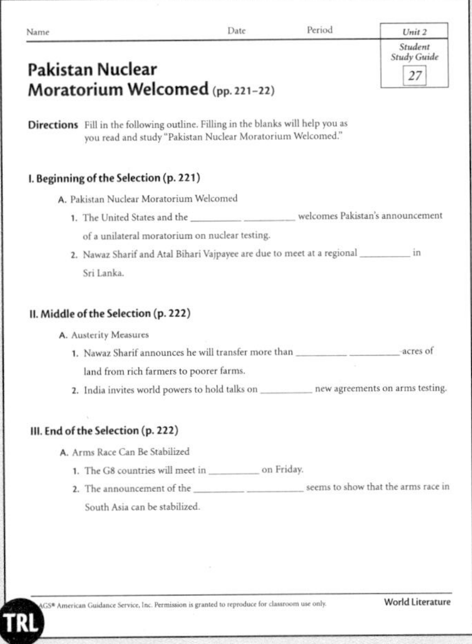

Name Date Period

Unit 2 *Student Study Guide* 27

Pakistan Nuclear Moratorium Welcomed (pp. 221–22)

Directions Fill in the following outline. Filling in the blanks will help you as you read and study "Pakistan Nuclear Moratorium Welcomed."

I. Beginning of the Selection (p. 221)

A. Pakistan Nuclear Moratorium Welcomed
1. The United States and the ________ ________ welcomes Pakistan's announcement of a unilateral moratorium on nuclear testing.
2. Nawaz Sharif and Atal Bihari Vajpayee are due to meet at a regional ________ in Sri Lanka.

II. Middle of the Selection (p. 222)

A. Austerity Measures
1. Nawaz Sharif announces he will transfer more than ________ ________ acres of land from rich farmers to poorer farms.
2. India invites world powers to hold talks on ________ new agreements on arms testing.

III. End of the Selection (p. 222)

A. Arms Race Can Be Stabilized
1. The G8 countries will meet in ________ on Friday.
2. The announcement of the ________ ________ seems to show that the arms race in South Asia can be stabilized.

 World Literature

TRL

Student Study Guide 27

Name Date Period

Unit 2 *Activity* 32

Pakistan Nuclear Moratorium Welcomed

Part A Directions In each blank choose the word or phrase from the Word Bank that best completes each sentence.

1. If only one country declares a stop to further testing, it is called a ________.
2. Actions taken to achieve a very simple way of living are called ________.
3. A "________ peace" was suggested by Prime Minister Nawaz Sharif of Pakistan.
4. The powerful group of major industrial countries is called the ________.
5. ________ first announced a moratorium on further nuclear testing.
6. After its tests, Pakistan stated its intention to build ________.
7. ________ were imposed on India and Pakistan after the testing.
8. The ultimate goal of all concerned was to ________ the region.
9. In Pakistan more than ________ acres of land were transferred from rich to poor farmers.
10. Nuclear explosions are also called ________.

Word Bank

austerity measures	detonations	durable	Economic sanctions	G8
India	nuclear missiles	one million	stabilize	unilateral moratorium

Part B Directions Read each sentence. Write *T* if the statement is true or *F* if it is false.

________ 1. Sri Lanka holds a similar position to Pakistan's prime minister.
________ 2. Pakistan was the first to announce a moratorium on nuclear testing.
________ 3. The testing in India and Pakistan added to the harmony between the countries.
________ 4. Nonproliferation means an attempt to cut down the number of nuclear weapons.
________ 5. Economic sanctions may include stopping trade or economic aid to a country.

 World Literature

TRL

Activity 32

Discussion Questions

A ASK Literary Element In reviewing past events, the BBC outlines responses of both Pakistan and India. Why might they do this? (This approach provides the fullest picture and helps readers see how and when events took place. It also is unbiased to either country.)

B ASK Critical Thinking Why would these nations meet to discuss other nations' conduct? (Answers might include that they feel the need to police world conduct for their own safety or that they are particularly alarmed by India and Pakistan's instability and want to create a joint policy.)

Environmental Connection

Nuclear war threatens millions of lives. But another threat is its long-term effects on the environment. Have students research and report on the effects of nuclear radiation and radioactive fallout. You may also wish to have students investigate accidents and system failures at nuclear energy facilities (such as that at Chernobyl, in the Ukraine) and the problems they have caused.

Austerity measures

Sanctions are actions that a country takes to punish another country's actions. Economic sanctions include stopping trade or economic aid.

A In response to the sanctions, Mr Sharif has unveiled a series of economic austerity measures. The measures, announced in a television address, include the transfer of more than one million acres of land from rich farmers to poorer farmers, and help for small businesses. Mr Sharif also said it was an honour for Pakistan to have joined the world's nuclear powers.

On May 21, India announced its own moratorium on nuclear testing, marking the end of its series of five nuclear test, and also invited world powers to hold talks on formalising new agreements on **arms** testing. Pakistan's nuclear **detonations,** set off to counteract the Indian explosions, were followed by statements of the country's **intention** to build nuclear missiles.

The *G8*, or Group of Eight, includes the world's major industrial countries. Officials from those countries often meet to discuss issues.

Arms race can be stabilised

Thursday's announcement came ahead of a meeting of **B** foreign ministers from the G8 countries who will discuss Pakistan and India's nuclear tests when they gather in London on Friday. Mr Sharif is hoping that the G8 leaders will not impose further measures.

The prime ministers of India and Pakistan shake hands as they meet to discuss nuclear issues.

A BBC correspondent said that the announcement of the unilateral moratorium seemed to be designed to show that the arms race in South Asia could be **stabilised** and that Islamabad was now showing the **restraint** that the international community has been calling for.

arms weapons

detonation an explosion

intention a plan to do something

restraint control over actions or feelings

stabilise (Amer. stabilize) to stop change; to make steady

Name Date Period

Unit 2 *Workbook* 32

Pakistan Nuclear Moratorium Welcomed

Part A Directions In each blank write the word or phrase from the Word Bank that best completes each sentence.

1. Actions taken to achieve a very simple way of living are called ________________.
2. ________________ first announced a moratorium on further nuclear testing.
3. After its tests, Pakistan stated its intention to build ________________.
4. If only one country declares a stop to further testing, it is called a ________________.
5. The powerful group of major industrial countries is called the ________________.
6. ________________ were imposed on India and Pakistan after the testing.
7. A "__________ peace" was suggested by Prime Minister Nawaz Sharif of Pakistan.
8. In Pakistan more than ________________ acres of land were transferred from rich to poor farmers.
9. Nuclear explosions are also called ________________.
10. The ultimate goal of all concerned was to ________________ the region.

Word Bank

austerity measures	detonations	durable	Economic sanctions	G8
India	nuclear missiles	one million	stabilize	unilateral moratorium

Part B Directions Read each sentence. Write *T* if the statement is true or *F* if it is false.

________ 1. Nonproliferation means an attempt to cut down the number of nuclear weapons.

________ 2. The testing in India and Pakistan added to the harmony between the countries.

________ 3. Economic sanctions may include stopping trade or economic aid to a country.

________ 4. Sri Lanka holds a similar position to Pakistan's prime minister.

________ 5. Pakistan was the first to announce a moratorium on nuclear testing.

 World Literature

TRL

Workbook 32

REVIEWING the SELECTION

Pakistan Nuclear Moratorium Welcomed

From the *BBC Online Network* (Friday, 12 June 1998)

Directions Write the answers to these questions using complete sentences.

Comprehension: Identifying Facts

1. What is a moratorium?
2. Which country's moratorium is announced in this report?
3. Which country tested nuclear weapons first—India or Pakistan?

Comprehension: Understanding Main Ideas

4. What was the main point of the announcement made by Pakistan's prime minister?
5. How did other countries and organizations react?
6. What other steps toward peace are India and Pakistan taking?

Understanding Literature: News Cycle

A major event such as a nuclear test sets off a cycle of news stories. This news cycle began with India's tests early in May. Newspapers around the world reacted. After the news story, they offered opinions in editorials. A few weeks later Pakistan also held nuclear tests. People reacted again. About two weeks later, Pakistan declared it would halt testing, This online report was on the BBC the next day.

7. Do the Internet and other electronic media make the news cycle shorter? How?
8. Read the section under the subhead "Arms race can be stabilised." How does this information explain the timing of the Pakistani announcement?

Critical Thinking

9. Reread the Pakistani prime minister's announcement on pages 210–212. Do you think Pakistan would have halted tests if India had not done so first? Why?
10. The information under the subhead "Austerity measures" is not news but happened weeks before. Why do you think the writer has included it in this article?

Writing on Your Own This story came from the Internet, but the BBC is known as a radio service. Rewrite the first section of this story as a radio announcement. Keep in mind that a radio news broadcast generally uses shorter sentences that are easy for listeners to understand.

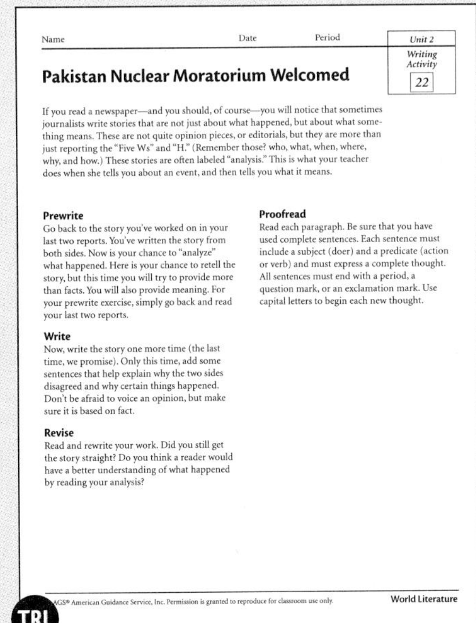

Name Date Period | *Unit 2* *Writing Activity* 22

Pakistan Nuclear Moratorium Welcomed

If you read a newspaper—and you should, of course—you will notice that sometimes journalists write stories that are not just about what happened, but about what something means. These are not quite opinion pieces, or editorials, but they are more than just reporting the "Five Ws" and "H." (Remember those? who, what, when, where, why, and how.) These stories are often labeled "analysis." This is what your teacher does when she tells you about an event, and then tells you what it means.

Prewrite
Go back to the story you've worked on in your last two reports. You've written the story from both sides. Now is your chance to "analyze" what happened. Here is your chance to retell the story, but this time you will try to provide more than facts. You will also provide meaning. For your prewrite exercise, simply go back and read your last two reports.

Write
Now, write the story one more time (the last time, we promise). Only this time, add some sentences that help explain why the two sides disagreed and why certain things happened. Don't be afraid to voice an opinion, but make sure it is based on fact.

Revise
Read and rewrite your work. Did you still get the story straight? Do you think a reader would have a better understanding of what happened by reading your analysis?

Proofread
Read each paragraph. Be sure that you have used complete sentences. Each sentence must include a subject (doer) and a predicate (action or verb) and must express a complete thought. All sentences must end with a period, a question mark, or an exclamation mark. Use capital letters to begin each new thought.

 World Literature

TRL

Writing Activity 22

Name Date Period | *Unit 2* *Selection Quiz* 21

Pakistan Nuclear Moratorium Welcomed

Directions Read the following statements. Circle the letter of the answer that correctly completes each sentence or that correctly answers each question.

1. At the beginning of the story, a unilateral moratorium on nuclear testing was announced by
   a. India. b. Pakistan. c. Afghanistan. d. Iraq.
2. The U.N. Secretary General is
   a. Kofi Annan. b. Cokie Roberts. c. Kofee Anon. d. K. Ofiannan.
3. Pakistan formed a nuclear pact with
   a. India. b. Pakistan. c. Afghanistan. d. Iraq.
4. Pakistan is hoping for a durable peace in
   a. India. b. Southeast Asia. c. South Asia. d. East Asia.
5. India's prime minister is
   a. Nawaz Sharif. b. Atal Bihari Vajpayee. c. Jawaharlal Nehru. d. Rabindranath Tagore.
6. The two prime ministers were to meet in
   a. Shangri-la. b. Taipan. c. New Delhi. d. Sri Lanka.
7. Pakistan planned to transfer __________ acres of land from rich to poor farmers.
   a. one thousand b. one million c. one billion d. one hundred million
8. How many nuclear tests did India perform before calling their own moratorium?
   a. five b. four c. six d. fifteen
9. The foreign ministers from the _________ countries were to discuss the nuclear testing by India and Pakistan.
   a. G7 b. Group of 7 c. 7G d. G8
10. The writer of this article is a correspondent from
   a. ABC. b. CBS. c. the BBC. d. CNN.

 World Literature

TRL

Selection Quiz 21

Reviewing the Selection

Answer Key

Comprehension: Identifying Facts

1. A moratorium is a temporary delay or pause in an action.

2. Pakistan has announced a moratorium.

3. India was first to test nuclear weapons.

Comprehension: Understanding Main Ideas

4. Sharif wanted to assure the world that it would not initiate an arms race or behave unstably.

5. Nations around the world seemed relieved.

6. They plan a meeting of prime ministers at a summit to discuss an agreement to end nuclear tests.

Understanding Literature: News Cycle

7. They report events instantaneously around the world, so there is no delay of days, as there once was, between international incidents and public awareness. This means public opinion and political reactions are also speedier.

8. The Pakistani and Indian governments want the Group of Eight (G8) to know they are working out their differences before the power-wielding nations meet to punish them further.

Critical Thinking

9. It seems unlikely that Pakistanis would have stopped their nuclear tests, since they feel threatened by India. In their point of view, the tests were essential to their survival.

10. Its inclusion reminds of the earlier, more defiant attitude of Pakistan and the vulnerability of the poor in that nation.

Writing on Your Own You may want to work through one or two sentences with students, helping them analyze ways to shorten and simplify sentence structure. Invite students to read their scripts aloud after they have practiced.

Selection Quiz

The Teacher's Resource Library includes a Selection Quiz for "Pakistan Nuclear Moratorium Welcomed" that may be given following the Selection Review.

Selection at a Glance

The Frightening Joy

From *De Volkskrant*

Building Atomic Security

Tomasz Wroblewski, From *Zycie Warszawy*

Student pages 224–227

Overview

Editorials from Dutch and Polish newspapers show how important this nuclear incident was to the world and give differing reactions to it.

Selection Summary

One editorial feels that the joyous response of Indians and Pakistanis to nuclear testing shows they are ignorant of what it means. A second recognizes that only having nuclear weapons as deterrents prevents the world from using them.

Objectives

- To understand the purpose of an editorial.
- To analyze editorial comments.

Audiocassette

Teacher's Resource Library TRL

- Vocabulary Workbook 22
- Selection Glossary 22
- Student Study Guide 28
- Activity 33
- Workbook 33
- Writing Activity 23
- Selection Quiz 22

INTRODUCING the SELECTIONS

The Frightening Joy

From *De Volkskrant* (Friday, 29 May 1998)

Building Atomic Security

Tomasz Wroblewski From *Zycie Warszawy* (Tuesday, 2 June 1998)

de Volkskrant

De Volkskrant
(established 1921)
Dutch

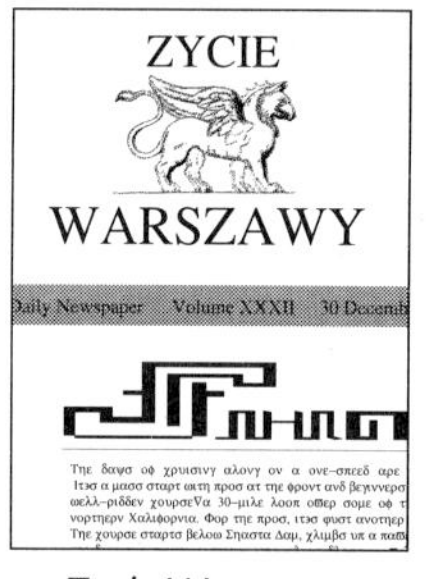
ZYCIE
WARSZAWY
Daily Newspaper Volume XXXII 30 Decemb

Zycie Warszawy
(established 1944)
Polish

About the Newspapers

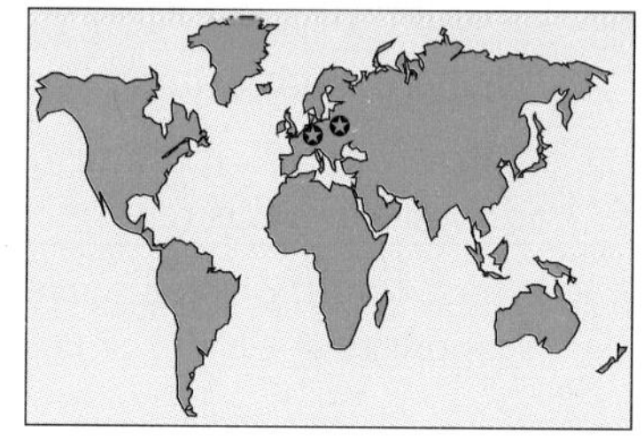

De Volkskrant is published in Amsterdam, the capital of the Netherlands. (In Dutch, its name means "People's newspaper.") It is the second largest paper in the city. It comes out in the mornings every day except Sunday.

More than twenty newspapers are published in Warsaw, the capital of Poland. Many of them belong to various political parties. They give the opinions of those parties. *Zycie Warszawy,* however, is an independent newspaper. Its name means "Warsaw Life." In terms of readership, it is one of the city's larger papers. More than 200,000 people read it on weekdays. About 330,000 read the Saturday edition.

About the Selections

As you have read, India held nuclear tests early in May. Pakistan answered with its own tests later in the month. At home, many Indians and Pakistanis were happy. The tests gave an image of national strength and pride. Others thought that the money should be spent to help the poor.

World reactions differed greatly. Many countries were shocked and afraid. The United States asked both countries to be careful. It urged them to join in halting nuclear tests. Other countries were pleased. India and Pakistan were making their own decisions. These selections are from editorials in newspapers in Europe. An **editorial** gives the opinion of the writer or the paper. These editorials appeared soon after the tests.

Literary Term

editorial a news writer's personal opinion about an event or topic

Setting the Stage for Reading

About the Newspapers

Have students read the text about the newspapers. Discuss why newspapers for cities so far from India and Pakistan might print editiorial comments about nuclear testing in these countries.

ASK How do you think a newspaper's political ownership affects its content? (Answers may include that it biases the paper in favor of that political party, that it causes the paper to lack objective balance in point of view, or that it limits the coverage and the types of events reported.)

About the Selections

Despite their opposing views, both of these editorials reinforce the idea that the entire world fears nuclear war.

Activate Prior Knowledge: Ask students to describe editorials or editorial cartoons they have read recently. Discuss the value of a public forum for expressing opinions about politics.

ASK Why wasn't the world alarmed about the nuclear testing that took place in the 1940s and 1950s? (Answers might include that it was secret before World War II, few realized how harmful its fallout would be, and it was assumed that another world war would not occur.)

The Frightening Joy

From *De Volkskrant*, Amsterdam

(Friday, 29 May 1998)

Despite the still-vivid memory of A-bombs falling on Japan, the world has been **perilously** close to the edge of nuclear war several times. Most frightening is the great joy in India **A** and Pakistan over these shows of national power, because it clearly demonstrates that the people do not understand the **gravity** of the danger....This is cheering on the way to Armageddon. **B**

As you read these two editorials, notice their different reactions to nuclear testing.

In the Bible, *Armageddon* is a great battle that is supposed to occur at the end of the world.

Indian Muslims shout slogans in favor of their prime minister's decision on nuclear testing.

gravity seriousness **perilously** dangerously

Reading Vocabulary TRL

Distribute the Selection Glossary page and have students preview the vocabulary words. Have students work in groups to brainstorm lists of words built from the same roots as the vocabulary words—e.g., *gravity, grave, gravitation.*

Motivation for Reading

Invite students to state their opinions about the Indian and Pakistani nuclear tests. Poll the class to see which opinion the majority holds.

Discussion Questions

Suggest that students use the comments in the margins of the student selections to focus their reading.

A ASK **Comprehension** Why is the Dutch reaction so different from the Indian and Pakistani citizens' reaction? (The Dutch writer realizes that nuclear tests tend to escalate into more serious nuclear buildups. The Asian people are only responding to a national pride issue, since their nations have been "second-class citizens" of the world for so long.)

B ASK **Literary Element** Explain that an allusion is a comparison that refers to someone or something famous in literature or history. What allusion does this paper use? Why? (It is an allusion to Armageddon, a biblical reference to the end of the world. It makes the point that nuclear war will destroy the world.)

Learning Styles

Visual Have students view the photograph on page 225 and describe the emotions of the men it pictures. Are there any details that suggest aggression? (raised fists; looks of determination on faces) Invite interested students to create a mural representing the reactions of India, Pakistan, Great Britain, Poland, and the Netherlands to the events covered by this series of news stories.

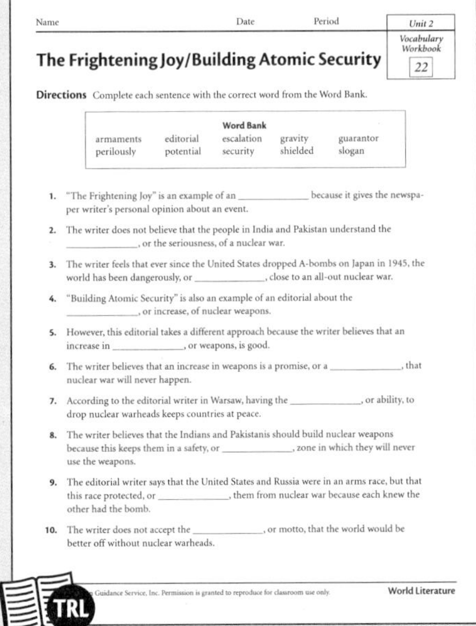

Name Date Period *Unit 2* *Vocabulary Workbook* 22

The Frightening Joy/Building Atomic Security

Directions Complete each sentence with the correct word from the Word Bank.

Word Bank				
armaments	editorial	escalation	gravity	guarantor
perilously	potential	security	shielded	slogan

1. "The Frightening Joy" is an example of an ____________ because it gives the newspaper writer's personal opinion about an event.
2. The writer does not believe that the people in India and Pakistan understand the ____________, or the seriousness, of a nuclear war.
3. The writer feels that ever since the United States dropped A-bombs on Japan in 1945, the world has been dangerously, or ____________, close to an all-out nuclear war.
4. "Building Atomic Security" is also an example of an editorial about the ____________, or increase, of nuclear weapons.
5. However, this editorial takes a different approach because the writer believes that an increase in ____________, or weapons, is good.
6. The writer believes that an increase in weapons is a promise, or a ____________, that nuclear war will never happen.
7. According to the editorial writer in Warsaw, having the ____________, or ability, to drop nuclear warheads keeps countries at peace.
8. The writer believes that the Indians and Pakistanis should build nuclear weapons because this keeps them in a safety, or ____________, zone in which they will never use the weapons.
9. The editorial writer says that the United States and Russia were in an arms race, but that this race protected, or ____________, them from nuclear war because each knew the other had the bomb.
10. The writer does not accept the ____________, or motto, that the world would be better off without nuclear warheads.

 World Literature

TRL

Vocabulary Workbook 22

Name Date Period *Unit 2* *Student Study Guide* 28

The Frightening Joy *and* Building Atomic Security (pp. 225–26)

Directions Fill in the following outline. Filling in the blanks will help you as you read and study "The Frightening Joy" and "Building Atomic Security."

I. The Frightening Joy (p. 225)

A. The Frightening Joy

1. The world has been dangerously close to __________ __________ several times.
2. India and Pakistan have shown great __________ over shows of national __________.
3. People cheer on the way to __________.

II. Building Atomic Security (p. 226)

A. Building Atomic Security

1. Nuclear __________ is the guarantor of peace.
2. Our fear of atomic __________ has protected us from World War III.
3. Americans and Russians have been building an atomic security zone for the past half __________.

 World Literature

TRL

Student Study Guide 28

Discussion Questions

A ASK Literary Element Explain that one way of showing attitude is through tone. A writer expresses a tone by the words he or she chooses. What tone is implied by the phrase "tired slogan"? (The attitude is one of impatience toward those who fear the nuclear tests.)

B ASK Comprehension Why does the author believe there has been no nuclear war? (Answers may include that people are too afraid of "atomic doom" to use their weapons or that nations have never intended to use the weapons they created, only to bluff others with them.)

C ASK Critical Thinking The buildup of nuclear weapons is called an "atomic security zone." Do you think this is a realistic description? (Answers may include that it credits all the governments of the world with too much rational thought and self control or that it overlooks human error.)

Building Atomic Security

Tomasz Wroblewski

From *Zycie Warszawy,* Warsaw

(Friday, 29 May 1998)

A There is a tired **slogan** that we all would be better off without nuclear warheads. The truth is that it is nuclear **potential,** not the lack of it, that is the **guarantor** of peace. **B** It is the **escalation** of **armaments** and fear of atomic doom, not common sense or disarmament, that have **shielded** us from World War III....Indians and Pakistanis in reality are doing nothing less than what Americans and Russians did **C** for the past half century—they are building an atomic **security** zone.

armaments weapons

escalation an increase or rapid growth

guarantor a person or thing that promises a certain result

potential the ability for action or growth in the future

security safety

shield to protect

slogan a saying or motto used by a group

Name Date Period

Unit 2 — Activity 33

The Frightening Joy *and* Building Atomic Security

Part A Directions In each blank choose the word or phrase from the Word Bank that best completes each sentence.

1. Some believe a great battle called ________________ will end the world.
2. The Polish writer calls the belief that we would be better off without nuclear warheads a ________________.
3. The Polish writer says the countries are building ________________.
4. The Dutch writer thinks the countries do not understand the ________________ of the danger.
5. The Polish writer compares the actions of Indians and Pakistanis to ________________ and Russians.
6. The Polish writer thinks ________________ of weapons has kept the world from starting War III.
7. The Dutch writer warns that we are ________________ to the edge of nuclear war.
8. The Polish writer reassures the reader that ________________ will prevent war.
9. India and Pakistan believed their tests were shows of national ________________.
10. The Dutch writer calls the ________________ of the countries frightening.

Word Bank				
Americans	an atomic security zone	Armageddon	escalation	gravity
joy	nuclear warheads	perilously close	power	tired slogan

Part B Directions Read each sentence. Write *T* if the statement is true or *F* if it is false.

________ 1. America and Russia held nuclear tests before India and Pakistan.
________ 2. Both writers agree the world would be better without nuclear warheads.
________ 3. The Polish writer has negative feelings about the testing in India and Pakistan.
________ 4. The Dutch writer says the bombing of Japan is still a vivid memory.
________ 5. According to the Polish writer, nuclear potential is a guarantor of peace.

 World Literature

TRL

Activity 33

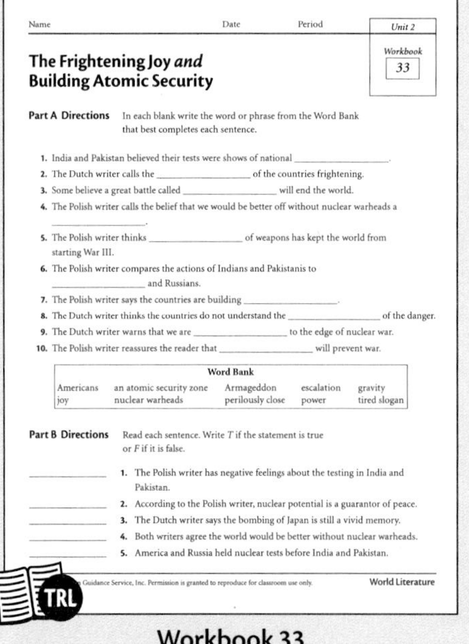

Name Date Period

Unit 2 — Workbook 33

The Frightening Joy *and* Building Atomic Security

Part A Directions In each blank write the word or phrase from the Word Bank that best completes each sentence.

1. India and Pakistan believed their tests were shows of national ________________.
2. The Dutch writer calls the ________________ of the countries frightening.
3. Some believe a great battle called ________________ will end the world.
4. The Polish writer calls the belief that we would be better off without nuclear warheads a ________________.
5. The Polish writer thinks ________________ of weapons has kept the world from starting War III.
6. The Polish writer compares the actions of Indians and Pakistanis to ________________ and Russians.
7. The Polish writer says the countries are building ________________.
8. The Dutch writer thinks the countries do not understand the ________________ of the danger.
9. The Dutch writer warns that we are ________________ to the edge of nuclear war.
10. The Polish writer reassures the reader that ________________ will prevent war.

Word Bank				
Americans	an atomic security zone	Armageddon	escalation	gravity
joy	nuclear warheads	perilously close	power	tired slogan

Part B Directions Read each sentence. Write *T* if the statement is true or *F* if it is false.

________ 1. The Polish writer has negative feelings about the testing in India and Pakistan.
________ 2. According to the Polish writer, nuclear potential is a guarantor of peace.
________ 3. The Dutch writer says the bombing of Japan is still a vivid memory.
________ 4. Both writers agree the world would be better without nuclear warheads.
________ 5. America and Russia held nuclear tests before India and Pakistan.

 World Literature

TRL

Workbook 33

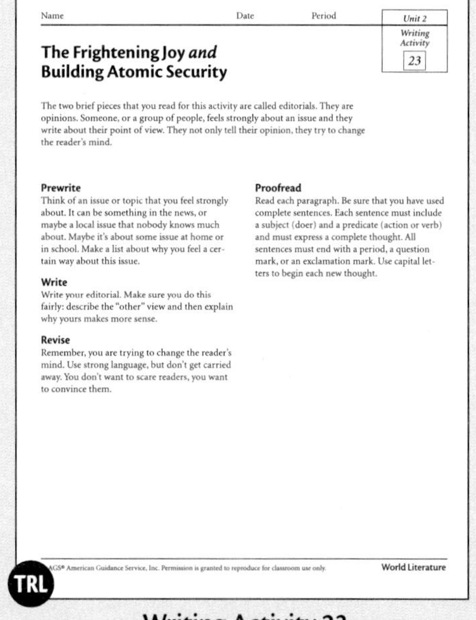

Name Date Period

Unit 2 — Writing Activity 23

The Frightening Joy *and* Building Atomic Security

The two brief pieces that you read for this activity are called editorials. They are opinions. Someone, or a group of people, feels strongly about an issue and they write about their point of view. They not only tell their opinion, they try to change the reader's mind.

Prewrite
Think of an issue or topic that you feel strongly about. It can be something in the news, or maybe a local issue that nobody knows much about. Maybe it's about some issue at home or in school. Make a list about why you feel a certain way about this issue.

Write
Write your editorial. Make sure you do this fairly: describe the "other" view and then explain why yours makes more sense.

Revise
Remember, you are trying to change the reader's mind. Use strong language, but don't get carried away. You don't want to scare readers, you want to convince them.

Proofread
Read each paragraph. Be sure that you have used complete sentences. Each sentence must include a subject (doer) and a predicate (action or verb) and must express a complete thought. All sentences must end with a period, a question mark, or an exclamation mark. Use capital letters to begin each new thought.

 World Literature

TRL

Writing Activity 23

REVIEWING the SELECTIONS The Frightening Joy and Building Atomic Security

Directions Write the answers to these questions using complete sentences.

Comprehension: Identifying Facts

1. How soon after Pakistan's tests did these editorials appear?
2. One paper says that having more weapons has actually prevented World War III. Which one?
3. Both editorials refer to historical events. What are they?

Comprehension: Understanding Main Ideas

4. What does the Dutch paper say that people in India do not understand?
5. What idea does the Polish paper call a "tired slogan"?
6. What is the Polish paper's opinion of disarmament?

Understanding Literature: Editorial

One feature of almost every newspaper is its editorial page. This page usually contains editorials and letters from readers. Often there is a political cartoon on the page, too. An editorial is a kind of essay. It deals with current issues and events—local or global. The opinions it gives are those of the writer or of the paper's owner. Like these two selections, an editorial is often about political views.

7. These newspapers are published far from India and Pakistan. Why was this event important enough for an editorial?
8. What does the title of the Dutch editorial mean?

Critical Thinking

9. Imagine a debate between the writers of these two pieces. What do you think they would say to each other?
10. Which of these opinions would be most welcome in India and Pakistan? Why?

Writing on Your Own These two European papers have completely different opinions about nuclear testing. Which point of view do you agree with? Imagine you are a resident of Amsterdam or Warsaw. Write a short letter to the editor of one of these newspapers. In your letter, explain why you agree or disagree with the point of view in the editorial.

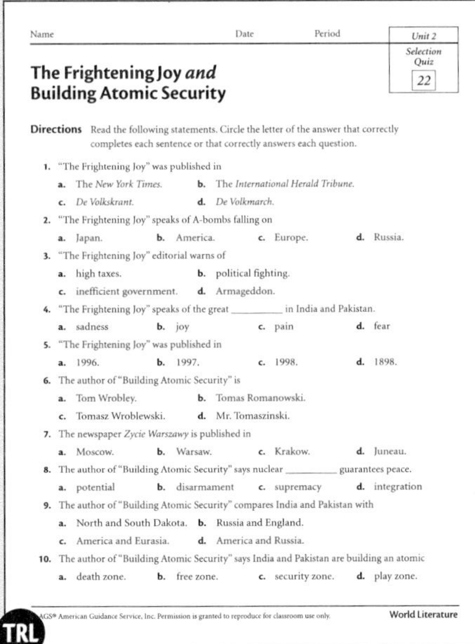

Name Date Period | *Unit 2* *Selection Quiz* 22

The Frightening Joy *and* Building Atomic Security

Directions Read the following statements. Circle the letter of the answer that correctly completes each sentence or that correctly answers each question.

1. "The Frightening Joy" was published in
   a. The *New York Times.* b. The *International Herald Tribune.* c. *De Volkskrant.* d. *De Volkmarch.*
2. "The Frightening Joy" speaks of A-bombs falling on
   a. Japan. b. America. c. Europe. d. Russia.
3. "The Frightening Joy" editorial warns of
   a. high taxes. b. political fighting. c. inefficient government. d. Armageddon.
4. "The Frightening Joy" speaks of the great ________ in India and Pakistan.
   a. sadness b. joy c. pain d. fear
5. "The Frightening Joy" was published in
   a. 1996. b. 1997. c. 1998. d. 1898.
6. The author of "Building Atomic Security" is
   a. Tom Wrobley. b. Tomas Romanowski. c. Tomasz Wroblewski. d. Mr. Tomaszinski.
7. The newspaper *Zycie Warszawy* is published in
   a. Moscow. b. Warsaw. c. Krakow. d. Juneau.
8. The author of "Building Atomic Security" says nuclear ________ guarantees peace.
   a. potential b. disarmament c. supremacy d. integration
9. The author of "Building Atomic Security" compares India and Pakistan with
   a. North and South Dakota. b. Russia and England. c. America and Eurasia. d. America and Russia.
10. The author of "Building Atomic Security" says India and Pakistan are building an atomic
   a. death zone. b. free zone. c. security zone. d. play zone.

 World Literature

TRL

Selection Quiz 22

Selection Quiz

The Teacher's Resource Library includes a Selection Quiz for "The Frightening Joy" and "Building Atomic Security" that may be given following the Selection Review.

Reviewing the Selection

Answer Key

Comprehension: Identifying Facts

1. The editorials appeared the next day.

2. The Polish paper feels they are a deterrent.

3. The Dutch paper refers to the bombing of Japan and the Bible's Armageddon; the Polish paper refers to stockpiling of weapons in the United States and Soviet Union.

Comprehension: Understanding Main Ideas

4. The Dutch writer does not believe Indians and Pakistanis understand that this power could destroy the world.

5. The Polish paper calls the statement that we should eliminate nuclear warheads for the good of the world a tired slogan.

6. Disarmament is considered a foolish, naïve idea; threats keep the peace.

Understanding Literature: Editorial

7. Nuclear weapons are so powerful and destructive that their use anywhere in the world threatens all other parts. For example, radiation could harm people thousands of miles from a nuclear blast.

8. The Asian attitude toward such a destructive capacity shows they lack the understanding needed to control nuclear arms responsibly.

Critical Thinking

9. The Dutch writer would say that armament demands sober intelligence and sophistication the Asians appear to lack; they risk the world with their short-sighted, emotional egos. The Polish writer would say that only a fool believes disarming nations will prevent them from warring; only having the potential to destroy an enemy prevents that enemy from attacking you.

10. The Polish opinion would be most popular in the East because these underdogs feel nuclear power makes them more secure and powerful, as though they cannot be bullied by the world.

Writing on Your Own Have students draft their statement of agreement or disagreement. Then have them list at least three reasons why they agree or disagree and provide evidence for each reason. They can use these notes to draft their letters.

Skills Lesson: Point of View

This skills lesson focuses on point of view, the perspective from which a story is told or an occurrence related. First-person point of view involves the writer (or speaker) in relating his or her own personal experience and vantage point, using "I." Third-person point of view involves a writer or speaker who describes and comments on events that happen to others, using "he" or "she."

Review Answers

1. Point of view is the storyteller's perspective and manner of communicating with readers.
2. Third-person point of view uses "he" and "she."
3. Journals use first-person point of view.
4. *Kaffir Boy* uses first-person point of view.
5. *The Last Seven Months of Anne Frank* is a biography.

Writing on Your Own Remind students to use specific details to describe the experience vividly and comment about their feelings to make their writing personal. Students should underline every use of the word *I* or *we* in their paragraphs.

Skills Lesson Point of View

Did you ever tell friends about something you did? You described people and places the way *you* saw them. You told the story from *your* point of view. In this unit, many of the authors told their stories as they remembered and lived them. They used a first-person point of view: "I."

Journals, diaries, and letters are almost always written from a first-person point of view. So are autobiographies. A biography is more complicated. Biography is usually written from a third-person point of view. The writer speaks of everyone as "he" or "she." At the same time, a biography often tries to show the point of view of the person who is its subject. In addition, the writer has a point of view toward the person in the biography. Many biographies give a good picture of the subject. Some, though, attack or criticize that person.

Anne Frank's diary gives her point of view:

> "Margot and I are getting a bit tired of our parents."

The reader sees Mark Mathabane's school and family through his eyes, too:

> "I ran, without stopping, all the way to the other end of the township where Granny lived. There I found my mother, her face swollen and bruised."

In *The Last Seven Months of Anne Frank*, the reader learns more about Anne Frank. At the same time, the women tell their own stories. Those take a first-person point of view:

> "He [Otto Frank] asked if I knew what had happened to his two daughters. I knew, but it was hard to get the words out of my mouth."

Review

1. What is point of view?
2. If a story refers to all the characters as "he" or "she," what is its point of view?
3. What is the usual point of view in a journal?
4. What is the point of view in Mark Mathabane's *Kaffir Boy?*
5. Is *The Last Seven Months of Anne Frank* a biography or autobiography?

Writing on Your Own Write a short paragraph about something you have done. Use the first-person point of view. Underline the words in the paragraph that show your point of view.

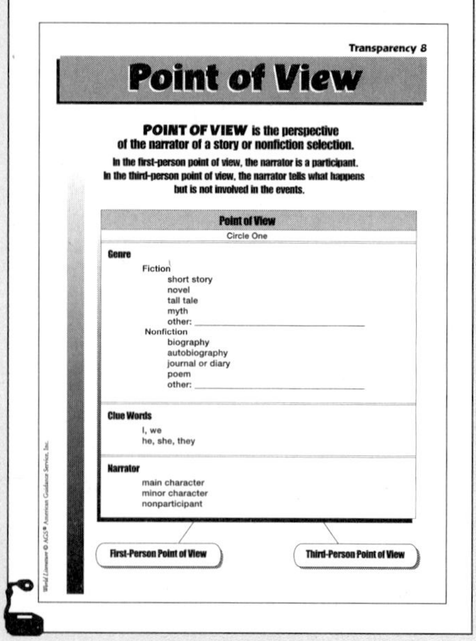

Transparency 8

Point of View

POINT OF VIEW is the perspective of the narrator of a story or nonfiction selection.

In the first-person point of view, the narrator is a participant. In the third-person point of view, the narrator tells what happens but is not involved in the events.

Point of View

Circle One

Genre

Fiction
- short story
- novel
- tall tale
- myth
- other: ____________

Nonfiction
- biography
- autobiography
- journal or diary
- poem
- other: ____________

Clue Words

I, we
he, she, they

Narrator

main character
minor character
nonparticipant

First-Person Point of View | **Third-Person Point of View**

Transparency 8

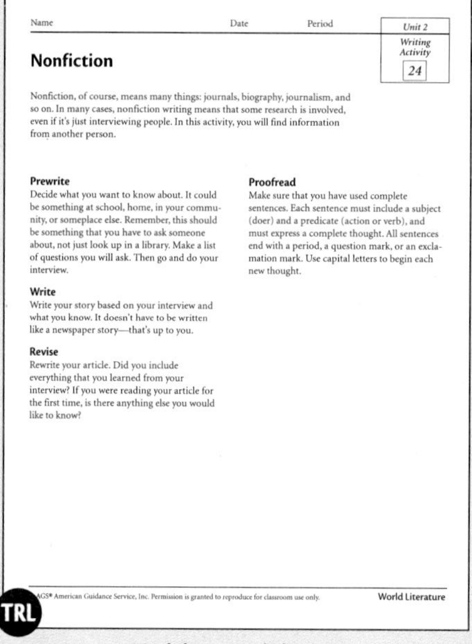

Name Date Period | *Unit 2* *Writing Activity* 24

Nonfiction

Nonfiction, of course, means many things: journals, biography, journalism, and so on. In many cases, nonfiction writing means that some research is involved, even if it's just interviewing people. In this activity, you will find information from another person.

Prewrite
Decide what you want to know about. It could be something at school, home, in your community, or someplace else. Remember, this should be something that you have to ask someone about, not just look up in a library. Make a list of questions you will ask. Then go and do your interview.

Write
Write your story based on your interview and what you know. It doesn't have to be written like a newspaper story—that's up to you.

Revise
Rewrite your article. Did you include everything that you learned from your interview? If you were reading your article for the first time, is there anything else you would like to know?

Proofread
Make sure that you have used complete sentences. Each sentence must include a subject (doer) and a predicate (action or verb), and must express a complete thought. All sentences end with a period, a question mark, or an exclamation mark. Use capital letters to begin each new thought.

 World Literature

TRL

Writing Activity 24

Name Date Period | *Unit 2* *Activity* 34 *page 1*

Unit Review

Part A Directions Circle the word or phrase in parentheses that best completes each sentence.

1. The story *(Kaffir Boy, China Men)* is set in New York City.
2. (Anne Frank, Indira Tagore) spent the final days of her life in a concentration camp.
3. (Autobiographies, Biographies) are written about a person, by that person.
4. Diaries, letters, and (journals, poems) are forms of very personal nonfiction.
5. Journalists write for newspapers and (politicians, magazines).

Part B Directions In each blank choose the word or phrase from the Word Bank that best completes each sentence.

1. The Indian author Tagore writes to his niece about ____________.
2. Ed, in the story *China Men*, named himself after ____________.
3. ____________ schooling is looked at closely in *By Any Other Name.*
4. Growing ____________ is the subject in *When Heaven and Earth Places.*
5. The real name of author Mark Twain was ____________.

Word Bank

Anglo-Indian	moonlight	rice
Samuel L. Clemens	Thomas Edison	

 World Literature

TRL

Activity 34, pages 1–2

UNIT 2 SUMMARY

Unit 2 contains several types of nonfiction writing. All are about real life and real people. But they are also different. Journals and diaries are private and personal. People tell their journals their secret thoughts and feelings. Letters can be personal, too.

Other nonfiction is written to be read by others. Biographies and autobiographies are about a person's life. Journalism is an account of real events. People write their own autobiographies. Someone else writes a person's biography. It may be about someone the writer knows. Or the writer may research someone he or she has never met.

Selections

- *Anne Frank: The Diary of a Young Girl* by Anne Frank. A Dutch Jewish girl's diary shows her thoughts during World War II.
- "Letter to Indira Tagore" by Rabindranath Tagore. The Indian Nobel Prize winner writes a letter to his niece about a moonlit night.
- "Letter to the Reverend J. H. Twichell" by Mark Twain. Twain writes to a friend about looking for a lost sock in the dark.
- *When Heaven and Earth Changed Places* by Le Ly Hayslip. A Vietnamese villager explains the importance of growing rice.
- "By Any Other Name" by Santha Rama Rau. Two Indian girls do not fit in at the British colonial school.
- *Kaffir Boy* by Mark Mathabane. A young black South African describes his life in a Johannesburg slum.
- *China Men* by Maxine Hong Kingston. Kingston's father, a Chinese immigrant, shows his wife New York City.
- *The Last Seven Months of Anne Frank* by Willy Lindwer. A Dutch filmmaker interviews women who knew the Frank family.

The journalism selections report reactions to nuclear tests:

- "Account Evened With India, Says PM" From *Dawn* (Pakistan)
- "Tests Are Nowhere Near India's: Fernandes" From *The Times of India* (India)
- "Pakistan Nuclear Moratorium Welcomed" From the *BBC Online Network* (Britain)
- "The Frightening Joy" From *De Volkskrant* (Netherlands)
- "Building Atomic Security" From *Zycie Warszawy* (Poland)

Unit Summary

As students read the selection descriptions on page 229 aloud, pose and discuss the following questions.

ASK Why is Anne Frank's diary so important to the world? (It reveals youthful idealism and struggle in a time of terrible, unforgettable oppression.)

ASK What does Tagore love about the moonlight? (It enlightens his spirit.)

ASK Why does Twain lose his temper? (His frustration builds up until an accident takes away his last bit of self-control.)

ASK Why do the Vietnamese give so much time and attention to growing rice? (They must if they are to eat, and they lack the machinery and technology to farm efficiently.)

ASK Why did the girls leave the school? (They could not stand being treated with condescension and contempt.)

ASK Why was going to school a matter of life or death for Mathabane? (If he did not go to school, he would be lost to the gang. Most gang youths wind up dead.)

ASK What does Ed love about the United States? (He loves its power, wealth, and technology as well as its freedom and opportunities.)

ASK What impression of the final months of the Frank family do these women give? (That it was horrifying.)

ASK What are the chief concerns of Pakistani Prime Minister Sharif? (to justify nuclear tests and to prepare the Pakistanis for hardships due to sanctions)

ASK What does Defense Minister Fernandes hope will happen next between Pakistan and India? (that they agree on a plan to avoid a nuclear arms race)

ASK What responses by India and Pakistan encouraged European nations? (Both nations declared a moratorium on nuclear testing and planned a summit.)

ASK Why is the idea of Indians and Pakistanis celebrating their nuclear power frightening to the Dutch writer? (They appear incapable of understanding how dangerous the situation is.)

ASK Why doesn't Tomasz Wroblewski find the Asian nuclear tests frightening? (He thinks those nations are merely establishing an "atomic security zone" to protect themselves from attack.)

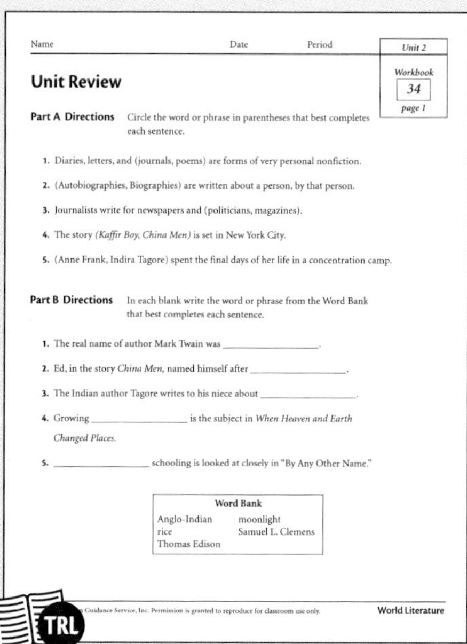

Name Date Period | Unit 2 | Workbook 34 page 1

Unit Review

Part A Directions Circle the word or phrase in parentheses that best completes each sentence.

1. Diaries, letters, and (journals, poems) are forms of very personal nonfiction.
2. (Autobiographies, Biographies) are written about a person, by that person.
3. Journalists write for newspapers and (politicians, magazines).
4. The story *(Kaffir Boy, China Men)* is set in New York City.
5. (Anne Frank, Indira Tagore) spent the final days of her life in a concentration camp.

Part B Directions In each blank write the word or phrase from the Word Bank that best completes each sentence.

1. The real name of author Mark Twain was ______________.
2. Ed, in the story *China Men*, named himself after ______________.
3. The Indian author Tagore writes to his niece about ______________.
4. Growing ______________ is the subject in *When Heaven and Earth Changed Places.*
5. ______________ schooling is looked at closely in "By Any Other Name."

Word Bank	
Anglo-Indian	moonlight
rice	Samuel L. Clemens
Thomas Edison	

 World Literature

TRL

Workbook 34, pages 1–2

Unit 2 Review

The Teacher's Resource Library includes two parallel forms of the Unit 2 Mastery Test. The difficulty level of the two forms is equivalent. You may wish to use one form as a pretest and the other form as a posttest.

Answer Key

Comprehension: Identifying Facts

1. Anne Frank; World War II and the Holocaust affected her life.

2. Mathabane grew up in South Africa.

3. One's own life story is called an autobiography.

4. Kingston wrote about her parents.

5. They discuss nuclear tests by India and Pakistan.

Comprehension: Understanding Main Ideas

6. Her diary provided Anne Frank with her only outlet for personal feelings and frustrations.

7. In *Kaffir Boy,* school turns the protagonist away from gangs and a life of self-destruction and toward education and survival. In "By Any Other Name," school causes two Indian girls to reject the British racist mindset.

8. Rice was their staple food; if the crop failed, they would starve.

9. Twain's letter is intimate in its humorously revealing self-portrait; Tagore's letter is personal in its inspirational description. Both letters are addressed to real people.

10. Pakistan's tests established the nation's capability to answer antagonist India's.

Understanding Literature: Setting

11. The time and place make his experience of the moonlight possible.

12. They see the Statue of Liberty, the Empire State Building, a public aquarium, and the most chic shopping areas. They react with admiration and awe; Kingston's father is happy, while her mother is homesick.

13. It is long past midnight in his hotel room in Munich, Germany.

14. *Kaffir Boy* is set in Alexandra, a black slum of Johannesburg. The bleak despair of conditions there makes his decision to go to school crucial.

UNIT 2 REVIEW

Directions Write the answers to these questions using complete sentences.

Comprehension: Identifying Facts

1. Two selections in this unit are about the same person. Who is that person? What historical events affected that person's life?
2. In what country did Mark Mathabane grow up?
3. What is the term for a person's life story written by that person?
4. About whom did Maxine Hong Kingston write this biography?
5. The newspaper articles and editorials in this unit all focus on one subject. What is that subject?

Comprehension: Understanding Main Ideas

6. Why is Anne Frank's diary so important to her?
7. How is school a turning point in *Kaffir Boy* and "By Any Other Name"?
8. Why was rice growing important in a Vietnamese village?
9. Compare the tone of the letters from Twain and Tagore. What makes these letters personal?
10. Why did Pakistan test nuclear weapons in late May 1998?

Understanding Literature: Setting

The time and place where a story take place are its setting. The settings in Unit 2 range from steamy rice paddies in Vietnam to the skyscrapers of New York. Setting includes time, too. *When* events take place is sometimes as important as *where.* The setting of Anne Frank's diary, for instance, is the crowded "secret annexe" in 1944, when she wrote down her thoughts.

11. Why is setting important in Tagore's letter to his niece?
12. The couple in *China Men* visit sights in New York. What do they see? How do they react?
13. What is the setting of Mark Twain's letter?
14. What is the setting of *Kaffir Boy?* How does it affect the story?
15. In which of this unit's selections is setting most important? Explain your choice.

Critical Thinking

16. In "By Any Other Name," what did the English teacher think of Indians? Give two examples.

17. Why do you think people still care about Anne Frank's story?

18. In *China Men*, Ed and his wife are both newcomers. Which will be happier in the United States? Why?

19. How did India react to Pakistan's nuclear tests? What did it show about the relationship between the countries?

20. Which of the people in this unit would you like to meet? Explain your choice.

Speak and Listen

Many selections in this unit are written in the first person. Choose part of one of these selections. Then practice reading it aloud. As you practice, think about who wrote it. What kind of gestures or expressions would he or she use? Read your selection to the class.

Beyond Words

Think back to a setting from this unit that you remember well. Draw a picture to illustrate the story and its setting. Add details from what you read. If you need to, research other details. For example, you might want to find out what kind of hats and clothes Vietnamese villagers wore in the 1960s. Write a caption to tell where and when your picture takes place.

Writing on Your Own

Think of a "turning point" event in your life. Did an event change things for you? (Remember the fight in *Kaffir Boy*.) Have rituals been important in your life? (Remember the rice growing in Le Ly Hayslip's village.) Write a section of your own autobiography. In it, explain the importance of this event in your life.

Test-Taking Tip

If you have trouble with a question on a test, go on to the next question. Come back to any you skipped.

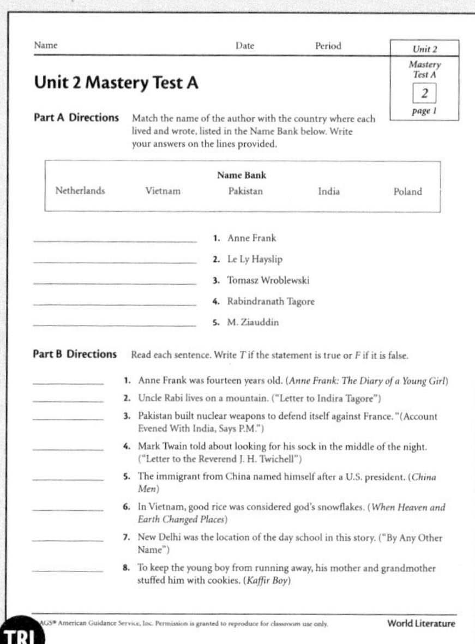

Name Date Period

Unit 2 Mastery Test A 2 *page 1*

Unit 2 Mastery Test A

Part A Directions Match the name of the author with the country where each lived and wrote, listed in the Name Bank below. Write your answers on the lines provided.

Name Bank

Netherlands Vietnam Pakistan India Poland

_______ 1. Anne Frank
_______ 2. Le Ly Hayslip
_______ 3. Tomasz Wroblewski
_______ 4. Rabindranath Tagore
_______ 5. M. Ziauddin

Part B Directions Read each sentence. Write *T* if the statement is true or *F* if it is false.

_______ 1. Anne Frank was fourteen years old. (*Anne Frank: The Diary of a Young Girl*)
_______ 2. Uncle Rabi lives on a mountain. ("Letter to Indira Tagore")
_______ 3. Pakistan built nuclear weapons to defend itself against France. "(Account Evened With India, Says P.M.")
_______ 4. Mark Twain told about looking for his sock in the middle of the night. ("Letter to the Reverend J. H. Twichell")
_______ 5. The immigrant from China named himself after a U.S. president. (*China Men*)
_______ 6. In Vietnam, good rice was considered god's snowflakes. (*When Heaven and Earth Changed Places*)
_______ 7. New Delhi was the location of the day school in this story. ("By Any Other Name")
_______ 8. To keep the young boy from running away, his mother and grandmother stuffed him with cookies. (*Kaffir Boy*)

 World Literature

TRL

Unit Mastery Test A, page 1

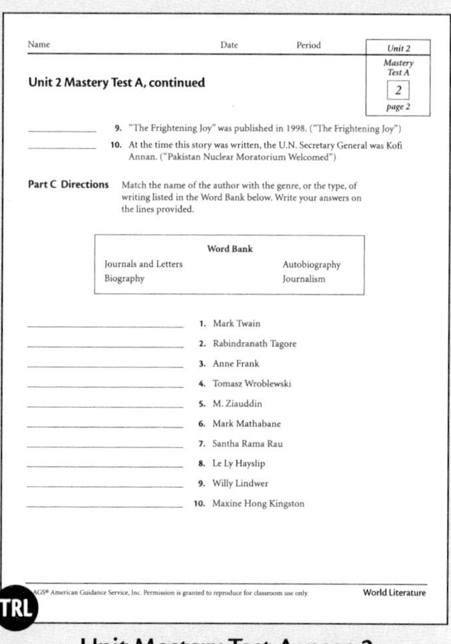

Name Date Period

Unit 2 Mastery Test A 2 *page 2*

Unit 2 Mastery Test A, continued

_______ 9. "The Frightening Joy" was published in 1998. ("The Frightening Joy")
_______ 10. At the time this story was written, the U.N. Secretary General was Kofi Annan. ("Pakistan Nuclear Moratorium Welcomed")

Part C Directions Match the name of the author with the genre, or the type, of writing listed in the Word Bank below. Write your answers on the lines provided.

Word Bank

Journals and Letters Autobiography
Biography Journalism

_______ 1. Mark Twain
_______ 2. Rabindranath Tagore
_______ 3. Anne Frank
_______ 4. Tomasz Wroblewski
_______ 5. M. Ziauddin
_______ 6. Mark Mathabane
_______ 7. Santha Rama Rau
_______ 8. Le Ly Hayslip
_______ 9. Willy Lindwer
_______ 10. Maxine Hong Kingston

 World Literature

TRL

Unit Mastery Test A, page 2

15. Answers may include *Anne Frank: The Diary of a Young Girl* or *Kaffir Boy*, both of whose settings establish the fate of the protagonist.

Critical Thinking

16. She thought their language and customs were not as "good" or "desirable" as those of the British. She gave the girls British versions of their names and made them sit far apart to take tests so they wouldn't cheat.

17. Her character showed bravery, strong values, and an unconquerable spirit in the face of horrific evil.

18. He will be happier, for he can take an active role in improving their lives and achieving dreams and will not be judged by appearance as much.

19. India discounted Pakistan's tests as insignificant. India is the more powerful nation of the two antagonists.

20. Answers may include Anne Frank, for her heroism; Mark Mathabane, for his achievement; or Le Ly Hayslip, for her wisdom and compassion.

Speak and Listen

Encourage students to understand the character they choose: What motivates him or her? How does he or she feel about the situation?

Beyond Words

Encourage students to include in their scenes or designs details that suggest time as well as place.

Writing on Your Own You may want to have students share their writings aloud or publish them in a class notebook.

UNIT 3 Planning Guide

Drama

	Student Pages	About the Author	About the Selection	Literary Terms	Reviewing the Selection	Writing on Your Own
	Selection Features					
■ ENGLAND From *Macbeth* by William Shakespeare	237–249	✔	✔	✔	✔	✔
■ SOUTH AFRICA From *"Master Harold" … and the Boys* by Athol Fugard	251–264	✔	✔	✔	✔	✔
■ SWEDEN *The Stronger* by August Strindberg	266–275	✔	✔	✔	✔	✔
■ SKILLS LESSON: Characterization; UNIT REVIEW	276, 278–279			✔		✔

Unit Features

Student Text
Drama
Classical Drama
Realistic Drama
Expressionistic Drama
Skills Lesson: Characterization
Unit Summary

Teacher's Resource Library
Activity 35: Drama
Workbook 35: Drama
Activity 36: Classical Drama
Workbook 36: Classical Drama
Activity 38: Realistic Drama
Workbook 38: Realistic Drama
Activity 40: Expressionistic Drama
Workbook 40: Expressionistic Drama

Teaching Strategies							Language Skills				Learning Styles					TRL Teacher's Resource Library					
Viewing the Art	Career Connection	Environmental Connection	Cross-Curricular Connection	Diversity Connection	Community Connection	Transparencies	Grammar	Literary Elements	Comprehension	Writing Connection	Auditory	Visual	Tactile/Kinesthetic	Group Learning	LEP/ESL	Vocabulary Workbook	Selection Glossary	Student Study Guide	Activities	Workbook	Writing Activities
238, 241	241		242				240	243	246	247	239	244		245		23	23	29	37	37	**25**
		255	254	260	262			252		259			254	261	256	24	24	30	39	39	**26**
269	268	269	271	270			273		272							25	25	31	41	41	**27**
						9													42	42	**28**

Assessment Features

Student Text

Unit 3 Review

Teacher's Resource Library

Activity 42: Unit 3 Review, pages 1–2
Workbook 42: Unit 3 Review, pages 1–2
Selection Quizzes 23–25
Unit 3 Mastery Tests A and B, pages 1–2
Midterm Mastery Test, pages 1–4

TRL Alternative Selection

The Alternative Selection can be found in the Teacher's Resource Library.

Alternative Selection 3:
Macbeth by William Shakespeare

Unit at a Glance

Unit 3: Drama

pages 232–279

Drama
pages 234–235

Selections

- ENGLAND From *Macbeth* by William Shakespeare, pages 237–249
- SOUTH AFRICA From *"Master Harold" ... and the Boys* by Athol Fugard, pages 251–264
- SWEDEN *The Stronger* by August Strindberg, pages 266–275

Unit Skills Lesson: Characterization page 276

Unit Summary page 277

Unit Review pages 278–279

Audiocassette

Transparency 9

Teacher's Resource Library TRL

- Activity 35 and 42, pages 1–2
- Workbook 35 and 42, pages 1–2
- Unit 3 Mastery Tests A and B, pages 1–2
- Midterm Mastery Test, pages 1–4

(Answer Keys for the Teacher's Resource Library begin on page 468 of this Teacher's Edition.)

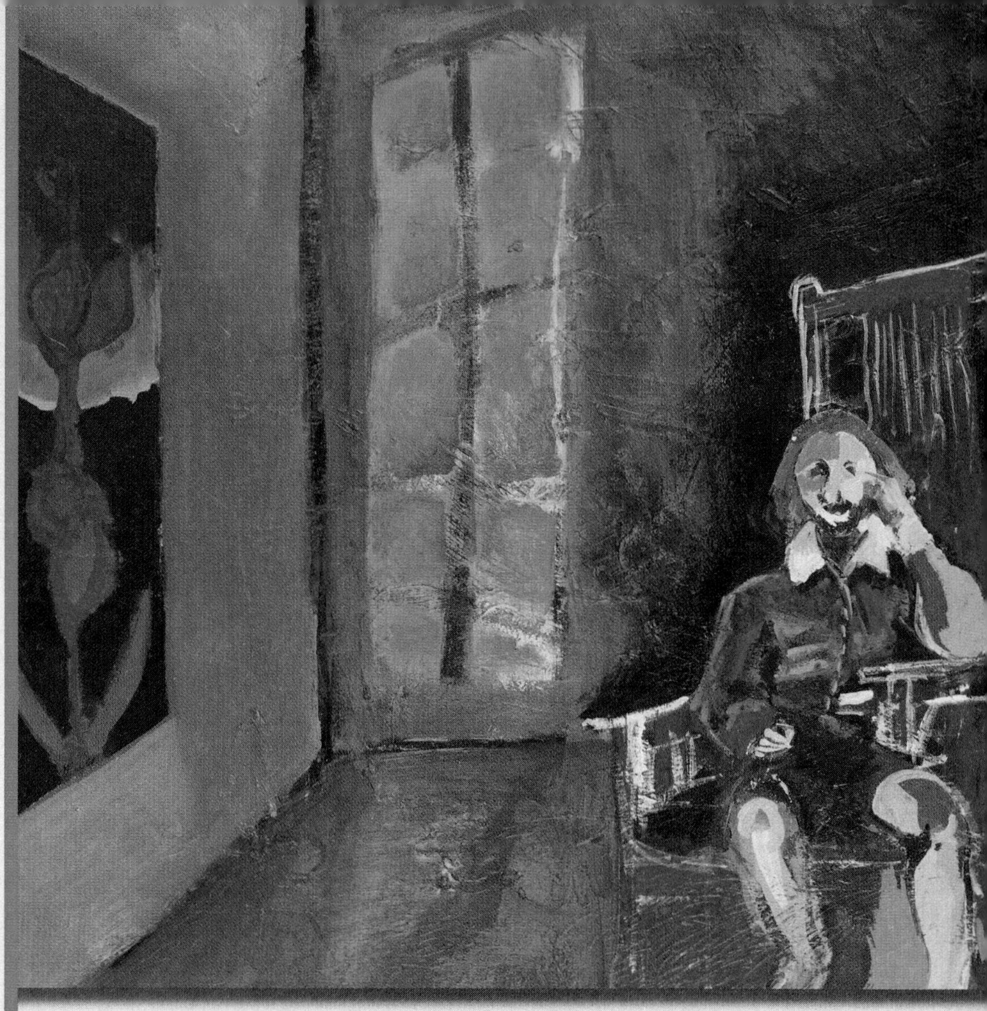

"Acting is not about dressing up...The whole essence of learning lines is to forget them so you can make them sound like you thought of them that instant."
—Glenda Jackson

"If it's a good script, I'll do it. And if it's a bad script, and they pay me enough, I'll do it."
—George Burns

Other Resources

Books for Teachers

Beard, Jocelyn A., ed. *Scenes from Classic Plays, 463 B.C. to 1970 A.D.* Newbury, VT: Smith and Kraus, 1993.

Hill, Philip G., ed. *Our Dramatic Heritage.* Rutherford, NJ: Fairleigh Dickinson University Press, 1983.

Books for Students

Chase, Mary. *Harvey: A Play in Three Acts.* New York: Dramatists Play Service, 1971.

Wilder, Thornton. *Our Town: A Play in Three Acts.* New York: Perennial Classics, 1998.

UNIT 3 *Drama*

The writer of a play is called a playwright. Playwrights draw on many different sources for their inspirations. They may write a play based on a historical event. They may take a story from their own experience. Or they may totally invent the story. No matter where it comes from, a story told in play format is enjoyable because we can see it, hear it, smell it, and feel it. A play shows us how someone else interprets a story. Watching a play brings an added dimension to the experience of reading it.

Unit 3 Selections — **Page**

Video

Dead Poets Society. (128 minutes) Burbank, CA: Touchstone Home Video, 1990.

Macbeth. New York: Time-Life Video, 1982. Series: The Shakespeare Plays.

Shakespeare of Stratford and London. (32 minutes) Washington, DC: National Geographic, 1978.

Software

Macbeth. New York: Voyager.

The Interactive Shakespeare Library: Macbeth. Princeton, NJ: Films for the Humanities and Sciences.

Introducing the Unit

Ask volunteers to read aloud the two quotations on page 232. Invite students to identify the writers if they can. (Glenda Jackson is a British actress who has appeared on stage and film; George Burns was a long-time radio, television, and movie actor in the United States.)

ASK What do you think Glenda Jackson means that the essence of learning lines is to forget them? (If you have learned the lines very well, you will not be self-conscious about having to remember them; then you can make them sound believable.)

ASK What does Burns's quotation tell you about the motivation of some actors? (Although they prefer to work with "good" scripts, they need to earn money and will do a "bad" script if necessary.)

Have students read page 233. Point out that plays are written to be performed for an audience. However, our enjoyment of plays includes reading them, whether or not we have the opportunity to see them on stage.

Review the Unit 3 selection genres and titles. Discuss what students know about the different types of drama.

Viewing the Art

Ask students to look at the painting on these two pages, *Shakespeare in His Study* by Michelle Puleo. Discuss with them whether they think the painting is realistic or the artist's impression of what Shakespeare and his study might have looked like. Point out that Shakespeare and his works are world famous.

ASK Why do you think a painter might choose Shakespeare in his study as a topic for a painting? (Answers will vary, but many students may suggest that the artist may have been moved by Shakespeare's works and wanted to immortalize him further by painting him.)

Drama

Ask students to read the text on pages 234–235, or have several share reading it aloud.

ASK Why will you not experience the complete play when you read it? (Because plays are meant to be presented on stage; in reading it, you miss experiencing the acting, the sets, the costumes, and so on.)

Point out that drama is one of the oldest forms of literature. Not only the Greeks, but also the ancient Egyptians before them, had some form of drama. Acting out stories is common children's play, and it may be from that impulse that drama began in many, many cultures early on. Forms of drama exist in early dance, as well. Often the origins of drama were based on religious stories used to teach moral principles. Ultimately, of course, drama evolved into the format we know as the play.

Tragedy is the oldest form of drama. Greek tragedy was usually based on gods and goddesses, heroes, and people's relationship to the gods. Modern tragedies, such as those by Eugene O'Neill, may be based on human faults of character and of the machinations of fate.

William Shakespeare is universally credited as the finest playwright of the English language. His plays are still produced routinely all over the world, even though modern audiences must sometimes struggle with understanding his language. Often Shakespeare's major characters are "larger than life" and have problems that ordinary people are unlikely to face. This is a characteristic of most classical tragedies.

ASK What is the main difference between a tragedy and a comedy? (The endings: a tragedy always ends "tragically," with the hero/protagonist destroyed in some manner. A comedy has a proverbial happy ending, with the effects of the plot not detrimental to the protagonist.)

UNIT 3 ■ DRAMA

A drama is a play that tells a story through dialogue and action performed by actors. Drama is an old form of literature. Dramatic plays started long ago as religious ceremonies in Greece. Gradually they became two distinct forms of drama: the tragedy and the comedy.

The protagonist is the main character in any drama. The antagonist is the opponent. In a tragedy, the antagonist destroys the protagonist. The antagonist could be the protagonist's own weaknesses. It could be another character's actions. The antagonist could also be a "bad guy," social injustice, or fate. A well-written tragedy offers its audience emotional release. It also reveals the workings of human nature. Shakespeare's Othello, for instance, is one of drama's greatest protagonists. The antagonist is an evil friend named Iago. Iago plays on Othello's jealousy and violent temper. Finally Othello destroys his wife, his career, and himself. The audience experiences Othello's grief as they identify with what he says and does.

A comedy is a play with a "happy ending." The conflict does not destroy the protagonist. The audience enjoys seeing the protagonist beat the antagonist. *Harvey,* for example, tells the story of Elwood P. Dowd. His best friend is Harvey, an invisible rabbit who is six feet tall. By the end of the play, Dowd has triumphed. He has avoided being sent to an institution for the insane. He has also convinced several other characters of Harvey's charms.

Tragic or comic, early drama followed a strict form. Greek dramas included a chorus. This was a group of actors who commented on and explained the action. Actors wore masks. Dialogue was spoken in verse. Verse is made up of word patterns that follow a definite, repeating rhythm and sometimes rhyme.

There are many forms of drama, from symbolist to naturalist to absurdist. This unit covers three forms of drama: classical, realistic, and expressionistic.

As you read, remember that you are not experiencing the complete play. Much of drama's power comes from the voices and movements of the cast. Scenery and costumes add to the effect. Reading the following selections aloud may help you get more of the feeling of a real play.

The following countries are represented in this unit: England, South Africa, and Sweden.

Draw students' attention to the world map on page 235 showing the countries represented in this unit.

ASK Which three countries are represented by the three plays in this unit? (England, South Africa, and Sweden)

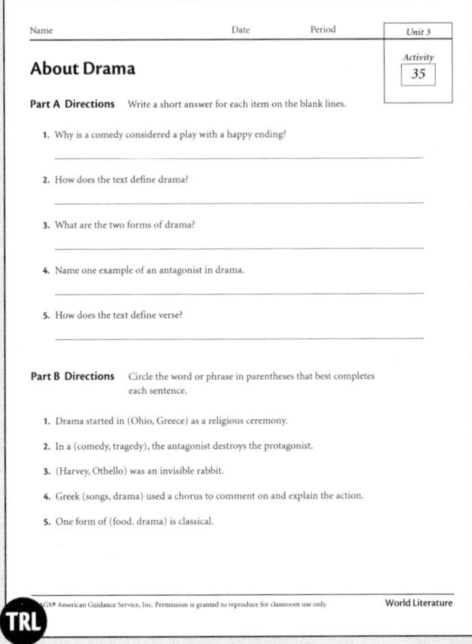

Name Date Period

Unit 3 Activity 35

About Drama

Part A Directions Write a short answer for each item on the blank lines.

1. Why is a comedy considered a play with a happy ending?
2. How does the text define drama?
3. What are the two forms of drama?
4. Name one example of an antagonist in drama.
5. How does the text define verse?

Part B Directions Circle the word or phrase in parentheses that best completes each sentence.

1. Drama started in (Ohio, Greece) as a religious ceremony.
2. In a (comedy, tragedy), the antagonist destroys the protagonist.
3. (Harvey, Othello) was an invisible rabbit.
4. Greek (songs, drama) used a chorus to comment on and explain the action.
5. One form of (food, drama) is classical.

 World Literature

TRL

Activity 35

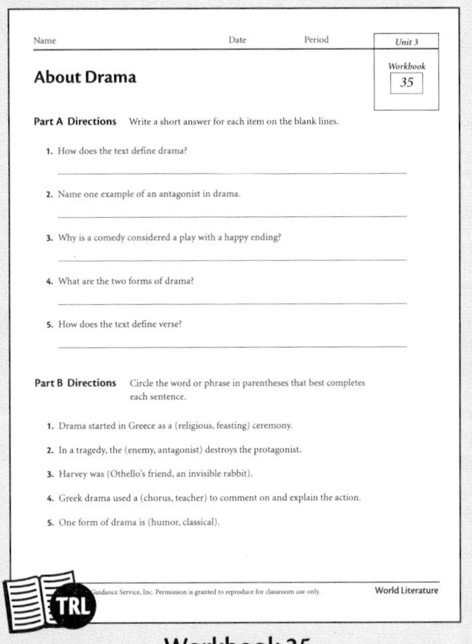

Name Date Period

Unit 3 Workbook 35

About Drama

Part A Directions Write a short answer for each item on the blank lines.

1. How does the text define drama?
2. Name one example of an antagonist in drama.
3. Why is a comedy considered a play with a happy ending?
4. What are the two forms of drama?
5. How does the text define verse?

Part B Directions Circle the word or phrase in parentheses that best completes each sentence.

1. Drama started in Greece as a (religious, feasting) ceremony.
2. In a tragedy, the (enemy, antagonist) destroys the protagonist.
3. Harvey was (Othello's friend, an invisible rabbit).
4. Greek drama used a (chorus, teacher) to comment on and explain the action.
5. One form of drama is (humor, classical).

 World Literature

TRL

Workbook 35

Classical Drama

Ask students to read the text on page 236, or have them take turns reading it aloud.

Draw their attention to the two quotations at the top of the page.

ASK What are the different attitudes toward Shakespeare expressed in the quotations? (One feels his influence is so profound as to "save the English-speaking world" and the other complains about having to "translate" his work.)

Point out that although the fact that Shakespeare wrote in blank verse might cause a problem with understanding the way the language is used, a greater part of the problem is that much of his language is now archaic. Explain that *archaic* means "out of date." You may need to further explain that as people use a language, they change it. Mention the timeliness of slang as an illustrative example that students may grasp easily.

Shakespeare wrote his plays over 300 years ago—ample time for the English language to grow and change rather significantly. Often the vocabulary words he uses had different meanings at that time or simply have been dropped from common usage today.

However, Shakespeare's talent for using language makes the effort to understand it worthwhile.

ASK What are some of the characteristics of classical drama? (plays about royalty or other important people; organized in five acts; written in blank verse)

Classical Drama

- "I think that in the end...Shakespeare and all he inspired...will save the English-speaking world." —Laurens van der Post
- "My brain is hurting. I have just had two pages of *Macbeth* to translate into English." —Sue Townsend

Ancient dramas in the Western world were written in the Greek and Latin languages. These are called "classical languages." When Shakespeare wrote during the sixteenth century, English-language drama had become what is now called classical drama. These plays were usually stories about royalty or other wealthy, important people.

Classical drama has five acts and is written in blank verse. Classical drama is divided into acts and scenes. These are similar to chapters in a book. Acts are separate sections that often involve changes in setting. Time may pass between acts. Each act consists of one or more scenes. The first and second acts introduce and develop the action or conflict. The third act features the climax. This is an event that triggers the comic or tragic ending. Acts four and five tie together the loose plot strands to create a neat ending.

Dialogue, or the words the characters speak, is often in a form called blank verse. Blank verse is written in iambic pentameter and does not rhyme. Iambic pentameter describes the beat, or rhythm, of a line of verse. It has five two-beat sounds per line. The emphasis falls on the even-numbered beats.

Shakespeare's plays are considered some of the best examples of classical drama ever written. Many playwrights of his time also wrote in this style. Plays of later times that follow the classical form are called neoclassical. (*Neo-* means "new.")

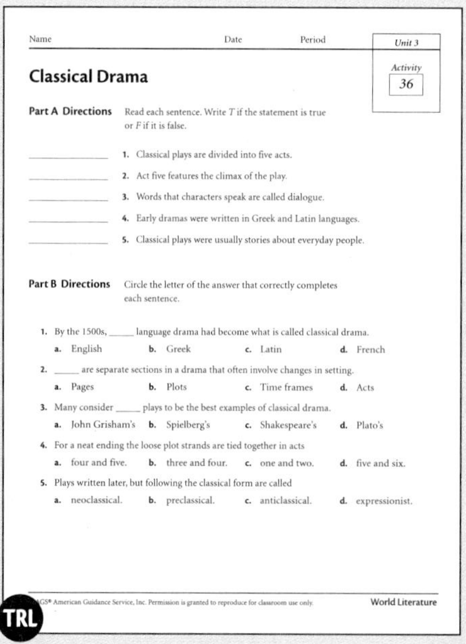

Name Date Period — Unit 3 — Activity 36

Classical Drama

Part A Directions Read each sentence. Write *T* if the statement is true or *F* if it is false.

______ 1. Classical plays are divided into five acts.
______ 2. Act five features the climax of the play.
______ 3. Words that characters speak are called dialogue.
______ 4. Early dramas were written in Greek and Latin languages.
______ 5. Classical plays were usually stories about everyday people.

Part B Directions Circle the letter of the answer that correctly completes each sentence.

1. By the 1500s, ____ language drama had become what is called classical drama.
   a. English b. Greek c. Latin d. French
2. ____ are separate sections in a drama that often involve changes in setting.
   a. Pages b. Plots c. Time frames d. Acts
3. Many consider ____ plays to be the best examples of classical drama.
   a. John Grisham's b. Spielberg's c. Shakespeare's d. Plato's
4. For a neat ending the loose plot strands are tied together in acts
   a. four and five. b. three and four. c. one and two. d. five and six.
5. Plays written later, but following the classical form are called
   a. neoclassical. b. preclassical. c. anticlassical. d. expressionist.

 World Literature

TRL

Activity 36

Name Date Period — Unit 3 — Workbook 36

Classical Drama

Part A Directions Read each sentence. Write *T* if the statement is true or *F* if it is false.

______ 1. Classical plays are divided into three acts.
______ 2. Act three features the climax of the play.
______ 3. Words that characters speak are called conversation.
______ 4. Early dramas were written in Greek and Hebrew languages.
______ 5. Classical plays were usually stories about royalty or important people.

Part B Directions Circle the letter of the answer that correctly completes each sentence.

1. By the 1500s, ____ language drama had become what is called classical drama.
   a. Greek b. English c. Latin d. French
2. ____ are separate sections in a drama that often involve changes in setting.
   a. Acts b. Plots c. Time frames d. Pages
3. Many consider ____ plays to be the best examples of classical drama.
   a. John Grisham's b. Spielberg's c. Plato's d. Shakespeare's
4. For a neat ending the loose plot strands are tied together in acts
   a. one and two. b. three and four. c. four and five. d. five and six.
5. Plays written later, but following the classical form are called
   a. preclassical. b. neoclassical. c. anticlassical. d. expressionist.

 World Literature

TRL

Workbook 36

INTRODUCING the SELECTION

Macbeth

William Shakespeare

William Shakespeare (1564–1616) English

About the Author

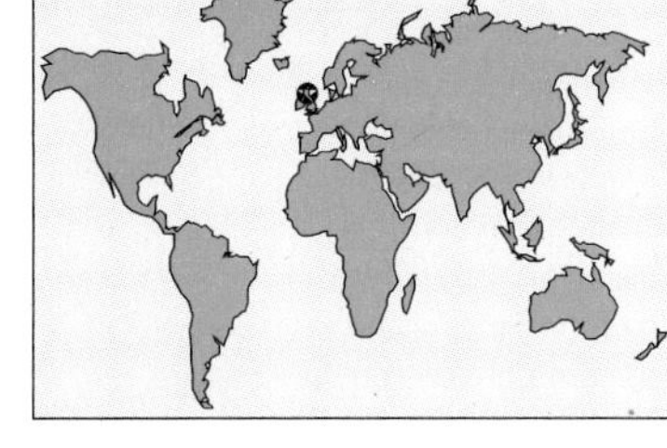

William Shakespeare was born in the small English town of Stratford-upon-Avon. He was well known as an actor and **playwright**. Shakespeare also wrote many **sonnets**. A sonnet is a fourteen-line poem, separated into three sections of four lines. The last two lines also rhyme.

Shakespeare used the classical five-act structure of a **drama**, or play. He used **blank verse**, a form of unrhymed poetry. Shakespeare based his plays on well-known stories. This is why most of them are set in far-off places or ancient times.

Literary Terms

blank verse unrhymed iambic pentameter

drama a play

playwright the author of a play

sonnet a fourteen-line poem divided into four sections, in iambic pentameter

About the Selection

Macbeth is a Scottish lord who wants to be king. At his wife's urging, he kills the rightful king. Macbeth then has his best friend, Banquo, killed. Banquo's son, Fleance, escapes. Having killed his friend, Macbeth is overcome by guilt. In the following scene, Macbeth and Lady Macbeth host a dinner party. During the party, Macbeth sees Banquo's ghost. He feels himself accused of murder. The guests see Macbeth speaking, but they do not see the ghost. They wonder if he has gone mad. It is the beginning of the end for Macbeth. *Macbeth* is a five-act play.

Some people find Shakespeare hard to understand. If you read the play aloud, the words come alive. A paraphrase has also been provided. This is a version of the scene that has been put in modern English. It will help you if you get stuck.

Selection at a Glance

Macbeth

William Shakespeare

Student pages 237–249

Overview

Macbeth is usually considered one of Shakespeare's greatest plays. Macbeth's tragedy is that he yields to the temptation of ambition and moves himself deeper and deeper into trouble. Elizabethan audiences may have therefore considered him more a villain than modern audiences do.

Selection Summary

Macbeth is one of William Shakespeare's best-known plays. Macbeth commits murder to become king but must struggle against guilt and his opponents.

Objectives

- To identify elements of classical drama.
- To understand characterization in drama.

Audiocassette 

Teacher's Resource Library 

- Vocabulary Workbook 23, pages 1–2
- Selection Glossary 23
- Student Study Guide 29, pages 1–2
- Activity 37
- Workbook 37
- Writing Activity 25
- Selection Quiz 23

Setting the Stage for Reading

About the Author

Ask students to read the text on page 237 and look at the portrait of William Shakespeare. Point out that Shakespeare is known around the world as the greatest playwright of the English language. The themes of his plays are universal, and the poetry of his language is unmatched—even when translated, as it has been, into many other languages. Shakespeare was clearly talented with the use of language and an astute student of human psychology and behavior.

ASK Why do you suppose Shakespeare chose to write plays instead of books or novels? (In Shakespeare's time, most people could not read. However, they could go to the theater and enjoy seeing a play.)

About the Selection

This selection is the entire Scene 4 of Act III of *Macbeth*. Previously, Macbeth and his wife, Lady Macbeth, have murdered Duncan, the king, in order for Macbeth to become king. Then Macbeth orders Banquo to be killed. It is at this point that the selection begins, as Macbeth and Lady Macbeth are having a feast with many nobles. Acknowledging the difficulty students are likely to have with reading Shakespeare, the selection provides a page-for-page paraphrase in modern English.

Activate Prior Knowledge: Ask students to recall seeing plays in various forms, including on television. Tell them that reading a play is like reading a script for a television program or movie.

ASK How is reading a play likely to be different from reading a story? (A play does not narrate a story but shows it in the actions and dialogue of the characters.)

Reading Vocabulary TRL

Help students preview the selection's vocabulary words by giving them copies of the Selection Glossary. Review the words and ask pairs of students to take turns saying the words and providing the matching definitions. These vocabulary terms are from the modern English version.

Motivation for Reading

Suggest that students visualize what the scene looks like as it begins: It is in a great hall of the king's castle during the Middle Ages, with a banquet prepared and ready for the royal couple and their grand guests.

Discussion Questions

Suggest that students use the marginal notes and questions in the student selection to help guide their reading.

A ASK Comprehension In 1040, Macbeth took the throne of Scotland as king after murdering King Duncan I. Those are the known facts on which Shakespeare based his play *Macbeth.* How does knowing that the play takes place in the eleventh century help you understand the characters and the action? (It clarifies the reasons for the rudimentary methods of communication and so on.)

B ASK Literary Element How can we tell what the characters are doing as they speak their dialogue? (Stage directions, presented here in italic type, explain the setting and movements of the actors.)

Viewing the Art

Edmund Dulac's painting of Macbeth looking down on the three Weird Sisters graces a promotional piece for a production of the play *Macbeth* at a London theater.

ASK How might such promotional artwork be used? (as the cover of programs or as posters or flyers used to advertise a play)

Shakespeare's Original

A Macbeth

William Shakespeare

This version of scene four from Act III of *Macbeth* appears as Shakespeare wrote it. It uses words that were common in England at the time. It is written in blank verse. As you read, compare it with the modern English version on the facing page.

Notes called *stage directions* describe where each scene is set. They tell the actors where and how to move.

The words following each character's name tell the character what to say. These speeches are called dialogue.

B *Act III, Scene 4: The hall of the palace.*
A banquet prepared. Enter Macbeth, Lady Macbeth, Ross, Lennox, Lords, and Attendant.

MACBETH. You know your own degrees, sit down at first
And last, the hearty welcome.

LORDS. Thanks to your majesty.

MACBETH. Ourself will mingle with society,
And play the humble host:
Our hostess keeps her state, but in best time
We will require her welcome.

LADY MACBETH. Pronounce it for me, sir, to all our friends,
For my heart speaks they are welcome.

First Murderer appears at the door

MACBETH. See, they encounter thee with their hearts' thanks.
Both sides are even: here I'll sit i'th' midst.
Be large in mirth, anon we'll drink a measure
The table round. *[turns to the door]*
There's blood upon thy face.

MURDERER. 'Tis Banquo's then.

MACBETH. 'Tis better thee without than he within.
Is he dispatched?

MURDERER. My lord, his throat is cut, that I did for him.

MACBETH. Thou art the best o'th' cut-throats! Yet he's good
That did the like for Fleance: if thou didst it,
thou art the nonpareil.

MURDERER. Most royal sir,
Fleance is 'scaped.

MACBETH. Then comes my fit again: I had else been perfect;
Whole as the marble, founded as the rock,
As broad and general as the casing air:
But now I am cabined, cribbed, confined, bound in
To saucy doubts and fears. But Banquo's safe?

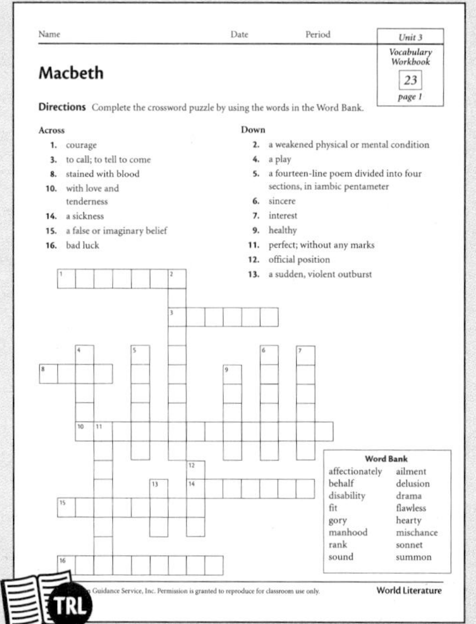

Name Date Period

Unit 3 *Vocabulary Workbook* 23 *page 1*

Macbeth

Directions Complete the crossword puzzle by using the words in the Word Bank.

Across
1. courage
3. to call; to tell to come
8. stained with blood
10. with love and tenderness
14. a sickness
15. a false or imaginary belief
16. bad luck

Down
2. a weakened physical or mental condition
4. a play
5. a fourteen-line poem divided into four sections, in iambic pentameter
6. sincere
7. interest
9. healthy
11. perfect; without any marks
12. official position
13. a sudden, violent outburst

Word Bank

affectionately	ailment
behalf	delusion
disability	drama
fit	flawless
gory	hearty
manhood	mischance
rank	sonnet
sound	summon

Guidance Service, Inc. Permission is granted to reproduce for classroom use only. World Literature

TRL Vocabulary Workbook 23, pages 1–2

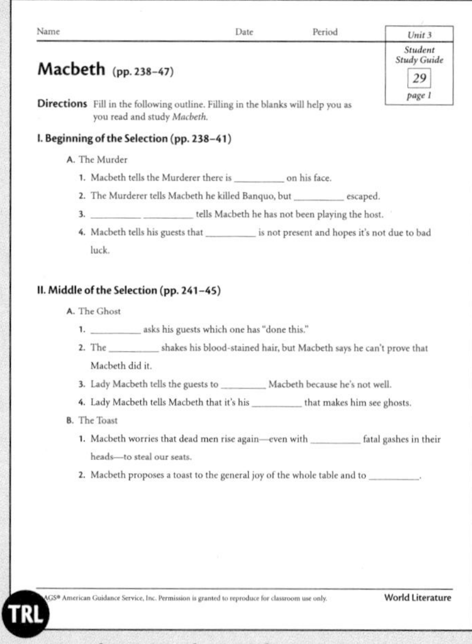

Name Date Period

Unit 3 *Student Study Guide* 29 *page 1*

Macbeth (pp. 238–47)

Directions Fill in the following outline. Filling in the blanks will help you as you read and study *Macbeth.*

I. Beginning of the Selection (pp. 238–41)

A. The Murder
1. Macbeth tells the Murderer there is __________ on his face.
2. The Murderer tells Macbeth he killed Banquo, but __________ escaped.
3. __________ __________ tells Macbeth he has not been playing the host.
4. Macbeth tells his guests that __________ is not present and hopes it's not due to bad luck.

II. Middle of the Selection (pp. 241–45)

A. The Ghost
1. __________ asks his guests which one has "done this."
2. The __________ shakes his blood-stained hair, but Macbeth says he can't prove that Macbeth did it.
3. Lady Macbeth tells the guests to __________ Macbeth because he's not well.
4. Lady Macbeth tells Macbeth that it's his __________ that makes him see ghosts.

B. The Toast
1. Macbeth worries that dead men rise again—even with __________ fatal gashes in their heads—to steal our seats.
2. Macbeth proposes a toast to the general joy of the whole table and to __________.

AGS® American Guidance Service, Inc. Permission is granted to reproduce for classroom use only. World Literature

TRL Student Study Guide 29, pages 1–2

Macbeth **C**

William Shakespeare

Modern English

Act 3, Scene 4. The hall of the palace.
A banquet has been prepared. Macbeth, Lady Macbeth, Ross, Lennox, Lords, and Attendants enter.

MACBETH — You know your **ranks**. Sit down accordingly. From the top table downward, I give you **hearty** welcome!

LORDS — Thanks to Your Majesty!

MACBETH — I'll **mingle** with the guests and play the humble host. Our hostess will stay seated. She'll welcome you at the proper time.

LADY MACBETH — Do so on my **behalf**, sir, to all our friends, for they are welcome with all my heart.

The Lords rise and bow. The First Murderer enters

MACBETH — [*To Lady Macbeth*] See—their heartfelt thanks are yours. [*He looks for a vacant seat*] Both sides are even. I'll sit here in the middle. [*He spots the Murderer*] Enjoy yourselves! We'll pass around the drinking cup just now! [*To the Murderer*] There's blood on your face. **D**

FIRST MURDERER — It's Banquo's then.

MACBETH — It's better outside you than inside him. Is he killed?

FIRST MURDERER — My lord, his throat is cut. That I did for him.

MACBETH — You are the best of cutthroats! Yet he's as good who did the same for Fleance. If you did it, you have no equal!

FIRST MURDERER — Most royal sir— Fleance escaped.

MACBETH — My illness comes back. I'd otherwise be **sound**. **Flawless** as marble. Solid as rock. As free and **liberated** as the air around us. Now I'm closed in, cramped, confined—the prisoner of nagging doubts and fears. But Banquo's fixed?

This version of *Macbeth* is written in modern English, the language we use today. Read it aloud to follow the action more easily. As you read, compare this version with the original. Find words and phrases that you know.

As Macbeth is walking among his seated guests, he sees the *First Murderer* at the doorway. The stage direction [*To the Murderer*] means they are speaking to each other in private. The audience, but not the guests, can hear their conversation.

Macbeth has ordered the murders of *Banquo* and his son, *Fleance*. He is pleased to know Banquo has been killed. He is upset that Fleance has escaped unhurt.

Macbeth wants to be sure that Banquo is dead. He asks the question again.

behalf interest
flawless perfect; without any marks
hearty sincere
liberated free from outside control
mingle to mix
rank official position
sound healthy

C ASK Comprehension Have students read the page 239 modern-English version of the part of the scene that is on page 238. How would you describe the differences between the two versions? (Obviously the language is different, and the modern version is therefore easier to understand. Some students may say that the modern version seems less poetic.)

D ASK Critical Thinking Why do you think Macbeth had Banquo killed? Why is he upset that Banquo's son Fleance escaped? (Banquo suspects Macbeth has ascended to the throne by killing Duncan. Therefore, Macbeth thinks Banquo is a threat to him and needs to be killed so that he cannot tell anyone of Macbeth's role in Duncan's death. As Banquo's son, Fleance is likely now to be an enemy of Macbeth as well.)

Learning Styles

Auditory Plays are an ideal medium for students who learn well auditorially. As students approach the reading of each page of this selection, assign the characters who have dialogue on the page to different students. After giving them an opportunity to read the page to themselves, have the "cast" members read their parts aloud. You may want to allow students to choose whether to read the original or modern English version of each page. Vary the "cast" with each pair of pages.

Name Date Period — Unit 3 — Activity 37

Macbeth

Part A Directions Match each item on the left with the correct item on the right. Write the correct letter on each line.

____ 1. displaced the mirth — a. Banquo's son
____ 2. to keep her state — b. bloody hair
____ 3. Banquo's safe — c. spoiled the enjoyment
____ 4. Fleance — d. stay seated
____ 5. gory locks — e. Banquo's dead

Part B Directions Write a short answer for each item on the blank lines.

1. What does Macbeth see that no one else at the banquet sees?
2. When Lady Macbeth asks, "Are you a man?" what is she really asking her husband?
3. What does Macbeth mean when he states "when the brains were out, the man would die"?
4. What does Lady Macbeth mean when she tells Macbeth, "Your noble friends do lack you"?
5. How do Macbeth and Lady Macbeth try to explain Macbeth's behavior?

 World Literature

TRL

Activity 37

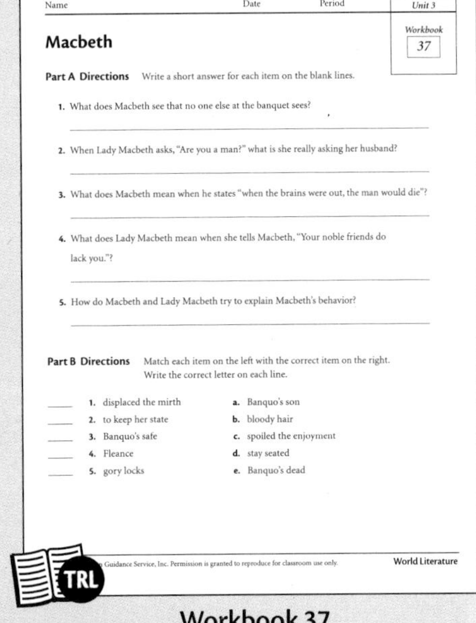

Name Date Period — Unit 3 — Workbook 37

Macbeth

Part A Directions Write a short answer for each item on the blank lines.

1. What does Macbeth see that no one else at the banquet sees?
2. When Lady Macbeth asks, "Are you a man?" what is she really asking her husband?
3. What does Macbeth mean when he states "when the brains were out, the man would die"?
4. What does Lady Macbeth mean when she tells Macbeth, "Your noble friends do lack you"?
5. How do Macbeth and Lady Macbeth try to explain Macbeth's behavior?

Part B Directions Match each item on the left with the correct item on the right. Write the correct letter on each line.

____ 1. displaced the mirth — a. Banquo's son
____ 2. to keep her state — b. bloody hair
____ 3. Banquo's safe — c. spoiled the enjoyment
____ 4. Fleance — d. stay seated
____ 5. gory locks — e. Banquo's dead

 World Literature

TRL

Workbook 37

Discussion Questions

A ASK Vocabulary In the second line of page 240, the murderer uses the word *trenchéd*, which has an accent over the second *e*. The written English language does not usually use accents. What do you think the accent indicates here? (That the *ed* should be pronounced as a separate syllable: instead of "trencht," the word should be pronounced as "trench-ed." This is done to maintain the rhythm or meter of the verse.)

B The dialogue between Macbeth and the murderer reveals that Macbeth is afraid of Fleance, although he thinks that Fleance has "No teeth for th' present," or is "harmless now."

C Comprehension According to Lady Macbeth, how does a feast differ from an ordinary meal? (by ceremony) What does she ask Macbeth to give? (a toast)

G Grammar

Word Study Shakespeare was clearly a man who loved language and the use of it. He is credited by many scholars as having the largest vocabulary of any English writer of his time. He loved to use new words and, in fact, sometimes made up words to suit his meaning as well as the requirements of his rhyme scheme. Word historians (etymologists) note that Shakespeare was the first to use in writing many English words such as *accommodation, assassination, frugal,* and *premeditated.*

Students may enjoy knowing that the pronunciation of many words differed in Shakespeare's day. Often, for example, a word like *flood* rhymed not only with *blood* but also with *mood* and *good*—a fact that is reflected still in the similarity of spellings among those words. Remind students that without radio, television, and telephones, people did not know how other speakers of their own language who lived far away sounded.

Encourage students to select one or more words from the play and research its word history.

What does the dialogue between Macbeth and the Murderer reveal?

B

A MURDERER. Ay, my good lord: safe in a ditch he bides,
With twenty trenchéd gashes on his head;
The least a death to nature.

MACBETH. Thanks for that:
There the grown serpent lies; the worm that's fled
Hath nature that in time will venom breed,
No teeth for th' present. Get thee gone; to-morrow
We'll hear ourselves again.

Murderer goes

C LADY MACBETH. My royal lord,
You do not give the cheer. The feast is sold
That is not often vouched, while 'tis a-making,
'Tis given with welcome: to feed were best at home;
From thence the sauce to meat is ceremony;
Meeting were bare without it.

The Ghost of Banquo appears, and sits in Macbeth's place

MACBETH. Sweet remembrancer!
Now good digestion wait on appetite,
And health on both!

LENNOX. May't please your highness sit?

MACBETH. Here had we now our country's honour roofed,
Were the graced person of our Banquo present;
Who may I rather challenge for unkindness
Then pity for mischance!

ROSS. His absence, sir,
Lays blame upon his promise. Please't your highness
To grace us with your royal company?

MACBETH. The table's full.

LENNOX. Here is a place reserved, sir.

MACBETH. Where?

LENNOX. Here, my good lord...What is't that moves your highness?

MACBETH. Which of you have done this?

LORDS. What, my good lord?

MACBETH. Thou canst not say I did it: never shake
Thy gory locks at me.

240 Unit 3 Drama

FIRST MURDERER	Yes, my good lord. Safe in a ditch he dwells, with twenty trench-like **gashes** in his head, the least of them fatal.
MACBETH	Thanks for that. The adult serpent's dead. The youngster that escaped has the makings of trouble, but he's harmless now. Go. Tomorrow we'll talk together again.

The First Murderer leaves

LADY MACBETH	My royal lord, you do not play the host! A tavern meal lacks welcoming **toasts**. Mere food alone is best consumed at home. What gives a feast its flavor is the ceremony. It's a poor feast without it.

The ghost of Banquo enters and sits in Macbeth's place

MACBETH	[***affectionately***] I'm glad you reminded me! [*To the company*] To appetites and good digestion! And health to both!
LENNOX	Do please sit, sir.
MACBETH	We'd have here under one roof the noblest in the land if our friend Banquo were present. I hope it's a case of thoughtlessness, not **mischance**.
ROSS	His absence, sir, is a **breach** of his promise. [*Indicating a seat*] Would Your Highness grace us with your royal company?
MACBETH	The table's full.
LENNOX	Here's a place reserved, sir.
MACBETH	Where?
LENNOX	Here, my good lord. What is upsetting Your Highness?
MACBETH **E**	[*pointing to the Ghost*] Which of you has done this?
LORDS	What, my good lord? [*The Ghost makes signals*]
MACBETH	You cannot say I did it! Don't shake your **gory locks** at me!

Lady Macbeth gently scolds Macbeth for deserting the banquet guests. She asks him to make a toast to start the banquet.

D Why do you think Macbeth calls attention to Banquo's absence from the banquet?

Lennox offers an empty chair to Macbeth. Only Macbeth can see the *Ghost* sitting in the chair. Macbeth's outburst upsets his guests.

affectionately with love and tenderness

breach a failure to live up to a promise

gash a long, deep cut

gory stained with blood

locks the hair of the head

mischance bad luck

toast a speech made along with a drink to honor someone

D Many students will see that by calling attention to Banquo's absence, Macbeth is demonstrating to his guests that he does not know where Banquo is—therefore trying to establish his innocence in the murder of Banquo, which he knows will eventually be discovered.

E ASK Critical Thinking Some people who have analyzed the play have interpreted the ghost of Banquo as Shakespeare's device to show Macbeth's guilty conscience. In other words, from the point of view of modern psychology it is Macbeth's guilty conscience affecting his mind, not literally Banquo's ghost. Do you think Macbeth's conscience could cause his reaction? (Many students will think that it could, although they will probably agree that the ghost is a more dramatic device.)

Career Connection

Many students in your class may have daydreamed of becoming actors, those who make drama come alive in theaters and on television and movie screens. Invite one or more local actors or drama teachers to address your class and provide students with some realistic insights into the field. Suggest that students prepare for such a visit by drafting questions and topics they would like addressed. If at all possible, arrange for interested students to visit a rehearsal of a play in production.

Viewing the Art

Macbeth Sees the Ghost of the Murdered Banquo by an unknown artist depicts Macbeth, dressed in regal attire, at the banquet.

ASK Why is Lennox directing Macbeth toward the "empty" chair? (He is offering Macbeth a seat at the table.) Why is Macbeth pointing at it? (He sees the ghost of Banquo at his place and is asking "Which of you has done this?")

Discussion Questions

A ASK Comprehension Does Banquo's ghost speak to Macbeth? Who else is aware of the ghost? (The ghost does not speak. No one else can see the ghost, although Lady Macbeth seems to sense what is going on.)

B ASK Literary Elements What does the stage direction in brackets that says "aside" mean? (That Lady Macbeth should say the words following the direction directly to Macbeth. In other words, only Macbeth and the audience of the play will hear her following words.)

Cross-Curricular Connection

History Duncan and Macbeth were real people, although Shakespeare's story about them has been considerably fictionalized. Invite interested students to do some research to find out what they can about the real Duncan and Macbeth and the early history of the Scottish throne. Ask them to report to the rest of the class the comparison between what they discovered and what Shakespeare wrote about the characters.

ROSS. Gentlemen, rise, his highness is not well.

A LADY MACBETH. Sit, worthy friends: my lord is often thus,
And hath been from his youth: pray you, keep seat,
The fit is momentary, upon a thought
He will again be well: if much you note him,
You shall offend him and extend his passion:
B Feed, and regard him not. *[aside]* Are you a man?

MACBETH. Ay, and a bold one, that dare look on that
Which might appal the devil.

LADY MACBETH. O proper stuff!
This is the very painting of your fear:
This is the air-drawn dagger which, you said,
Led you to Duncan. O, these flaws and starts
(Imposter to true fear) would well become
A woman's story at a winter's fire,
Authorized by her grandam. Shame itself!
Why do you make such faces? When all's done,
You look but on a stool.

MACBETH. Prithee, see there! behold! look! lo! how say you?
Why what care I? If thou canst nod, speak too.
If charnel-houses and our graves must send
Those that we bury back, our monuments
Shall be the maws of kites.

The Ghost vanishes

LADY MACBETH. What! quite unmanned in folly?

MACBETH. If I stand here, I saw him.

LADY MACBETH. Fie, for shame!

MACBETH. Blood hath been shed ere now, i'th' olden time,
Ere humane statute purged the gentle weal;
Ay, and since too, murders have been performed
Too terrible for the ear: the time has been,
That, when the brains were out, the man would die,
And there an end: but now they rise again,
With twenty mortal murders on their crowns,
And push us from our stools. This is more strange
Than such a murder is.

LADY MACBETH. My worthy lord,
Your noble friends do lack you.

242 Unit 3 Drama

Ross	Gentlemen, rise. His Highness is not well.	
Lady Macbeth	Sit, good friends. My lord is often like this and has been since his youth. Please, stay in your seats. The **fit** will soon pass. He'll be well again in a moment. If you take too much notice, you'll offend him and extend his fit. Eat up, and ignore him. [*To Macbeth, angrily*] Are you a man? **C**	Lady Macbeth tries to turn attention away from Macbeth. She says that he often has this kind of *fit*. In fact, she knows what he has done. She is afraid others may guess his crimes by watching his behavior.
Macbeth	Yes, and a bold one, that dares to look at what might scare the devil.	
Lady Macbeth	Oh, really! This is a fear of your imagination. This is that air-borne dagger which you said led you to Duncan! Oh, these fits and **starts**—these fake fears—would better suit an old wife's tale told at a winter fireside. Shame on you! Why are you making such faces? When all is said and done, you are only looking at a stool! **D**	Earlier in the play, Macbeth describes a vision in which he see a *dagger* covered in blood. It is hanging in midair and pointing toward Duncan's room. He says it was a sign telling him to kill the king.
Macbeth	See there—look! There! Now what do you say? [*To the Ghost*] Why, what do I care? If you can nod, speak too! If graves and tombs will send back those we bury, we'd better feed our corpses to the vultures!	

The Ghost disappears

Lady Macbeth	Is your foolishness taking away your **manhood**?	Remember, only Macbeth (and the audience) can see the Ghost.
Macbeth	As sure as I stand here, I saw him!	
Lady Macbeth	What nonsense!	
Macbeth	[*To himself*] Blood has been shed before now, in the old days before just laws reformed society. Yes, and since then, too, murders have been **committed**, too terrible to hear about. There was a time when smashed brains meant the man would die, and that was that. But now men rise again, with twenty fatal gashes in their heads, and steal our seats. This is stranger than murder.	
Lady Macbeth	My worthy lord. Your noble friends are missing you.	

commit to do or perform

fit a sudden, violent outburst

manhood courage

start a quick, jerking movement

C ASK Critical Thinking Why does Lady Macbeth tell the guests that Macbeth often has this kind of fit, or strange behavior? (She wants to try to provide an explanation for his bizarre actions and pretend that it is common behavior in order to have the guests assume that this is not anything they should be alarmed about. She is thinking fast to make excuses for his behavior so the guests will not be suspicious of him.)

D ASK Comprehension Remember that Duncan was the king of Scotland whom Macbeth murdered in order to gain the throne for himself. Macbeth's guilty conscience has been working since even before that murder. Before the deed was done, Macbeth tried to justify his planned action. In Scene 1 of Act II, Macbeth has a famous and often-quoted speech in which he says,

"Is this a dagger which I see before me,
The handle toward my hand? Come, let me clutch thee. . . ."

What favor does Macbeth think the vision of the dagger does for him? (He interprets this vision as a command to carry out his murder of Duncan.)

Literary Elements

Foreshadowing Sometimes a writer plants clues or hints about what will happen later in the story. This is called *foreshadowing*. Sometimes just the general mood or tone of a story can be thought of as foreshadowing, too. This is certainly true with *Macbeth*, as is made clear in this scene of Banquo's ghost. The fact that Macbeth sees the ghost and is so deeply affected by it as to risk the suspicions of the people at the banquet certainly bodes ill for Macbeth in the rest of the story. In fact, Macbeth's strange behavior at the banquet gets more bizarre as the scene proceeds, foreshadowing his later degeneration. His last words in this scene (on page 247) are a clear example of foreshadowing—here he directly states that his "delusions are beginner's fear" and he has only just begun. The audience is thus forewarned that his murderous deeds will continue.

Ask small groups of students to discuss why the foreshadowing intentionally makes it clear to the audience that Macbeth has doomed himself and that his situation will not improve. How does this affect the movement of the play?

Discussion Questions

A ASK Comprehension At the top of the page, why does Macbeth say "I have a strange infirmity"? (He suddenly becomes aware that he must explain his peculiar behavior, and he does so by agreeing with Lady Macbeth's excuse by stating that he is subject to such "fits.")

B ASK Critical Thinking How do you suppose the guests at the banquet feel about now? (They may be bewildered by Macbeth's behavior, but probably none are yet suspicious of its cause. They may not be surprised to observe people behaving strangely.)

C ASK Literary Element What simile does Macbeth use to compare the effect of the ghost's appearance? What does he mean by the simile? (The appearance overcomes him "like a summer's cloud." The ghost's appearance ruins the banquet and darkens the mood in the same way that a summer storm darkens the sky and ruins the day.)

Learning Styles

Visual Macbeth's speech to the ghost in the middle of page 245 provides a good opportunity for visually oriented students. Suggest that students make a point of trying to see the pictures in their mind that are described in the speech (the rugged Russian bear, armor-plated rhinoceros, wild tiger, baby girl, and the ghost itself). Read the speech aloud to students, or invite a capable volunteer to do so.

Have students prepare a chart identifying the images that would not frighten Macbeth and the image that does. Then have them use the chart to discuss the following questions: How are the nonfrightening images alike? What do they have in common? How do they differ from the frightening image? Why is Macbeth fearful of the one frightening image? You may want to help students realize that Macbeth is saying that it is the form of the ghost that frightens him, and that if the ghost took any other form, it would not affect him.

MACBETH. I do forget.
A Do not muse at me, my most worthy friends;
I have a strange infirmity, which is nothing
To those that know me. Come, love and health to all;
Then I'll sit down. Give me some wine, fill full.

The Ghost reappears

I drink to th' general joy o'th' whole table,
And to our dear friend Banquo, whom we miss;
Would he were here! to all, and him we thirst,
B And all to all!

LORDS. Our duties, and the pledge.

MACBETH. Avaunt! and quit my sight! let the earth hide thee!
Thy bones are marrowless, thy blood is cold;
Thou hast no speculation in those eyes
Which thou dost glare with!

LADY MACBETH. Think of this, good peers,
But as a thing of custom: 'tis no other;
Only it spoils the pleasure of the time.

MACBETH. What man dare, I dare:
Approach thou like the ruggéd Russian bear,
The armed rhinoceros, or th'Hyrcan tiger,
Take any shape but that, and my firm nerves
Shall never tremble: or be alive again,
And dare me to the desert with thy sword;
If trembling I inhabit then, protest me
The baby of a girl. Hence, horrible shadow!
Unreal mock'ry, hence! *[The Ghost vanishes]*
Why, so; being gone,
I am a man again. Pray you, sit still.

LADY MACBETH. You have displaced the mirth, broke the good meeting,
With most admired disorder.

MACBETH. Can such things be,
C And overcome us like a summer's cloud,
Without our special wonder? You make me strange
Even to the disposition that I owe,
When now I think you can behold such sights,
And keep the natural ruby of your cheeks,
When mine is blanched with fear.

MACBETH [*Recovering*] I'm forgetting. [*To the guests*] Don't **brood** over me, my most worthy friends. I have a strange **disability**, which is nothing to those who know me. Come! [*Raising his glass*] Love and health to all! Then I'll sit down. Give me some wine. Fill it up!

The Ghost returns

I drink to the general joy of the whole table, and to our dear friend Banquo, who is not present. Would he were here! [*Proposing a toast*] To all, and to him we lack, and health to everyone!

LORDS Our duties, and the toast!

MACBETH [*Seeing the* Ghost] Go away! **Quit** my sight! Back to your grave! Your bones are marrowless, your blood is cold. You have no power of seeing in those glaring eyes!

LADY MACBETH Think of this, good noblemen, as a **chronic ailment**. That's what it is. Unfortunately, it upsets things.

MACBETH [*To the Ghost*] Whatever man dares, I dare! Approach me like a rugged Russian bear, an armor-plated rhinoceros, or a wild tiger! Take any shape but your own, and my firm nerves will never tremble. Or come alive again, and dare me to the desert with your sword! If I fall to trembling then, call me a baby girl! **Begone**, horrible shadow! Unreal mockery, begone! [*The Ghost goes*]
Why, then. Once it is gone, I am a man again. [*To the guests*] Please—keep your seats.

LADY MACBETH [***Reproaching** him*] You've spoiled the enjoyment—destroyed the atmosphere—with your ridiculous behavior!

MACBETH Can such things happen— **E**
like a cloud spoiling a summer's day—without astonishing us? You make me doubt myself. You can behold such sights and keep the natural color of your cheeks. Mine turn white with fear.

Lady Macbeth finally succeeds in getting Macbeth's attention. He realizes he needs to explain his odd behavior.

D Why does Macbeth *propose a toast* to Banquo?

When Macbeth begins to rave again, Lady Macbeth makes an excuse for it.

ailment a sickness

begone a command meaning "go away"

brood to think moodily about something

chronic continuing for a long time

disability a weakened physical or mental condition

quit to leave

reproach to scold; to blame

D Macbeth probably proposes a toast to Banquo for the same reason that earlier (on page 241) he called attention to Banquo's absence—he wants everyone in the banquet hall to believe that he truly misses Banquo and is puzzled by his absence.

E ASK Critical Thinking What do you think might happen to Macbeth? Why? (Answers will vary, but most students should remember that this is a tragedy, and therefore Macbeth as the protagonist is likely to have an unhappy end.)

Learning Styles

Group Learning Students are likely to understand the scene best if they have an opportunity to actually act it out. Invite volunteers to take the parts of the characters. It is not necessary for students to memorize their parts; reading them aloud will suffice. However, all will benefit from a rehearsal or two, which can help them get a better sense of timing and expression. You may want to appoint a director or act as director yourself in order to make sure the scene flows well. Then have students perform the scene for an audience of the rest of the class. You may want to mention that this kind of reading a play aloud by actors is routinely done at the beginning of professional play rehearsals.

Discussion Questions

A ASK Critical Thinking Why does Lady Macbeth insist that all the guests leave so quickly? (She realizes that Macbeth's odd behavior will not change, so she thinks that the guests will become more and more suspicious if they stay and observe more of it.)

B ASK Critical Thinking What do you think the sentence "Blood will have blood" means? (Once blood has been shed violently, it will cause more blood to be shed.)

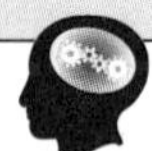

Comprehension

Predicting Mention to students that one way they can help themselves be better readers is to predict what will happen next in what they read. To do this, they need to pay attention to clues in what they are reading. Their predictions may not always match the way the story actually turns out—many mystery authors, for example, delight in giving readers false clues. But it helps to think about what is likely to happen next.

Invite discussion about what is likely to happen in *Macbeth* after this scene. Let students speculate in any way that seems logical and that they can defend.

ROSS. What sights, my lord?

A LADY MACBETH. I pray you, speak not; he grows worse and worse;
Question enrages him: at once, good night.
Stand not upon the order of your going,
But go at once.

LENNOX. Good night, and better health
Attend his majesty!

LADY MACBETH. A kind good night to all! *[They leave]*

B MACBETH. It will have blood; they say, blood will have blood:
Stones have been known to move and trees to speak;
Augures and understood relations have
By maggot-pies and choughs and rooks brought forth
The secret'st man of blood. ... What is the night?

LADY MACBETH. Almost at odds with morning, which is which.

MACBETH. How say'st thou, that Macduff denies his person
At our great bidding?

LADY MACBETH. Did you send to him, sir?

MACBETH. I hear it by the way; but I will send:
There's not a one of them but in his house
I keep a servant fee'd. I will to-morrow
(And betimes I will) to the Weïrd Sisters:
More shall they speak; for now I am bent to know,
By the worst means, and worst. For mine own good
All causes shall give way: I am in blood
Stepped in so far that, should I wade no more,
Returning were as tedious as go o'er:
Strange things I have in head that will to hand,
Which must be acted ere they may be scanned.

LADY MACBETH. You lack the season of all natures, sleep.

MACBETH. Come, we'll to sleep. My strange and self-abuse
Is the initiate fear that wants hard use:
We are yet but young in deed.

They go

246 Unit 3 Drama

ROSS What sights, my lord?

LADY MACBETH Please don't say anything. He gets worse and worse. Questions enrage him. Now, goodnight! No ceremonial leave-taking. Go at once.

LENNOX Good night, and may His Majesty enjoy better health.

LADY MACBETH A kind goodnight to all! *[She hustles them out]*

MACBETH It will have blood. They say, "Blood will have blood." Gravestones have been known to move, and trees to speak. Magpies, crows and ravens have spotted the most secretive of murderers. What time of night is it?

LADY MACBETH Almost morning. It's hard to tell the difference.

MACBETH What do you make of Macduff ignoring our invitation?

LADY MACBETH Did you **summon** him, sir?

MACBETH I hear rumors. But I'll summon him all right. I keep a spy in all their houses. Early tomorrow, I'll go to the Weird Sisters. They must tell me more. I must know the worst, by whatever means. Nothing shall stand in the way of my interests. My path has been so bloody, stopping now and going back would be no easier than going forward. I have some projects in my head that need action first and thought later. They must be done before they are thought of.

LADY MACBETH You lack what all creatures need—sleep.

MACBETH Come, we'll go to sleep. My **delusions** are beginner's fear. I need experience. We've only just started.

They go

C *Ross* asks Macbeth what he saw. Why does Lady Macbeth interrupt?

Macduff is a nobleman who opposed Macbeth's choice as king. He also discovered the body of murdered King Duncan. He is suspicious about who really murdered him.

The *Weird Sisters* are witches who appeared at the beginning of the play. They predicted that Macbeth would be king. Macbeth wants to see them now to learn what will happen in his future.

D Macbeth believes that he is afraid because he's new to crime and violence. He says that, as he carries out more bloody deeds, he'll become used to it.

delusion a false or imaginary belief

summon to call; to tell to come

Drama Unit 3 **247**

C Lady Macbeth interrupts when Ross asks Macbeth what he saw because she is afraid Macbeth will reveal something he shouldn't. She does not want Ross or any of the other guests to become suspicious of Macbeth.

D ASK Critical Thinking Do you believe, like Macbeth, that he will become used to carrying out crime and violence? (Answers may vary, but the truth of the play is that, of course, he does behave with increasingly more murderous violence. Students may also volunteer that he has less to lose as he commits more and more violence.)

Writing Connection

Recall with students the speculation they discussed about possible ways the story of *Macbeth* ends. Let them review the discussion briefly. Ask students to write a paragraph or two explaining what they think will happen as the story ends. Allow free rein here based on what they know from this scene. Do not expect them to know or develop the actual story. You may want to allow groups of two or three students to work together to develop the remainder of the plot, with each student concentrating on one major character such as Macbeth, Lady Macbeth, Fleance, Banquo's ghost, or Macduff.

Reviewing the Selection

Answer Key

Comprehension: Identifying Facts

1. The setting is the hall of the palace with a banquet prepared.

2. Attending the banquet are Macbeth, Lady Macbeth, Ross, Lennox, and other lords and attendants.

3. The First Murderer interrupts Macbeth.

4. The Murderer has killed Banquo, which we know because he admits that it is Banquo's blood Macbeth sees on his face.

5. Fleance is Banquo's son. Fleance has escaped the murderers.

6. Lady Macbeth reminds Macbeth to pay attention to his guests by suggesting that he give them a formal welcome.

7. Macbeth sees a ghost.

8. It is the ghost of Banquo according to the stage directions.

9. Lady Macbeth says that Macbeth exhibits such behavior occasionally and no one should worry about it.

10. Macbeth wants to ask the Weird Sisters for advice because they predicted that he would be king.

Comprehension: Understanding Main Ideas

11. Lady Macbeth calls Macbeth away to protect him from the suspicions of the banquet guests.

12. Macbeth talks as if Banquo were alive in order to persuade people that he knows nothing of Banquo's death.

13. Macbeth sees the ghost because he is guilty of Banquo's murder.

14. In asking "Which of you has done this?," Macbeth accuses his guests of playing a trick on him by putting someone in his seat who looks like Banquo. This upsets the guests, who cannot see Banquo's ghost, because they do not understand what he means.

15. Lady Macbeth asks "Are you a man?" in order to find out if Macbeth still has the senses of a man or if he has gone crazy.

16. Macbeth wants to think of the ghost as something completely unreal that is merely making fun of him.

17. The quotation means that Macbeth is doubting himself. He may think that Lady Macbeth is unmoved by the sight of the ghost, when she, in fact, does not see it at all and so is unmoved while he is frightened.

18. Macbeth is suspicious that Macduff is now his enemy and is working against him.

19. Other possible indications that Macbeth is unstable are that he has spies in the houses of those he thinks are enemies and that he now believes the Weird Sisters will foretell his future.

20. He means that he must act without thinking, for if he thinks about things first, he will not act at all.

REVIEWING the SELECTION

Macbeth

William Shakespeare

Directions Write the answers to these questions using complete sentences.

Comprehension: Identifying Facts

1. What is the setting for the scene?
2. Who is attending the banquet?
3. Who interrupts Macbeth as he is greeting his guests?
4. Who has the Murderer killed? How do you know?
5. Who is Fleance? What has happened to him?
6. Who reminds Macbeth to pay attention to his guests? What does she ask him to do?
7. Who sees a ghost?
8. Whose ghost is it? How do you know?
9. How does Lady Macbeth explain Macbeth's odd behavior?
10. Whom does Macbeth want to ask for advice? Why?

Comprehension: Understanding Main Ideas

11. Why does Lady Macbeth call Macbeth away from his conversation with the Murderer?
12. Macbeth knows that Banquo is dead. Still, he talks about him as if he were alive. Why?
13. Macbeth is the only character who sees the ghost. Why?
14. Macbeth says, "Which of you has done this?" What does he mean? Why does this upset the guests?
15. Why does Lady Macbeth ask, "Are you a man?"
16. Why does Macbeth call the ghost a mockery?
17. Macbeth says to Lady Macbeth, "You can behold such sights and keep the natural color of your cheeks. Mine turn white with fear." What does he mean?
18. Macduff is not at the banquet. Why does this worry Macbeth?
19. We know that Macbeth is seeing things—a dagger in midair and a ghost at the table. What else does he do that might mean he is mentally unstable?
20. Macbeth says he has projects in mind that "need action first and thought later." What does he mean?

Understanding Literature: Drama

A drama is a play. In a drama the story is told by actors performing for an audience. The author of a drama is called a playwright. He or she writes dialogue to tell the actors what to say. The playwright also writes stage directions that describe the setting. They tell the actors what to do and how to do it. Stage directions tell actors when to enter and exit. They may describe movements or tone of voice, too.

21. Look at the stage directions in the modern English version of the scene from *Macbeth*. Which one tells us that only the Murderer can hear Macbeth?
22. Which stage direction tells Lady Macbeth to speak as if she is annoyed with Macbeth?
23. Which stage direction shows that Macbeth is about to propose a toast?
24. Look at the dialogue near the end of the scene. Lennox says, "Good night, and may His Majesty enjoy better health." To whom is he speaking?
25. Lady Macbeth says, "A kind goodnight to all!" Who does she mean?

Critical Thinking

During the course of this scene, Lady Macbeth seems uneasy. She criticizes Macbeth's behavior. She tries to get him to act normally. Finally, she ends the banquet early.

26. Do you think her first line in the scene is fitting for a queen? Why or why not?
27. Look at her next lines. Are they fitting? Why or why not?
28. How does she try to reassure the guests?
29. Later she says, "Shame on you! Why are you making such faces?" Why has her tone changed?
30. Look at her last line. How do you think she feels about Macbeth?

Writing on Your Own The Ghost in this scene from *Macbeth* does not have any lines. If he did, what do you think he would say? Write two lines of dialogue for his first appearance. Write another two lines of dialogue for his second appearance.

Understanding Literature: Drama

21. The stage direction [*To the Murderer*] on page 239 indicates that Macbeth speaks only to the Murderer.

22. Near the top of page 243, the stage direction [*To Macbeth, angrily*] tells Lady Macbeth to speak as if she is annoyed with Macbeth.

23. On page 241, the direction [*To the company*] indicates that Macbeth is addressing the whole group and is about to make a toast.

24. He is speaking to Lady Macbeth.

25. She is addressing the whole group of guests who are leaving, but she also probably means that she hopes Macbeth will also have a good night.

Critical Thinking

26. Her first line (on pages 238–239) seems to be fitting for a queen; in it, she bids the king to welcome their guests with all her heart.

27. Her next lines (on pages 240–241) have her scolding Macbeth for not playing the host properly. This may not be fitting behavior for a queen.

28. She tries to reassure the guests by explaining that such "fits" by Macbeth are routine and nothing to worry about.

29. Her tone has changed because she is getting more and more worried that Macbeth's behavior will give the guests reason to be suspicious of him and his role in Duncan's and Banquo's deaths.

30. She is tender and affectionate, as well as concerned, when she suggests that what Macbeth needs is sleep.

Writing on Your Own Remind students that the ghost is visible only to Macbeth, so any lines of dialogue the ghost speaks must be addressed only to Macbeth.

Selection Quiz

The Teacher's Resource Library includes a Selection Quiz for *Macbeth* that may be given following the Selection Review.

Name Date Period

Unit 3 *Writing Activity* 25

Macbeth

Let's pretend that you are Shakespeare. Don't worry, you don't have to write like him, but try to think like him. One reason Shakespeare's plays are still interesting is he wrote good stories—there was murder, treachery, and comedy, as well as beautiful language. In other words, Shakespeare had good ideas for plays. This will be your job: to think of a good idea for a classical play.

Prewrite
Jot down some ideas for a play. Think of setting your play among kings and queens—people find royalty interesting. Is someone killed in your play? Does someone try to come to power? Does someone fall in love? Is someone falsely accused?

Also, write the words *Act 1, Act 2, Act 3, Act 4,* and *Act 5* on a piece of paper.

Write
Now, next to *Act 3,* write the main action of the play. If Lord Fred gets murdered in the play, then you would write that next to *Act 3.* If Lord Fred becomes king and that's the main action of the play, write it in Act 3. So far, so good.

Finish the other Acts. For Acts 1 and 2, write actions that lead to the big event in Act 3. And for the Acts 4 and 5, list actions that bring your play to an end. Remember, these are simple statements describing what happens. Don't write long paragraphs.

Revise
Read through your Acts. Does the action make sense? Do you think this would be a good play?

Proofread
Pay attention to capital letters, misspellings, and punctuation. Don't worry so much about complete sentences because you are simply sketching ideas for a play.

 World Literature

TRL

Writing Activity 25

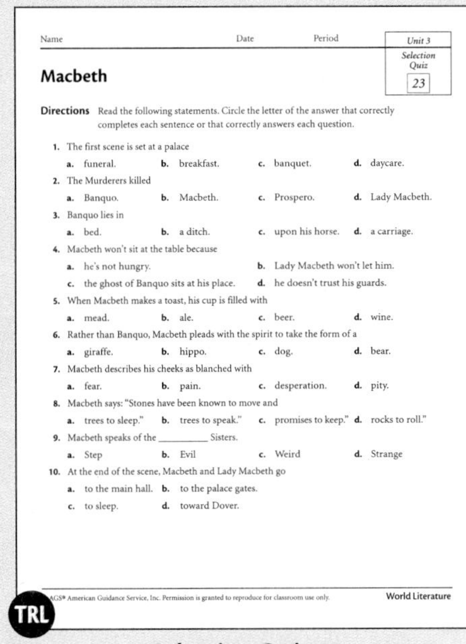

Name Date Period

Unit 3 *Selection Quiz* 23

Macbeth

Directions Read the following statements. Circle the letter of the answer that correctly completes each sentence or that correctly answers each question.

1. The first scene is set at a palace
   a. funeral. b. breakfast. c. banquet. d. daycare.
2. The Murderers killed
   a. Banquo. b. Macbeth. c. Prospero. d. Lady Macbeth.
3. Banquo lies in
   a. bed. b. a ditch. c. upon his horse. d. a carriage.
4. Macbeth won't sit at the table because
   a. he's not hungry. b. Lady Macbeth won't let him.
   c. the ghost of Banquo sits at his place. d. he doesn't trust his guards.
5. When Macbeth makes a toast, his cup is filled with
   a. mead. b. ale. c. beer. d. wine.
6. Rather than Banquo, Macbeth pleads with the spirit to take the form of a
   a. giraffe. b. hippo. c. dog. d. bear.
7. Macbeth describes his cheeks as blanched with
   a. fear. b. pain. c. desperation. d. pity.
8. Macbeth says: "Stones have been known to move and
   a. trees to sleep." b. trees to speak." c. promises to keep." d. rocks to roll."
9. Macbeth speaks of the __________ Sisters.
   a. Step b. Evil c. Weird d. Strange
10. At the end of the scene, Macbeth and Lady Macbeth go
    a. to the main hall. b. to the palace gates.
    c. to sleep. d. toward Dover.

 World Literature

TRL

Selection Quiz 23

Realistic Drama

Ask students to read the text on page 250, or have them take turns reading it aloud. Draw attention to the two quotations at the top of the page and invite discussion of the two views of acting.

ASK Why might acting naturally be the "most difficult performance in the world" for an actor? (It must be hard to say lines in such a casual way as to make them sound natural.)

ASK What do you think the other quote means? (Many students might think that an actor may feel that he or she "comes to life" as an actor only while performing. Others might suggest that an actor "comes to life" as someone else during a performance.)

Realistic drama is probably much more familiar to modern audiences, particularly students, than classical drama is. Although their quality as real dramatic literature may be debatable, many situation comedies and other nonnews television shows can be described as realistic drama, for example.

The evolution from classical to realistic drama may have been a reflection of cultural change. In Shakespeare's time, for instance, few people could read; going to plays gave them a picture of the world that existed outside of their own narrow experience. They were often enthralled by stories of royalty and the machinations of the fates. As audiences became more knowledgeable about the world through modern communication, their interest turned to the kinds of literature that reflected their own lives, problems, and culture.

Many playwrights of realistic drama were heavily influenced by Henrik Ibsen, who essentially invented the form with *A Doll's House* in 1879. He emphasized not only realistic problems and topics but also a natural approach to both his subject matter and his characters. The problems of his plots reflected the real problems of real people. Other playwrights around the world became inspired to write similarly, many exposing in their work genuine social problems as well as people's problems with one another, their work, and their society.

Realistic Drama

- "The most difficult performance in the world is acting naturally, isn't it?" —Angela Carter
- "We [actors] are born at the rise of the curtain and we die with its fall...." —Micheál MacLiammóir

As drama developed, many rules changed or disappeared. Students and audiences still study and enjoy classical drama. But other kinds of plays speak just as strongly to audiences. A pioneer of realistic drama in the late 1800s was Henrik Ibsen of Norway. Realistic drama was a strong force in the theater in the 1950s. A realistic drama tells a story just as it might happen in real life. The characters speak in everyday language, not in verse. They are ordinary people rather than royalty or millionaires. Their problems center on job and family. The play is set in an average home and neighborhood. Many television dramas would be considered realistic. Modern American writers in the realistic style include Arthur Miller and William Inge.

Even Shakespeare's dramas have moments that might be called realistic. These moments usually concern the poor or minor characters. They do not speak in verse but in normal language. They face everyday problems and events.

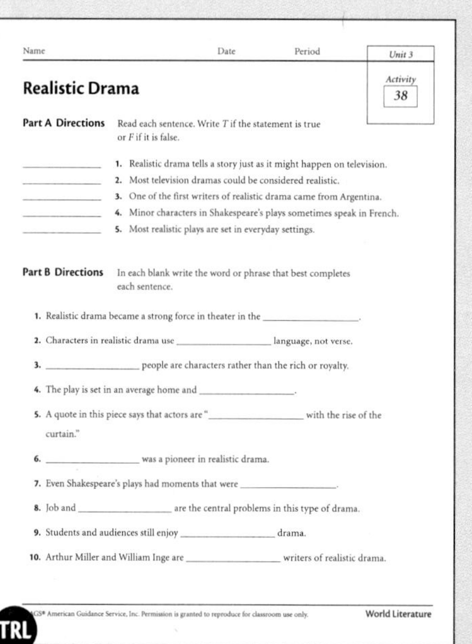

Name Date Period — *Unit 3* *Activity* 38

Realistic Drama

Part A Directions Read each sentence. Write *T* if the statement is true or *F* if it is false.

_____ 1. Realistic drama tells a story just as it might happen on television.
_____ 2. Most television dramas could be considered realistic.
_____ 3. One of the first writers of realistic drama came from Argentina.
_____ 4. Minor characters in Shakespeare's plays sometimes speak in French.
_____ 5. Most realistic plays are set in everyday settings.

Part B Directions In each blank write the word or phrase that best completes each sentence.

1. Realistic drama became a strong force in theater in the _____.
2. Characters in realistic drama use _____ language, not verse.
3. _____ people are characters rather than the rich or royalty.
4. The play is set in an average home and _____.
5. A quote in this piece says that actors are "_____ with the rise of the curtain."
6. _____ was a pioneer in realistic drama.
7. Even Shakespeare's plays had moments that were _____.
8. Job and _____ are the central problems in this type of drama.
9. Students and audiences still enjoy _____ drama.
10. Arthur Miller and William Inge are _____ writers of realistic drama.

 World Literature

TRL

Activity 38

Name Date Period — *Unit 3* *Workbook* 38

Realistic Drama

Part A Directions In each blank write the word or phrase that best completes each sentence.

1. Realistic drama became a strong force in theater in the _____.
2. Characters in realistic drama use _____ language, not verse.
3. _____ people are characters rather than the rich or royalty.
4. The play is set in an average home and _____.
5. A quote in this piece says that actors are "_____ with the rise of the curtain."
6. _____ was a pioneer in realistic drama.
7. Even Shakespeare's plays had moments that were _____.
8. Job and _____ are the central problems in this type of drama.
9. Students and audiences still enjoy _____ drama.
10. Arthur Miller and William Inge are _____ writers of realistic drama.

Part B Directions Read each sentence. Write *T* if the statement is true or *F* if it is false.

_____ 1. Realistic drama tells a story just as it might happen in real life.
_____ 2. Most television dramas could be considered realistic.
_____ 3. One of the first writers of realistic drama came from Norway.
_____ 4. Minor characters in Shakespeare's plays sometimes speak in realistic language.
_____ 5. Most realistic plays are set in castles.

 World Literature

TRL

Workbook 38

INTRODUCING the SELECTION

"Master Harold" ... and the Boys

Athol Fugard

Athol Fugard
(1932–)
South African

About the Author

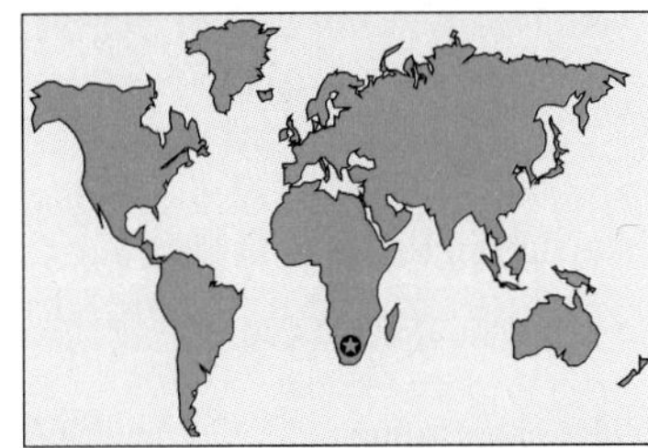

Athol Fugard was born in Middleburg, South Africa. His plays focus on the politics of South Africa. Often their subject is *apartheid.* Apartheid was a government policy in South Africa for many years. It kept blacks and whites strictly separated. It denied black South Africans many rights. Fugard's works show the destruction apartheid caused. But they also show how the human spirit can win over hatred. Fugard has acted in, written, and directed many plays. Some of his other works are *A Lesson from Aloes, Boesman and Lena, Sizwe Banzi Is Dead,* and *The Blood Knot.*

Literary Term

realistic drama a play that tells a story just as it might happen in real life

About the Selection

Fugard wrote *"Master Harold" ... and the Boys* in 1982. This drama shows people affected by apartheid. It is a **realistic drama** about South Africans. It tells a story about everyday life. Hally (short for Harold) is the teenage son of a white, middle-class family. They own a restaurant. He goes to a private school where he is an average student. Sam and Willie are black waiters in the restaurant. They have known Hally since he was a child. Sam has become a sort of foster father to Hally. Hally's own father is an alcoholic and an embarrassment to him.

The following selection is in two parts. In the first part Hally and Sam remember an extraordinary day together when Hally was a child. The second part shows how apartheid could ruin even the best relationships between blacks and whites. Despite their problems, Sam and Hally may be able to learn from each other. Maybe their relationship will be stronger. There is hope for the future.

Selection at a Glance

"Master Harold" ... and the Boys

Athol Fugard

Student pages 251–264

Overview

"Master Harold" ... and the Boys, like most of Athol Fugard's work, demonstrates the tragic effects of apartheid on the people forced to live under its dictates. The play, written in 1982, is based on an incident from Fugard's boyhood in South Africa.

Selection Summary

In *"Master Harold" ... and the Boys* by Athol Fugard, the attitudes of apartheid threaten the friendship between a white boy and the black man who is like a father to him.

Objectives

- To read and understand an example of realistic drama.
- To understand a culture as depicted by the characters in a drama.

Audiocassette 

Teacher's Resource Library TRL

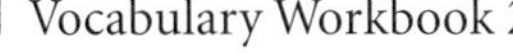

- Vocabulary Workbook 24
- Selection Glossary 24
- Student Study Guide 30, pages 1–3
- Activity 39, pages 1–2
- Workbook 39, pages 1–2
- Writing Activity 26
- Selection Quiz 24

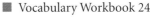

Setting the Stage for Reading

About the Author

Have students read the text and look at the picture of Athol Fugard. Explain that Fugard's most noted works emphasize the capacity of the human spirit to survive many injustices, usually those of apartheid in his native country of South Africa. In 1963, Fugard, who is white, helped found the first successful nonwhite theater group in South Africa. He has been an actor and director as well as a playwright.

ASK Why might a white playwright who is deeply disturbed by apartheid decide to get involved with a nonwhite theater group? (The theater was the medium in which he felt comfortable to bring his strong views to audiences' attention.)

About the Selection

Much of Fugard's work concentrates on the effects of apartheid on the human beings who lived under its influence. In this play, a lonely white boy has developed a close friendship with a black man who has fulfilled some of the fatherly role the boy needs. As the boy grows older and more aware of his status as a white person, he is torn between exerting that power and staying loyal to his appreciative memory of the role the black man has played in his life.

Activate Prior Knowledge: Discuss apartheid with students, making sure they understand the extreme limitations the policy exerted over the lives of blacks.

ASK What might it have been like to live under apartheid as a black person? as a white person? (Answers are likely to focus on the repression blacks experienced and the advantages and perhaps guilt whites experienced.)

Reading Vocabulary TRL

Help students preview the selection's vocabulary words by giving them copies of the Selection Glossary. Have pairs of students take turns making up a sentence using one of the words.

Motivation for Reading

Tell students that this selection will demand that they think about what it might be like in very different circumstances than those they are used to. Suggest that they keep in mind what they have learned about apartheid as they read this play.

Discussion Questions

Suggest that students use the notes in the margin of the student text to help guide and focus their reading of the play.

A Literary Element The setting of a play is its time and place. What is the setting of this play? (A tea room restaurant in South Africa on a wet and windy afternoon in 1950.)

B ASK Critical Thinking How might you describe the relationship between Sam and Hally after reading just the first page of the dialogue between them? (They seem to be old friends who feel affection for each other.)

"MASTER HAROLD" ... AND THE BOYS

ATHOL FUGARD

This scene is from a one-act play. All the action takes place in one act. There are no breaks or scene changes. As you read, look for the events and speeches that makes this play realistic.

Hally is a seventeen-year-old white boy dressed in a school uniform. Sam and Willie are black men in their thirties. They are wearing white waiters' coats.

Time: 1950

A *Place: The St. George's Park Tea Room on a wet and windy afternoon in Port Elizabeth, South Africa.*

HALLY Come on, guess. If your memory is so good, you must remember it as well.

SAM We got up to a lot of tricks in there, Hally.

HALLY This one was special, Sam.

SAM I'm listening.

HALLY It started off looking like another of those useless nothing-to-do afternoons. I'd already been down to Main Street looking for adventure, but nothing had happened. I didn't feel like climbing trees in the Donkin Park or pretending I was a private eye and following a stranger ... so as usual: See what's cooking in Sam's room. This time it was you on the floor. You had two thin pieces of wood and you were smoothing them down with a knife. It didn't look particularly interesting, but when I asked you what you were doing, you just said, "Wait and see, Hally. Wait ... and **B** see" ... in that secret sort of way of yours, so I knew

Literary Elements

Flashback Like foreshadowing, flashback is a literary technique in which a writer takes the audience into another time of the action. A flashback is, as its name implies, a look back at something that previously happened. Readers must pick up clues planted by the writer to discover that the "action" has moved to a previous time.

On page 252, Hally flashes back to the memory of an incident he and Sam shared some years previously. Have students look for clues to the flashback. (Among the clues are Hally's initial comment about memory and Sam's response that they "got up to a lot of tricks" together. The main signal to the flashback comes at the beginning of Hally's long speech at the end of this page, when he says "It started off ..." Another clue is his use of the past tense, indicating that it is over and done with now.)

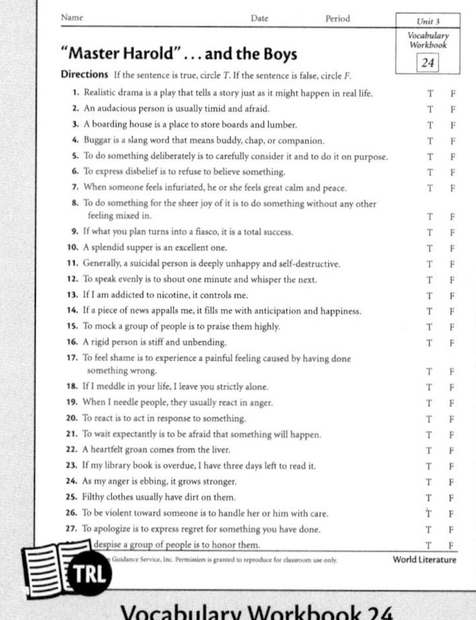

Name Date Period

Unit 3 *Vocabulary Workbook* 24

"Master Harold" . . . and the Boys

Directions If the sentence is true, circle *T*. If the sentence is false, circle *F*.

1. Realistic drama is a play that tells a story just as it might happen in real life. T F
2. An audacious person is usually timid and afraid. T F
3. A boarding house is a place to store boards and lumber. T F
4. Buggar is a slang word that means buddy, chap, or companion. T F
5. To do something deliberately is to carefully consider it and to do it on purpose. T F
6. To express disbelief is to refuse to believe something. T F
7. When someone feels infuriated, he or she feels great calm and peace. T F
8. To do something for the sheer joy of it is to do something without any other feeling mixed in. T F
9. If what you plan turns into a fiasco, it is a total success. T F
10. A splendid supper is an excellent one. T F
11. Generally, a suicidal person is deeply unhappy and self-destructive. T F
12. To speak evenly is to shout one minute and whisper the next. T F
13. If I am addicted to nicotine, it controls me. T F
14. If a piece of news appalls me, it fills me with anticipation and happiness. T F
15. To mock a group of people is to praise them highly. T F
16. A rigid person is stiff and unbending. T F
17. To feel shame is to experience a painful feeling caused by having done something wrong. T F
18. If I meddle in your life, I leave you strictly alone. T F
19. When I needle people, they usually react in anger. T F
20. To react is to act in response to something. T F
21. To wait expectantly is to be afraid that something will happen. T F
22. A heartfelt groan comes from the liver. T F
23. If my library book is overdue, I have three days left to read it. T F
24. As my anger is ebbing, it grows stronger. T F
25. Filthy clothes usually have dirt on them. T F
26. To be violent toward someone is to handle her or him with care. T F
27. To apologize is to express regret for something you have done. T F

despise a group of people is to honor them. T F

 World Literature

Vocabulary Workbook 24

there was a surprise coming. You teased me, you **bugger**, by being **deliberately** slow and not answering my questions!

(Sam laughs)

C And whistling while you worked away! God, it was **infuriating**! I could have brained you! It was only when you tied them together in a cross and put that down on the brown paper that I realized what you were doing. "Sam is making a kite?" And when I asked you and you said "Yes" ... ! *(Shaking his head with **disbelief**)* The **sheer audacity** of it took my **E** breath away. I mean, seriously, what ... does a black man know about flying a kite? I'll be honest with you, Sam, I had no hopes for it. If you think I was excited and happy, you got another guess coming. In fact, I was ... scared that we were going to make fools of ourselves. When we left the **boarding house** to go up onto the hill, I was praying quietly that there wouldn't be any other kids around to laugh at us.

Earlier, we learned that, as a young boy, Hally often visited Sam and Willie at home in the Jubilee Boardinghouse. During these visits, Sam and Hally talked about his schoolwork. They learned a lot from each other.

D What does this remark show you about South Africa at this time?

SAM (*Enjoying the memory as much as Hally*) Ja, I could see that.

Ja means "yes."

HALLY I made it obvious, did I?

SAM Ja. You refused to carry it.

HALLY Do you blame me? Can you remember what the poor thing looked like? Tomato-box wood and brown paper! Flour and water for glue! Two of my mother's old stockings for a tail, and then all those bits and pieces of string you made me tie together so that we could fly it! ... No, that was now only asking for a miracle to happen.

F Why did Sam have to use old, used materials to build the kite?

SAM Then the big argument when I told you to hold the string and run with it when I let go.

audacity boldness; daring

boarding house a place to live where one pays for a room and meals

bugger a slang word meaning companion or chap

deliberately carefully considered; on purpose

disbelief a refusal to believe

infuriating causing great anger

sheer pure; not mixed with anything

C ASK Vocabulary Point out to students that *slang* is a word or words used in informal, nonstandard ways. In the sentence, "I could have brained you," *brained* is a slang term. What do you think it means? (hit on the head)

D Hally's remark shows his assumption that a black man could not know anything about flying a kite, nor that it was proper for a black man to do so. The remark displays the casual racism that Hally had been brought up with.

E ASK Vocabulary Explain to students that an idiom is a phrase or expression with a meaning that cannot be understood by knowing the meaning of the individual words. The phrase "took my breath away" is an idiom. What does it mean? (astonished, surprised, dumbfounded, amazed)

F Sam had to use old materials to build the kite because they were all he had. Implied here, too, are two other situations: Sam is willing to use whatever he has to make something for Hally, and he could not afford to buy better materials for the project.

Name Date Period

Unit 3 *Student Study Guide* 30 *page 1*

"Master Harold" . . . and the Boys (pp. 252–62)

Directions Fill in the following outline. Filling in the blanks will help you as you read and study *"Master Harold" . . . and the Boys.*

I. Beginning of the Selection (pp. 252–56)

A. Making the Kite

1. Hally remembers an afternoon that happened when he was a young boy after going to __________ room to see what was cooking.
2. When Sam ties the pieces of wood in a __________ and puts it on brown paper, Hally realizes that Sam is making a __________.
3. Hally hopes there won't be any __________ around when they go up the hill to fly the kite.
4. The kite is made from tomato-box wood, brown paper, old __________, and bits of string tied together.

B. Flying the Kite

1. When Hally starts to __________, he feels something alive behind him at the end of the string, tugging as if it wants to be __________.
2. Hally lets the kite have more __________ until he's just holding a piece of __________.
3. Hally is a little __________ to look after the kite by himself, but Sam has __________ to do.
4. Sam can't __________ __________ he made the kite.
5. Hally says it's time to make another kite, but it wouldn't be a good day to fly it because it's __________.

II. Middle of the Selection (pp. 256–59)

A. The Argument

1. Sam tells Hally to stop because it's his __________ he's talking about.
2. Sam tells Hally to take back his words and ask for __________.
3. Hally tells Sam that nobody knows how he's __________.

 World Literature

TRL

Student Study Guide 30, pages 1–3

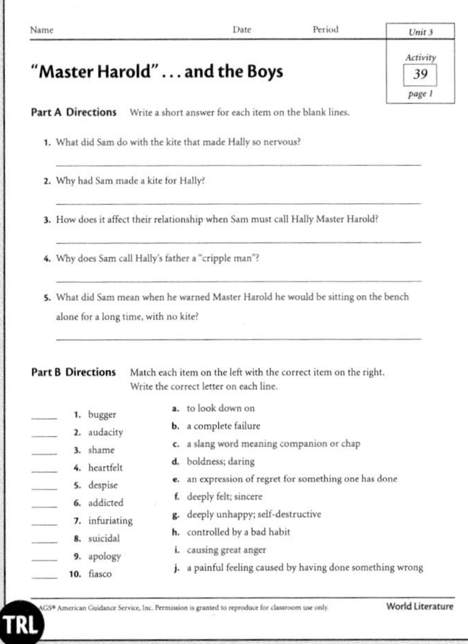

Name Date Period

Unit 3 *Activity* 39 *page 1*

"Master Harold" . . . and the Boys

Part A Directions Write a short answer for each item on the blank lines.

1. What did Sam do with the kite that made Hally so nervous?
2. Why had Sam made a kite for Hally?
3. How does it affect their relationship when Sam must call Hally Master Harold?
4. Why does Sam call Hally's father a "cripple man"?
5. What did Sam mean when he warned Master Harold he would be sitting on the bench alone for a long time, with no kite?

Part B Directions Match each item on the left with the correct item on the right. Write the correct letter on each line.

____	1. bugger	a. to look down on
____	2. audacity	b. a complete failure
____	3. shame	c. a slang word meaning companion or chap
____	4. heartfelt	d. boldness; daring
____	5. despise	e. an expression of regret for something one has done
____	6. addicted	f. deeply felt; sincere
____	7. infuriating	g. deeply unhappy; self-destructive
____	8. suicidal	h. controlled by a bad habit
____	9. apology	i. causing great anger
____	10. fiasco	j. a painful feeling caused by having done something wrong

 World Literature

TRL

Activity 39, pages 1–2

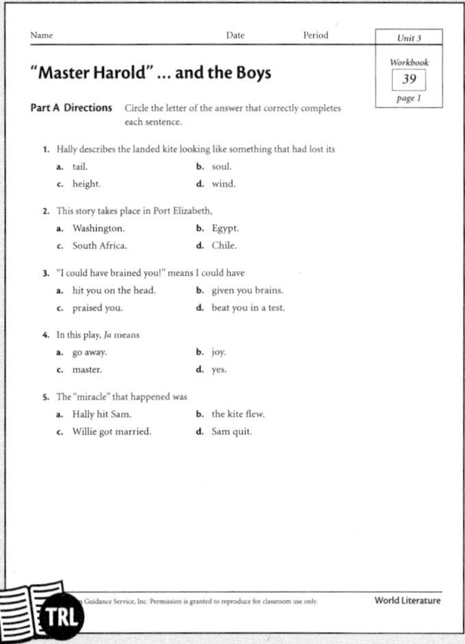

Name Date Period

Unit 3 *Workbook* 39 *page 1*

"Master Harold" ... and the Boys

Part A Directions Circle the letter of the answer that correctly completes each sentence.

1. Hally describes the landed kite looking like something that had lost its
   a. tail. b. soul.
   c. height. d. wind.
2. This story takes place in Port Elizabeth,
   a. Washington. b. Egypt.
   c. South Africa. d. Chile.
3. "I could have brained you!" means I could have
   a. hit you on the head. b. given you brains.
   c. praised you. d. beat you in a test.
4. In this play, *Ja* means
   a. go away. b. joy.
   c. master. d. yes.
5. The "miracle" that happened was
   a. Hally hit Sam. b. the kite flew.
   c. Willie got married. d. Sam quit.

 World Literature

TRL

Workbook 39, pages 1–2

Discussion Questions

A ASK Critical Thinking Hally is remembering this scene from his childhood with great delight, and Sam is recalling it with him. As you visualize the scene with Hally and Sam, consider why it surprised Hally that the kite actually flew. (Hally thought the kite was so crudely made that he didn't expect it to actually work.)

B ASK Literary Elements What does it reveal about the character of Hally that he shares the credit for the kite flying even though he had nothing to do with building it and didn't know how to go about launching it? (It shows that Hally assumed that Sam would be incapable of doing such a thing on his own, despite the evidence to the contrary. It is another subtle but real clue to the racism Hally has been brought up to believe in.)

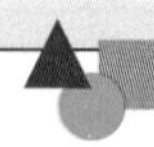

Learning Styles

Tactile/Kinesthetic Students may gain some understanding of Hally's changing emotions during the kite-flying episode by acting it out. A volunteer may assume the role of Hally and physically demonstrate through mime his initial reaction to the kite, his refusal to carry it, his reluctant try to get it to fly, his ultimate success, and the remainder of the scene. If possible, you might also have students make their own kites, using the same type of materials Sam did. They can try to fly their kites as well.

HALLY I was prepared to run, all right, but straight back to the boarding house.

SAM (*Knowing what's coming*) So what happened?

HALLY Come on, Sam, you remember it as well as I do.

SAM I want to hear it from you.

(*Hally pauses. He wants to be as accurate as possible*)

HALLY You went up a little distance from me down the hill, you held it up ready to let it go. ... "This is it," I thought. "Like everything else in my life, here comes another **fiasco**." Then you shouted, "Go, Hally!" and I started to run. (*Another pause*) I don't know how to describe it, Sam. Ja! The miracle happened! I was running, waiting for it to crash to the ground, but instead suddenly there was something alive behind me at the end of the string, tugging at it as if it wanted to be free. I looked back ... (*Shakes his head*) **A** ... I still can't believe my eyes. It was flying! Looping around and trying to climb even higher into the sky. You shouted to me to let it have more string. I did, until there was none left and I was just holding that piece of wood we had tied it to. You came up and joined me. You were laughing.

SAM So were you. And shouting, "It works, Sam! We've done it!"

HALLY **B** And we had! I was so proud of us! It was the most **splendid** thing I had ever seen. I wished there were hundreds of kids around to watch us. The part that scared me, though, was when you showed me how to make it dive down to the ground and then just when it was on the point of crashing, swoop up again!

SAM You didn't want to try it yourself.

fiasco a complete failure

splendid glorious; excellent

Cross-Curricular Connection

Science Invite scientifically minded students to explore what makes a kite fly, including the most successful kite designs, materials, weather for flying, and so on. Ask them to report to the class the results of their research. You may want to encourage them to experiment with designs and, if possible, demonstrate their successes.

HALLY Of course not! I would have been **suicidal** if anything had happened to it. Watching you do it made me nervous enough. I was quite happy just to see it up there with its tail fluttering behind it. You left me after that, didn't you? You explained how to get it down, we tied it to the bench so that I could sit and watch it, and you went away. I wanted you to stay, you know. I was a little scared of having to look after it by myself.

SAM **C** (*Quietly*) I had work to do, Hally.

HALLY It was sort of sad bringing it down, Sam. And it looked sad again when it was lying there on the ground. Like something that had lost its soul. Just tomato-box wood, brown paper and two of my mother's old stockings! But, ... I'll never forget that first moment when I saw it up there. I had a stiff neck the next day from looking up so much.

Notice the stage directions in this play. They often tell the actors exactly how to look or move.

(*Sam laughs. Hally turns to him with a question he never thought of asking before*)

Why did you make that kite, Sam?

SAM (***Evenly***) I can't remember.

HALLY Truly?

SAM Too long ago, Hally.

HALLY **D** Ja, I suppose it was. It's time for another one, you know.

SAM Why do you say that?

HALLY Because it feels like that. Wouldn't be a good day to fly it, though.

evenly without a change in tone

suicidal deeply unhappy; self-destructive

C ASK Literary Elements The stage directions tell us that Sam speaks "quietly" and later "evenly." How do those directions help you realize what Sam's reactions to Hally are? (Sam is being realistic and calm, despite Hally's excitement at the memory of the kite flying. His calmness implies that his memory of the scene may be somewhat different than Hally's.)

D ASK Vocabulary The word *ja*, meaning "yes," reflects the Afrikaans language spoken by white Dutch settlers of South Africa that is probably Hally's native language. The word is pronounced "yah." Since the play is written in English and not Afrikaans, why do you suppose the author has his characters say "ja" instead of "yes"? (Accept answers students can defend. Some may say that the use of the word reminds audiences of the location of the play.)

Environmental Connection

Hally and Sam flew their kite in what apparently was a public park (though, as we learn later in the play, it was a whites-only park). Discuss with students the role parks can play in the lives of people. Draw their attention to several of the national parks in the United States as well as local town or city parks. Encourage discussion of why parks are important. You may want to address with students the issue of restricting access to some national parks as one way of preserving them.

Discussion Questions

A ASK Comprehension As the scene shifts near the top of this page, it is clear that Sam and Hally are having an argument of some sort. What do you think they have been talking about? (Apparently Hally has been seriously criticizing his father, and Sam is cautioning him not to do so.)

B Willie's manner of speaking is more deferential and less familiar with Hally. Sam and Hally are old friends and have had an intimate almost father-son relationship. Willie has not been part of that. Although Willie is a very minor character, he is important to the play to show the usual subservient behavior of blacks in the presence of whites.

Learning Styles

LEP/ESL Help students understand that ellipses have several different uses in English writing. They are used to indicate that copy has been omitted from quoted text. They are also used with dialogue to indicate fragmented, faltering speech patterns. The speech pattern may be interrupted by indecisiveness or uncertainty.

Throughout the play, ellipses are used to show interrupted speech. For example, Sam hesitates before he identifies Hally's father as a "cripple man." Sam most likely wanted to stop and think of the right words to use to describe Hally's father so that he would not offend Hally or demean Hally's father. Help students identify reasons why ellipses are used to indicate interrupted speech on these pages.

The brackets, [ ], indicate that something has been added to let you know what has happened in the part of the play that has been omitted in this excerpt.

SAM — No. You can't fly kites on rainy days.

[*Later, Sam and Hally are arguing about Hally's father. Hally seems both to hate and love his father, who is* ***addicted*** *to alcohol.*]

A

SAM — (*Almost shouting*) Stop now!

HALLY — (*Suddenly* ***appalled*** *by how far he has gone*) Why?

SAM — Hally? It's your father you're talking about.

HALLY — So?

SAM — Do you know what you've been saying?

(*Hally can't answer. He is* ***rigid*** *with* ***shame****. Sam speaks to him sternly*)

No, Hally, you mustn't do it. Take back those words and ask for forgiveness! It's a terrible sin for a son to **mock** his father with jokes like that. You'll be punished if you carry on. Your father is your father, even if he is a ... cripple man.

B
Why is Willie's manner of speaking different from Sam's and Hally's?

WILLIE — Yes, Master Hally. Is true what Sam say.

SAM — I understand how you are feeling, Hally, but even so ...

HALLY — No, you don't!

SAM — I think I do.

HALLY — And I'm telling you you don't. Nobody does.

(*Speaking carefully as his shame turns to rage at Sam*)

It's your turn to be careful, Sam. Very careful! You're treading on dangerous ground. Leave me and my father alone.

SAM — I'm not the one who's been saying things about him.

HALLY — What goes on between me and my Dad is none of your business!

SAM — Then don't tell me about it. If that's all you've got to say about him, I don't want to hear.

addicted controlled by a bad habit

appalled filled with horror or dismay

mock to make fun of

rigid stiff

shame a painful feeling caused by having done something wrong

(*For a moment Hally is at a loss for a response*)

HALLY Just get on with your bloody work and shut up.

SAM Swearing at me won't help you.

HALLY Yes, it does! Mind your own ... business and shut up!

SAM Okay. If that's the way you want it, I'll stop trying. **C**

(*He turns away. This infuriates Hally even more*)

HALLY Good. Because what you've been trying to do is **meddle** in something you know nothing about. All that concerns you in here, Sam, is to try and do what you get paid for—keep the place clean and serve the customers. In plain words, just get on with your job. My mother is right. She's always warning me about allowing you to get too familiar. Well, this time you've gone too far. It's going to stop right now. **D**

(*No response from Sam*)

You're only a servant in here, and don't forget it.

(*Still no response. Hally is trying hard to get one*)

And as far as my father is concerned, all you need to remember is that he is your boss.

SAM (***Needled** at last*) No, he isn't. I get paid by your mother.

HALL Don't argue with me, Sam!

SAM Then don't say he's my boss.

Bloody is a British swear word used to give the next word strong emphasis.

meddle to interfere **needled** made angry

C ASK Critical Thinking Sam says he will "stop trying." What has he been trying to do? (He has tried to calm Hally down and prevent him from talking and feeling negatively toward his father. In this way, Sam has still been acting fatherly and trying to teach Hally about the right thing to do.)

D ASK Comprehension Why is Hally insulting Sam and reminding him that their relationship is that of a servant and his master rather than that of old friends? (Hally is feeling defensive because Sam has made him feel guilty for insulting his father. He is so upset that he is trying to tip the balance of their whole relationship. Some students may see that Hally is confused about the conflict between what he has learned about his role as a white man in apartheid and his affectionate relationship with a black man.)

Discussion Questions

A Sam is warning Hally not to go too far in his insulting talk. He is afraid that Hally will continue to insult him to the point that he will have to remove himself from the affectionate relationship they have always shared. He knows that will hurt them both.

B ASK Comprehension Why does Sam say "quietly and very carefully" that he may never again call Hally anything but "Master Harold"? (He knows that Hally is now defining himself as the white boss in a racist society, which will force Sam to play the role of the black subservient. Sam knows that will change their relationship forever, symbolized by his never again feeling free to call Hally anything but "Master Harold.")

HALLY He's a white man and that's good enough for you.

SAM I'll try to forget you said that.

HALLY Don't! Because you won't be doing me a favor if you do. I'm telling you to remember it.

A

Remember that Sam is older than Hally. Why is Sam warning Hally? What is he afraid will happen?

(*A pause. Sam pulls himself together and makes one last effort*)

SAM Hally, Hally ... ! Come on now. Let's stop before it's too late. You're right. We *are* on dangerous ground. If we're not careful, somebody is going to get hurt.

HALLY It won't be me.

SAM Don't be so sure.

HALLY I don't know what you're talking about, Sam.

SAM Yes, you do.

HALLY (*Furious*) ... I wish you would stop trying to tell me what I do and what I don't know.

(*Sam gives up. He turns to Willie*)

SAM Let's finish up.

This stage direction tells Sam to act very angry when Hally grabs him.

HALLY Don't turn your back on me! I haven't finished talking.

(*He grabs Sam by the arm and tries to make him turn around. Sam* ***reacts*** *with a flash of anger*)

SAM Don't do that, Hally! (*Facing the boy*) All right, I'm listening. Well? What do you want to say to me?

HALLY (*Pause as Hally looks for something to say*) To begin with, why don't you also start calling me Master Harold, like Willie.

SAM Do you mean that?

HALLY Why ... do you think I said it?

SAM And if I don't?

HALLY You might just lose your job.

B SAM (*Quietly and very carefully*) If you make me say it once, I'll never call you anything else again.

react act as in response to something

HALLY So? (*The boy confronts the man*) Is that meant to be a threat?

SAM Just telling you what will happen if you make me do that. You must decide what it means to you.

HALLY Well, I have. It's good news. Because that is exactly what Master Harold wants from now on. Think of it as a little lesson in respect, Sam, that's long **overdue**, and I hope you remember it as well as you do your geography. I can tell you now that somebody who will be glad to hear I've finally given it to you will be my Dad. Yes! He agrees with my Mom. He's always going on about it as well. "You must teach the boys to show you more respect, my son." **C**

C Why does Hally's father refer to Sam and Willie as *the boys*?

SAM So now you can stop complaining about going home. Everybody is going to be happy tonight.

HALLY That's perfectly correct. You see, you mustn't get the wrong idea about me and my Dad, Sam. We also have our good times together. ...

SAM ... Come, Willie, let's finish up and go.

(*Sam and Willie start to tidy up the tea room. Hally doesn't move. He waits for a moment when Sam passes him*)

HALLY (*Quietly*) Sam ...

(*Sam stops and looks* ***expectantly*** *at the boy. Hally spits in his face.* **D** *A long and* ***heartfelt*** *groan from Willie. For a few seconds Sam* **E** *doesn't move*)

SAM (*Taking out a handkerchief and wiping his face*) It's all right, Willie.

(*To Hally*)

Ja, well, you've done it ... Master Harold. Yes, I'll start calling you that from now on. It won't be difficult anymore. You've hurt yourself, Master Harold. I saw it coming, I warned you, but you wouldn't listen. You've just hurt yourself *bad*. And you're a coward, Master

expectantly eagerly waiting to hear or see something

heartfelt deeply felt; sincere

overdue past due

C The fact that Hally's father refers to the black men as "boys" clearly shows his racist attitude toward them as inferior, not smart enough or capable enough to be treated as the grown men they are.

D ASK Critical Thinking Why did Hally spit in Sam's face? (It is a supreme insult, and Hally apparently felt that he needed to exert his superiority over Sam by doing something really horrible and extreme.)

E ASK Critical Thinking Why does Willie groan when Hally spits at Sam? (Willie is horrified at Hally's behavior but, more importantly, afraid of Sam's reaction. If Sam retaliates in any way he would be in a great deal of trouble and could lose his job, his freedom, or even his life.)

Writing Connection

Point out that realistic drama might be fun for students to write. Suggest that they work in small groups of three or four to develop a situation with two to four characters. They may find it fruitful to extemporaneously act out the situation as they think the characters would behave and speak. Then they can recall what "worked" and what they think they should alter before they write their final draft. Have them work together to write the scene. Volunteer groups may want to present their work by acting out the scene for the rest of the class.

Discussion Questions

A Hally has just spit in Sam's face, which is a gross insult. Sam tells Hally he should be spitting in his father's face rather than Sam's. By that he means that it is his father Hally is really so angry at, not Sam. However, Sam is also saying that if Hally doesn't understand that, Hally is therefore ending the relationship with Sam that he has known. Hally's white skin protects him because it makes him the superior person in any interaction with blacks under the system of apartheid. It also protects him because any assault on him by a black would be considered the black person's fault, no matter what the white person had done to the black person.

B ASK Vocabulary What does *boet* mean? Why do you think Willie calls Sam "Boet Sam"? (*Boet* means "brother," so Willie is calling Sam "Brother Sam." He may do this regularly or he may be simply saying it here to remind Sam that Willie is on his side, like a brother, during this confrontation.)

What just happened here? What does Sam mean? How does Hally's white skin protect him?

A

Harold. The face you should be spitting in is your father's ... but you used mine, because you think you're safe inside your fair skin ...

(*Pause, then moving* **violently** *toward Hally*) Should I hit him, Willie?

Boet is an expression meaning "brother" or a close friend.

B

WILLIE (*Stopping Sam*) No, Boet Sam.

SAM (*Violently*) Why not?

WILLIE It won't help, Boet Sam.

SAM I don't want to help! I want to hurt him.

WILLIE You also hurt yourself.

SAM And if he had done it to you, Willie?

WILLIE Me? Spit at me like I was a dog? (*A thought that had not occurred to him before. He looks at Hally*) Ja. Then I want to hit him. I want to hit him hard!

(*A dangerous few seconds as the men stand staring at the boy. Willie turns away, shaking his head*)

But maybe all I do is go cry at the back. He's little boy, Boet Sam. Little *white* boy. Long trousers now, but he's still little boy.

SAM (*His violence* **ebbing** *away into defeat as quickly as it flooded*) You're right. So go on, then: groan again, Willie. You do it better than me. (*To Hally*) You don't know all of what you've just done ... Master Harold. It's not just that you've made me feel dirtier than I've ever been in my life ... I mean, how do I wash off yours and your father's **filth**? ... I've also failed. A long time ago I promised myself I was going to try and do something, but you've just shown me ... Master Harold ... that I've failed. ...

HALLY (*Great pain*) I love him, Sam.

ebbing fading away; becoming less

filth foul matter; dirt

violently with strong physical force or rough action

Diversity Connection

The history of apartheid in South Africa is somewhat different from the history of racism in the United States. In South Africa, white Dutch settlers came to an area populated by black people and dominated the native people by imposing strict rules and regulations to keep them subservient and separate. In the United States, of course, black people were brought into the country as enslaved people. However, in both cases the result was similar—white people developed a policy of antiblack behavior and attitudes that included separatism. In both countries such clear-cut separatism is no longer legal; however, vestiges of racist and separatist attitudes and behavior still exist.

Encourage students to compare and contrast the systems of apartheid in South Africa and segregation in the United States or to investigate the roles of individuals, such as Nelson Mandela, Martin Luther King, Jr., and Rosa Parks, who helped end the legal acceptance of these systems.

SAM I know you do. That's why I tried to stop you from saying these things about him. It would have been so simple if you could have just **despised** him for being a weak man. But he's your father. You love him and you're ashamed of him. You're ashamed of so much! ... And now that's going to include yourself. That was the promise I made to myself: to try and stop that happening. (*Pause*) After we got him to bed you came back with me to my room and sat in a corner and carried on just looking down at the ground. And for days after that! You hadn't done anything wrong, but you went around as if you owed the world an **apology** for being alive. I didn't like seeing that! That's not the way a boy grows up to be a man! ... But the one person who should have been teaching you what that means was the cause of your shame. If **C** you really want to know, that's why I made you that kite. I wanted you to look up, be proud of something, of yourself ... (*Bitter smile at the memory*) ... And you certainly were that when I left you with it up there on the hill. Oh, ja ... something else! ... If you ever do write it as a short story, there *was* a twist in our ending. I couldn't sit down there and stay with you. It was a "Whites Only" bench. You were too young, too excited to notice then. But not anymore. If you're not careful ... Master Harold ... you're going to be sitting up there by yourself for a **D** long time to come, and there won't be a kite in the sky. (*Sam has got nothing more to say. He exits into the kitchen, taking off his waiter's jacket*)

Now we know why Sam built the kite for Hally. He wanted to give him a reason to look up. He didn't want Hally to feel that he had to look down because he was ashamed of his father.

(*Hally goes behind the counter and collects the few coins in the cash register. As he starts to leave ...*)

SAM Don't forget the comic books.

apology an expression of regret for something one has done

despise to look down on

C ASK Comprehension What was Sam's motive in building the kite for Hally? (to help Hally be proud of himself; to "have a reason to look up" and not always hang his head in shame over his father)

D ASK Critical Thinking What does Sam's long speech on this page reveal about him and about his past with Hally? (It shows that Sam has always tried to be a father to Hally, to teach him, to encourage him to believe in himself. It also reveals to Hally that the reason he couldn't stay with Hally the day of the kite-flying was that, as a black man, he could not sit on the whites-only bench Hally sat down on. This is more than a small detail: it exposes the fact of apartheid again interfering with the relationship between them. The speech also shows that Sam is getting tired of putting up with Hally's new and ugly behavior toward him. He is exerting his own dignity by refusing to take it any more.)

Learning Styles

Group Learning As with *Macbeth* and any drama, students may understand it best by acting it out. Have volunteers play the three parts—Hally, Sam, and Willie. Encourage the three students to rehearse together to develop their own sense of timing and expression. They can read their dialogue rather than memorize it. You may want to act as "narrator" who reads the stage directions aloud at the appropriate spots so the actors can concentrate only on the dialogue.

A Sam is willing to take the first step toward reconciliation because he remembers that his role has always been to be the fatherly leader in their relationship and he should act that way again.

B Sam is clearly hoping that the "better weather tomorrow" also means a better relationship between himself and Hally in the future. He hopes that Hally will rise above the influence of apartheid and "stand up and walk away from it."

Community Connection

If at all possible, arrange for your class to see the performance of a play. Perhaps your school has a drama class or club that performs. A community theater or even professional theater may allow your group to attend a rehearsal for free or a regular performance for a reduced rate. The three plays in this unit, like most dramatic works, were intended to be presented in theaters before live audiences. Students will have a different experience in a theater than they do watching a movie or a television show. You can add to their experience by arranging for them to have a copy of a script to read and/or to meet one or more of the actors in the play.

(Hally returns to the counter and puts them in his case. He starts to leave again)

A
Why is Sam willing to take the first step to heal the damage done to their relationship?

SAM (*To the retreating back of the boy*) Stop ... Hally...

(Hally stops, but doesn't turn to face him)

Hally... I've got no right to tell you what being a man means if I don't behave like one myself, and I'm not doing so well at that this afternoon. Should we try again, Hally?

HALLY Try what?

SAM Fly another kite, I suppose. It worked once, and this time I need it as much as you do.

B
Sam says he's hoping for *better weather tomorrow.* What else is he hoping tomorrow will bring?

HALLY It's still raining, Sam. You can't fly kites on rainy days, remember.

SAM So what do we do? Hope for better weather tomorrow?

HALLY (*Hopeless gesture*) I don't know. I don't know anything anymore.

SAM You sure of that, Hally? Because it would be pretty hopeless if that was true. It would mean nothing has been learnt in here this afternoon, and there was a ... a lot of teaching going on ... one way or the other. But anyway, I don't believe you. I reckon there's one thing you know. You don't *have* to sit up there by yourself. You know what that bench means now, and you can leave it any time you choose. All you've got to do is stand up and walk away from it.

REVIEWING the SELECTION

"Master Harold" ... and the Boys

Athol Fugard

Directions Write the answers to these questions using complete sentences.

Comprehension: Identifying Facts

1. Sam made a surprise for Hally. What was it?
2. Hally says a miracle happened. What was it?
3. What reason does Sam give for leaving Hally and the kite?
4. What did Sam use to make the kite?
5. How does Hally feel about his father?
6. Why does Hally get mad at Sam?
7. Hally tells Sam to "just get on with your job." What is Sam's job?
8. According to Hally, who is Sam's boss? According to Sam, who is his boss?
9. Hally tells Sam to call him by a different name. What is it?
10. Who else will be glad that Hally is asking respect from Sam?

Comprehension: Understanding Main Ideas

11. Why was Hally surprised that Sam knew how to fly a kite?
12. Why did Hally refuse to carry the kite?
13. Hally says that Sam was being "too familiar." What does this mean?
14. Hally tells Sam to call him Master Harold. What is the significance of this?
15. Why does Sam start to move violently toward Hally?
16. Willie describes Hally by saying, "Long trousers now, but he's still little boy." What does he mean?
17. Sam says that he's failed. How did he fail?
18. Why is Hally ashamed of his father?
19. What was the real reason why Sam left Hally alone with the kite?
20. What does Sam apologize for?

Review Continued on Next Page

Reviewing the Selection

Answer Key

Comprehension: Identifying Facts

1. Sam made a kite to surprise Hally.

2. The miracle Hally says happened was that the kite flew.

3. Near the beginning of the play, Sam tells Hally the reason he left was that he had work to do. At the end of the play, he confesses that the real reason was that Hally was sitting on a "whites-only" bench where Sam would not be allowed.

4. Sam used tomato-box wood, brown paper, flour-and-water glue, and two of Hally's mother's old stockings to make the kite.

5. Hally is ashamed of his father.

6. Hally gets mad at Sam because Sam tries to tell him not to insult his own father.

7. Sam's job is working as a waiter in the restaurant owned by Hally's family.

8. Hally tells Sam that Hally's father is Sam's boss. Sam says that it is Hally's mother who is his boss.

9. Hally tells Sam to call him "Master Harold."

10. Hally's father will be glad that Hally is demanding respect from Sam.

Comprehension: Understanding Main Ideas

11. Hally was surprised because the racist attitude he has grown up with has led him to expect black men not to be capable of very much.

12. Hally refused to carry the kite because he thought it looked so odd.

13. To Hally, being "too familiar" meant that Sam was acting like a close family friend instead of like a servant.

14. If Sam is calling Hally "Master Harold," it means that Sam must treat Hally formally as his master rather than informally as his friend.

15. Sam is very hurt and angry at Hally's sudden change of attitude toward him. He reacts violently when Hally grabs his arm and scolds him.

16. Hally no longer wears the short pants that little boys do in their society, but he is still acting like a little boy as opposed to a mature man.

17. Sam feels he failed to teach Hally to rise above apartheid because Hally is acting as if he suddenly wants to be the master and have Sam be the servant.

18. Hally's father is an alcoholic, and Hally is ashamed of him for it.

19. He could not sit on the bench where Hally was because the bench was for "whites only."

20. Sam apologizes for allowing himself to get angry with Hally and not acting toward Hally like a man.

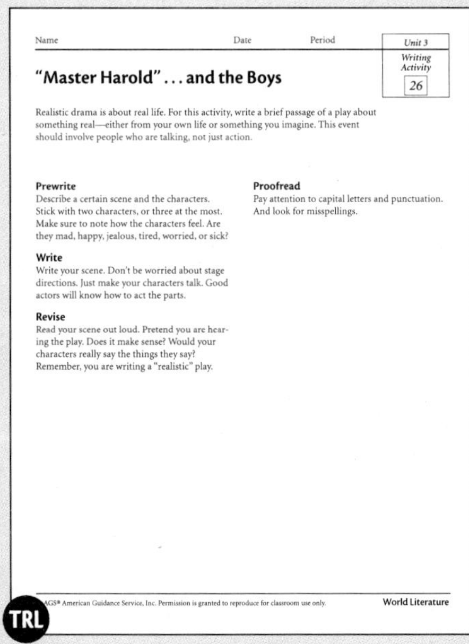

Name Date Period

Unit 3 *Writing Activity* 26

"Master Harold" . . . and the Boys

Realistic drama is about real life. For this activity, write a brief passage of a play about something real—either from your own life or something you imagine. This event should involve people who are talking, not just action.

Prewrite
Describe a certain scene and the characters. Stick with two characters, or three at the most. Make sure to note how the characters feel. Are they mad, happy, jealous, tired, worried, or sick?

Write
Write your scene. Don't be worried about stage directions. Just make your characters talk. Good actors will know how to act the parts.

Revise
Read your scene out loud. Pretend you are hearing the play. Does it make sense? Would your characters really say the things they say? Remember, you are writing a "realistic" play.

Proofread
Pay attention to capital letters and punctuation. And look for misspellings.

 World Literature

TRL

Writing Activity 26

Understanding Literature: Realistic Drama

21. The play is set in 1950 in a restaurant in South Africa. It seems very realistic.

22. The characters are dressed as real people, with Hally in his school uniform and the two black men in the uniforms of waiters in the restaurant.

23. The action is realistic. Real people would talk and act this way.

24. Hally's problems are very real. They include dealing with his mixed feelings about his father. He is also having a serious problem deciding how to act as a white man reflecting apartheid when he has been strongly influenced by an affectionate black man to think beyond the boundaries of apartheid.

25. The play taking place in one act means it takes place in approximately the time it would take real people to have this conversation. That supports its sense of realism.

Critical Thinking

26. He wanted to make Hally feel better about himself, to believe that he could be successful at something.

27. Sam plays the role of the father in Hally's life, because Hally's real father does not.

28. Sam has probably learned to speak English well because he has been around people who do.

29. Apartheid has virtually defined the relationship between the two because Sam has always worked so hard to help Hally rise above it; yet Hally is deeply affected by it as it defines the culture around him.

30. Answers may vary. Some students may feel that there is hope for the relationship to regain its affection. Others may feel that Hally's actions in the second scene have done permanent damage to the friendship.

Writing on Your Own You may want to allow some students to write their paragraphs mainly about the role Nelson Mandela played in the changes in South Africa. Others might concentrate on the apartheid system itself, and the way it has changed. Still others might want to compare the South Africa depicted in the play to the South Africa of today.

REVIEWING the SELECTION

"Master Harold" ... and the Boys

(Continued)

Understanding Literature: Realistic Drama

"Master Harold"...and the Boys is a realistic drama. It's a play that tells a story as it might have happened in real life. A realistic drama must have a believable setting. It must have realistic characters who must say and do realistic things. The audience watching a realistic drama should believe that they are watching a slice of life.

21. What is the setting of this play? Is it realistic?
22. Read the description of how the three characters are dressed. Do they look like real people? Why or why not?
23. Look at the action in the play. Is it realistic? Why or why not?
24. Is Hally troubled by real problems? What are they?
25. *"Master Harold"...and the Boys* is a play in one act. How might that make it seem more realistic?

Critical Thinking

26. What was Sam's real reason for making the kite for Hally?
27. What role does Sam play in Hally's life?
28. How do you think Sam has learned to speak English well?
29. How has apartheid affected the relationship between Sam and Hally?
30. Do you think there's hope for the future of Sam and Hally's friendship?

Writing on Your Own This play is set in 1950. South Africa has undergone many changes since then. Ask your librarian or teacher for recent articles about South Africa. Look for information about apartheid and a man named Nelson Mandela. What has happened to the apartheid system? Write a paragraph describing the changes.

Selection Quiz

The Teacher's Resource Library includes a Selection Quiz for *"Master Harold"... and the Boys* that may be given following the Selection Review.

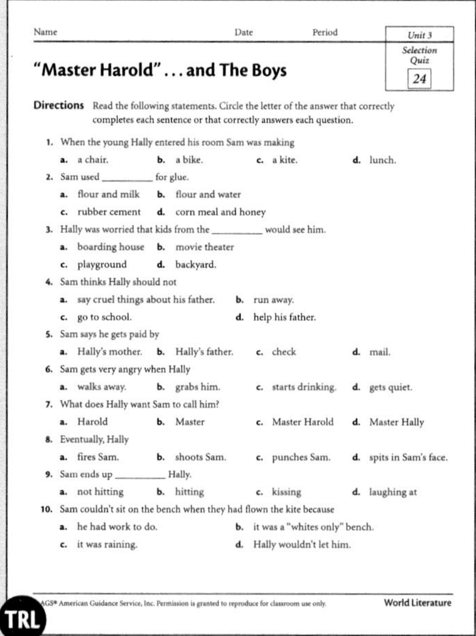

Name Date Period

Unit 3 Selection Quiz 24

"Master Harold" . . . and The Boys

Directions Read the following statements. Circle the letter of the answer that correctly completes each sentence or that correctly answers each question.

1. When the young Hally entered his room Sam was making
   a. a chair. b. a bike. c. a kite. d. lunch.
2. Sam used __________ for glue.
   a. flour and milk b. flour and water
   c. rubber cement d. corn meal and honey
3. Hally was worried that kids from the __________ would see him.
   a. boarding house b. movie theater
   c. playground d. backyard.
4. Sam thinks Hally should not
   a. say cruel things about his father. b. run away.
   c. go to school. d. help his father.
5. Sam says he gets paid by
   a. Hally's mother. b. Hally's father. c. check d. mail.
6. Sam gets very angry when Hally
   a. walks away. b. grabs him. c. starts drinking. d. gets quiet.
7. What does Hally want Sam to call him?
   a. Harold b. Master c. Master Harold d. Master Hally
8. Eventually, Hally
   a. fires Sam. b. shoots Sam. c. punches Sam. d. spits in Sam's face.
9. Sam ends up __________ Hally.
   a. not hitting b. hitting c. kissing d. laughing at
10. Sam couldn't sit on the bench when they had flown the kite because
    a. he had work to do. b. it was a "whites only" bench.
    c. it was raining. d. Hally wouldn't let him.

 World Literature

TRL

Selection Quiz 24

Expressionistic Drama

- "We reason deeply when we forcibly feel." —Mary Wollstonecraft
- "He who is sorrowful can force himself to smile, but he who is glad cannot weep." —Selma Lagerlöf

Expressionistic drama began in Europe and became most popular after 1900. Writers exaggerated a character's inner feelings. Expressionistic playwrights did not want to present events realistically. They tried to increase the audience's emotional participation in other ways. These writers used lighting, staging, design, and directing in new ways. In Eugene O'Neill's *Strange Interlude*, for example, the protagonist is split into two characters. The split shows the conflict between the character's public and private nature. Thornton Wilder's *Our Town* uses a narrator, as a realistic play might. But only very little scenery is used to move the action. Samuel Beckett's *Waiting for Godot* emphasizes the frustration of human existence. The characters wait and wait, but Godot never appears.

Expressionistic Drama

Ask students to read page 265. You may prefer to have them take turns reading it aloud.

Draw their attention to the quotations at the top of the page.

ASK What relationship do you think these two quotations have to the topic of expressionistic drama? (Both quotations address the issues of deeply felt feelings and their expression, which is the basic theme of expressionistic drama.)

Expressionistic drama emphasizes characters' feelings and the impact of events in an often dramatically exaggerated way, as the examples mentioned demonstrate. The dramatists' intent is usually not to show a "slice of life," as in realistic drama, but rather to focus attention on the main theme through some unusual method of staging, characterization, or other aspect of the presentation.

ASK How does expressionistic drama differ from classical drama and from realistic drama? (Expressionistic drama does not have the formal structure, language, or characters typical of classical drama—those features may be anything the dramatist chooses in order to make his or her thematic point. Nor does expressionistic drama tell its story as if it might be observed happening in real life—the hallmark of realistic drama.)

Name Date Period Unit 3 Activity 40

Expressionistic Drama

Part A Directions Read each sentence. Write *T* if the statement is true or *F* if it is false.

_____ 1. Expressionistic playwrights wanted to present events realistically.

_____ 2. A split inside the protagonist (*Strange Interlude*) is between good and bad.

_____ 3. *Our Town* uses very little scenery to move the action.

_____ 4. Samuel Beckett writes about the frustration of human experience.

_____ 5. In *Waiting for Godot*, Godot shows up late.

Part B Directions In each blank choose the word or phrase from the Word Bank that best completes each sentence.

1. O'Neill's _____ has a protagonist split into two characters.
2. Characters' exaggerated inner _____ are found in expressionistic drama.
3. _____ is where expressionistic drama began.
4. In expressionistic dramas, the playwrights try to increase the audience's _____ participation.
5. Writers of expressionistic drama use lighting, _____, and design in new ways.

Word Bank: emotional, Europe, feelings, staging, *Strange Interlude*

 World Literature

TRL

Activity 40

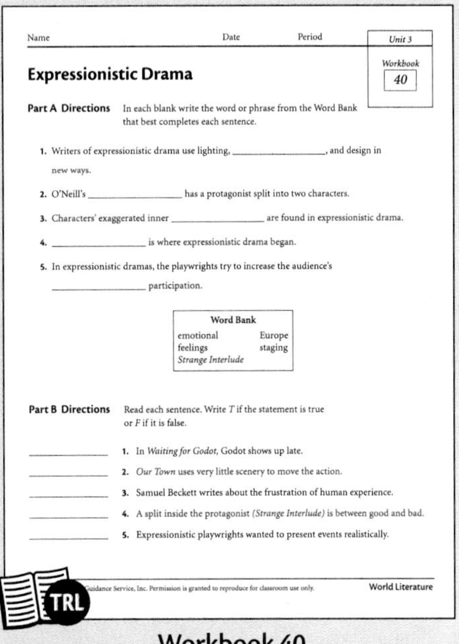

Name Date Period Unit 3 Workbook 40

Expressionistic Drama

Part A Directions In each blank write the word or phrase from the Word Bank that best completes each sentence.

1. Writers of expressionistic drama use lighting, _____, and design in new ways.
2. O'Neill's _____ has a protagonist split into two characters.
3. Characters' exaggerated inner _____ are found in expressionistic drama.
4. _____ is where expressionistic drama began.
5. In expressionistic dramas, the playwrights try to increase the audience's _____ participation.

Word Bank: emotional, Europe, feelings, staging, *Strange Interlude*

Part B Directions Read each sentence. Write *T* if the statement is true or *F* if it is false.

_____ 1. In *Waiting for Godot*, Godot shows up late.

_____ 2. *Our Town* uses very little scenery to move the action.

_____ 3. Samuel Beckett writes about the frustration of human experience.

_____ 4. A split inside the protagonist (*Strange Interlude*) is between good and bad.

_____ 5. Expressionistic playwrights wanted to present events realistically.

 World Literature

TRL

Workbook 40

Selection at a Glance

The Stronger

August Strindberg
(translated by Ants Oras)

Student pages 266–275

Overview

August Strindberg is often considered to be Sweden's greatest writer. He is internationally acknowledged as a major literary innovator and the originator of expressionistic drama.

Selection Summary

The Stronger by August Strindberg is a play in which only one character speaks. Strindberg explores the inner thoughts of Mme. X as she realizes something about her marriage.

Objectives

- To understand and appreciate expressionistic drama.
- To understand some conventions of written drama.

Audiocassette

Teacher's Resource Library TRL

- Vocabulary Workbook 25
- Selection Glossary 25
- Student Study Guide 31, pages 1–2
- Activity 41
- Workbook 41
- Writing Activity 27
- Selection Quiz 25

INTRODUCING the SELECTION

The Stronger

August Strindberg (translated by Ants Oras)

August Strindberg
(1849–1912)
Swedish

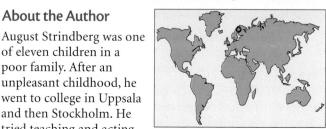

Literary Terms

expressionistic drama a play that seems realistic but changes some elements for dramatic effect

prop a piece of equipment used on stage during a play

About the Author

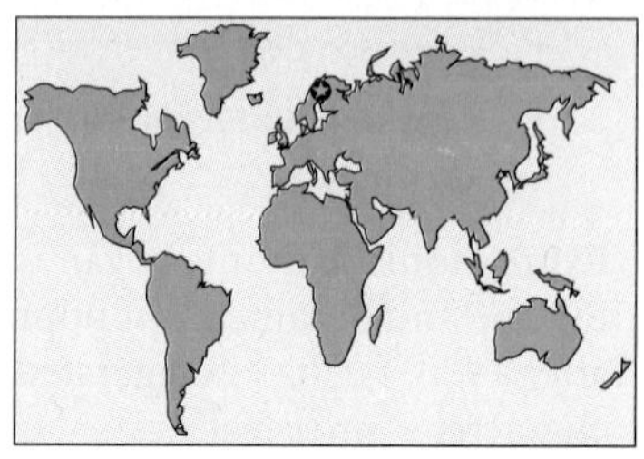

August Strindberg was one of eleven children in a poor family. After an unpleasant childhood, he went to college in Uppsala and then Stockholm. He tried teaching and acting. Then he went back to his studies. He received a cash award from the King of Sweden and began writing. One of his plays earned him a job at the Royal Library. He wrote many short stories, novels, and plays. Strindberg's plays often show conflicts between men and women. One of his most famous plays is *Miss Julie*. Strindberg's late plays inspired other expressionistic playwrights.

About the Selection

Strindberg's works range from naturalistic to expressionistic. **Expressionistic drama** is not meant to be realistic. It may seem realistic but changes some elements for dramatic effect. As Strindberg grew older, his works depended more and more on dialogue. He used fewer **props** and stage directions. A prop (short for "property") is a piece of equipment used on stage to help the story. *The Stronger* is one result of this trend. The play breaks away from many of the usual forms of drama. One of the main characters never speaks. She seems to be present only so the other woman is not speaking to herself. This play presents psychological conflict only by the words spoken

Setting the Stage for Reading

About the Author

Have students read the text and look at Strindberg's picture. Point out that Strindberg's mother died when he was thirteen, and his father remarried. This event contributed to his unhappy adolescence. While at the University of Uppsala, he lived in terrible poverty and loneliness and was forced to leave to earn money. He taught school and acted as a private tutor. He wanted to be an actor but was just too shy. In 1869 he began to write, and he felt "as if a long pain were over."

ASK Why might a painfully shy and unhappy man find that "a long pain" was over once he began to write? (Perhaps writing gave him the ability to express his feelings in ways he couldn't do otherwise.)

About the Selection

Many of Strindberg's works, like this play, express his pessimistic views about the relationships between men and women. Strindberg's troubled life included three marriages, all of which began happily but ended bitterly.

Activate Prior Knowledge: Discuss examples of monologues that students have experienced.

ASK How does a stand-up comic or another kind of monologuist communicate dialogue with another person? (The artist may act as if listening to another person or comment on what must be another person's words or actions.)

THE STRONGER

August Strindberg

PERSONS
MME. X, *actress, married* **A**
MLLE. Y, *actress, single*
A Waitress

A corner in a ladies' café; two small iron tables, a red velvet sofa and some chairs. Mme. X enters in winter clothing, wearing a hat and a cloak and carrying a fine Japanese basket on her arm. Mlle. Y sits with a half-empty beer bottle in front of her, reading an illustrated paper, then changing it for another.

MME. X: How are you, little Amelie?—You're sitting alone here on Christmas Eve like a **disconsolate** old bachelor.

(*Mlle. Y looks up from the paper, nods, goes on reading.*)

MME. X: You know, I am **heartily** sorry to see you like this, alone, all alone in a café on Christmas Eve. I feel quite as sorry as that evening in a Paris restaurant when I saw a bridal party, with the bride sitting and reading a comic paper and the groom playing **billiards** with the witnesses. Goodness, I thought, with such a beginning how is this to continue and to end!

He played billiards on his wedding evening!—Yes, and she read a comic paper! Well, but that is hardly the same situation as here.

B
Mme. X is the abbreviation for Madame X. *Mlle. Y* is the abbreviation for Mademoiselle Y. These are French titles of address. The first is for a married woman and the second for an unmarried one.

As you read, think about why the author did not give specific names to his characters.

The *witnesses* were the wedding guests. They sign, or witness, a paper that makes the wedding legal.

billiards a game similar to pool, played with a cue and solid balls on a large oblong table with raised edges

disconsolate very sad

heartily with enthusiasm

Reading Vocabulary TRL

Help students preview the selection's vocabulary words by giving them copies of the Selection Glossary. Have students work in small groups in which one student chooses one of the words at random. The group member who defines the word correctly can choose another word for the group to define. Groups should continue until all words have been defined correctly.

Motivation for Reading

Point out to students that people often reveal themselves and their emotions by what they say. Suggest they read *The Stronger* not only to find out how Mme. X feels but what kind of person she is and what has happened in her life as shown by what she says in the play.

Discussion Questions

Use the questions and comments in the margins of the student selection to help students focus and check their reading.

A ASK Literary Elements What makes you think that it is important to the play that the two women are both actresses, with one married and the other unmarried? (The author is very careful to identify them this way at the beginning of the play.)

B ASK Vocabulary What are the English equivalents of the titles *Mme.* and *Mlle.?* (We use *Mrs.* like *Mme.* to indicate a married woman and *Miss* like *Mlle.* as a title for an unmarried woman. We also use the title *Ms.*, which does not identify the marital status of a woman.)

Name Date Period

Unit 3
Vocabulary Workbook
25

The Stronger

Directions Each set of sentences contains two underlined definitions. Below the set are three words. Circle the one undefined word.

1. Mme. X thinks that Mlle. Y looks very sad sitting in the café. X believe that Y is sad because she greatly wishes to be acting in the theater again.
   longs disconsolate props
2. Y looks at X scornfully. Mme. X says that Y is wrong in believing that X eased her out of the theater with her secret schemes.
   abhors contemptuously intrigues
3. X shows Y some slippers with embroidered tulips and admits that she intensely dislikes tulips. Her husband wears them in a current of air.
   abhors chiffonier draught
4. X's husband calls his servants remarkably stupid persons. He thinks their work is too bad to be described.
   longs morons unspeakable
5. Mme. X begins to speak in a sadly thoughtful way. She says that there is something unpleasant and disturbing in the air when Y visits her home.
   discordant christening pensively
6. Mme. X realizes that an intense friendship flared up between Y and Mme. X's husband. X admits that she learned her strong feelings from Y.
   violent passions fiancé
7. Mme. X rages that Y's soul moved like a worm into her own. X was left with only the outer skin of herself.
   malice rind slithered
8. X says that Y fascinated her with her black eyes. She accuses Y of looking in the newspaper for stories about people who feel miserable.
   bewitched slithered wretched
9. X says that Y is full of ill will because her feelings are hurt. She accuses Y of being a person who steers a ship who plans to shipwreck everyone.
   bewitch malice pilot
10. X says that she will not be mean despite the fact that Y had an affair with her husband. She says that Y's emotions no longer appeal to X's husband.
    petty affections pilots

 World Literature

TRL

Vocabulary Workbook 25

Name Date Period

Unit 3
Student Study Guide
31
page 1

The Stronger (pp. 267–73)

Directions Fill in the following outline. Filling in the blanks will help you as you read and study *The Stronger.*

I. Beginning of the Selection (pp. 267–68)

A. Mlle. Y and Mme. X
   1. Mlle. Y is sitting alone on ________ Eve.
   2. Mme. X once saw a bridal party in which the bride sat and read a comic paper while the groom played ________ with the witnesses.
   3. The waitress brings Mme. X a cup of hot ________.

B. Presents
   1. Last Christmas, Mlle. Y felt happy in the ________ with her fiancé's parents.
   2. Mme. X feels that a ________ is the best of all things, next to the theater.
   3. Mme. X bought a ________ for Lisa and a pop gun for ________.
   4. Mme. X would be less surprised if Mlle. Y was ________ her.

II. Middle of the Selection (pp. 268–71)

A. The Slippers
   1. Mme. X's husband wants ________ on everything.
   2. Mme. X makes the slippers walk along the ________ to show how her husband looks when he walks.
   3. Mme. X says her husband is ________ to her.

B. The Accusation
   1. Women are ________ about Mme. X's husband, perhaps because he is in the ________ department.
   2. Mme. X invites Mlle. Y to come to their house in the ________ to show that she's not cross with them.
   3. When Mme. X first met Mlle. Y, she was ________ of her.

 World Literature

TRL

Student Study Guide 31, pages 1–2

Discussion Questions

A Mlle. Y apparently has not been married despite her celebration with a fiancé last Christmas. It seems that the wedding did not take place.

B ASK Vocabulary How do we know that the word *piglet* means "baby pig"? (The ending *-let* is a diminutive, or clue that the word means something little.)

C Mme. X refers to her children as her piglets.

D ASK Comprehension Who is Mme. X's "old man"? What is his name? (Her "old man" is her husband, whose name is Bob.)

Career Connection

Students may be familiar with the job of waiting on tables in a restaurant as the waitress does when she brings hot chocolate to Mme. X. Many people use such jobs to support themselves while they are studying to become something else—famously, for example, actors and students. However, careers in restaurant management as well as in other aspects of food service are often lucrative, though they usually demand hard work and long hours. Often they do not require a college education. You may want to have students visit a local restaurant and discuss career or job opportunities with the manager and/or chef. Make sure that students find out what kinds of preparation are required for positions in food service.

(The Waitress enters, places a cup of hot chocolate before Mme. X and goes out.)

Mme. X: I tell you what, Amelie! Now I really believe you would have done better to have kept him. Remember, I was the first to urge you "Forgive him!" Don't you recall it?—You could have been married to him, with a home of your own. Don't you remember last Christmas, how happy you felt out in the country with your **fiancé**'s parents; How you praised the happiness of a home and how you **longed** to get away from the theater?—Yes, darling Amelie, a home is the best of all things—next to the theater—a home and some brats too—but that you wouldn't understand.

A What seems to have happened in Mlle. Y's personal life?

*(Mlle. Y looks **contemptuous.**)*

Mme. X: *(drinks a few spoonfuls from her cup, opens her basket and shows her Christmas presents)*: Now you'll see **B** what I've bought for my piglets. *(Shows a doll)* Look at this. This is for Lisa. Look how it rolls its eyes and turns its neck. There! And here is Maja's pop gun. *(Loads it and shoots at Mlle. Y.)*

C Who is Mme. X referring to as her *piglets*?

(Mlle. Y makes a scared gesture.)

Mme. X: Did this startle you? Did you fear I'd shoot you? What?—Good heavens, I don't believe you could possibly have thought that. I'd be less surprised if you were shooting me, since I got in your way—I know you can't forget that—although I was completely innocent. You still believe I eased you out of the theater with my **intrigues**, but I didn't! I didn't, even though you think I did!—But what is the use of telling you, for you still believe I did it. *(Takes out a pair of* **D** *embroidered slippers)* And these are for my old man. With tulips embroidered, by myself—I **abhor** tulips, you understand, but he wants tulips on everything.

abhor to dislike intensely; to find disgusting

fiancé a French term meaning a man engaged to be married

longed greatly wished for

contemptuous showing scorn

intrigue a secret or underhanded scheme

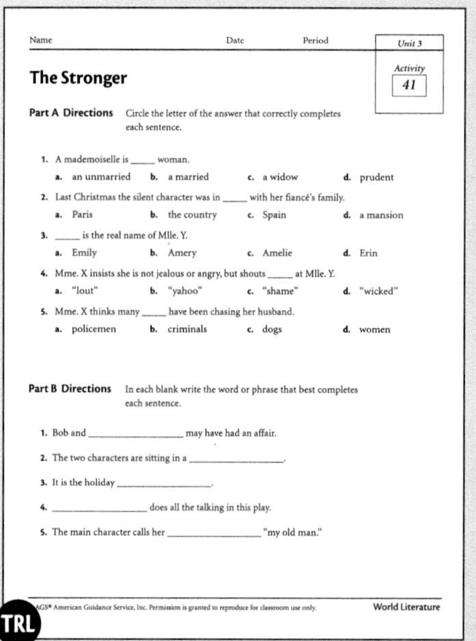

Name Date Period

Unit 3 Activity 41

The Stronger

Part A Directions Circle the letter of the answer that correctly completes each sentence.

1. A mademoiselle is _____ woman.
   a. an unmarried b. a married c. a widow d. prudent
2. Last Christmas the silent character was in _____ with her fiancé's family.
   a. Paris b. the country c. Spain d. a mansion
3. _____ is the real name of Mlle. Y.
   a. Emily b. Amery c. Amelie d. Erin
4. Mme. X insists she is not jealous or angry, but shouts _____ at Mlle. Y.
   a. "lout" b. "yahoo" c. "shame" d. "wicked"
5. Mme. X thinks many _____ have been chasing her husband.
   a. policemen b. criminals c. dogs d. women

Part B Directions In each blank write the word or phrase that best completes each sentence.

1. Bob and _________________ may have had an affair.
2. The two characters are sitting in a _________________.
3. It is the holiday _________________.
4. _________________ does all the talking in this play.
5. The main character calls her _________________ "my old man."

 World Literature

TRL

Activity 41

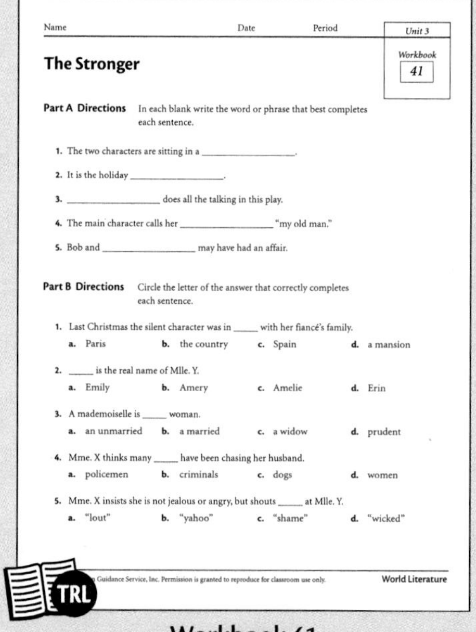

Name Date Period

Unit 3 Workbook 41

The Stronger

Part A Directions In each blank write the word or phrase that best completes each sentence.

1. The two characters are sitting in a _________________.
2. It is the holiday _________________.
3. _________________ does all the talking in this play.
4. The main character calls her _________________ "my old man."
5. Bob and _________________ may have had an affair.

Part B Directions Circle the letter of the answer that correctly completes each sentence.

1. Last Christmas the silent character was in _____ with her fiancé's family.
   a. Paris b. the country c. Spain d. a mansion
2. _____ is the real name of Mlle. Y.
   a. Emily b. Amery c. Amelie d. Erin
3. A mademoiselle is _____ woman.
   a. an unmarried b. a married c. a widow d. prudent
4. Mme. X thinks many _____ have been chasing her husband.
   a. policemen b. criminals c. dogs d. women
5. Mme. X insists she is not jealous or angry, but shouts _____ at Mlle. Y.
   a. "lout" b. "yahoo" c. "shame" d. "wicked"

 World Literature

TRL

Workbook 41

(*Mlle. Y looks up from her paper ironically and with some curiosity.*)

MME. X: (*puts a hand in each slipper*) Look how small Bob's feet are. Well? And you ought to see how daintily he walks. You've never seen him in his slippers. **F**

E Irony is the use of words or expressions that say one thing but mean another. Is Mlle. Y really interested in what Mme. X is saying?

(*Mme. Y laughs aloud.*)

MME. X: Look, I'll show you. (*Makes the slippers walk along the table.*)

(*Mlle. Y laughs aloud.*)

MME. X: Now look, and when he is out of sorts he stamps with his foot like this. "What!...Those servants, they'll never learn how to make coffee! Goodness! Now those **morons** haven't clipped the lamp wick properly." And then there's a **draught** from the floor and his feet freeze: "Blast it, how cold it is, and these **unspeakable** idiots can't keep the fire going." (*Rubs one slipper's sole against the other's upper.*)

This play was written before electricity was used for lights. A daily duty for a house servant was to trim the *wicks* in the oil-burning lamps. The wicks were tightly woven fibers that drew the fuel to the flame. A neatly trimmed wick ensured a steady light

(*Mlle. Y bursts out laughing.*)

MME. X: And then he comes home and has to search for his slippers, which Marie has put under the **chiffonier** ...Oh, but it is sinful to sit thus and make a fool of one's old man. Whatever he is, he is nice, a decent little fellow—you ought to've had such a husband, Amelie.—Why are you laughing! Why? Why?—And look here, I know he is faithful to me; yes, I do know that, for he told me himself . . . What are you grinning at?...When I was on my Norway tour, that nasty Frédérique came and tried to seduce him—Could you imagine such an infamy? (*Pause.*) But I'd have

chiffonier a high chest of drawers, often with a mirror

moron a remarkably stupid person

unspeakable too bad to be described

draught (Amer. draft) a current of air

E Mlle. Y acts as if she really doesn't care much about whatever Mme. X says or does.

F ASK Critical Thinking Do you think Mlle. Y has ever met Mme. X's husband, Bob? (Probably. Mme. X remarks that Mlle. Y has "never seen him in his slippers," indicating that she has seen him, but in more formal attire.)

Viewing the Art

Draw students' attention to the quilt pictured on this page. It is *Tulips in a Vase,* a cotton quilt by Mrs. Elizabeth Loehr. Encourage discussion of quilts as an art form, pointing out that in past times women's creativity was often channeled to practical things for the home.

ASK Why do you think this quilt was chosen to illustrate this page? (Perhaps because the quilt is an example of handwork depicting tulips, something mentioned in the text.) You may wish to point out that tulips and rosmaling are typical folk art motifs and styles in Sweden and elsewhere.

Environmental Connection

Before electricity, oil and coal were used for heat and light, and coal was also used extensively in industry. Air pollution, though not regularly acknowledged as such, was a serious problem both inside homes and factories and in the air outside. Suggest that students find out more about the impact of electricity on everyday life and whether it solved the problem of air pollution.

Discussion Questions

A The author may be giving the direction as an indication that Mme. X is thinking something through, and perhaps is coming to a conclusion that she may, after all, know why she and Mlle. Y seem always to be at loggerheads with each other.

B ASK Critical Thinking What do you think might have happened in the past between these two women? (It seems they were both in the theater and met each other socially as well. Apparently Mme. X feels somewhat guilty for something she did that brought Mlle. Y some problems with staying in the theater.)

Diversity Connection

Through the beginning of the twentieth century, it was common for upper-middle-class as well as upper-class people to have servants in their homes. The servants were usually people from lower-class homes who were relatively uneducated. This type of lifestyle has essentially disappeared. In the story, Mme. X's husband is described as being very critical of his servants' performance.

Encourage students to discuss what it must have been like to live in a house and be a servant expected to carry out such duties and be treated in this way. Extend the discussion to include what it might be like to live in a house when you were a family member who enjoyed the service of servants who carried out all household tasks.

scratched out her eyes if she'd come near me after my return! (*Pause.*) What a good thing Bob told me about it himself rather than let me hear it through gossip! (*Pause.*) But Frédérique was not the only one, believe me! I don't know why, but the women are positively crazy about my husband—perhaps they think he has some say about theater engagements because he is in the government department!—Who knows but you yourself may have been chasing him!—I never trusted you more than just so much—but now I do know he doesn't care for you, and I always thought you were bearing him some grudge.

(*Pause. They view each other, both embarrassed.*)

A

Rallentando is an Italian musical term meaning a gradually decreasing tempo or speed. It is used here as a stage direction. It tells the character to speak the rest of the line more slowly. Why does the author give this direction?

MME. X: Come to see us in the evening, Amelie, and show you aren't cross with us, at least not with me! I don't know why, but it is so uncomfortable to be **at loggerheads** with you, of all people. Possibly because I got in your way that time—(*rallentando*) or—I just don't know why in particular!

B

(*Pause. Mlle. Y gazes curiously at Mme. X.*)

MME. X: (***pensively***) Our acquaintance was such an odd one—when I first saw you I was afraid of you, so afraid that I couldn't risk letting you out of my sight; whenever I came or went I was always near you—I couldn't afford to have you for an enemy, so I became your friend. But there was always something **discordant** in the air when you came to our home, for I saw my husband couldn't stand you—it all felt somehow awkward, like ill-fitting clothes—and I did what I could to make him take to you but to no purpose—until you got yourself engaged to be married! Then a **violent** friendship flared up so that for a moment it looked as though the two of you had only now ventured to show your real

at loggerheads an expression meaning "quarreling"

discordant unpleasant; disturbing

pensively in a sadly thoughtful way

violent intense

270 *Unit 3 Drama*

feelings because you were safe—and so what?—What happened?—I wasn't jealous—how queer!—And I recall the **christening** when you stood godmother to our baby—I made Bob kiss you—and he did, but you were so confused—that is to say, I didn't notice at the time—haven't thought about it since—not once until—this moment. (*Gets up furiously.*)

Why are you silent? You haven't said a word all this time, you've only let me sit and talk. You've been sitting and staring and making me unwind all these thoughts which lay like raw silk in their cocoon—thoughts—maybe suspicious ones—let me see.—Why did you break off your engagement? Why haven't you been to our house since that happened? Why aren't you coming to see us tonight?

Silkworms spin raw silk threads into a *cocoon* about their bodies. Unraveling a cocoon is a difficult, time-consuming task. Mme. X is finding it difficult to unravel her thoughts.

(*Mlle. Y seems on the point of speaking.*)

MME. X: Be quiet! You needn't say a word, for now I grasp it all myself. It was because—because—because!—Yes indeed!—Every bit of it falls into its place! That's it!—Shame! Shame! I won't sit at the same table with you. (*Moves her things to the other table.*) **C** **D**

So that was why I had to embroider tulips on his slippers although I hate tulips—because you like them! That was why—(*throws the slippers on the floor*)—that was why we had to spend the summer on Lake Mälar—because you couldn't bear the sea at Saltsiö; that was why my son had to be christened Eskil—because such was the name of your father; that was why I had to wear your colors, read your authors, eat your favorite dishes, drink your drinks—your chocolate, for example; that was why—Oh, my God—this is frightful to think of, frightful!—Everything came from you to me, even your **passions** and

Lake Mälar is near Stockholm, Sweden. It is a popular resort area.

christening a ceremony for naming and baptizing a child

passion a strong feeling for or about something

C ASK Comprehension What is happening to Mme. X as she talks here? (She is gradually coming to realize something as she talks about Mlle. Y and her husband.)

D ASK Comprehension By the time Mme. X gets to the part of her speech at the bottom of this page, what has she figured out? (That there has been some sort of love affair between her own husband and Mlle. Y, and that Mlle. Y has had a great influence on Mme. X's husband.)

Cross-Curricular Connection

Science The production of silk thread has been carried out in the same way for centuries. The silkworm is actually the caterpillar, or larva of a moth called *Bombyx mori.* These moths are carefully cultivated by silk farmers.

Ask students to do some research to discover more about the process of producing silk, from the laying of the eggs that become the silkworms to the production of silk cloth. They may also be interested in the history of silk making, which may have begun as long as 4000 years ago in China.

Discussion Questions

A ASK Literary Element What simile does the author use to describe how Mlle. Y's soul slithered into Mme. X's? What other similes does the author use? Why do you think writers use similes? ("Your soul slithered into mine like a worm into an apple." The author uses many other similes including "you lay like a snake ...," and "you lay like an enormous crab." Writers use similes to make an idea clear or simply to use poetic language.)

B ASK Critical Thinking How has Mme. X's mood changed since she first entered the café? (Then she seemed calm and superior to Mlle. Y and somewhat sorry for Mlle. Y. Now she is angry and deeply disturbed as her own thoughts have brought her to some painful realizations about the role of Mlle. Y in her life.)

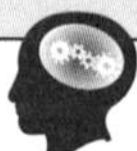

Comprehension

Inference Point out to students that often writers do not give detailed information to describe what a person, place, or event is like. They do, however, provide small pieces of information that provide clues that readers can use to make inferences.

Throughout the play *The Stronger,* Mme. X delivers a monologue in which she is speaking to a character seen but not heard. What Mlle. Y is feeling and thinking can only be inferred by the reader through Mme. X's reactions to her and stage directions. Ask students to write a short character sketch of Mlle. Y based on inferences drawn from the clues given in the play. Encourage students to share their sketches with the class and discuss what clues they used to make their inferences.

A addictions!—Your soul **slithered** into mine like a worm into an apple, eating and eating, digging and digging, until all that was left was a **rind** with some black, messy substance inside! I wanted to escape from you but couldn't; you lay like a snake **bewitching** me with your black eyes—I felt how my wings rose only to drag me down; I lay with tied feet in the water, and the harder my hands struck out, the more I worked myself down, down right to the bottom where you lay like an enormous crab in order to grip me with your claws—and this is where I now am.

B Shame, shame! How I hate you, how I hate you, how I hate you! Yet you only sit, silent, calm, uncaring; not caring whether the moon is waxing or waning, whether it is Christmas or New Year's, whether people are happy or unhappy; incapable of love or hatred; rigid like a stork over a mousehole—unable to grab your quarry, unable to chase it, yet well able to wait until it comes into your clutches. Here you sit in your corner—do you know that it is because of you that it's called the Rat-trap?—Here you scan your paper to find out whether anybody has got into trouble or is **wretched** or must give up the theater; here you sit, watching out for victims, calculating your chances like a **pilot** planning a shipwreck, and collecting your tribute!

Poor Amelie, do you know that I pity you because you are unhappy, unhappy like a hurt beast and full of **malice** because you are hurt?—I can't feel angry with you although I would like to—you are the cornered one after all—well yes, that affair with Bob, why

When the moon is *waxing,* it is growing gradually larger. When the moon is *waning,* it is becoming gradually smaller.

When Mme. X says Mlle. Y is like a *stork,* she's using a *simile.* A simile is a figure of speech that makes a comparison using *like* or *as.*

bewitch to fascinate
malice ill will
pilot a person who steers a ship
rind the outer skin or coating of a thing
slither to move along by gliding, as a snake
wretched miserable; very unhappy

should I bother about it?—In what way does it harm me?—And whether it was you or somebody else who taught me to drink chocolate, what of it? (*Drinks a spoonful from her cup; knowingly*) After all, chocolate is good for one's health. And if I learned from you how to dress—*tant mieux*—that only strengthened my husband's affection for me—and so you lost what I won—Yes, there are indications that you really have lost him. Yet of course, you intended me to fade out of the picture—as you have done, sitting here as you do and regretting what you did—but look here, I just won't do it!—We **shan't** be **petty**, don't you agree? And why should I take only what no one else wants!

Tant mieux is a French expression meaning "so much the better."

Perhaps, all things considered, I may indeed be the stronger—for you never got anything out of me, you only gave—and now I am like that thief—as you woke up you found I had all the things you missed. **C**

How else could it come about that everything turned worthless and barren in your hand? With all your tulips and fine **affections** you never managed to keep a man's love—as I have done; you never learned the art of living from your writers, as I did; nor did you ever get any little Eskil of your own, even though Eskil is the name of your father!

And why are you always silent, silent, silent? Yes, I mistook this for strength; but perhaps all it meant was that you hadn't anything to say—that you never were able to think a thought. (*Gets up and takes the slippers from the floor*) Now I'm going home—with the tulips—*your* tulips! You were unable to learn anything from people—unable to bend—and so you snapped like a dry stalk—but I won't snap. **D**

Thanks ever so much, Amelie, for all your kind lessons; thanks for teaching my husband how to love! Now I'm going home to love him. (*Goes.*)

affections emotions or feelings | **petty** mean; small | **shan't** a short form of shall not

C ASK Critical Thinking Mme. X identifies herself as the stronger of the two women. Do you agree that she is? (Answers may vary; some argument could be made for either woman to be the stronger in their relationship, both past and present. Make sure students can support their opinions with evidence from the play.)

D ASK Literary Element Why do you think the author has Mlle. Y in the play at all without letting her speak? (It may be that it is her very presence that prompts Mme. X to go through her own analysis of the situation of their relationship.)

G Grammar

Use of Dashes Point out to students that Mme. X's monologue, particularly on this page, is peppered with dashes. Explain that a dash indicates a break or pause in a sentence. It may be used instead of a colon or parenthesis. When used as parentheses are, dashes appear in pairs to set off an "aside," or thought that interrupts the main thought of the sentence. As with Mme. X's speech, dashes are often used to indicate a speaker's hesitation or change of thought. Have a volunteer read the second paragraph aloud twice—the first time pausing at the dashes and the second time not pausing. Discuss how the dash provides a dramatic pause that enhances the monologue.

Encourage students to work in small groups to write dialogue for a short scene. Have them include dashes to indicate a comment that is an aside, a hesitation in speech, or a change in thought.

Reviewing the Selection

Answer Key

Comprehension: Identifying Facts

1. The play is set in a small café, probably in the late 1800s.

2. The three characters are Mme. X, Mlle. Y, and the waitress.

3. The waitress and Mlle. Y never speak.

4. Mme. X is drinking hot chocolate.

5. Mlle. Y spent last Christmas in the country with her fiancé's parents.

6. Mme. X has a doll and a pop gun in her basket; they are for her children.

7. Mme. X has embroidered tulips on her husband's slippers because he insisted—and later Mme. X realizes that was because Mlle. Y. loves tulips.

8. Apparently Mlle. Y's plans to marry have fallen through.

9. Mlle. Y is the godmother.

10. Mme. X gets up from her table and moves her things to another table. She is very angry at Mlle. Y at that point and wants to get away from her.

Comprehension: Understanding Main Ideas

11. They seem to think that because he is in government service he has some control over the theater.

12. It seemed to Mme. X that Mlle. Y and Mme. X's husband behaved very awkwardly. Mme. X felt it was because they could not stand each other.

13. Mme. X's husband seemed to develop a friendship with Mlle. Y.

14. Some of the many things Mme. X has done to please her husband include embroidering tulips on his slippers, spending the summer where Mlle. Y wanted to be, naming her son after Mlle. Y's father, wearing colors that Mlle. Y liked, and so on.

15. These actions pleased him because they were exactly what Mlle. Y liked.

16. Mme. X compares Mlle. Y to a worm, a snake, a crab, and a stork.

17. Such comparisons help us realize that Mme. X thinks Mlle. Y is a very slimy, unpleasant person, because that is how most of us feel about these animals.

REVIEWING the SELECTION

The Stronger

August Strindberg

Directions Write the answers to these questions using complete sentences.

Comprehension: Identifying Facts

1. What is the setting of the play? Remember that setting includes both time and place.
2. Who are the three characters?
3. Which two of the actors never speak?
4. What is Mme. X drinking?
5. Where did Mlle. Y spend last Christmas?
6. What gifts does Mme. X have in her basket? Who are they for?
7. What has Mme. X embroidered on her husband's slippers? Why?
8. What has happened to Mlle. Y's plans to marry?
9. Who is the godmother for Mme. X's son?
10. A stage direction near the middle of the play tells Mme. X to move. Why does she move? Where does she move to?

Comprehension: Understanding Main Ideas

11. Why are other actresses attracted to Mme. X's husband?
12. Why was Mme. X once uneasy when Mlle. Y visited her home? How did she explain it at the time?
13. How did the behavior of Mme. X's husband change when Mlle. Y got engaged?
14. Mme. X has done a number of things to please her husband. List them.
15. Why did these actions please him?
16. Mme. X compares Mlle. Y to several living creatures. List them.
17. Do these comparisons help you understand how Mme. X feels about Mlle. Y? How?
18. How does Mlle. Y react to Mme. X's accusations?
19. Mme. X says the café is called the Rat-trap because of Mlle. Y. What does she mean?
20. What does Mme. X decide to do?

18. Mlle. Y does not seem to react at all to the accusations.

19. She means that because Mlle. Y spends a lot of time there, she is perhaps trapping other people as well as Mme. X.

20. Mme. X decides to go home to her husband, to be a good wife, and to enjoy her life.

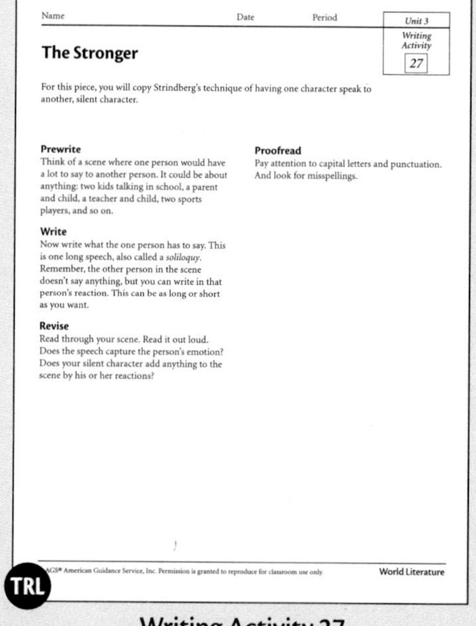

Name Date Period | *Unit 3* *Writing Activity* *27*

The Stronger

For this piece, you will copy Strindberg's technique of having one character speak to another, silent character.

Prewrite
Think of a scene where one person would have a lot to say to another person. It could be about anything: two kids talking in school, a parent and child, a teacher and child, two sports players, and so on.

Write
Now write what the one person has to say. This is one long speech, also called a *soliloquy*. Remember, the other person in the scene doesn't say anything, but you can write in that person's reaction. This can be as long or short as you want.

Revise
Read through your scene. Read it out loud. Does the speech capture the person's emotion? Does your silent character add anything to the scene by his or her reactions?

Proofread
Pay attention to capital letters and punctuation. And look for misspellings.

 World Literature

TRL

Writing Activity 27

Understanding Literature: Expressionistic Drama

The Stronger is an example of expressionistic drama. An expressionistic drama is a play that seems realistic but that changes some elements for dramatic effect. Strindberg, the author of this play, was one of the first playwrights to write in this style. In this play, he uses characters in a new way.

21. What is unusual about the characters' names?
22. Why does Strindberg use these names?
23. What is unusual about the dialogue in the play?
24. Why do you think Strindberg has only one character speak?
25. Think about the title. Who is, finally, the stronger? Explain.

Critical Thinking

26. What do you know about Mme. X's husband?
27. What do you know about Mme. X's marriage?
28. What do you think happened between Mlle. Y and Mme. X's husband?
29. Do you think Mme. X's imagination has run wild? Why or why not?
30. How do you think Mme. X will act when she gets home? Why?

Writing on Your Own Imagine that you are Mlle. Y. Reread the part of the play just before the stage direction, "Mlle. Y seems on the point of speaking." Why does she decide not to speak? What thoughts are in her mind? Write your response.

Name Date Period

Unit 3 *Selection Quiz* 25

The Stronger

Directions Read the following statements. Circle the letter of the answer that correctly completes each sentence or that correctly answers each question.

1. *The Stronger* takes place on
   a. Christmas Day. **b.** Thanksgiving. **c.** Christmas Eve. **d.** New Year's.
2. Mlle. Y is drinking
   a. wine. **b.** beer. **c.** coffee. **d.** tea.
3. When Mme. X refers to her "piglets" she means her
   a. sisters. **b.** dogs. **c.** barnyard friends. **d.** children.
4. Mme. X's husband loves __________. Mme. X hates them.
   a. pickles **b.** daisies **c.** tulips **d.** roses
5. Who tried to seduce Mme. X's husband?
   a. Amy **b.** Frédérique **c.** Genviève **d.** Susanne
6. Mme. X recalls when Mlle. Y kissed X's husband at
   a. her baby's christening. **b.** the mall.
   c. their wedding. **d.** Christmas dinner.
7. Mme. X realizes that her son is named after Mlle. Y's
   a. son. **b.** father. **c.** brother. **d.** uncle.
8. Mme. X compares Mlle. Y to a _________ gripping with her claws.
   a. lobster **b.** monster **c.** crayfish **d.** crab
9. Mme. X ends up __________ Mlle. Y.
   a. pitying **b.** hitting **c.** killing **d.** whipping
10. Mme. X thanks Mlle. Y for
    a. the hot chocolate. **b.** teaching her husband how to love.
    c. teaching her husband how to dress. **d.** for speaking so much.

 World Literature

TRL

Selection Quiz 25

Selection Quiz

The Teacher's Resource Library includes a Selection Quiz for *The Stronger* that may be given following the Selection Review.

Understanding Literature: Expressionistic Drama

21. It is unusual that the characters do not have realistic names, but are rather known by anonymous letters *X* and *Y*.

22. He may have used these names to indicate that the two characters could be any two women.

23. It is unusual that there really is no dialogue—instead the play is a monologue, with all the words being spoken by one person.

24. He probably has only one person speak because he is showing the development of the one character, spurred by the other.

25. Answers may vary. Most students may feel that Mme. X is really the stronger, since she survives the emotional war over her husband and seems committed to pursuing her relationship with him, while Mlle. Y ends up without him. Others may feel that Mlle. Y is the stronger because she had such deep influence over the life of Mme. X.

Critical Thinking

26. He works in a government office, has had many women try to seduce him, has had an affair with Mlle. Y, and has allowed her to influence his life with his wife.

27. Her marriage has had its difficulties, particularly with her husband's affair with Mlle. Y and that woman's influence over him. However, she is relatively happy and has two children. And her marriage seems to be lasting.

28. They had a love affair.

29. Most students will think that Mme. X has really stumbled on the truth as she was thinking this through rather than letting her imagination run wild.

30. Mme. X will probably act like a happy wife when she gets home, because she has realized that despite the painful affair her husband had with Mlle. Y, Mme. X is still married and happy with her husband.

Writing on Your Own Point out that the stage direction is on page 271. Suggest that students consider what they know from the whole play as they think about why Mlle. Y chose not to speak here.

Skills Lesson: Characterization

This Skills Lesson focuses on the ways a playwright shows the audience the personality of a play's characters.

Review Answers

1. Plays begin with a physical description of the characters for two reasons: first, if readers are going to perform in the play, they need to know the playwright's vision of the type of person for each character, and, secondly, someone who is merely reading the play should have a mental picture of the character as the playwright envisioned him or her.

2. Willie's manner of speech reveals that he is a follower, especially of Sam.

3. Mlle. Y's behavior reveals that she is a person of little conscience.

4. Mme. X's dialogue reveals that she has been complacent but suddenly realizes something painful about her life that she decides to rise above.

5. Answers will vary. Make sure students can defend their ideas with evidence from the plays.

Writing on Your Own Students who have difficulty writing may benefit from working with others who have chosen the same character. Allow the small groups to brainstorm about the character before they write their own paragraphs individually.

Skills Lesson Characterization

Characterization is the way a writer develops characters by revealing their personality traits. In a play, physical descriptions help reveal characters. What characters say and do shows still more about them. What others say about them adds to the characterization. And how others react to them reveals still more.

When we first see a character, we develop an idea about who he or she is. This is based simply on how the actor looks and moves. We learn more about the character as we listen to dialogue. We begin to form an opinion about the person based on what we hear. These are external clues. They are things we can see and hear. Playwrights use such external clues to reveal what the internal person is really like.

For example, in *Macbeth,* Shakespeare shows little by little that Macbeth is going mad. As Macbeth is planning how to murder King Duncan, he sees a vision of a blood-stained dagger hanging in midair. It points toward Duncan's sleeping chamber. After the murder of Banquo, Macbeth sees and talks to his ghost. At the end of that same scene, Macbeth tells us he has spies in the homes of noblemen. He's now afraid to trust anyone. He wants the advice of the Weird Sisters. He believes they can foretell the future. Shakespeare shows us through Macbeth's words and actions that he is gradually losing his mind.

Review

1. Why do you think most plays begin with a physical description of the characters?
2. In *"Master Harold"...and the Boys,* what does Willie's manner of speech reveal about him?
3. In "*The Stronger,*" what does Mlle. Y's behavior reveal about her?
4. What does Mme. X's dialogue reveal about her?
5. Who is the least likable character in the plays in this unit? Why?

Writing on Your Own Choose one of the characters from the plays in this unit. Write one paragraph describing the character. Be sure to answer these questions. How does the person look, move, and speak? How does the person behave toward others? How do others react to this person?

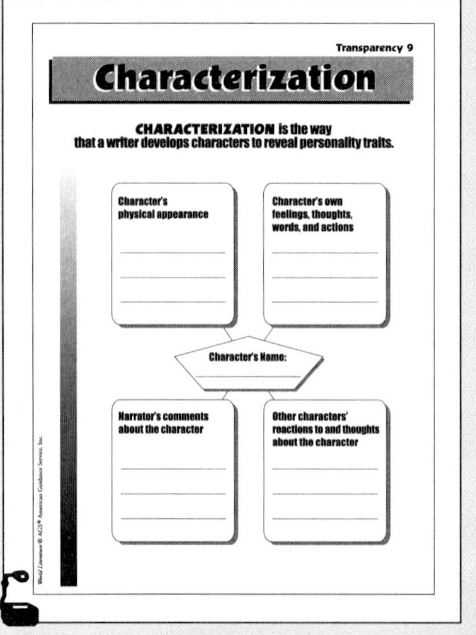

Transparency 9

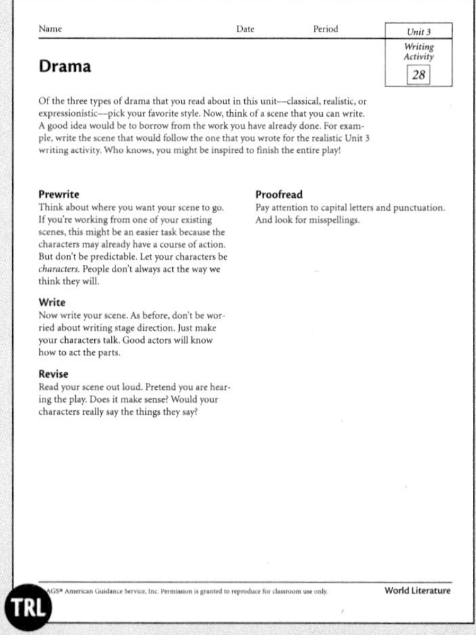

Name Date Period

Unit 3 Writing Activity 28

Drama

Of the three types of drama that you read about in this unit—classical, realistic, or expressionistic—pick your favorite style. Now, think of a scene that you can write. A good idea would be to borrow from the work you have already done. For example, write the scene that would follow the one that you wrote for the realistic Unit 3 writing activity. Who knows, you might be inspired to finish the entire play!

Prewrite
Think about where you want your scene to go. If you're working from one of your existing scenes, this might be an easier task because the characters may already have a course of action. But don't be predictable. Let your characters be *characters.* People don't always act the way we think they will.

Write
Now write your scene. As before, don't be worried about writing stage direction. Just make your characters talk. Good actors will know how to act the parts.

Revise
Read your scene out loud. Pretend you are hearing the play. Does it make sense? Would your characters really say the things they say?

Proofread
Pay attention to capital letters and punctuation. And look for misspellings.

 World Literature

TRL

Writing Activity 28

UNIT 3 SUMMARY

In Unit 3 you read three types of plays. Shakespeare's *Macbeth* is called a classical drama. Fugard's *"Master Harold"...and the Boys* is a realistic play. Strindberg's *The Stronger* is an expressionistic drama.

These different types of plays have much in common with each other. For instance, each of the playwrights describes a setting. They tell us when and where a play takes place. All plays have stage directions. Actors follow these directions to know when and how to speak and move. Characters, the people in a story, are essential in a play. So is dialogue, the conversations between the characters. Playwrights use more than just words to tell a story. They skillfully bring together setting, stage directions, characters, and dialogue.

Playwrights use these elements differently depending on the type of play they're writing. For example, the dialogue in classical drama is written in blank verse. The dialogue in a realistic play or expressionistic drama is written in everyday language. The settings of classical dramas are sometimes places where you'd find royalty and nobility. Or they may be imaginary places from myths and legends. In contrast, the settings for realistic plays are ordinary, real life places. In expressionistic drama, one of these elements may be changed or exaggerated for a special effect. In realistic drama, each element is carefully used to create a story just as it might have happened in real life.

Selections

- *Macbeth* by William Shakespeare. In one of Shakespeare's best-known plays, Macbeth commits murder to become king but must struggle against guilt and his opponents.
- *"Master Harold"...and the Boys* by Athol Fugard. The attitudes of apartheid threaten the friendship between a white boy and the black man who is like a father to him.
- *The Stronger* by August Strindberg. In a play in which only one character speaks, Strindberg explores the inner thoughts of Mme. X as she realizes something about her marriage.

Unit Summary

Have students read page 277 and recall that *Macbeth* is an example of a classical drama, *"Master Harold" ... and the Boys* is a realistic drama, and *The Stronger* is an example of an expressionistic drama.

ASK What are some reasons we know that *Macbeth* is a classical drama? (It is written in blank verse and is about royal people.)

ASK What identifies *"Master Harold"... and the Boys* as realistic drama? (Its dialogue and characters seem true to life; the people speak and act as real people would.)

ASK How do you know that *The Stronger* is expressionistic drama? (Although it seems to be about realistic people, it is very unrealistic that one of the characters would never speak. Such exaggeration for effect is typical of expressionistic drama.)

Name Date Period Unit 3 *Activity* 42 *page 1*

Unit Review

Part A Directions Write a short answer for each item on the blank lines.

1. What are some of the limitations of settings in plays?
2. Name one of the two types of drama.
3. How have the characters changed from Shakespeare's time to modern drama?
4. What one characteristic most separates expressionistic drama from classical and realistic drama?
5. Name one of the four common elements playwrights use in all forms of drama.

Part B Directions Read each sentence. Write *T* if the statement is true or *F* if it is false.

_______ 1. *"Master Harold" . . . and the Boys* is about the principal of a boys' college.
_______ 2. Characterization is the term for the words spoken in a play.
_______ 3. The main character in *Macbeth* sees a bloody ax floating in front of him.
_______ 4. Action in *The Stronger* takes place on Yom Kippur.
_______ 5. In all three plays the setting has something to do with food being served.

 World Literature

TRL

Activity 42, pages 1–2

Name Date Period Unit 3 *Workbook* 42 *page 1*

Unit Review

Part A Directions In each blank write the word or phrase from the Word Bank that best completes each sentence.

1. Characterization reveals _______ traits about each character.
2. _______ descriptions also help reveal characters.
3. Things the reader can see and hear about a character are called _______.
4. In _______ the main character is slowly going mad.
5. Dialogue in classical drama is written in _______.
6. _______ language is used in expressionistic drama.
7. A setting in a classical drama may be an _______ place from myths or legends.
8. _______ drama carefully selects each element to create a story as if it was real life.
9. In *"Master Harold"* the attitudes of _______ are critical to the story.
10. Only one character speaks in the play _______.

Word Bank	
apartheid	blank verse
Everyday	external clues
imaginary	*Macbeth*
personality	Physical
Realistic	*The Stronger*

 World Literature

TRL

Workbook 42, pages 1–2

The Teacher's Resource Library includes two parallel forms of the Unit 3 Mastery Test. The difficulty level of the two forms is equivalent. You may wish to use one form as a pretest and the other form as a posttest.

Midterm Mastery Test

The Teacher's Resource Library includes the Midterm Mastery Test. This test is pictured on page 465 of the Teacher's Edition. The Midterm Mastery Test assesses the major learning objectives for Units 1 through 3.

Answer Key

Comprehension: Identifying Facts

1. Banquo is murdered in *Macbeth.*

2. The play is set in South Africa in 1950.

3. The words the characters in a play say are called dialogue.

4. The ghost of Banquo is a character in *Macbeth.*

5. Shakespeare wrote *Macbeth* about 400 years ago.

Comprehension: Understanding Main Ideas

6. Classical drama is written in blank verse, has five acts divided into scenes, and is about royalty or other important people.

7. *"Master Harold"... and the Boys* focuses on apartheid and its effects.

8. He sees a vision of a dagger pointing toward Duncan's room, and he sees the ghost of Banquo. Both visions indicate that Macbeth is so tormented by guilt that he is slowly going mad.

9. Sam is fond of Hally because he has watched him grow up and has helped him by acting fatherly toward him.

10. Mlle. Y thinks Mme. X is being silly to think this way about a home, in part because Mlle. Y does not have a home and has, in fact, disrupted the home through an affair with Mme X's husband.

Understanding Literature: Setting

11. Props would include the costumes of the royal couple and their guests, the table set for the banquet, chairs for the table, some evidence of food and drink with plates and goblets, and so on.

12. A café is a public place, where characters can meet.

13. *Macbeth* must be set in a certain period because it is written about that period of history. *"Master Harold"... and the Boys* must be set in the time when apartheid was still the rule of the land in South Africa.

14. The interaction between the characters may be timeless, although certain aspects of their lives belong to a certain time.

UNIT 3 REVIEW

Directions Write the answers to these questions using complete sentences.

Comprehension Identifying Facts

1. Who is murdered in one of the plays? In which play?
2. What country is the setting for *"Master Harold"...and the Boys*? What year is it set in?
3. What is the term for the words the characters in a play say?
4. Which play has a ghost as a character?
5. How long ago did Shakespeare write *Macbeth*?

Comprehension: Understanding Main Ideas

6. What is a classical drama? List at least three elements.
7. What play focuses on apartheid and its effects?
8. Macbeth sees two visions. What are they? What do they mean?
9. Why is Sam so fond of Hally?
10. When Mme. X. says "a home is the best of all things," Mlle. Y looks contemptuous? Why?

Understanding Literature: Setting

The setting—the time and place—in a play is very different from the setting in a story. In a story, the setting can be anything a writer can imagine and describe with words. The setting in a play, though, is limited to what can be shown or represented on a stage. The stage sets in Shakespeare's day were small and quite simple. The audience had to imagine things such as battles. Stage sets now can be much more elaborate and creative. Still, a playwright must tell the story within the limits of a stage.

11. The objects on stage in a play are called "properties," or "props." What props are needed for the stage setting in the scene from *Macbeth*? Remember to include costumes, too.
12. Two of the plays have similar settings—a café or a restaurant. Why does a café make a good setting?
13. Two of the plays must be set in a certain period of time. Which ones? Why?
14. Strindberg sets his play on Christmas Eve. However, he doesn't name a year. Is the play timeless? Why?

15. Which playwright provides the most details about the setting? How does this contribute to your understanding and enjoyment of the play?

Critical Thinking

16. Do you think Fugard used *"Master Harold"...and the Boys* to show his attitude toward apartheid? How?
17. Although you read these plays, they were written to be performed. How would your experience be different if you were in a theater audience?
18. Why do you think Shakespeare continues to be popular with audiences?
19. What do realistic drama and expressionistic drama have in common?
20. Identify the play in the unit you liked best. Explain the reasons for your choice.

Speak and Listen

Choose a short segment of dialogue between two characters from Shakespeare's original of *Macbeth*. Work with a partner. Read the dialogue aloud. Practice putting the emphasis on certain words to convey meaning. Refer to the paraphrase. It will help you understand the passage. Present the scene to the class.

Beyond Words

Plays are often advertised on playbills or small posters. Design and produce a playbill for one of the plays that includes the name of the play and the playwright. Suppose that the play is being done by your school's drama club. Use a drawing or graphic to draw attention to the poster.

Writing on Your Own Newspapers and magazines publish reviews of play performances. These reviews are written by theater critics who have seen the play. The reviews are their opinions about the play's dialogue, the actors' work, and the stage sets. Imagine that you've just seen a production of one of the plays in this unit. Choose one of the above topics and write a review about it. Tell your opinion.

Test-Taking Tip

Studying together in small groups and asking questions of one another is one way to review material for tests.

15. Shakespeare provides many details about the setting of his plays, and *Macbeth* is no exception. The details help the reader understand the impact of the time and place on the people and the action.

Critical Thinking

16. Fugard clearly used the play to show how horrible he thinks apartheid is. He shows how a white boy becomes nasty, for example, as he grows up to realize that in the view of apartheid he is superior to his old black friends.

17. Answers may vary, but students should realize that hearing the words and watching real people say them and interact with each other is a very different experience from reading.

18. Shakespeare's stories are timeless, his insights into people are universal, and his language is poetry.

19. They both involve people who are like real, ordinary people, involved in ordinary situations.

20. Answers will vary, but students should defend their choices with logical reasons.

Speak and Listen

Remind students that they should not pause at the end of a line of blank verse unless it shows by use of punctuation that a pause is required. Despite the unfamiliarity of the words, they should strive to make the dialogue sound as realistic as possible.

Beyond Words

If possible, display several playbills that you or colleagues have collected. Have students identify the copy on the playbill samples as well as their graphics.

Writing on Your Own Before students write their reviews, you may want to provide them with several examples from local newspapers or from national newsmagazines as models. Point out that a review needs to tell readers something about the play other than just the reviewer's opinion.

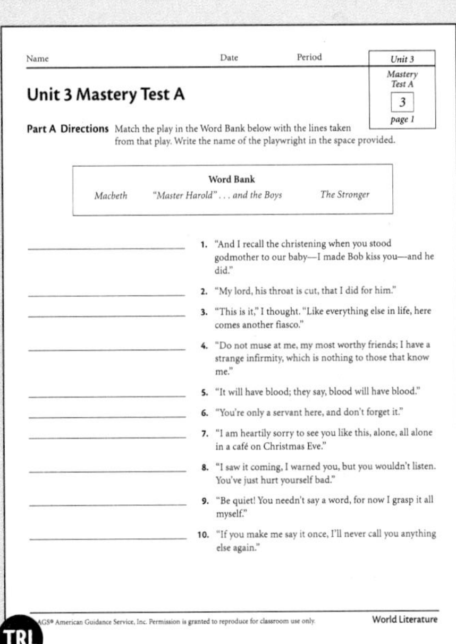

Name Date Period | *Unit 3* *Mastery Test A* 3 *page 1*

Unit 3 Mastery Test A

Part A Directions Match the play in the Word Bank below with the lines taken from that play. Write the name of the playwright in the space provided.

Word Bank
Macbeth *"Master Harold" . . . and the Boys* *The Stronger*

1. "And I recall the christening when you stood godmother to our baby—I made Bob kiss you—and he did."
2. "My lord, his throat is cut, that I did for him."
3. "This is it," I thought. "Like everything else in life, here comes another fiasco."
4. "Do not muse at me, my most worthy friends; I have a strange infirmity, which is nothing to those that know me."
5. "It will have blood; they say, blood will have blood."
6. "You're only a servant here, and don't forget it."
7. "I am heartily sorry to see you like this, alone, all alone in a café on Christmas Eve."
8. "I saw it coming, I warned you, but you wouldn't listen. You've just hurt yourself bad."
9. "Be quiet! You needn't say a word, for now I grasp it all myself."
10. "If you make me say it once, I'll never call you anything else again."

 World Literature

TRL

Unit Mastery Test A, page 1

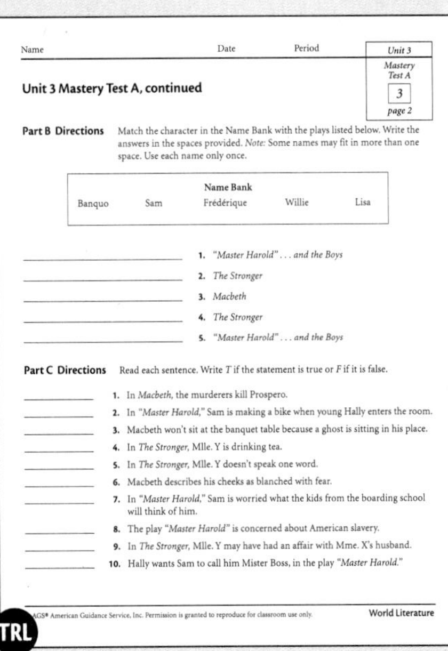

Name Date Period | *Unit 3* *Mastery Test A* 3 *page 2*

Unit 3 Mastery Test A, continued

Part B Directions Match the character in the Name Bank with the plays listed below. Write the answers in the spaces provided. *Note:* Some names may fit in more than one space. Use each name only once.

Name Bank
Banquo Sam Frédérique Willie Lisa

1. *"Master Harold" . . . and the Boys*
2. *The Stronger*
3. *Macbeth*
4. *The Stronger*
5. *"Master Harold" . . . and the Boys*

Part C Directions Read each sentence. Write *T* if the statement is true or *F* if it is false.

1. In *Macbeth*, the murderers kill Prospero.
2. In *"Master Harold,"* Sam is making a bike when young Hally enters the room.
3. Macbeth won't sit at the banquet table because a ghost is sitting in his place.
4. In *The Stronger*, Mlle. Y is drinking tea.
5. In *The Stronger*, Mlle. Y doesn't speak one word.
6. Macbeth describes his cheeks as blanched with fear.
7. In *"Master Harold,"* Sam is worried what the kids from the boarding school will think of him.
8. The play *"Master Harold"* is concerned about American slavery.
9. In *The Stronger*, Mlle. Y may have had an affair with Mme. X's husband.
10. Hally wants Sam to call him Mister Boss, in the play *"Master Harold."*

 World Literature

TRL

Unit Mastery Test A, page 2

UNIT 4 Planning Guide

Poetry

	Student Pages	About the Author	About the Selection	Literary Terms	Reviewing the Selection	Writing on Your Own
■ ISRAEL "The Diameter of the Bomb" by Yehuda Amichai	284–286	✔	✔	✔	✔	✔
■ CHINA "Taking Leave of a Friend" by Li Po	287–289	✔	✔	✔	✔	✔
■ VIETNAM "Thoughts of Hanoi" by Nguyen Thi Vinh	290–292	✔	✔	✔	✔	✔
■ PHILIPPINES "Mindoro" by Ramón Sunico	293–296	✔	✔	✔	✔	✔
■ CHILE "Ode to a Pair of Socks" by Pablo Neruda	297–300	✔	✔	✔	✔	✔
■ JAPAN Three Haiku Basho, Kikaku, and Anonymous	301–303	✔	✔	✔	✔	✔
■ WALES "Do Not Go Gentle Into That Good Night" by Dylan Thomas	304–307	✔	✔	✔	✔	✔
■ SKILLS LESSON: Style; UNIT REVIEW	308, 310–311			✔		✔

Selection Features

Unit Features

Student Text

Poetry
Skills Lesson: Style
Unit Summary

Teacher's Resource Library

Activity 43: Poetry
Workbook 43: Poetry

Assessment Features

Student Text

Unit 4 Review

Teacher's Resource Library

Activity 51: Unit 4 Review, pages 1–2
Workbook 51: Unit 4 Review, pages 1–2
Selection Quizzes 26–32
Unit 4 Mastery Tests A and B, pages 1–2

Teaching Strategies							Language Skills				Learning Styles					TRL Teacher's Resource Library					
Viewing the Art	Career Connection	Environmental Connection	Cross-Curricular Connection	Diversity Connection	Community Connection	Transparencies	Grammar	Literary Elements	Comprehension	Writing Connection	Auditory	Visual	Tactile/Kinesthetic	Group Learning	LEP/ESL	Vocabulary Workbook	Selection Glossary	Student Study Guide	Activities	Workbook	Writing Activities
			285													26	26	32	44	44	**29**
				288												26	27	33	45	45	**30**
							292			292		292				27	28	34	46	46	**31**
		294									295		295			27	29	35	47	47	**32**
					299			299							299	28	30	36	48	48	**33**
302																28	31	37	49	49	**34**
	306								306					306		28	32	38	50	50	**35**
						10													51	51	**36**

Unit at a Glance

Unit 4: Poetry

pages 280–311

Poetry
pages 282–283

Selections

- ISRAEL "The Diameter of the Bomb" by Yehuda Amichai, pages 284–286
- CHINA "Taking Leave of a Friend" by Li Po, pages 287–289
- VIETNAM "Thoughts of Hanoi" by Nguyen Thi Vinh, pages 290–292
- PHILIPPINES "Mindoro" by Ramón Sunico, pages 293-296
- CHILE "Ode to a Pair of Socks" by Pablo Neruda, pages 297–300
- JAPAN Three Haiku, pages 301–303 Basho, Kikaku, and Anonymous, page 302
- WALES "Do Not Go Gentle Into That Good Night" by Dylan Thomas, pages 304–307

Unit Skills Lesson: Style
page 308

Unit Summary page 309

Unit Review pages 310–311

Audiocassette

Transparency 10

Teacher's Resource Library TRL

- Activity 43 and 51, pages 1–2
- Workbook 43 and 51, pages 1–2
- Unit 4 Mastery Tests A and B, pages 1–2

(Answer Keys for the Teacher's Resource Library begin on page 468 of this Teacher's Edition.)

"As honey sweetens/the mouth readily/a poem should make sense/right away."
—Atakuri Molla

"To read a poem is to hear it with our eyes; to hear it is to see it with our ears."
—Octavio Paz

"There is the view that poetry should improve your life. I think people confuse it with the Salvation Army."
—John Ashbery

Other Resources

Books for Teachers

Abramson, Glenda. *The Writing of Yehuda Amichai: A Thematic Approach.* Albany, NY: State University of New York Press, 1989.

Davies, James A., ed. *A Reference Companion to Dylan Thomas.* Westport, CT: Greenwood Publishing Group, 1998.

Higginson, William J. *Haiku Handbook: How to Write, Share, and Teach Haiku.* New York: Kodansha, 1992.

Teitelboim, Volodia, and Beverly J. Delong-Tonelli (trans.). *Neruda: An Intimate Biography.* Austin: University of Texas Press, 1991.

Books for Students

Amichai, Yehuda. *The Selected Poetry of Yehuda Amichai.* Trans. Chana Bloch and Stephen Mitchell. Berkeley, CA: University of California Press, 1996.

Neruda, Pablo. *The Book of Questions.* Port Townsend, WA: Copper Canyon Press, 1991.

Thomas, Dylan. *A Child's Christmas in Wales.* New York: New Directions, 1995.

UNIT 4 *Poetry*

People who love poetry find it exciting and vivid. They like the images and emotions that are packed into a few lines. Others may find it hard to pull out the meaning of the poem. They may never read it aloud to hear the rhyme and rhythm. They may not realize that songs they love are also poetry. This unit has a variety of poems. Some will be easy to understand, others will not. It's okay for people to disagree about what a poem means. To enjoy a poem, relax. Slow down. Don't try to get all the ideas at once. Read it aloud more than once. Think about the images. Enjoy.

Video

The Japanese Way of Life. (25 minutes) Chatsworth, CA: AIMS Multimedia.

Poetry Hall of Fame: Volume 4. (60 minutes) Botsford, CT: Filmic Archives.

Yo Soy Pablo Neruda. (28 minutes) Princeton, NJ: Films for the Humanities and Sciences.

Software

Astonishing Asia. CD-ROM. Fairfield, CT: Queue, Inc.

China: Home of the Dragon. CD-ROM. Pound Ridge, NY: Orange Cherry New Media.

History and Culture of China. CD-ROM. Fairfield, CT: Queue, Inc.

Introducing the Unit

Invite volunteers to read the quotations on page 280. Have students choose one that is closest to their own attitude toward poems they have read and explain their feelings.

ASK What similarities do Molla and Paz share in their expectations of poetry? (They rely on appeal to the senses and suggest that poetry has an immediate awakening impact.)

ASK What does the comparison with honey suggest about poems? (Answers may include that the effects of "sampling" honey and poetry should be felt immediately or that poems are delightful, to be savored, and have an immediate impact.)

ASK In what sense can eyes hear and ears see? (Answers should suggest that Paz is speaking figuratively; poetry stimulates the simultaneous and heightened use of all the senses.)

ASK Which quote focuses most on the reader's expectations? (John Ashbery's)

ASK What advice do you think Ashbery would give to someone about to read his poems? (He might advise: "Relax and enjoy. Be open and let the poems talk to you, but do not expect a sermon.")

Read aloud the paragraph on page 281. Have students list some favorite songs with puzzling lyrics. Discuss different meanings the songs might have. Remind students that poems generally suggest rather than state main ideas.

Review the Unit 4 selection titles. Discuss the moods and images they bring to mind.

Viewing the Art

Night View of Saru-Hashi in Koshu is by an unknown artist. The simple lines, geometric shapes, and colors provide a serene, tranquil setting. The arch bridge, one of the oldest forms of bridges, gracefully unites the land and divides the night sky from the water below.

ASK What geometric shapes are easily distinguishable in the artwork? (circles, triangles, and rectangles)

Poetry

Ask students to silently read the text on pages 282 and 283, or have students take turns reading aloud.

Encourage students to name and recite portions of songs and poems they know that have a strong pattern of rhyme or rhythm. Discuss what these elements add to the piece. Point out that humans have a basic reaction to music. This response may be related to experience of nature, seasons, and life itself, which all have definite rhythms to their cycles. It also reflects people's joy in language and its sounds.

ASK What are some symbols that have a powerful effect on you? What do you think is the value of including symbols in poems? (Students may mention school colors, flags, religious symbols, handshakes, or many other objects or actions. They may suggest the power of symbols to communicate strong emotions and complex ideas in a single word or simple images.)

ASK What are the connotations of a word? Why are they important in a poem? (Connotations are the associations we have with a word beyond its dictionary meaning. Students may suggest that they are important because they assure that each word in a poem will have personal, emotional impact related to experiences.)

Ask students to name the types of poems with which they are familiar. Invite volunteers to further describe or share examples of sonnets, haiku, limericks, free verse, or other forms of poetry. Explain that a *villanelle* is a French verse form 19 lines long, using only two rhymes; it has five stanzas of three lines each and a final one of four lines.

Students may be familiar with the *Odyssey* and the *Iliad* as stories but not realize that they are poems. Explain that these adventure stories were written as poems partly so the singer-poet could memorize long passages more easily.

Poetry packs the most feeling into the least space. The writer of a poem is called a poet. A poet usually expresses ideas within the limits of a specific poetic form. Classical poets developed many different combinations of rhyme, rhythm, and length. Rhyme is the use of words with the same vowel and end sounds. Rhythm is the beat. It is a regular pattern of stress on certain syllables.

Good poetry proves the saying that a picture is worth a thousand words. Poets often use a carefully chosen symbol. A symbol can be a person, place, thing, or event. It stands for something else. By using a familiar symbol, the poet communicates the emotions and facts connected with it. A flying bird, for instance, may stand for freedom. In another poem, a bird may stand for fate, or doom. For years, the wall that divided Berlin was a strong symbol. It stood for cruel separation. The 1989 fall of the Berlin Wall, though, brought people back together. It meant harmony.

Word choice is important in poetry. This is because the words must fit a certain rhythm or rhyme. At the same time, it must create an image. For example, a poet might write about people walking or moving along the Berlin Wall. But the poet would be more likely to choose other words that strengthen that symbol. Look at the connotations—the images or emotion connected to words—of *boiling, bubbling,* or *surging.* They suggest moving water—many people stood in the rain and made toasts to freedom. They also suggest the disorder that large numbers of people can cause.

Poems can be divided into many different genres, or types. Early poems were usually songs to a deity. Others were epics, long stories written in verse. They were sung or chanted aloud. Gradually, other forms developed. A popular genre in English was the sonnet. It is a fourteen-line poem in iambic pentameter. It has any one of several rhyme schemes (patterns of rhyming words). Haiku is a traditional Japanese poetic form. A haiku has seventeen unrhymed syllables. Humorous subjects appear in limericks. Free verse often doesn't rhyme. Serious poets may attempt a villanelle.

Explain that iambic pentameter describes the length of lines (10 syllables) and their rhythm (every other syllable is accented). This meter is said to come closest to imitating human speech.

Poems can also be grouped by purpose. Elegies, for example, are poems that mourn someone's death. Poems may be grouped by a literary technique. Robert Browning wrote dramatic monologues. In those poems, a character reveals personality by talking to the reader. Today's poets use simpler forms. Some poets may combine several genres in new ways.

All poems use some kind of rhythmic pattern. They express an idea, impression, or emotion. In this unit, notice the wide range of forms. Look at their relationship to the idea of the poem. Also, remember that enjoying a good poem may take time and effort. Sometimes reading a poem out loud adds to your appreciation. The more you think about a good poem, the better it becomes.

The following countries are represented in this unit: Israel, China, Vietnam, the Philippines, Chile, Japan, and Wales.

ASK What other categories of "purpose" poems, besides elegies, can you name? (Answers may include odes, or poems that praise a subject, ballads, narrative poems, love poems, and awakening poems, or poems celebrating a sudden insight.)

Point out that *monologue* is related to *dialogue*. The former describes a solitary speaker; the latter, two or more people speaking to each other.

ASK What does the term *dramatic monologue* suggest about these poems? (Answers may suggest that dramatic monologues are like plays for one person, that they are suspenseful, or that they relate a conflict or story.)

Be sure students understand that a poem is more than its purpose and richer than its form. It is above everything else a means of sharing an extraordinary experience at a basic level, common to all people. A love poem written five hundred years ago is just as moving today as it was then because everyone desires to love and be loved. Poetry focuses on universal truths and values by sharing the common experiences of people.

Poetry's musical nature can best be appreciated when read aloud. Encourage students to read the poems in this unit aloud. Remind them that a poem does not reveal all its meanings and enjoyment on a first or even a second reading. Reading poetry requires patience and thought.

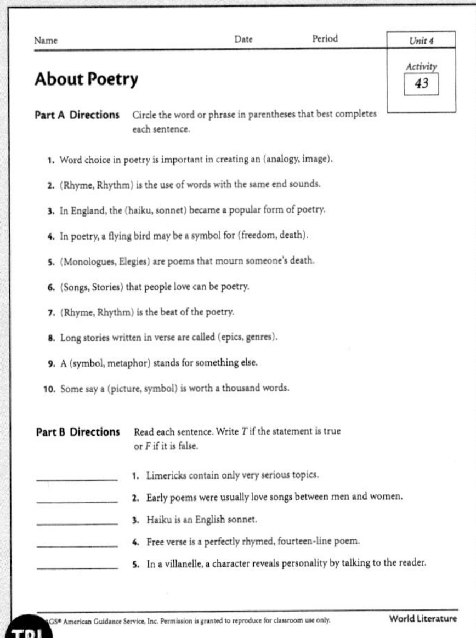

Name Date Period *Unit 4* *Activity* 43

About Poetry

Part A Directions Circle the word or phrase in parentheses that best completes each sentence.

1. Word choice in poetry is important in creating an (analogy, image).
2. (Rhyme, Rhythm) is the use of words with the same end sounds.
3. In England, the (haiku, sonnet) became a popular form of poetry.
4. In poetry, a flying bird may be a symbol for (freedom, death).
5. (Monologues, Elegies) are poems that mourn someone's death.
6. (Songs, Stories) that people love can be poetry.
7. (Rhyme, Rhythm) is the beat of the poetry.
8. Long stories written in verse are called (epics, genres).
9. A (symbol, metaphor) stands for something else.
10. Some say a (picture, symbol) is worth a thousand words.

Part B Directions Read each sentence. Write *T* if the statement is true or *F* if it is false.

_______ 1. Limericks contain only very serious topics.
_______ 2. Early poems were usually love songs between men and women.
_______ 3. Haiku is an English sonnet.
_______ 4. Free verse is a perfectly rhymed, fourteen-line poem.
_______ 5. In a villanelle, a character reveals personality by talking to the reader.

 World Literature

TRL

Activity 43

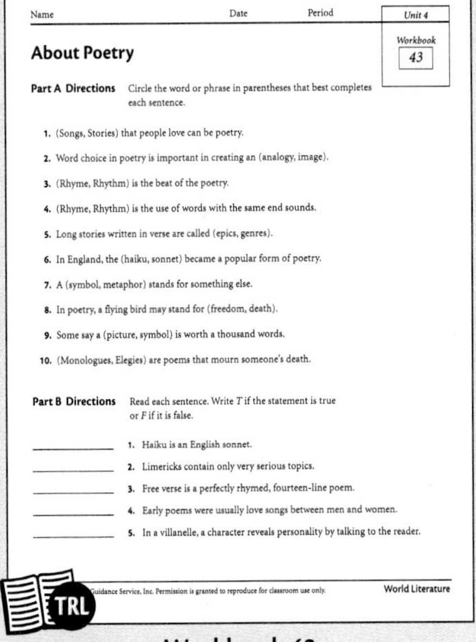

Name Date Period *Unit 4* *Workbook* 43

About Poetry

Part A Directions Circle the word or phrase in parentheses that best completes each sentence.

1. (Songs, Stories) that people love can be poetry.
2. Word choice in poetry is important in creating an (analogy, image).
3. (Rhyme, Rhythm) is the beat of the poetry.
4. (Rhyme, Rhythm) is the use of words with the same end sounds.
5. Long stories written in verse are called (epics, genres).
6. In England, the (haiku, sonnet) became a popular form of poetry.
7. A (symbol, metaphor) stands for something else.
8. In poetry, a flying bird may stand for (freedom, death).
9. Some say a (picture, symbol) is worth a thousand words.
10. (Monologues, Elegies) are poems that mourn someone's death.

Part B Directions Read each sentence. Write *T* if the statement is true or *F* if it is false.

_______ 1. Haiku is an English sonnet.
_______ 2. Limericks contain only very serious topics.
_______ 3. Free verse is a perfectly rhymed, fourteen-line poem.
_______ 4. Early poems were usually love songs between men and women.
_______ 5. In a villanelle, a character reveals personality by talking to the reader.

 World Literature

TRL

Workbook 43

Selection at a Glance

The Diameter of the Bomb

Yehuda Amichai (translated by Chana Bloch)

Student pages 284–286

Overview

Amichai has published eleven volumes of poetry, two novels, and a book of short stories. This poem appears in his *Selected Poetry,* which is translated into English.

Selection Summary

In "The Diameter of the Bomb," Yehuda Amichai shows how one tragic event has a widespread effect.

Objectives

- To understand the conversational nature of free verse.
- To identify and analyze symbols and connotations that connect a reader emotionally to a poem.

Audiocassette

Teacher's Resource Library TRL

- Vocabulary Workbook 26
- Selection Glossary 26
- Student Study Guide 32
- Activity 44
- Workbook 44
- Writing Activity 29
- Selection Quiz 26

INTRODUCING the SELECTION

The Diameter of the Bomb

Yehuda Amichai (translated by Chana Bloch)

Yehuda Amichai
(1924–)
Israeli

About the Author

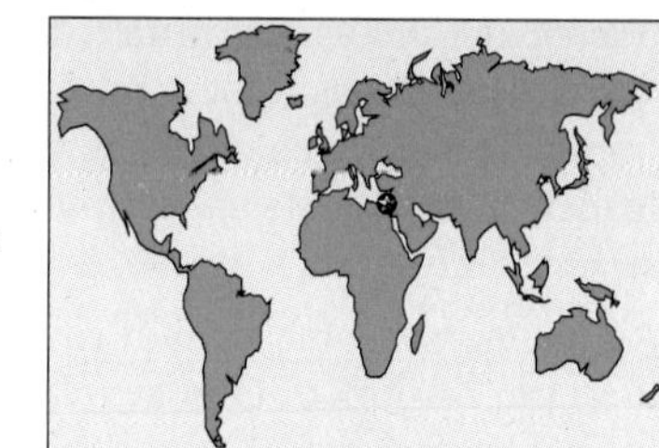

Yehuda Amichai is one of modern Israel's most important writers. He was born in Würzburg, Germany, to a Jewish family. After Hitler came to power in 1936, they moved to Jerusalem. Amichai served in the British army during World War II. He later fought for independence with the Israeli army. He began to publish poetry in magazines in the 1940s. He also has written novels, short stories, and plays. Many of these works have won awards. His works have been translated into more than twenty languages. The focus of Amichai's poetry is often on modern living. He writes in the Hebrew language used by the Israeli people in everyday life.

Literary Terms

free verse poetry that uses actual speech patterns for the rhythms of sound and does not have a strict rhyming pattern or regular line length

symbol a person, place, or thing that represents an idea or thought

About the Selection

"The Diameter of the Bomb" shows how one event connects to many others. The explosion of a bomb reaches only a certain distance Yet its effects may be felt far beyond that circle. Like many modern poets, Amichai uses free verse. **Free verse** is poetry that doesn't rhyme. Notice how the poem begins with phrases that could be taken from the newspaper. It quickly becomes more personal. Amichai uses many **symbols** to help the reader connect emotionally with the subject. Symbols are persons or objects that stand for an idea. They speak to a reader's emotions. What emotions do you feel when you read words like *graveyard* or *howl of orphans?* Look for other symbols as you read.

Setting the Stage for Reading

About the Author

Yehuda Amichai is internationally renowned as well as important to Israel. Israel's "master poet" has created in verse a portrait of modern Jewish life in Israel. His perspective of World War II helps him explore the present problems and perspectives of Israelis.

ASK Why might having fought in World War II have made Amichai determined to tell his people's story? (Answers may mention the destructiveness of that war and the intent of the Nazis to destroy the Jewish people. It is natural to want to preserve and explain that which is precious.)

About the Selection

The poem has a deceptive simplicity in its factual, even-handed presentation. Like the expanding effects of the bomb, its implications spread like waves.

Activate Prior Knowledge: Ask students to explain what a circle stands for. (Some may mention completeness or wholeness or "sets" of things)

ASK Why might the explosion of a bomb make us think of circles? (The shape of the bomb and the way in which its impact spreads are circular as are the circles of family and friends affected by a bomb and the shape of the earth itself.)

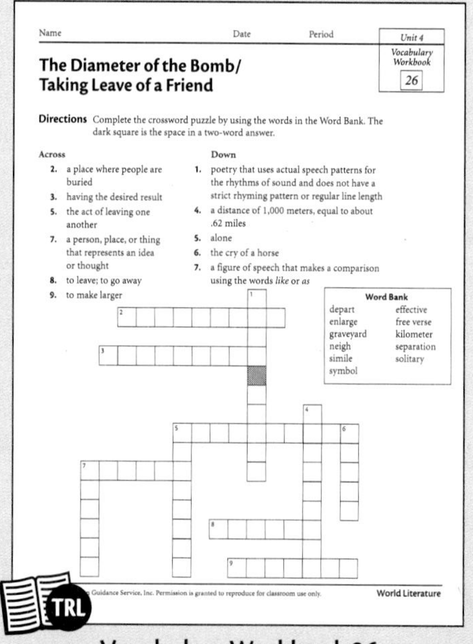

Name Date Period

Unit 4
Vocabulary Workbook 26

The Diameter of the Bomb/ Taking Leave of a Friend

Directions Complete the crossword puzzle by using the words in the Word Bank. The dark square is the space in a two-word answer.

Across

2. a place where people are buried
3. having the desired result
5. the act of leaving one another
7. a person, place, or thing that represents an idea or thought
8. to leave; to go away
9. to make larger

Down

1. poetry that uses actual speech patterns for the rhythms of sound and does not have a strict rhyming pattern or regular line length
4. a distance of 1,000 meters, equal to about .62 miles
5. alone
6. the cry of a horse
7. a figure of speech that makes a comparison using the words *like* or *as*

Word Bank

depart	effective
enlarge	free verse
graveyard	kilometer
neigh	separation
simile	solitary
symbol	

World Literature

Vocabulary Workbook 26

The Diameter of the Bomb

Yehuda Amichai

The diameter of the bomb was thirty centimeters
and the diameter of its **effective** range about seven meters,
with four dead and eleven wounded.

And around these, in a larger circle **A**
of pain and time, two hospitals are scattered
and one **graveyard**. But the young woman
who was buried in the city she came from,
at a distance of more than a hundred
kilometers,
enlarges the circle considerably,
and the **solitary** man mourning her death
at the distant shores of a country far across the sea
includes the entire world in the circle.
And I won't even mention the howl of orphans
that reaches up to the throne of God and
beyond, making
a circle with no end and no God.

As you read, look for symbols used by the poet.

The poet measures distances using the metric system. One hundred *centimeters* equals one *meter.* A meter is equal to about 39 inches, slightly longer than a yard. Later he refers to *kilometers,* a distance of 1,000 meters.

B Why is the man now alone?

effective having the desired result

enlarge to make larger

graveyard a place where people are buried

kilometer a distance of 1000 meters, equal to about .62 miles.

solitary alone

Reading Vocabulary TRL

Review the words on the Selection Glossary page. Use each in a question for students to answer.

Motivation for Reading

Have students describe an explosion. List their adjectives and have them read the poem to identify additional adjectives that describe a bomb's effects.

Discussion Questions

Point out the comments and question in the margin. Students should use them to better understand the poem.

A ASK Comprehension What is happening to the circle described by the poet? (It enlarges to include more and more people.)

B The man is alone because his wife was killed in the explosion.

Cross-Curricular Connection

Mathematics Have students read the marginal note about the metric system and make a table on the board, showing the relationship of millimeters, centimeters, meters, and kilometers. Challenge students to convert the measurements in the poem into other metric units—e.g., 7 meters = 700 cm or 7000 mm.

Name Date Period | *Unit 4* *Student Study Guide* 32

The Diameter of the Bomb (p. 285)

Directions Fill in the following outline. Filling in the blanks will help you as you read and study "The Diameter of the Bomb."

I. Beginning of the Selection (p. 285)

A. First Stanza
1. The diameter of the bomb is __________ centimeters.
2. The diameter of the bomb's effective range is about seven __________.
3. __________ people died from the bomb.

II. Middle of the Selection (p. 285)

A. Second Stanza
1. Two __________ and one graveyard make the circle larger.
2. A young woman is __________ in the city she came from.
3. A solitary man __________ her death.

III. End of the Selection (p. 285)

A. Third Stanza
1. The solitary man lives on the distant __________ of a country across the sea.
2. The __________ of orphans reach up to the throne of God.
3. The __________ has no end and no God.

 World Literature

TRL

Student Study Guide 32

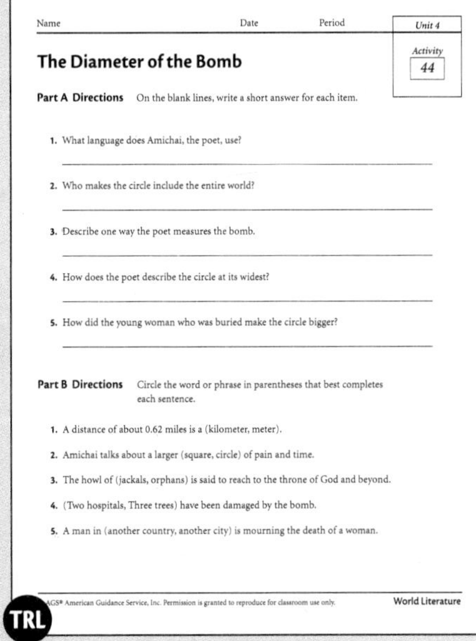

Name Date Period | *Unit 4* *Activity* 44

The Diameter of the Bomb

Part A Directions On the blank lines, write a short answer for each item.

1. What language does Amichai, the poet, use?
2. Who makes the circle include the entire world?
3. Describe one way the poet measures the bomb.
4. How does the poet describe the circle at its widest?
5. How did the young woman who was buried make the circle bigger?

Part B Directions Circle the word or phrase in parentheses that best completes each sentence.

1. A distance of about 0.62 miles is a (kilometer, meter).
2. Amichai talks about a larger (square, circle) of pain and time.
3. The howl of (jackals, orphans) is said to reach to the throne of God and beyond.
4. (Two hospitals, Three trees) have been damaged by the bomb.
5. A man in (another country, another city) is mourning the death of a woman.

 World Literature

TRL

Activity 44

Name Date Period | *Unit 4* *Workbook* 44

The Diameter of the Bomb

Part A Directions Write a short answer for each item on the blank lines.

1. What language does Amichai use?
2. How does the poet describe the circle at its widest?
3. Who makes the circle include the entire world?
4. How did the young woman who was buried make the circle bigger?
5. Describe one way the poet measures the

Part B Directions Circle the word or phrase in parentheses that best completes each sentence.

1. A distance of about .62 miles is a (kilometer, meter).
2. (Two hospitals, Three people) have been damaged by the bomb.
3. Amichai talks about a larger (square, circle) of pain and time.
4. A man in (another country, another city) is mourning the death of a woman.
5. The howl of (jackals, orphans) is said to reach to the throne of God and beyond.

 World Literature

TRL

Workbook 44

Poetry Unit 4 **285**

Reviewing the Selection

Answer Key

Comprehension: Identifying Facts

1. The bomb is 30 cm in diameter. Its blast reaches 7 m.

2. She is buried in her hometown, about 100 km distant from where the bomb exploded; because that is where she came from.

3. Four are killed; 11 are wounded.

Comprehension: Understanding Main Ideas

4. The wounded are transported to the hospitals, spreading the area that those affected by the blast occupy.

5. A relative in another nation far away mourns for the young woman, bringing the world into the picture.

6. Orphans were created by the bomb, so their parents must have been killed.

Understanding Literature: Free Verse

7. Students may respond that they enjoy free verse because it is like "talk." Others may prefer the familiarity of strict rhythm and rhyme.

8. Because it focuses intently on the emotional wounds and the spiritual questions raised by terrorism, the piece ends with an intensity one expects of poetry.

Critical Thinking

9. It forces the reader to consider how the violent act of bombing destroys much more than the lives of those next to the bomb; it shatters lives, changes the world, and resonates all the way to heaven.

10. Students may think the poet refers to a specific bombing but ends by showing how the effects of all bombings are similar.

Writing on Your Own Encourage students to make a flow chart on scratch paper. In the center, they can write the event they have in mind. Then they can write down related events and use arrows and lines to show which events caused which others to happen. Remind students to use transitional words such as *then, as a result,* and *consequently* in their paragraphs.

Selection Quiz

The Teacher's Resource Library includes a Selection Quiz for "The Diameter of the Bomb" that may be given following the Selection Review.

REVIEWING the SELECTION

The Diameter of the Bomb

Yehuda Amichai

Directions Write the answers to these questions using complete sentences.

Comprehension: Identifying Facts

1. What is the diameter of the bomb? What is its real range?
2. Where is one woman buried? Why is she buried there?
3. How many people are killed and wounded?

Comprehension: Understanding Main Ideas

4. How do the two hospitals create a larger circle around the bomb?
5. Who brings the entire world into the circle?
6. How do you know that some of those killed were parents? Explain.

Understanding Literature: Free Verse

"The Diameter of the Bomb" is written in free verse. It does not have a strict rhyme pattern. It does not have regular line lengths. It is written as though the poet were talking.

7. Do you like free verse? Why or why not?
8. Do you think that the last part of the poem is more "poetic" than the first part? Why or why not?

Critical Thinking

9. Explain what "The Diameter of the Bomb" is about.
10. Do you think the poet is thinking of one event? Or could this bombing occur anywhere?

Writing on Your Own Think of an event that happened at your school or in the world. Write a paragraph telling how one event leads to another.

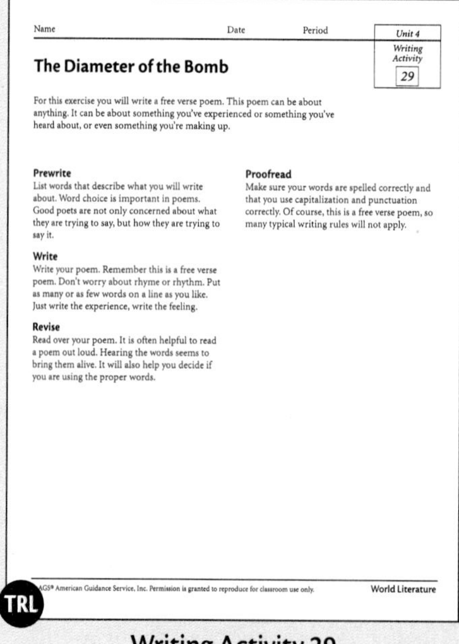

Name Date Period

Unit 4 Writing Activity 29

The Diameter of the Bomb

For this exercise you will write a free verse poem. This poem can be about anything. It can be about something you've experienced or something you've heard about, or even something you're making up.

Prewrite
List words that describe what you will write about. Word choice is important in poems. Good poets are not only concerned about what they are trying to say, but how they are trying to say it.

Write
Write your poem. Remember this is a free verse poem. Don't worry about rhyme or rhythm. Put as many or as few words on a line as you like. Just write the experience, write the feeling.

Revise
Read over your poem. It is often helpful to read a poem out loud. Hearing the words seems to bring them alive. It will also help you decide if you are using the proper words.

Proofread
Make sure your words are spelled correctly and that you use capitalization and punctuation correctly. Of course, this is a free verse poem, so many typical writing rules will not apply.

 World Literature

TRL

Writing Activity 29

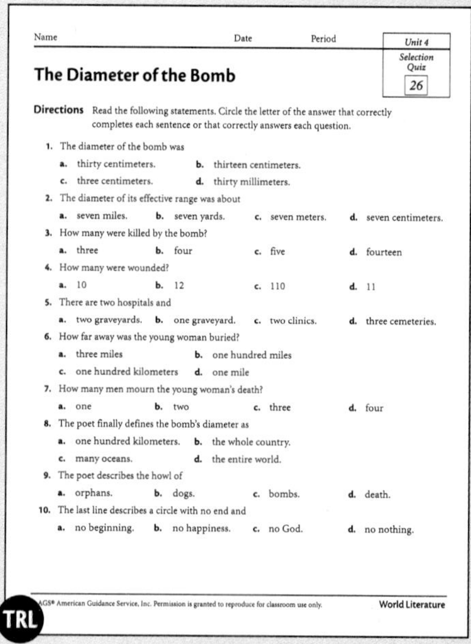

Name Date Period

Unit 4 Selection Quiz 26

The Diameter of the Bomb

Directions Read the following statements. Circle the letter of the answer that correctly completes each sentence or that correctly answers each question.

1. The diameter of the bomb was
   a. thirty centimeters. b. thirteen centimeters. c. three centimeters. d. thirty millimeters.
2. The diameter of its effective range was about
   a. seven miles. b. seven yards. c. seven meters. d. seven centimeters.
3. How many were killed by the bomb?
   a. three b. four c. five d. fourteen
4. How many were wounded?
   a. 10 b. 12 c. 110 d. 11
5. There are two hospitals and
   a. two graveyards. b. one graveyard. c. two clinics. d. three cemeteries.
6. How far away was the young woman buried?
   a. three miles b. one hundred miles c. one hundred kilometers d. one mile
7. How many men mourn the young woman's death?
   a. one b. two c. three d. four
8. The poet finally defines the bomb's diameter as
   a. one hundred kilometers. b. the whole country. c. many oceans. d. the entire world.
9. The poet describes the howl of
   a. orphans. b. dogs. c. bombs. d. death.
10. The last line describes a circle with no end and
    a. no beginning. b. no happiness. c. no God. d. no nothing.

 World Literature

TRL

Selection Quiz 26

INTRODUCING the SELECTION

Taking Leave of a Friend

Li Po (translated by Ezra Pound)

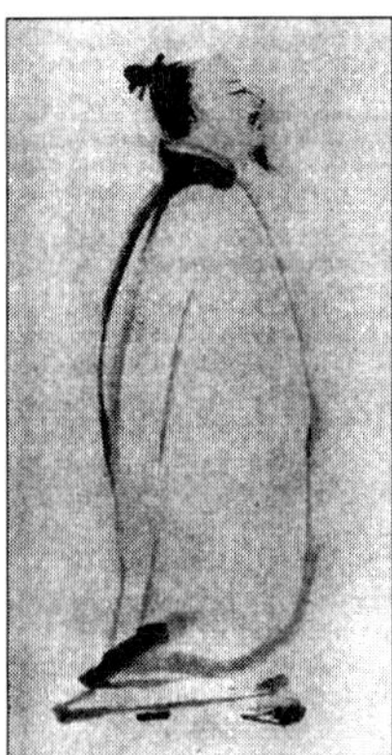

Li Po
(701–762)
Chinese

Literary Term

simile a figure of speech that makes a comparison using the words *like* or *as*

About the Author

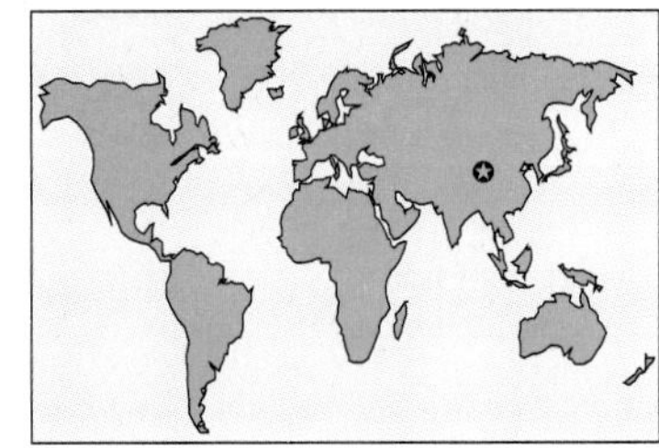

Li Po lived more than 1,200 years ago, but is considered one of China's greatest poets. He was a popular poet in his lifetime, too. (His name is sometimes spelled Li Bo.) He was born in what is now Szechwan, in western China. Li Po spent much of his life traveling across China. In about 742, he worked as a poet at the court of the Chinese emperor, then he went traveling again. He became a poet for one of the emperor's sons, Prince Lin. Later this caused him political trouble. Li Po spent some time in prison but was pardoned.

Ezra Pound was a well-known American poet. He had a strong influence on English and American poetry in the early 1900s. While living in Paris in the 1920s, Pound translated from Italian, Chinese, and Japanese literature. *Personae,* from which "Taking Leave of a Friend" comes, was published in 1909.

About the Selection

Li Po probably wrote about a thousand poems. He followed traditional Chinese forms. As in this poem, he often wrote about nature, friendship, and the passing of time. He also speaks of traveling and living in the mountains. You can see these themes in "Taking Leave of a Friend." This poem uses **similes.** A simile is a figure of speech that makes a comparison using the words *like* or *as.* Look for similes as you read the selection. Think about how Li Po feels as he and his friend say good-bye.

Selection at a Glance

Taking Leave of a Friend

Li Po (translated by Ezra Pound)

Student pages 287–289

Overview

The poet paints a vivid picture of the mountainous surroundings where friends part. The beauty and severity of their environment echo the feelings of love and loss within each friend.

Selection Summary

In "Taking Leave of a Friend," Li Po, a Chinese poet of the eighth century, looks at two friends parting.

Objectives

- To identify and define similes in poetry.
- To comprehend state of mind from descriptive details.

Audiocassette 

Teacher's Resource Library TRL

- Vocabulary Workbook 26
- Selection Glossary 27
- Student Study Guide 33
- Activity 45
- Workbook 45
- Writing Activity 30
- Selection Quiz 27

Setting the Stage for Reading

About the Author

Li Po was a Taoist; *Taoism* is a philosophy that urges a simple, unselfish lifestyle. Li Po's verse is beloved for its vitality, musical quality, imagery, and beautiful language.

ASK Why might a poet who spent a lot of time traveling hundreds of years ago make good observations about nature? (Answers might point out that travel would be on foot or horse, necessarily slow, and force one to experience nature up close, using all the senses.)

About the Selection

The interweaving of striking natural detail and small, telling gestures make this poem's theme of parting poignant and immediate.

Activate Prior Knowledge: Ask students to list factors that would make travel in the mountains difficult.

ASK Remind students that setting includes time as well as place. Why might parting be so emotional for friends, given this setting? (Answers might include that they must now face hardships alone, may be separated for years, or likely will never meet again.)

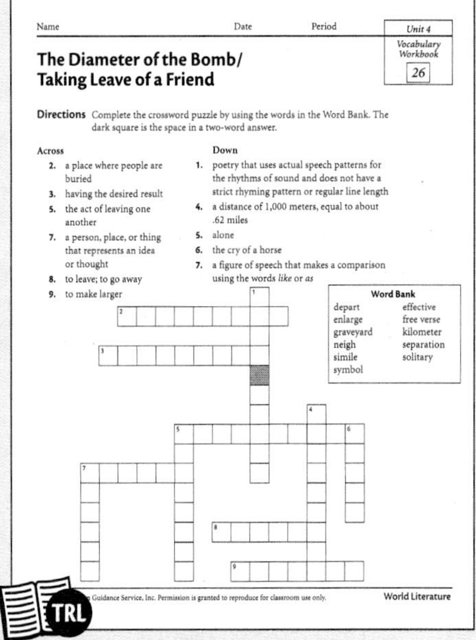

Name Date Period

Unit 4 — *Vocabulary Workbook* 26

The Diameter of the Bomb/ Taking Leave of a Friend

Directions Complete the crossword puzzle by using the words in the Word Bank. The dark square is the space in a two-word answer.

Across

2. a place where people are buried
3. having the desired result
5. the act of leaving one another
7. a person, place, or thing that represents an idea or thought
8. to leave; to go away
9. to make larger

Down

1. poetry that uses actual speech patterns for the rhythms of sound and does not have a strict rhyming pattern or regular line length
4. a distance of 1,000 meters, equal to about .62 miles
5. alone
6. the cry of a horse
7. a figure of speech that makes a comparison using the words *like* or *as*

Word Bank

depart	effective
enlarge	free verse
graveyard	kilometer
neigh	separation
simile	solitary
symbol	

World Literature

TRL

Vocabulary Workbook 26

Reading Vocabulary TRL

Review the words on the Selection Glossary page to be sure students know them. Invite students to use the words in sentences.

Motivation for Reading

Have students recall a difficult good-bye and its setting. Ask them to read the poem to discover how the speaker feels about saying good-bye.

Discussion Questions

Have students read the comment and question in the margin to help them set a purpose for reading.

A His mind is compared to a floating cloud.

B ASK Literary Element Why are these similes suited to the setting? (They compare thoughts and emotions to natural things in the scene.)

Diversity Connection

The Chinese have the custom of bowing as they greet one another or depart, much as Americans have the custom of shaking hands upon meeting and leaving. Suggest that students investigate other examples of cultural differences.

Taking Leave of a Friend

Li Po

As you read, notice how the poet pictures nature.

Blue mountains to the north of the walls,
White river winding about them:
Here we must make **separation**
And go out through a thousand miles
of dead grass.

A What does the writer say his mind is like?

Mind like a floating wide cloud,
B Sunset like the parting of old acquaintances
Who bow over their clasped hands at a distance.
Our horses **neigh** to each other
as we are **departing**.

depart to leave; to go away

neigh the cry of a horse

separation the act of leaving one another

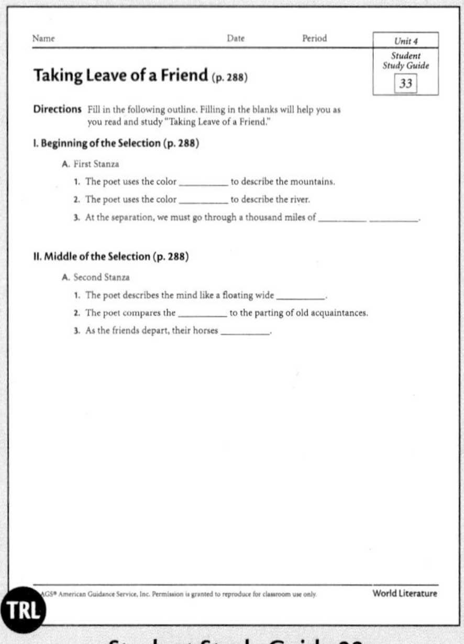

Name Date Period | *Unit 4* *Student Study Guide* 33

Taking Leave of a Friend (p. 288)

Directions Fill in the following outline. Filling in the blanks will help you as you read and study "Taking Leave of a Friend."

I. Beginning of the Selection (p. 288)

A. First Stanza

1. The poet uses the color __________ to describe the mountains.
2. The poet uses the color __________ to describe the river.
3. At the separation, we must go through a thousand miles of __________ __________.

II. Middle of the Selection (p. 288)

A. Second Stanza

1. The poet describes the mind like a floating wide __________.
2. The poet compares the __________ to the parting of old acquaintances.
3. As the friends depart, their horses __________.

TRL Student Study Guide 33

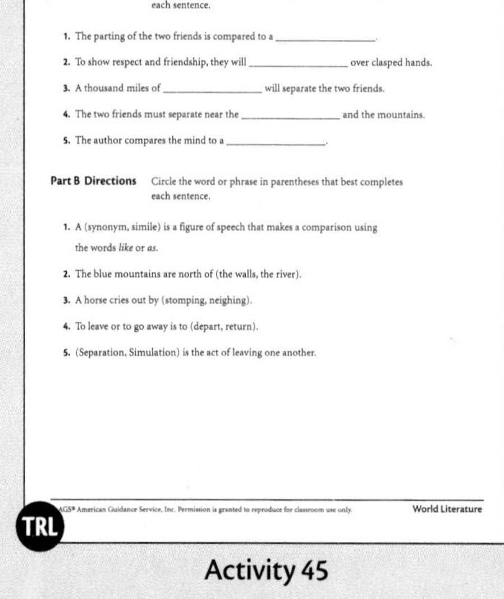

Name Date Period | *Unit 4* *Activity* 45

Taking Leave of a Friend

Part A Directions In each blank, write the word or phrase that best completes each sentence.

1. The parting of the two friends is compared to a __________________.
2. To show respect and friendship, they will __________________ over clasped hands.
3. A thousand miles of __________________ will separate the two friends.
4. The two friends must separate near the __________________ and the mountains.
5. The author compares the mind to a __________________.

Part B Directions Circle the word or phrase in parentheses that best completes each sentence.

1. A (synonym, simile) is a figure of speech that makes a comparison using the words *like* or *as*.
2. The blue mountains are north of (the walls, the river).
3. A horse cries out by (stomping, neighing).
4. To leave or to go away is to (depart, return).
5. (Separation, Simulation) is the act of leaving one another.

TRL Activity 45

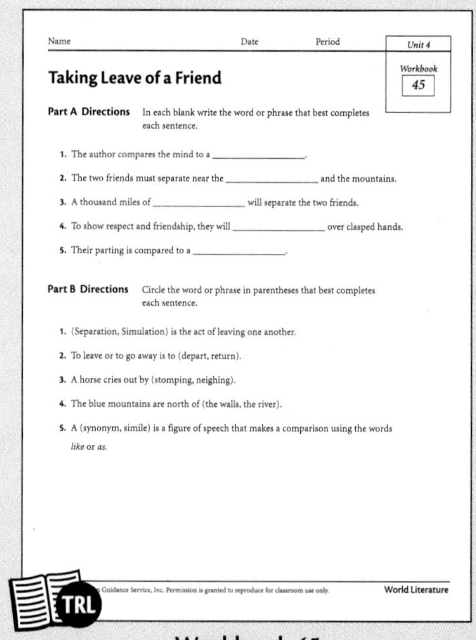

Name Date Period | *Unit 4* *Workbook* 45

Taking Leave of a Friend

Part A Directions In each blank write the word or phrase that best completes each sentence.

1. The author compares the mind to a __________________.
2. The two friends must separate near the __________________ and the mountains.
3. A thousand miles of __________________ will separate the two friends.
4. To show respect and friendship, they will __________________ over clasped hands.
5. Their parting is compared to a __________________.

Part B Directions Circle the word or phrase in parentheses that best completes each sentence.

1. (Separation, Simulation) is the act of leaving one another.
2. To leave or to go away is to (depart, return).
3. A horse cries out by (stomping, neighing).
4. The blue mountains are north of (the walls, the river).
5. A (synonym, simile) is a figure of speech that makes a comparison using the words *like* or *as*.

TRL Workbook 45

REVIEWING the SELECTION

Taking Leave of a Friend

Li Po

Directions Write the answers to these questions using complete sentences.

Comprehension: Identifying Facts

1. What color do the mountains seem to be?
2. Describe the rest of the scene where this occurs.
3. What do the horses do?

Comprehension: Understanding Main Ideas

4. Does the title of the poem give the main idea? Explain.
5. How far apart will the friends be? What words show this?
6. What action shows that the friends want to be in touch as long as they can?

Understanding Literature: Similes

A simile is a figure of speech that compares two things. For example, you might say, "A smile is *like* a sunny day." That is a clue to help you find a simile. A simile uses the words *like* or *as*.

7. What does the poet compare to a cloud?
8. What does he say is like a sunset?

Critical Thinking

9. Is this a truly sad poem? Why or why not?
10. Is the place where the friends part a pleasant one? Explain.

Writing on Your Own Imagine you are one of the two friends in this poem. Write a paragraph or a short poem about how you feel at this time. Tell how you feel about leaving your friend. You might also tell where you are going and what your trip will be like.

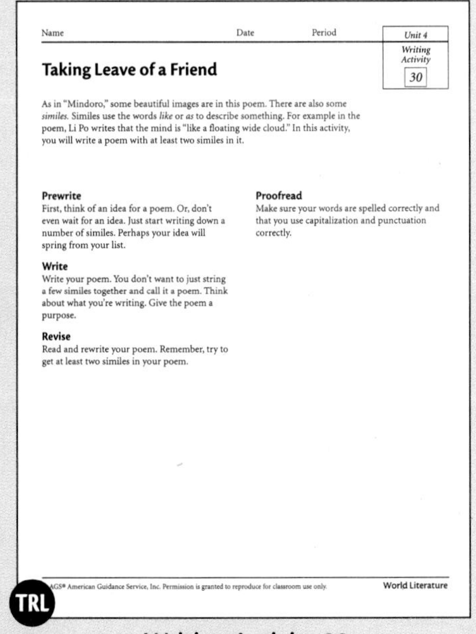

Name Date Period

Unit 4 *Writing Activity* 30

Taking Leave of a Friend

As in "Mindoro," some beautiful images are in this poem. There are also some *similes*. Similes use the words *like* or *as* to describe something. For example in the poem, Li Po writes that the mind is "like a floating wide cloud." In this activity, you will write a poem with at least two similes in it.

Prewrite
First, think of an idea for a poem. Or, don't even wait for an idea. Just start writing down a number of similes. Perhaps your idea will spring from your list.

Write
Write your poem. You don't want to just string a few similes together and call it a poem. Think about what you're writing. Give the poem a purpose.

Revise
Read and rewrite your poem. Remember, try to get at least two similes in your poem.

Proofread
Make sure your words are spelled correctly and that you use capitalization and punctuation correctly.

 World Literature

TRL

Writing Activity 30

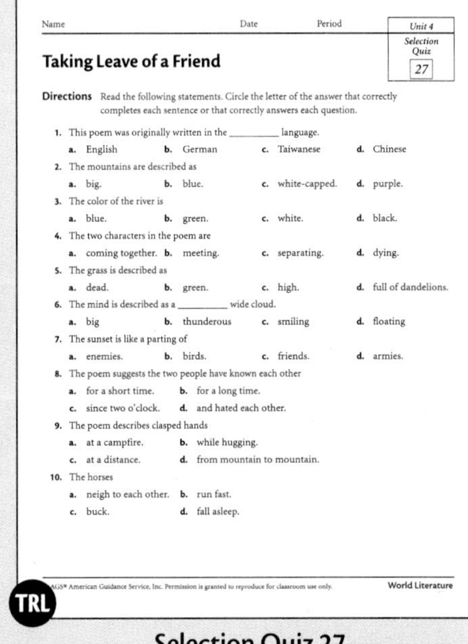

Name Date Period

Unit 4 *Selection Quiz* 27

Taking Leave of a Friend

Directions Read the following statements. Circle the letter of the answer that correctly completes each sentence or that correctly answers each question.

1. This poem was originally written in the ________ language.
   a. English b. German c. Taiwanese d. Chinese
2. The mountains are described as
   a. big. b. blue. c. white-capped. d. purple.
3. The color of the river is
   a. blue. b. green. c. white. d. black.
4. The two characters in the poem are
   a. coming together. b. meeting. c. separating. d. dying.
5. The grass is described as
   a. dead. b. green. c. high. d. full of dandelions.
6. The mind is described as a ________ wide cloud.
   a. big b. thunderous c. smiling d. floating
7. The sunset is like a parting of
   a. enemies. b. birds. c. friends. d. armies.
8. The poem suggests the two people have known each other
   a. for a short time. b. for a long time.
   c. since two o'clock. d. and hated each other.
9. The poem describes clasped hands
   a. at a campfire. b. while hugging.
   c. at a distance. d. from mountain to mountain.
10. The horses
    a. neigh to each other. b. run fast.
    c. buck. d. fall asleep.

 World Literature

TRL

Selection Quiz 27

Reviewing the Selection

Answer Key

Comprehension: Identifying Facts

1. The distant mountains appear blue.

2. A white river rushes past the mountains, dry plains stretch away into the distance, and the sun sets amid floating clouds.

3. They neigh to each other across the space that separates.

Comprehension: Understanding Main Ideas

4. The title gives the complete context, so that the poem need not explain, merely describe.

5. They will be a thousand miles apart, represented by the "thousand miles of dead grass" that separate.

6. As they ride in opposite directions, they pause, turn, and bow as long as they can see each other.

Understanding Literature: Similes

7. He compares his mind to a floating cloud.

8. He compares the parting to a sunset.

Critical Thinking

9. The poem is poignant. Students may cite the "dead" appearance of the distance between them, the mind that is "floating" instead of focused, the coming darkness, and the horses calling to one another at a distance.

10. The setting has a severe beauty, but suggests isolation and loss.

Writing on Your Own Encourage students to refer to the poem as they make notes for their paragraphs and draw details of setting into their explanations. Remind them that to communicate feelings in writing requires vivid, concrete details.

Selection Quiz

The Teacher's Resource Library includes a Selection Quiz for "Taking Leave of a Friend" that may be given following the Selection Review.

Selection at a Glance

Thoughts of Hanoi

Nguyen Thi Vinh (translated by Nguyen Ngoc Bich with Burton Raffel and W. S. Merwin)

Student pages 290–292

Overview

This poem gives local flavor and color of Vietnam as it touches on the universal heartaches of civil war. The speaker remembers Hanoi as it was years ago. He fears that it is changed and mourns that he cannot return and is separated from his own people.

Selection Summary

In "Thoughts of Hanoi," Nguyen Thi Vinh from Vietnam looks back at the city before war split the country.

Objectives

- To identify personification in a poem.
- To identify and analyze images in two poems.

Audiocassette 

Teacher's Resource Library TRL

- Vocabulary Workbook 27
- Selection Glossary 28
- Student Study Guide 34
- Activity 46
- Workbook 46
- Writing Activity 31
- Selection Quiz 28

INTRODUCING the SELECTION

Thoughts of Hanoi

Nguyen Thi Vinh (translated by Nguyen Ngoc Bich with Burton Raffel and W. S. Merwin)

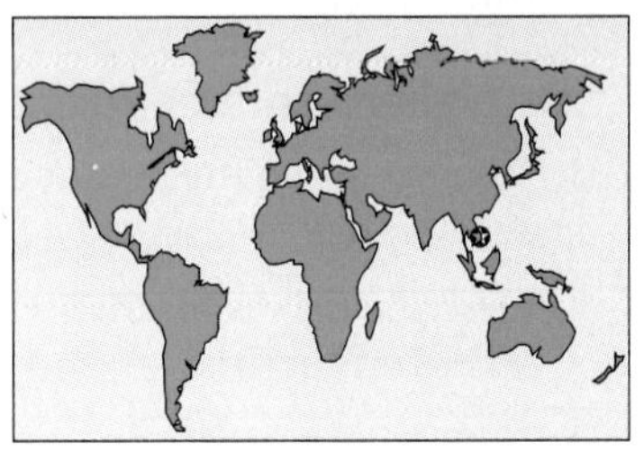

About the Author

Nguyen Thi Vinh was born in 1924. She was one of a group of writers in South Vietnam who became known in the early 1960s. She has written a novel and short stories as well as poetry. These works reflect her experiences of the many years of war in Vietnam.

About the Selection

After the end of World War II, Vietnam suffered years of civil war. In 1954 the country was split in two. Communists ruled the north. A republic governed the south. In "Thoughts of Hanoi" Nguyen Thi Vinh looks back to a time before the country was divided. (Hanoi was then the capital city.) The poem is a sort of **elegy**, a sad poem about someone's death. The poem does not mourn a specific person's death. But the author asks whether some familiar things still exist in the city. The poem speaks to a childhood friend, now on the other side in the war. The author uses **personification** for Hanoi. The city is given human characteristics. It almost becomes a character in itself. It seems that Nguyen fears that the Hanoi of the past is dead.

Literary Terms

elegy a poem that mourns someone's death

personification giving human characteristics to a nonhuman object

Setting the Stage for Reading

About the Author

Have students look at the map and locate Vietnam. It is bordered by Cambodia, Laos, China, and the South China Sea. The war that divided Vietnam lasted from 1954 until 1975. Hanoi, the capital city, lies in the north; when she wrote this poem, Nguyen Thi Vinh lived in South Vietnam.

ASK Why do you think Nguyen Thi Vinh felt such sadness about Hanoi? (Answers may include that she could no longer go there because of the war, that it had been damaged by fighting, or that it symbolizes the division of her country and its people.)

About the Selection

The poet has chosen images and a form that focus attention on beloved details of daily life in Hanoi. The staggered lines that describe children at work and play suggest joyful energy.

Activate Prior Knowledge: Remind students that war, including the American Civil War, has often forced relatives and friends into battle against one another.

ASK Why do you think Nguyen Thi Vinh personified Hanoi in her poem? (Answers may include because it is living and beloved to her or to help readers see it as she does.)

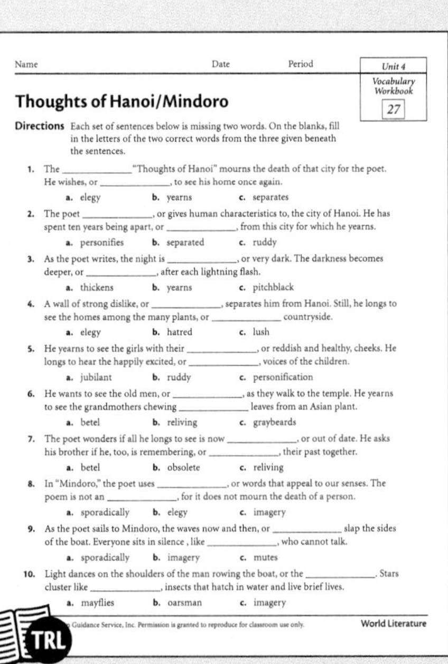

Name ______ Date ______ Period ______

Unit 4 *Vocabulary Workbook* 27

Thoughts of Hanoi/Mindoro

Directions Each set of sentences below is missing two words. On the blanks, fill in the letters of the two correct words from the three given beneath the sentences.

1. The ______ "Thoughts of Hanoi" mourns the death of that city for the poet. He wishes, or ______, to see his home once again.
   a. elegy b. yearns c. separates
2. The poet ______, or gives human characteristics to, the city of Hanoi. He has spent ten years being apart, or ______, from this city for which he yearns.
   a. personifies b. separated c. ruddy
3. As the poet writes, the night is ______, or very dark. The darkness becomes deeper, or ______, after each lightning flash.
   a. thickens b. yearns c. pitchblack
4. A wall of strong dislike, or ______, separates him from Hanoi. Still, he longs to see the homes among the many plants, or ______ countryside.
   a. elegy b. hatred c. lush
5. He yearns to see the girls with their ______, or reddish and healthy, cheeks. He longs to hear the happily excited, or ______, voices of the children.
   a. jubilant b. ruddy c. personification
6. He wants to see the old men, or ______, as they walk to the temple. He yearns to see the grandmothers chewing ______ leaves from an Asian plant.
   a. betel b. reliving c. graybeards
7. The poet wonders if all he longs to see is now ______, or out of date. He asks his brother if he, too, is remembering, or ______, their past together.
   a. betel b. obsolete c. reliving
8. In "Mindoro," the poet uses ______, or words that appeal to our senses. The poem is not an ______, for it does not mourn the death of a person.
   a. sporadically b. elegy c. imagery
9. As the poet sails to Mindoro, the waves now and then, or ______ slap the sides of the boat. Everyone sits in silence , like ______, who cannot talk.
   a. sporadically b. imagery c. mutes
10. Light dances on the shoulders of the man rowing the boat, or the ______. Stars cluster like ______, insects that hatch in water and live brief lives.
   a. mayflies b. oarsman c. imagery

 World Literature

TRL

Vocabulary Workbook 27

Thoughts of Hanoi

Nguyen Thi Vinh

The night is deep and chill **A**
as in early autumn. **Pitchblack,**
it **thickens** after each lightning flash.
I dream of Hanoi:
Co-ngu Road
ten years of **separation**
the way back sliced by a frontier of **hatred.**

I want to bury the past
to burn the future
still I **yearn**
still I fear
those endless nights
waiting for dawn.

Brother,
how is Hang Dao now?
How is Ngoc Son temple?
Do the trains still run
each day from Hanoi
to the neighboring towns?
To Bac-ninh, Cam-giang, Yen-bai,
the small villages, islands
of brown thatch in a **lush** green sea? **B**

The girls
bright eyes
ruddy cheeks
four-piece dresses
raven-bill scarves
sowing harvesting
spinning weaving
all year round,

As you read, notice what the poet is remembering.

Hanoi was the French colonial capital of Vietnam before the country was divided. It then became the capital of Communist North Vietnam.

Ngoc Son ("Jade Mountain") temple is on an island in a lake in the center of Hanoi.

The poet names some of the towns near Hanoi.

hatred strong dislike or hate

lush having lots of plants

pitchblack very dark; as dark as tar

ruddy having a healthy, reddish color

separation the state of being apart

thicken to become deeper or denser

yearn to wish for deeply

Reading Vocabulary TRL

Distribute the Selection Glossary page and assign words to pairs of students. Have them choose a way, such as illustration, dialogue, or pantomime, to demonstrate the word meanings.

Motivation for Reading

Ask students to imagine that they have been forced to leave their home, or their country, and cannot return. What would they miss the most?

Discussion Questions

Suggest that students use the marginal comments and question to help them understand the poem.

A ASK Literary Element Remind students that an image is a word picture that creates a feeling. What feeling is created by this image of night? (Feelings of dread and fear are associated with the night; hatred is connected with the lightning.)

B ASK Comprehension What is Vietnam like, judging from these images? (It is a tropical country with lush plant growth year round.)

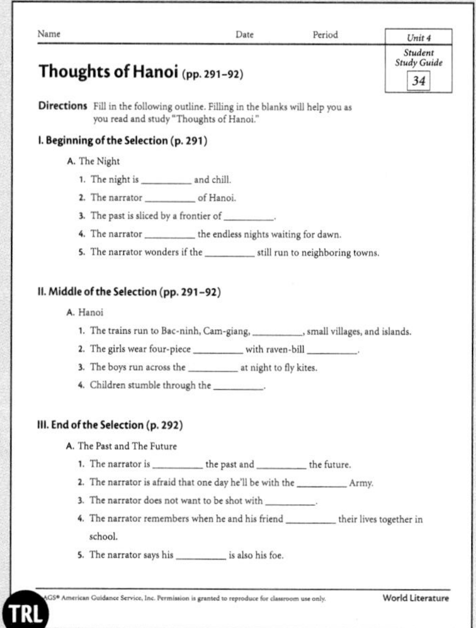

Name Date Period

Unit 4 Student Study Guide 34

Thoughts of Hanoi (pp. 291–92)

Directions Fill in the following outline. Filling in the blanks will help you as you read and study "Thoughts of Hanoi."

I. Beginning of the Selection (p. 291)

A. The Night

1. The night is ________ and chill.
2. The narrator ________ of Hanoi.
3. The past is sliced by a frontier of ________.
4. The narrator ________ the endless nights waiting for dawn.
5. The narrator wonders if the ________ still run to neighboring towns.

II. Middle of the Selection (pp. 291–92)

A. Hanoi

1. The trains run to Bac-ninh, Cam-giang, ________, small villages, and islands.
2. The girls wear four-piece ________ with raven-bill ________.
3. The boys run across the ________ at night to fly kites.
4. Children stumble through the ________.

III. End of the Selection (p. 292)

A. The Past and The Future

1. The narrator is ________ the past and ________ the future.
2. The narrator is afraid that one day he'll be with the ________ Army.
3. The narrator does not want to be shot with ________.
4. The narrator remembers when he and his friend ________ their lives together in school.
5. The narrator says his ________ is also his foe.

 World Literature

TRL

Student Study Guide 34

Name Date Period

Unit 4 Activity 46

Thoughts of Hanoi

Part A Directions On the blank lines, write a short answer for each item.

1. The past and future are described two different ways in this poem, once near the beginning and once near the end. What is one of those ways?
2. How is the land that separated the poet and friend described?
3. What does the poet fear most in this poem?
4. How does the poet describe the small villages remembered from the past?
5. What do the bright-eyed girls of the village do?

Part B Directions Read each sentence. Write *T* if the statement is true or *F* if it is false.

________ 1. The author remembers planes leaving daily from Hanoi.
________ 2. To wish deeply for something is to yearn for it.
________ 3. Throughout the poem the author calls the friend "brother."
________ 4. Graybeards are the older males of the villages.
________ 5. If something is obsolete, it is out of date.

 World Literature

TRL

Activity 46

Name Date Period

Unit 4 Workbook 46

Thoughts of Hanoi

Part A Directions Write a short answer for each item on the blank lines.

1. How does the poet describe the small villages he remembers?
2. What do the bright eyed girls of the village do?
3. The past and future are described two different ways in this poem, once near the beginning and once near the end. What is one of those ways?
4. How does the poet describe the land that separated him from his friend?
5. What does the poet fear most in this poem?

Part B Directions Read each sentence. Write *T* if the statement is true or *F* if it is false.

________ 1. Graybeards are the older males of the villages.
________ 2. If something is obsolete, it is out of date.
________ 3. The author remembers planes leaving daily from Hanoi.
________ 4. To wish deeply for something is to yearn for it.
________ 5. The author calls his friend brother throughout the poem.

 World Literature

TRL

Workbook 46

Poetry Unit 4 **291**

Discussion Questions

A ASK Comprehension How does the speaker's memory of Hanoi differ from his present feeling about it, as shown in the opening lines of the poem? (The sun shines, the sky is clear, and people are relaxed and happy, whereas the present is cold, black, "thick," and charged with hatred.)

B ASK Critical Thinking Why does the speaker focus on the past and the future? (The present is too harsh and unpleasant to think about.)

C ASK Comprehension What does the speaker plead for? (He wants the hatred between them to stop.)

D They are old friends now on opposite sides in a war; i.e., they chose to be friends but are forced to be foes.

Writing Connection

Point out the many questions in "Thoughts of Hanoi." Have students comment on their effect. (Answers may include that they suggest the speaker is anxious and out of touch, create a feeling of uncertainty, or make readers think about things that worry the speaker.) Explain that a writer may pose questions to focus our attention on important issues and make us think about how we would answer.

Ask students to write a letter to someone with whom they have had a disagreement, telling how they feel now and asking this person questions they feel are important.

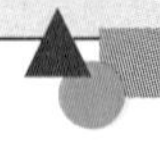

Learning Styles

Visual The poem provides rich imagery that enables a reader to visualize the country and people of Vietnam. Suggest that visually oriented students depict the images by cutting pictures from old magazines or drawing them to create a bulletin board display for the poem.

Ploughing is another spelling of the word *plowing*.

the boys
ploughing
transplanting
in the fields
in their shops
running across
the meadow at evening
to fly kites
and sing alternating songs.
A Stainless blue sky,
jubilant voices of children
stumbling through the alphabet,
village **graybeards** strolling to the temple,
grandmothers basking in twilight sun,
chewing **betel** leaves
while the children run—

Brother,
how is all that now?
Or is it **obsolete**?
B Are you like me,
reliving the past,
imagining the future?
Do you count me as a friend
or am I the enemy in your eyes?
Brother, I am afraid
that one day I'll be with the March-North Army
meeting you on your way to the South.
I might be the one to shoot you then
or you me
C but please
not with hatred.

For don't you remember how it was,
you and I in school together,
plotting our lives together?
Those roots go deep!

Brother, we are men,
conscious of more
than material needs.
How can this happen to us
my friend
my foe?

D Why does the speaker in the poem call the person both his *friend* and his *foe*?

betel an Asian plant whose leaves are chewed

graybeards old men

jubilant happily excited

obsolete out of date

reliving living over again; remembering

292 *Unit 4 Poetry*

Grammar

Direct Address On line 14, the speaker of the poem directly addresses the childhood friend as "Brother." Have students note that the direct address is separated from the rest of the sentence by a comma.

Have students look for and note other examples of direct address in the poem. (lines 47, 55, and 66.)

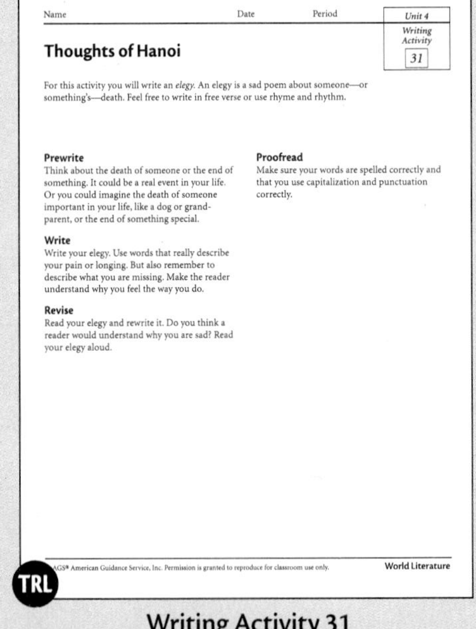

Name Date Period | Unit 4 *Writing Activity* 31

Thoughts of Hanoi

For this activity you will write an *elegy*. An elegy is a sad poem about someone—or something's—death. Feel free to write in free verse or use rhyme and rhythm.

Prewrite
Think about the death of someone or the end of something. It could be a real event in your life. Or you could imagine the death of someone important in your life, like a dog or grandparent, or the end of something special.

Write
Write your elegy. Use words that really describe your pain or longing. But also remember to describe what you are missing. Make the reader understand why you feel the way you do.

Revise
Read your elegy and rewrite it. Do you think a reader would understand why you are sad? Read your elegy aloud.

Proofread
Make sure your words are spelled correctly and that you use capitalization and punctuation correctly.

 World Literature

TRL

Writing Activity 31

INTRODUCING the SELECTION

Mindoro

Ramón Sunico

About the Author

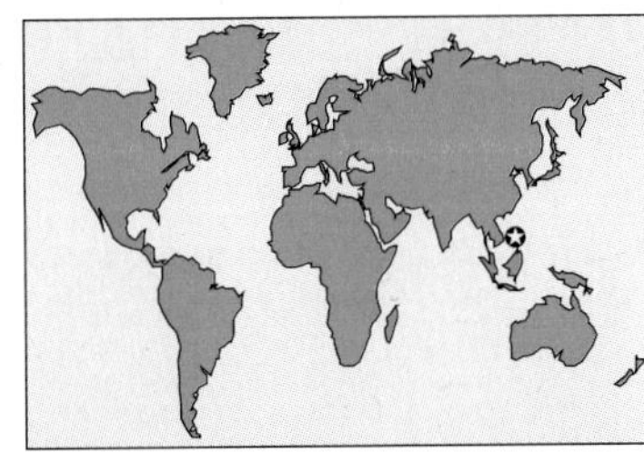

Ramón Sunico was born in 1955 in the Philippines. He was a teacher and is now a publisher. (He is also called "RayVi.") Sunico manages Cacho Publishing House in Manila, Philippines. His company has published fiction and books on medicine and law. He is now especially interested in books for children. He has translated stories from English, German, and Filipino. Sunico wants books to tackle present-day issues. His company publishes stories with themes such as relationships, the environment, and dealing with handicaps.

Literary Term

imagery pictures created by words; the use of words that appeal to the senses

About the Selection

The **imagery** in this poem contrasts with that in "Thoughts of Hanoi." Imagery is pictures created by words. Sunico uses quiet images to show a scene of beauty from the Philippine island of Mindoro. Nguyen remembered a city that was gone. "Mindoro" celebrates a living island. It uses images of nature, such as mayflies. Look for images that tell you about the life of people here. Is that life hard or easy?

Selection at a Glance

Mindoro

Ramón C. Sunico

Student pages 293–296

Overview

Mindoro is one of the smaller islands in the island nation of the Philippines. It is mountainous and tropical.

Selection Summary

In "Mindoro," Ramón Sunico, a modern Filipino poet, describes a sunset near an island.

Objectives

- To analyze images and the senses to which they appeal.
- To grasp the feelings about a place suggested by the description of it.

Audiocassette 

Teacher's Resource Library TRL

- Vocabulary Workbook 27
- Selection Glossary 29
- Student Study Guide 35
- Activity 47
- Workbook 47
- Writing Activity 32
- Selection Quiz 29

Setting the Stage for Reading

About the Author

Among the children's books that Sunico has translated and published are legends and myths such as "Why It Rains" and "The Boy Who Ate Stars." He is also trying to resurrect a secret language used for centuries by Filipino women to express their hidden sadness over oppression.

ASK Why might Sunico want to bring back the secret language for his people? (Answers may include that he sees it is still needed, for his people's lives are still hard or that it is a part of their culture and history.)

About the Selection

The poem suggests subtly that life means hard work, poverty, and closeness to nature for the fishers.

Activate Prior Knowledge: Point out to students that Mindoro lies close to the equator. Have them identify the kind of climate one would expect there. (It should be hot and very rainy for part of each year.)

ASK Why do you think many people regard a tropical island as a "paradise"? (Answers may include the rest, warmth, beaches, quiet, and exotic plants and animals that many imagine will be found there.)

Name Date Period | *Unit 4* *Vocabulary Workbook* 27

Thoughts of Hanoi/Mindoro

Directions Each set of sentences below is missing two words. On the blanks, fill in the letters of the two correct words from the three given beneath the sentences.

1. The ______________ "Thoughts of Hanoi" mourns the death of that city for the poet. He wishes, or ______________, to see his home once again.
   a. elegy b. yearns c. separates
2. The poet ______________, or gives human characteristics to, the city of Hanoi. He has spent ten years being apart, or ______________, from this city for which he yearns.
   a. personifies b. separated c. ruddy
3. As the poet writes, the night is ______________, or very dark. The darkness becomes deeper, or ______________, after each lightning flash.
   a. thickens b. yearns c. pitchblack
4. A wall of strong dislike, or ______________, separates him from Hanoi. Still, he longs to see the homes among the many plants, or ______________ countryside.
   a. elegy b. hatred c. lush
5. He yearns to see the girls with their ______________, or reddish and healthy, cheeks. He longs to hear the happily excited, or ______________, voices of the children.
   a. jubilant b. ruddy c. personification
6. He wants to see the old men, or ______________, as they walk to the temple. He yearns to see the grandmothers chewing ______________ leaves from an Asian plant.
   a. betel b. reliving c. graybeards
7. The poet wonders if all he longs to see is now ______________, or out of date. He asks his brother if he, too, is remembering, or ______________, their past together.
   a. betel b. obsolete c. reliving
8. In "Mindoro," the poet uses ______________, or words that appeal to our senses. The poem is not an ______________, for it does not mourn the death of a person.
   a. sporadically b. elegy c. imagery
9. As the poet sails to Mindoro, the waves now and then, or ______________ slap the sides of the boat. Everyone sits in silence , like ______________, who cannot talk.
   a. sporadically b. imagery c. mutes
10. Light dances on the shoulders of the man rowing the boat, or the ______________. Stars cluster like ______________, insects that hatch in water and live brief lives.
    a. mayflies b. oarsman c. imagery

 World Literature

TRL **Vocabulary Workbook 27**

Reading Vocabulary TRL

Use the Selection Glossary page to review vocabulary. Ask students to write a context sentence for each word.

Motivation for Reading

Ask students what sunset means to them. Invite volunteers to describe sunsets they have seen. Have students read the poem to learn what sunset means to the fishers of Mindoro.

Discussion Questions

Have students use the marginal questions and comments to focus their reading.

A ASK Comprehension What does the poem describe in the first lines? (It describes a sunset over the ocean.)

B ASK Literary Element What does the phrase "blood light" suggest about sunset and about the fishers? (It suggests redness, danger, life in nature, and the importance of daylight to the fishers' lives.)

Environmental Connection

Fishing is one industry important to people in many island nations and coastal towns. At the same time, many worry that pollution and over-fishing are harming the ocean environment. Have students research and report on the environmental issues involving the ocean and their implications for fishers and other people who rely on the ocean for their livelihood.

Mindoro

Ramón C. Sunico

Notice how the poet describes the setting. Think about what the images mean.

A The sun dissolves:
some pieces float
on the green sea
which hurries to darkness.

B The blood light flickers
while **sporadically**
a wave
slaps against the side of our slippery boat.

sporadically happening now and then

Name Date Period

Unit 4 *Student Study Guide* 35

Mindoro (pp. 294–95)

Directions Fill in the following outline. Filling in the blanks will help you as you read and study "Mindoro."

I. Beginning of the Selection (pp. 294–95)

A. The Sunset

1. As the sun ________, some pieces float.
2. The green sea hurries to ________.
3. Waves sporadically ________ against the side of the boat.
4. The last-light dances on the shoulders of the ________.

I. Middle of the Selection (p. 295)

A. The Night

1. The stars begin to ________.
2. The poet compares the call of land to the sharpness of a ________.
3. Dinner is ________ at the rented home.

III. End of the Selection (p. 295)

A. Riding Along

1. The people are ________ as they ride on the boat.
2. On the boaters' left is the ________.
3. On the boaters' right are the ________ of Mindoro.

 World Literature

TRL

Student Study Guide 35

Name Date Period

Unit 4 *Activity* 47

Mindoro

Part A Directions Match each item on the left with the correct item on the right. Write the correct letter on each line.

____	1. oarsman	a.	pictures created by words
____	2. sporadically	b.	not speaking
____	3. imagery	c.	an insect that hatches and only lives a few days
____	4. mayfly	d.	the man rowing a boat
____	5. mute	e.	happening now and then

Part B Directions In each blank, write the word or phrase that best completes each sentence.

1. Colors from the setting sun are ________ that dance on the oarsman's shoulders.
2. The author says he and his companions are ________, riding in the boat.
3. "________ flickering" is another way the sunset is described in this poem.
4. The sun is described as ________ and pieces of it float on the sea.
5. No one is paying attention to the stars as they ________.

 World Literature

TRL

Activity 47

The red threads
of last-light
dance
on the shoulders of our **oarsman.**

No one notices **D**
the stars
begin
to cluster like **mayflies.**

The call
of land
to us
is sharper than a fishhook: **E**
the rented
home
and dinner steaming.

We are
all **mutes**
riding along on this boat.

To the left
the sea
slices the afternoon in two.

To the right
the mountains of Mindoro ripen.

mayfly an insect that hatches in the water and only lives a few days

mute a person who can't talk

oarsman the man rowing a boat

C

Last-light is a poetic term for the last rays of the sun. What color is the light?

F

Why do you think everyone in the boat is quiet?

C The light is red.

D ASK Literary Element Point out the simile in lines 14–16 and ask students to identify its parts. (Stars are compared to mayflies.)

E ASK Critical Thinking Why do you think the poet compares the fishers' desire to get back to land to a fishhook? (The fishers' longing to get back to the comforts of home is as painful as being stuck by a hook.)

F Answers may include that they are too tired and hungry to talk or that they are enjoying the beauty of the sunset.

Learning Styles

Tactile/Kinesthetic Have students work in small groups to create dioramas of the scene presented in the poem. Encourage them to find out through research what kinds of fishing boats to depict.

Learning Styles

Auditory Encourage students with strong auditory skills to develop a musical background for an oral reading of the poem. Suggest that they choose music that will complement the mood and tone of the poem.

Name Date Period

Unit 4 *Workbook* 47

Mindoro

Part A Directions Match each item on the left with the correct item on the right. Write the correct letter on each line.

____ 1. mayfly a. pictures created by words

____ 2. oarsman b. not speaking

____ 3. sporadically c. an insect that hatches and only lives a few days

____ 4. imagery d. the man rowing a boat

____ 5. mute e. happening now and then

Part B Directions In each blank write the word or phrase that best completes each sentence.

1. The sun is described as ________ and pieces of it float on the sea.
2. Colors from the setting sun are ________ that dance on the oarsman's shoulders.
3. The author says he and his companions are ________, riding in the boat.
4. ________ flickering is another way the sunset is described in this poem.
5. No one is paying attention to the stars as they ________.

 World Literature

TRL

Workbook 47

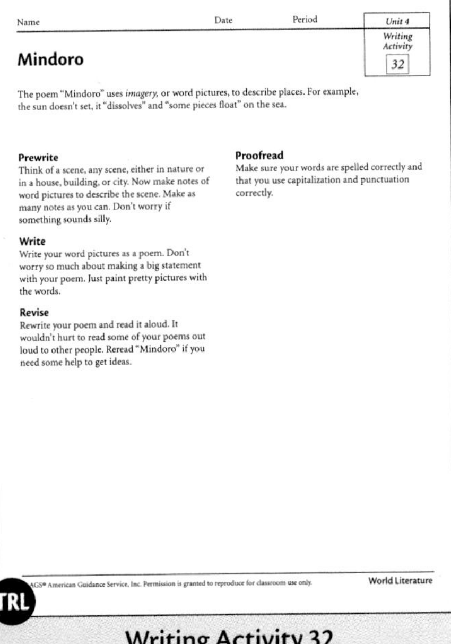

Name Date Period

Unit 4 *Writing Activity* 32

Mindoro

The poem "Mindoro" uses *imagery,* or word pictures, to describe places. For example, the sun doesn't set, it "dissolves" and "some pieces float" on the sea.

Prewrite
Think of a scene, any scene, either in nature or in a house, building, or city. Now make notes of word pictures to describe the scene. Make as many notes as you can. Don't worry if something sounds silly.

Write
Write your word pictures as a poem. Don't worry so much about making a big statement with your poem. Just paint pretty pictures with the words.

Revise
Rewrite your poem and read it aloud. It wouldn't hurt to read some of your poems out loud to other people. Reread "Mindoro" if you need some help to get ideas.

Proofread
Make sure your words are spelled correctly and that you use capitalization and punctuation correctly.

 World Literature

TRL

Writing Activity 32

Reviewing the Selections

Answer Key

Comprehension: Identifying Facts

1. Students may mention brilliantly dressed girls at work and play; boys working, playing, and singing songs; or people out enjoying the twilight.

2. It is sunset.

3. They are traveling by rowboat.

Comprehension: Understanding Main Ideas

4. The poet is for South Vietnam but would prefer that north and south be reunited and at peace.

5. They were close childhood friends and studied together at school.

6. They are thinking about getting home to food and rest.

Understanding Literature: Imagery

7. They are compared to islands in the thick, green jungle. The people as described have energy, simplicity, and serenity.

8. The three images of setting sun (lines 1–12) appeal primarily to the sense of sight and secondarily to the sense of touch.

Critical Thinking

9. Students may suggest titles such as "Island Home," "Fishers Going Home," or "Day's End." Accept any reasons students can justify through the poem's details and theme.

10. Answers may include homesick for places left behind, nostalgic for past days that won't return, or yearning for peace and friendship.

Writing on Your Own Encourage students to include details that appeal to as many senses as possible in their sentences. Have them begin their writing process by freewriting whatever phrases about the place pop into mind.

Selection Quiz

The Teacher's Resource Library includes Selection Quizzes for "Thoughts of Hanoi" and "Mindoro" that may be given following the Selection Review.

REVIEWING the SELECTIONS

Thoughts of Hanoi
Nguyen Thi Vinh

Mindoro
Ramón Sunico

Directions Write the answers to these questions using complete sentences.

Comprehension: Identifying Facts

1. Name two specific things the poet remembers about the city of Hanoi.
2. What time of day is it in the poem "Mindoro"?
3. In "Mindoro," how are the poet and his friends traveling?

Comprehension: Understanding Main Ideas

4. "Thoughts of Hanoi" is about the conflict between North and South Vietnam. Which side is the poet on?
5. How does the poet know the other person in "Thoughts of Hanoi"?
6. In "Mindoro," what are the people thinking about?

Understanding Literature: Imagery

Poets use imagery to create a picture with words. Images usually appeal to the senses—sight, smell, hearing, or touch. Imagery can touch the reader's feelings. It can also help the reader share what the poet is imagining.

7. Look at "Thoughts of Hanoi." What image does the poet use for the small villages?
8. Look at "Mindoro." Name one of the images of the sunset. What sense does this image appeal to?

Critical Thinking

9. What would be another good title for "Mindoro"? Why?
10. How does "Thoughts of Hanoi" make you feel?

Writing on Your Own Think about a place that means a lot to you. Write one or two sentences about that place. Use imagery to compare it to something else. You might think about a place you enjoyed going when you were a child. Can you remember a sight, or sound, or smell? Try to make others share that feeling.

296 *Unit 4 Poetry*

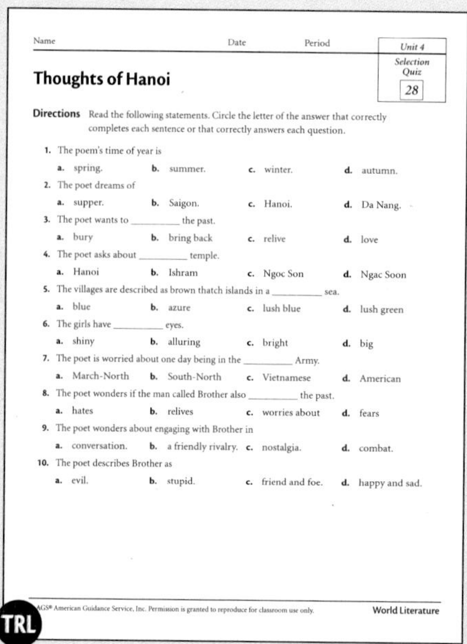

Name Date Period

Unit 4 Selection Quiz 28

Thoughts of Hanoi

Directions Read the following statements. Circle the letter of the answer that correctly completes each sentence or that correctly answers each question.

1. The poem's time of year is
   a. spring. b. summer. c. winter. d. autumn.
2. The poet dreams of
   a. supper. b. Saigon. c. Hanoi. d. Da Nang.
3. The poet wants to ________ the past.
   a. bury b. bring back c. relive d. love
4. The poet asks about ________ temple.
   a. Hanoi b. Ishram c. Ngoc Son d. Ngac Soon
5. The villages are described as brown thatch islands in a ________ sea.
   a. blue b. azure c. lush blue d. lush green
6. The girls have ________ eyes.
   a. shiny b. alluring c. bright d. big
7. The poet is worried about one day being in the ________ Army.
   a. March-North b. South-North c. Vietnamese d. American
8. The poet wonders if the man called Brother also ________ the past.
   a. hates b. relives c. worries about d. fears
9. The poet wonders about engaging with Brother in
   a. conversation. b. a friendly rivalry. c. nostalgia. d. combat.
10. The poet describes Brother as
    a. evil. b. stupid. c. friend and foe. d. happy and sad.

 World Literature

TRL

Selection Quiz 28

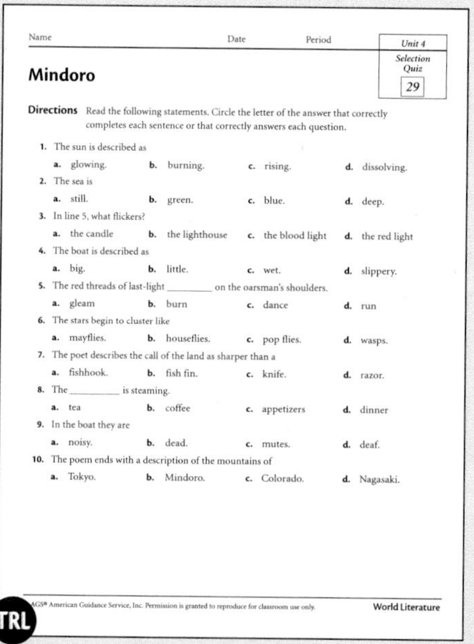

Name Date Period

Unit 4 Selection Quiz 29

Mindoro

Directions Read the following statements. Circle the letter of the answer that correctly completes each sentence or that correctly answers each question.

1. The sun is described as
   a. glowing. b. burning. c. rising. d. dissolving.
2. The sea is
   a. still. b. green. c. blue. d. deep.
3. In line 5, what flickers?
   a. the candle b. the lighthouse c. the blood light d. the red light
4. The boat is described as
   a. big. b. little. c. wet. d. slippery.
5. The red threads of last-light ________ on the oarsman's shoulders.
   a. gleam b. burn c. dance d. run
6. The stars begin to cluster like
   a. mayflies. b. houseflies. c. pop flies. d. wasps.
7. The poet describes the call of the land as sharper than a
   a. fishhook. b. fish fin. c. knife. d. razor.
8. The ________ is steaming.
   a. tea b. coffee c. appetizers d. dinner
9. In the boat they are
   a. noisy. b. dead. c. mutes. d. deaf.
10. The poem ends with a description of the mountains of
    a. Tokyo. b. Mindoro. c. Colorado. d. Nagasaki.

 World Literature

TRL

Selection Quiz 29

INTRODUCING the SELECTION

Ode to a Pair of Socks

Pablo Neruda (translated by Ken Krabbenhoft)

Pablo Neruda
(1904–1973)
Chilean

Literary Terms

figurative language language that makes a comparison and is not meant to be taken literally

surrealism a writing style that has a dreamlike quality

About the Author

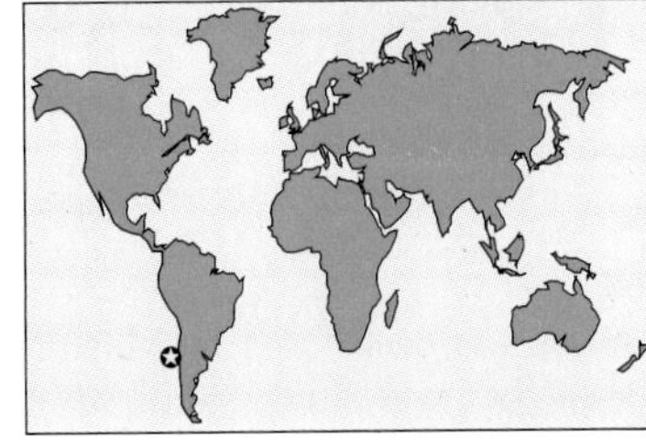

Pablo Neruda was born in Parral, in the rainy southern part of Chile. (His real name was Neftalí Ricardo Reyes y Basoalto.) During his career he became Latin America's best-known poet. A book of poems, published in 1924, made him famous. It was called *Twenty Love Poems and a Song of Despair.* At the same time, Neruda worked as a diplomat. This work took him all over the world. Over the years, he wrote many books of poetry. One major work is *Canto General,* published in 1950. In 1971 he received the Nobel Prize for Literature. Neruda was active in Chilean politics and the government of Salvador Allende. He was ambassador to France from 1970 to 1972. He died in 1973 in Santiago, Chile.

About the Selection

One critic calls Neruda "many poets in one." His poetry changed during his lifetime. He began as a symbolist poet. He moved from there to surrealism. **Surrealism** is a writing style with a dreamlike quality. Surrealist writers use whatever words come into their mind. They do not change what they write. They believe that their readers will follow these free-flowing thoughts.

In the 1950s, Neruda began to write more realistically. He looked at everyday objects and saw wonder in them. He wrote several books of odes to ordinary things. An ode is a poem in praise of something. Some of Neruda's odes were to laziness, to an onion, and to a storm. The following poem is one of those odes. As you will see, Neruda looks at objects in a unique way. He describes them with **figurative language.** He makes comparisons that are not meant to be taken literally. This ode comes from *Odes to Common Things* (a translation published in 1994).

Poetry Unit 4 **297**

Selection at a Glance

Ode to a Pair of Socks

Pablo Neruda (translated by Ken Krabbenhoft)

Student pages 297–300

Overview

Neruda's odes to ordinary things are among his most beloved poems worldwide. They reflect the more relaxed mastery and rich sense of humor of his later years, after a period of intense political activism.

Selection Summary

In "Ode to a Pair of Socks," Nobel prize-winning poet Pablo Neruda describes the joy of getting a pair of hand-knit socks.

Objectives

- To identify similes and metaphors in a poem.
- To understand how figurative language reveals wonder in the ordinary.

Audiocassette 

Teacher's Resource Library 

- Vocabulary Workbook 28
- Selection Glossary 30
- Student Study Guide 36
- Activity 48
- Workbook 48
- Writing Activity 33
- Selection Quiz 30

Setting the Stage for Reading

About the Author

Throughout his long career, Neruda evolved his style toward greater simplicity. Whether his subjects were his concerns for the peoples of the world or views of the things around him, Neruda never failed to find extraordinary qualities and worth in them.

ASK Why do you think Neruda was active in world politics? (Answers may include that his viewpoint and vision made him eager to work for peace and a possible end to suffering or that he believed this was a good way to make a difference.)

About the Selection

The ode's power lies in its clear comparisons and joyful tone. Having realized the extraordinary nature of the socks, Neruda decides to use them.

Activate Prior Knowledge: Have students describe an object or event they have heard praised in public. Why was it praised? What kind of language did the speaker use? Discuss the qualities that students find praiseworthy.

ASK Is most of the poetry you have read about ordinary or special things and people? (Answers may include that most poems praise special beauty or great deeds or that poems about ordinary things make them seem special.)

Reading Vocabulary TRL

Use the Selection Glossary page to help students become familiar with new words. Pair students and have partners demonstrate what each means for the class.

Motivation for Reading

Ask students why and when they would find an article of clothing inspiring and uplifting. What might make a pair of socks special?

Discussion Questions

Point out the marginal notes and questions. Suggest that students answer the questions after they have read the entire poem.

A The poet's tone is both humorous and admiring.

B ASK Literary Element What does this comparison suggest about the color and texture of the socks? (Threads of brilliant gold or yellow are knit into them; they are soft.) What do mentions of sunset and sheepskin suggest the speaker values about the socks? (He values the connection their making and materials have with nature.)

C ASK Comprehension How do the speaker's feet appear to him, compared to the socks? (His feet seem ugly and unworthy of the "heavenly socks.")

Ode to a Pair of Socks

Pablo Neruda

A As you read, think about the mood of the poem. Is the poet serious or teasing?

Maru Mori brought me
a pair
of socks
that she knit with her
shepherd's hands.
Two socks as soft
as rabbit fur.
I thrust my feet
inside them
B as if they were
two
little boxes
knit
from threads
of sunset
and sheepskin.

My feet were
two woolen
fish
in those **outrageous** socks,
two **gangly**,
navy-blue sharks
impaled
on a golden thread,
two giant blackbirds,
two cannons:
thus
were my feet
honored
by
those
heavenly
socks.
They were
so beautiful
C I found my feet
unlovable
for the very first time,
like two **crusty** old
firemen, firemen
unworthy
of that embroidered
fire,
those **incandescent**
socks.

crusty gruff; stern in manner

gangly tall, thin, and ungraceful

impaled speared; stuck on a sharp stick

incandescent glowing; very bright

outrageous extreme

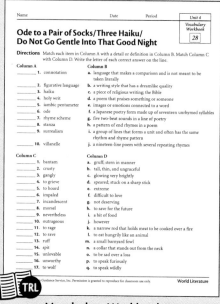

unlovable difficult to love

unworthy not deserving

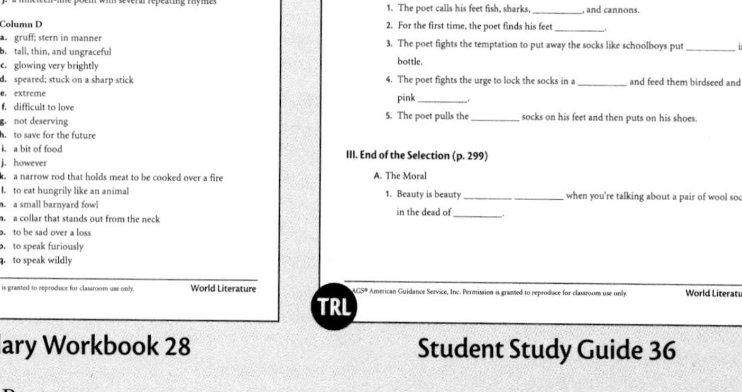

Name Date Period — Unit 4 Vocabulary Workbook 28

Ode to a Pair of Socks/Three Haiku/ Do Not Go Gentle Into That Good Night

Directions Match each item in Column A with a detail or definition in Column B. Match Column C with Column D. Write the letter of each correct answer on the line.

Column A	Column B
____ 1. connotation	a. language that makes a comparison and is not meant to be taken literally
____ 2. figurative language	b. a writing style that has a dreamlike quality
____ 3. haiku	c. a piece of religious writing; the Bible
____ 4. holy writ	d. a poem that praises something or someone
____ 5. iambic pentameter	e. images or emotions connected to a word
____ 6. ode	f. a Japanese poetry form made up of seventeen unrhymed syllables
____ 7. rhyme scheme	g. five two-beat sounds in a line of poetry
____ 8. stanza	h. a pattern of end rhymes in a poem
____ 9. surrealism	i. a group of lines that forms a unit and often has the same rhythm and rhyme pattern
____ 10. villanelle	j. a nineteen-line poem with several repeating rhymes

Column C	Column D
____ 1. bantam	a. gruff; stern in manner
____ 2. crusty	b. tall, thin, and ungraceful
____ 3. gangly	c. glowing very brightly
____ 4. to grieve	d. speared; stuck on a sharp stick
____ 5. to hoard	e. extreme
____ 6. impaled	f. difficult to love
____ 7. incandescent	g. not deserving
____ 8. morsel	h. to save for the future
____ 9. nevertheless	i. a bit of food
____ 10. outrageous	j. however
____ 11. to rage	k. a narrow rod that holds meat to be cooked over a fire
____ 12. to rave	l. to eat hungrily like an animal
____ 13. ruff	m. a small barnyard fowl
____ 14. spit	n. a collar that stands out from the neck
____ 15. unlovable	o. to be sad over a loss
____ 16. unworthy	p. to speak furiously
____ 17. to wolf	q. to speak wildly

 World Literature

TRL

Vocabulary Workbook 28

Name Date Period — Unit 4 Student Study Guide 36

Ode to a Pair of Socks (pp. 298–99)

Directions Fill in the following outline. Filling in the blanks will help you as you read and study "Ode to a Pair of Socks."

I. Beginning of the Selection (p. 298)

A. Receiving the Socks

1. ________ ________ is a shepherd.
2. The socks are soft as ________ fur.
3. The poet thrusts his feet in the socks as if they were knit from threads of ________ and ________.

II. Middle of the Selection (pp. 298–99)

A. The Feet and the Socks

1. The poet calls his feet fish, sharks, ________, and cannons.
2. For the first time, the poet finds his feet ________.
3. The poet fights the temptation to put away the socks like schoolboys put ________ in a bottle.
4. The poet fights the urge to lock the socks in a ________ and feed them birdseed and pink ________.
5. The poet pulls the ________ socks on his feet and then puts on his shoes.

III. End of the Selection (p. 299)

A. The Moral

1. Beauty is beauty ________ ________ when you're talking about a pair of wool socks in the dead of ________.

 World Literature

TRL

Student Study Guide 36

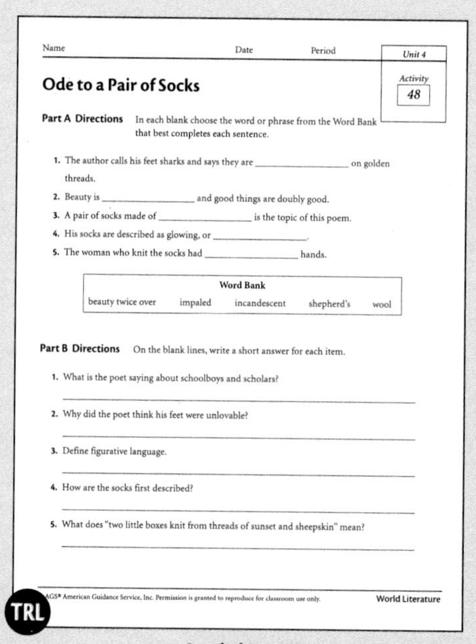

Name Date Period — Unit 4 Activity 48

Ode to a Pair of Socks

Part A Directions In each blank choose the word or phrase from the Word Bank that best completes each sentence.

1. The author calls his feet sharks and says they are ________ on golden threads.
2. Beauty is ________ and good things are doubly good.
3. A pair of socks made of ________ is the topic of this poem.
4. His socks are described as glowing, or ________.
5. The woman who knit the socks had ________ hands.

Word Bank				
beauty twice over	impaled	incandescent	shepherd's	wool

Part B Directions On the blank lines, write a short answer for each item.

1. What is the poet saying about schoolboys and scholars?
2. Why did the poet think his feet were unlovable?
3. Define figurative language.
4. How are the socks first described?
5. What does "two little boxes knit from threads of sunset and sheepskin" mean?

 World Literature

TRL

Activity 48

Nevertheless
I fought
the sharp temptation
to put them away
the way schoolboys
put
fireflies in a bottle,
the way scholars
hoard
holy writ.
I fought **F**
the mad urge
to lock them
in a golden
cage
and feed them birdseed
and **morsels** of pink melon
every day.
Like jungle
explorers
who deliver a young deer
of the rarest species
to the roasting **spit**
then **wolf** it down
in shame,
I stretched
my feet forward
and pulled on
those
gorgeous
socks,
and over them
my shoes.

So this is
the moral of my **ode**:
beauty is beauty
twice over
and good things are doubly
good
when you're talking about a
pair of wool
socks
in the dead of winter.

D What does the poet first think about doing with the new socks? What does he do instead?

E Why might socks be *doubly good* in winter?

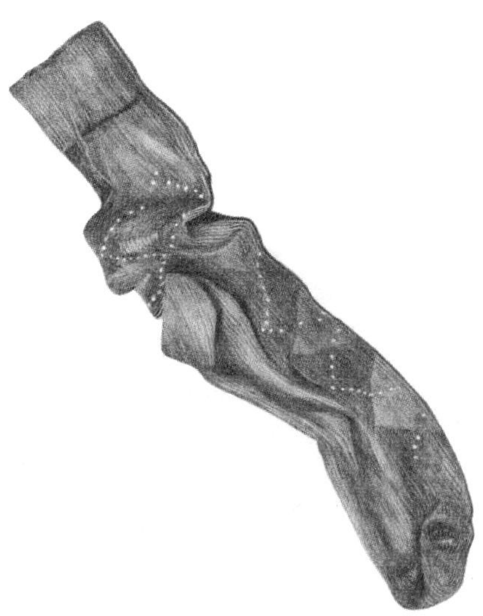

hoard to save for the future

holy writ a piece of religious writing; the Bible

morsel a bit of food

nevertheless however

ode a poem that praises something or someone

spit a narrow rod that holds meat to be cooked over a fire

wolf to eat hungrily, like an animal

D He thinks he should save them, put them away. Instead he puts them on.

E They are not only beautiful and comfortable, they also keep his feet warm.

F ASK Critical Thinking Why might the speaker feel the urge to treat these socks like precious birds? Why might he at the same time think it is "mad" to lock them away? (They seem beautiful and rare to him; they seem to take on a life of their own. He realizes that putting them away is a waste, that they were made to be enjoyed and admired each day.)

Literary Elements

Similes and Metaphors Have students work in small groups to identify all of the similes and metaphors in the poem. Remind them, if necessary, that a simile compares unlike objects by using the word *like* or *as;* metaphors compare the objects by directly identifying one thing as another. Ask members of the group to then discuss the comparisons and the effect of these literary devices on mood and meaning in the poem. Have each group share with the class its analysis.

Community Connection

Knitting is a craft that many people enjoy. Ask students to find out whether there are any knitting classes or clubs in their community. If so, invite someone from a club or class to provide a demonstration for students. The home arts teacher or the proprietor of a crafts store may also be able to help you contact someone for a demonstration.

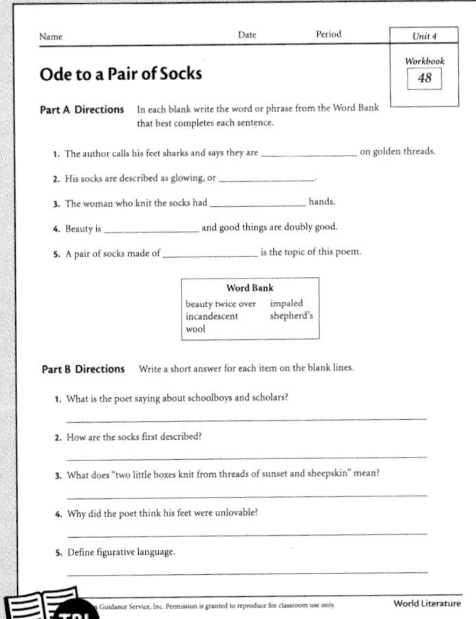

Name Date Period | *Unit 4* | *Workbook* 48

Ode to a Pair of Socks

Part A Directions In each blank write the word or phrase from the Word Bank that best completes each sentence.

1. The author calls his feet sharks and says they are ________________ on golden threads.
2. His socks are described as glowing, or ________________.
3. The woman who knit the socks had ________________ hands.
4. Beauty is ________________ and good things are doubly good.
5. A pair of socks made of ________________ is the topic of this poem.

Word Bank
beauty twice over
incandescent
wool
impaled
shepherd's

Part B Directions Write a short answer for each item on the blank lines.

1. What is the poet saying about schoolboys and scholars?
2. How are the socks first described?
3. What does "two little boxes knit from threads of sunset and sheepskin" mean?
4. Why did the poet think his feet were unlovable?
5. Define figurative language.

 World Literature

TRL

Workbook 48

Learning Styles

LEP/ESL Students whose first language is Spanish or Spanish-language students may enjoy reading Neruda's work in its original language. Suggest that students read "Ode to a Pair of Socks" in Spanish and compare it to the English version. The Spanish version is available in the dual Spanish/English edition of *Odes to Common Things.* How are the versions of the poem alike and different? Is anything lost in the translation? Encourage students to present their comparison to the class.

Reviewing the Selection

Answer Key

Comprehension: Identifying Facts

1. They are given to him by a woman, Maru Mori, who herds sheep.
2. They are made of wool.
3. He wears them for everyday use.

Comprehension: Understanding Main Ideas

4. They are ugly in comparison to the socks.
5. Their beauty and uniqueness seem too special to "waste" on his ugly feet or on daily wear.
6. He says that "beauty is beauty twice over"—perhaps meaning that the beautiful object admired and put to its proper use is a blessing multiplied.

Understanding Literature: Figurative Language

7. He compares his feet to navy blue sharks, giant blackbirds, cannons, and crusty old firemen.
8. He compares them to "little boxes knit from threads of sunset and sheepskin."

Critical Thinking

9. Answers may include that she felt honored and delighted that her gift had so pleased the recipient and that he had found her work so exquisite.
10. Some students may find Neruda's humor and wild imaginativeness compelling. Others may enjoy his commonsense wisdom.

Writing on Your Own Encourage students to include details that appeal to the senses and figurative language in their responses. These details and comparisons should help reveal feelings.

Selection Quiz

The Teacher's Resource Library includes a Selection Quiz for "Ode to a Pair of Socks" that may be given following the Selection Review.

REVIEWING the SELECTION

Ode to a Pair of Socks

Pablo Neruda

Directions Write the answers to these questions using complete sentences.

Comprehension: Identifying Facts

1. How does Neruda get the socks?
2. What are the socks made of?
3. What does the poet finally do with the socks?

Comprehension: Main Idea

4. Why do the poet's feet suddenly seem "unlovable"?
5. Why does the poet think about putting the socks away?
6. What does the poet say about beauty in his moral?

Understanding Literature: Figurative Language

Figurative language is language that makes a comparison but is not meant to be taken literally. It is also called a "figure of speech." Two kinds of figurative language are *similes* and *metaphors.* Both make comparisons. A simile uses *like* or *as.* A metaphor says one thing *is* another. For example, Neruda says, "My feet were two woolen fish." Clearly, this isn't a literal comparison. His feet aren't fish. But the words make a picture so that you see the object differently. Poets often use figurative language.

7. Besides fish, Neruda compares his feet to other things. Name two of them.
8. When the poet first gets the socks, he compares them to something. Write the words he uses about the socks themselves.

Critical Thinking

9. How do you think the knitter felt about this poem? Explain.
10. From this poem, do you think you would like to know Pablo Neruda? Why or why not?

Writing on Your Own Think of something ordinary that you like. Think about how it makes you feel. Write a short poem or paragraph about it. Tell what it is and how it makes you feel.

300 Unit 4 Poetry

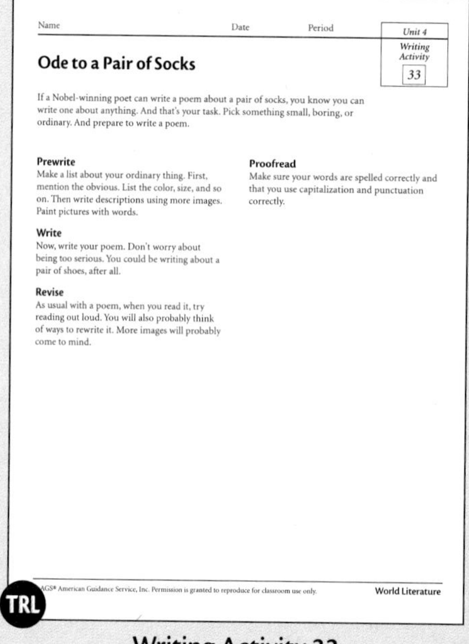
Name Date Period

Unit 4 Writing Activity 33

Ode to a Pair of Socks

If a Nobel-winning poet can write a poem about a pair of socks, you know you can write one about anything. And that's your task. Pick something small, boring, or ordinary. And prepare to write a poem.

Prewrite
Make a list about your ordinary thing. First, mention the obvious. List the color, size, and so on. Then write descriptions using more images. Paint pictures with words.

Write
Now, write your poem. Don't worry about being too serious. You could be writing about a pair of shoes, after all.

Revise
As usual with a poem, when you read it, try reading out loud. You will also probably think of ways to rewrite it. More images will probably come to mind.

Proofread
Make sure your words are spelled correctly and that you use capitalization and punctuation correctly.

 World Literature

TRL

Writing Activity 33

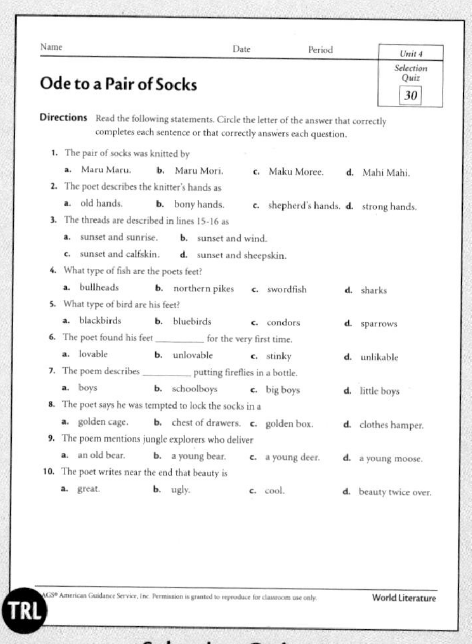
Name Date Period

Unit 4 Selection Quiz 30

Ode to a Pair of Socks

Directions Read the following statements. Circle the letter of the answer that correctly completes each sentence or that correctly answers each question.

1. The pair of socks was knitted by
   a. Maru Maru. b. Maru Mori. c. Maku Moree. d. Mahi Mahi.
2. The poet describes the knitter's hands as
   a. old hands. b. bony hands. c. shepherd's hands. d. strong hands.
3. The threads are described in lines 15-16 as
   a. sunset and sunrise. b. sunset and wind.
   c. sunset and calfskin. d. sunset and sheepskin.
4. What type of fish are the poets feet?
   a. bullheads b. northern pikes c. swordfish d. sharks
5. What type of bird are his feet?
   a. blackbirds b. bluebirds c. condors d. sparrows
6. The poet found his feet __________ for the very first time.
   a. lovable b. unlovable c. stinky d. unlikable
7. The poem describes __________ putting fireflies in a bottle.
   a. boys b. schoolboys c. big boys d. little boys
8. The poet says he was tempted to lock the socks in a
   a. golden cage. b. chest of drawers. c. golden box. d. clothes hamper.
9. The poem mentions jungle explorers who deliver
   a. an old bear. b. a young bear. c. a young deer. d. a young moose.
10. The poet writes near the end that beauty is
   a. great. b. ugly. c. cool. d. beauty twice over.

 World Literature

TRL

Selection Quiz 30

INTRODUCING the SELECTION

Three Haiku

Basho (translated by Olivia Gray)

Kikaku (translated by Harry Behn)

Anonymous (translated by Harry Behn)

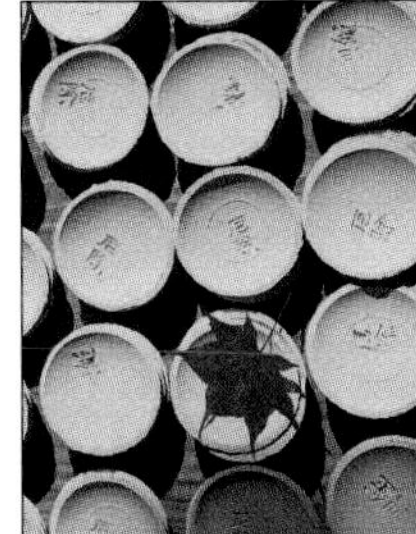

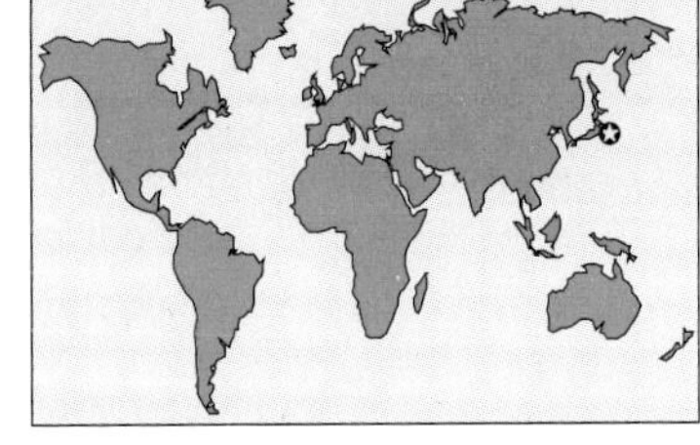

About the Authors

Basho made **haiku** a respected poetry form in Japan.He was born in 1644 into a samurai family. Until his early twenties he served as a samurai warrior. Among samurai, writing poetry was an admired skill. Later, Basho turned entirely to writing and teaching. He used different pen names. His pen name *Basho* comes from a kind of banana tree that grew near where he lived.

Takarai Kikaku was born in 1661. He became one of Basho's students. Some of Kikaku's works have been put to music. Writing poetry was so important in Japanese society that poets competed. Basho and Kikaku often wrote verses on the same themes. Often they answered each other's verses. One story says that they were sitting in a garden together when Basho wrote the first haiku that follows.

Literary Terms

connotation images or emotions connected to a word

haiku a Japanese poetry form, made of seventeen unrhymed syllables

About the Selections

These poems are traditional Japanese haiku. In Japanese, a haiku has seventeen unrhymed syllables. (Translations may not follow this rule.) Still, of all poems, haiku use the most symbols. That is because they are so short. They use words and symbols to call up feelings in the reader. They also depend on **connotations**. Those are the feelings and images connected with a word.

Selection at a Glance

Three Haiku

Basho (translated by Olivia Gray)
Kikaku and Anonymous (translated by Harry Behn)

Student pages 301–303

Overview

These haiku suggest scenes or moods powerfully in just a few words. Their simplicity is deceptive and profound. Their words are carefully chosen to open many associations for the reader.

Selection Summary

The "Three Haiku" by Basho, Kikaku, and an unknown poet are traditional Japanese poems. They give three quick "snapshots": a frog by a pool, a cocky rooster, and a small singing bird.

Objectives

- To note the characteristics of haiku, such as natural images and strong suggestion.
- To identify the mood created by images.

Audiocassette

Teacher's Resource Library TRL

- Vocabulary Workbook 28
- Selection Glossary 31
- Student Study Guide 37
- Activity 49
- Workbook 49
- Writing Activity 34
- Selection Quiz 31

Setting the Stage for Reading

About the Author

Basho traveled often and widely in Japan. On his last trip (1694), as he lay dying in Osaka, he wrote a haiku that indicated he was still thinking of traveling and writing. At the time of his death, Basho had more than 2000 students.

ASK Why do you think Basho and Kikaku, teacher and student, sometimes wrote together and often answered each other's haiku? (Answers may include that this was one form of instruction, that they had formed a close bond, or that haiku is a public rather than a private expression.)

About the Selection

Each haiku tries to express a single and complete mood through highly suggestive language and to create a fresh view of a subject drawn from daily life.

Activate Prior Knowledge: Many students will have some experience with haiku. Ask them to share what they know about the form and recite haiku they have enjoyed.

ASK Haiku often includes words that suggest the season or time of day—since these times carry many associations. What season is suggested by cherry blossoms? By mosquitoes? (spring and summer)

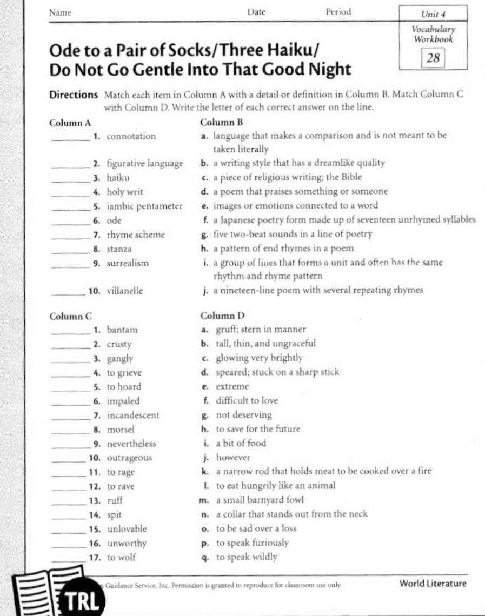

Name Date Period

Unit 4 *Vocabulary Workbook* 28

Ode to a Pair of Socks/Three Haiku/ Do Not Go Gentle Into That Good Night

Directions Match each item in Column A with a detail or definition in Column B. Match Column C with Column D. Write the letter of each correct answer on the line.

Column A	Column B
______ 1. connotation	a. language that makes a comparison and is not meant to be taken literally
______ 2. figurative language	b. a writing style that has a dreamlike quality
______ 3. haiku	c. a piece of religious writing; the Bible
______ 4. holy writ	d. a poem that praises something or someone
______ 5. iambic pentameter	e. images or emotions connected to a word
______ 6. ode	f. a Japanese poetry form made up of seventeen unrhymed syllables
______ 7. rhyme scheme	g. five two-beat sounds in a line of poetry
______ 8. stanza	h. a pattern of end rhymes in a poem
______ 9. surrealism	i. a group of lines that forms a unit and often has the same rhythm and rhyme pattern
______ 10. villanelle	j. a nineteen-line poem with several repeating rhymes

Column C	Column D
______ 1. bantam	a. gruff; stern in manner
______ 2. crusty	b. tall, thin, and ungraceful
______ 3. gangly	c. glowing very brightly
______ 4. to grieve	d. speared; stuck on a sharp stick
______ 5. to hoard	e. extreme
______ 6. impaled	f. difficult to love
______ 7. incandescent	g. not deserving
______ 8. morsel	h. to save for the future
______ 9. nevertheless	i. a bit of food
______ 10. outrageous	j. however
______ 11. to rage	k. a narrow rod that holds meat to be cooked over a fire
______ 12. to rave	l. to eat hungrily like an animal
______ 13. ruff	m. a small barnyard fowl
______ 14. spit	n. a collar that stands out from the neck
______ 15. unlovable	o. to be sad over a loss
______ 16. unworthy	p. to speak furiously
______ 17. to wolf	q. to speak wildly

 World Literature

TRL

Vocabulary Workbook 28

Reading Vocabulary TRL

Use the Selection Glossary page to be sure students can visualize the rooster in the second haiku.

Motivation for Reading

Write on the board "Less is more." Explain that to the Japanese poet, it is valuable to say less and suggest more, so that the reader participates imaginatively in creating meaning.

Discussion Questions

Have students read the marginal comment and question as they read.

A ASK Critical Thinking What do you think an "ancient pool" looks like? How does the splash of the frog contrast this? (Answers may suggest that it is deep, quiet, and surrounded by lush growth. A leaping frog adds energy and a certain humor to the scene.)

B The mood is humorous.

Viewing the Art

Bird and Magnolia are by Nakabayashi Chikuto. The simple painting focuses on the beauty of nature much as the Three Haiku do.

ASK How is the painting like the haiku here? (The painting and the haiku focus on the beauty of nature.)

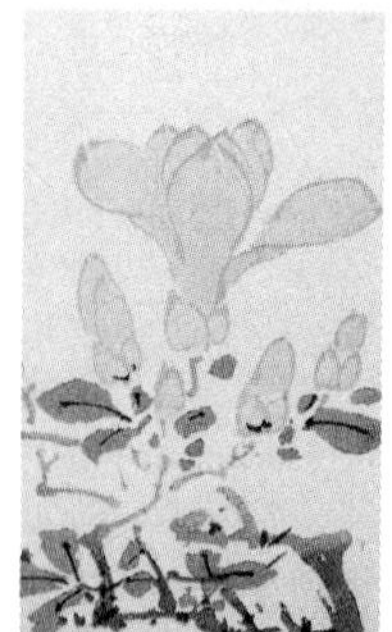

Three Haiku

Basho, Kikaku, Anonymous

A As you read, note the form of the poems.

Ancient pool. Sound
of a frog's leap—
Splissssshhhhh. . . .

—Basho

B What is the mood of this poem?

A **bantam** rooster
spreading his **ruff** of feathers
thinks he's a lion!

—Kikaku

Small bird, forgive me.
I'll hear the end of your song
in some other world.

—Anonymous

bantam a small barnyard fowl

ruff a collar that stands out from the neck

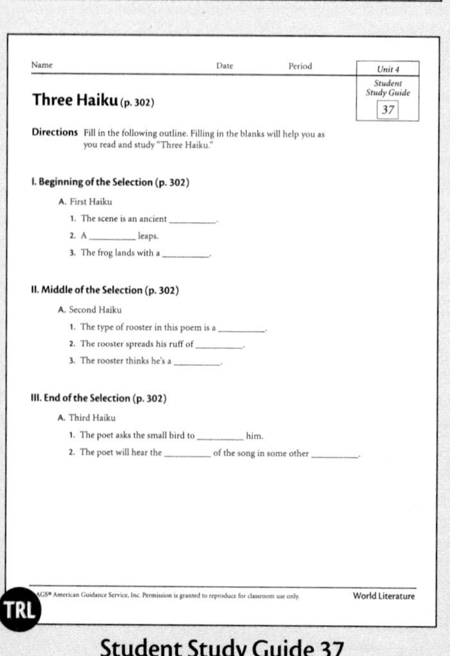

Name Date Period

Unit 4 — *Student Study Guide* 37

Three Haiku (p. 302)

Directions Fill in the following outline. Filling in the blanks will help you as you read and study "Three Haiku."

I. Beginning of the Selection (p. 302)

A. First Haiku

1. The scene is an ancient ________.
2. A ________ leaps.
3. The frog lands with a ________.

II. Middle of the Selection (p. 302)

A. Second Haiku

1. The type of rooster in this poem is a ________.
2. The rooster spreads his ruff of ________.
3. The rooster thinks he's a ________.

III. End of the Selection (p. 302)

A. Third Haiku

1. The poet asks the small bird to ________ him.
2. The poet will hear the ________ of the song in some other ________.

 World Literature

TRL **Student Study Guide 37**

Name Date Period

Unit 4 — *Activity* 49

Three Haiku

Part A Directions In each blank, write the word or phrase that best completes each sentence.

1. An ________ is the setting in the first haiku.
2. In the third haiku, the poet asks the bird to ________.
3. A small barnyard fowl is called a ________.
4. The ________ thinks it is a lion.
5. In some other ________, the poet will hear the end of the bird's song.

Part B Directions Read each sentence. Write *T* if the statement is true or *F* if it is false.

________ 1. Kikaku taught Basho how to write haiku.
________ 2. Basho is a pen name which means bold.
________ 3. A ruff of feathers is a scraggly tail on a bird.
________ 4. The three animals in these haiku are a lion, a frog, and a songbird.
________ 5. Before Basho wrote poetry full time, he was a samurai warrior.

 World Literature

TRL **Activity 49**

Name Date Period

Unit 4 — *Workbook* 49

Three Haiku

Part A Directions In each blank write the word or phrase that best completes each sentence.

1. In the third haiku, the poet asks the bird to ________.
2. A small barnyard fowl is called a ________.
3. An ________ is the setting in the first haiku.
4. The ________ thinks it is a lion.
5. In some other ________, the poet will hear the end of the bird's song.

Part B Directions Read each sentence. Write *T* if the statement is true or *F* if it is false.

________ 1. Basho is a pen name which means bold.
________ 2. A ruff of feathers is a scraggly tail on a bird.
________ 3. Kikaku taught Basho how to write haiku.
________ 4. The three animals in these haiku are a lion, a frog, and a songbird.
________ 5. Before Basho wrote poetry full time, he was a samurai warrior.

 World Literature

TRL **Workbook 49**

REVIEWING the SELECTION

Three Haiku

Basho, Kikaku, Anonymous

Directions Write the answers to these questions using complete sentences.

Comprehension: Identifying Facts

1. Name the three animals in the three poems.
2. What does the rooster think he is?
3. What is the setting of the haiku by Basho?

Comprehension: Understanding Main Ideas

4. What makes the "Splish" sound in the first poem?
5. How does the rooster try to look impressive?
6. What does the poet ask the small bird to do?

Understanding Literature: Haiku

Haiku is a Japanese poetry form. It has a strict style. Usually, a haiku is three lines long. The first line has five syllables. The middle line has seven syllables. The last line has five syllables. (When a haiku is translated from Japanese, the syllable count may not be the same.) A haiku uses images and the power of suggestion to create emotion. Usually it draws images from nature. It may give a "snapshot" of a single image.

7. All three of these haiku draw from nature. Explain.
8. The haiku by Basho uses images that contrast. Explain what kind of mood this creates.

Critical Thinking

9. How does the poet make the rooster seem funny?
10. Which haiku do you like best? Why?

Writing on Your Own Think of an image from nature. Write a haiku to show that image. Try to create a certain mood in your poem.

Reviewing the Selection

Answer Key

Comprehension: Identifying Facts

1. A frog, a bantam rooster, and a songbird are the poems' subjects.

2. The rooster has the fierce attitude of a lion.

3. It is set beside an ancient pond.

Comprehension: Understanding Main Ideas

4. A frog makes the sound as it jumps into the water.

5. It puffs out the ruff of feathers at its neck.

6. He asks forgiveness for not being able to listen to the bird's song.

Understanding Literature: Haiku

7. The settings are all outdoors, and the subjects are all animals—two wild and one domestic.

8. The contrast between the serenity and beauty of the ancient pond and the freshness and informality of the frog's leap create surprise and wake up the reader.

Critical Thinking

9. He points out how the rooster's fighting spirit and aggressive attitude are much bigger than its size warrants.

10. Some students may prefer the humor of the bantam rooster; others may be drawn to the emotion and suggestion of death in the third. A few may enjoy the way meaning moves out in widening circles from Basho's simple poem.

Writing on Your Own Explain that it may be easier to suggest a mood by focusing on an image or symbol which calls up strong emotions in them. Suggest that students use the 5/7/5 syllable rule loosely, to ensure economy, but not force their language just to create exactly 17 syllables.

Selection Quiz

The Teacher's Resource Library includes a Selection Quiz for "Three Haiku" that may be given following the Selection Review.

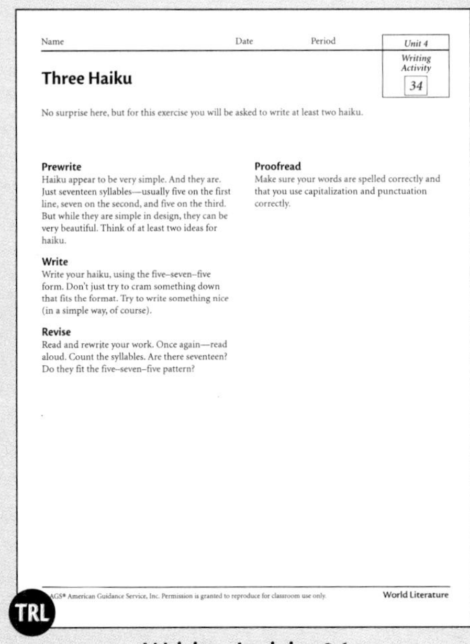

Name Date Period

Unit 4 *Writing Activity* *34*

Three Haiku

No surprise here, but for this exercise you will be asked to write at least two haiku.

Prewrite
Haiku appear to be very simple. And they are. Just seventeen syllables—usually five on the first line, seven on the second, and five on the third. But while they are simple in design, they can be very beautiful. Think of at least two ideas for haiku.

Write
Write your haiku, using the five–seven–five form. Don't just try to cram something down that fits the format. Try to write something nice (in a simple way, of course).

Revise
Read and rewrite your work. Once again—read aloud. Count the syllables. Are there seventeen? Do they fit the five–seven–five pattern?

Proofread
Make sure your words are spelled correctly and that you use capitalization and punctuation correctly.

 World Literature

TRL

Writing Activity 34

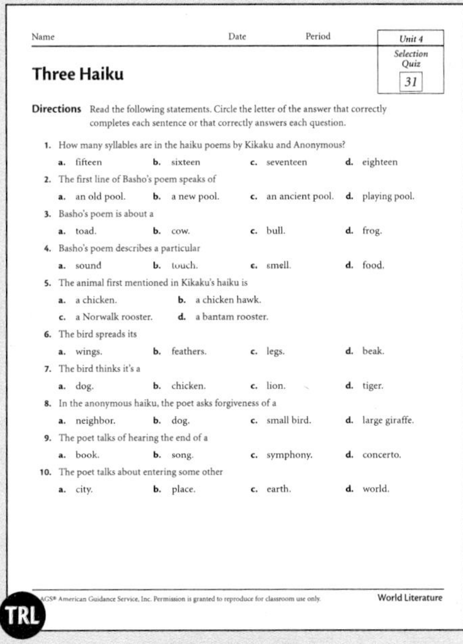

Name Date Period

Unit 4 *Selection Quiz* *31*

Three Haiku

Directions Read the following statements. Circle the letter of the answer that correctly completes each sentence or that correctly answers each question.

1. How many syllables are in the haiku poems by Kikaku and Anonymous?
   a. fifteen b. sixteen c. seventeen d. eighteen
2. The first line of Basho's poem speaks of
   a. an old pool. b. a new pool. c. an ancient pool. d. playing pool.
3. Basho's poem is about a
   a. toad. b. cow. c. bull. d. frog.
4. Basho's poem describes a particular
   a. sound b. touch. c. smell. d. food.
5. The animal first mentioned in Kikaku's haiku is
   a. a chicken. b. a chicken hawk. c. a Norwalk rooster. d. a bantam rooster.
6. The bird spreads its
   a. wings. b. feathers. c. legs. d. beak.
7. The bird thinks it's a
   a. dog. b. chicken. c. lion. d. tiger.
8. In the anonymous haiku, the poet asks forgiveness of a
   a. neighbor. b. dog. c. small bird. d. large giraffe.
9. The poet talks of hearing the end of a
   a. book. b. song. c. symphony. d. concerto.
10. The poet talks about entering some other
   a. city. b. place. c. earth. d. world.

 World Literature

TRL

Selection Quiz 31

Selection at a Glance

Do Not Go Gentle Into That Good Night

Dylan Thomas

Student pages 304–307

Overview

"Do Not Go Gentle Into That Good Night" is typical of Thomas's poetry in its personal subject matter, its intensely lyrical sound and rhythm, and its dense imagery, focused on the cycle of birth and death.

Selection Summary

In "Do Not Go Gentle Into That Good Night," Dylan Thomas, a Welsh poet, talks about fighting against death.

Objectives

- To identify rhyme and understand rhyme scheme.
- To identify iambic pentameter rhythm.

Audiocassette 

Teacher's Resource Library TRL

- Vocabulary Workbook 28
- Selection Glossary 32
- Student Study Guide 38
- Activity 50
- Workbook 50
- Writing Activity 35
- Selection Quiz 32

INTRODUCING the SELECTION

Do Not Go Gentle Into That Good Night

Dylan Thomas

Dylan Thomas
(1914–1953)
Welsh

About the Author

Dylan Thomas was born in 1914 in Swansea, in southwest Wales. He left school when he was sixteen and worked as a newspaper reporter. Thomas began writing poetry early. His first book of poems was published when he was twenty. His poetry shows an intense energy and love of life. He used language and rhythm musically. Thomas' short stories and plays also show a love of words. The radio play *Under Milk Wood* describes a day in a Welsh village. Audiences loved to hear Thomas read his own works aloud. He made several tours in the United States in the 1950s.

Literary Terms

iambic pentameter five two-beat sounds in a line of poetry

rhyme scheme a pattern of end rhymes in a poem

stanza a group of lines that forms a unit and often has the same rhythm and rhyme pattern

villanelle a nineteen-line poem with several repeating rhymes

About the Selection

"Do Not Go Gentle Into That Good Night" is a fine example of a villanelle. A **villanelle** is a form used in France in the 1500s. It has nineteen rhymed lines. They follow a pattern of repeating rhymes. The poem is split into five **stanzas** of three lines and one stanza of four lines. (A stanza is a group of lines that form a unit in a poem.) Look at the **rhyme scheme**, or pattern of end rhymes. Notice how many rhymes there are. "Do Not Go Gentle" also uses **iambic pentameter**. Iambic pentameter describes the beat, or rhythm, of a line of verse. Each line has five two-beat sounds. The emphasis falls on the even-numbered beats.

Setting the Stage for Reading

About the Author

Have students read the text and look at the photo. *Dylan* means "tide" in Welsh, and Thomas lived up to the name in his intensity both in his work and personal presence. Witty and fun-loving, he had many friends. He read his work in a booming Welsh voice. When he died at 39, he was recognized as one of the best young poets of the English language.

ASK Why do you think a person who loves life and words might write poetry with strong rhyme and rhythm? (Answers may include that these song-like elements enhance words and intensify emotions.)

About the Selection

Point out that line 1 is repeated in lines 6, 12, and 18. Line 3 is repeated in lines 9, 15, and 19. In effect, a villanelle has eight lines that are essentially refrain.

Activate Prior Knowledge: Ask students to name and recite lines from poems they remember. They are likely to remember them because of their strong imagery, rhythm, and sound effects.

ASK Why might a poem about death focus on night? (Answers might include that night is a symbol for death or that darkness, like death, contains the unknown.)

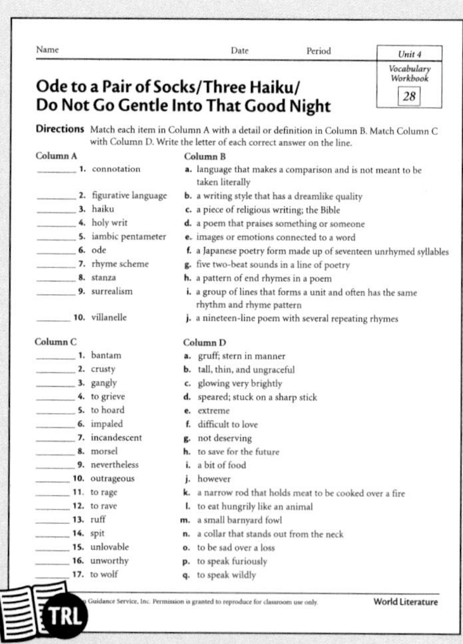

Name ________ Date ________ Period ________

Unit 4 — *Vocabulary Workbook* 28

Ode to a Pair of Socks/Three Haiku/ Do Not Go Gentle Into That Good Night

Directions Match each item in Column A with a detail or definition in Column B. Match Column C with Column D. Write the letter of each correct answer on the line.

Column A	Column B
______ 1. connotation	a. language that makes a comparison and is not meant to be taken literally
______ 2. figurative language	b. a writing style that has a dreamlike quality
______ 3. haiku	c. a piece of religious writing; the Bible
______ 4. holy writ	d. a poem that praises something or someone
______ 5. iambic pentameter	e. images or emotions connected to a word
______ 6. ode	f. a Japanese poetry form made up of seventeen unrhymed syllables
______ 7. rhyme scheme	g. five two-beat sounds in a line of poetry
______ 8. stanza	h. a pattern of end rhymes in a poem
______ 9. surrealism	i. a group of lines that forms a unit and often has the same rhythm and rhyme pattern
______ 10. villanelle	j. a nineteen-line poem with several repeating rhymes

Column C	Column D
______ 1. bantam	a. gruff; stern in manner
______ 2. crusty	b. tall, thin, and ungraceful
______ 3. gangly	c. glowing very brightly
______ 4. to grieve	d. speared; stuck on a sharp stick
______ 5. to hoard	e. extreme
______ 6. impaled	f. difficult to love
______ 7. incandescent	g. not deserving
______ 8. morsel	h. to save for the future
______ 9. nevertheless	i. a bit of food
______ 10. outrageous	j. however
______ 11. to rage	k. a narrow rod that holds meat to be cooked over a fire
______ 12. to rave	l. to eat hungrily like an animal
______ 13. ruff	m. a small barnyard fowl
______ 14. spit	n. a collar that stands out from the neck
______ 15. unlovable	o. to be sad over a loss
______ 16. unworthy	p. to speak furiously
______ 17. to wolf	q. to speak wildly

World Literature

TRL

Vocabulary Workbook 28

Do Not Go Gentle Into That Good Night

Dylan Thomas

Do not go gentle into that good night,
Old age should burn and **rave** at close of day;
Rage, rage against the dying of the light.

Though wise men at their end know dark is right, **A**
Because their words had forked no lightning they
Do not go gentle into that good night.

Good men, the last wave by, crying how bright
Their frail deeds might have danced in a green bay, **B**
Rage, rage against the dying of the light.

Wild men who caught and sang the sun in flight,
And learn, too late, they **grieved** it on its way,
Do not go gentle into that good night.

As you read, notice the rhyme scheme.

Thomas is using *gentle* as an adverb instead of *gently.*

Forked no lightning means that their words had not lit up the world, like a lightning flash.

grieve to cause harm or sadness

rage to speak furiously

rave to speak wildly

Reading Vocabulary TRL

After students have studied the Selection Glossary page, invite volunteers to pantomime the meaning of each term.

Motivation for Reading

Ask students what they believe a person thinks about when near death. Invite volunteers to state some goals they hope to achieve in their lifetime.

Discussion Questions

Suggest that students answer the question on page 306 after they finish reading the poem.

A ASK Comprehension These lines report that wise men know that death (dark) must come (is right); why are they still unwilling to die without a struggle? (They had not done enough in word or action to enlighten the world or change it.)

B ASK Literary Element This metaphor compares the "deeds" of good men to waves in a "green bay." As the last wave passes, why are they not satisfied? (They see that they could have done more good; their acts seem frail to them.)

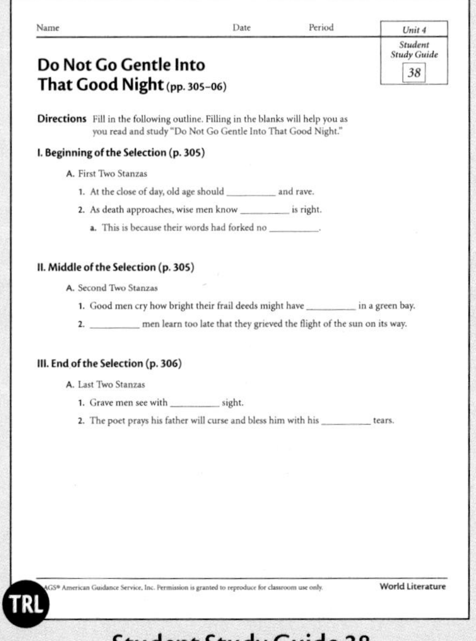

Name Date Period Unit 4 Student Study Guide 38

Do Not Go Gentle Into That Good Night (pp. 305–06)

Directions Fill in the following outline. Filling in the blanks will help you as you read and study "Do Not Go Gentle Into That Good Night."

I. Beginning of the Selection (p. 305)

A. First Two Stanzas

1. At the close of day, old age should __________ and rave.
2. As death approaches, wise men know __________ is right.
   a. This is because their words had forked no __________.

II. Middle of the Selection (p. 305)

A. Second Two Stanzas

1. Good men cry how bright their frail deeds might have __________ in a green bay.
2. __________ men learn too late that they grieved the flight of the sun on its way.

III. End of the Selection (p. 306)

A. Last Two Stanzas

1. Grave men see with __________ sight.
2. The poet prays his father will curse and bless him with his __________ tears.

 World Literature

TRL

Student Study Guide 38

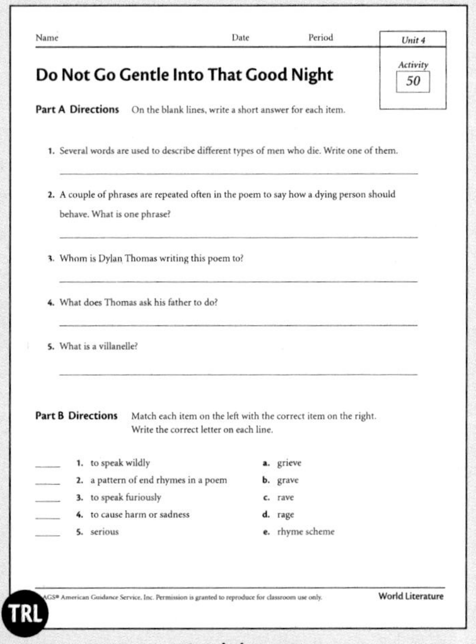

Name Date Period Unit 4 Activity 50

Do Not Go Gentle Into That Good Night

Part A Directions On the blank lines, write a short answer for each item.

1. Several words are used to describe different types of men who die. Write one of them.
2. A couple of phrases are repeated often in the poem to say how a dying person should behave. What is one phrase?
3. Whom is Dylan Thomas writing this poem to?
4. What does Thomas ask his father to do?
5. What is a villanelle?

Part B Directions Match each item on the left with the correct item on the right. Write the correct letter on each line.

____	1. to speak wildly	a. grieve
____	2. a pattern of end rhymes in a poem	b. grave
____	3. to speak furiously	c. rave
____	4. to cause harm or sadness	d. rage
____	5. serious	e. rhyme scheme

 World Literature

TRL

Activity 50

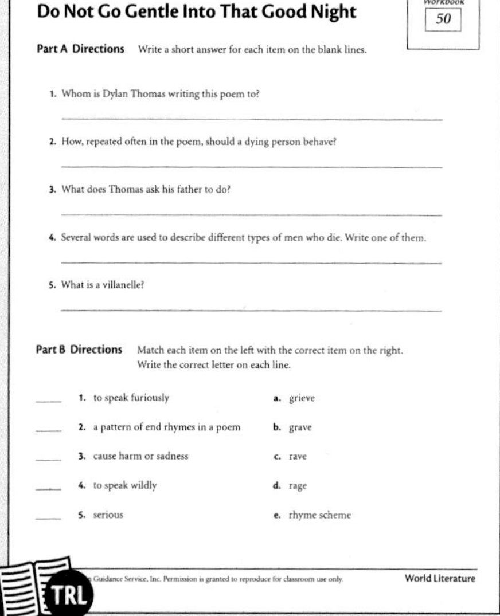

Name Date Period Unit 4 Workbook 50

Do Not Go Gentle Into That Good Night

Part A Directions Write a short answer for each item on the blank lines.

1. Whom is Dylan Thomas writing this poem to?
2. How, repeated often in the poem, should a dying person behave?
3. What does Thomas ask his father to do?
4. Several words are used to describe different types of men who die. Write one of them.
5. What is a villanelle?

Part B Directions Match each item on the left with the correct item on the right. Write the correct letter on each line.

____	1. to speak furiously	a. grieve
____	2. a pattern of end rhymes in a poem	b. grave
____	3. cause harm or sadness	c. rave
____	4. to speak wildly	d. rage
____	5. serious	e. rhyme scheme

 World Literature

TRL

Workbook 50

Discussion Questions

A ASK Literary Element Explain that irony exists when the writer gives a meaning to words that is the opposite of their usual sense. What irony does Thomas introduce in lines 13–14? (The sight of the dying men is blinding ["dazzling"]; sightless eyes are filled with light [blaze like meteors]. He suggests that one sees, or understands, most clearly just when sight, and life, are about to be taken away.)

B ASK Comprehension Why does the speaker address his father? What is the "sad height"? (He realizes his father is near death—which makes him seem distant and which saddens both of them.)

C He wants his father to fight to hold on to life for as long as possible. Although there is good in death ("good night"), the speaker hopes his father will focus all his remaining energy on living.

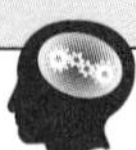

Comprehension

Compare and Contrast Each stanza of the poem identifies different types of individuals. Through comparison and contrast students can gain insight into how, though different, the individuals have a common bond of clinging to life. Suggest that students compare and contrast the types of individuals—wise, good, wild, and grave. How would their lives be different? What does each do at the end of life? What do they have in common?

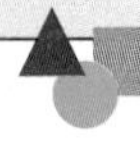

Learning Styles

Group Learning Have students work in small groups to read and summarize a short story by Dylan Thomas or his radio play. Suggest that the students present their summary to the class as well as prepare a choral reading of part of the story or play.

Grave means "serious" here.

A Grave men, near death, who see with blinding sight
Blind eyes could blaze like meteors and be gay,
Rage, rage against the dying of the light.

How does the poet want his father to feel about dying?

B And you, my father, there on the sad height,
Curse, bless, me now with your fierce tears, I pray.
Do not go gentle into that good night.
Rage, rage against the dying of the light.

C

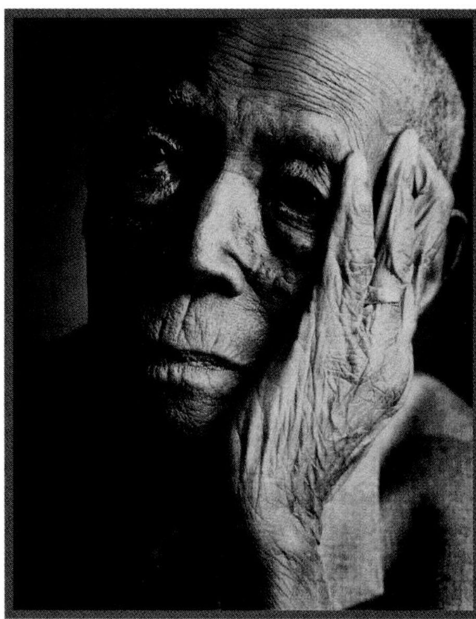

Career Connection

Dylan Thomas advises the aged to resist death and live as fully as they can. As the elderly population of the United States grows, careers in care of the elderly have grown as well. From gerontologists, doctors specializing in the care of the elderly, to assisted-living managers, to physical therapists, care givers are needed to meet the needs of the elderly. Arrange for students to visit a hospital wing devoted to elderly care or an assisted-living complex. Explore what types of careers are available and their educational and personal requirements.

306 *Unit 4 Poetry*

REVIEWING the SELECTION

Do Not Go Gentle Into That Good Night

Dylan Thomas

Directions Write the answers to these questions using complete sentences.

Comprehension: Identifying Facts

1. How does the poet say that people should behave when death is near?
2. What four kinds of men does the poet name?
3. To whom is Thomas writing this poem?

Comprehension: Understanding Main Ideas

4. What do wise men know at their end?
5. What is the main idea of the poem as a whole?
6. What does the poet think that serious people will regret?

Understanding Literature: Rhyme Scheme

The term *rhyme scheme* means the pattern of rhymes. This poem is a villanelle. In this form of poetry, the first five stanzas have three lines. The first and third lines rhyme. This rhyme scheme, or pattern, is *aba.* The letter *a* stands for the lines whose last words rhyme with *night.* In the last stanza, the first, third and fourth lines rhyme. The last stanza is *abaa.*

7. Look at the third stanza. What two words rhyme?
8. Look at the second line of each stanza. What rhyming words do you find at the ends of the lines?

Critical Thinking

9. What regrets keep both wise men and good men from dying quietly?
10. How do you think the poet feels about his father? Explain.

Writing on Your Own Do you agree with the poet about what a dying person should do? Why or why not? Write a paragraph telling your own outlook.

Reviewing the Selection

Answer Key

Comprehension: Identifying Facts

1. Instead of quietly accepting death, they should fight to stay alive as long as possible.

2. He names wise men, good men, wild men, and grave men.

3. He speaks to his father, who is dying.

Comprehension: Understanding Main Ideas

4. They know that "dark is right"—i.e., death cannot be avoided.

5. The poet advises the living to hold onto life in order to accomplish more and fulfill what they dreamed of doing, not to meekly submit to death.

6. They will regret that they were not more lighthearted in their approach to life, for it might have brought more light into their lives.

Understanding Literature: Rhyme Scheme

7. *Bright* and *light* rhyme.

8. The rhyming words of middle lines are *day, they, bay, way, gay,* and *pray.*

Critical Thinking

9. All find the achievements of their lives unsatisfactory. The wise regret that their words weren't wiser. The good regret that their deeds were not great enough. The wild men regret that their wild flights came to nothing. The serious regret the poverty of joy in their lives.

10. The intensity of his imperatives show that the speaker cares deeply for his father. Students may say that the poet thinks of his father as a strong, vigorous man.

Writing on Your Own Ask students to compose a topic sentence that states their opinion clearly. Then have them list the reasons they think as they do.

Selection Quiz

The Teacher's Resource Library includes a Selection Quiz for "Do Not Go Gentle Into That Good Night" that may be given following the Selection Review.

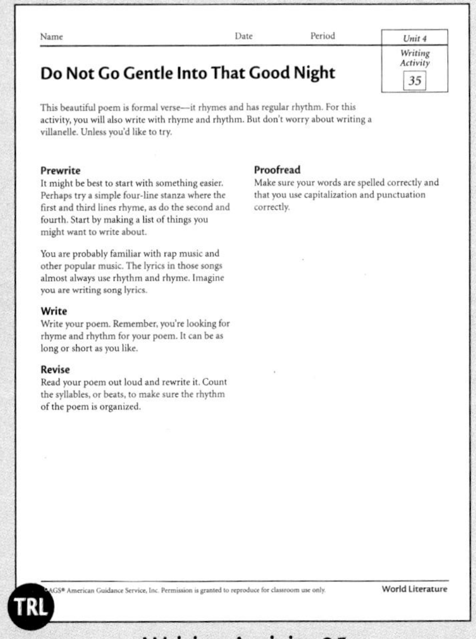

Name Date Period

Unit 4 *Writing Activity* 35

Do Not Go Gentle Into That Good Night

This beautiful poem is formal verse—it rhymes and has regular rhythm. For this activity, you will also write with rhyme and rhythm. But don't worry about writing a villanelle. Unless you'd like to try.

Prewrite
It might be best to start with something easier. Perhaps try a simple four-line stanza where the first and third lines rhyme, as do the second and fourth. Start by making a list of things you might want to write about.

You are probably familiar with rap music and other popular music. The lyrics in those songs almost always use rhythm and rhyme. Imagine you are writing song lyrics.

Write
Write your poem. Remember, you're looking for rhyme and rhythm for your poem. It can be as long or short as you like.

Revise
Read your poem out loud and rewrite it. Count the syllables, or beats, to make sure the rhythm of the poem is organized.

Proofread
Make sure your words are spelled correctly and that you use capitalization and punctuation correctly.

 World Literature

TRL

Writing Activity 35

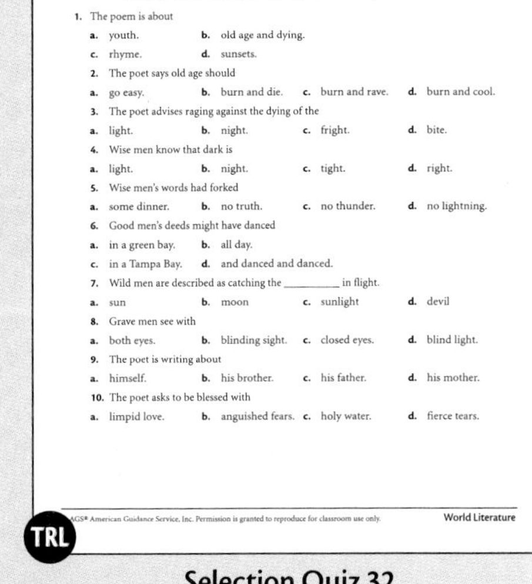

Name Date Period

Unit 4 *Selection Quiz* 32

Do Not Go Gentle Into That Good Night

Directions Read the following statements. Circle the letter of the answer that correctly completes each sentence or that correctly answers each question.

1. The poem is about
   a. youth. b. old age and dying.
   c. rhyme. d. sunsets.
2. The poet says old age should
   a. go easy. b. burn and die. c. burn and rave. d. burn and cool.
3. The poet advises raging against the dying of the
   a. light. b. night. c. fright. d. bite.
4. Wise men know that dark is
   a. light. b. night. c. tight. d. right.
5. Wise men's words had forked
   a. some dinner. b. no truth. c. no thunder. d. no lightning.
6. Good men's deeds might have danced
   a. in a green bay. b. all day.
   c. in a Tampa Bay. d. and danced and danced.
7. Wild men are described as catching the __________ in flight.
   a. sun b. moon c. sunlight d. devil
8. Grave men see with
   a. both eyes. b. blinding sight. c. closed eyes. d. blind light.
9. The poet is writing about
   a. himself. b. his brother. c. his father. d. his mother.
10. The poet asks to be blessed with
   a. limpid love. b. anguished fears. c. holy water. d. fierce tears.

 World Literature

TRL

Selection Quiz 32

Skills Lesson: Style

There are no cut and dried categories of style. A writer's style is unique because it combines diction, sentence structure, imagery, rhythm, repetition, emphasis, arrangement of ideas, etc., into a voice that is like no other. Style is what results from combining the ideas to be formed and expressed with the writer's individuality.

Review Answers

1. Style is an author's way of writing that expresses his or her ideas and personality.
2. Style expresses the author's thoughts and attitudes toward those thoughts. In a real sense, style mirrors "who the writer is."
3. "Do Not Go Gentle" expresses fierce energy and emotion about the death of a loved one; it reveals the poet's love of life. "Mindoro" expresses quiet love for the beauty of a place; it reveals the poet's vision of his land as mysterious and whole.
4. All of these poems compress vivid images of nature into a small space and suggest human emotions without stating them.
5. Answers may suggest that rhymed verse is most musical, free verse most natural, and haiku most inspirational.

You may want to review several poems with students, reading them aloud and pointing out different poetic devices: imagery, figurative language, format, rhyme, etc. Encourage students to write about an experience or attitude that is real and deeply felt.

Style

Style is an author's way of writing. It includes not only what the writer says but also the way he or she says it. These examples show two different styles:

> The thief lied.
>
> That rascal was never on friendly terms with the truth.

The first sentence is serious and factual. The second is in a humorous style. The author seems amused but not bothered by the other person's lies.

The poems in this unit have many styles. In "The Diameter of the Bomb," Yehuda Amichai begins on a low key. His words could almost come from a police report:

> The diameter of the bomb was
> thirty centimeters
> and the diameter of its effective
> range about seven meters,
> with four dead and eleven wounded.

By the ending, though, his deep outrage at this tragedy shows:

> And I won't even mention the howl
> of orphans
> that reaches up to the throne of
> God and
> beyond, making
> a circle with no end and no God.

Pablo Neruda writes about a pair of socks. His style is not ordinary, though. His style is to have fun with them.

> I fought
> the mad urge
> to lock them in a golden
> cage
> and feed them birdseed
> and morsels of pink melon
> every day.

Review

1. What is style?
2. Does style give you a sense of who the writer is? Why or why not?
3. How are the styles of "Do Not Go Gentle Into That Good Night" and "Mindoro" different?
4. Describe how "Taking Leave of a Friend" and the three haiku are alike in style.
5. Which do you prefer, free verse, haiku, or rhymed verses? Explain.

Writing on Your Own Think about the poems you read. Write your own poem. You can use free verse, haiku, or rhymed lines. You might choose something serious or something funny on any subject.

308 *Unit 4 Poetry*

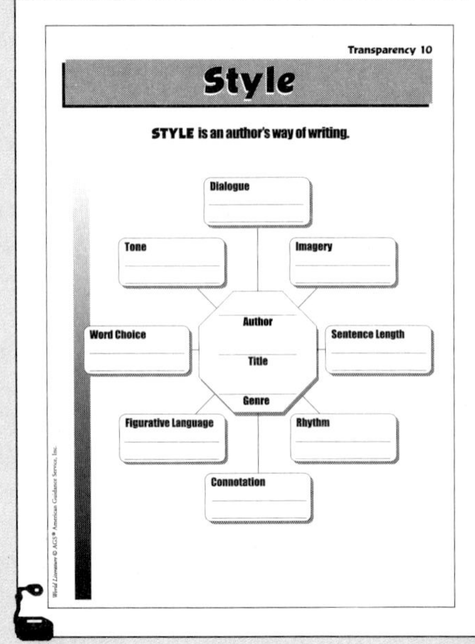

Transparency 10

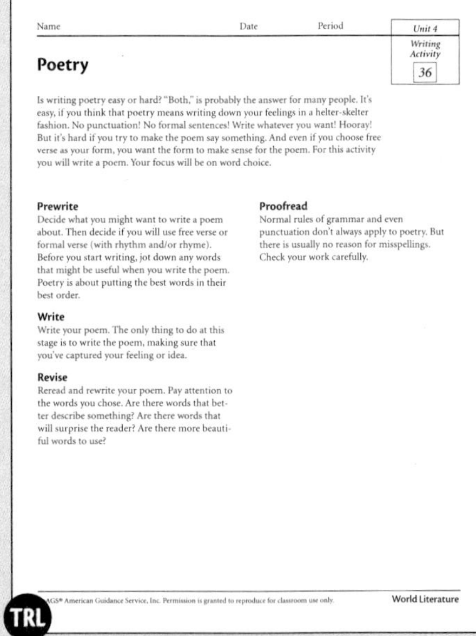

Name Date Period | Unit 4 Writing Activity 36

Poetry

Is writing poetry easy or hard? "Both," is probably the answer for many people. It's easy, if you think that poetry means writing down your feelings in a helter-skelter fashion. No punctuation! No formal sentences! Write whatever you want! Hooray! But it's hard if you try to make the poem say something. And even if you choose free verse as your form, you want the form to make sense for the poem. For this activity you will write a poem. Your focus will be on word choice.

Prewrite
Decide what you might want to write a poem about. Then decide if you will use free verse or formal verse (with rhythm and/or rhyme). Before you start writing, jot down any words that might be useful when you write the poem. Poetry is about putting the best words in their best order.

Write
Write your poem. The only thing to do at this stage is to write the poem, making sure that you've captured your feeling or idea.

Revise
Reread and rewrite your poem. Pay attention to the words you chose. Are there words that better describe something? Are there words that will surprise the reader? Are there more beautiful words to use?

Proofread
Normal rules of grammar and even punctuation don't always apply to poetry. But there is usually no reason for misspellings. Check your work carefully.

World Literature

Writing Activity 36

UNIT 4 SUMMARY

A poem packs a lot of meaning into few words. The words must fit certain rhythms or rhyme schemes. They must create images. In this you read poetry from seven countries. The poems cover a time span from the eighth century to the twentieth century.

Poems belong to many forms. These depend on length and meter, or rhythm. For instance, a sonnet has fourteen lines and a certain meter. A haiku has three lines and seventeen syllables. Free verse doesn't rhyme. Blank verse is unrhymed verse with five beats in a line. (Shakespeare's plays are in blank verse.) Some poets combine traditional forms to create new forms.

Poems can also be grouped by their purpose. An *ode* is a poem of praise. Some odes praise beautiful landscapes. Others salute great athletes. An *elegy* mourns a death.

You may think that poetry is not as easy to read as prose. Keep in mind that a poem is like the words of a song. It can help to read a poem aloud.

Selections

- "The Diameter of the Bomb" by Yehuda Amichai. An Israeli poet shows how one tragic event has a widespread effect.
- "Taking Leave of a Friend" by Li Po. A Chinese poet of the eighth century looks at two friends parting.
- "Thoughts of Hanoi" by Nguyen Thi Vinh. A poet from Vietnam looks back at the city before war split the country.
- "Mindoro" by Ram n Sunico. A modern Filipino poet describes sunset near an island.
- "Ode to a Pair of Socks" by Pablo Neruda. A Nobel prize-winner describes the joy of getting a pair of hand-knit socks.
- "Three Haiku" by Basho, Kikaku, and an unknown poet. Three very short poems are in a traditional Japanese form. They give three quick "snapshots:" a frog by a pool, a cocky rooster, and a small singing bird.
- "Do Not Go Gentle Into That Good Night" by Dylan Thomas. A Welsh poet talks about fighting against death.

Unit Summary

Ask volunteers to read the paragraphs and selection descriptions on page 309. After each paragraph, ask students to comment about what they learned in the unit. Discuss the following questions for each selection.

ASK Why does Amichai feel outrage about the small bomb he describes? (It caused so much senseless death, destruction, and sorrow.)

ASK What shows the friends are sad to say good-bye in Li Po's poem? (They keep each other in sight as long as possible. Their horses, which must be used to being together, neigh to each other.)

ASK To whom is Nguyen Thi Vinh's speaker talking and why? (He is speaking to a friend who lives in North Vietnam, enemy territory, because he fears their common history and roots have been lost to the war.)

ASK To what senses do the images in "Mindoro" appeal? Why? (Visual and touch: the spectacle of the sunset and the tiredness of the fishermen make sight and touch most suitable to communicate the experience.)

ASK Why does the speaker in Neruda's poem find the socks "heavenly"? (They are beautiful to him and he appreciates the effort of their maker.)

ASK How does each haiku create a "snapshot" of nature? (It focuses on one scene with a single, powerful image.)

ASK Why does the speaker in Thomas's poem say one should not give in to death meekly? (He feels that life should be as long as possible so that each person can accomplish more and understand better what life is for.)

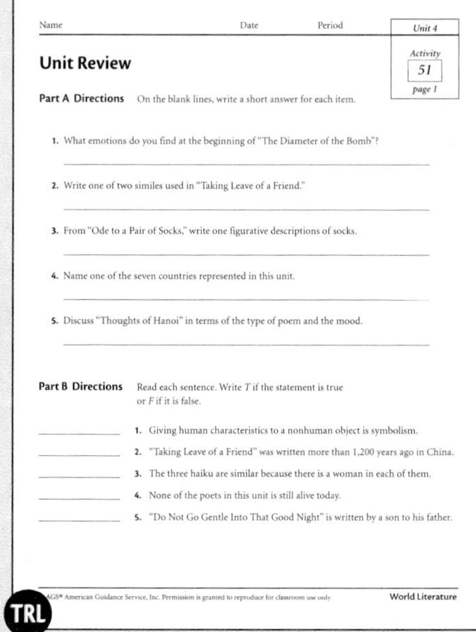

Name Date Period | *Unit 4* *Activity* 51 *page 1*

Unit Review

Part A Directions On the blank lines, write a short answer for each item.

1. What emotions do you find at the beginning of "The Diameter of the Bomb"?
2. Write one of two similes used in "Taking Leave of a Friend."
3. From "Ode to a Pair of Socks," write one figurative descriptions of socks.
4. Name one of the seven countries represented in this unit.
5. Discuss "Thoughts of Hanoi" in terms of the type of poem and the mood.

Part B Directions Read each sentence. Write *T* if the statement is true or *F* if it is false.

_____ 1. Giving human characteristics to a nonhuman object is symbolism.
_____ 2. "Taking Leave of a Friend" was written more than 1,200 years ago in China.
_____ 3. The three haiku are similar because there is a woman in each of them.
_____ 4. None of the poets in this unit is still alive today.
_____ 5. "Do Not Go Gentle Into That Good Night" is written by a son to his father.

 World Literature

TRL

Activity 51, pages 1–2

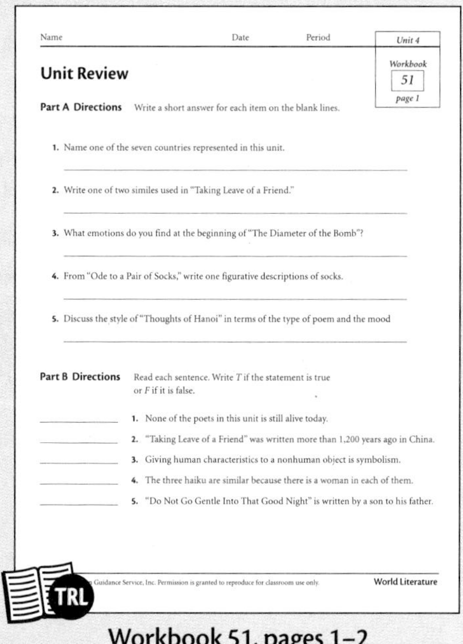

Name Date Period | *Unit 4* *Workbook* 51 *page 1*

Unit Review

Part A Directions Write a short answer for each item on the blank lines.

1. Name one of the seven countries represented in this unit.
2. Write one of two similes used in "Taking Leave of a Friend."
3. What emotions do you find at the beginning of "The Diameter of the Bomb"?
4. From "Ode to a Pair of Socks," write one figurative descriptions of socks.
5. Discuss the style of "Thoughts of Hanoi" in terms of the type of poem and the mood

Part B Directions Read each sentence. Write *T* if the statement is true or *F* if it is false.

_____ 1. None of the poets in this unit is still alive today.
_____ 2. "Taking Leave of a Friend" was written more than 1,200 years ago in China.
_____ 3. Giving human characteristics to a nonhuman object is symbolism.
_____ 4. The three haiku are similar because there is a woman in each of them.
_____ 5. "Do Not Go Gentle Into That Good Night" is written by a son to his father.

 World Literature

TRL

Workbook 51, pages 1–2

Unit 3 Review

The Teacher's Resource Library includes two parallel forms of the Unit 4 Mastery Test. The difficulty level of the two forms is equivalent. You may wish to use one form as a pretest and the other form as a posttest.

Answer Key

Comprehension: Identifying Facts

1. The poetry form is free verse.

2. Haiku is the Japanese poetry form.

3. Dylan Thomas uses traditional rhyming in his villanelle "Do Not Go Gentle Into That Good Night."

4. Pablo Neruda wrote odes to ordinary things.

5. Ramón Sunico writes about Mindoro, an island of the Philippines.

Comprehension: Understanding Main Ideas

6. "The Diameter of the Bomb," "Do Not Go Gentle Into That Good Night," or "Thoughts of Hanoi" are solemn or grim in tone and subject matter. "Taking Leave of a Friend," "Mindoro," and the final haiku touch on moving subjects and are handled with thoughtful rather than light attention.

7. "Ode to a Pair of Socks" and the first two haiku take a humorous view.

8. Both poems discuss the destruction, pain, and sorrow caused by war. "The Diameter of the Bomb" condemns it in a tone of outrage, focusing on one incident. "Thoughts of Hanoi" recalls with gentle sadness how Hanoi and people's relationships used to be.

9. He loves and is awed by the gift of hand-knitted woolen socks.

10. It is set in nature, with mountains and river as a backdrop.

Understanding Literature: Mood

11. Mood is atmosphere, or the feeling created in literature through word choices and images.

12. It begins sounding neutral and journalistic; it ends with outrage.

13. Answers may include the absurd image of the cocky little rooster, causing laughter; the splish of the leaping frog, introducing freshness; or the lovely song of the bird, creating longing.

14. Students may point to images of the sunset on the water or mountains or the stars in the darkening sky, creating a peaceful mood.

15. "Thoughts of Hanoi" is nostalgic and pleading. Students may cite words such as "how is Hang Dao now?" "don't you remember," "lush," "stainless," "jubilant," basking," and "please."

UNIT 4 REVIEW

Directions Write the answers to these questions using complete sentences.

Comprehension: Identifying Facts

1. What poetry form is used in "The Diameter of the Bomb"?
2. What is the name of the Japanese poetry form in this unit?
3. One of these selections has a traditional rhyming form. Which is it? Who wrote it?
4. Name a poet who wrote odes to everyday things.
5. What country does Ram n Sunico write about?

Comprehension: Understanding Main Ideas

6. Name two poems in this unit that are about serious things.
7. Name two poems that are happy or funny.
8. Compare and contrast "Thoughts of Hanoi" and "The Diameter of the Bomb." How are they alike and different?
9. What gift does Pablo Neruda receive? How does he feel about that gift?
10. What is the setting of "Taking Leave of a Friend"?

Understanding Literature: Mood

Mood is the feeling that a piece of writing causes. Even within a short piece, the mood may change. That gives a change of pace. Still, the work has an overall feeling. Images are one thing that set a mood. The image of feet as gangly navy-blue sharks adds to a playful mood in Neruda's "Ode." Word choices are another way to create mood. Words such as burn and rage help create the mood of "Do Not Go Gentle Into That Good Night."

11. What is mood?
12. Think about "The Diameter of the Bomb." How does the mood change from the beginning to the end of the poem?
13. Choose one of the three haiku. Explain how an image creates the mood.
14. What are some of the images in "Mindoro"? What mood do they create?
15. What is the mood of "Thoughts of Hanoi"? Name three words or phrases that help create this mood.

Critical Thinking

16. Think of the images used in the poems in this unit. Name the image you like best. Tell why you like it.

17. The poem "Taking Leave of a Friend" was written over 1,200 years ago. Tell why people might like it so much that we still read it.

18. Dylan Thomas's poem has a pattern of rhyme and meter. Do you think this makes the poem more powerful? Why or why not?

19. What is your favorite poem from this unit? Explain your choice.

20. If you could meet one of these poets, which one would it be? Explain your choice.

Speak and Listen

Think of a poem you like. It could be one from this unit. It could be one you find in the library. Read the poem to yourself several times, then practice reading the poem aloud. Read the poem to the class when you can read it well. Explain to the class what the poem means to you.

Beyond Words

Images are very important in poetry. Choose one image you like from the poems in this unit. Draw a picture to show what that image suggests to you. Your drawing can be realistic. It can also just suggest an image. For example, you might just use color to show the image. Your drawing might barely suggest a tree or boat.

Writing on Your Own

Think about how a poem is like and not like a short story. Write an essay comparing poems with short stories. Tell how they are alike and different. You might want to name a poem from this unit that tells a story. Compare it with a short story on the same theme. Or you might name a poem that does not tell a story. Write about how it is like or different from a short story.

Test-Taking Tip

Before you begin a test, look it over quickly. Try to set aside enough time to complete each section.

Critical Thinking

16. Accept all answers that provide reasons based on accurate perception of the image and involve the senses.

17. Sadness at parting is a universal experience that touches all people in all times.

18. Students may point out that Thomas has used rhythm and rhyme to make his emotional appeal more dramatic and lyrical.

19. Accept any choice for which students offer reasons based on analysis of the poem's subject, images, craft, or mood.

20. In evaluating students' choice of poet, analyze reasons for how well they show understanding of the poet's themes and perspectives or life experiences.

Speak and Listen

Encourage students to read their poems with expression, but naturally, so that they do not overemphasize poetic devices.

Beyond Words

Point out that realism and detail may not be most important to communicating poetic ideas. Discuss ways that line and color choices can reinforce the mood created by words in poetry.

Writing on Your Own Have students select a poem and a story to use as examples throughout their comparison essay. Help them create a table comparing the same elements before they write their drafts.

Name ______ Date ______ Period ______

Unit 4 Mastery Test A 4 *page 1*

Unit 4 Mastery Test A

Part A Directions Match the poem in the Poem Bank below with the lines taken from the poem. Write the name of the poem in the space provided. *Note:* You do not need to write the whole name of the poem, but enough to identify it.

Poem Bank

"The Diameter of the Bomb"
"Thoughts of Hanoi"
"Ode to a Pair of Socks"
"Do Not Go Gentle Into That Good Night"
"Taking Leave of a Friend"
"Mindoro"
"Three Haiku"

______ 1. And you, my father, there on the sad height

______ 2. Like jungle/ explorers/ who deliver a young deer

______ 3. And I won't even mention the howl of orphans

______ 4. Do you count me as a friend/ or am I the enemy in your eyes?

______ 5. To the left/ the sea/ slices the afternoon in two

______ 6. My feet were/ two woolen/ fish

______ 7. Small bird, forgive me

______ 8. Rage, rage against the dying of the light

______ 9. I want to bury the past/ to burn the future

______ 10. Mind like a floating wide cloud

 World Literature

TRL

Unit Mastery Test A, page 1

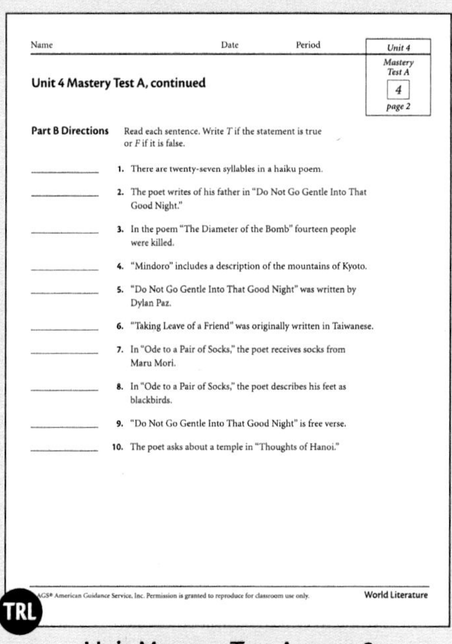

Name ______ Date ______ Period ______

Unit 4 Mastery Test A 4 *page 2*

Unit 4 Mastery Test A, continued

Part B Directions Read each sentence. Write *T* if the statement is true or *F* if it is false.

______ 1. There are twenty-seven syllables in a haiku poem.

______ 2. The poet writes of his father in "Do Not Go Gentle Into That Good Night."

______ 3. In the poem "The Diameter of the Bomb" fourteen people were killed.

______ 4. "Mindoro" includes a description of the mountains of Kyoto.

______ 5. "Do Not Go Gentle Into That Good Night" was written by Dylan Paz.

______ 6. "Taking Leave of a Friend" was originally written in Taiwanese.

______ 7. In "Ode to a Pair of Socks," the poet receives socks from Maru Mori.

______ 8. In "Ode to a Pair of Socks," the poet describes his feet as blackbirds.

______ 9. "Do Not Go Gentle Into That Good Night" is free verse.

______ 10. The poet asks about a temple in "Thoughts of Hanoi."

 World Literature

TRL

Unit Mastery Test A, page 2

UNIT 5 Planning Guide

Persuasive Literature

	Student Pages	About the Author	About the Selection	Literary Terms	Reviewing the Selection	Writing on Your Own
■ FRANCE "Letter to the English" by Joan of Arc	317–319	✔	✔	✔	✔	✔
■ RUSSIA "Nobel Lecture" by Alexander Solzhenitsyn	320–334	✔	✔	✔	✔	✔
■ UNITED STATES "The Gettysburg Address" by Abraham Lincoln	335–336	✔	✔	✔	✔	✔
■ UNITED STATES "Inaugural Address" by John F. Kennedy	337–342	✔	✔	✔	✔	✔
■ FRANCE "Of Repentance" by Michel de Montaigne	344–346	✔	✔	✔	✔	✔
■ ANTIGUA From *A Small Place* by Jamaica Kincaid	347–361	✔	✔	✔	✔	✔
■ SKILLS LESSON: Setting; UNIT REVIEW	362, 364–365			✔		✔

(Column group heading: Selection Features)

Unit Features

Student Text
Persuasive Literature
Speeches
Essays
Skills Lesson: Setting
Unit Summary

Teacher's Resource Library
Activity 52: Persuasive Literature
Workbook 52: Persuasive Literature
Activity 53: Speeches
Workbook 53: Speeches
Activity 58: Essays
Workbook 58: Essays

Assessment Features

Student Text
Unit 5 Review

Teacher's Resource Library
Activity 61: Unit 5 Review, pages 1–2
Workbook 61: Unit 5 Review, pages 1–2
Selection Quizzes 33–38
Unit 5 Mastery Tests A and B, pages 1–2

Teaching Strategies							Language Skills				Learning Styles					TRL Teacher's Resource Library					
Viewing the Art	Career Connection	Environmental Connection	Cross-Curricular Connection	Diversity Connection	Community Connection	Transparencies	Grammar	Literary Elements	Comprehension	Writing Connection	Auditory	Visual	Tactile/Kinesthetic	Group Learning	LEP/ESL	Vocabulary Workbook	Selection Glossary	Student Study Guide	Activities	Workbook	Writing Activities
318																29	33	39	54	54	37
			321	326				322	324	325		328	331		323	30	34	40	55	55	38
																31	35	41	56	56	39
	341						340	341	339		340					31	36	42	57	57	40
345																32	37	43	59	59	41
		349, 356	348, 354	350, 352	351			352	351, 353					355, 358		32	38	44	60	60	42
						11													61	61	43

Unit at a Glance

Unit 5: Persuasive Literature

pages 312–365

Persuasive Literature
pages 314–315

Selections
- FRANCE "Letter to the English" by Joan of Arc, pages 317–319
- RUSSIA "Nobel Lecture" by Alexander Solzhenitsyn, pages 320–334
- UNITED STATES "The Gettysburg Address" by Abraham Lincoln, pages 335– 336
- UNITED STATES "Inaugural Address" by John F. Kennedy, pages 337–342
- FRANCE "Of Repentance" by Michel de Montaigne, pages 344–346
- ANTIGUA From *A Small Place* by Jamaica Kincaid, pages 347–361

Unit Skills Lesson: Setting
page 362

Unit Summary page 363

Unit Review pages 364–365

Audiocassette

Transparency 11

Teacher's Resource Library TRL
- Activity 52 and 61, pages 1–2
- Workbook 52 and 61, pages 1–2
- Unit 5 Mastery Tests A and B, pages 1–2

(Answer Keys for the Teacher's Resource Library begin on page 468 of this Teacher's Edition.)

"There is nothing that you may not get people to believe if you will only tell it them loud enough and often enough."
—Ouida

"Folks don't like to have somebody around knowin' more than they do ... You're not gonna change any of them by talkin' right ... and when they don't want to learn there's nothing you can do but keep your mouth shut or talk their language."
—Harper Lee

Other Resources

Books for Teachers

Lincoln, Abraham. (Andrew Delbanco, ed.) *The Portable Abraham Lincoln.* New York: Viking, 1992.

Solzhenitsyn, Aleksandr. *August 1914: The Red Wheel.* New York: Farrar, Straus & Giroux, 1989.

Books for Students

Freedman, Russell. *Lincoln: A Photobiography*. Boston: Houghton Mifflin, 1987.

Garden, Nancy. *Dove & Sword: A Novel of Joan of Arc.* New York: Farrar, Straus & Giroux, 1995.

Hansen, Joyce. *Between Two Fires: Black Soldiers in the Civil War.* Danbury, CT: Franklin Watts, 1993.

Kort, Michael. *The Rise and Fall of the Soviet Union.* Danbury, CT: Franklin Watts, 1992.

UNIT 5 *Persuasive Literature*

You see or hear persuasive writing every day. Think about ads, speeches, and editorials. Their purpose is to persuade. Ads are all around. Many people do not like this. They think that people are being led to buy, buy, buy. They feel the ads persuade us all too well. Some people think ads are fine. They show us choices. They say all media help us share ideas. Some people think this is good.

In this unit, you will read two forms of persuasive writing. They are speeches and essays. You will also see that persuasive writing has long been a part of literature.

Introducing the Unit

Read aloud the quotations on page 312. Explain that both Ouida and Harper Lee were authors of fiction, but they explored very different subject matter. Ouida wrote extravagant romances about fashionable European life. Harper Lee focused on social conditions in the American South.

ASK What are both speakers saying about language? How do the speaker's messages differ? (Both say that language can be used to convince people. Ouida feels one need only make oneself heard, loudly and often. Lee, on the other hand, feels that persuasion is more difficult than that. One must speak the language that people want to hear.)

Explain that the selections in this unit all share the same purpose: to persuade. Some of the selections are speeches and others are essays. The selections are drawn from many different phases of history.

Review the Unit 5 selection genres and titles. Discuss the purposes of speeches and essays.

Viewing the Art

Have students look at the painting on page 312. *Joan of Arc Leaving Vaucouleurs, 23 February 1429* was painted by Jean Jaques Scherrer. Explain that Joan was a French peasant girl who felt that God called her to lead the French army against England during the Hundred Years' War. She left Vaucouleurs dressed in men's clothing and accompanied by six armed men.

ASK What does the painter accomplish by placing Joan in the center of the painting far above all the other figures? (Her piety is suggested. She appears brave, larger than life, and capable of leading.)

Video

The Fragile Balance (1955–1961). (24 minutes.) Chatsworth, CA: AIMS Multimedia.

The Rise and Fall of the Soviet Union. (25 minutes.) Washington, DC: National Geographic.

Software

Atlas of U.S. Presidents. CD-ROM. Fairfield, CT: Queue, Inc.

The Civil War: Two Views. CD-ROM. Pound Ridge, NY: Orange Cherry New Media.

History and Culture of France. CD-ROM. Fairfield, CT: Queue, Inc.

Persuasive Literature

Ask students to silently read the text on page 314 and to view the map on page 315.

Persuasive literature, whether fiction or nonfiction, is designed to influence opinions and sometimes actions. Persuasive nonfiction—essays, proclamations and other letters, speeches—often bolsters arguments with supportive facts. The writer may appeal to the logic, emotions, beliefs, values, and attitudes of the intended audience. At the same time, nonfiction works, like fictional literature, may use literary techniques and devices to help sway opinion.

ASK What is the main purpose of persuasive literature? (to influence opinion)

ASK What forms can persuasive literature take? (It can be found in all genres: poems, novels, plays, and a variety of nonfiction works.)

ASK Persuasion has motivated some writers to create great works of fictional literature. What are some of these works and their purposes? ("The Faerie Queene" to flatter Elizabeth I; *Uncle Tom's Cabin* to turn the American public against slavery; "The Crucible" to object to McCarthyism; *The Gulag Archipelago* to expose the evils of Russian prisons.)

ASK Most persuasive writing is nonfiction. What literary techniques are used by creators of nonfiction persuasive works? (Among the techniques used are metaphor and irony.)

UNIT 5 ■ PERSUASIVE LITERATURE

Literary works written mainly to influence opinion are persuasive. The purpose of persuasive writing is more important than its form. Because of that, persuasive writing is found in all genres, or types of writing. In the 1500s, Edmund Spenser wrote a poem, "The Faerie Queene." Its purpose was to flatter Elizabeth I of England as both a ruler and a woman. In the 1850s, Harriet Beecher Stowe wrote the novel *Uncle Tom's Cabin.* (A novel is a longer work of fiction.) With her book, Stowe tried to turn the American public against slavery. During the 1950s Arthur Miller wrote the play "The Crucible." It tried to expose the American anti–Communist hysteria. The play showed McCarthyism as a destructive force like the Salem witch hunts three hundred years earlier. The Russian writer Alexander Solzhenitsyn wrote a series of novels, *The Gulag Archipelago.* He meant to expose the evils and inhumanity of the Soviet prison system.

Poems, novels, and plays written to persuade are not always great literature. Besides, you have read those genres elsewhere in *World Literature.* For those reasons the selections in this unit are nonfiction, as is most persuasive writing. The authors of these selections criticize, reassure, threaten, praise, argue with, and inspire their audiences. Nonetheless, they do use literary techniques. For example, the speeches by Lincoln and Kennedy use metaphors. A metaphor is a figure of speech that says one thing *is* something else. For example, "My love *is* a rose." Jamaica Kincaid uses irony. This form uses words that seem to say one thing but mean the opposite.

As you read, notice the language, imagery, and organization of these selections. Though some were written long ago, they are models that present-day authors still imitate.

The following countries are represented in this unit: France, Russia, the United States, and Antigua.

Have students view the map and read the caption. Tell students that in this unit they will read persuasive works by individuals from each of the countries labeled on the map. You might also explain that the works are drawn from many different periods of history. The speech by Joan of Arc, from France, was delivered in the early 1400s. The other works range from the 1500s to the late 1900s.

ASK On which continent is France located? (Europe)

ASK Which of the countries represented in this unit are located in the Northern Hemisphere? (The United States, Antigua, France, and Russia are all in the Northern Hemisphere.)

Name ____ Date ____ Period ____ *Unit 5* *Activity* 52

Persuasive Literature

Part A Directions On the blank lines, write a short answer for each item.

1. Define persuasive literature.
2. What is a metaphor?
3. In the nonfiction pieces of this unit, what do the authors do for their audiences?
4. Name one of the two forms of persuasive writing covered in this unit.
5. How do some people think advertising helps us?

Part B Directions In each blank, write the word or phrase that best completes each sentence.

1. Novels and plays written to persuade are not always great ________.
2. You see persuasive writing every day in ads and ________.
3. ________ uses words that seem to say one thing but mean the opposite.
4. Some people think that ads lead people to ________, and that this is not good.
5. All ________, or types of writing, include persuasive writing.

 World Literature

TRL

Activity 52

Name ____ Date ____ Period ____ *Unit 5* *Workbook* 52

Persuasive Literature

Part A Directions Write a short answer for each item on the blank lines.

1. What is a metaphor?
2. Name one of the two forms of persuasive writing covered in this unit.
3. How do some people think advertising helps us?
4. Define persuasive literature.
5. In the nonfiction pieces of this unit, what do the authors do for their audiences?

Part B Directions In each blank write the word or phrase that best completes each sentence.

1. You see persuasive writing every day in ads and ________.
2. Some people think that ads lead people to ________, and that this is not good.
3. All ________, or types of writing, include persuasive writing.
4. Novels and plays written to persuade are not always great ________.
5. ________ uses words that seem to say one thing but mean the opposite.

 World Literature

TRL

Workbook 52

Speeches

Ask students to silently read the text and quotations on page 316. Explain that Peggy Noonan was a member of former President Ronald Reagan's staff. She wrote a book titled *What I Saw at the Revolution: A Political Life in the Reagan Era.* Charlotte Perkins Gilman was a member of the women's movement in the United States in the late nineteenth and early twentieth century. Her most noted works include *Women in Economics*, in which she urged women to gain economic independence through work outside the home, and a play entitled *The Yellow Wallpaper.*

ASK What power does Noonan attribute to speeches? (They can enliven even the dullest minds.)

ASK According to Gilman, what do audiences like to hear? (They prefer light topics with plenty of jokes.)

ASK What are some kinds of speeches and when are they delivered? (Proclamations are letters about important events; they are read aloud. Speeches are given at trials and other important events.)

ASK Do speakers usually deliver speeches off the tops of their heads? (No, speeches are usually written before they're delivered.)

Speeches

- "A speech reminds us that words ... have the power to make dance the dullest beanbag of a heart." —Peggy Noonan
- "Audiences are always better pleased with a smart retort, some joke or epigram, than with any amount of reasoning." —Charlotte Perkins Gilman

Speeches are usually written. But they are meant to be spoken to an audience. They respond to an event or occasion. One kind of speech is a proclamation, a letter about important events meant to be read out loud. Trials and other events are also good times for a speech. Speeches work best when they are read out loud. Hearing a good speech, an audience can enjoy its sound as well as its ideas and images.

The occasions for these speeches have passed. Their audiences are gone. Yet the form and content of each still "speaks" to similar events today. Speakers all around the world often still quote from these selections.

316 *Unit 5 Persuasive Literature*

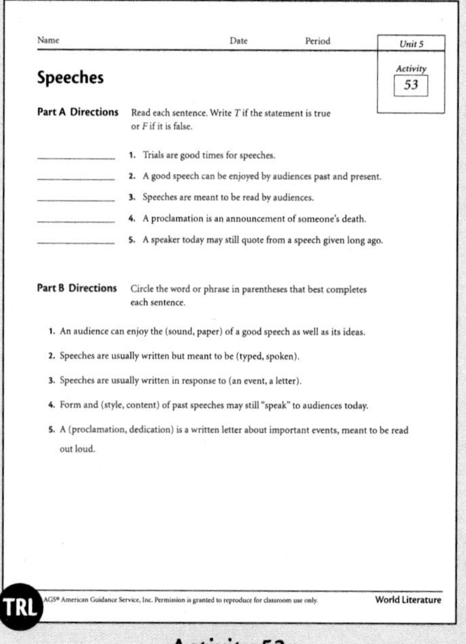
Name Date Period | Unit 5 Activity 53

Speeches

Part A Directions Read each sentence. Write *T* if the statement is true or *F* if it is false.

_______ 1. Trials are good times for speeches.
_______ 2. A good speech can be enjoyed by audiences past and present.
_______ 3. Speeches are meant to be read by audiences.
_______ 4. A proclamation is an announcement of someone's death.
_______ 5. A speaker today may still quote from a speech given long ago.

Part B Directions Circle the word or phrase in parentheses that best completes each sentence.

1. An audience can enjoy the (sound, paper) of a good speech as well as its ideas.
2. Speeches are usually written but meant to be (typed, spoken).
3. Speeches are usually written in response to (an event, a letter).
4. Form and (style, content) of past speeches may still "speak" to audiences today.
5. A (proclamation, dedication) is a written letter about important events, meant to be read out loud.

TRL ©AGS® American Guidance Service, Inc. Permission is granted to reproduce for classroom use only. World Literature

Activity 53

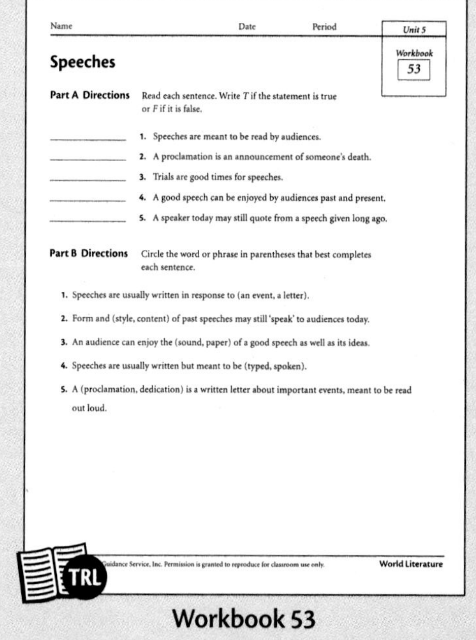
Name Date Period | Unit 5 Workbook 53

Speeches

Part A Directions Read each sentence. Write *T* if the statement is true or *F* if it is false.

_______ 1. Speeches are meant to be read by audiences.
_______ 2. A proclamation is an announcement of someone's death.
_______ 3. Trials are good times for speeches.
_______ 4. A good speech can be enjoyed by audiences past and present.
_______ 5. A speaker today may still quote from a speech given long ago.

Part B Directions Circle the word or phrase in parentheses that best completes each sentence.

1. Speeches are usually written in response to (an event, a letter).
2. Form and (style, content) of past speeches may still 'speak' to audiences today.
3. An audience can enjoy the (sound, paper) of a good speech as well as its ideas.
4. Speeches are usually written but meant to be (typed, spoken).
5. A (proclamation, dedication) is a written letter about important events, meant to be read out loud.

TRL ...uidance Service, Inc. Permission is granted to reproduce for classroom use only. World Literature

Workbook 53

INTRODUCING the SELECTION

Letter to the English

Joan of Arc (translated by Willard Trask)

Joan of Arc
(1412–1431)
French

Literary Term

proclamation a letter about important events meant to be read aloud

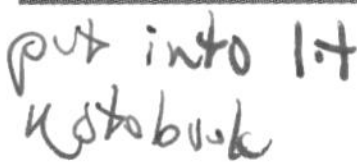

About the Speaker

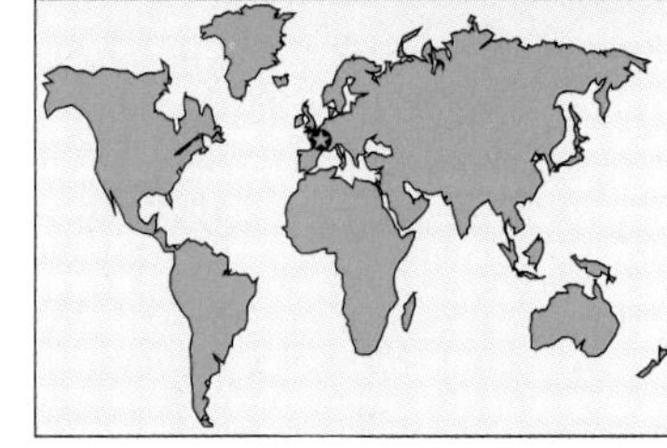

Joan of Arc was the uneducated daughter of a farmer. France and England had been at war, on and off, for many years. Now the English held most of France, including Paris. At age thirteen, Joan began to hear voices. She believed they were saints with a message from God. The voices told her to support the young French king, Charles VII, and help him drive the English out. Joan eventually convinced the king to let her lead an army to Orléans. The city was under attack by the English. Joan inspired the French troops to drive the English away. After that victory, Charles VII was officially crowned.

Soon after, French enemies turned Joan over to the English. A church court convicted her as a heretic, a questioner of the faith. Joan was burned at the stake in Rouen in May 1431. Joan is a national heroine in France today.

About the Selection

The following selection is a **proclamation.** A proclamation is a letter that is read aloud. It may then posted where it can be studied. Most people in the 1400s could not read. So they got the news by hearing it read out loud. A proclamation is the old version of a news broadcast.

This letter was addressed to the English, but Joan knew that the French would also hear it. It was delivered just before the planned attack.

Selection at a Glance

Letter to the English

Joan of Arc (translated by Willard Trask)

Student pages 317–319

Overview

Joan of Arc's proclamation, or announcement, was meant to be read aloud. Proclamations were read aloud before a large audience and then posted in a public area. Those who were able to read could then further scrutinize the text.

Selection Summary

In her "Letter to the English," Joan of Arc, a French heroine, sends a proclamation that warns the English to leave France.

Objectives

- To read and understand a proclamation.
- To identify the intended audience.

Audiocassette 

Teacher's Resource Library 

- Vocabulary Workbook 29
- Selection Glossary 33
- Student Study Guide 39
- Activity 54
- Workbook 54
- Writing Activity 37
- Selection Quiz 33

Setting the Stage for Reading

About the Author

Ask students to read the text and look at the painting. Joan of Arc was only sixteen when she heard voices that led her to Vaucouleurs, where she asked the captain of the garrison for permission to join the army.

ASK Why do you think Joan was able to convince the king to let her lead an army? Would Joan of Arc be taken seriously today? (Charles was moved by her piety and her resolution. Today some people might believe Joan of Arc, but the authorities would never allow her to intervene in government affairs.)

About the Selection

Before the battle of Orléans, Joan dictated her letter of defiance to the English. Her determination and inspiration encouraged the French, who defeated the English at Orléans.

Activate Prior Knowledge: Have students discuss other proclamations they have read or heard about. Suggest that they discuss the situations in which these proclamations were made.

ASK In what kinds of contemporary situations might people write proclamations? (Proclamations might be written, delivered, and posted during political protests, strikes, or political campaigns.)

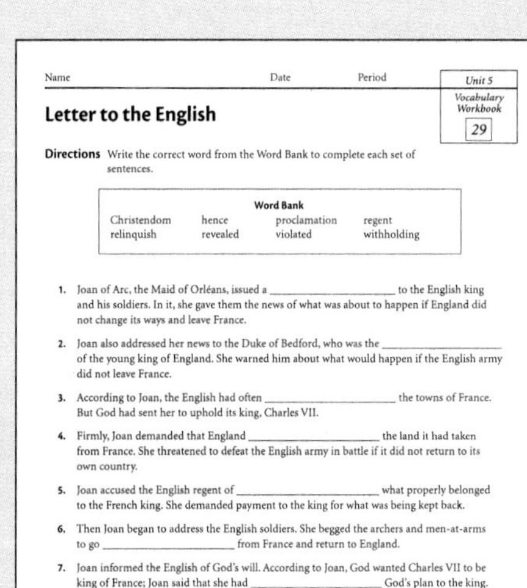

Name Date Period | *Unit 5* *Vocabulary Workbook* 29

Letter to the English

Directions Write the correct word from the Word Bank to complete each set of sentences.

Word Bank			
Christendom	hence	proclamation	regent
relinquish	revealed	violated	withholding

1. Joan of Arc, the Maid of Orléans, issued a ______________ to the English king and his soldiers. In it, she gave them the news of what was about to happen if England did not change its ways and leave France.
2. Joan also addressed her news to the Duke of Bedford, who was the ______________ of the young king of England. She warned him about what would happen if the English army did not leave France.
3. According to Joan, the English had often ______________ the towns of France. But God had sent her to uphold its king, Charles VII.
4. Firmly, Joan demanded that England ______________ the land it had taken from France. She threatened to defeat the English army in battle if it did not return to its own country.
5. Joan accused the English regent of ______________ what properly belonged to the French king. She demanded payment to the king for what was being kept back.
6. Then Joan began to address the English soldiers. She begged the archers and men-at-arms to go ______________ from France and return to England.
7. Joan informed the English of God's will. According to Joan, God wanted Charles VII to be king of France; Joan said that she had ______________ God's plan to the king.
8. Joan, the Maid of Orléans, begged the Regent of England to leave France. She insisted that if he did not do so, he would be destroyed. She believed that what she was doing for France would be the best thing that had ever been done for ______________.

 World Literature

Vocabulary Workbook 29

Reading Vocabulary TRL

Help students preview the selection's vocabulary by giving them copies of the Selection Glossary. Have students take turns using the words in sentences.

Motivation for Reading

What does sixteen-year-old Joan of Arc threaten to do if the English do not make peace in Orléans? Encourage students to find out by reading the proclamation.

Discussion Questions

Suggest that students use the marginal notes to guide their reading.

A ASK Comprehension What is the purpose of Joan's speech? (She is requesting the English to surrender all the land they have violated in France.)

Viewing the Art

Joan of Arc Enters Orléans by an unknown artist shows Joan entering Orléans, where she won a decisive victory.

ASK How are the illustrations of Joan on pages 312 and 318 alike and different? (Answers may include both show a confident Joan astride a horse. One shows her as she prepares to leave for battle, and the other depicts her entering Orléans, which she regained for France.)

Letter to the English

Joan of Arc

As you read, note to whom Joan addresses her speech.

The English *king,* Henry VI, was only a child. The *Duke of Bedford* was his uncle.

Blood royal refers to the claim that Charles was the true heir to the French throne.

Nill is an old word meaning "will not."

A King of England, and you, Duke of Bedford, who call yourself **Regent** of the Kingdom of France ... Do justice to the King of Heaven; surrender to the Maid, who is sent here from God, King of Heaven, the keys of all the good towns you have taken and **violated** in France. She is come from God to uphold the blood royal. She is ready to make peace if you will do justice, **relinquishing** France and paying for what you have **withheld.**

As to you, you archers and men-at-arms, gentle and others, who are before the town of Orléans, go **hence** into your own country in God's name; and if you do not so, expect to hear news of the Maid, who will shortly come to see you, to your very great damage.

King of England, if you do not do so, I am a commander, and in whatever place in France I come upon your men, I will make them leave it, will they or nill they; and if they will not yield obedience, I will have them all slain. I am sent here from God, King of Heaven, to put you, hand to hand, out of all France. Yet if they will yield obedience, I will grant them mercy.

And think not otherwise: for you shall not hold the Kingdom of France from God, King of Heaven, Saint Mary's son, but King Charles shall hold it, the true heir. For so God, King of Heaven, wills it; and so it has been **revealed** to him by the Maid, and he shall enter Paris with a fair company.

If you will not believe this news from God and the Maid, wherever we find you, there we shall strike; and we shall raise such a battle-cry as there has not been in France in a thousand years, if you will not do justice. And know surely that the King of Heaven will send more strength to the Maid than you can bring against her and her good soldiers in any assault. And when the blows begin, it shall be seen whose right is the better before the God of Heaven.

You, Duke of Bedford: The Maid prays and beseeches you not to bring on your own destruction. If you will do her justice, you may yet come in her company there where the French shall do the fairest deed that ever was done for **Christendom.** So answer if you will make peace in the city of Orléans. And if you do not so, consider your great danger speedily.

Christendom all Christians
hence from here
regent one who rules in place of a king
relinquish to release or let go
reveal to show
violate to ruin by force
withhold to keep back

Name ______ Date ______ Period ______ Unit 5 Student Study Guide 39

Letter to the English (p. 318)

Directions Fill in the following outline. Filling in the blanks will help you as you read and study "Letter to the English."

I. Beginning of the Selection (p. 318)

A. Paragraphs One and Two
1. Joan addresses King of ______ and Duke of ______.
2. Joan refers to herself as the ______.
3. Joan is ready to make ______ if they do justice by releasing ______ and paying what they've withheld.
4. To the archers and men-at-arms, Joan tells them to go back to their own countries in ______ name.
5. If the men do not leave, they will hear from the Maid at very great ______.

II. Middle of the Selection (p. 318)

A. Paragraphs Three and Four
1. If Joan comes across any of the King of England's men in France, she will make them leave or have them ______.
2. Joan says she was sent here from ______ to put you out of all France.
3. God wills King ______ to hold the Kingdom of France.

III. End of the Selection (p. 318)

A. Paragraphs Five and Six
1. Joan says that the King of Heaven will send her more ______ than they can bring against her and her good soldiers.
2. If the Duke of Bedford does the Maid justice, he can expect the French to do the fairest deed ever done for ______.

 World Literature

TRL Student Study Guide 39

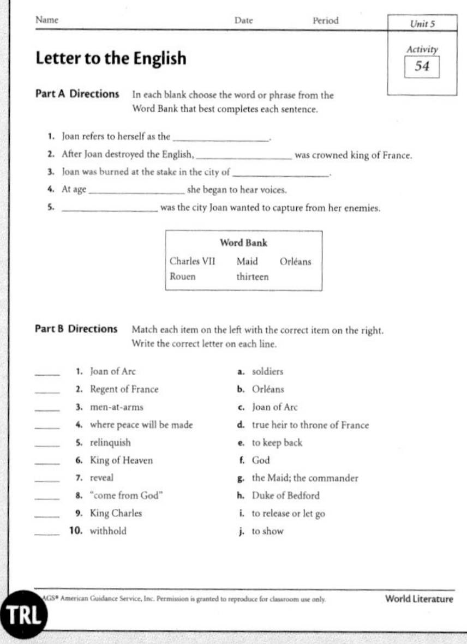

Name ______ Date ______ Period ______ Unit 5 Activity 54

Letter to the English

Part A Directions In each blank choose the word or phrase from the Word Bank that best completes each sentence.

1. Joan refers to herself as the ______.
2. After Joan destroyed the English, ______ was crowned king of France.
3. Joan was burned at the stake in the city of ______.
4. At age ______ she began to hear voices.
5. ______ was the city Joan wanted to capture from her enemies.

Word Bank		
Charles VII	Maid	Orléans
Rouen	thirteen	

Part B Directions Match each item on the left with the correct item on the right. Write the correct letter on each line.

____ 1. Joan of Arc		a. soldiers
____ 2. Regent of France		b. Orléans
____ 3. men-at-arms		c. Joan of Arc
____ 4. where peace will be made		d. true heir to throne of France
____ 5. relinquish		e. to keep back
____ 6. King of Heaven		f. God
____ 7. reveal		g. the Maid; the commander
____ 8. "come from God"		h. Duke of Bedford
____ 9. King Charles		i. to release or let go
____ 10. withhold		j. to show

 World Literature

TRL Activity 54

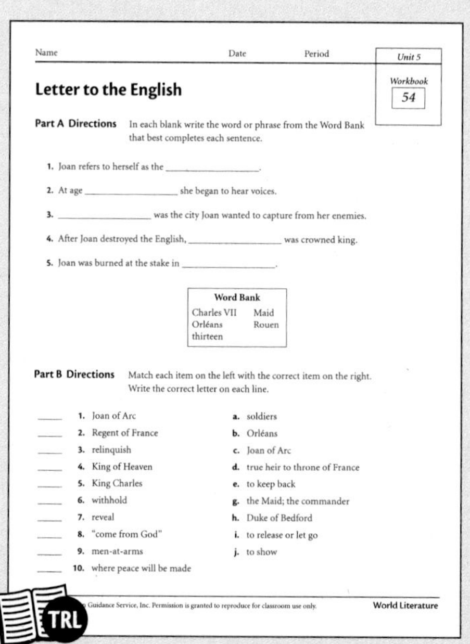

Name ______ Date ______ Period ______ Unit 5 Workbook 54

Letter to the English

Part A Directions In each blank write the word or phrase from the Word Bank that best completes each sentence.

1. Joan refers to herself as the ______.
2. At age ______ she began to hear voices.
3. ______ was the city Joan wanted to capture from her enemies.
4. After Joan destroyed the English, ______ was crowned king.
5. Joan was burned at the stake in ______.

Word Bank	
Charles VII	Maid
Orléans	Rouen
thirteen	

Part B Directions Match each item on the left with the correct item on the right. Write the correct letter on each line.

____ 1. Joan of Arc	a. soldiers
____ 2. Regent of France	b. Orléans
____ 3. relinquish	c. Joan of Arc
____ 4. King of Heaven	d. true heir to throne of France
____ 5. King Charles	e. to keep back
____ 6. withhold	g. the Maid; the commander
____ 7. reveal	h. Duke of Bedford
____ 8. "come from God"	i. to release or let go
____ 9. men-at-arms	j. to show
____ 10. where peace will be made	

 World Literature

TRL Workbook 54

REVIEWING the SELECTION

Letter to the English

Joan of Arc

Directions Write the answers to these questions using complete sentences.

Comprehension: Identifying Facts

1. What two people does Joan address at the beginning of her letter?
2. Who does Joan say has sent her to lead this battle?
3. What is Joan's main goal for France?

Comprehension: Understanding Main Ideas

4. What does Joan demand that the English do if they want peace?
5. What reason does Joan give for stating that Charles should be king?
6. Why does Joan believe she and her troops will win this battle?

Understanding Literature: Proclamation

A proclamation is a letter that is read aloud. It is then published or posted where it can be read. Joan wrote her proclamation over five hundred years ago, when most people could not read. The proclamation was read aloud to them. Today, most people can read. News is spread by television and radio. Yet proclamations are still used. They may be used to celebrate events. The mayor of a town may issue a proclamation to honor a good citizen or the opening of a new school.

7. Joan threatens the English. How does her proclamation show that she would rather they left on their own?
8. Why do you think Joan addresses one part of her letter to the English soldiers?

Critical Thinking

9. How do you think the English leaders reacted to this letter? What about ordinary soldiers?
10. Joan died for her beliefs. Do you think from this letter that she perhaps expected to?

Writing on Your Own Think of someone you would like to honor. Write a proclamation to declare a certain day that person's day. You might have a day to honor a teacher or a sports hero. Open by directing the letter to a person or group. (For instance: "Students of the Blank School.") Then state why the person is being honored. Also tell when the day is.

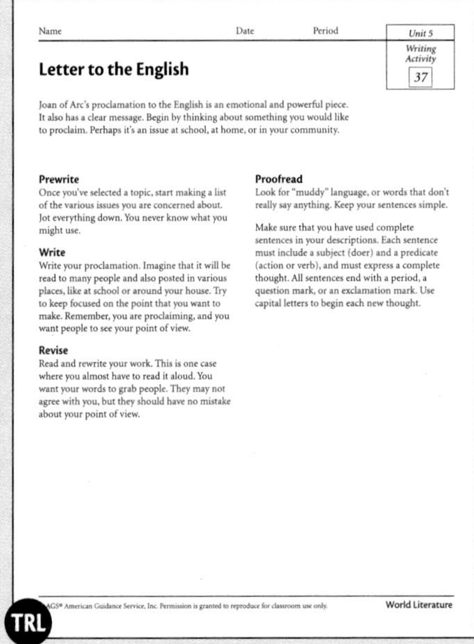

Name Date Period | *Unit 5 Writing Activity* 37

Letter to the English

Joan of Arc's proclamation to the English is an emotional and powerful piece. It also has a clear message. Begin by thinking about something you would like to proclaim. Perhaps it's an issue at school, at home, or in your community.

Prewrite
Once you've selected a topic, start making a list of the various issues you are concerned about. Jot everything down. You never know what you might use.

Write
Write your proclamation. Imagine that it will be read to many people and also posted in various places, like at school or around your house. Try to keep focused on the point that you want to make. Remember, you are proclaiming, and you want people to see your point of view.

Revise
Read and rewrite your work. This is one case where you almost have to read it aloud. You want your words to grab people. They may not agree with you, but they should have no mistake about your point of view.

Proofread
Look for "muddy" language, or words that don't really say anything. Keep your sentences simple.

Make sure that you have used complete sentences in your descriptions. Each sentence must include a subject (doer) and a predicate (action or verb), and must express a complete thought. All sentences end with a period, a question mark, or an exclamation mark. Use capital letters to begin each new thought.

 World Literature

TRL

Writing Activity 37

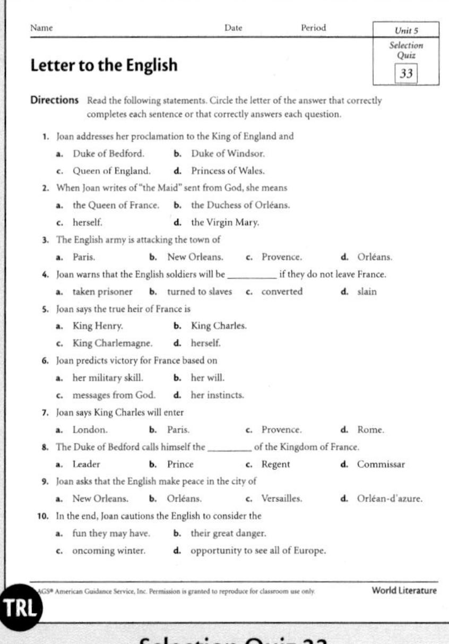

Name Date Period | *Unit 5 Selection Quiz* 33

Letter to the English

Directions Read the following statements. Circle the letter of the answer that correctly completes each sentence or that correctly answers each question.

1. Joan addresses her proclamation to the King of England and
   a. Duke of Bedford. b. Duke of Windsor. c. Queen of England. d. Princess of Wales.
2. When Joan writes of "the Maid" sent from God, she means
   a. the Queen of France. b. the Duchess of Orléans. c. herself. d. the Virgin Mary.
3. The English army is attacking the town of
   a. Paris. b. New Orleans. c. Provence. d. Orléans.
4. Joan warns that the English soldiers will be ________ if they do not leave France.
   a. taken prisoner b. turned to slaves c. converted d. slain
5. Joan says the true heir of France is
   a. King Henry. b. King Charles. c. King Charlemagne. d. herself.
6. Joan predicts victory for France based on
   a. her military skill. b. her will. c. messages from God. d. her instincts.
7. Joan says King Charles will enter
   a. London. b. Paris. c. Provence. d. Rome.
8. The Duke of Bedford calls himself the ________ of the Kingdom of France.
   a. Leader b. Prince c. Regent d. Commissar
9. Joan asks that the English make peace in the city of
   a. New Orleans. b. Orléans. c. Versailles. d. Orléan-d'azure.
10. In the end, Joan cautions the English to consider the
   a. fun they may have. b. their great danger. c. oncoming winter. d. opportunity to see all of Europe.

 World Literature

TRL

Selection Quiz 33

Reviewing the Selection

Answer Key

Comprehension: Identifying Facts

1. Joan addresses the King of England and the Duke of Bedford.

2. God has sent her to lead this battle.

3. Her main goal is to place France into the hands of King Charles.

Comprehension: Understanding Main Ideas

4. She demands that the English leave France and relinquish the land they have taken.

5. God wills that Charles be crowned king.

6. They will win because God divines it.

Understanding Literature: Proclamation

7. Because she believes her purpose is holy, she would rather not slay the English but have them leave France voluntarily.

8. She wants the soldiers to understand that while her plea is directed to the King of England, her wrath will be directed at them. Knowing this, they might heed her warning.

Critical Thinking

9. Answers might propose that the English leaders laughed at Joan's proclamation. They may have even thought she was a lunatic. Soldiers, out of self-interest, perhaps took her threats more seriously.

10. Answers might suggest that the proclamation expresses confidence and strength of purpose. Because she had deep faith in God and was convinced that she was doing rightly, she might not have imagined she would die as a heretic.

Writing on Your Own Encourage students to model their proclamations on Joan's. They should explicitly address the audience and explain their purpose in detail.

Selection Quiz

The Teacher's Resource Library includes a Selection Quiz for "Letter to the English" that may be given following the Selection Review.

Selection at a Glance

Nobel Lecture

Alexander Solzhenitsyn

Student pages 320–334

Overview

"Nobel Lecture" was written by Alexander Solzhenitsyn after he learned he'd won the Nobel Prize for Literature in 1970. Fearful of leaving Russia, Solzhenitsyn did not travel to Sweden to receive his award, but he sent a speech that was read in his absence.

Selection Summary

On winning the Nobel Prize, Solzhenitsyn, a Russian writer, gives his view of the importance of world literature.

Objectives

- To read and understand a persuasive speech
- To identify persuasive elements in a speech

Audiocassette

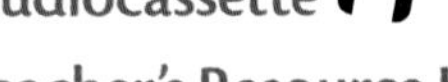

Teacher's Resource Library

- Vocabulary Workbook 30, pages 1–4
- Selection Glossary 34
- Student Study Guide 40, pages 1–2
- Activity 55, pages 1–2
- Workbook 55, pages 1–2
- Writing Activity 38
- Selection Quiz 34

INTRODUCING the SELECTION

Nobel Lecture

Alexander Solzhenitsyn

Alexander Solzhenitsyn (1918–) Russian

Literary Term

persuasive meant to influence

About the Speaker

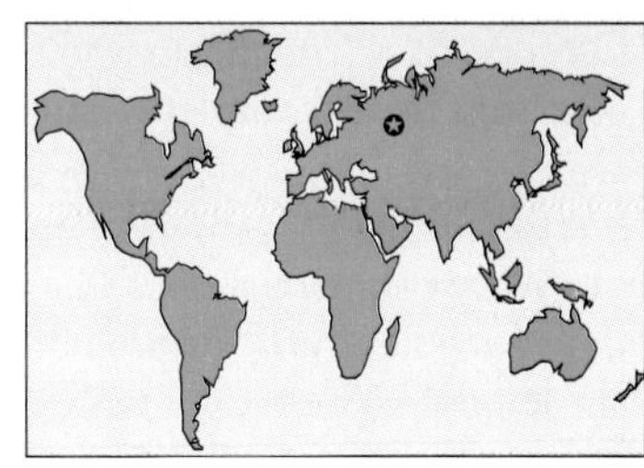

Alexander Solzhenitsyn was born in Kislovodsk, Russia. In World War II he fought in the Soviet army. After the war, Solzhenitsyn was arrested for writing critical remarks about Josef Stalin. (Stalin was the leader of the Soviet Union.) Solzhenitsyn spent eight years in prisons. This was the background for his first novel, *One Day in the Life of Ivan Denisovich*. A few years later, though, the government no longer let him publish. In 1969 Solzhenitsyn was kicked out of the Soviet Writers Union. The next year he won the Nobel Prize for Literature.

In 1973 the first part of *The Gulag Archipelago* was published in France. It exposed the Soviet prison system. Solzhenitsyn was arrested and then exiled. He lived in the United States for some years. In 1994, after the Soviet Union collapsed, Solzhenitsyn returned to live in Russia.

About the Selection

This is Solzhenitsyn's Nobel Prize speech, but he never gave it. In 1970, he was afraid to go to Sweden, where the prizes are given. He thought Russian officials would not let him return home. The speech was read in his absence. Solzhenitsyn tries to persuade others to stand up for truth. But he knows what the cost of standing up can be. This makes his speech doubly **persuasive**. It is meant to influence others. He not only speaks persuasively, but his own life is persuasive. We know he has lived by his words.

Setting the Stage for Reading

About the Author

Ask students to read the text and look at the photo. With the publication in 1962 of his short novel *One Day in the Life of Ivan Denisovich,* Solzhenitsyn became a literary superstar in Russia and around the world. However, when Nikita Khrushchev fell from power in 1964 and repressive government policies once again squelched artistic activities, Solzhenitsyn lost the favor he had briefly enjoyed. He responded by becoming an ardent opponent of repressive policies.

Activate Prior Knowledge: Explain that after World War II, the Soviet Union under Joseph Stalin was an extremely repressive society. Government policies inhibited freedom of expression. Have students recall anything they have read or heard about life in the Soviet Union between World War II and the 1990s.

ASK How do you think repressive government policies affected Solzhenitsyn's creativity? (Policies that were intended to squelch creative expression actually inspired Solzhenitsyn's work.)

About the Selection

This speech was sent to Sweden to be read in Solzhenitsyn's absence. He appeals to writers everywhere to take up the cause of truth. His words are persuasive, but more so are the facts of his life.

ASK What are the advantages of using one's own life as supporting evidence in a persuasive speech? (Doing so increases the speaker's credibility and makes his or her words highly convincing.)

Nobel Lecture

Alexander Solzhenitsyn

From time **immemorial** man has been made in such a way **A** that his vision of the world, so long as it has not been instilled under hypnosis, his motivations and scale of values, his actions and intentions are determined by his personal and group experience of life. As the Russian saying goes, "Do not believe your brother, believe your own crooked eye." And that is the most sound basis for an understanding of the world around us and of human conduct in it. And during the long **epochs** when our world lay spread out in mystery and wilderness, before it became **encroached** by common lines of communication, before it was transformed into a single, **convulsively pulsating** lump—men, relying on experience, ruled without mishap within their limited areas, within their communities, within their societies, and finally on their national territories. At that time it was possible for individual human beings to perceive and accept a general scale of values, to distinguish between what is considered normal, what incredible; what is cruel and what lies beyond the boundaries of wickedness; what is honesty, what **deceit**. And although the scattered peoples led extremely different lives and their social values were often strikingly at odds, just as their systems of weights and measures did not agree, still these **discrepancies** surprised only occasional travellers, were reported in journals under the name of wonders, and bore no danger to mankind which was not yet one.

But now during the past few decades, imperceptibly, suddenly, mankind has become one—hopefully one and

Solzhenitsyn begins by talking about culture. As you read, watch for where he begins to talk about writing.

Solzhenitsyn uses *man* and *mankind* to mean all people, men and women.

convulsively shaking violently

deceit a trick

discrepancy a difference; a conflict

encroached gradually entered or occupied

epoch a long period of history

immemorial beyond the limits of memory

pulsating moving in a regular rhythm

Reading Vocabulary 

Help students preview the selection's vocabulary by giving them copies of the Selection Glossary. Ask pairs of students to take turns providing definitions of the terms.

Motivation for Reading

Encourage students to imagine life in a country where the government censors and controls artistic expression. What would everyday life be like in a land with total control of the arts by the government?

Discussion Questions

As students read the selection, suggest that they read and consider the questions and comments in the margins of the student selection.

A ASK Critical Thinking What generalization about humans does Solzhenitsyn make? (People's actions have always been determined by their individual and group experiences.)

Cross-Curricular Connection

History The Soviet Union officially came into existence when Russia, a communist regime, joined with other Republics in 1922. For about seventy years, the Communists controlled the country, often through extreme repression. Encourage groups of students to build their background knowledge of the Soviet Union through research reports, which they present to the class. Different groups might choose different topics to provide an overview of the Union of Soviet Socialist Republics.

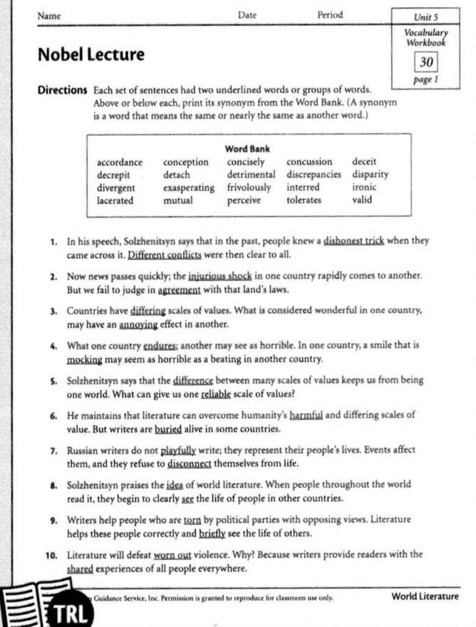

Name Date Period

Unit 5 — Vocabulary Workbook 30 — page 1

Nobel Lecture

Directions Each set of sentences had two underlined words or groups of words. Above or below each, print its synonym from the Word Bank. (A synonym is a word that means the same or nearly the same as another word.)

Word Bank

accordance	conception	concisely	concussion	deceit
decrepit	detach	detrimental	discrepancies	disparity
divergent	exasperating	frivolously	interred	ironic
lacerated	mutual	perceive	tolerates	valid

1. In his speech, Solzhenitsyn says that in the past, people knew a dishonest trick when they came across it. Different conflicts were then clear to all.
2. Now news passes quickly; the injurious shock in one country rapidly comes to another. But we fail to judge in agreement with that land's laws.
3. Countries have differing scales of values. What is considered wonderful in one country, may have an annoying effect in another.
4. What one country endures; another may see as horrible. In one country, a smile that is mocking may seem as horrible as a beating in another country.
5. Solzhenitsyn says that the difference between many scales of values keeps us from being one world. What can give us one reliable scale of values?
6. He maintains that literature can overcome humanity's harmful and differing scales of value. But writers are buried alive in some countries.
7. Russian writers do not playfully write; they represent their people's lives. Events affect them, and they refuse to disconnect themselves from life.
8. Solzhenitsyn praises the idea of world literature. When people throughout the world read it, they begin to clearly see the life of people in other countries.
9. Writers help people who are torn by political parties with opposing views. Literature helps these people correctly and briefly see the life of others.
10. Literature will defeat worn out violence. Why? Because writers provide readers with the shared experiences of all people everywhere.

 World Literature

Vocabulary Workbook 30, pages 1–4

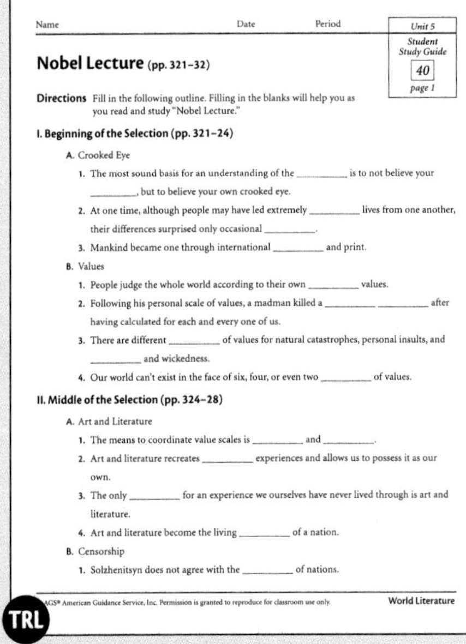

Name Date Period

Unit 5 — Student Study Guide 40 — page 1

Nobel Lecture (pp. 321–32)

Directions Fill in the following outline. Filling in the blanks will help you as you read and study "Nobel Lecture."

I. Beginning of the Selection (pp. 321–24)

A. Crooked Eye
1. The most sound basis for an understanding of the ________ is to not believe your ________, but to believe your own crooked eye.
2. At one time, although people may have led extremely ________ lives from one another, their differences surprised only occasional ________.
3. Mankind became one through international ________ and print.

B. Values
1. People judge the whole world according to their own ________ values.
2. Following his personal scale of values, a madman killed a ________ ________ after having calculated for each and every one of us.
3. There are different ________ of values for natural catastrophes, personal insults, and ________ and wickedness.
4. Our world can't exist in the face of six, four, or even two ________ of values.

II. Middle of the Selection (pp. 324–28)

A. Art and Literature
1. The means to coordinate value scales is ________ and ________.
2. Art and literature recreates ________ experiences and allows us to possess it as our own.
3. The only ________ for an experience we ourselves have never lived through is art and literature.
4. Art and literature become the living ________ of a nation.

B. Censorship
1. Solzhenitsyn does not agree with the ________ of nations.

 World Literature

Student Study Guide 40, pages 1–2

Discussion Questions

A Today satellite communications allow international broadcast and print to spread news swiftly around the globe. Some news events are simultaneously broadcast in many nations; however, most news is broadcast within hours of the actual event.

B ASK Critical Thinking How do people in various parts of the world evaluate news they receive from faraway nations? According to Solzhenitsyn, what is the problem with this? (People evaluate what they read and hear according to their own longstanding scales of value. This may lead to misinterpretation of events and misunderstanding among societies.)

Literary Elements

Metaphor Solzhenitsyn uses a metaphor to describe the amount of news we receive as "an avalanche of events [that] descends upon us." Remind students that a metaphor is an illustrative comparison made between two things without the use of the word *like* or *as*. Ask students to discuss whether they agree with this metaphor. Encourage them to illustrate the metaphor in a political cartoon style.

dangerously one—so that the **concussions** and inflammations of one of its parts are almost instantaneously passed on to others, sometimes lacking in any kind of necessary immunity. Mankind has become one, but not steadfastly one as communities or even nations used to be; not united through years of **mutual** experience, neither through possession of a single eye, affectionately called crooked, nor yet through a common native language, but, surpassing all barriers, through international broadcasting and print. An avalanche of events descends upon us—in one minute half the world hears of their splash. But the yardstick by which to measure those events and to **evaluate** them in **accordance** with the laws of unfamiliar parts of the world—this is not and cannot be conveyed via soundwaves and in newspaper columns. For these yardsticks were matured and **assimilated** over too many years of too specific conditions in individual countries and societies; they cannot be exchanged in midair. **B** In the various parts of the world men apply their own hard-earned values to events, and they judge stubbornly, confidently, only according to their own scales of values and never according to any others.

Solzhenitsyn refers back to the Russian saying in the first paragraph.

A How does the world hear about international events so fast? Do you think he really means one minute?

And if there are not many such different scales of values in the world, there are at least several; one for evaluating events near at hand, another for events far away; aging societies possess one, young societies another; unsuccessful people one, successful people another. The **divergent** scales of values scream in **discordance**, they dazzle and daze us, and in order that it might not be painful we steer clear of all other values, as though from insanity, as though from

accordance agreement
assimilate to take in
concussion a shock; an injury
discordance a harsh, confused sound
divergent drawing apart; differing
evaluate to judge the worth of
mutual shared

322 Unit 5 Persuasive Literature

Name Date Period Unit 5

Nobel Lecture Activity 55 page 1

Part A Directions On the blank lines, write a short answer for each item.

1. Solzhenitsyn describes world literature as having special powers. What is one power?
2. Who or what does Solzhenitsyn say can coordinate different scales of values?
3. What does Solzhenitsyn mean when he says, "A man with two hearts is not for this world"?
4. Give one example of the different scales of values people use to judge the world.
5. How is the power of literature to unite different scales of values described?

Part B Directions Read each sentence. Write *T* if the statement is true or *F* if it is false.

_____ 1. Art can help one nation understand another nation.
_____ 2. In some places beatings are forgiven as an unfortunate joke.
_____ 3. Solzhenitsyn was loved by the government of the Soviet Union.
_____ 4. The term "scales of values" is used to describe how money is weighed in countries.
_____ 5. Humanity has become one through religious beliefs.

©AGS® American Guidance Service, Inc. Permission is granted to reproduce for classroom use only. World Literature

TRL

Activity 55, pages 1–2

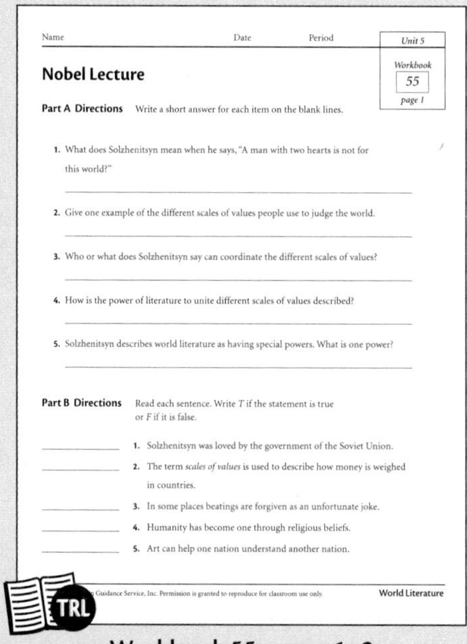

Name Date Period Unit 5

Nobel Lecture Workbook 55 page 1

Part A Directions Write a short answer for each item on the blank lines.

1. What does Solzhenitsyn mean when he says, "A man with two hearts is not for this world?"
2. Give one example of the different scales of values people use to judge the world.
3. Who or what does Solzhenitsyn say can coordinate the different scales of values?
4. How is the power of literature to unite different scales of values described?
5. Solzhenitsyn describes world literature as having special powers. What is one power?

Part B Directions Read each sentence. Write *T* if the statement is true or *F* if it is false.

_____ 1. Solzhenitsyn was loved by the government of the Soviet Union.
_____ 2. The term *scales of values* is used to describe how money is weighed in countries.
_____ 3. In some places beatings are forgiven as an unfortunate joke.
_____ 4. Humanity has become one through religious beliefs.
_____ 5. Art can help one nation understand another nation.

Guidance Service, Inc. Permission is granted to reproduce for classroom use only. World Literature

TRL

Workbook 55, pages 1–2

illusion, and we confidently judge the whole world according to our own home values. Which is why we take for the greater, more painful and less bearable disaster not that which is in fact greater, more painful and less bearable, but that which lies closest to us. Everything which is further away, which does not threaten this very day to invade our threshold—with all its groans, its stifled cries, its destroyed lives, even if it involves millions of victims—this we consider on the whole to be perfectly bearable and of **tolerable** proportions.

C Which events and disasters attract people's attention most?

In one part of the world, not so long ago, under persecutions not inferior to those of the ancient Romans', hundreds of thousands of silent Christians gave up their lives for their belief in God. In the other hemisphere a certain madman, **D** (and no doubt he is not alone), speeds across the ocean to DELIVER us from religion—with a thrust of steel into the high priest! He has calculated for each and every one of us according to his personal scale of values!

Words in capital letters are emphasized more than others.

That which from a distance, according to one scale of values, appears as enviable and flourishing freedom, at close quarters, and according to other values, is felt to be infuriating **constraint** calling for buses to be overthrown. That which in one part of the world might represent a dream of incredible prosperity, in another has the **exasperating** effect of wild **exploitation** demanding immediate strike. There are different scales of values for natural catastrophes: a flood craving two hundred thousand lives seems less significant than our local accident. There are different scales of values for personal insults: sometimes even an **ironic** smile or a **dismissive** gesture is **humiliating**, while for others cruel beatings are forgiven as an unfortunate joke. There are different scales of values for punishment and wickedness: according to one, a month's arrest, banishment to the country, or an isolation-cell where one is fed on white rolls

constraint force that limits freedom of thought or action

dismissive in a manner that discards or sends away

exasperating annoying

exploitation the unfair use of something for selfish reasons

humiliating causing shame or loss of dignity

ironic mocking

tolerable able to be endured

C The events and disasters that most attract our attention are those that lie closest to us.

D ASK Comprehension What are some examples of how differing scales of values affect people's interpretations of events? (A "certain madman" delivers people from religion according to his own scale of values. At the same time those people might feel themselves robbed of their religion. What one person sees as freedom, another experiences as constraint. One person's dream of prosperity is another's nightmare of exploitation.)

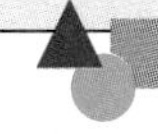

Learning Styles

LEP/ESL Solzhenitsyn identifies the many differences in cultural values including something as simple as gestures. Involve students who have experienced differing cultures to discuss how body language, as well as spoken language, differs across cultures. For example, in Japan making eye contact while talking is a breach of etiquette, but in the United States making eye contact is good manners. Invite students to share the meanings of different gestures and how those same gestures carry different meanings in various societies.

Discussion Questions

A Solzhenitsyn points out that people have two sets of values: one set for themselves and their own society and another set for those who live in remote corners of the world and about whom they know next to nothing.

B ASK Comprehension Ask students to summarize what Solzhenitsyn has said up to this point. (People have an inherent defect: they understand only their personal life experiences. Therefore, people quite naturally misunderstand another person's distant grief. The danger is this: in a world full of people, our inability to comprehend one another will divide us.)

C ASK Literary Element Explain that an analogy makes a comparison between two things based on certain resemblances they share. To what does Solzhenitsyn compare humans' duality of values? (to a man with two hearts)

D ASK Critical Thinking What techniques does Solzhenitsyn use in the last paragraph on this page to engage his listeners? (He uses repetition; he asks question after question starting with the words "Who will.")

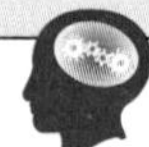

Comprehension

Summarizing Summarizing, or identifying main ideas, is a useful strategy that will help students better understand the ideas Solzhenitsyn is developing in his speech. Suggest that students work with partners to read and summarize in a few short phrases or sentences each paragraph in the speech. Their summary can serve as a review and study aid. Alternatively, have students complete Student Study Guide 40 as they read.

White rolls and milk are used as symbols for "soft" prison treatment.

A What different sets of values does the writer contrast? Notice the results he discusses in the next paragraph.

and milk, shatters the imagination and fills the newspaper columns with rage. While according to another, prison sentences of twenty-five years, isolation-cells where the walls are covered with ice and the prisoners stripped to their underclothes, lunatic asylums for the sane, and countless unreasonable people who for some reason will keep running away, shot on the frontiers—all this is common and accepted. While the mind is especially at peace concerning that exotic part of the world about which we know virtually nothing, from which we do not even receive news of events, but only the trivial, out-of-date guesses of a few correspondents.

B Yet we cannot reproach human vision for this duality, for this **dumbfounded** incomprehension of another man's distant grief, man is just made that way. But for the whole of mankind, compressed into a single lump, such mutual **incomprehension** presents the threat of **imminent** and violent destruction. One world, one mankind cannot exist in the face of six, four or even two scales of values: we shall be torn apart by this **disparity** of rhythm, this disparity of vibrations.

C A man with two hearts is not for this world, neither shall we be able to live side by side on one Earth.

Notice that the writer restates the question in several ways. He is leading up to an answer.

D But who will co-ordinate these value scales, and how? Who will create for mankind one system of interpretation, **valid** for good and evil deeds, for the unbearable and the bearable, as they are **differentiated** today? Who will make clear to mankind what is really heavy and intolerable and what only grazes the skin locally? Who will direct the anger to that which is most terrible and not to that which is nearer? Who might succeed in transferring such an understanding beyond the limits of his own human experience? Who might succeed in impressing upon a **bigoted**, stubborn human creature the distant joy and grief of others, an understanding of dimensions and deceptions which he himself has never

bigoted stubbornly holding a belief and disliking those who disagree

differentiate to show a difference between

disparity difference

dumbfounded stunned into silence

imminent about to happen

incomprehension lack of understanding

valid reliable

experienced? Propaganda, constraint, scientific proof—all are useless. But fortunately there does exist such a means in our world! That means is art. That means is literature.

They can perform a miracle: they can overcome man's **detrimental** peculiarity of learning only from personal experience so that the experience of other people passes him by in vain. From man to man, as he completes his brief spell on Earth, art transfers the whole weight of an unfamiliar, lifelong experience with all its burdens, its colours, its sap of life; it recreates in the flesh an unknown experience and allows us to possess it as our own.

E How do art and literature help people understand others' values?

And even more, much more than that; both countries and whole continents repeat each other's mistakes with time lapses which can amount to centuries. Then, one would think, it would all be so obvious! But no; that which some nations have already experienced, considered and rejected, is suddenly discovered by others to be the latest word. And here again, the only substitute for an experience we ourselves have never lived through is art, literature. They possess a wonderful ability: beyond distinctions of language, custom, social structure, they can convey the life experience of one whole nation to another. To an inexperienced nation they can convey a harsh national trial lasting many decades, at best sparing an entire nation from a superfluous, or mistaken, or even **disastrous** course, thereby **curtailing** the **meanderings** of human history. It is this great and noble property of art that I urgently recall to you today from the Nobel **tribune**. **F**

And literature conveys **irrefutable** condensed experience in yet another **invaluable** direction; namely, from generation to generation. Thus it becomes the living memory of the nation. Thus it preserves and kindles within itself the flame of her spent history, in a form which is safe from deformation and

curtail to cut short

detrimental harmful

disastrous causing disaster

invaluable beyond price

irrefutable impossible to prove wrong

meandering going along a winding course

tribune a platform from which to speak to a group

E Art can recreate life in its most intimate details, allowing one person to read or see another person's experiences—to live someone else's life and know it firsthand. Art is a substitute for experience.

F ASK Comprehension What effect can art have on life? (Because it can act as a substitute for experience, art can convey the life of a whole nation to another, allowing a young nation to avoid the disastrous mistakes the older nation made, and thus helping the young nation find a swift course to success.)

Writing Connection

Have students write a short paragraph in which they use the propaganda technique of repetition. They may opt to repeat questions, as Solzhenitsyn did, or they may repeat statements, as Martin Luther King, Jr., did in his "I Have a Dream" speech by repeating the phrase "I have a dream." Explain that repetition is simply a matter of repeating phrases that have a similar construction. Students may wish to begin each of their sentences with the same word or phrase.

Discussion Questions

A ASK Critical Thinking Is Solzhenitsyn a credible source of information about censorship? Why do you believe he knows what he's talking about? (Yes, he comes from a nation that censored its literature; he knows the authors he names; his own work has been censored by the government.)

B Censorship not only violates personal freedom, it destroys the heart of a nation and its memory. It divides members of a nation from one another: robbing them of language, preventing them from communicating, depriving them of understanding.

Diversity Connection

Solzhenitsyn says he's against the concept of the melting pot—a metaphor that was long used to describe the United States. Solzhenitsyn says our differences make the world a colorful and interesting place to live—in short, he believes we should celebrate our differences. This attitude aligns with the currently popular metaphor depicting the United States as a mosaic. Invite students to discuss the differences between the two metaphors: melting pot and mosaic.

Solzhenitsyn says that the lessons of art and literature can be passed from country to country. They can also be passed down through history.

slander. In this way literature, together with language, protects the soul of the nation.

(In recent times it has been fashionable to talk of the levelling of nations, of the disappearance of different races in the melting-pot of **contemporary** civilization. I do not agree with this opinion, but its discussion remains another question. Here it is merely fitting to say that the disappearance of nations would have **impoverished** us no less than if all men had become alike, with one personality and one face. Nations are the wealth of mankind, its **collective** personalities; the very least of them wears its own special colours and bears within itself a special **facet** of divine intention.)

A But woe to that nation whose literature is disturbed by the **intervention** of power. Because that is not just a violation against "freedom of print," it is the closing down of the heart of the nation, a slashing to pieces of its memory. The nation ceases to be mindful of itself, it is deprived of its spiritual unity, and despite a supposedly common language, **compatriots** suddenly cease to understand one another. Silent generations grow old and die without ever having talked about themselves, either to each other or to their descendants. When writers such as Achmatova and Zamjatin—**interred** alive throughout their lives—are condemned to create in silence until they die, never hearing the echo of their written words, then that is not only their personal tragedy, but a sorrow to the whole nation, a danger to the whole nation.

B What does Solzhenitsyn say are the effects of censorship? Anna *Achmatova* was a Russian poet whose works were attacked by authorities. Yevgeny *Zamjatin* was another writer whose books were banned.

In some cases moreover—when as a result of such a silence the whole of history ceases to be understood in its entirety—it is a danger to the whole of mankind.

At various times and in various countries there have arisen heated, angry and exquisite debates as to whether art and the

collective grouped together

compatriot a person from one's own country

contemporary living at the same time

facet one part or angle

impoverish to make poor

interred buried

intervention an act of interfering

326 *Unit 5 Persuasive Literature*

artist should be free to live for themselves, or whether they should be for ever mindful of their duty towards society and serve it albeit in an unprejudiced way. For me there is no **dilemma**, but I shall refrain from raising once again the train of arguments. One of the most brilliant addresses on this **C** subject was actually Albert Camus' Nobel speech, and I would happily subscribe to his conclusions. Indeed, Russian literature has for several decades **manifested** an **inclination** not to become too lost in contemplation of itself, not to flutter about too **frivolously**. I am not ashamed to continue this tradition to the best of my ability. Russian literature has long been familiar with the notions that a writer can do much within his society, and that it is his duty to do so.

Camus, a French writer, won the 1957 Nobel Prize.

Let us not violate the RIGHT of the artist to express exclusively his own experiences and **introspections**, disregarding everything that happens in the world beyond. Let us not DEMAND of the artist, but—reproach, beg, urge and **entice** him—that we may be allowed to do. After all, only in part does he himself **D** develop his talent; the greater part of it is blown into him at birth as a finished product, and the gift of talent imposes responsibility on his free will. Let us assume that the artist does not OWE anybody anything: nevertheless, it is painful to see how, by retiring into his self-made worlds or the spaces of his subjective whims, he CAN surrender the real world into the hands of men who are **mercenary**, if not worthless, if not insane. ...

dilemma a situation that requires a difficult choice

entice to tempt

frivolously not seriously; playfully

inclination a leaning toward something

introspection examining one's own thoughts

manifest to show

mercenary concerned only with making money

C ASK Literary Element Explain that an *allusion* is an implied or indirect reference. Explain that Solzhenitsyn refers directly to a speech given by Albert Camus, however, he doesn't discuss the speech in any detail. To what in Camus' speech does Solzhenitsyn allude? What does he say about the reference? (He alludes to the conclusions Camus made in a speech by saying he "would happily subscribe to" them.)

D ASK Critical Thinking What is Solzhenitsyn saying about the artist's role in society? (The artist doesn't owe society anything. But he does have a responsibility, at least to himself, to use his God-given gifts, which have the potential to make the world a better place.)

Discussion Questions

A ASK **Comprehension** What is the main idea of the second paragraph? (The writer cannot stand outside of society and its evils; he is an accomplice to any evil committed by his fellow citizens.)

B The writer vicariously partakes in all life's events. When terrible things happen, the writer feels responsible.

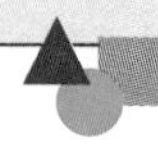

Learning Styles

Visual Solzhenitsyn identifies the place and role of writers. Suggest that students make a two-column chart in which they identify the place and roles writers do not have, according to Solzhenitsyn, in one column with those they do have in another. This organizational graphic will help students better understand what is being said in the speech about the role of writers.

What then is the place and role of the writer in this cruel, **dynamic**, split world on the brink of its ten destructions? After all we have nothing to do with letting off rockets, we do not even push the lowliest of hand-carts, we are quite scorned by those who respect only material power. Is it not natural for us too to step back, to lose faith in the steadfastness of goodness, in the **indivisibility** of truth, and to just impart to the world our bitter, **detached** observations: how mankind has become hopelessly corrupt, how men have **degenerated**, and how difficult it is for the few beautiful and refined souls to live amongst them? **A**

But we have not even **recourse** to this flight. Anyone who has once taken up the WORD can never again evade it; a writer is not the detached judge of his compatriots and contemporaries, he is an accomplice to all the evil committed in his native land or by his countrymen. And if the tanks of his fatherland have flooded the asphalt of a foreign capital with blood, then the brown spots have slapped against the face of the writer forever. And if one fatal night they suffocated his sleeping, trusting Friend, then the palms of the writer bear the bruises from that rope. And if his young fellow citizens breezily declare the superiority of **depravity** over honest work, if they give themselves over to drugs or seize hostages, then their stink mingles with the breath of the writer.

B How is a writer affected by terrible events?

Shall we have the **temerity** to declare that we are not responsible for the sores of the present-day world?

However, I am cheered by a vital awareness of WORLD LITERATURE as of a single huge heart, beating out the cares

degenerate to become much worse

depravity a wicked act

detached not connected

dynamic full of energy; changing

indivisibility state of not being able to be divided

recourse something to turn to for help

temerity foolish boldness

328 *Unit 5 Persuasive Literature*

and troubles of our world, albeit presented and **perceived** differently in each of its corners.

C What symbol does Solzhenitsyn choose for world literature?

Apart from age-old national literatures there existed, even in past ages, the **conception** of world literature as an **anthology** skirting the heights of the national literatures, and as the sum total of mutual literary influences. But there occurred a lapse **D** in time: readers and writers became acquainted with writers of other tongues only after a time lapse, sometimes lasting centuries, so that mutual influences were also delayed and the anthology of national literary heights was revealed only in the eyes of descendants, not of contemporaries.

But today, between the writers of one country and the writers and readers of another, there is a **reciprocity** if not instantaneous then almost so. I experience this with myself. Those of my books which, alas, have not been printed in my own country have soon found a responsive, worldwide audience, despite hurried and often bad translations. Such distinguished western writers as Heinrich Böll have undertaken critical **analysis** of them. All these **E** last years, when my work and freedom have not come crashing down, when contrary to the laws of gravity they have hung suspended as though on air, as though on NOTHING—on the invisible dumb **tension** of a sympathetic public **membrane**; then it was with grateful warmth, and quite unexpectedly for myself, that I learnt of the further support of the international brotherhood of writers. On my fiftieth birthday I was astonished to receive congratulations from well-known western writers. No pressure on me came to pass by unnoticed. During my dangerous weeks of exclusion from the Writers' Union the WALL OF DEFENCE advanced by the world's prominent writers protected me from worse persecutions; and Norwegian writers and artists hospitably prepared a roof for me, in the event of my threatened exile being put into effect. Finally even the advancement of my name for the Nobel Prize was raised not in

analysis a study of how parts fit together
anthology a collection of writings
conception an idea; a mental picture
membrane a thin layer of material
perceived seen; known through the senses
reciprocity an equal exchange
tension the condition of being stretched

C Solzhenitsyn symbolizes world literature with the image of a single huge and beating heart.

D ASK Comprehension How does access to the "world literature" of the past compare to the access to contemporary world literature? (In the past writers separated by distance learned of one another's work only after great lapses of time. Now, hurried translations allow writers in different countries instant access to one another's work.)

E ASK Comprehension How does Solzhenitsyn support his claim that contemporary literature swiftly finds a worldwide audience? (He shares his personal experience, explaining that when his work wasn't well-received in his home country, he was surprised to discover that he had a supportive international audience who congratulated him on his birthday, protected him from persecution, prepared a home for him in the event of his exile, and nominated him for the Nobel Prize.)

Discussion Questions

A Mauriac's support of Solzhenitsyn shows that writers have begun to form an international community that provides protection, support, and fellowship.

B ASK Critical Thinking According to Solzhenitsyn what is the solution to the problems of the world? (He says, "salvation lies in everyone making everything his or her business.")

C ASK Critical Thinking How can literature serve as leader in world unity? (Writers of literature have been among the first to recognized the unity and common characteristics of humans and can espouse it through their writing.)

D ASK Comprehension What is the author's purpose in this speech? (He wants to persuade his audience—writers—to expose the world's problems, bring people together, and better the world.)

Mauriac was a French writer who won the Nobel Prize in 1952. How does this kind of support help prove the writer's point about world literature?
A

the country where I live and write, but by François Mauriac and his colleagues. And later still entire national writers' unions have expressed their support for me.

Thus I have understood and felt that world literature is no longer an abstract anthology, nor a generalization invented by literary historians; it is rather a certain common body and a common spirit, a living heartfelt unity reflecting the growing unity of mankind. State frontiers still turn crimson, heated by electric wire and bursts of machine fire; and various ministries of internal affairs still think that literature too is an "internal affair" falling under their **jurisdiction**; newspaper headlines still display: "No right to interfere in our internal affairs!"
B Whereas there are no INTERNAL AFFAIRS left on our crowded Earth! And mankind's sole **salvation** lies in everyone making everything his business; in the people of the East being vitally concerned with what is thought in the West, the people of the West vitally concerned with what goes on in the East.
C And literature, as one of the most sensitive, responsive instruments possessed by the human creature, has been one of the first to adopt, to assimilate, to catch hold of this feeling of a growing unity of mankind. And so I turn with confidence to the world literature of today—to hundreds of friends whom I have never met in the flesh and whom I may never see.

D Friends! Let us try to help if we are worth anything at all! Who from time immemorial has **constituted** the uniting, not the dividing, strength in your countries, **lacerated** by discordant parties, movements, **castes** and groups? There in its **essence** is the position of writers: expressers of their native language—the chief binding force of the nation, of the very earth its people occupy, and at best of its national spirit.

I believe that world literature has it in its power to help mankind, in these its troubled hours, to see itself as it really is, notwithstanding the **indoctrinations** of prejudiced people and

caste a social class

constitute to make up

essence the basic quality of something

indoctrination the teaching of a certain point of view

jurisdiction the area where one has authority

lacerated torn

salvation rescue from evil or problems

parties. World literature has it in its power to convey condensed experience from one land to another so that we might cease to be split and dazzled, that the different scales of values might be made to agree, and one nation learn correctly and **concisely** the true history of another with such strength of recognition and painful awareness as it had itself experienced the same, and thus might it be spared from repeating the same cruel mistakes. And perhaps under such conditions we artists will be able to cultivate within ourselves a field of vision to embrace the WHOLE WORLD: in the centre observing like any other human being that which lies nearby, at the edges we shall begin to draw in that which is happening in the rest of the world. And we shall **correlate**, and we shall observe world proportions.

Centre is the British spelling of *center.*

And who, if not writers, are to pass judgment—not only on **E** their unsuccessful governments, (in some states this is the easiest way to earn one's bread, the occupation of any man who is not lazy), but also on the people themselves, in their cowardly humiliation or self-satisfied weakness? Who is to pass judgment on the light-weight sprints of youth, and on the young pirates **brandishing** their knives?

We shall be told: what can literature possibly do against the ruthless **onslaught** of open violence? But let us not forget that violence does not live alone and is not capable of living alone: it is necessarily interwoven with falsehood. Between them lies the most **intimate**, the deepest of natural bonds. Violence finds its only refuge in falsehood, falsehood its only support in violence. Any man who has once **acclaimed** violence as his METHOD must **inexorably** choose falsehood as

F How are violence and lies connected?

acclaim to praise

brandish to wave in a threatening way

concisely briefly

correlate to show a relationship

inexorably in a way that will not be stopped

intimate very close

onslaught an attack

E ASK Critical Thinking What group of people does Solzhenitsyn call upon to pass judgment on all things that occur in the world? (writers everywhere)

F Lies support violence. Any person who chooses a violent path can only support his actions by using lies as his founding principle.

Learning Styles

Tactile/Kinesthetic Ask students who excel at tactile/kinesthetic interpretations to create an image though artwork or a tableau depicting the role of the artist as described in the following sentence from page 331: "And perhaps under such conditions we artists will be able to cultivate within ourselves a field of vision to embrace the WHOLE WORLD: in the centre observing like any other human being that which lies nearby, at the edges we shall begin to draw in that which is happening in the rest of the world."

Discussion Questions

A ASK **Comprehension** What point is Solzhenitsyn making in the second paragraph? (Art can destroy falsehood.)

B ASK **Comprehension** What will happen to violence when falsehood is destroyed? (People will see violence in all its ugliness, will no longer accept it, and will call for its end.)

C He believes that truth, however small compared to other evils, has the power to outweigh evil and even to make it disappear. Taken literally, the statement breaks the law of the conservation of mass and energy, but the statement describes good and evil, which cannot be expected to conform to scientific laws.

his PRINCIPLE. At its birth violence acts openly and even with pride. But no sooner does it become strong, firmly established, than it senses the **rarefaction** of the air around it and it cannot continue to exist without descending into a fog of lies, clothing them in sweet talk. It does not always, not necessarily, openly throttle the throat, more often it demands from its subjects only an oath of allegiance to falsehood, only **complicity** in falsehood.

A And the simple step of a simple courageous man is not to **partake** in falsehood, not to support false actions! Let THAT enter the world, let it even reign in the world—but not with my help. But writers and artists can achieve more: they can CONQUER FALSEHOOD! In the struggle with falsehood art always did win and it always does win! Openly, irrefutably for everyone! Falsehood can hold out against much in this world, but not against art.

B And no sooner will falsehood be **dispersed** than the nakedness of violence will be revealed in all its ugliness—and violence, **decrepit**, will fall.

That is why, my friends, I believe that we are able to help the world in its white-hot hour. Not by making the excuse of possessing no weapons, and not by giving ourselves over to a frivolous life—but by going to war!

Proverbs about truth are well-loved in Russian. They give steady and sometimes striking expression to the **not inconsiderable** harsh national experience:

C He refers to the scientific principle that matter and energy can neither be created nor destroyed. How does his statement break that law?

ONE WORD OF TRUTH SHALL OUTWEIGH THE WHOLE WORLD.

And it is here, on an imaginary fantasy, a **breach** of the principle of the conservation of mass and energy, that I base both my own activity and my appeal to the writers of the whole world.

breach a break

complicity state of being involved in a wrong action

decrepit worn out

disperse to scatter in different directions

not inconsiderable important enough to demand attention

partake to share; to take part

rarefaction the state of being thin or less dense

Nobel Lecture

Alexander Solzhenitsyn

Directions Write the answers to these questions using complete sentences.

Comprehension: Identifying Facts

1. What, according to Solzhenitsyn, has decided people's view of the world in the past?
2. What change has quickly made people become one?
3. How do different scales of value affect how people see a disaster?
4. What does he say can make one person feel another's joy or grief?
5. How do art and literature affect nations?
6. How does censorship affect a country?
7. In what ways did the world's writers help Solzhenitsyn?
8. Who suggested Solzhenitsyn for a Nobel Prize?
9. What power does world literature have?
10. What is the relationship between violence and lying?

Comprehension: Understanding Main Ideas

11. In earlier times, why didn't it matter that groups had different values?
12. Why do different sets of values matter more today?
13. How does literature extend people's experience?
14. What is the debate over the role of the artist?
15. What happens if artists do not speak out?
16. Why is a single heart a good symbol for world literature?
17. How did the actions of other writers help protect Solzhenitsyn?
18. Why can a country no longer have "internal affairs"?
19. What has world literature become?
20. How do writers and artists fight falsehood?

Review Continued on Next Page

Reviewing the Selection

Answer Key

Comprehension: Identifying Facts

1. People's views were decided by their own personal experiences.

2. The speed at which we now communicate has made people become one.

3. People put less weight on disasters that don't immediately affect them.

4. Literature can help people experience one another's joy and grief.

5. Art and literature can help nations understand and know each other.

6. Censorship robs a country of its language, its memory, and its unity.

7. The world's writers supported his work, congratulated and encouraged him, rallied behind him so that he might not suffer persecution, prepared a home for him in the event of his exile, and nominated him for the Nobel Prize.

8. François Mauriac nominated Solzhenitsyn.

9. World literature can conquer falsehood.

10. Lies are the only support for violence.

Comprehension: Understanding Main Ideas

11. The different values of groups mattered little in the past because groups remained isolated from one another.

12. Different sets of values matter today because people interact with and judge one another.

13. Literature can act as a substitute for experience, helping people sympathize with others' trials and triumphs.

14. Does the artist owe anything to society?

15. If artists do not speak out, no one will pass judgment on the actions of governments and individuals.

16. A single heart represents the purpose of world literature—to unify all people by allowing them to share/experience one another's lives.

17. The actions of other writers helped make Solzhenitsyn an important figure in the world literature scene, thereby deterring his opponents from harming him.

18. A country can no longer have internal affairs because the actions of one nation affect every nation.

19. World literature has become a world unifier.

20. Writers and artists fight falsehood by exposing it. Once exposed, falsehood dies.

Understanding Literature: Persuasive Writing

21. The "Nobel Lecture" was written as an address to writers everywhere. The author hoped to persuade them to use writing as a means of bettering the world.

22. Solzhenitsyn expects writers to be self-sacrificing in their work, not to write simply about their own private concerns but to write about matters urgent to humanity.

23. His speech is hopeful in that it expresses confidence that art can conquer falsehood and violence, unite nations, and better the lives of everyone.

24. The writer is trying to persuade other writers and artists as well as all people to think about their actions and the way they view the world.

25. Solzhenitsyn has probably influenced many people because his works are popular and he won the highest honor a writer can earn.

Critical Thinking

26. Students may write that the speech would inspire them and encourage them to take action and fight censorship.

27. He sent the speech because he had something important to say.

28. Students may have trouble understanding why Solzhenitsyn wanted to stay in a country that censored him and made his life difficult. Some students may come to understand that he wanted to stay in Russia because he needed to make a difference there. He felt obligated to use his talents to expose the evils of the government, to conquer falsehood, and to help the people.

29. If students agree that artists can change the world, they should support their opinion with examples.

30. Students should explain their opinions by agreeing with or contesting points Solzhenitsyn made in his speech.

Writing on Your Own In addition to outlining the main points, students can include supporting details in their outlines. Review with students the standard format of an outline.

Selection Quiz

The Teacher's Resource Library includes a Selection Quiz for "Nobel Lecture" that may be given following the Selection Review.

REVIEWING the SELECTION

Nobel Lecture

(Continued)

Understanding Literature: Persuasive Writing

Persuasive writing is writing that tries to change another's mind. This kind of writing can take many forms. Sometimes drama, poetry, short stories, or novels are persuasive. Usually persuasive writing is some form of nonfiction. Solzhenitsyn's speech is a form of persuasive writing.

21. Why was the "Nobel Lecture" written?
22. What does Solzhenitsyn expect of other writers and artists?
23. Would you say this speech is hopeful? Why or why not?
24. Whom do you think the writer is trying to persuade?
25. Do you think the writer influenced others? Explain.

Critical Thinking

26. Imagine you are a writer in a country that suppresses or censors writers. How would you feel about this speech?
27. Solzhenitsyn could not attend the Nobel ceremonies. Why do you think he sent this speech?
28. If you had been Solzhenitsyn, would you have gone back to Russia? Explain.
29. Do you agree that writers can change the world? Why or why not?
30. Did you like this speech? Why or why not?

Writing on Your Own An outline can help you understand a subject. Make an outline of the Nobel lecture. Your outline can list the main idea of each paragraph or section.

Name Date Period

Unit 5 *Writing Activity* 38

Nobel Lecture

You'll use Solzhenitsyn's speech against itself for this activity. Write a brief speech that is opposed to his view. Imagine that you are a government official, probably Communist, who disagrees with Solzhenitsyn.

Prewrite
Make a list of points that counter Solzhenitsyn's argument. You may find this difficult to do if you agree with him, but try hard. This will give you an idea of what propagandists do and the role they have had in societies throughout time. Propagandists try to show that someone else is wrong, even if they have to lie to do it.

Write
Write your piece. Explain why Solzhenitsyn is wrong and you are right. You want to do two things in this piece: knock Solzhenitsyn down and build up the government's viewpoint. But try not to lie, if you can help it.

Revise
Read and rewrite your piece. Since this is propaganda, it does not need to be beautiful prose. But is it strong? Nobody should misunderstand your viewpoint—you speak for the government.

Proofread
Make sure that you have used complete sentences in your descriptions. Each sentence must include a subject (doer) and a predicate (action or verb), and must express a complete thought. All sentences end with a period, a question mark, or an exclamation mark. Use capital letters to begin each new thought.

 World Literature

TRL

Writing Activity 38

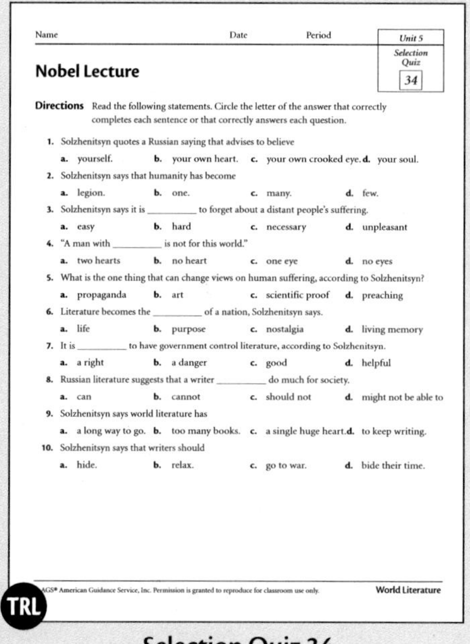

Name Date Period

Unit 5 *Selection Quiz* 34

Nobel Lecture

Directions Read the following statements. Circle the letter of the answer that correctly completes each sentence or that correctly answers each question.

1. Solzhenitsyn quotes a Russian saying that advises to believe
   a. yourself. b. your own heart. c. your own crooked eye. d. your soul.
2. Solzhenitsyn says that humanity has become
   a. legion. b. one. c. many. d. few.
3. Solzhenitsyn says it is __________ to forget about a distant people's suffering.
   a. easy b. hard c. necessary d. unpleasant
4. "A man with __________ is not for this world."
   a. two hearts b. no heart c. one eye d. no eyes
5. What is the one thing that can change views on human suffering, according to Solzhenitsyn?
   a. propaganda b. art c. scientific proof d. preaching
6. Literature becomes the __________ of a nation, Solzhenitsyn says.
   a. life b. purpose c. nostalgia d. living memory
7. It is __________ to have government control literature, according to Solzhenitsyn.
   a. a right b. a danger c. good d. helpful
8. Russian literature suggests that a writer __________ do much for society.
   a. can b. cannot c. should not d. might not be able to
9. Solzhenitsyn says world literature has
   a. a long way to go. b. too many books. c. a single huge heart. d. to keep writing.
10. Solzhenitsyn says that writers should
    a. hide. b. relax. c. go to war. d. bide their time.

 World Literature

TRL

Selection Quiz 34

INTRODUCING the SELECTION

The Gettysburg Address

Abraham Lincoln

Abraham Lincoln (1809–1865) American

About the Speaker

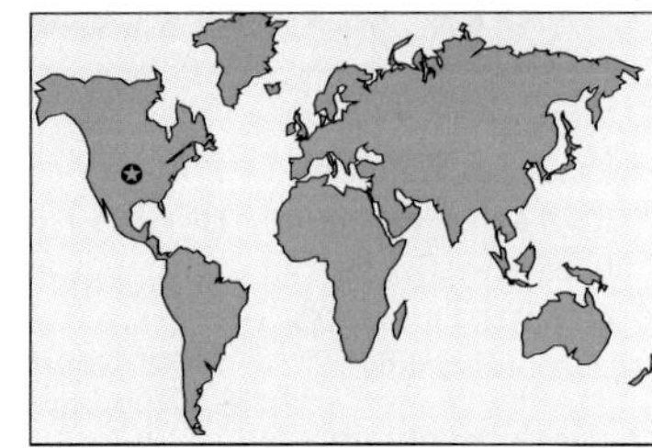

Abraham Lincoln was born in Kentucky and grew up in Indiana. As a young man, he moved to a small town in Illinois. Lincoln educated himself by reading a lot.

Lincoln tried many jobs. Then his speaking skills led him into politics. His campaign debates put Lincoln in the national spotlight as a spokesman against slavery. In 1860 the new Republican party named him its candidate for President. He won the election.

Soon after the election, the Civil War began. The struggle to save the Union claimed most of Lincoln's attention. Many moving words about democracy and freedom come from his **speeches** during this time. Speeches are works meant to be spoken out loud. In 1865 Lincoln was shot and killed while watching a play.

Literary Term

speech a written work meant to be read aloud

About the Selection

During the first two years of the Civil War, the Union army lost several major battles. In July 1863 they won their first big victory against the Confederate army. The battle was near Gettysburg, Pennsylvania. More than eleven thousand soldiers died there. In November 1863, the Union decided to keep part of the Gettysburg battlefield as a cemetery. Lincoln was asked to speak. His three-minute address disappointed some who heard it. Today it is considered one of the world's great speeches.

Selection at a Glance

The Gettysburg Address

Abraham Lincoln

Student pages 335–336

Overview

"The Gettysburg Address" was delivered on November 19, 1863, at the site of a major Civil War battle during the dedication of the National Cemetery at Gettysburg, Pennsylvania. The main speech of the day, by Edward Everett, was two hours long. Following that, Lincoln's three-minute speech disappointed some listeners.

Selection Summary

In "The Gettysburg Address," President Abraham Lincoln speaks to dedicate a cemetery at the site of the Battle of Gettysburg.

Objectives

- To read and understand a speech.
- To identify and understand metaphor in a speech.

Audiocassette 

Teacher's Resource Library 

- Vocabulary Workbook 31, pages 1–2
- Selection Glossary 35
- Student Study Guide 41
- Activity 56
- Workbook 56
- Writing Activity 39
- Selection Quiz 35

Setting the Stage for Reading

Remind students that Abraham Lincoln was the sixteenth President of the United States, most noted for preserving the Union during the Civil War and bringing about the emancipation of the slaves.

Activate Prior Knowledge: Abraham Lincoln is a legendary figure who is deemed a hero both at home and abroad. Have students recall anything they have read or heard previously about Lincoln.

ASK How do you think Lincoln's experiences as a young man affected the type of leader he became? (Lincoln was the epitome of a self-made man who believed in his country's greatness.)

About the Selection

"The Gettysburg Address," despite the criticism it immediately received, soon was recognized as an oratory masterpiece. In fact on the day following its deliverance, Edward Everett, the best-known orator of the time, said this about Lincoln's address. "I wish I could flatter myself that I had come as near to the central idea of the occasion in two hours as you did in two minutes."

ASK What are the advantages of saying a lot with just a few words? (Being able to sum up a big issue in a few words reveals mental acuity. Listeners are likely to remember every word of brief, meaningful speeches.)

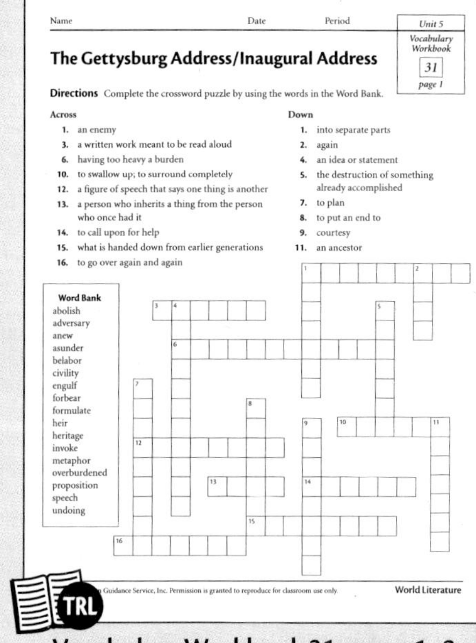

Name Date Period

Unit 5 *Vocabulary Workbook* 31 *page 1*

The Gettysburg Address/Inaugural Address

Directions Complete the crossword puzzle by using the words in the Word Bank.

Across

1. an enemy
3. a written work meant to be read aloud
6. having too heavy a burden
10. to swallow up; to surround completely
12. a figure of speech that says one thing is another
13. a person who inherits a thing from the person who once had it
14. to call upon for help
15. what is handed down from earlier generations
16. to go over again and again

Down

1. into separate parts
2. again
4. an idea or statement
5. the destruction of something already accomplished
7. to plan
8. to put an end to
9. courtesy
11. an ancestor

Word Bank

abolish, adversary, anew, asunder, belabor, civility, engulf, forbear, formulate, heir, heritage, invoke, metaphor, overburdened, proposition, speech, undoing

 World Literature

Vocabulary Workbook 31, pages 1–2

Reading Vocabulary TRL

Help students preview the selection's vocabulary by taking a few moments to discuss each word and its definition.

Motivation for Reading

Encourage students to consider whether a speech at an important event should be long to do justice to the occasion.

Discussion Questions

Ask students to answer the question in the student text marginal note after reading the entire speech.

A Lincoln was wrong in saying that the world would not remember his speech. It ranks among the world's most-noted and often-quoted speeches.

The Gettysburg Address

Abraham Lincoln

As you read, watch for patterns that add interest to a speech. Also watch for phrases that sound familiar.

A *score* is twenty years. *Four score and seven* would equal eighty-seven years.

Four score and seven years ago our fathers brought forth on this continent, a new nation, **conceived** in liberty, and dedicated to the **proposition** that all men are created equal.

Now we are engaged in a great civil war, testing whether that nation, or any nation so conceived and so dedicated, can long endure. We are met on a great battlefield of that war. We have come to dedicate a portion of that field, as a final resting place for those who here gave their lives that that nation might live. It is altogether fitting and proper that we should do this.

A

Was Lincoln right that the world would not notice or remember this talk?

But in a larger sense, we cannot dedicate—we cannot **consecrate**—we cannot **hallow**—this ground. The brave men, living and dead, who struggled here, have consecrated it, far above our poor power to add or **detract**. The world will little note, nor long remember, what we say here, but it can never forget what they did here. It is for us the living, rather, to be dedicated here to the unfinished work which they who fought here have thus far so nobly advanced.

It is rather for us to be here dedicated to the great task remaining before us—that from these honored dead we may take increased devotion to that cause for which they gave the last full **measure** of devotion—that we here highly resolve that these dead shall not have died in vain—that this nation, under God, shall have a new birth of freedom—and that government of the people, by the people, for the people, shall not perish from the earth.

conceive to form in the mind

consecrate to dedicate to a serious purpose

detract to take away

hallow to set apart as holy

measure an amount

proposition an idea or statement

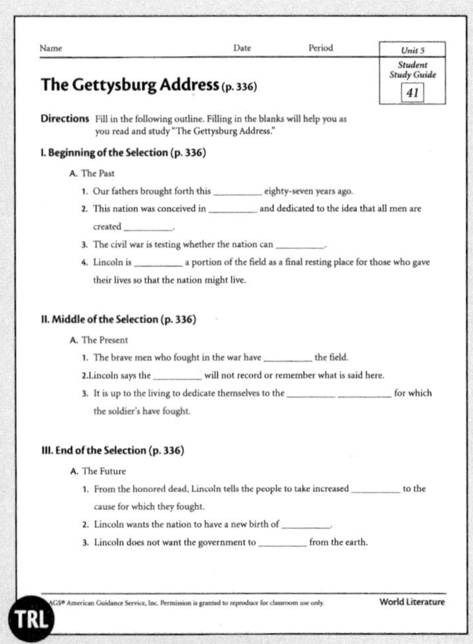
Name Date Period Unit 5 Student Study Guide 41

The Gettysburg Address (p. 336)

Directions Fill in the following outline. Filling in the blanks will help you as you read and study "The Gettysburg Address."

I. Beginning of the Selection (p. 336)

A. The Past

1. Our fathers brought forth this ________ eighty-seven years ago.
2. This nation was conceived in ________ and dedicated to the idea that all men are created ________.
3. The civil war is testing whether the nation can ________.
4. Lincoln is ________ a portion of the field as a final resting place for those who gave their lives so that the nation might live.

II. Middle of the Selection (p. 336)

A. The Present

1. The brave men who fought in the war have ________ the field.
2. Lincoln says the ________ will not record or remember what is said here.
3. It is up to the living to dedicate themselves to the ________ ________ for which the soldier's have fought.

III. End of the Selection (p. 336)

A. The Future

1. From the honored dead, Lincoln tells the people to take increased ________ to the cause for which they fought.
2. Lincoln wants the nation to have a new birth of ________.
3. Lincoln does not want the government to ________ from the earth.

 World Literature

TRL

Student Study Guide 41

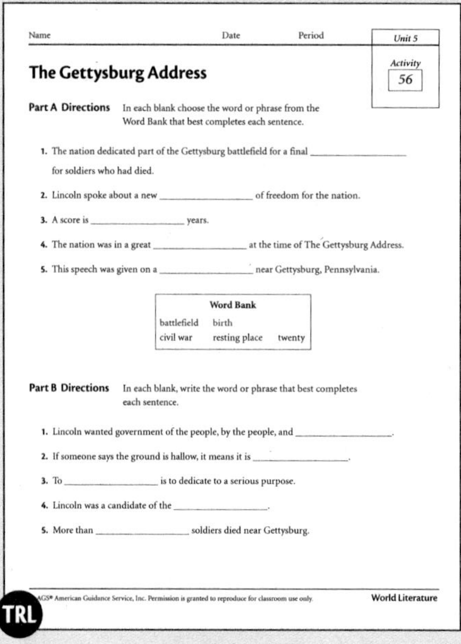
Name Date Period Unit 5 Activity 56

The Gettysburg Address

Part A Directions In each blank choose the word or phrase from the Word Bank that best completes each sentence.

1. The nation dedicated part of the Gettysburg battlefield for a final ________ for soldiers who had died.
2. Lincoln spoke about a new ________ of freedom for the nation.
3. A score is ________ years.
4. The nation was in a great ________ at the time of The Gettysburg Address.
5. This speech was given on a ________ near Gettysburg, Pennsylvania.

Word Bank		
battlefield	birth	
civil war	resting place	twenty

Part B Directions In each blank, write the word or phrase that best completes each sentence.

1. Lincoln wanted government of the people, by the people, and ________.
2. If someone says the ground is hallow, it means it is ________.
3. To ________ is to dedicate to a serious purpose.
4. Lincoln was a candidate of the ________.
5. More than ________ soldiers died near Gettysburg.

 World Literature

TRL

Activity 56

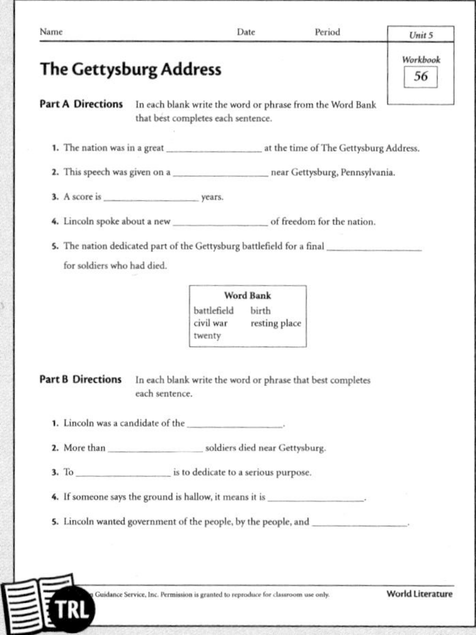
Name Date Period Unit 5 Workbook 56

The Gettysburg Address

Part A Directions In each blank write the word or phrase from the Word Bank that best completes each sentence.

1. The nation was in a great ________ at the time of The Gettysburg Address.
2. This speech was given on a ________ near Gettysburg, Pennsylvania.
3. A score is ________ years.
4. Lincoln spoke about a new ________ of freedom for the nation.
5. The nation dedicated part of the Gettysburg battlefield for a final ________ for soldiers who had died.

Word Bank	
battlefield	birth
civil war	resting place
twenty	

Part B Directions In each blank write the word or phrase that best completes each sentence.

1. Lincoln was a candidate of the ________.
2. More than ________ soldiers died near Gettysburg.
3. To ________ is to dedicate to a serious purpose.
4. If someone says the ground is hallow, it means it is ________.
5. Lincoln wanted government of the people, by the people, and ________.

 World Literature

TRL

Workbook 56

INTRODUCING the SELECTION

Inaugural Address

John F. Kennedy

John Fitzgerald Kennedy (1917–1963) American

Literary Term

metaphor a figure of speech that says one thing *is* another

About the Speaker

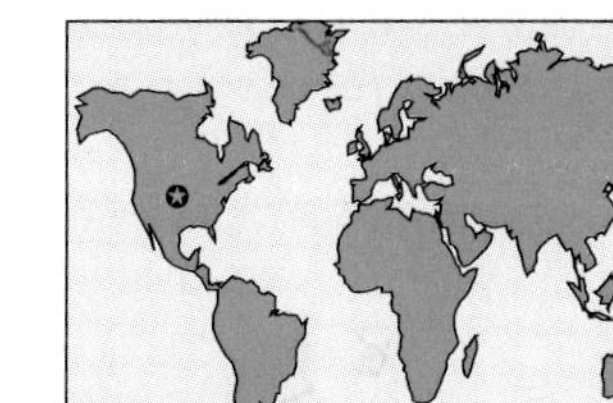

Born in Massachusetts, John F. Kennedy was the second son of a wealthy Irish Catholic family. Kennedy was educated in private schools and graduated from Harvard. He served in the navy during World War II. He then went into politics. In 1952 he won a seat in the Senate. Kennedy's work in the Senate and his quick-witted speaking style drew the attention of Democratic leaders. So did his book *Profiles in Courage*. He was named to run for president in 1960. Kennedy appeared confident during presidential debates on national TV. He convinced the American public that his religion and inexperience with foreign policy were not serious problems. He narrowly defeated Richard Nixon to become the thirty-fifth U.S. president. Kennedy was shot and killed in November 1963.

About the Selection

Kennedy won the 1960 election for several reasons. People thought he would bring the energy of youth to the presidency. Nixon was only a few years older. But he had been Dwight Eisenhower's vice president. People associated him with the Korean War, McCarthyism, and other bad memories. Kennedy campaigned as a new kind of politician. He wanted to represent the poor and young as well as the rich and established. An inaugural address is the speech given when a President is inaugurated, or sworn in. This speech was given in Washington on January 20, 1961. Note that Kennedy also uses **metaphor** in his address.

Selection at a Glance

Inaugural Address

John F. Kennedy

Student pages 337–342

Overview

During his presidential campaign, John F. Kennedy's slogan was "Let's get this country moving again." In his memorable "Inaugural Address," he lays out his famous challenge to the people: "Ask not what your country can do for you—ask what you can do for your country."

Selection Summary

After being sworn in as President of the United States, the new President, John F. Kennedy, addresses the country and the world by delivering his "Inaugural Address."

Objectives

- To read and understand an inaugural address.
- To identify metaphors in the speech.

Audiocassette 

Teacher's Resource Library 

- Vocabulary Workbook 31, pages 1–2
- Selection Glossary 36
- Student Study Guide 42
- Activity 57
- Workbook 57
- Writing Activity 40
- Selection Quiz 36

Setting the Stage for Reading

About the Author

Explain that John F. Kennedy captured the American imagination with his glamour and wealth, his charisma and wit, his intelligent wife and charming children, and his assemblage of Harvard intellectuals.

Activate Prior Knowledge: Point out that John F. Kennedy's mystique grew after his tragic and untimely death. Ask students to discuss what they already have read or heard about John F. Kennedy and his family.

ASK Why do you think religion was a factor in the 1960 presidential election? (Kennedy was a Roman Catholic, and the country had never had a Catholic President.)

About the Selection

John F. Kennedy had a winning oratory record. His inaugural address came on the wake of a series of televised debates through which he demonstrated his grasp of the issues. His inaugural address touches upon the key issues of the day: the economy, closing the missile gap, and preventing the spread of communism.

ASK What do you think Kennedy meant when he challenged Americans to "Ask not what your country can do for you—ask what you can do for your country"? (Students may suggest that Kennedy was challenging Americans to serve their nation in a variety of ways to help make the entire world a better place to live.)

Reading Vocabulary TRL

Help students preview the selection's vocabulary words by giving them copies of the Selection Glossary. Suggest that each student write at least five sentences with contextual meanings for selected vocabulary words.

Motivation for Reading

Ask students to read the address to find out what the President saw as the role of the United States in the world.

Discussion Questions

Suggest that students answer the question in the margin of the student selection after reading the entire speech.

A Critical Thinking What is the first revolution that Kennedy is referring to? (He is referring to the American Revolution in which the British American colonies gained their independence from Great Britain.)

B Kennedy is referring to atomic weapons.

C ASK Comprehension What is Kennedy saying about U.S. foreign policy? (The United States is not merely concerned with its own liberty, it will support any nation in the fight for liberty.)

Inaugural Address
John F. Kennedy

As you read, watch for passages that show Kennedy means his words for the entire world.

Kennedy uses the word man *to mean all humans, men and women.*

B *What does he mean by* the power to abolish all forms of human life*?*

Tempered *means strengthened.*

The world is very different now. For man holds in his mortal hands the power to **abolish** all forms of human poverty and all forms of human life. And yet the same revolutionary beliefs for which our **forebears** fought are still at issue around the globe—the belief that the rights of man come not from the generosity of the state but from the hand of God.

A We dare not forget today that we are the **heirs** of that first revolution. Let the word go forth from this time and place, to friend and foe alike, that the torch has been passed to a new generation of Americans—born in this century, tempered by war, **disciplined** by a hard and bitter peace, proud of our ancient **heritage**—and unwilling to witness or permit the slow **undoing** of those human rights to which this nation has always been committed, and to which we are committed today at home and around the world.

C Let every nation know, whether it wishes us well or ill, that we shall pay any price, bear any burden, meet any hardship, support any friend, oppose any foe to assure the **survival** and the success of liberty.

This much we pledge—and more.

To those old allies whose cultural and spiritual origins we share, we pledge the loyalty of faithful friends. United, there is little we cannot do in a host of new cooperative ventures.

abolish to put an end to

disciplined trained to act according to certain rules

forebear an ancestor

heir person who inherits a thing from the person who once had it

heritage what is handed down from earlier generations

survival the act of staying in existence

undoing the destruction of something already accomplished

338 *Unit 5 Persuasive Literature*

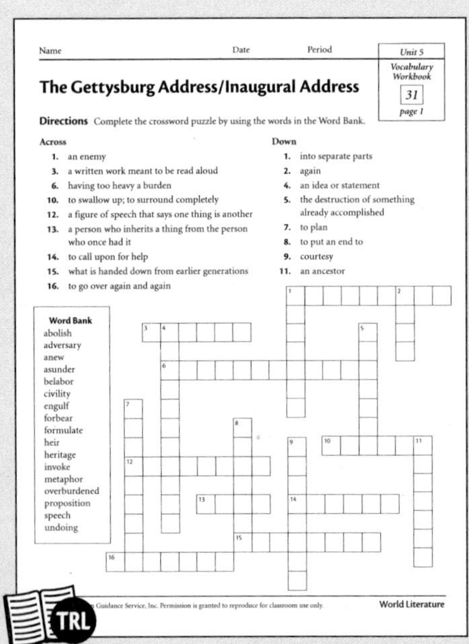
Name Date Period

Unit 5 *Vocabulary Workbook* 31 *page 1*

The Gettysburg Address/Inaugural Address

Directions Complete the crossword puzzle by using the words in the Word Bank.

Across

1. an enemy
3. a written work meant to be read aloud
6. having too heavy a burden
10. to swallow up; to surround completely
12. a figure of speech that says one thing is another
13. a person who inherits a thing from the person who once had it
14. to call upon for help
15. what is handed down from earlier generations
16. to go over again and again

Down

1. into separate parts
2. again
4. an idea or statement
5. the destruction of something already accomplished
7. to plan
8. to put an end to
9. courtesy
11. an ancestor

Word Bank
abolish
adversary
anew
asunder
belabor
civility
engulf
forbear
formulate
heir
heritage
invoke
metaphor
overburdened
proposition
speech
undoing

Guidance Service, Inc. Permission is granted to reproduce for classroom use only. World Literature

Vocabulary Workbook 31, pages 1–2

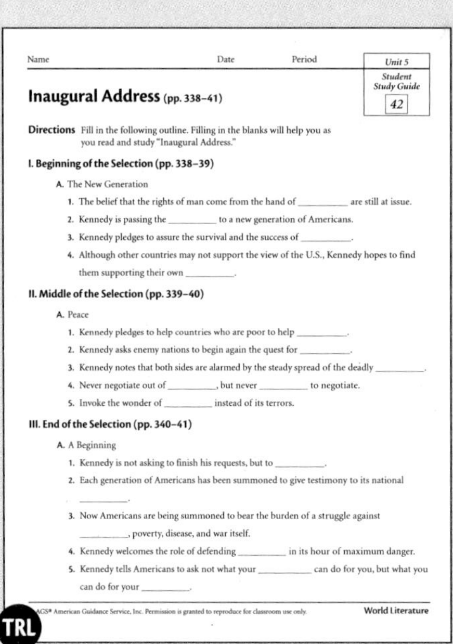
Name Date Period

Unit 5 *Student Study Guide* 42

Inaugural Address (pp. 338–41)

Directions Fill in the following outline. Filling in the blanks will help you as you read and study "Inaugural Address."

I. Beginning of the Selection (pp. 338–39)

A. The New Generation
1. The belief that the rights of man come from the hand of __________ are still at issue.
2. Kennedy is passing the __________ to a new generation of Americans.
3. Kennedy pledges to assure the survival and the success of __________.
4. Although other countries may not support the view of the U.S., Kennedy hopes to find them supporting their own __________.

II. Middle of the Selection (pp. 339–40)

A. Peace
1. Kennedy pledges to help countries who are poor to help __________.
2. Kennedy asks enemy nations to begin again the quest for __________.
3. Kennedy notes that both sides are alarmed by the steady spread of the deadly __________.
4. Never negotiate out of __________, but never __________ to negotiate.
5. Invoke the wonder of __________ instead of its terrors.

III. End of the Selection (pp. 340–41)

A. A Beginning
1. Kennedy is not asking to finish his requests, but to __________.
2. Each generation of Americans has been summoned to give testimony to its national __________.
3. Now Americans are being summoned to bear the burden of a struggle against __________, poverty, disease, and war itself.
4. Kennedy welcomes the role of defending __________ in its hour of maximum danger.
5. Kennedy tells Americans to ask not what your __________ can do for you, but what you can do for your __________.

AGS® American Guidance Service, Inc. Permission is granted to reproduce for classroom use only. World Literature

Student Study Guide 42

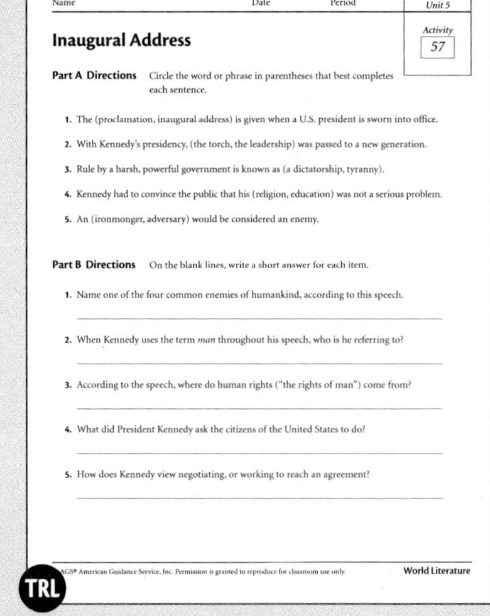
Name Date Period

Unit 5 *Activity* 57

Inaugural Address

Part A Directions Circle the word or phrase in parentheses that best completes each sentence.

1. The (proclamation, inaugural address) is given when a U.S. president is sworn into office.
2. With Kennedy's presidency, (the torch, the leadership) was passed to a new generation.
3. Rule by a harsh, powerful government is known as (a dictatorship, tyranny).
4. Kennedy had to convince the public that his (religion, education) was not a serious problem.
5. An (ironmonger, adversary) would be considered an enemy.

Part B Directions On the blank lines, write a short answer for each item.

1. Name one of the four common enemies of humankind, according to this speech.
2. When Kennedy uses the term *man* throughout his speech, who is he referring to?
3. According to the speech, where do human rights ("the rights of man") come from?
4. What did President Kennedy ask the citizens of the United States to do?
5. How does Kennedy view negotiating, or working to reach an agreement?

AGS® American Guidance Service, Inc. Permission is granted to reproduce for classroom use only. World Literature

Activity 57

Divided, there is little we can do—for we dare not meet a powerful challenge at odds and split **asunder**.

To those new states whom we welcome to the ranks of the free, we pledge our word that one form of colonial control shall not have passed away merely to be replaced by a far more iron **tyranny**. We shall not always expect to find them supporting our view. But we shall always hope to find them strongly supporting their own freedom—and to remember that, in the past, those who foolishly sought power by riding the back of the tiger ended up inside. **D**

A number of countries in Africa and Asia had recently become independent of *colonial* rule.

John Kennedy delivers his inaugural speech.

To those peoples in the huts and villages of half the globe struggling to break the bonds of mass misery, we pledge our best efforts to help them help themselves, for whatever period is required—not because the Communists may be doing it, not because we seek their votes, but because it is right. If a free society cannot help the many who are poor, it cannot save the few who are rich. ...

Finally, to those nations who would make themselves our **adversary**, we offer not a pledge but a request: that both sides begin **anew** the quest for peace, before the dark powers of destruction **unleashed** by science **engulf** all humanity in planned or accidental self-destruction. **E**

F What *dark powers of destruction* had science let loose in this period?

We dare not tempt them with weakness. For only when our arms are sufficient beyond doubt can we be certain beyond doubt that they will never be employed.

adversary an enemy

anew again

asunder into separate parts

engulf to swallow up; to surround completely

tyranny rule by a harsh, powerful government

unleashed let loose; released

D ASK Comprehension Summarize what Kennedy means by the statement "those who foolishly sought power by riding the back of the tiger ended up inside"? (He's warning nations who have new governments not to seek power by supporting those who appear to be most ferociously powerful, for they lose all freedom when the powerful take over complete control.)

E ASK Critical Thinking What is Kennedy, as spokesperson of the United States, offering the world? (He's extending a peace offering.)

F Atomic weapons are the dark powers of destruction that science let loose.

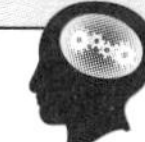

Comprehension

Comparing and Contrasting
Kennedy compares the right reason for helping the struggling people of the earth with the wrong reason. According to him, the wrong reason to pledge ourselves to a struggling nation is because the Communists are doing the same thing. Helping struggling nations should not be motivated by fear of communism; it should be motivated by our understanding of what is right.

ASK According to Kennedy, why should the United States help struggling nations? (Because it's the right thing to do.) What are we helping these struggling nations achieve? (freedom)

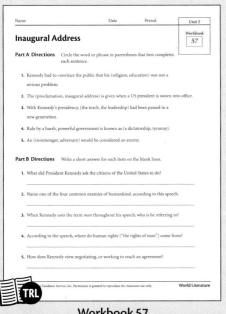

Name Date Period Unit 5 Workbook 57

Inaugural Address

Part A Directions Circle the word or phrase in parentheses that best completes each sentence.

1. Kennedy had to convince the public that his (religion, education) was not a serious problem.
2. The (proclamation, inaugural address) is given when a US president is sworn into office.
3. With Kennedy's presidency, (the torch, the leadership) had been passed to a new generation.
4. Rule by a harsh, powerful government is known as (a dictatorship, tyranny).
5. An (ironmonger, adversary) would be considered an enemy.

Part B Directions Write a short answer for each item on the blank lines.

1. What did President Kennedy ask the citizens of the United States to do?
2. Name one of the four common enemies of humankind, according to this speech.
3. When Kennedy uses the term *man* throughout his speech, who is he referring to?
4. According to the speech, where do human rights ("the rights of man") come from?
5. How does Kennedy view negotiating, or working to reach an agreement?

 World Literature

TRL

Workbook 57

Discussion Questions

A ASK Critical Thinking What two great and powerful nations is Kennedy talking about here? (The United States and the Soviet Union)

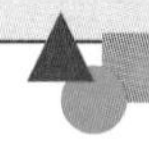

Learning Styles

Auditory Kennedy's speech was written to be read aloud. Students who have a keen ear for speech may enjoy reading aloud Kennedy's address. Invite a student who excels at oral reading or drama to read aloud the speech, stressing the repeated phrases such as "Let us" and "Let both sides." Record presentations and make the recordings available in a listening center for independent use. After the student has read the speech, pose the following questions.

ASK What phrases were repeated? (Let us; Let both sides)

ASK How did this repetition affect you as a listener? (Students will have various responses. For example, a student might say that he or she thought the repetition created a rhythm that was very captivating, almost hypnotic, and moving.)

Grammar

Let's and Lets The verb *to let* means "to allow or permit." Students probably use the word *lets* often in their everyday speech. For example, a student might say "I'll come to your party if my mom *lets* me." Explain to students that the words *let us* can be joined together to form the contraction *let's*. In his speech, Kennedy said, "So let us begin anew."

ASK How can you rephrase Kennedy's statement using a contraction instead of the words *let us*? (So let's begin anew.)

A But neither can two great and powerful groups of nations take comfort from our present course—both sides **overburdened** by the cost of modern weapons, both rightly alarmed by the steady spread of the deadly atom, yet both racing to alter that uncertain balance of terror that stays the hand of mankind's final war.

Kennedy takes the oath of office.

So let us begin anew—remembering on both sides that **civility** is not a sign of weakness, and sincerity is always subject to proof. Let us never **negotiate** out of fear. But let us never fear to negotiate.

Let both sides explore what problems unite us instead of **belaboring** those problems which divide us.

Let both sides, for the first time, **formulate** serious and precise proposals for the inspection and control of arms—and bring the absolute power to destroy other nations under the absolute control of all nations.

Let both sides seek to **invoke** the wonders of science instead of its terrors. Together let us explore the stars, conquer the deserts, **eradicate** disease, tap the ocean depths and encourage the arts and commerce.

All this will not be finished in the first 100 days. Nor will it be finished in the first 1,000 days, nor in the life of this Administration, nor even perhaps in our lifetime on this planet. But let us begin.

belaboring going over again and again
civility courtesy
eradicate to get rid of
formulate to plan
invoke to call upon for help
negotiate to work to reach agreement
overburdened having too heavy a burden

In your hands, my fellow citizens, more than mine, will rest the final success or failure of our course. Since this country **B** was founded, each generation of Americans has been summoned to give testimony to its national loyalty. The graves of young Americans who answered the call to service surround the globe.

Now the trumpet summons us again—not as a call to bear arms, though arms we need—not as a call to battle, though **embattled** we are—but a call to bear the burden of a long twilight struggle year in and year out, "rejoicing in hope, patient in **tribulation**"—a struggle against the common enemies of man: tyranny, poverty, disease and war itself.

Can we forge against these enemies a grand and **global alliance**, north and south, east and west, that can assure a more fruitful life for all mankind? Will you join in that historic effort?

In the long history of the world, only a few generations have been granted the role of defending freedom in its hour of **maximum** danger. I do not shrink from this responsibility—I welcome it. I do not believe that any of us would exchange places with any other people or any other generation. The energy, the faith, the devotion which we bring to this **endeavor** will light our country and all who serve it—and the glow from that fire can truly light the world.

And so, my fellow Americans: ask not what your country can do for you—ask what you can do for your country.

C How does this statement make the speech especially effective? What was Kennedy asking people to do?

My fellow citizens of the world: ask not what America will do for you, but what together we can do for the freedom of man.

embattled ready for battle

endeavor a sincere attempt

global alliance an agreement among world nations

maximum the greatest possible

tribulation suffering

B ASK Comprehension What does Kennedy mean by a testimony of loyalty? (He's talking about going to war.)

C Kennedy's final statements are effective because they draw each and every American into the destiny of the United States. He assigns a purpose to every common citizen and reminds Americans that they play the most important role, which is flattering and empowering considering the lack of influence people often feel when it comes to their relationship with their country. He is asking people to live up to the privilege and responsibility of freedom.

Literary Elements

Metaphor Remind students that a metaphor is a comparison between two things made without the use of the word *like* or *as*. It says one thing is another thing. Point out the metaphor in this sentence: "The energy, the faith, the devotion which we bring to this endeavor will light our country and all who serve it—and the glow from that fire can truly light the world." Ask what Kennedy is likening American energy, faith, and devotion to. (a warming fire)

Career Connection

Many Americans took Kennedy's challenge by joining the Peace Corps—a volunteer program established by the Kennedy administration. The corps trains men and women to serve in other countries where they help solve problems through education, example, and working together with the people for two years. Students may wish to investigate the Peace Corps or other service organizations such as the Red Cross as ways of beginning their careers. Suggest that students look at the opportunities, responsibilities, and educational requirements as well as the mission and goals of such organizations.

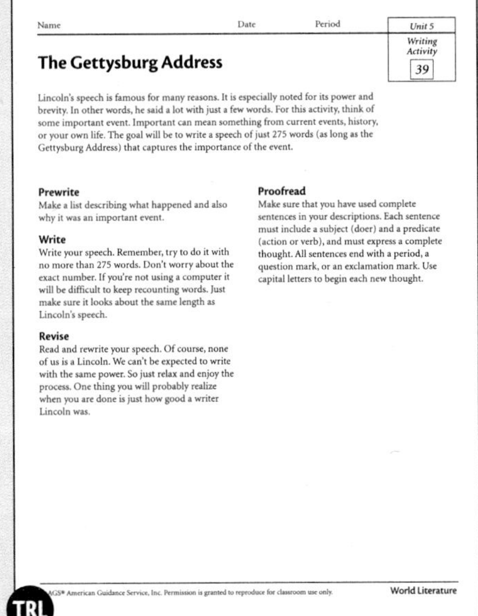

Name Date Period

Unit 5 *Writing Activity* 39

The Gettysburg Address

Lincoln's speech is famous for many reasons. It is especially noted for its power and brevity. In other words, he said a lot with just a few words. For this activity, think of some important event. Important can mean something from current events, history, or your own life. The goal will be to write a speech of just 275 words (as long as the Gettysburg Address) that captures the importance of the event.

Prewrite
Make a list describing what happened and also why it was an important event.

Write
Write your speech. Remember, try to do it with no more than 275 words. Don't worry about the exact number. If you're not using a computer it will be difficult to keep recounting words. Just make sure it looks about the same length as Lincoln's speech.

Revise
Read and rewrite your speech. Of course, none of us is a Lincoln. We can't be expected to write with the same power. So just relax and enjoy the process. One thing you will probably realize when you are done is just how good a writer Lincoln was.

Proofread
Make sure that you have used complete sentences in your descriptions. Each sentence must include a subject (doer) and a predicate (action or verb), and must express a complete thought. All sentences end with a period, a question mark, or an exclamation mark. Use capital letters to begin each new thought.

 World Literature

TRL

Writing Activity 39

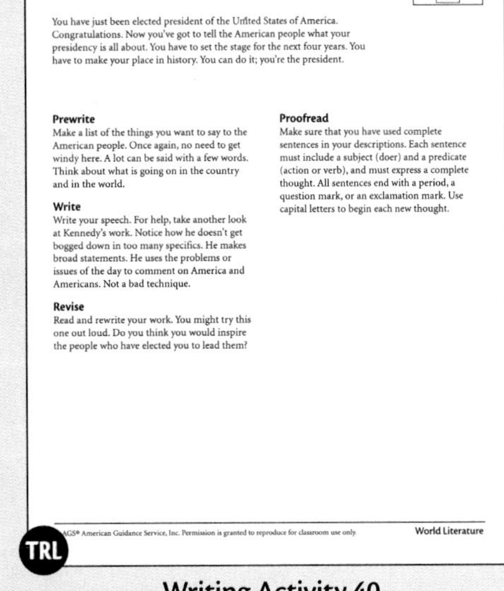

Name Date Period

Unit 5 *Writing Activity* 40

Inaugural Address

You have just been elected president of the United States of America. Congratulations. Now you've got to tell the American people what your presidency is all about. You have to set the stage for the next four years. You have to make your place in history. You can do it; you're the president.

Prewrite
Make a list of the things you want to say to the American people. Once again, no need to get windy here. A lot can be said with a few words. Think about what is going on in the country and in the world.

Write
Write your speech. For help, take another look at Kennedy's work. Notice how he doesn't get bogged down in too many specifics. He makes broad statements. He uses the problems or issues of the day to comment on America and Americans. Not a bad technique.

Revise
Read and rewrite your work. You might try this one out loud. Do you think you would inspire the people who have elected you to lead them?

Proofread
Make sure that you have used complete sentences in your descriptions. Each sentence must include a subject (doer) and a predicate (action or verb), and must express a complete thought. All sentences end with a period, a question mark, or an exclamation mark. Use capital letters to begin each new thought.

 World Literature

TRL

Writing Activity 40

Reviewing the Selection

Answer Key

Comprehension: Identifying Facts

1. Lincoln spoke at Gettysburg eighty-seven years after the nation was formed.

2. The existence of the United States was being tested by the Civil War.

3. Kennedy's speech was delivered on the day he was inaugurated as President.

Comprehension: Understanding Main Ideas

4. Lincoln asks his audience to have increased devotion to the United States.

5. Kennedy names tyranny, poverty, disease, and war as the enemies of all the world.

6. Kennedy asks Americans to do what they can for their country.

Understanding Literature: Metaphor

7. He is describing the birth of our nation. He uses a birth metaphor when he says, "our fathers brought forth," and "conceived in liberty."

8. Kennedy says that the energy of the American people can be like a fire that lights up all the world. He compares patriotism to a trumpet call.

Critical Thinking

9. He sent enemies a message of peace and cooperation. The United States is on more friendly terms with former enemies; we have arms control agreements; we explore space together; we tackle problems, such as pollution, together.

10. Students should support their opinions with details from the speech. They might mention such things as emotional language, repetition, and appealing to the audience.

Students might prepare a list of positive statements to use in their paragraphs. Some may write that the speakers avoid negativity by balancing negative points with inspirational suggestions.

Selection Quiz

The Teacher's Resource Library includes a Selection Quiz for Abraham Lincoln's "Gettysburg Address" and John F. Kennedy's "Inaugural Address" that may be given following the Selection Review.

REVIEWING the SELECTIONS

The Gettysburg Address

Abraham Lincoln

Inaugural Address

John F. Kennedy

Directions Write the answers to these questions using complete sentences.

Comprehension: Identifying Facts

1. How long after the United States became a nation did Lincoln speak at Gettysburg?
2. Why does Lincoln say that the existence of the United States is being tested?
3. What is the occasion for Kennedy's speech?

Comprehension: Understanding Main Ideas

Lincoln and Kennedy make requests of the audience.

4. What does Lincoln ask of his audience?
5. What things does Kennedy name as the real enemies of all the world?
6. What does Kennedy ask of the American people?

Understanding Literature: Metaphor

A metaphor is a figure of speech that says one thing is another. For example, "love is a thunderstorm" is a metaphor. It compares a thunderstorm to being in love. (The writer seems to be in a stormy romance.) Both speeches contain metaphors, although Kennedy's address uses more.

7. In the first paragraph of the Gettysburg Address, Lincoln uses metaphors about birth. What is he describing? Name one metaphor he uses.
8. Explain a metaphor about sound or light in the Kennedy speech.

Critical Thinking

9. What message did Kennedy send to America's enemies? Have any of his goals been reached in the time that has passed?
10. Choose one of the speeches. Tell why you think it is persuasive.

Writing on Your Own Both speeches discuss serious events. Yet they do not seem negative or depressing. Write a paragraph to explain how the speakers avoid negative emotions.

342 *Unit 5 Persuasive Literature*

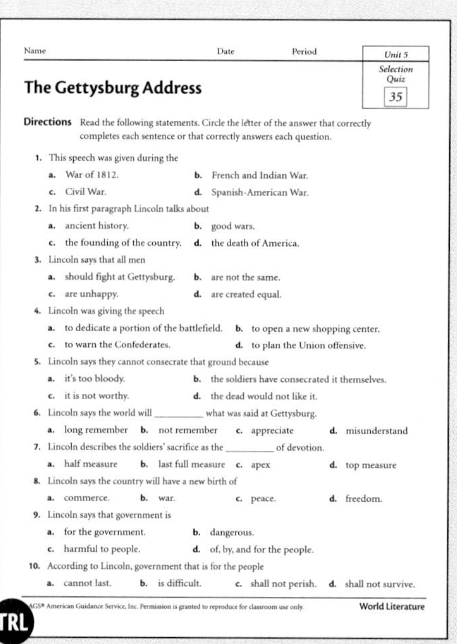

Name Date Period

Unit 5 Selection Quiz 35

The Gettysburg Address

Directions Read the following statements. Circle the letter of the answer that correctly completes each sentence or that correctly answers each question.

1. This speech was given during the
   a. War of 1812. b. French and Indian War.
   c. Civil War. d. Spanish-American War.
2. In his first paragraph Lincoln talks about
   a. ancient history. b. good wars.
   c. the founding of the country. d. the death of America.
3. Lincoln says that all men
   a. should fight at Gettysburg. b. are not the same.
   c. are unhappy. d. are created equal.
4. Lincoln was giving the speech
   a. to dedicate a portion of the battlefield. b. to open a new shopping center.
   c. to warn the Confederates. d. to plan the Union offensive.
5. Lincoln says they cannot consecrate that ground because
   a. it's too bloody. b. the soldiers have consecrated it themselves.
   c. it is not worthy. d. the dead would not like it.
6. Lincoln says the world will __________ what was said at Gettysburg.
   a. long remember b. not remember c. appreciate d. misunderstand
7. Lincoln describes the soldiers' sacrifice as the __________ of devotion.
   a. half measure b. last full measure c. apex d. top measure
8. Lincoln says the country will have a new birth of
   a. commerce. b. war. c. peace. d. freedom.
9. Lincoln says that government is
   a. for the government. b. dangerous.
   c. harmful to people. d. of, by, and for the people.
10. According to Lincoln, government that is for the people
    a. cannot last. b. is difficult. c. shall not perish. d. shall not survive.

 World Literature

TRL

Selection Quiz 35

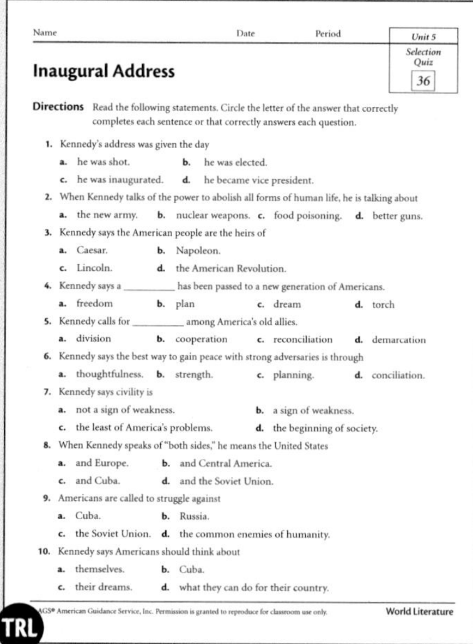

Name Date Period

Unit 5 Selection Quiz 36

Inaugural Address

Directions Read the following statements. Circle the letter of the answer that correctly completes each sentence or that correctly answers each question.

1. Kennedy's address was given the day
   a. he was shot. b. he was elected.
   c. he was inaugurated. d. he became vice president.
2. When Kennedy talks of the power to abolish all forms of human life, he is talking about
   a. the new army. b. nuclear weapons. c. food poisoning. d. better guns.
3. Kennedy says the American people are the heirs of
   a. Caesar. b. Napoleon.
   c. Lincoln. d. the American Revolution.
4. Kennedy says a __________ has been passed to a new generation of Americans.
   a. freedom b. plan c. dream d. torch
5. Kennedy calls for __________ among America's old allies.
   a. division b. cooperation c. reconciliation d. demarcation
6. Kennedy says the best way to gain peace with strong adversaries is through
   a. thoughtfulness. b. strength. c. planning. d. conciliation.
7. Kennedy says civility is
   a. not a sign of weakness. b. a sign of weakness.
   c. the least of America's problems. d. the beginning of society.
8. When Kennedy speaks of "both sides," he means the United States
   a. and Europe. b. and Central America.
   c. and Cuba. d. and the Soviet Union.
9. Americans are called to struggle against
   a. Cuba. b. Russia.
   c. the Soviet Union. d. the common enemies of humanity.
10. Kennedy says Americans should think about
    a. themselves. b. Cuba.
    c. their dreams. d. what they can do for their country.

 World Literature

TRL

Selection Quiz 36

Essays

- "An essay... has a minimum of one anecdote and one universal idea." —Carol Bly
- "The more opinions you have, the less you see." —Wim Wenders

A writer explaining a personal point of view is writing an essay. An essay may be about a basic issue or current event. In either case, the writer will present facts as he or she understands them. The writer's talents and limitations affect what is written.

Essays have existed from the beginning of literature. Plato, a Greek philosopher of long ago, wrote dialogues. These imaginary conversations showed his ideas about truth, beauty, and government. Around 1450, the printing press was introduced into Europe. It then became easier to publish essays. This helped many thinkers of the 1500s to the 1800s become famous interpreters of their societies. They include Michel de Montaigne, Thomas Paine, and Ralph Waldo Emerson.

By the 1700s and 1800s many people could afford to buy books and newspapers. Also, more people could read. This meant many new readers. Essayists began to write opinion articles. They wrote their ideas about many things, from gossip to literary criticism. This trend continues today. Newspaper editorials and advice columns are kinds of essays. The essay also still exists in the form of regular columns in newspapers and magazines.

What makes modern essayists popular? It may be their point of view, writing style, or both. They are not the final authority on any subject. But their ideas are useful. They can help readers form their own opinions.

Essays

Ask students to silently read the text on page 343. Essays are literary works on a particular topic. They are often short and present personal points of view.

Direct students' attention to the quotations. You might want to explain that an anecdote is an illustrative story.

ASK According to the Carol Bly's criteria, do you think an essay would be easy to write? (Perhaps it's not difficult to come up with an anecdote, but coming up with an interesting one can be a task. Furthermore, not everyone knows universal truths. To write an essay takes considerable contemplation and knowledge.)

ASK How can Wim Wenders's statement be paraphrased? (Opinionated people have their minds made up about many things, so they're unlikely to look inquisitively at the world. They risk not noticing some of the greatest wonders of life.)

Name Date Period | *Unit 5* | *Activity* 58

Essays

Part A Directions In each blank, write the word or phrase that best completes each sentence.

1. By the ________ hundreds, many people could read.
2. Around 1450, the ________ was introduced in Europe.
3. Regular ________ in newspapers and magazines are essays.
4. The writer's ________ may limit and affect what is written.
5. An essay is written from a ________ point of view.

Part B Directions Read each sentence. Write *T* if the statement is true or *F* if it is false.

________ 1. Reading an essay may help the reader form an opinion.
________ 2. During the 1700s and 1800s essayists began to write speeches.
________ 3. Essays may present facts about a current event as the writer understands them.
________ 4. The writing style of an essayist may make his or her writing popular.
________ 5. Newspaper editorials are a kind of essay.

 World Literature

TRL

Activity 58

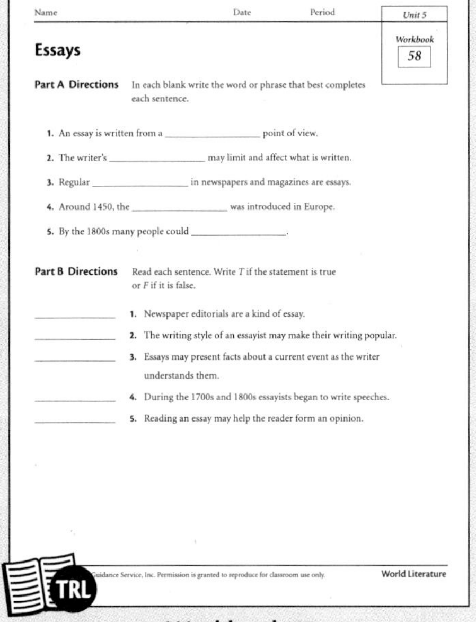
Name Date Period | *Unit 5* | *Workbook* 58

Essays

Part A Directions In each blank write the word or phrase that best completes each sentence.

1. An essay is written from a ________ point of view.
2. The writer's ________ may limit and affect what is written.
3. Regular ________ in newspapers and magazines are essays.
4. Around 1450, the ________ was introduced in Europe.
5. By the 1800s many people could ________.

Part B Directions Read each sentence. Write *T* if the statement is true or *F* if it is false.

________ 1. Newspaper editorials are a kind of essay.
________ 2. The writing style of an essayist may make their writing popular.
________ 3. Essays may present facts about a current event as the writer understands them.
________ 4. During the 1700s and 1800s essayists began to write speeches.
________ 5. Reading an essay may help the reader form an opinion.

 World Literature

TRL

Workbook 58

Selection at a Glance

Of Repentance

Michel de Montaigne (translated by J. M. Cohen)

Student pages 344–346

Overview

Michel de Montaigne's "Of Repentance" appeared in his third book of essays, published in 1588. In the essay, he maintains the objective distance he came to be known for and which is attested to by his motto, "I stand back."

Selection Summary

In "Of Repentance," Michel de Montaigne, a French essayist, tells the story of a man known as the Thief.

Objectives

- To read and understand an essay.
- To identify the author's point of view in an essay.

Audiocassette 

Teacher's Resource Library TRL

- Vocabulary Workbook 32, pages 1–3
- Selection Glossary 37
- Student Study Guide 43
- Activity 59
- Workbook 59
- Writing Activity 41
- Selection Quiz 37

INTRODUCING the SELECTION

Of Repentance

Michel de Montaigne (translated by J. M. Cohen)

Michel de Montaigne (1533–1592) French

About the Author

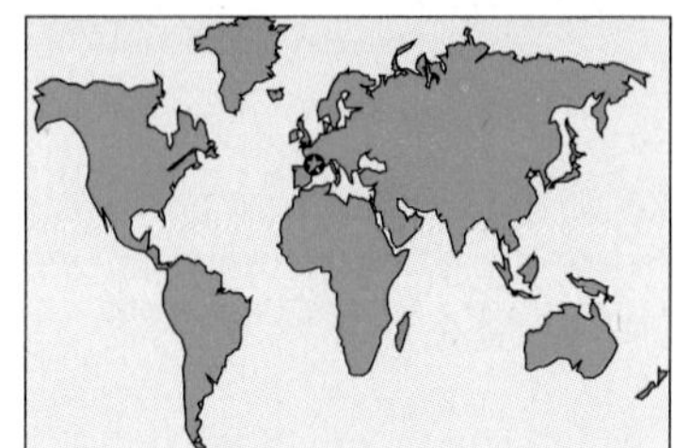

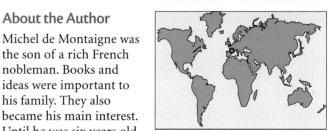

Michel de Montaigne was the son of a rich French nobleman. Books and ideas were important to his family. They also became his main interest. Until he was six years old, Montaigne heard and was taught to speak only Latin. He came to know that language well. Montaigne practiced law for several years. Then in 1571 his father died. He left Montaigne his share of the family money. Montaigne retired. He spent the rest of his life happily pursuing things that interested him, especially writing. His **essays,** or comments on society, show that he was a thoughtful man and a keen observer. An essay is a piece of writing that show's a writer's opinions on some basic or current issue.

Literary Terms

essay a written work that shows a writer's opinions on some basic or current issue

style an author's way of writing

About the Selection

Montaigne filled three books with his essays. They are detached, amused, lively observations on life. His early works tend to imitate the thoughts of the classic writers he must have studied. As he matured, he developed his own literary **style,** or way of writing. His writing is graceful and personal. His essays about friendship, education, and religion reflect his own experiences—his travels, the unrest of the French religious wars, the loss of a close friend. He gradually developed the habit of watching and learning from the world around him. "I stand back" was his official motto. "Of Repentance" is part of his third book of essays. It was published in 1588.

Setting the Stage for Reading

About the Author

Michel de Montaigne was afforded a luxury that many writers today only dream of: thanks to the inheritance he received from his father, he was able to quit his job and focus his attention exclusively on writing.

ASK What qualifications did Montaigne have as an essayist? (He was well-read, highly educated, and fluent in the law—all of which suggest that he had the intelligence and thoughtfulness to be a keen observer of society.)

About the Selection

"Of Repentance" is a brief essay told in parable form. Explain that a parable is a short story that illustrates a moral attitude.

Activate Prior Knowledge: Have students discuss other stories or essays dealing with a morals or values.

ASK About what topics might contemporary essayists write short essays similar to Montaigne's "Of Repentance"? (Students may name any number of topics: the right to bear arms, violence, vanity, fame, rage, honesty, trust, truthfulness, excellence, and so on.)

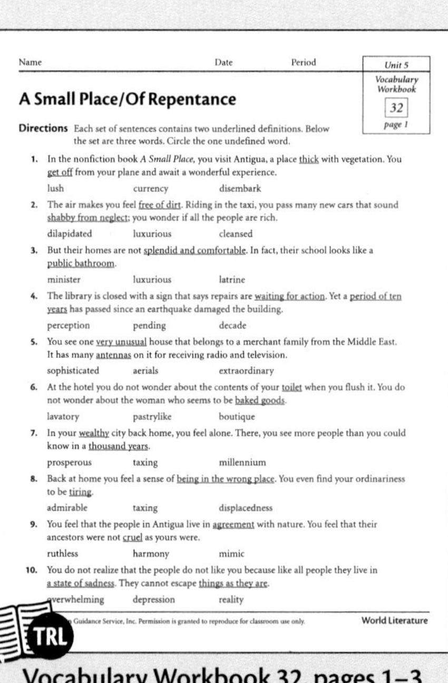

Name Date Period | *Unit 5* *Vocabulary Workbook* 32 *page 1*

A Small Place/Of Repentance

Directions Each set of sentences contains two underlined definitions. Below the set are three words. Circle the one undefined word.

1. In the nonfiction book *A Small Place,* you visit Antigua, a place thick with vegetation. You get off from your plane and await a wonderful experience.
   lush currency disembark
2. The air makes you feel free of dirt. Riding in the taxi, you pass many new cars that sound shabby from neglect; you wonder if all the people are rich.
   dilapidated luxurious cleansed
3. But their homes are not splendid and comfortable. In fact, their school looks like a public bathroom.
   minister luxurious latrine
4. The library is closed with a sign that says repairs are waiting for action. Yet a period of ten years has passed since an earthquake damaged the building.
   perception pending decade
5. You see one very unusual house that belongs to a merchant family from the Middle East. It has many antennas on it for receiving radio and television.
   sophisticated aerials extraordinary
6. At the hotel you do not wonder about the contents of your toilet when you flush it. You do not wonder about the woman who seems to be baked goods.
   lavatory pastrylike boutique
7. In your wealthy city back home, you feel alone. There, you see more people than you could know in a thousand years.
   prosperous taxing millennium
8. Back at home you feel a sense of being in the wrong place. You even find your ordinariness to be tiring.
   admirable taxing displacedness
9. You feel that the people in Antigua live in agreement with nature. You feel that their ancestors were not cruel as yours were.
   ruthless harmony mimic
10. You do not realize that the people do not like you because like all people they live in a state of sadness. They cannot escape things as they are.
    overwhelming depression reality

 World Literature

TRL Vocabulary Workbook 32, pages 1–3

Of Repentance

Michel de Montaigne

The other day, when I was on the estate of a kinsman of mine in Armagnac, I saw a peasant whom everybody called *The Thief.* He told us his story, which was like this: Born a beggar, and realizing that if he were to earn his living by the work of his hands, he would never succeed in securing himself against want, he decided to become a thief; and thanks to his physical strength, he practised his trade quite safely throughout his youth. He gathered his harvest and his **vintage** from other men's lands, but at such great distances and in such great stacks that no one could conceive how one man could carry away so much on his shoulders in a single night. And he took care, besides, to **equalize** and distribute the damage that he caused, so as to **minimize** the loss to each individual. Now, in his old age, he is rich for a man of his condition, thanks to his trade, which he openly confesses. And to **reconcile** God to his winnings, he has made it, he said, his daily task to **compensate** the heirs of the men he robbed by voluntary gifts. If he does not complete his task—for to do it all at once is beyond him—he will, he says, leave it as a charge to his heirs, to repay them according to the wrong he did to each, which is known to him alone. From his account, whether true or false, it seems that this man regards theft as a dishonest action, and hates it, though less than he hates poverty. He **repents** of it quite simply, but in so far as it was thus **counterbalanced** and compensated, he does not repent of it.

A

As you read, think about what the thief has to repent. What is Montaigne's attitude toward him?

Armagnac is a region in southwestern France.

Do you think the man repents or not?

B

compensate to repay

counterbalance to use one act to make up for another

equalize to make equal

minimize to make as small as possible

reconcile to bring into agreement

repent to feel sorry for an action

vintage a crop of grapes grown for wine

Reading Vocabulary TRL

Help students preview the vocabulary with the Selection Glossary. Invite students to use the words in sentences.

Motivation for Reading

How does one who is sorry for his or her actions behave? Encourage students to consider this question as they read.

Discussion Questions

Suggest that students first read the entire essay before trying to answer the questions in the margins.

A Montaigne's attitude, or tone, toward the thief seems neutral.

B Students who think the thief is truly sorry may find their proof in the fact that the thief is concerned with compensation. Others might explain that he is not so sorry that he's willing to return to poverty or go to prison.

Viewing the Art

Paul Cezanne, a French painter of the late 1800s and early 1900s, was well-known for his landscapes of the countryside near his home. Shown is his painting *Meadow and Trees.*

ASK How does the painting support the essay? (The essay takes place in rural France and the painting depicts a rural French scene.)

Name Date Period | *Unit 5* | *Student Study Guide* 43

Of Repentance (p. 345)

Directions Fill in the following outline. Filling in the blanks will help you as you read and study "Of Repentance."

I. Beginning of the Selection (p. 345)

A. Youth

1. The thief was born a __________.
2. The thief realizes if he earns his living by the work of his __________, he will not succeed in securing himself against __________.
3. The thief practices his trade safely throughout his youth, due to his __________.

II. Middle of the Selection (p. 345)

A. Life of a Thief

1. The thief gathers his __________ and his vintage from other men's lands.
2. The thief takes so much and travels such long distances that people wonder how one man can carry so much on his __________ in a single night.
3. The thief has made it his __________ __________ to compensate the heirs of the men he robbed by giving them gifts.

III. End of the Selection (p. 345)

A. Payment

1. If the thief does not complete his task, he will leave it to his __________ to repay them.
2. The thief regards theft as a __________ action.
3. The thief hates __________ more than theft.
4. He repents theft, yet he does not __________ it.

 World Literature

TRL

Student Study Guide 43

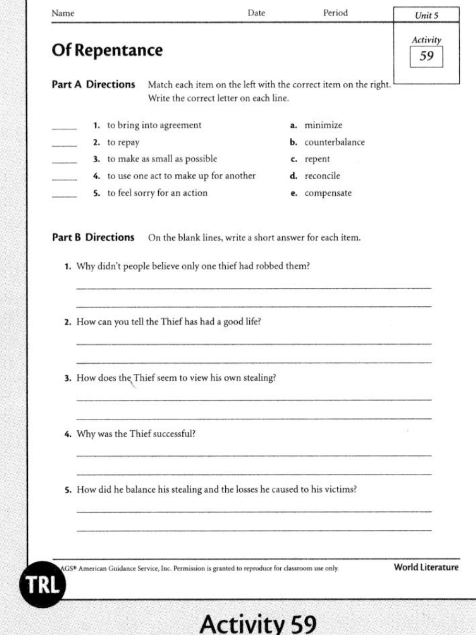

Name Date Period | *Unit 5* | *Activity* 59

Of Repentance

Part A Directions Match each item on the left with the correct item on the right. Write the correct letter on each line.

_____	1. to bring into agreement	a. minimize
_____	2. to repay	b. counterbalance
_____	3. to make as small as possible	c. repent
_____	4. to use one act to make up for another	d. reconcile
_____	5. to feel sorry for an action	e. compensate

Part B Directions On the blank lines, write a short answer for each item.

1. Why didn't people believe only one thief had robbed them?
2. How can you tell the Thief has had a good life?
3. How does the Thief seem to view his own stealing?
4. Why was the Thief successful?
5. How did he balance his stealing and the losses he caused to his victims?

 World Literature

TRL

Activity 59

Name Date Period | *Unit 5* | *Workbook* 59

Of Repentance

Part A Directions Match each item on the left with the correct item on the right. Write the correct letter on each line.

_____	1. to use one act to make up for another	a. minimize
_____	2. to feel sorry for an action	b. counterbalance
_____	3. to bring into agreement	c. repent
_____	4. to repay	d. reconcile
_____	5. to make as small as possible	e. compensate

Part B Directions Write a short answer for each item on the blank lines.

1. Why was the Thief successful?
2. How did he balance his stealing and the losses he caused to his victims?
3. Why didn't people believe only one thief had robbed them?
4. How can you tell the Thief has had a good life?
5. How does the Thief seem to view his own stealing?

 World Literature

TRL

Workbook 59

Reviewing the Selection

Answer Key

Comprehension: Identifying Facts

1. He decided to steal rather than labor.

2. No one believed that one person could be strong enough to carry such great quantities such great distances in a single night.

3. He tries to make up for stealing by giving gifts to the heirs of those from whom he stole.

Comprehension: Understanding Main Ideas

4. Stealing was a good career because it would lift him up from poverty, which laboring would not have done.

5. If he dies without paying everyone back, the Thief will charge his heirs with the task of repayment.

6. He's sorry he had to steal to become rich, which is why he wants to pay back the people he robbed.

Understanding Literature: Essays

7. Montaigne met the Thief on the estate of one of his own relatives.

8. Montaigne seems skeptical of the Thief's story and questions the sincerity of his repentance.

Critical Thinking

9. A,c; B, a; C, b

10. Students should explain their opinions by referring to the essay and citing examples from their own experience.

Students may want to use an idea web to record possible examples in a brainstorming session before they begin writing. Suggest they develop their paragraph around one example.

Selection Quiz

The Teacher's Resource Library includes a Selection Quiz for "Of Repentance" that may be given following the Selection Review.

REVIEWING the SELECTION

Of Repentance

Michel de Montaigne

Directions Write the answers to these questions using complete sentences.

Comprehension: Identifying Facts

1. How did the Thief decide to make his living as a young man?
2. Why didn't anyone believe that the Thief had stolen their crops?
3. How has the Thief tried to make up for stealing?

Comprehension: Understanding Main Ideas

4. Explain why the Thief decided that stealing would be a good career for him.
5. What will the Thief do if he still hasn't paid everyone back by the time he dies?
6. Does the Thief regret his actions as a young man?

Understanding Literature: Essays

An essay is a comment on some part of society. It may be about a basic issue or something in the news. It gives the writer's point of view on the subject.

7. What is Montaigne's personal connection with the Thief?
8. Explain what you think is Montaigne's attitude toward the Thief.

Critical Thinking

9. Montaigne seems to say that people may feel one way about a general principle. But they may act differently in a specific case. Match each general principle with its specific example.

   A. being on time
   B. honesty
   C. minimum drinking age of twenty-one

   a. cheating on a test
   b. drinking champagne on prom night
   c. choosing to catch a late bus to school

10. Do you like or dislike the person called "the Thief"? Why or why not?

Writing on Your Own Pick one of the pairs in question 9. Write a paragraph to explain why people can believe in a general principle but act in a different way.

346 *Unit 5 Persuasive Literature*

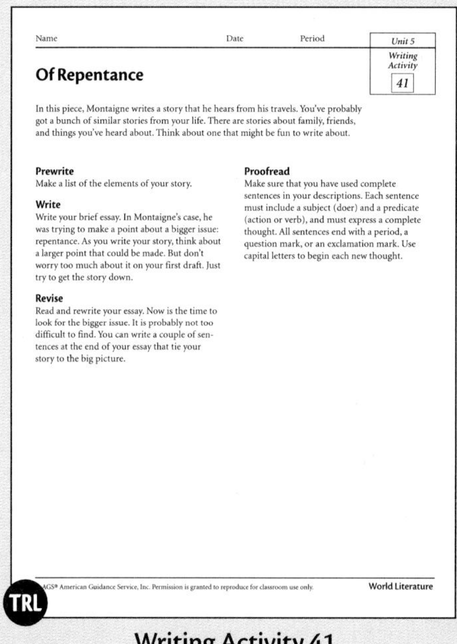
Name Date Period | *Unit 5* *Writing Activity* 41

Of Repentance

In this piece, Montaigne writes a story that he hears from his travels. You've probably got a bunch of similar stories from your life. There are stories about family, friends, and things you've heard about. Think about one that might be fun to write about.

Prewrite
Make a list of the elements of your story.

Write
Write your brief essay. In Montaigne's case, he was trying to make a point about a bigger issue: repentance. As you write your story, think about a larger point that could be made. But don't worry too much about it on your first draft. Just try to get the story down.

Revise
Read and rewrite your essay. Now is the time to look for the bigger issue. It is probably not too difficult to find. You can write a couple of sentences at the end of your essay that tie your story to the big picture.

Proofread
Make sure that you have used complete sentences in your descriptions. Each sentence must include a subject (doer) and a predicate (action or verb), and must express a complete thought. All sentences end with a period, a question mark, or an exclamation mark. Use capital letters to begin each new thought.

 World Literature

TRL

Writing Activity 41

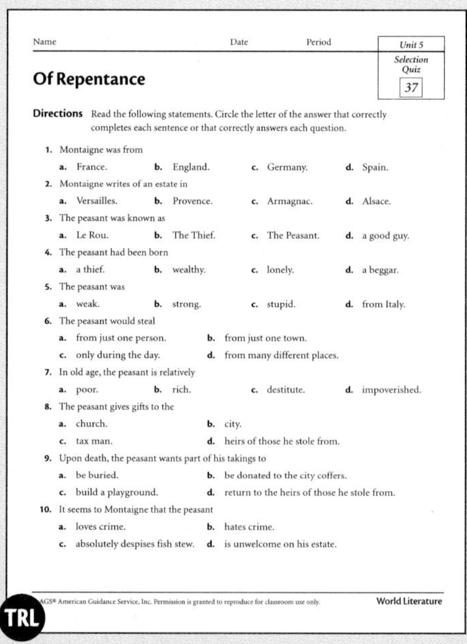
Name Date Period | *Unit 5* *Selection Quiz* 37

Of Repentance

Directions Read the following statements. Circle the letter of the answer that correctly completes each sentence or that correctly answers each question.

1. Montaigne was from
   a. France. b. England. c. Germany. d. Spain.
2. Montaigne writes of an estate in
   a. Versailles. b. Provence. c. Armagnac. d. Alsace.
3. The peasant was known as
   a. Le Rou. b. The Thief. c. The Peasant. d. a good guy.
4. The peasant had been born
   a. a thief. b. wealthy. c. lonely. d. a beggar.
5. The peasant was
   a. weak. b. strong. c. stupid. d. from Italy.
6. The peasant would steal
   a. from just one person. b. from just one town.
   c. only during the day. d. from many different places.
7. In old age, the peasant is relatively
   a. poor. b. rich. c. destitute. d. impoverished.
8. The peasant gives gifts to the
   a. church. b. city.
   c. tax man. d. heirs of those he stole from.
9. Upon death, the peasant wants part of his takings to
   a. be buried. b. be donated to the city coffers.
   c. build a playground. d. return to the heirs of those he stole from.
10. It seems to Montaigne that the peasant
   a. loves crime. b. hates crime.
   c. absolutely despises fish stew. d. is unwelcome on his estate.

©AGS® American Guidance Service, Inc. Permission is granted to reproduce for classroom use only. World Literature

TRL

Selection Quiz 37

INTRODUCING the SELECTION

A Small Place

Jamaica Kincaid

Jamaica Kincaid (1949–) Antiguan

About the Author

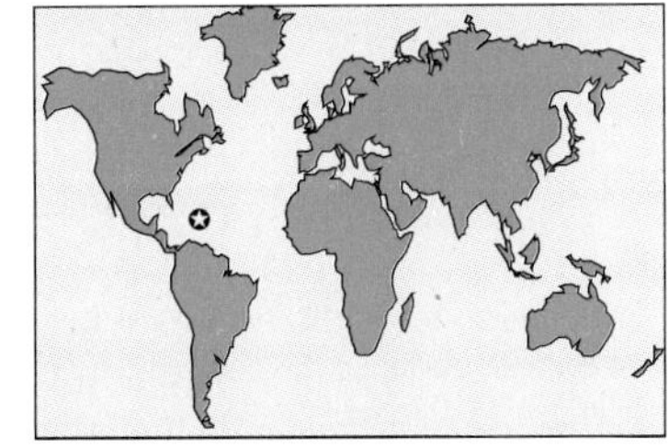

Jamaica Kincaid was born in St. John's, Antigua, an island in the West Indies. She grew up on this "small place" but left for New York City when she was sixteen. Her original name was Elaine Potter Richardson. She changed it when she became a writer. She wanted her name to reflect her Caribbean heritage. Kincaid's first novel, *Annie John,* was published in 1985. It is based on her own childhood. She has also written short stories. She has been a staff writer for *The New Yorker* magazine. Many of Kincaid's works are concerned with colonial control and corruption. Her opinions may sting, but they certainly get her readers' attention.

Literary Terms

irony using words that seem to say one thing but mean the opposite

tone the attitude an author takes toward a subject

About the Selection

A Small Place is a nonfiction book about Antigua. It was published in 1988. In this chapter, the writer tries to persuade tourists to think about their effect on the island. She argues that they carry on the tradition of foreign control. They help to destroy the local culture. She points out many ways that the islanders have been forced to change. The **tone** of her writing, or the attitude she takes toward her topic, is often angry and biting. She also uses **irony** to help make her point. Irony is the use of words that say one thing but really mean the opposite. Kincaid makes a powerful argument. She makes her readers think about what they are doing when they travel.

Selection at a Glance

A Small Place

Jamaica Kincaid

Student pages 347–361

Overview

A Small Place is an ironic essay that explores the ugliness of tourism and attacks those individuals who choose to impose themselves upon the impoverished residents of small places like Antigua.

Selection Summary

In this chapter from *A Small Place,* Jamaica Kincaid takes an ironic look at tourists who come to the island of Antigua.

Objectives

- To read and understand an essay.
- To identify the author's tone.

Audiocassette 

Teacher's Resource Library 

- Vocabulary Workbook 32, pages 1–3
- Selection Glossary 38
- Student Study Guide 44, pages 1–2
- Activity 60, pages 1–2
- Workbook 60, pages 1–2
- Writing Activity 42
- Selection Quiz 38

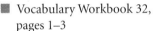

Setting the Stage for Reading

About the Author

Jamaica Kincaid is a prolific Antigua-born author whose work appears frequently in *The New Yorker.* Her given name was Elaine Richardson, but she changed it to better reflect her Caribbean heritage.

ASK What does Jamaica Kincaid's name say about her self-concept? (She has a strong sense of herself as a Caribbean woman and is so proud of her heritage that she chose a name that conveys her identity to the world.)

About the Selection

The selection students are about to read is a chapter from Kincaid's nonfiction book titled *A Small Place.* The story's angry, bitter tone grows out of the author's belief that tourism carries on the tradition of foreign control and exploitation in the Caribbean.

Activate Prior Knowledge: Invite students to discuss their personal experiences as tourists or with tourists.

ASK What aspects of tourism are ugly? (Students may name some of the following points: tourists may have more available resources than local residents; they may demand special services since they are on vacation; they may think that the local culture is less sophisticated than their own.)

Reading Vocabulary TRL

Help students preview the vocabulary by giving them copies of the Selection Glossary. Encourage student pairs to take turns reading and defining the terms.

Motivation for Reading

What do some local people in the Caribbean think of vacationers? Read this selection to find out.

Discussion Questions

Suggest that students use the comments and questions in the margins of the student text to focus their reading.

A Kincaid's first paragraph is rather benign, so students may not initially detect her ironic way of expressing anger.

B ASK **Critical Thinking** Why might the Prime Minister of an island nation that depends on tourism for much of its national income name the airport after himself? (The airport is one of the country's most important public buildings and is the only one that beach-bound tourists may ever see.)

A Small Place

Jamaica Kincaid

A
How do you think the writer feels about tourists? As you read, look for clues.

The island of *Antigua* is in the Caribbean Sea, east of Puerto Rico.

Aeroplane is the British spelling of *airplane.* Other British spellings, such as *favour* and *colour,* are used later.

If you go to Antigua as a tourist, this is what you will see. If you come by aeroplane, you will land at the V. C. Bird International Airport. Vere Cornwall (V. C.) Bird is the Prime Minister of Antigua. You may be the sort of tourist **B** who would wonder why a Prime Minister would want an airport named after him—why not a school, why not a hospital, why not some great public monument? You are a tourist and you have not yet seen a school in Antigua, you have not yet seen the hospital in Antigua, you have not yet seen a public monument in Antigua. As your plane descends to land, you might say, What a beautiful island Antigua is—more beautiful than any of the other islands you have seen, and they were very beautiful, in their way, but they were much too green, much too **lush** with vegetation, which indicated to you, the tourist, that they got quite a bit of rainfall, and rain is the very thing that you, just now, do not want, for you are thinking of the hard and cold and dark and long days you spent working in North America (or, worse, Europe), earning some money so that you could stay in this place (Antigua) where the sun always shines and where the climate is deliciously hot and dry for the four to ten days you are going to be staying there; and since you are on your

This is Nelson Dockyard in Antigua.

lush growing thick with plants

Cross-Curricular Connection

Social Studies In the 1990s, Antigua suffered a number of blows. In 1994 Prime Minister Vere Cornwall Bird retired and his son Lester Bird took over leadership. Soon thereafter, Lester's younger brother, Ivor, was found guilty of possessing illegal drugs but was given a surprisingly light sentence. Crimes against tourists forced the government to institute police and army patrols of tourist areas. In September of 1995, Hurricane Luis struck a heavy blow to Antigua causing approximately $300 million dollars worth of damage. In 1998, another hurricane, Georges, rolled over the island.

ASK What impact do you think these setbacks had on tourism? (Tourists may have been reluctant to visit the nation that had suffered natural and social disasters.)

holiday, since you are a tourist, the thought of what it might be like for someone who had to live day in, day out in a **C** place that suffers constantly from drought, and so has to watch carefully every drop of fresh water used (while at the same time surrounded by a sea and an ocean—the Caribbean Sea on one side, the Atlantic Ocean on the other), must never cross your mind.

You **disembark** from your plane. You go through customs. Since you are a tourist, a North American or European—to be **frank,** white—and not an Antiguan black returning to Antigua from Europe or North America with cardboard boxes of much needed cheap clothes and food for relatives, you move through customs swiftly, you move through customs with ease. Your bags are not searched. You emerge from customs into the hot, clean air: immediately you feel **cleansed,** immediately you feel blessed (which is to say special); you feel free. You see a man, a taxi driver; you ask him to take you to your destination; he **quotes** you a price. You immediately think that the price is in the local **currency,** for you are a tourist and you are familiar with these things (rates of exchange) and you feel even more free, for things seem so cheap, but then your driver ends by saying, "In U.S. currency." You may say, "Hmmmm, do you have a formal sheet that lists official prices and destinations?" Your driver obeys the law and shows you the sheet, and he apologises for the **incredible** mistake he has made in quoting you a price off the top of his head which is so vastly different (favouring him) from the one listed. You are driven to your hotel by this taxi driver in his taxi, a brand-new Japanese-made vehicle. The road on which you are travelling is a very bad road, very much in need of repair. You are feeling wonderful, so you say, "Oh, what a marvellous change these bad roads are from the splendid

Customs is the official process for inspecting what people bring into a country.

D
Why would the tourist say bad roads are *a marvellous change*? What does this remark show about the tourist?

cleansed clean; free of dirt

currency the form of money a country uses

disembark to get out of a craft, such as a boat or plane

frank bluntly honest

incredible too unlikely to be believed

quote to state or offer a price

C ASK Critical Thinking When Kincaid says, "since you are a tourist, the thought of what it might be like for someone who had to live day in, day out in a place that suffers constantly from drought … must never cross your mind," what message does she want readers to get? (She is pointing out that what tourists like about Antigua—sunshine and warm weather—comes at the expense of the local people who desperately need rain for fresh water. She wants readers to understand that Antigua is not paradise.)

D Tourists can be inappropriately enthusiastic about tokens of poverty that they encounter at their destinations. Tourists, glutted by the comforts of life in wealthy powerful nations, see a certain charm in shoeless children, dilapidated cars, water pumps, unpaved roads, and other absences of progress. This attitude shows how inconsiderate tourists can be. Their attitudes would probably change dramatically if they asked themselves, "Could I live like this—for the rest of my life?"

Environmental Connection

Antigua lacks forests, mountains, and rivers and suffers, as Kincaid points out, constantly from droughts. Temperatures hover year-long at around 81° F, and only about 40 inches of rain fall annually. Antigua lies in the path of the hurricanes that often wreak havoc in the West Indies. Suggest that students investigate the demands tourism places on the environment. For example, uses of precious resources such as water and waste disposal.

Name Date Period

Unit 5
Vocabulary Workbook
32
page 1

A Small Place/Of Repentance

Directions Each set of sentences contains two underlined definitions. Below the set are three words. Circle the one undefined word.

1. In the nonfiction book *A Small Place*, you visit Antigua, a place thick with vegetation. You get off from your plane and await a wonderful experience.
   lush currency disembark
2. The air makes you feel free of dirt. Riding in the taxi, you pass many new cars that sound shabby from neglect; you wonder if all the people are rich.
   dilapidated luxurious cleansed
3. But their homes are not splendid and comfortable. In fact, their school looks like a public bathroom.
   minister luxurious latrine
4. The library is closed with a sign that says repairs are waiting for action. Yet a period of ten years has passed since an earthquake damaged the building.
   perception pending decade
5. You see one very unusual house that belongs to a merchant family from the Middle East. It has many antennas on it for receiving radio and television.
   sophisticated aerials extraordinary
6. At the hotel you do not wonder about the contents of your toilet when you flush it. You do not wonder about the woman who seems to be baked goods.
   lavatory pastrylike boutique
7. In your wealthy city back home, you feel alone. There, you see more people than you could know in a thousand years.
   prosperous taxing millennium
8. Back at home you feel a sense of being in the wrong place. You even find your ordinariness to be tiring.
   admirable taxing displacedness
9. You feel that the people in Antigua live in agreement with nature. You feel that their ancestors were not cruel as yours were.
   ruthless harmony mimic
10. You do not realize that the people do not like you because like all people they live in a state of sadness. They cannot escape things as they are.
   overwhelming depression reality

 World Literature

TRL

Vocabulary Workbook 32, pages 1–3

Name Date Period

Unit 5
Student Study Guide
44
page 1

A Small Place (pp. 348–59)

Directions Fill in the following outline. Filling in the blanks will help you as you read and study *A Small Place*.

I. Beginning of the Selection (pp. 348–52)

A. Airport
1. The international airport in Antigua is named after Vere __________ __________.
2. A vacationer in Antigua may not think about what it's like for someone who has to watch carefully every drop of fresh __________ used.
3. A vacationer in Antigua will move through __________ with ease.

B. Roads
1. The roads in Antigua are in much need of __________.
2. All the cars in Antigua are __________-made; there are no American cars.
3. Antiguans use __________ gas in their cars.
4. The two main car dealerships in Antigua are owned in part or outright by __________ in government.
5. Antiguans refer to doctors as "the three __________."

II. Middle of the Selection (pp. 352–55)

A. History
1. An __________ in 1974 damaged the library in Antigua.
2. Antigua is __________ miles long and __________ miles wide.
3. When Kincaid talks about "the West," she means Europe and North America __________ its conquest and settlement by Europeans.

B. The Wealthy
1. The vacationer passes the Prime Minister's Office, the __________ Building, and the American Embassy.

 World Literature

TRL

Student Study Guide 44, pages 1–2

Persuasive Literature Unit 5 **349**

Discussion Questions

A ASK Critical Thinking Twice Kincaid has said, "Or, worse, Europe." What does this parenthetical comment suggest about her opinion of Europeans? (She has plenty of ire for North American tourists, but she thinks Europeans are even worse than Americans. She does not, however, support her opinion with any explanation or evidence, so she risks having readers think she harbors unjustified bias against Europeans.)

B ASK Critical Thinking What effect is achieved by the repetition of the statement "you are on your holiday; you are a tourist"? (Addressing the audience directly and using repetition are two common and effective propaganda techniques. By repeating the statement she forces readers to start thinking about it: Why does she keep saying that? Does she have a problem with that?)

Diversity Connection

English settlers colonized Antigua in 1632. These colonists imported large numbers of African slaves to work on sugar plantations. The slaves were freed in 1834 and became self-reliant sailors, hunters, and fishers. The majority of Antiguans today are descendants of African slaves. Because of Antigua's British colonial history, English is the official language, and most Antiguans are Christians.

A highways I am used to in North America." (Or, worse, Europe.) Your driver is reckless; he is a dangerous man who drives in the middle of the road when he thinks no other cars are coming in the opposite direction, passes other cars on blind curves that run uphill, drives at sixty miles an hour on narrow, curving roads when the road sign, a rusting, beat-up thing left over from colonial days, says 40 MPH.

B This might frighten you (you are on your holiday; you are a tourist); this might excite you (you are on your holiday; you are a tourist), though if you are from New York and take taxis you are used to this style of driving; most of the taxi drivers in New York are from places in the world like this. You are looking out the window (because you want to get your money's worth); you notice that all the cars you see are brand-new, or almost brand-new, and that they are all Japanese-made. There are no American cars in Antigua—no new ones, at any rate; none that were manufactured in the last ten years. You continue to look at the cars and you say to yourself, Why, they look brand-new, but they have an awful sound, like an old car—a very old, **dilapidated** car. How to account for that? Well, possibly it's because they use leaded gasoline in these brand-new cars whose engines were built to use non-leaded gasoline, but you mustn't ask the person driving the car if this is so, because he or she has never heard of unleaded gasoline. You look closely at the car; you see that it's a model of a Japanese car that you might hesitate to buy; it's a model that's very expensive; it's a model that's quite impractical for a person who has to work as hard as you do and who watches every penny you earn so that you can afford this holiday you are on. How do they afford such a car? And do they live in a **luxurious** house to match such a car? Well, no. You will be surprised, then, to see that most likely the person driving this brand-new car filled with the

dilapidated shabby from neglect

luxurious quite splendid and comfortable

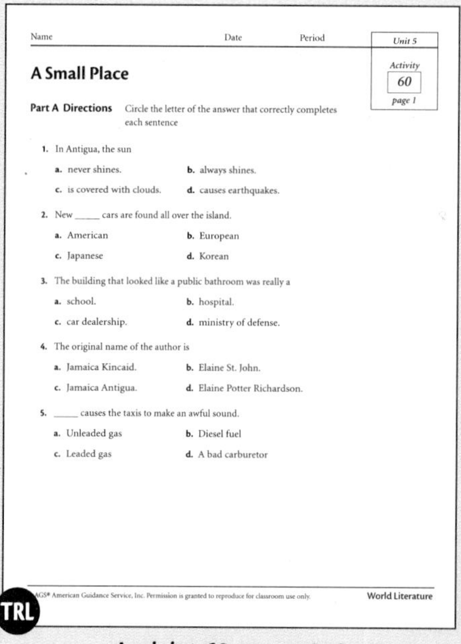

Name Date Period Unit 5 Activity 60 page 1

A Small Place

Part A Directions Circle the letter of the answer that correctly completes each sentence.

1. In Antigua, the sun
   a. never shines. b. always shines.
   c. is covered with clouds. d. causes earthquakes.
2. New ____ cars are found all over the island.
   a. American b. European
   c. Japanese d. Korean
3. The building that looked like a public bathroom was really a
   a. school. b. hospital.
   c. car dealership. d. ministry of defense.
4. The original name of the author is
   a. Jamaica Kincaid. b. Elaine St. John.
   c. Jamaica Antigua. d. Elaine Potter Richardson.
5. ____ causes the taxis to make an awful sound.
   a. Unleaded gas b. Diesel fuel
   c. Leaded gas d. A bad carburetor

©AGS® American Guidance Service, Inc. Permission is granted to reproduce for classroom use only. World Literature

TRL

Activity 60, pages 1–2

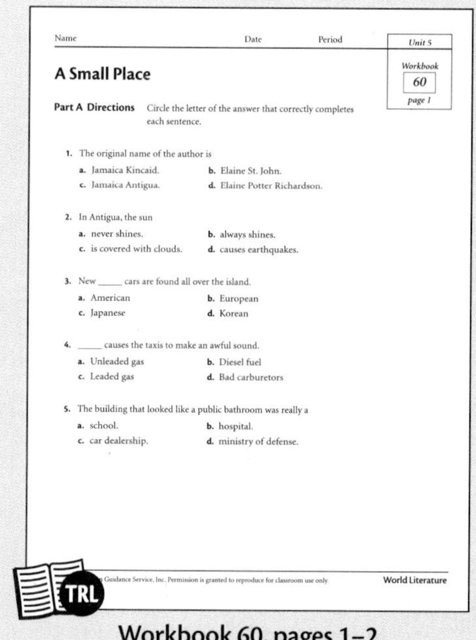

Name Date Period Unit 5 Workbook 60 page 1

A Small Place

Part A Directions Circle the letter of the answer that correctly completes each sentence.

1. The original name of the author is
   a. Jamaica Kincaid. b. Elaine St. John.
   c. Jamaica Antigua. d. Elaine Potter Richardson.
2. In Antigua, the sun
   a. never shines. b. always shines.
   c. is covered with clouds. d. causes earthquakes.
3. New ____ cars are found all over the island.
   a. American b. European
   c. Japanese d. Korean
4. ____ causes the taxis to make an awful sound.
   a. Unleaded gas b. Diesel fuel
   c. Leaded gas d. Bad carburetors
5. The building that looked like a public bathroom was really a
   a. school. b. hospital.
   c. car dealership. d. ministry of defense.

Guidance Service, Inc. Permission is granted to reproduce for classroom use only. World Literature

TRL

Workbook 60, pages 1–2

wrong gas lives in a house that, in comparison, is far beneath the **status** of the car; and if you were to ask why you would be told that the banks are encouraged by the government to make loans available for cars, but loans for houses not so easily available; and if you ask again why, you will be told that the two main car dealerships in Antigua are owned in part or outright by **ministers** in government. Oh, but you are on holiday and the sight of these brand-new cars driven by people who may or may not have really passed their driving test (there was once a **scandal** about driving licences for sale) would not really stir up these thoughts in you. You pass a building sitting in a sea of dust and you think, It's some **latrines** for people just passing by, but when you look again you see the building has written on it PIGOTT'S SCHOOL. You pass the hospital, the Holberton Hospital, and how wrong you are not to think about this, for though you are a tourist on your holiday, what if your heart should miss a few beats? What if a blood vessel in your neck should break? What if one of those people driving those brand-new cars filled with the wrong gas fails to pass safely while going uphill on a curve and you are in the car going in the opposite direction? Will you be comforted to know that the hospital is staffed with doctors that no actual Antiguan trusts; that Antiguans

C
Have you changed your mind about the writer's opinion of the tourist? Why or why not?

latrine a small building used for a public bathroom

minister a high government official

scandal talk about a public disgrace or action

status social position relative to others

C Initially her tone seemed observant, accommodating, even sympathetic of the tourist experience. However, it is now quite clear that her statements are laden with irony. Her opinion of tourists, in fact, is harshly critical.

Community Connection

Kincaid describes the inadequacies of the facilities for such social and welfare institutions as the school, hospital, and library. These are important facilities in most communities. Suggest that students identify the schools, hospitals, and libraries in their own and nearby communities. What are the physical facilities like? What kinds of programs are available through the institutions? How important are the institutions to the community? How would visitors to the community perceive the facilities?

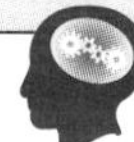

Comprehension

Cause-Effect Relationships Help students understand the cause-effect relationship between the fact that government ministers own car dealerships and the expensive Japanese cars that so many Antiguans drive. Help students complete cause-effect statements such as the following: Because government ministers own car dealerships, they have urged local banks to make auto loans available to people. The ministers' actions have had the following effect: many Antiguans have taken out large loans so that they could buy expensive cars from the minister-owned dealerships. In the end, the government ministers profit.

Discussion Questions

A No one wants to receive medical care from Antiguan doctors. However, officials can afford to fly to the United States when they need medical care, while the average Antiguan has only two options, to see the local doctors or to forego all medical treatment.

Literary Elements

Irony Kincaid uses irony when she says one thing but means another. For example when she writes, "we Antiguans, for I am one, have a great sense of things, and the more meaningful the thing, the more meaningless we make it," she is being ironic.

ASK What is the meaning of Kincaid's statement? (Students may interpret her comment as self-deprecatory, implying that Antiguans do not have a great sense of things, that they trivialize major tragedies.)

Diversity Connection

Different cultures do have different attitudes toward time. For example, in the Philippines punctuality can be considered rude. If a party is scheduled to begin at six o'clock, only an ill-mannered person would arrive promptly at six; anyone with good sense would naturally arrive about an hour late. So, tourists to foreign lands are not wrong to question the local perception of time. Kincaid, however, exaggerates that idea by suggesting that a tourist might think Antiguan time is slow by twelve years. Encourage students who have visited or come from other cultures to discuss how perceptions of such aspects of life as time are like or unlike those in the United States.

A
What is the difference between medical care for officials and for ordinary people?

always say about the doctors, "I don't want them near me"; that Antiguans refer to them not as doctors but as "the three men" (there are three of them); that when the Minister of Health himself doesn't feel well he takes the first plane to New York to see a real doctor; that if any one of the ministers in government needs medical care he flies to New York to get it?

It's a good thing that you brought your own books with you, for you couldn't just go to the library and borrow some. Antigua used to have a splendid library, but in The Earthquake (everyone talks about it that way—The Earthquake; we Antiguans, for I am one, have a great sense of things, and the more meaningful the thing, the more meaningless we make it) the library building was damaged. This was in 1974, and soon after that a sign was placed on the front of the building saying, THIS BUILDING WAS DAMAGED IN THE EARTHQUAKE OF 1974. REPAIRS ARE **PENDING**. The sign hangs there, and hangs there more than a **decade** later, with its **unfulfilled** promise of repair, and you might see this as a sort of quaintness on the part of these islanders, these people descended from slaves—what a strange, unusual **perception** of time they have. REPAIRS ARE PENDING, and here it is many years later, but perhaps in a world that is twelve miles long and nine miles wide (the size of Antigua) twelve years and twelve minutes and twelve days are all the same. The library is one of those splendid old buildings from colonial times, and the sign telling of the repairs is a splendid old sign from colonial times. Not very long after The Earthquake Antigua got its independence from Britain, making Antigua a state in its own right, and Antiguans are so proud of this that each year,

decade a period of ten years

pending not yet decided; waiting for action

perception a way of seeing or observing

unfulfilled not finished; not completed

to mark the day, they go to church and thank God, a British **B** God, for this. But you should not think of the confusion that must lie in all that and you must not think of the damaged library. You have brought your own books with you, and among them is one of those new books about economic history, one of those books explaining how the West (meaning Europe and North America after its conquest and settlement by Europeans) got rich: the West **C** got rich not from the free (free—in this case meaning got-for-nothing) and then undervalued labour, for generations, of the people like me you see walking around you in Antigua but from the **ingenuity** of small shopkeepers in Sheffield and Yorkshire and Lancashire, or wherever; and what a great part the invention of the wristwatch played in it, for there was nothing noble-minded men could not do when they discovered they could slap time on their wrists just like that (isn't that the last straw; for not only did we have to suffer the **unspeakableness** of slavery, but the satisfaction to be had from "We made you bastards rich" is taken away, too), and so you needn't let that slightly funny feeling you have from time to time about **exploitation**, **oppression**, **domination** develop into full-fledged unease, **discomfort**; you could ruin your holiday. They are not responsible for what you have; you owe them nothing; in fact, you did them a big favour, and you can provide one hundred examples. For here you are now, passing by Government House. And here you are now, passing by the Prime Minister's Office and the Parliament Building, and overlooking these, with a splendid view of St. John's Harbour, the American **Embassy**. If it were not for you, they would not have Government House, and Prime Minister's Office, and Parliament Building and embassy of powerful country. Now you are

Sheffield, Yorkshire, and *Lancashire* are in England. English settlers used slave labor to grow sugar on Antigua.

discomfort the feeling of being uneasy or not comfortable

domination control or rule of one person or group by another

exploitation the use of a person or resource for selfish purposes

ingenuity cleverness; inventive skill

oppression strict rule or control through the use of force

unspeakableness a condition too bad to be described

B ASK Critical Thinking What does Kincaid really mean when she says "you should not think of the confusion that must lie in all that and you must not think of the damaged library"? (She's being ironic again. What she really means is that tourists should think about the colonial history of Antigua and the confusion it causes; they should think about the library still in ruin twelve years after an earthquake and wonder why something hasn't been done about it.)

C ASK Comprehension According to this passage, what are some character traits of Europeans and North Americans? How do those traits affect their behavior? (They are brutal, selfish, unrepentant, satisfied, and dishonest. They were able to ruthlessly exploit Africans to make themselves rich, and now they are so satisfied with their wealth that they can't let themselves think about the bloody cost by which that wealth was attained. They lie to themselves and to the world so that they don't have to feel sorrow or guilt, which allows them to remain comfortable.)

Comprehension

Identifying Supporting Details Kincaid here lists details that North Americans and Europeans use when asserting that they are not responsible for the situation of people such as the Antiguans, or the Indians, or the Jamaicans, or the Haitians.

ASK What evidence do former colonists of Antigua cite to prove that they have helped, not harmed, Antigua? (We built a Government House, a Prime Minister's Office, and a Parliament Building. We dredged St. John's Harbor so seafaring ships could bring you tourists, we built an American Embassy, we brought you our God.)

Discussion Questions

A ASK Critical Thinking The author describes the mansion as being the color of old cow dung. What does her word choice reveal about her opinion of the mansion or its inhabitants? (The negative connotation of her words suggest that she dislikes the mansion.)

B ASK Critical Thinking The author describes how the Middle Eastern family worked their way up to a position of extreme wealth and power. Then she says "Antiguans hate them." Why might the family be hated? (Because they're getting rich at the expense of the Antiguans by charging outrageous rent on their properties. Plus, some Antiguans might feel jealous that this family who started with nothing is now very rich.)

Cross-Curricular Connection

History It is pointed out that Antigua is a member of the Commonwealth of Nations, formerly called the "British Commonwealth." The Commonwealth is an association of free nations composed of Great Britain and several of its former colonies. Members of the Commonwealth maintain friendly ties and acknowledge the British monarch as the symbolic head of their association. Other members of the Commonwealth include India, Pakistan (who left in 1972 and rejoined in 1989), Australia, New Zealand, Canada, Cyprus, Jamaica, Kenya, Malta, Dominica, Zimbabwe, and Belize. Ask students to locate the nations of the Commonwealth on the world map on pages 418–419 or on a globe.

A passing a mansion, an **extraordinary** house painted the colour of old cow dung, with more **aerials** and antennas attached to it than you will see even at the American Embassy. The people who live in this house are a merchant family who came to Antigua from the Middle East less than twenty years ago. When this family first came to Antigua, they sold dry goods door to door from suitcases they carried on their backs. Now they own a lot of Antigua; they **B** regularly lend money to the government, they build enormous (for Antigua), ugly (for Antigua), concrete buildings in Antigua's capital, St. John's, which the government then rents for huge sums of money; a member of their family is the Antiguan Ambassador to Syria; Antiguans hate them. Not far from this mansion is another mansion, the home of a drug smuggler. Everybody knows he's a drug smuggler, and if just as you were driving by he stepped out of his door your driver might point him out to you as the **notorious** person that he is, for this drug smuggler is so rich people say he buys cars in tens—ten of this one, ten of that one—and that he bought a house (another mansion) near Five Islands, contents included, with cash he carried in a suitcase: three hundred and fifty thousand American dollars, and, to the surprise of the seller of the house, lots of American dollars were left over. Overlooking the drug smuggler's mansion is yet another mansion, and leading up to it is the best paved road in all of Antigua—even better than the road that was paved for the Queen's visit in 1985 (when the Queen came, all the roads that she would travel on were paved anew, so that the Queen might have been left with the impression that riding in a car in Antigua was a pleasant experience). In this mansion lives a woman **sophisticated** people in Antigua call Evita. She is a notorious woman. She's young and beautiful and the

Antigua is a member of the British Commonwealth, whose head is the *Queen* of England.

aerial an antenna for receiving radio or TV

extraordinary very unusual

notorious famous for bad activities

sophisticated having a broad knowledge of the world

girlfriend of somebody very high up in the government. Evita is notorious because her relationship with this high government official has made her the owner of **boutiques** and property and given her a say in cabinet meetings, and all sorts of other privileges such a relationship would bring a beautiful young woman.

C What do you think Kincaid is saying about wealthy people in Antigua?

Oh, but by now you are tired of all this looking, and you **D** want to reach your destination—your hotel, your room. You long to **refresh** yourself; you long to eat some nice **lobster**, some nice local food. You take a bath, you brush your teeth. You get dressed again; as you get dressed, you look out the window. That water—have you ever seen anything like it? Far out, to the horizon, the colour of the water is navy-blue; nearer, the water is the colour of the North American sky. From there to the shore, the water is pale, silvery, clear, so clear that you can see its pinkish-white sand bottom. Oh, what beauty! Oh, what beauty! You have never seen anything like this. You are so excited. You breathe shallow. You breathe deep. You see a beautiful boy skimming the water, godlike, on a Windsurfer. You see an incredibly unattractive, fat, **pastrylike**-fleshed woman enjoying a walk on the beautiful sand, with a man, an incredibly unattractive, fat, pastrylike-fleshed man; you see the pleasure they're taking in their surroundings. Still standing, looking out the window, you see yourself lying on the beach, enjoying the amazing sun (a sun so powerful and yet so beautiful, the way it is always overhead as if on permanent guard, ready to stamp out any cloud that dares to darken and so empty rain on you and ruin your holiday; a sun that is your personal friend). You see yourself taking a walk on that beach. You see yourself meeting new people (only they are new in a very limited way, for they are people just like you). You see yourself

E Of the people just described, which are probably Antiguan and which probably tourists? How does the writer feel about them?

boutique a small shop that sells special, often expensive, goods

lobster a sea animal that is used for food

pastrylike looking like baked goods made of dough

refresh to make less tired, as if by resting or eating

C Kincaid is implying a certain amount of corruption among Antigua's wealthy and that much of their wealth was gotten in questionable ways, if not outright illegally.

D ASK Comprehension How does the author's tone change from the beginning of the paragraph to the end? (In the beginning the writing is lovely and refreshing, but toward the paragraph's end her tone grows negative and she focuses on ugliness.)

E The beautiful boy is probably an Antiguan. The fat, unattractive man and woman with pastrylike flesh are tourists. The author obviously feels disgusted by them.

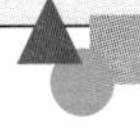

Learning Styles

Group Learning Suggest that students work in small groups to create two posters—one as a tourism promotional poster and one as a campaign poster for a person hoping to improve living conditions in Antigua. Remind students that the messages and illustrations on the posters would be quite different. The tourism poster would focus on positive aspects of the nation whereas the campaign poster would focus on the needs of the nation. After students display the posters, discuss how they biased both posters to promote particular viewpoints.

Discussion Questions

A ASK **Comprehension** What is the author's purpose in saying "it would amaze even you to know the number of black slaves this ocean has swallowed up"? (In part she may be going for shock value, trying to further repulse her audience. But actually she's making an important point: if Antigua uses the ocean as its garbage can, the dirty deed was learned from colonizers who tossed not just human waste but human beings into the water.)

B Up to this point she has listed several characteristics of tourists that prove their ugliness—not necessarily a physical ugliness, but a spiritual one stemming from the fact that they are using this island and perpetuating the colonial mentality.

Environmental Connection

Human sewage, like any waste, can be a useful fertilizer. However if sewage is spewed into the environment faster than it can be broken down, it becomes a dangerous pollutant. The absence of wastewater treatment and disposal systems creates great risks to public health. Coastal waters could become oxygen deficient and polluted with pathogenic bacteria, industrial wastes, and toxic chemicals.

If possible, arrange for students to tour a waste management plant or invite a waste management engineer to speak to the class about the importance and techniques of proper waste management.

eating some delicious, locally grown food. You see yourself, you see yourself ... You must not wonder what exactly happened to the contents of your **lavatory** when you flushed it. You must not wonder where your bathwater went when you pulled out the stopper. You must not wonder what happened when you brushed your teeth. Oh, it might all end up in the water you are thinking of taking a swim in; the contents of your lavatory might, just might, graze gently against your ankle as you wade carefree in the water, for you see, in Antigua, there is no proper sewage-disposal system. But the Caribbean Sea is very big and the Atlantic Ocean is even bigger; it would amaze even you to know the number of black slaves this ocean has swallowed up. When you sit down to eat your delicious meal, it's better that you don't know that most of what you are eating came off a plane from Miami. And before it got on a plane in Miami, who knows where it came from? A good guess is that it came from a place like Antigua first, where it was grown dirt-cheap, went to Miami, and came back. There is a world of something in this, but I can't go into it right now.

She means that waste water is piped into the ocean.

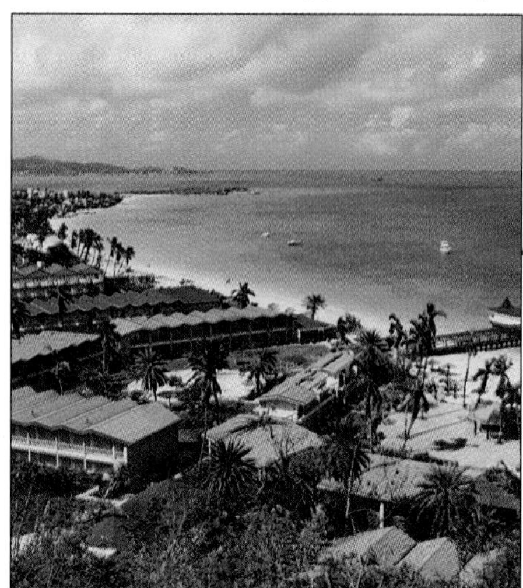

This is Dickinson Bay, Antigua, after Hurricane Georges, 1998.

A

B

How does the writer prove her claim that tourists are ugly? Does she mean ugly to look at?

The thing you have always suspected about yourself the minute you become a tourist is true: A tourist is an ugly human being. You are not an ugly person all the time; you are not an ugly person ordinarily; you are not an ugly person day to day. From day to day, you are a nice person. From day to

lavatory a bathroom

day, all the people who are supposed to love you on the whole do. From day to day, as you walk down a busy street in the **C** large and modern and **prosperous** city in which you work and live, dismayed, puzzled (a **cliché**, but only a cliché can explain you) at how alone you feel in this crowd, how awful it is to go unnoticed, how awful it is to go unloved, even as you are surrounded by more people than you could possibly get to know in a lifetime that lasted for **millennia**, and then out of the corner of your eye you see someone looking at you and absolute pleasure is written all over that person's face, and then you realise that you are not as revolting a presence as you think you are (for that look just told you so). And so, ordinarily, you are a nice person, an attractive person, a person capable of drawing to yourself the affection of other people (people just like you), a person at home in your own skin (sort of; I mean, in a way; I mean, your dismay and puzzlement are natural to you, because people like you just **D** seem to be like that, and so many of the things people like you find **admirable** about yourselves—the things you think about, the things you think really define you—seem rooted in these feelings): a person at home in your own house (and all its nice house things), with its nice back yard (and its nice back-yard things), at home on your street, your church, in community activities, your job, at home with your family, your relatives, your friends—you are a whole person. But one day, when you are sitting somewhere, alone in that crowd, and that awful feeling of **displacedness** comes over you, and really, as an ordinary person you are not well equipped to look too far inward and set yourself aright, because being ordinary is already so **taxing**, and being ordinary takes all you have out of you, and though the words "I must get away" do not actually pass across your lips, you make a leap from being that nice blob just sitting like a boob in your **amniotic sac** of the **E**

admirable worth admiration

amniotic sac a pouch that holds a developing baby before it is born

cliché an expression or idea that has been used over and over

displacedness a state of being out of place or in the wrong place

millennium a period of one thousand years

prosperous successful; wealthy

taxing tiring; difficult

C ASK Critical Thinking Are the author's comments in this passage facts or opinions? (Her comments reflect her opinions and notions about the everyday life of a "typical" tourist. She offers no proof that her statements are based on factual evidence or thorough research.)

D ASK Comprehension Kincaid keeps referring to "people like you." What characteristics do those people have in common? (They have nice houses with nice things and nice back yards; they live in a state of dismay and puzzlement; they enjoy their neighbors and go to church and community activities; they have jobs, friends, and family.)

E ASK Critical Thinking What is the author saying about modern experience when she describes it as an amniotic sac. (She's saying it shelters people and provides them with all their needs. It also keeps them from recognizing what goes on in the "real world outside.")

Discussion Questions

A ASK Critical Thinking Why does the author describe Antigua as "heaps of death and ruin"? (She is referring to the poverty of the nation, the rundown condition of its buildings and infrastructure, and the poor health and hard lives of its people.)

B ASK Comprehension What is the difference between Kincaid's ancestors and the ancestors of white tourists? (Antiguan ancestors were not clever or ruthless in the same way as the white people's ancestors. If Africans had been more like white people, then quite likely the whites would now be the ones living in poverty on Caribbean islands, and the black would be prospering in modern society.)

Learning Styles

Group Learning Have groups of students discuss what they know about tourism. Students may share any experiences they have had as tourists or as locals in a place descended upon by flocks of tourists. You might get students started by posing the following questions. Some economies including American resort towns and Antigua are built almost entirely on tourism. How, then, can Kincaid be so critical of tourism? Would her country really be better off without tourists?

A modern experience to being a person visiting heaps of death and ruin and feeling alive and inspired at the sight of it; to being a person lying on some faraway beach, your stilled body stinking and glistening in the sand, looking like something first forgotten, then remembered, then not important enough to go back for; to being a person marvelling at the **harmony** (ordinarily, what you would say is the backwardness) and the union these other people (and they are other people) have with nature. And you look at the things they can do with a piece of ordinary cloth, the things they fashion out of cheap, **vulgarly** colored (to you) twine, the way they squat down over a hole they have made in the ground, the hole itself is something to marvel at, and since you are being an ugly **B** person this ugly but joyful thought will swell inside you: their ancestors were not clever in the way yours were and not **ruthless** in the way yours were, for then would it not be you who would be in harmony with nature and backwards in that charming way? An ugly thing, that is what you are when you become a tourist, an ugly, empty thing, a stupid thing, a piece of rubbish pausing here and there to gaze at this and taste that, and it will never occur to you that the people who inhabit the place in which you have just paused cannot stand you, that behind their closed doors they laugh at your strangeness (you do not look the way they look); the physical sight of you does not please them; you have bad manners (it is their custom to eat their food with their hands; you try eating their way, you look silly; you try eating the way you always eat, you look silly); they do not like the way you speak (you have an accent); they collapse helpless from laughter, **mimicking** the way they imagine you must look as you carry out some everyday bodily **function**. They do not like you. *They do not like me!* That thought never actually occurs to you. Still, you feel a little uneasy. Still, you feel a little foolish.

function a normal use or activity

harmony a pleasant agreement in feeling or actions

mimic to copy closely

ruthless cruel; without mercy

vulgarly in bad taste; crudely

Still, you feel a little out of place. But the **banality** of your own life is very real to you; it drove you to this extreme, spending your days and your nights in the company of people who despise you, people you do not like really, people you would not want to have as your actual neighbour. And so you must devote yourself to puzzling out how much of what you are told is really, really true (Is ground-up bottle glass in **C** peanut sauce really a delicacy around here, or will it do just what you think ground-up bottle glass will do? Is this rare, **multicoloured**, snout-mouthed fish really an **aphrodisiac**, or will it cause you to fall asleep permanently?). Oh, the hard work all of this is, and is it any wonder, then, that on your return home you feel the need of a long rest, so that you can recover from your life as a tourist?

That the native does not like the tourist is not hard to explain. For every native of every place is a potential tourist, and every tourist is a native of somewhere. Every native everywhere lives a life of **overwhelming** and crushing banality and boredom and desperation and **depression**, and every deed, good and bad, is an attempt to forget this. Every native would like to find a way out, every native would like a rest, every native would like a tour. But some natives—most natives in the world—cannot go anywhere. They are too poor. They are too poor to go anywhere. They are too poor to escape the **reality** of their lives; and they are too poor to live properly in the place where they live, which is the very place you, the tourist, want to go—so when the natives see you, the tourist, they envy you, they envy your ability to leave your own banality and boredom, they envy your ability to turn their own banality and boredom into a source of pleasure for yourself.

D
Do you think the writer is sometimes a tourist herself? How does she feel about that?

aphrodisiac a food or drug that brings about sexual desire

banality the quality of having little meaning

depression a state of sadness

multicoloured (Amer. multicolored) having many colors

overwhelming crushing; destructive

reality things as they actually exist

C ASK Critical Thinking What would you think if you were visiting a place and the locals told you things like this? (The outrageous questions make it clear that a person is an object of ridicule.)

D The only way that Kincaid could write such a scathing essay with any credibility is if she had firsthand experience both as a tourist and as a native in a place visited by tourists. She probably feels ugly about her own experiences as a tourist but accepts them as necessary reprieves from the boredom of everyday life.

Reviewing the Selection

Answer Key

Comprehension: Identifying Facts

1. Hot, sunny, dry weather is normal.

2. They use leaded gas in cars built to take unleaded gas.

3. They can get auto loans but not home loans.

4. The book is an economic history, explaining how the West got rich by exploiting enslaved people.

5. Officials go to New York when they need doctors.

6. Pigott's School looks like a latrine.

7. The library closed in 1974 after an earthquake.

8. The drug smuggler has a mansion and he's above the law. The criminal activities of the wealthy are ignored.

9. The Antiguans were the slaves of British plantation owners.

10. Native Antiguans hate tourists.

Comprehension: Understanding Main Ideas

11. The driver is reckless, the roads are bad, and you might get overcharged.

12. Tourists love the fact that the sun shines every day of their vacation. However, for residents of Antigua the lack of water is a source of hardship.

13. Tourists breeze through customs while Antiguans are delayed and searched.

14. A tourist should worry about the hospital because he or she might require medical attention.

15. Mostly corrupt, brutal, or immoral people have gotten rich in Antigua.

16. The ocean water is polluted with raw sewage.

17. The writer reveals corruption by explaining why so many people drive expensive cars. Government officials urge banks to dole out big auto loans so that people can buy expensive cars from dealerships owned by those very same government officials.

18. Tourists only meet other tourists.

19. The tourists can tell themselves that colonialism has benefited Antigua.

20. Most Antiguans are too poor to ever leave Antigua.

REVIEWING the SELECTION

A Small Place

Jamaica Kincaid

Directions Write the answers to these questions using complete sentences.

Comprehension: Identifying Facts

1. What kind of weather is usual in Antigua?
2. Why do many cars in Antigua have an awful sound?
3. Why do Antiguans have better cars than houses?
4. What is the subject of one of the books the tourist brings?
5. Where does the Minister of Health go to see a doctor?
6. What does Pigott's School look like?
7. When did the library close for repairs? Why did it close?
8. What is one sign that the drug smuggler is rich?
9. How were Antiguans treated by the British long ago?
10. How do most native Antiguans feel about tourists?

Comprehension: Understanding Main Ideas

11. What are the problems with taking a taxi in Antigua?
12. Why is Antigua's lack of rainfall a joy for tourists and a problem for the native Antiguans?
13. How is going through customs different for tourists than for the native Antiguans?
14. Why should a tourist worry about the condition of the hospital in Antigua?
15. What sorts of people have gotten rich in Antigua?
16. What is wrong with the beautiful ocean water around the island?
17. How does the writer show that the government is corrupt? Give an example.
18. Why are the new people a tourist meets not really new?
19. How does the writer suggest that the tourist get rid of guilt feelings about the way the native Antiguans were treated?
20. Why can't most native Antiguans be tourists at some time?

360 Unit 5 Persuasive Literature

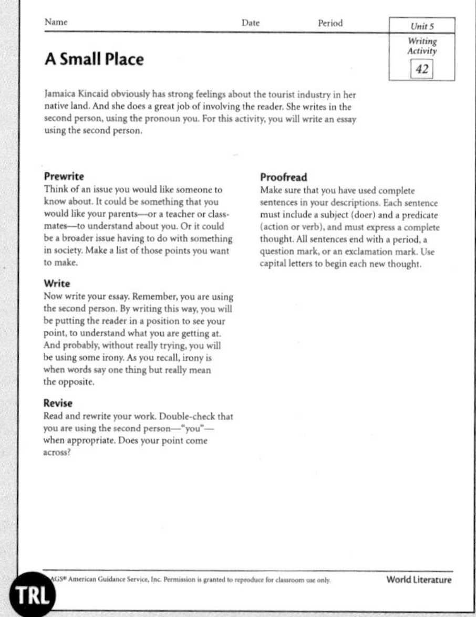

Name Date Period

Unit 5 Writing Activity 42

A Small Place

Jamaica Kincaid obviously has strong feelings about the tourist industry in her native land. And she does a great job of involving the reader. She writes in the second person, using the pronoun you. For this activity, you will write an essay using the second person.

Prewrite
Think of an issue you would like someone to know about. It could be something that you would like your parents—or a teacher or classmates—to understand about you. Or it could be a broader issue having to do with something in society. Make a list of those points you want to make.

Write
Now write your essay. Remember, you are using the second person. By writing this way, you will be putting the reader in a position to see your point, to understand what you are getting at. And probably, without really trying, you will be using some irony. As you recall, irony is when words say one thing but really mean the opposite.

Revise
Read and rewrite your work. Double-check that you are using the second person—"you"—when appropriate. Does your point come across?

Proofread
Make sure that you have used complete sentences in your descriptions. Each sentence must include a subject (doer) and a predicate (action or verb), and must express a complete thought. All sentences end with a period, a question mark, or an exclamation mark. Use capital letters to begin each new thought.

 World Literature

TRL

Writing Activity 42

Understanding Literature: Tone

Tone is the attitude the author takes toward a subject. The tone may be humorous, affectionate, or optimistic. It might be bitter, angry, or depressed. The tone may shift at certain points in the writing. One thing that affects the tone of *A Small Place* is that the author's use of irony. Irony is using words that seem to say one thing but mean something else.

21. What is the tone of *A Small Place*?
22. What is ironic about tourists being pleased the island is not too lush?
23. Name another contrast between what the tourist sees and what the reality is.
24. How does Kincaid explain why people want to be tourists?
25. What do you think is the harshest thing the author says?

Critical Thinking

26. How does reading this selection make you feel? Explain.
27. Why do you think that only the airport is named for the Prime Minister?
28. How do you think the writer wants readers to respond to this piece?
29. Kincaid is from Antigua. She now lives in New York City. Is she a good spokesperson for Antigua? Why or why not?
30. Is the writer suggesting that people never travel? Explain.

Writing on Your Own Think of a place that you know well. Think of how it would look to a tourist. Think of what you know of that a tourist wouldn't see. Write a paragraph about the place. Tell what the tourist sees and what more there is to the picture.

Name Date Period | Unit 5 Selection Quiz 38

A Small Place

Directions Read the following statements. Circle the letter of the answer that correctly completes each sentence or that correctly answers each question.

1. Kincaid writes about
   a. Jamaica. b. Puerto Rico. c. the Virgin Islands. d. Antigua.
2. The airport is named after the
   a. President. b. founder. c. Prime Minister. d. airline company.
3. The taxi driver asks for a ________ cab fare at first.
   a. low b. high c. bargain-basement d. false
4. Most of the cars are brand-new ________ models.
   a. American b. Japanese c. German d. Bavarian
5. Antiguans ________ their doctors.
   a. trust b. do not trust c. truly love d. don't understand
6. Antigua is
   a. nine kilometers long and twelve kilometers wide.
   b. nine miles wide and twelve miles long.
   c. nine miles all around.
   d. twelve miles all around.
7. When did the earthquake strike Antigua?
   a. 1964 b. 1975 c. 1974 d. 1908
8. Kincaid says a tourist is
   a. a good thing. b. good for the country being visited.
   c. a beautiful person. d. an ugly human being.
9. The native Antiguans ________ the tourists.
   a. appreciate b. love c. adore d. do not like
10. Most natives, Kincaid says,
   a. are happy. b. are travelers.
   c. are too poor to travel. d. love tourists.

 World Literature

TRL

Selection Quiz 38

Selection Quiz

The Teacher's Resource Library includes a Selection Quiz for *A Small Place* that may be given following the Selection Review.

Understanding Literature: Tone

21. The tone is harsh and angry.

22. Tourist pleasure in Antigua's sunny, dry weather overlooks the fact the island is continually ravaged by drought.

23. The tourist sees beautiful, clear, blue water, which is actually polluted with sewage.

24. People want to be tourists because they are miserable in their "real" existence and want to get away from it.

25. The harshest thing the author says is "The thing you have always suspected about yourself the minute you become a tourist is true: A tourist is an ugly human being." Also harsh is "only a cliché can explain you."

Critical Thinking

26. Students may explain that the selection made them feel uneasy about traveling. Other students may have felt outrage at Kincaid's accusative tone since, after all, Antigua's economy depends on tourism.

27. Perhaps the airport is the only building that the government values.

28. She wants readers to feel remorse, to reconsider the idea of tourism, and to take a greater interest in the reality of "tourist" havens.

29. Students may feel that Kincaid is not a good spokesperson for Antigua. They may question what she is doing to improve Antigua. Other students might think Kincaid is qualified to write as she does because she has an insider's point of view.

30. The essay is urging people who travel to be conscientious travelers, to learn about the culture they're visiting, too see the whole picture, and to be compassionate without being condescending.

Writing on Your Own Encourage students to use Kincaid's essay as a model, but explain that they need not adopt an angry tone in their paragraphs; they can have a playful, a serious, or an ominous tone as they see fit. Students should not write exclusively about the picturesque aspects of their place, they should create a complete picture. In prewriting, suggest that students choose an organizational technique for their paragraph.

Skills Lesson: Setting

This Skills Lesson focuses on the effects of setting in persuasive writing. Remind students that place and time combine to establish setting.

Review Answers

1. The setting of a piece of writing includes details about the time and place.

2. Time and place matter in Joan of Arc's letter because it addresses events that occurred at a specific historic moment and place. Without setting, her letter would have existed in a void and been meaningless.

3. In Kennedy's inaugural address, time is more important than place.

4. The setting of Montaigne's piece makes the Thief's story possible because only at that time and in those fields would he have been able to commit those specific acts of larceny.

5. Students' answers will vary. Some students may have found the setting in Kincaid's essay most interesting because it was more vivid that the settings of the other selections.

Writing on Your Own In prewriting, encourage students to settle upon a specific occasion for their speech. Help them get started by brainstorming a list of events at which speeches are given.

Skills Lesson Setting

The setting of a piece of writing includes time and place. Writers of scary stories can create a setting that sets your heart beating. You turn the page fast to see what will happen next. Writers of history stories try to take you back to other times. They use touches such as these:

> "The airplane circled the wheat field like a great moth. Its canvas wings shone white. The engine whined with insect sharpness."

Setting can be important in speeches and essays, too. For example, Lincoln says:

> "Now we are engaged in a great civil war. ..." "We are met on a great battlefield of that war. ..." "... a final resting place for those who here gave their lives. ..."

The setting has a serious meaning. Without this place, there would have been no speech.

Setting is at the heart of Jamaica Kinkaid's writing on Antigua. She draws a savage comparison. It is between the beauty tourists see and the natives' poverty.

> "From there to the shore, the water is pale, silvery clear, so clear that you can see its pinkish-white sand bottom. Oh, what beauty!"

Compare that with:

> "You must not wonder what exactly happened to the contents of your lavatory when you flushed it. ... Oh, it might all end up in the water you are thinking of taking a swim in ... in Antigua there is no proper sewage-disposal system."

Review

1. What is setting?
2. Why do time and place matter in Joan of Arc's letter?
3. Name a selection in this unit in which you think time is more important than place.
4. How does the setting in long-ago rural France make the Thief's story possible?
5. Which setting did you find most interesting? Explain.

Writing on Your Own Think of an event at which you might make a speech. (You might choose a school event, a sports dinner, or a family occasion.) Write a few sentences to start a speech for that audience. First explain the time and place of the event. Then begin to give your own thoughts about it.

362 Unit 5 Persuasive Literature

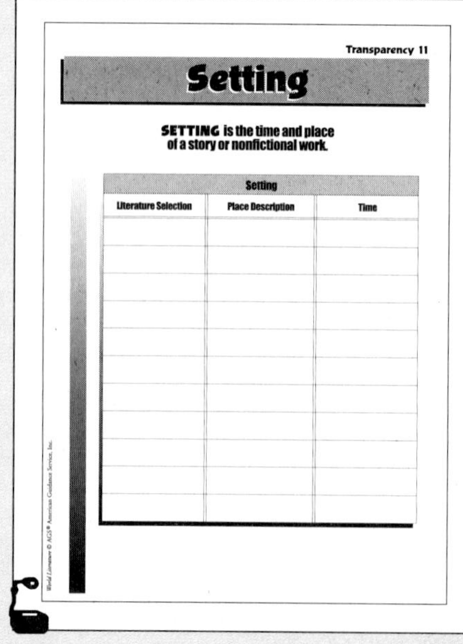

Transparency 11

Setting

SETTING is the time and place of a story or nonfictional work.

Setting		
Literature Selection	Place Description	Time

Transparency 11

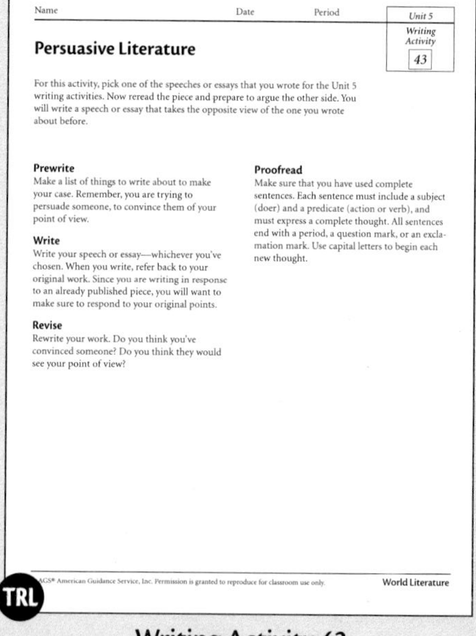

Name Date Period

Unit 5 Writing Activity 43

Persuasive Literature

For this activity, pick one of the speeches or essays that you wrote for the Unit 5 writing activities. Now reread the piece and prepare to argue the other side. You will write a speech or essay that takes the opposite view of the one you wrote about before.

Prewrite
Make a list of things to write about to make your case. Remember, you are trying to persuade someone, to convince them of your point of view.

Write
Write your speech or essay—whichever you've chosen. When you write, refer back to your original work. Since you are writing in response to an already published piece, you will want to make sure to respond to your original points.

Revise
Rewrite your work. Do you think you've convinced someone? Do you think they would see your point of view?

Proofread
Make sure that you have used complete sentences. Each sentence must include a subject (doer) and a predicate (action or verb), and must express a complete thought. All sentences end with a period, a question mark, or an exclamation mark. Use capital letters to begin each new thought.

World Literature

TRL

Writing Activity 43

UNIT 5 SUMMARY

In this unit you read examples of persuasive writing. Persuasive writing is meant to influence opinion. The selections in this unit are all nonfiction. Most persuasive writing is in that form. Examples of persuasive writing in fiction can be found in other parts of this book.

This unit includes speeches and essays. Speeches are given for many reasons. They are meant for a special audience. They are in response to some event or occasion. Even when written, a speech is meant to be heard. You will find it helpful to read the speeches out loud. You may find recordings of some.

Essays give a writer's personal point of view. They may be written about a basic issue or a current event. The writer presents the facts as she or he sees them. The writer's way of thinking shapes the essay. So does the writer's style, or way of writing.

Selections

- "Letter to the English" by Joan of Arc. The French heroine sends a proclamation that warns the English to leave France.
- "Nobel Lecture" by Alexander Solzhenitsyn. On winning the Nobel Prize, the Russian writer gives his view of the importance of world literature.
- "The Gettysburg Address" by Abraham Lincoln. The President speaks to dedicate a cemetery at the site of the Battle of Gettysburg.
- "Inaugural Address" by John F. Kennedy. After being sworn in as President of the United States, the new President addresses the country and the world.
- "Of Repentance" by Michel de Montaigne. The French essayist tells the story of a man known as the Thief.
- *A Small Place* by Jamaica Kincaid. A chapter from her book takes an ironic look at tourists who come to the island of Antigua.

Unit Summary

Have students take turns reading the selection descriptions on page 363 and describing what they remember from each selection.

ASK What threat does Joan of Arc make to the English? (Leave France or expect blood to spill.)

ASK What evil does Solzhenitsyn say writers have the power to conquer? (falsehood)

ASK What does Abraham Lincoln call upon his listeners to do? (to reaffirm their devotion to the propositions set forth in the Declaration of Independence and resolve that the United States would not perish)

ASK What key point does John F. Kennedy make to the American people at the end of his inaugural address? (Ask what you can do for your country.)

ASK What does the Thief do to make amends for all that he stole? (He gives gifts to the heirs of the landowners he stole from.)

ASK What does Kincaid say motivates people to become tourists in other lands? (They desire to escape the misery of their life at home.)

Name Date Period | *Unit 5* | *Activity* 61 *page 1*

Unit Review

Part A Directions Circle the word or phrase in parentheses that best completes each sentence.

1. (Persuasive writings, Monologues) are meant to influence people's opinions.
2. The personal point of view of the writer is shared in an (elegy, essay).
3. A (poem, speech) is meant to be said or read out loud to an audience.
4. The (style, setting) of a piece of writing includes time and place.
5. A writer's style and (way of thinking, punctuation) affect how an essay is written.

Part B Directions On the blank lines, write a short answer for each item.

1. In their speeches, what did Lincoln and Kennedy ask of the citizens of the United States?
2. What kind of power does world literature have, according to Solzhenitsyn?
3. Why does Joan of Arc think she will be successful against the English?
4. What do you learn about the main character in "Of Repentance"?
5. How does Jamaica Kincaid let you know how she feels about tourists?

 World Literature

TRL

Activity 61, Pages 1–2

Name Date Period | *Unit 5* | *Workbook* 61 *page 1*

Unit Review

Part A Directions Circle the word or phrase in parentheses that best completes each sentence.

1. The (style, setting) of a piece of writing includes time and place.
2. (Persuasive writings, Monologues) are meant to influence people's opinions.
3. The personal point of view of the writer is shared in an (elegy, essay).
4. A (poem, speech) is meant to be said or read out loud to an audience.
5. A writer's style and (way of thinking, punctuation) affect how an essay is written.

Part B Directions Write a short answer for each item on the blank lines.

1. What do you learn about the main character in "Of Repentance"?
2. What did Lincoln and Kennedy, in their speeches, ask of the citizens of this nation?
3. What kind of power does world literature have, according to Solzhenitsyn?
4. Why does Joan of Arc think she will be successful against the English?
5. How does Jamaica Kincaid let you know how she feels about tourists?

 World Literature

TRL

Workbook 61, Pages 1–2

Unit 5 Review

The Teacher's Resource Library includes two parallel forms of the Unit 5 Mastery Test. The difficulty level of the two forms is equivalent. You may wish to use one form as a pretest and the other form as a posttest.

Answer Key

Comprehension: Identifying Facts

1. "Letter to the English" and "Of Repentance" are from France.

2. Solzhenitsyn's (Russia) Nobel Lecture and JFK's (USA) inaugural address were written during the cold war.

3. Speeches and essays are presented.

4. Montaigne wrote an essay.

5. Solzhenitsyn's lecture was read at the Nobel Prize ceremony.

Comprehension: Understanding Main Ideas

6. He asks for artists to take up the cause of truth in the hopes of conquering falsehood in all the world.

7. The principle of repentance and remorse is discussed.

8. Joan of Arc wants to inspire the English to leave France and return occupied territory to the French.

9. Lincoln and Kennedy both challenge the American people to express their devotion for their country by taking patriotic action.

10. *A Small Place* is really about the ravages of colonialism.

Understanding Literature: Essays, Letters, Speeches

11. All are nonfiction.

12. A speech is meant to be read aloud and is usually for some special event.

13. It is a letter but it was read aloud and then posted in a public place for all to see.

UNIT 5 REVIEW

Directions Write the answers to these questions using complete sentences.

Comprehension Identifying Facts

1. Which two selections are from France?
2. Two selections were written during the Cold War. Identify them and tell what countries their authors are from.
3. Two forms of persuasive writing are used in this unit. What are they?
4. What literary form does Montaigne use in "Of Repentance"?
5. What was the occasion for Solzhenitsyn's speech?

Comprehension: Understanding Main Ideas

6. What is the main thing Solzhenitsyn asks for in "Nobel Lecture"?
7. What principle is discussed in "Of Repentance"?
8. What does Joan of Arc want to accomplish with her speech?
9. How are Lincoln's and Kennedy's speeches alike? Name one way.
10. *A Small Place* at first seems to be about travel. What is it really about?

Understanding Literature: Essays, Letters, Speeches

Essays, letters, and speeches are nonfiction. (Sometimes a fiction writer uses a series of letters. This is a literary device. They are not real letters.) An essay is a written work that shows a writer's opinions on some issue. A letter contains thoughts and feelings written to a certain person. Most letters are personal. Some letters are meant for the public. A speech is usually written. But it is meant to be read aloud. It is meant for a special event. Some essays and speeches are meant to persuade. Their writers try to influence the opinion of the reader. Writers of essays and speeches use the same devices that are used in fiction. Such devices in this unit include metaphor and irony.

11. What do essays, letters, and speeches have in common?
12. How is a speech different from a letter or essay?
13. "Letter to the English" is called both a speech and a letter. Explain why both labels can be right.

14. In which essay in the unit does the writer seem more personally involved?

15. All of the selections in this unit are called persuasive writing. Which selection do you think is the most persuasive?

Critical Thinking

16. Do you think the speeches have the same effect being read as they would being spoken?

17. Choose one of the selections. Explain why it is still being read.

18. Choose two of the writers in this unit. Compare their styles of writing.

19. Which selection in this unit do you like least? Why?

20. Which selection do you think asks the most of its audience? Explain.

Speak and Listen

Choose a speech from this unit or find one in the library. You can also search the Internet. If you don't find one you like, write your own. After you choose a speech, practice reading it. Then read it out loud in class.

Beyond Words

Find pictures of some of the speakers or places from this unit. You might find them in textbooks. You might use magazines or the Internet. Copy the pictures, then cut them out. Put them on a flat surface to make a collage. (A collage is a piece of art made by pasting objects on a surface.) You do not have to find exactly the places or people that are in the unit. But they should be things that suggest the ideas of the speeches or essays.

Writing on Your Own

Think about the beliefs or wishes expressed in this unit. Each writer had strong ideas about something that was important to him or her.

Do you think their writing would have been as good if they had not had strong ideas? Write an essay about one of the writers. Tell what belief the writer had. Do you think that belief made the writing stronger? Explain why you feel the way you do.

Test-Taking Tip

Read the test directions twice. Sometimes they will give you a hint. For example, the directions may remind you to look for the best answer.

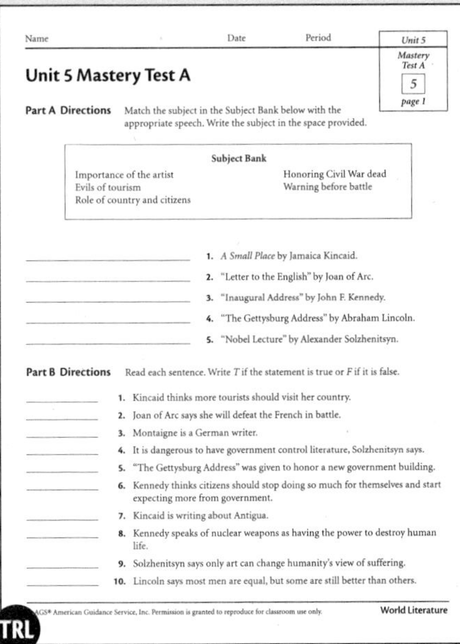

Name Date Period

Unit 5 Mastery Test A 5 page 1

Unit 5 Mastery Test A

Part A Directions Match the subject in the Subject Bank below with the appropriate speech. Write the subject in the space provided.

Subject Bank

Importance of the artist
Evils of tourism
Role of country and citizens
Honoring Civil War dead
Warning before battle

1. *A Small Place* by Jamaica Kincaid.
2. "Letter to the English" by Joan of Arc.
3. "Inaugural Address" by John F. Kennedy.
4. "The Gettysburg Address" by Abraham Lincoln.
5. "Nobel Lecture" by Alexander Solzhenitsyn.

Part B Directions Read each sentence. Write *T* if the statement is true or *F* if it is false.

1. Kincaid thinks more tourists should visit her country.
2. Joan of Arc says she will defeat the French in battle.
3. Montaigne is a German writer.
4. It is dangerous to have government control literature, Solzhenitsyn says.
5. "The Gettysburg Address" was given to honor a new government building.
6. Kennedy thinks citizens should stop doing so much for themselves and start expecting more from government.
7. Kincaid is writing about Antigua.
8. Kennedy speaks of nuclear weapons as having the power to destroy human life.
9. Solzhenitsyn says only art can change humanity's view of suffering.
10. Lincoln says most men are equal, but some are still better than others.

 World Literature

TRL

Unit Mastery Test A, page 1

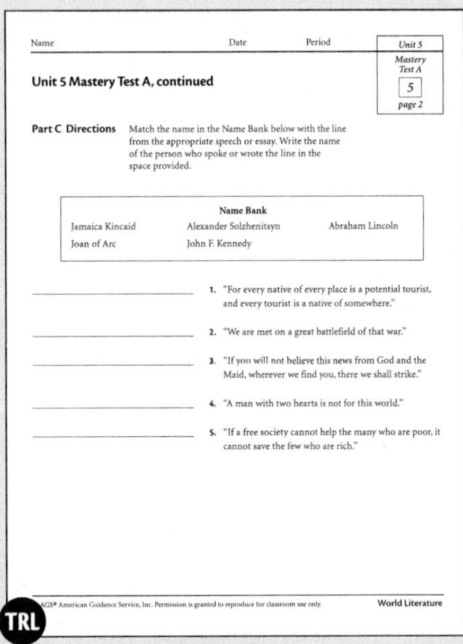

Name Date Period

Unit 5 Mastery Test A 5 page 2

Unit 5 Mastery Test A, continued

Part C Directions Match the name in the Name Bank below with the line from the appropriate speech or essay. Write the name of the person who spoke or wrote the line in the space provided.

Name Bank

Jamaica Kincaid
Alexander Solzhenitsyn
Abraham Lincoln
Joan of Arc
John F. Kennedy

1. "For every native of every place is a potential tourist, and every tourist is a native of somewhere."
2. "We are met on a great battlefield of that war."
3. "If you will not believe this news from God and the Maid, wherever we find you, there we shall strike."
4. "A man with two hearts is not for this world."
5. "If a free society cannot help the many who are poor, it cannot save the few who are rich."

 World Literature

TRL

Unit Mastery Test A, page 2

14. Kincaid seems more personally involved in her topic than Montaigne was in his.

15. Students answers will vary. Any answer is correct as long as it is supported with details from the selection and personal insights.

Critical Thinking

16. The speeches are probably more powerful when spoken.

17. Students may choose to explain any one of the selections. In their explanations, they should draw out the key points that make the selection exceptional and explain why the selection has stood the test of time.

18. Students may compare any two authors. For example, a student might explain that Montaigne stands at a distance from his subject matter and writes a very cool, objective piece. Solzhenitsyn, however, is quite impassioned and rouses his audience's emotions.

19. Students must support their answers with reasons.

20. Students may choose any selection, but they must be able to explain their answer. Evaluate how carefully they have thought out their decision and how well they support their opinion.

Speak and Listen

Remind students that delivering a speech is not the same as reading aloud. Encourage students not to read their speeches word for word. Suggest that they write notes on index cards and only glance at their notes during their delivery.

Beyond Words

In addition to pictures, students can make drawings and designs on their collages. They can also write captions or words that express ideas or emotions.

Writing on Your Own Students may wish to identify examples from the selection to use in their essays. Suggest that they write the examples on note cards, making sure to include the page reference as well as the quotation.

UNIT 6 Planning Guide

Humorous Literature

	Student Pages	About the Author	About the Selection	Literary Terms	Reviewing the Selection	Writing on Your Own
	Selection Features					
■ IRELAND "A Modest Proposal" by Jonathan Swift	371–376	✔	✔	✔	✔	✔
■ ARGENTINA "Cup Inanity and Patriotic Profanity" by Andrew Graham-Yooll, From the *Buenos Aires Herald*	377–381	✔	✔	✔	✔	✔
■ UNITED STATES "Staying at a Japanese Inn: Peace, Tranquillity, Insects" by Dave Barry	383–388	✔	✔	✔	✔	✔
■ UNITED STATES "Why Can't We Have Our Own Apartment?" by Erma Bombeck	389–392	✔	✔	✔	✔	✔
■ AUSTRIA "Lohengrin" by Leo Slezak	394–400	✔	✔	✔	✔	✔
■ UKRAINE "A Wedding Without Musicians" by Sholom Aleichem	401–409	✔	✔	✔	✔	✔
■ SKILLS LESSON: Dialogue; UNIT REVIEW	410, 412–413			✔		✔

Unit Features

Student Text
Humorous Literature
Satire
Columns
Stories
Skills Lesson: Dialogue
Unit Summary

Teacher's Resource Library
Activity 62: Humorous Literature
Workbook 62: Humorous Literature
Activity 63: Satire
Workbook 63: Satire
Activity 66: Columns
Workbook 66: Columns
Activity 69: Stories
Workbook 69: Stories

Assessment Features

Student Text
Unit 6 Review

Teacher's Resource Library
Activity 72: Unit 6 Review, pages 1–2
Workbook 72: Unit 6 Review, pages 1–2
Selection Quizzes 39–44
Unit 6 Mastery Tests A and B, pages 1–2
Final Mastery Test, pages 1–6

Teaching Strategies							Language Skills				Learning Styles					TRL Teacher's Resource Library					
Viewing the Art	Career Connection	Environmental Connection	Cross-Curricular Connection	Diversity Connection	Community Connection	Transparencies	Grammar	Literary Elements	Comprehension	Writing Connection	Auditory	Visual	Tactile/Kinesthetic	Group Learning	LEP/ESL	Vocabulary Workbook	Selection Glossary	Student Study Guide	Activities	Workbook	Writing Activities
375			372	372	373		374		374						375	33	39	45	64	64	44
	379	380														34	40	46	65	65	45
				385	386								387			35	41	47	67	67	46
									391	391	390					36	42	48	68	68	47
			395, 396					397				398		399		36	43	49	70	70	48
			403	404			406	404			405					37	44	50	71	71	49
						12													72	72	50

Unit at a Glance

Unit 6: Humorous Literature
pages 366–413

Humorous Literature
pages 368–369

Selections
- IRELAND "A Modest Proposal" by Jonathan Swift, pages 371–376
- ARGENTINA "Cup Inanity and Patriotic Profanity" by Andrew Graham-Yooll, From the *Buenos Aires Herald,* pages 377–381
- UNITED STATES "Staying at a Japanese Inn: Peace, Tranquillity, Insects" by Dave Barry, pages 383–388
- UNITED STATES "Why Can't We Have Our Own Apartment?" by Erma Bombeck, pages 389–392
- AUSTRIA "Lohengrin" by Leo Slezak, pages 394–400
- UKRAINE "A Wedding Without Musicians" by Sholom Aleichem, pages 401–409

Unit Skills Lesson: Dialogue
page 410

Unit Summary page 411

Unit Review pages 412–413

Audiocassette

Transparency 12

Teacher's Resource Library TRL
- Activity 62 and 72, pages 1–2
- Workbook 62 and 72, pages 1–2
- Writing Activity 50
- Unit 6 Mastery Tests A and B, pages 1–2
- Final Mastery Test, pages 1–6

(Answer Keys for the Teacher's Resource Library begin on page 468 of this Teacher's Edition.)

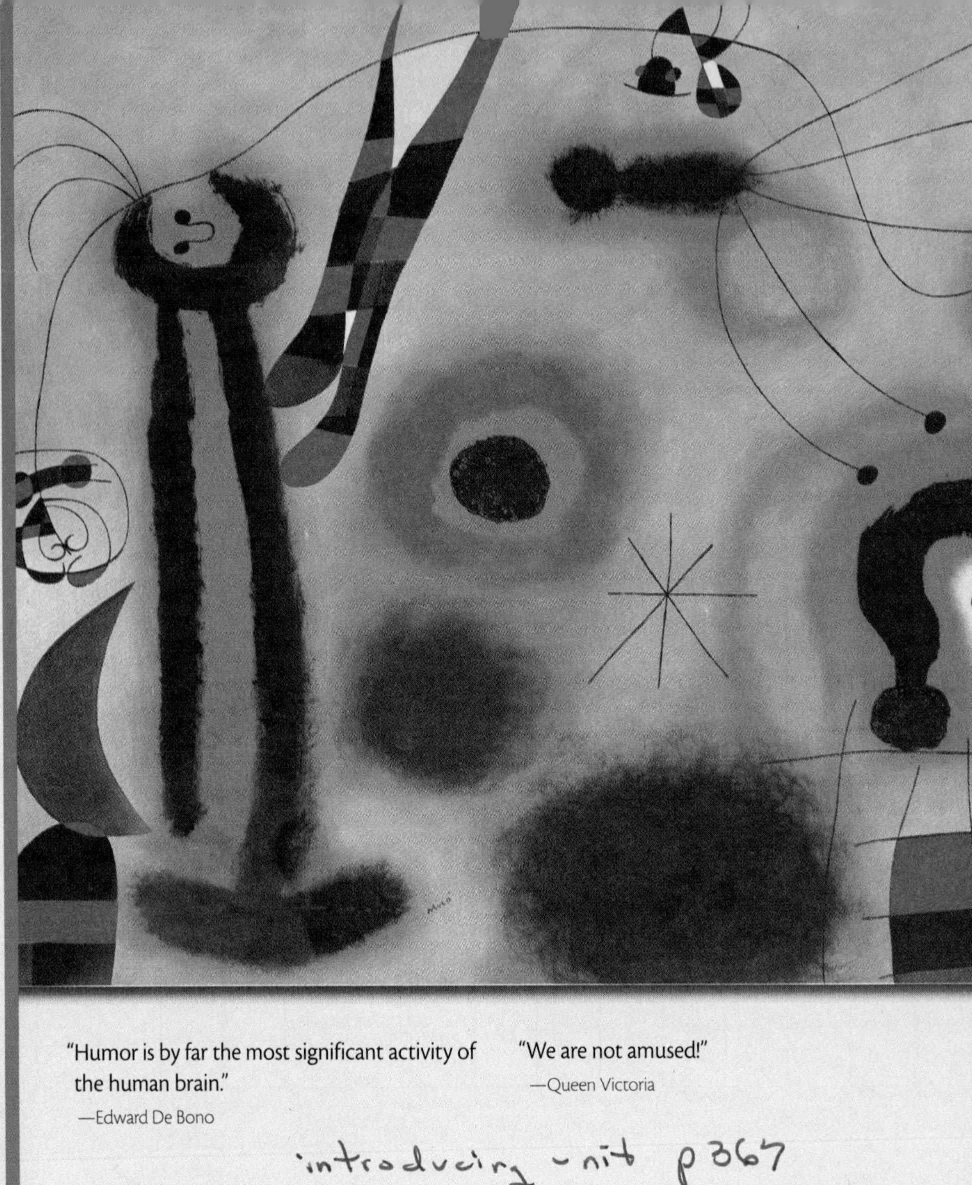

"Humor is by far the most significant activity of the human brain."
—Edward De Bono

"We are not amused!"
—Queen Victoria

introducing unit p367

Other Resources

Books for Teachers

Fakih, Kimberly Olson. *The Literature of Delight: A Critical Guide to Humorous Books for Children.* New Providence, NJ: R. R. Bowker, 1993.

Ford, Gerald. *Humor and the Presidency.* New York: Arbor House, 1987.

Gardner, Gerald C. *All the Presidents' Wits: The Power of Political Humor.* New York: Morrow, 1986.

Books for Students

Bombeck, Erma. *Forever, Erma: Best-Loved Writing from America's Favorite.* Thorndike, ME: Thorndike Press, 1997.

Peck, Richard. *Those Summer Girls I Never Met.* New York: Delacorte Press, 1988.

Jonathan Swift. *Gulliver's Travels.* New York: Penguin USA, 1997

Twain, Mark. *The Celebrated Jumping Frog of Calaveras County, and Other Sketches.* New York: Oxford University Press, 1996.

UNIT 6 Humorous Literature

We all like to laugh. Some writers write in ways that make us laugh. Still, not all those writers are just having fun with human nature. Some use wit as a way to get readers to read about serious problems. Beneath the wit of their work is a bite. They hope their readers will see that something in the world needs to be changed.

The works you will read are told in several ways. Some quickly make it clear that they are just for fun. Others are told with a straight face. At first you might not be sure that you are reading humor. You may want to read some selections more than once. The next reading may show you a funny spot that you missed the first time.

Unit 6 Selections — Page

Introducing the Unit

Have volunteers read the quotations on page 366. Encourage a brief discussion about humor. Invite students to agree or disagree with De Bono's quotation. You may want to point out that Queen Victoria was known to be stern and solemn—and, as Queen of England, always referred to herself as "we" instead of "I." This is the "royal we."

ASK What makes something funny? (Answers may include slapstick pratfalls, ridicule, exaggeration, and so on.) Let students share their own opinions of what is funny. Help them realize that many people, including comedians, have spent time analyzing humor—and had difficulty doing so.

Explain that humor is universal. People in all cultures laugh. However, people from different cultures and different times may find different things funny.

ASK How can humorous writing be more than just funny? (It may show people serious problems and inspire them to find solutions.)

Review the Unit 6 selection genres and titles. Discuss what students know about the different genres.

Viewing the Art

Direct students' attention to the painting on these two pages, and identify it as *Libellula con le Ali Rosse All'inseguimento di un Serpente Che Striscia Come una Spirale, Etc.*, ("Dragonfly With Red Wings in Pursuit of a Snake That Crawls Like a Spiral") by Joan Miró (pronounced *hwahn mee ROH*). Miró was a Spanish painter who lived from 1893 to 1983. He is known for the humor, playfulness, and color in his abstract work. He was a leader of the surrealist art movement. He visited the United States in 1947 and became a major influence on American abstract painting.

ASK Do you think Miró intended this painting to seem humorous? What makes you think so? (Most students will agree that the artist intended to delight his audience.)

Video

Animal Farm. Botsford, CT: Filmic Archives, 1954

An Argentine Journey. (3-part series) Princeton, NJ: Films for the Humanities and Sciences

Bill Cosby in Aesop's Fables. Irvine, CA: Karl Lorimar Home Video, 1986.

The Mouse That Roared. Burbank, CA: RCA/Columbia Pictures Home Video, 1993.

Gulliver's Travels. Botsford, CT: Filmic Archives, 1997

Software

Twain's World for Windows. (CD-ROM) IBM PC and Compatibles; Macintosh. Bureau of Electronic Publishing.

Humorous Literature

Ask students to read the text on page 368, or have several share reading it aloud.

ASK Why do people write humorous literature? (Humor writers try to be funny. Sometimes they only want to entertain their readers. Other writers want to use humor to draw attention to problems. Still others may use such techniques as exaggeration to point out people's ridiculous behavior.)

You may want to remind students that the work of people who write humor doesn't always end up in print. Many humor writers do scripts for television or movies. Some write (and may perform, as well) monologues for stand-up comedians.

ASK What might be part of the motive for someone to write and perform as a stand-up comedian? (to entertain and to attract attention)

ASK How is humor sometimes connected to anger? (Some humorists are so angry about a situation that they make fun of it as a way to encourage people to do something about it.)

Humorous literature is created to be funny. Some humor comes from feeling better than someone who makes a mistake. We laugh at the stuffy banker who slips on a banana peel. She is lying on the sidewalk and we aren't. Other humor comes from the unexpected—a sudden reversal of events. We laugh because we expect the banker to sit on a leather chair, not the sidewalk. Whatever our reasons, laughter is the reaction a humorist wants. A humorist is someone who writes funny works. The humorist may write a light piece to pass the time. Or the humorist may poke fun at human behavior with the idea of changing it. In either case, the desire to be funny is more important than the form of expression the writer chooses.

The tone of humor depends on how angry human behavior has made the humorist. Some writers may let the reader sit back and enjoy someone (even the writer) slipping on a banana peel. Or the writer may inspire us to rush out and pick up the banana peel before someone else slips.

Humor can take almost any literary form. Neil Simon's early plays were comedies poking fun at the stress-filled lives of New Yorkers. The French writer Molière wrote many humorous plays with a serious point. Ogden Nash and Edward Lear wrote funny poems. The Unit 6 selections are grouped into three forms of humorous writing: satire, columns, and stories.

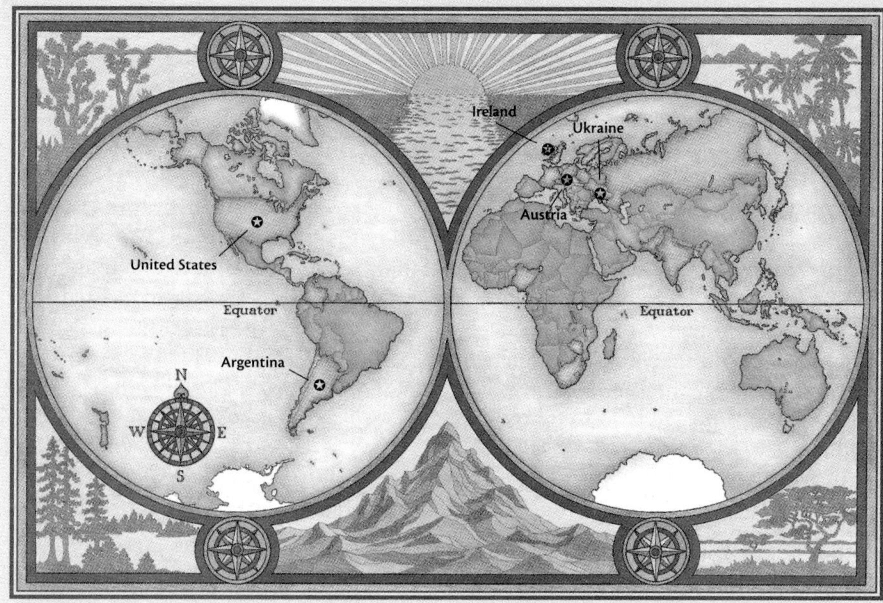

The following countries are represented in this unit: Ireland, Argentina, the United States, Austria, and Ukraine.

Draw students' attention to the world map on page 369 showing the countries represented in this unit.

ASK Why do you think selections are not included from such places as China or India? (Perhaps because humorous writing from cultures so different from our own might be difficult to understand. Also, of course, not every culture can be represented in one unit of this book.)

Name _______ Date _______ Period _______ *Unit 6* *Activity* 62

About Humorous Literature

Part A Directions Read each sentence. Write *T* if the statement is true or *F* if it is false.

_______ 1. Humor is written by a humorist.
_______ 2. Humor may be written in most literary forms.
_______ 3. Humorous literature is created to be challenging.
_______ 4. Beneath the wit of some work is a bite.
_______ 5. A writer of humor may inspire us to make changes in our lives.

Part B Directions In each blank, write the word or phrase that best completes each sentence.

1. Sometimes _______ is used to get readers to read about serious problems.
2. Humorous writings may be light or may _______ at human behavior with the idea of changing it.
3. Writers of humor have fun with _______ nature.
4. Humor can come from the _______, a sudden reversal of events.
5. The _______ of humor depends on how angry human behavior has made the writer.

 World Literature

TRL

Activity 62

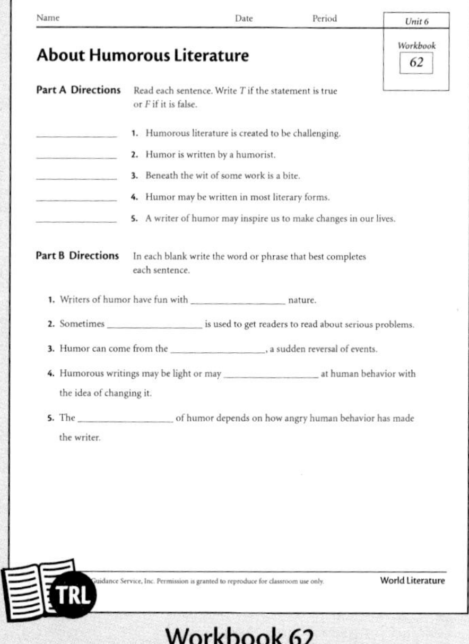
Name _______ Date _______ Period _______ *Unit 6* *Workbook* 62

About Humorous Literature

Part A Directions Read each sentence. Write *T* if the statement is true or *F* if it is false.

_______ 1. Humorous literature is created to be challenging.
_______ 2. Humor is written by a humorist.
_______ 3. Beneath the wit of some work is a bite.
_______ 4. Humor may be written in most literary forms.
_______ 5. A writer of humor may inspire us to make changes in our lives.

Part B Directions In each blank write the word or phrase that best completes each sentence.

1. Writers of humor have fun with _______ nature.
2. Sometimes _______ is used to get readers to read about serious problems.
3. Humor can come from the _______, a sudden reversal of events.
4. Humorous writings may be light or may _______ at human behavior with the idea of changing it.
5. The _______ of humor depends on how angry human behavior has made the writer.

 World Literature

TRL

Workbook 62

Satire

Ask students to read the text on page 370, or have them take turns reading it aloud.

ASK What is satire? (a type of literary humor that makes fun of foolishness or evil)

Discuss the quotations at the top of the page. Invite students to provide their own interpretation of Mme. Roland's remark about finding "amusement in killing flies."

ASK What do you think Quentin Crisp's attitude toward life might be? (He may think life is funny. Or he may believe that people do not see the foolishness of their own and others' behavior.)

Remind students that the two following selections are both identified as satire.

ASK What are you likely to find in the following two selections? Why? (Because they are identified as satires, the two selections will probably be based on the anger of the writers at a situation they see around them. The writers probably hope to prompt people to change some behavior as a result of their ridicule.)

Satire

- "A fondness for satire indicates a mind pleased with irritating others; for myself, I never could find amusement in killing flies." —Mme. Marie-Jeanne Roland
- "If you describe things exactly as they are, you will be thought of as a satirist." —Quentin Crisp

One of the oldest forms of literary humor is satire. Satire is humor that makes fun of foolishness or evil. Writers who decide to challenge others' behavior can become angry. They can try to make people laugh at those actions. Or they can do both. Satire is a way for a writer to be angry while making people laugh at evil or foolish acts.

The talents of certain writers are well suited to satire. Geoffrey Chaucer's *Canterbury Tales* are one example. These stories and character portraits from the 1300s use satire throughout. Other well-known satirists include Mark Twain, François Rabelais, and Charles Dickens.

Satire requires an ability to describe human behavior accurately and vividly. A satirist sees tiny traits and behaviors. Careful word choice goes into using irony, puns, and other literary techniques. Above all, a writer using satire must have a strong sense of right and wrong. The writer must understand the difference between what society says is okay and what it knows is right. Satirists try to remind their readers of basic truths that are often ignored. Many satirists are very angry at what they see. One of the following selections is a reaction to social injustice. The other shows anger at foolish behavior.

370 *Unit 6 Humorous Literature*

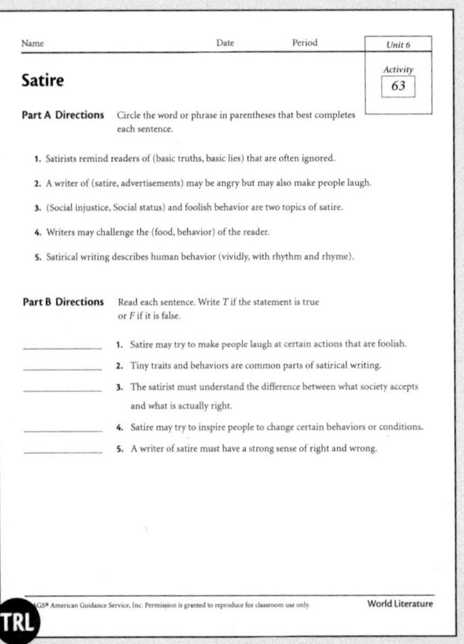

Name Date Period Unit 6 Activity 63

Satire

Part A Directions Circle the word or phrase in parentheses that best completes each sentence.

1. Satirists remind readers of (basic truths, basic lies) that are often ignored.
2. A writer of (satire, advertisements) may be angry but may also make people laugh.
3. (Social injustice, Social status) and foolish behavior are two topics of satire.
4. Writers may challenge the (food, behavior) of the reader.
5. Satirical writing describes human behavior (vividly, with rhythm and rhyme).

Part B Directions Read each sentence. Write *T* if the statement is true or *F* if it is false.

_____ 1. Satire may try to make people laugh at certain actions that are foolish.
_____ 2. Tiny traits and behaviors are common parts of satirical writing.
_____ 3. The satirist must understand the difference between what society accepts and what is actually right.
_____ 4. Satire may try to inspire people to change certain behaviors or conditions.
_____ 5. A writer of satire must have a strong sense of right and wrong.

 World Literature

TRL

Activity 63

Name Date Period Unit 6 Workbook 63

Satire

Part A Directions Circle the word or phrase in parentheses that best completes each sentence.

1. Satirists remind readers of (basic truths, basic lies) that are often ignored.
2. Writers may challenge the (food, behavior) of the reader.
3. A writer of (satire, advertisements) angry but may also make people laugh.
4. Satirical writing describes human behavior (vividly, with rhythm and rhyme).
5. (Social injustice, Social status) and foolish behavior are two topics used in satire.

Part B Directions Read each sentence. Write *T* if the statement is true or *F* if it is false.

_____ 1. Satire may try to make people laugh at certain actions that are foolish.
_____ 2. Satire may try to inspire people to change certain behaviors or conditions.
_____ 3. Tiny traits and behaviors are common parts of satirical writing.
_____ 4. A writer of satire must have a strong sense of right and wrong.
_____ 5. The satirist must understand the difference between what society accepts and what is right.

 World Literature

TRL

Workbook 63

INTRODUCING the SELECTION

A Modest Proposal

Jonathan Swift

Jonathan Swift (1667–1745) Irish

Literary Terms

pamphlet a short printed essay about a specific problem

satire humorous writing that makes fun of foolishness or evil

tone the attitude an author takes toward a subject

About the Author

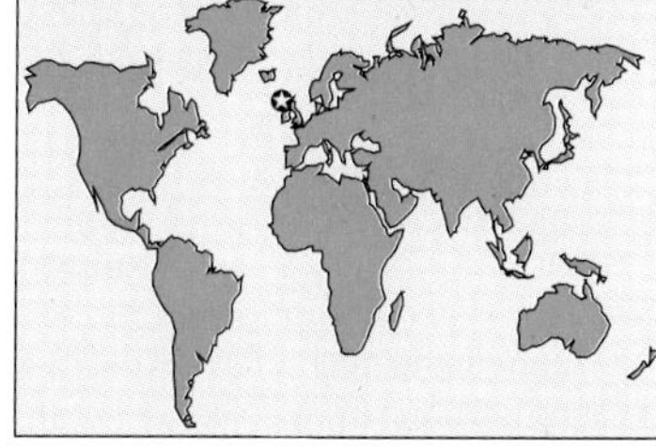

Though his parents were English, Jonathan Swift was born in Dublin, Ireland. Swift became an Anglican priest in 1695. For the rest of his life he served in churches in England or Ireland. Swift was named dean of the cathedral in Dublin in 1713. He settled there and wrote some of his greatest works.

His religious training gave Swift a perfect background for **satire**. Satire is humor that makes fun of foolishness or evil. Swift's literary career began with a satire about religion. His interest in English politics led him to write **pamphlets** about current public problems. A pamphlet is a short printed essay about a specific problem. Swift's most famous work, *Gulliver's Travels* (1726), combines Swift's political and moral views. This work is considered a model of satire.

About the Selection

Swift wrote "A Modest Proposal" in 1729. In it he reveals the terrible poverty of the Irish people. He also satirizes the English attitude toward them. The innocent **tone** of "A Modest Proposal" fooled many people. Tone is the attitude an author takes toward a subject. Thinking he was serious, many readers of Swift's time were angry at him. He does not seriously suggest that the English want to cook and eat Irish babies for lunch. But he does want to show that their indifference and contempt toward the Irish are just as evil. Beneath Swift's seeming sincerity lies the deep anger of a morally outraged man.

Selection at a Glance

A Modest Proposal

Jonathan Swift

Student pages 371–376

Overview

"A Modest Proposal" is almost as well known as Jonathan Swift's most famous work, *Gulliver's Travels.* Although many people are familiar with *Gulliver's Travels,* some do not realize that it too was written to be a satire, not simply a fantastic imaginary adventure. It is easier to understand the satirical purpose of "A Modest Proposal," however, especially at the point in the essay in which Swift begins to explain the idea of eating children!

Selection Summary

In "A Modest Proposal," Jonathan Swift makes an outrageous suggestion for dealing with poverty in Ireland.

Objectives

- To identify some of the elements of satire.
- To appreciate the humor of a satirical piece.

Audiocassette 

Teacher's Resource Library 

- Vocabulary Workbook 33, pages 1–2
- Selection Glossary 39
- Student Study Guide 45
- Activity 64, pages 1–2
- Workbook 64, pages 1–2
- Writing Activity 44
- Selection Quiz 39

Setting the Stage for Reading

About the Author

Have students read the text of page 371 and look at the painting of Jonathan Swift. Point out that although Swift is a well-known writer, he was also a working Anglican priest for most of his life.

ASK Why might a priest be inspired to write satire? (A priest might be especially knowledgeable about the difficulties of people's lives. A priest also might be especially shocked and angry at the mistreatment of people.)

About the Selection

As is often typical of satire, this essay seems to be realistic and reasonable with some exaggerated exceptions that reveal its satirical purpose.

Activate Prior Knowledge: Discuss the definition of satire. Invite students to share examples of satire they have read or seen in movies or on television.

ASK How might the title of the essay, "A Modest Proposal," be satirical? (One element of satire is exaggeration; here the author is providing an outlandish and bizarre proposal. Calling it "modest" is contradictory, funny, and exaggerated.)

Reading Vocabulary TRL

Help students preview the selection's vocabulary words by giving them copies of the Selection Glossary. Review the words and ask pairs of students to take turns saying the words and providing the matching definitions.

Motivation for Reading

Suggest that students think of attitudes or behavior that they find cruel and outrageous. Mention that they may find in Swift's essay a model they themselves could use to address those issues.

Discussion Questions

Suggest that students answer the questions in the margins of the student selection as they read the selection.

A Swift does seem to be appealing to common sense, and that is likely to prompt his readers to take him seriously.

B ASK Literary Element A common element of satire is to seem reasonable while attracting the reader into more and more outlandish ideas. How do you think that technique can draw readers into the satire? (By making them believe what they are reading is sensible, the exaggerations of later comments will be all the more shocking.)

A Modest Proposal

Jonathan Swift

As you read, look for ways the writer sets up the satire. Remember that he is writing from an Irish point of view.

A Modest Proposal FOR PREVENTING THE CHILDREN OF POOR PEOPLE IN IRELAND FROM BEING A BURDEN TO THEIR PARENTS OR COUNTRY, AND FOR MAKING THEM BENEFICIAL TO THE PUBLIC

It is a melancholy object to those who walk through this great town or travel in the country, when they see the streets, the roads, and cabin doors, crowded with beggars of the female-sex, followed by three, four, or six children, all in rags and **importuning** every passenger for an **alms.** These mothers, instead of being able to work for their honest livelihood, are forced to employ all their time in strolling to beg **sustenance** for their helpless infants, who, as they grow up, either turn thieves for want of work, or leave their dear native country to fight for the Pretender in Spain, or sell themselves to the Barbadoes.

Some poor people became soldiers for pay. Others went as servants to Caribbean islands.

I think it is agreed by all parties that this **prodigious** number of children in the arms or on the backs, or at the heels of their mothers, and frequently of their fathers, is in the present **deplorable** state of the kingdom a very great additional **grievance**; and therefore whoever could find out a fair, cheap, and easy method of making these children sound, useful members of the **commonwealth** would deserve so well of the public as to have his statue set up for a preserver of the nation. **B**

A Does Swift seem to appeal to common sense at this point? Might this tempt you to take him seriously?

alms charity; a handout

commonwealth the community as a whole; the nation

deplorable terrible

grievance something to complain about

importuning begging

prodigious enormous

sustenance something that supports life, especially food

Cross-Curricular Connection

History Jonathan Swift wrote "A Modest Proposal" in 1729, three years after he wrote his famous book *Gulliver's Travels.* Although he attacked the attitude of the English toward the Irish in "A Modest Proposal," he also wanted to inspire the Irish people to improve their situation themselves. Encourage interested students to do some research to find out about life in Ireland in the early 1700s. What was life like in the city of Dublin? How did that compare to the life of people who lived away from the city?

Diversity Connection

The Irish also suffered discrimination when many emigrated to the United States a century or so after Swift's essay. You may want to invite students to discuss other examples of discrimination against a people of one nation by the people of another. Extend the discussion to the impact of such discrimination on the people of both sides.

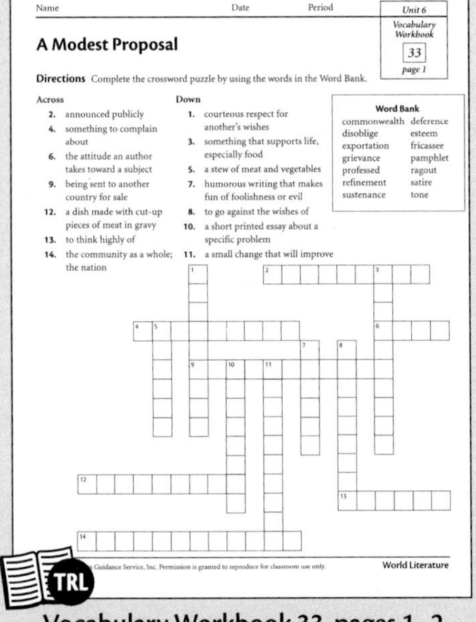

Name Date Period

Unit 6 *Vocabulary Workbook* 33 *page 1*

A Modest Proposal

Directions Complete the crossword puzzle by using the words in the Word Bank.

Across
2. announced publicly
4. something to complain about
6. the attitude an author takes toward a subject
9. being sent to another country for sale
12. a dish made with cut-up pieces of meat in gravy
13. to think highly of
14. the community as a whole; the nation

Down
1. courteous respect for another's wishes
3. something that supports life, especially food
5. a stew of meat and vegetables
7. humorous writing that makes fun of foolishness or evil
8. to go against the wishes of
10. a short printed essay about a specific problem
11. a small change that will improve

Word Bank

commonwealth	deference
disoblige	esteem
exportation	fricassee
grievance	pamphlet
professed	ragout
refinement	satire
sustenance	tone

World Literature

TRL Vocabulary Workbook 33, pages 1–2

But my intention is very far from being confined to provide only for the children of **professed** beggars; it is of a much greater extent, and shall take in the whole number of infants at a certain age who are born of parents in effect as little able to support them as those who demand our charity in the streets.

As to my own part, having turned my thoughts for many years upon this important subject and maturely weighed the several schemes of other projectors, I have always found them grossly mistaken in their computation. It is true, a child just dropped from its dam may be supported by her milk for a solar year, with little other nourishment; at most not above the value of two shillings, which the mother may certainly get, or the value in scraps, by her lawful occupation of begging; and it is exactly at one year old that I propose to provide for them in such a manner as instead of being a charge upon their parents or the parish, or wanting food and **raiment** for the rest of their lives, they shall on the contrary contribute to the feeding, and partly to the clothing, of many thousands....

I am assured by our merchants that a boy or a girl before twelve years old is no salable commodity; and even when they come to this age they will not yield above three pounds, or three pounds and half a crown at most on the Exchange; which cannot turn to account either to the parents or the kingdom, the charge of **nutriment** and rags having been at least four times that value.

I shall now humbly propose my own thoughts, which I hope will not be liable to the least objection.

I have been assured by a very knowing American of my acquaintance in London, that a young healthy child well nursed is at a year old a most delicious, nourishing, and **wholesome** food, whether stewed, roasted, baked, or boiled; and I make no doubt that it will equally serve in a **fricassee** or a **ragout**. **D**

I do therefore humbly offer it to public consideration that of the hundred and twenty thousand children, already **computed**, twenty thousand may be reserved for breed, whereof only one-

The writer refers to the Irish as if they were animals. *Dam* is a word usually used for mother animals such as sheep. A *shilling* is an old English coin, worth only a small amount.

C
How could a child be a *salable commodity*? Is Swift suggesting that people don't see children as real human beings? A *pound* and *half a crown* are units of money.

The writer uses the word *humbly* the same way he offers a "modest proposal." He is actually about to propose something shocking—in a satiric way.

compute to count

fricassee a dish made with cut-up pieces of meat in gravy

nutriment food

professed announced publicly

ragout a stew of meat and vegetables

raiment clothing

wholesome healthful

C A child, as a laborer, is a source of income, or a salable commodity. Yes, Swift no doubt was implying that people (the English, in this case) did not see children as real human beings. This is another subtle way a writer can communicate his or her point—by choice of loaded words.

D ASK Critical Thinking What does Swift's mention of the American imply about the American's habits? (The American has evidently eaten young children.)

Community Connection

Swift described many Irish as being homeless and having to earn a living by begging in the streets. Help students contact a local homeless shelter. Have them find out roughly how many people are homeless in their own community and what kinds of help are available to them.

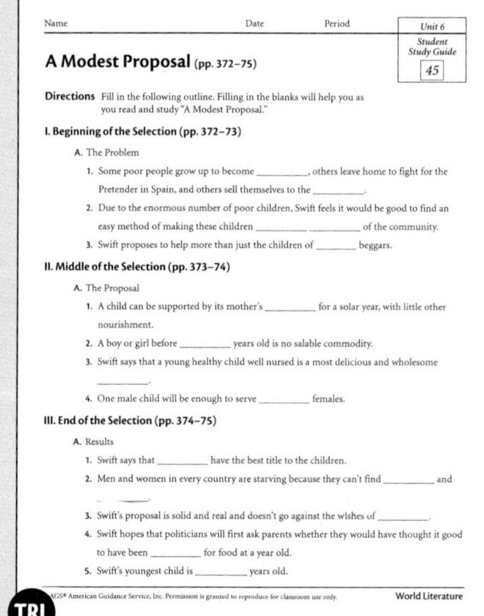

Name Date Period | Unit 6 | Student Study Guide 45

A Modest Proposal (pp. 372–75)

Directions Fill in the following outline. Filling in the blanks will help you as you read and study "A Modest Proposal."

I. Beginning of the Selection (pp. 372–73)

A. The Problem

1. Some poor people grow up to become __________, others leave home to fight for the Pretender in Spain, and others sell themselves to the __________.
2. Due to the enormous number of poor children, Swift feels it would be good to find an easy method of making these children __________ __________ of the community.
3. Swift proposes to help more than just the children of _______ beggars.

II. Middle of the Selection (pp. 373–74)

A. The Proposal

1. A child can be supported by its mother's __________ for a solar year, with little other nourishment.
2. A boy or girl before __________ years old is no salable commodity.
3. Swift says that a young healthy child well nursed is a most delicious and wholesome __________.
4. One male child will be enough to serve __________ females.

III. End of the Selection (pp. 374–75)

A. Results

1. Swift says that __________ have the best title to the children.
2. Men and women in every country are starving because they can't find __________ and __________.
3. Swift's proposal is solid and real and doesn't go against the wishes of __________.
4. Swift hopes that politicians will first ask parents whether they would have thought it good to have been __________ for food at a year old.
5. Swift's youngest child is __________ years old.

 World Literature

TRL

Student Study Guide 45

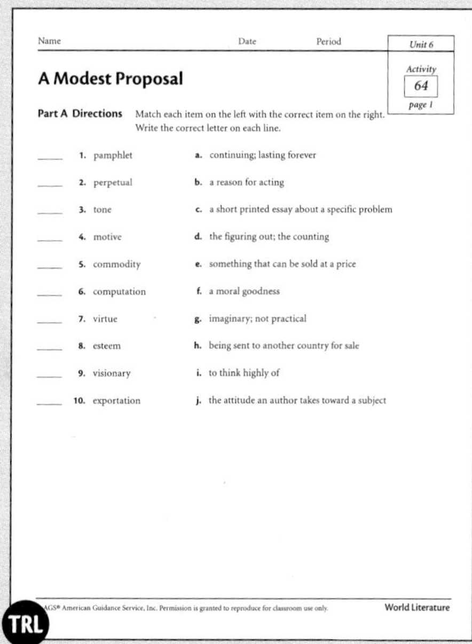

Name Date Period | Unit 6 | Activity 64 page 1

A Modest Proposal

Part A Directions Match each item on the left with the correct item on the right. Write the correct letter on each line.

____ 1. pamphlet — a. continuing; lasting forever
____ 2. perpetual — b. a reason for acting
____ 3. tone — c. a short printed essay about a specific problem
____ 4. motive — d. the figuring out; the counting
____ 5. commodity — e. something that can be sold at a price
____ 6. computation — f. a moral goodness
____ 7. virtue — g. imaginary; not practical
____ 8. esteem — h. being sent to another country for sale
____ 9. visionary — i. to think highly of
____ 10. exportation — j. the attitude an author takes toward a subject

 World Literature

TRL

Activity 64, pages 1–2

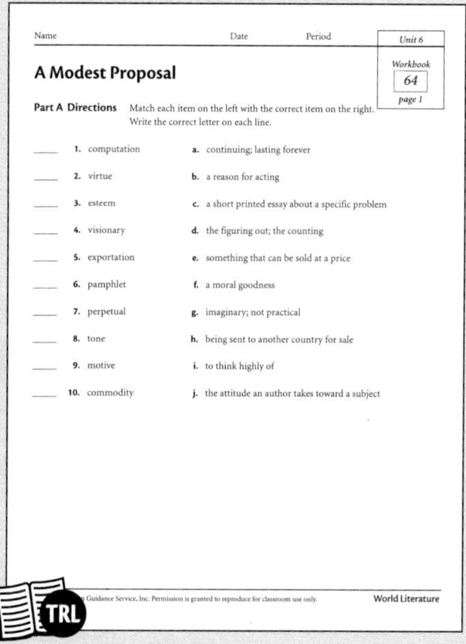

Name Date Period | Unit 6 | Workbook 64 page 1

A Modest Proposal

Part A Directions Match each item on the left with the correct item on the right. Write the correct letter on each line.

____ 1. computation — a. continuing; lasting forever
____ 2. virtue — b. a reason for acting
____ 3. esteem — c. a short printed essay about a specific problem
____ 4. visionary — d. the figuring out; the counting
____ 5. exportation — e. something that can be sold at a price
____ 6. pamphlet — f. a moral goodness
____ 7. perpetual — g. imaginary; not practical
____ 8. tone — h. being sent to another country for sale
____ 9. motive — i. to think highly of
____ 10. commodity — j. the attitude an author takes toward a subject

 World Literature

TRL

Workbook 64, pages 1–2

Discussion Questions

A Landlords have "devoured" the parents by demanding more rent than they know people can pay. Swift is very angry at this unfair behavior. He finds the landlords greedy, selfish human beings without a sense of fairness.

B ASK Comprehension Why can't people pay their rent or for food? (They cannot earn enough money because they are not able to find work.)

Grammar

Ellipses Some students may be unfamiliar with ellipses, or the three dots in a row that stand for something left out of quoted material. Point out the example in the third paragraph on page 374. Explain that the ellipses at the end of the paragraph indicate that Jonathan Swift wrote more material at this point in the essay than is included here. To show that something has been left out, the ellipses have been inserted. Explain that a period follows the end of the last sentence, and then the three dots of the ellipses—so it looks like four dots here. Ellipses can also be used in the middle of a sentence to indicate that something has been omitted. In that case, only three dots are used. Interested students may want to find a copy of the complete text of "A Modest Proposal" to see what has been cut from the copy here.

fourth part be males, which is more than we allow sheep, black cattle, or swine; and my reason is that these children are seldom the fruits of marriage, a **circumstance** not much regarded by our savages, therefore one male will be sufficient to serve four females. That the remaining hundred thousand may at a year old be offered in sale to the persons of quality and fortune through the kingdom, always advising the mother to let them suck plentifully in the last month, so as to render them plump and fat for a good table. A child will make two dishes at an entertainment for friends; and when the family dines alone, the **fore** or hind quarter will make a reasonable dish, and seasoned with a little pepper or salt will be very good boiled on the fourth day, especially in winter.

Persons of quality means those in the upper classes.

A In what way have the landlords already *devoured* the parents? What is Swift's attitude toward the English landlords?

I have reckoned upon a medium that a child just born will weigh twelve pounds, and in a solar year if **tolerably** nursed increaseth to twenty-eight pounds.

I grant this food will be somewhat dear, and therefore very proper for landlords, who, as they have already devoured most of the parents, seem to have the best title to the children....

Butchers we may be assured will not be wanting; although I rather recommend buying the children alive, and dressing them hot from the knife as we do roasting pigs.

A very worthy person, a true lover of his country, and whose virtues I highly **esteem**, was lately pleased in **discoursing** on this matter to offer a **refinement** upon my scheme. He said that many gentlemen of this kingdom, having of late destroyed their deer, he conceived that the want of venison might be well supplied by the bodies of young lads and maidens, not exceeding fourteen years of age nor under twelve, so great a number of both sexes in every **B** county being now ready to starve for want of work and service; and these to be disposed of by their parents, if alive, or otherwise by their nearest relations. But with due **deference** to so excellent a friend and so deserving a patriot, I cannot be altogether in his sentiments; for as to the males, my American acquaintance assured me from frequent experience that their flesh was

This is Swift's real point, that people are starving because of lack of work.

circumstance an event; a situation

deference courteous respect for another's wishes

discourse to discuss

esteem to think highly of

fore the front part

refinement a small change that will improve

tolerably sufficiently; enough

374 Unit 6 Humorous Literature

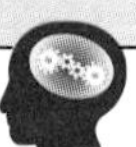

Comprehension

Differentiating Between Fact and Fiction The exaggerations in "A Modest Proposal" are fictional. However, many were based on the facts that Swift observed. Suggest that students make up a two-column chart with one column headed "Facts" and the other headed "Fiction." Remind them that a fact is something that can be proved to be true. Let small groups work together to list several examples of facts and of fiction in the selection. Then have the groups compare their work and make a class chart.

ASK Are there more facts or more fictional statements in the selection? (more fiction) Why do you think that is so? (because it was Swift's purpose to exaggerate some ideas, or to make them fictional, in order to make his purpose clear)

generally tough and lean, like that of our schoolboys, by continual exercise, and their taste disagreeable; and to fatten them would not answer the charge....

But as to myself, having been wearied out for many years with offering vain, idle, **visionary** thoughts, and at length utterly despairing of success, I fortunately fell upon this proposal, which, as it is wholly new, so it hath something solid and real, of no expense and little trouble, full in our own power, and whereby we can **incur** no danger in ***disobliging*** England. For this kind of commodity will not bear **exportation,** the flesh being of too tender a consistence to admit a long continuance in salt, *although perhaps I could name a country which would be glad to eat up our whole nation without it....*

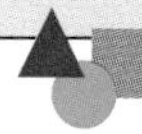

Swift shows special bitterness here. What is he saying about England's "appetite"?

I desire those politicians who dislike my overture, and may perhaps be so bold to attempt an answer, that they will first ask the parents of these mortals whether they would not at this day think it a great happiness to have been sold for food at a year old in the manner I prescribe, and thereby have avoided such a perpetual scene of misfortunes as they have since gone through by the oppression of landlords, the impossibility of paying rent without money or trade, the want of common sustenance, with neither house nor clothes to cover them from the **inclemencies** of the weather, and the most **inevitable** prospect of **entailing** the like or greater miseries upon their breed for ever.

D

How does it help the satire to include the real facts here?

I profess, in the sincerity of my heart, that I have not the least personal interest in endeavoring to promote this necessary work, having no other motive than the *public good of my country, by advancing our trade, providing for infants, relieving the poor, and giving some pleasure to the rich.* I have no children by which I can propose to get a single penny; the youngest being nine years old, and my wife past child-bearing.

E

How does the final paragraph contribute to the satire?

disoblige to go against the wishes of

entailing resulting in

exportation being sent to another country for sale

inclemency storms; discomforts

incur to bring upon oneself

inevitable sure to happen

visionary imaginary; not practical

Viewing the Art

Vincent van Gogh painted *The Potato Eaters* in 1885. It reflects much of his work from the early years when he painted mostly still lifes, landscapes, and peasant scenes. In *The Potato Eaters,* van Gogh uses his artistic talents to express social criticism about the plight of the peasants.

ASK How does van Gogh's use of color contribute to the effect of the painting? (The dark colors help convey the idea of a dreary, dull world in which little light or pleasantness is available to peasants forced to subsist on low incomes and menial work.)

C Swift clearly feels that England's insatiable "appetite" will completely devour all of Ireland.

D Contrasting the exaggerations of satire with some real facts only emphasizes the exaggerations.

E The final paragraph contributes to the satire by including both facts and exaggerations—capped by Swift's last sentence explaining why he himself will not be able to make the sacrifices he suggests for others. This is a humorous, satirical, final twist.

Learning Styles

LEP/ESL Some students may be unfamiliar with the use of italics for special emphasis. Point out to them the italics in the second paragraph on this page. Read the paragraph out loud to students, emphasizing with tone of voice the italicized word and clause. Then read it again, this time without emphasis. Such a demonstration can help students understand how to "hear" as they read, following the cues provided by the writer. Then have students follow your model and read aloud the final paragraph on the page, paying special attention to the italics.

ASK Why should you pay attention to clues such as italics when you read? (to help yourself understand what the author wanted to emphasize)

Reviewing the Selection

Answer Key

Comprehension: Identifying Facts

1. Most parents beg on the streets.

2. Children a year old could be eaten.

3. Older children would not be suitable because they would cost more to feed and clothe than they could be sold for.

Comprehension: Understanding Main Ideas

4. Swift is writing about the English who did not hire Irish people or pay fair wages. He is also disturbed about landlords who demanded high rents that they knew their tenants could not pay.

5. This meat would be suitable for English landlords because the landlords "have already devoured most of the parents" by making it impossible for them to survive.

6. Swift claims the English "would be glad to eat up our whole nation."

Understanding Literature: Satire

7. Irony is the saying of one thing while meaning the opposite. There are many examples in the selection, beginning with the use of the word *modest* in its title. Another example is the food being "proper for landlords, who, . . . seem to have the best title to the children."

8. Swift suggests that Americans have similarly brutal attitudes when he mentions that it was an American who suggested that a young child makes a good meal.

Critical Thinking

9. Two possible examples are (a) his description of the plight of mothers followed by their children in rags and (b) the paragraph on page 375 that describes the plight of the Irish.

10. He explains that he cannot make money from this scheme as he has no children.

Writing on Your Own Suggest that students limit their paragraphs to a single idea about Swift's motivation. If desired, students can then compare their individual ideas in a discussion.

Selection Quiz

The Teacher's Resource Library includes a Selection Quiz for "A Modest Proposal" that may be given following the Selection Review.

REVIEWING the SELECTION

A Modest Proposal

Jonathan Swift

Directions Write the answers to these questions using complete sentences.

Comprehension: Identifying Facts

1. How do the parents of most of the children in this satire make a living?
2. At what age does the satire suggest that children be sold for eating?
3. Why are older children not suitable for this use?

Comprehension: Understanding Main Ideas

4. What problems in Ireland is Swift actually writing about?
5. Why does Swift say that this meat would be suitable for English landlords?
6. Why does Swift say that his proposal won't bother the English?

Understanding Literature: Satire

Satire is humor that pokes fun at foolishness or evil. Although it is a kind of humor, satire seldom makes the reader laugh. The writer is often angry about the topic. It is clear in this piece that Swift is angry and bitter.

7. Satire usually uses heavy irony. Find an ironic statement in this satire.
8. Swift tosses out a few specific insults in this work. What does he suggest about Americans?

Critical Thinking

9. Quote one statement in which Swift reveals his strong feelings about the tragedy of Ireland's poor.
10. At the end, Swift again pretends to be a well-meaning observer. What does he say to show he will not make money from his scheme?

Writing on Your Own Reread the paragraph in the introduction about Swift's background. Write one paragraph to explain how it might have made him angry about the problems of the Irish.

376 *Unit 6 Humorous Literature*

Name Date Period

Unit 6 Writing Activity 44

A Modest Proposal

No surprise here, but for this activity you will write a satire. And you're lucky. Satire is fun, and it's also an opportunity to make a point about something. Perhaps you can dig back to some of your other activities and choose a topic you've already written about.

Prewrite
For this part of the activity, think about how you can write in a humorous way about something serious. Pick a subject and make a list of ways you can discuss it in a humorous way. Satire makes fun of something, so be mindful of that when you make your list.

Write
Write your article. Remember, you want to have fun but also make a point. Refer back to "A Modest Proposal" if you need inspiration or need to be reminded how effective satire can be. And don't worry about being too outrageous: It would be hard to be more outrageous than Swift.

Revise
Read and rewrite your work. If it's funny—and you've made fun of something—and you've got your point across, then your satire probably works.

Proofread
Make sure that you have used complete sentences in your descriptions. Each sentence must include a subject (doer) and a predicate (action or verb), and must express a complete thought. All sentences end with a period, a question mark, or an exclamation mark. Use capital letters to begin each new thought.

 World Literature

TRL

Writing Activity 44

Name Date Period

Unit 6 Selection Quiz 39

A Modest Proposal

Directions Read the following statements. Circle the letter of the answer that correctly completes each sentence or that correctly answers each question.

1. Swift begins by writing of the __________ of Irish mothers.
   a. happiness b. wealth c. grand prospects d. poverty
2. These mothers are forced to
   a. beg. b. sing. c. close their doors. d. go to college.
3. Swift says something must be done about
   a. all the poor Irish children. b. the awful weather.
   c. the educational system. d. too much taxes.
4. How old are children in Swift's proposal?
   a. ten months b. one year c. two years d. ten years
5. Swift proposes that Irish children become
   a. a source of food. b. smarter. c. Englishmen. d. Americans.
6. Swift thinks English __________ would be the best customers for the children.
   a. dukes b. princes c. peasants d. landlords
7. Swift refers to __________ acquaintance who helped him in this regard.
   a. an American b. a Russian c. a German d. a Spanish
8. At one point, Swift proposes to replace __________ with young lads and maidens.
   a. beef b. pork c. venison d. bread
9. When Swift suggests there is a country willing to eat up all of Ireland, he means
   a. America. b. England. c. Russia. d. Germany.
10. Swift makes his proposal for
    a. the "public good." b. his private gain.
    c. the private good of marketers. d. the butcher industry.

 World Literature

TRL

Selection Quiz 39

INTRODUCING the SELECTION

Cup Inanity and Patriotic Profanity

Andrew Graham-Yooll, From the *Buenos Aires Herald* (July 2, 1998)

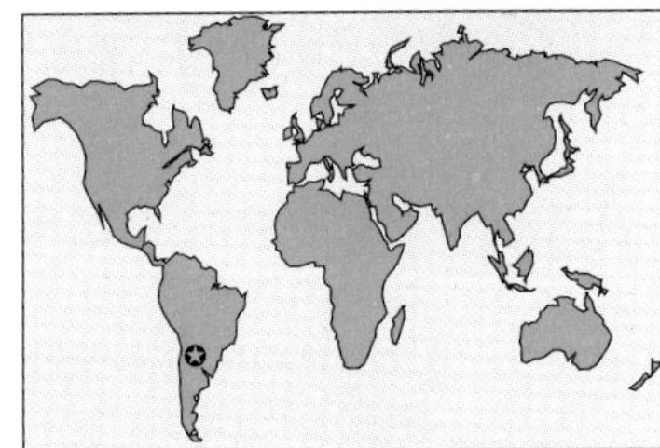

Buenos Aires Herald (established 1876) Argentinian

Literary Terms

editorial a news writer's personal opinion about an event or topic

sarcasm a heavy, sometimes mean-spirited kind of irony

About the Newspaper

The *Buenos Aires Herald* is Argentina's only English-language daily newspaper. William Cathcart, from Scotland, founded the *Herald* in 1876. The *Herald* has survived wars, government repression, terrorism, and economic crises. Over the years, it has become known for independent, biting **editorials.** Most news stories simply state and analyze the facts. An editorial, though, gives a news writer's opinion about an event. Today the *Herald* can be found on the Internet. Its address is http://www.buenosairesherald.com.

About the Selection

Argentina and Great Britain have had a love-hate relationship for years. Argentina was a Spanish colony but also had many settlers from Britain. Britain and Argentina fought a short war in 1982. Argentina lost. This made relations worse. In 1998, Argentina beat Great Britain during the World Cup soccer matches. Many Argentinians saw the victory as revenge for the war. (However, France was the winner of the World Cup.)

Both English and Argentinians are known for "soccer hooligans"—sometimes called "yobs." These fans often start fights over games. They justify their bad behavior by calling it "patriotism." In this editorial, the writer uses **sarcasm**, a heavy kind of irony, to show his dislike of their behavior.

Selection at a Glance

Cup Inanity and Patriotic Profanity

Andrew Graham-Yooll
From the *Buenos Aires Herald*

Student pages 377–381

Overview

Modern newspapers and newsmagazines are the source of some current examples of satire. Sometimes such writing is found in editorials, as in the next selection.

Selection Summary

Andrew Graham-Yooll views the behavior of soccer fans celebrating a victory.

Objectives

- To read and understand an example of modern satire.
- To understand the use of sarcasm in satire.

Audiocassette 

Teacher's Resource Library TRL

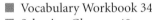

- Vocabulary Workbook 34
- Selection Glossary 40
- Student Study Guide 46
- Activity 65
- Workbook 65
- Writing Activity 45
- Selection Quiz 40

Setting the Stage for Reading

About the Newspaper

Ask students to read the text and locate Buenos Aires, Argentina, on the small world map. Explain that all newspapers have special pages on which they present "editorials," or summaries of the paper's official position and opinion on timely issues. The authors of editorials are usually not identified, but most often they are members of the newspaper's editorial board—a group of experienced newspaper writers who together develop the paper's editorial stance.

ASK Why might a newspaper have and express opinions the way an individual person does? (in order to influence its readers)

About the Selection

Explain to students that Argentina is one of many countries whose people love soccer and have many soccer competitions. Soccer teams from various countries meet in the World Cup soccer matches held once every four years. For soccer fans, the World Cup is like the World Series of American baseball and the football Super Bowl all rolled into one.

Activate Prior Knowledge: Discuss with students examples they provide of heated and partisan audiences for athletic contests, in both amateur and professional sports.

ASK How might fans behave foolishly at a baseball, basketball, or football game? (Some might intrude on others by shouting, pushing, or insulting the opposite team; by getting into fights with other people in the stands; by throwing trash onto the playing field.)

Reading Vocabulary TRL

Help students preview the selection's vocabulary words by giving them copies of the Selection Glossary. Have pairs of students take turns making up a sentence using one of the words.

Motivation for Reading

Ask students if they have ever been annoyed by the behavior of fans of sports teams. Invite them to read this editorial to find out how one person felt about such bad behavior and what he did about it.

Discussion Questions

Suggest that students read the whole selection before they try to find the answers to notes in the margin of the student text.

A The Argentinean team wanted to be rid of the blame and guilt they felt as a result of losing the war with Britain. Note that part of the writer's point is that a game should not spur the same level of patriotic fervor that a war does.

B ASK **Comprehension** How does the explanatory note about Maradoña help you understand the text reference to him? (Without the note, one would not know what the "hand of God" incident involving Maradoña's hand was.)

Cup Inanity and Patriotic Profanity

Andrew Graham-Yooll,

From the *Buenos Aires Herald* (Thursday, July 2, 1998)

As you read, note the author's tone and point of view.

A What *vindication* might the Argentine team want?

B *Maradoña*, an Argentine soccer star, scored a goal in 1986 in a game against England. He used his hands illegally.

The Dutch team did beat Argentina later.

Argentina won the World Cup in 1978. That year the government arrested, tortured, and killed thousands of Argentinians.

What a wonderful victory for Argentina's soccer squad. **Self-congratulatory commentary** yesterday was also packed full of **plaudits** for the dozen or so **millionaires** who had taken such an outstanding step for the well-being of a nation.

Celebration was everywhere and the **significance** of beating England referred to patriotic **vindication** and other such inanities which filled every inch of air and available screen space. In truth, it helped Argentina to **definitively** overcome the "hand of God" incident in the 1986 World Cup involving Diego Armando Maradoña's paw, but victory was a squeak, and secured against a ten-man team. For a sense of sporting balance, it was OK. Balance requires, of course, that the Dutch thrash Argentina on Saturday.

Even if the national team wins, please, not another 1978, when people were being tortured in Sierra Chica prison while the patriotic mob were screaming their support for the tormentors in Government House. A few people may still be able to remember that: 1978 was also described as a sporting event.

commentary an explanation; a series of remarks

definitively finally; completely

millionaire a person with at least one million dollars

plaudits strong praise

self-congratulatory giving praise to oneself

significance the meaning; the importance

vindication proof that clears away blame or guilt

Name Date Period

Unit 6 *Vocabulary Workbook* 34

Cup Inanity and Patriotic Profanity

Directions Match each item in Column A with a detail or definition in Column B. Match Column C with Column D. Write the letter of each correct answer on the line.

Column A	Column B
______ 1. banality	a. a news writer's personal opinion about an event or topic
______ 2. commentary	b. an explanation
______ 3. consumption	c. completely
______ 4. debased	d. lowered in worth
______ 5. definitively	e. the period of time that something lasts
______ 6. dictatorial	f. a flag
______ 7. disciplinarian	g. dirty
______ 8. duration	h. an insulting word or phrase
______ 9. editorial	i. a person who strictly carries out rules
______ 10. ensign	j. having the powers of a strong, single ruler
______ 11. epithet	k. buying
______ 12. grubby	l. the quality of having little meaning

Column C	Column D
______ 1. makeshift	a. a heavy, sometimes mean-spirited kind of irony
______ 2. millionaire	b. a person with at least one million dollars
______ 3. onslaught	c. strong praise
______ 4. pensioner	d. giving praise to oneself
______ 5. plaudits	e. the importance of something
______ 6. racist	f. proof that clears away blame or guilt
______ 7. sarcasm	g. a temporary substitute
______ 8. self-congratulatory	h. a person who receives pay after retiring
______ 9. significance	i. referring to another race in an insulting way
______ 10. ungovernable	j. not possible to control
______ 11. vindication	k. a violent attack or charge

 World Literature

TRL

Vocabulary Workbook 34

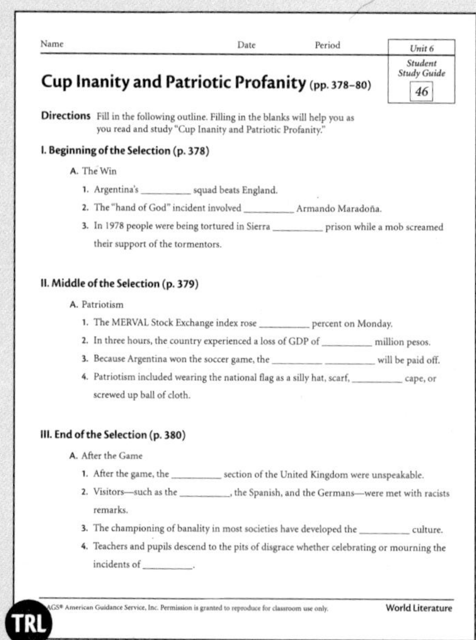

Name Date Period

Unit 6 *Student Study Guide* 46

Cup Inanity and Patriotic Profanity (pp. 378–80)

Directions Fill in the following outline. Filling in the blanks will help you as you read and study "Cup Inanity and Patriotic Profanity."

I. Beginning of the Selection (p. 378)

A. The Win

1. Argentina's ________ squad beats England.
2. The "hand of God" incident involved ________ Armando Maradoña.
3. In 1978 people were being tortured in Sierra ________ prison while a mob screamed their support of the tormentors.

II. Middle of the Selection (p. 379)

A. Patriotism

1. The MERVAL Stock Exchange index rose ________ percent on Monday.
2. In three hours, the country experienced a loss of GDP of ________ million pesos.
3. Because Argentina won the soccer game, the ________ ________ will be paid off.
4. Patriotism included wearing the national flag as a silly hat, scarf, ________ cape, or screwed up ball of cloth.

III. End of the Selection (p. 380)

A. After the Game

1. After the game, the ________ section of the United Kingdom were unspeakable.
2. Visitors—such as the ________, the Spanish, and the Germans—were met with racists remarks.
3. The championing of banality in most societies have developed the ________ culture.
4. Teachers and pupils descend to the pits of disgrace whether celebrating or mourning the incidents of ________.

 World Literature

TRL

Student Study Guide 46

However, Tuesday must have been really good for Argentina. The MERVAL Stock Exchange index rose four percent yesterday. And it had risen just under half a point just before the match started, against an average six months of decline. **C**

For the **duration** of the match, three hours all told, the country froze, with a loss of GDP of 230 million pesos, according to Perfil newspaper.

That hardly matters. As a result of Tuesday's score we are all going to be so patriotic that we can assume that the foreign debt will be paid off shortly, there will be no more poor in Argentina, unemployment will be something entirely unknown (and easily forgotten), **pensioners** will have a decent retirement, cheques with the relief for the small-holders who have lost everything outside Goya will be in the post tomorrow. And the Wizard of Oz will be made President on July 31.... **D**

The *peso* is the unit of money in Argentina. *GDP* stands for *Gross Domestic Product,* a measure of a country's economy.

Cheque is another spelling of *check.* Other British-style spellings, such as *centre,* are used later in the article.

On Tuesday patriotism meant filling the streets with litter from waste bins emptied out of office windows. The patriotic rubbish blocked drains and spread a carpet of filth over the city centre's streets. Patriotism was to wear the national **ensign** as a silly hat, scarf, Superman cape, screwed up ball of cloth....Patriotism was to trail this **makeshift** dress along the street, turning it **grubby** not in triumph but in neglect. Patriotism was to wave bottles of beer until they had been drunk dry and then fling the empty so as to smash a store window. Patriotism involves yelling **racist** insults presented as patriotic slogans, and using the most **debased** language to describe people who are different.

French police arrest an English hooligan before the World Cup match between England and Argentina in 1998.

debased lowered in worth

duration the period of time that something lasts

ensign a flag

grubby dirty

makeshift a temporary substitute

pensioner a person who receives pay after retiring

racist referring to another race in an insulting way

C ASK Comprehension Part of the irony in the editorial is that the writer points out rather sarcastically that fans assume a cause-effect relationship between the winning of a game and other circumstances. What is one example in the first paragraph on this page? (The stock exchange index rose for the first time in six months after the game had begun.) Is it likely that the match would have caused the stock to rise? Why or why not? (Probably not. People buying and selling stocks in companies are carrying out business too serious to be influenced by the outcome of a game.) Explain to students that Argentina is one of many countries whose people love soccer. There are many soccer competitions, culminating in the World Cup soccer matches held once every four years.

D ASK Critical Thinking How does the exaggeration in the third paragraph contribute to the satire? (It shows that any cause-effect relationship between the outcome of the game and other national affairs is clearly ridiculous to assume.)

Career Connection

Some students, especially those who have had some success with their writing, may be interested in careers as news writers for newspapers, magazines, or television. If possible, invite a local news writer to address interested students. Make sure students prepare in advance for the visit by listing questions they want to ask and information they want to find out.

Name Date Period Unit 6 Activity 65

Cup Inanity and Patriotic Profanity

Part A Directions In each blank choose the word or phrase from the Word Bank that best completes each sentence.

1. In England and Argentina, crowds sometimes gather in ________ after a game.
2. Comments that are ________ insult people who are from another race.
3. ________ is proof that clears away blame or guilt.
4. A person called a ________ receives pay after retiring from a job.
5. Another word for an athletic game or contest is ________.

Word Bank		
match	pensioner	pubs
racist	Vindication	

Part B Directions On the blank lines, write a short answer for each item.

1. What is a yob and why do yobs exist?
2. How does the author sarcastically describe "patriotic actions" by citizens, after the soccer match was won?
3. The author lists many positive things that will happen because of the win. Name two.
4. What two events were going on at the same time in 1978, in Argentina?
5. Define the term *sarcasm.*

 World Literature

TRL

Activity 65

Name Date Period Unit 6 Workbook 65

Cup Inanity and Patriotic Profanity

Part A Directions In each blank write the word or phrase from the Word Bank that best completes each sentence.

1. ________ is proof that clears away blame or guilt.
2. A person called a ________ receives pay after retiring from their job.
3. Comments that are ________ insult people who are from another race.
4. In England and Argentina, crowds sometimes gather in ________ after a game.
5. Another word for an athletic game or contest is ________.

Word Bank	
match	pensioner
pubs	racist
Vindication	

Part B Directions Write a short answer for each item on the blank lines.

1. The author lists many patriotic actions that will happen because of the win. Name two.
2. What two events were going on at the same time in 1978, in Argentina?
3. How does the author sarcastically describe patriotic behavior by citizens, after the win?
4. What is a *yob* and why do yobs exist?
5. Define the term *sarcasm.*

 World Literature

TRL

Workbook 65

Discussion Questions

A ASK Vocabulary The word *horde* is usually used to describe a group of animals moving together, such as a horde of horses. How does the writer's use of such a word in the first line on this page compare with Swift's use of the word *dam* to refer to a woman who has just borne a child? (Both writers intended to compare the human beings to animals. However, Swift wanted to show that one group of people thought of another group as animals. In this editorial, the writer wants the readers to think of this group of people—the soccer fans—as animals because of their behavior.)

B ASK Literary Elements Irony means making statements with exactly the opposite usual meaning of the words. For example, a person might complain that he or she needs something "the way I need a hole in the head." Obviously such a statement means that the person does *not* need whatever it is. Sarcasm is irony with a mean streak. Both devices are common in satire. Ask students to find an example of irony and an example of sarcasm in the selection. (Answers will vary. Examples of irony: the title phrase "patriotic profanity" or "patriotism meant filling the streets with litter. …" Examples of sarcasm: "the many applications of a limited language education" and "always room to praise the good administration of places such as Turkey or Saudi Arabia. …")

A No soccer horde has a monopoly on this behaviour and none is exempted.

Winston Churchill, or some other English worthy, once said that the British were **ungovernable**, except in war. And after the battle they were unspeakable.

This was much the case in many pubs throughout the English section of the United Kingdom yesterday.

French, Spanish, Germans and other visitors in England, who wanted to join in what they thought was sporting revelry (they obviously did not understand the natives), met with barrage after **onslaught** of drunken abuse and racist **epithets**
B which illustrated the many applications of a limited language education.

Yob is a slang expression for a hooligan or street criminal.

This sentence shows irony. Governments in *Turkey* and *Saudi Arabia* exert strict control.

The factors that have helped develop the yob culture, in Britain, Argentina, and wherever, are not the relaxation of rules, as some **disciplinarians** wish to have it, but the championing of **banality** in most societies that are described as advanced capitalist states—which is where the enterprising sell banality for mass **consumption**. (The so-called less-advanced societies are irrelevant here as they are mostly repressed by **dictatorial** rule of varying degrees of severity. However, there is always room to praise the good administration of places such as Turkey or Saudi Arabia, for example.)

Cricket, rugby, and soccer are all games that were taken to British colonies such as the *West Indies*.

Anyway, the magnificent Argentine victory on Tuesday provided the confirmation that the English inventors of many sports get thrashed by their pupils (by West Indians in cricket, South Africans in rugby, Argentines in soccer, and so on) with great regularity. And that confirms nothing more than that teachers and pupils descend to the pits of disgrace whether celebrating or mourning the incidents of wargames.

banality the quality of having little meaning

consumption buying

dictatorial having the powers of a strong, single ruler

disciplinarian a person who strictly carries out rules

epithet an insulting word or phrase

onslaught a violent attack or charge

ungovernable not possible to control

Environmental Connection

The rampaging behavior of the soccer fans described in this editorial included such actions as emptying wastebaskets out of office windows and throwing empty beer bottles to smash store windows. Discuss with students what the streets must have been like after the fans left. Ask students to consider how uncomfortable it would be for people to move through neighborhoods littered like this. Encourage them to discuss who cleans up these messes, who pays to clean up the mess, and who should. Help them conclude that we are all responsible for keeping our world clean.

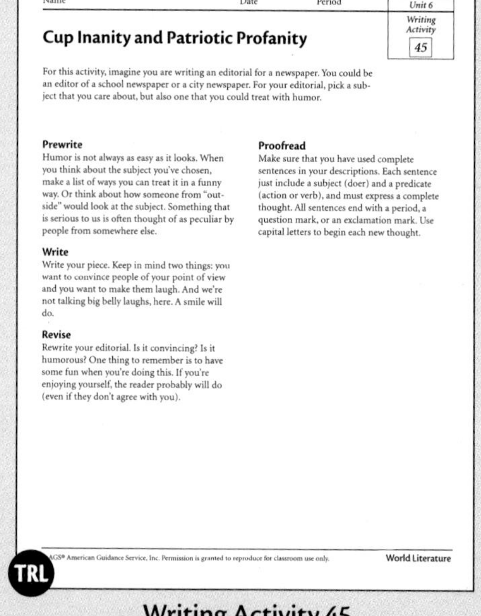

Name Date Period

Unit 6 *Writing Activity* 45

Cup Inanity and Patriotic Profanity

For this activity, imagine you are writing an editorial for a newspaper. You could be an editor of a school newspaper or a city newspaper. For your editorial, pick a subject that you care about, but also one that you could treat with humor.

Prewrite
Humor is not always as easy as it looks. When you think about the subject you've chosen, make a list of ways you can treat it in a funny way. Or think about how someone from "outside" would look at the subject. Something that is serious to us is often thought of as peculiar by people from somewhere else.

Write
Write your piece. Keep in mind two things: you want to convince people of your point of view and you want to make them laugh. And we're not talking big belly laughs, here. A smile will do.

Revise
Rewrite your editorial. Is it convincing? Is it humorous? One thing to remember is to have some fun when you're doing this. If you're enjoying yourself, the reader probably will do (even if they don't agree with you).

Proofread
Make sure that you have used complete sentences in your descriptions. Each sentence just include a subject (doer) and a predicate (action or verb), and must express a complete thought. All sentences end with a period, a question mark, or an exclamation mark. Use capital letters to begin each new thought.

 World Literature

TRL

Writing Activity 45

REVIEWING the SELECTION Cup Inanity and Patriotic Profanity

Andrew Graham-Yooll, From the *Buenos Aires Herald* (July 2, 1998)

Directions Write the answers to these questions using complete sentences.

Comprehension: Identifying Facts

1. What victory is being celebrated?
2. What happened in the Argentine economy after the match?
3. What were some of the actions of "patriotic" Argentinian soccer fans?

Comprehension: Understanding Main Ideas

4. What does the writer think causes the "yob culture"?
5. Where is the "yob culture" found?
6. When the writer speaks of "wargames," what does he mean?

Understanding Literature: Sarcasm

Sarcasm is a heavy, sometimes mean-spirited kind of irony. It can be personal and meant to hurt. Even the title of this editorial shows the author's harsh opinion.

7. The author pokes fun at the importance of the win by exaggerating its wonderful effects. What are some of the things he says will happen?
8. The writer describes foreigners in England trying to join in the *sporting revelry.* How is this phrase sarcastic?

Critical Thinking

9. In what ways did the losers and winners act the same after the match?
10. Explain the writer's comparison of two events in 1978. What is his point?

Writing on Your Own Think of some way you have seen people behave in public. Have you seen behavior that is mean or stupid? Write an editorial making fun of this type of behavior. Talk about groups only. Do not write about individuals.

Name Date Period | *Unit 6* *Selection Quiz* 40

Cup Inanity and Patriotic Profanity

Directions Read the following statements. Circle the letter of the answer that correctly completes each sentence or that correctly answers each question.

1. In the opening paragraph, the writer refers to Argentina's soccer squad as
   a. a bunch of hooligans. b. fops and yops. c. stars. d. a dozen or so millionaires.
2. Argentina's victory over England was hailed by many as
   a. fate. b. patriotic vindication. c. patriotic vilification. d. luck.
3. The writer refers to former Argentina star Diego
   a. Adona. b. Madonna. c. Digamo. d. Maradoña.
4. The writer asks people not to forget the year ________, when government torture occurred during the soccer celebrations.
   a. 1988 b. 1978 c. 1998 d. 1908
5. Which stock exchange rose after Argentina won?
   a. Dow Jones b. NASDAQ c. MERVAL d. Nikkei
6. During the match the country lost ________ of GDP, according to one newspaper.
   a. 2 percent b. 230 million pesos c. $3,000,000 d. 23 million pesos
7. The British are only governable during ________, the writer quotes someone as saying.
   a. holiday b. peace c. war d. weekends
8. The English, in their pubs, were
   a. laughing with foreigners. b. yelling at foreigners. c. feeding foreigners. d. giving foreigners money.
9. The writer worries about the championing of
   a. banality. b. America. c. England. d. civility.
10. The writer says that England always ________ at sports they invent.
   a. wins b. loses c. shouts d. celebrates

 World Literature

TRL

Selection Quiz 40

Selection Quiz

The Teacher's Resource Library includes a Selection Quiz for "Cup Inanity and Patriotic Profanity" that may be given following the Selection Review.

Reviewing the Selection

Answer Key

Comprehension: Identifying Facts

1. The victory being celebrated is the victory of Argentina over Great Britain in the World Cup soccer matches.

2. The stock market rose.

3. They dumped waste bins out of office windows, wore silly clothing, threw empty beer bottles through store windows, and shouted racist insults at people who were different from themselves.

Comprehension: Understanding Main Ideas

4. He thinks the "yob culture" is the result of the "championing of banality," or oversupporting activities such as soccer matches that have little important meaning.

5. It is found in Britain, Argentina, and other places, particularly those with soccer teams.

6. He feels that soccer fans blow the importance of the games way out of proportion—to the level of war.

Understanding Literature: Sarcasm

7. Among other things, he says the soccer win will result in the foreign debt being paid off, the elimination of poverty and unemployment, and so on.

8. The phrase is sarcastic because there is nothing of good sportsmanship in the celebration of the soccer fans.

Critical Thinking

9. The losers and the winners all joined the rowdy behavior.

10. He compares the 1978 victory of Argentina in the World Cup to the fact that in 1978 the government abused thousands of Argentineans. He hopes sarcastically that the current soccer victory will not result in similar "celebrations." Here he is also implying the kind of outrageous cause and effect that underscores the apparent seriousness with which the soccer fans connect the soccer victory to patriotism.

Suggest that students try to use examples of sarcasm and irony in their own editorials. Emphasize that, as the writer of this editorial did, they should write about the behavior of a group of people, not about individuals.

Columns

Ask students to read page 382. You may want to have several volunteers share reading the page aloud to the rest of the class.

Discuss the two quotations at the top of the page. Encourage students to theorize about the connection of the quotations to what they have been reading. How is it likely that "many true words are spoken in jest" in such things as newspaper columns and elsewhere? (Let discussion range; many students will see that humorists and comedians often illuminate the truth with humor.)

Invite volunteers to talk about being a "weird little kid" and how that background might help an adult be a writer. Students may recognize Katherine Paterson as a writer of books they have read such as *The Bridge to Terabithia* or *The Great Gilly Hopkins.* If so, invite them to comment on how the quotation seems to fit what they think they know of her from having read her books.

Point out to students that not all columnists are humor writers. However, all columnists express their own opinions and points of view in their columns. That is one important reason why a writer's column has a byline, which helps make it clear to readers that whatever is said in a column is the responsibility of the writer, not of the newspaper or magazine in which the column appears.

ASK What examples of columns have you read? (Answers will vary. Suggest that students bring examples to class of columns they have liked from various periodicals. These can be shared on a bulletin-board display or in a class period of oral readings.)

Columns

- "Many true words are spoken in jest." —Dinah Maria Mulock Craik
- "There are few things, apparently, more helpful to a writer than having once been a weird little kid." —Katherine Paterson

Columns are articles that appear regularly in periodicals. Their authors receive a by-line. A by-line tells who wrote an article. Columns are a popular form of humor. Hundreds of men and women write on the local level or for wider readership. They write about a range of topics. Columnists like Dave Barry began as local writers. But they became so popular that their articles now appear all over the world. Yet their columns still retain a local flavor. This appeals to many readers.

Following are selections by two columnists who write from the viewpoint of the average person. They struggle with parenting, work, and home repair. Readers recognize and share the stress of these activities. They enjoy relieving their tensions with a good laugh. This wide appeal has made these columns extremely popular, in America and abroad.

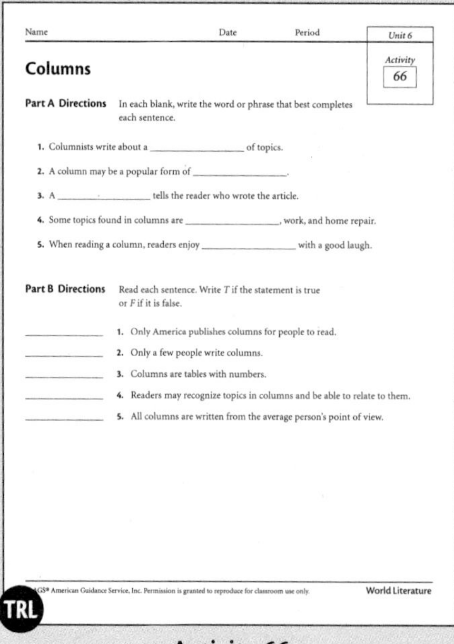

Name Date Period | *Unit 6* | *Activity* 66

Columns

Part A Directions In each blank, write the word or phrase that best completes each sentence.

1. Columnists write about a ____________ of topics.
2. A column may be a popular form of ____________.
3. A ____________ tells the reader who wrote the article.
4. Some topics found in columns are ____________, work, and home repair.
5. When reading a column, readers enjoy ____________ with a good laugh.

Part B Directions Read each sentence. Write *T* if the statement is true or *F* if it is false.

____ 1. Only America publishes columns for people to read.
____ 2. Only a few people write columns.
____ 3. Columns are tables with numbers.
____ 4. Readers may recognize topics in columns and be able to relate to them.
____ 5. All columns are written from the average person's point of view.

 World Literature

TRL

Activity 66

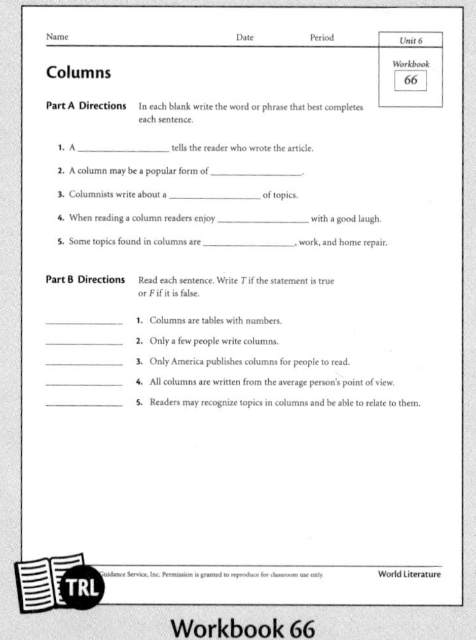

Name Date Period | *Unit 6* | *Workbook* 66

Columns

Part A Directions In each blank write the word or phrase that best completes each sentence.

1. A ____________ tells the reader who wrote the article.
2. A column may be a popular form of ____________.
3. Columnists write about a ____________ of topics.
4. When reading a column readers enjoy ____________ with a good laugh.
5. Some topics found in columns are ____________, work, and home repair.

Part B Directions Read each sentence. Write *T* if the statement is true or *F* if it is false.

____ 1. Columns are tables with numbers.
____ 2. Only a few people write columns.
____ 3. Only America publishes columns for people to read.
____ 4. All columns are written from the average person's point of view.
____ 5. Readers may recognize topics in columns and be able to relate to them.

 World Literature

TRL

Workbook 66

INTRODUCING the SELECTION

Staying at a Japanese Inn: Peace, Tranquillity, Insects

Dave Barry

Dave Barry
(1948–)
American

Literary Terms

column a regularly appearing article in a periodical

exaggeration a use of words to make something seem worse than it is; stretching the truth to a great extent

stereotype a simplified idea about another person

About the Author

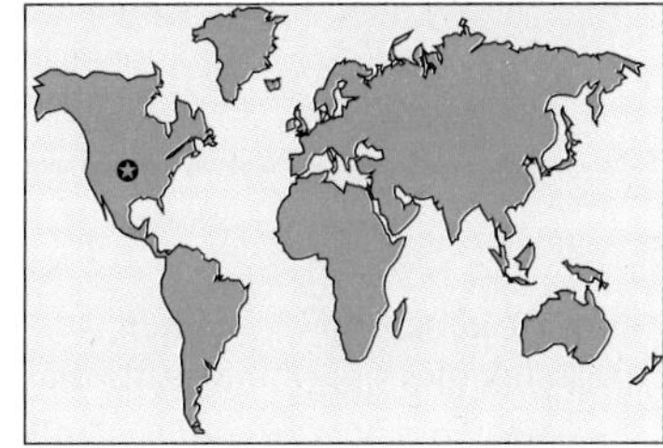

Dave Barry began his career writing for a small Pennsylvania newspaper. He later took a job with the Associated Press in Philadelphia and taught classes on writing. Soon, he began writing a weekly humor **column**. Impressed, the *Miami Herald* newspaper offered him a staff position. Subjects for Barry's column have included hopeless attempts at home repair, battles with the hardy plants and animals of the tropics, and more. Barry won the Pulitzer Prize for journalism in 1988. He now lives and writes in Miami.

About the Selection

Dave Barry's column is syndicated by the Knight-Ridder News Service. This means it appears weekly in newspapers all over America. Many of his columns concentrate on his own family's experiences. Barry traveled to Japan with his wife, Beth, and their son, Robby. *Dave Barry Does Japan* is about his experiences. The book uses cultural differences between the United States and Japan as the basis for humor. In this selection from the book, Barry uses many techniques to make us laugh. He uses **exaggeration** to make things seem worse or more extreme than they are. But he doesn't poke fun only at the Japanese. Barry uses American **stereotypes** about Japanese culture as a mirror to show us our own faults. A stereotype is a simplified idea about another person. At the same time, he shows stereotypes about Americans. Barry also uses sarcasm, but only lightly, to entertain.

Selection at a Glance

Staying at a Japanese Inn: Peace, Tranquillity, Insects

Dave Barry

Student pages 383–388

Overview

Dave Barry writes humorous columns that occasionally are satirical. He is one of many columnists who depend on their particularly wry and funny view of the world to entertain their readers.

Selection Summary

In "Staying at a Japanese Inn: Peace, Tranquillity, Insects," Dave Barry tells about trying to fit into a different culture.

Objectives

- To appreciate the humor in a newspaper column.
- To understand the use of exaggeration in humor.

Audiocassette 

Teacher's Resource Library TRL

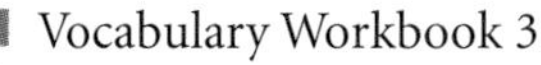

- Vocabulary Workbook 35
- Selection Glossary 41
- Student Study Guide 47
- Activity 67, pages 1–2
- Workbook 67, pages 1–2
- Writing Activity 46
- Selection Quiz 41

Setting the Stage for Reading

About the Author

Ask students to read the text and look at the picture. Mention that humor columnists like Dave Barry often are people who simply have a funny outlook on life and use that viewpoint in their writing. Barry's columns are very popular, so his type of humor is clearly appreciated by many people. In the early 1990s, the television show *Dave's World* was loosely based on Dave Barry's life.

ASK How might Barry's writing show the kind of person he is? (His personality and attitude toward life show in his columns; he clearly finds humor in daily events.)

About the Selection

Newspaper columns such as Dave Barry's are limited by space, and columnists quickly learn to write columns that are always about the same length. This particular selection, however, is a bit longer than a usual column because it is an excerpt from a book.

Activate Prior Knowledge: Invite students to describe other humorous columns they have read.

ASK How might cultural differences result in funny experiences? (As one example illustrates, awkward attempts to use other languages often lead to humorous misunderstandings.)

Reading Vocabulary TRL

Help students preview the selection's vocabulary words by giving them copies of the Selection Glossary. Have students work in small groups. One student chooses one of the words at random. The group member who defines the word correctly can choose another word for the group to define. Groups should continue until all words have been defined correctly.

Motivation for Reading

Invite students to imagine that they are visiting Japan. What unusual situations do they think they might encounter as they try to live for several days in this different culture? Suggest that they read the selection to find out how the Barry family's experience compares to what they imagine.

Discussion Questions

Use the questions in the margins of the student selection to help students focus and check their reading.

A ASK Literary Elements Is Barry exaggerating when he explains what his family said to the Japanese ladies? (probably; apparently they used some Japanese words but were not quite sure what they meant)

Staying at a Japanese Inn: Peace, Tranquillity, Insects

Dave Barry

As you read, note how the author uses exaggeration.

Kyoto is a city in Japan known for its beautiful sites. **A**

When we arrived in Kyoto, we took a cab to our inn, which was a **traditional** type of Japanese inn called a *ryokan.*[1] When we pulled up in front, three women in **kimonos** came out and began bowing and saying things in Japanese and picking up our luggage. Using our Japanese skills, we said "thank you" or possibly "good night," and we bowed, and they bowed some more, which was not easy for them to do while holding our luggage, and then we started to go into the inn, at which point the women started speaking excitedly and pointing at our shoes.

Japan has a thing about shoes. You can wear them into stores and **westernized** hotels and restaurants, but you're not supposed to wear them into homes or traditional inns. You're supposed to take your shoes off at the door and put on slippers. And then if you go to the bathroom, you're supposed to take off *those* slippers and put on *another* pair of slippers, which are just for the bathroom. This custom may seem silly, but there's a sound reason for it: It keeps foreigners confused. At least that's what it did for us. I was always forgetting to change **footwear**, plus the slippers were always too small for me, so to keep my feet in them, I had to kind of **mince** around.

Following the baggage-carrying *ryokan* ladies, I minced with Beth and Robby to our room, which was in the very simple, very

[1] Literally, "type of inn."

footwear anything worn on the feet

kimono a long, loose robe with wide sleeves and tied with a sash

mince to walk with very short steps

traditional referring to customs followed for many years

westernized influenced by European or American ways

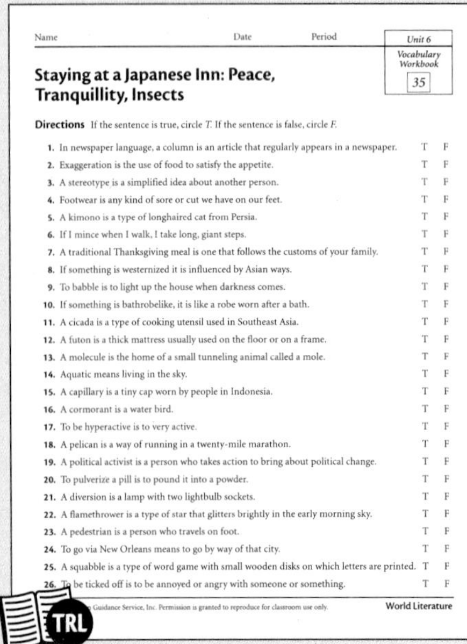

Name Date Period | Unit 6 Vocabulary Workbook 35

Staying at a Japanese Inn: Peace, Tranquillity, Insects

Directions If the sentence is true, circle *T.* If the sentence is false, circle *F.*

1. In newspaper language, a column is an article that regularly appears in a newspaper. T F
2. Exaggeration is the use of food to satisfy the appetite. T F
3. A stereotype is a simplified idea about another person. T F
4. Footwear is any kind of sore or cut we have on our feet. T F
5. A kimono is a type of longhaired cat from Persia. T F
6. If I mince when I walk, I take long, giant steps. T F
7. A traditional Thanksgiving meal is one that follows the customs of your family. T F
8. If something is westernized it is influenced by Asian ways. T F
9. To babble is to light up the house when darkness comes. T F
10. If something is bathrobelike, it is like a robe worn after a bath. T F
11. A cicada is a type of cooking utensil used in Southeast Asia. T F
12. A futon is a thick mattress usually used on the floor or on a frame. T F
13. A molecule is the home of a small tunneling animal called a mole. T F
14. Aquatic means living in the sky. T F
15. A capillary is a tiny cap worn by people in Indonesia. T F
16. A cormorant is a water bird. T F
17. To be hyperactive is to very active. T F
18. A pelican is a way of running in a twenty-mile marathon. T F
19. A political activist is a person who takes action to bring about political change. T F
20. To pulverize a pill is to pound it into a powder. T F
21. A diversion is a lamp with two lightbulb sockets. T F
22. A flamethrower is a type of star that glitters brightly in the early morning sky. T F
23. A pedestrian is a person who travels on foot. T F
24. To go via New Orleans means to go by way of that city. T F
25. A squabble is a type of word game with small wooden disks on which letters are printed. T F
26. To be ticked off is to be annoyed or angry with someone or something. T F

Guidance Service, Inc. Permission is granted to reproduce for classroom use only. World Literature

TRL

Vocabulary Workbook 35

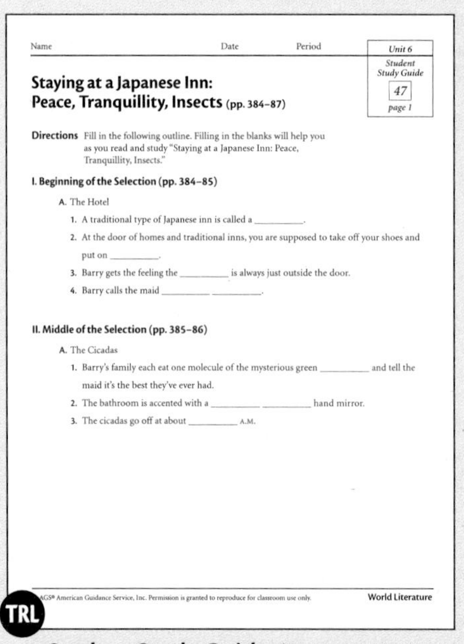

Name Date Period | Unit 6 Student Study Guide 47 page 1

Staying at a Japanese Inn: Peace, Tranquillity, Insects (pp. 384–87)

Directions Fill in the following outline. Filling in the blanks will help you as you read and study "Staying at a Japanese Inn: Peace, Tranquillity, Insects."

I. Beginning of the Selection (pp. 384–85)

A. The Hotel

1. A traditional type of Japanese inn is called a ________.
2. At the door of homes and traditional inns, you are supposed to take off your shoes and put on ________.
3. Barry gets the feeling the ________ is always just outside the door.
4. Barry calls the maid ________ ________.

II. Middle of the Selection (pp. 385–86)

A. The Cicadas

1. Barry's family each eat one molecule of the mysterious green ________ and tell the maid it's the best they've ever had.
2. The bathroom is accented with a ________ ________ hand mirror.
3. The cicadas go off at about ________ A.M.

AGS® American Guidance Service, Inc. Permission is granted to reproduce for classroom use only. World Literature

TRL

Student Study Guide 47, pages 1–2

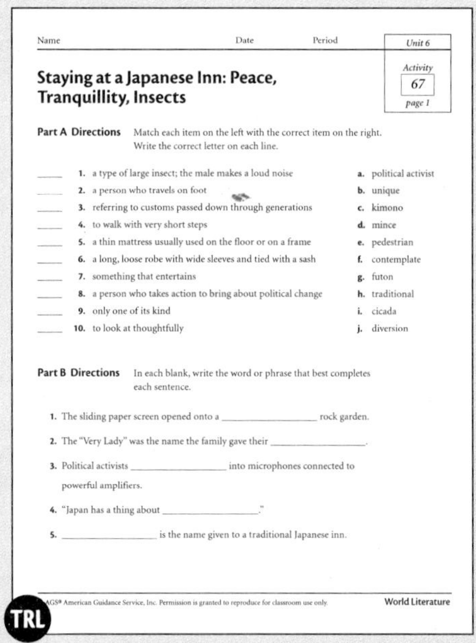

Name Date Period | Unit 6 Activity 67 page 1

Staying at a Japanese Inn: Peace, Tranquillity, Insects

Part A Directions Match each item on the left with the correct item on the right. Write the correct letter on each line.

____	1. a type of large insect; the male makes a loud noise	a. political activist
____	2. a person who travels on foot	b. unique
____	3. referring to customs passed down through generations	c. kimono
____	4. to walk with very short steps	d. mince
____	5. a thin mattress usually used on the floor or on a frame	e. pedestrian
____	6. a long, loose robe with wide sleeves and tied with a sash	f. contemplate
____	7. something that entertains	g. futon
____	8. a person who takes action to bring about political change	h. traditional
____	9. only one of its kind	i. cicada
____	10. to look at thoughtfully	j. diversion

Part B Directions In each blank, write the word or phrase that best completes each sentence.

1. The sliding paper screen opened onto a ________ rock garden.
2. The "Very Lady" was the name the family gave their ________.
3. Political activists ________ into microphones connected to powerful amplifiers.
4. "Japan has a thing about ________."
5. ________ is the name given to a traditional Japanese inn.

AGS® American Guidance Service, Inc. Permission is granted to reproduce for classroom use only. World Literature

TRL

Activity 67, pages 1–2

beautiful Japanese style, everything in light-colored wood. There was a sliding paper screen that opened up into a little **cicada**-infested rock garden with a brook **babbling** through it. The room had no beds or bureaus or chairs, only straw floor mats and a low table. In a *ryokan,* when you want to sleep, a maid comes in and puts down some **futons** for you. In fact, the maid comes in a lot; you got the feeling she was always just outside the door, day and night, ready to come in and do something for you. Our maid, who was wearing a kimono and a beeper, came in about thirty seconds after we arrived....

She said "*Hai domo!*" to us a lot. As far as I was able to determine, "*Hai domo!*" means "Yes, very!" We came to think of her as the Very Lady.

B

Do you think *hai domo* really means, *Yes, very!*?

She gestured to indicate that we should kneel with her around the low table, then she welcomed us to the *ryokan* **via** a nice little traditional ceremony wherein she poured us some tea and served us some kind of mysterious green substance. We smiled and bowed and drank the tea, and we each ate about one **molecule** of the green substance, and we smiled some more to indicate that it was the best darned mysterious green substance we had ever eaten and we would almost surely be wolfing it down later on.

C

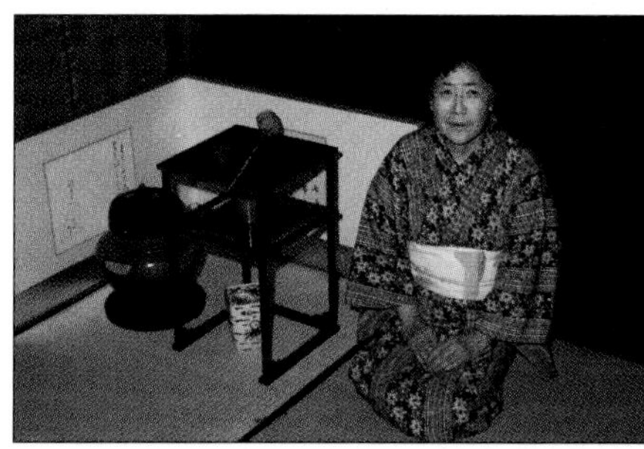

The traditional Japanese tea ceremony is called Chado.

Then the Very Lady showed us, via ancient traditional *ryokan* hand gestures, how to operate the TV remote control. She also showed us the bathroom, which was, like the rest of the inn, done in the beautiful, simple Japanese style, with lots of light-colored wood, accented by a Woody Woodpecker hand mirror.[2] The maid also showed us our *yukata,* which are lightweight **bathrobelike** garments that you're supposed to wear while you stroll (or, in my case, mince) around

---

[2] Here is another interesting ryokan bathroom fact: There was never any shampoo, but every day there were three new toothbrushes.

babble to make a low, quiet sound like water

bathrobelike like a robe worn after a bath

cicada a type of large insect; the males make a loud, humming noise

futon a thin mattress usually used on the floor or on a frame

molecule a tiny bit

via by way of

B *Hai domo* may not mean "Yes, very!" Most students will likely agree that Barry says this to point out the humor in trying to communicate in another language, just as he did on the previous page when he spoke of his family not quite knowing what they were saying in Japanese.

C ASK Critical Thinking Why do you suppose Barry refers to the snack his family was offered as "mysterious green substance"? (Again, he is trying to be funny, yet they probably really did not quite know what it was.)

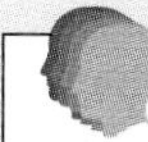

Diversity Connection

Small differences between cultural ways of doing things have often been both difficult and humorous for the people undergoing them. Ask volunteers for examples from their own or their family's experiences in moving from one culture to another or in visiting another culture. You may want to point out that because the United States is a "country of immigrants," many families have had to adjust to a new culture as they have moved to this country, either recently or several generations ago.

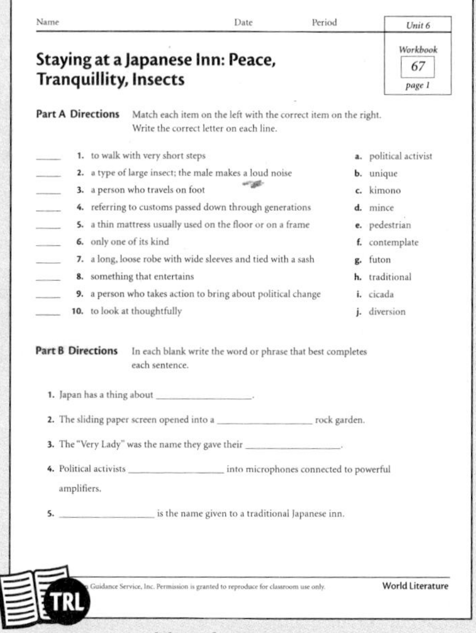

Name ____ Date ____ Period ____

Unit 6 — *Workbook* 67 *page 1*

Staying at a Japanese Inn: Peace, Tranquillity, Insects

Part A Directions Match each item on the left with the correct item on the right. Write the correct letter on each line.

____	**1.** to walk with very short steps	**a.**	political activist
____	**2.** a type of large insect; the male makes a loud noise	**b.**	unique
____	**3.** a person who travels on foot	**c.**	kimono
____	**4.** referring to customs passed down through generations	**d.**	mince
____	**5.** a thin mattress usually used on the floor or on a frame	**e.**	pedestrian
____	**6.** only one of its kind	**f.**	contemplate
____	**7.** a long, loose robe with wide sleeves and tied with a sash	**g.**	futon
____	**8.** something that entertains	**h.**	traditional
____	**9.** a person who takes action to bring about political change	**i.**	cicada
____	**10.** to look at thoughtfully	**j.**	diversion

Part B Directions In each blank write the word or phrase that best completes each sentence.

1. Japan has a thing about ____________.
2. The sliding paper screen opened into a ____________ rock garden.
3. The "Very Lady" was the name they gave their ____________.
4. Political activists ____________ into microphones connected to powerful amplifiers.
5. ____________ is the name given to a traditional Japanese inn.

 World Literature

TRL

Workbook 67, pages 1–2

Humorous Literature Unit 6 **385**

Discussion Questions

A Barry contrasts the peace-inducing surroundings of the Japanese *ryokan* with the harried pace of an American shopping mall as a way of making a humorous comment on the clash of cultures. In this case, the clash is not only of cultures but of times. Modern Japan is also a place of shopping malls and hyperactivity. However, America has no ancient tradition of quiet places designed for contemplation, as the Japanese do.

B Barry is using exaggeration when he mentions that the cicadas had amplifiers. In the following paragraph, he again implies the lack of understanding between Japanese and English when he stumbles over the meaning of the word *cormorant,* confusing it probably with *cornet* (a type of trumpet). Actually, *cormorant* is an English word—which makes this even funnier: Barry is so persuaded that Japanese words are confusing that he finds an English word in a Japanese setting confusing!

Community Connection

Political activists are part of most societies. Ask students to name local examples as well as others worldwide that they know of. Suggest people who walk on picket lines or protesters who hold up signs at meetings as several possible American examples. Invite students to compare these activities with those of the Japanese political activists Barry describes. What effect are these activities likely to have on people observing them? (In many cases, people are annoyed by such activities rather than persuaded, as the activists hope.)

A How does Barry poke fun at ancient cultures meeting modern times in this paragraph?

B What kind of humor is Barry using here?

the *ryokan.* The idea is that you become extremely relaxed and contemplate the rock garden and listen to the brook babble and the cicadas chatter until you achieve total inner peace. Or, if you are a typical **hyperactive** American suburban mall-oriented family like us, you go stark raving mad.

Maybe the problem was that the cicadas went off at about 4:30 a.m. and apparently had gotten hold of small but powerful amplifiers. So between them and the sudden unexpected appearances of the Very Lady, we never got quite enough sleep in the *ryokan....*

Another interesting thing to do in the Kyoto area is go see the **cormorant** fishing. This is a unique and traditional and weird method of catching fish using cormorants, which are a type of musical instrument similar to the trumpet.

No, just kidding. Cormorants are a type of **aquatic** bird sort of like **pelicans.** They're used in a centuries-old nighttime fishing technique still practiced in a few places, including a town near Kyoto called Uji. We took a train out there one evening, and found it to be a pleasant little river village, nice and peaceful except for a man at the train station shouting angrily over a huge truck-mounted public-address system. That's what **political activists** do in Japan: They shout angrily at you over powerful amplifiers turned up loud enough to **pulverize** concrete. As a persuasive technique, this leaves much to be desired. We saw quite a few of these trucks in Tokyo, and nobody paid any attention; everybody just walked briskly past.

This is smart. If you stood still and listened, you'd be deaf as a tire iron within minutes. So if the activists ever *did* attract any followers, they'd have a...time carrying out whatever political actions they had in mind:

"WE MUST STRENGTHEN OUR MILITARY!"

"WHAT DID HE SAY?"

"HE SAYS HE WANTS TO LENGTHEN OUR **CAPILLARIES**."

"NO, THANKS, I ALREADY ATE."

aquatic living in or one water

capillary a tiny blood vessel

cormorant a water bird

hyperactive very active

pelican a large bird whose bill has a pouch that holds fish

political activist a person who takes action to bring about political change

pulverize to pound into a powder

Anyway, we walked briskly away from the angry shouting man at the Uji station, and I asked a **pedestrian** for directions, using the international symbol for cormorant fishing, which is when you have one hand pretend to be a cormorant and swoop down on the other hand, which is pretending to be a fish.

He aimed us toward the river, where we found fishermen preparing some long, narrow wooden boats. At the end of each boat was a pole sticking out over the water; suspended from this was a wire basket in which the fishermen had built a log fire. The purpose of the fire is to attract the fish, although why a creature who lives under water would be attracted to fire is beyond me. Perhaps these are unusually stupid fish.

When night had fallen and the fires were burning brightly, the fishermen brought out some baskets, three per boat, each one containing two cormorants. The men put leashes around each bird's neck, looped so that the bird could get a fish into its mouth but not swallow it. Then the men pushed off from shore and started drifting down the river, two men controlling each boat and a third man in front, near the burning basket, holding leashes attached to the six cormorants, who swam around and **squabbled** with each other. **D**

At first this approach didn't look terribly practical; my impression was that it would be a lot less trouble to try to scoop up the fish with trumpets. But it turned out that cormorants, once they stopped squabbling, did a pretty good job. They'd disappear under water, and every third or fourth time they'd come up with a fish. Whenever this happened, the leash man would haul the cormorant in, snatch the fish away, and shove the cormorant back out. You'd think eventually the cormorants would get **ticked off** about this, maybe start plotting acts of revenge....But I guess the cormorants aren't a whole lot smarter than the fish.

Still, it made for a pleasant evening's **diversion**, a uniquely Japanese experience, and we were in a good mood as we headed back to our little Kyoto *ryokan,* with its peaceful babbling brook and its cheerfully chattering cicadas. Someday I will go back and kill them with a **flamethrower**.

C
Could the scene at the *Uji station* happen in the United States?

diversion something that entertains

flamethrower a military weapon that sends out a stream of burning fuel

pedestrian a person who travels on foot

squabble to quarrel; to argue about something small

ticked off a slang term meaning to be annoyed or angry

C Students may agree that the political activity at the train station could happen in the United States. And it would be possible for people from another country to ask their way in a United States train station by using gestures.

D ASK Comprehension Why do you think some Japanese catch fish by using cormorants as Barry describes? (Probably just to please tourists; it is an inefficient and slow method to get fish when modern techniques are available. However, it is historic and picturesque.)

Learning Styles

Tactile/Kinesthetic Students whose dominant learning modality is tactile/kinesthetic will appreciate the way Barry asked a pedestrian for directions to the cormorant fishing. Invite volunteers to demonstrate Barry's gestures. Similarly, students can pantomime several scenes in Barry's story, such as Barry putting on the too-small slippers and walking in them, the tea ceremony, and so on.

Humorous Literature Unit 6 **387**

Reviewing the Selection

Answer Key

Comprehension: Identifying Facts

1. Some features of a typical Japanese inn include the demand that guests wear slippers instead of shoes; furnishings of straw mats and low tables; and futons brought in for sleeping only at night.

2. In a traditional inn people sleep on mats called futons.

3. Cormorants are birds used to catch fish.

Comprehension: Understanding Main Ideas

4. The Japanese custom requires people to leave their shoes outside and wear slippers when inside a house.

5. The Japanese method of relaxation is to enjoy the rock garden, the brook, and the cicadas. This didn't work well for the Barrys, who are typical Americans used to a hectic pace of life.

6. There are several examples of old meeting new, particularly across cultures. One is the method of relaxation. Another is the tea ceremony. Perhaps the most colorful is the cormorant fishing.

Understanding Literature: Exaggeration

7. Barry says they had apparently "gotten hold of small but powerful amplifiers."

8. Barry says he will go back to Japan someday and kill the cicadas with flamethrowers.

Critical Thinking

9. One conflict in the story is between the expectations of the Barry family and the way the inn is operated. For example, the cicadas bothered the Barrys but were clearly assumed to be a nice touch for the inn.

10. Most students will have found the story humorous. Encourage them to explain what they found funny.

Writing on Your Own Suggest that students consider an American custom that a visitor from a foreign country might notice right away, as the Barrys noticed the Japanese custom about shoes.

Selection Quiz

The Teacher's Resource Library includes a Selection Quiz for "Staying at a Japanese Inn: Peace, Tranquillity, Insects" that may be given following the Selection Review.

REVIEWING the SELECTION

Staying at a Japanese Inn: Peace, Tranquillity, Insects

Dave Barry

Directions Write the answers to these questions using complete sentences.

Comprehension: Identifying Facts

1. What are the features of a typical Japanese inn?
2. What do you sleep on in a traditional inn?
3. What are cormorants, and how are they used in Japan?

Comprehension: Understanding Main Ideas

4. Describe the Japanese custom about shoes.
5. How well does the Japanese method of relaxing work for the Barrys? Why or why not?
6. Give an example of old meeting new in this story.

Understanding Literature: Exaggeration

Exaggeration is a special use of words. It makes something seem far better or worse than it really is. It stretches the truth to a great extent. Exaggeration is common in everyday speech. Here are some examples: "He eats everything in sight." "You've grown as tall as a tree."

7. How does Barry exaggerate the noise the cicadas make?
8. Give one more example of exaggeration in this column.

Critical Thinking

9. Several conflicts are shown in this story. Describe one.
10. Did you think this story was funny? Why or why not?

Writing on Your Own Think of a typical American custom. Choose something small, like the Japanese custom with shoes. Imagine how this custom might look to someone from another country. Write a description of it from that point of view. Use exaggeration.

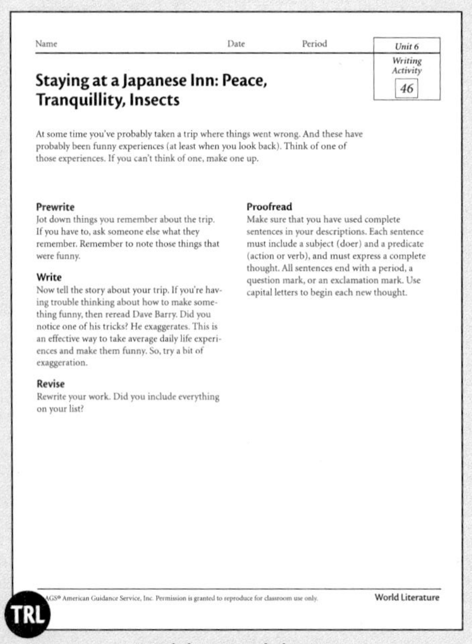

Name Date Period | *Unit 6* *Writing Activity* 46

Staying at a Japanese Inn: Peace, Tranquillity, Insects

At some time you've probably taken a trip where things went wrong. And these have probably been funny experiences (at least when you look back). Think of one of those experiences. If you can't think of one, make one up.

Prewrite
Jot down things you remember about the trip. If you have to, ask someone else what they remember. Remember to note those things that were funny.

Write
Now tell the story about your trip. If you're having trouble thinking about how to make something funny, then reread Dave Barry. Did you notice one of his tricks? He exaggerates. This is an effective way to take average daily life experiences and make them funny. So, try a bit of exaggeration.

Revise
Rewrite your work. Did you include everything on your list?

Proofread
Make sure that you have used complete sentences in your descriptions. Each sentence must include a subject (doer) and a predicate (action or verb), and must express a complete thought. All sentences end with a period, a question mark, or an exclamation mark. Use capital letters to begin each new thought.

 World Literature

TRL

Writing Activity 46

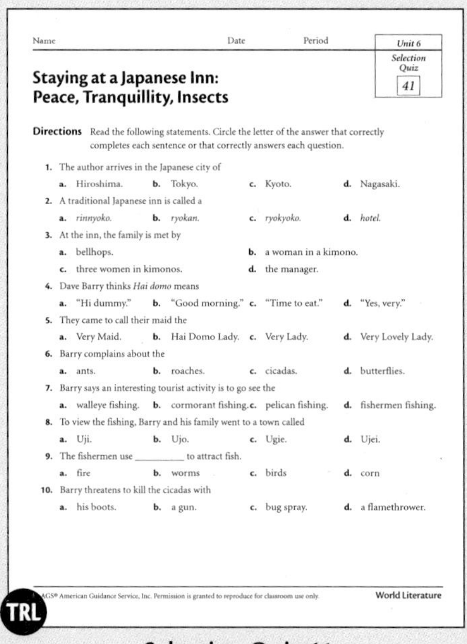

Name Date Period | *Unit 6* *Selection Quiz* 41

Staying at a Japanese Inn: Peace, Tranquillity, Insects

Directions Read the following statements. Circle the letter of the answer that correctly completes each sentence or that correctly answers each question.

1. The author arrives in the Japanese city of
   a. Hiroshima. b. Tokyo. c. Kyoto. d. Nagasaki.
2. A traditional Japanese inn is called a
   a. *rinnyoko.* b. *ryokan.* c. *ryokyoko.* d. *hotel.*
3. At the inn, the family is met by
   a. bellhops. b. a woman in a kimono. c. three women in kimonos. d. the manager.
4. Dave Barry thinks *Hai domo* means
   a. "Hi dummy." b. "Good morning." c. "Time to eat." d. "Yes, very."
5. They came to call their maid the
   a. Very Maid. b. Hai Domo Lady. c. Very Lady. d. Very Lovely Lady.
6. Barry complains about the
   a. ants. b. roaches. c. cicadas. d. butterflies.
7. Barry says an interesting tourist activity is to go see the
   a. walleye fishing. b. cormorant fishing. c. pelican fishing. d. fishermen fishing.
8. To view the fishing, Barry and his family went to a town called
   a. Uji. b. Ujo. c. Ugie. d. Ujei.
9. The fishermen use ________ to attract fish.
   a. fire b. worms c. birds d. corn
10. Barry threatens to kill the cicadas with
   a. his boots. b. a gun. c. bug spray. d. a flamethrower.

 World Literature

TRL

Selection Quiz 41

INTRODUCING the SELECTION

Why Can't We Have Our Own Apartment?

Erma Bombeck

Erma Bombeck
(1927–1996)
American

Literary Term

theme the main idea of a literary work

About the Author

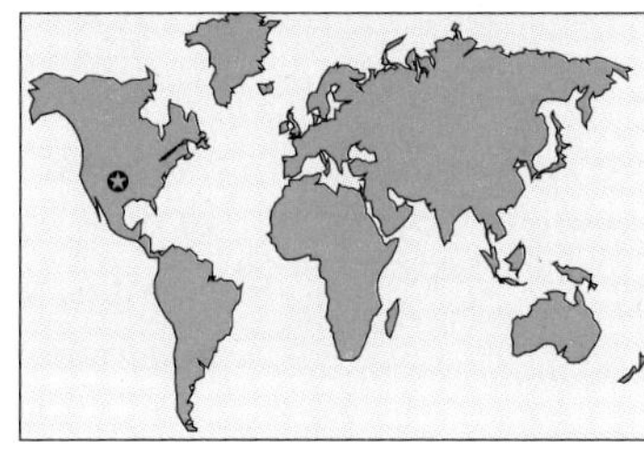

Erma Bombeck grew up, went to college, married a teacher, and started a family. She found family concerns amusing, boring, and frustrating. As her family grew, she began sharing her feelings in newspapers. In 1964 she began to write a humor column for a weekly paper in suburban Dayton, Ohio. The next year her column moved to a larger newspaper. Soon it was syndicated, or distributed to newspapers all over the country. Bombeck's column, "At Wit's End," appeared several times a week. Some six hundred papers carried it.

Bombeck survived the Great Depression. That may have helped her develop her sense of humor. Her humor has amused millions of readers. Bombeck collected her impressions in several best-selling books. The titles of them are jokes themselves. Some of her most popular books are *Just Wait Until You Have Children* and *The Grass Is Always Greener Over the Septic Tank*.

About the Selection

The following selection is from *If Life Is a Bowl of Cherries—What Am I Doing in the Pits?* It was published in 1978. Bombeck writes as a middle-aged parent and homemaker. She deals with the challenges and irritations of grown children. Her basic **themes,** or topics, are the small questions of daily family life. A theme is the main idea of a literary work.

Selection at a Glance

Why Can't We Have Our Own Apartment?

Erma Bombeck

Student pages 389–392

Overview

Like fellow columnist Dave Barry, Erma Bombeck saw humor in everyday life. Her perspective was a bit different, however—she wrote mainly about life as a homemaker and parent. Her humor resonated with so many people that her columns and books were immensely popular.

Selection Summary

In "Why Can't We Have Our Own Apartment?," parents switch roles with children and ask to move out.

Objectives

- To understand the theme of a literary work.
- To see how role reversal can be both humorous and enlightening.

Audiocassette 

Teacher's Resource Library 

- Vocabulary Workbook 36, pages 1–2
- Selection Glossary 42
- Student Study Guide 48
- Activity 68
- Workbook 68
- Writing Activity 47
- Selection Quiz 42

Setting the Stage for Reading

About the Author

Ask students to read the text and look at the picture. Explain that for many years Erma Bombeck's newspaper columns and books were extremely popular. She put her unique humorous twist on the daily life experiences of millions of people.

ASK Why do you suppose readers enjoyed Bombeck's humor about daily life? (They could identify with the situations and the fact that she could put a humorous twist on things they didn't necessarily find funny.)

About the Selection

Bombeck had a good ear for dialogue, which shows in this column when the parents and teenagers talk about the parents' desire to move out and get their own apartment. Because some of the humor lies in the role reversal, the words of the teenagers and the parents are more likely to have been those of the opposite roles.

Activate Prior Knowledge: Invite students to think about situations in which they and adults might trade places.

ASK What would it be like if we changed places? How would you like to teach the class? What might be humorous about the exchange if I were the student? (Answers will vary, but lead students, if necessary, to emphasize the potential humor in such a situation.)

Reading Vocabulary TRL

Help students preview the selection's vocabulary words by giving them copies of the Selection Glossary. Review the words by having pairs of students take turns saying sentences using the words.

Motivation for Reading

Suggest that students read the column to discover the humor in parents acting like teenagers and vice-versa.

Discussion Questions

Suggest that students use the questions in the margins of the student selection to check their understanding as they read.

A ASK Literary Elements You may want to remind students that the theme of a piece of writing is its main idea. As they read, suggest they consider what the column is really about to identify its theme. From the title of the column, what do you think might be its theme? (Someone wants to move into their own apartment, presumably away from the family.)

B ASK Comprehension Who is having the conversation? (Two parents and their three children, who are all apparently teenagers.)

Learning Styles

Auditory Because this short column is mainly dialogue, it provides a perfect opportunity for auditory learners to act it out. Ask volunteers to play the five parts and divide up the dialogue. Invite a sixth to read the narrative. Then have the "cast" read their parts. Encourage students to read with expression as they think the characters would have sounded.

A Why Can't We Have Our Own Apartment?

Erma Bombeck

As you read, think about the theme of the column. Keep track of who is saying each line.

We knew the kids would take it the wrong way, but we had to do it anyway.

B "Children," we said, "your father and I want to get our own apartment."

One looked up from his homework and the other two even turned down the volume on the TV set. "What are you saying?"

"We are saying we'd like to move out and be on our own for a while."

"But why?" asked our daughter. "Aren't you happy here? You have your own room and the run of the house."

"I know, but a lot of parents our age are striking out on their own."

"It'll be expensive," said our son. "Have you thought about **utilities** and phone bills and newspapers and a hundred little things you take for granted around here?"

"We've thought it all through."

"Spit it out," said our daughter. "What's bothering you about living with us? Did we ask too much? What did we ask you to do? Only cook, make beds, do laundry, take care of the

utility a household service, such as electricity, telephone, or water

Name Date Period

Unit 6 *Vocabulary Workbook* 36 *page 1*

Why Can't We Have Our Own Apartment?/Lohengrin

Directions For each definition below, circle the word being defined.

1. A ____________ is the main idea of a literary work.
   satire setting theme
2. A ____________ is a household service, such as electricity, telephone, or water.
   utility appliance suite
3. In "Why Can't We Have Our Own Apartment?" Bombeck tells her children that she wants to move out and to take with her a few small ____________, or pieces of household equipment, such as a toaster.
   utilities appliances suites
4. She also wants to take her bedroom ____________, which is the matched set of furniture in her bedroom.
   appliance suite linens
5. Finally, she wants to take some ____________, or household goods made of cloth, such as sheets and towels.
   appliances stereos linens
6. She wants to leave so that she can play her ____________, or sound equipment, without the children complaining.
   stereo appliance suite
7. A piece of writing that is ____________ tells about the author's life.
   autobiographical biographical parody
8. A ____________ is an exaggerated look at a situation
   setting biography parody
9. In "Lohengrin," Slezak makes fun of the opera he starred in and ____________, or makes known, the somewhat amusing plot of the opera.
   complicates sues reveals
10. He says that operas tend to be ____________ and that the audience must pay close attention to figure out what is going on.
    complicated parody archduke
11. The canary in an opera may turn out to be the ____________ of royal rank, who had been changed into a bird because of someone's jealousy.
    archduke random complicate

 World Literature

TRL

Vocabulary Workbook 36, pages 1–2

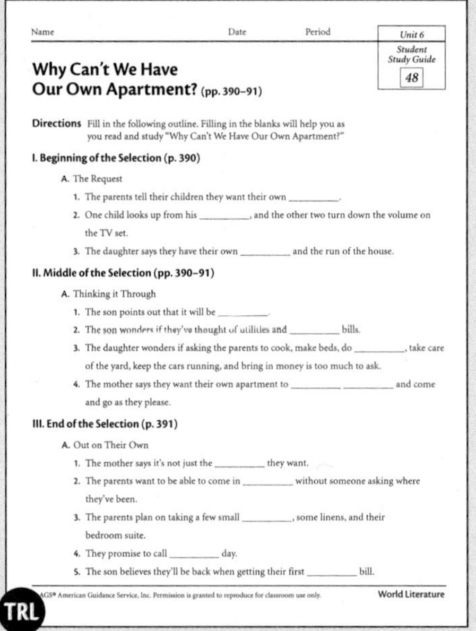

Name Date Period

Unit 6 *Student Study Guide* 48

Why Can't We Have Our Own Apartment? (pp. 390–91)

Directions Fill in the following outline. Filling in the blanks will help you as you read and study "Why Can't We Have Our Own Apartment?"

I. Beginning of the Selection (p. 390)

A. The Request
1. The parents tell their children they want their own __________.
2. One child looks up from his __________, and the other two turn down the volume on the TV set.
3. The daughter says they have their own __________ and the run of the house.

II. Middle of the Selection (pp. 390–91)

A. Thinking it Through
1. The son points out that it will be __________.
2. The son wonders if they've thought of utilities and __________ bills.
3. The daughter wonders if asking the parents to cook, make beds, do __________, take care of the yard, keep the cars running, and bring in money is too much to ask.
4. The mother says they want their own apartment to __________ __________ and come and go as they please.

III. End of the Selection (p. 391)

A. Out on Their Own
1. The mother says it's not just the __________ they want.
2. The parents want to be able to come in __________ without someone asking where they've been.
3. The parents plan on taking a few small __________, some linens, and their bedroom suite.
4. They promise to call __________ day.
5. The son believes they'll be back when getting their first __________ bill.

 World Literature

TRL

Student Study Guide 48

yard, keep the cars in running order and bring in the money. Was that so hard?"

"It's not that," I said gently. "It's just that we want to fix up **D** our own apartment and come and go as we please."

"If it's your car you wanted, why didn't you say so? We could make arrangements."

"It's not just the car. We want to be able to play our **stereos** when we want to and come in late without someone saying, 'Where have you been?' and invite people over without other people hanging around eating our chip dip."

"What will you do for furniture?"

"We don't need all that much. We'll just take a few small **appliances**, some **linens**, our bedroom **suite**, the typewriter, the luggage, the card table and chairs, the old TV you never use, and some pots and pans and a few tables and chairs."

"You'll call everyday?"

We nodded.

As we headed for the car I heard one son whisper sadly, "Wait till they get their first utility bill. They'll be back."

What family member would you expect to say what the daughter is saying? **C**

appliance a piece of household equipment, such as a toaster, stove, or microwave

linens household goods made of cloth, such as sheets and towels

stereo sound equipment, often used to play music

suite a matched set of furniture

C A parent would be expected to say what the daughter does regarding what could be so hard about living at home.

D ASK Critical Thinking Contrast the parents in the column to ordinary parents of teenagers. How are they alike? How are they different? (The parents in the column are behaving the way most teenagers do when they demand that they be allowed to move into their own apartment because they want to be independent. So they are not behaving much like ordinary parents.)

Writing Connection

The column is made up almost entirely of dialogue. Point out to students the importance of properly using quotation marks and words that identify the speaker when they write dialogue. Suggest they look carefully at some of the techniques used by Bombeck in the column, including (1) a different speaker's words always begin a new paragraph, (2) a speaker's words are always enclosed in quotation marks, (3) words identifying the speaker are provided, especially when necessary for clarity. Words identifying the speaker are separated from the quotation marks by a comma.

You may want to allow pairs of students to work together to write a dialogue between two people in order to practice using these devices.

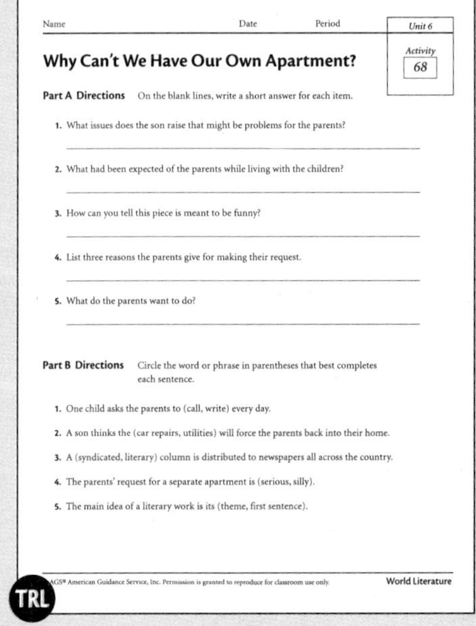

Name Date Period Unit 6 Activity 68

Why Can't We Have Our Own Apartment?

Part A Directions On the blank lines, write a short answer for each item.

1. What issues does the son raise that might be problems for the parents?
2. What had been expected of the parents while living with the children?
3. How can you tell this piece is meant to be funny?
4. List three reasons the parents give for making their request.
5. What do the parents want to do?

Part B Directions Circle the word or phrase in parentheses that best completes each sentence.

1. One child asks the parents to (call, write) every day.
2. A son thinks the (car repairs, utilities) will force the parents back into their home.
3. A (syndicated, literary) column is distributed to newspapers all across the country.
4. The parents' request for a separate apartment is (serious, silly).
5. The main idea of a literary work is its (theme, first sentence).

 World Literature

TRL

Activity 68

Name Date Period Unit 6 Workbook 68

Why Can't We Have Our Own Apartment?

Part A Directions Write a short answer for each item on the blank lines.

1. How can you tell this piece is meant to be funny?
2. What do the parents want to do?
3. List three reasons the parents give for making their request.
4. What issues does the son raise that might be problems for the parents?
5. What had been expected of the parents while living with the children?

Part B Directions Circle the word or phrase in parentheses that best completes each sentence.

1. A (syndicated, literary) column is distributed to newspapers all across the country.
2. The main idea of a literary work is its (theme, first sentence).
3. The parents' request for a separate apartment is (serious, silly).
4. One child asks the parents to (call, write) every day.
5. A son thinks the (car repairs, utilities) will force the parents back into their home.

 World Literature

TRL

Workbook 68

Comprehension

Inferring Time Relationships Introducing the Selection on page 389 states that this selection is from a book published in 1978. Ask students what clues they can pick up throughout the selection that tell them the column was written over twenty years ago. If necessary, help them point out dated examples of daily life such as playing "stereos," eating "chip dip," and using a typewriter.

Reviewing the Selection

Answer Key

Comprehension: Identifying Facts

1. The family members include two parents and three children. One child is a daughter, another a son. We're not sure whether the third child is a son or a daughter.

2. The parents want to move out and have an apartment of their own.

3. Their son points out that it will be expensive and that they must think of utility bills and other things they take for granted while they are living at home.

Comprehension: Understanding Main Ideas

4. More typically it is teenagers who wish they could move out and have their own place, and adult parents who caution them that it would not be as simple and carefree as they think.

5. Bombeck's children must have complained about wanting to come and go as they please, using the car, playing their stereos whenever they want, coming in late without criticism, and inviting friends over whenever they want.

6. The parents expect to take a few items of furniture including some small appliances and an old TV.

Understanding Literature: Theme

7. The theme, or main idea, of this piece is the desire for independence.

8. Bombeck makes the theme funny through the device of role reversal. It is funny to think that parents might want to be independent of their teenaged children.

Critical Thinking

9. Apparently the Bombeck children have frequently wanted to use the family car.

10. Answers will vary, but many students will find the role reversal itself very funny.

Tell students to try to make their point of view humorous as they write their sentences.

Selection Quiz

The Teacher's Resource Library includes a Selection Quiz for "Why Can't We Have Our Own Apartment?" that may be given following the Selection Review.

REVIEWING the SELECTION

Why Can't We Have Our Own Apartment?

Erma Bombeck

Directions Write the answers to these questions using complete sentences.

Comprehension: Identifying Facts

1. Who are the family members featured in this column?
2. What do the parents want to do?
3. What problems does the son raise?

Comprehension: Understanding Main Ideas

4. How are roles reversed in this story?
5. What are some of the things the children must have complained about?
6. What kinds of things do the parents plan to take with them?

Understanding Literature: Theme

Theme is the main idea of a literary work. The theme may be a large question, such as what is the meaning of life. It may be an idea or motive such as love, greed, or ambition. A theme can also be simpler ideas, such as the quirks of everyday living.

7. What is the theme of this piece?
8. How does the writer make her treatment of the theme funny?

Critical Thinking

9. What can you conclude about the use of the car in this family?
10. What part of this piece did you find funniest? Explain.

Writing on Your Own In this piece, Bombeck describes a scene that may be like something she actually thought about doing in her family. Think of something you might like to do about your family life but never have done. Write a few sentences telling what you want to do. Tell why you want to do it and whether you think you might really do it.

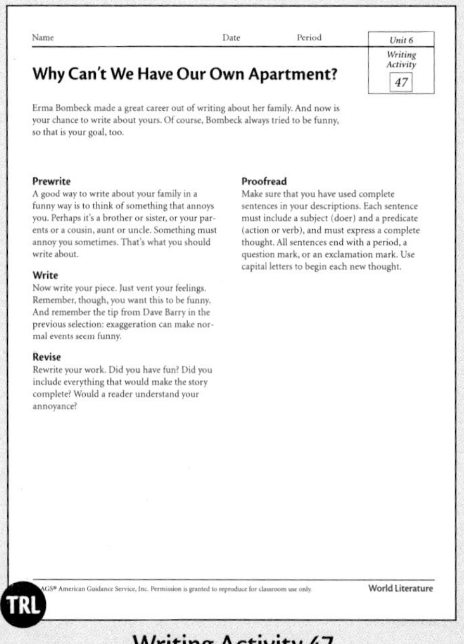
Name Date Period | *Unit 6* *Writing Activity* 47

Why Can't We Have Our Own Apartment?

Erma Bombeck made a great career out of writing about her family. And now is your chance to write about yours. Of course, Bombeck always tried to be funny, so that is your goal, too.

Prewrite
A good way to write about your family in a funny way is to think of something that annoys you. Perhaps it's a brother or sister, or your parents or a cousin, aunt or uncle. Something must annoy you sometimes. That's what you should write about.

Write
Now write your piece. Just vent your feelings. Remember, though, you want this to be funny. And remember the tip from Dave Barry in the previous selection: exaggeration can make normal events seem funny.

Revise
Rewrite your work. Did you have fun? Did you include everything that would make the story complete? Would a reader understand your annoyance?

Proofread
Make sure that you have used complete sentences in your descriptions. Each sentence must include a subject (doer) and a predicate (action or verb), and must express a complete thought. All sentences end with a period, a question mark, or an exclamation mark. Use capital letters to begin each new thought.

 World Literature

TRL

Writing Activity 47

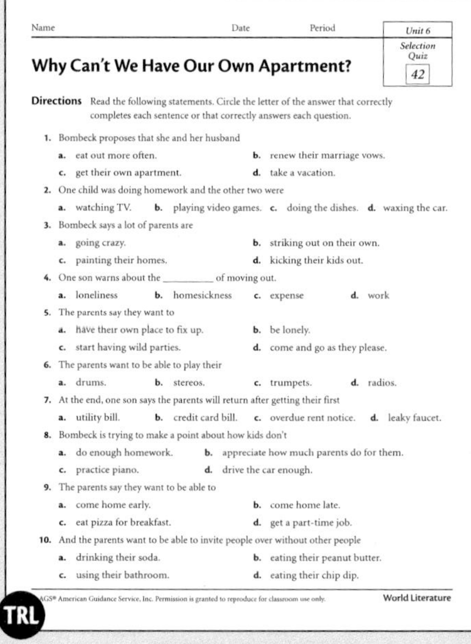
Name Date Period | *Unit 6* *Selection Quiz* 42

Why Can't We Have Our Own Apartment?

Directions Read the following statements. Circle the letter of the answer that correctly completes each sentence or that correctly answers each question.

1. Bombeck proposes that she and her husband
   a. eat out more often. b. renew their marriage vows. c. get their own apartment. d. take a vacation.
2. One child was doing homework and the other two were
   a. watching TV. b. playing video games. c. doing the dishes. d. waxing the car.
3. Bombeck says a lot of parents are
   a. going crazy. b. striking out on their own. c. painting their homes. d. kicking their kids out.
4. One son warns about the ________ of moving out.
   a. loneliness b. homesickness c. expense d. work
5. The parents say they want to
   a. have their own place to fix up. b. be lonely. c. start having wild parties. d. come and go as they please.
6. The parents want to be able to play their
   a. drums. b. stereos. c. trumpets. d. radios.
7. At the end, one son says the parents will return after getting their first
   a. utility bill. b. credit card bill. c. overdue rent notice. d. leaky faucet.
8. Bombeck is trying to make a point about how kids don't
   a. do enough homework. b. appreciate how much parents do for them. c. practice piano. d. drive the car enough.
9. The parents say they want to be able to
   a. come home early. b. come home late. c. eat pizza for breakfast. d. get a part-time job.
10. And the parents want to be able to invite people over without other people
   a. drinking their soda. b. eating their peanut butter. c. using their bathroom. d. eating their chip dip.

 World Literature

TRL

Selection Quiz 42

Stories

- "My function as a writer is not story-telling but truth-telling: to make things plain." —Laura Riding Jackson
- "There have been great societies that did not use the wheel, but there have been no societies that did not tell stories." —Ursula K. Le Guin

Humorous stories can be either fiction or nonfiction. In either case, their main purpose is to amuse. Many anecdotes, or short stories, are meant to be humorous. If a funny story is fairly short and ends with a punchline, it is called a joke. If someone tells a longer story in person, it is usually called a monologue or a routine. Performers on television, radio, and recordings often deliver monologues as part of their act. Humorous stories are long enough not to depend on a big finish. Their details and plot are often funnier than their punchlines or points. They often make us laugh at ourselves as well as their characters and situations.

The following selections find humor in different situations. One pokes fun at "high culture." The other makes us chuckle at everyday human behavior.

Stories

Direct students to read page 393 to themselves, or have a volunteer read the page aloud to the class.

ASK What's the difference between a humorous story and a joke? (A joke is short and ends with a punch line.)

Invite students to discuss the two quotations at the top of the page. Ask how students think a writer of fiction could consider herself or himself someone who tells the truth and makes things plain. (Students may see that writers often illuminate the truth of human nature whether the specifics are factual or not.)

Point out that Ursula K. LeGuin is right—all societies, no matter how primitive, tell and have told stories. You may want to encourage some further discussion. Mention the existence of myths and legends that we know people told before recorded history in many cultures. Students may know of some examples to share with the group.

Even before people developed writing systems, they told stories. Often the purpose of these stories was simply to share the values of the culture and the ways to deal with universal human feelings. Often the stories attempted to explain natural phenomena. Myths dealt with profound questions about how the world came to be and the powers that governed the world and the people in it. Other stories recounted the marvelous tales of heroes and their adventures.

Such stories were told by parents to their children, by local leaders to their communities, and by elders during ceremonies. People grew up hearing and knowing the stories. They passed them along to succeeding generations.

Often such stories included humorous aspects. The stories were, after all, a significant part of available entertainment. And people often remember something that is funny. That makes it easier to tell the story to someone else.

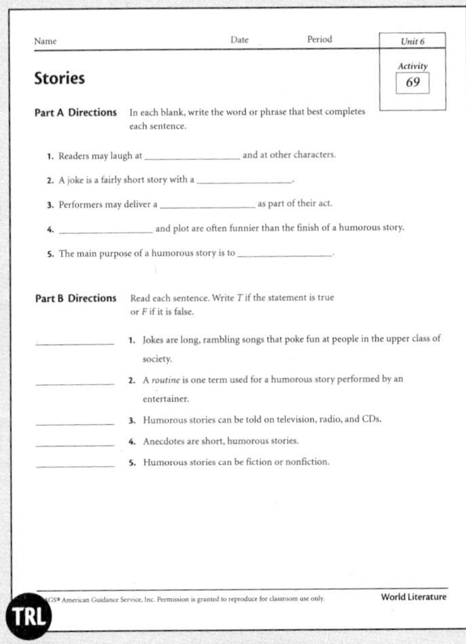

Name Date Period Unit 6 Activity 69

Stories

Part A Directions In each blank, write the word or phrase that best completes each sentence.

1. Readers may laugh at ______ and at other characters.
2. A joke is a fairly short story with a ______.
3. Performers may deliver a ______ as part of their act.
4. ______ and plot are often funnier than the finish of a humorous story.
5. The main purpose of a humorous story is to ______.

Part B Directions Read each sentence. Write *T* if the statement is true or *F* if it is false.

______ 1. Jokes are long, rambling songs that poke fun at people in the upper class of society.
______ 2. A *routine* is one term used for a humorous story performed by an entertainer.
______ 3. Humorous stories can be told on television, radio, and CDs.
______ 4. Anecdotes are short, humorous stories.
______ 5. Humorous stories can be fiction or nonfiction.

 World Literature

TRL

Activity 69

Name Date Period Unit 6 Workbook 69

Stories

Part A Directions In each blank write the word or phrase that best completes each sentence.

1. The main purpose of a humorous story is to ______.
2. A joke is a fairly short story with a ______.
3. ______ and plot are often funnier than the finish of a humorous story.
4. Readers may laugh at ______ and at other characters.
5. Performers may deliver a ______ as part of their act.

Part B Directions Read each sentence. Write *T* if the statement is true or *F* if it is false.

______ 1. Humorous stories can be fiction or nonfiction.
______ 2. A *routine* is one term used for a humorous story performed by an entertainer.
______ 3. Anecdotes are short, humorous stories.
______ 4. Jokes poke fun at people in the upper class of society.
______ 5. Humorous stories can be told on television, radio, and CDs.

 World Literature

TRL

Workbook 69

Selection at a Glance

Lohengrin

Leo Slezak
(translated by Charles E. Pederson)

Student pages 394–400

Overview

"Grand" opera has often been the subject of parody and jokes. Often the real humor of these parodies is appreciated best by those most familiar with the operas. However, even those who have never heard or heard of Richard Wagner's opera *Lohengrin* can appreciate this parody of it written by a knowledgeable cast member.

Selection Summary

In "Lohengrin," Leo Slezak makes the story of an opera sound absurd.

Objectives

- To read and understand a parody.
- To appreciate the humor of parody.

Audiocassette 

Teacher's Resource Library TRL

- Vocabulary Workbook 36, pages 1–2
- Selection Glossary 43
- Student Study Guide 49
- Activity 70
- Workbook 70
- Writing Activity 48
- Selection Quiz 43

INTRODUCING the SELECTION

Lohengrin

Leo Slezak (translated by Charles E. Pederson)

Leo Slezak
(1873–1946)
Austrian

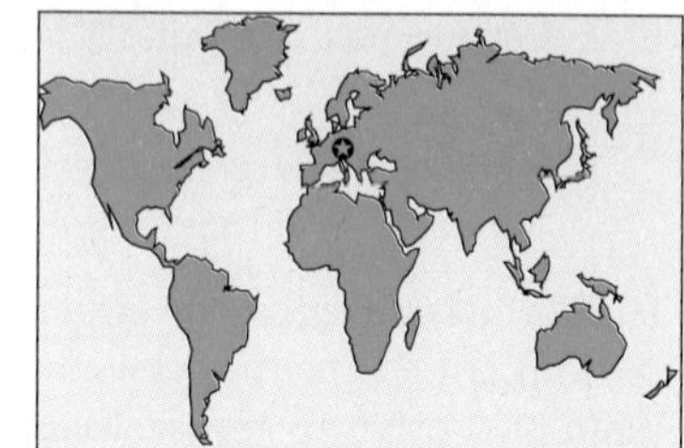

About the Author

Leo Slezak was born in Moravia, then part of Austria (now the Czech Republic). Having a beautiful voice, he soon began to sing opera. In 1896 he sang his first leading role—as Lohengrin. He sang for many years with the Vienna Royal Opera (Hofoperntheater) and the famous conductor Gustav Mahler. In 1900 he sang *Lohengrin* at Covent Garden in London. His first American performance was as Otello at the Metropolitan Opera in New York in 1909. His singing career lasted until 1933. Slezak was also a gifted and witty writer. He wrote several comic **autobiographies,** or books about his own life. He also acted in films.

Literary Terms

autobiography a story about a person's life written by that person

parody an exaggerated look at a situation

About the Selection

Leo Slezak sang many operatic roles in his long career. Still, he could see that many people find opera hard to understand. He uses this knowledge in his writing. He is supposed to have said about the opera *Il Trovatore:* "Even I don't get what's going on in this one!" He wrote a popular book that is a **parody** of opera guidebooks.

The opera *Lohengrin* was written by German composer Richard Wagner. Its first performance was in 1850. Wagner based the story of the "Swan Knight" on several legends from the Middle Ages. In the following selection, Slezak quickly outlines the action of the opera. (Remember that the part of Lohengrin was his own most famous role.) This parody exaggerates the funny aspects of both plot and character.

Setting the Stage for Reading

About the Author

Leo Slezak was a gifted tenor and comedian. He made his European operatic debut in *Lohengrin* in 1896. He later abandoned his operatic career and began acting in comedic films.

ASK How might a sense of humor be useful to an opera singer who also wrote an autobiography? (It could help him entertain his readers with a humorous perspective.)

About the Selection

Lohengrin is a well-known opera by Richard Wagner (pronounced VOG ner), a German composer who lived from 1813 to 1883. He wrote many operas, often based on ancient myths. He is noted for his beautiful melodies. Many people are familiar with the lovely "Wedding March" from the opera *Lohengrin,* though they may not realize its origin.

Activate Prior Knowledge: Ask students to recall what they know of opera or other kinds of musical theater in which people sing at least some of their dialogue.

ASK Why do you suppose an opera singer would want to make fun of opera? (possibly because he knew operas so well he knew how to make them funny)

Lohengrin

Leo Slezak

It's a **complicated** matter, so pay careful attention, or you may **A** never figure out what is going on.

As you read, notice how Slezak uses parody. He exaggerates the action and the story of the opera.

As background you must know that long ago, magic was all the rage. In those days, people—mostly princes—were changed into all kinds of animals. It often happened that you might think you had a genuine canary from the Harz mountains, and then one **B** day it would **reveal** itself to be a charmed **archduke**, whom some miserable, jealous fairy had changed into a bird....

The *Hartz* (spelled *Harz* in German) *mountains* are a region of Germany famous for legends. "Hartz Mountain" is also a breed of canary.

As the curtain rises, the stage is spotted with men. (I can hear you correcting me now. "You should say people," you say, but truly it is a bunch of men.) They are **randomly** beating their swords on their shields and singing.

King Heinrich, wearing a long false beard, sits beneath a large oak, holding court.

Telramund, an upper-class noble, has brought a **lawsuit** against Elsa von Brabant, maintaining that she killed her brother, little Gottfried.

The king does not believe Telramund, and it's not true anyway.

Elsa is called forward and questioned. She denies having done it.

Who is telling the truth? Telramund or Elsa?

I almost forgot to mention that Telramund is married. His wife is named Mrs. Ortrud. She's a truly gloomy woman, and actually she forced Telramund to bring the suit.

C
Think about the time and place of this opera. Is there something silly about the name *Mrs. Ortrud*?

archduke a royal rank equal to that of a prince

complicated not easy to understand

lawsuit a complaint brought before a court of law

randomly without a definite pattern or plan

reveal to make known

Reading Vocabulary 

Help students preview the selection's vocabulary words by giving them copies of the Selection Glossary. Suggest that students make up a sentence for each Glossary word.

Motivation for Reading

Ask students if they have ever listened to a comedian make fun of a situation that was not originally intended to be funny. Point out that this selection does that by making fun of an opera. Make sure students understand that they do not have to know anything about the opera to appreciate the humor in this parody. Suggest they read it to be entertained.

Discussion Questions

Suggest that students use the questions in the margins of the student selection to focus and review their reading.

A ASK Literary Element What is funny about the very first line? (the idea that it is possible for someone to never be able to figure out what is going on in an opera)

B ASK Comprehension What are the several meanings the writer uses for the phrase "Harz mountains"? (those mountains in Germany famous for legends, plus the breed of canary, plus the fact that a canary might be real in the story or might be a magically transformed person)

C Students may find the name humorous, partly because characters in fairy tales and legends usually don't have "Mrs." or "Mr." in front of their names.

Cross-Curricular Connection

Music If possible, share part of the opera *Lohengrin* with students. You may want to invite a local music teacher or opera student to provide highlights of the music. They might also contribute some insights into the appeal of opera. You might play a selection or two from a recording, perhaps the "Wedding March" or an aria of the character of Lohengrin to show students what Slezak would have sung during a performance.

Discussion Questions

A ASK Vocabulary The phrase "days of yore" is very outdated and used very seldom except in storytelling. Why do you think the author uses it here? (to make clear that this opera is based on an old and fanciful story)

B The author suggests that the swan leaves because Lohengrin sings a quarter note flat—a distinction hardly noticeable to most listeners.

C Many stories end with all loose ends tied up and everyone settled and happy. Most students will agree that Act I has this kind of happy ending.

Cross-Curricular Connection

Math Point out to students that the acts of the opera are identified by Roman numerals—Acts I, II, and III. Invite students to list Roman numerals as far as they can. (Lists can usually be found in dictionaries, among other sources.) Ask students to identify other ways in which we use Roman numerals. (to identify page numbers at the front of some books, in outlines, in references to Articles of the Constitution, and so on)

Days of yore is a phrase like "once upon a time." It means a time long past.

A In days of yore, "trial by battle" was also all the rage. If it could not be proved who was guilty or innocent, two men were allowed to fight it out. The loser was guilty. Seems like a **dubious** way to go about it.

Still, Telramund challenges anyone to strike for Elsa's honor.

Even though none of the knights thinks Elsa capable of such mean behavior, no one leaps to her defense, **despite** repeated blasts on the announcement trumpet. The king orders the trumpet to be blasted once more.

Suddenly a shining knight is seen in the distance, standing in a boat pulled by a snow-white swan.

The chorus of men shouts in confusion, pointing at the knight and looking in a sick way at the orchestra conductor. That apparently does not help, since everyone has different ideas about what's going on—what the Latin scholar calls "tohu vabohu."

Tohu vabohu is actually a Hebrew term meaning "chaos."

Lohengrin enters, spotlights hit him from all sides, and he sings the Swan Song a quarter note flat. The swan, hearing this, swims away.

What is the author suggesting about why the swan leaves? **B**

Now comes the interesting part.

You can actually hear Telramund trembling, but he doesn't give up. He can't, since giving up is not written into the script.

First, Lohengrin goes to Elsa and asks would she like him to fight for her and would she consider marrying him, though only on condition that she never ask who he is and where he comes from.

What? Not to know with whom one has the pleasure? The nerve!

She vows never to ask, he goes over and defeats Telramund but spares his life, Mrs. Ortrud flies into a rage, Elsa flings herself on the neck of the Nameless One, the men beat their swords on their shields with joy, the king strokes his false beard, blesses the couple's **union**, and the curtain falls.

C Does this seem like a good spot for a happy ending?

That's Act I.

despite in spite of

dubious causing doubt as to worth or truth

union a marriage

Name Date Period

Unit 6
Vocabulary Workbook
36
page 1

Why Can't We Have Our Own Apartment?/Lohengrin

Directions For each definition below, circle the word being defined.

1. A __________ is the main idea of a literary work.
   satire setting theme
2. A __________ is a household service, such as electricity, telephone, or water.
   utility appliance suite
3. In "Why Can't We Have Our Own Apartment?" Bombeck tells her children that she wants to move out and to take with her a few small __________, or pieces of household equipment, such as a toaster.
   utilities appliances suites
4. She also wants to take her bedroom __________, which is the matched set of furniture in her bedroom.
   appliance suite linens
5. Finally, she wants to take some __________, or household goods made of cloth, such as sheets and towels.
   appliances stereos linens
6. She wants to leave so that she can play her __________, or sound equipment, without the children complaining.
   stereo appliance suite
7. A piece of writing that is __________ tells about the author's life.
   autobiographical biographical parody
8. A __________ is an exaggerated look at a situation
   setting biography parody
9. In "Lohengrin," Slezak makes fun of the opera he starred in and __________, or makes known, the somewhat amusing plot of the opera.
   complicates sues reveals
10. He says that operas tend to be __________ and that the audience must pay close attention to figure out what is going on.
    complicated parody archduke
11. The canary in an opera may turn out to be the __________ of royal rank, who had been changed into a bird because of someone's jealousy.
    archduke random complicate

 World Literature

TRL Vocabulary Workbook 36, pages 1–2

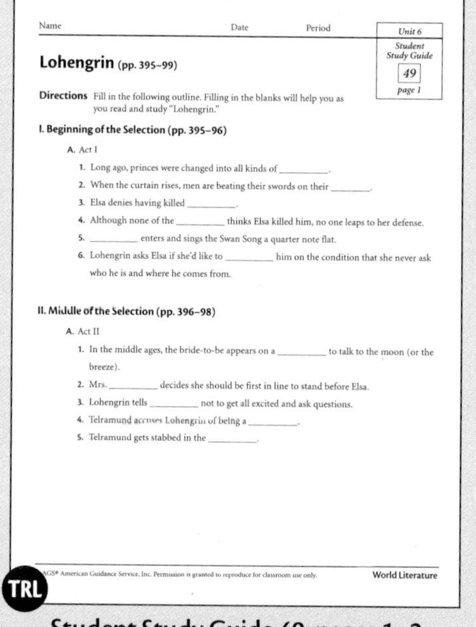

Name Date Period

Unit 6
Student Study Guide
49
page 1

Lohengrin (pp. 395–99)

Directions Fill in the following outline. Filling in the blanks will help you as you read and study "Lohengrin."

I. Beginning of the Selection (pp. 395–96)

A. Act I

1. Long ago, princes were changed into all kinds of __________.
2. When the curtain rises, men are beating their swords on their __________.
3. Elsa denies having killed __________.
4. Although none of the __________ thinks Elsa killed him, no one leaps to her defense.
5. __________ enters and sings the Swan Song a quarter note flat.
6. Lohengrin asks Elsa if she'd like to __________ him on the condition that she never ask who he is and where he comes from.

II. Middle of the Selection (pp. 396–98)

A. Act II

1. In the middle ages, the bride-to-be appears on a __________ to talk to the moon (or the breeze).
2. Mrs. __________ decides she should be first in line to stand before Elsa.
3. Lohengrin tells __________ not to get all excited and ask questions.
4. Telramund accuses Lohengrin of being a __________.
5. Telramund gets stabbed in the __________.

 World Literature

TRL Student Study Guide 49, pages 1–2

Act II opens in the dark.

From a corner come **unnaturally** long **criticisms** and **mutual** accusations. Mrs. Ortrud and Telramund are arguing. He calls her "companion of his disgrace." She is also unfriendly to him.

After much back and forth, they decide to make Elsa curious and turn her against Lohengrin. **D**

On the night before a wedding in the middle ages, the bride-to-be apparently always appeared on a balcony to talk to the moon, or if no moon was available, to the breeze.

Today such exaggerated gestures are simply not done, plus people would think you're cracked if you acted that way.

Cracked is a slang word for "crazy."

While the bride-to-be **gabs** with the breeze, Mrs. Ortrud—below the balcony—sighs so loudly that Elsa can't help but hear her. She goes down, scoops up Mrs. Ortrud from the doorway, and brings her back inside the palace.

If that isn't the dumbest thing she could do, I don't know what is.

The most experienced women in the chorus have the part of maidens in the bridal train. They scatter flowers. The men occupy themselves with marching and singing in **syncopation**. Everyone strides majestically to the church. Suddenly Mrs. Ortrud shoves her way to stand before Elsa, claiming that she should be first in line.

The author uses *experienced* to refer to both their acting experience and, ironically, their age.

This causes great excitement. In the midst of it come the king and Lohengrin. Lohengrin immediately sizes up the situation, lightning bolts shooting from his eyes. Going to Elsa, he takes her aside and tells her not to get all excited and go asking him any questions, otherwise he would have to leave at once. Elsa says that of course she has no such thoughts and is so happy even to be marrying him at all. He presses her to his chest and they stride on to the church. **E**

At the last moment, Telramund leaps from behind a pillar and scolds Lohengrin. He accuses Lohengrin of being a **sorcerer** and

criticism a judgment that finds fault

gab a slang word meaning to talk; to chatter

mutual shared in common

sorcerer a wizard

syncopation a musical accent not on the usual beat

unnaturally unusually; in an unexpected way

D ASK Literary Element An important aspect of parody is exaggeration. What are several examples of exaggeration on this page? (a bride-to-be always appearing on a balcony to talk to the moon or a breeze; Mrs. Ortrud sighing so loudly that Elsa hears her up on the balcony; lightning bolts shooting from Lohengrin's eyes)

E ASK Critical Thinking Lohengrin, the groom, demands that his bride, Elsa, not ask him any questions about who he is or anything about him. The author says that "of course Elsa has no such thoughts and is so happy even to be marrying him at all." What view of women's role in marriage do you think Wagner is reflecting here? Why? (It was typical both in Wagner's time and in the fairy tale type of stories he used for his operas that women did not have basic rights; often married women were assumed to be the property of their husbands.)

Literary Elements

Literary Devices A technique or device that Slezak uses here is another common element of humorous monologues: the narrator steps outside of the action to comment upon it. Often these "asides" are meant to be humorous in themselves, but they also serve to remind audience members that the author is an observer just as they are.

ASK Why might the narrator consider Elsa's bringing Mrs. Ortrud back into the palace "the dumbest thing"? (Mrs. Ortrud was trying to turn Elsa against her fiancé, Lohengrin.

Name Date Period — Unit 6 — *Activity* 70

Lohengrin

Part A Directions Match each item on the left with the correct item on the right. Write the correct letter on each line.

____ 1. a statement that a person has done something wrong — a. unrealistic
____ 2. not likely to happen in real life — b. accusation
____ 3. not easy to understand — c. complicated
____ 4. a complaint brought before a court of law — d. visa
____ 5. a paper that permits a person to enter a country — e. lawsuit

Part B Directions Circle the word or phrase in parentheses that best completes each sentence.

1. When a character swoons, she (faints, dances lightly about the room).
2. Lohengrin is considered (a shining knight, a strange freak).
3. (Marriage, Magic) was all the rage at the time this story takes place.
4. (Elsa, Mrs. Ortrud) turns out to be the guilty one in the end.
5. Throughout the story, men keep beating their swords (on their shields, on each other).

Part C Directions Read each sentence. Write *T* if the statement is true or *F* if it is false.

____ 1. Lohengrin shoots lightning bolts from his eyes, sometimes killing people.
____ 2. In trial by battle, the loser is the guilty one.
____ 3. The swan turns out to be Elsa's younger brother Gottfried.
____ 4. Telramund wants to quit after he sees Lohengrin, but the script won't let him.
____ 5. Elsa breaks her promise to Lohengrin and asks who he is.

 World Literature

TRL

Activity 70

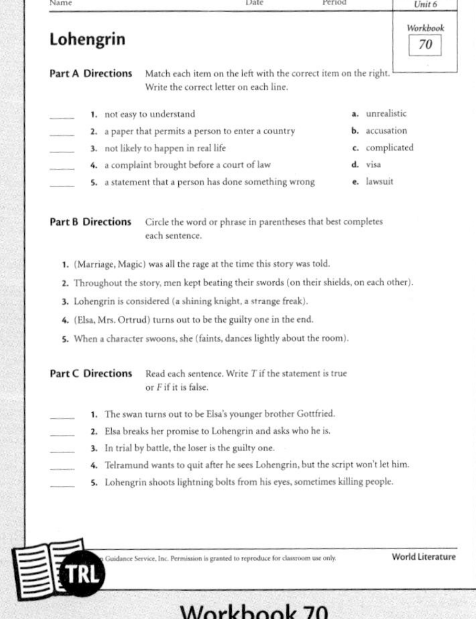

Name Date Period — Unit 6 — *Workbook* 70

Lohengrin

Part A Directions Match each item on the left with the correct item on the right. Write the correct letter on each line.

____ 1. not easy to understand — a. unrealistic
____ 2. a paper that permits a person to enter a country — b. accusation
____ 3. not likely to happen in real life — c. complicated
____ 4. a complaint brought before a court of law — d. visa
____ 5. a statement that a person has done something wrong — e. lawsuit

Part B Directions Circle the word or phrase in parentheses that best completes each sentence.

1. (Marriage, Magic) was all the rage at the time this story was told.
2. Throughout the story, men kept beating their swords (on their shields, on each other).
3. Lohengrin is considered (a shining knight, a strange freak).
4. (Elsa, Mrs. Ortrud) turns out to be the guilty one in the end.
5. When a character swoons, she (faints, dances lightly about the room).

Part C Directions Read each sentence. Write *T* if the statement is true or *F* if it is false.

____ 1. The swan turns out to be Elsa's younger brother Gottfried.
____ 2. Elsa breaks her promise to Lohengrin and asks who he is.
____ 3. In trial by battle, the loser is the guilty one.
____ 4. Telramund wants to quit after he sees Lohengrin, but the script won't let him.
____ 5. Lohengrin shoots lightning bolts from his eyes, sometimes killing people.

 World Literature

TRL

Workbook 70

Humorous Literature Unit 6 **397**

Discussion Questions

A Most students will agree that Act II has a happy ending.

B Students' visualizations of the bridal chamber's furnishings will vary, but all should imply a sense of discomfort.

C The comparison of Elsa's tears to boric acid makes them seem exaggerated.

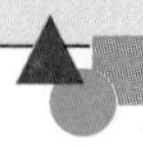

Learning Styles

Visual Opera is a visual art as well as a musical and dramatic one. Students who learn visually may benefit from seeing some opera settings of *Lohengrin.* Encourage interested students to find examples through videos, television productions, library books about operas, the Internet, or by writing the Metropolitan Opera in New York or the Lyric Opera of Chicago—or other opera companies—for information from opera programs. Students may enjoy sharing the results.

notes that the whole situation stinks—a lot. He goes on to question any person who rides around on swans, who sends swans away, whom no one can ask who one is, and where are his ID, his papers, his **visa**! Telramund declares the whole business of the trial by battle to be nonsense and wants a new hearing.

To be brief, Telramund is upset—with good reason, he feels.

But once a judgment has been made in someone's favor, that person can legally do anything. Telramund gets a stab in the stomach and is tossed aside.

A
Does this seem like a good spot for a happy ending?

Lohengrin and Elsa resume their interrupted striding to the church, the men beat their swords on their shields with joy, and under the approving nods of the king, the curtain falls.

Act III—The Bridal Chamber

Lohengrin and Elsa are **ushered** in by the king, who—with some winks and a few practical words of advice—leaves again.

B
What do you picture as the room's furnishings?

The room's furnishings alone tell the audience it's not going to be a pleasant wedding night.

Lohengrin sings for such a long time that, to get him to stop, Elsa finally asks him who he is. The fatal bomb explodes. On top of that, Telramund enters to kill Lohengrin. He misses his thrust and falls to the floor, struck dead by lightning bolts from Lohengrin's eyes.

He is cleared away.

C
Boric acid is a salty solution used in medicine. What is the effect of comparing Elsa's tears to boric acid?

Lohengrin says nothing to Elsa. He has to speak to the king first. Another of Lohengrin's mean tricks. As Elsa's tears fall like boric acid, the curtain falls.

Change of scenery. Same scene as Act I.

The king appears on horseback. The horse expresses its inner feelings, while the men beat their swords on their shields with eagerness, shouting for victory. It's off to war for them, each one panting for a hero's death.

Lohengrin is to lead a **battalion**. He enters and says he can't go with them. To his good luck, Elsa has asked him the forbidden question and he has to go home now.

The men beat their swords on their shields with despair.

battalion a large group of soldiers

usher to show people the way

visa a paper that permits a person to enter a country

398 *Unit 6 Humorous Literature*

Elsa is brought in. She **swoons**. In this opera, she seems only to stride or swoon.

Lohengrin strikes a **pose** and sings the tale of the Holy Grail. He has no evidence for what he's singing, only a lot of **unprovable** stuff for which no review board in the world would let him out of the army. But everyone present believes him. Maybe they do only because it's late and no one wants to **prolong** the performance by **pressing** him for details or getting into a debate.

The *Holy Grail* is said by legend to be the cup used by Jesus at the Last Supper. Many knights of old went in search of it.

As Elsa gasps for breath, Lohengrin says good-bye, giving her a horn, a ring, and a sword. She is supposed to learn to play the horn, she should save the ring, and give the sword to her brother.

Talk about confusing!

Lohengrin leaves.

The men beat their swords on their shields with sadness.

Suddenly, Mrs. Ortrud appears again. She just won't go away. She cries that it was she who turned Elsa's brother into a swan, that she was guilty the entire time.

Lohengrin blasts a hole in her with the lightning from his eyes. She dies.

The swan dives, and from the water leaps an exaggeratedly attractive boy—a prince. He hugs Elsa. It's little brother Gottfried!

With no animal to pull his boat, Lohengrin can't leave. Then a handy dove comes and carries him off—although that seems just a little **unrealistic**.

D
What is funny about saying the dove is *unrealistic*?

Elsa swoons and screams, and the curtain falls—thank heavens, because it is late indeed. The opera is over!

pose a position taken on purpose, as to have a picture taken

press to ask in an urgent way

prolong to make last longer

swoon to faint

unprovable not possible to prove

unrealistic not likely to happen in real life

D Saying the dove is unrealistic is a funny remark because the dove is a tiny detail in a whole opera of unrealistic characters and situations.

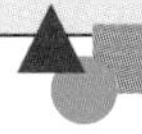

Learning Styles

Group Learning Students may enjoy putting on a parody version of the story of *Lohengrin.* There are many summaries available of operas that can give them a more complete version of the actual story of the opera than is in Slezak's version. A well-known source is *The Concise Oxford Dictionary of Opera* (London: Oxford University Press, 1972), probably available in most libraries. Have students work together to cast the story and devise their own dialogue, exaggerating the situations and dialogue. They can perform the parody for any audience: their own class, other classes, or even parents' night.

Reviewing the Selection

Answer Key

Comprehension: Identifying Facts

1. Elsa is accused of killing her brother.

2. He arrives in a boat pulled by a swan.

3. In the end, the swan turns into Elsa's brother, Gottfried.

Comprehension: Understanding Main Ideas

4. Lohengrin and Telramund fight over Elsa's honor. Telramund has accused her of murdering her brother and Lohengrin wins the fight.

5. Lohengrin tells Elsa that she must never ask who he is or where he has come from. In Act II, he explains that if she asks he will have to leave at once.

6. Mrs. Ortrud and Lohegrin caused most of the trouble. She turns Elsa's brother into the swan and encourages Telramund to bring the lawsuit against Elsa. He makes an unusual request and exhibits strange behavior.

Understanding Literature: Parody

7. Slezak exaggerates the actions of the chorus. Later he says that the oldest and most experienced women in the chorus play young maidens.

8. Slezak makes Lohengrin appear somewhat incompetent and foolish. He accuses Lohengrin of playing mean tricks. He also says Lohengrin escapes going to battle because he has to go home after Elsa asks him the forbidden question.

Critical Thinking

9. Students may choose other parts of the story to illustrate how complicated it is; make sure they can defend their choices.

10. Answers will vary, but ask students to defend their opinions with answers based on the content of the selection.

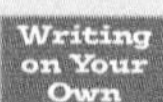

Operas are staged for an audience, and set designers devise the way the stage looks. Encourage students to draw sketches to accompany their descriptions.

Selection Quiz

The Teacher's Resource Library includes a Selection Quiz for "Lohengrin" that may be given following the Selection Review.

REVIEWING the SELECTION

Lohengrin

Leo Slezak

Directions Write the answers to these questions using complete sentences.

Comprehension: Identifying Facts

1. What does the lawsuit against Elsa accuse her of doing?
2. How does Lohengrin arrive?
3. What does the swan turn into at the end?

Comprehension: Understanding Main Ideas

4. Why do Lohengrin and Telramund fight? Who wins?
5. What does Lohengrin tell Elsa she must never do? What will happen if she does?
6. Who has actually caused most of the trouble in the opera? How?

Understanding Literature: Parody

Parody is an exaggerated look at a situation. It may be a tongue-in-cheek imitation of a person, event, or serious work of literature. A parody picks out certain features of the work. Then it exaggerates them. You also may have heard a parody of a well-known song or poem.

7. How does Slezak use parody to make fun of the chorus?
8. How does Slezak make fun of the hero, Lohengrin?

Critical Thinking

9. The author opens by saying the opera is complicated. Name a part of the story where he makes it sound as complicated as possible.
10. Did you enjoy this parody? Why or why not?

Writing on Your Own Think about staging the opera *Lohengrin.* Choose one part that would be hard to stage. Use your imagination to tell how you might stage it.

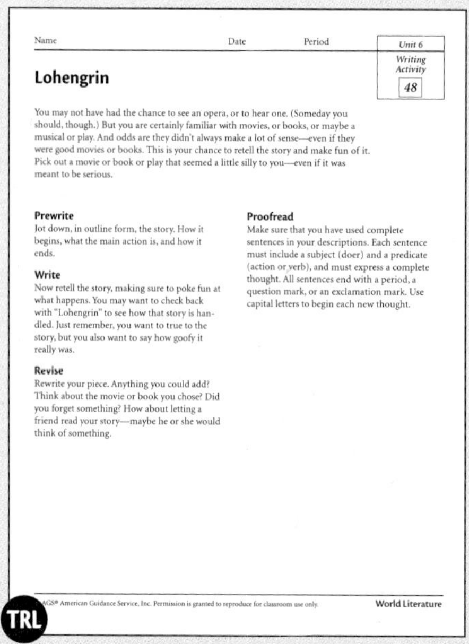

Name Date Period

Unit 6 *Writing Activity* 48

Lohengrin

You may not have had the chance to see an opera, or to hear one. (Someday you should, though.) But you are certainly familiar with movies, or books, or maybe a musical or play. And odds are they didn't always make a lot of sense—even if they were good movies or books. This is your chance to retell the story and make fun of it. Pick out a movie or book or play that seemed a little silly to you—even if it was meant to be serious.

Prewrite
Jot down, in outline form, the story. How it begins, what the main action is, and how it ends.

Write
Now retell the story, making sure to poke fun at what happens. You may want to check back with "Lohengrin" to see how that story is handled. Just remember, you want to true to the story, but you also want to say how goofy it really was.

Revise
Rewrite your piece. Anything you could add? Think about the movie or book you chose? Did you forget something? How about letting a friend read your story—maybe he or she would think of something.

Proofread
Make sure that you have used complete sentences in your descriptions. Each sentence must include a subject (doer) and a predicate (action or verb), and must express a complete thought. All sentences end with a period, a question mark, or an exclamation mark. Use capital letters to begin each new thought.

 World Literature

TRL

Writing Activity 48

Name Date Period

Unit 6 *Selection Quiz* 43

Lohengrin

Directions Read the following statements. Circle the letter of the answer that correctly completes each sentence or that correctly answers each question.

1. At the time the story took place, _________ was all the rage.
   a. the Twist b. reading c. magic d. ballroom dancing
2. King _________ sits under an oak tree at the beginning of the opera.
   a. Henry b. Edward c. Charles d. Heinrich
3. Telramund accuses _________ of murdering Gottfried.
   a. Lisa b. Carmen c. Elisa d. Elsa
4. A knight arrives, in a boat pulled by
   a. a swan. b. a dolphin. c. a walleye. d. a smaller boat.
5. The knight in the boat is
   a. Don Giovanni. b. Don José. c. Tristan. d. Lohengrin.
6. Lohengrin asks Elsa to marry him and never to
   a. leave him. b. ask who he is and where he is from.
   c. invite her mother to live with them. d. travel to the Blue Mountain.
7. Act II opens with Mrs. Ortrud arguing with
   a. Elsa. b. King Heinrich. c. Lohengrin. d. Telramund.
8. On their wedding night, Elsa
   a. faints. b. runs away.
   c. asks Lohengrin who he is. d. doesn't speak.
9. Lohengrin kills Telramund with
   a. his sword. b. lightning bolts from his eyes.
   c. a gun. d. a lance.
10. The swan from Lohengrin's boat
   a. drowns. b. turns into Gottfried.
   c. turns into King Heinrich. d. sings a beautiful little aria.

 World Literature

TRL

Selection Quiz 43

INTRODUCING the SELECTION

A Wedding Without Musicians

Sholom Aleichem

Sholom Aleichem
(1859–1916)
Ukrainian

Literary Terms

anecdote a short, funny story

humorist someone who writes funny works

irony the use of words that seem to say one thing but mean the opposite

About the Author

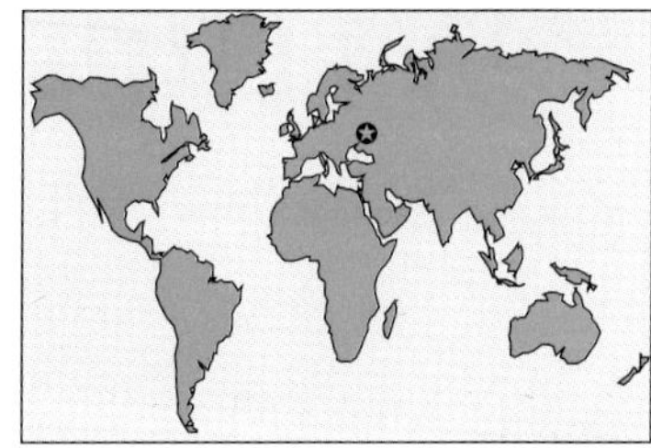

Sholom Aleichem was born Sholem (or Solomon) Rabinowitz in Pereyaslav, Ukraine. (Ukraine was then part of the Russian Empire.) He was a short-story writer, dramatist, and **humorist,** or someone who writes funny works. At first he taught and wrote in Russian and Hebrew. Then he began to write in Yiddish. That is the traditional language of Eastern European Jews. His pen name comes from a traditional Hebrew greeting for old friends. By 1894 he used that name all the time. He left Russia in 1905 and later moved to the United States.

Sholom Aleichem's works often describe the simple life of small-town Jews. He wrote more than forty books of novels and stories. Many have been translated into English. They include *Stempenyu*, *Inside Kasrilevke*, and *The Old Country*. The play and movie of *Fiddler on the Roof* are based on Aleichem's stories in *Tevye the Dairyman*.

About the Selection

Jews faced serious hardships in Russia and the Ukraine in the 1800s. They could live only in certain places. They were kept out of schools and jobs. In spite of this, Aleichem looks at his characters and situations with humor and **irony.** Irony is using words to mean the opposite of what they seem to say. "A Wedding Without Musicians" comes from a collection called *The Railroad Stories* (1911). It is typical of Aleichem's tales. It is written like a story someone is telling aloud. It is almost like a long **anecdote,** a short, funny story.

Selection at a Glance

A Wedding Without Musicians

Sholom Aleichem

Student pages 401–409

Overview

Like Leo Slezak in "Lohengrin," Sholom Aleichem makes situations that are not inherently funny seem humorous. Slezak parodies an opera. Aleichem parodies a much more serious situation—discrimination and violence against Jewish people.

Selection Summary

In "A Wedding Without Musicians," part of a train doesn't arrive, and it is a good thing for Jews in a small village.

Objectives

- To appreciate an anecdote as one type of humorous writing.
- To appreciate that a humorous parody can be based on a serious situation.

Audiocassette 

Teacher's Resource Library 

- Vocabulary Workbook 37, pages 1–2
- Selection Glossary 44
- Student Study Guide 50
- Activity 71
- Workbook 71
- Writing Activity 49
- Selection Quiz 44

Setting the Stage for Reading

About the Author

Have students read the text and look at the picture of Sholom Aleichem. Explain that Aleichem is famous for his stories of "laughter through tears." He wrote many stories as well as novels and plays, always about the Jewish experience in western Russia as well as Jewish immigration to the United States. He himself immigrated to the United States two years before his death.

ASK Why do you think Aleichem wrote often about the "simple life of small-town Jews?" (probably because that is what he knew best)

About the Selection

Discrimination against Jews was extreme in Russia and Ukraine in the 1800s, often leading to violence against them that seemed to be calmly accepted, if not joined, by most non-Jews. Aleichem's gentle humor pokes fun at the most terrible of situations, a testimony to the survival of the Jewish spirit.

Activate Prior Knowledge: Ask students familiar with the movie or play *Fiddler on the Roof* briefly to summarize it for the class.

ASK Why might Aleichem write stories so that they sounded as if someone was simply telling them aloud? (This was probably a familiar format to his Jewish audience in Russia and the Ukraine of the late 1800s.)

Reading Vocabulary TRL

Help students preview the selection's vocabulary words by giving them copies of the Selection Glossary. Have pairs of students work together to define the words.

Motivation for Reading

Discuss with students what "a wedding without musicians" might be like. (dull, incomplete, and without joy and pizzazz) Tell them this story is not about weddings or musicians. Suggest they read the story to find out why the author gave it what seems to be an unrelated title.

Discussion Questions

Suggest that students use the questions in the margins of the student selection as discussion prompts.

A ASK Literary Elements What elements give the story the flavor of an oral story or monologue? (the first-person narrative sprinkled with such comments as "the last time I told you..." and the conversational tone of the language)

B ASK Comprehension Pogroms were a violent expression of extreme discrimination and racism against the Jews. How do you think it was possible for Aleichem to write about such happenings with humor? (Writing might have been his way of helping himself and others try to retain a sense of perspective to protect themselves as much as possible.)

A Wedding Without Musicians

Sholom Aleichem

As you read, note the details in this anecdote.

The *Straggler Special* is a local train. The writer is referring to an earlier story about the same train.

A The last time I told you about our **Straggler** Special, I described the miracle of *Hashono Rabo.* This time I shall tell you about another miracle in which the Straggler Special figured, how thanks to the Straggler Special the town of Heissin was saved from a terrible fate.

This took place during the days of the Constitution when **reprisals** against the Jews were going on everywhere. Though I must tell you that we Jews of Heissin have never **B** been afraid of **pogroms**. Why? Simply because there is no one in our town who can carry out a pogrom. Of course you can imagine that if we looked very hard we could find one or two volunteers who wouldn't deny themselves the pleasure of **ventilating** us a little, that is, breaking our bones or burning down our houses. For example, when reports of pogroms began drifting in, the few squires, who are enemies of our people, wrote **confidential** letters to the proper authorities, saying it might be a good idea if "something were done" in Heissin also; but since there was no one here to do it, would they be so kind as to send help, in other words, would they **dispatch** some "people" as quickly as possible.

Pogroms—mob attacks against Jews—happened fairly often in Russia under the tsars. They were especially serious from the 1880s to the early 1900s. The government did little to stop pogroms.

confidential meant to be secret

dispatch to send off quickly to a place

pogrom an organized attack on a group (Russian for "riot")

reprisal an act of force in revenge for an assumed wrong

straggler something that lags behind the others

ventilate to put in motion; to blow away

402 Unit 6 Humorous Literature

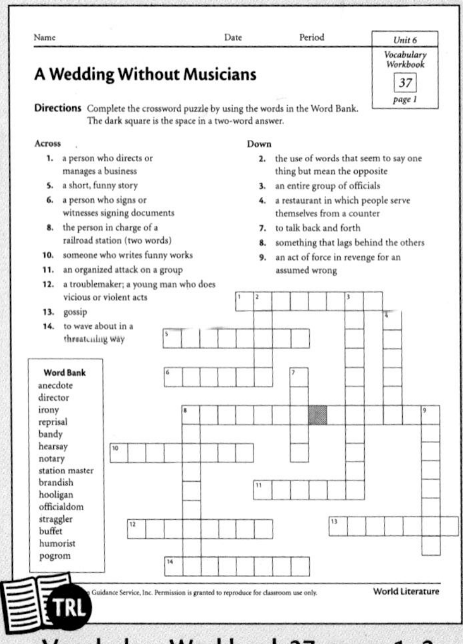

Name Date Period

Unit 6 Vocabulary Workbook 37 page 1

A Wedding Without Musicians

Directions Complete the crossword puzzle by using the words in the Word Bank. The dark square is the space in a two-word answer.

Across

1. a person who directs or manages a business
5. a short, funny story
6. a person who signs or witnesses signing documents
8. the person in charge of a railroad station (two words)
10. someone who writes funny works
11. an organized attack on a group
12. a troublemaker; a young man who does vicious or violent acts
13. gossip
14. to wave about in a threatening way

Down

2. the use of words that seem to say one thing but mean the opposite
3. an entire group of officials
4. a restaurant in which people serve themselves from a counter
7. to talk back and forth
8. something that lags behind the others
9. an act of force in revenge for an assumed wrong

Word Bank
anecdote
director
irony
reprisal
bandy
hearsay
notary
station master
brandish
hooligan
officialdom
straggler
buffet
humorist
pogrom

World Literature

Vocabulary Workbook 37, pages 1–2

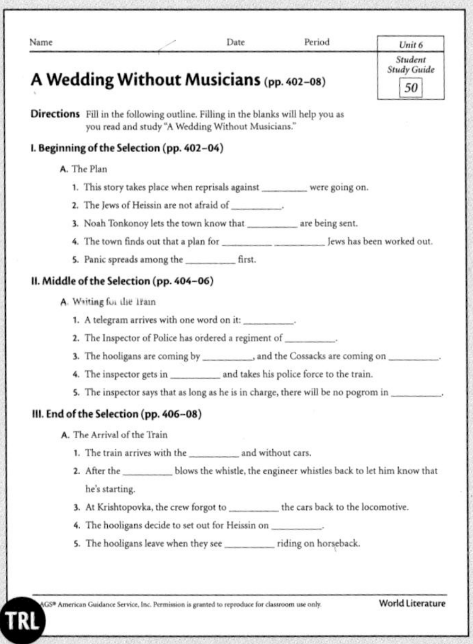

Name Date Period

Unit 6 Student Study Guide 50

A Wedding Without Musicians (pp. 402–08)

Directions Fill in the following outline. Filling in the blanks will help you as you read and study "A Wedding Without Musicians."

I. Beginning of the Selection (pp. 402–04)

A. The Plan

1. This story takes place when reprisals against _________ were going on.
2. The Jews of Heissin are not afraid of _________.
3. Noah Tonkonoy lets the town know that _________ are being sent.
4. The town finds out that a plan for _________ _________ Jews has been worked out.
5. Panic spreads among the _________ first.

II. Middle of the Selection (pp. 404–06)

A. Waiting for the Train

1. A telegram arrives with one word on it: _________.
2. The Inspector of Police has ordered a regiment of _________.
3. The hooligans are coming by _________, and the Cossacks are coming on _________.
4. The inspector gets in _________ and takes his police force to the train.
5. The inspector says that as long as he is in charge, there will be no pogrom in _________.

III. End of the Selection (pp. 406–08)

A. The Arrival of the Train

1. The train arrives with the _________ and without cars.
2. After the _________ blows the whistle, the engineer whistles back to let him know that he's starting.
3. At Krishtopovka, the crew forgot to _________ the cars back to the locomotive.
4. The hooligans decide to set out for Heissin on _________.
5. The hooligans leave when they see _________ riding on horseback.

World Literature

Student Study Guide 50

And before another twenty-four hours had passed a reply came, also confidentially, that "people" were being sent. From where? From Zhmerinko, from Kazatin, Razdilno, Popelno and other such places that had distinguished themselves in beating up Jews. Do you want to know how we learned of this deep secret? We found it out through our regular source of news, Noah Tonkonoy. Noah Tonkonoy is **C** a man whom God has **endowed** with a pair of extra-long legs and he uses them to good purpose. He never rests and he is seldom to be found at home. He is always busy with a thousand things and most of these things have to do with other people's business rather than his own. By trade he is a printer, and because he is the only printer in Heissin he knows all the squires and the police and has dealings with **officialdom** and is in on all their secrets.

Noah Tonkonoy spread the good news all over town. He told **D** the secret to one person at a time, in strictest confidence, of course, saying, "I am telling this only to you. I wouldn't tell it to anyone else." And that was how the whole town became aware of the fact that a mob of **hooligans** was on the way, and that a plan for beating up Jews had been worked out. The plan told exactly when they would start, on which day, at which hour, and from which point, and by what means—everything to the last detail.

You can imagine what terror this struck in our hearts. Panic spread quickly. And among whom do you think it spread first? Among the poor, of course. It's a peculiar thing about poor people. When a rich man is afraid of a pogrom, you can understand why. He is afraid, poor fellow, that he will be turned into a **pauper**. But those of you who are already paupers, what are you afraid of? What have you got to lose? But you should have seen how they bundled up their

endow to provide with a talent or quality

hooligan a troublemaker; a young man who does vicious or violent acts

officialdom an entire group of officials

pauper a very poor person

C ASK Literary Element What kind of character is Noah Tonkonoy? (He is funny, both in looks and in actions. Yet he plays an important role in his community and in the story.)

D ASK Literary Element Aleichem says that "Noah Tonkonoy spread the good news all over town" when he told everyone people were arriving to carry out a pogrom against the Jews in town. How is this phrase an example of irony? (It says the opposite of what is meant—an impending pogrom would be terrible and frightening news.)

Cross-Curricular Connection

History Have students illuminate through research the history of the Jews during the time when Aleichem wrote his stories. Let students extend their research into the continuing discrimination against the Jews that culminated in the horrors of the Holocaust during World War II. You may want to invite discussion about stereotyping and unfair treatment of people based on racist attitudes.

Name Date Period | Unit 6 | Activity 71

A Wedding Without Musicians

Part A Directions On the blank lines, write a short answer for each item.

1. Why were the Jews afraid of pogroms?
2. Why was Noah Tonkonoy called the walking newspaper?
3. How did the townspeople try to stop from being beaten up?
4. What turned out to be a real "hero" in this story?
5. What language does the author's name come from and what does it mean?

Part B Directions In each blank, write the word or phrase that best completes each sentence.

1. Heavy ________ caused the cars to be left behind when the locomotive left.
2. ________ were ordered to come from a nearby town to help stop the pogrom.
3. Aleichem talks about breaking bones and burning houses, calling it ________.
4. The title, "A Wedding Without Musicians," refers to a ________ without hooligans.
5. At the end of the story the author compares the hooligans to ________.

 World Literature

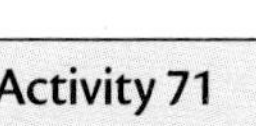

Activity 71

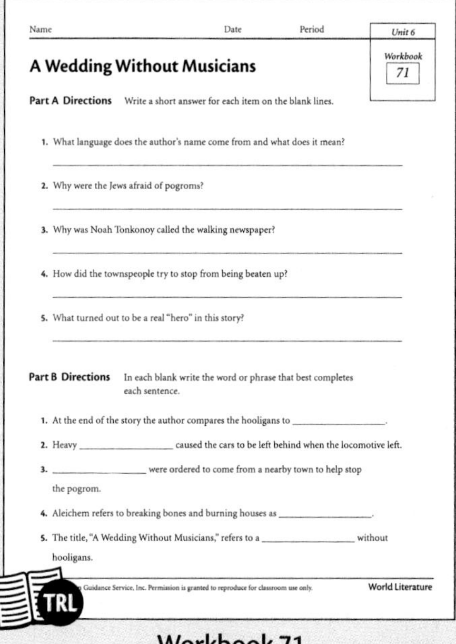

Name Date Period | Unit 6 | Workbook 71

A Wedding Without Musicians

Part A Directions Write a short answer for each item on the blank lines.

1. What language does the author's name come from and what does it mean?
2. Why were the Jews afraid of pogroms?
3. Why was Noah Tonkonoy called the walking newspaper?
4. How did the townspeople try to stop from being beaten up?
5. What turned out to be a real "hero" in this story?

Part B Directions In each blank write the word or phrase that best completes each sentence.

1. At the end of the story the author compares the hooligans to ________.
2. Heavy ________ caused the cars to be left behind when the locomotive left.
3. ________ were ordered to come from a nearby town to help stop the pogrom.
4. Aleichem refers to breaking bones and burning houses as ________.
5. The title, "A Wedding Without Musicians," refers to a ________ without hooligans.

 World Literature

Workbook 71

Discussion Questions

A The inspector would "accept a gift" that was essentially a bribe to do what the giver asked of him, in this case to protect the Jews of the town against the hooligans.

Literary Elements

Similes and Metaphors Figurative language compares things that are basically not alike except in the way they are being compared. Two common examples used often by writers are similes and metaphors. A simile uses the word *like* or the word *as* in the comparison: "the ice was like a sheet of glass." A metaphor does not use the word *like* or *as*. Instead, it describes one thing as having the qualities of another: "the ice was a sheet of glass." Help students find examples of both in the story. (several metaphors: "a jewel of a fellow," "our walking newspaper," on page 404; "it was a wedding without musicians," page 407; several similes: "as regular as a clock," page 405; "like rats in a famine," and "like ice in summer," page 408.)

Diversity Connection

Genocide is the word used to describe an organized extermination or murder of an entire people. The Jews have been victimized by attempts at genocide throughout their history. Recent examples include the Russian pogroms of the late 1800s of which Aleichem writes and the German Holocaust during World War II, during which close to six million European Jews were systematically rounded up and killed.

Ask students to find out about examples of genocide in the present-day world. Encourage discussion about whether there is any way for the rest of the world to prevent such atrocities.

Running hither and yon is an expression using old words for "here and there."

children and packed up their **belongings** and began running hither and yon, looking for a place to hide. Where can a person hide? This one hides in a friendly peasant's cellar, another in the **Notary's** attic, a third in the **Director's** office at the factory. Everyone finds a spot for himself.

He is wondering if a Jew can trust a non-Jew in this circumstance.

I was the only one in town who wasn't anxious to hide. I am not boasting about my bravery. But this is the way I see it: what's the sense of being afraid of a pogrom? I don't say that I am a hero. I might have been willing to hide too, when the hour of **reckoning** came. But I asked myself first, "How can I be sure that during the slaughter the friendly peasant in whose cellar I was hiding, or the Notary, or the Director of the factory himself, wouldn't...." You understand. And all that aside, how can you leave a town wide open like that? It's no trick to run away. You have to see about doing something. But, alas, what can a Jew do? He appeals to a friendly official. And that is just what we did.

A What do you think it means that the Inspector would *accept a gift*?

In every town there is at least one friendly official you can appeal to. We had one too, the Inspector of Police, a jewel of a fellow, willing to listen to us and willing to accept a gift on occasion. We went to the Inspector with the proper gifts and asked for his protection. He reassured us at once. He told us to go home and sleep in peace. Nothing would happen. Sounds good, doesn't it? But we still had our walking newspaper, Noah, who was broadcasting another secret through the length and **breadth** of the town. The secret was that a telegram had just arrived. He swore by everything holy that he had seen it himself. What was in that telegram? Only one word—*Yediem.* An ugly word. It means simply, "We are coming." We ran back to the Inspector. "Your honor," we told him, "it looks bad." "What looks bad?" he asked, and we told him, "A telegram has just arrived." "From

belongings personal possessions

breadth the width

director a person who directs or manages a business

notary a notary public; a person who signs or witnesses signing documents

reckoning paying or settling what is owed

where?" We told him. "And what does it say?" We told him, "*Yediem.*" At this he burst out laughing. "You are big fools," he said. "Only yesterday I ordered a regiment of Cossacks from Tolchin."

Cossacks made up special military units in the Russian army.

When we heard this we breathed more easily. When a Jew hears that a Cossack is coming, he takes courage, he can face the world again. The question remained: who would arrive first, the Cossacks from Tolchin, or the hooligans from Zhmerinko? Common sense told us that the hooligans would arrive first, because they were coming by train, while the Cossacks were coming on horseback. But we pinned all our hopes on the Straggler Special. God is merciful. He would surely perform a miracle and the Straggler would be at least a few hours late. This wasn't too much to hope for, since it happened nearly every day. But this one time it looked as though the miracle wouldn't take place. The Straggler kept going from station to station as regular as a clock. You can imagine how we felt when we learned, confidentially, of course, through Noah Tonkonoy, that a telegram had arrived from the last station, from Krishtopovka. *Yediem,* it said, and not just *yediem*—but *yediem* with a *hurrah!* in front of it. **B**

Naturally we took this last bit of news straight to the Inspector. We begged him not to rely on the Cossacks who might or might not arrive from Tolchin sometime, but to send police to the station, at least for the sake of appearances, so that our enemies wouldn't think that we were completely at their mercy. The Inspector listened to our pleas. He did what we asked, and more. He got himself up in full uniform, with all his orders and medals, and took the whole police force, that is the **gendarme** and his assistant, to the station with him to meet the train. **C**

D
How big is the town's police force?

gendarme a police officer

B ASK Comprehension Why did the Jews in town think the Straggler Special could save them? (because the train was famous for being late, which would mean that its passengers, the hooligans, would arrive after the Cossacks)

C ASK Critical Thinking Why did the Jews think that having the police at the station might help them? (They thought the police force in the station might intimidate or frighten the hooligans when they got off the train. Of course, part of the humor of the story lies in the fact that the police force consisted of only two people.)

D The town's police force was made up of two people—the gendarme (the Inspector) and his assistant.

Learning Styles

Auditory Aleichem's style is to write his stories as though they are being told aloud by a storyteller. This medium will appeal to students who learn well auditorially. Ask a volunteer to tell the story aloud in his or her own words, giving vocal expression and gestures to communicate.

Discussion Questions

A ASK **Comprehension** Everyone dreaded the arrival of the Straggler Special. What startling and funny thing became apparent when it arrived? (The locomotive arrived without any railroad cars behind it.)

Grammar

Paragraphs Remind students that when they write they should group related sentences together into paragraphs. Usually a new paragraph is indicated by indenting the first sentence or, as shown in this book, by separating the paragraphs with extra space. Neither way is more correct than the other as long as the beginning of a new paragraph is clear to the reader.

But our enemies weren't asleep either. They also put on their full dress uniforms, complete with ribbons and medals, took a couple of priests along, and also came to meet the train. The Inspector asked them sternly, "What are you doing here?" And they asked him the same question, "What are you doing here?" They **bandied** words back and forth, and the Inspector let them know in no uncertain terms that their trouble was for nothing. As long as he was in charge, there would be no pogrom in Heissin. They listened, smiled knowingly, and answered with **insolence**, "We shall see."

Just then a train whistle was heard from the distance. The sound struck terror to our hearts. We waited for another whistle to blow and after that for the shouts of "Hurrah!" What would happen after the Hurrah! we knew only too well from **hearsay**. We waited, but heard nothing more. What had happened? The sort of thing that could only happen to our Straggler Special.

When the Straggler Special drew into the station, the engineer stopped the locomotive, stepped out calmly and made his way toward the **buffet**. We met him halfway. "Well, my good fellow, and where are the cars?" "Which cars?"
A "Can't you see that you are here with the locomotive and without cars?"

bandy to talk back and forth

buffet a restaurant in which people serve themselves from a counter

hearsay gossip

insolence a rude or insulting attitude

406 Unit 6 Humorous Literature

He stared at us. "What do I care about the cars? They are the business of the crew." "Where is the crew?" "How should I know where the crew is? The conductor blows the whistle when he is ready and I whistle back to let him know that I am starting, and off we go. I don't have an extra pair of eyes in back of my head to see what's going on behind me." That was his story and according to that he was right. But right or wrong, there stood the Straggler Special without cars and without passengers. In other words, it was a wedding without musicians. **D**

B

What do you think of the engineer's attitude? **C**

Later we learned that a band of hooligans had been on the way to Heissin, all of them **handpicked** youths, armed to the teeth with clubs and knives and other weapons. Their spirits were high and **liquor** flowed freely. At the last station, Krishtopovka, they invited the crew to join them and treated everybody to drinks—the conductor, the fireman, the gendarmes. But in the midst of this **revelry** they forgot one little detail, to **couple** the cars back to the locomotive. And so the locomotive went off at the usual time to Heissin and the rest of the Straggler Special remained standing in Krishtopovka.

Neither the hooligans nor the other passengers nor the crew noticed that they were standing still. They continued to empty bottle after bottle and to make merry, until the **station master** suddenly noticed that the locomotive had

couple to attach; to link together

handpicked chosen carefully

liquor a strong alcoholic drink

revelry a loud celebration

station master the person in charge of a railroad station

B ASK Literary Element How does the engineer's attitude contribute to the humor of the story? (It adds to the improbability of the situation.)

C Most students should see that the engineer was being extremely literal about his responsibilities, interpreting them to extend only to driving the locomotive rather than getting the whole train to its destination.

D ASK Critical Thinking What does the author compare the Straggler Special without cars and passengers to? (a wedding without musicians) Why do you think this is or is not a good title for the story? (Many students will feel that this is a good title because it emphasizes the humor of the incomplete train and the whole tone of the story with the unexpected happening at every turn.)

Discussion Questions

A ASK Literary Elements Remember that a simile is a comparison that uses the word *like* or *as.* What are two examples of similes in the second paragraph on this page? (like rats in a famine, like ice in summer)

B It is ironic that the Straggler Special saved the day by not delivering its passengers the way it should. Nothing in the story seemed to work quite the way it was expected to, and the Straggler Special was no exception. The author's final comment serves to sum up the humor of the story.

Raising a *hue and cry* means to make a great protest or a great noise.

gone off and left the cars behind. He spread the alarm, the crew came tumbling out. A hue and cry was raised. The hooligans blamed the crew, the crew blamed the hooligans, but what good did it do? At last they decided that the only thing to do was to set out for Heissin on foot. They took heart and began marching toward Heissin, singing and shouting as they went.

And so they arrived in their usual good form, singing and yelling and **brandishing** their clubs. But it was already too late. In the streets of Heissin the Cossacks from Tolchin were riding up and down on horseback with whips in their hands. Within half an hour not one of the hooligans **A** remained in town. They ran off like rats in a **famine**, they melted like ice in summer.

B What is ironic about the Straggler Special as a hero? How does this add to the anecdote?

Now, I ask you, didn't the Straggler Special deserve to be showered with gold, or at least written up?

brandish to wave about in a threatening way

famine a severe lack of food

REVIEWING the SELECTION

A Wedding Without Musicians

Sholom Aleichem

Directions Write the answers to these questions using complete sentences.

Comprehension: Identifying Facts

1. How do the townspeople first hear about the planned pogrom?
2. What does the telegram say? What do people think it means?
3. What public official is a friend to the Jews in the town?

Comprehension: Understanding Main Ideas

4. Why are the hooligans coming to town?
5. Why are people relieved to know the hooligans are coming by train?
6. How do the Cossacks manage to arrive before the hooligans?

Understanding Literature: Anecdote

An anecdote is a short, funny story. An anecdote has a single point. It may touch on some part of a person's personality. It may focus on a single idea. It can give us a fuller picture of a person. It can make an abstract concept more solid. This story includes more details and is a bit longer than a typical anecdote. It is still a short, funny story.

7. How does the story begin?
8. Why is the Straggler Special a strange hero?

Critical Thinking

9. Cruel treatment was a serious problem for Jews in Russia. Why do you think anyone would tell funny stories about it?
10. Did you like this story? Why or why not?

Writing on Your Own Write a brief outline of the story. Tell what happens at the beginning of the story. Then write the events in the middle. Finally, tell how it ends.

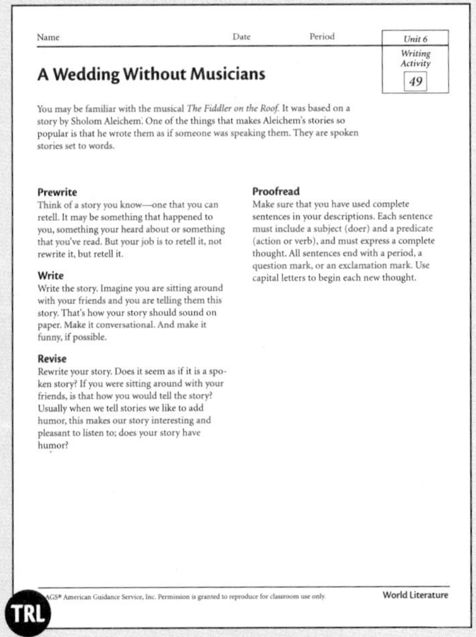

Name Date Period

Unit 6 Writing Activity 49

A Wedding Without Musicians

You may be familiar with the musical *The Fiddler on the Roof.* It was based on a story by Sholom Aleichem. One of the things that makes Aleichem's stories so popular is that he wrote them as if someone was speaking them. They are spoken stories set to words.

Prewrite
Think of a story you know—one that you can retell. It may be something that happened to you, something your heard about or something that you've read. But your job is to retell it, not rewrite it, but retell it.

Write
Write the story. Imagine you are sitting around with your friends and you are telling them this story. That's how your story should sound on paper. Make it conversational. And make it funny, if possible.

Revise
Rewrite your story. Does it seem as if it is a spoken story? If you were sitting around with your friends, is that how you would tell the story? Usually when we tell stories we like to add humor, this makes our story interesting and pleasant to listen to; does your story have humor?

Proofread
Make sure that you have used complete sentences in your descriptions. Each sentence must include a subject (doer) and a predicate (action or verb), and must express a complete thought. All sentences end with a period, a question mark, or an exclamation mark. Use capital letters to begin each new thought.

 World Literature

TRL

Writing Activity 49

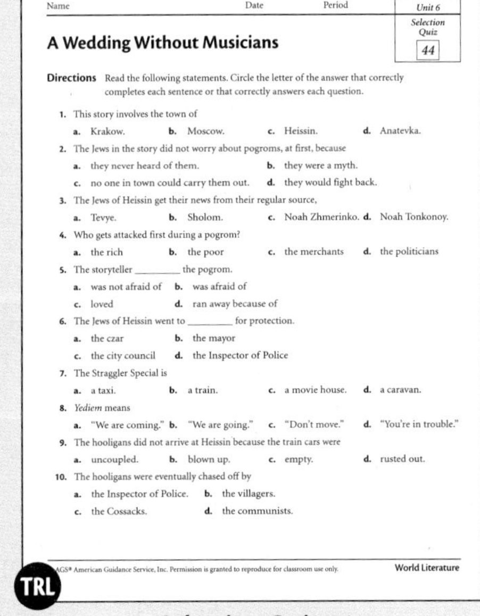

Name Date Period

Unit 6 Selection Quiz 44

A Wedding Without Musicians

Directions Read the following statements. Circle the letter of the answer that correctly completes each sentence or that correctly answers each question.

1. This story involves the town of
   a. Krakow. b. Moscow. c. Heissin. d. Anatevka.
2. The Jews in the story did not worry about pogroms, at first, because
   a. they never heard of them. b. they were a myth.
   c. no one in town could carry them out. d. they would fight back.
3. The Jews of Heissin get their news from their regular source,
   a. Tevye. b. Sholom. c. Noah Zhmerinko. d. Noah Tonkonoy.
4. Who gets attacked first during a pogrom?
   a. the rich b. the poor c. the merchants d. the politicians
5. The storyteller ________ the pogrom.
   a. was not afraid of b. was afraid of
   c. loved d. ran away because of
6. The Jews of Heissin went to ________ for protection.
   a. the czar b. the mayor
   c. the city council d. the Inspector of Police
7. The Straggler Special is
   a. a taxi. b. a train. c. a movie house. d. a caravan.
8. *Yediem* means
   a. "We are coming." b. "We are going." c. "Don't move." d. "You're in trouble."
9. The hooligans did not arrive at Heissin because the train cars were
   a. uncoupled. b. blown up. c. empty. d. rusted out.
10. The hooligans were eventually chased off by
    a. the Inspector of Police. b. the villagers.
    c. the Cossacks. d. the communists.

 World Literature

TRL

Selection Quiz 44

Reviewing the Selection

Answer Key

Comprehension: Identifying Facts

1. The townspeople first hear of the planned pogrom through their "walking newspaper," Noah Tonkonoy.

2. The telegram says simply, "Yediem," which means "We are coming." People think it means the hooligans who will carry out the pogrom are coming.

3. The Inspector of Police is a friend to the Jews in the town.

Comprehension: Understanding Main Ideas

4. The hooligans are coming to town to carry out the pogrom against the Jews.

5. People are relieved to know the hooligans are arriving by train because they know the train never runs on time. This means, they think, that the Cossacks who will defend them will arrive first.

6. The Cossacks manage to arrive before the hooligans because the train engineer leaves the cars containing the hooligans in another station.

Understanding Literature: Anecdote

7. The story begins as though the author is simply telling another story about the Straggler Special.

8. The Straggler Special saved the Jews in town by being its incompetent self.

Critical Thinking

9. Answers may vary, but many students will see that keeping a sense of humor in the face of tragedy may be one way to cope with the problem. It also displays a unique Jewish humor that can find something laughable in such serious problems.

10. Answers will vary, but many students will enjoy the humor of the story.

Writing on Your Own You may want to review the outline format with students before they begin so they recall the use of capital and lowercase Roman numerals and capital and lowercase letters. Their outlines should not go into more detail than that.

Selection Quiz

The Teacher's Resource Library includes a Selection Quiz for "A Wedding Without Musicians" that may be given following the Selection Review.

Skills Lesson: Dialogue

This Skills Lesson focuses on the conventions of written dialogue as well as authors' intent in using dialogue.

Review Answers

1. Dialogue shows the exact words spoken by a character.

2. A writer uses dialogue to show what characters are thinking and how they relate to each other.

3. You can recognize dialogue by the quotation marks that surround each character's exact words.

4. Bombeck's dialogue adds to the humor of her piece because the dialogue of the parents and the children seems to be reversed.

5. The effect of the dialogue in Aleichem's story is to underscore the scene, showing that the characters are out of breath as they talk.

Writing on Your Own Students may find that working in pairs is helpful in writing dialogue. Suggest that each pair devise a situation in which two people would be talking to each other, imagine that they are the two people, and say what they think the people would say to each other. Then they can write the dialogue.

Skills Lesson Dialogue

Dialogue is the conversation between characters in a story. It gives their exact words. It lets readers know what characters are thinking. Dialogue also shows how characters relate to one another.

There are two ways in which dialogue is special. Quotation marks go around the speaker's words. Usually, another phrase tells who is speaking. Here is an example.

> "Stop right there!" the police officer yelled.
>
> "Not on your life," Lance whispered.

"Stop right there!" is what the officer said. "Not on your life," is what Lance said. The phrase *the police officer yelled* shows the officer is speaking. *Lance whispered* shows Lance is speaking.

Almost all of "Why Can't We Have Our Own Apartment?" is in dialogue. It's easy to tell who is speaking. The exact words of the parents and children play a large part in the humor. Each seems to say what you would expect the other to say. Here is an example.

> "But why?" asked our daughter. "Aren't you happy here? You have your own room and the run of the house."
>
> "I know, but a lot of parents our age are striking out on their own."

This example is from "A Wedding Without Musicians." The short sentences make the characters sound out of breath.

> "Your honor," we told him, "it looks bad." "What looks bad?" he asked, and we told him, "A telegram has just arrived." "From where?" We told him. "And what does it say?" We told him, "*Yediem*."

Review

1. What does dialogue show?
2. Why does a writer use dialogue?
3. How can you recognize dialogue?
4. How does Bombeck's dialogue add to the humor?
5. What is the effect of the dialogue in the Aleichem story?

Writing on Your Own Write a dialogue between two characters. Include words to show who is speaking. Put quotation marks around the speaker's exact words.

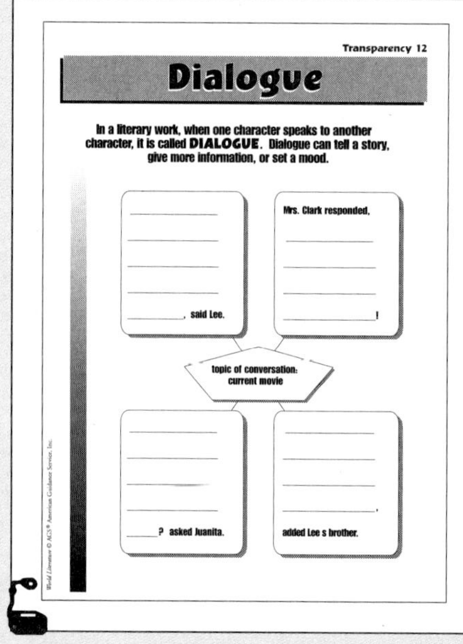

Transparency 12

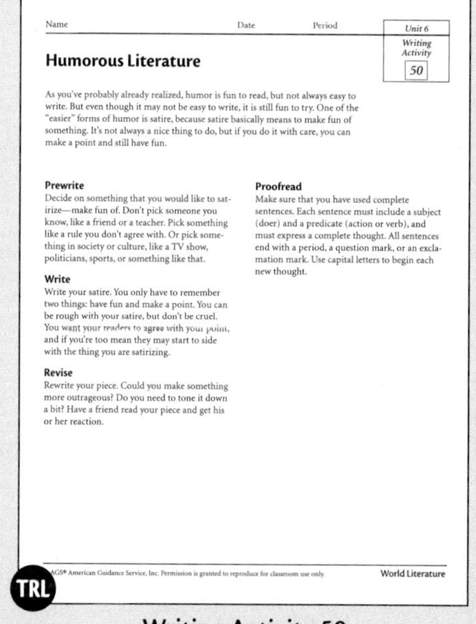

Name Date Period

Unit 6 *Writing Activity* 50

Humorous Literature

As you've probably already realized, humor is fun to read, but not always easy to write. But even though it may not be easy to write, it is still fun to try. One of the "easier" forms of humor is satire, because satire basically means to make fun of something. It's not always a nice thing to do, but if you do it with care, you can make a point and still have fun.

Prewrite
Decide on something that you would like to satirize—make fun of. Don't pick someone you know, like a friend or a teacher. Pick something like a rule you don't agree with. Or pick something in society or culture, like a TV show, politicians, sports, or something like that.

Write
Write your satire. You only have to remember two things: have fun and make a point. You can be rough with your satire, but don't be cruel. You want your readers to agree with your point, and if you're too mean they may start to side with the thing you are satirizing.

Revise
Rewrite your piece. Could you make something more outrageous? Do you need to tone it down a bit? Have a friend read your piece and get his or her reaction.

Proofread
Make sure that you have used complete sentences. Each sentence must include a subject (doer) and a predicate (action or verb), and must express a complete thought. All sentences end with a period, a question mark, or an exclamation mark. Use capital letters to begin each new thought.

 World Literature

TRL

Writing Activity 50

410 *Unit 6 Humorous Literature*

UNIT 6 SUMMARY

In Unit 6 you read examples of different kinds of humorous writing. Some are funny because the writers describe funny situations. Not all the pieces are just for fun, though. Some authors use humor to make a serious point. Satire and irony are ways of using humor. Satire can be very serious while it is humorous.

Jonathan Swift and Andrew Graham-Yooll use humor in a serious way. They write about something that made them angry. Their words may make us laugh. They can also make us uncomfortable. They let us see how ridiculous or awful a situation is. Sholom Aleichem makes fun of those who were mistreating the Jews. The other three writers intend for us to laugh in a different way. Dave Barry makes fun of himself. Leo Slezak makes fun of an opera story. Erma Bombeck turns a family story upside down.

Humor in writing can serve several purposes. You probably did not laugh out loud at the satires by Swift and Graham-Yooll. The story by Sholom Aleichem is set in a serious situation. But it might have made you smile. The Barry, Bombeck, and Slezak stories probably made you laugh. They were written to entertain.

Selections

- "A Modest Proposal" by Jonathan Swift. Swift makes an outrageous suggestion for dealing with poverty in Ireland.
- "Cup Inanity and Patriotic Profanity" by Andrew Graham-Yooll. The writer views the behavior of soccer fans celebrating a victory.
- "Staying at a Japanese Inn: Peace, Tranquillity, Insects" by Dave Barry. Barry tells about trying to fit into a different culture.
- "Why Can't We Have Our Own Apartment?" by Erma Bombeck. Parents switch roles with children and ask to move out.
- "Lohengrin" by Leo Slezak. Slezak makes the story of an opera sound absurd.
- "A Wedding Without Musicians" by Sholom Aleichem. Part of a train doesn't arrive, and it is a good thing for Jews in a small village.

Unit Summary

Direct students to read the page. Then ask volunteers to read the selection descriptions and explain how each one fits into the classification of "humorous literature."

ASK What was outrageous about Swift's suggestion? (He made the extreme and outrageous suggestion that the Irish sell their children to the English to use for food.)

ASK What didn't Andrew Graham-Yooll like about the behavior of soccer fans after a game? (The fans pretended they were being patriotic when they looted, broke windows, and carried out other examples of unsavory behavior.)

ASK What can be funny about people of one culture meeting people of another, as shown in Dave Barry's column? (People can misunderstand not only language but gestures and habits.)

ASK How do you know that Erma Bombeck's column was intended just to be humorous? (It is based on her knowledge of families, but the situation it describes is extremely unrealistic.)

ASK What makes the opera *Lohengrin* an easy target for Slezak's parody? (The story of the opera is already complicated and absurd although it apparently is not intended to be funny.)

ASK Why is it a good thing that the train through the town of Heissin is unreliable? (The fact that something went wrong saved the Jews in the town.)

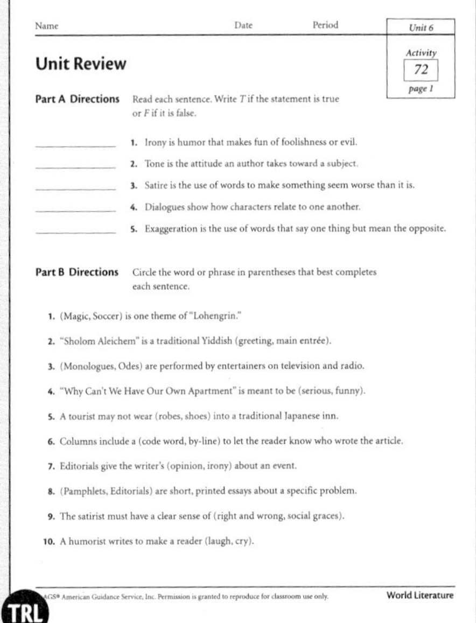

Name Date Period | *Unit 6* | *Activity* 72 *page 1*

Unit Review

Part A Directions Read each sentence. Write *T* if the statement is true or *F* if it is false.

_______ **1.** Irony is humor that makes fun of foolishness or evil.
_______ **2.** Tone is the attitude an author takes toward a subject.
_______ **3.** Satire is the use of words to make something seem worse than it is.
_______ **4.** Dialogues show how characters relate to one another.
_______ **5.** Exaggeration is the use of words that say one thing but mean the opposite.

Part B Directions Circle the word or phrase in parentheses that best completes each sentence.

1. (Magic, Soccer) is one theme of "Lohengrin."
2. "Sholom Aleichem" is a traditional Yiddish (greeting, main entrée).
3. (Monologues, Odes) are performed by entertainers on television and radio.
4. "Why Can't We Have Our Own Apartment" is meant to be (serious, funny).
5. A tourist may not wear (robes, shoes) into a traditional Japanese inn.
6. Columns include a (code word, by-line) to let the reader know who wrote the article.
7. Editorials give the writer's (opinion, irony) about an event.
8. (Pamphlets, Editorials) are short, printed essays about a specific problem.
9. The satirist must have a clear sense of (right and wrong, social graces).
10. A humorist writes to make a reader (laugh, cry).

 World Literature

TRL

Activity 72, pages 1–2

Name Date Period | *Unit 6* | *Workbook* 72 *page 1*

Unit Review

Part A Directions Read each sentence. Write *T* if the statement is true or *F* if it is false.

_______ **1.** Exaggeration is the use of words that say one thing but mean the opposite.
_______ **2.** Dialogues show how characters relate to one another.
_______ **3.** Satire is the use of words to make something seem worse than it is.
_______ **4.** Tone is the attitude an author takes toward a subject.
_______ **5.** Irony is humor that makes fun of foolishness or evil.

Part B Directions Circle the word or phrase in parentheses that best completes each sentence.

1. A humorist writes to make a reader (laugh, cry).
2. The satirist must have a clear sense of (right and wrong, social graces).
3. (Pamphlets, Editorials) are short printed essays about a specific problem.
4. Editorials give the writer's (opinion, irony) about an event.
5. Columns include a (code word, by-line) to let the reader know who wrote the article.
6. A tourist may not wear (robes, shoes) into a traditional Japanese inn.
7. "Why Can't We Have Our Own Apartment" is meant to be (serious, funny).
8. (Monologues, Odes) are performed by entertainers on television and radio.
9. "Sholom Aleichem" is a traditional Yiddish (greeting, main entrée).
10. (Magic, Soccer) is the main theme of "Lohengrin."

 World Literature

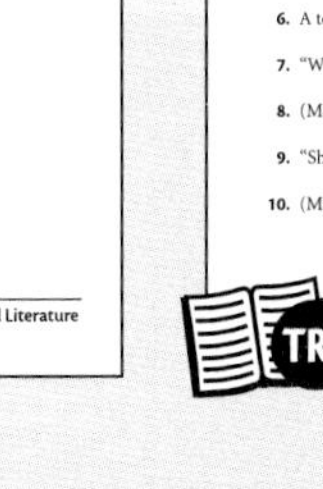

Workbook 72, pages 1–2

Humorous Literature Unit 6 **411**

Unit 6 Review

The Teacher's Resource Library includes two parallel forms of the Unit 6 Mastery Test. The difficulty level of the two forms is equivalent. You may wish to use one form as a pretest and the other form as a posttest.

Final Mastery Test

The Teacher's Resource Library includes the Final Mastery Test. This test is pictured on pages 466–467 of the Teacher's Edition. The Final Mastery Test assesses the major learning objectives for Units 1 through 6, with emphasis on Units 4 through 6.

Answer Key

Comprehension: Identifying Facts

1. A work that makes fun of evil or foolishness is called satire. The two in this unit are "A Modest Proposal" and "Cup Inanity and Patriotic Profanity."

2. Dave Barry and his family visited Japan.

3. Sholom Aleichem writes about Jewish life in the early 1900s.

4. A humorist is a person who writes funny works.

5. "Lohengrin" is a parody that makes fun of the story of an opera.

Comprehension: Understanding Main Ideas

6. "A Modest Proposal" addresses the serious situation of English mistreatment of the Irish people.

7. The Jews in "A Wedding Without Musicians" are threatened with a pogrom—an organized attack.

8. The selections by Barry, Bombeck, and Slezak are all meant just to amuse. Students should understand that each one has no other purpose.

9. "A Modest Proposal" and "Cup Inanity and Patriotic Profanity" are intended to affect the reader's opinion. Students should see that these writers want readers to change their own behavior and perhaps that of others.

10. Graham-Yooll's tone is sarcastic; he holds the soccer fans up to ridicule.

UNIT 6 REVIEW

Directions Write the answers to these questions using complete sentences.

Comprehension Identifying Facts

1. What is the term for a work that makes fun of evil or foolishness? Name one from this unit.
2. What country did Dave Barry and his family visit?
3. Which author writes about Jewish life in the early 1900s?
4. What is a humorist?
5. Which selection is a parody? What does it parody?

Comprehension: Understanding Main Ideas

6. What is the serious social situation discussed in "A Modest Proposal"?
7. What danger threatens the Jews of Heissin in "A Wedding Without Musicians"?
8. Name a selection that is meant just to amuse. Explain your choice.
9. Name a selection that is meant to affect the reader's opinion. Explain your choice.
10. What is the tone of Graham-Yooll's editorial?

Understanding Literature: Irony and Exaggeration

Irony is the use of words that seem to say one thing but mean the opposite. Exaggeration is the use of words to make something seem worse than it is. It stretches the truth. In this unit, the authors use irony and exaggeration to be funny. Several of them also turn this type of humor to a serious purpose.

11. How does the writer of "Cup Inanity and Patriotic Profanity" exaggerate the effects of a soccer victory on Argentina?
12. What is ironic about the way the printer tells secrets in "A Wedding Without Musicians"?
13. How does Dave Barry use exaggeration in describing the political activist?
14. What is ironic about the title "Why Can't We Have Our Own Apartment?"
15. Give another example of exaggeration from one of the selections.

Understanding Literature: Irony and Exaggeration

11. The writer of "Cup Inanity and Patriotic Profanity" exaggerates the effects of the soccer victory on Argentina by suggesting that the fans believe the victory affected the rise in the stock market, will cause the foreign debt to paid off, and so on.

12. It is ironic that a printer whose job it is to print news distributes it mainly by telling people privately what the news is.

13. Barry exaggerates the political activists by saying that their persuasive techniques include shouting angrily and loudly.

14. The irony in the title "Why Can't We Have Our Own Apartment?" lies in the fact that the assumed speaker of the question is a teenager; however, in the column the speaker is a parent.

15. Answers will vary, as there are many examples of exaggeration in these selections, from Swift's description of an American eating babies to Barry's wanting to kill the cicadas with flamethrowers and Slezak's description of the swan leaving because Lohengrin sings a quarter note flat.

Critical Thinking

16. Do you think you would enjoy the opera *Lohengrin*? Does reading the parody make a difference? Explain.
17. Which author do you think has the gloomiest view of life? Explain.
18. What is ironic about a humorist having a gloomy view of life?
19. Erma Bombeck and Johnathan Swift have very different writing styles. Describe the differences.
20. Which selection did you like most? Why?

Speak and Listen

Go to the library. Find a short humorous work of literature. You may want to look for humorous poems or anecdotes. You might want to choose a monologue like those used by stand-up comics. Read the piece to yourself until you feel comfortable reading it. Then read it to the class. Or you might learn it well enough to tell it rather than reading it.

Beyond Words

Work with classmates. Look for cartoons that tell a funny story without using words. Make copies of the cartoons. Then make a bulletin board display of them.

Writing on Your Own Think of a funny TV show that you like. What is in the show that makes it funny to you? What kind of humor does it use? Write a paragraph explaining why you like the show.

Test-Taking Tip

When taking a short-answer test, first answer the questions you know. Then go back to spend time on the questions you are less sure of.

Critical Thinking

16. Students' opinions about enjoying the opera will vary. Their explanations should reflect what they read in the parody.

17. Answers will vary, but perhaps Swift shows the gloomiest view.

18. The irony lies in the contrast between humor and gloom. However, many satirists like Swift and Graham-Yooll have both.

19. Bombeck writes in a breezy style, using a great deal of dialogue to describe what seems to be an ordinary family scene. Swift, on the other hand, writes very formally.

20. Answers will vary, but students should be able to defend their opinions with descriptions of the selections.

Speak and Listen

Encourage students to find a humorous piece that fits their own personality and that they can be comfortable reading or telling aloud. Tell them to try to read or tell the selection the way they think the writer would have wanted it to sound.

Beyond Words

You may want to allow gifted students to add to the bulletin-board display examples of their own cartoons or wordless humor.

Writing on Your Own Encourage students to watch one particular episode of their favorite program and incorporate specific examples of its humor into their paragraphs.

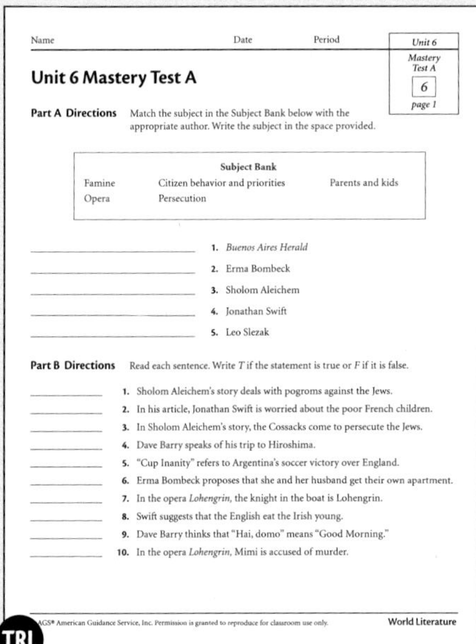

Name Date Period | *Unit 6 Mastery Test A* 6 *page 1*

Unit 6 Mastery Test A

Part A Directions Match the subject in the Subject Bank below with the appropriate author. Write the subject in the space provided.

Subject Bank		
Famine	Citizen behavior and priorities	Parents and kids
Opera	Persecution	

______ 1. *Buenos Aires Herald*
______ 2. Erma Bombeck
______ 3. Sholom Aleichem
______ 4. Jonathan Swift
______ 5. Leo Slezak

Part B Directions Read each sentence. Write *T* if the statement is true or *F* if it is false.

______ 1. Sholom Aleichem's story deals with pogroms against the Jews.
______ 2. In his article, Jonathan Swift is worried about the poor French children.
______ 3. In Sholom Aleichem's story, the Cossacks come to persecute the Jews.
______ 4. Dave Barry speaks of his trip to Hiroshima.
______ 5. "Cup Inanity" refers to Argentina's soccer victory over England.
______ 6. Erma Bombeck proposes that she and her husband get their own apartment.
______ 7. In the opera *Lohengrin,* the knight in the boat is Lohengrin.
______ 8. Swift suggests that the English eat the Irish young.
______ 9. Dave Barry thinks that "Hai, domo" means "Good Morning."
______ 10. In the opera *Lohengrin,* Mimi is accused of murder.

 World Literature

TRL

Unit Mastery Test A, page 1

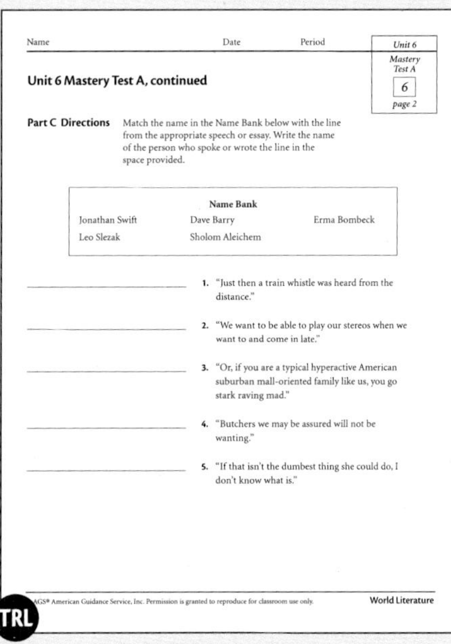

Name Date Period | *Unit 6 Mastery Test A* 6 *page 2*

Unit 6 Mastery Test A, continued

Part C Directions Match the name in the Name Bank below with the line from the appropriate speech or essay. Write the name of the person who spoke or wrote the line in the space provided.

Name Bank		
Jonathan Swift	Dave Barry	Erma Bombeck
Leo Slezak	Sholom Aleichem	

______ 1. "Just then a train whistle was heard from the distance."
______ 2. "We want to be able to play our stereos when we want to and come in late."
______ 3. "Or, if you are a typical hyperactive American suburban mall-oriented family like us, you go stark raving mad."
______ 4. "Butchers we may be assured will not be wanting."
______ 5. "If that isn't the dumbest thing she could do, I don't know what is."

 World Literature

TRL

Unit Mastery Test A, page 2

Correcting Common Writing Mistakes

1. Make subjects and verbs agree

- Singular subject must have a singular verb.
- Plural subjects must have plural verbs.
- Compound subjects must have plural verbs.

2. Make pronouns agree with antecedents

- In gender:
  –Replace the name of a male person with a masculine pronoun.
  –Replace the name of a female person with a feminine pronoun.
  –Replace singular names with *it* or *its.*
  –Replace plural names with *they, them,* or *their.*
- In number:
  –Make the pronoun singular if its antecedent is singular.
  –Make the pronoun plural if its antecedent is plural.

3. Capitalize proper nouns and proper adjectives

- Capitalize proper nouns.
- Capitalize the first word of any sentence or title.
- Capitalize the names of languages.
- Capitalize the pronoun *I.*
- Capitalize all proper adjectives.

4. Use correct verb tenses

- Action verbs tell what someone did.
- State-of-being verbs express the condition of the subject.
- Helping verbs help the main verb express tense, or time.
  –Use one main verb in a verb phrase.
  –Use helping verbs in a verb phrase.
  –Use the main verb last in a verb phrase.
- Make sure the verb tenses are logical.
- Use the same verb tenses if the actions occurred at the same time.
- Use different verb tenses if the actions occurred at different times.

5. Use and spell verb forms correctly

- Form the past tense of a regular verb by adding *-ed* or *-d.*
- Use the past participle to form the past perfect tenses.

6. Use and spell possessives and plurals correctly

- Use a possessive noun to show ownership or a relationship between two things.
- Make a singular noun possessive by adding an apostrophe (') and the letter *s.*
- Make a plural noun possessive by adding only an apostrophe.
- Add both an apostrophe and the letter *s* if the plural noun does not end in an *s.*

7. Avoid run-on sentences

- Begin sentences with a capital letter.
- End each sentence with a period, question mark, or exclamation point.
- Do not end a sentence or separate two sentences with a comma.
- Use a comma plus a conjunction to connect two complete ideas.

8. Avoid sentence fragments

- Make sure each sentence has a subject and a verb that express a complete idea.
- Use a subject and a predicate.
- Do not capitalize the first word of a phrase that does not begin a new idea.

414 *Appendix A Writing Tips*

Paragraphs

The Three Parts of a Paragraph

1. The topic sentence

The topic sentence states the main idea in a paragraph. It is usually the first sentence of a paragraph. It lets the reader know what your paragraph is going to be about. The topic sentence should get the reader's attention. It should make the reader want to read the rest of your paragraph.

Ask yourself these questions to help you write your topic sentence:

- What is the purpose of my paragraph?
- What is the main point I want to make?
- Why am I writing this paragraph?
- What will this paragraph be about?

2. The body

The body of a paragraph is the group of sentences that tell more about your main idea. It supports the point of view of your topic sentence. The body can include:

- Facts
- Details
- Explanations
- Reasons
- Examples
- Illustrations

3. The conclusion or summary

The last sentence of a paragraph is a conclusion or a summary. A conclusion is a judgment. It is based on the facts that you presented in your paragraph. Your conclusion must make sense.

A summary is a statement that briefly repeats the main ideas of your paragraph. It repeats your idea or ideas in slightly different words. It does not add new information.

The Purposes of a Paragraph

Every paragraph has one of five purposes. The five purposes are:

1. To give information or facts

Facts are included in all three parts of a paragraph. You may gather facts by reading, listening, or observing.

2. To explain your ideas

You may use this kind of paragraph to:

- Make something clear
- Help someone understand an idea
- Give the meaning of something
- Give reasons for something

3. To ask for information

In this kind of paragraph, make your questions clear and specific. That way, you get specific answers.

4. To persuade

This kind of paragraph helps you to convince someone to act or believe a certain way. You must be sure of what you are saying, then you can persuade someone.

5. To tell a story

You can tell an imaginary or true story in this kind of paragraph. A true story should follow the order in which things happened.

Checklist for Proofreading and Revising

✔Use this checklist to proofread and revise your papers.

Check your paper

- ❑ Do I have a meaningful title?
- ❑ Do I have a conclusion or a summary at the end?

Check your paragraphs

- ❑ Do I start every paragraph on a new line?
- ❑ Is the first line of every paragraph indented?
- ❑ Does my first sentence (topic sentence) in every paragraph explain the main idea of my paragraph? Does it attract my reader's attention well?
- ❑ Do sentences in the middle of my paragraphs support the main idea?
- ❑ Do I include facts, details, explanations, reasons, examples, or illustrations to support my main idea?
- ❑ Do I need to take out any sentences that do not relate to my main idea?

Check your sentences

- ❑ Do I capitalize the first word of every sentence?
- ❑ Do I end every sentence with the correct punctuation mark?
- ❑ Do I express a complete idea in every sentence?
- ❑ Do my pronouns all have clear antecedents?
- ❑ Do I have any run-on sentences that I need to correct?
- ❑ Can I improve my sentences?
- ❑ Can I add adjectives, adverbs, or prepositional phrases?
- ❑ Can I combine short, related ideas into longer, more varied sentences?

Check your verbs

- ❑ Do I have a subject and a verb in every sentence?
- ❑ Do my subject and verb agree in every sentence?
- ❑ Is my verb tense logical in every sentence?
- ❑ Is my verb tense consistent in every sentence?
- ❑ Are my irregular verbs correct?

Check your punctuation and capitalization

- ❑ Did I capitalize all my proper nouns and proper adjectives?
- ❑ Did I capitalize and punctuate all my direct quotations correctly?
- ❑ Did I use a comma to separate words in a series?

Check your spelling

- ❑ Did I choose the correct spelling for each homonym?
- ❑ Did I use an apostrophe only in contractions and possessive nouns?
- ❑ Did I spell every plural noun correctly?
- ❑ Did I spell all words with *ie* or *ei* correctly?
- ❑ Did I drop the silent *e* before adding an ending beginning with a vowel?
- ❑ Did I double the final consonant before adding an ending?

Planning and Writing Reports

Plan the report

- Choose a broad subject you would like to explore.
- Select a topic in that subject area.
- Find out how much information is in the library about your topic.
- Limit your topic so that you have enough information to write a complete report.
- Write a title for your report.
- List your subtopics, or the parts of your larger topic.

Find information

- Go to the library to find information on your topic.
- Look in the library catalog for books that have useful information.
- Check almanacs, encyclopedias, atlases, or other sources in the library reference section.
- Check *The Reader's Guide to Periodical Literature* for magazines with information you could use.
- Take notes on the information you find.
- Use index cards.
- Start each card with this information about the source you find facts in:
  –authors' names
  –book or article and magazine title
  –page numbers
  –volume numbers
  –date of publication
- Copy all the information that you may need.
- Copy any quotations exactly as they are printed.
- Use a different card for each source.

Get organized

- Put your note cards in order by topic and subtopic.
- Choose an order that seems suitable for your topics.
- Do not use notes that seem not to fit anywhere.
- List your main topics.
- Write a final topic outline.

Write your report

- Write your report using note cards and an outline.
- Begin your report with a topic paragraph stating the main idea.
- Use your own words to write the ideas you found in your sources (paraphrase).
- Write an author's exact words if you use direct quotations.
- Name the author or source of any direct quotations you use.
- Repeat your main ideas in a summary paragraph at the end.
- Proofread your report.
- Revise and rewrite it as needed.
- Include a title page at the front of your report.

Prepare a bibliography

- Use the bibliographic information on your note cards.
- Put your cards in alphabetical order.
- Include a blank page after your bibliography.

World Map

ARCTIC OCEAN
Beaufort Sea
Baffin Bay
GREENLAND
Bering Sea
Gulf of Alaska
CANADA
Hudson Bay
Labrador Sea
NORTH AMERICA
NORTH PACIFIC OCEAN
UNITED STATES OF AMERICA
NORTH ATLANTIC OCEAN
CANARY ISLANDS
MEXICO
Gulf of Mexico
THE BAHAMAS
WESTERN SAHARA
CUBA
DOMINICAN REPUBLIC
HAWAII
PUERTO RICO (U.S.)
BELIZE
HONDURAS
HAITI
Caribbean Sea
SENEGAL
GUATEMALA
EL SALVADOR
THE GAMBIA
GUINEA-BISSAU
PANAMA
NICARAGUA
GUINEA
VENEZUELA
GUYANA
COSTA RICA
SURINAME
SIERRA LEONE
FRENCH GUIANA
COLOMBIA
0° Equator
ECUADOR
SOUTH AMERICA
PERU
BRAZIL
BOLIVIA
PARAGUAY
SOUTH PACIFIC OCEAN
CHILE
ARGENTINA
URUGUAY
N
W
E
S
FALKLAND ISLANDS (U.K.)
SOUTH GEORGIA ISLAND (U.K.)
80°N
60°N
40°N
20°N
20°S
40°S
60°S
80°S
160°W
140°W
120°W
100°W
80°W
60°W
40°W
20°W

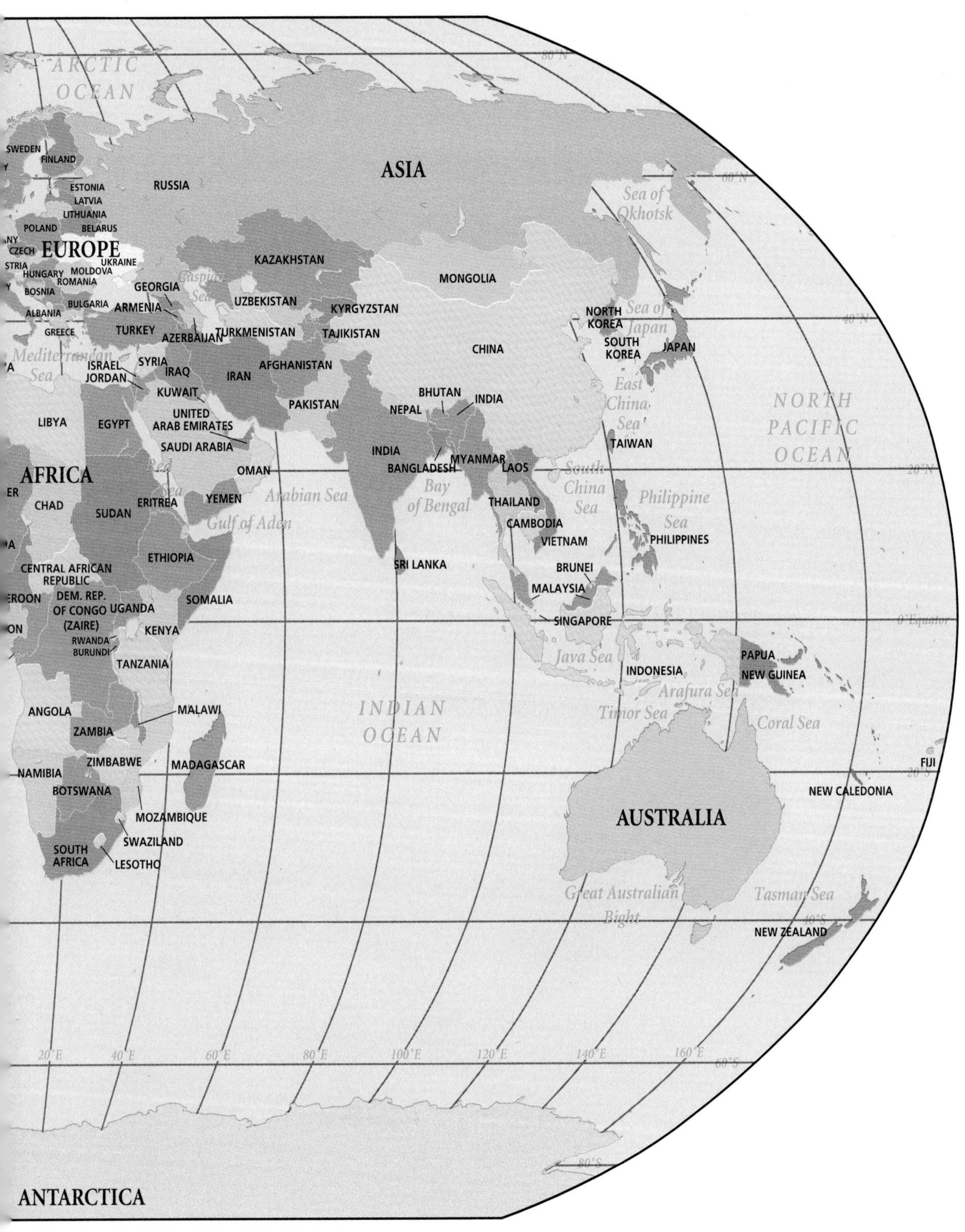

ARCTIC OCEAN
80°N
ASIA
SWEDEN
FINLAND
RUSSIA
ESTONIA
LATVIA
LITHUANIA
POLAND
BELARUS
EUROPE
CZECH
UKRAINE
HUNGARY
MOLDOVA
ROMANIA
BOSNIA
BULGARIA
ALBANIA
GREECE
GEORGIA
ARMENIA
TURKEY
AZERBAIJAN
Caspian Sea
KAZAKHSTAN
UZBEKISTAN
TURKMENISTAN
KYRGYZSTAN
TAJIKISTAN
MONGOLIA
CHINA
Sea of Okhotsk
60°N
Sea of Japan
NORTH KOREA
SOUTH KOREA
JAPAN
40°N
Mediterranean Sea
ISRAEL
JORDAN
SYRIA
IRAQ
IRAN
AFGHANISTAN
KUWAIT
PAKISTAN
BHUTAN
NEPAL
INDIA
UNITED ARAB EMIRATES
SAUDI ARABIA
LIBYA
EGYPT
East China Sea
TAIWAN
NORTH PACIFIC OCEAN
AFRICA
OMAN
Red Sea
BANGLADESH
MYANMAR
LAOS
South China Sea
20°N
CHAD
SUDAN
ERITREA
YEMEN
Arabian Sea
Bay of Bengal
THAILAND
Philippine Sea
Gulf of Aden
CAMBODIA
VIETNAM
PHILIPPINES
ETHIOPIA
SRI LANKA
BRUNEI
CENTRAL AFRICAN REPUBLIC
MALAYSIA
DEM. REP. OF CONGO (ZAIRE)
UGANDA
SOMALIA
SINGAPORE
0° Equator
KENYA
RWANDA
BURUNDI
Java Sea
PAPUA NEW GUINEA
TANZANIA
INDONESIA
Arafura Sea
ANGOLA
MALAWI
INDIAN OCEAN
Timor Sea
Coral Sea
ZAMBIA
ZIMBABWE
MADAGASCAR
FIJI
NAMIBIA
20°S
BOTSWANA
NEW CALEDONIA
MOZAMBIQUE
AUSTRALIA
SWAZILAND
SOUTH AFRICA
LESOTHO
Great Australian Bight
Tasman Sea
40°S
NEW ZEALAND
20°E
40°E
60°E
80°E
100°E
120°E
140°E
160°E
60°S
80°S
ANTARCTICA

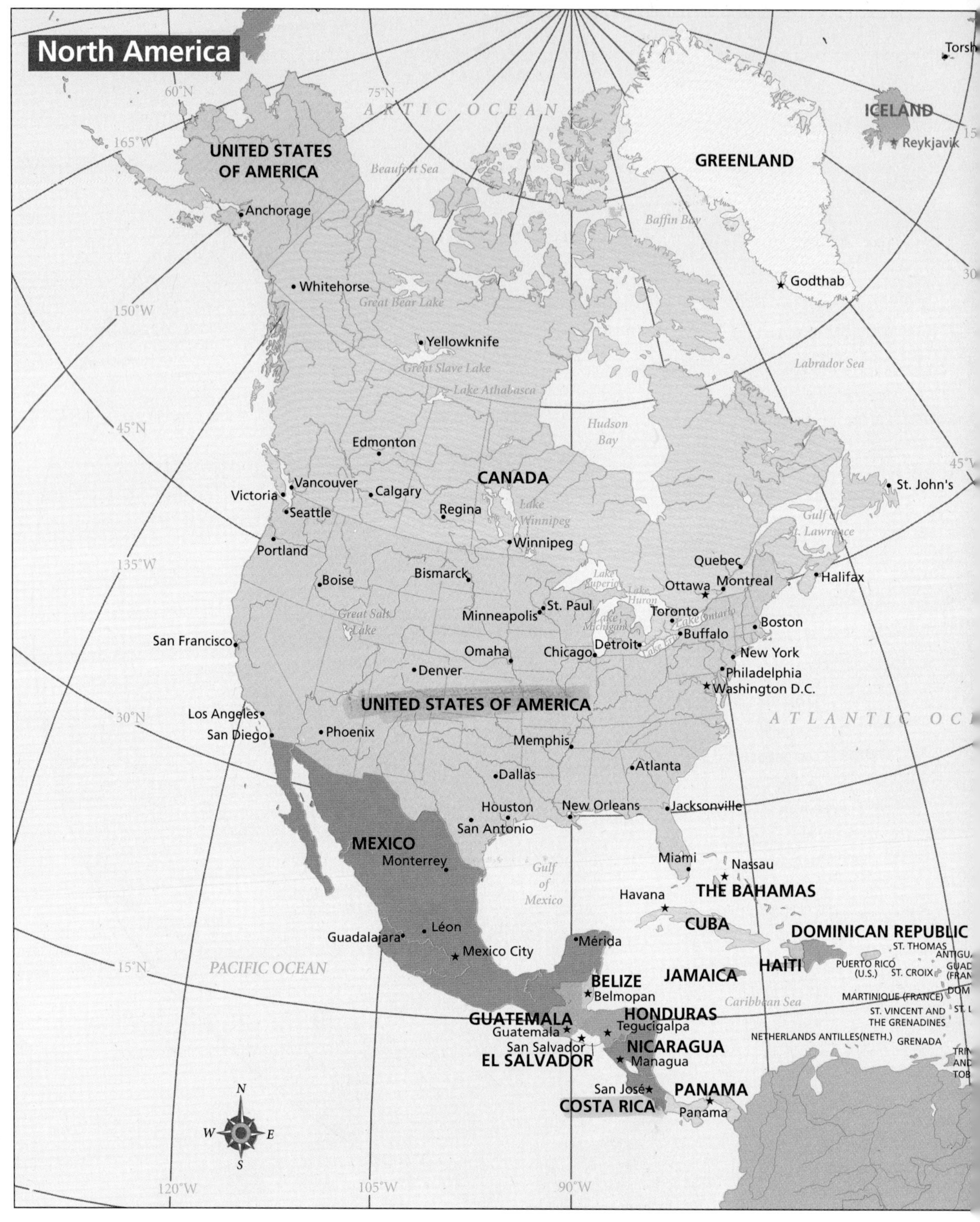

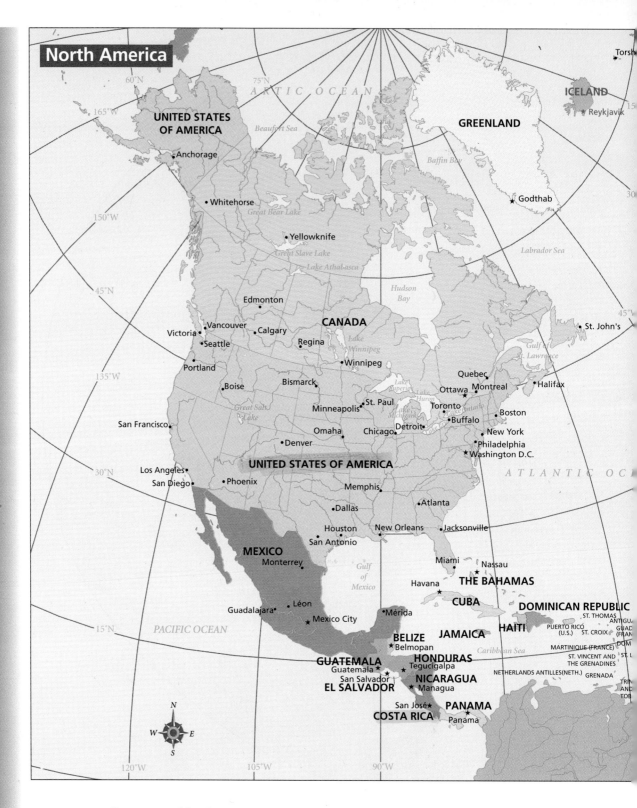

North America
ARTIC OCEAN
60°N
75°N
165°W
150°W
135°W
45°N
30°N
15°N
120°W
105°W
90°W
UNITED STATES OF AMERICA
Beaufort Sea
Anchorage
Whitehorse
Great Bear Lake
Yellowknife
Great Slave Lake
Lake Athabasca
Edmonton
Vancouver
Victoria
Seattle
Calgary
CANADA
Regina
Lake Winnipeg
Winnipeg
Portland
Boise
Bismarck
Hudson Bay
GREENLAND
Baffin Bay
Godthab
Labrador Sea
ICELAND
Reykjavik
St. John's
Gulf of St. Lawrence
Quebec
Montreal
Ottawa
Halifax
Lake Superior
Lake Huron
Lake Michigan
Lake Ontario
Lake Erie
Toronto
Buffalo
Boston
St. Paul
Minneapolis
Great Salt Lake
San Francisco
Omaha
Chicago
Detroit
New York
Philadelphia
Washington D.C.
Denver
UNITED STATES OF AMERICA
Los Angeles
San Diego
Phoenix
Memphis
Atlanta
Dallas
Houston
San Antonio
New Orleans
Jacksonville
ATLANTIC
MEXICO
Monterrey
Gulf of Mexico
Miami
Nassau
THE BAHAMAS
Havana
CUBA
DOMINICAN REPUBLIC
ST. THOMAS
PUERTO RICO (U.S.)
ST. CROIX
HAITI
JAMAICA
Léon
Guadalajara
Mexico City
Mérida
PACIFIC OCEAN
BELIZE
Belmopan
Caribbean Sea
MARTINIQUE (FRANCE)
ST. VINCENT AND THE GRENADINES
GRENADA
NETHERLANDS ANTILLES(NETH.)
GUATEMALA
Guatemala
HONDURAS
Tegucigalpa
San Salvador
EL SALVADOR
NICARAGUA
Managua
San José
COSTA RICA
PANAMA
Panama
N
S
E
W

South America
Caribbean Sea
ST. LUCIA
GRENADA
Managua
San José
Panama
Barranquilla
Caracas
Valencia
VENEZUELA
Cúcuta
Medellín
Bogotá
Puerto Ayacucho
COLOMBIA
Mitú
Georgetown
Paramaribo
GUYANA
SURINAME
Cayenne
FRENCH
GUIANA
Macapá
Quito
ECUADOR
Galápagos
Islands
Guayaquil
Belém
Santarém
Fortaleza
Teresina
Talara
PERU
Trujillo
Porto Velho
Recife
Maceió
Aracaju
BRAZIL
Barreiras
Salvador
Huánuco
Lima
Ica
Cuzco
BOLIVIA
La Paz
Santa Cruz
Sucre
Brásilia
Goiânia
Iquique
Rio de Janeiro
São Paulo
PACIFIC OCEAN
Antofagasta
PARAGUAY
Asunción
CHILE
Córdoba
Rosario
Santiago
URUGUAY
Buenos Aires
Montevideo
Concepción
ARGENTINA
ATLANTIC OCEAN
Valdivia
Puerto Montt
N
W
E
S
Comodoro Rivadavia
FALKLAND ISLANDS
(U.K.)
SOUTH GEORGIA ISLAND
(U.K.)
90°W
80°W
70°W
60°W
50°W
40°W

Europe
15°W
0°
15°E
45°E
60°N
45°N
Reykjavik
ICELAND
Norwegian Sea
Faroe Islands
NORTH ATLANTIC OCEAN
SWEDEN
FINLAND
RUSSIA
NORWAY
Gulf of Bothnia
Helsinki
Oslo
Stockholm
Tallinn
ESTONIA
Baltic Sea
SCOTLAND
North Sea
Moscow
LATVIA
Riga
Belfast
DENMARK
Copenhagen
LITHUANIA
Vilnius
IRELAND
Dublin
Minsk
NETHERLANDS
BELARUS
WALES
U. K.
Amsterdam
London
Berlin
Warsaw
Brussels
GERMANY
POLAND
English Channel
BELGIUM
Kiev
UKRAINE
LUX.
Prague
CZECH REP.
Ostrava
Paris
SLOVAKIA
MOLDOVA
Vienna
Bratislava
FRANCE
Bern
AUSTRIA
Budapest
Chisinau
SWITZERLAND
HUNGARY
ROMANIA
Bay of Biscay
SLOVENIA
Zagreb
Black Sea
Monte Carlo
BOSNIA AND HERZEGOVINA
Belgrade
Bucharest
MONACO
CROATIA
Sarajevo
BULGARIA
Varna
ITALY
Adriatic Sea
SERBIA
Sofia
ANDORRA
PORTUGAL
Madrid
Corsica
Rome
MACEDONIA
Skopje
Ankara
Lisbon
SPAIN
Tiranë
ALBANIA
Sardinia
Aegean Sea
Balearic Islands
Tyrrhenian Sea
GREECE
Athens
Gibraltar
Algiers
Ionian Sea
Rabat
Tunis
N
Valletta
MALTA
W
E
S
Mediterranean Sea
Tripoli
Alexandria

Africa
Lisbon
SPAIN
Cordoba
Gibraltar
GREECE
Athens
Algiers
Tunis
MALTA
Nicosia
CYPRUS
Casablanca
Rabat
MOROCCO
TUNISIA
Tripoli
Mediterranean Sea
Damascus
Baghdad
Amman
Alexandria
Cairo
ALGERIA
LIBYA
EGYPT
Riyadh
Red Sea
MAURITANIA
Nouakchott
MALI
NIGER
ERITREA
Asmara
Khartoum
YEMEN
SENEGAL
Niamey
CHAD
Bamako
Ouagadougou
N'Djamena
SUDAN
BURKINA FASO
Djibouti
GUINEA
BENIN
NIGERIA
Addis Ababa
SOMALIA
IVORY COAST
Yamoussoukro
Abuja
ETHIOPIA
CENTRAL AFRICAN REPUBLIC
GHANA
Porto-Novo
Monrovia
Abidjan
CAMEROON
Bangui
LIBERIA
Accra
TOGO
Yaoundé
EQUATORIAL GUINEA
DEMOCRATIC REPUBLIC OF CONGO (ZAIRE)
UGANDA
Kampala
Mogadishu
SÃO TOME & PRINCIPE
Libreville
GABON
CONGO
KENYA
Nairobi
RWANDA
Bujumbura
BURUNDI
Brazzaville
Kinshasa
TANZANIA
Dar es Salaam
Luanda
Likasi
COMOROS
MALAWI
ANGOLA
ZAMBIA
Lusaka
Lilongwe
ATLANTIC OCEAN
Harare
MOZAMBIQUE
MADAGASCAR
Antananarivo
MAURITIUS
Port Loui
ZIMBABWE
Bulawayo
REUNION
NAMIBIA
Windhoek
BOTSWANA
Gaborone
Pretoria
Maputo
Mbabane
SWAZILAND
LESOTHO
Bloemfontein
Durban
Maseru
SOUTH AFRICA
Cape Town
N
W
E
S
10°W
0°
10°E
20°E
30°E
40°E
50°E

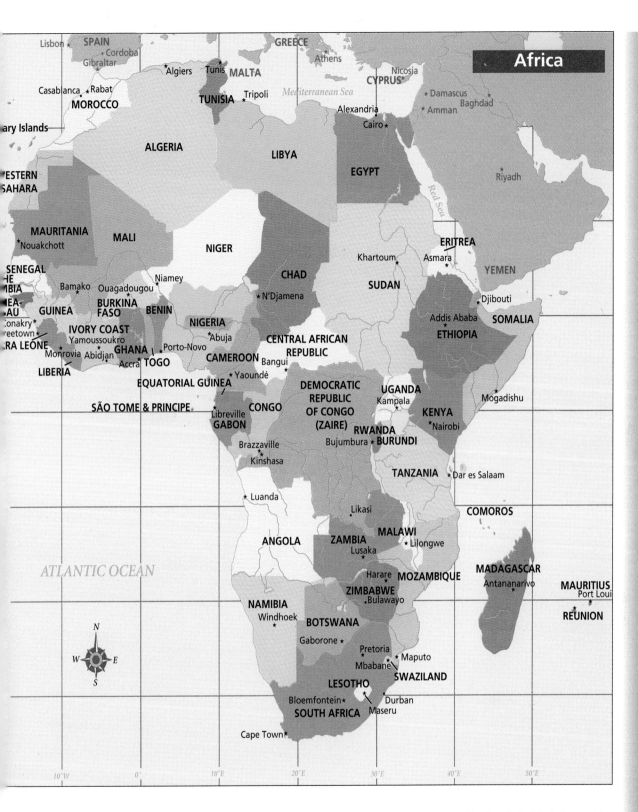

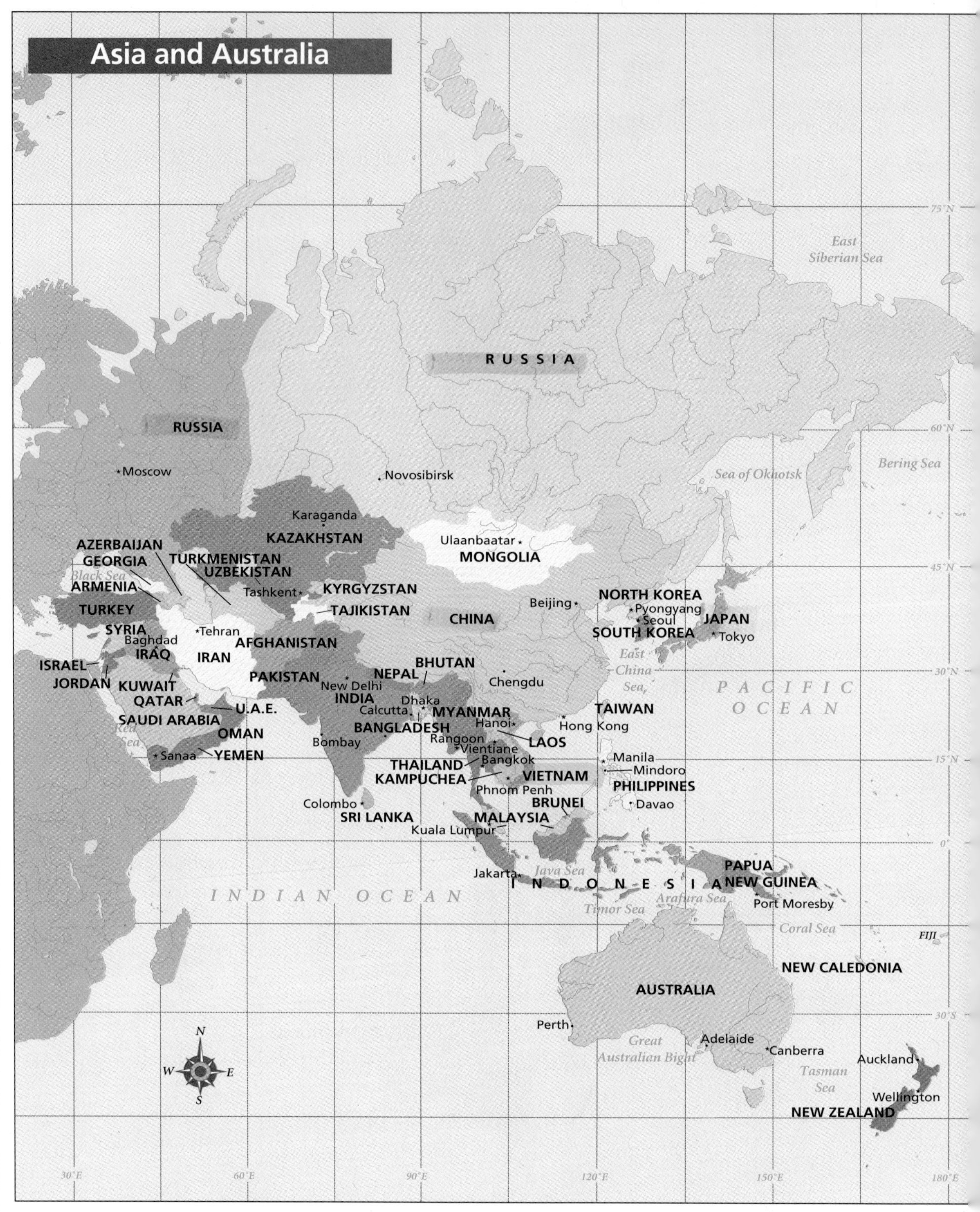
Asia and Australia
RUSSIA
RUSSIA
Moscow
Novosibirsk
East Siberian Sea
Bering Sea
Sea of Okhotsk
Karaganda
KAZAKHSTAN
Ulaanbaatar
MONGOLIA
AZERBAIJAN
GEORGIA
TURKMENISTAN
UZBEKISTAN
Black Sea
ARMENIA
Tashkent
KYRGYZSTAN
TURKEY
TAJIKISTAN
CHINA
Beijing
NORTH KOREA
Pyongyang
Seoul
SOUTH KOREA
JAPAN
Tokyo
SYRIA
Tehran
Baghdad
IRAQ
IRAN
AFGHANISTAN
ISRAEL
JORDAN
KUWAIT
QATAR
U.A.E.
SAUDI ARABIA
OMAN
Red Sea
Sanaa
YEMEN
PAKISTAN
New Delhi
NEPAL
BHUTAN
Chengdu
East China Sea
PACIFIC OCEAN
INDIA
Dhaka
Calcutta
MYANMAR
BANGLADESH
TAIWAN
Hanoi
Hong Kong
Bombay
Rangoon
Vientiane
LAOS
THAILAND
Bangkok
KAMPUCHEA
VIETNAM
Manila
Mindoro
PHILIPPINES
Phnom Penh
Colombo
SRI LANKA
BRUNEI
Davao
MALAYSIA
Kuala Lumpur
Jakarta
Java Sea
INDONESIA
PAPUA NEW GUINEA
Port Moresby
INDIAN OCEAN
Arafura Sea
Timor Sea
Coral Sea
FIJI
NEW CALEDONIA
AUSTRALIA
Perth
Great Australian Bight
Adelaide
Canberra
Auckland
Tasman Sea
Wellington
NEW ZEALAND
N
W
E
S
75°N
60°N
45°N
30°N
15°N
0°
30°S
30°E
60°E
90°E
120°E
150°E
180°E

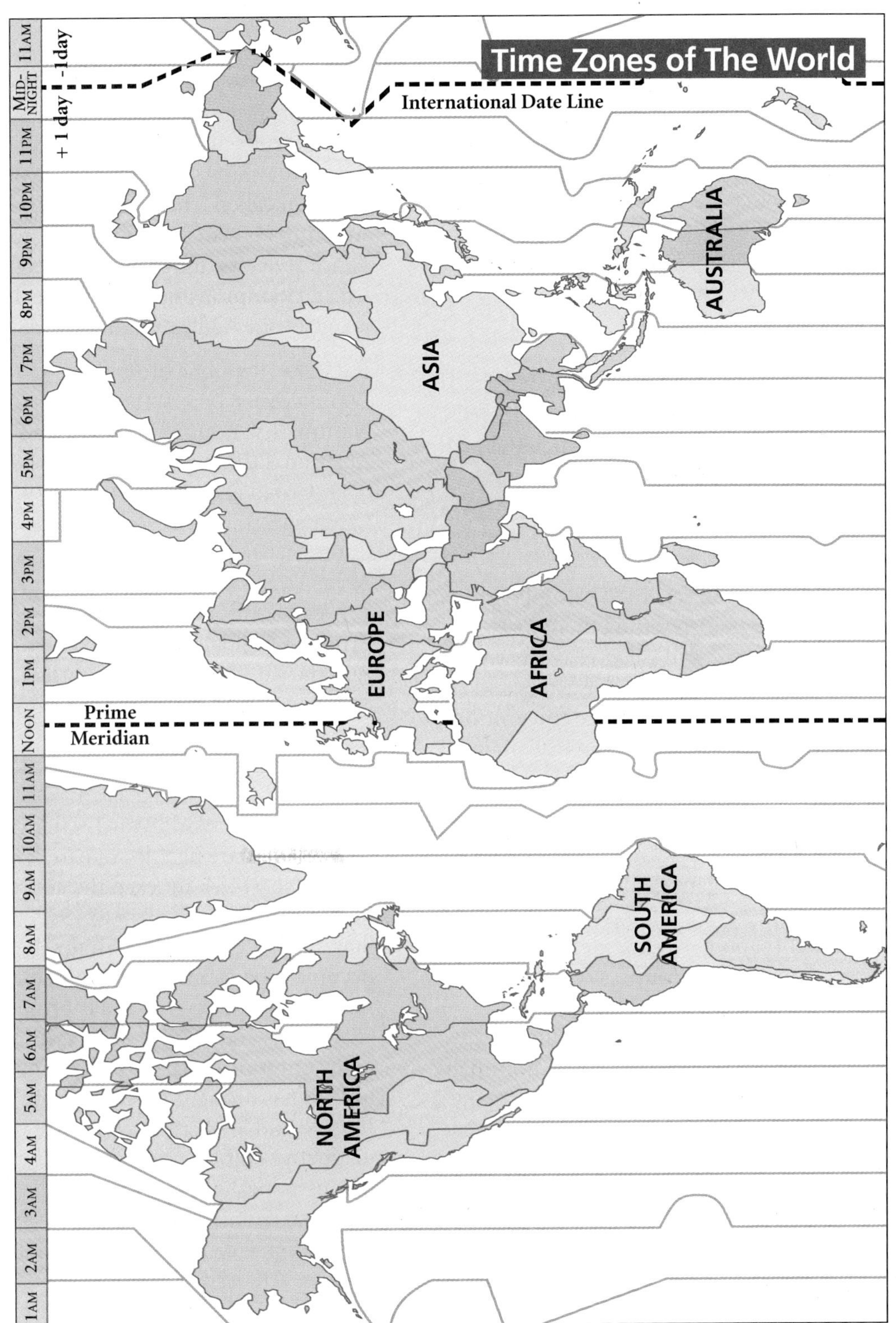
Time Zones of The World
International Date Line
+ 1 day
-1day
Prime Meridian
1AM
2AM
3AM
4AM
5AM
6AM
7AM
8AM
9AM
10AM
11AM
NOON
1PM
2PM
3PM
4PM
5PM
6PM
7PM
8PM
9PM
10PM
11PM
MID-NIGHT
11AM
NORTH AMERICA
SOUTH AMERICA
EUROPE
AFRICA
ASIA
AUSTRALIA

Student Passport to World Cultures

Adapted from ***Information Please Almanac, New York Times 1998 Almanac,*** and ***AGS Survey of World Cultures.*** Information on Wales adapted from Robert Evans (e-mail: Robert.Evans@cs.cf. ac.uk). Information on Sweden ©1994-98 by Antti Lahelma and Johan Olofsson, used by permission. (http:/www.lysator.liu.se/nordic/scnfaq73.html)

Antigua and Barbuda

Population: 65,647 (1996 estimated). **Nationality:** noun: Antiguan(s); adjective: Antiguan. **Ethnic groups:** mostly black African origin; British, Portuguese, Lebanese, Syrian. **Languages:** English (official), local dialects. **Religions:** Anglican, other Protestants, some Roman Catholic. **Area:** 170 sq. mi. (440 sq km); about 2.5 times larger than Washington, DC.

Profile: Columbus claimed Antigua for Spain in 1493. The British settled there in 1632, growing tobacco and sugar. Slavery was outlawed in 1834. Natural disasters and the closing of industries hindered the economy in the 1800s. Today, tourism is the main industry. Barbuda has recently tried to break away because of political and cultural differences.

Argentina (Argentine Republic)

Population: 34,672,997 (1996 estimated). **Nationality:** noun: Argentine(s); adjective: Argentine. **Ethnic groups:** White, mestizo, Indian, and other nonwhite groups. **Languages:** Spanish, English, Italian, German, French. **Religions:** 90% nominally Roman Catholic (less than 20% practicing), 2% Protestant, 2% Jewish, 6% other. **Area:** 1,068,298 sq. mi. (2,766,890 sq km); about three-tenths the size of the United States.

Profile: Argentina is the second largest and the southernmost country in South America. While generally temperate, the varying altitudes create different climates. Among its many natural resources are petroleum products, uranium, timber, beef, pork, fish, cotton, fruits, wool and cereals. Because Argentina ships so much grain worldwide, it has been called "the granary of the world." Argentina is also known for its musical and dance style, the tango, and for its frequent world championships in polo. Its literacy rate is one of the highest in the world.

Austria (Republic of Austria)

Population: 8,023,244 (1996 estimated) **Nationality:** noun: Austrian(s); adjective: Austrian. **Ethnic groups:** 99.4% German, 0.3% Croatian, 0.2% Slovene, 0.1% other. **Languages:** German. **Religions:** 85% Roman Catholic, 6% Protestant, 9% none or other. **Area:** 32,377 sq. mi. (83,855 sq km); its size is between South Carolina and Maine.

Profile: Originally conquered by the Romans Austria was united under Charlemagne and later became part of the Habsburg empire. Part of the country was overrun by the Turks several times, the last being in the late 1600s. The killing of Archduke Franz Ferdinand in 1914 triggered World War I. After the war, the Austrian empire had disappeared, replaced by a republic. Hitler annexed the country before World War II. From 1945 to 1955, the United States, the USSR, Great Britain, and France occupied the country. Then it became a neutral democracy. Austria is proud of its mountains and natural beauty. Its people enjoy outdoor sports such as skiing. Its rich history has brought together many cultures of Eastern and Western Europe. The result is a distinctive culture unlike those of other German-speaking countries. Today, Austria is a neutral country, allowing it to act as an international center of government and politics. Yet, despite its international flavor, Austria holds its rural heritage dear.

Student Passport to World Cultures

Chile (Republic of Chile)
Population: 14,508,158 (1997 estimated). **Nationality:** noun: Chilean(s); adjective: Chilean. **Ethnic groups:** European and European-Indian, Indian, other. **Language:** Spanish. **Religions:** 89% Roman Catholic, 11% Protestant, small Jewish population. **Area:** 292,259 sq. mi. (756,950 sq km); slightly larger than Texas.
Profile: Chile is sometimes called the "Shoestring Nation" because it is ten times as long as it is wide. In the north, it is warm; in the south, cold. The Andes mountains are a tourist attraction for fishers, skiers, and others. Although Chile's farmlands are fertile due to mountain runoff, it cannot produce enough food to feed its people. Mineral deposits are the country's main source of income.

China (People's Republic of China)
Population: 1,221,591,778 (1997 estimated). **Nationality:** noun: Chinese (singular and plural); adjective: Chinese. **Ethnic groups:** Han Chinese; Zhuang, Uygur, Hui, Yi, Tibetan, Miao, Manchu, Mongol, Buyi, Korean, and numerous others. **Languages:** Standard Chinese or Mandarin (Putonghua based on the Beijing dialect); Yue (Cantonese), Wu (Shanghainese), Minbei (Fuzho), Minnan (Hokkien-Taiwanese), Xiang, Gan, Hakka dialects, and minority languages (see "Ethnic groups"). **Religions:** officially atheist, but traditionally pragmatic and eclectic; Taoism, Buddhism, 2-3% Muslim, 1% Christian. **Area:** 3,705,392 sq. mi. (9,596,960 sq km); its size is between the United States and Canada.
Profile: China has one of the world's oldest civilizations. With more than a billion citizens, it has the largest population in the world. Until the early 1900s, China was ruled by dynasties. During this time, the Chinese people made many important contributions to civilization. When the last dynasty failed, China became a republic. However, since 1949, the government has been ruled by the Communist Party. The arts have always been important in China. Evidence appears in beautiful porcelain and landscape painting, for example, as well as in the writings of Confucius.

Colombia (Republic of Colombia)
Population: 37,418,290 (1997 estimated). **Nationality:** noun: Colombian(s), adjective: Colombian. **Ethnic groups:** mestizo, white, mulatto, black, other. **Language:** Spanish. **Religions:** 95% Roman Catholic. **Area:** 439,734 sq. mi. (1,138,910 sq km); between Texas and Alaska.
Profile: In the early 1800s, Colombia originally was part of Gran Colombia, which included the modern-day countries of Ecuador, Panama, Venezuela, and Colombia. Its climate varies from the swampy Pacific coast—the rainiest in South America—to the cold, high mountain ranges in the west. Colombia holds first place for the production of mild coffee. Although the government has remained fairly stable, illegal trafficking in drugs has caused many problems.

England. *See* United Kingdom.

France (French Republic)
Population: 58,609,285 (1997 estimated). **Nationality:** noun: Frenchman (men), Frenchwoman (women), French (collective plural); adjective: French. **Ethnic groups:** Celtic and Latin with Teutonic, Slavic, North African, Indochinese, and Basque minorities. **Languages:** French (100% of population); rapidly declining regional dialects (Provençal, Breton, Alsatian, Corsican,

Catalan, Basque, Flemish). **Religions:** 90% Roman Catholic, 2% Protestant, 1% Jewish, 1% Muslim (North African workers), 6% unaffiliated. **Area:** 176,460 sq. mi. (457,030 sq km); its size is between California and Texas. **Profile:** France, the largest country in Western Europe, has a varied geography and climate. Its culture stretches back thousands of years. Contributors include the Celts, Romans, and Germanic peoples who once invaded this land. Strong leaders such as Charlemagne, Louis XIV, and Napoleon brought France to a position of world importance. The French today have maintained their appreciation of the arts. They delight in preparing and cooking food. A high standard of living gives them time to enjoy family life, another important part of their culture. Sports, such as soccer and bicycling, are popular.

Germany (Federal Republic of Germany) **Population:** 82,071,765 (1997 estimated). **Nationality:** noun: German(s); adjective: German. **Ethnic groups:** German, Turkish, other. **Languages:** German. **Religions:** 45% Protestant, 37% Roman Catholic, 18% unaffiliated or other. **Area:** 137,803 sq. mi. (356,910 sq km); about the size of Virginia and North and South Carolina combined. **Profile:** Germany, a central European nation, has historically been a strong military power in Europe. As part of the Holy Roman Empire and Prussia, it controlled the cultures of the lands it invaded. Germany and Adolf Hitler's Third Reich were defeated in World War II, and the country was divided into East and West Germany. Even divided, the people spoke the same language and many practiced the same Christian faith. They formally agreed to reunite in 1990. Since then, Germany has had to deal with many problems brought on by the complex process of reunifying, including finding ways to finance industrial improvements in the former East Germany. A reunified Germany draws from the country's past. It includes a love of outdoor sports, regional costumes worn on special occasions, and foods that were first prepared before modern-day refrigeration.

Great Britain. *See* United Kingdom.

India (Republic of India) **Population:** 966,783,171 (1997 estimated). **Nationality:** noun: Indian(s); adjective: Indian. **Ethnic groups:** Indo-Aryan, Dravidian, Mongoloid and others. **Languages:** Hindi, English, and fourteen other official languages; twenty-four languages spoken by a million or more persons each; numerous other languages and dialects; Hindi is the national language and primary tongue of 30% of the people; English enjoys associate status but is the most important language for national, political, and commercial communication; Hindustani, a variant of Hindi/Urdu, is spoken throughout northern India. **Religions:** 80% Hindu, 14% Muslim, 2.4% Christian, 2% Sikh. **Area:** 1,269,340 sq. mi. (3,287,590 sq km); slightly more than one-third the size of the United States. **Profile:** The Indus River valley was home to the first Indians. They had a well-developed civilization; it was one of the oldest in the world. As invaders conquered India, the civilization weakened. Europeans came to India around 1600. Among them were the British, who formed the British East India Trading Company. The company grew until it gave the British almost complete control of India for centuries. After many years of struggle, India finally became an independent nation in 1947. Today, India is a democratic republic. Most of its people are Hindus. This means that its customs and traditions are based on the Hindu religion. The most famous of India's beautiful temples and mosques is the Taj Mahal.

Ireland

Population: 3,606,952 (1996 estimated). **Nationality:** noun: Irishman (men), Irishwoman (women), Irish (collective plural); adjective: Irish. **Ethnic groups:** Celtic with English minority. **Languages:** Irish (Gaelic) and English (official); English widely spoken. **Religions:** 93% Roman Catholic, 3% Anglican, 4% other. **Area:** 27,135 sq. mi. (70,280 sq km); slightly larger than West Virginia.

Profile: In the 400s St. Patrick converted Ireland, at first a collection of warring Celtic chieftainships, to Christianity. It was first invaded by the Vikings in the 800s. Although joined with England in 1800 by the Act of Union, Ireland was not well represented in the British parliament. In 1949 Ireland severed all ties to the British crown and became a fully independent republic. Since then its history has been dominated by economic problems and "The Troubles." In this anti-British violence, the Irish Republican Army, a guerrilla group, has attempted to drive the British troops from Northern Ireland. Ireland's cultural contributions are strongest in literature. Consider the writings of Jonathan Swift, George Bernard Shaw, William Butler Yeats and James Joyce. The most important national holiday in Ireland is Saint Patrick's Day, March 17.

Israel (State of Israel)

Population: 5,534,672 (1997 estimated). **Nationality:** noun: Israeli(s); adjective: Israeli. **Ethnic groups:** Jewish, non-Jewish (mostly Arab). **Languages:** Hebrew (official), Arab (official for Arab minority); English most widely used foreign language. **Religions:** 82% Judaism, 14% Islam (mostly Sunni Muslim), 2% Christian, 2% Druze or other. **Area:** 8,019 sq. mi. (20,770 sq km); slightly larger than Massachusetts.

Profile: The Jewish people, led by Moses, escaped slavery in Egypt and set up a kingdom along the Mediterranean Sea. Through the years, the numbers of Jews living in Palestine (as the area was called) decreased as the Arab population increased. After World War I, the Jews began resettling in Palestine. During World War II, millions of Jews fled to Palestine to avoid the Holocaust. In 1948 the United Nations divided Palestine into two states, one for the Jews and one for the Arabs. The Israeli people, who come from all parts of the world, are bound together by the Jewish religion. They are set apart from their neighbors by language, religion, and customs. They tend to be literate, skilled, and hardworking. Border fights continue between Israel and its Arab neighbors. Many people on both sides have been killed. Israel is short of water and fertile land. Its farms are typically on the coast, where the climate is pleasant and there is enough rainfall for farming. The main crops are olives, grapes, and citrus fruits, especially lemons and oranges.

Japan

Population: 125,732,794 (1997 estimated). **Nationality:** noun: Japanese (singular, plural); adjective: Japanese. **Ethnic groups:**

Japanese, other (mostly Korean). **Language:** Japanese. **Religions:** most Japanese observe both Shinto and Buddhist rites; about 16% belong to other faiths, including 0.8% Christian. **Area:** 145,882 sq. mi. (377,835 sq km); slightly larger than Montana.
Profile: Japan is a mountainous country made up of four main islands. In its early years, powerful families or military leaders ruled. Under the leadership of Emperor Mutsuhitos, many advancements were made. A constitution was written and a two-house Parliament established. Japan was destroyed during World War II. But with the help of the United States and others, it rebuilt its industries and government. Today, Japan is a high-technology, industrial country. Though Western influence is strong, the Japanese maintain their own culture. Education is especially important to them.

Netherlands (Kingdom of the Netherlands)
Population: 15,649,729 (1997 estimated). **Nationality:** noun: Dutchman (men), Dutchwoman (women); adjective: Dutch. **Ethnic groups:** Dutch, Moroccans, Turks, and other. **Languages:** Dutch (official). **Religions:** 34% Roman Catholic, 25% Protestant, 36% unaffiliated, 3% Muslim. **Area:** 14,413 sq. mi. (37,330 sq km); 1.3 times size of Maryland.
Profile: During the Holy Roman Empire, the Netherlands was originally the low-lying area near the mouths of the Rhine, Meuse, and Scheldt rivers in northwestern Europe. Despite its small size, the Netherlands became a world power in the 1600s. It maintained extraordinary influence and prestige in European affairs into the 1900s. While devastated by World War II, political stability allowed a dramatic postwar recovery. Today, its main crops are grains, potatoes, sugar beets, livestock; its natural resources include natural gas, crude oil, and fertile soil. The Netherlands are famous for flower farming, especially tulips.

Nigeria (Federal Republic of Nigeria)
Population: 107,129,469 (1997 estimated). **Nationality:** noun: Nigerian(s), adjective: Nigerian. **Ethnic groups:** 250 tribal groups; Hausa and Fulani in north, Yoruba in southwest, and Ibos in southeast make up 65% of population. **Languages:** English (official); Hausa, Yoruba, Ibo, Fulani, and several other languages also widely used. **Religions:** 50% Muslim, 40% Christian, 10% indigenous beliefs. **Area:** 356,668 sq. mi. (923,770 sq km); about 1.3 times the size of Texas.
Profile: Nigeria's history goes back around 2,000 years. It is the most populated country in Africa. It is also one of the richest countries in Africa, with mineral resources and large oil deposits on the Niger River. There is also coal in the river's delta. But most Nigerians are farmers. Since Nigerians tend to speak English and love movies, most movies are in English. Its four ethnic groups distrust one another. In 1967 a civil war broke out when one group tried to set up an independent country, Biafra. The war ended in 1970 with the Biafrans' defeat.

Pakistan (Islamic Republic of Pakistan)
Population: 132,185,299 (1997 estimated). **Nationality:** noun: Pakistani(s), adjective: Pakistani. **Ethnic groups:** Punjabi, Sindhi, Pashtun (Pathun), Baloch, Juhajir (immigrants from India and their descendants). **Languages:** Urdu and English (official); total spoken languages: 48% Punjabi, 12% Sindhi, 10% Siraiki, 8% Pashtu, 8% Urdu, 3% Balochi. **Religions:** 97% Muslim

(77% Sunni, 20% Shi'a); 3% Christian, Hindu, and other. **Area:** 310,401 sq. mi. (803,940 sq km); about twice the size of California.
Profile: Around 350 B.C. Alexander the Great made the middle of the Indus River valley—what is now Pakistan—part of his empire. Arab invaders brought the religion of Islam at the start of the 700s. Ever since, the region has been deeply committed to Islam. Pakistan remains a strong Islamic country. Wheat, rice, cotton and tobacco—its main crops—are grown in the Indus River valley; livestock is farmed in the drier areas of the north and west. Pakistan's natural resources include land, extensive natural gas reserves, some crude oil, coal, and iron ore. Its industry is limited to textiles and food processing. Seeking a balance of power with India, Pakistan tested nuclear weapons in 1998.

Philippines (Republic of the Philippines)

Population: 76,103,564 (1997 estimated). **Nationality:** noun: Filipino(s); adjective: Philippine. **Ethnic groups:** Christian Malay, Muslim Malay, Chinese, other. **Languages:** Filipino (based on Tagalog) and English (both official). **Religions:** 83% Roman Catholic, 9% Protestant, 5% Muslim, 3% Buddhist and other. **Area:** 115,830 sq. mi. (300,000 sq km); slightly larger than Arizona.
Profile: The Philippine islands were controlled by the Spanish from around 1500 to 1898. As a result, Christianity became the main religion, in particular, Roman Catholicism. Control passed to the United States after the Spanish-American War in 1898. Of the 7,000 islands in the Philippines, only about 700 are inhabited. Many have rich soil and natural resources. The islands' tropical climate is good for farming and lumbering. The people are mostly Filipinos, a mixture of Malaysian, Spanish, Chinese, Indian, and Arabian heritage. Many Filipinos work for the wealthy farmers who own most of the land.

Poland (Republic of Poland)

Population: 38,615,239 (1997 estimated). **Nationality:** noun: Pole(s), adjective: Polish. **Ethnic groups:** Polish, German, Ukranian, Byelorussian. **Language:** Polish. **Religions:** 95% Roman Catholic (about 75% practicing), 5% Eastern Orthodox, Protestant, and other. **Area:** 120,726 sq. mi. (312,680 sq km); about the size of Virginia and North and South Carolina combined.
Profile: Poland and its strong culture have developed over many centuries. One influence is its early Slavic culture. Another is its varied geography and climate, and a long history of conflict. Both still color Polish life today. Early on, Poland had much power. Then it ceased to exist as a nation. But culture has kept the Poles unified over the years. Today, this cultural unity is bringing Poland a renewed sense of independence. Once a Communist nation, today it is a democratic republic. Poles enjoy a common language and a rich history of contributions to the arts and sciences.

Russia (Russian Federation)

Population: 147,305,569 (1997). **Nationality:** noun: Russian(s), adjective: Russian. **Ethnic groups:** Russian, Tartar, Ukranian, Chuvash. **Languages:** Russian (official), ethnic languages. **Religions:** Russian Orthodox, Muslim. **Area:** 6,592,745 sq. mi. (17,075,200 sq km); almost twice the size of the United States.
Profile: In the 800s, the Russian state began in the city of Kiev. In the 1200s Mongol invaders destroyed Kiev. The tsars ruled Russia from Moscow until 1917 when the Communists took over. Mikhail Gorbachev tried to reform

Communist society in 1985. But the democratic movement took control with Boris Yeltsin as its leader. In December 1991 the Soviet Union broke into separate republics, and the Commonwealth of Independent States came into being. They comprise fifteen separate, independent countries. The largest is Russia, or "Great Russia." It has more than half the population and about three-quarters of the land of the old Soviet Union. The Commonwealth's chief crops are grain, potatoes, sugar beets, vegetables, and sunflowers; its natural resources include coal, petroleum, natural gas, gold, and iron; its major industries are the extraction and processing of raw materials, and machine-building, from rolling mills to high-performance aircraft. Russia measures about 6,000 miles from western to eastern border. Within these borders is a great variety of climate, from frozen Siberia to the arid southwest. Much of the country is in the northern latitudes. More than half the Commonwealth is flat with rolling hills. Russia also has a great diversity of people. More than 100 distinct languages are spoken and many religious faiths are followed. The culture of Russia is old and deep. It has excelled in classical music, literature, ballet, and art. Russia has also produced many great scientists.

South Africa (Republic of South Africa)

Population: 42,327,458 (1997 estimated). **Nationality:** noun: South African(s), adjective: South African. **Ethnic groups:** black, white, Indian, other. **Languages:** Afrikaans, English, Zulu, Xhosa, Sotho, Ndebele, Pedi, Swazi, Tsonga, Venda, Tswana (all official). **Religions:** most whites and about 60% of blacks are Christian; roughly 60% of Indians are Hindu, 2% Muslim, 28.5% traditional beliefs. **Area:** 471,444 sq. mi. (1,221,040 sq km); its size is between Texas and Alaska. **Profile:** The Dutch settled the republic of South Africa, at the southern end of Africa, in the 1600s. It consists of four provinces: the Cape, Natal, Orange Free State, and the Transvaal. Except for a narrow coastal plain, the country is mostly a great plateau, including grasslands, savanna, and desert. South Africa's well-developed economy produces 40% of the manufactured goods of Africa, 50% of its minerals, and 20% of its farm products. It is the wealthiest nation in Africa. In 1948 apartheid (or "separate development") became official government policy. However, in May 1996, South Africa did away with apartheid and became a democracy. It is now under the leadership of Nelson Mandela.

South Korea (Republic of Korea)

Population: 45,948,811 (1997 estimated). **Nationality:** noun: Korean (s); adjective: Korean. **Ethnic groups:** homogenous; small Chinese minority (about 20,000). **Languages:** Korean; English widely taught in high school. **Religions:** 48.6% Christian, 47.4% Buddhism, 3% Confucianism; pervasive folk religion. **Area:** 38,023 sq. mi. (98,480 sq km); its size is between Indiana and Kentucky. **Profile:** Korea, a peninsula between China and Japan, was invaded many times by both countries. Japan ruled it from 1910 to 1945. Today, Korea is no longer one country. It is divided into North Korea, ruled by Communists, and South Korea, a republic. The Korean alphabet is considered highly scientific. The Korean lifestyle reflects the teachings of Confucius. South Korea, which has twice as many people as North Korea, is a modern, industrial, democratic nation. South Korea's chief crops are rice, barley, vegetables, legumes, chickens, pigs, and cattle. Its natural resources include coal, tungsten, and graphite. Major industries include electronics, automobiles, chemicals, and shipbuilding.

Sweden (Kingdom of Sweden)

Population: 8,865,051 (1997). **Nationality:** noun: Swede(s), adjective: Swedish. **Ethnic groups:** homogenous white population; small Lappish minority; about 12% foreign-born or first-generation immigrants (Finns, Yugoslavs, Danes, Norwegians, Greeks, Turks). **Languages:** Swedish, small Lapp- and Finnish-speaking minorities. **Religions:** 94% Evangelical Lutheran, 1.5% Roman Catholic, 4.5% other. **Area:** 173,731 sq. mi. (449,964 sq km); slightly larger than California.

Profile: The earliest Swedes were the Svear. They dominated a trading empire in the 900s. Sweden is long and narrow. Its terrain is mostly flat or gently rolling lowlands; there are mountains in the north and west. Nature is special to the Swedes. While Sweden has different climates, it tends to be cool in the summer and cold in the winter. The country's chief crops are grain, sugar beets, potatoes, meat, and milk; its natural resources include iron ore, zinc, lead, copper, silver, timber, uranium, and hydropower. Swedes are industrious and work hard to improve their society.

Switzerland (Swiss Confederation)

Population: 7,240,463 (1997 estimated). **Nationality:** noun: Swiss (singular, plural), adjective: Swiss. **Ethnic groups:** German, French, Italian, Romansch, other. **Languages:** total population: 63.7% German, 19.2% French, 7.6% Italian, 0.6% Romansch, 8.9% other. **Religions:** 46.7% Catholic, 40% Protestant. **Area:** 15,942 sq. mi. (41,290 sq km); its size is between Maryland and West Virginia.

Profile: Switzerland is a landlocked country in the middle of Europe. It is famous for its neutrality in the two world wars and for its mountains, the Alps. In its early years, Switzerland was a Roman province called Helvetia. It came into its present form around 1300, with the formation of the Swiss League. Now the league numbers twenty cantons (states) and six half-cantons. Switzerland has one of the highest standards of living in Europe. Its major industries are machinery, chemicals, and watchmaking.

Ukraine (Republic of Ukraine)

Population: 50,447,719 (1997 estimated). **Nationality:** noun: Ukranian(s); adjective: Ukranian. **Ethnic groups:** Ukranian, Russian, Jewish. **Languages:** Ukranian (official), Russian, Romanian, Polish, Hungarian. **Religions:** Christian: Ukranian Orthodox, Ukranian Autocephalous Orthodox, Ukranian Catholic, Protestant; Judaism, Islam. **Area:** 233,089 sq. mi. (603,700 sq km); about twice the size of Arizona.

Profile: The Ukraine is the third largest country in the Commonwealth of Independent States (Russia) and the most densely populated of the former Soviet republics. Established in the 800s, Ukraine is the heartland of ancient Russia and the center for Ukranian Orthodox religion. Its people are called East Slavs or "Little Russians." Kiev, the capital and cultural center of the Ukraine, is considered the Mother of Russian cities. It is an ancient Christian city with many cathedrals and monuments that date back to the eleventh and twelfth centuries. The Ukraine contributes beets, grain, coal, and iron to the Commonwealth.

Student Passport to World Cultures

United Kingdom (United Kingdom of Great Britain and Northern Ireland)
Population: 57,591,677 (1997 estimated). **Nationality:** noun: Briton(s), British (collective plural); adjective: British. **Ethnic groups:** English, Scottish, Irish, Welsh, Ulster, West Indian, Indian, Pakistani, other. **Languages:** English, Welsh, Scottish form of Gaelic. **Religions:** 27 million Anglican; 5.3 million Roman Catholic; 2.0 million Presbyterian; 760,000 Methodist; 450,000 Jewish. **Area:** 94,525 sq. mi. (244,820 sq km); slightly smaller than Oregon.
Profile: Many factors have shaped British culture. Its four countries (England, Scotland, Wales, and Ireland) share a varied geography and a mild, wet climate. The rich British culture has roots in invaders' cultures. These include Celts, Romans, Vikings, and French. Britain has shared its culture with many other countries. This includes the United States and other former colonies. Many countries use the principles of law and government developed in Britain. The Industrial Revolution begun in Great Britain changed most world cultures. Many British writers are loved all over the world. Today, Britain has emerged from two world wars as a modern industrial power. The British enjoy a high level of social support from the government. Everyday life in Britain includes typically British sports like rugby and cricket, unique customs, and excellent schools.

United States of America
Population: 267,954,764 (1997 estimated). **Nationality:** noun: American(s); adjective: American. **Ethnic groups:** white, black, Asian or Pacific Islander, American Indian, Eskimo, or Aleut. **Languages:** English; large Spanish-speaking minority. **Religions:** 56% Protestant, 28% Roman Catholic, 10% none, 2% Jewish, 4% other. **Area:** 3,618,770 sq. mi. (9,372,610 sq km); fourth-largest country.
Profile: The United States is one of the largest and strongest countries in the world. Its geography changes greatly from the Pacific Ocean on the west coast to the Atlantic Ocean on the east coast. Deserts, forests, mountains, and plains are all included. The United States is an international economic leader. It is the world's second-largest producer, and number-one exporter, of grain. Other natural resources include coal, copper, lead, uranium, gold, iron, nickel, silver, crude oil, natural gas, and timber. Major industries in the United States include petroleum, steel, motor vehicles, aerospace, telecommunications, chemicals, electronics, food processing, consumer goods, fishing, lumber, and mining.

Vietnam (Socialist Republic of Vietnam)
Population: 75,123,880 (1997 estimated). **Nationality:** noun: Vietnamese (singular, plural); adjective: Vietnamese. **Ethnic groups:** Vietnamese, Chinese; ethnic minorities include Muong, Thai, Meo, Khmer, Man, Cham, other mountain groups. **Languages:** Vietnamese (official), French, Chinese, English, Khmer, ethnic languages (Mon-Khmer and Malayo-Polynesian). **Religions:** Buddhist, Confucian, Taoist, Roman Catholic. **Area:** 127,243 sq. mi. (329,560 sq km); about the size of Virginia and North and South Carolina combined.
Profile: The Chinese first ruled the Vietnamese by the year 111. In the 1800s, the French ruled them. With the French withdrawal in 1954, Vietnam was divided into North and South. The two countries fought for over a decade. The United States and the Soviet Union were also involved. In 1975 North and South Vietnam were reunited

under Communist rule. The Vietnamese people have borrowed traditions from China, France, and India. They tend to be shy. They greet people with a slight bow and with the palms of their hands open. The teachings of Confucius have influenced the rural people, and they live simply. Vietnam's chief crops are rice, corn, potatoes, rubber, soybeans, and coffee. Its major industries are food processing, textiles, and machine-building.

Wales (Constituent Principality of the United Kingdom of Great Britain and Northern Ireland)
Profile: The history of Wales involves many struggles. Some invaders came from inside Britain and some from outside. The land has been controlled by Romans, Saxons, Picts, Vikings, and Norman French. Finally, in 1536, the Act of Union made it a principality within Britain. Wales's climate is temperate. Its terrain includes high plateaus with mountain ranges cut through by river valleys. It is a land of small farms. In the mountains and moors, sheep farming is a major occupation. Along the coast, dairy and mixed farming are the rule. Among Wales's old heavy industries, even coal mining has almost ceased in Wales. *See also* United Kingdom.

Zimbabwe (Republic of Zimbabwe)
Population: 11,423,175 (1997 estimated).
Nationality: noun: Zimbabwean(s); adjective: Zimbabwean. **Ethnic groups:** African (Shona, Ndebele, other), white, mixed and Asian.
Languages: English (official), ChiShona, Si Ndebele. **Religions:** 50% syncretic (part Christian, part indigenous beliefs), 25% Christian, 24% indigenous beliefs, 1% Muslim.
Area: 150,803 sq. mi. (390,580 sq km); slightly larger than Montana.
Profile: In 1880 Englishman Cecil Rhodes forced the Matabele, a Bantu ethnic group, to surrender ownership of their land to the British. These lands were combined with what is now Zambia. Together they were called Rhodesia. At the end of the 1800s, the countries were divided into Northern and Southern Rhodesia. After black Africans defeated Rhodesia's white supremacy regime in 1980, Southern Rhodesia became the independent country of Zimbabwe. (Northern Rhodesia became Zambia.) The middle of Zimbabwe is a high plateau; the edges are lowlands. The climate is mild and the soil rich. Most people farm. Since the tsetse fly is not a problem, herders raise cattle and sheep for meat. Zimbabwe's chief crops are tobacco, corn, tea, sugar, and cotton. Its natural resources are coal, chromium ore, asbestos, gold, and nickel. The major industries are mining, steel, clothing, and footwear manufacturing.

Handbook of Literary Terms

A

act the separate sections of a play

action what goes on in a story

alliteration the repetition of initial consonant sounds

allusion something referring to a historical event, a person, a place, or a work of literature

almanac a calendar and date book

anecdote a short, funny story

animal imagery a literary device that uses animal-like descriptions to tell about a person

antagonist a person or thing in the story struggling against the main character

aphorism a wise and clever saying

assonance the repetition of vowel sounds

autobiography a person's life story written by that person

B

ballad a simple song that often uses a refrain and sometimes uses rhyme and is passed from person to person

biography a person's life story told by someone else

blank verse unrhymed iambic pentameter

by-line a line in a news article that tells who wrote it

C

character a person in a story

characterization the way a writer develops characters by revealing personality traits

chorus a group of actors who comment on and explain the action in a play

classical drama the rules that define the form of a play

climax an event that triggers the comic or tragic ending of a play

column a regularly appearing article in a periodical

comedy a play with a nontragic ending

coming-of-age story a story that tells how a young person matures

conflict a struggle the main character of a story has

connotation images or emotions connected to a word

consonance the repetition of consonant sounds usually within the context of several words

contemporary current or recent literature

couplet a rhyming pair

D

denouement the resolution to a story

detective story a story in which the main character solves a crime

dialect a regional variety of a language

436 *Handbook of Literary Terms*

dialogue the conversation among characters in a story; the words that characters in a play speak

diary a record of personal events, thoughts, or private feelings

drama a play

dramatic monologue a poem in which a character talks to the reader

E

editorial a news writer's personal opinion about an event or topic

elegy a poem that mourns someone's death

end rhyme a feature of a poem or song in which the last words of two lines rhyme with one another

epic a long story written in verse

essay a written work that shows a writer's opinions on some basic or current issue

exaggeration a use of words to make something seem worse than it is; stretching the truth to a great extent

excerpt a short passage from a longer piece of writing

expressionistic drama a play that may seem realistic but that changes some elements for dramatic effect

F

fable a short story or poem with a moral, often with animals who act like humans

fantasy stories in which wizards and other creatures participate

feature story a news story that analyzes the effect and importance of an event

fiction writing that is imaginative and designed to entertain

figurative language language that makes a comparison and is not meant to be taken literally

first person written as if someone is telling the story

flashback a look into the past at some point in a story

folktale a story that has been handed down from one generation to another

free verse poetry that does not have a strict rhyming pattern or regular line length, and uses actual speech patterns for the rhythms of sound

G

genre a kind of literature

ghost writer someone paid to write a person's autobiography and let that person take the credit

Handbook of Literary Terms 437

Handbook of Literary Terms

H

haiku a Japanese poetry form, made of seventeen unrhymed syllables

Harlem Renaissance a literary movement within modern literature that focuses on African American pride

historical fiction writing that draws on factual events of history

humor literature created to be funny

humorist someone who writes funny works

hyperbole a gross exaggeration

I

iambic pentameter five two-beat sounds in a line of poetry

image a word or phrase that appeals to the senses and allows the reader to picture events

imagery pictures created by words; the use of words that appeal to the senses

immediate news stories on TV and in newspapers as the event happens

Internet a worldwide network of computers that speak a common language

irony the use of words that seem to say one thing but mean the opposite

J

joke a short story that ends with a punchline

journal writing that records a writer's first impressions about a subject

journalism the gathering and communicating of news to the public

L

legend a traditional story that once was told orally and was handed down from one generation to another

letter impressions and feelings written to a specific person

limerick a humorous five-line poem

local color a kind of writing that reflects the way people speak, dress, and behave, and the customs popular in certain places

lullaby a soothing song or poem sung to a baby

M

metaphor a figure of speech that says one thing *is* another; a figure of speech that makes a comparison

modernism a literary movement in the twentieth century that focuses on trying to explain the many changes of the modern world

monologue a longer story told in person

438 *Handbook of Literary Terms*

mood the feeling that writing creates

moral a message in a story

myth a story that explains how some things in the natural world came to be

N

narrator the teller of a story

naturalism a literary movement that focuses on the survival of the fittest against nature and features characters as being helpless against events that are beyond human control and understanding

neoclassical recent plays written in the classical form

news cycle the length of time between the publishing of a news item and an update or reaction to the item

news story the first reports of an event; mainly covers the bare facts

nonfiction writing about real people and events

novel fiction that is book-length and has more plot and character details than a short story

O

onomatopoeia the use of a word to imitate a sound

P

pamphlet a short printed essay about a specific problem; it has no cover or has a paper cover

parody an exaggerated look at a situation

pen name a false name used for writing

personal essay a kind of writing that explores the author's opinion of a topic in a light and often entertaining way

personification giving human characteristics to a nonhuman object

persuasive meant to influence

playwright the author of a play

plot the series of events in a story

poem a short piece of literature that usually has rhythm and paints powerful or beautiful impressions with words

point of view the position from which the author or storyteller tells the story

proclamation letters about important events meant to be read aloud

prop piece of equipment used on stage during a play

prose written language that is not verse

prose poem an open form of poetry that is written as prose rather than as traditional poetry

protagonist the main character in a story

pun humorous use of words or phrases

Handbook of Literary Terms **439**

R

realism a literary movement in which authors write about life as it is, not as they wish it to be

realistic drama a play that tells a story just as it might happen in real life

refrain the repetition of words or phrases to create mood or emphasis

regionalism a word or phrase that comes from a particular area

requiem a prayer for the dead; a work that has been written in honor of the dead

rhyme words with the same vowel and ending sounds

rhyme scheme a pattern of end rhymes in a poem

rhythm a regular pattern of stressed and unstressed syllables

rising action the buildup of excitement in a story

romanticism a literary movement marked by the excitement of learning, the sense of hopefulness, the spirit of individual freedom, strong morals, deeply personal thoughts, emotional sincerity, an interest in nature, and an interest in the unusual and the original

routine a longer story that a storyteller uses over and over in a live performance

S

sarcasm a heavy, sometimes mean-spirited kind of irony

satire humorous writing that makes fun of foolishness or evil

"sci-fi" a kind of science fiction that predicts what the future might be like

science fiction a type of literature that deals with people, places, and events that could not happen in our reality

semiautobiography a story based on a person's life written by that person, with some events changed

sequence the order of events in a literary work

setting the time and place in a story

short story a brief prose narrative

sidebar research and analysis of a news story

simile a figure of speech that makes a comparison using the words *like* or *as*

sketch a brief writing that often runs from subject to subject and is often humorous

sonnet a fourteen-line poem divided into four sections, in iambic pentameter

speech a written work meant to be read aloud

spiritual a religious and emotional song developed among enslaved Africans in the South during the middle of the 1800s

440 *Handbook of Literary Terms*

stanza a group of lines that forms a unit and often has the same rhythm and rhyme pattern

stereotype a simplified idea about another person or group

stream of consciousness a writing technique that develops the plot by allowing the reader to see how and what the characters are thinking

style an author's way of writing

subtitle a second, less important title under the first that gives more information about the writing

surrealism a writing style that is meant to be understood by a reader's subconscious

symbol a person, place, or thing that represents an idea or thought

symbolism the larger meaning of a person, place, or object

T

theme the main idea of a literary work

third person a point of view that refers to characters as "he" or "she" and expresses some characters' thoughts

tone the attitude an author takes toward a subject

tragedy a play in which the main character is destroyed

transcendentalism a literary movement in which the spiritual world has greater value than the material world and the individual is of great importance

turning point a story about an experience that changes a literary character's life

V

verse word patterns that follow definite rhythm and rhyme

villanelle a nineteen-line poem with several repeating rhymes

W

Web site a place on the Internet where information is published

Handbook of Literary Terms **441**

Glossary

abandoned no longer lived in, 127
abhor to dislike intensely; to find disgusting, 268
abject humble; without self-respect, 114; miserable, 212
abolish to put an end to, 338
abreast side by side; in an even line, 181
abruptly suddenly; all of a sudden, 89, 132
abstinence stopping oneself from doing something; self-denial, 96
abstract not practical; not related to real life, 112
acclaim to praise, 331
accordance agreement, 169, 322
accost to approach and speak to in challenging way, 186
adamant refusing to change or move, 38
addicted controlled by a bad habit, 256
adequately well enough, 163
administer to manage, 68
admirable worth admiration, 357
admonish to warn; to scold with a warning, 180
adolescent a teenager or young person, 146
adversary an enemy, 339
aerial an antenna for receiving radio or TV, 354
affected artificial; assumed to impress others, 146
affectionate showing loving, fond feelings for someone, 144
affectionately with love and tenderness, 241
affections emotions or feelings, 273
affluent rich; having plenty of money, 111
aflame burning, 48
agenda a list of things to be done, 210
agitation strong emotion; disturbance, 25
ailment a sickness; an illness, 45, 245
air to discuss in public, 217
alarming frightening, 218
alms charity; a hand-out, 372
ambling slow-moving, 93
amiable friendly, 53
amniotic sac a pouch that holds a developing baby before it is born, 357
ample enough to satisfy, 186
amusement entertainment, 63
analysis a study of how parts fit together, 329
analyzing examining; studying the parts of, 40
anew again, 339
antedate to come before, 60
anthology a collection of writings, 329
anticipated expected, 210
aphrodisiac a food or drug that brings about sexual desire, 359
apology an expression of regret for something one has done, 261
appalled filled with horror or dismay, 256
apparent easily understood, 171
appliance a piece of household equipment, such as a toaster, stove, or microwave, 391
application a way to use something, 215
appropriations public money to be spent on certain things, 57
aptitude a natural ability or talent, 72
aquatic living in or on water, 386
archduke a royal rank equal to that of a prince, 395
aright correctly, 97
aristocratic of high social class, 27; noble or superior in appearance, 204
armaments weapons, 226
arms weapons, 222
arrogant overly proud in a self-important way, 41
arsenal a storehouse for weapons, 218
artillery branch of the military armed with large guns, 27
askew to one side, 95
assault to attack, 47
assimilate to take in, 322
assimilation being taken in by a group, 109
associating being with; keeping company, 113
asunder into separate parts, 339
at loggerheads an expression meaning "quarreling," 270
audacity boldness; daring, 253
austere stern and serious, 182
averted looking away, 26; turned away, 131
babble to make a low, quiet sound like water, 385
baboon a large monkey, 28
backbreaking very difficult, 217
backtrack to go back the way one came, 188
baffled confused, 166
balk to stop and refuse to go, 177
banality the quality of having little meaning, 359, 380
bandy to talk back and forth, 406
bantam a small barnyard fowl, 302
bathrobelike like a robe worn after a bath, 385
battalion a large group of soldiers, 398
bawling crying loudly, 180
beckon to summon by gesturing, 178
begone a command meaning "go away," 245
behalf interest, 239
belaboring going over again and again, 340
belligerent marked by hostile or warlike behavior, 189
belongings personal possessions, 404
beneficial doing good; helpful, 121
benzene a colorless, flammable liquid, 176
bequeath to give to, as in a will, 27
betel an Asian plant whose leaves are chewed, 292
bewitch to fascinate, 272
bigoted stubbornly holding a belief and disliking those who disagree, 324
billiards a game similar to pool, played with a cue and solid balls on a large oblong table with raised edges, 267
blanch to turn pale, 30
blockade something that stops movement in and out of an area, 212
blurt to say suddenly and without thinking, 179
boarding house a place to live where one pays for a room and meals, 253
bosom the breast of a human, 192
bottleneck something that slows progress, 62
boutique a small shop that sells special, often expensive, goods, 355

442 *Glossary*

Glossary

brandish to wave about in a threatening way, 331, 408
breach a failure to live up to a promise, 241; a break, 332
breadth width; extent, 130, 404
breakthrough a major accomplishment, 61
breeching strap of harness behind a horse's rear legs, 95
brood to think moodily about something, 245
buffet a restaurant in which people serve themselves from a counter, 407
bugger a slang word meaning companion or chap, 253
burr a rough or prickly covering around a nut, 128
cadence a rhythm of speech, 58
calculate to plan, 48
calculation a mathematical process or answer, 67
calligraphy fine handwriting, 70
candelabra a candle holder with several branches, 44
capability the ability to do something, 211
capillary a tiny blood vessel, 386
capricious acting on impulse; hard to predict, 59
captivate to fascinate; to interest deeply, 176
caress a gentle touch, 101
caste a social class, 330
catastrophic terrible, 58
celestial heavenly, 36
ceremoniously with formal ceremony, 44
certify to confirm that standards have been met, 72
champagne a sparkling white wine made in France, 45
charitable generous, 109
cheetah a wild spotted cat, 28
cherished kept fondly in mind, 147
chestnut a type of tree that has nuts enclosed in a prickly casing, 127
chiffonier a high chest of drawers, often with a mirror, 269
Christendom all Christianity; the land in which most people are Christians, 318
christening a ceremony for naming and baptizing a child, 271
chronic constant; continuing for a long time, 114, 245
cicada a type of large insect; the males make a loud, humming noise, 385
cipher a zero, 53
circumstance an event; a situation, 374
circumstances conditions, 63; the way someone lives, 145
circumstantial depending on the surrounding conditions, 46
civil service civilian workers of the government, 166
civility courtesy, 340
clanging ringing, 30
cleansed clean; free of dirt, 349
cliché an expression or idea that has been used over and over, 357
client a customer; a person for whom one does a professional service, 24
clod a lump or chunk of dirt, 160
coincidence an accident that makes events seem related, 46
collective grouped together, 326
commentary an explanation; a series of remarks, 378
commiserate to express sorrow and sympathy, 120
commit to do or perform, 42, 243
commonwealth the community as a whole; the nation, 372
communion a sharing of feelings, 163
compass limited area, 94
compatriot a person from one's own country, 326
compel to force, 63
compelling forceful, 186
compensate to repay, 345
competitive involving the effort to win, 169
compile to put together information into a record, 75
completion ending, 210
compliance yielding to a demand, 184
complicated not simple; not easy to understand, 56, 78, 395
complicity state of being involved in a wrong action, 332
compose to make quiet or calm, 38
comprehensive knowing, 25
compulsion the force or reason behind an action, 212
compute to find a number; to work mathematical problems, 54; to count, 373
concealment a state of being hidden, 39
concede to give up, 42
conceive to form in the mind, 336
conception an idea; a mental picture, 329
concisely briefly, 331
concussion a shock; an injury, 322
condescension an attitude of being better than someone else, 37
confidential meant to be secret, 402
confirm to give proof, 203
conflict a battle; the fighting, 127
confounded confused; puzzled, 181
congregate to collect or gather, 187
conjecture a guess, 44
conscientious careful to do things right, 70, 102
consecrate to dedicate to a serious purpose, 336
consequence importance, 29
consequently as a result, 53
conservative not liking change, 59
constellation a pattern of stars that form a picture, 72
constitute to make up, 330
constraint force that limits freedom of thought or action, 323
constructively helpfully, 221
consumption the process of eating or drinking, 70; buying, 380
contemplate to look at thoughtfully, 180
contemporary living at the same time, 326
contemptuous showing scorn, 268
contemptuously with scorn, 46
context the setting or situation, 216
contorted twisted; hard to follow, 151
contradict to say both one thing and its opposite, 57
contrivance a mechanical device, 60
convent a community of nuns, 110
convey to bring or carry, 160
convict to find guilty, 42
convulsed shaken or pulled jerkily, 30
convulsively shaking violently, 321
coolie an unskilled worker who does odd jobs, 171
cope to manage successfully, 166
coppice a dense growth of bushes; a small wood, 96
cormorant a water bird, 386

Glossary **443**

Glossary

coroner the official who decides the cause of death, 32
correlate to show a relationship, 331
corrugate to wrinkle, 55
corrupt dishonest, 210
corrupt to spoil; to make less honest or moral, 112
cosmopolitan including people from many places, 117
coterie a group of people who meet often, 180
counterbalance to use one act to make up for another, 345
couple to attach; to link together, 407
courtesy an act of politeness, 169
courtyard an open space surrounded by buildings or walls, 43
coverage the way something is reported in newspapers or on television, 68
cowed frightened by threats, 129
credence belief; proof, 186
criminologist a person who studies crime and criminal behavior, 38
criticism a judgment that finds fault, 397
cruelty something that causes pain or suffering, 148
crusty gruff; stern in manner, 298
cubicle a small room, 182
currency the form of money a country uses, 349
curry a food dish seasoned with curry powder, 169
curtail to cut short, 325
dash to run quickly, 128
data information, 57, 68
deadening making less intense or lively, 151
debark to get off, as from a ship, 80
debased lowered in worth, 379
decade a period of ten years, 352
deceit a trick, 321
decrepit worn out, 332
deduction an answer found by reasoning, 24
defensive done to defend oneself, 211
deference courteous respect for another's wishes, 122, 374
definitively finally; completely, 378
defray to pay the costs, 26
degenerate to become much worse, 328
deliberately slowly; with care, 43; carefully considered; on purpose, 215, 253
delicacy a rare or special food, 45; a special, enjoyable food, 188
delicious delightful, 154
delusion a false or imaginary belief, 247
depart to leave; to go away, 288
deplorable terrible, 372
deployment the spreading of troops or weapons in a larger area, 218
depravity a wicked act, 328
depression a state of sadness, 359
deserted empty, 172
designate to select for a role, 71
despise to look down on, 261
despite in spite of, 212, 396
destiny fate; a person's fate or future, 105, 192
detached not connected, 328
detachment a small military unit of soldiers, 128
deterrent something that prevents or discourages an action, 217
detonation an explosion, 222
detract to take away, 336
detrimental harmful, 325
development growth; progress, 215
dictatorial having the powers of a strong, single ruler, 380
differentiate to show a difference between, 324
dilapidated shabby from neglect, 350
dilemma a situation that requires a difficult choice, 327
director a person who directs or manages a business, 404
disability a weakened physical or mental condition, 245
disastrous causing disaster, 325
disbelief a refusal to believe, 253
disburse to pay out or hand out, 72
disciplinarian a person who strictly carries out rules, 380
discipline punishment given as a correction, 185
disciplined trained to act according to certain rules, 338
discomfort the feeling of being uneasy or not comfortable, 353
disconcertingly in an upsetting way, 119
disconsolate very sad, 267
discord arguments, disagreements, 205
discordance a harsh, confused sound, 322
discordant unpleasant; disturbing, 270
discourse to discuss, 374
discrepancy a difference; a conflict, 321
disembark to get out of a craft, such as a boat or plane, 349
disfigured marred or spoiled, 188
disinfection getting rid of germs that can cause diseases, 78
dismissive in a manner that discards or sends away, 323
disoblige to go against the wishes of, 375
disparity difference, 324
dispatch to send out, 78; to send off quickly to a place, 402
dispel to make disappear, 32
dispensable not necessary, 63
disperse to scatter in different directions, 332
displacedness a state of being out of place or in the wrong place, 357
disputation a discussion or debate, 151
disrupt to upset or interfere, 112
dissolute wicked; of bad character, 26
dissuade to persuade someone not to take a certain action, 212
dissuasion discouraging someone from an action, 120
distinguished appearing important or famous, 203
distorted twisted, 38
divergent drawing apart; differing, 322
diversion something that entertains, 387
divert to turn aside, 59
divine coming from a god, 163
dog-cart a cart pulled by one horse with room for two passengers, 25
domination control or rule of one person or group by another, 353
draught (Amer. draft) a current of air, 269
dubious causing doubt as to worth or truth, 396

444 *Glossary*

Glossary

dumbfounded stunned into silence, 324
dunce a stupid person, 118
duration the period of time that something lasts, 379
dynamic full of energy; changing, 328
dystrophy illness caused by poor nutrition, 71
eavesdrop to listen secretly, 113
ebbing fading away; becoming less, 260
eccentrically oddly, not in an expected way, 71
ecliptic circle formed where the plane of earth's orbit and another object cross, 71
effective having the desired result, 285
electric eel a long, thin fish that can produce an electric current, 198
eliminate to get rid of, 62
embalm to preserve, 179
embattled locked in a struggle, 53; ready for battle, 341
embrace to adopt; to welcome, 190
emit to send out, 102
emotionally with strong feelings, 204
enclosure an area inside a fence or wall, 43
encroached gradually entered or occupied, 321
endeavor a sincere attempt, 341
endow to provide with a talent or quality, 403
engulf to swallow up; to surround completely, 339
enlarge to make larger, 285
ensign a flag, 379
entailing resulting in, 375
enthuse to show excitement or interest, 114
entice to tempt, 327
epithet an insulting word or phrase, 380
epoch a long period of history, 321
equality state of being equal, 62
equalize to make equal, 345
equivalent something that is equal, 58
eradicate to get rid of, 340
escalation an increase or rapid growth, 226
essence the basic quality of something, 330
esteem to think highly of, 374
etherealization making things lighter, 60
eucalyptus a tall tree with strong-smelling leaves, 171
evader a person who avoids doing something, 210
evaluate to judge the worth of, 322
evenly without a change in tone, 255
exaggerate to make something greater or more serious than it really is, 146
exasperating annoying, 323
excessive too much, 122
excursion a trip; an expedition, 74, 104
executive the branch of government that carries out the laws, 217
exigency something demanding immediate attention, 63
existential based on real experience, 205
expectantly eagerly waiting to hear or see something, 259
expenditure spending, 211
expletive a curse, 155
explicitness a very frank or clear statement, 113
exploitation the unfair use of a person or resource for selfish purposes, 323, 353
exportation being sent to another country for sale, 375
extinguish to put out, 151
extraneous not necessary, 73
extraordinary remarkable; very unusual, 167, 354
facet one part or angle, 326
faltering hesitating in movement, 48
famine a severe lack of food, 408
fancy imagination, 95
federation an association of states, 57
feign to pretend, 102
fervent showing deep feeling, 109
fiancé a French term meaning a man engaged to be married, 268
fiasco a complete failure, 254
fickle not faithful; not reliable, 159
filth foul matter; dirt, 260
financial having to do with money, 111
finery elegant, dressy clothing, 197
finite limited, 58
fit a sudden violent outburst, 243
fitful restless, 38
flamethrower a military weapon that sends out a stream of burning fuel, 387
flawless perfect; without any marks, 239
flicker to give off unsteady light, 47
fluently using language easily, 119
fodder dry food for farm animals, 129
footwear anything worn on the feet, 384
foppishly vainly; overly proud of one's looks, 182
fore the front part, 374
forebear an ancestor, 338
formalise (Amer. formalize) to make official; to sign an agreement, 221
formalities official rules; customs, 80
formulate to plan, 340
forsaken abandoned; left alone, 123
forthwith immediately, 211
fortnight a period of two weeks, 28
foyer an entrance hall, 43
fragrance sweetness of smell, 171
frank bluntly honest, 349
frenzy a wild excitement, 88
fricassee a dish made with cut-up pieces of meat in gravy, 373
frivolously not seriously; playfully, 327
function a normal use or activity, 358
function to work properly, 73
fundamentals the basics, 62
futon a thin mattress usually used on the floor or on a frame, 385
gab a slang word meaning to talk; to chatter, 397
gangly tall, thin, and ungraceful, 298
garnish to add extras to a serving of food, 46
gash a long deep cut, 241
gemstone a jewel, 163
gendarme a police officer, 406
gender sex; male or female, 71
gild to cover with gold, 36
glimmer to give off a dim light, 54
global alliance an agreement among world nations, 341
global worldwide, 217

Glossary **445**

Glossary

glorified made to seem more important than is really true, 38
glorify to give honor or high praise, 111
Gold Mountain Chinese immigrants' name for the United States, 198
gory stained with blood, 241
gourd a kind of vegetable that grows on a vine, 127
graveyard a place where people are buried, 285
gravity seriousness, 47, 225
graybeards old men, 292
grievance something to complain about, 372
grieve to cause harm or sadness, 305
grubby dirty, 379
grudgingly unwillingly, 122
guarantor a person or thing that promises a certain result, 226
haggard looking worn because of worry, 25; looking thin and tired, 57
hallow to set apart as holy, 336
handpicked chosen carefully, 407
harmony agreement, 146; a pleasant agreement in feeling or actions, 358
hastily quickly, 90
hatred strong dislike or hate, 291
hazard something dangerous, 73
headmistress female principal of a school, 166
hearsay gossip, 406
heartfelt deeply felt; sincere, 259
heartily with enthusiasm, 267
hearty sincere, 239
hectic confused; full of fast activity, 177
heighten to make more intense, 161
heir person who inherits something from the person who once had it, 338
hence from this time, 185; from here, 318
herbalist a person who makes medicines from herbs, 121
heritage what is handed down from earlier generations, 338
hesitate to hold back, 131
Hindi languages widely spoken in India, 167
hoard to save for the future, 299
holster a case for a pistol, 100
holy writ a piece of religious writing; the Bible, 299
homily a sermon, 120
hooligan a troublemaker; a young man who does vicious or violent acts, 403
hornswoggling tricking someone, 56
hospitality the friendly treatment of guests, 28
hostile angrily opposed to, 122
hubbub confusion, 30
humidity the amount of moisture in the air, 69
humiliating causing shame or loss of dignity, 323
humiliation the state of being disgraced or shamed, 186
hydroponics a method of growing plants in water, 60
hyperactive very active, 386
hypothesis an idea that needs to be proved, 44
idealism belief that things can be perfect, 111
identical exactly the same, 47
illiterate not knowing how to read or write, 192
illusionist a magician, 54
immemorial beyond the limits of memory, 321
imminent about to happen, 324
immortal one who lives forever, 199
impaled speared; stuck on a sharp stick, 298
impasse a road with no way out, 45
impassive not moving; not showing any feeling, 37
impending about to happen, 30
impenetrable thick; not possible to get through, 39; not able to be pierced or broken, 58
imperative commanding, 54
impetuous hasty; quick to act, 36
impingement the act of intruding or disturbing, 59
implore to beg, 123
importuning begging, 372
impoverish to make poor, 326
improvise to invent or put together on the spur of the moment, 79
in earnest sincere, 154
inability lack of ability, 166
incalculable not possible to measure in advance, 58
incandescent glowing; very bright, 298
incapable without the ability, 121
incarnation the solid or human form of an idea, 46
incessantly continuing without stopping, 36, 145
incision a thin cut, 105
inclemency storms; discomforts, 375
inclination a leaning toward something, 327
incomprehensible not capable of being understood, 168
incomprehension lack of understanding, 324
incredible too unlikely to be believed, 349
incredulously in surprise; not believing, 112
incur to bring upon oneself, 375
indifferent not caring one way or another, 42, 68
indignity an insult; shameful treatment, 38
indistinct not clear, 95
indivisibility state of not being able to be divided, 328
indoctrination the teaching of a certain point of view, 330
induce to persuade, 37
ineligible not qualified, 184
ineradicable impossible to erase or remove, 104
inevitable sure to happen, 96, 375
inevitably in a way that can't be prevented, 43
inexorably in a way that can't be stopped, 40, 331
inexplicable not possible to explain, 129
infectious capable of causing infection, 205
infer to conclude, 205
infinitely without any limits, 120
inflexible stiff; rigid, 102
infuriating causing great anger, 253
ingenuity cleverness; inventive skill, 353
inkling a hint; a suggestion, 183
innermost most personal; deepest, 147
inscrutable mysterious; hard to understand, 37
insignificant small; not important, 151
insolence a rude or insulting attitude, 406

446 *Glossary*

Glossary

insular limited in outlook and experience, 167
integer a whole number such as 1, 2, 3, 61
integrity completeness, 210
intellectual having to do with the mind, 61
intensify to become stronger, 27
intensity strength, 210
intention aim; a plan to do something, 97, 222
interject to insert a remark, 189
interminable endless, 154
internship a time of supervised training, 72
interred buried, 326
intervene to come in between, 187
intervention an act of interfering, 326
intimate very close, 331
intimidated frightened, 166
intone to speak in a chant, 114
intricate complex; difficult to arrange, 178
intrigue a secret or underhanded scheme, 268
introspection examining one's own thoughts, 327
intruder a person who breaks in, 39
intuition a way of knowing without proof, 24, 61
invaluable beyond price, 325
invasion an entering by force, 130
inventory the stock of supplies, 68
investigation a study to get facts, 24
invoke to call upon for help, 340
ironic mocking, 323
irrefutable impossible to prove wrong, 325
irritating annoying, 112
isolated kept apart from others, 205
jasmine a vine or bush with fragrant flowers, 170
jubilant happily excited, 292
jurisdiction the area where one has authority, 330
karma fate; destiny, 160
kilometer a distance of 1,000 meters, equal to about .62 miles, 285
kimono a long, loose robe with wide sleeves and tied with a sash, 384
kohl dark powder used as eye makeup, 168
laborious requiring long, hard work, 163
lacerated torn, 330
laden loaded with; heavy, 62
lamentation a cry of grief or sorrow, 186
landscape a stretch of land forming a single scene, 89
latrine an outdoor toilet, 110; a small building used for a public bathroom, 351
latter the second of two things mentioned, 145
lavatory a bathroom, 356
lavishly generously; using more than is necessary, 179
lawsuit a complaint brought before a court of law, 395
leasehold property held by lease, 96
leave a vacation; permission to be away from work, 117
leech a blood-sucking worm, 161
lethargy drowsiness; slowness, 114
liberated free from outside control, 239
limb a leg or arm, 178
linens household goods made of cloth, such as sheets and towels, 391
lingering lasting a long time; staying on, 90
liquor a strong alcoholic drink, 407
loathing intense dislike, 31
loathsome disgusting, 31
lobster a sea animal that is used for food, 355
locks the hair of the head, 241
lofty high, 127
logical reasonable, 24
longed greatly wished for, 268
loophole a way out of a difficult problem or situation, 37, 110
lot fate; state in life, 190
lush having lots of plants, 291; growing thick with plants, 348
luxurious quite splendid and comfortable, 350
magnitude greatness; importance, 192
maintaining declaring, insisting, 216
makeshift a temporary substitute, 379
malice ill will, 272
mallet a short-handled, heavy hammer, 160
maneuver a change in course or position, 79
manhood courage, 243
mania an intense, almost insane, excitement, 27
manifest to show, 327
manifold of many kinds, 26
manipulate to handle or manage, 59
manipulation the action of controlling or operating, 76
manner kinds, 198
manor the main house on an estate, 28
manure animal waste used as fertilizer, 161
massive huge, 211
matriarch a woman who rules a family, 179
mature to become fully grown, 160
maximum the greatest possible amount, 109, 341
mayfly an insect that hatches in the water and only lives a few days, 295
mayonnaise a thick salad dressing, 45
meandering going along a winding course, 325
measure an amount, 336
meddle to interfere, 257
membrane a thin layer of material, 329
mercenary concerned only with making money, 327
merciless cruel; without mercy, 94
metropolis a city, 24
militarisation (Amer. militarization) the process of being taken over or used by the military, 216
millennium a period of one thousand years, 357
millet a cereal grain whose small seeds are used for food, 188
millionaire a person with at least one million dollars, 378
mimic to copy closely, 358
mince to walk with very short steps, 384
mingle to mix, 239
minimize to make as small as possible, 345
minister a high government official, 351
minutely paying attention to small details, 184

Glossary **447**

mirage an optical illusion; something you see that is not really there, 151
mischance bad luck, 241
misery great pain, 148
mission a task; an assignment, 129
misunderstand to fail to understand correctly, 145
mock to make fun of, 256
mocking laughing in disgust and anger, 151
molecule a tiny bit, 385
momentary brief, 41
monitor to measure with an instrument or device, 218
monotonous dull, boring, 76
monotony sameness, 161
monsoon seasonal winds that bring rain to southern Asia, 159
mores traditional customs, 189
moron a remarkably stupid person, 269
morose gloomy, 27
morsel a bit of food, 299
motive the reason for an action, 37
multicoloured (Amer. multicolored) having many colors, 359
murderer someone who kills another person, 104
murderess a woman who kills someone, 121
mute a person who can't talk, 295
mutilated cut up; damaged, 101, 122
mutual shared in common, 206, 322, 397
needled made angry, 257
negligence carelessness, 72
negotiate to work to reach agreement, 340
negotiations discussions leading to an agreement, 119
neigh the cry of a horse, 288
nevertheless all the same, 121; however, 299
norm the usual pattern, 221
not inconsiderable important enough to demand attention, 332
notary a notary public; a person who signs or witnesses signing documents, 404
notorious famous for bad activities, 354
nurture to care for, 159

nutrient food needed for growth, 163
nutriment food, 373
oarsman the man rowing a boat, 295
obeisance a respectful gesture or attitude, 114
oblivious not aware; not noticing, 40
obscenities curses, 187
obsolete out of date, 292
obstinate stubborn, 111
obstinately stubbornly, 121
occupant a person who lives or stays in a certain place, 31
ode a poem that praises something or someone, 299
officialdom an entire group of officials, 403
onslaught an attack, 331; a violent attack or charge, 380
openly publicly; in front of others, 204
oppression strict rule or control through the use of force, 353
option a choice, 215
oracle a person who gives wise advice, 176
originate to begin, 53
outrageous extreme, 298
outset the beginning, 24
overburdened having too heavy a burden, 340
overdue past due, 259
overjoyed delighted; very happy, 94
overpowering powerful; too strong to resist, 40
overwhelming crushing; destructive, 359
overwhelmingly with strength impossible to resist, 63
painstaking very careful, 55
palatial elaborate; like a palace, 211
palpitate to beat rapidly, 168
paradoxically self-contradictory, 184
parapet a railing along the edge of a roof or wall, 28
parcel an area of land, 161
parching very dry, 119
parsonage a house where a church minister lives, 31
partake to share; to take part, 332
participant one who takes part in something, 67
passion a strong feeling for or about something, 271
pastor a Christian minister, 118
pastrylike looking like baked goods made of dough, 355

pauper a very poor person, 403
pedestrian a person walking or traveling on foot, 43, 387
peevishness annoyance; bad temper, 172
pelican a large bird whose bill has a pouch that holds fish, 386
pending not yet decided; waiting for action, 352
penetrate to force or find a way into, 40
pensioner a person who receives pay after retiring, 379
pensively in a sadly thoughtful way, 270
perceived seen; known through the senses, 329
perceptible able to be seen or heard, 39
perception a way of seeing or observing, 352
perfunctorily without thought or care, 122
perilously dangerously, 225
perpetrate to carry out, 27
persevere to carry on in spite of difficulties, 122
perseveringly keeping at something in spite of difficulties, 190
peruse to read carefully, 184
petitioner one who asks for help, 154
petty mean; small, 273
philosophy a basic theory; a viewpoint, 176
pilchard a small fish related to the herring, 176
pilot a person who steers a ship, 272
pitch completely black, 154
pitchblack very dark; as dark as tar, 291
pitiable causing a feeling of pity, 25
placative calming; ready to ease another person's mind, 60
placidly calmly, 53
plague the sudden arrival of something destructive; a nuisance, 159
plaudits strong praise, 378
plight serious problem, 96
pogrom an organized attack on a group (Russian for "riot"), 402
poised held up; balanced, 103
political activist a person who takes action to bring about political change, 386

448 *Glossary*

Glossary

pollination transfer of pollen to make plants fertile, 70
pool to combine one's money with others in a group project, 197
pose a position taken on purpose, as to have a picture taken, 399
postmonsoon after the rainy season, 167
potential the ability for action or growth in the future, 226
precarious dangerous, 58; insecure, 166
precipice a steep cliff, 36
precisely exactly, 78
precision exactness, 102
precocious showing ability at an earlier age than usual, 109
predetermination deciding in advance, 71
predicament a difficult situation, 47
prejudice an unfair strong feeling toward a group, 113; feeling of hatred for a particular group, 146
premature earlier than expected, 25
preposterous absurd, 47
press to ask in an urgent way, 399
pretext an excuse for not doing something, 190
prig a person who is easily offended, 130
primitive simple or crude, 78, 197
priority order of importance, 176
privacy state of being alone, away from others, 63
privy an outhouse, 182
procedure a way of doing something, 73
proceedings series of events, 168
prodigious enormous, 372
profane not holy or sacred, 155
professed announced publicly, 373
profoundly deeply, 48
profusely in large amounts, 44
prolong to make last longer, 399
proposition an idea or statement, 336
proprietor the owner of a business, 86
prosperous successful; wealthy, 357
protestation a strong objection, 179
protruding sticking out, 31
psychic having to do with mind and spirit, 72
psychoneurotic having mental problems, 73
pulsating moving in a regular rhythm, 321
pulverize to pound into a powder, 386
pumice a light rock from a volcano, 74
puncture a small hole caused by a sharp object, 32
purge to cleanse; to purify, 177
pyramid a figure with four triangles for sides, 74
qualification an ability that suits a person for a certain task, 119
quench to satisfy; to put out, 86
quit to leave, 245
quote to state or offer a price, 349
racist referring to another race in an insulting way, 379
rage to speak furiously, 305
ragout a stew of meat and vegetables, 373
raiment clothing, 373
random by chance; without purpose, 56
randomly without a definite pattern or plan, 395
rank official position, 239
rapidity speed, 32
rarefaction the state of being thin or less dense, 332
rash bold; hasty, 120
rasp to scrape with a harsh sound, 102
rational based on reason, 59
rave to speak wildly, 305
razor an instrument used for shaving, 89, 100
re-enactment acting out something that happened once before, 123
react to act as in response to something, 258
reality things as they actually exist, 359
rebel to go against rules or authority, 206
recalcitrant stubborn; resisting authority, 62
recall to call back; to remember, 32, 128
receptive ready to accept, 161
reciprocate to respond to another's actions, 221
reciprocity an equal exchange, 329
reckoning paying or settling what is owed, 404
recollection something remembered, 186
reconcile to bring into agreement, 345
reconstruction the rebuilding of something, 59
recourse something to turn to for help, 328
recurrent repeated, 47
red-handed in the act of doing something wrong, 44
refinement a small change that will improve, 374
refresh to make less tired, as if by resting or eating, 355
regent a person who temporarily rules in place of a king, 318
regretful remembering with sorrow or grief, 181
reign to rule or dominate, 145
rejuvenate to restore youth or energy, 104
relentlessly without yielding, 93
reliable to be trusted, 71
relinquish to release or let go, 318
reliving living over again; remembering, 292
reluctant not willing, 77
reluctantly unwillingly, 177
remorse regret for having done something harmful, 123
repent to feel sorry for an action, 345
reprisal an act of force in revenge for an assumed wrong, 402
reproach to scold; to blame, 245
requisitioned demanded, required, 206
resourceful able to find ways to get things done, 199
restive hard to handle, 89
restless never still or motionless, 144
restraint control over actions or feelings, 222
reveal to show, 32, 318; to make known, 395
revelry a loud celebration, 407
reverberate to echo, 44
revere to honor and respect, 176
rigid stiff, 171, 256
rigmarole nonsense, 56
rind the outer skin or coating of a thing, 272
ritual a series of acts done in a traditional order, 162
rotation the motion of a planet turning around its axis, 67

Glossary **449**

rouge reddish powder used to add color to the face, 197
rounds a pattern of assigned duties, 69
ruckus a noisy disturbance, 131
ruddy having a healthy, reddish color, 291
rude rough; crudely made, 87
ruefully expressing regret or pity, 182
ruff a collar that stands out from the neck, 302
ruthless cruel; without mercy, 32, 358
sabotage to damage on purpose, 36
sackcloth rough, coarse cloth, 96
sage a wise person, 199
salvation rescue; a way out of danger, 45; rescue from evil or problems, 330
sanity soundness of mind, 189
sarcastically mockingly, 109
sari a draped outer garment of lightweight cloth traditionally worn by Indian women, 170
satanic devilish; evil, 43
savor to taste, 46
say-so the right to decide, 205
scandal talk about a public disgrace or action, 351
sceptical (Amer. skeptical) doubting, 110
scoff to show scorn, 189
scropbrush a brush to scrub with, 177
scrutinize to examine carefully, 36
scuttle a pail for carrying coal, 181
sear to burn, 28
security safety, 29, 216, 226
sedan a closed automobile with front and back seats, 41
sedately calmly; with dignity, 170
seismology the study of earthquakes, 217
self-congratulatory giving praise to oneself, 378
self-regulating making adjustments without outside help, 69
sensual pleasing to the senses, 161
separation the act of leaving one another, 288; the state of being apart, 291
serum a liquid containing medicine, 76
shame a painful feeling caused by having done something wrong, 256
shan't a short form of shall not, 273
sheer pure; not mixed with anything, 253
shield to protect, 226
shielding hiding, 202
short circuit a break in an electric current, 39
shun to avoid, 190
shuttle to go back and forth, 46
siesta a rest, usually taken after the noonday meal, 169
significance meaning; importance, 190, 206, 378
sisal a long, strong durable white fiber used to make ropes and twine, 178
skeptically with doubt, 61
skirmish a conflict or dispute, 187
slither to move along by gliding, as a snake, 272
slogan a saying or motto used by a group, 226
smoke out to find; to make known, 53
snare a trap, 131
solely only, 211
solitary alone, 285
sophisticated having a broad knowledge of the world, 354
sorcerer a wizard, 397
sordid dirty; selfish, 57
sorghum cereal grain ground into fine meal or made into a sweet syrup, 188
sound healthy, 239
spatter to splash, 25
specific particular, 62
specimen an example of a group of things, 131
speedily quickly, 31
spine a thorn, 129
spit a narrow rod that holds meat to be cooked over a fire, 299
splendid glorious; excellent, 254
sporadically happening now and then, 294
sprint to run a short distance at top speed, 170
sputum spit, 78
squabble to quarrel; to argue about something small, 387
squeegee a tool used to scrape water from a flat surface, 197
stabilise (Amer. stabilize) to stop change; to make steady, 222
start a quick, jerking movement, 243
station master the person in charge of a railroad station, 407
status social position relative to others, 351
stealthiness secretive actions, 154
steeped soaked; thoroughly covered, 41
stereo sound equipment, often used to play music, 391
sterile free from germs, 68
stifle to hold back, 130
stifled choked or smothered, 145
straggler something that lags behind the others, 402
strategic related to military planning, 215
stricken struck; strongly affected, 30
strop a strip of leather used for sharpening razors, 100
stubble short, stiff growth, 129
stylus a sharp pointed tool, 54
subside to become quiet, 56
succession the act of following in order, 41
successive following, 26
succumb to give in to, 110
suffocation suffering from not having enough air, 73
suicidal deeply unhappy; self-destructive, 255
suite a matched set of furniture, 391
sullenly in a gloomy or sulky way, 77
summon to call; to tell to come, 247
superb of unusually high quality, 144
superfluous more than needed, 78
survival the act of staying in existence, 338
survive to stay alive, 114; to go on living, 203
suspicious arousing distrust, 130
sustenance something that supports life, especially food, 372
swathe to wrap with a band of material, 181
sway influence, 192
swoon to faint, 399
syncopation a musical accent not on the usual beat, 397
taboo forbidden by social customs, 189
taken aback startled, 128

450 *Glossary*

Glossary

tangential a point or line that touches, but doesn't cross, another, 73
taro a plant grown for its edible, starchy root, 159
taxing tiring; difficult, 357
temerity foolish boldness, 328
tendency a pattern of doing things a certain way, 77
tension an uneasy or angry relationship, 221; the condition of being stretched, 329
tentatively with hesitation, 113
tepid slightly warm, 170
terrestrial referring to the earth and its people, 57
theological related to the study of religion, 121
thicken to become deeper or denser, 291
thrash to beat or strike, 199
threshold an entrance or beginning, 218
tiara a small crown, 26
ticked off a slang term meaning to be annoyed or angry, 387
till to make land ready for growing crops, 130
tirade a long, violent, scolding speech, 187
tirelessly constantly; without stopping, 40
to wit an expression meaning "that is to say,"154
toast a speech made along with a drink to honor someone, 241
togs clothes, 178
tolerable able to be endured, 323
tolerably sufficiently; enough, 374
tonga a wagon, 171
touched affected, 204
traditional referring to customs followed for many years, 384
trait a quality of character; a peculiarity, 177
tranquillity calm, 148
transcribe to make a copy of, 77
transplant to lift and replant in another area, 160
tribulation suffering, 341
tribune a platform from which to speak to a group, 325
trireme an ancient Greek or Roman warship, 60
trivial not important, 26
tuft a small clump of hair, 102
tussle to struggle; to wrestle, 179
tyrannous unfair; severe; cruel, 185
tyranny rule by a harsh, powerful government, 339
unaccountably mysteriously; without explanation, 94
unbearable painful; hard to endure, 203
uncluttered empty; not filled with things, 198
undoing the destruction of something already accomplished, 338
unfulfilled not finished; not completed, 352
ungodly wicked or outrageous, 178
ungovernable not possible to control, 380
unhealthy dangerous, risky, 206
unhindered not prevented or stopped, 205
unilateral involving only one side in an issue, 221
union a marriage, 396
unleashed let loose; released, 339
unlovable difficult to love, 298
unnaturally unusually; in an unexpected way, 397
unprovable not possible to prove, 399
unrealistic not likely to happen in real life, 399
unsolicited not requested, 181
unspeakable too bad to be described, 269
unspeakableness a condition too bad to be described, 353
unsuspecting trusting; not suspicious, 87
unworthy not deserving, 298
uphold to maintain; to keep, 148
usher to conduct; to escort, 182; to show people the way, 398
utility a household service, such as electricity, telephone, or water, 390
valid completely acceptable; genuine, 167; reliable, 324
veal cutlet a thin slice of meat, 45
vehemently with strong emotion, 120; forcefully; violently, 189
veld the South African grassland, 180
ventilate to put in motion; to blow away, 402
ventilator a passage in a house that air is blown through, 31
veranda a roofed porch extending along the outside of a building, 167
via by way of, 385
vindication proof that clears away blame or guilt, 378
vintage a crop of grapes grown for wine, 345
violate to ruin by force, 318
violent hard; with great physical force, 39; intense, 270
violently with strong physical force or rough action, 260
visa a paper that permits a person to enter a country, 398
visionary imaginary; not practical, 375
visualize to imagine, 40
vital very important and necessary, 76
void a feeling of emptiness, 190
vulgarly in bad taste; crudely, 358
waning growing smaller, as the visible part of the moon, 70
warhead the front part of a missile or bomb that contains the explosive, 218
waver to be unsure, 147
weaponry different types of weapons seen as a group, 216
wen a small growth on the skin, 127
westernized influenced by European or American ways, 384
wethers sheep, 96
whereas while at the same time, 109
wholesome healthful, 373
widower a man whose wife has died, 130
wiry slender yet muscular, 182
withhold to keep back, 318
wizened dried up; wrinkled, 170, 180
woe misfortune; great sorrow, 87
wolf to eat hungrily, like an animal, 299
wrench to jerk, 39
wretched worthless; seen with scorn, 29; miserable; very unhappy, 272
writhe to twist as in pain, 30
yearn to wish for deeply, 291
ziggurat an ancient tower built something like a pyramid, 60

Glossary **451**

Index of Authors and Titles

452 *Index of Authors and Titles*

Index of Authors and Titles

Index of Authors and Titles **453**

Index of Selections by Country

454 *Index of Selections by Country*

Index of Selections by Country

Index of Fine Art

Index

456 *Index*

Index

Index **457**

458 *Index*

Index

Index **459**

Index

460 *Index*

Index **461**

Acknowledgments

Acknowledgment is made for permission to reprint or record the following copyrighted material. Every effort has been made to determine copyright owners. In the case of any omissions, the publisher will be pleased to make suitable acknowledgments in future editions.

Pages 24-32: "The Adventure of the Speckled Band" from *The Complete Sherlock Holmes* by Sir Arthur Conan Doyle. Reprinted by permission of Sir Arthur Conan Doyle Copyright holders.

Pages 36-48: "Death Arrives on Schedule" by Hansjörg Martin, trans. by Charles E. Pederson. From *Blut an der Manschette,* ©1974 Hansjörg Martin. Used by permission of Rowohlt Verlag, Reinbek, Germany.

Pages 53-63: "The Feeling of Power" From THE BEST SCIENCE FICTION OF ISAAC ASIMOV by Isaac Asimov. Copyright © 1986 by Nightfall, Inc. Used by permission of Doubleday, a division of Bantam Doubleday Dell Publishing Group, Inc

Pages 67-81: "The Expedition" ("Die Expedition") by Rudolf Lorenzen, trans. by Charles E. Pederson. Reprinted by permission of Herbach & Haase Literarische Agentur.

Pages 86-90: "The Cegua," From *Short and Shivery: Thirty Chilling Tales* by Robert D. San Souci Illus. by Katherine Coville. Copyright ©1987 by Robert D. San Souci. Used by permission of Bantam Doubleday Dell Books for Young Readers.

Pages 93-97: From "Master and Man" by Leo Tolstoy from *Master and Man and Other Stories* trans. by Paul Foote (Penguin Classics, 1977) copyright © Paul Foote, 1977. Reproduced by permission of Penguin Books Ltd.

Pages 100-105: "Just Lather, That's All" by Hernando Téllez, trans. by Donald A. Yates from *Contemporary Latin American Short Stories* edited by Pat McNees. Reprinted by permission of Donald A. Yates and the estate of Beatriz Téllez.

Pages 109-114: From *Nervous Conditions* by Tsitsi Dangarembga. (Seattle: Seal Press, 1988) pp. 178-183. Used with permission.

Pages 117-123: Text: "Marriage Is a Private Affair" from *Girls at War and Other Stories* by Chinua Achebe. Copyright ©1972, 1973. Used by permission of Doubleday, a division of Bantam Doubleday Dell Publishing Group, Inc. and Harold Ober Associates Incorporated. **Audio:** "Marriage Is a Private Affair" from *Girls at War and Other Stories* by Chinua Achebe. Copyright © 1972 by Chinua Achebe. Reprinted by permission of Harold Ober Associates Incorporated.

Pages 127-132: "Cranes," From *Shadows of a Sound* ©1990 by Hwang Sun-won. Published by Mercury House, San Francisco, CA and reprinted by permission.

Pages 144-148: From *The Diary of a Young Girl: The Definitive Edition* by Anne Frank. Otto H. Frank & Mirjam Pressler, Editors, translated by Susan Massotty. Translation copyright ©1995 by Doubleday, a division of Bantam Doubleday Dell Publishing Group, Inc. Used by permission of Doubleday, a division of Bantam Doubleday Dell Publishing Group, Inc.

Page 151: "Letter to Indira Tagore," from *Rabindranath Tagore: An Anthology,* Krishna Dutta and Andrew Robinson eds./trans. (New York, 1997, St. Martin's Press.) Reprinted by permission of Andrew Robinson.

Pages 158-163: Text: From *When Heaven and Earth Changed Places* by Le Ly Hayslip. Copyright © 1989 by Le Ly Hayslip and Charles Jay Wurts. Used by permission of Doubleday, a division of Bantam Doubleday Dell Publishing Group, Inc. **Audio:** From *When Heaven and Earth Changed Places* by Le Ly Hayslip. Copyright © 1989 by Le Ly Hayslip with Jay Wurts. Reprinted by permission of Le Ly Hayslip, Jay Wurts and the Sandra Dijkstra Literary Agency.

Pages 166-172: "By Any Other Name" from *Gifts of Passage* by Santha Rama Rau. Copyright 1951 by Santha Rama Rau. Copyright renewed ©1979 by Santha Rama Rau. Reprinted by permission of HarperCollins Publishers, Inc. "By Any Other Name" originally appeared in *The New Yorker.*

Pages 176-192: Text: Reprinted with permission of Simon & Schuster from *Kaffir Boy* by Mark Mathabane. Copyright © 1986 by Mark Mathabane. **Audio:** Reproduced with the permission of Fifi Oscard Agency, Inc., from *Kaffir Boy* by Mark Mathabane. Copyright © 1986 by Mark Mathabane.

Pages 197-199: "The Father from China" from *China Men* by Maxine Hong Kingston. Copyright ©1980 by Maxine Hong Kingston. Reprinted by permission of Alfred A. Knopf Inc.

Pages 202-206: From *The Last Seven Months of Anne Frank* by Willy Lindwer translated by Alison Meersschaert. Copyright © 1991 by Willy Lindwer. Reprinted by permission of Pantheon Books, a division of Random House, Inc.

Pages 210-212: "Account Evened With India, Says PM: Pakistan Opts to Go Nuclear" by M. Ziauddin from *The Dawn* (Pakistan) 29 May 1998. Reprinted by permission.

Pages 215-218: "Tests Are Nowhere Near India's: Fernandes" from *The Times of India,* June 1,1998. Reprinted by arrangement with The Times of India and The Press Trust of India. No part of this may be reproduced, reprinted, transmitted or stored in any form or medium without

462 *Acknowledgments*

Acknowledgments

permission of the publishers, Bennett, Coleman & Co. Ltd, New Delhi, India.

Pages 221-222: "Pakistan Nuclear Moratorium Welcomed" from BBC Online Network, Friday, June 12, 1998. Reprinted by permission of BBC News Online. www.bbc.co.uk/news.

Page 225: "The Frightening Joy" from *DeVolkskrant* as appeared in World Press Review Vol. 45, Issue 8, August 1998. Reprinted by permission.

Page 226: "Building Atomic Security" by Tomasz Wroblewski as appeared in *World Press Review* Vol. 45, Issue 8, August 1998. Reprinted by permission.

Pages 238-246: "Macbeth" Act 3, Scene 4 from *The Complete Works of William Shakespeare* by William Shakespeare, the Cambridge text established by John Dover Wilson. Copyright ©The Cambridge text of the complete works of William Shakespeare. Cambridge University Press 1921, 1922, 1923, 1924, 1926, 1928, 1929, 1930, 1931, 1934, 1936, 1939, 1946, 1947, 1949, 1950, 1952, 1954, 1955, 1956, 1957, 1960, 1962, 1966. Reprinted with the permission of Cambridge University Press.

Pages 239-247: From *Shakespeare Made Easy: Macbeth* by William Shakespeare, edited and translated by Alan Durband. Copyright © 1984 Alan Durband. Reprinted by permission of Hutchinson & Co. Ltd and Barron's Educational Series, Inc.

Pages 252-262: From *"Master Harold"... and the Boys* by Athol Fugard. Copyright ©1982 by Athol Fugard. Reprinted by permission of Alfred A. Knopf, Inc.

Pages 267-273: *The Stronger,* by August Strindberg, trans. by Ants Oras. Translation ©Ants Oras.

Page 285: "The Diameter of the Bomb" from *The Selected Poetry of Yehuda Amichai* by Yehuda Amichai edited and trans. by Chana Bloch and Stephen Mitchell. Copyright ©1996 The Regents of the University of California. Reprinted by permission of The Regents of the University of California and Chana Bloch.

Page 288: "Taking Leave of a Friend" by Li Po from *Personae* by Ezra Pound. Copyright ©1926 by Ezra Pound. Reprinted by permission of New Directions Publishing Corp.

Page 291-292: "Thoughts of Hanoi" from *A Thousand Years of Vietnamese Poetry* by Nguyen Thi Vinh, trans. by Nguyen Ngoc Bich with Burton Raffel and W. S. Mervin, ©1974. Reprinted by permission of The Asia Society.

Pages 294-295: "Mindoro" by Ramón C. Sunico from *This Same Sky* by Naomi Shihab Nye. Reprinted by permission of Ramón C. Sunico.

Pages 298-299: "Ode to a Pair of Socks" from *Odes to Common Things* by Pablo Neruda. Copyright ©1994 by Pablo Neruda and Pablo Neruda Fundacion (Odes in Spanish); Compilation and Illustrations ©by Ferris Cook; Odes (English translation) ©by Ken Krabbenhoft. By permission of Little, Brown and Company.

Page 302: Japanese haiku translated by Harry Behn. From *More Cricket Songs.* Copyright ©1971 Harry Behn. Used by permission of Marian Reiner.

Pages 305-306: "Do Not Go Gentle Into That Good Night" by Dylan Thomas, from *The Poems of Dylan Thomas.* Copyright © 1952 by Dylan Thomas. Reprinted by permission of New Directions Publishing Corp. Also from *Collected Poems* by Dylan Thomas. Reprinted by permission of David Higham Associates.

Page 318: "Letter to the English," From *Joan of Arc In Her Own Words* translated by Willard Trask. Copyright ©1996. Reprinted by permission of Books & Co./Turtle Point.

Pages 321-332: "Nobel Lecture" by Alexander Solzhenitsyn. ©The Nobel Foundation 1970. Reprinted by permission of The Nobel Foundation.

Page 345: From "On Repentance" from *Essays* by Michel de Montaigne, trans. by J. M. Cohen (Penguin Classics, 1958) copyright © J. M. Cohen, 1958. Reproduced by permission of Penguin Books Ltd.

Pages 348-359: Text: Excerpt from *A Small Place* by Jamaica Kincaid. Reprinted by permission of Farrar, Straus & Giroux, Inc. **Audio:** Excerpt from *A Small Place* by Jamaica Kincaid. Copyright © 1988 by Jamaica Kincaid, recorded with the permission of The Wylie Agency, Inc.

Pages 378-380: "Cup Inanity and Patriotic Profanity" by Andrew Graham-Yooll, "On Thursday" column, July 2, 1998, *Buenos Aires Herald,* (Founded 1876). Reprinted by permission of the author.

Pages 384-387: "Japanese Inns: Peace, Tranquillity, Insects," From *Dave Barry Does Japan* by Dave Barry. Copyright © 1992 by Dave Barry. Reprinted by permission of Random House, Inc.

Pages 390-391: "Why Can't We Have Our Own Apartment?" From *If Life Is a Bowl of Cherries, What Am I Doing in the Pits?* by Erma Bombeck. Reprinted by permission of The Aaron M. Priest Literary Agency, Inc.

Pages 395-399: "Lohengrin" by Leo Slezak, trans. by Charles E. Pederson. From *Der Wortbruch* by Leo Slezak. Copyright ©1927, 1959 by Rowohlt Verlag GmbH, Reinbek bei

Acknowledgments **463**

Acknowledgments

Hamburg. Reprinted by permission of Sanford J. Greenburger Associates.

Pages 402-408: "A Wedding Without Musicians," reprinted from *Tevye's Daughters* by Sholom Aleichem. Copyright ©1949 by the children of Sholom Aleichem and Crown Publishers, Inc. Copyrights renewed 1977 by Crown Publishers, Inc. Reprinted by permission of Crown Publishers, Inc.

Images

Page 10, David Young-Wolff/PhotoEdit; p. 16 (top), Tony Freeman/PhotoEdit; p.16 (bottom), Myrleen Ferguson Cate/PhotoEdit; p. 18, Private Collection/John Kaufmann/SuperStock; p. 21, Judy King; p. 23, Brown Brothers; pp. 28, 29, 31, Rachel Taylor; p. 35, Carl Purcell/Corbis; pp. 37, 42, 46, PhotoDisc ©1999; p. 52, Brown Brothers; p. 54, James Harrington/Tony Stone Images; p. 55 Biondo Productions/Gamma Liaisons; p. 66, Carl Purcell/Corbis; p. 68, ©Tony Stone Images; p. 71, ©PHOTRI; p. 85, Robert D. San Souci; pp. 87, 89 Jeff Spackman; p. 92, The Granger Collection, New York; p. 94, Josef Mensing Gallery, Hamm-Rhynern/Bridgeman Art Library, London/ SuperStock; p. 99, Gran Enciclopedie de Colombia; p. 100, ©Estate of Ilya Bolotowsky/Licensed by VAGA, New York, NY; p. 103, Kactus Foto/SuperStock; p. 108, The Women's Press, U.K.; p. 110, Reuters/Corbis-Bettmann; p. 111, ©Mark Peters/Gamma Liaison; p. 116, ©Steve Miller/New York Times; p. 118, Mike Wells/Tony Stone Worldwide; p. 126, Courtesy of the Korean Cultural Center, NY; p. 127, Underwood & Underwood/Corbis-Bettman; p. 132, Christie's Images/SuperStock; p. 138, Private collection/Beth Hinckley/ SuperStock; p. 141, Judy King; p. 143, ©SuperStock; pp. 145, 148, Associated Press/Worldwide; p. 150, The Granger Collection, New York; p. 151, Ben Edwards/Tony Stone Worldwide; p. 153, Brown Brothers; p. 155, Joel Iskowitz; p. 158, ©Alain Buu/Gamma; p. 159, Associate Press/Worldwide; p. 160, UPI/Corbis-Bettmann; p. 165, Archive Photos; pp. 166, 170, Sandy Rabinowitz; p. 175, Musee des Arts Africains et Oceaniens Paris/Explorer, Paris/SuperStock; pp. 177, 180, Hajima Ota; 183, Private Collection/Mathabane; 187, Jeanne Montassamy-Ashe; p. 196, Nancy Crampton; p. 199, Associated Press/Worldwide; pp. 201, 202, 205, 206, H. Pick-Goslar Foundation; p. 209, Rachel Taylor; p. 210, Saeed Ahmed/Associated Press/Worldwide; p. 214, Rachel Taylor; p. 218, Ajit Kumar/ Associated Press/Worldwide; p. 220, ©Bob Clarke/Liaison International; p. 222, Agence France Presse; p. 224, Rachel Taylor; p. 225, Ajit Kumar/Associated Press/Worldwide; p. 232, Michelle Puleo/SuperStock; p. 235, Judy King; p. 237, National Portrait Gallery, London/SuperStock; p. 238, ©Victoria & Albert Museum, London/Art Resource, NY; p. 241, A.K.G., Berlin/SuperStock; p. 242, Corbis-Bettmann; p. 251, ©Archive Photos; p. 255, ©1983 Gerry Goodstein; p. 257, Archive Photos; p. 266, Brown Brothers; p. 269, National Museum of American Art, Washington DC/Art Resource, NY; p. 272, ©Stock Montage, Inc.; p. 280, David David Gallery, Philadelphia/David David Gallery/SuperStock; p. 283, Judy King; p. 284, Nancy Crampton; p. 285, Ian O'Leary/Tony Stone Images; p. 287, Liang Kai, by permission of China Span; p. 288, ©Bill Mitchell; p. 290, ©SuperStock; p. 291, Mark Lewis/Tony Stone Images; p. 292, Hugh Sitton/Tony Stone Images; p. 293, S. Vilder/SuperStock; p. 294, Randa Bishop/ Tony Stone Images; p. 297, UPI/Corbis-Bettmann; pp. 298-299, From "ODES TO COMMON THINGS" by Pablo Neruda. copyright ©1994 by Pablo Neruda and Pablo Neruda Foundation (Odes in Spanish); 1994 by Ferris Cook (Compilation and illustrations); 1994 by Ken Krabbenhoft (Odes in English-Translation). by permission of Little, Brown and Company; p. 301, ©T. Iwamiya/PPS; p. 302, from "A Haiku Garden" by Stephen Addiss with Fumiko and Akira Yamamoto, 1996/Weatherhill; p. 304, The Granger Collection, New York; p. 306, Terry Vine/Tony Stone Images; p. 312, Giraudon/Art Resource, NY; p. 315, Judy King; p. 317, Christie's Images/SuperStock; p. 318, Stock Montage/ SuperStock; p. 320, The Granger Collection, New York; p. 322, George Haling/Tony Stone Images; p. 327, Lori Adamski Peek/Tony Stone Images; p. 328, Ron Sangha/Tony Stone Images; p. 331, Paul Chesley/Tony Stone Images; p. 335, Brown Brothers; pp. 336, 337, The Granger Collection, New York; pp. 339, 340, Associated Press/Worldwide; p. 344, The Granger Collection, New York; p. 345, Christie's Images/ SuperStock; p. 347, ©Neal Boenzi, New York Times; p. 348, Allan Aflack Courtesy of the Antigua Tourism Board; p. 351, Cosmo Condina/Tony Stone Images; p. 356, Allan Aflack Courtesy of the Antigua Tourism Board; p. 366, ©1999 Artists Rights Society (ARS), New York/ADAGP, Paris; p. 369, Judy King; p. 370, The Granger Collection, New York; p. 371, ©Stock Montage, Inc.; p. 375, Stedelijk Museum, Amsterdam, Holland; p. 377, Rachel Taylor; p. 379, Agence France Presse/ Corbis-Bettmann; p. 383, ©SAGA 1991/Frank Capri/Archive Photos; p. 385, ©Adrian Bradshaw; p. 389, Frank Capri/ Archive Photos; p. 391, Guy Porfirio; p. 394, Brown Brothers; pp. 396, 397, 399, Karen Lafoya; p. 401, ©Archive Photos; pp. 406, 407, 408, Carole Katchen

464 *Acknowledgments*

Midterm Mastery Test

Name Date Period

Units 1–3
Midterm Mastery Test
page 1

Midterm Mastery Test

Part A Directions Read the names of authors listed in the box below. Then, read the information about each author. Write the name of the author being described on each line provided.

Arthur Conan Doyle	Le Ly Hayslip
William Shakespeare	Robert D. San Souci
Leo Tolstoy	August Strindberg
Anne Frank	Chinua Achebe
Hwang Sun-won	Rabindranath Tagore

_______ **1.** Kept a diary while in hiding during World War II.

_______ **2.** Swedish playwright who wrote in the expressionistic style.

_______ **3.** A classical dramatist from England, some say the greatest playwright ever.

_______ **4.** This writer from India is well known for the many letters he has written.

_______ **5.** One of the great Russian writers, author of *War and Peace.*

_______ **6.** Creator of the character Sherlock Holmes.

_______ **7.** Korean author who writes of the Korean War.

_______ **8.** Vietnamese autobiography author who writes of the effect of the Vietnam War on the people.

_______ **9.** Wrote an adventure story about a beautiful woman who is transformed into a fearful beast.

_______ **10.** This African writer from Nigeria has written many stories about the conflicts between tribal custom and new ways.

 World Literature

Midterm Mastery Test, page 1

Name Date Period

Units 1–3
Midterm Mastery Test
page 2

Midterm Mastery Test, continued

Part B Directions Read the words in the box below. Then, read the numbered words and write the word from the box next to the word it most closely resembles in meaning. Write the word on the line provided.

Affectionate	Illusionist	Reliable
Beckoning	Mock	Siesta
Deposition	Overdue	Superb
Deduction	Placidly	Tedious
Hastily	Primitive	Wretched

_______ **1.** Simple

_______ **2.** Miserable

_______ **3.** Quickly

_______ **4.** Hatred

_______ **5.** Magician

_______ **6.** Trustworthy

_______ **7.** Loving

_______ **8.** Great

_______ **9.** Conclusion

_______ **10.** Boring

_______ **11.** Calmly

_______ **12.** Rest

_______ **13.** Statement

_______ **14.** Tardy

_______ **15.** Calling

Part C Directions Read each sentence. Write *T* if the statement is true or *F* if it is false.

_______ **1.** In *The Stronger,* Mlle. Y has many speaking lines.

_______ **2.** Sherlock Holmes's partner was named Dr. Watson. ("The Adventure of the Speckled Band")

_______ **3.** Macbeth won't sit at the banquet table because a cat is sitting in his place.

_______ **4.** Nyasha thinks Tambudzai should attend the local school. (*Nervous Conditions*)

 World Literature

Midterm Mastery Test, page 2

Name Date Period

Units 1–3
Midterm Mastery Test
page 3

Midterm Mastery Test, continued

_______ **5.** To keep a young boy from running away, his mother and grandmother tied him up. (*Kaffir Boy*)

_______ **6.** Nnaemeka's girlfriend is Nanoo. ("Marriage Is a Private Affair")

_______ **7.** The line of latitude separating North and South Korea is the Twenty-Eighth Parallel. ("Cranes")

_______ **8.** In Vietnam, good rice was considered god's gemstones. (*When Heaven and Earth Changed Places*)

_______ **9.** New Delhi was the location of the day school in this story. ("By Any Other Name")

_______ **10.** "The Frightening Joy" was published in 1908. ("The Frightening Joy")

_______ **11.** The immigrant from China named himself after a US inventor. (*China Men*)

_______ **12.** In *Macbeth,* the murderers killed Banquo.

_______ **13.** Leisegang is the retired police inspector. ("Death Arrives on Schedule")

_______ **14.** In *"Master Harold" . . . and the Boys* Sam was making a kite when young Hally entered the room.

_______ **15.** In *The Stronger,* Mlle. Y is drinking beer.

Part D Directions Answer the following questions. Write your answers in complete sentences on the lines provided.

1. What is expressionistic drama?

2. Why did Pakistan develop nuclear weapons?

 World Literature

Midterm Mastery Test, page 3

Name Date Period

Units 1–3
Midterm Mastery Test
page 4

Midterm Mastery Test, continued

3. What is the "frightening joy" described in *De Volkskrant?*

4. How was the murder committed in "The Adventure of the Speckled Band."

5. In "The Cegua," why did the innkeeper warn the man not travel alone at night?

6. What season is Tolstoy's "Master and Man" set in?

7. Why was Anne Frank's family in hiding?

8. Why does the barber want to kill Captain Torres in "Just Lather, That's All"?

9. Why is Macbeth unable to sit at the banquet table?

10. In Asimov's "The Feeling of Power," why are people learning to do math by hand?

 World Literature

Midterm Mastery Test, page 4

Final Mastery Test

Name Date Period

Units 1–6 *Final Mastery Test page 1*

Final Mastery Test

Part A Directions Read the names of authors listed in the box below. Then, read the information about each author. Write the name of the author being described on each line provided.

Abraham Lincoln	Isaac Asimov	Mark Twain
Alexander Solzhenitsyn	Jamaica Kincaid	Michel de Montaigne
Athol Fugard	Jonathan Swift	Pablo Neruda
Dylan Thomas	Leo Slezak	Sholom Aleichem
Hansjörg Martin	Mark Mathabane	

______ 1. An Irish satirist and a cleric.

______ 2. An American humorist who wrote of life on the Mississippi, among other things.

______ 3. Gave a brief, famous speech on an important battlefield.

______ 4. Newspaper columnist who has won a Pulitzer prize for his humorous writing.

______ 5. German detective story writer.

______ 6. Wrote of Jewish village life, often in a humorous way.

______ 7. Opera performer turned writer.

______ 8. Nobel winner who spoke of the importance of art in society.

______ 9. Welsh poet who wrote of his father's coming death.

______ 10. South African writer who told of growing up with apartheid.

______ 11. South African playwright who wrote of apartheid.

______ 12. Chilean poet who won the Nobel Prize for Literature.

 World Literature

Final Mastery Test, page 1

Name Date Period

Units 1–6 *Final Mastery Test page 2*

Final Mastery Test, continued

______ 13. French essayist.

______ 14. Born in Antigua and opposed to tourism in home country.

______ 15. American science fiction writer who has written many books, both fiction and nonfiction.

Part B Directions Read the words in the box below. Then, read the numbered words and write the word from the box next to the word it most closely resembles in meaning. Write the word on the line provided.

Chaos	Famine	Tidbit
Duration	Horde	Venison
Endowed	Persuasive	
Exaggeration	Plaudits	

______ 1. A small bit of knowledge

______ 2. Deer meat

______ 3. Praise

______ 4. Span

______ 5. Unruly mob

______ 6. Overstatement

______ 7. Convincing

______ 8. Disorder

______ 9. Gifted

______ 10. Lack of food

 World Literature

Final Mastery Test, page 2

Name Date Period

Units 1–6 *Final Mastery Test page 3*

Final Mastery Test, continued

Part C Directions Read each sentence. Write *T* if the statement is true and *F* if it is false.

______ 1. The play *"Master Harold" . . . and the Boys* is concerned about apartheid.

______ 2. There are seventeen syllables in a haiku poem.

______ 3. In the poem "The Diameter of the Bomb," four people were killed.

______ 4. "Do Not Go Gentle Into That Good Night" was written by Dylan Thomas.

______ 5. Kincaid thinks tourism is harmful to her home country.

______ 6. The poet writes of his mother in "Do Not Go Gentle Into That Good Night."

______ 7. It is good to have government control literature, Solzhenitsyn says.

______ 8. The Gettysburg Address was given to honor those fallen in battle.

______ 9. Joan of Arc says she will defeat the English in battle.

______ 10. Kennedy thinks citizens should ask what they can do for their country, rather than just asking for more things from their country.

______ 11. Sholom Aleichem's story deals with pogroms against Orthodox Christians.

______ 12. Dave Barry writes of his trip to Kyoto.

______ 13. Hally wants Sam to call him Master Harold, in the play *"Master Harold" . . . and the Boys.*

______ 14. In Sholom Aleichem's story, the Cossacks come to protect the Jews.

______ 15. "Cup Inanity" refers to Argentina's soccer victory over California.

______ 16. Swift suggests that the English eat Irish potatoes.

______ 17. Lincoln says all men are created equal.

______ 18. "Do Not Go Gentle Into That Good Night" is a villanelle.

______ 19. Anne Frank was thirty-four years old at the time her diary entries were written.

______ 20. "Mindoro" includes a description of the mountains of Nova Scotia.

 World Literature

Final Mastery Test, page 3

Name Date Period

Units 1–6 *Final Mastery Test page 4*

Final Mastery Test, continued

______ 21. Uncle Rabi lives on a boat.

______ 22. Pakistan builds nuclear weapons to defend itself against India.

______ 23. Mark Twain tells about looking for his cane in the middle of the night.

______ 24. In *The Stronger,* Mlle. Y has an affair with Mme. X.

______ 25. In his article, Jonathan Swift is worried about poor Irish children.

Part D Directions Read the words in the box below. Then, read the numbered words and write the word from the box next to the word that is most *opposite* in meaning. Write the word on the line provided.

Departing	Monopoly	Perpetual	Theme
Distant	Mute	Sowing	
Incandescent	Absolute	Sustenance	

______ 1. Close

______ 2. Harvesting

______ 3. Vocal

______ 4. Arriving

______ 5. Dull

______ 6. Hunger

______ 7. Momentary

______ 8. Many

______ 9. Incomplete

______ 10. Pointless

 World Literature

Final Mastery Test, page 4

Final Mastery Test

Name Date Period

Units 1–6
Final Mastery Test
page 5

Final Mastery Test, continued

Part E Directions Answer the following questions. Write your answers in complete sentences on the lines provided.

1. Why does Jonathan Swift propose that the English eat the Irish young?
2. How big is the diameter of the bomb described in Amichai's poem?
3. Who does Solzhenitsyn call to stand against governmental tyranny?
4. Why does Erma Bombeck say that she and her husband are planning to move out?
5. How can The Thief in Montaigne's essay continue to steal if he hates doing it?
6. Why does Dylan Thomas tell his father to rage against the night?
7. Of the three haiku poems included in the poetry section, which is your favorite? Briefly explain why.

 World Literature

Final Mastery Test, page 5

Name Date Period

Units 1–6
Final Mastery Test
page 6

Final Mastery Test, continued

8. Why does John Kennedy say that the United States must remain strong?
9. Why does Joan of Arc think she will prevail against the English?
10. In Aleichem's description of Jewish village life, why do you think the Jews are persecuted?
11. Why does the *Buenos Aires Herald* write an editorial about soccer?
12. Jamaica Kincaid is upset about tourism in her homeland. Do you agree or disagree with her? Briefly explain.
13. Why do you think Macbeth is afraid of Banquo's ghost?
14. Why do you think the Chinese immigrant chose to name himself after an American inventor?
15. Like the characters in "The Expedition," would you like to take a space journey knowing that you would not return to earth alive? Briefly explain.

 World Literature

Final Mastery Test, page 6

Teacher's Resource Library Answer Key

Activities

Activity 1—About Fiction
Part A: 1. F **2.** T **3.** F **4.** T **5.** F

Part B: 1. c **2.** c **3.** d **4.** a **5.** b

Activity 2—Detective Stories
Part A: 1. F **2.** T **3.** F **4.** F **5.** T **6.** F **7.** F **8.** T **9.** F **10.** T

Part B: 1. protagonist **2.** bullets **3.** temptations **4.** separated **5.** questions

Activity 3—The Adventure of the Speckled Band
Part A: 1. c **2.** a **3.** c **4.** b **5.** c **6.** c **7.** a

Part B: 1. 1900 **2.** a detective **3.** Dr. Watson **4.** married **5.** sister **6.** India **7.** snake **8.** room

Part C: 1. a fan club **2.** home; rooms **3.** blacksmith **4.** Roylott **5.** sister **6.** pistol **7.** murderer; killer **8.** 1883 **9.** clang **10.** India

Activity 4—Death Arrives on Schedule
Part A: 1. b **2.** a **3.** i **4.** l **5.** f **6.** j **7.** d **8.** e **9.** g **10.** c **11.** k **12.** h

Part B: 1. a novel **2.** the theme **3.** criminal **4.** Leisegang's **5.** German **6.** Hafermass **7.** a film producer **8.** bad luck

Part C:
Across **2.** Hamburg **5.** Death **6.** Retired **9.** Pistol **10.** Leg

Down **1.** Fir tree **3.** Algernissen **4.** Broker **7.** Rental **8.** Dining

Activity 5—Science Fiction
1. F **2.** F **3.** F **4.** F **5.** F **6.** F **7.** F **8.** F **9.** F **10.** F **11.** T **12.** T **13.** T **14.** T **15.** F

Activity 6—The Feeling of Power
Part A: 1. Russia **2.** "laws" **3.** Deneb **4.** multiply **5.** The government

Part B: 1. c **2.** g **3.** a **4.** e **5.** f **6.** b **7.** d

Part C: 1. F **2.** F **3.** F **4.** F **5.** T **6.** T **7.** F **8.** F

Part D: 1. future **2.** Computers **3.** kills, depolarizes **4.** Technician **5.** General Weider

Activity 7—The Expedition
Part A: 1. Cerberus **2.** Eight **3.** Galaxis **4.** Astraea **5.** Olaf **6.** heavenly bodies

Part B: 1. F **2.** F **3.** T **4.** F **5.** F **6.** F **7.** F

Part C: 1. c **2.** c **3.** a **4.** c **5.** a **6.** c **7.** a

Activity 8—Adventure
1. b **2.** a **3.** a **4.** d **5.** c **6.** a **7.** b **8.** c **9.** d **10.** a

Activity 9—The Cegua
Part A: 1. b **2.** f **3.** j **4.** a **5.** d **6.** e **7.** g **8.** h **9.** i **10.** c

Part B: 1. setting **2.** quench **3.** setting **4.** Costa Rica **5.** the Cegua

Activity 10—Master and Man
Part A: 1. Russia **2.** Crimean **3.** 1870s **4.** Vasilii Andreich **5.** servant **6.** horse **7.** never **8.** snowdrift **9.** circle **10.** numb

Part B: 1. F **2.** T **3.** F **4.** F **5.** F

Activity 11—Just Lather, That's All
Part A: 1. e **2.** b **3.** a **4.** h **5.** c **6.** g **7.** f **8.** i **9.** d **10.** j

Part B: 1. barber, rebel **2.** Torres **3.** captain **4.** school **5.** murderer

Activity 12—Turning Points
Part A: 1. young **2.** turning point **3.** first-person **4.** coming-of-age **5.** ending

Part B: 1. T **2.** T **3.** T **4.** T **5.** T

Activity 13—Nervous Conditions
Part A:
Across **3.** Nyasha **5.** Tsitsi **6.** Dangarembga **7.** Uncle **9.** Nuns **10.** Maiguru

Down **1.** An education **2.** Marriage **4.** Aunt **5.** Tambudzai **8.** Convent

Activity 14—Marriage Is a Private Affair
Part A: 1. T **2.** T **3.** F **4.** F **5.** F

Part B: 1. conflict **2.** Lagos **3.** traditional **4.** a Christian **5.** surprised **6.** eight **7.** grandsons

Part C: 1. b **2.** c **3.** d **4.** a **5.** b **6.** b **7.** d **8.** c

Activity 15—Cranes
Part A: 1. f **2.** i **3.** j **4.** h **5.** g **6.** b **7.** d **8.** a **9.** e **10.** c

Activity 16—Unit Review
Part A: Answers will vary, but examples follow. **1.** The main job of the protagonist is to look for clues and solve a crime. **2.** Westerns, war stories, and spy stories could be called adventure fiction. **3.** Humans are not able to send people so far away. **4.** Characters are people, animals, or things in a story. The setting is the time and place of a story. Plot is the action that takes place in a story. **5.** Science fiction deals with people and events that did not happen; these stories are usually set in the future. **6.** There

are still many places in the world where marriages are arranged. There are parents who do not accept the people their children marry. **7.** In our world we know people can think and do math, but we are trying to get computers to do everything. In the world of "The Feeling of Power," computers do everything, and the people are finding out that they themselves can think and do math in their heads. **8.** Turning point stories include an experience that changes a character's life. **9.** Accept answers that have reasons behind them. Yes: because the captain was his enemy; because the captain was killing all his friends. No: because then the barber would be a killer; because then someone would come to kill the barber; because things would only get worse for everyone. **10.** A man falls in love with another's wife. He decides to kill the man. He gets on one train to establish an alibi. He secretly gets off to meet the man he's to kill. They go on a different train. The one kills the other. The killer meets the first train at a station down the line. He pretends he never left that train. He is caught because his fellow passenger on the train is a retired police inspector. He became suspicious over the killer's behavior.

Part B: **1.** c **2.** g **3.** f **4.** b **5.** i **6.** j **7.** h **8.** a **9.** e **10.** d

Activity 17—About Nonfiction
Part A: **1.** letters **2.** real **3.** diary **4.** Biographies **5.** magazines

Part B: **1.** journal **2.** genres **3.** what **4.** interested **5.** feelings **6.** autobiography **7.** Feature **8.** Internet **9.** book **10.** resource

Activity 18—Journals and Letters
Part A: **1.** T **2.** T **3.** T **4.** F **5.** T

Part B: Answers will vary, but examples follow. **1.** The telephone and computer are more often being used for communication these days. **2.** A diary is like an imaginary friend. **3.** The events and people have usually been changed. **4.** Jacqueline Kennedy Onassis said, "I want to live my life, not record it." **5.** A journal focuses more on events, sights, or ideas. A diary focuses on feelings.

Activity 19—Anne Frank: The Diary of a Young Girl
Part A: **1.** a teenager **2.** the Netherlands **3.** Otto Frank **4.** Amsterdam **5.** Kitty **6.** the attic **7.** were Jews

Part B: **1.** T **2.** F **3.** F **4.** T **5.** F **6.** T **7.** F **8.** F

Activity 20—Letter to Indira Tagore
Part A: **1.** F **2.** T **3.** F **4.** T **5.** T **6.** T **7.** F **8.** F

Part B: **1.** knighted **2.** school **3.** painter **4.** bored **5.** heavens **6.** insignificant **7.** moonlight

Activity 21—Letter to the Rev. J. H. Twichell
Part A: **1.** F **2.** F **3.** T **4.** F **5.** F

Part B: **1.** a **2.** b **3.** a **4.** c **5.** a

Activity 22—Autobiography
Part A: **1.** d **2.** a **3.** b **4.** b **5.** c

Part B: **1.** F **2.** T **3.** F **4.** T **5.** F

Activity 23—When Heaven and Earth Changed Places
Part A: **1.** c **2.** d **3.** a **4.** e **5.** b

Part B: **1.** T **2.** T **3.** F **4.** T **5.** T

Part C:
Across **1.** sprout **4.** peace **6.** rice **8.** muddy **9.** beetle

Down **2.** transplant **3.** fertilize **4.** paddy **7.** children

Activity 24—By Any Other Name
Part A: **1.** f **2.** a **3.** e **4.** d **5.** c **6.** b

Part B: **1.** F **2.** T **3.** F **4.** F **5.** F **6.** F **7.** T

Part C: **1.** valid **2.** personality **3.** in the back **4.** cry **5.** siesta **6.** walls **7.** angry

Activity 25—Kaffir Boy
Part A: Answers will vary, but examples follow. **1.** The only hope a black South African had to get a decent job was to have an education. **2.** He thought it was exciting, adventurous and full of surprises; also a *tsotsi* didn't go to school. **3.** His mother stood up to the father and said Johannes was going to get an education. **4.** She hoped they would both have education [go to school] some day. **5.** Apartheid was a government policy used to keep whites and blacks apart.

Part B: **1.** T **2.** T **3.** F **4.** T **5.** F

Part C: **1.** inclination **2.** matriarchs **3.** philosophy **4.** survival **5.** birth certificate **6.** admonished **7.** knife **8.** owned **9.** Venda **10.** half-half

Activity 26—Biography
Part A: **1.** c **2.** b **3.** a **4.** b **5.** d

Part B: **1.** T **2.** F **3.** T **4.** F **5.** T

Activity 27—China Men
Part A: **1.** China **2.** rouge **3.** Gold Mountain **4.** pierced ears **5.** finery

Part B: **1.** silk **2.** washing windows **3.** cotton gloves **4.** yellow skin **5.** uncluttered **6.** his city **7.** hair **8.** saint **9.** blonde women **10.** aquarium

Teacher's Resource Library Answer Key

Activity 28—The Last Seven Months of Anne Frank
Part A: **1.** c **2.** d **3.** e **4.** a **5.** b **6.** g **7.** h **8.** f **9.** c **10.** i

Part B: **1.** typhus **2.** thirteenth **3.** writer **4.** nurse **5.** Otto

Activity 29—Journalism
Part A: **1.** fairly **2.** right **3.** short articles **4.** Feature **5.** communicating

Part B: **1.** F **2.** F **3.** T **4.** T **5.** T

Activity 30—Account Evened With India, Says PM
Part A: **1.** T **2.** T **3.** F **4.** T **5.** F

Part B: Answers will vary, but examples follow. **1.** Those who had borrowed billions of rupees from the banks. **2.** He said the tests were held in the interest of national security and integrity. **3.** He threatened the tax evaders and corrupt tax collectors. **4.** India had proven it harbored strong expansionist ambitions. India had tested nuclear weapons before Pakistan. **5.** Official buildings would be turned into schools, hospitals, women's universities, or sold.

Activity 31—Tests Are Nowhere Near India's: Fernandes
Part A: **1.** nuclear tests **2.** India **3.** nuclear **4.** earthquakes **5.** missiles

Part B: **1.** f **2.** i **3.** h **4.** c **5.** d **6.** b **7.** a **8.** g **7.**e **10.** j

Activity 32—Pakistan Nuclear Moratorium Welcomed
Part A: **1.** unilateral moratorium **2.** austerity measures **3.** durable **4.** G8 **5.** India **6.** nuclear missiles **7.** Economic sanctions **8.** stabilize **9.** one million **10.** detonations

Part B: **1.** F **2.** T **3.** F **4.** T **5.** T

Activity 33—The Frightening Joy and Building Atomic Security
Part A: **1.** Armageddon **2.** tired slogan **3.** an atomic security zone **4.** gravity **5.** Americans **6.** escalation **7.** perilously close **8.** nuclear warheads **9.** power **10.** joy

Part B: **1.** T **2.** F **3.** F **4.** T **5.** T

Activity 34—Unit Review
Part A: **1.** China Men **2.** Anne Frank **3.** Autobiographies **4.** journals **5.** magazines

Part B: **1.** moonlight **2.** Thomas Edison **3.** Anglo-Indian **4.** rice **5.** Samuel L. Clemens

Part C: **1.** i **2.** j **3.** f **4.** d **5.** b **6.** c **7.** e **8.** g **9.** a **10.** h

Workbook Activity 35—About Drama
Part A: Answers will vary, but examples follow. **1.** In a comedy the audience enjoys seeing the protagonist beat the antagonist. **2.** Drama tells a story through dialogue and action performed by actors. **3.** The two forms of drama are tragedy and comedy. **4.** Antagonists can be a character in the play, social injustice, a protagonist's own weaknesses, or fate. **5.** Verse is made up of word patterns that follow a definite, repeating rhythm and sometimes rhyme.

Part B: **1.** Greece **2.** tragedy **3.** Harvey **4.** drama **5.** drama

Workbook Activity 36—Classical Drama
Part A: **1.** T **2.** F **3.** T **4.** T **5.** F

Part B: **1.** a **2.** d **3.** c **4.** a **5.** a

Workbook Activity 37—Macbeth
Part A: **1.** c **2.** d **3.** e **4.** a **5.** b

Part B: Answers will vary, but examples follow. **1.** He sees the ghost of Banquo. **2.** She's asking if his foolishness has robbed him of his manhood. **3.** There was a time when smashed brains meant a man would die. **4.** She is reminding him his noble friends are missing him and his presence at the table. **5.** They explain that he has had a strange disability since early childhood.

Workbook Activity 38—Realistic Drama
Part A: **1.** F **2.** T **3.** F **4.** F **5.** T
Part B: **1.** 1950s **2.** everyday **3.** Ordinary **4.** neighborhood **5.** born **6.** Henrik Ibsen **7.** realistic **8.** family **9.** classical **10.** American

Workbook Activity 39— "Master Harold" . . . and the Boys
Part A: Answers will vary, but examples follow. **1.** Sam allowed the kite to dive down close to the ground, as if to crash, then pulled it up again. **2.** Sam wanted Hally to look up and be proud of something, to be proud of himself. **3.** Sam had been like a father to Hally, now he would be a servant to him. **4.** Hally's father was addicted to alcohol [was an alcoholic]. **5.** Sam wanted Hally to understand he could choose to be separated from South African blacks the rest of his life.

Part B: **1.** c **2.** d **3.** j **4.** f **5.** a **6.** h **7.** i **8.** g **9.** e **10.** b

Part C: **1.** a **2.** d **3.** c **4.** b **5.** b

Workbook Activity 40—Expressionistic Drama
Part A: **1.** F: Expressionistic playwrights did not want to present events realistically. **2.** F: The split in *Strange Interlude* is between the character's public and private nature. **3.** T **4.** T **5.** F: In *Waiting for Godot,* Godot never appears.

Part B: **1.** emotional **2.** staging **3.** *Strange Interlude* **4.** feelings **5.** Europe

Workbook Activity 41—The Stronger

Part A: **1.** a **2.** b **3.** c **4.** c **5.** d

Part B: **1.** MLLE. Y **2.** ladies' café **3.** Christmas Eve **4.** MME. X **5.** husband

Workbook Activity 42—Unit 3 Review

Part A: Answers will vary, but examples follow. **1.** Settings are limited to what can be shown or represented on the actual stage. **2.** Tragedy and comedy. In tragedy, the antagonist (bad guy, enemy) usually destroys the protagonist (good guy, hero). Comedy gives the reader a happy ending and the protagonist usually wins over the antagonist. **3.** Characters used to be mostly nobility and important people; now they can be anyone. **4.** The changing or exaggerating of character or setting is found in expressionistic drama. **5.** The four elements are setting, stage directions, characters, and dialogue.

Part C: **1.** personality **2.** Physical **3.** external clues **4.** *Macbeth* **5.** blank verse **6.** Everyday **7.** imaginary **8.** Realistic **9.** apartheid **10.** *The Stronger*

Part B: **1.** F: "*Master Harold*" is about apartheid in Africa and friendship between white and black people. **2.** F: Dialogue is the term for the words spoken in a play. **3.** F: The main character in *Macbeth* sees a ghost and a bloody knife floating in front of him. **4.** F: Action in *The Stronger* takes place on Christmas Eve. **5.** T: café, restaurant, and banquet hall

Activity 43—About Poetry

Part A: **1.** image **2.** Rhyme **3.** sonnet **4.** freedom **5.** Elegies **6.** Songs **7.** Rhythm **8.** epics **9.** symbol **10.** picture

Part B: **1.** F: Humorous subjects appear in limericks. **2.** F: Early poems were usually songs to a deity. **3.** F: Haiku is a traditional Japanese poetic form. **4.** F: Free verse often doesn't rhyme. **5.** F: In a dramatic monologue a character reveals personality by talking to the reader.

Activity 44—The Diameter of the Bomb

Part A: Answers will vary, but examples follow. **1.** He writes in the Hebrew language. **2.** The solitary man mourning the death of the young woman who was killed. **3.** The bomb is thirty centimeters; its effective range is about seven meters; it has left four dead and eleven wounded. **4.** It is a circle with no end and no God. **5.** Her graveyard includes more people in the bomb's damage.

Part B: **1.** kilometer **2.** circle **3.** orphans **4.** Two hospitals **5.** another country

Activity 45—Taking Leave of a Friend

Part A: **1.** sunset **2.** bow **3.** dead grass **4.** river **5.** floating wide cloud

Part B: **1.** simile **2.** the walls **3.** neighing **4.** depart **5.** Separation

Activity 46—Thoughts of Hanoi

Part A: Answers will vary, but examples follow. **1.** First the author says she wants to bury the past and burn the future. Later in the poem she asks her friend if he is reliving the past and imagining the future. **2.** She calls the land a frontier of hatred. **3.** The author fears she will march against her friend and kill him, or be killed by him. **4.** The small villages are islands of brown thatch in a lush green sea. **5.** The girls sow, harvest, spin, and weave.

Part B: **1.** F: The author remembers trains leaving daily from Hanoi. **2.** T **3.** T **4.** T **5.** T

Activity 47—Mindoro

Part A: **1.** d **2.** e **3.** a **4.** c **5.** b

Part B: **1.** red threads **2.** mutes **3.** Blood light **4.** dissolving **5.** cluster like mayflies

Activity 48—Ode to a Pair of Socks

Part A: **1.** impaled **2.** beauty twice over **3.** wool **4.** incandescent **5.** shepherd's

Part B: Answers will vary, but examples follow. **1.** They both hide things away so others would not see them. Schoolboys put fireflies in a bottle and scholars hoard holy writ. **2.** He thought the socks were too beautiful to be put on his feet. **3.** Figurative language makes a comparison and is not meant to be taken literally. **4.** Two socks as soft as rabbit fur. **5.** The socks were colorful and soft.

Activity 49—Three Haiku

Part A: **1.** ancient pool **2.** forgive him **3.** bantam **4.** rooster **5.** world

Part B: **1.** F: Basho taught Kikaku how to write haiku. **2.** F: Basho comes from a kind of banana tree that grew near where the author lived. **3.** F: A ruff of feathers is a collar that stands out from the neck. **4.** F: The three animals in these haiku are a rooster, a frog, and a songbird. **5.** T

Activity 50—Do Not Go Gentle Into That Good Night

Part A: Answers will vary, but examples follow. **1.** The men are described as wise, good, wild, and grave. **2.** "Rage, rage against the dying of the light" or "Do not go gentle into that good night." **3.** He is writing to his father, who is dying. **4.** To curse him, to be angry, to cry out; to fight against dying. **5.** A villanelle is a form of poetry with nineteen lines and several repeating rhymes, used in France in the 1500s.

Part B: 1. c 2. e 3. c 4. a 5. b

Activity 51—Unit 4 Review

Part A: Answers will vary, but examples follow. **1.** This poem starts like a matter-of-fact news report, very little emotion. **2.** Two similes are "Mind like a floating wide cloud," and "Sunset like the parting of old acquaintances." **3.** Two descriptions of the socks are "two little boxes knit from threads of sunset and sheepskin," and "embroidered fire, those incandescent socks." **4.** Countries represented in this unit include Israel, China, Vietnam, the Philippines, Chile, Japan, and Wales. **5.** This poem is a sort of elegy that mourns deaths in Vietnam. The mood changes many times during the poem to include anger, sadness, remembering happy times, and confusion about the future.

Part B: **1.** F: When giving human characteristics to a nonhuman object is personification. **2.** T **3.** F: The three haiku are similar because there is an animal in each of them. **4.** F: Three of the authors in this unit are still alive. **5.** T

Part C: **1.** c **2.** j **3.** b **4.** i **5.** d **6.** h **7.** f **8.** e **9.** g **10.** a

Activity 52—Persuasive Literature

Part A: Answers will vary, but examples follow. **1.** Persuasive literature is written mainly to influence opinion. **2.** A metaphor is a figure of speech that says one thing is something else. **3.** The authors criticize, reassure, threaten, praise, argue with, and inspire their audiences. **4.** This unit covers speeches and essays. **5.** Advertising shows us choices and shares ideas.

Part B: **1.** literature **2.** editorials **3.** irony **4.** buy **5.** genres

Activity 53—Speeches

Part A: **1.** T **2.** T **3.** F: Speeches are meant to be spoken; heard by audiences. **4.** F: A proclamation is a letter about important events meant to be read out loud. **5.** T

Part B: **1.** sound **2.** spoken **3.** an event **4.** content **5.** proclamation

Activity 54—Letter to the English

Part A: **1.** the Maid **2.** Charles VII **3.** Rouen **4.** thirteen **5.** Orléans

Part B: **1.** g **2.** h **3.** a **4.** b **5.** i **6.** f **7.** j **8.** c **9.** d **10.** e

Activity 55—Nobel Lecture

Part A: Answers will vary, but examples follow. **1.** World literature has power to convey experiences from one land to another, to make different scales of values agree, and to allow one nation to learn correctly the true history of another nation and perhaps prevent themselves from making the same mistakes. **2.** Solzhenitsyn says art and literature can coordinate different scales of values. **3.** Existing with different scales of values is difficult; people will be torn apart by these differences. **4.** The scales of values include one for evaluating events near at hand, another for events far away; one for aging societies, one for young societies; and unsuccessful and successful people each have one. **5.** Literature is able to convey experiences from one generation to another; it becomes the living memory of a nation.

Part B: **1.** T **2.** T **3.** F: The Soviet government put him in prison and exiled him from Russia for years. **4.** F: The term "scales of values" describes how people judge other people and nations. **5.** F: Humanity has become one through international broadcasting and print.

Part C: **1.** i **2.** h **3.** c **4.** g **5.** f **6.** b **7.** e **8.** a **9.** j **10.** d

Activity 56—The Gettysburg Address

Part A: **1.** resting place **2.** birth **3.** twenty **4.** civil war **5.** battlefield

Part B: **1.** for the people **2.** holy **3.** consecrate **4.** new Republican party **5.** eleven thousand

Activity 57—Inaugural Address

Part A: **1.** inaugural address **2.** the torch **3.** tyranny **4.** religion **5.** adversary

Part B: Answers will vary, but examples follow. **1.** The common enemies of humankind are tyranny, poverty, disease, and war. **2.** The term *man* really means all of humanity, all people. **3.** They come not from the generosity of the state but from the hand of God. **4.** He asked the citizens of the United States to ask not what the United States will do for them, but what together all can do for the freedom of the world. **5.** He thinks we should never negotiate out of fear, but never fear to negotiate.

Activity 58—Essays

Part A: **1.** eighteen **2.** printing press **3.** columns **4.** talents **5.** personal

Part B: **1.** T **2.** F: During the 1700s and 1800s essayists began to write opinion articles. **3.** T **4.** T **5.** T

Activity 59—Of Repentance

Part A: **1.** d **2.** e **3.** a **4.** b **5.** c

Part B: Answers will vary, but examples follow. **1.** The Thief took large loads each night and carried them great distances. **2.** He is now paying back the people he robbed, with voluntary gifts. **3.** He seems to think it is dishonest and hates it, but he hated his own poverty more. **4.** The

Thief was successful due to his physical strength in his youth. **5.** He stole from many places so that no one would have a large loss.

Activity 60—A Small Place

Part A: 1. b **2.** c **3.** a **4.** d **5.** c

Part B: 1. backward **2.** water; sea **3.** twelve **4.** native **5.** drug smuggler

Part C: 1. customs **2.** dilapidated **3.** British God **4.** Antigua **5.** hospital

Activity 61—Unit 5 Review

Part A: 1. Persuasive writings **2.** essay **3.** speech **4.** setting **5.** way of thinking

Part B: Answers will vary, but examples follow. **1.** They both ask the United States to remember what has gone before and to continue to work forward, complete tasks begun, and never forget those who laid the foundation. **2.** World literature is a common bond between peoples of the earth, it shares a common spirit, helps people learn about each other and care about what happens in other parts of the world, and is generally a uniting power for all people. (or) World literature has power to convey experiences from one land to another, to make different scales of values agree, and to allow one nation to learn correctly the true history of another nation and perhaps prevent them from making the same mistakes. **3.** Joan of Arc believes she will be successful because she has heard voices and directions she believes come directly from God. **4.** The main character was very poor, he was a thief, he gained quite a bit of wealth from his stealing, he repented from his wrongdoing, and gave voluntary gifts back to those he had stolen from. **5.** Jamaica Kincaid takes an attitude immediately in the tone of her writing, which is angry and sarcastic. She also uses irony. She says, "A tourist is an ugly human being."

Part C: 1. proclamations **2.** evaluate **3.** humiliating **4.** metaphor **5.** bigot **6.** negotiate **7.** repent **8.** dilapidated **9.** consecrated **10.** extraordinary

Activity 62—About Humorous Literature

Part A: 1. T **2.** T **3.** F: Humorous literature is created to be funny. **4.** T **5.** T

Part B: 1. wit **2.** poke fun **3.** human **4.** unexpected **5.** tone

Activity 63—Satire

Part A: 1. basic truths **2.** satire **3.** Social injustice **4.** behavior **5.** vividly

Part B: 1. T **2.** T **3.** T **4.** T **5.** T

Activity 64—A Modest Proposal

Part A: 1. c **2.** a **3.** j **4.** b **5.** e **6.** d **7.** f **8.** i **9.** g **10.** h

Part B: Answers will vary, but examples follow. **1.** Poor children ("savages") usually do not feel marriage is important and so one male could serve four females. **2.** He says they deserve first choice of the children because the landlords have already devoured most of their parents. **3.** Because they are poor all their lives, it would be better to be dead than to live a life of misfortune and misery. **4.** Swift's proposes that Irish children be fed and fattened until one year old and then sold as a product for people to eat. **5.** To become thieves or leave their native country.

Activity 65—Cup Inanity and Patriotic Profanity

Part A: 1. pubs **2.** racist **3.** Vindication **4.** pensioner **5.** match

Part B: Answers will vary, but examples follow. **1.** A yob is slang for street criminal or hooligan. The author says yobs exist because capitalist states encourage (champion) them. **2.** "Patriotic actions" included filling the streets with litter, wearing the national flag (ensign) on a silly hat or cape, waving bottles of beer and throwing them through store windows, yelling racist insults, and using bad language (swearing). **3.** The list includes foreign debt will be paid off, there will be no more poor in Argentina, unemployment will be something unknown, pensioners will have a decent retirement, relief checks for those outside Goya will be in the mail tomorrow, and the Wizard of Oz will be made president. **4.** In 1978 a mob was screaming their support for the government because the national team won, and people were arrested, tortured, and killed by the same government. **5.** Sarcasm is a heavy, sometimes mean-spirited kind of irony.

Teacher's Resource Library Answer Key

Activity 66—Columns

Part A: **1.** range **2.** humor **3.** by-line **4.** parenting **5.** relieving tension

Part B: **1.** F: Many countries around the world publish columns for people to read. **2.** F: Hundreds of women and men write columns. **3.** F: Columns are articles that appear regularly in periodicals. **4.** T **5.** F: Some columns are written from the average person's point of view.

Activity 67—Staying at a Japanese Inn: Peace, Tranquillity, Insects

Part A: **1.** i **2.** e **3.** h **4.** d **5.** g **6.** c **7.** j **8.** a **9.** b **10.** f

Part B: **1.** cicada-infested **2.** maid **3.** shout angrily **4.** shoes **5.** Ryokan

Part C: **1.** F: The room had no beds or chairs. **2.** F: Cormorants are waterbirds similar to pelicans. **3.** F: There is no international symbol for fishing. **4.** F: At the inn, guests must put on one set of slippers for the main room and one set for the bathroom. **5.** F: Cormorant fishers fish by using a wire basket with a log fire to attract the fish.

Part D: **1.** stupid **2.** Tea **3.** peace **4.** neck **5.** beeper

Activity 68—Why Can't We Have Our Own Apartment?

Part A: Answers will vary, but examples follow. **1.** Some issues include utilities, phone bills, newspapers, and furniture. **2.** They were expected to cook, make beds, do laundry, take care of the yard, keep the cars running, and bring in the money. **3.** Children usually ask parents about moving out and having their own place. This column is backward. **4.** Reasons for leaving include fix up the apartment as they please, play stereos when they want, come in late without being questioned, invite people over and not have someone hanging around, and use of the car. **5.** The parents want to move out and get their own apartment.

Part B: **1.** call **2.** utilities **3.** syndicated **4.** silly **5.** theme

Activity 69—Stories

Part A: **1.** themselves **2.** punchline **3.** monologue **4.** Details **5.** amuse

Part B: **1.** F: A joke is a short funny story about anything, and it ends in a punchline. **2.** T **3.** T **4.** T **5.** T

Activity 70—Lohengrin

Part A: **1.** b **2.** a **3.** c **4.** e **5.** d

Part B: **1.** faints **2.** a shining knight **3.** Magic **4.** Mrs. Ortrud **5.** on their shields

Part C: **1.** T **2.** T **3.** T **4.** T **5.** T

Activity 71—A Wedding Without Musicians

Part A: Answers will vary, but examples follow.
1. Pogroms were organized mob attacks against the Jews, and sometimes the government encouraged them.
2. Noah was a printer and a busybody who knew all the news and secrets, and he ran around the town telling everyone about them. **3.** They offered gifts to the Inspector of Police and asked for help. **4.** The Straggler Special was a hero when it came to town with no cars attached. **5.** "Sholom Aleichem" comes from Yiddish; it is a traditional Hebrew greeting.

Part B: **1.** drinking; partying **2.** Cossacks **3.** ventilating **4.** pogrom; fight **5.** rats in a famine; ice in summer

Activity 72—Unit 6 Review

Part A: **1.** F: Satire is humor that makes fun of foolishness or evil. **2.** T **3.** F: Exaggeration is the use of words to make something seem worse than it is. **4.** T **5.** F: Irony is the use of words that say one thing but mean the opposite.

Part B: **1.** Magic **2.** greeting **3.** Monologues **4.** funny **5.** shoes **6.** by-line **7.** opinion **8.** Pamphlets **9.** right and wrong **10.** laugh

Part C: Answers will vary, but examples follow. **1.** This story teaches the reader that Jews sometimes were beaten for no reason and often the government did nothing to stop it, their homes and possessions were destroyed, and they had to bribe local officials to help them.
2. Lohengrin makes her promise never to ask who he is or where he comes from. **3.** Barry points fun at both American tourists and Japanese traditions. **4.** Graham-Yooll describes the government as being praised because of the soccer team winning, while at the same time arresting and torturing people. **5.** Swift wants the reader to understand how awfully the Irish are treated by the British; that the British have indifference and contempt toward the Irish.

Teacher's Resource Library Answer Key

Workbook

Workbook 1—About Fiction

Part A: **1.** T **2.** T **3.** F: Novels are longer works of fiction. **4.** F: Plot is the action in the story. **5.** F: The three elements of fiction are character, plot, and setting.

Part B: **1.** c **2.** d **3.** c **4.** b **5.** a

Workbook 2—Detective Stories

Part A: **1.** whodunits **2.** protagonist **3.** innocent **4.** antagonist **5.** decency

Part B: **1.** F: The detective is usually called the protagonist. **2.** F: Detectives dodge bullets and plunge into fights. **3.** T **4.** F: Detectives find criminals, question them, and may even punish them. **5.** F: In today's detective stories, the main character is in the middle of the action.

Workbook 3—The Adventure of the Speckled Band

Part A: **1.** c **2.** f **3.** e **4.** h **5.** a **6.** i **7.** d **8.** g **9.** j **10.** b

Part B: **1.** first **2.** stepfather **3.** cheetah **4.** whistle or a low, clear whistle **5.** Dr. Roylott

Part C: Answers will vary, but examples follow. **1.** "She was young and beautiful and very dead." **2.** Holmes had helped a friend. **3.** She was getting married, and she would be taking her money with her. **4.** The snake passed through an air duct (ventilator) in the house. **5.** She was getting married [and her sister had been killed right before she was to marry].

Part D: **1.** F: Helen was about to be married; Julia had been killed when she was about to marry. **2.** F: A horse pulls a dog-cart. **3.** T **4.** F: Dr. Roylott killed Julia to keep her money. **5.** F: They lived in Calcutta, India, before moving to England.

Workbook 4—Death Arrives on Schedule

Part A:

Across **2.** Hamburg **5.** Death **6.** Retired **9.** Pistol **10.** Leg

Down **1.** Fir tree **3.** Algernissen **4.** Broker **7.** Rental **8.** Dining

Part B: **1.** a **2.** d **3.** g **4.** h **5.** e **6.** i **7.** k **8.** f **9.** c **10.** l **11.** j **12.** b

Part C: **1.** theme **2.** novel **3.** German **4.** bad luck **5.** Leisegang's **6.** a film producer **7.** Hafermass **8.** criminal

Workbook 5—Science Fiction

Part A: **1.** c **2.** a **3.** d **4.** b **5.** c

Part B: **1.** T **2.** T **3.** T **4.** T **5.** F: Science Fiction usually has its own section in bookstores.

Workbook 6—The Feeling of Power

Part A: Answers will vary, but examples follow. **1.** Humans are dispensable. **2.** Irony is using an idea or image in the opposite way from its ordinary meaning. **3.** earth and Deneb **4.** Aub did not want his discovery used for war. **5.** Graphitics comes from the European word *grapho* meaning to write.

Part B: **1.** F: Asimov was born in Russia. **2.** F: The arms race was between the United States and the Soviet Union. **3.** F: Myron Aub was the technician who discovered graphitics. **4.** T **5.** F: Earth was at war with the Denebians.

Part C: **1.** computers **2.** mathematics **3.** computing **4.** human **5.** powerful

Part D: **1.** b **2.** e **3.** i **4.** g **5.** c **6.** j **7.** a **8.** d **9.** f **10.** h

Workbook 7—The Expedition

Part A: **1.** b **2.** e **3.** d **4.** a **5.** c

Part B: **1.** being bored **2.** radio **3.** Astraea **4.** dystrophy **5.** engineer **6.** any of these: geography, history, foreign language, art, literature **7.** plants **8.** killed himself **9.** make entries in the logbook; keep the logbook **10.** mentally handicapped

Part C: **1.** F: Vera, Bruno, Melanie, and Olaf were the original team of four. **2.** T **3.** F: Olaf died first. **4.** T **5.** T

Workbook 8—Adventure

Part A: **1.** plot **2.** Dangerous **3.** computer **4.** wits **5.** Symbolism

Part B: **1.** a **2.** b **3.** c **4.** d **5.** a

Workbook 9—The Cegua

Part A: **1.** setting **2.** quench **3.** landscape **4.** Costa Rica **5.** the Cegua

Part B: Answers will vary, but examples follow. **1.** Other regionalisms include habits, folk tales, and customs. **2.** A *cantina* is a tavern. It comes from Spanish. **3.** The Cegua first appears as a beautiful woman. **4.** As a monster, the Cegua has a horse's head, fangs, fiery eyes, and sulfur breath. **5.** The young man did not believe the story about the Cegua.

Workbook 10—Master and Man

Part A: **1.** c **2.** e **3.** g **4.** a **5.** j **6.** b **7.** i **8.** f **9.** d **10.** h

Part B: **1.** naturalism **2.** snow storm **3.** wormwood **4.** his horse; Dapple **5.** hoof prints

Workbook 11—Just Lather, That's All

1. b **2.** c **3.** a **4.** b c **5.** c **6.** d **7.** a **8.** c **9.** d **10.** a

Teacher's Resource Library Answer Key

Workbook 12—Turning Points

Part A: **1.** ending **2.** turning point **3.** first-person **4.** coming of age **5.** young

Part B: **1.** T **2.** T **3.** T **4.** T **5.** T

Workbook 13—Nervous Conditions

Part A: **1.** Rhodesia **2.** Tambudzai **3.** accept any of these: education, equipment, teachers, food, furniture, everything **4.** assimilation **5.** loose

Part B: **1.** d **2.** e **3.** f **4.** a **5.** j **6.** h **7.** i **8.** b **9.** c **10.** g

Workbook 14—Marriage Is a Private Affair

Part A: Answers will vary, but examples follow. **1.** She is from the city and he is from a small, rural village. **2.** Ugoye was an "Amazon" and a "dunce." **3.** He asks his father's forgiveness because he broke the tradition and went against his father's beliefs. **4.** A wife needs to be of good character and have a Christian background. **5.** "It has never been heard." (never been done before) **6.** He suggests using an herbalist and a medicine named Amalile. **7.** Okeke cuts the wife out of the picture and sends it back to his son. **8.** Nene keeps a better home than most of them. **9.** Nature sends the first rain of the year. **10.** He wants to see his grandsons; he regrets how he behaved.

Part B: **1.** discussions **2.** an herbalist **3.** perseveres **4.** remorse **5.** forsaken

Workbook 15—Cranes

Part A: **1.** fear **2.** Public Peace Office **3.** Song-sam **4.** Thirty-Eighth Parallel **5.** grown up in the same village

Part B: **1.** T **2.** F: Song-sam had left his family, Tok-jae had stayed. **3.** F: Song-sam volunteered because he and Tok-jae had been boyhood friends. **4.** F: Song-sam had cried. **5.** T

Part C: **1.** killed **2.** a hard worker **3.** close **4.** family; parents, wife and children **5.** the crane

Workbook 16—Unit 1 Review

Part A: Answers will vary, but examples follow. **1.** Science fiction deals with people and events that did not happen; these stories are usually set in the future. **2.** The main job of the protagonist is to look for clues and solve a crime. **3.** Turning-point stories include an experience that changes a character's life. **4.** Westerns, war stories, and spy stories could be called adventure fiction. **5.** Characters are people, animals, or things in a story. The setting is the time and place of a story. Plot is the action that takes place in a story. **6.** Humans are not able to send people so far away. **7.** There are still many places in the world where marriages are arranged. There are parents who do not accept the people their children marry. **8.** A man falls in love with another's wife. He decides to kill the man. He gets on one train to establish an alibi. He secretly gets off to meet the man he's to kill. They go on a different train. The one kills the other. The killer meets the first train at a station down the line. He pretends he never left that train. He is caught because his fellow passenger on the train is a retired police inspector. He became suspicious over the killer's behavior. **9.** Accept answers that have reasons behind them: Yes: because the captain was his enemy; because the captain was killing all his friends. No: because then the barber would be a killer; because then someone would come to kill the barber; because things would only get worse for everyone. **10.** In our world we know people can think and do math, but we are trying to get computers to do everything. In the world of "The Feeling of Power," computers do everything, and the people are finding out that they themselves can think and do math in their heads.

Part B: **1.** e **2.** h **3.** g **4.** f **5.** b **6.** i **7.** j **8.** a **9.** d **10.** c

Workbook 17—About Nonfiction

Part A: **1.** real **2.** diary **3.** biographies **4.** magazines **5.** letters

Part B: **1.** genres **2.** "what" **3.** feelings **4.** autobiography **5.** feature **6.** journal **7.** interested **8.** book **9.** resource **10.** Internet

Workbook 18—Journals and Letters

Part A: **1.** T **2.** T **3.** T **4.** T **5.** F: A diary is personal and expresses private feelings.

Part B: Answers will vary, but examples follow **1.** A diary is like an imaginary friend. **2.** The events and people have usually been changed. **3.** Jacqueline Kennedy Onassis said, "I want to live my life, not record it." **4.** A journal focuses more on events, sights, or ideas. A diary focuses on feelings. **5.** The telephone and computer are more often being used for communication these days.

Workbook 19—Anne Frank: The Diary of a Young Girl

Part A: **1.** g **2.** c **3.** f **4.** j **5.** e **6.** d **7.** i **8.** b **9.** a **10.** h

Part B: **1.** Peter **2.** crazy **3.** "Kitty" **4.** youth, or adolescence **5.** truth

Workbook 20—Letter to Indira Tagore

Part A: Answers will vary, but examples follow. **1.** Personification is giving human characteristics to nonhuman things. **2.** Tagore just notices the moon when he turns out the lamp. **3.** He has been reading critical essays and refers to them as artificial discussions and a book of empty wordiness. **4.** The heavens are waiting for him soundlessly outside all the time, without protest. **5.** He wants to enjoy the moonlight; to read by the moonlight; or to continue to notice the heavens above him in the evenings.

Part B: **1.** T **2.** F: A mirage is an illusion; something you think you see that is really not there. **3.** T **4.** F: If you mock someone, you laugh at him or her in disgust or in anger. **5.** T

Workbook 21—Letter to the Reverend J. H. Twichell

Part A: **1.** delicious **2.** expletives **3.** pawing **4.** stealthiness **5.** breakfast **6.** dark **7.** praying **8.** 3 A.M. **9.** wash-bowl **10.** pen name

Part B: **1.** sympathetic **2.** two hours **3.** Livy **4.** sock **5.** club

Workbook 22—About Autobiography

Part A: **1.** a **2.** d **3.** b **4.** c **5.** b

Part B: **1.** their life **2.** "told" **3.** view **4.** important **5.** mistakes

Workbook 23—When Heaven and Earth Changed Places

Part A: **1.** j **2.** d **3.** g **4.** e **5.** i **6.** h **7.** a **8.** b **9.** f **10.** c

Part B: **1.** Twice **2.** monsoon **3.** scarecrows **4.** grass **5.** karma

Part C: Answers will vary, but examples follow. **1.** The soil was right when a handful of watery mud would ooze through their fingers like soup. **2.** The women transplanted the rice stalks, bending over for hours in knee-deep, muddy water. Women and children also pulled weeds in the standing water and mud of the fields. **3.** Hayslip says, "The labors and rituals of the harvest defined the other half of our existence." **4.** The stalks were tied in bundles and used to fix roofs or to kindle fires. **5.** Parents must never strike children, no matter how naughty they've been, while they are eating rice. The parents might receive divine punishment if they do.

Workbook 24—By Any Other Name

Part A: **1.** F: Curry is a food dish seasoned with curry powder. **2.** F: A sari is a draped outer garment of cloth traditionally worn by Indian women. **3.** F: The term *coolie* refers to an unskilled worker who does odd jobs. Curry refers to a dish of food heavily seasoned. **4.** F: Veranda is a roofed porch extending along the outside of a building. **5.** F: Hindi is a group of languages widely spoken in India.

Part B: **1.** valid **2.** personality **3.** in the back **4.** cry **5.** siesta

Part C: **1.** limited **2.** Santha **3.** Pamela **4.** Nalini **5.** nanny **6.** too hard **7.** friendship **8.** cheat **9.** stay home **10.** Cynthia

Workbook 25—Kaffir Boy

Part A: Answers will vary, but examples follow. **1.** Apartheid was a government policy used to keep whites and blacks apart. **2.** The only hope a black South African had to get a decent job was to have an education. **3.** He thought it was exciting, adventurous, and full of surprises; also a tsotsi didn't go to school. **4.** His mother stood up to the father and said Johannes was going to get an education. **5.** She hoped they would both have education [go to school] someday.

Part B: **1.** F: Mr. Mathabane thought a white man's education was a waste of time for his black son. **2.** T **3.** T **4.** T **5.** F: The grandmother had no money because her husband had taken it all and left her.

Part C: **1.** matriarchs **2.** philosophy **3.** survival **4.** inclination **5.** admonished **6.** knife **7.** birth certificate **8.** Venda **9.** half-half **10.** owned

Workbook 26—Biography

Part A: **1.** a **2.** c **3.** b **4.** d **5.** b

Part B: **1.** F: An autobiography is written by the subject. **2.** T **3.** F: The author relies on conversations with others and may not write about thoughts or feelings of the subject. **4.** T **5.** T

Workbook 27—China Men

Part A: **1.** finery **2.** pierced **3.** rouge **4.** Gold Mountain **5.** China

Part B: **1.** washing windows **2.** cotton gloves **3.** yellow skin **4.** silk **5.** his city **6.** hair **7.** uncluttered **8.** blondes **9.** aquarium **10.** saint

Workbook 28—The Last Seven Months of Anne Frank

Part A: **1.** c **2.** d **3.** e **4.** a **5.** b **6.** g **7.** h **8.** f **9.** j **10.** i

Part B: **1.** thirteenth **2.** writer **3.** nurse **4.** Otto **5.** typhus

Workbook 29—Journalism

Part A: **1.** F: "Breaking news" is immediate news, covered as it happens. **2.** F: A Web site is material put on the Internet for people to read. **3.** T **4.** T **5.** T

Part B: **1.** right **2.** fairly **3.** short articles **4.** communicating **5.** Feature

Teacher's Resource Library Answer Key

Workbook 30—Account Evened With India, Says PM

Part A: **1.** exclusive club **2.** India **3.** Sanctions **4.** security **5.** America

Part B: Answers will vary, but examples follow. **1.** He said the tests were held in the interest of national security and integrity. **2.** He threatened the tax evaders and corrupt tax collectors. **3.** Official buildings would be turned into schools, hospitals, women's universities, or sold. **4.** Those who had borrowed billions of rupees from the banks. **5.** India had proven it harbored strong expansionist ambitions. India had tested nuclear weapons before Pakistan.

Workbook 31—Tests Are Nowhere Near India's: Fernandes

Part A: **1.** T **2.** T **3.** F: Only the Prime Minister of India will have a finger on the button. **4.** T **5.** T

Part B: **1.** c **2.** f **3.** i **4.** h **5.** b **6.** d **7.** j **8.** a **9.** g **10.** e

Workbook 32—Pakistan Nuclear Moratorium Welcomed

Part A: **1.** austerity measures **2.** India **3.** nuclear missiles **4.** unilateral moratorium **5.** G8 **6.** Economic sanctions **7.** durable **8.** one million **9.** [nuclear] detonations **10.** stabilize

Part B: **1.** T **2.** F: The testing added to the tensions between the countries. **3.** T **4.** F: Atal Bihari Vajpayee is India's counterpart to Pakistan's prime minister. **5.** F: India was the first to announce a moratorium on nuclear testing.

Workbook 33—The Frightening Joy and Building Atomic Security

Part A: **1.** power **2.** joy **3.** Armageddon **4.** tired slogan **5.** escalation **6.** Americans **7.** an atomic security zone **8.** gravity **9.** perilously close **10.** nuclear warheads

Part B: **1.** F: The Polish writer sees the testing as helping to prevent war. **2.** T **3.** T **4.** F: Only the Dutch writer feels this way; the Polish writer does not feel this way. **5.** T

Workbook 34—Unit 2 Review

Part A: **1.** journals **2.** Autobiographies **3.** magazines **4.** China Men **5.** Anne Frank

Part B: **1.** Samuel L. Clemens **2.** Thomas Edison **3.** moonlight **4.** rice **5.** Anglo-Indian

Part C: **1.** c **2.** e **3.** g **4.** a **5.** h **6.** i **7.** j **8.** f **9.** d **10.** b

Workbook 35—About Drama

Part A: Answers will vary, but examples follow. **1.** Drama tells a story through dialogue and action performed by actors. **2.** Antagonists can be a character in the play, social injustice, a protagonist's own weaknesses, or fate. **3.** In a comedy the audience enjoys seeing the protagonist beat the antagonist. **4.** The two forms of drama are tragedy and comedy. **5.** Verse is made up of word patterns that follow a definite, repeating rhythm and sometimes rhyme.

Part B: **1.** religious **2.** antagonist **3.** an invisible rabbit **4.** chorus **5.** classical

Workbook 36—Classical Drama

Part A: **1.** F: Classical plays are divided into five acts. **2.** T **3.** F: The words that characters speak are called dialogue. **4.** F: Early dramas were written in the Greek and Latin languages. **5.** T

Part B: **1.** b **2.** a **3.** d **4.** c **5.** b

Workbook 37—Macbeth

Part A: Answers will vary, but examples follow. **1.** He sees the ghost of Banquo. **2.** She's asking if his foolishness has robbed him of his manhood. **3.** There was a time when smashed brains meant a man would die. **4.** She is reminding him his noble friends are missing him and his presence at the table. **5.** They explain that he has had a strange disability since early childhood.

Part B: **1.** c **2.** d **3.** e **4.** a **5.** b

Workbook 38—Realistic Drama

Part A: **1.** 1950s **2.** everyday **3.** Ordinary **4.** neighborhood **5.** born **6.** Henrik Ibsen **7.** realistic **8.** family **9.** classical **10.** American

Part B: **1.** T **2.** T **3.** T **4.** T **5.** F: Most of the plays are set in average homes and neighborhoods.

Workbook 39—"Master Harold"... and the Boys

Part A: **1.** b **2.** c **3.** a **4.** d **5.** b

Part B: **1.** c **2.** d **3.** j **4.** f **5.** a **6.** h **7.** i **8.** g **9.** e **10.** b

Part C: Answers will vary, but examples follow. **1.** Sam allowed the kite to dive down close to the ground, as if to crash, then pulled it up again. **2.** Sam wanted Hally to look up and be proud of something, to be proud of himself. **3.** Sam had been like a father to Hally, now he would be a servant to him. **4.** Hally's father was addicted to alcohol [was an alcoholic]. **5.** Sam wanted Hally to understand he could choose to be separated from South African blacks for the rest of his life.

Workbook 40—Expressionistic Drama

Part A: **1.** staging **2.** *Strange Interlude* **3.** feelings **4.** Europe **5.** emotional

Teacher's Resource Library Answer Key

Part B: **1.** F: In *Waiting for Godot,* Godot never appears. **2.** T **3.** T **4.** F: The split in *Strange Interlude* is between the character's public and private nature. **5.** F: Expressionistic playwrights did not want to present events realistically.

Workbook 41—The Stronger

Part A: **1.** ladies' café **2.** Christmas Eve **3.** MME. X **4.** husband **5.** MLLE. Y

Part B: **1.** b **2.** c **3.** a **4.** d **5.** c

Workbook 42—Unit 3 Review

Part A: **1.** personality **2.** Physical **3.** external clues **4.** Macbeth **5.** blank verse **6.** Everyday 7. imaginary **8.** Realistic **9.** apartheid **10.** *The Stronger*

Part B: **1.** F: *"Master Harold"* is about apartheid in Africa and friendship between white and black people. **2.** F: Dialogue is the term for the words spoken in a play. **3.** F: The main character in *Macbeth* sees a ghost and a bloody knife floating in front of him. **4.** F: Action in *The Stronger* takes place on Christmas Eve. **5.** T: café, restaurant, and banquet hall

Part C: Answers will vary, but examples follow. **1.** Settings are limited to what can be shown or represented on the actual stage. **2.** Tragedy and comedy. In tragedy, the antagonist (bad guy, enemy) usually destroys the protagonist (good guy, hero). Comedy gives the reader a happy ending and the protagonist usually wins over the antagonist. **3.** Characters used to be mostly nobility and important people; now they can be anyone. **4.** The changing or exaggerating of character or setting is found in expressionistic drama. **5.** The four elements are setting, stage directions, characters, and dialogue.

Workbook 43—About Poetry

Part A: **1.** Songs **2.** image **3.** Rhythm **4.** Rhyme **5.** epics **6.** sonnet **7.** symbol **8.** freedom **9.** picture **10.** Elegies

Part B: **1.** F: Haiku is a traditional Japanese poetic form. **2.** F: Humorous subjects appear in limericks. **3.** F: Free verse often doesn't rhyme. **4.** F: Early poems were usually songs to a deity. **5.** F: In a dramatic monologue a character reveals personality by talking to the reader.

Workbook 44—The Diameter of the Bomb

Part A: Answers will vary, but examples follow. **1.** He writes in the Hebrew language. **2.** It is a circle with no end and no God. **3.** The solitary man mourning the death of the young woman who was killed. **4.** Her graveyard includes more people in the bomb's damage. **5.** The bomb is thirty centimeters; its effective range is about seven meters; it has left four dead and eleven wounded.

Part B: **1.** kilometer **2.** Two hospitals **3.** circle **4.** another country **5.** orphans

Workbook 45—Taking Leave of a Friend

Part A: **1.** floating wide cloud **2.** river **3.** dead grass **4.** bow **5.** sunset

Part B: **1.** Separation **2.** depart **3.** neighing **4.** the walls **5.** simile

Workbook 46—Thoughts of Hanoi

Part A: Answers will vary, but examples follow. **1.** The small villages are islands of brown thatch in a lush green sea. **2.** The girls sow, harvest, spin, and weave. **3.** First the author says he wants to bury the past and burn the future. Later in the poem he asks his friend if he is reliving the past and imagining the future. **4.** He calls the land a frontier of hatred. **5.** The author fears he will march against his friend and kill him, or be killed by him.

Part B: **1.** T **2.** T **3.** F: The author remembers trains leaving daily from Hanoi. **4.** T **5.** True

Workbook 47—Mindoro

Part A: **1.** c **2.** d **3.** e **4.** a **5.** b

Part B: **1.** dissolving **2.** red threads **3.** mutes **4.** Blood light **5.** cluster like mayflies

Workbook 48—Ode to a Pair of Socks

Part A: **1.** impaled **2.** incandescent **3.** shepherd's **4.** beauty twice over **5.** wool

Part B: Answers will vary, but examples follow. **1.** They both hid things away so others would not see them. Schoolboys put fireflies in a bottle and scholars hoard holy writ. **2.** Two socks as soft as rabbit fur. **3.** The socks were colorful and soft. **4.** He thought the socks were so beautiful, they were too nice to be put on his feet. **5.** Figurative language makes a comparison and is not meant to be taken literally.

Workbook 49—Three Haiku

Part A: **1.** forgive him **2.** bantam **3.** ancient pool **4.** rooster **5.** world

Part B: **1.** F: Basho comes from a kind of banana tree that grew near where the author lived. **2.** F: A ruff of feathers is a collar that stands out from the neck. **3.** F: Basho taught Kikaku how to write haiku. **4.** F: The three animals in these Haiku are a rooster, a frog, and a songbird. **5.** T

Teacher's Resource Library Answer Key

Workbook 50—Do Not Go Gentle Into That Good Night

Part A: Answers will vary, but examples follow. **1.** He is writing to his father who is dying. **2.** "Rage, rage against the dying of the light." or "Do not go gentle into that good night." **3.** To curse him, to be angry, to cry out; to fight against dying. **4.** The men are described as wise, good, wild, and grave. **5.** A villanelle is a form of poetry used in France in the 1500s, with nineteen lines, and several repeating rhymes.

Part B: 1. c **2.** e **3.** a **4.** c **5.** b

Workbook 51—Unit 4 Review

Part A: Answers will vary, but examples follow. **1.** Countries represented in this unit include Israel, China, Vietnam, the Philippines, Chile, Japan, and Wales. **2.** Two similes are "Mind like a floating wide cloud," and "Sunset like the parting of old acquaintances." **3.** This poem starts like a matter-of-fact news report, very little emotion. **4.** Two descriptions of the socks are two little boxes knit from threads of sunset and sheepskin, and embroidered fire, those incandescent socks. **5.** This poem is a sort of elegy that mourns deaths in Vietnam. The mood changes many times during the poem to include anger, sadness, remembering happy times, and confusion about the future.

Part B: 1. F: Three of the authors in this unit are still alive. **2.** T **3.** F: When you give human characteristics to a nonhuman object that is personification. **4.** F: The three haiku are similar because there is an animal in each of them. **5.** True

Part C: 1. h **2.** f **3.** j **4.** b **5.** c **6.** i **7.** d **8.** e **9.** a **10.** g

Workbook 52—Persuasive Literature

Part A: Answers will vary, but examples follow. **1.** A metaphor is a figure of speech that says one thing is something else. **2.** This unit covers speeches and essays. **3.** Advertising shows us choices and shares ideas. **4.** Literary works written mainly to influence opinion are persuasive. **5.** The authors criticize, reassure, threaten, praise, argue with, and inspire their audiences.

Part B: 1. editorials **2.** buy **3.** genres **4.** literature **5.** irony

Workbook 53—Speeches

Part A: 1. F: Speeches are meant to be spoken; heard by audiences. **2.** F: A proclamation is a letter about important events meant to be read out loud. **3.** T **4.** T **5.** T

Part B: 1. an event **2.** content **3.** sound **4.** spoken **5.** proclamation

Workbook 54—Letter to the English

Part A: 1. the Maid **2.** thirteen **3.** Orléans **4.** Charles VII **5.** Rouen

Part B: 1. g **2.** h **3.** i **4.** f **5.** d **6.** e **7.** j **8.** c **9.** a **10.** b

Workbook 55—Nobel Lecture

Part A: Answers will vary, but examples follow. **1.** Existing with all the different scales of values is difficult; people will be torn apart by these differences. **2.** The scales of values include one for evaluating events near at hand, another for events far away; one for aging societies, one for young societies; and unsuccessful and successful people each have one. **3.** The author says art and literature can coordinate the different scales of values. **4.** Literature is able to convey experiences from one generation to another; it becomes the living memory of a nation. **5.** World literature has power to convey experiences from one land to another, to make the different scales of values agree, and to allow one nation to learn correctly the true history of another nation and perhaps prevent them from making the same mistakes.

Part B: 1. F: Solzhenitsyn was in prison and exiled from Russia for years. **2.** F: The term scales of values describes how people judge other people and nations. **3.** T **4.** F: Humanity has become one through international broadcasting and print. **5.** T

Part C: 1. c **2.** g **3.** h **4.** f **5.** i **6.** a **7.** j **8.** e **9.** d **10.** b

Workbook 56—The Gettysburg Address

Part A: 1. civil war **2.** battlefield **3.** twenty **4.** birth **5.** resting place

Part B: 1. new Republican party **2.** eleven thousand **3.** consecrate **4.** holy **5.** for the people

Workbook 57—Inaugural Address

Part A: 1. religion **2.** inaugural address **3.** the torch **4.** tyranny **5.** adversary

Part B: Answers will vary, but examples follow. **1.** He asked the citizens of the United States to ask not what the United States will do for them, but what together all can do for the freedom of the world. **2.** The common enemies of humankind are tyranny, poverty, disease, and war. **3.** The term *man* really means all of mankind, all people. **4.** They come not from the generosity of the state but from the hand of God. **5.** He thinks we should never negotiate out of fear, but never fear to negotiate.

Teacher's Resource Library Answer Key

Workbook 58—Essays

Part A: **1.** personal **2.** talents **3.** columns **4.** printing press **5.** read

Part B: **1.** T **2.** T **3.** T **4.** F: During the 1700s and 1800s essayists began to write opinion articles. **5.** T

Workbook 59—Of Repentance

Part A: **1.** b **2.** c **3.** d **4.** e **5.** a

Part B: Answers will vary, but examples follow. **1.** The Thief was successful due to his physical strength in his youth. **2.** He stole from many places so that no one would have a large loss. **3.** The thief took large loads each night and carried them great distances. **4.** He is now paying back the people he robbed, with voluntary gifts. **5.** He seems to think it is dishonest and hates it, but he hated his own poverty more.

Workbook 60—A Small Place

Part A: **1.** d **2.** b **3.** c **4.** c **5.** a

Part B: **1.** native **2.** backward **3.** water; sea **4.** drug smuggler **5.** twelve

Part C: **1.** Antigua **2.** customs **3.** dilapidated **4.** hospital **5.** British God

Workbook 61—Unit 5 Review

Part A: **1.** setting **2.** Persuasive writings **3.** essay **4.** speech **5.** way of thinking

Part B: Answers will vary, but examples follow. **1.** The main character was very poor, he was a thief, he gained quite a bit of wealth from his stealing, he repented from his wrongdoing, and gave voluntary gifts back to those he had stolen from. **2.** They both ask the nation to remember what has gone before and to continue the work forward, complete tasks begun, and never forget those who laid the foundation. **3.** World literature is a common bond between peoples of the earth, it shares a common spirit, helps people learn about each other and care about what happens in other parts of the world, and is generally a uniting power for all people. (or) World literature has power to convey experiences from one land to another, to make the different scales of values agree, and to allow one nation to learn correctly the true history of another nation and perhaps prevent them from making the same mistakes. **4.** Joan of Arc believes she will be successful because she has heard voices and directions she believes come directly from God. **5.** Jamaica Kincaid takes an attitude immediately in the tone of her writing, which is angry and sarcastic. She also uses irony. She says, "A tourist is an ugly human being."

Part C: **1.** metaphor **2.** proclamations **3.** evaluate **4.** humiliating **5.** bigot **6.** consecrated **7.** negotiate **8.** repent **9.** dilapidated **10.** extraordinary

Workbook 62—About Humorous Literature

Part A: **1.** F: Humorous literature is created to be funny. **2.** T **3.** T **4.** T **5.** T

Part B: **1.** human **2.** wit **3.** unexpected **4.** poke fun **5.** tone

Workbook 63—Satire

Part A: **1.** basic truths **2.** behavior **3.** satire **4.** vividly **5.** Social injustice

Part B: **1.** T **2.** T **3.** T **4.** T **5.** T

Workbook 64—A Modest Proposal

Part A: **1.** d **2.** f **3.** i **4.** g **5.** h **6.** c **7.** a **8.** j **9.** b **10.** e

Part B: Answers will vary, but examples follow. **1.** Swift's proposal is that Irish children be fed and fattened until one year old and then sold as a product for people to eat, **2.** To become thieves or leave their native country. **3.** Poor children ("savages") usually do not feel marriage is important and so one male could serve four females. **4.** He says they deserve first choice of the children because the landlords have already devoured most of their parents. **5.** Because they are poor all their lives, it would be better to be dead than to live a life of misfortune and misery.

Workbook 65—Cup Inanity and Patriotic Profanity

Part A: **1.** Vindication **2.** pensioner **3.** racist **4.** pubs **5.** match

Part B: Answers will vary, but examples follow. **1.** The list includes foreign debt will be paid off, there will be no more poor in Argentina, unemployment will be something unknown, pensioners will have a decent retirement, relief checks for those outside Goya will be in the mail tomorrow, and the Wizard of Oz will be made president. **2.** In 1978 a mob was screaming their support for the government because the national team won, and people were arrested, tortured, and killed by the same government. **3.** "Patriotic actions" included filling the streets with litter, wearing the national ensign on a silly hat or cape, waving bottles of beer and throwing them through store windows, yelling racist insults, and using bad language (swearing). **4.** A yob is slang for street criminal or hooligan. The author says yobs exist because capitalist states encourage (champion) them. **5.** Sarcasm is a heavy, sometimes mean-spirited kind of irony.

Teacher's Resource Library Answer Key

Workbook 66—Columns

Part A: **1.** by-line **2.** humor **3.** range **4.** relieving tension **5.** parenting

Part B: **1.** F: Columns are articles that appear regularly in periodicals. **2.** F: Hundreds of women and men write columns. **3.** F: Many countries around the world publish columns for people to read. **4.** F: Some columns are written from the average person's point of view. **5.** T

Workbook 67—Staying at a Japanese Inn: Peace, Tranquillity, Insects

Part A: **1.** d **2.** i **3.** e **4.** h **5.** g **6.** b **7.** c **8.** j **9.** a **10.** f

Part B: **1.** shoes **2.** cicada-infested **3.** maid **4.** shout angrily **5.** Ryokan

Part C: **1.** F: At the inn, guests must put on one set of slippers for the main room and one set for the bathroom. **2.** F: The room had no beds or chairs. **3.** F: Cormorants are waterbirds similar to pelicans. **4.** F: There is no international symbol for fishing that uses hands fluttering. **5.** F: Cormorant fishers fish by using a wire basket with a log fire to attract the fish.

Part D: **1.** neck **2.** stupid **3.** tea **4.** peace **5.** beeper

Workbook 68—Why Can't We Have Our Own Apartment?

Part A: Answers will vary, but examples follow. **1.** Children usually ask parents about moving out and having their own place. This column is backward. **2.** The parents want to move out and get their own apartment. **3.** Reasons for leaving include fix up the apartment as they please, play stereos when they want, come in late without being questioned, invite people over and not have someone hanging around, and use of the car. **4.** Some issues include utilities, phone bills, newspapers, and furniture. **5.** They were expected to cook, make beds, do laundry, take care of the yard, keep the cars running, and bring in the money.

Part B: **1.** syndicated **2.** theme **3.** silly **4.** call **5.** utilities

Workbook 69—Stories

Part A: **1.** amuse **2.** punchline **3.** Details **4.** themselves **5.** monologue

Part B: **1.** T **2.** T **3.** T **4.** F: A joke is a short funny story about anything, and it ends in a punchline. **5.** T

Workbook 70—Lohengrin

Part A: **1.** c **2.** d **3.** a **4.** e **5.** b

Part B: **1.** Magic **2.** on their shields **3.** a shining knight **4.** Mrs. Ortrud **5.** faints

Part C: **1.** T **2.** T **3.** T **4.** T **5.** T

Workbook 71—A Wedding Without Musicians

Part A: Answers will vary, but examples follow. **1.** The name comes from Yiddish; it is a traditional Hebrew greeting. **2.** Pogroms were organized mob attacks against the Jews, and sometimes the government encouraged them. **3.** Noah was a printer and a busybody who knew all the news and secrets, and he ran around the town telling everyone about them. **4.** They offered gifts to the Inspector of Police and asked for help. **5.** The Straggler Special was a hero when it came to town with no cars attached.

Part B: **1.** rats in a famine; ice in summer **2.** drinking; partying **3.** Cossacks **4.** ventilating **5.** pogrom; fight

Workbook 72—Unit 6 Review

Part A: **1.** F: Irony is the use of words that say one thing but mean the opposite. **2.** T **3.** F: Exaggeration is the use of words to make something seem worse than it is. **4.** T **5.** F: Satire is humor that makes fun of foolishness or evil.

Part B: **1.** laugh **2.** right and wrong **3.** Pamphlets **4.** opinion **5.** by-line **6.** shoes **7.** funny **8.** Monologues **9.** greeting **10.** Magic

Part C: Answers will vary, but examples follow. **1.** Swift wants the reader to understand how awfully the Irish are treated by the British; that the British have indifference and contempt toward the Irish. **2.** Graham-Yooll describes the government as being praised because of the soccer team winning, while at the same time arresting and torturing people. **3.** Barry points fun at American tourists and Japanese traditions. **4.** Lohengrin makes her promise never to ask who is he or where he comes from. **5.** This story teaches the reader that Jews sometimes were beaten for no reason and usually the government did nothing to stop it, their homes and possessions were destroyed, and they had to bribe local officials to help them.

Teacher's Resource Library Answer Key

Vocabulary Workbook

Vocabulary Workbook 1—The Adventure of the Speckled Band, page 1

1. setting 2. client 3. intuition 4. trivial 5. mania 6. bequeathed 7. cheetah 8. writhe 9. parsonage 10. coroner

Vocabulary Workbook 1—The Adventure of the Speckled Band, page 2

Column A: 1. c 2. b 3. f 4. g 5. k 6. l 7. a 8. e 9. j 10. h 11. d 12. i 13. m

Column C: 1. a 2. d 3. c 4. e 5. m 6. g 7. i 8. l 9. j 10. h 11. k 12. f 13. b

Vocabulary Workbook 1—The Adventure of the Speckled Band, page 3

Across 5. baboon 6. protruding 7. client 10. investigation 11. cheetah 12. mania 13. dispel 14. averted 15. aristocratic

Down 1. coroner 2. convulsed 3. manor 4. dog-cart 8. pitiable 9. manifold 10. intuition

Vocabulary Workbook 2—Death Arrives on Schedule, page 1

Across 1. masculine 4. development 5. foresee 6. hale 7. ignition 9. merit

Down 2. inconvenience 3. rental 4. deposition 8. curt

Vocabulary Workbook 2—Death Arrives on Schedule, page 2

1. exclusive 2. aggressive 3. favorable 4. bungalow 5. compartment 6. registration 7. retrieve 8. originate 9. invest

Vocabulary Workbook 2—Death Arrives on Schedule, page 3

1. j 2. a 3. n 4. i 5. g 6. l 7. f 8. k 9. c 10. d 11. m 12. h 13. b 14. e 15. q 16. p 17. o

Vocabulary Workbook 3—The Feeling of Power, page 1

1. amiable 2. stylus 3. glimmer 4. random 5. haggard 6. divert 7. reconstruction 8. hydroponics 9. bottleneck 10. overwhelmingly

Vocabulary Workbook 3—The Feeling of Power, page 2

Column A: 1. c 2. e 3. g 4. i 5. l 6. m 7. k 8. a 9. j 10. h 11. f 12. d 13. b

Column C: 1. c 2. e 3. a 4. g 5. i 6. k 7. m 8. l 9. j 10. h 11. f 12. b 13. d

Vocabulary Workbook 3—The Feeling of Power, page 3

Column A: 1. c 2. j 3. b 4. e 5. f 6. a 7. g 8. i 9. h 10. d

Column C: 1. a 2. b 3. c 4. j 5. f 6. d 7. g 8. i 9. h 10. e

Vocabulary Workbook 4—The Expedition, page 1

Across 2. suffocation 3. psychic 6. humidity 8. denouement 9. rotation 10. vital 11. serum 12. data 13. sterile

Down 1. pschoneurotic 3. protagonist 4. hazard 5. coverage 7. indifferent

Vocabulary Workbook 4—The Expedition, page 2

1. a, b 2. c, b 3. c, a 4. a, b 5. b, c 6. b, a 7. c, a 8. b, a 9. a, b 10. a, b

Vocabulary Workbook 4—The Expedition, page 3

1. T 2. F 3. F 4. F 5. F 6. T 7. F 8. T 9. T 10. T 11. T 12. T 13. F 14. F 15. T 16. T 17. F 18. F 19. F 20. T 21. T 22. T 23. T 24. F 25. T 26. F 27. T 28. T 29. F 30. T

Vocabulary Workbook 5—The Cegua

1. action 2. setting 3. regionalism 4. proprietor 5. quench 6. rude 7. woe 8. unsuspecting 9. frenzy 10. restive 11. landscape 12. abruptly 13. razor 14. hastily 15. lingered

Vocabulary Workbook 6—Master and Man

1. a, b 2. c, b 3. a, c 4. c, b 5. b, c 6. c, b 7. a, c 8. a, b 9. b, c 10. a, c

Vocabulary Workbook 7—Just Lather, That's All

1. holster 2. razor 3. strop 4. conscientious 5. rasps 6. tuft 7. emits 8. incising 9. excursion 10. ineradicable

Vocabulary Workbook 8—Nervous Conditions

1. T 2. T 3. T 4. T 5. T 6. F 7. F 8. F 9. F 10. T 11. F 12. T 13. F 14. F 15. T 16. T 17. F 18. F 19. T 20. F 21. T 22. T 23. T 24. F 25. F 26. T 27. T 28. F 29. F 30. F

Vocabulary Workbook 9—Marriage Is a Private Affair, page 1

1. third-person 2. fluently 3. negotiations 4. disconcerted 5. qualification 6. vehemently 7. theological 8. herbalist 9. murderess, nevertheless 10. excessive 11. deference 12. perfunctorily 13. re-enactment

Teacher's Resource Library Answer Key

Vocabulary Workbook 9—Marriage Is a Private Affair, page 2
Column A: 1. b 2. e 3. h 4. i 5. d 6. f 7. a 8. j 9. c 10. g

Column B: 1. b 2. e 3. i 4. g 5. a 6. h 7. d 8. j 9. f 10. c

Vocabulary Workbook 10—Cranes
1. F 2. T 3. T 4. F 5. T 6. F 7. T 8. F 9. F 10. F 11. T 12. T 13. T 14. T 15. F 16. T 17. T 18. F 19. T 20. F 21. T 22. T 23. F 24. F 25. F 26. T 27. F 28. T 29. T 30. T

Vocabulary Workbook 11—Anne Frank: The Diary of a Young Girl
1. restless 2. circumstances 3. stifled 4. superb 5. reigned 6. adolescent 7. innermost 8. misunderstood 9. uphold 10. precise

Vocabulary Workbook 12—Letter to Indira Tagore
Part A: 1. b 2. f 3. e 4. i 5. h 6. d 7. g 8. c 9. a

Part B: 1. d 2. a 3. c 4. e 5. b

Vocabulary Workbook 13—Letter to the Rev. J. H. Twichell
Across 2. pen name 3. profane 4. to wit 6. interminable 9. pitch 10. expletive

Down 1. delicious 2. pun 3. petitioner 5. stealthiness 6. in earnest 7. satire 8. theme

Vocabulary Workbook 14—When Heaven and Earth Changed Places
1. T 2. F 3. F 4. F 5. T 6. T 7. T 8. F 9. F 10. T 11. T 12. T 13. F 14. F 15. F 16. T 17. F 18. F 19. F 20. T 21. F 22. T 23. T 24. F 25. T 26. F 27. F

Vocabulary Workbook 15—By Any Other Name, page 1
1. c, a 2. a, b 3. c, a 4. c, a 5. b, a 6. c, a 7. b, a 8. c, a 9. a, b 10. c, a

Vocabulary Workbook 15—By Any Other Name, page 2
1. baffled, cope 2. inability, intimidated 3. precariously, extraordinary 4. valid, palpitating 5. courteous, accordance 6. siesta, wizened 7. sedately, sprinted 8. tepid, rigid 9. fragrance, tongas 10. deserted, peevishness

Vocabulary Workbook 16—Kaffir Boy, page 1
Column A: 1. d 2. e 3. a 4. i 5. f 6. j 7. h 8. b 9. g 10. c

Column C: 1. e 2. j 3. f 4. a 5. i 6. d 7. h 8. g 9. c 10. b

Vocabulary Workbook 16—Kaffir Boy, page 2
Column A: 1. c 2. d 3. g 4. h 5. i 6. a 7. f 8. e 9. j 10. b

Column C: 1. h 2. b 3. g 4. c 5. a 6. d 7. i 8. j 9. f 10. e

Vocabulary Workbook 16—Kaffir Boy, page 3
1. setting 2. oracle 3. pilchard 4. limbs 5. velds 6. swathe 7. abreast 8. austere 9. compliance 10. paradoxically

Vocabulary Workbook 16—Kaffir Boy, page 4
1. b, c 2. a, b 3. c, b 4. a, c 5. b, a 6. c, a 7. a, b 8. a, b 9. c, b 10. c, b

Vocabulary Workbook 17—China Men
Part A: 1. b 2. l 3. e 4. g 5. f 6. d 7. j 8. k 9. m 10. i 11. h 12. a 13. c 14. n

Part B: Sentences will vary.

Vocabulary Workbook 18—The Last Seven Months of Anne Frank
1. confirm 2. distinguished 3. survive 4. touched 5. openly 6. inferred 7. existential 8. isolated 9. required 10. requisitioned

Vocabulary Workbook 19—Account Evened With India, Says PM
1. T 2. F 3. T 4. F 5. F 6. F 7. F 8. T 9. T 10. T 11. T 12. F 13. F 14. F 15. T 16. F 17. F 18. T 19. T 20. T 21. T

Vocabulary Workbook 20—Tests Are Nowhere Near India's: Fernandes
Column A: 1. e 2. b 3. c 4. g 5. f 6. d 7. a

Column C: 1. d 2. g 3. b 4. f 5. e 6. c 7. h 8. a

Column E: 1. h 2. f 3. a 4. c 5. g 6. d 7. e 8. b

Vocabulary Workbook 21—Pakistan Nuclear Moratorium Welcomed
Across 1. restraint 3. norm 8. constructively 9. intentioin 10. formalise 11. stabilise

Down 2. arms 3. news cycle 4. detonation 5. tension 6. unilateral 7. reciprocate

Teacher's Resource Library Answer Key

Vocabulary Workbook 22—The Frightening Joy/ Building Atomic Security
1. editorial **2.** gravity **3.** perilously **4.** escalation **5.** armaments **6.** guarantor **7.** potential **8.** security **9.** shielded **10.** slogan

Vocabulary Workbook 23—Macbeth, page 1
Across 1. manhood **3.** summon **8.** gory **10.** affectionately **14.** ailment **15.** delusion **16.** mischance

Down 2. disability **4.** drama **5.** sonnet **6.** hearty **7.** behalf **9.** sound **11.** flawless **12.** rank **13.** fit

Vocabulary Workbook 23—Macbeth, page 2
1. k **2.** a **3.** e **4.** l **5.** m **6.** i **7.** f **8.** c **9.** g **10.** d **11.** b **12.** n **13.** o **14.** j **15.** h

Vocabulary Workbook 24—"Master Harold"... and the Boys
1. T **2.** F **3.** F **4.** T **5.** T **6.** T **7.** F **8.** T **9.** F **10.** T **11.** T **12.** F **13.** T **14.** F **15.** F **16.** T **17.** T **18.** F **19.** T **20.** T **21.** F **22.** F **23.** F **24.** F **25.** T **26.** F **27.** T **28.** F

Vocabulary Workbook 25—The Stronger
1. props **2.** abhors **3.** chiffonier **4.** longs **5.** christening **6.** fiancé **7.** malice **8.** slithered **9.** bewitch **10.** pilots

Vocabulary Workbook 26—The Diameter of the Bomb, Taking Leave of a Friend
Across 2. graveyard **3.** effective **4.** separation **7.** symbol **8.** depart **9.** enlarge

Down 1. free verse **4.** kilometer **5.** solitary **6.** neigh **7.** simile

Vocabulary Workbook 27—Thoughts of Hanoi, Mindoro
1. a, b **2.** a, b **3.** c, a **4.** b, c **5.** b, a **6.** c, a **7.** b, c **8.** c, b **9.** a, c **10.** b, a

Vocabulary Workbook 28— Ode to a Pair of Socks, Three Haiku, Do Not Go Gentle Into That Good Night
Column A: 1. e **2.** a **3.** f **4.** c **5.** g **6.** d **7.** h **8.** i **9.** b **10.** j

Column C: 1. m **2.** a **3.** b **4.** o **5.** h **6.** d **7.** c **8.** i **9.** j **10.** e **11.** p **12.** q **13.** n **14.** k **15.** f **16.** g **17.** l

Vocabulary Workbook 29—Letter to the English
1. proclamation **2.** regent **3.** violated **4.** relinquish **5.** withholding **6.** hence **7.** revealed **8.** Christendom

Vocabulary Workbook 30—Nobel Lecture, page 1
1. deceit, discrepancies **2.** concussion, accordance **3.** divergent, exasperating **4.** tolerates, ironic **5.** disparity, valid **6.** detrimental, interred **7.** frivolously, detach **8.** conception, perceive **9.** lacerated, concisely **10.** decrepit, mutual

Vocabulary Workbook 30—Nobel Lecture, page 2
Column A: 1. f **2.** i **3.** e **4.** j **5.** c **6.** b **7.** a **8.** h **9.** g **10.** d

Column B: 1. b **2.** f **3.** h **4.** j **5.** i **6.** a **7.** g **8.** d **9.** c **10.** e

Vocabulary Workbook 30—Nobel Lecture, page 3
1. deceits **2.** ironic **3.** assimilate **4.** bigoted **5.** tribune **6.** collective **7.** depravity **8.** recourse **9.** tension **10.** intimate

Vocabulary Workbook 30—Nobel Lecture, page 4
1. T **2.** F **3.** F **4.** T **5.** T **6.** F **7.** F **8.** F **9.** F **10.** F **11.** T **12.** F **13.** T **14.** F **15.** F **16.** T **17.** T **18.** T **19.** T **20.** F **21.** F **22.** F **23.** F

Vocabulary Workbook 31—The Gettysburg Address/Inaugural Address, page 1
Across 1. adversary **3.** speech **6.** overburdened **10.** engulf **12.** metaphor **13.** heir **14.** invoke **15.** heritage **16.** belabor

Down 1. asunder **2.** anew **4.** proposition **5.** undoing **7.** formulate **8.** abolish **9.** civility **11.** forbear

Vocabulary Workbook 31—The Gettysburg Address/Inaugural Address, page 2
1. c **2.** a, b **3.** c, a **4.** a, b **5.** c, a **6.** b, c **7.** a, b **8.** c, b **9.** b

Vocabulary Workbook 32—A Small Place/Of Repentance, page 1
1. currency **2.** luxurious **3.** minister **4.** perception **5.** sophisticated **6.** boutique **7.** taxing **8.** admirable **9.** mimic **10.** overwhelming

Vocabulary Workbook 32—A Small Place/Of Repentance, page 2
Column A: 1. h **2.** g **3.** c **4.** j **5.** d **6.** a **7.** e **8.** f **9.** i **10.** b

Column C: 1. b **2.** j **3.** c **4.** g **5.** d **6.** a **7.** e **8.** h **9.** f **10.** i

Teacher's Resource Library Answer Key

Vocabulary Workbook 32—A Small Place/Of Repentance, page 3
1. F 2. T 3. T 4. T 5. T 6. T 7. T 8. F 9. T 10. F 11. F 12. F 13. T 14. F 15. F 16. T 17. F 18. F 19. T 20. T 21. F

Vocabulary Workbook 33—A Modest Proposal, page 1
Across 2. professed 4. grievance 6. tone 9. exportation 12. fricassee 13. esteem 14. commonwealth

Down 1. deference 3. sustenance 5. ragout 7. satire 8. disoblige 10. pamphlet 11. refinement

Vocabulary Workbook 33—A Modest Proposal, page 2
1. alms, importune 2. prodigious, deplorable 3. raiment 4. nutriment, wholesome 5. computes, circumstance 6. fore, tolerably 7. discoursing 8. visionary, incur 9. inclemency, inevitable 10. entails

Vocabulary Workbook 34—Cup Inanity and Patriotic Profanity
Column A: 1. l 2. b 3. k 4. d 5. c 6. j 7. i 8. e 9. a 10. f 11. h 12. g

Column C: 1. g 2. b 3. k 4. h 5. c 6. i 7. a 8. d 9. e 10. j 11. f

Vocabulary Workbook 35—Staying at a Japanese Inn: Peace, Tranquillity, Insects
1. T 2. F 3. T 4. F 5. F 6. F 7. T 8. F 9. F 10. T 11. F 12. T 13. F 14. F 15. F 16. T 17. T 18. F 19. T 20. T 21. F 22. F 23. T 24. T 25. F 26. T

Vocabulary Workbook 36—Why Can't We Have Our Own Apartment?/Lohengrin, page 1
1. theme 2. utility 3. appliances 4. suite 5. linens 6. stereo 7. autobiographical 8. parody 9. reveals 10. complicated 11. archduke

Vocabulary Workbook 36—Why Can't We Have Our Own Apartment?/Lohengrin, page 2
1. archduke 2. union 3. gab 4. sorcerers 5. reveals 6. battalion 7. posing 8. presses 9. swoon 10. visa

Vocabulary Workbook 37—A Wedding Without Musicians, page 1
Across 1. director 5. anecdote 6. notary 8. station master 10. humorist 11. progrom 12. hooligan 13. hearsay 14. brandish

Down 2. irony 3. officialdom 4. buffet 7. bandy 8. straggler 9. reprisal

Vocabulary Workbook 37—A Wedding Without Musicians, page 2
1. a, b 2. c, a 3. b, c 4. b, c 5. a, c 6. b, a 7. c, b 8. b, a

Student Study Guides

Student Study Guides 1–6

These activities are to be used with pages 10–15 in this text.

Student Study Guide 7

I.
- A.
  1. seven
  2. sitting-room
  3. deductions
- B.
  1. gray; frightened
  2. dog-cart; train
  3. Farintosh
     a. Farintosh; tiara
  4. Stoner

II.
- A.
  1. stepfather; Roylotts
  2. butler
  3. Julia; two
  4. Stoke Moran
  5. cheetah
- B.
  1. two
  2. whistle
  3. locked; unlocked
  4. band; speckled band

III.
- A.
  1. pain
  2. brownish speckles
  3. swamp adder
- B.
  1. ventilator
  2. whistle
  3. clang; safe
  4. hiss; ventilator

Student Study Guide 8

I.
- A.
  1. possesses; Loni Leisegang
  2. unimportant
  3. aggressive
  4. rich aggressors
- B.
  1. Helfried Leisegang
  2. whiskey; driver's license
  3. Loni; suited
  4. almost perfect
  5. kill

II.
- A.
  1. property; car
  2. Leisegang; train
  3. whiskeys; sleep
  4. suitcase; loads
  5. boards; Munich
- B.
  1. traveling
  2. suitcase; staying
  3. smoke
  4. gets off
- C.
  1. platform
  2. dark; sunglasses
  3. Nienburg
  4. car
  5. suspicious
  6. shoots; Leisegang

III.

A.

1. trees
2. Hannover
3. station
4. express
5. breakfast; fir needle

B.

1. compartment
2. sleeping
3. express
4. sleep; toilet
5. Würzburg
6. gun
7. Hamburg; police

C.

1. deposition
2. newspaper
3. surprised; sunny; jacket
4. leave; different
5. Hannover; jacket; sun
6. compartment; time
7. searched; ticket; recently
8. Hafermass

D.

1. killing
2. film producer; dies

Student Study Guide 9

I.

A.

1. Weider; Brant
2. Technician
3. nine
4. seventeen
5. seven; three

II.

A.

1. hornswoggling
2. any
3. Terrestrial Federation
4. week

B.

1. human thought
2. Project Number
3. Aub
4. guarantee

III.

A.

1. railroads
2. lost art
3. decimal
4. square root

B.

1. graphitics
2. uncomfortable
3. man
4. protein-depolarizer
5. Shuman
6. power

Teacher's Resource Library Answer Key

Student Study Guide 10

I.

A.

1. methane
2. results
3. diapers
4. bored

B.

1. Halifax
2. humidity
3. Mars
4. calligraphy

C.

1. plants
2. birth control
3. liver
4. neglects

D.

1. panic attacks
2. logbook
3. emergency; child
4. ammoniac gas
5. holiday

II.

A.

1. $C_6H_{12}O_6$
2. ball
3. Lyride
4. Capricornus

B.

1. radio
2. down; pardoned
3. thirty-nine
4. random; laugh
5. warmer

C.

1. land
2. Wellington
3. Astraea
4. technical
5. moon
6. old people

Student Study Guide 11

I.

A.

1. ranch
2. fool
3. mad
4. woman
   a. red; sulfur

II.

A.

1. wind; leaves
2. dark; deep
3. Bagaces
4. doesn't answer
5. pursuing

III.

A.

1. coat; teeth
2. pale
3. dogs bark
4. senseless
5. frighten children

Student Study Guide 12

I.

A.

1. hut
2. wilderness
3. wormwood
4. right; left

II.

A.

1. wormwood; circle
2. Dapple
3. cheer; help
4. behind; face

III.

A.

1. collapses
2. right
3. Nicholas; candles
4. shafts

Teacher's Resource Library Answer Key

Student Study Guide 13

I.
- A.
  1. military cap
  2. sympathy
  3. mutilated

II.
- A.
  1. target practice
  2. rebel; barber
  3. six
  4. 2:20
  5. pore; blood

III.
- A.
  1. enemy
  2. alive; shaved
  3. body; hide
  4. kill

Student Study Guide 14

I.
- A.
  1. evils; advantages
  2. mission
  3. convent

II.
- A.
  1. chances
  2. boy
  3. decent; decent
     - a. principle

III.
- A.
  1. corrupted
  2. prejudiced
  3. never; convent
  4. New Year's
  5. Babamukuru
  6. Nyamarira

Student Study Guide 15

I.
- A.
  1. dad
  2. letter; shock

II.
- A.
  1. Ugoye Nweke
  2. love her
  3. character; Christian
- B.
  1. Girls'
  2. eat
  3. spoke; tongue
  4. native doctor

III.
- A.
  1. Nene
  2. women
  3. sons
  4. sleeps

Student Study Guide 16

I.
- A.
  1. children
  2. Public Peace
  3. pumpkin
  4. smoke

II.
- A.
  1. killed
  2. dirt
  3. Shorty

III.
- A.
  1. father
  2. farmer
  3. Demilitarized Zone

B.
  1. crane
     - a. Seoul
  2. crane
  3. autumn

Teacher's Resource Library Answer Key

Student Study Guide 17

I.
- A.
  1. attic
  2. common sense
  3. Peter

II.
- A.
  1. Mummy
  2. read
  3. kisses
  4. Skew-wiff
  5. person
  6. admiration

III.
- A.
  1. opinions
  2. ideals; truth
  3. peace; tranquillity

Student Study Guide 18

I.
- A.
  1. 1895
  2. boat; reading
  3. poetry
  4. mirage

II.
- A.
  1. spirit; demon
  2. bed
  3. moonlight

III.
- A.
  1. empty wordiness
  2. unenlightened
  3. concealing; advertising
  4. lamp

Student Study Guide 19

I.
- A.
  1. 26
  2. breakfast
  3. butcher
     a. swear

II.
- A.
  1. 3
     a. 2
  2. Livy
  3. Blame that sock
  4. stronger; stronger
     a. sit; floor

III.
- A.
  1. window
  2. half an hour
  3. wash-bowl
  4. Livy; club

Teacher's Resource Library Answer Key

Student Study Guide 20

I.

A.

1. May
2. Ky La
3. god; messenger
    a. mixed up
    b. beetle

II.

A.

1. paddies; stalks
2. mud; soup
3. hands; rice; earth
4. manure; animal

III.

A.

1. rolling
2. March
3. Mother Earth
4. themselves; soldiers
5. strike; communion

Student Study Guide 21

I.

A.

1. Zorinabad
2. Pamela; Cynthia
3. civil service
4. Mother's

B.

1. personality
2. whitewashed; matting
3. cotton
4. name

II.

A.

1. lizard
2. Indian
    a. curry
3. siesta

B.

1. indoors; outside
2. winning
3. catching

III.

A.

1. Ayah
2. apple
3. sandwiches
4. cook's

B.

1. Nalini
2. home
3. Indian; cheat
4. Cynthia

Teacher's Resource Library Answer Key

Student Study Guide 22

I.

- A.
  1. school
  2. rebel
  3. baths
- B.
  1. Bushy
  2. stained; black
  3. pig's
  4. door; window
- C.
  1. hands
  2. bad influence
  3. coal; infant
     - a. knife

II.

- A.
  1. books; papers
  2. untie
  3. canes
- B.
  1. year
  2. pass
  3. Venda
  4. Shangaan
  5. two

III.

- A.
  1. freedom
  2. mother
  3. obscenities
  4. swollen; bruised
- B.
  1. school
     - a. white man's
  2. leave
  3. selling
  4. father
  5. decent job
  6. good; proud
  7. school; keep

Student Study Guide 23

I.

- A.
  1. windows
  2. cotton gloves
  3. earrings; powder

II.

- A.
  1. upswept
  2. Empire State Building
     - a. everything

III.

- A.
  1. blondes
  2. eels; talking
  3. Tom Edison
  4. inventor

Student Study Guide 24

I.

- A.
  1. books
  2. diary
  3. Margot

II.

- A.
  1. crosses
  2. Annie
- B.
  1. Street
  2. Westerbork
  3. knew

III.

- A.
  1. Anne
  2. mother
  3. typhus

Teacher's Resource Library Answer Key

Student Study Guide 25

I.

- A.
  1. integrity
  2. national agenda

II.

- A.
  1. schools
  2. rupees
  3. China

III.

- A.
  1. economic blockade
  2. Clinton; five
  3. India; 1971

Student Study Guide 26

I.

- A.
  1. low-intensity
  2. hydrogen
  3. nuclear science
  4. testing

II.

- A.
  1. weapon race
  2. button
  3. deterrent
  4. echo

III.

- A.
  1. Hiroshima
  2. earthquakes
  3. warheads; missile
  4. small

Student Study Guide 27

I.

- A.
  1. United Nations
  2. summit

II.

- A.
  1. one million
  2. formalising

III.

- A.
  1. London
  2. unilateral moratorium

Student Study Guide 28

I.

- A.
  1. nuclear war
  2. joy; power
  3. Armageddon

II.

- A.
  1. potential
  2. doom
  3. century

Teacher's Resource Library Answer Key

Student Study Guide 29

I.

- A.
  1. blood
  2. Fleance
  3. Lady Macbeth
  4. Banquo

II.

- A.
  1. Macbeth
  2. ghost
  3. ignore
  4. imagination
- B.
  1. twenty
  2. Banquo

III.

- A.
  1. blood
  2. shape
  3. atmosphere
- B.
  1. Ross; go
  2. blood
  3. Macduff
  4. Weird
  5. beginner's

Student Study Guide 30

I.

- A.
  1. Sam's
  2. cross; kite
  3. kids
  4. stockings
- B.
  1. run; free
  2. string; wood
  3. scared; work
  4. remember why
  5. raining

II.

- A.
  1. father
  2. forgiveness
  3. feeling
  4. Dad
  5. shut up
- B.
  1. mother
  2. mother
  3. white man
  4. Sam
  5. Master Harold
     - a. once

III.

- A.
  1. boys
  2. face
  3. father
  4. Willie
  5. dirtier
- B.
  1. ashamed
  2. proud
  3. Whites
  4. tomorrow
  5. stand up

Teacher's Resource Library Answer Key

Student Study Guide 31

I.
- A.
  1. Christmas
  2. billiards
  3. chocolate
- B.
  1. country
  2. home
  3. doll; Maja
  4. shooting

II.
- A.
  1. tulips
  2. table
  3. faithful
- B.
  1. crazy; government
  2. evening
  3. afraid
  4. friendship
  5. godmother
  6. engagement

III.
- A.
  1. speaking
  2. table
  3. father
  4. soul
  5. stork
  6. Rat-trap
- B.
  1. angry
  2. fade
  3. thief
  4. strength
  5. love

Student Study Guide 32

I.
- A.
  1. thirty
  2. meters
  3. Four

II.
- A.
  1. hospitals
  2. buried
  3. mourns

III.
- A.
  1. shores
  2. howl
  3. circle

Student Study Guide 33

I.
- A.
  1. blue
  2. white
  3. dead grass

II.
- A.
  1. cloud
  2. sunset
  3. neigh

Teacher's Resource Library Answer Key

Student Study Guide 34

I.

A.

1. deep
2. dreams
3. hatred
4. fears
5. trains

II.

A.

1. Yen-bai
2. dresses; scarves
3. meadow
4. alphabet

III.

A.

1. reliving; imagining
2. March-North
3. hatred
4. plotted
5. friend

Student Study Guide 35

I.

A.

1. dissolves
2. darkness
3. slap
4. oarsman

II.

A.

1. cluster
2. fishhook
3. steaming

III.

A.

1. mute
2. sea
3. mountains

Student Study Guide 36

I.

A.

1. Maru Mori
2. rabbit
3. sunset; sheepskin

II.

A.

1. blackbirds
2. unlovable
3. fireflies
4. cage; melon
5. gorgeous

III.

A.

1. twice over; winter

Student Study Guide 37

I.

A.

1. pool
2. frog
3. splissssshhhhh

II.

A.

1. bantam
2. feathers
3. lion

III.

A.

1. forgive
2. end; world

Teacher's Resource Library Answer Key

Student Study Guide 38

I.
- A.
  1. burn
  2. dark
     a. lightning

II.
- A.
  1. danced
  2. Wild

III.
- A.
  1. blinding
  2. fierce

Student Study Guide 39

I.
- A.
  1. England; Bedford
  2. Maid
  3. peace; France
  4. God's
  5. damage

II.
- A.
  1. slain
  2. God
  3. Charles

III.
- A.
  1. strength
  2. Christendom

Student Study Guide 40

I.
- A.
  1. world; brother
  2. different; travellers
  3. broadcasting
- B.
  1. home
  2. high priest
  3. scales; punishment
  4. scales

II.
- A.
  1. art; literature
  2. unknown
  3. substitute
  4. memory
- B.
  1. levelling
  2. mankind
  3. society
- C.
  1. owe
  2. material
  3. evil

III.
- A.
  1. instantaneous
  2. Mauriac
  3. body; spirit
- B.
  1. binding
  2. history
  3. judgment
- C.
  1. refuge; support
  2. conquer
  3. war

Teacher's Resource Library Answer Key

Student Study Guide 41

I.

A.

1. nation
2. liberty; equal
3. endure
4. dedicating

II.

A.

1. consecrated
2. world
3. unfinished work

III.

A.

1. devotion
2. freedom
3. perish

Student Study Guide 42

I.

A.

1. God
2. torch
3. liberty
4. freedom

II.

A.

1. themselves
2. peace
3. atom
4. fear; fear
5. science

III.

A.

1. begin
2. loyalty
3. tyranny
4. freedom
5. country; country

Student Study Guide 43

I.

A.

1. beggar
2. hands; want
3. strength

II.

A.

1. harvest
2. shoulders
3. daily task

III.

A.

1. heirs
2. dishonest
3. poverty
4. repent

Teacher's Resource Library Answer Key

Student Study Guide 44

I.

A.

1. Cornwall Bird
2. water
3. customs

B.

1. repair
2. Japanese
3. leaded
4. ministers
5. men

II.

A.

1. earthquake
2. twelve; nine
3. after

B.

1. Parliament
2. merchant; twenty
3. Queen

III.

A.

1. pinkish-white
2. people
3. sewage-disposal
4. Miami

B.

1. human being
2. nice; affection
3. inspired; ruin
4. laugh
5. rest
6. natives; poor

Student Study Guide 45

I.

A.

1. thieves; Barbadoes
2. useful members
3. professed

II.

A.

1. milk
2. twelve
3. food
4. four

III.

A.

1. landlords
2. work; service
3. England
4. sold
5. nine

Student Study Guide 46

I.

A.

1. soccer
2. Diego
3. Chica

II.

A.

1. four
2. 230
3. foreign debt
4. Superman

III.

A.

1. English
2. French
3. yob
4. wargames

Teacher's Resource Library Answer Key

Student Study Guide 47

I.

A.

1. ryokan
2. slippers
3. maid
4. Very Lady

II.

A.

1. substance
2. Woody Woodpecker
3. 4:30

III.

A.

1. aquatic
2. Uji
3. international symbol
4. fire
5. three
6. revenge
7. kill

Student Study Guide 48

I.

A.

1. apartment
2. homework
3. room

II.

A.

1. expensive
2. phone
3. laundry
4. fix up

III.

A.

1. car
2. late
3. appliances
4. every
5. utility

Student Study Guide 49

I.

A.

1. animals
2. shields
3. Gottfried
4. knights
5. Lohengrin
6. marry

II.

A.

1. balcony
2. Ortrud
3. Elsa
4. sorcerer
5. stomach

III.

A.

1. lightning bolts
2. home
3. Holy Grail
4. swan
5. dove

Teacher's Resource Library Answer Key

Student Study Guide 50

I.

- A.
    1. Jews
    2. pogroms
    3. people
    4. beating up
    5. poor

II.

- A.
    1. Yediem
    2. Cossacks
    3. train; horseback
    4. uniform
    5. Heissin

III.

- A.
    1. locomotive
    2. conductor
    3. couple
- 4. foot
- 5. Cossacks

Teacher's Resource Library Answer Key

Selection Quizzes

Selection Quiz 1—The Adventure of the Speckled Band
1. b 2. a 3. b 4. d 5. a 6. d 7. c 8. b 9. d 10. a

Selection Quiz 2—Death Arrives on Schedule
1. c 2. c 3. a 4. b 5. a 6. b 7. b 8. c 9. d 10. a

Selection Quiz 3—The Feeling of Power
1. c 2. d 3. a 4. c 5. b 6. c 7. a 8. d 9. b 10. d

Selection Quiz 4—The Expedition
1. c 2. a 3. c 4. a 5. c 6. c 7. d 8. c 9. d 10. c

Selection Quiz 5—The Cegua
1. c 2. b 3. c 4. d 5. a 6. a 7. c 8. a 9. c 10. b

Selection Quiz 6—Master and Man
1. b 2. c 3. b 4. c 5. d 6. c 7. d 8. b 9. a 10. b

Selection Quiz 7—Just Lather, That's All
1. c 2. a 3. c 4. d 5. c 6. c 7. a 8. c 9. d 10. c

Selection Quiz 8—Nervous Conditions
1. b 2. c 3. c 4. d 5. c 6. d 7. d 8. a 9. d 10. b

Selection Quiz 9—Marriage Is a Private Affair
1. d 2. d 3. a 4. a 5. d 6. a 7. d 8. a 9. b 10. a

Selection Quiz 10—Cranes
1. c 2. a 3. a 4. c 5. d 6. a 7. b 8. d 9. a 10. d

Selection Quiz 11—Anne Frank: The Diary of a Young Girl
1. c 2. a 3. d 4. d 5. c 6. a 7. b 8. c 9. d 10. a

Selection Quiz 12—Letter to Indira Tagore
1. d 2. c 3. d 4. a 5. b 6. a 7. d 8. b 9. b 10. c

Selection Quiz 13—Letter to the Rev J. H. Twichell
1. d 2. b 3. c 4. a 5. c 6. a 7. b 8. d 9. a 10. d

Selection Quiz 14—When Heaven and Earth Changed Places
1. c 2. b 3. a 4. d 5. a 6. b 7. c 8. d 9. d 10. a

Selection Quiz 15—By Any Other Name
1. c 2. a 3. d 4. b 5. d 6. c 7. b 8. c 9. d 10. b

Selection Quiz 16—Kaffir Boy
1. a 2. d 3. c 4. a 5. c 6. b 7. c 8. d 9. a 10. b

Selection Quiz 17—China Men
1. b 2. a 3. b 4. c 5. c 6. d 7. c 8. a 9. d 10. c

Selection Quiz 18—The Last Seven Months of Anne Frank
1. c 2. b 3. b 4. d 5. c 6. a 7. b 8. b 9. b 10. c

Selection Quiz 19—Account Evened With India, Says PM
1. c 2. a 3. d 4. b 5. c 6. d 7. b 8. c 9. d 10. c

Selection Quiz 20—Tests Are Nowhere Near India's: Fernandes
1. b 2. b 3. a 4. d 5. c 6. a 7. b 8. c 9. d 10. a

Selection Quiz 21—Pakistan Nuclear Moratorium Welcomed
1. b 2. a 3. a 4. c 5. b 6. d 7. b 8. a 9. d 10. c

Selection Quiz 22—The Frightening Joy and Building Atomic Security
1. c 2. a 3. d 4. b 5. c 6. c 7. b 8. a 9. d 10. c

Selection Quiz 23—Macbeth
1. c 2. a 3. b 4. c 5. d 6. d 7. a 8. b 9. c 10. c

Selection Quiz 24 —"Master Harold" ... and the Boys
1. c 2. b 3. a 4. a 5. a 6. b 7. c 8. d 9. a 10. b

Selection Quiz 25 The Stronger
1. c 2. b 3. d 4. c 5. b 6. a 7. b 8. d 9. a 10. b

Selection Quiz 26—The Diameter of the Bomb
1. a 2. c 3. b 4. d 5. b 6. c 7. a 8. d 9. a 10. c

Selection Quiz 27—Taking Leave of a Friend
1. d 2. b 3. c 4. c 5. a 6. d 7. c 8. b 9. c 10. a

Selection Quiz 28—Thoughts of Hanoi
1. d 2. c 3. a 4. c 5. d 6. c 7. a 8. b 9. d 10. c

Selection Quiz 29—Mindoro
1. d 2. b 3. c 4. d 5. c 6. a 7. a 8. d 9. c 10. b

Selection Quiz 30—Ode to a Pair of Socks
1. b 2. c 3. d 4. d 5. a 6. b 7. b 8. a 9. c 10. d

Selection Quiz 31—Three Haiku
1. c 2. c 3. d 4. a 5. d 6. b 7. c 8. c 9. b 10. d

Selection Quiz 32—Do Not Go Gentle Into That Good Night
1. b 2. c 3. a 4. d 5. d 6. a 7. a 8. b 9. c 10. d

Selection Quiz 33—Letter to the English
1. a 2. c 3. d 4. d 5. b 6. c 7. b 8. c 9. b 10. b

Selection Quiz 34—Nobel Lecture
1. c 2. b 3. a 4. a 5. b 6. d 7. b 8. a 9. c 10. c

Selection Quiz 35—The Gettysburg Address
1. c 2. c 3. d 4. a 5. b 6. b 7. b 8. d 9. d 10. c

Selection Quiz 36—Inaugural Address
1. c 2. b 3. d 4. d 5. b 6. b 7. a 8. d 9. d 10. d

Selection Quiz 37—Of Repentance
1. a 2. c 3. b 4. d 5. b 6. d 7. b 8. d 9. d 10. a

Selection Quiz 38—A Small Place
1. d 2. c 3. b 4. b 5. b 6. b 7. c 8. d 9. d 10. c

Selection Quiz 39—A Modest Proposal
1. d 2. a 3. a 4. b 5. a 6. d 7. a 8. c 9. b 10. a

Selection Quiz 40—Cup Inanity and Patriotic Profanity
1. d 2. b 3. d 4. b 5. c 6. b 7. c 8. b 9. a 10. b

Selection Quiz 41—Staying at a Japanese Inn: Peace, Tranquillity, Insects
1. c 2. b 3. c 4. d 5. c 6. c 7. b 8. a 9. a 10. d

Selection Quiz 42—Why Can't We Have Our Own Apartment?
1. c 2. a 3. b 4. c 5. d 6. b 7. a 8. b 9. b 10. d

Selection Quiz 43—Lohengrin
1. c 2. d 3. d 4. a 5. d 6. b 7. d 8. c 9. b 10. b

Selection Quiz 44—A Wedding Without Musicians
1. c 2. c 3. d 4. b 5. a 6. d 7. b 8. a 9. a 10. c

Teacher's Resource Library Answer Key

Unit Mastery Tests

Unit 1 Mastery Test A

Part A: **1.** Sherlock Holmes **2.** Tschanz **3.** Shuman **4.** Bruno **5.** a señorita H **6.** Vasilii Andreich **7.** Captain Torres **8.** Tambudzai **9.** Nnaemeka **10.** Song-sam

Part B: **1.** Turning Point **2.** Adventure **3.** Science Fiction **4.** Detective Story **5.** Turning Point **6.** Adventure **7.** Science Fiction **8.** Detective Story **9.** Turning Point **10.** Adventure

Part C: **1.** F **2.** T **3.** F **4.** T **5.** T

Unit 1 Mastery Test B

Part A: **1.** Vasilii Andreich **2.** Captain Torres **3.** Tambudzai **4.** Nnaemeka **5.** Song-sam **6.** Sherlock Holmes **7.** Tschanz **8.** Shuman **9.** Bruno **10.** a señorita

Part B: **1.** Adventure **2.** Science Fiction **3.** Detective Story **4.** Turning Point **5.** Adventure **6.** Turning Point **7.** Adventure **8.** Science Fiction **9.** Detective Story **10.** Turning Point

Part C: **1.** F **2.** T **3.** F **4.** T **5.** T

Unit 2 Mastery Test A

Part A: **1.** Netherlands **2.** Vietnam **3.** Poland **4.** India **5.** Pakistan

Part B: **1.** T **2.** F **3.** F **4.** T **5.** F **6.** F **7.** F **8.** F **9.** T **10.** T

Part C: **1.** Journals and Letters **2.** Journals and Letters **3.** Journals and Letters **4.** Journalism **5.** Journalism **6.** Autobiography **7.** Autobiography **8.** Autobiography **9.** Biography **10.** Biography

Unit 2 Mastery Test B

Part A: **1.** India **2.** Pakistan **3.** Netherlands **4.** Vietnam **5.** Poland

Part B: **1.** F **2.** T **3.** T **4.** F **5.** F **6.** F **7.** F **8.** F **9.** T **10.** T

Part C: **1.** Journals and Letters **2.** Journalism **3.** Journals and Letters **4.** Journals and Letters **5.** Autobiography **6.** Autobiography **7.** Journalism **8.** Autobiography **9.** Biography **10.** Biography

Unit 3 Mastery Test A

Part A: **1.** *The Stronger* **2.** *Macbeth* **3.** *"Master Harold"* **4.** *Macbeth* **5.** *Macbeth* **6.** *"Master Harold"* **7.** *The Stronger* **8.** *"Master Harold"* **9.** *The Stronger* **10.** *"Master Harold"*

Part B: **1.** Sam or Willie **2.** Lisa or Frédérique **3.** Banquo **4.** Lisa or Frédérique **5.** Sam or Willie

Part C: **1.** F **2.** F **3.** T **4.** F **5.** T **6.** T **7.** T **8.** F **9.** T **10.** F

Unit 3 Mastery Test B

Part A: **1.** *"Master Harold"* **2.** *The Stronger* **3.** *"Master Harold"* **4.** *The Stronger* **5.** *"Master Harold"* **6.** *The Stronger* **7.** *Macbeth* **8.** *"Master Harold"* **9.** *Macbeth* **10.** *Macbeth*

Part B: **1.** Banquo **2.** Lisa or Frédérique **3.** Sam or Willie **4.** Sam or Willie **5.** Lisa or Frédérique

Part C: **1.** T **2.** T **3.** F **4.** T **5.** F **6.** F **7.** F **8.** T **9.** F **10.** T

Unit 4 Mastery Test A

Part A: **1.** "Do Not Go Gentle Into That Good Night" **2.** "Ode to a Pair of Socks" **3.** "The Diameter of the Bomb" **4.** "Thoughts of Hanoi" **5.** "Mindoro" **6.** "Ode to a Pair of Socks" **7.** "Three Haiku" **8.** "Do Not Go Gentle Into That Good Night" **9.** "Thoughts of Hanoi" **10.** "Taking Leave of a Friend"

Part B: **1.** F **2.** T **3.** F **4.** F **5.** F **6.** F **7.** T **8.** T **9.** F **10.** T

Unit 4 Mastery Test B

Part A: **1.** "Ode to a Pair of Socks" **2.** "Three Haiku" **3.** "Do Not Go Gentle Into That Good Night" **4.** "Thoughts of Hanoi **5.** "Taking Leave of a Friend" **6.** "Do Not Go Gentle Into That Good Night" **7.** "Ode to a Pair of Socks" **8.** "The Diameter of the Bomb" **9.** "Thoughts of Hanoi" **10.** "Mindoro"

Part B: **1.** F **2.** T **3.** T **4.** F **5.** T **6.** F **7.** T **8.** F **9.** F **10.** F

Teacher's Resource Library Answer Key

Unit 5 Mastery Test A

Part A: **1.** Evils of tourism **2.** Ultimatum before battle **3.** Role of country and citizens **4.** Honoring Civil War dead **5.** Importance of the artist

Part B: **1.** F **2.** F **3.** F **4.** T **5.** F **6.** F **7.** T **8.** T **9.** T **10.** F

Part C: **1.** Jamaica Kincaid **2.** Abraham Lincoln **3.** Joan of Arc **4.** Alexander Solzhenitsyn **5.** John F. Kennedy

Unit 5 Mastery Test B

Part A: **1.** Role of country and citizens **2.** Honoring Civil War dead **3.** Importance of the artist **4.** Evils of tourism **5.** Ultimatum before battle

Part B: **1.** F **2.** T **3.** T **4.** T **5.** F **6.** F **7.** F **8.** F **9.** T **10.** F

Part C: **1.** Joan of Arc **2.** Alexander Solzhenitsyn **3.** John F. Kennedy **4.** Jamaica Kincaid **5.** Abraham Lincoln

Unit 6 Mastery Test A

Part A: **1.** Citizen behavior and priorities **2.** Parents and kids **3.** Persecution **4.** Famine **5.** Opera

Part B: **1.** T **2.** F **3.** F **4.** F **5.** T **6.** T **7.** T **8.** T **9.** F **10.** F

Part C: **1.** Sholom Aleichem **2.** Erma Bombeck **3.** Dave Barry **4.** Jonathan Swift **5.** Leo Slezak

Unit 6 Mastery Test B

Part A: **1.** Persecution **2.** Famine **3.** Opera **4.** Citizen behavior and priorities **5.** Parents and kids

Part B: **1.** T **2.** T **3.** T **4.** F **5.** F **6.** T **7.** F **8.** F **9.** F **10.** T

Part C: **1.** Dave Barry **2.** Jonathan Swift **3.** Leo Slezak **4.** Sholom Aleichem **5.** Erma Bombeck

Midterm Mastery Test

Part A: **1.** Anne Frank **2.** August Strindberg **3.** William Shakespeare **4.** Rabindranath Tagore **5.** Leo Tolstoy **6.** Arthur Conan Doyle **7.** Hwang Sun-won **8.** Le Ly Hyslip **9.** Robert D. San Souci **10.** Chinua Achebe

Part B: **1.** Primitive **2.** Wretched **3.** Hastily **4.** Deposition **5.** Illusionist **6.** Reliable **7.** Affectionate **8.** Superb **9.** Deduction **10.** Tedious **11.** Placidly **12.** Siesta **13.** Mock **14.** Overdue **15.** Beckoning

Part C: **1.** F **2.** T **3.** F **4.** T **5.** T **6.** F **7.** F **8.** T **9.** F **10.** F **11.** T **12.** T **13.** F **14.** T **15.** T

Part D: Answers may vary. Some suggestions follow. **1.** Expressionistic drama is a play that seems realistic but changes reality for dramatic effect. **2.** Pakistan wanted to protect itself from India, which also developed nuclear weapons. **3.** The frightening joy countries feel about gaining nuclear weapons is offset by the frightening prospect of Armageddon. **4.** Murder was committed with a poisonous snake. **5.** The man should not travel alone because he might meet the Cegua, a terrible creature. **6.** *Master and Man* takes place during the winter. **7.** The Frank family was hiding because they were Jews, under persecution from the Nazis during World War II. **8.** The barber thinks about killing the captain because he is responsible for capturing and executing fourteen revolutionaries, and the barber is a secret revolutionary. **9.** Macbeth can't sit at the table because he is haunted by the ghost of Banquo. **10.** They learn to do math by hand so they can regain control and power over computers.

Final Mastery Test

Part A: **1.** Jonathan Swift **2.** Mark Twain **3.** Abraham Lincoln **4.** Dave Barry **5.** Hansjörg Martin **6.** Sholom Aleichem **7.** Leo Slezak **8.** Alexander Solzhenitsyn **9.** Dylan Thomas **10.** Mark Mathabane **11.** Athol Fugard **12.** Pablo Neruda **13.** Michel de Montaigne **14.** Jamaica Kincaid **15.** Isaac Asimov

Part B: **1.** Tidbit **2.** Venison **3.** Plaudits **4.** Duration **5.** Horde **6.** Exaggeration **7.** Persuasive **8.** Chaos **9.** Endowed **10.** Famine

Part C: **1.** T **2.** T **3.** T **4.** T **5.** T **6.** F **7.** F **8.** T **9.** T **10.** T **11.** F **12.** T **13.** T **14.** T **15.** F **16.** F **17.** T **18.** T **19.** F **20.** F **21.** T **22.** T **23.** F **24.** F **25.** T

Part D: **1.** Distant **2.** Sowing **3.** Mute **4.** Departing **5.** Incandescent **6.** Sustenance **7.** Perpetual **8.** Monopoly **9.** Absolute **10.** Theme

Part E: **1.** To make a point about the starving Irish. He used satire to raise concern for the Irish people. **2.** The impact of the bomb spreads across the entire world. **3.** He calls on writers to stand guard against government oppression. **4.** Because their kids do not appreciate how much they do for them. **5.** It has become his way of life, the way he earns a living. **6.** Because he does not want his father to give in to death, but wants him to fight to stay alive. **7.** Open ended. **8.** Because the United States was concerned about the Russian nuclear threat. Without strength, the United States could not have peace, he said. **9.** Because she believed God was her partner, her guide, her inspiration. **10.** Open ended. **11.** It was upset about how people got carried away with the game and connected it to patriotism and other things. **12.** Open ended. **13.** Because he feels guilty. **14.** Open ended. **15.** Open ended.

AGS

Teacher Questionnaire

Attention Teachers! As publishers of *World Literature,* we would like your help in making this textbook more valuable to you. Please take a few minutes to fill out this survey. Your feedback will help us to better serve you and your students.

1) What is your position and major area of responsibility? ____________

____

____

2) Briefly describe your setting:

____ regular education ____ special education ____ adult basic education

____ community college ____ university ____ other ____________

3) The enrollment in your classroom includes students with the following (check all that apply):

____ at-risk for failure ____ low reading ability ____ behavior problems

____ learning disabilities ____ ESL ____ other ____________

4) Grade level of your students: ____________

5) Racial/ethnic groups represented in your classes (check all that apply):

____ African-American ____ Asian ____ Caucasian ____ Hispanic

____ Native American ____ Other

6) School Location:

____ urban ____ suburban ____ rural ____ other ____________

7) What reaction did your students have to the materials? (Include comments about the cover design, lesson format, illustrations, etc.)

____

____

____

8) What features in the student text helped your students the most?

____

____

____

OVER ➤

9) What features in the student text helped your students the least? Please include suggestions for changing these to make the text more relevant.

____

____

____

10) How did you use the Teacher's Edition and support materials, and what features did you find to be the most helpful?

____

____

____

11) What activity from the program did your students benefit from the most? Please briefly explain.

____

____

____

12) Optional: Share an activity that you used to teach the materials in your classroom that enhanced the learning and motivation of your students.

____

____

____

Several activities will be selected to be included in future editions. Please include your name, address, and phone number so we may contact you for permission and possible payment to use the material. Thank you!

▼ **fold in thirds and tape shut at the top** ▼

Name: ______________

School: ______________

Address: ______________

City/State/ZIP: ______________

Phone: ______________

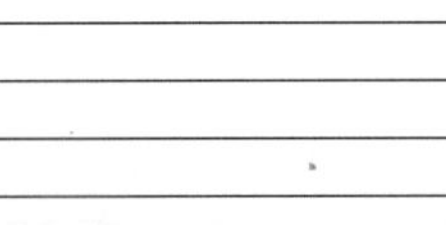

NO POSTAGE NECESSARY IF MAILED IN THE UNITED STATES

BUSINESS REPLY MAIL

FIRST-CLASS MAIL PERMIT NO.12 CIRCLE PINES MN

POSTAGE WILL BE PAID BY ADDRESSEE

AGS

ATTN MARKETING SUPPORT
AMERICAN GUIDANCE SERVICE, INC.
4201 WOODLAND ROAD
PO BOX 99
CIRCLE PINES MN 55014-9923